COMPLETE GUIDE TO
CRUISING
& CRUISE SHIPS 2002

by Douglas Ward
President
The Maritime Evaluations Group (MEG)

Berlitz Publishing Company, Inc.
Princeton   Mexico City   London   Eschborn   Singapore

Berlitz Trademark Reg. U.S. Patent Office and other countries
Marca Registrada

Cover design: Tonya Hallman
Cover photo: *Royal Princess* courtesy of Hans Blohm/Masterfile
Back cover photos: *Queen Elizabeth 2* (left), *Europa* (middle), and *Crystal Symphony* (right) courtesy of Douglas Ward
Layout: Media Content Marketing, Inc.

Although the publisher tries to insure the accuracy of all the information in this book, changes are inevitable and errors may result. The publisher cannot be responsible for any resulting loss, inconvenience, or injury. If you find an error in this guide, please let the editors know by writing to Berlitz Publishing Company, 400 Alexander Park, Princeton, NJ 08540-6306.

ISBN 2-8315-7840-X

Printed in Canada

Publisher's Note: The Maritime Evaluations Group (MEG) has evaluated cruise ships since 1980, issuing annual reports on the world's best cruise fleet. All professional opinions and ratings are strictly those of the author and not of the publisher, Berlitz, which makes this survey available in bookstores.

CONTENTS

STOP PRESS

The very nature of a book such as this, which contains so much factual information, is subject to constant change, just as many parts of the cruise industry itself constantly change. The book is up-to-date and as accurate as possible, until July 2001, when it was completed, although last-minute changes received are noted below.

↪ Golden Sun Cruises' *Aegean Spirit* was renamed *Ocean Glory I* as this book was completed, but was plagued with problems that resulted in the ship's arrest and withdrawal from service. Golden Sun Cruises has been disbanded.

↪ Fred Olsen Cruise Lines purchased the former *Crown Dynasty* in April 2001. The ship has been renamed *Braemar* and, after an extensive refurbishment, is now being used for fly-cruises specifically aimed at British passengers. *Braemar* starts operating at the beginning of the winter season, 2001.

↪ P&O Cruises' *Arcadia* will become an adults-only (no children allowed) ship starting May 2002.

↪ As this book was being completed, Spain's tour operator Pullmantur purchased two ships formerly operated by Premier Cruise Lines: *Oceanic* (formerly Premier Cruise Lines' *Big Red Boat I*) for the Spanish-speaking market.

↪ In November 2001 Royal Caribbean International's *Viking Serenade* will be renamed *Island Escape* and transferred to the new, UK-based cruise line Island — a joint venture between the UK's First Choice Holidays and Royal Caribbean International. The ship, which will commence cruising in March 2002, will operate 7-day Caribbean cruises in the winter and 7-day Mediterranean cruises in the summer.

↪ As this book was being completed, Seabourn Cruise Line announced the sale of its two smallest ships, *Seabourn Goddess I* and *Seabourn Goddess II* to a Norwegian cruise company.

↪ In spring 2002 *Seabourn Sun* will be transferred to Holland America Line after the ship's scheduled winter around-the-world cruise. The ship will then undergo some refurbishment, and public rooms will be renamed *Prinsendam* before entering service in June 2002 in Europe.

↪ In spring 2002 *Westerdam* will leave the Holland America Line fleet and will be transferred to Costa Cruises to replace the ageing *Costa Riviera*. Westerdam is scheduled to enter service in June 2002. The ship's new name is *Costa Europa*.

↪ In spring 2002, *Crown Princess* will be transferred from Princess Cruises to Seetours (Germany). The ship's new name was unknown at press time, although the project name was *Tosca*.

↪ In summer 2002, Star Cruises' *SuperStar Aries* will be moved to Orient Lines, a company it owns, and will be renamed *Ocean Voyager*. As such, the ship will operate long-distance itineraries throughout the world, including an annual around-the-world cruise (the first is scheduled for 2003).

↪ In fall 2002, *Ocean Princess* will be transferred from the Princess Cruises fleet to UK-based P&O Cruises. The ship will be renamed *Oceana*.

↪ In fall 2002, *Pacific Princess* will be withdrawn from the Princess Cruises fleet. The ship is expected to operate under the California-based Grand Circle Cruises banner.

FROM THE AUTHOR

Ever since my first transatlantic crossing, in July 1965, aboard Cunard Line's 83,673-ton ocean liner RMS Queen Elizabeth (then the largest passenger ship in the world), I have been captivated by passenger ships and the sea. Today, after more than 4,800 days at sea, involving participation in more than 850 cruises, 150 transatlantic crossings, and countless Panama Canal transits, shipyard visits, ship christenings, and maiden voyages, I am even more fascinated by and absorbed in every aspect of cruising and cruise ships.

Don't be land bound when you can be cruise bound! Speak to anyone who has taken a cruise — they'll be enthusiastic in their praise. So will you — that is, if you choose the right ship, for the right reasons. This book is intended to be a comprehensive source of information about cruising and the ships that offer to take you away from the pressures, stresses, and confines of daily life ashore.

When you first look into taking a cruise, you will be confronted by an enormous and bewildering choice. Don't panic. Simply read through this book carefully. At the end you will be nearer to making the right choice and you will leave for your cruise as well informed as most specialists in the industry! In fact, any professional cruise sales agent will find this book a valuable reference source about ships and cruising.

From time to time, the media reports on criminal aspects of the cruise industry, such as rape and environmental pollution. The international cruise industry, which consists of more than 90 ocean-going cruise operators carrying over ten million passengers each year, provides an extremely safe and hassle-free way to take a vacation. In fact, with less than 100 cases of alleged rape among more than ten million passengers, the statistics are truly exemplary.

The major players in the North American cruise industry (North America is where the offenses occurred) have together set a "zero-tolerance" of any crimes committed aboard ships calling on US ports and are empowered to report any such instances to the Federal Bureau of Investigation.

With regards to environmental dumping, yes, there have been instances where a crew has not followed company guidelines. The result has been fines of astounding magnitude — far more than have ever been doled out to industrial companies on land.

So, I implore you to treat the few isolated incidents with caution, reserve, and an open mind, and to look at the big picture. Cruising is the most affordable, safe, and highly romantic way to take a vacation. If only the rest of the world were so.

This book is a tribute to everyone who has made my seafaring experiences possible, and a thank you to all the cruise lines for their excellent cooperation.

Douglas Ward
June 2001

HOW TO USE THIS BOOK

The book is divided into two sections. Part One introduces you to the world of cruising, helps you define what you are looking for in a cruise vacation and what kind of accommodation to choose, and provides valuable advice on what to know before you go. It provides a look at life aboard ship and how to get the best from it; the cuisine; nautical terminology; amusing anecdotes; the ship's hierarchy; and advice about going ashore. Alternative cruises, such as expedition cruises, sail-cruise ships, coastal and river cruises, and freighters, are discussed, too, culminating with that ultimate travel experience: the around-the-world cruise.

Part Two contains profiles of 269 oceangoing cruise vessels. From large to small, from unabashed luxury to ships for the budget-minded, old and new: They are all here. The ratings and evaluations are a painstaking documentation of my personal work. I travel constantly throughout the world, and I am "at sea" for more than nine months each year.

The attraction of cruising is in the variety of products and choices available. This book is intended to help you make informed decisions, given the enormous differences between ships, service standards, and cruise lines today.

The evaluations of cruise ships in this book have been made objectively without bias, partiality, or prejudice. In almost all instances, the ships have been visited recently by the author or one of his team members in order to update earlier ratings or to assess current status. Passenger comments and feedback are also taken into account in the final evaluations.

Most of the statistical information contained in the profiles in Part Two was supplied and checked by the cruise lines and ship owners. Any errors or updated information should be sent to the author at the address below.

The author's constant cruise and ship inspection schedule means that he is very seldom on land, and regrets that he is no longer able to answer any written letters sent by mail:

Mr. Douglas Ward
The Maritime Evaluations Group
Canada House
1 Carrick Way
New Milton
Hampshire BH25 6UD
ENGLAND

WHY TAKE A CRUISE?

WHY IS A CRUISE VACATION SO POPULAR?

Over 10 million people are not likely to be wrong (that's how many people took a cruise last year)! Cruising is popular today because it takes you away from the pressures and strains of contemporary life by offering an escape from reality. Cruise ships are really self-contained resorts, without the crime, which can take you to several destinations in the space of just a few days.

The sea has always been a source of adventure, excitement, romance, and wonder. It is beneficial and therapeutic, and, because you pay in advance, you know what you will spend on your vacation without any hidden surprises. There is no traffic (except when you go ashore in ports of call), and no pollution. The hassles of ordinary travel are almost eliminated in one pleasant little package. It's no wonder that 85 percent of passengers want to go again. And again. And again.

Warning: Cruising Is Addictive!

MORE REASONS: THE SIGHTS

The sights, the sights! Some of the world's most beautiful sights and places are seen best from the decks of cruise ships. Indeed, there's simply no other way to see the awe-inspiring beauty of Antarctica, Alaska's Inside Passage and its glaciers, the Galapagos Islands, the Panama Canal, or Vietnam's haunting Halong Bay. Up-close and personal is just one of the reasons that cruising is such a valuable experience.

ISN'T CRUISING EXPENSIVE?

Compare what it would cost on land to have all of your meals and entertainment provided, as well as transportation, fitness and sports facilities, social activities, educational talks, parties, and other functions, and you will soon realize the incredible value of a cruise. Further, a ship is a destination in itself, which moves to other destinations. No land-based resort could ever do that! Simply give yourself a vacation budget, and go to your professional travel supplier with it. The rest, as they say, will be taken care of.

JUST WHO TAKES A CRUISE?

Those who are single, couples, families with children of all ages (including single parents and grandparents), honeymooners, second- or third-time honeymooners, groups of friends, and college buddies are all passengers. In fact, today's passengers are likely to be your next-door neighbors.

WHERE CAN I GO ON A CRUISE?

There are over 30,000 different cruises to choose from each year, and more than 500 cruise destinations in the world. A cruise can also take you to places inaccessible by almost any other means, such as Antarctica, the North Cape, the South Sea islands, and so on.

BUT ISN'T CRUISING FOR OLD PEOPLE?

Nothing could be further from the truth. The average age of passengers gets younger each year. Although those of silver years have found cruising to be a very safe way to travel the world, the average age of first-time passengers is now well under 40. Remember that even wrinkly old people can have fun, too, and many of them have more get-up-and-go than some people under the age of 40!

IF A SEVEN-DAY CRUISE IS ADVERTISED FOR $400 PER PERSON, IS THIS TOO GOOD TO BE TRUE?

As a rule, yes! Consider that a decent hotel room in New York costs at least $200 per night (plus taxes) without meals or entertainment; it stands to reason that something is not quite as it seems. Before booking, read the fine print. Look at all the additional costs such as tips to cabin and dining room stewards, shore excursions, drinks (plus a 15 percent gratuity), plus getting to and from the ship. That $400 per person could well be for a four-berth cabin adjacent to the ship's laundry or above the disco, but in any event, not in a desirable location (just like a $50 hotel room in New York).

WON'T I GET BORED?

Men usually ask this. But get them aboard, and it is almost guaranteed that there won't be enough time in the day to do all the things they want to do (as long as you choose the right ship, for the right

1

reasons). There are more things to do aboard today's ships than there are on almost any Caribbean island. So, whether you want to lie back and be pampered or go nonstop, you can do it on a cruise.

WHY DOES IT COST MORE TO CRUISE IN EUROPE AND THE FAR EAST THAN IN THE CARIBBEAN?
The answer is twofold:
1) Almost all aspects of operations, including fuel costs, port charges, air transportation, and supplying food to the ships, are much higher in Europe.
2) Cruise companies can make more money (called yield) than in the cut-price Caribbean, where sun, sea, and sand are the principal attractions. In Europe, sight-seeing, architecture, culture, and other things are part of a more enriching cruise experience.

CAN I LEARN ABOUT COMPUTERS WHILE ON A CRUISE?
Absolutely. Crystal Cruises, Cunard Line, and Seabourn Cruise Line are examples of cruise lines that provide computers and lectures. Computer Learning Centers aboard *Crystal Harmony*, *Crystal Symphony* and *QE2* each have almost two-dozen computer workstations or laptops for class use.

CAN I GET/SEND E-MAIL ON BOARD?
Yes and no: It depends on your service provider. Aboard most ships, e-mail facilities have now been added to some degree or other. Several ships now sport an Internet café, or Internet Centers. For many companies, e-mail has now become an important revenue generator. One cruise ship, Europa (Hapag-Lloyd Cruises) even has a full personal computer in every cabin, while some other ships have installed computers in their most expensive suites.

CAN I DINE WHEN I WANT TO?
Yes, you can — well, almost. Most of the major cruise lines have introduced what is termed "flexible dining" whereby you can choose (with some limitations) when you want to eat, and with whom you dine. Just like going out to restaurants ashore, reservations may be required, and occupants of the most expensive suites will get priority.

IS CRUISING FOR SINGLES?
Yes. A cruise vacation is ideal for those traveling alone (over 25 percent of all passengers are solo travelers), because it is easy to meet other people in a noncompetitive environment. Many ships also have dedicated cabins for singles as well as special add-on rates for single occupancy of double cabins. Some cruise lines will find a cabin mate for you to share with, if you so desire. However, be aware that in cabins that have three or four berths, personal privacy will be non-existent!

ARE CRUISES FOR HONEYMOONERS?
Absolutely! In fact, a cruise is the ideal setting for romance, shipboard weddings (these can be arranged in some ports, depending on local regulations), receptions, and honeymoons. Most decisions are already made for you so all you have to do is show up. Most ships have accommodation in double-, queen-, or king-sized beds, too. And for those on a second honeymoon, many ships now perform a "renewal of vows" ceremony (some ships charge for this, some do not).

ARE CRUISES FOR CHILDREN, TOO?
Oh, yes! In fact, a cruise provides families with more quality time than any other type of vacation (family cruising is the largest growth segment in the cruise industry). Activities are tailored to various age groups (even Disney has cruise ships dedicated to families and children). In addition, a cruise is educational, allows children to interact in a safe, crime-free environment, and takes them to destinations in comfortable and familiar surroundings. In fact, kids have such a good time aboard ship and ashore, you will have difficulty getting them home after the cruise (if you choose the right ship). And you as parents (or single parent) will get time to enjoy life, too.

CAN I FIND A QUIET, SERENE CRUISE, AWAY FROM CHILDREN AND NOISE?
Yes, indeed. If you don't like crowds, noise, or long lines, there are some beautiful small ships ready to cater to your every whim. Perhaps a sail-cruise vessel or a river or barge cruise could also provide the right antidote. There are so many choices. Companies with ships that are totally child-free include: Renaissance Cruises, Saga Cruises, Swan Hellenic Cruises.

IS THERE A CRUISE WITH NO PORTS OF CALL?

Yes, but it is not really a cruise. It is a transatlantic crossing, from New York to Southampton, England, aboard Cunard Line's *Queen Elizabeth 2*. While I have been advising cruise lines for years that a ship doing occasional three-, four-, or seven-day cruises to nowhere would be welcomed by many repeat passengers, no cruise line has yet taken the initiative. Many passengers are so "allergic" to places that are really tourist rip-off destinations that they really want nothing more than to be aboard a ship at sea, with all the comforts of home.

ARE THERE DIFFERENT CLASSES ABOARD SHIP?

Not really. Gone are the class distinctions and the pretensions of formality of the past. Differences are now found mainly in the type of accommodation chosen; in the price you pay for a larger cabin (or suite), the location of your cabin (or suite), and whether or not you have butler service.

ISN'T IT DIFFICULT TO FIND ONE'S WAY AROUND LARGE SHIPS?

Well, it can take at least a few hours, or a day or so. However, in general, remember that decks are horizontal, while stairs are vertical. The rest comes naturally, with practice.

CAN I GO SHOPPING IN PORTS OF CALL?

Yes, you can. Many passengers with a black belt in shopping engage in "retail therapy" when visiting ports of call such as Dubai, Hong Kong, Singapore, St. Martin, and St. Thomas, among so many others. Just remember that you will have to carry all those purchases home at the end of your cruise, as the luggage companies know well enough.

AREN'T ALL SHIPS AND CRUISES SIMILAR?

Indeed, no! Far from it! Look through this book and you will see that ships range from under 200 ft (60.9 m) to over 1,000 ft (304 m) in length. They carry from under 100 to almost 4,000 passengers; facilities, food, and service vary according to the size of the ship. Ambience ranges from ultra-casual to very formal (starchy and reserved). Entertainment ranges from amateur dramatics to full-fledged high-tech production shows, from the corner cabaret to a world-famous headliner.

AS A REPEAT PASSENGER WHO LIKES LARGE SHIPS, IT IS DIFFICULT TO ESCAPE FROM CONSTANT NOISE. WHAT DO YOU SUGGEST?

I understand your problem. Simply contact the hotel manager and let him (or her) know that volume levels are unacceptable and to please do something about it. If enough people do this, things will have to change for the better. Or you could take earplugs!

HOW PREGNANT CAN I BE WHEN I TAKE A CRUISE?

No worries: You can be very pregnant. Typically, most cruise lines will not allow a mother-to-be to cruise past their 28th week of pregnancy. You may be required to produce a doctor's certificate, and you should let your doctor know that you are planning a cruise.

AS A REPEAT PASSENGER, I'VE NOTICED STANDARDS DROPPING. WHY?

Well, prices are the same (or lower) than they were ten years ago, but operational and crew costs have risen considerably. Somewhere along the line, something has to give. It is usually in the small details that cruise lines think passengers will not notice, like food quality.

WHERE DID ALL THE MONEY GO?

Apart from the cruise fare, which you know before you go, there could be other incidentals such as government taxes, port charges, air ticket tax. Once on board, extra costs will typically include drinks, mini-bar items, cappuccino and espresso coffees, shore excursions, sending or receiving e-mail, health spa treatments, casino gaming, photographs, laundry/dry-cleaning, babysitting services, wine tasting, bottled water placed in your cabin, and the services of the medical department.

A cruise aboard a ship belonging to one of the major cruise lines (Carnival Cruise Lines, Celebrity Cruises, Costa Cruises, Holland America Line, Norwegian Cruise Line, Princess Cruises, Royal Caribbean International, Star Cruises) could be compared to buying a car, whereby automobile manufacturers offer a basic model at a set price and add on optional extras. These cruise lines will tell you that income generated on board helps to keep the basic cost of a cruise reasonable.

WHERE TO?

With so many destinations available to cruise ships, there is almost certainly a ship to take you wherever you want to go. Because itineraries vary widely, depending on each ship and cruise, it is wise to make as many comparisons as you can by reading the cruise brochures for descriptions of the ports of call.

Several ships may offer the same or similar itineraries simply because these have been successfully tried and tested. Narrow the choice further by noting the time spent at each port, and whether the ship actually docks in port or lies at anchor. Then, compare the size of each vessel and its facilities.

CARIBBEAN CRUISES

There are over 7,000 islands in the Caribbean Sea, although many are small or uninhabited. Caribbean cruises are usually destination-intensive cruises in a warm, sunny climate that cram between four and eight ports into one week, depending on whether you sail from a Florida port or from a port already in the Caribbean, such as Barbados or San Juan. This means you could be visiting at least one port a day, with little time at sea for relaxation (the original "port-a-cabin"). This kind of "island hopping" leaves little time to explore a destination before you have to be back on board. Although you see a lot of places in a week, by the end of the cruise you may need another week to unwind. Note: June–November is hurricane season in the Caribbean (including the Bahamas and Florida).

→ **Eastern Caribbean** cruises typically include ports such as Barbados, Dominica, Martinique, Puerto Rico, St. Croix, St. Kitts, St. Martin, and St. Thomas.
→ **Western Caribbean** cruises typically include ports such as Calica, Cozumel, Grand Cayman, and Playa del Carmen.
→ **Southern Caribbean** cruises typically include ports such as Antigua, Aruba, Barbados, La Guaira (Caracas), and Grenada.

PRIVATE ISLANDS

Several cruise lines with Bahamas/Caribbean itineraries feature a "private island" (also called an "out-island"). This is a small island close to Nassau in The Bahamas outfitted with all the ingredients to make an all-day beach party a "nice day out." Also available are watersports, SCUBA, snorkeling, crystal-clear waters, warm sands, even a hammock or two, and, possibly a massage in a beach cabana. There are no reservations to make, no tickets to buy, and no hassles with taxis. If you're looking for a "desert island" fix, however, be aware that you may be sharing your private island with over 2,000 other travelers.

Norwegian Cruise Line was the first to feature a private island in 1977. Today, Disney Cruise Line, whose first ship debuted in July 1998, has the most extensive facilities of all on its private island (which is wholly owned, not leased, like all others).

Cruise ships line up, ready to cruise from the port of Miami.

Some private islands change names depending on the day of the week, and what ship is in. Beaches that look idyllic for 200 passengers can prove extremely noisy and crowded with 2,000 or more passengers from a large ship anchored for a "Beach Barbecue." Cruise lines have their own names for these islands. For example: Castaway Cay (Disney Cruise Line), Catalina Island (Celebrity Cruises), Coco Cay (Royal Caribbean International), Little Stirrup Cay (Norwegian Cruise Line), Half Moon Cay (Holland America Line), Princess Cay (Princess Cruises), and Serena Cay (Costa Cruises).

One bonus is that a "private island" will not be cluttered with hawkers and hustlers, as are so many Caribbean beaches. And, because they are private, there is security, and no fear of passengers being mugged, as occurs on some islands.

Private island beach days are not all-inclusive, however, and attract high prices for snorkel gear (and mandatory swim vest), pleasure craft, and "banana" boat fun rides; it has become yet another way for cruise lines to increase revenue. However, it costs a lot of money to develop a private island. Examples: Disney Cruise Line spent $25 million developing and outfitting Castaway Cay (formerly known as Gorda Cay), while Holland America Line spent $16 million developing Half Moon Cay.

EUROPE/MEDITERRANEAN CRUISES

Traveling within Europe (including the Baltic, Black Sea, Mediterranean, and Norwegian fjord areas) makes economic sense. European/Mediterranean cruises are popular because so many of Europe's major cosmopolitan cities — Amsterdam, Barcelona, Copenhagen, Genoa, Helsinki, Lisbon, London, Monte Carlo, Nice, Oslo, St. Petersburg, Stockholm, and Venice — are on the water. It is far less expensive to take a cruise than to fly and stay in decent hotels (and have to pay for food and transport).

→ You will not have to try to speak or understand different languages when you are aboard ship as you would ashore (if you choose the right ship).
→ Aboard ship you use a single currency.
→ A wide variety of shore excursions are available.
→ Lecture programs provide you with insights before stepping ashore. Small ships are arguably better than large ships, as they can obtain berthing space (large ships may have to anchor in more of the smaller ports, so it can take time to get to and from shore — a frustrating incon-

5

venience). Note that many Greek islands are only accessible by shore tender. When looking at itineraries, one company may give you more time ashore than another company, so compare the brochures.

ALASKA CRUISES

For a real cold rush, try an Alaskan cruise. They are popular because:

→ They offer the best way to see Alaska's magnificent shoreline and glaciers.
→ It is a vast, relatively unexplored region.
→ There is a wide range of shore excursions to choose from, including many floatplane and heli-copter tours.
→ There is an extensive array of excursions to add to your cruise. These can include "dome car" rail journeys to Denali National Park to see North America's highest peak — Mt. McKinley.
→ Pre- and post-cruise journeys to Banff and Jasper National Parks can be made from Vancouver.

There are two popular cruise routes:

→ **The Inside Passage Route**, which usually includes visits to tidewater glaciers, such as those found in Glacier Bay's Hubbard Glacier or Tracy Arm (just two of the fifteen active glaciers along the 62-mile-long Glacier Bay coastline). Typical ports of call might include Juneau, Ketchikan, Skagway, and Haines.
→ **The Glacier Route**, which usually includes the Gulf of Alaska during a seven-day, one-way cruise between Vancouver and Anchorage. Typical ports of call might include Seward, Sitka, and Valdez.

Two of the major cruise lines, Holland America Line and Princess Cruises, have such comprehensive facilities ashore (hotels, tour buses, and even trains) that they are committed to Alaska for many years. Holland America Line-Westours and Princess Tours (a division of Princess Cruises) have, between them, invested over $300 million in Alaska; Holland America Line-Westours is the state's largest private employer. Other lines depend on what's left of the local transportation for their land tours. In 2001, for example, Holland America Line took 115,000 passengers to Alaska, while Princess Cruises took 180,000.

Some ships anchor rather than dock in some ports of call, due to the limited amount of docking space. Many cruise brochures unfortunately do not indicate which ports are known to be anchor (tender) ports.

Sadly, there is now so much congestion in many of the small Alaska ports (over 700,000 cruise passengers visited Alaska in 2001), where several large ships may be in port on any given day, that avoiding crowded streets is an unpleasant part of the cruise experience. Even nature is retreating; with more humans around, wildlife is becoming harder to spot. And some of the same shops can now be found in Alaska as well as in the Caribbean.

For those of a more adventurous nature, consider one of the more unusual Alaska cruises to the far north, around the Pribilof Islands (superb for bird watching) and into the Bering Sea.

TRANSCANAL CRUISES

Transcanal cruises take you through the Panama Canal, constructed by the United States after the failure of a French effort started by Ferdinand de Lesseps. The French labored for twenty years, beginning in 1880, but disease and financial problems defeated them. The United States took over the building effort in 1904 and the waterway opened just ten years later on 15 August, 1914. The Panama Canal runs from northwest to southeast, and the best way to experience this engineering wonder is from the deck of a cruise ship. Control of the canal passed from the US government to Panama in 2000. A widening of the canal and new locks, to be built between 2002 and 2010, at a cost of more than $4 billion, will enable those 'post-Panamax' ships (such as Adventure of the Seas, Carnival Destiny, Carnival Triumph, Carnival Victory, Explorer of the Seas, Golden Princess, Grand Princess, Star Princess, and Voyager of the Seas) to pass through the canal.

Cruising from the Caribbean to the Pacific, a ship is lifted 85 ft (26 m) in a continuous flight of three steps at Gatun Locks to Gatun Lake, through which it will travel to Gaillard Cut where the Canal slices through the Continental Divide. It will be lowered at Pedro Miguel Locks 31 ft (9.4 m) in one step to Miraflores Lake, then the remaining two steps to sea level at Miraflores Locks before passing into the Pacific Ocean. Ships move through the locks under their own power guided by towing locomotives. The 50-mile (80 km) trip across the Isthmus of Panama takes about 9 hours.

Panama Canal cruises typically depart from Ft. Lauderdale or San Juan, calling at one or two Caribbean islands before entering the canal and ending in Acapulco, Los Angeles, or San Francisco.

AUSTRALASIA AND ORIENT CRUISES

If you like the idea of cruising in Australasia, Southeast Asia, or the Orient and you live in Europe or North America, be aware that the flying time to get to your port of embarkation and ship will be long. It is advisable to arrive at least two days before the cruise, as time changes and jet lag can be severe. The area has so much to offer that it is worth taking a cruise of at least fourteen days to make the most of it.

Choose an itinerary that is appealing to you, and then read about the proposed destinations and their attractions. Your cruise or travel agent will be able to provide you with some of the essential background on destinations and help you select an itinerary. Australia, New Zealand, the islands of the South Pacific, Hong Kong, China, Japan, Indonesia, Malaysia, Singapore, and Thailand offer superb cruise destinations.

WHERE TO?

Today's cruise ships do indeed roam all over the world. For the sake of simplicity, some of the major cruise areas are grouped together on the following pages, together with the names of the companies and, in most cases, the cruise lines that will take you there.

Cruise lines with several ships tend to switch ships to operate certain itineraries from year to year; thus, the names of ships are not provided. When it was compiled, the list was as accurate as was possible, given the fact that many companies had not released their full itineraries for 2002.

WHEN IS THE BEST CRUISE SEASON?

MONTH	Alaska	Amazon	Antarctica	Arctic/Greenland	Around Great Britain	Around South America	Australia/New Zealand	Bahamas	Bermuda	Black Sea	Caribbean
January		★	★			★	✪	★			★
February		★	★			★	★	★			★
March		★				★	★	★			★
April								★		★	★
May					★			★	★	★	★
June	★				★			✧	★	★	✧
July	★			★	★			✧	★	★	✧
August	★				★			✧	★	★	✧
September	★				★			✧	★	✧	✧
October						★	★	✧	★		✧
November			★			★	★	✧			✧
December		★	★			★	✪	★			★

Key:

★ = this is the best cruise season

✧ = this is hurricane season, which can mean unpredictable weather patterns in this region

✪ = this is cyclone season, which can mean unpredictable weather patterns in this region

Egypt/Israel	Galapagos Islands	Mediterranean	Mexican Riviera/US West Coast	New England/Canada	North Cape/Norwegian Fjords/Iceland	Northwest Passage	Red Sea/East Africa/Indian Ocean	South Pacific	Southeast Asia	US East Coast	World Cruises
★			★				★	✪	★		★
★			★				★	✪	★		★
★			★				★		★		★
★	★							★			★
	★							★		★	
	★				★			★		★	
	★				★	★		★		★	
	★		★		★	★		★		★	
	★		★					★		★	
★	★		★				★		★	★	
★		★					★		★		
★		★					★	✪	★		★

WHERE TO?

Key:
X = Frequent and infrequent calls
Y = Year-round calls

See NOTES on page 16

	Alaska	Antarctica	Amazon	Arabian Gulf (Red Sea)	Around Africa	Around Britain	Around South America	Around the World	Atlantic Isles (Canary Isles/Madeira)	Australia/New Zealand/South Pacific	Bahamas	Bermuda (summer season contract)
Abercrombie & Kent	X	X								X		
Aida Cruises												
Airtours Sun Cruises			X							X		
Alaska's Glacier Bay Cruises	X											
American Canadian Caribbean Line												
American Cruise Lines												
American Hawaii Cruises												
Canodros												
Carnival Cruise Lines	X										Y	
Celebrity Cruises	X						X				Y	X
Classic International Cruises												
Classical Cruises												
Clipper Cruise Line	X	X	X				X	X				
Club Med Cruises									X			
Costa Cruises									X			
Croatia Cruise Lines												
Cruise West	X											
Crystal Cruises	X		X	X			X	X	X	X		
Cunard Line			X			X	X	X	X	X		
Delphin Seereisen			X				X	X				
Delta Queen Coastal Cruises	X											
Disney Cruise Line											Y	
Dreamline Cruises							X	X	X			
Festival Cruises/First European Cruises									X			
Fred Olsen Cruise Lines			X		X				X			
Galapagos Cruises												
Golden Sun Cruises												
Great Lakes Cruises												
Hapag-Lloyd Cruises	X	X	X	X	X	X	X	X		X		
Hebridean Island Cruises						X						
Holland America Line	X						X	X	X	X	Y	
Imperial Majesty Cruise Line											Y	
Island												
Islas Galapagos y Turismos												

Canada/New England	Caribbean	Caribbean (including Cuba)	Chilean Fjords/Patagonia	Europe (Eastern, including Black Sea)	Europe (Mediterranean)	Galapagos Islands	Great Lakes Region (USA/CANADA)	Greek Islands	Hawaii	Indian Ocean	Mexican Riviera (3, 4, and 7-day cruises)	North Cape/Baltic Sea	Northwest Passage	South America (east coast)	Southeast Asia	Tahiti and her islands	Transatlantic Crossing	U.S. Coastal Cruises	Charter/Roaming (Varied) Itineraries
			X	X	X	Y	X					X							
	X				X														
	X			X	X					X							X		
X	X														X			X	
																		Y	
									Y										
				Y															
X	Y							X			Y								
Y				X	X		X	X				X		X			X		
	X				X							X		X					
	X				X		X												
X	X		X		X									X	X			X	
	X															X		X	
	X			X	X			X				X		X			X		
				X	X														
X	X				X					X	X	X		X	X		X		
X	X				X					X	X	X		X	X		X		
X	X	X										X		X					
					X														X
			X	X	X							X		X			X		
	X			X	X			X									X		
X	X	X			X							X		X			X		
						Y													
				X	X			X											
					X														
X	X	X		X	X		X	X		X	X	X		X	X		X		
					X			X		X									
X	Y				X						X			X	X	X	X		
	X				X														
						Y													

11

WHERE TO?

	Alaska	Antarctica	Amazon	Arabian Gulf (Red Sea)	Around Africa	Around Britain	Around South America	Around the World	Atlantic Isles (Canary Isles/Madeira)	Australia/New Zealand/South Pacific	Bahamas	Bermuda (summer season contract)
Kristina Cruises												
Lindblad Expeditions	X											
Louis Cruise Lines												
Majestic International Cruises												
Mano Maritime												
Mediterranean Shipping Cruises					X							
Metropolitan Touring												
Mitsui OSK Passenger Line								X				
New Paradise Cruises												
Noble Caledonia		X	X			X						
Norwegian Cruise Line	X										Y	X
Nouvelle Frontieres												
NYK Cruise Line								X		X		
Orient Lines		X						X		X		
P&O Cruises				X					X	X		
P&O Cruises (Australia)										Y		
Peace Boat								X				
Phoenix Seereisen	X		X	X	X		X	X	X	X		
Plantours & Partner			X		X	X		X	X			
Ponant Cruises			X									
Princess Cruises	X		X				X	X	X	X	Y	X
Pullmantur Cruises												
Quark Expeditions		X										
Radisson Seven Seas Cruises		X	X				X	X	X	Y		
Regal Cruises								X				
Renaissance Cruises												
Royal Caribbean International	X						X			X	Y	X
Royal Olympic Cruises			X	X			X					
Saga Cruises								X				
St. Helena Shipping							X					
Sea Cloud Cruises												
Seabourn Cruise Line	X		X				X	X		X		
Seetours			X				X	X	X			
Silversea Cruises			X				X	X	X	X		
Society Expeditions	X	X					X	X				

Canada/New England	Caribbean	Caribbean (including Cuba)	Chilean Fjords/Patagonia	Europe (Eastern, including Black Sea)	Europe (Mediterranean)	Galapagos Islands	Great Lakes Region (USA/CANADA)	Greek Islands	Hawaii	Indian Ocean	Mexican Riviera (3, 4, and 7-day cruises)	North Cape/Baltic Sea	Northwest Passage	South America (east coast)	Southeast Asia	Tahiti and her islands	Transatlantic Crossing	U.S. Coastal Cruises	Charter/Roaming (Varied) Itineraries
									X			X							
		Y			Y														
				X				X											
				X															
				X															
	X			X	X					X		X				X			
						Y													
															Y				X
					Y														
			X	X				X		X					X				
X	Y				X				W							X			
	Y																		
										X					Y				
		X			X			X		X				X	X		X		
X	X				X			X		X		X					X		
																			X
X	X				X			X		X		X		X					
	X				X			X				X					X		
	X				X			X											
X	Y				X				X	X		X	X	X	X		X		
	X				X														
			X										X	X					
X	X			X	X					X		X		X	X	Y	X		
X	X																		
					Y			X								Y			
X	Y				X					X	X	Y	X		X	X		X	
	X				X			X						X			X		
					X			X		X					X		X		
	X				X												X		
X	X				X			X	X	X		X		X	X		X		
X	X				X							X		X	X		X		X
X	X		X		X			X		X		X		X	X		X		
			X																

WHERE TO?

	Alaska	Antarctica	Amazon	Arabian Gulf (Red Sea)	Around Africa	Around Britain	Around South America	Around the World	Atlantic Isles (Canary Isles/Madeira)	Australia/New Zealand/South Pacific	Bahamas	Bermuda (summer season contract)
Spanish Cruise Line												
Star Clippers									X			
Star Cruises			X							X		
Star Line Cruises												
Swan Hellenic Cruises			X		X							
Thomson Cruises			X						X			
Transocean Tours	X	X					X	X	X	X		
United States Lines												
Valtur Tourism												
Venus Cruise (Japan Cruise Line)	X									X		
Windjammer Barefoot Cruises												
Windstar Cruises										X		
World Explorer Cruises	X											

Canada/New England	Caribbean	Caribbean (including Cuba)	Chilean Fjords/Patagonia	Europe (Eastern, including Black Sea)	Europe (Mediterranean)	Galapagos Islands	Great Lakes Region (USA/CANADA)	Greek Islands	Hawaii	Indian Ocean	Mexican Riviera (3, 4, and 7-day cruises)	North Cape/Baltic Sea	Northwest Passage	South America (east coast)	Southeast Asia	Tahiti and her islands	Transatlantic Crossing	U.S. Coastal Cruises	Charter/Roaming (Varied) Itineraries
	X				X														
	X				X										X		X		
															Y				
					X					X									
								X		X		X			X				
	X				X					X							X		
X	X	X			X			X		X			X	X	X		X		
									Y										
		Y																	
															Y				
Y																			
	X				X										X		X		

NOTES FOR WHERE TO? CHART

Bahamas: Only those ships that feature year-round cruises to the Bahamas are included.

Bermuda (summer): Only the five cruise lines (featuring five ships) that have long-term Bermuda government contracts for weekly summer season cruises to Bermuda are listed here, although several other companies operate cruises that include Bermuda infrequently throughout the year.

New England/Canada: These cruises are typically seven-day northbound voyages between New York and Montreal or southbound voyages from Montreal to New York. Of course, these can be combined to make a 14-day round-trip voyage.

Caribbean: Note that there are several more companies than those listed here whose ships visit the Caribbean infrequently, but their schedules are seldom known far enough in advance to be included.

Alaska: These cruises are operated between May and September only.

Mexican Riviera Year-Round (three/four/seven days): Ships based on the US West Coast.

Hawaii: A number of cruise lines have ships that call at Hawaii, and some now cruise from there on a regular basis, although the archaic US Cabotage laws still linger. The Passenger Services Act (known commonly as the Jones Act) states that only US flag ships (there are only two major ocean-going US-flagged ships at present – American Hawaii Cruises' *Independence*, and United States Lines' *Patriot*) can embark and disembark passengers in US ports without first going to a foreign port (a US flag ship is one that is registered in the United States).

Antarctica: The Antarctic is not a place for normal cruise ships (evacuation in the event of an emergency would prove virtually impossible). To operate in this region, where ice can easily crush a ship within the hour should the weather deteriorate (as it often does), a ship must have an "ice-strengthened" or "ice-hardened" hull capable of breaking through pack ice in the formative stage. Rubber-inflatable Zodiac landing craft are used for venturing ashore (there are no docks on the Antarctic continent). The austral summer is the only time ships can travel to the Antarctic Peninsula, where many nations have their research stations, because the ice is so dense during the winter months that the continent (which, at its smallest, is the size of North America) swells to twice its summer size.

Roaming Ships: Cruise lines with "roaming" ships constantly roam around the world, mostly on non-repeating itineraries of varying cruise lengths.

Part One:
THE WORLD OF CRUISING

MS Nordkapp; courtesy Norwegian Coastal Voyage Inc.

YOUR FIRST CRUISE: WHAT TO EXPECT

Make sure you have your passport and any visas required (in some countries — such as the People's Republic of China, or Russia — you might go ashore on organized excursions under a group visa). Pack any medication you may need, and advise family members and friends where you are going.

With anticipation and excitement running high, if you've never been on a cruise before, allow me to take you through a typical initial embarkation process.

You already have been sent your cruise tickets and documents by the cruise line or your travel agent. A typical document package might include:

→ Flight ticket
→ Cruise ticket
→ Luggage tags
→ Embarkation card (to fill out before you get to the embarkation point)
→ Discount coupons for the shops on board
→ Bon Voyage gift selection form

→ Bon Voyage gift selection form
→ Shore excursion brochure
→ Onboard credit account form
→ Guide to services on board
→ Ship's telephone and fax contact numbers
→ Coupon for tuxedo rental

Assume that you've arrived at the airport closest to your ship's embarkation point, and retrieved your luggage. It is probable that there will be a representative from the cruise line waiting, holding a sign that says "Condor Cruise Lines" or something similar. You will be asked to place your luggage in a cluster together with those of other passengers on the same flight as you, or with passengers on other flights arriving at roughly the same time.

Alternatively, you could have perhaps driven to the port of embarkation (or taken a limousine, train, or specially chartered bus). Once there, you would hand over your luggage to a representative of the cruise line or to a baggage handler (who will probably expect a tip, even for moving it a few feet).

In any case (no pun intended), the next time you see your luggage should be aboard your ship, where it will be delivered to your cabin. Now, let's proceed to the check-in point.

Go to the registration (check-in) area in the terminal building. For large ships, numerous desks will be set up (with the alphabet split into several parts), probably with lines of people at each of them. Go to the desk that displays the first letter of your surname, wait in line (having filled out all embarkation, registration, and immigration documents), and then check in. If your accommodation is designated as a "suite," there should be a separate check-in facility (called "gold card service").

If you are cruising from a US port and you are a non-US citizen or "Resident Alien," you will go to a separate desk to check in (*Note*: Do not buy duty-free liquor to take on board — it will not be allowed by the cruise line and will be confiscated until the last day of the cruise). You will be asked for your passport, which you deposit with the check-in personnel (be sure to ask for a receipt — it is, after all, a valuable document). If you are cruising from any other port in the world that is not a US port, be advised that each country has its own check-in requirements, setups, and procedures (passport control and inspection, for example). In any event, once you've checked in, you will be only a few steps away from your ship and cruise.

Documents in hand, you will probably go through a security-screening device, for both your person and hand luggage (just like at airports). Next, you'll walk a few paces towards the gangway. This may be a covered, airport-type gangway, or an open gangway (hopefully with a net underneath it in case you drop something over the side). The gangway could be flat, or you may have to walk up (or down) an incline, depending on the location of the gangway, the tide, or other local conditions. As you approach the gangway you will probably be greeted by the ship's photographers, a snap-happy team ready to take your photograph, bedraggled as you may appear after having flown or otherwise traveled for hours. If you do not want your photograph taken, say "no" firmly, and proceed.

Once on the gangway, you will feel a heightened sense of anticipation. At the ship end of the gangway, you will find a decorated (hopefully) entrance and the comfortable feel of air-conditioning if the weather is hot. The ship's cruise staff will welcome you aboard. Give them your cabin number, and a steward should magically appear to take your carry-on luggage from you and take you directly to your cabin. At last you've arrived.

The door to your cabin should be unlocked and open. If it is locked, ask the steward to obtain the key to open the door. Aboard the newest ships, you will probably be handed an electronically

Bon Voyage!

coded key card, which you insert into the door lock. Once inside the cabin, put down your personal effects and take a good look. Is it clean? Is it tidy? Are the beds properly made? Check under them to make sure the floor is clean (on one cruise I found a pair of red ladies shoes, but, alas, no lady to go with them!). Make sure there is ice in the ice container. Check the bathroom, bathtub (if there is one), or shower. Make sure there are towels and soap. If all is clean and shipshape, fine.

If there are problems, bring them to the attention of your cabin steward immediately. Or call the purser's office (or reception desk), and explain the problem, then quietly but firmly request that someone in a supervisory position see you to resolve it. The housekeeping in cruise ships is generally very good, but sometimes when "turnaround" time is tight, when passengers disembark in the morning and new passengers embark in the afternoon, little things get overlooked. They shouldn't, but they do (just as in any hotel ashore).

One thing you should also do immediately is to remember the telephone number for the ship's hospital, doctor, or for medical emergencies, just so you know how to call for help should any medical emergency arise.

Your luggage probably will not have arrived yet (especially if it is a ship carrying more than 500 passengers) so don't sit in the cabin waiting for it. Once you've oriented yourself with the cabin and its features, put your hand luggage away somewhere, and, deck plan in hand, take a walk, around the ship.

Familiarize yourself with the layout of the ship. Learn which way is forward, which way is aft, and how to reach your cabin from the main stairways. This is also a good time to learn how to get from your cabin to the outside decks in an emergency. A Passenger Lifeboat Drill typically takes place before the ship sails. This means that the drill will not disturb your cruise (or your sleep) as it would if it were held the next morning. Regulations dictate that a drill must take place within 24 hours after the ship sails from the embarkation port.

After the drill (you'll find your lifejacket in the cabin and directions to your assembly station will be posted on the back of the cabin door), you can take off the lifejacket and relax. By now, your luggage probably will have arrived.

Unpack, then go out on deck just before the ship sails. It's always a magical moment, and a good time to meet some new faces. Now, enjoy yourself. You're on a wonderful cruise vacation. No cares. No hassle. No hype. Just you (and perhaps a loved one) and that bracing sea air. You'll soon be ready for that first night's dinner. It is simply amazing how the sea air gives you an appetite, although there's no truth to the rumor that the sea air seems to shrink your clothes by the end of the cruise.

19

CRUISING FOR FREQUENT PASSENGERS: WHAT'S NEW

The cruise industry is buoyant, and the introduction of new ships continues at a dizzying rate. More than 40 new ships are scheduled for delivery between January 2002 and December 2005, at a cost of more than $15 billion, fueled by the continuing increase in demand for high-value cruise vacations.

New ships incorporate the latest in sophisticated high-tech electronic navigation and safety equipment, recent advances in propulsion technology and the best in advanced ship design and construction, offering passengers an unprecedented number of options, choice of facilities, and dining and entertainment experiences.

Late 2000 saw the introduction of the world's largest cruise vessel to date: Royal Caribbean International's 137,308-ton *Explorer of the Seas* (sister to the 137,300-ton *Voyager of the Seas*, introduced in 1999), a floating leisure playground aimed at the standard cruise marketplace. Is bigger better? That's up to the individual to decide, but it is rather like being in a large shopping mall environment as opposed to a smaller boutique environment, or "all-inclusive" versus "all exclusive" cruising.

PROPULSION

The latest ships are now powered by gas turbines, or by diesel-electric or diesel-mechanical propulsion systems that propel them at speeds of up to 28 knots (only Cunard Line's *QE2*, with a top speed of more than 30 knots, is faster).

A new technology is now incorporated into propulsion design, the "pod" system. Briefly, pods, which resemble huge outboard motors, replace internal electric propulsion motors, shaft lines, rudders and their machinery, and are compact, self-contained units that typically weigh about 170 tons each. Pod units pull, rather than push, a ship through the water. When going ahead, pod units face with the propeller forward (ships can go astern either by rotating the pods 180 degrees or by reversing the thrust). A vessel's turning circle diameter is reduced considerably, and vibration at the ship's stern is virtually eliminated.

New ships will incorporate everything that is seen to be environmentally friendly, such as "enviro-engines" that provide power without visible smoke, "enviro-laundries," — maybe even "enviro-entertainment"! How about "enviro-passengers?"

EXTERIORS

The indented, cascading after-decks of ships such as *Aurora*, *Oriana*, *Norwegian Leo*, and *SuperStar Virgo* are both stunning and practical — overlooking aft pool areas. Other cruise ships take the "block" approach and fill in stern areas with cabins that have an aft-facing view (*Carnival Destiny*, *Carnival Triumph*, *Carnival Victory*, for example), or multilevel dining rooms with huge expanses of glass windows (*Century*, *Galaxy*, *Infinity*, *Mercury*, *Millennium*, and *Summit*, for example), or other public rooms and facilities.

The most instantly recognizable exterior is that of *AIDAcara*, with huge bold red lips and brown eyes adorning her prow. Other ships now have huge slogans painted on their white sides (Royal Caribbean International's slogan "Like No Vacation On Earth" for example).

INTERIORS

Retro is in and contemporary is out, as interior designers change tack to create luxurious, welcoming interiors reminiscent of Europe's grand hotels, particularly in the small and mid-size ships, where the sense of intimacy can be genuinely established.

Large ships have interiors that include such things as multi-deck-high atriums, large theaters complete with revolving stages, hydraulic orchestra pits, huge scenery stowage spaces, Internet cafés, computer learning centers, and in-cabin interactive television — not to mention billiard (pool) tables that self correct aboard a moving ship. Some ships feature two atrium lobbies instead of one (*Carnival Destiny*, *Carnival Triumph*, *Carnival Victory*, *Galaxy*, and *Mercury*), while the industry's largest ships, namely Royal Caribbean International's *Explorer of the Seas* and *Voyager of the Seas* feature a large horizontal, rather than a vertical atrium — reminiscent of a city shopping walkway. These are extremely popular.

As for contemporary, among the most stunning, bold, and graphic interiors are those that are found in the ships of Carnival Cruise Lines. Somehow, lilac neon, fiber optics, mosaics, and multicolored carpeting go together here although they never would in any setting other than a Las Vegas hotel. It is all a feast for the eyes and mind (entertainment architecture, as the interior designer calls it), but for many (especially for European passengers) it could be sensory overload (but a good advertisement for the fiber optic and lighting industries).

Ships have become instant floating art museums (some are better than others), with collections of artwork costing several million dollars per ship. For example: $12 million (*Voyager of the Seas*); $6 million (*Vision of the Seas*); $4 million (*Enchantment of the Seas*); $3.8 million (*Century*); $3 million (*Galaxy*); $2.5 million (*Sun Princess*); $2 million (*Veendam*); $1 million (*AIDAcara, Inspiration*). However, it is not the money spent that's important; it is the fact that artwork now forms a more important integral part of the physical interior decor than ever before, and particularly so with large ships, with ever larger wall spaces to cover.

COMPUTER-DRIVEN CRUISING

Can you send and/or receive e-mails when aboard your cruise ship? Yes, you can, aboard some ships — but at a price. As an example, Crystal Cruises imposes a set-up charge of $5, plus $3 for each page of e-mail messages. Many ships now boast Internet cafés, where you can do coffee and e-mail — typically at a cost of $0.75–$1 per minute.

Most cruise lines have web sites on the Internet (see *Appendices* in Part Two). Computers link almost all departments and functions aboard the latest ships, and (somewhat inflexible) interactive television systems let you order wine, arrange shore excursions, play casino games, go shopping, and order pay-per-view movies, all from the comfort of your cabin. Computers cannot yet pour you a drink, although you can order one, accompanied by a light snack. But, order a croissant with your breakfast and the "point and select" system won't bother to ask whether you'd like it warm or cold. Oh well, that's technology for you; as long as you are a "standard" photofit passenger, it'll work for you. Otherwise, call room service (sort of defeats the purpose, doesn't it?).

FLOATING SPAS

Health and fitness spas are among the hottest passenger (revenue) facilities in the latest cruise ships, with more space than ever devoted to them. The basic sauna, steam room, and massage facilities have evolved into huge, specially designed spas that include the latest in high-tech muscle exercising, aerobic and weight-training machines. There are also relaxation treatments, such as hydrotherapy and thalassotherapy baths, jet blitz, rasul (graduated steam and all-over body mud cleansing), seaweed wraps, and hot and cold stone massage.

Ships with large spas locate them on the uppermost decks of the latest ships, and feature large floor-to-ceiling ocean-view windows. Treatment rooms (some will have integral showers) are flexible and can be adapted to incorporate the latest trends, gimmicks, and themes. Traditional Japanese design elements, including a rock garden and shoji screens, provide a serene environment in the AquaSpas aboard *Century, Galaxy, Mercury, Millennium* and *Summit*. Or, how about a 30-person coed sauna, with a large glass wall overlooking the port side (*AIDAcara*)?

FOR SMOKERS

Cigar smoking is in vogue, and special cigar bars and lounges have been created aboard several ships, including: *Adventure of the Seas, Century, Crystal Harmony, Crystal Symphony, Europa, Explorer of the Seas, Galaxy, Horizon, Infinity, Mercury, Millennium, Mistral, Norwegian Leo, Norwegian Sky, Seven Seas Mariner, SuperStar Virgo, Summit, Voyager of the Seas,* and *Zenith*.

FOR NONSMOKERS

Carnival Cruise Lines' Paradise was the first cruise ship to be entirely nonsmoking (even the shipyard workers who built the ship were not allowed to smoke — officially). Think you can smoke anyway? Forget it — there's a fine if you do (crew and other passengers can detect cigarette smoke within five miles). You will be fined $250 and asked to leave at the next port (at your expense). All Renaissance Cruises' R-class ships, *R One, R Two, R Three, R Four, R Five, R Six, R Seven,* and *R Eight* are all totally nonsmoking, including cabins, all public rooms and areas, and open decks (there is a smoking room for the crew). Further, nonsmokers will be pleased to learn that many ships now feature totally nonsmoking dining rooms and show lounges.

21

DINING AND SERVICE

→ What's hot (no pun intended!)? Several ships now pay homage to past transatlantic liners of the past in the decor of their dining rooms or alternative restaurants; examples include the Normandie Restaurant aboard *Carnival Pride*, the Olympic Restaurant aboard *Millennium*, and the United States Restaurant aboard *Infinity*. More will no doubt follow. I expect several ships to start charging for better dining experiences. Many new ships now feature flexible dining and 24-hour casual eateries, so that you can eat when you want. Although the concept is good, the delivery often is not (it is typically self-service eating, and not the dining experience most passengers envisage). Also hot (in culinary-speak) is the fact that several cruise lines have aligned themselves with well-known brand names ashore in order to provide an "authenticity" to their product, and to produce a "wow" effect. Examples include Crystal Cruises (Valentino); Radisson Seven Seas Cruises (Le Cordon Bleu); and Silversea Cruises (Relais & Chateaux).

→ Two-deck-high dining rooms are back in vogue: *Amsterdam, Century, Carnival Spirit, Costa Atlantica, Dawn Princess, Galaxy, Legend of the Seas, Infinity, Maasdam, Mercury, Millennium, Nordic Empress, Rotterdam, Ryndam, Splendour of the Seas, Statendam, Sun Princess, Veendam,* and *Volendam* have them. Not to be outdone, *Adventurer of the Seas, Explorer of the Seas,* and *Voyager of the Seas* (plus two others on order) have dining halls that are three decks high.

→ Some ships, such as *Norwegian Star, SuperStar Leo,* and *SuperStar Virgo* feature as many as 10 different restaurants and eateries, some incur an extra charge — just like going out ashore.

WHAT'S NOT SO HOT

→ Floating resorts that travel by night and are in port during the day provide little connection with the sea and nature. Almost everything is designed to keep passengers *inside* the ship (to spend money, increasing onboard revenue and shareholders' dividends).

→ Entertainment — either production shows or cabaret acts — it's all so much the same no matter what ship you are aboard. It's time for more creative thinking.

→ The latest breed of aggressive, so-called "cruise directors" who insist on interposing themselves into every part of your cruise, day and night. Public address systems are consistently overused by these bouncy youngsters, and are too loud, which hardly makes for a restful cruise. Some of these cruise directors may make excellent cheerleaders, but they seem unable to communicate with anyone over the age of 25!

→ Then there's homogenous accommodation. As identically sized standard cabins are the same shape and layout (good for incentive planners, but not for individual passengers), they also tend to be the same colors: eggshell white, off-white, or computer-colored beige! Although such colors are welcome after days in the sun, they quickly become tedious on voyages over long stretches of water. Only bold bedspreads or the occasional color prints that adorn a spare wall bring relief. Plain ceilings are also boring. Close to useless are wall-mounted hair dryers (which have poor directed pressure) in modular bathrooms; they should, instead, be located in the vanity desk or dressing area.

→ Calling passengers "guests" is confusing, nautically incorrect (a guest in one's house doesn't pay), and cannot be translated into some languages. Passengers pay to be aboard ship. Ships are different from hotels, and should remain so. They provide a nautical experience and move through water; passengers have cabins and suites and decks, not floors. However, several cruise lines think they are in the hotel business, as hoteliers and accountants run them, not shipping people

→ The use of "hotel-speak" is further invading the industry. Royal Caribbean International, for example, now calls its in-cabin refrigerators "Automatic Refreshment Centers."

→ Two things that have almost disappeared: streamers and free champagne, formerly provided at bon voyage parties on deck on sailing day (exception: world cruises and Japanese-registered cruise ships). Instead, waiters hustle you to buy a "bon voyage" cocktail, or some "Bahamaramamaslammer" in a polystyrene sports cup! The little goodies, such as travel bags and extensive personal amenity kits, have been taken away by the bean counters of many of the world's cruise lines, believing that passengers won't notice. Believe me, they do.

→ As for food, note that ships that operate seven-day cruises repeat menu cycles each week. So, if, for example, you take two back-to-back seven-day Eastern and Western Caribbean cruises, the menu may be repeated for the second week (as will the whole entertainment program and the cruise director's spiel, jokes, and activities).

→ Cruise ship food and service standards have suffered more lately due to deep discounting. Ships carrying over 1,000 passengers cannot seem to deliver what is portrayed in the cruise brochures consistently. Also, because of the acute shortage of waiters who speak good English (the majority of passengers are North American), many cruise lines have had to train personnel from Caribbean basin, Central American countries, and eastern Europe, and their command of the language is often less than adequate.

→ One thing that should go pier-side is the amateurish, intrusive "Baked Alaska Parade." Popular with first-time passengers, it is old hat for many. It's time the cruise lines were more creative. The industry should also find a better way to sing "Happy Birthday" than the present waiter-induced chant that always seems to sound like a funeral dirge!

→ In the seven-day cruise market (particularly from US ports) disembarkation is still an untidy and hostile process. Passengers are unceremoniously dumped ashore, with little help after the trying procedures of locating their luggage and going through customs inspection. Poor representation once they get to their respective airports for check-in may be an added ordeal. Of particular concern is the fact that the same procedure applies to all passengers, whether they are in the finest penthouse suite or the smallest interior (no-view) cabin. The final impression of these seven-day cruises, therefore, is poor. Worst disembarkation ports: Ft. Lauderdale, Los Angeles, Miami, and San Juan.

ENVIRONMENTAL CONCERNS

Cruise ships refine oil, treat human waste, and incinerate garbage, but that's not enough today, as pressure continues to mount for clean oceans. Engine emissions are now subject to the provisions of Marpol Annexe VI.

Cruise ships and their operating companies also have a unique position among all shipping interests. They are not likely to damage the ocean environment as compared with oil tankers, although spillage of any kind is regrettable.

Other environmental concerns involve the condition of the air aboard ships. Of particular note is the fact that a ship's air-conditioning system can provide an ideal site for mold growth such as that found in the aerospora group (including *Cladosporium* sp.). Thus, it is vital that cruise lines not skimp on maintenance, and the replacement of filters and other items in air-conditioning systems is very important.

CRUISING: A BACKGROUNDER

DID YOU KNOW...?

...that the first vessel built exclusively for cruising was Hamburg-Amerika Line's two-funnel yacht, the 4,409-tonne *Princessin Victoria Luise*? This luxury ship even included a private suite for the German kaiser.

...that the first ship to be fitted with real stabilizers (not an autogyro device) was the Peninsular & Oriental Steam Navigation Company's 1949-built 24,215-tonne *Chusan*?

...that the first consecrated oceangoing Roman Catholic chapel aboard a passenger ship was in Compagnie Generale Transatlantique's *Ile de France* of 1928?

...that the latest life rafts called Hydrostatic Release Units (HRU), designed in Britain and approved by the Royal Navy, are now compulsory on all British-registered ships? Briefly, an HRU is capable of automatically releasing a life raft from its mountings when a ship sinks (even *after* it sinks) but can also be operated manually at the installation point, saving precious time in an emergency.

Although the first cruises (actually "pleasure voyages") really started in the early 1800s, it was not until around 1960 that the modern-day cruise industry began, following the demise of transatlantic ocean liner crossings.

In June 1958, the first commercial jet aircraft flew across the Atlantic and forever altered the economics of transatlantic travel. It was the last year in which more passengers crossed the North Atlantic by sea than by air. In the early 1960s, passenger-shipping directories listed over 100 passenger lines. Until the mid-1960s, it was cheaper to cross the Atlantic by ship than by plane, but the appearance of the jet aircraft changed that rapidly, particularly with the introduction of jumbo jets in the early 1970s. In 1962, more than one million people crossed the North Atlantic by ship; in 1970, that number was down to 250,000.

The success of the jumbo jets created a fleet of unprofitable and out-of-work passenger liners that appeared doomed for the scrap heap. Even the famous big "Queens," noted for their regular weekly transatlantic service, found themselves at risk. Cunard White Star Line's *Queen Mary* (81,000-tonnes) was withdrawn in September 1967. Sister ship *Queen Elizabeth*, at 83,673-tonnes the largest passenger liner ever built (until 1996), made her final crossing in October 1968 (I sailed the final voyage aboard this great ship).

Transatlantic shipping companies searched for new ways to employ their aging vessels, but few survived the fast growth of the jet aircraft. Ships were sold for a fraction of their value. Many lines went out of business and ships were scrapped. Those that survived attempted to mix transatlantic crossings with voyages south to the sun. The Caribbean (including the Bahamas) became appealing, cruising became an alternative, and an entire new industry was born, with new lines being formed exclusively for cruising.

Then came smaller, more specialized ships, capable of getting into the tiny ports of developing Caribbean islands (there were no commercial airlines taking vacationers to the Caribbean then, and few hotels), which were built to carry a sufficient number of passengers in a single class arrangement.

Instead of cruising long distances south from more northerly ports such as New York, companies established their headquarters in Florida. This not only avoided the cold weather, choppy seas, and expense of the northern ports but also saved fuel costs with shorter runs to the Caribbean. Cruising was reborn. California became the base for cruises to the Mexican Riviera, and Vancouver on Canada's west coast became the focus for summer cruises to Alaska.

Flying passengers to embarkation ports was the next logical step, and soon a working relationship emerged between the cruise lines and the airlines. Air/sea and "sail 'n' stay" packages thrived — joint cruise and hotel vacations with inclusive pricing. Cruising became an integrated part of tourism, with ships and hotels offering comfort and relaxation, and airlines providing quick access.

*Royal Caribbean International's **Voyager of the Seas** has a unique design.*

Some of the old liners came out of mothballs, purchased by emerging cruise lines and refurbished for warm-weather cruising operations, often with their interiors redesigned and refitted. During the late 1970s, the modern cruise industry grew at a rapid rate.

CRUISING TODAY

Today's cruise concept hasn't changed much from that of earlier days, although it has been improved, refined, expanded, and packaged for ease of consumption. No longer the domain of affluent, retired people, the industry today is vibrant and alive with passengers of every age and socio-economic background. Cruising is no longer the shipping business, but the hospitality industry (although some cruise ship staff appear to be in the hostility industry).

New ships are generally larger than their counterparts of yesteryear, yet cabin size has become "standardized" to provide more space for entertainment and other public facilities. Today's ships boast air conditioning to keep heat and humidity out; stabilizers to keep the ship on an even keel; a high level of maintenance, safety, and hygiene; and more emphasis on health and fitness facilities.

Cruise ship design has moved from the traditional, classic, rounded profiles of the past (example: *Queen Elizabeth 2*) to the extremely boxy shapes with squared-off sterns and towering super-structures today (example: *Millennium*). Although ship lovers lament these design changes, they have resulted from the need to fit as much as possible in the space provided (you can squeeze more in a square box than you can in a round one, although it may be less aesthetically appealing). Form follows function, and ships have changed from ocean transportation to giant floating vacation resorts.

Although ships have long been devoted to eating and relaxation in comfort (promulgating the maxim "Traveling slowly unwinds you faster"), ships today offer more activities, and more learning and life-enriching experiences than before. And there are many more places you can visit on a cruise: from Antarctica to Acapulco, Bermuda to Bergen, Dakar to Dominica, Shanghai to St. Thomas, or if you prefer, perhaps nowhere at all.

The cruise industry is a $15-billion business worldwide and growing. It provides employment to a growing number, both directly (there are over 100,000 shipboard officers, staff, and crew, as well as about 15,000 employees in cruise company offices), and indirectly (suppliers of foodstuffs and mechanical and electrical parts, port agents, transport companies, destinations, airlines, railways, hotels, car rental companies).

In 2000, more than 10 million people worldwide took a cruise, packaged and sold by cruise lines through tour operators and travel agents. The most recent (2000) breakdown of passengers by nationality choosing to take an oceangoing cruise vacation is provided below (taken from figures supplied by the Maritime Evaluations Group):

United States	6,900,000
UK*	800,000
Asia (not including Japan)	800,000
Germany	283,000
Canada	300,000
Italy	250,000
Australasia	200,000
Japan	200,000
France	223,000
Rest of Europe	250,000
Cyprus**	75,000
Freighter Passengers	3,000
TOTAL	**10,284,000**

*This figure includes 120,000 British passengers who took a two- to seven-day cruise from Cyprus in conjunction with a resort/hotel stay.
**Local Cyprus market.
Note: The above numbers do not include river cruise passengers.

CONSTRUCTING A MODERN CRUISE SHIP

More than any other type of vessel, a cruise ship has to fulfill fantasies and satisfy exotic imaginations. It is the job of the shipyard to take those fantasies and turn them into a steel ship without unduly straining the laws of naval architecture and safety regulations, not to mention budgets.

Although no perfect cruise ship exists, turning owners' dreams and concepts into ships that embody those ideals is the job of specialized marine architects and shipyards, as well as consultants, interior designers, and a mass of specialist suppliers. Computers have simplified this complex process, although shipboard management and operations personnel often become frustrated with designers who are more idealistic than they are practical. Ships represent a compromise between ideals and restrictions of space and finance, the solution being to design ships for specific areas and conditions of service.

Ships used to be constructed in huge building docks, from the keel (backbone) up. Today, ships are built in huge sections, then joined together in an assembly area (as many as fifty or more sections for a large ship). The sections may not even be constructed in the shipyard, but they will be assembled there.

Formerly, passenger spaces were slotted in wherever there was space within a given hull. Today, computers provide highly targeted ship design, enabling a new ship to be built within two years instead of within the four or five years it took in the 1950s.

The maximum noise and vibration levels allowable in the accommodation spaces and recreational areas are stipulated in any owner's contract with the shipyard. Vibration tests are carried out once a ship is built and launched, using a finite method element of evaluation; this embraces analyses of prime sources of noise and excitation, namely the ship's propellers and main engines.

Prefabricated cabin modules, including *in situ* bathrooms complete with toilets and all plumbing, are used today. When the steel structure of the relevant deck is ready, with main lines and insulation installed, cabin modules are then affixed to the deck, and power lines and sanitary plumbing are swiftly connected. All waste and power connections, together with hot/cold water mixing valves, are arranged in the service area of the bathroom and can be reached from the passageway outside the cabin for maintenance.

CRUISING TOMORROW

Current thinking in ship design follows two distinct paths: large ships or smaller ships.

→ Large ships, where the "economy of scale" helps the operator to keep the cost per passengers down. Three companies (Carnival Cruise Lines, Princess Cruises, and Royal Caribbean International) have ships measuring over 100,000 tonnes, capable of carrying over 3,000 passengers, with the "bigger is better" principle being pursued for all it's worth. These ships are, however, limited to the Caribbean, being too wide to transit the Panama Canal (non-Panamax).

→ On small ships, where the "small is exclusive" concept has gained a strong foothold, particularly in the luxury category. Cruise lines offer high-quality ships of low capacity, which can provide a highly personalized range of quality services.

Other cruise lines have expanded by "stretching" their ships. This is accomplished literally by cutting a ship in half, and inserting a newly constructed midsection, thus instantly increasing capacity, adding more accommodation and public rooms, while maintaining the same draft. "Stretched" ships include: *Black Watch* (ex-*Royal Viking Star*), *Carousel* (ex-*Nordic Prince*), *Costa Classica*, *Norwegian Dream* (ex-*Dreamward*), *Norwegian Majesty* (ex-*Royal Majesty*), *Norwegian Star* (ex-*Royal Viking Sea*), *Norwegian Wind* (ex-*Windward*), *Sundream* (ex-*Song of Norway*), and *Westerdam* (ex-*Homeric*).

Whatever direction the design of cruise vessels takes in the future, ships are becoming increasingly environmentally friendly. With growing concern, particularly in eco-sensitive areas such as Alaska and the South Pacific, better safeguards against environmental pollution and damage are being built into the vessels.

The cruise industry is fast approaching "zero discharge," whereby nothing is discharged into the world's oceans at any time. This is an easier objective to attain for the latest batch of ships, while older ships have a more difficult time achieving zero discharge due to outdated equipment.

Relax by the pool aboard **SuperStar Virgo** *(Star Cruises).*

CHOOSING YOUR SHIP AND CRUISE

So, you've decided your next vacation will be a cruise. Good choice! But the decisions do not stop there. Bombarded with glossy cruise literature tempting you with every imaginable lure and overly prolific use of the phrases "five-star luxury," "gourmet dining," and "fabulous destinations," selecting the right ship can be a chore.

There are different ships to suit different needs. Despite constant cruise company claims that theirs has been named the "Best Cruise Line" or "Best Cruise Ship," *there really is no such thing* — only what's good, and right, for you.

Most shipowners want to be a "luxury" cruise operator, and most passengers want to sail aboard one of the top-rated "luxury" ships. But few operators can deliver a five-star ship, product, and crew.

WHAT A CRUISE IS

A cruise is a vacation. It is an antidote to (and escape from) the stress and strain of life ashore. It offers you a chance to relax and unwind in comfortable surroundings, with attentive service, good food, and a ship that changes the scenery for you. It is virtually a hassle-free and, more importantly, a crime-free vacation. You never have to make blind choices. Everything's close at hand, and there are always polite people to help you.

WHAT A CRUISE IS NOT

Some cruises simply aren't relaxing, despite cruise brochures proclaiming that "you can do as much or as little as you want to." For example, large ships that carry 3,000 or more passengers tend to cram lots of passengers into small cabins and provide nonstop activities that do little but insult the intelligence and assault the wallet.

Price is, of course, the key factor for most people. The cost of a cruise provides a useful guideline to the ambience, type of passengers, and degree of luxury, food, and service that you will likely find on board.

The amount you are prepared to spend will determine the size, location, and style of shipboard accommodation you get. Be wary of cruise lines that offer huge discounts — it either means that the product was unrealistically priced at source or that there will be a reduction in quality somewhere. Ships are as individual as fingerprints: each one can change its "personality" from cruise to cruise, depending on the character of the passengers (and crew).

Passengers encompass all types of personalities and lifestyles, from affluent, reserved, and mature to active, athletic, fun-loving, and youthful, family-oriented, conservation-minded, adventurous, or wild fun seekers. They may be well traveled, or honeymooners on their first cruise, or veteran passengers who cruise several times a year.

HOW LONG?

The standard of luxury, comfort, and service is generally in direct proportion to the length of the cruise. To operate long, low-density voyages, cruise lines must charge high rates to cover the extensive preparations, high food and transportation costs, port operations, fuel, and other expenditures. The length of cruise you choose will depend on the time and money at your disposal and the degree of comfort you are seeking.

The popular standard length of a cruise is seven days, although cruises can vary from two-day party cruises to a slow exotic voyage around the world of up to 180 days. If you are new to cruising and want to "get your feet wet," try a short cruise first.

WHICH SHIP?

Because cruise ships can be self-sufficient resorts, there really is a cruise line, cruise, and ship to suit virtually all tastes, so it is important to take into account your own personality and vacation requirements when selecting a ship.

Ships are measured (not weighed) in gross register tons (grt) and come in three principal size categories, as follows:

Small Ships: for up to 500 passengers (typically measure 2,000–25,000 tons)

Mid-Size Ships: for 500–1,000 passengers (typically measure 25,000–50,000 tons)

Large Ships: for over 1,000 passengers (typically measure 50,000–150,000 tons)

Ships in the harbor at St. Thomas, US Virgin Islands.

Whatever the physical dimensions, all cruise ships provide the same basic ingredients: accommodation, activities, entertainment, plenty of food, good service, and ports of call. However, some do it much better than others (and charge more, accordingly).

SPACE
To get an idea of the amount of the space around you, look at the Passenger Space Ratio given for each ship in Part Two (tonnage divided by number of passengers).

Passenger Space Ratio:
→ 50 and above — the ultimate
→ 30 to 50 — very spacious
→ 20 to 30 — reasonably spacious
→ 10 to 20 — moderate to high density
→ 10 or below — extremely cramped

SMALL SHIPS (UP TO 500 PASSENGERS)
Choose a small ship for an intimate cruise experience and a small number of passengers. Some of the most exclusive cruise ships in the world belong in this group (but so do most of the coastal vessels with basic, unpretentious amenities, sail-cruise ships, and the expedition-style cruise vessels that take passengers to see nature).

Choose this size ship if you do not need much entertainment, large ship facilities, gambling casinos, or several restaurants — also if you do not like to wait in lines for anything. If you want to swim in the late evening, or have champagne in the Jacuzzi at midnight, it is easier aboard small ships than aboard larger ships, where more rigid programs provide the kind of inflexible schedules that passengers detest.

Small Ships: Advantages
→ More like small inns than mega-resorts.
→ Easy to find your way around, and signage is usually clear and concise.
→ At their best in warm weather areas.

29

→ Capable of truly catering to the highest degree of culinary excellence, with fresh foods cooked individually to order.

→ Most provide an "open seating" in the dining room; this means that you can sit with whomever you wish, whenever you wish, for all meals.

→ Provide a totally unstructured lifestyle, offering a level of service not found aboard most of the larger ships, and no or almost no announcements.

→ Provide an "open bridge" policy, allowing passengers to go to the navigational bridge at almost any time (except during difficult maneuvers and in cases of difficult weather conditions).

→ Some small ships have a hydraulic marina water sports platform located at the stern and carry equipment such as jet skis, Windsurfers, a water ski powerboat, and scuba and snorkeling gear.

→ When the ship is at anchor, going ashore is easy and speedy, with a continuous tender service.

Small Ships: Disadvantages

→ Do not have the bulk, length, or beam to sail well in open seas in inclement weather conditions.

→ Do not have the range of public rooms or open spaces that large ships can provide. Options for entertainment, therefore, are limited.

MID-SIZE SHIPS (500–1,000 PASSENGERS)

Choose a mid-size ship if you want to be among up to 1,000 passengers. They are well suited to the smaller ports of the Aegean and Mediterranean, and are more maneuverable than larger ships. Several of these ships operate around-the-world cruises and other long-distance cruising itineraries to exotic destinations not really feasible aboard many of the ships in the small or large ship categories.

There is a big difference in the amount of space available. Cabins vary from large "penthouse suites" complete with butler service to tiny inside cabins.

These ships will generally be more stable at sea than those in the "small ships" category, due to their increased size and draft. They provide more facilities, more entertainment, and more dining options. There is some entertainment, and more structured activities than small ships, but less than large ships.

Mid-Size Ships: Advantages

→ They are neither too large, nor too small, but often strike a happy balance in terms of size and facilities.

→ It is an easy matter to find one's way around.

→ They generally sail well in areas of inclement weather, being neither high-sided like the large ships, nor too shallow draft like some of the small ships.

→ Lines seldom form (except for ships that are approaching 1,000 passengers), but if they do, they are likely to be short.

→ They appear more like traditional ships than most of the larger vessels, which tend to be more "boxy" in shape and profile.

Mid-Size Ships: Disadvantages

→ They do not offer as wide a range of public rooms and facilities as do large ships.

→ Few have large show lounges for large-scale production shows; hence entertainment tends to be more of the cabaret variety.

LARGE SHIPS (1,000–2,000 PASSENGERS)

Choose a large ship if you enjoy being with lots of other people, in a large-scale city environment, and you are out to have a good time. If you are sociable and like to experience plenty of entertainment and dining (no, make that eating) options, these ships will provide a well packaged standard or premium cruise vacation experience, usually in a seven-day cruise. Aboard large cruise ships, it is the interaction between passengers and crew that will determine a good, or not-so-good, or completely indifferent cruise experience.

Large ships have extensive facilities and programs for families with children of all ages. But if you meet someone on the first day and want to meet them again, make sure you appoint a place and time, or you may not see them again (apart from the size of the ship, they may be at a different meal seating). These ships have a highly structured array of activities and passenger participation events each day, together with large entertainment venues, and the most lavish production shows at sea.

It is in the standard of service, entertainment, lecture programs, level of communication, and finesse in dining services that really can move these ships into high rating categories, but they must be exceptional to do so. Choose higher-priced suite accommodation and you get better service levels than lower-grade accommodation.

Large ships are run on a highly programmed basis. It is difficult, for example, to go swimming in the late evening or after dinner (decks are cleaned and pools are often netted over by 6pm — too early). Having champagne delivered to outdoor hot tubs late at night is virtually impossible. Large ships have lost the flexibility for which cruise ships were once known, and have become victims of company "policy" legislation and insurance regulations. So many large ship passengers feel they are participants in "conveyor-belt" cruising.

Choose a large ship if you enjoy being with lots of other people, in a large-scale city environment, out to have a good time. If you are sociable, and like to experience plenty of entertainment and dining options, these ships will certainly provide a well-packaged standard or premium cruise vacation experience, usually in a seven-day cruise.

These ships have extensive facilities and programs for families with children of all ages. But if you meet someone on the first day and want to meet them again, make sure you appoint a place and time, or you may not see them again (apart from the size of the ship, they may be at a different meal seating). These ships have a highly structured array of activities and passenger participation events each day, together with large entertainment venues, and the most lavish production shows at sea.

It is in the standard of service, entertainment, lecture programs, level of communication, and finesse in dining services that really can move these ships into high rating categories, but they must be exceptional to do so. Choose higher-priced suite accommodation and you get better service levels than lower-grade accommodation.

Large ships are run on a highly programmed basis. It is difficult, for example, to go swimming in the late evening, or after dinner (decks are cleaned and pools are netted over by 6:00pm — too early). Having champagne delivered to outdoor hot tubs late at night is virtually impossible. Large ships have lost the flexibility for which cruise ships were once known, and have become victims of company "policy" legislation and insurance regulations. So many large ship passengers feel they are participants in "conveyor-belt" cruising.

Large Ships: Advantages

→ Have the widest range of public rooms and facilities, often a wraparound promenade deck outdoors, and more space (but more passengers).
→ Generally better flexibility in dining options.
→ The newest ships have state-of-the-art electronic interactive entertainment facilities and options (good for those into computers and high-tech gadgetry).
→ Generally sail well in open seas in inclement weather conditions.
→ There are more facilities and activities for people of all ages, particularly designed for families with children.

Large Ships: Disadvantages

→ Trying to find your way around the ship can prove frustrating.
→ There are probably lines to wait in: for embarkation, the purser's office (information desk), elevators, informal buffet meals, fast food grills, shore tenders, shore excursions, immigration, and disembarkation.
→ They resemble floating hotels (but with constant announcements), and so many items cost extra. Actually, they are more like retail parks surrounded by cabins.
→ Signage is often confusing; there will be a lack of elevators at peak times.
→ The larger the ship, the more impersonal the service (unless you have "butler" service in a penthouse suite).
→ You will probably have to use a sign-up sheet to use gymnasium equipment such as treadmills or exercise bicycles.
→ There are too many announcements (they could be in several languages).
→ Dining room staff is so programmed to provide speedy service, it is almost impossible to sit and dine in leisurely fashion.
→ Food may well be rather bland (cooking for 2,000 is not quite the same as cooking for a little dinner party of twenty).
→ Telephoning room service can be frustrating, particularly in those ships with automatic telephone answering systems that state "your call will be answered by room service personnel in the order it was received."

Courtesy Douglas Ward

*The classic design of **Queen Elizabeth 2** (Cunard Line).*

→ Room service breakfast is not generally available on the day of disembarkation.
→ Swimming pools are often closed in the early evening; some take the deck chairs away, or strap them up so they can't be used.
→ The in-cabin music aboard the latest batch of ships is supplied through the television set, and it may be impossible to turn off the picture (so much for quiet, romantic late-night music, and darkened cabins).
→ When the ship is at anchor, you will need to stand in line, or wait in a lounge, for a "tender ticket" — then wait until your ticket number is called — to go ashore by ship-to-shore craft. This can take an hour or more! Getting back on board could take some time, too, and you could be standing out in the hot sun for a long time.
→ Some large ships have only two main staircases. In the event of an emergency, the evacuation of more than 2,000 passengers could prove difficult.

THE BIG EIGHT CRUISE LINES

All eight offer one thing: a well-packaged cruise (generally of seven days) that includes interesting itineraries, plenty of food, reasonable service, and a good selection of entertainment and production shows (mostly by the use of technical effects and great lighting). The ships also provide large casinos, shopping malls, and extensive spa and fitness facilities. Most ask you to pay port taxes, insurance, gratuities to staff over and above the cruise fare, and for many additional items.

The lines differ in the facilities, space, food, and service featured, together with subtle differences in the delivery of the cruise product. Here are some of the positive and negative differences among the Big Eight cruise lines. Note that changes, upgrading and downgrading of products and services, may have occurred since this book was completed.

Carnival Cruise Lines

This is the largest and most successful cruise line in the world. It specializes in cruises for the young at heart, with plenty of upbeat music, and passenger participation games typically found in an adult summer camp atmosphere. While some of the activities could be taken to be potentially degrading, they are nevertheless well liked by passengers who associate such activities with "fun," the line's theme. All the ships have incredibly imaginative multicolored, very upbeat decor (each ship has its own decor theme).

32

Carnival does not try to sell itself as an "upmarket" cruise line and consistently delivers exactly what its brochures say, for which there is a huge, growing first-time cruise audience. However, the company provides a well-packaged cruise vacation, with smart new ships that have the latest high-tech entertainment facilities and features. Shore excursions are booked via in-cabin ("Fun Vision") television systems.

With almost identical large ships, the company does a fine job of providing almost nonstop activities. If you do not mind drinks in plastic glasses (on deck) and basic hamburger/hot dog and other fast foods in abundance, this line provides them almost round-the-clock (pizzas are available 24 hours a day). The company provides excellent "dazzle and sizzle" production shows and a lot of nighttime entertainment options for party people, as well as some excellent children's programming (ideal for young families).

Carnival features "Total Choice" dining aboard all its ships — you choose any of four seating times for dinner (5:45pm; 6:30pm; 8pm; and 8:45pm — note that this gives you just 45 minutes to "dine")! Although the menu choice looks good, the actual cuisine delivered is quite non-memorable. But if you like pizzas, the largest ships in the fleet serve an average of 800 pizzas per day, so it should give you some idea of what passengers can expect from their dining experience. All ships also have a serve-yourself casual Lido Buffet — for breakfast, lunch and dinner — so you don't need to dress to go to the formal dining rooms.

The cabins throughout the fleet are a decent size. Carnival will help you have fun all the way, but do not expect the finesse or attentition to small details you might find with some of the lesser-known lines. Major sources of passenger complaints include embarkation and disembarkation (shore-side staff), and the large number of security staff aboard ship (these complaints are also true of Royal Caribbean International).

The company has grown dramatically over the last few years and has improved its product substantially. In 1996, the company introduced a "Vacation Guarantee" program (the first of its kind in the industry) to great success, particularly for first-time passengers who do not know whether they will enjoy cruising (few passengers ever consider leaving the cruise).

Celebrity Cruises

Celebrity Cruises has established an outstanding reputation for its cuisine, particularly in the dining rooms, with their formal service. All meals are made from scratch, and no pre-packaged, boxed, or pre-prepared items are used at all, which is an admirable achievement, and different from all others in the Big Eight group. The sauces accompanying the main dishes, in particular, are excellent. Thus, there is a good degree of taste that is often lacking aboard the larger, standard market ships of today. The waiters (many of them from Eastern European countries) are well trained and it is generally easy to communicate with them. There are several tables for two in the dining room, although dining room chairs do not have armrests and would be more comfortable with them.

Another reason this line provides a high-quality cruise experience is the fact that each ship simply has much more staff than other ships of comparable size and passenger number. This is particularly noticeable in the housekeeping and food and beverage departments. As a result, the line delivers passengers with a superior product. The artwork in the latest ships in the fleet is also rather stunning, and comprises what is probably the most attractive collection of contemporary art in the cruise industry today.

Two ships in its present six-ship fleet (*Horizon* and *Zenith*) have complete wraparound teak promenade decks, while *Century*, *Galaxy*, *Infinity*, *Mercury*, *Millennium*, and *Summit* do not. The ships are always spotlessly clean, and constant vacuuming and polishing take place around the clock. There are more cleaners and service personnel aboard Celebrity Cruises' ships (per passenger) than in any of the other Big Eight cruise lines. In fact, there are more crew members per passenger than aboard any of the others in the Big Eight cruise lines. It is the line's commitment to providing a superior product that fully justifies the additional expenditure on all the details and staff necessary.

At present, the high standards established by Celebrity Cruises are to be continued under new owner Royal Caribbean International. At present, however, the standard of food and its delivery remain the very best of any of the Big Eight cruise lines.

Costa Cruises

This company specializes in cruises for Europeans (or passengers with European tastes), and particularly Italians (during the summer European season). The ships have a definite European "feel" to them, in their decor and manner of product delivery, which is very laid back.

33

The food is really standard hotel banquet fare, disappointing and non-memorable, as is the service, which displays little or no finesse (it is hard to find an Italian waiter anywhere — something the company was once known for). The company does, however, present good Italian pasta dishes, which are always popular, and, on formal nights, dining by candlelight. But there are no wine waiters! The self-serve buffets are particularly poor and arguably the worst of all the Big Eight.

The cabins tend to be on the mean side in size, but the decor is fresh and upbeat, and the bathrooms are very practical units (some ships have sliding doors), an excellent alternative to those that open inward, taking space from the bathroom).

What is good is the variety of public rooms, lounges, and bars, many of which provide fairly intimate spaces. The entertainment and shows are geared toward the international passengers found aboard almost any ship in the fleet. Costa Cruises is the only company to have a chapel aboard each of its ships, with Roman Catholic Mass featured daily. Carnival Corporation, parent company of Costa Cruises, purchased part of the company in 1997, and the rest in 2000.

Holland America Line
This line features teakwood outdoor promenade decks fleet-wide, whereas most other cruise lines feature artificial grass or some other form of indoor-outdoor carpeting. The ships are very clean and well maintained.

The food is adequate, though not memorable, but the food quality, presentation, and service have become very standardized in recent years, and ingredients are mostly from pre-packaged goods, although the menu variety looks reasonable. Dining room service is too fast but provided by friendly, almost always-smiling Indonesian waiters whose communication skills leave much to be desired. The company does, however, offer cappuccino and espresso coffees, and free ice cream during certain hours of the day aboard its ships, as well as hot hors d'oeuvres in all bars — something other major lines seem to have dropped, or charge extra for.

When it comes to buffets, there are more canned fruits (liked by many older passengers because they are soft) used by this line than by Celebrity Cruises or Princess Cruises, but about the same amount as found aboard the ships of Costa Cruises or Norwegian Cruise Line.

The company's claim to "five-star" ships in its brochures is erroneous and misleading. The ships are extremely pleasant and have an elegant "feel" to them, with some fine, somewhat eclectic artwork from the Dutch East and West Indies. What is excellent is the fact that social dancing is always on the menu. This is something that older passengers, in particular, enjoy. However, communication with many of the smiling staff can prove frustrating, and passenger care (for which Holland America Line used to be well known) has now become quite mediocre.

The suites and cabins are of good proportions, and come nicely equipped. They are quite comfortable, and Holland America Line also provides a good array of personal toiletry amenities. An additional bonus item is a canvas tote bag provided for all passengers, which is a nice extra and useful for shopping or for going to the beach.

Carnival Corporation, the parent company of Carnival Cruise Lines, wholly owns Holland America Line.

Norwegian Cruise Line
This line provides a good product for a youthful, active, sports-minded audience. Most of the staff is from the Caribbean basin, and, in general, do not have the finesse of those ships that have a greater percentage of European staff. The cabins are reasonably attractive and functional, although closet and drawer space is very limited in the newest ships.

NCL now features freestyle dining, whereby you turn up and a table will be found for you — so you can change tables every night, and dine with whom you want (not available in all restaurants in all ships)! Dining room cuisine is generally not memorable, however, but lighter fare is available in a "bistro" setting aboard all ships in the fleet for those that want to "eat and run" and not bother with the more formal dining room setting. Sports fans will find sports bars and memorabilia aboard these ships — good for those young-at-heart fans and devotees.

As for entertainment, the production shows are of the colorful, well-choreographed, slightly belittling, noisy, high-energy type. Norwegian Cruise Line was purchased in 2000 by Star Cruises.

Princess Cruises
Despite billing itself as "The Love Boat," Princess Cruises has only a few tables for two in the dining rooms of *Dawn Princess*, *Grand Princess*, *Ocean Princess*, *Sea Princess*, and *Sun Princess*.

Princess Cruises was once known for its good dining room food but today it is very much run-of-the-mill fare and quite non-memorable. Sadly, there are no longer any wine waiters in the dining room, and the table waiters are now expected to serve wine. However, the casual dining options have become much improved, particularly in the Horizon Court, although plastic plates are used.

Princess Cruises has also introduced freestyle dining, where you turn up and a table will be found for you (not available in all restaurants in all ships), so you can change tables every night, and dine with whom you want!

The cabins are generally of generous proportions (exceptions: *Dawn Princess*, *Sea Princess*, and *Sun Princess*) and are reasonably well designed. They are well- equipped and comfortable, with warm decor and practical bathrooms. All ships have Filipino cabin staff (there are exceptions) and some European staff in front-line service areas.

The company's Shore Excursion Program is arguably the best run of any of the Big Eight companies. Entertainment tends to be very traditional, with a mix of elegant production shows and the usual cabaret acts, but volume levels often increase beyond bearable. The company now charges for so many extra items that the product has, like that of other large lines, turned into almost all-exclusive cruising. The UK-based P&O Group, which also owns Aida Cruises, P&O Cruises, and P&O Cruises (Australia), wholly owns Princess Cruises.

Royal Caribbean International

Brilliance of the Seas, *Enchantment of the Seas*, *Grandeur of the Seas*, *Legend of the Seas*, *Radiance of the Seas*, *Rhapsody of the Seas*, *Splendour of the Seas*, and *Vision of the Seas* have slightly larger cabins than in the older ships *Majesty of the Seas*, *Monarch of the Seas*, and *Sovereign of the Seas*.

The company places more emphasis than most on passenger participation activities, such as Art Auctions, Passenger Talent Show, Masquerade Parade, Country & Western Jamboree, and so on. It is all very predictable, and the same programming is featured aboard all its ships, because it is tried, tested, and proven, if perhaps a little "old hat" by now.

Although Royal Caribbean International's food is of approximately the same standard as that aboard Carnival Cruise Line ships, Carnival's ships have larger cabins, as do the ships of Celebrity Cruises, Holland America Line, and Princess Cruises. French, Italian, Oriental, Caribbean, and American are the main themes for the menus for different nights. Wine lovers should note that there are no vintages on the wine lists (because they are all so young).

The ships are shapely, with well-rounded sterns, and interesting design profiles that make them instantly recognizable. Most ships feature a trademark Viking Crown Lounge, set around the funnel stack, either in front of it or part way up it. Large, brightly lit casinos are provided, as are shopping galleries that passengers have to walk through in order to get almost anywhere else. It is all cleverly designed to extract maximum revenue from you — in a nice way, of course.

Royal Caribbean International also owns Celebrity Cruises, although the two brands are thankfully kept separate as far as the onboard product (particularly the food and service) is concerned.

Star Cruises

The company, established in 1994, has a diverse fleet of ships and caters to many nationalities and types of passengers, but markets principally to Australians, Europeans (particularly British and German), Indians, and Southeast Asians. Star Cruises operates in the Pan-Asia region.

Since its inception as an operator of ships primarily for casino gaming, the company has partly made the transition into a "normal" cruise line (although casino gaming remains an important part of the entertainment facilities). The intention is to have twelve ships, one for each sign of the zodiac. Passengers book in one of two classes: "Balcony Class" and "Non-Balcony Class."

Star Pisces operates short cruises for serious casino players, while *MegaStar Aries*, and *MegaStar Capricorn* are two small and finely outfitted luxury ships for VIP club members, private charters, and for testing new routes (and are thus not suitable for inclusion in this book).

The purpose-built new, large ships *SuperStar Leo* and *SuperStar Virgo* (which have many restaurants and dining spots and more entertainment for the company's activity-oriented Asian vacationers) are all fine cruise ships.

Star Cruises is the only cruise line to have its own simulator center, an outstanding training facility for its Scandinavian navigation officers. Star Cruises' parent company, Genting Berhad, owns a string of land-based resorts and hotels, huge tracts of land for development, and other interests including entertainment, aviation, power stations, oil and gas units, and rubber and palm oil plantations.

This cruise line is young, but is now the third largest cruise company in the world (Star Cruises

THE BIG EIGHT CRUISE LINES

A look at this chart shows just what cruise lines do (or do not) provide in your cabin and bathroom

Cruise line	Carnival Cruise Lines		Celebrity Cruises		Costa Cruises	
	Standard Cabins	Suites	Standard Cabins	Suites	Cabins	Suites
CABIN						
Bed Linen: Duvets (not sheets/blankets)	No	No	No	Yes	No	No
Bed Linen: 100% Cotton	No	No	No	No	Yes	Yes
Bed Linen: 50% Cotton/50% Polyester	Yes	Yes	Yes	Yes	No	No
Pillowcases: 100% Cotton	No	No	No	No	No	No
Towels: 100% Cotton	No	No	Yes	Yes	Yes	Yes
Towels: 86% Cotton/14% Polyester	Yes	Yes	No	No	No	No
Non-Allergenic Pillows	No	No	No	No	Yes (2)	Yes (2)
Fresh Fruit Bowl	No	No	No	Yes	Yes (2)	Yes (2)
Fresh Flowers	No	No	No	Yes	Yes (2)	Yes (2)
Telephone	Yes	Yes	Yes	Yes	Yes	Yes
Personal Safe	Yes	Yes	Yes	Yes	Yes	Yes
Personalized Stationery	No	No	No	Yes	No	No
Television	Yes	Yes	Yes	Yes	Yes	Yes
VCR Player	No	Yes	No	Yes	No	No
CD Player	No	No	No	Yes (7)	No	No
Shoe Shine	No	No	No	Yes	Yes	Yes
Continental Breakfast	Yes	Yes	Yes	Yes	Yes	Yes
Full In-Cabin Breakfast/Lunch/Dinner Service	No	No	Yes	Yes	No	Yes
Complimentary Espresso/Cappuccino Coffees	Yes	Yes	No	Yes	No	No
Free Local Newspaper in Port (when available)	No	No	No	Yes	No	No
Complimentary Pressing Service (First 24 Hours)	No	No	No	Yes	No	Yes
CABIN BATHROOM						
Real Glasses in Bathroom	Yes	Yes	Yes	Yes	Yes	Yes
Plastic Glasses in Bathroom	No	No	No	No	No	No
Soap/Shampoo Dispenser Unit	No	No	No	No	Yes (3)	Yes (3)
Soap	Yes	Yes	Yes	Yes	Yes	Yes
Shampoo	No	No	No	No	Yes	Yes
Conditioner	No	No	No	No	Yes	Yes
Combined Shampoo/Conditioner	Yes	Yes	Yes	Yes	No	No
Foaming Bath Oil	No	No	No	Yes	No	No
Hand Lotion	No	Yes	Yes	Yes	Yes	Yes
Mouthwash	No	No	No	Yes	No	No
Shower Cap	No	No	No	Yes	Yes	Yes
Loofah Sponge	No	No	No	Yes	No	No
Hair dryer	Yes (8)	Yes (8)	Yes	Yes	Yes	Yes
Weight Scale	No	No	No	Yes	No	No
Bathrobes	Yes (9)	Yes	No	Yes	No	Yes
Shaving/Make-Up Mirror	No	No	No	Yes	No	No

KEY

(1) = Selected suites only

(2) = On request only

(3) = In the shower unit only : *Costa Victoria*

(4) = On back-to-back cruises only (turnaround day)

(5) = Deluxe cabins only

(6) = Royal Suite only

(7) = Penthouse Suite only

(8) = *Carnival Destiny, Carnival Triumph, Carnival*

Holland America Line		Norwegian Cruise Line		Princess Cruises		Royal Caribbean International		Star Cruises (10)	
Standard Cabins	Suites	Standard Cabins	Suites	Standard Cabins	Suites	Standard Cabins	Suites	Standard Cabins	Suites (Balcony Class)
No	No	No	No	No	No	No	No	Yes	No
No	No	On request	On request	No	No	Yes (11)	No	Yes	Yes
Yes	Yes	Yes	Yes	Yes	Yes	Yes	Yes	No	No
No	No	No	No	No	No	Yes (11)	No	Yes	Yes
No	No	Yes	Yes	Yes	Yes	Yes	Yes	Yes	Yes
Yes	Yes	No	No	No	No	No	No	No	No
No	No	No	No	Yes	Yes	Yes	Yes	No	No
Yes	Yes	Yes (2)	Yes	Yes	Yes	No	No	No	Yes
Yes	Yes	No	Yes	No	Yes	No	No	No	Yes
Yes	Yes	Yes	Yes	Yes	Yes	Yes	Yes	Yes	Yes
No	Yes	No	Yes	Yes	Yes	Yes	Yes	Yes	Yes
No	Yes	No	No	No	No	No	No	No	No
Yes	Yes	Yes	Yes	Yes	Yes	Yes	Yes	Yes	Yes
No	Yes	No	Yes (1)	No	No	No	Yes (6)	No	Yes
No	No	No	Yes (1)	No	No	No	Yes (6)	No	Yes
No	No	No	No	No	Yes	No	No	No	No
Yes	Yes	Yes	Yes	Yes	Yes	Yes	Yes	No	Yes
Yes	Yes	Yes	Yes	Yes	Yes	Yes	Yes	No	No
No	No	No	No	No	No	No	No	No	Yes
No	No	No	No	Yes (4)	Yes (4)	No	No	No	Yes (2)
No	Yes	No	No	No	No	No	No		
Yes	Yes	Yes	Yes	Yes	Yes	Yes	Yes	Yes	Yes
No	No	No	No	No	No	No	No	No	No
No	No	No	No	No	No	No	No	No	No
Yes	Yes	Yes	Yes	Yes	Yes	Yes	Yes	Yes	Yes
No	No	No	No	Yes	Yes	Yes	Yes	No	Yes
No	No	No	No	Yes	Yes	No	Yes (5)	No	Yes
Yes	No	Yes	Yes	No	No	No	No	Yes	No
No	Yes	No	Yes (1)	No	No	No	No	No	Yes
Yes	Yes	Yes	Yes	Yes	Yes	No	Yes (5)	No	Yes
No	No	No	No	No	No	No	No	No	Yes
Yes	Yes	Yes	Yes	Yes (2)	Yes (2)	Yes	Yes	Yes	Yes
No	No	No	No	No	No	No	No	No	No
No	Yes	Yes	Yes	Yes	Yes	No	No	Yes	Yes
No	No	No	Yes (1)	No	No	No	No	No	Yes
No	Yes	No	Yes	Yes	Yes	No	Yes	No	Yes
No	No	No	No	No	No	No	No	No	Yes

(9) = All outside-view suites and cabins
(all ships)
(10) = *SuperStar Leo* and *SuperStar Virgo* only
(11) = *Brilliance of the Seas* and *Radiance of the Seas* only

wholly owns Norwegian Cruise Line and Orient Lines). Although service levels and finesse are inconsistent, and the company often moves its ships to different base ports and changes itineraries on short notice, the hospitality aboard the ships is very good, as is the choice of food available for many different ethnic nationalities.

New vs. Old Ships

A ship built before 1980 is considered old. Yet, many passengers like older ships. Although it is inevitable that some older tonnage cannot match the latest in high-tech ships, it should be noted that ships today are not constructed to the same high standards, or with the same loving care, as they were in the past.

New Ships: Advantages

→ Incorporate the latest in high-tech electronic equipment and the best in advanced ship design and construction.
→ Meet the latest safety and operating standards as laid down by the international maritime conventions.
→ Feature more public room space, with public rooms and lounges built out to the sides of the hull (enclosed promenade decks are no longer regarded as essential).
→ Offer more standardized cabin layouts and fewer categories.
→ Are more fuel-efficient.
→ Have a shallower draft, which makes it easier for them to enter and leave ports.
→ Have bow and stern thrusters, so they seldom require tug assistance in many ports, thus reducing operating costs.
→ Have plumbing and air-conditioning systems that are new and work.
→ Have diesel engines mounted on rubber to minimize vibration.
→ Are usually fitted with the latest submersible lifeboats.

New Ships: Disadvantages

→ Do not "take the weather" as well as older ships (the experience of sailing across the North Atlantic in November on one of the new large ships can be unforgettable). Because of their shallow draft, these ships roll, even when there is the slightest puff of wind.
→ Tend to have smaller standard cabins, which can mean narrow, short beds.
→ Have thin hulls and therefore do not withstand the bangs and dents as well as older, more heavily plated vessels.
→ Have decor made mostly from synthetic materials (due to stringent regulations) and, therefore, could cause problems for those passengers who are sensitive to such materials.
→ Have toilets of the powerful vacuum suction "barking dog" type.
→ Are powered mainly by diesel (or diesel-electric) engines, which inevitably cause some vibration; although on the latest vessels, the engines are mounted on pliable, floating rubber cushions and are, therefore, virtually vibration-free.
→ Have cabin windows that are completely sealed instead of portholes that can be opened.

Older Ships (pre-1970): Advantages

→ Have strong, plated hulls (often riveted) that can withstand tremendously hard wear and tear; they "take the weather" well.
→ Have large cabins with long, wide beds/berths, due to the fact that passengers of yesteryear needed more space, given that voyages were much longer.
→ Have a wide range of cabin sizes, shapes, and grades that are more suited to those families traveling with children.
→ Have toilets that are of the "gentle flush" variety instead of the powerful "barking dog" vacuum toilets found aboard newer ships.
→ Are powered by steam turbines, which are virtually free of vibration or noise and are considerably quieter and smoother in operation than modern vessels.
→ Have portholes that, in many instances, actually open.
→ Have interiors that are built from more traditional materials such as wood and brass, with less use of synthetic fibers (less likely to affect anyone who is allergic to synthetics).
→ Have deep drafts that help them to achieve a smooth ride in the open seas.

Older Ships (pre-1970): Advantages

→ Are not so fuel efficient and, therefore, are more expensive to operate than the new ships.

→ Need a larger crew, because of the more awkward, labor-intensive layouts of the ships.

→ Have a deep draft (necessary for a smooth ride) but need tugs to negotiate ports and tight berths.

→ Have increasing difficulty in complying with the current international fire, safety, and environmental regulations.

→ Are usually fitted with older-type open lifeboats.

→ Ten years or older are more likely to have plumbing and air-conditioning problems in cabins and public areas.

THE CREW

You can estimate the standard of service by looking at the crew-to-passenger ratio (provided in the ship profiles in Part Two). The best service levels are aboard ships that have a ratio of one crew member to every two passengers, or higher. The best ships in the world, from the point of view of crew living and working conditions, also tend to be the most expensive ones (the adage "you get what you pay for" tends to be true).

Most ships now have multinational crews, although there may be one or two exceptions. The crew mixture gives the impression of a ship being like a miniature United Nations. If the crew is happy, the ship will be happy, too, and passengers will sense it.

MAIDEN/INAUGURAL VOYAGES

There is an element of excitement in taking the maiden voyage of a new cruise ship, or in joining the inaugural voyage of a recently refurbished, reconstructed, or stretched vessel.

If you have a degree of tolerance and you are not bothered by some inconvenience, slow or nonexistent service in the dining room, fine; otherwise, wait until the ship has been in service for at least three months. Then again, if you book a cruise on the third or fourth voyage, and there is a delay in the ship's introduction, you could find yourself on the maiden voyage! One thing is certain — any maiden voyage is a collector's item, but Murphy's Law prevails: "If anything can go wrong, it will." For example:

→ A strike, fire, or shipyard bankruptcy are possible causes of delay to a new ship.

→ Service aboard new or recently refurbished ships (or a new cruise line) is likely to be uncertain at best and could be a complete disaster. An existing cruise line may use experienced crew from its other vessels to help "bring out" a new ship, but they may be unfamiliar with the ship's layout and may have problems training other staff.

→ Plumbing and electrical items tend to cause the most problems, particularly aboard reconstructed and refurbished vessels. Examples: toilets that do not flush or do not stop flushing; faucets incorrectly marked, where "hot" really means "cold"; room thermostats mistakenly fitted with reverse wiring; televisions, audio channels, lights, and electronic card key locks that do not work; electrical outlets incorrectly indicated; and "automatic" telephones that refuse to function.

→ The galley (kitchen) of a new ship causes perhaps the most consternation. Even if everything works and the executive chef has ordered the right supplies, they could be anywhere other than where they should be. Imagine if they forgot to load the seasoning, or if the eggs arrived shell-shocked!

→ "Software" items such as menus, postcards, writing paper, or remote control units for television and/or video systems, door keys, towels, pillowcases, glassware, and perhaps even toilet paper may be missing, lost in the bowels of the ship, or simply not ordered.

→ In the entertainment department, items such as spare spotlight bulbs may not be in stock. Or there may be no hooks in the dressing rooms to hang costumes on (many older ships do not even have dressing rooms). Or what if the pianos arrived damaged, or "flip" charts for the lecturers didn't show up? Manuals for high-tech sound and lighting equipment may be in a foreign language.

THEME CRUISES

If there's a theme, there's probably a cruise to suit. Each year, an ever richer variety of theme cruises is available, with many cultural, ecological, and educational subjects.

Typical theme cruise topics include: Adventure, Antiques, Archaeological, Art Lovers, Astronomy, Backgammon, Ballroom and Latin Dancing, Big Band, Blues Festival, Bridge, Chess Tournament, Chocoholics, Classical Music, Computer Science, Cosmetology, Country and Western, Diet and Nutrition, Educational, Exploration, Fashion, Film Festival, Food and Wine, Gardening, Holistic Health, Gay/Lesbian, Jazz Festival, Maiden Voyage, Movie Buffs, Murder Mystery, Naturist/Nude, Octoberfest, Ornithology (Bird Watching), Photography, Scottish Dancing, Sequence Dancing, Singles, Steamboat Race, Superbowl, Theatrical, and Wine Tasting.

SIGNS YOU'VE CHOSEN THE WRONG SHIP

➡ When, just after you've embarked, a waiter hands you a drink in a tall plastic glass from a whole tray of drinks of identical color and froth, then gives you a bill to sign without having the courtesy to say "Welcome Aboard."

➡ When the so-called "luxury" cabin you booked has walls so thin you can hear your neighbors combing their hair.

➡ When what the brochure describes as a "full bathtub" actually means "a large sink" located at floor level.

➡ When you wanted a quiet, restful cruise, but your travel agent booked you aboard a ship with 300 baseball fans and provided them all with signed baseball bats and boom boxes for their use on deck (solution: read this book thoroughly first)!

➡ When you packed your tuxedo, but other passengers take "formal" attire to mean clean cut-off jeans and a less stained T-shirt. Check the brochure carefully.

➡ When the "medical facility" is in fact located in the purser's office and consists of a box of adhesive bandages with directions for their use in a foreign language.

➡ When the gymnasium equipment is kept in the restaurant manager's office.

➡ When you have a cabin with an "obstructed view" (this will usually mean there is a lifeboat hanging outside it!), and it is next to or below the disco. Or the laundry. Or the garbage disposal facility. Or the anchor!

➡ When the "fresh selected greens" on the menu means a sprig of parsley on the entree plate, at every lunch and dinner seating (boring even on a three-day cruise).

➡ When the cruise director tries to sell passengers a watch, or a piece of art, over the ship's public address system.

➡ When front-row seats at a rock concert would be quieter than a poolside deck chair at midday.

➡ When you hear *Achy-Breaky Heart*, *Mary Ann*, the *Macarena*, or *Yellow Bird* ten times during the first day.

➡ When you have to buy shin pads to prevent injury from the 600 children that try to run you down in the passageways.

➡ When the cruise brochure shows your cabin with flowers and champagne, but you get neither. If you want them, you get a bill and the flowers will never be watered anyway.

➡ When the bottled water on your dining room table comes with a bill ever so quickly if you dare to open the bottle.

➡ When "fresh catch of the day" on the menu means that the fish is so old that it would be best used as a door stop.

➡ When the brochure says "Butler Service," but you have to clean your own shoes, get your own ice, and still tip twice the amount you would for an "ordinary" cabin steward.

➡ When the Beer Drinking or Hog Calling Contest, Knobby Knees Contest, and Pajama Bingo are listed as "enrichment lectures."

➡ When the "fresh-squeezed orange juice" you just ordered means fresh-squeezed, but last week, or the week before that, on land, and then poured into industrial-size containers, before transfer to your polystyrene plastic cup on deck.

➡ When the brochure says tipping is not required, but your waiter and cabin steward tell you otherwise and threaten they will break your kneecaps if you do not hand them something that approaches what to you is a large sum of money.

➡ When the cruise director thoughtfully telephones you at 2:30am to tell you that the bingo jackpot is up to $1000!

➡ When, on the final day, the words "early breakfast" means 5:00am, and "vacate your cabin by 7:30am" means you must spend about three hours sitting in the show lounge waiting for disembarkation, with 500 available seats, your hand luggage, and 2,000 other passengers, probably playing bingo.

→ When the Lifeboat Drill consists of a crew member who hands you a lifejacket and asks you to teach him how to wear it, and what the whistle is for.

→ When you are out on deck, you look up and notice a big hole in the bottom of one or more of the ship's lifeboats.

→ When the cabin steward tries to sell you a time-share in his uncle's coal mine in wherever he is from, at a greatly reduced price, or says you must go without soap and towels for a week.

→ When the proclaimed "five-course gourmet meal" in the dining room turns out to be four courses of salty chicken soup and a potato.

→ When the "Deck Buffet" literally means that there are no tables and chairs, only the deck, to eat off.

→ When the brochure shows photos of smiling young couples, but you and your spouse/partner are the only ones under 80.

→ When the library is located in the engine room.

→ When the captain tells you he is really a concert pianist and his diploma is for the piano, not navigation.

ACCOMMODATION

DID YOU KNOW...?

...that the first "en suite" rooms (with private bathroom in cabin) were on board Cunard Line's *Campania* of 1893?

...that the first liner to offer private terraces with their first-class suites was *Normandie* in 1935 (the Trouville Suite had four bedrooms as well as its own private terrace)?

...that the first single-berth cabins built as such were aboard Cunard Line's *Campania* of 1893?

...that the first ships to feature private balconies were the *Saturnia* and *Vulcania* in the early 1900s?

...that the first ship to be fitted with interior plumbing was the 6,283-ton *Normandie* of 1883?

...that the first ship to be fitted with an internal electric lighting system was aboard the Inman liner *City of Berlin* in 1879?

...that cruising today is not the same as it was in the nineteenth century? On the first cruise ships there was little entertainment, and passengers had to clean their own cabins! Orders enforced on all ships sailing from Great Britain in 1849, for example, instructed all passengers to be in their beds by 10pm!

You should feel at home when at sea, so it is important to choose the right accommodation for your needs. Like houses ashore, all cabins have good and not-so-good points. Choose wisely, for if you find your cabin (incorrectly called a "stateroom" by some companies) is too small when you get to the ship, it may be impossible to change it or to upgrade, as the ship could very well be completely full.

Cruise lines designate cabins only when deposits have been received (they may, however, guarantee the grade and rate requested). If this is not done automatically, or if you come across a disclaimer such as one spotted recently — "All cabin assignments are confirmed upon embarkation of the vessel" — get a guarantee in writing that your cabin will not be changed upon embarkation.

There are three main types of accommodation, but many variations on each theme:
- **Suites:** (the largest living spaces, typically with a private balcony); and "junior" suites (with or without private balcony)
- **Outside-view cabins**: a large picture window or one or more portholes (with or without private balcony)
- **Interior (no-view) cabins:** so called because there is no window or porthole, although there could be an inner "courtyard" view.

PRIVATE BALCONIES

Balconies are in. A private balcony (or "veranda" or "terrace") is just that. It is a balcony (or mini-terrace) adjoining your cabin where you can sit, enjoy the view, dine, or even have a massage or sex. These add another dimension to your home away from home. There's something very civilized (if slightly antisocial) about sitting on one's balcony sipping champagne, or having breakfast "a la deck" in some exotic place. It is also pleasant to get fresh air and to escape cold (air-conditioned) cabins. The value of a private balcony, for which you pay a premium, comes into its own in warm weather areas. One thing is almost certain: Once you have a private balcony, you'll be hooked. Balconies are like cruises. They are totally addictive! Indeed, some ships have enough private balconies for more than 800 budding Juliets to be wooed by their Romeos.

Some private balconies are not so private, however. Balconies not separated by full floor-to-ceiling partitions (examples: *Carnival Destiny*, *Carnival Triumph*, *Carnival Victory*, *Maasdam*, *Norway*, *Oriana*, *Ryndam*, *Seven Seas Mariner*, *Statendam*, and *Veendam*) don't quite cut it. You could get noise or smoke from your neighbor, but when all things are in your favor, a balcony is a wonderful extra. Some ships have balconies with full floor-to-ceiling privacy partitions and an outside light (examples: *Century*, *Galaxy*, *Mercury*, and *Radisson Diamond*). *Note*: Some partitions in Century, Galaxy, and Mercury are full, some are partial, depending on deck and location. Another downside of private balconies is that you cannot escape the loud music being played on the open swimming pool deck atop the ship — particularly annoying when "island night" goes on until the early morning hours and you just want to sit quietly on the balcony.

Some suites with forward-facing private balconies may not be so good, as the wind speed can make them all but unusable. And when the ship drops anchor in ports of call, the noise pollution can be deafening.

All private balconies have railings to lean on, but the balconies in some ships have solid steel plates between railing and deck, so you cannot look out to sea when you are seated (examples: *Costa Classica*, *Costa Romantica*, *Dawn Princess*, and *Sun Princess*). Better are those ships with balconies that have clear glass (examples: *Aurora*, *Brilliance of the Seas*, *Century*, *Galaxy*, *Mercury*, *Nordic Empress*, and *Radiance of the Seas*) or horizontal bars.

HOW MUCH?

→ The amount you pay for accommodation is directly related to the size of the cabin, its location, and the facilities and services provided.

→ There are no set standards, each line implementing its own system according to ship size, age, construction, and profit potential.

→ Most cruise lines *do not* give cabin sizes in their brochures, but you will find the size range in the ship profiles in Part Two of this book.

→ If this is your first cruise, choose the most expensive cabin you can afford. If it is too small (and most cabins are small), the cruise might fall short of your expectations.

→ It is arguably better to book a low-grade cabin on a good ship than book a high-grade cabin on a poor ship.

Courtesy Douglas Ward

A selection of personal amenities is provided in top suite accommodations.

➜ If you are in a party of three or more and do not mind sharing a cabin, you will achieve a substantial saving per person, so you may be able to book a higher-grade cabin without paying extra.

CABIN SIZES

Cabins are like miniature hotel rooms and provide more or less the same facilities, except space. Ships necessarily have space limitations and utilize space efficiently. Viewed by most owners and designers as little more than a convenient place for passengers to sleep, shower, and change, cabin space is often compromised in favor of large public rooms and open areas. In some of the smaller interior (no-view) and outside cabins, changing clothes is a challenge; and to take a shower, you need to be an acrobat!

The latest ships come with more standardized cabin sizes, because they are made in modular form (I, and others, consider 170 sq ft (15.7 sq m) to be the *minimum* acceptable size for a "standard" cabin today). They all have integrated bathrooms (mostly made from noncombustible phenolic-glass-reinforced plastics) fitted into the ship during construction.

Older (pre-1970) ships had more spacious cabins (there were more days at sea, fewer ports of call, and fewer entertainment rooms). This encouraged many to spend a great deal of time in their cabins, often entertaining other passengers. It would be wise to ask your travel agent for the dimensions of the cabin you have selected.

CABIN LOCATION

➜ An "outside-view" cabin is recommended for first-time passengers (an "inside" cabin has no portholes or windows, making it more difficult to orient you or to gauge the weather or time).

➜ Cabins located in the center of a ship are more stable and tend to be noise- and vibration-free. Ships powered by diesel engines (this applies to most new and modern vessels) create and transmit some vibration, especially at the stern.

➜ Take into account personal habits when choosing the location of your cabin. For example, if you like to go to bed early, avoid a cabin close to the disco. If you have trouble walking, choose a cabin close to the elevator.

➜ Generally, the higher the deck, the higher the cabin price, and the better the service. This is an inheritance from transoceanic times, when upper-deck cabins and suites were sunnier and warmer.

➜ Cabins at the bow (front) of a ship are slightly crescent-shaped, given that the outer wall follows the curvature of the ship's hull. But they can be exposed to early morning noises, such as the anchor being dropped at ports where the ship cannot dock.

➜ Cabins with interconnecting doors are fine for families or close friends, but the wall between them is usually thin, so you can plainly hear anything that's being said next door.

➜ Many brochures now indicate cabins that have "obstructed-views." Cabins on lower decks are closer to engine noise and heat, especially at the aft of the vessel and around the engine casing. Be aware that in many older ships, elevators will probably not operate to the lowermost decks.

FACILITIES

Cabins provide some, or all, of the following:

➜ Private bathroom (generally small and compact) fitted with shower, wash basin, and toilet. Higher-grade cabins and suites may have full-size bathtubs. Some even have a whirlpool bath and/or bidet, a hair dryer, and more space.

➜ Electrical outlets for personal appliances, usually 110 and/or 220 volts.

➜ Multichannel radio, television (regular satellite channels or closed circuit), and VCR or DVD player.

➜ Two beds or a lower and upper berth (possibly, another one or two upper berths) or a double-, queen-, or king-size bed. In some ships, twin beds can be pushed together to form a double.

➜ Telephone, for intercabin or ship-to-shore communication.

➜ Depending on cabin size, a chair, or chair and table, or sofa and table, or even a separate lounge/sitting area (higher accommodation grades).

➜ Refrigerator and bar (higher accommodation grades).

➜ Vanity/desk unit with chair or stool.

➜ Personal safe.

➜ Closet space, some drawer space, plus storage room under beds for suitcases.

➜ Bedside night stand/table unit.

A cabin on board ***Hebridean Princess*** *(Hebridean Island Cruises).*

- Towels, soap, shampoo, and conditioner. (Many ships, particularly the "upscale" ones, provide a greater selection of items.)

Many first-time passengers are surprised to find their cabin has twin beds. Double beds are a comparative rarity except in the higher-priced suites. Aboard some ships you will find upper and lower berths. A "berth" is a nautical term for a bed held in a wooden or metal frame. A "Pullman berth" tucks away out of sight during the day, usually into the bulkhead or ceiling. You climb up a short ladder to get into an upper berth.

THE SUITE LIFE

Suites are the most luxurious and spacious of all shipboard accommodation, and typically come with butler service (butlers are the bringers of comfort and life's little extras). A suite (literally a "suite of rooms") should be a minimum of 400 sq ft (37.1 sq m), and comprise a lounge or sitting room separated from a bedroom by a solid door (not just a curtain); a bedroom with a large bed; one or more bathrooms, and an abundance of closet, drawer, and other storage space. Be advised, however, that many cruise lines inaccurately describe some accommodation as suites, when in fact they are simply nothing more than a large cabin with a curtain that divides sitting and sleeping areas.

Some ships have whole decks or sections of decks devoted to suites. Cruise lines know that some passengers will pay handsomely to stay in the best and quietest accommodation. They will also expect the best service and preferential treatment throughout the ship.

Suites are best on long voyages with several days at sea. Be aware that in large ships (those carrying more than 1,000 passengers), there may be a whole deck or two devoted to penthouses and suites, but you will have to share the rest of the ship with those in lower-priced accommodation. That means there is no preferential seating in the showroom, the dining rooms, or on sunbathing decks. You may, however, get separate check-in facilities and preferential treatment upon disembarkation, but your luggage will be lumped together with that of everyone else (not so "suite"!).

TYPICAL CABIN LAYOUT

The following rates are typical of those you can expect to pay for (a) a seven-day and (b) a ten-day Caribbean cruise aboard a modern cruise ship. The rates are per person and include free roundtrip airfare or low-cost air add-ons from principal North American gateways.

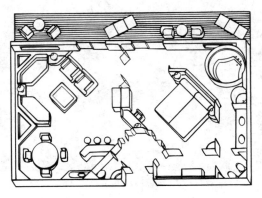

Luxury outside suite with private verandahh, separate lounge area, vanity area, extra-large double or queen-sized bed, bathroom with tub, shower, and extensive closet and storage space.
(a) $2,250 (b) $4,000

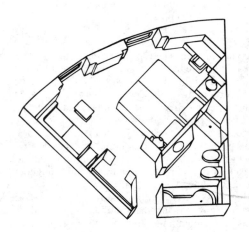

Deluxe outside cabin with lounge area, double or twin beds, bathroom with tub, shower, and ample closet and storage space.
(a) $2,250 (b) $2,850

Note that in some ships, third- and fourth-person berths are available for families or friends wishing to share. The upper Pullman berths, not shown on these cabin layouts, are recessed into the wall above the lower beds.

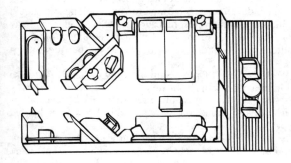

Large outside double with bed and convertible daytime sofabed, bathroom with shower, and good closet space.
(a) $1,750 (b) $2,450

Standard outside double with twin beds (plus a possible upper third/fourth berth), small sitting area, bathroom with shower, and reasonable closet space.
(a) $1,450 (b) $1,975

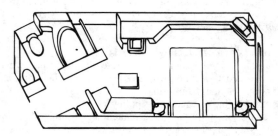

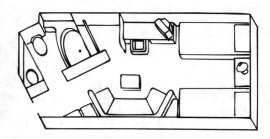

Inside double with two lower beds that may convert into daytime sofabeds (plus a possible upper third/fourth berth), bathroom with shower, and fair closet space.
(a) $1,250 (b) 1,750

47

BOOKING YOUR CRUISE

THE INTERNET
While the Internet may be a good resource tool, it is not the place to book your cruise, unless you know exactly what you want (in which case, the US-based <www.expedia.com> is a good place to go). Questions cannot be asked, and most of the information provided by the cruise companies is strictly marketing hype. Most sites providing cruise ship reviews have something to sell, and the sound-byte information provided can be misleading.

TRAVEL AGENTS
Travel agents do not generally charge for their services, although they do earn a commission from cruise lines for booking their clients on a cruise. Consider a travel agent as your business advisor, and not merely as a ticket agent. He/she will handle all matters relevant to your booking and should have the latest information on changes of itinerary, cruise fares, fuel surcharges, discounts, and any other related items, including insurance in case you have to cancel prior to sailing. Most travel agents are linked into cruise line computer systems and have access to all the pertinent ship-board information.

There is *no* "Best Cruise Line in the World" or "Best Cruise Ship" — only the ship and cruise that's right *for you*. Your travel agent should find exactly the *right ship* for *your needs* and *lifestyle*. Some sell only a limited number of cruises and are known as "preferred suppliers," because they receive special "overrides" on top of their normal commission (they probably know their limited number of ships well, however).

If *you* have chosen a ship and cruise, be firm and book exactly what you want, or change agencies. In the UK, look for a member of the Guild of Professional Cruise Agents. PSARA (Passenger Shipping Association of Retail Agents) provides in-depth agent training in the UK, as well as a full "bonding" scheme to protect passengers from failed cruise lines. In the US, look for a member of NACOA (National Association of Cruise Oriented Agencies), or a CLIA (Cruise Lines International Association) affiliated agency.

Questions to Ask Your Travel Agent
➝ Is air transportation included in the cabin rate quoted? If not, what will be the extra cost?
➝ What other extra costs will be involved? These can include port charges, insurance, gratuities, shore excursions, laundry, and drinks.
➝ What is the cruise line's cancellation policy?
➝ If I want to make changes to my air arrangements, routing, dates, and so on, will the insurance policy cover everything in case of missed or canceled flights?
➝ Does your agency deal with only one, or several different insurance companies?
➝ Does the cruise line offer advance booking discounts or other incentives?
➝ Do you have preferred suppliers, or do you book any cruise on any cruise ship?
➝ Have you sailed aboard the ship I want to book, or that you are recommending?
➝ Is your agency bonded and insured? If so, by whom?
➝ If you book the shore excursions offered and recommended by the cruise line, is insurance coverage provided?

RESERVATIONS
Plan ahead and book early. After choosing a ship, cruise, date, and cabin, you pay a deposit that is roughly 10 percent for long cruises, 20 percent for short cruises (most cruise lines ask for a set amount). The balance is normally payable 45 to 60 days prior to departure. For a late reservation, you pay in full when space is confirmed (when booking via the Internet, for example). Cruise lines reserve the right to change prices in the event of tax increases, fluctuating rates of exchange, fuel surcharges, or other costs beyond their control.

When you make your reservation, also make special dining requests known: seating preference, smoking or nonsmoking sections.

After the line has received full payment, your cruise ticket will be issued, along with baggage tags and other items. Check your documents when they arrive. In these days of automation, it is prudent to make sure that the ship, date, and cruise details you paid for are correctly noted. Also verify any connecting flight times.

EXTRA COSTS

Cruise brochures boldly proclaim that "everything's included," but in most cases you will find this is not strictly true. In fact, for some cruises "all-exclusive" would be a more appropriate term. Make sure you know what you're paying for before booking a crusie.

Your fare covers the ship as transportation, your cabin, meals, entertainment, activities, and service on board; it typically does not include alcoholic beverages, laundry, dry cleaning or valet services, shore excursions, meals ashore, gratuities, port charges, cancellation insurance, optional onboard activities such as skeet shooting, bingo, or casino gambling.

Expect to spend about $25 per day per person on extras, plus another $10–$12 per day per person in gratuities. Genuine exceptions can be found in some small ships (those carrying fewer than 500 passengers) where just about everything is included.

Typical Extra-Cost Items:

Baby-sitting (per hour)	$5
Bottled Water	$2.50–$7 (per bottle)
Cappuccino/Espresso	$1.50–$2.50
Cartoon Character Bedtime "Tuck-In" Service	$20
Wash One Shirt	$1.50–$3
Dry-Clean Dress	$3–$7.50
Dry-Clean Jacket	$4–$8
E-Mail	$3 per page
Golf Simulator	$15 (30 minutes)
Hair Wash/Set	$17–$28
Haircut (men)	$20
Ice Cream	$1–$3.75
In-cabin Movies	$6.95-$12.95
Laundry Soap	$0.50–1.50
Massage	$1.50-plus per minute (plus tip)
Satellite Phone/Fax	$6.95–15 per minute
Send an e-mail	$0.75 per minute
Sodas (soft drinks)	$1–$2
Souvenir Photo	$6–$8
Trapshooting (three or five shots)	$5, $8
Video Postcard	$4.95–$6.95
Wine/Cheese Tasting	$10–$15
Wine with Dinner	$7–$500

Calculate the total cost of your cruise (not including any extra-cost services you might decide you want once on board) with the help of your travel agent. Here are the approximate prices per person for a typical seven-day cruise aboard a well-rated mid-size or large cruise ship, based on an outside-view two-bed cabin:

Cruise fare	$1,200
Port charges	$100 (if not included)
Gratuities	$50
Total per person	**$1,350**

This is under $200 per person per day. For this price, you wouldn't even get a decent hotel room in London, New York, Tokyo, or Venice!

DISCOUNTS AND INCENTIVES

→ Book ahead to get the best discounts (discounts decrease closer to the cruise date).

→ You may be able to reserve a cabin grade, but not a specific cabin — "tba" (to be assigned). Some lines will accept this arrangement and may even upgrade you.

→ It is useful to know that the first cabins to be sold out are usually those at minimum and maximum rates. *Note*: Premium rates apply during Christmas/New Year cruises.

→ Some cruise lines have "frequent passenger" clubs. Members are first to be notified of any special offers being made. Discounts can frequently be high, so it is worth belonging, especially if you like cruising with a particular line.

CANCELLATIONS AND REFUNDS

Do take out full cancellation insurance (if it is not included), as cruises (and air transportation to/from them) must be paid in full before your tickets are issued. Without such insurance, if you cancel at the last minute (even for medical reasons) you could lose the whole fare. Insurance coverage can be obtained from your travel agent, and paying by credit card makes sense (you'll probably get your money back in case the travel agency goes out of business). Also, beware of policies sold by the cruise lines — they may well be no good if the cruise line goes out of business (several cruise lines have become defunct in the past few years).

Cruise lines usually accept cancellations more than 30 days before sailing, but all charge full fare if you do not turn up on sailing day, whatever the reason. Other cancellation fees depend on the cruise and length of trip. Curiously, many lines do not return port taxes, which are not part of the cruise fare.

MEDICAL INSURANCE

Whether you intend to travel overseas or cruise down a local river, and your present medical insurance does not cover you, you should look into extra coverage for your cruise. A "passenger protection program" will be offered by the cruise line, and the charge for it will appear on your final invoice unless you decline. It is worth every penny, and it typically covers such things as evacuation by air ambulance, high-limit baggage, baggage transfers, personal liability, and missed departure.

PORT TAXES/HANDLING CHARGES

These are assessed by individual port authorities and are generally shown in the brochure. Port charges form part of the final payment, although they can be changed at any time up to the day of embarkation.

AIR/SEA PACKAGES

When your cruise fare includes "free air" (as in a one-way or round-trip air ticket), note that airline arrangements usually cannot be changed without paying a premium, as cruise lines often book group space on aircraft to obtain the lowest rates.

If you *do* make changes, remember that in the event of the airline canceling your flight, *the cruise line is under no obligation* to help you or return your cruise fare if you do not reach the ship on time. If you are flying to a foreign country you should allow extra time (particularly in the winter) to cover the risk that any airline connections may be delayed or canceled.

Airlines often use a frustrating "hub-and-spoke" system, which can prove frustrating. Because of changes to air schedules, cruise and air tickets may not be sent to passengers until a few days before the cruise.

In Europe, air/sea packages generally start at a major metropolitan airport; some include first-class rail travel from outlying districts. In the United States, many cruise lines include connecting flights from small suburban airports as part of the whole package.

Most cruise lines offer the flexibility of jetting out to join a ship in one port and flying home from another. An advantage is that you only have to check your baggage once at the departure airport. The baggage transfer from plane to ship is handled for you.

Note: This does not include intercontinental fly/cruises, where you must claim your baggage at the airport on arrival in order to clear it though customs.

Although the cruise package may state "free air," there is no such thing as a free air ticket. The cost of the airfare is simply hidden in the overall cruise fare. However, air tickets are not always included. Some cruise lines simply do not believe in increasing their rates to cover "free air," or they simply may wish to avoid subsidizing airline tickets. These are, for the most part, the upscale lines that operate long-distance cruises to more exotic destinations.

CRUISE CUISINE

that there is an unwritten rule called "Ward's Third Law of Gluttony," which states that passengers will eat precisely twice as much food as they need from breakfast and luncheon buffets, then add a lettuce leaf or two at dinner to justify the guilt complex brought about by over-consumption?

...that the liner *Amerika* in 1938 was the first ship to have an alternative restaurant open separately from the dining saloons? It was named the Ritz Carlton.

...that the first à la carte restaurant aboard a passenger ship was in the German ship *Amerika* of 1905?

...that the longest bar on any cruise ship is aboard *AIDAcara*? The bar is 195 ft (59.5 m) long.

...that a whole county in Iowa raises all its beef cattle for Carnival Cruise Lines?

...that *Legend of the Seas* was christened with the world's largest bottle of champagne? It had to be specially made, and was a "Sovereign-size" bottle (the equivalent of 34 bottles) of Moet & Chandon champagne.

...that the United States Line's *Manhattan* in 1931 was the first ship to have a cocktail named after it — perhaps the only ship with that distinction?

...that 2,000 Methuselah-sized bottles (the equivalent of 12 bottles) of Cristal champagne were made specially for Crystal Cruises' passengers to purchase for the eve of the year 2000 (the millennium)? The cost — $2000 each!

Dining is typically the single most talked- and written-about aspect of the cruise experience. There is a thrill of anticipation that comes with dining out in a fine restaurant. The same is true aboard ship, where dining in elegant, friendly, and comfortable surroundings stimulates an appetite sharpened by the bracing sea air. Some passengers do carry abundance therapy to the limit, however.

Attention to presentation, quality, and choice of menu in the honored tradition of the transatlantic luxury liners has made cruise ships justly famous. Cruise lines know that you will spend more time eating on board than doing anything else, so their intention is to cater well to your palate, within the confines of a predetermined budget.

The "intelligent standardization" of the food operation and menus translates to cost-effectiveness in the process of food budgeting for any cruise line. Being able to rationalize expenditure *and* provide maximum passenger satisfaction is, therefore, almost a science today. Quite simply, *you get what you pay for*. Aboard low-priced cruises, you will get portion-controlled frozen food that has been reheated. To get fresh food (particularly fresh fish and the best cuts of meats), cruise lines must pay significantly more, adding to the cruise price.

Cruise lines put maximum effort into telling passengers how good their food is, often to the point of being unable to deliver what is shown in the brochures. Not all meals aboard all ships are gourmet affairs by any stretch of the imagination. In general, cruise cuisine compares favorably with the kind of "banquet" food served in a standard hotel or family restaurant, in other words, almost tasteless.

Most ships cannot offer a real "gourmet" experience because the galley (ship's kitchen) may be striving to turn out hundreds of meals at the same time. What you will find is a good selection of palatable, pleasing, and complete meals served in comfortable surroundings, in the company of good friends (and you do not have to do the cooking!). Maybe you will even dine by candlelight, a pleasant way to spend any evening.

Experienced passengers who "collect" cruises have seen it, smelled it, and tasted it all before aboard ships: real rubber duck-fowl (foul) food, fit only to be stuffed, painted, and used as children's toys in their bathtubs! Talk about rock-hard lobster, fish with the elasticity of a baseball bat, inedible year-old shrimp, veterinarian-rejected chicken, and grenade-quality meats. Not to mention teary-eyed or hammer-proof cheese, soggy salty crackers, unripe fruits, and coffee that looks (and tastes) like army surplus paint! Or yellow-green leaves that are either garnish or a poor excuse for salad! Sadly, it is all there, in the cruise industry's global cafeteria.

Most ships feature self-serve buffets for breakfast and luncheon, one of the effects of discounted fares (because less staff are required). Strangely, passengers do not seem to mind lining up for self-service food (this somehow reminds me of school lunches). But while buffets look fine when they are fresh, after a few minutes of passengers serving themselves, they do not. And, one learns soon enough that the otherwise sweet little old ladies can become ruthlessly competitive at buffet opening time! Passengers should not have to play guessing games when it comes to food, but many cruise lines forget to put labels on food items, which slows down any buffet line. Labels on salad dressings, sauces, and cheeses would be particularly useful.

Passengers have different preferences and tastes. Some like their food plain, while some like it spicy; some like *nouvelle cuisine*, some like meat and potatoes (and lots of it). Some try new things, some stick with the same old stuff. It is all a matter of personal taste. Cruise lines tend to cater to general tastes. The best ships offer food cooked more or less individually to your liking. Some people are accustomed to drinking coffee out of polystyrene plastic cups and eating food off of paper plates at home. Others wouldn't dream of doing that and expect fine dining, with food served on fine china, just as they do at home.

If you are left-handed, tell your waiter at your first meal exactly how you want your cutlery placed and to make sure that tea or coffee cup handles are turned in the correct direction. (This is impossible with a fish knife, of course!). It would be better if right- or left-hand preferences were established when you book, and the cruise lines informed the ship.

Menus are displayed outside the dining room each day so that you can preview each meal. Suite occupants have menus delivered. When looking at the menu, one thing you will never have to do is to consider the price: It is all included.

HEALTHY EATING

With more emphasis placed on low-cholesterol and low-salt diets today, most ships have "spa" menus with calorie-filled sauces replaced by spa cuisine. Some cruise lines include basic nutritional information, such as the calorie count and fat, protein, and carbohydrate content, on their

*The large selection of teas aboard Aida Cruises' **Aida**.*

"spa" menus, or for selected "light" items on their regular menus (mostly for dinner, seldom for breakfast or lunch).

If you are vegetarian, vegan, macrobiotic, counting calories, or want a salt-free, sugar-restricted, low-fat, low-cholesterol, or any other diet, advise your travel agent at the time of booking, and get the cruise line to confirm that the ship can actually handle your dietary requirements. *Note*: Cruise ship food does tend to be liberally sprinkled with salt, and vegetables are often cooked with sauces containing dairy products, salt, and sugar.

THE DINING ROOM
Aboard many ships, the running and staffing of dining rooms is contracted to a specialist maritime catering organization. Ships that cruise in waters away from their home country find that professional catering companies do an excellent job. The quality is generally to a good standard. However, ships that control their own catering staff and food are often those that go to great lengths to ensure that their passengers are satisfied.

DINING ROOM STAFF
The restaurant manager (also known as the Maître d' Hotel — not to be confused with the ship's Hotel Manager) is an experienced host, with shrewd perceptions about compatibility. It is his responsibility to seat you with compatible fellow passengers. If a table reservation has been arranged prior to boarding, you will find a table assignment/seating card in your cabin when you embark. If not, make your reservation with the restaurant manager or one of his assistants immediately after you embark.

Unless you are with your own family or group of friends, you will be seated next to strangers. Tables for two are a rarity; most tables seat four, six, or eight. It is a good idea to ask to be seated at a larger table, because if you are a couple seated at a table for four and you do not get along with your table partners, there is no one else to talk to. And remember, if the ship is full, it may be difficult to change tables once the cruise has started.

If you are unhappy with any aspect of the dining room operation, the sooner you tell someone the better. Do not wait until the cruise is over to send a scathing letter to the cruise line, for then it is too late to do anything positive.

The best waiters are those trained in European hotels or hotel/catering schools. These qualified individuals excel in fine service. They will learn your likes and dislikes quickly. They normally work aboard the best ships, where dignified professionalism is expected and living conditions are good.

SMOKING/NONSMOKING
Many ships have totally nonsmoking dining rooms, while some provide smoking (cigarettes only, not cigars or pipes) and nonsmoking sections. Nonsmokers who wish to sit in a no-smoking area should tell the restaurant manager when reserving a table. Note that at open seating breakfasts and luncheons in the dining room (or informal buffet dining area), smokers and nonsmokers may be seated close together.

THE CAPTAIN'S TABLE
The captain usually occupies a large table in or near the center of the dining room on "formal" nights. The table seats eight or more people picked from the passenger or "commend" list by the hotel manager. If you are invited to the captain's table it is gracious to accept and you will have the chance to ask all the questions you like about shipboard life.

WHICH SEATING?
→ **Open Seating**: Also called Freestyle Dining, or Personal Choice Dining, this simply means that you can sit at *any* available table, with whomever *you* wish, at *whatever time* you choose (within dining room opening hours).
→ **Single Seating**: you can choose *when* you wish to eat (within dining room hours) but have an assigned table for the cruise.
→ **Two Seatings**: you are assigned (or choose) one of two seatings, early or late. Typical meal times for two-seating ships are:
    a) Breakfast: 6:30am/8:30am   b) Lunch:noon/1:30pm   c) Dinner:6:30pm/8:30pm
→ **Four Seatings:** you choose the time (at present, only Carnival Cruise Lines operates four seatings). Dinner is at 5:30pm/6:45pm/7:30pm or 8:45pm.

Note: Some ships that operate in Europe (the Mediterranean) or South America will probably have later meal times. Dinner hours may also vary when the ship is in port to allow for the timing of shore excursions.

A TYPICAL DAY

From morning till night (and beyond), food is offered to the point of overkill, even aboard the most modest cruise ship.

→ 6am: hot coffee and tea on deck for early risers.

→ Full breakfast: typically with as many as 60 different items, in the main dining room. For a more casual meal, you can serve yourself buffet-style at an indoor/outdoor deck café (the choice may be more restricted than in the main dining room, yet adequate).

→ Lunchtime: with service in the dining room, buffet-style at an informal café, or at a separate grill for hot dogs and hamburgers, and a pizzeria, where everything is cooked right in front of you but usually presented with less style than at a fast food restaurant.

→ 4pm: Afternoon tea, in the British tradition, complete with finger sandwiches and cakes. This may be served in one of the main lounges to the accompaniment of live music (it may even be a "tea-dance") or recorded classical music.

→ Dinner: the main event of the evening, and apart from the casualness of the first and last nights, it is formal in style.

→ Midnight Buffet: without a doubt the most famous of all shipboard meals. They are grand spreads, often based around a different theme each night, (seafood, Oriental, tropical fruit fantasy, chocoholic, etc.). There may be a Gala Midnight Buffet (usually on the penultimate evening), for which the chefs pull out all the stops.

PLATE SERVICE VS. SILVER SERVICE

Plate Service: When the food is presented as a complete dish, it is as the chef wants it to look; color combinations, the size of the component parts, and their positioning on the plate. All are important. In most cruise ships, "plate service" is now the norm. It works well and means that most people seated at a table will be served at the same time and can eat together, rather than let their food become cold, as can be the case with silver service.

Silver Service: When the component parts are brought to the table separately, so that the diner, not the chef, can choose what goes on the plate and in what proportion. Silver service is best when there is plenty of time (few cruise ships provide silver service today). What some cruise lines class as silver service is actually silver service of vegetables only, with the main item, be it fish, fowl, or meat, already positioned on the plate.

NATIONAL DIFFERENCES

The different nationalities among passengers present their own special needs and requirements. Some examples:

→ Asian, British, German, and other European passengers like boiled eggs served in real china eggcups for breakfast. North Americans rarely eat boiled eggs, and most often put the eggs into a bowl and eat them with a fork.

→ German passengers tend to prefer breads (especially dark breads) and a wide variety of cheeses for breakfast and lunch. They tend to like yellow (not white) potatoes. They also have an obvious liking for German draught or bottled beers rather than American canned beers.

→ French passengers have a liking for soft, not flaky, croissants, and may request brioche and confitures.

→ Japanese passengers like "bento box," breakfasts of salmon and eel, and vegetable pickles, as well as Japanese rice, which is very different from Chinese rice.

→ Southern Italians like to have red sauce with just about everything, while northern Italians like less of the red sauces and more white sauces and flavorings, such as garlic, with their pasta.

→ Australian passengers need "vegemite" to spread on bread and toast.

→ Many North Americans like weak coffee with everything, often before, during, and after a meal. This is why, even on the most upscale ships, sugar is placed on tables (also for iced tea). North Americans tend to eat and run, whereas Europeans, for example, like to dine in a more leisurely fashion, treating mealtimes as a social occasion.

→ Most passengers agree that cruise coffee is appalling, but often it is simply the chlorinated water that gives it a different taste. Europeans prefer strong coffee, usually made from the coffee beans of African countries like Kenya. North Americans usually drink the coffee from Colombia or Jamaica.

→ European tea drinkers like to drink tea out of tea cups, not coffee or sports mugs (very few cruise ships know how to make a decent cup of tea, so British passengers in particular should be aware of this).

THE EXECUTIVE CHEF

The executive chef plans the menus, orders the food, organizes his staff, and arranges all the meals on the menus. He makes sure that menus are not repeated, even on long cruises. On some cruises, he works with guest chefs from restaurants ashore to offer tastes of regional cuisine. He may also purchase fish, seafood, fruit, and various other local produce in "wayside" ports and incorporate them into the menu with a "special of the day" announcement.

THE GALLEY

The galley ("kitchen" for landlubbers) is the heart of all food preparation on board. At any time of the day or night, there is plenty of activity, whether it is baking fresh bread at 2am, making meals and snacks for passengers and crew around the clock, or decorating a special birthday cake. The staff, from executive chef to pot-washer, all work together as a team, each designated a specific role, with little room for error.

The galley and preparation areas consist of the following sections (the names in parentheses are the French names given to the person who is the specialist in the area of expertise):

Fish Preparation Area *(Poisonnier)*: This area contains freezers and a fully equipped preparation room, where fish is cleaned and cut to size before it is sent to the galley.

Meat Preparation Area *(Butcher/Rotisseur):* This area contains separate freezers for meat and poultry. Their temperatures are kept at approximately 10°F. There are also defrosting areas (35°F to 40°F). Meat and poultry are sliced and portioned before being sent to the galley.

Vegetable Preparation Area *(Entremetier):* Vegetables are cleaned and prepared in this area.

Sauce Preparation Area *(Saucier):* This is where the sauces are prepared.

Soup Preparation Area *(Potagier):* Soups are made in huge tureens.

Cold Kitchen *(Garde Manger):* This is the area where all cold dishes and salads are prepared, from the simplest sandwich (for room service, for example) to the works of art that grace the buffets. The area is well equipped with mixing machines, slicing machines, and refrigeration cabinets where prepared dishes are stored until required.

Bakery and Pastry Shop *(Baker):* This area provides the raw ingredients for preparing food, and contains dough mixers, refrigerators, proving ovens, ovens, and containers in all manner of shapes and sizes. Dessert items, pastries, sweets, and other confectionery are prepared and made here.

Pantry: This is where cheese and fruits are prepared, and where sandwiches are made.

Dishwashing Area: This area contains huge conveyor-belt dishwashing machines. Wash and rinse temperatures are carefully controlled to comply with public health regulations. This is where all the cooking utensils are scrubbed and cleaned, and where the silverware is scrupulously polished.

HYGIENE STANDARDS

Galley equipment is in almost constant use, and regular inspections and maintenance help detect potential problems. There is continual cleaning of equipment, utensils, bulkheads, floors, and hands.

Cruise ships sailing from or visiting US ports are subject to sanitation inspections. These are voluntary, not mandatory inspections, based on forty-two inspection items, undertaken by the United States Public Health (USPH) Department of Health and Human Services, under the auspices of the Centers for Disease Control. The cruise line pays for each ship inspection. A similar process takes place in Britain under the Port Health Authority, which has even more stringent guidelines.

A tour of the galley proves to be a highlight for some passengers, when a ship's insurance company permits. A video of *Behind the Scenes*, for use on in-cabin television, may be provided instead.

In accordance with internationally accepted standards, all potable water brought on board, or produced by distillation aboard cruise ships, should contain a free chlorine or bromine residual equal to or greater than 0.2 ppm (parts per million). This is why drinking water served in the dining room often tastes of chlorine.

WASTE DISPOSAL

Cruise ships must be capable of efficient handling of garbage and waste materials, as trash generated by passengers and crew must be managed, stored, and disposed of efficiently and economically. The larger the ship, the more waste is created, and the greater the need for reliable disposal systems.

Trash includes bottles, cans, corrugated cartons, fabrics, foodstuffs, paper products, plastic containers, as well as medical waste, sludge oil, wet waste, and so on. The sheer magnitude of waste materials can be highly problematic, especially on long cruises. If solid waste is not burnable, or cannot be disposed of overboard (this must be biodegradable), it must be stored for later off-loading and disposal on land.

Although the latest breed of cruise ships is equipped with "zero-discharge" facilities, many older cruise ships still have a way to go when it comes to garbage handling. One method of dealing with food waste is to send it to a waste-pulping machine that has been partially filled with water. Cutting mechanisms reduce the waste and allow it to pass through a special sizing ring to be pumped directly overboard or into a holding tank or an incinerator when the ship is within three-mile limits.

Whichever method of waste disposal is chosen, it, as well as the ship, must meet the extremely stringent demands of Annex V of MARPOL 73/78 international regulations.

CAVIAR AND CHAMPAGNE

Although it might seem like it from menu descriptions, most ships do not serve Beluga caviar, but the less expensive and more widely available Sevruga and Sevruga Malossol (low-salt) caviar. Even more widely served aboard the standard cruise ships is Norwegian lumpfish "caviar." If you are partial to the best caviar, you might want to know that Cunard's *QE2* is reputed to be the world's largest single buyer of caviar after the Russian and the Ukrainian governments.

Those who have not tasted good caviar may find it very salty. That's because the eggs are taken fresh from a sleeping female sturgeon (it takes about 20 years for a female beluga sturgeon to mature). The eggs are passed through a screen to separate them from other fibrous matter, then mixed with salt, which acts as a preservative and promotes the taste. The more salt added, the better the caviar is preserved; the less salt added, the finer the taste.

The two countries that produce most of the world's caviar are Iran and Russia. In general, Russian caviar is more highly salted than caviar from Iran. And just as each vineyard produces different wines, so each fishery will produce different-tasting caviar.

The Caspian Sea is the spawning ground for 90 percent of the world's caviar-producing sturgeon. There are three types that are fished for caviar.

→ The *beluga* is hardest to find and the most expensive. It can weigh 1,500 pounds. One fish can yield up to 20 pounds of caviar, and its eggs are the largest and most delicate.

→ The second most desirable caviar fish is the *ossetra*. This takes about 13 years to mature, and weighs up to about 40 pounds. These are the most durable eggs (they are also smaller).

→ The third caviar fish is the *severuga*, which weighs about six pounds. It also has small eggs.

Caviar is a natural accompaniment for good champagne, but good champagne doesn't come cheap. Champagne-making is a real art (in France itself, the production of Champagne is restricted to a very small geographic area). It is bottled in many sizes, ranging from the minute to the ridiculously huge.

The three main grape-growing districts in Champagne are: the *Montagne de Reims*, the *Vallée de la Marne*, and the *Côtes des Blancs*. The first two mainly grow the dark pinot-noir and pinot-meunier grapes; the latter grows the white chardonnay variety (all are used in making champagne). Removing the husks before full fermentation prevents the dark grapes from coloring the wine red. If pink champagne is required, the skins are left in the grape mix for a longer time to add color.

Although the Champagne area has been producing wines of renown for a long time, its vintners were unable to keep their bubbles from fizzling out until a monk in the Abbey of Hautvilliers, whose name was Dom Perignon, came up with the solution. The bubbles — escaping carbonic acid gas — had always escaped, until Dom Perignon devised a bottle capable of containing the champagne without it exploding from the bottle, a common occurrence in local cellars. The legacy of this clever monk is that the champagne bottle is the strongest bottle made today. Its thickness is concentrated

*A lovely presentation of breakfast from room service aboard **Silver Cloud**.*

around the bottle's base and shoulders. Dom Perignon's bottle was aided by the coincidental development of the cork.

Even after his work, champagne was not the elixir enjoyed today. It was cloudy due to residual sediment (dead yeast cells). Its bubbles, therefore, could not be truly relished visually until la Veuve Cliquot (the Widow Cliquot) devised the system of *remuage* in the nineteenth century. Rather than laying the bottles down horizontally for their period of aging, she put them in a special rack, called a *pupitre*, which held them at a 45-degree angle, with the neck of the bottle facing down. Each day, the bottles are given a short, sharp, quarter turn to shake the sediment that settles in the neck of the bottle.

Once this is complete, a process called *dégorgement* freezes the neck of the bottle. It is then uncorked and internal pressure ejects the ice containing the sediment. Obviously, this means that the bottle is a little less than totally full, so the champagne is topped up with what is called the *dosage*, which is a sweet champagne liqueur. After the dosage is added, the permanent cork is forced in and wired up. The bottles then remain in the cellar of the winery until they are ordered. Each bottle is then washed and labeled prior to being shipped for sale.

BIG EIGHT CUISINE COMPARISONS

These scores are compiled from evaluations and ratings accumulated over a period of years, and are based on established standards of food and service delivery within the hospitality industry.

	Carnival Cruise Lines	Celebrity Cruises	Costa Cruises	Holland America Line	Norwegian Cruise Line	Princess Cruises	Royal Caribbean International	Star Cruises
Food: Dining Room/Cuisine	6.3	8.6	6.4	7.2	6.2	7.2	7.1	7.0
Food: Buffets/Informal Dining	6.0	8.1	5.7	6.1	5.7	6.5	6.4	6.7
Food: Quality of Ingredients	6.0	8.7	6.2	7.1	6.3	6.9	6.9	8.0
Food: Afternoon Tea/Snacks	4.2	7.1	5.1	5.6	4.8	5.9	5.4	5.6
Wine List:	6.6	8.2	5.6	6.0	6.1	6.6	6.1	6.4
Overall Food Score	5.82	8.14	5.80	6.40	5.82	6.62	6.38	6.74
Service: Dining Rooms	5.8	8.3	6.1	7.0	6.7	7.3	7.2	7.1
Service: Bars	6.8	8.0	6.4	7.1	6.8	7.5	7.3	6.8
Service: Cabins	6.6	8.1	6.8	7.4	6.4	7.5	7.3	7.2
Service: Open Decks	6.0	7.6	5.8	6.6	6.2	6.8	6.4	6.0
Service: Wines	5.3	8.0	5.3	6.1	6.4	6.2	6.1	7.1
Overall Service Score	6.10	8.00	6.08	6.84	6.50	7.06	6.80	6.84
COMBINED FOOD AND SERVICE SCORE	5.96	8.07	5.94	6.62	6.16	6.84	6.59	6.79

Key:
Below 5: Unacceptable food   6 - 7: Acceptable to good, not memorable   8 - 9: Excellent, many memorable meals
5 - 6: Adequate, but only just   7 - 8: Very good, some meals memorable   9 -10: Outstanding – best at sea

CRUISING FOR THE PHYSICALLY CHALLENGED

The *advantages* of a cruise for the physically challenged are many:

→ Good place for relaxation and self-renewal.
→ Pure air at sea (no smog, no pollen).
→ No packing and unpacking.
→ Spacious public rooms.
→ Excellent medical facilities close by.
→ Specialized dietary requirements can be catered to.
→ The staff will generally be very helpful.
→ Varied entertainment.
→ Gambling (but, as yet, no wheelchair-accessible gaming tables or slot machines).
→ Security (no crime on board).
→ Different ports of call.

The *disadvantages* of a cruise for the physically challenged are:

→ Very few ships have access-help lifts installed at their swimming pools (exception: P&O Cruises) or thalassotherapy pools or shore tenders (exception: Holland America Line).
→ Unless cabins are specifically designed for the physically challenged, problem areas include the entrance, furniture configuration, closet hanging rails, and beds.
→ Cabin bathrooms: doors that open inward are useless; the grab bars, wheel-in shower stall, toiletries cabinet should be at an accessible height.
→ Elevator doorways: the width of the door is important for wheelchair passengers; controls are often not at a height suitable for operation from a wheelchair (except in the newer ships).
→ Sometimes having to wait behind hordes of able-bodied passengers who really do not need to use the elevators.
→ Access to outside decks is not often provided through electric-eye doors that open and close automatically. Rather it is provided through doorways that have to be opened manually.

Cruise lines, port authorities, airlines, and various allied services are slowly improving their facilities for the physically challenged. Not all are in wheelchairs, of course, but all have needs that the cruise industry is (slowly) working to accommodate. Few cruise line brochures show photographs of passengers in wheelchairs (Princess Cruises is an exception).

The design of ships has traditionally worked against the mobility-limited. To keep water out or to prevent water escaping from a flooded cabin or public area, raised edges (known as "coamings" or "lips") are often placed in doorways and across exit pathways. Also, cabin doorways are often not wide enough to accommodate even a standard wheelchair. A "standard" cabin door is about 24 inches (60.9 cm) wide.

Cabins designed for the mobility-limited typically have doors that are about 30 inches (76.2 cm) wide. "Standard" bathroom doors are normally only about 22 inches (55.8 cm) wide, whereas those designed for wheelchairs are about 28–30 inches (71.1–76.2 cm) wide. Ask your travel agent to confirm the width of cabin and bathroom doors. Remember to allow for the fact that your knuckles on either side of a wheelchair can add to the width of your wheelchair. Beds in cabins for the physically challenged aboard most ships are not equipped with a "panic" button, adjacent to a bedside light switch (*Carnival Destiny*, *Carnival Triumph*, and *Carnival Victory* are examples of ships that have them installed).

Bathroom doors are a particular problem, and the door itself, whether it opens outward into the cabin or inward into the bathroom, only compounds the problems of maneuvering a wheelchair within a cramped space. Four cabins for the physically challenged in the *QE2*, however, have electrically operated sliding doors into the bathroom, a completely level entrance into both cabin and bathroom, and remote-controlled lights, curtains, and doors, as well as a door intercom and alarm.

Bathrooms in many older ships are normally small and full of plumbing fixtures, often at odd angles, awkward when moving about from the confines of a wheelchair. The bathrooms aboard new ships are more accessible, but the plumbing is often located beneath the complete prefabricated module, making the floor higher than in the cabin, meaning a ramp must be fitted in order to wheel in.

Some cruise lines, if given advance notice, will remove a bathroom door and replace it with a hanging fabric curtain. Many will provide ramps for the bathroom doorway, where a sill or "lip" is encountered.

It was once the policy of almost all cruise lines to discourage the mobility-limited from taking a cruise or traveling anywhere by ship for reasons of safety, insurance, and legal liability. But a cruise is the ideal holiday for the physically challenged, as it provides a relaxed environment with plenty of social contact, organized entertainment, and activities. Despite most brochures declaring that they accept wheelchairs, few ships are well fitted to accommodate them. Some cruise lines openly state that all public restrooms and cabin bathrooms are inaccessible to wheelchair-bound passengers.

What about safety? Curiously, only three cruise ships currently provide direct access ramps to the lifeboats; they are *Crystal Harmony*, *Crystal Symphony*, and *Europa*.

The list at the end of this chapter pertains to all the ships presented in Part Two and provides a guide as to their accessibility. The author, or one of his staff, personally wheels around each ship to check mobility and maneuvering problems.

Once you've decided on your ship and cruise, the next step is to select your accommodation. There are many grades of cabin, depending on size, facilities, and location. Choose a cruise line that permits you to select a specific cabin, rather than one that merely allows you to designate a price category, then assigns you a cabin immediately prior to your departure date or, worse still, actually at embarkation.

Cabins: What They Should Include:
→ No "lip" or threshold at the cabin door, which should be a minimum of 35 inches wide (89.0 cm).
→ Bedside "panic" button linked to the navigation bridge (which is manned 24 hours a day).
→ Enough space to maneuver a wheelchair between entrance, bed, closet, and bathroom.
→ Closet with "pull down" clothes rail.
→ Telephone mounted at wheelchair height (not high up on wall).
→ Mirrors useable when seated in a wheelchair (full-length).
→ Safe or lockable drawer that is reachable at wheelchair height.
→ Convenient electrical outlet for battery charger (for electronic wheelchair users)

Bathrooms: What They Should Include:
→ Outward opening door.
→ No "lip" at bathroom door.
→ No "lip" into shower stall.
→ Shower stall (with detachable showerhead located at head height when seated in a wheelchair).
→ Shower chair that folds up when not in use, and grab rails.
→ Grab rails for toilet.
→ Toilet with electric automatic seat pad cleaner.
→ Sink at low enough height for wheelchair to move up close.
→ Emergency (panic) button in or adjacent to shower (for falls).

The following tips will help you choose wisely:
→ If the ship does not have any specially equipped cabins for the physically challenged, book the best outside cabin in your price range or choose another ship. However, be careful as you may find that even cruise brochures that state that a ship has "wheelchair accessible" cabins fail to say whether the wheelchair will fit through the *bathroom* door, or whether there is a "lip" at the door. Find out whether the wheelchair can fit into the shower area. Get your travel agent to check, and recheck the details. Do not take "I think so" as an answer. Get specific measurements.
→ Choose a cabin that is close to an elevator. Not all elevators go to all decks, so check the deck plan carefully. Smaller and older vessels may not even have elevators, making access to many areas, including the dining room, difficult or almost impossible.
→ Avoid, at all costs, a cabin down a little alleyway shared by several other cabins, even if the price is attractive. The space along these alleyways is extremely limited and entering one of these cabins in a wheelchair is likely to be a frustrating experience.
→ Cabins located amidships are less affected by vessel motion, so choose something in the middle of the ship if you are concerned about rough seas, no matter how infrequently they might occur.
→ The larger (and therefore the more expensive) the cabin, the more room you will have to maneuver in. Nowhere does this assume more importance than in the bathroom.

➝ If your budget allows, pick a cabin with a bath rather than just a shower, because there will be considerably more room, especially if you are unable to stand comfortably.

➝ Meals in some ships may be served in your cabin, on special request. This is a decided advantage should you wish to avoid dressing for every meal. There are, however, few ships that have enough actual space in the cabin for dining tables.

➝ If you want to join other passengers in the dining room and your ship offers two fixed-time seatings for meals, choose the second rather than the first. Then you can linger over your dinner, secure in the knowledge that the waiter will not try to rush you.

➝ Space at dining room tables can be somewhat limited in many ships. When making table reservations, therefore, tell the restaurant manager that you would like a table that leaves plenty of room for your wheelchair, so that it doesn't become an obstacle for the waiters and leaves plenty of room for them — or other passengers — to get past.

➝ Find a travel agent who knows your needs and understands your requirements, but follow up on all aspects of the booking yourself so that there will be no slip-ups when the day arrives for you to travel.

➝ Make sure that the cabin you booked is so stated on the final passenger ticket contract. Also make sure that the contract specifically states that if, for any reason, the cabin is not available, that you will get a full refund and transportation back home as well as any reimbursement for any hotel bills incurred.

➝ Take your own wheelchair with you, as ships carry only a limited number of wheelchairs; these are provided for emergency hospital use only. An alternative is to rent an electric wheelchair, which can be delivered to the ship on your sailing date.

➝ If you live near the port of embarkation, arrange to visit the ship yourself to check its suitability for your accessibility requirements (most cruise lines will be helpful in this regard).

Hanging rails in the closets on most ships are positioned too high for someone who is wheelchair-bound to reach (even the latest ships seem to repeat this basic error). Many cruise ships, however, have cabins specially fitted out to suit the mobility-limited, in which this and similar problem areas have been dealt with. They are typically fitted with roll-in closets and have a pull-down facility to bring your clothes down to any height you want.

Elevators are a constant source of difficulty for wheelchair passengers. Often the control buttons are located far too high to reach, especially those for upper decks.

Doors on upper decks that open onto a Promenade or Lido Deck are very strong, are difficult to handle, and have high sills. Unless you are ambulatory, or can get out of your wheelchair, these doors can be a source of annoyance, even if there is help at hand, as they open inward or outward (they should ideally be electrically operated sliding doors).

Advise any airline you might be traveling with of any special needs well ahead of time so that arrangements can be made to accommodate you without last-minute problems.

Advise the cruise line repeatedly of the need for proper transfer facilities, in particular buses or vans with wheelchair ramps.

EMBARKATION

Even if you've alerted the airline and arranged your travel according to your needs, there is still one problem to surmount when you arrive at the cruise embarkation port to join your ship: the actual boarding. If you embark at ground level, the gangway to the ship may be level or inclined. It will depend on the embarkation deck of the ship and/or the tide in the port. Alternatively, you may be required to embark from an upper level of a terminal, in which case the gangway could well be of the floating loading-bridge type, like those used at major airports. Some have flat floors; others may have raised lips spaced every three feet (awkward to negotiate in a wheelchair, especially if the gangway is made steeper by a rising tide).

TENDERING

Cruise lines should (but don't always) provide an anchor emblem in brochures for those ports of call where a ship will be at anchor instead of alongside. If the ship is at anchor, be prepared for an interesting but safe experience. The crew will lower you and your wheelchair into a waiting tender (ship-to-shore launch) and then, after a short boat-ride, lift you out again onto a rigged gangway or integral platform. If the sea is calm, this maneuver proceeds uneventfully; if the sea is choppy, your embarkation could vary from exciting to harrowing. Fortunately (or not) this type of embarkation is rare unless you are leaving a busy port with several ships all sailing the same day. Holland America

Line is currently the only company that has made its shore tenders accessible to wheelchair passengers, with a special boarding ramp and scissor lift so that wheelchair passengers can see out of the shore tender's windows.

WHEELCHAIRS

Wheelchair passengers with limited mobility should use a collapsible wheelchair. By limited mobility, I mean a person able to get out of the wheelchair and step over a sill or walk with a cane, crutches, or other walking device.

The chart that follows indicates the best cruise ships for wheelchair accessibility. Remember to ask questions before you make a reservation. Examples:

→ Does the cruise line's travel insurance (with a cancellation/trip interruption) cover you for any injuries while you are aboard ship?

→ Are any public rooms or public decks aboard the ship inaccessible to wheelchairs (for instance, it is sometimes difficult to obtain access to the outdoor swimming pool deck)?

→ Will you be guaranteed a good viewing place in the main showroom from where you can see the shows if seated in a wheelchair?

→ Will special transportation be provided to transfer you from airport to ship?

→ If you need a collapsible wheelchair, can this be provided by the cruise line?

→ Are passengers required to sign a medical release?

→ Do passengers need a doctor's note to qualify for a cabin for the physically challenged?

→ Will crew be on hand to help, or must the passengers rely on their own traveling companions for help?

→ Are the ship's tenders accessible to wheelchairs?

→ How do you get from your cabin to the lifeboats (which may be up or down several decks) in an emergency if the elevators are out of action and cannot be used?

WAIVERS

Passengers who do not require wheelchairs but are challenged in other ways, such as those who have impaired sight, hearing, or speech, present their own particular requirements. Many of these can be avoided if the person is accompanied by an able-bodied companion experienced in attending to their special needs. In any event, some cruise lines require physically challenged passengers to sign a waiver.

HEARING IMPAIRED

Many people suffer from hearing loss. Those affected should be aware of problems aboard ship:

→ Hearing the announcements on the public address system.

→ Use of the telephone.

→ Poor acoustics in key areas (for example, boarding shore tenders).

Take a spare battery for your hearing aid. More new ships have cabins specially fitted with colored signs to help those who are hearing impaired. *Crystal Cruises' Crystal Harmony* and *Crystal Symphony*, and *Celebrity Cruises' Century, Galaxy,* and *Mercury* are fitted with movie theaters with special headsets for the hearing impaired.

Many ships make life difficult for the hearing impaired, with constant, irritating, and repetitive announcements. It is often difficult for the hearing impaired to distinguish important or useful announcements from those that are of little or no importance.

Finally, when going ashore, particularly on organized excursions, be aware that most destinations are simply not equipped to handle the hearing impaired.

SHIPS RATED FOR WHEELCHAIR ACCESSIBILITY

Ship	Suitability Level	Ship	Suitability Level
Adventure of the Seas	A	Crystal Harmony	A
Aegean I	D	Crystal Symphony	A
Aegean Spirit	D	Dalmacija	D
AIDAcara	B	Dawn Princess	A
AIDAvita	B	Delphin	D
Akademik Sergey Vavilov	D	Disney Magic	B
Albatros	D	Disney Wonder	B
Ambasador I	D	Ecstasy	C
American Eagle	D	Elation	C
Amsterdam	B	Enchantment of the Seas	B
Arcadia (Golden Sun Cruises)	D	Endeavour	D
Arcadia (P&O Cruises)	B	Europa	B
Arion	D	European Star	B
Astor	C	European Vision	B
Astoria	C	Explorer	D
Asuka	C	Explorer of the Seas	A
Atalante	D	Fantasy	C
Aurora	A	Fascination	C
Ausonia	D	Finnmarken	B
Azur	D	Flamenco	D
Black Prince	D	Flying Cloud	D
Black Watch	C	Fuji Maru	D
Bolero	D	Funchal	D
Bremen	D	Galapagos Explorer II	D
Brilliance of the Seas	B	Galaxy	B
Calypso	D	Golden Princess	A
Cape Cod Light	D	Grand Princess	A
Cape May Light	D	Grande Caribe	D
Carnival Destiny	B	Grande Mariner	D
Carnival Legend	B	Grandeur of the Seas	B
Carnival Pride	B	Hanseatic	D
Carnival Spirit	B	Harald Jarl	D
Carnival Triumph	B	Hebridean Princess	D
Carnival Victory	B	Hebridean Spirit	D
Caronia	C	Holiday	D
Carousel	D	Horizon	B
Celebration	D	Imagination	C
Century	B	Independence	D
Clelia II	D	Infinity	A
Clipper Adventurer	D	Inspiration	C
Clipper Odyssey	C	Jubilee	D
Club Med 2	D	Kapitan Dranitsyn	D
C. Columbus	C	Kapitan Khlebnikov	D
Costa Allegra	D	Kong Harald	C
Costa Atlantica	B	Kristina Regina	D
Costa Classica	B	Le Levant	D
Costa Marina	D	Le Ponant	D
Costa Riviera	D	Legacy	D
Costa Romantica	B	Legend of the Seas	B
Costa Tropicale	D	Lofoten	D
Costa Victoria	B	Maasdam	B
Crown Odyssey	B	Majesty of the Seas	C
Crown Princess	B	Mandalay	D

SHIPS RATED FOR WHEELCHAIR ACCESSIBILITY

Ship	Suitability Level	Ship	Suitability Level
Marco Polo	C	Professor Multanovskiy	D
Maxim Gorkiy	D	Queen Elizabeth 2	B
Melody	C	R One	B
Mercury	B	R Two	B
Midnatsol	C	R Three	B
Millennium	A	R Four	B
Minerva	C	R Five	B
Mistral	C	R Six	B
Monarch of the Seas	C	R Seven	B
Monterey	D	R Eight	B
Nantucket Clipper	D	Radiance of the Seas	B
Narvik	C	Radisson Diamond	C
Niagara Prince	D	Regal Empress	D
Nippon Maru	C	Regal Princess	B
Noordam	C	Renaissance Seven	D
Nordic Empress	C	Renaissance Eight	D
Nordkapp	C	Rhapsody	D
Nordlys	C	Rhapsody of the Seas	B
Nordnorge	C	Richard With	C
Norway	B	Rotterdam	A
Norwegian Dream	C	Royal Clipper	D
Norwegian Majesty	D	Royal Princess	B
Norwegian Sea	D	Royal Star	D
Norwegian Sky	B	Ryndam	C
Norwegian Star	B	Saga Rose	C
Norwegian Sun	B	St. Helena	D
Norwegian Wind	C	Sapphire	D
Oceana	C	Seabourn Goddess I	D
OceanBreeze	D	Seabourn Goddess II	D
Ocean Majesty	D	Seabourn Legend	D
Ocean Princess	A	Seabourn Pride	D
Olvia	D	Seabourn Spirit	D
Olympia Countess	D	Seabourn Sun	A
Olympia Explorer	C	Sea Bird	D
Olympia Voyager	C	Sea Cloud	D
Oriana	B	Sea Cloud II	D
Orient Venus	D	Sea Lion	D
Pacific Princess	C	Sea Princess	A
Pacific Sky	C	Seawing	D
Pacific Venus	C	Sensation	C
Paradise	C	Serenade	D
Patriot	C	Seven Seas Mariner	A
Paul Gauguin	C	Seven Seas Navigator	B
Polaris	D	Silver Cloud	C
Polarlys	C	Silver Shadow	A
Polynesia	D	Silver Star	D
Princesa Amorosa	D	Silver Whisper	A
Princesa Cypria	D	Silver Wind	C
Princesa Marissa	D	Song of Flower	D
Princesa Victoria	D	Sovereign of the Seas	C
Princess Danae	D	Sovetskiy Soyuz	D
Professor Khromov	D	Spirit of '98	D
Professor Molchanov	D	Spirit of Alaska	D

63

SHIPS RATED FOR WHEELCHAIR ACCESSIBILITY

Ship	Suitability Level	Ship	Suitability Level
Spirit of Columbus	D	*Van Gogh*	D
Spirit of Discovery	D	*Veendam*	C
Spirit of Endeavour	D	*Vesteralen*	D
Spirit of Glacier Bay	D	*Victoria*	C
Spirit of Oceanus	D	*Viking Bordeaux*	D
Splendour of the Seas	B	*Viking Serenade*	D
Star Clipper	D	*Vision of the Seas*	B
Star Flyer	D	*Vistamar*	D
Star Pisces	D	*Volendam*	B
Star Princess	A	*Voyager of the Seas*	A
Statendam	C	*Westerdam*	C
Stella Oceanis	D	*Wilderness Adventurer*	D
Stella Solaris	D	*Wilderness Discoverer*	D
Summit	A	*Wind Song*	D
Sunbird	C	*Wind Spirit*	D
Sundream	D	*Wind Star*	D
Sun Princess	A	*Wind Surf*	C
SuperStar Aries	B	*World Renaissance*	D
SuperStar Gemini	C	*Yamal*	D
SuperStar Leo	B	*Yankee Clipper*	D
SuperStar Taurus	D	*Yorktown Clipper*	D
SuperStar Virgo	B	*Zaandam*	B
Switzerland	D	*Zenith*	B
The Emerald	D		
The Iris	D		
The World of ResidenSea	A		
Topaz	D		
Triton	D		
Universe Explorer	D		
Valtur Prima	D		

Notes

    A) Recommended as most suitable for wheelchair passengers
    B) Reasonably accessible for wheelchair passengers
    C) Moderately accessible for wheelchair passengers
    D) Not suitable for wheelchair passengers

    1) The following ships of Carnival Cruise Lines have double-width entertainment deck promenades that are good for wheelchair passengers, but the public restrooms are not accessible. In addition, although the cabin bathrooms are equipped with shower stalls and grab rails, the bathrooms have a steel "lip" and are, thus, neither suitable nor accessible when stepping out of a wheelchair: *Celebration, Ecstasy, Elation, Fantasy, Fascination, Holiday, Imagination, Inspiration, Jubilee, Paradise, Sensation.*

    2) *Crystal Harmony* and *Crystal Symphony* (Crystal Cruises) are the only ships presently in operation that provide special access ramps from an accommodation deck directly to the ship's lifeboats.

    3) *Regal Princess* (Princess Cruises) has large outside cabins for the physically challenged, although they have lifeboat-obstructed views.

CRUISING FOR ROMANTICS

DID YOU KNOW...?

...that motion pictures' most famous on-screen odd couple, Jack Lemmon and Walter Matthau, teamed up to be gentlemen dance hosts aboard a Caribbean cruise ship, in a film released in the US in July 1997? Called *Out to Sea*, the film also stars Gloria DeHaven, Dyan Cannon, Hal Linden, Alexander Powers, and Brent Spiner. The "cruise ship" interior was filmed at Raleigh Studios in Hollywood.

...that Epirotiki Line's *Jupiter* was used to carry the 61 finalists of the Miss Universe contest in 1976 (Epirotiki Line is now part of Royal Olympic Cruises)?

...that on Valentine's Day in 1998, some 5,000 couples renewed their vows aboard the ships of Princess Cruises?

Back in 1932, Warner Bros. released the film *One Way Passage*, a bittersweet story starring Kay Francis and William Powell. Remember the shipboard romance between Bette Davis and Paul Henried in the film *Now, Voyager*? Or Irene Dunne and Charles Boyer in *An Affair to Remember*? All involved oceangoing passenger ships and romance. Then there was *Gentlemen Prefer Blondes*, in which Marilyn Monroe and Jane Russell starred. In the early 1950s, Howard Hughes presented Jane Russell in an RKO movie called *The French Line*, which depicted life on board one of the great ocean liners of the time — the *ss Liberté* — as being exciting, frivolous, promiscuous, and romantic! The movie was, in fact, made on board the great ship. Today that same romantic attraction is still very much in vogue. In 1997, Kate Winslet and Leonardo DiCaprio showed young love and its great adventure aboard a stricken ocean liner on its maiden voyage across the North Atlantic, in the major Hollywood blockbuster *Titanic*.

While you may not believe in mermaids, romance does happen. With more and more people traveling alone, the possibility of a shipboard romance affords a special attraction. More than two million cruise passengers (more than 25 percent of all cruise passengers) traveled as singles in 2001. About 25 percent of all calls to travel agents are made by singles and single parents. Cruise lines are just waking up to this fact and are trying to help by providing special programs for single passengers. Some cruise lines or tour operators advertise special cruises for singles, but remember that the age range could be anything from 7 to 70.

Make no mistake about it, the world of cruising is made for couples. Singles are an expensive afterthought. Some singles are turned off to cruising because most cruise lines charge a single occupancy supplement for anyone traveling alone. The most precious commodity aboard any cruise ship is space. Every square foot must be used for essential facilities or revenue-earning areas. Since a single cabin is often as large as a double and uses the same electrical wiring, plumbing, and fixtures — and thus is just as expensive to build — cruise lines naturally feel justified in charging supplements or premiums for those who are occupying single cabins.

Single cabins are often among the most expensive, when compared with the per-person rates for double occupancy cabins. From the point of view of the crew, it takes as much time to clean a single cabin as it does a double. And there is only one tip instead of two.

SINGLE SUPPLEMENTS

If you want to travel alone and not share a cabin you can pay either a flat rate for the cabin or a single "supplement" if you occupy a double cabin. Some lines charge a fixed amount — $250, for instance — as a supplement, no matter what cabin category, ship, itinerary, or length of cruise you require. Single supplements, or solo occupancy rates, vary between lines, and sometimes between ships. Check with your travel agent for the latest rates.

GUARANTEED SINGLE RATES

Although some singles travel with friends or family, many others like to travel alone. For this reason, cruise lines have established several programs to accommodate them. One is the

65

"Guaranteed Single" rate, which provides a set price without having to be concerned about which cabin to choose. Some cruise lines have guaranteed singles' rates, but the line and *not* the passenger picks the cabin. If the line does not find a roommate, the single passenger may get the cabin to himself/herself at no extra charge.

GUARANTEED SHARE PROGRAMS

A "Guaranteed Share" program allows you to pay the normal double-occupancy rate, but the cruise line will find another passenger of the same sex to share the double cabin with you. Some cruise lines do not advertise a guaranteed share program in their brochures but will often try to accommodate such bookings, particularly when demand for space is light. You could book a guaranteed share basis cabin only to find that you end up with a cabin to yourself. As cruise lines are apt to change such things at short notice, it is best to check with your travel agent for the latest rates, and read the fine print.

CRUISING FOR SINGLE WOMEN

Any single woman can take a cruise vacation knowing that she is going to be as safe — if not safer — than she would be in any major vacation destination, but that does not mean that a cruise ship is a totally safe, completely hassle-free environment. Common sense should be the rule. Undoubtedly though, cruising is a great way to relax, and if you are seeking that special someone, cruising somehow brings people closer together.

There is always someone to talk to, be they couples or other singles, and cruising is not a "meat market" where you are always under observation. The easiest way to meet other singles, however, is to participate in scheduled activities. Be a little assertive, and get the cruise director or cruise staff to introduce you to other singles.

In the dining room, ask the restaurant manager to seat you with other singles, or a mix of singles and couples. Note that there is often a dearth of single black men (they simply have not discovered cruising yet).

If you are looking for romance, however, beware of the lure of the uniform. In considering an easy affair or fling with a ship's officer (or member of the crew), remember that they get to see new faces every week (or every cruise), and thus the possible risk of sexually transmitted diseases should be borne in mind.

GENTLEMEN CRUISE HOSTS

The female-to-male passenger ratio is high (as much as eight-to-one on world cruises and other long voyages), especially for passengers of middle to senior years, so some cruise lines provide male social hosts, specially recruited as dance and bridge partners, and company during social functions. First used to good effect aboard Cunard Line's *QE2* in the late 1970s, gentlemen hosts are now employed by a great number of cruise lines (particularly those carrying a large number of elderly passengers).

They generally host a table in the dining room, appear as dance partners at all cocktail parties and dance classes, and accompany women on shore excursions. These gentlemen, usually over 55 years of age and retired, are outgoing, mingle well, are well groomed, and enjoy cruise ships and traveling around the world almost free of charge.

If you think you would like such a job, do remember that you'll have to dance for several hours most nights, and dance just about every kind of dance well! Crystal Cruises, Cunard Line, Holland America Line, and Silversea Cruises, among others, provide gentlemen hosts, especially on the longer voyages and world cruises.

THE LOVE BOAT CONNECTION

Two famous television shows, *The Love Boat* (US) and *Traumschiff* (Germany), have given a tremendous boost to the concept of cruising as the ultimate romantic vacation, although what is shown on the screen does not quite correspond to reality. Indeed, the real captain of one ship, when asked the difference between his job and that of the captain of *The Love Boat*, remarked: "On TV they can do a retake if things are not right the first time around, whereas I have to get it right the first time!"

Ships are indeed romantic places (watching the blockbuster Hollywood movie *Titanic*, released in 1997, should convince you). There is nothing quite like standing on the aft deck of a cruise ship with your love — your hair blowing in the breeze — as you sail over the moonlit waters to yet another discovery. Of course, a full moon only occurs once a month, so check the calendar to make sure the timing of your moonlit cruise is perfect. And should the weather fail you, the ship itself offers many romantic settings.

There is no doubt that cruises provide excellent opportunities for meeting people of similar interests. So if you are looking for romance, and if you choose the right ship, the odds are definately in your favor.

GETTING MARRIED ABOARD SHIP

As in all those old black-and-white movies, a ship's captain can indeed marry you when at sea (unless the ship's country of registry prohibits, or does not recognize, such marriages), although in practice, this service is rarely offered by cruise lines today. You would need to inquire in your country of domicile (or residence) whether such a marriage is legal, and ascertain what paperwork and blood tests are required. The onus to provide the *validity* of such a marriage is yours. The captain could be sued and perhaps held criminally liable if he marries a couple that are not legally entitled to be married (for example, an underage male or female who do not have the consent of a parent or guardian, or if one or both parties are not legally divorced).

It is a simple matter to arrange to get married aboard almost any cruise ship when the ship is alongside in port, provided you take along your own registered minister. American Hawaii Cruises, Carnival Cruise Lines, Holland America Line, and Princess Cruises, among others, offer wedding packages. These include the services of a minister to marry you, wedding cake, champagne, bridal bouquet and matching boutonniere for the bridal party, a band to perform at the ceremony, and an album of wedding photos. Carnival Cruise Lines' program includes a marriage ceremony on a beach in Grand Cayman or St. Thomas. Princess Cruises offers weddings on a beach in St. Thomas (price range $525–$1,175 per package). Or you could arrange a romantic wedding Disney-style on its private island, Castaway Cay.

Princess Cruises features weddings aboard *Grand Princess*, in the first oceangoing wedding chapel aboard a contemporary cruise vessel, performed by the ship's captain (the wedding is legal because of the ship's registry, in Bermuda). There are three packages, Pearl, Emerald, and Diamond; the cost is $1400, $1800, and $2400, respectively. A Wedding Coordinator at the line handles all the details for you. And what could be better way than to be married aboard ship and have your honeymoon aboard, too!

Even if you can't get married aboard ship, you could have your wedding reception aboard one. Many cruise lines offer outstanding facilities and provide complete services to help you plan your reception. Contact the Director of Hotel Services at the cruise line of your choice. The cruise line should go out of its way to help, especially if you follow the reception with a honeymoon cruise.

UK-based passengers should know that P&O Cruises hosts a series of cruises called the "Red-Letter Anniversary Collection" for those celebrating 10, 15, 20, 25, 30, 35, 40, 45, 50, 55, or 60 years of marriage. Gifts you will receive with the compliments of P&O Cruises include a brass carriage clock, leather photograph album, free car parking at Southampton, or free first-class rail travel from anywhere in the UK (make sure to check with your travel agent for the latest and correct details).

A cruise also makes a fine, no-worry honeymoon vacation (perhaps that should read a "no worrymoon" vacation), and a delightful belated honeymoon getaway if you had no time to spare when you were married. You will feel as if you are in the middle of a movie set as you sail away to fairytale places, though actually, the ship is a destination in itself.

RENEWAL OF VOWS

There has recently been an upsurge in cruise lines performing "renewal of vows" ceremonies. A cruise is a wonderful setting for reaffirming to one's partner the strength of commitment. A handful of ships have a small chapel where this ceremony can take place; otherwise it can be anywhere aboard ship (a most romantic time is at sunrise or sunset on the open deck). The renewal of vows ceremony is conducted by the ship's captain and a nondenominational text reaffirms the love and trust between "partners, lifetime friends, and companions."

Although some companies, such as Carnival Cruise Lines, Celebrity Cruises, Holland America Line, and Princess Cruises, have complete packages for purchase, which include music, champagne, hors d'oeuvres, certificate, corsages for the women, and so on, most other companies do not charge (yet). The ship's photographer usually records the event (it is a revenue-generating photo opportunity) and will have special photo albums embossed with the cruise line's logo.

CRUISING FOR HONEYMOONERS

Cruising is popular as a honeymoon vacation. The advantages are obvious: You pack and unpack only once; it is a hassle-free and crime-free environment; and you get special attention, if you want it. It is also easy to budget in advance, as one price often includes airfare, cruise, food, entertainment, several destinations, shore excursions, and pre- and post-cruise hotel stays. Once you are married, some cruise lines often offer discounts to entice you to book a future (anniversary) cruise. Just think, no cooking meals, everything will be done for you. You can think of the crew as your very own service and kitchen staff.

Although no ship as yet provides bridal suites (hint, hint), many ships do provide cabins with queen-sized or double beds. Some, but by no means all, also provide tables for two in the dining room.

Some cruise ships feature Sunday departures, so couples can plan a Saturday wedding and reception before traveling to their ship. Pre- and post-cruise hotel accommodation can also be arranged.

Most large ships accommodate honeymoon couples well; however, if you want to plan a more private, intimate honeymoon, try one of the smaller, yacht-like cruise vessels such as those of Seabourn Cruise Line, Radisson Seven Seas Cruises, Silversea Cruises, or Windstar Cruises.

And what could be more romantic for honeymooners than to stroll by themselves on deck, to the forward part of the ship, above the ship's bridge. This is the quietest (except perhaps for some wind noise) and most dimly lit part of the ship, and an ideal spot for stargazing and romancing.

Cruise lines offer a variety of honeymoon packages, just as hotels and resorts on land do. Although not all cruise lines provide all services, typically they might include:

→ Private captain's cocktail party for honeymooners.
→ Tables for two in the dining room.
→ Set of crystal champagne or wine glasses.
→ Honeymoon photograph with the captain, and photo album.
→ Complimentary champagne (imported or domestic) or wine.
→ Honeymoon cruise certificate.
→ Champagne and caviar for breakfast.
→ Flowers in your suite or cabin.
→ Complimentary cake.
→ Special T-shirts.

Finally:

→ Remember to take a copy of your marriage license or certificate, for immigration (or marriage) purposes, as your passports will not yet have been amended.
→ Remember to allow extra in your budget for things like shipboard gratuities (tips), shore excursions, and spending money ashore.
→ If you want to sleep in a large bed next to your loved one, check with your travel agent and cruise line to make sure the cabin you have booked has such a bed. Better still, book a suite. But check and double-check to avoid disappointment.
→ If you need to take your wedding gown aboard for a planned wedding somewhere along the way — in Hawaii or Bermuda, for example — there is usually space to hang it in the dressing room next to the stage in the main showroom, especially on larger ships.

CRUISING FOR FAMILIES

Yes, you *can* take children on a cruise. In fact, once you get them aboard, you will hardly see them at all, if you choose the right ship and cruise. Families can do different things on a cruise, and parents do not have to be concerned about the whereabouts of their children. Where else can you go out for a night on the town without having to drive, and be home in a moment should the baby-sitter need you?

Dad can sleep in. Mom can go swimming and join an aerobics class. The kids can join in the organized activities that go on all day long. Whether you share a cabin with them or whether they have their own separate but adjoining cabin, there will be plenty to keep them occupied. Aboard several ships that cruise in the Caribbean, you will even find favorite life-sized cartoon characters.

Some cruise lines have token family programs, with limited activities and only a couple of general-al staff allocated to look after children, even though their brochures might claim otherwise. But cruise lines that are really serious about family cruise programs dedicate complete teams of children's and "tweens and teens" counselors, who run special programs that are off-limits to adults. They also have facilities such as high chairs in the dining room, cots, and real playrooms. Most children's entertainment is designed to run simultaneously with adult programs. For those cruising with very young children, baby-sitting services may also be available. For example, *QE2* has real children's nurses and even trained English National Nursing Examination Board-qualified nannies. *Arcadia, Aurora,* and *Oriana* have a "night nursery" for children of two to five years of age, so parents can go "out on the town" while the staff takes care of their offspring.

Parents, of course, have long realized that children cost more as they age. For example, children under two years travel free on most cruise lines (and airlines). If they are over two, they cost money.

There is little doubt that families who cruise together stay together! There is no better vacation for families than a ship cruise, especially at holiday time, whether it is at Christmas and New Year, Easter, or during the long summer school vacation. Active parents can have the best of all worlds, family togetherness, social contact, and privacy. Cruise ships provide a very safe, crime-free, encapsulated environment, and give junior passengers a lot of freedom without parents having to be concerned about where their children are at all times. Cruising has never been more child-friendly or affordable.

A cruise also allows junior passengers a chance to meet and play with others in their own age group. And because the days aboard are long, youngsters will also be able to spend time with their parents or grandparents, as well as with their peers.

A cruise for children is an educational experience. They will tour the ship's bridge, meet senior officers and learn about the navigation, radar, and communications equipment, as well as being able to see how the ship operates. They will be exposed to different environments, experience many types of food, travel to and explore new places, and participate in any number of exciting activities.

Cruise ships can be full of kids, or they can provide quiet moments. But aboard the busiest ships, adults will rarely get to use the swimming pools alone as they will be overcome with children having a truly good time. One good thing about a ship's swimming pool for kids, however, is the fact that there is no sand to get in their eyes (or anywhere else)!

Many cruise lines, recognizing the needs of families, have added a whole variety of children's programs to their daily activities. Some ships have separate swimming pools and play areas for children, as well as junior discos, video rooms, and teen centers.

69

Cruise lines serious about children divide them into five distinct age groups, with various names to match, according to cruise line and program: Toddlers (ages 2–4); Juniors (ages 5–7); Intermediate (ages 8–10); Tweens (ages 11–13); and Teens (ages 14–17). Notably, it often seems to be children under twelve who get the most from a cruise vacation.

DISNEY GOES CRUISING

In late July 1998, Disney Cruise Line entered the family cruise market with a big splash. The giant entertainment and theme park company introduced the first of two large ships (each has two funnels) that cater specifically to families with children. The two ships, *Disney Magic* and *Disney Wonder*, are family cruise ships that cater to 1,750 adults and up to 1,000 children, with the whole of the Disney organization to draw from for the shipboard entertainment program. For more comments, see *Disney Magic* and *Disney Wonder* in Part Two.

GENERAL INFORMATION

Parents with babies can rest assured that they will find selected baby foods on board ships that cater to children (along with cribs and high chairs, but do ask your travel agent to check first). If you need something out of the ordinary, or that special brand of baby food, do let your travel agent know well in advance. Most cruise lines are accommodating and will do their best to obtain what is needed, provided enough notice is given. Parents using organic baby foods, such as those obtained from health food stores, should be aware that cruise lines buy their supplies from major general food suppliers and not the smaller specialized food houses.

Although many ships have full programs for children during days at sea, these may be limited when the ship is in port. Ships expect you to take your children with you on organized excursions, and sometimes (though not always) there are special prices for children. If the ship has a playroom, it might be wise to find out if it is open and supervised on all days of the cruise. Do not expect your travel agent to know everything. Either ask the agent to find the answers to your questions, or do some research yourself.

When going ashore, remember that if you want to take your children swimming or to the beach, it is wise to phone ahead to a local hotel with a beach or pool. Whether it is in the Caribbean, the Mediterranean, or the Orient, most hotels will be delighted to show off their property, hoping for future business.

Some cruise ships in the Caribbean area have the use of a "private" island for a day. A lifeguard will be on duty, and there will be water sports and snorkeling equipment you can rent. Remember, however, that the beaches on some "private" islands are fine for 200 passengers, but with 2,000 they become crowded, and standing in line for beach barbecues and changing and toilet facilities becomes a necessary part of the experience.

Although the sun and sea might attract juniors to the warm waters of the Caribbean, children aged seven and over will find a Baltic, Black Sea, or Mediterranean cruise a delight. They will also have a fine introduction to history, languages, and different cultures.

CHILDREN'S RATES

Most cruise lines offer special rates for children sharing their parents' cabin. The cost is often lower than third and fourth person share rates. To get the best possible rates, however, it is wise to book early. And do not overlook booking an interior (no-view) cabin; you will rarely be in it anyway.

You should note that, although many adult cruise rates include airfare, most children's rates do not! Also, although some lines say children sail "free," they must in fact pay port taxes as well as airfare. The cruise line will get the airfare at the best rate, so there is no need to shop around for the lowest fare.

Unless they have plenty of things to keep them occupied, even the most placid and well-behaved children can become bored and restless. So try to choose a cruise where there are lots of other children, as they will be best equipped to provide the required entertainment.

SINGLE PARENTS

Single parents traveling with children will have their own special needs, and need not feel left out, either. They will feel more secure than in any hotel. In fact, a cruise provides a safe, convenient way for any single parent and child to be together but also have their own space and, in some cases, a guarantee of peer companionship for the child. A handful of cruise lines so far have introduced their versions of the "Single Parent Plan." This offers an economical way for single parents to take their children on a cruise, with parent and child sharing a two-berth cabin, or parent and children sharing a three-berth cabin. Single parents will pay approximately one-third the normal single-person rate for their children, and there will be plenty of activities for both parent and children to enjoy.

CHILDREN-FRIENDLY CRUISE LINES

The following cruise lines and ships have been selected by the author for their excellent programs and care (not all ships of a particular cruise line have been chosen):

→Aida Cruises (*AIDAcara, AIDAvita*)
→Carnival Cruise Lines (*Carnival Destiny, Carnival Legend, Carnival Pride, Carnival Spirit, Carnival Triumph, Carnival Victory, Ecstasy, Elation, Fantasy, Fascination, Imagination, Inspiration, Paradise, Sensation*)
→Celebrity Cruises (*Century, Galaxy, Infinity, Mercury, Millennium, Summit*)
→Cunard Line (*Queen Elizabeth 2*)
→Disney Cruise Line (*Disney Magic, Disney Wonder*)
→Norwegian Cruise Line (*Norway, Norwegian Sky, Norwegian Sun*)
→P&O Cruises (*Aurora, Oriana*)
→Royal Caribbean International (*Adventure of the Seas, Brilliance of the Seas, Explorer of the Seas, Radiance of the Seas, Voyager of the Seas*)
→Star Cruises (*Star Pisces, SuperStar Leo, SuperStar Virgo*)
→Thomson Cruises (*Emerald, Topaz*)

FAMILY REUNIONS

A cruise can provide the ideal place for a family reunion (either with or without children). Here are some tips to take into account when planning one.

→Let your travel agent do the planning and make all the arrangements (ask for a group discount if the total in your group adds up to more than 15). Make sure that together you choose the right cruise line, for the right reasons.

→ Book 12 months in advance if possible, so that you can arrange cabins close to each other (remember to arrange for everyone to be at the same dinner seating, if the ship operates two seatings).

→If anyone in the group has a birthday or anniversary, tell your travel agent to arrange a special cake (most cruise lines do not charge extra for this). Special private parties can also be arranged, although there will be an additional cost. If the group is not too large, you may be able to request to dine at the captain's table.

→Arrange shore excursions as a group (in some ports, private arrangements may prove unbeatable).

→Finally, get everything in writing (particularly cabin assignments and locations).

Children love the sense of adventure cruising offers.

BEFORE YOU GO

BAGGAGE

→ There is generally no limit to the amount of personal baggage you can take on your cruise (towels, soap, shampoo, and shower caps are provided aboard most cruise ships). Do allow extra space for purchases on the cruise.

→ Tag your luggage with your name, ship, cabin number, sailing date, and port of embarkation (tags are provided by the cruise line with your tickets). Baggage transfers from airport to ship are generally smooth and problem-free when handled by the cruise line.

→ Liability for loss or damage to baggage is contained in the passenger contract (part of your ticket). Do take out insurance (the policy should extend from the date of departure until two or three days after your return home).

CLOTHING

If you think you might not wear it, don't take it, as closet space aboard many ships is at a premium. So, unless you are on an extended cruise, keep your luggage to a minimum.

For cruises to tropical areas, where the weather is warm to hot with high humidity, casual wear should include plenty of lightweight cottons and other natural fibers. Synthetic materials do not "breathe" as well and often retain heat. Clothes should, however, be as opaque as possible to counteract the ultraviolet rays of the sun. Take a lightweight cotton sweater or windbreaker for the evenings, when the ship's air-conditioning will seem even more powerful after a day in the sun. Pack sunglasses and a hat. Rainstorms in the tropics are infrequent and do not last long, but they can give you a good soaking, so take inexpensive, lightweight rainwear for excursions.

The same is true for cruises to the Mediterranean, Greek Isles, or North Africa, although there will be little or no humidity for most of the year. Certain areas may be dusty as well as dry. In these latitudes, the weather can be changeable and might be cool in the evenings from October to March, so take extra sweaters and a windbreaker.

For cruises to Alaska, the North Cape, or the Norwegian fjords, take some warm comfortable clothing layers, plus a raincoat or parka for the northernmost port calls. Cruises to Alaska and the

Courtesy Douglas Ward

Carnival Destiny *(Carnival Cruise Lines) makes week-long cruises to the Caribbean.*

Land of the Midnight Sun are operated during the peak summer months, when temperatures are pleasant and the weather is less likely to be inclement. Unless you are traveling to northern ports such as St. Petersburg during winter, you will not need thermal underwear. However, you will need it — and an overcoat — if you are taking an adventure cruise to the Antarctic Peninsula or through the Northwest Passage.

In destinations with a strong religious tradition, like Venezuela, Haiti, the Dominican Republic, Colombia, and countries in the Far East, note that shorts or bare shoulders may cause local offense, so cover up.

Aboard ship, dress rules are relaxed during the day, but in the evening what you wear should be tasteful. Men should take a blazer or sports jacket and ties for the dining room and for any "informal" occasions. Transatlantic crossings are normally more elegant and require formal attire.

For formal nights (usually two out of seven), women can wear a long evening gown, elegant cocktail dress, or a smart pants suit. Gentlemen are expected to wear either a tuxedo or dark business suit and tie. These "rules" are less rigid on short and moderately priced cruises. If you are the athletic type, pack sportswear (and gym shoes) for the gymnasium or aerobics classes.

No matter where in the world you are traveling, comfortable low- or flat-heeled shoes are a *must* for women, except for formal nights. Light, airy walking shoes are best. If you are in the Caribbean or Pan-Pacific region and you are not used to heat and humidity, your ankles may swell, so tight shoes are not recommended. Rubber soles are best for walking on the deck of a ship.

→ **Formal**: Tuxedo, dinner jacket or dark suit for men; evening gown or other appropriate formal attire for women.

→ **Informal:** Jacket and tie for men; cocktail dress, dressy pantsuit, or the like for women.

→**Casual Elegance:** Long trousers (no shorts or jeans), proper collared and sleeved shirt (gentlemen); skirt or slacks and top for women.

→**Casual Relaxed:** Slacks and sweater or an open shirt (no tie) for men (no beach wear or muscle shirts); a blouse with skirt, slacks, or similar comfortable attire for women. Shoes are always required.

DOCUMENTS

A passport is the most practical proof of your citizenship and identification. Visas are required for some countries (allow time to obtain these). On most cruises, you will hand in your passport to the purser upon embarkation. This helps the ship to clear customs and immigration inspection on arrival in ports of call. Your passport will be returned prior to the ship's arrival in the port of disembarkation.

FLYING...AND JET LAG

Several cruise lines have "air deviation" desks that enable you to change your air flights and connections, for an additional fee (typically $25–$50 per person).

Modern air travel is fast and efficient. Even experienced travelers, however, may occasionally find that the stress of international travel persists long after the flight is over.

Eastbound flights seem to cause more pronounced jet lag than westbound flights. Jet aircraft are generally pressurized to some 8,000 feet (2,400 meters) in altitude, causing discomfort in the ears and the stomach, and swollen feet. A few precautions should reduce the less pleasant effects of flying around the world. Plan as far in advance of your cruise as you possibly can. Take a daytime flight, so that you can arrive at, or close to, your normal bedtime. Try to be as quiet as possible prior to flying, and allow for another five hours of rest after any flight that crosses more than five time zones.

Note: Babies and small children are less affected by changes in time because of their shorter sleeping and waking cycles, but adults generally need more time to adjust. The only way to experience a flight without jet lag is to fly the *Concorde* (London or Paris–New York or New York–London or Paris). At Mach-2 speed, such a flight does not produce the symptoms of jet lag.

MEDICATION

Take any medicine and other medical supplies that you need, plus spare eyeglasses or contact lenses. In many countries it may be difficult to find certain medicines. Others may be sold under different names. If you are taking a long cruise, ask your doctor for names of alternatives, in case the medicine you are taking is not available.

The ship's pharmacy will stock certain standard remedies, but do not expect a supply of the more unusual or obscure medicines. Remember to take along a doctor's prescription for any medication, especially when you are flying into foreign countries to join a ship, as customs may be difficult without documentation, particularly in the Far East.

Also, be advised that if you run out of your medication and you need to get a supply aboard ship, most ships will require that you see the doctor, even if you have a prescription. There is a charge for each visit, plus the cost of any medication.

Let spouses/companions also carry a supply of your medicine and medical supplies. Do not pack medication in any luggage to be checked in when flying, but take it in your carry-on.

MONEY MATTERS

Most cruise ships operate primarily in US dollars (or Euros) but a few operate in other currencies. Major credit cards and travelers' checks are accepted on board (few lines take personal checks). You sign for drinks and other assorted services, as part of the "cashless cruising" policy. Some large ships now have ATM cash machines.

PETS

Pets are not allowed aboard cruise ships (although a handful of cargo-passenger ships still carry them), with two exceptions. The first is aboard the scheduled transatlantic services of the *QE2*, which has 16 air-conditioned kennels (plus a genuine British lamppost and New York fire hydrant) and cat containers, plus several special cages for birds. The second is aboard the scheduled South Atlantic service from England to Cape Town and the Ascension Islands aboard *St. Helena*.

PHOTOGRAPHY

It is hard to find any situation more ideal for photography than a cruise. Your photographs enable you to share your memories with others at home. Here are some tips:

→ Use low-speed film in tropical areas such as the Caribbean or South Pacific (high-speed film is easily damaged by heat). Take plenty of film with you; standard sizes are available in the ship's shop, but the selection is limited. If you purchase film during a port visit, try to buy from an air-conditioned store, and check the expiration date.

→ Keep film cool, as the latent image on exposed film is fragile and easily affected by heat. There will be professional photographers on board who may develop film for you, for a fee (print film only).

→ When taking photographs in ports of call, respect the wishes of local inhabitants. Ask permission to photograph someone close-up. Most will smile and tell you to go ahead. But some people are superstitious or afraid of having their picture taken and will shy away from you. Do not press the point.

LIFE ABOARD

TOP 30 PET PEEVES (MINE AND THOSE OF OTHER PASSENGERS)

→ Passengers who do not possess a credit card (particularly older Asian passengers) are made to feel inferior at the check-in/embarkation desks, particularly in the United States. Some cruise lines have the temerity to ask for a $500 deposit in cash, just for the "privilege" of securing an onboard charge card. No hotel on land does this. Simply refuse, and say that if you cannot trust me, then refund my cruise fare.

→ Aboard the large, high-tech ships, getting Cabin Services, or the "Guest Relations Desk," or the Operator to answer the telephone can be an exercise in frustration, that taxes one patience

→ Aboard many ships, 15 percent is automatically added to wine bills. Thus, a wine waiter makes much more money on a more expensive bottle of wine, whether he knows anything about that wine (or how to decant and serve it, for example) or not. For doing just the same job for a wine costing $125 as for a wine costing $15 he makes a lot more. Therefore, insist on adding your own gratuity, and politely refuse to be told how much you have to tip.

→ Cruise brochures that use models provide the anticipation of an onboard product that a ship cannot always deliver; the result is disappointment for passengers. Some cruise brochures state that their ship has a "small ship feel, big ship choice" when it really caters to more than 1,000 passengers (often more than 2,000).

→ Constant and repetitive announcements for bingo, horse racing, and the latest gizmo sale in the shops are incredibly irritating.

→ Any announcement that is repeated. Any announcement that is repeated.

→ Flowers in one's cabin that are never watered or refreshed by the steward.

→ Bathrobes provided but never changed for the duration of the cruise.

→ Skimpy towels.

→ Mini-bar/refrigerators that do not provide limes and lemons for drinks.

→ Remote control units that need a instruction manual to understand their operation for turning on the television and getting a video player to work.

→ In-cabin announcements at any time, except for emergencies (they are completely unnecessary for programmed events and shore excursions).

→ Garnishes, when "parsley with everything" seems to be the rule of the seagoing entree experience.

→ Baked Alaska parades.

→ Paper, plastic, or polystyrene plastic cups for drinks of any kind.

→ Paper napkins for meals or informal buffets (they should be linen or cotton).

→ Plastic plates (often too small) for buffets.

→ Buffets where only cold plates are available, even for hot food items.

→ Repetitious breakfast and luncheon buffets and uncreative displays.

→ "Elevator" music playing continuously in passageways and on open decks (even worse: soft rock music).

→ Artwork placed aboard ships, when the cruise line does not care or know enough about it to place the name of the artist and the year of creation alongside, whether it be a painting or a sculpture.

→ Shopping lecturers, shopping videos, art auctions, and carpet auctions.

→ Shore-side porters who take your bags when you get off the bus, or out of your car, then stand there until you tip them before they move your bags or drop them (worst ports: Ft. Lauderdale and Miami).

→ Cabin stewards/stewardesses who place small folded pieces of paper in cabin door frames to show when their passengers have left their cabins.

→ Audiovisual technicians who think that the volume level of the show should equal that for a rock concert for 250,000 people.

→ Bands scheduled to play in a lounge that do not start playing until passengers walk in and sit down.

→ Private island days, when the tender ride to get to the island is longer than the flight to get to the ship.

⇢ Ships that ask you to settle your shipboard account before the morning of disembarkation.
⇢ Long lines and waiting periods for disembarkation.

AIR-CONDITIONING

Cabin temperature can be regulated by an individually controlled thermostat, so you can adjust it to suit yourself. Public room temperatures are controlled automatically. Air temperatures are often kept cooler than you may be used to.

ART AUCTIONS

Aboard many large and mid-size ships, art auctions form part of the entertainment. They are fun participation events, but don't expect to purchase an heirloom, as most of the art pieces are pure drivel. It's funny how so many identical pieces can be found aboard so many other ships!

BABY-SITTING

In some ships, stewards, stewardesses, and other staff may be available as sitters for an hourly charge. Make arrangements at the purser's office.

BEAUTY SALON/BARBER SHOP

Make appointments as soon after boarding as possible (particularly on short cruises). Appointment times fill up rapidly, particularly before social events such as a captain's cocktail party. Charges are comparable to those ashore. Typical services: haircut for men and women, styling, permanent waving, coloring, manicure, pedicure, and leg waxing.

BRIDGE VISITS

Check the *Daily Program* for navigation bridge visits. In some ships, bridge visits are not allowed for insurance and security reasons. In others, although personal visits are forbidden, a Behind the Scenes video on how the ship is run may be shown on the cabin television system.

CASHLESS CRUISING

It is now the norm to cruise cash-free, and to settle your account with one payment (by cash or credit card) prior to disembarking on the last day. Often this is arranged by making an imprint of a credit card prior to embarkation, permitting you to sign for everything. Before the end of the cruise, a detailed statement is delivered to your cabin. Some cruise lines may discontinue their "cashless" system for the last day of the cruise, which can be most irritating. *Note*: Ships visiting a "private island" on a Bahamas/Caribbean itinerary will probably ask you to pay cash for beverages, watersports/SCUBA gear, and other items purchased ashore.

CASINO

While most passengers do not choose a cruise in order to gamble, many cruise ships have casinos, with a range of table games (typically blackjack or 21, Caribbean stud poker, roulette, craps, and baccarat). Playing chips and cash change are available from the cashier or from banknote acceptance machines. Children under 18 are not allowed in the casino. The casino will be closed in port due to international customs regulations, and taking photographs in the casino is usually forbidden. German- and Japanese-registered ships are not permitted to operate casinos that give cash prizes.

Most cruise lines show videos that give information on how to play the various table games, as well as free lessons to entice players. Remember that casinos provide entertainment rather than a hard-core gambling environment.

COMMENT CARDS

On the last day of the cruise you are asked to fill out a company "comment card." Some cruise lines offer "incentives" such as a bottle of champagne. Be honest when you fill out this form, it serves as a means of communication between you and the cruise line. Pressure from staff to write "excellent" for everything is rampant aboard cruise ships. But if there *have* been problems with the service or any other aspect of your cruise, do say so.

COMMUNICATIONS

Most ships now have a direct-dial satellite telephone system. In addition, all ships are given an inter-

nationally recognized call sign, made up of a combination of several letters and digits. When the ship is at sea, you can call from your cabin (or the ship's radio room) to anywhere in the world:
→ via radiotelephone (a slight/moderate background noise might be noticed).
→ via satellite (which will be as clear as your own home phone).
Direct dial satellite calls (this service started in 1986) are more expensive, but are completed instantly. Some ships also have credit card telephones located in public areas; these also connect instantly, via satellite. Satellite calls can also be made when the ship is in port (radiotelephone calls cannot). Satellite telephone calls cost between $5 and $15 per minute, depending on the type of communications equipment the ship carries (the latest systems are digital). Calls are charged to your onboard account.
Your relatives and friends can reach you by calling the High Seas Operator in most countries (in the United States, dial 1-800-SEA-CALL). The operator will need the name of the ship, together with the ocean code (Atlantic is 871; Pacific is 872; and the Indian Ocean is 873).

CRUISESPEAK

The following terminology is used aboard today's cruise ships. The correct nautical terminology is given, while the words that follow are what many cruise lines now use:
Cabin Service: Room Service
Passenger: Guest
Purser's Office: Guest Relations Desk or Front Office
Cabin: Penthouse Suite, Junior Suite, Stateroom, or Room

CUSTOMS REGULATIONS

All countries vary in the duty-free allowances granted by their own customs service, but you will be informed aboard your cruise ship of the allowable amounts for your nationality and residency.

DAILY PROGRAM

The *Daily Program* contains a list of the day's activities, entertainment, and social events. It is normally delivered to your cabin the evening before the day that it covers. Read it carefully, so that you know what, when, and where things are happening.

*Being aboard **Crystal Harmony** (Crystal Cruises) is like cruising in a grand hotel.*

DEATH AT SEA

What happens if someone dies at sea? Typically, it happens more on long cruises, where passengers are generally older. Bodies are put in a special refrigeration unit for removal at the port of disembarkation, or the body can be flown home from a wayward port of call (more complicated, owing to the paperwork). Note that flying a body home usually involves a large expense. A burial at sea can also be arranged aboard ship (some people have a body cremated at home, return to their favorite cruise ship, and have the ashes scattered at sea).

DEPARTURE TAX

If you are disembarking in a foreign port and flying home, be advised that there could be a departure tax to pay (in local currency) at the airport.

DISEMBARKATION

During the final part of your cruise, the cruise director will give an informal talk on customs, immigration, and disembarkation (sometimes called "debarkation") procedures. The night before your ship reaches its final destination, you will be given a customs form to fill out. Any duty-free items bought from the shop on board must be included in your allowance (save the receipts in case a customs officer wishes to see them).

The night before arrival, place your main baggage outside your cabin on retiring (or before 4am). It will be collected and off-loaded on arrival. Leave out fragile items, liquor, and the clothes you intend to wear for disembarkation and onward travel (it is amazing just how many people pack everything, only to find they are in an embarrassing position on disembarkation day). Anything left in your cabin will be considered hand luggage to be hand-carried off when you leave.

On disembarkation day, breakfast will typically be early. It might be better to miss breakfast and sleep later, providing announcements on the ship's public address system do not wake you (it may be possible to turn off such announcements). Even worse than early breakfast is the fact that you will be commanded (requested, if you are lucky) to leave your cabin early, only to wait in crowded public rooms — sometimes for hours. To add insult to injury, your cabin steward (after he has received his tip, of course) will knock on the door to take the sheets off the bed so the cabin can be made up for the incoming passengers. Cruise aboard the smaller "upscale" ships and this will not happen.

Before leaving the ship, remember to claim any items you have placed in the ship's safety deposit boxes and leave your cabin key in your cabin. Passengers cannot go ashore until all baggage has been off-loaded, and customs and/or immigration inspections or pre-inspections have been carried out. In most ports, this takes two to three hours after arrival. It is wise to leave at least three hours from the time of arrival to catch a connecting flight or other transportation. Once off the ship, you will identify your baggage on the pier before going through customs inspection (delays are usually minimal). Porters may be there to assist you.

ENGINE ROOM

In almost all passenger ships, the engine room is off-limits to passengers, and visits are not allowed, for insurance and security reasons. In some ships, a technical information leaflet may be available. On others, a *Behind the Scenes* video may be shown on the cabin television system. For more specific or detailed information, contact a member of the ship's engineering staff via the purser's office.

GIFT SHOPS

The gift shop/boutique/drugstore will offer a selection of souvenirs, gifts, toiletries, and duty-free items, as well as a basic stock of essential items. You will find duty-free items, such as perfumes, watches, and so on, very competitively priced, and buying onboard ship may save you the hassle of shopping ashore. Opening hours are posted at the store and in the *Daily Program*.

HEALTH/FITNESS/SPA FACILITIES

The latest ships have elaborate spas where (for an extra fee) whole days of treatments are on offer. Stress reducing and relaxation treatments are practiced combined with the use of seawater, which contains minerals, micronutrients, and vitamins. Massages might include Swedish remedial massage, shiatsu, and aromatherapy treatments. Aboard some ships you can even get a massage on your private balcony.

LAUNCH (TENDER) SERVICES

Enclosed or open motor launches (called "tenders") are employed on those occasions when your cruise ship is unable to berth at a port or island. In such cases, a regular launch service is operated between ship and shore for the duration of the port call. Details of the launch service will be provided in the *Daily Program*. When stepping on or off a tender, remember to extend "forearm to forearm" to the person assisting you. Do not grip their hands because this simply has the effect of immobilizing the helper.

LAUNDERETTE

Some ships are fitted with self-service launderettes, equipped with washers, dryers, and ironing facilities (there may be a charge for laundry detergent and for use of the machines).

LAUNDRY AND DRY CLEANING

Most ships offer a full laundry and pressing service. Some ships may also offer dry-cleaning facilities. A detailed list of services (and prices) can be found in your cabin. Your steward will collect and deliver your laundry or dry cleaning.

LIBRARY

Most cruise ships have a library offering a good selection of books, reference material, and periodicals. A small deposit (refundable on return of the book) is sometimes required when you borrow a book. Note that aboard the small luxury ships, the library is open 24 hours a day, and no deposit is required. Aboard large ships, you will probably find that the library is open only a couple of hours each morning and afternoon. *Aurora*, *Oriana* and *QE2* are examples of ships with full-time, qualified librarians (aboard most other ships a member of the cruise staff or entertainment staff — with no knowledge of books or authors works the library). The library is where you will find games like Scrabble, backgammon, and chess.

LIFEBOAT DRILL

There have been few recent incidents requiring the evacuation of passengers, although two cruise ships have been totally lost following collisions (*Jupiter*, 1988, and *Royal Pacific*, 1992). Travel by ship, however, remains one of the safest means of transportation. Even so, it cannot be stressed enough that attendance at lifeboat drill is not only required but makes sense, and participation is mandatory. You must, at the very least, know your boat station and how to get to it in the event of an emergency.

If others are lighthearted about the drill, do not let that affect your seriousness of purpose. Be sure to note your exit and escape pathways and learn how to put on your lifejacket correctly. The drill takes no more than 15 minutes of your time and is a good investment in playing safe (in 1992, the cruise ship *Royal Pacific sank* in 16 minutes following a collision).

A Passenger Lifeboat Drill *must* be conducted on board within 24 hours of leaving the embarkation port (within 6 hours would be more desirable). You will hear an announcement from the bridge, which goes something like this: "Ladies and Gentlemen, may I have your attention, please. This is the captain speaking to you from the bridge. In 15 minutes time, the ship's alarm bells will signal emergency lifeboat drill for all passengers. This is a mandatory drill, conducted in accordance with the requirements of the *Safety of Life at Sea Convention*. There can be no exceptions."

The typical announcement will continue:

"The emergency signal is a succession of seven or more short blasts followed by one long blast of the ship's whistle, supplemented by the ringing of the electric gongs throughout the ship. On hearing this signal, you should make your way quickly but quietly to your cabin, put on warm clothing and your lifejacket, then follow the signs to your emergency boat station, where you will be kept fully informed over the loudspeakers through which I am speaking to you now."

LOST PROPERTY

Contact the purser's office immediately if you lose or find something on the ship. Notices regarding lost and found property may be posted on the bulletin boards.

MAIL

You can buy stamps and mail letters aboard most ships. Some ships use the postal privileges and stamps of their flag of registration, while others buy local stamps at ports of call. Mail is usually taken ashore by the ship's port agent just before the ship sails for the next port. A list of port agents and mailing addresses will be sent with your tickets and documents before you leave for your cruise, so you can advise friends and family how to send mail to you.

MASSAGE
Make appointments for a massage as soon after embarkation as possible, in order to obtain the time and day of your choice. Larger ships have more staff and offer more flexibility in appointment times. The cost averages about $2 per minute. In some ships, a massage service is available in your cabin (or on your private balcony), if it is large enough to accommodate a portable massage table.

MEDICAL SERVICES
Except for ships registered in England or Norway, there are *no* mandatory international maritime requirements for cruise lines to carry a licensed physician or to have hospital facilities aboard. However, in general, all ships carrying over 50 passengers *do* have hospital facilities and *do* carry at least one licensed doctor aboard ship (ships registered in England and Norway have both, without exception). Usually, there is a reasonably equipped hospital in miniature, although the standard of medical practice and of the physicians themselves may vary from line to line. Most shipboard doctors are generalists; there are no cardiologists or neurosurgeons. Doctors are often employed as outside contractors and therefore will charge for use of their services, including seasickness shots (except for Russian and Ukrainian registered vessels, where medical services are free). UK passengers should note that ships fall outside the UK National Health Service scheme.

Regrettably, many cruise lines place a low priority on providing medical services (there are, however, some exceptions). Most shipboard physicians are not certified in trauma treatment or medical evacuation procedures, for example. Most ships that cater to North American passengers tend to carry doctors licensed in the United States, Canada, or Britain, but aboard many other ships, doctors come from a variety of countries and disciplines. Some medical organizations, such as the American College of Emergency Physicians, have created a special division for cruise medicine.

Cunard Line's *QE2*, which carries 2,921 passengers and crew, has a fully equipped hospital with one surgeon, one doctor, a staff of six nurses, and two medical orderlies; contrast this with Carnival's *Sensation*, which carries up to 3,514 passengers and crew, with just one doctor and two nurses.

There is wide variation between standards and equipment. Obviously, any ship that features long-distance cruises, with several days at sea, should have better medical facilities and a better qualified staff than one that is engaged in a standard seven-day Caribbean cruise, with a port of call to make almost every day.

There is, at present, no agreed industry-wide standard relating to the standard of medical certification that is required by cruise ships. Most ship doctors are necessarily of the general practice type, but often, short-term contracts can mean poor continuity and differing standards.

Ideally, a ship's medical staff should be certified in Advanced Cardiac Life Support. The minimal standard medical equipment should include:
→ Examination room
→ Isolation ward/bed
→ X-ray machine (to verify the existence of broken or fractured bones)
→ Cardiac monitor (EKG) and defibrillator
→ Oxygen-saturation monitor (to determine a patient's blood-oxygen level)
→ External pacemaker
→ Oxygen, suction, and ventilators
→ Hematology analyzer
→ Culture incubator
→ Mobile trolley intensive care unit
Note: Any existing health problems that require treatment on board must be reported at the time of booking.

MOVIES
In most cruise ships a dedicated movie theater is an essential part of the ship's public-room facilities. The movies are recent, often selected by the cruise line from a special licensed film- or video-leasing service. Many of the latest ships have replaced or supplemented the ship's movie theater with television sets and video players in each cabin.

NEWS AND SPORTS BULLETINS
The world's news and sports results are reported in the ship's newspaper or placed on the bulletin board that is normally located near the purser's office or in the library. For sports results not listed, ask at the purser's office; it may be possible for the office to obtain the results for you.

PASSENGER LISTS
All ships of yesteryear provided passenger lists with each passenger's name and hometown or region. Today, only a handful of companies carry on the tradition (perhaps some passengers are traveling with someone they should not!).

PHOTOGRAPHS
Professional photographers take pictures of passengers throughout the cruise, including their arrival on board. They cover all main events and social functions, such as the captain's cocktail party. The photographs can be viewed without any obligation to purchase (the price is likely to be in excess of $6 for a postcard-sized color photograph).

POSTCARDS AND WRITING PAPER
These are available from the writing room, library, purser's office, or your room steward. Aboard many ships, they are available for a modest sum.

PURSER'S OFFICE
This is also known as the reception office, guest relations, or information desk. Centrally located, this is the nerve center of the ship for general passenger information and problems. Opening hours are posted outside the office and given in the *Daily Program*. In some ships, the purser's office is open 24 hours a day.

RELIGIOUS SERVICES
Interdenominational services are conducted on board, usually by the captain or staff captain. A few older ships (and Costa Cruises' ships) have a small private chapel. Denominational services may be offered by specially invited or fellow-passenger members of the clergy.

Courtesy Norwegian Coastal Voyage Inc.

Take in unique vistas of nature while enjoying a comfortable cruise.

ROOM SERVICE

Beverages and snacks are available at most hours. Liquor is normally limited to the hours when the ship's bars are open. Your room steward will advise you of the services that are offered. There is no charge for room service.

SAFETY FIRST

In an increasingly regulated world, the importance of safety cannot be overplayed. The training of crew in relation to safety and security has become extremely important — so much so that new international regulations are due to come into force that will require all crew to undergo basic safety training before they are allowed to join and work aboard any cruise ship. No longer will crew be recruited with the intention of providing on-the-job training.

Safeguards for passengers include lifeboats and life rafts. Since the introduction of the 1983 amendments to Chapter III of the *Safety of Life at Sea* (SOLAS) *Convention 1974* (which came into effect in 1980), much attention has been given to safety. The SOLAS conventions are subscribed to by all member countries of the United Nations, under the auspices of the International Maritime Organization (IMO).

All cruise ships built since 1 July 1986, must have either totally enclosed or partially enclosed lifeboats (only ships built before this date are allowed to have open lifeboats). These have diesel engines that will still operate when the lifeboat is inverted.

The 1990 SOLAS standards on stability and fire protection (mandating the enclosing of all stairways and the installation of sprinkler and smoke detection systems and "low-location" lighting) for all new ship construction took effect on October 1997. Existing ships have another five years to comply (the retrofitting of sprinkler systems in particular is an expensive measure that may not be considered viable by owners of older ships).

October 1, 1997, was the deadline whereby all cruise ships must:
→ Use smoke detectors and smoke alarms in all passenger cabins, corridors, stairway enclosures, and other public spaces.
→ Have and use low-level lighting showing routes of escape (such as in corridors and stairways).
→ Make all fire doors throughout the ship controllable from the ship's navigation bridge, and their status displayed thereon.
→ Make all fire doors that are held open by hinges capable of release from a remote location.
→ Use a general emergency alarm that is audible in all cabins.
In 2010, the use of combustible materials in cruise ship construction (allowed under the previous SOLAS 60 regulations) will be forbidden.

The crew attends frequent emergency drills, the lifeboat equipment is regularly tested, and the fire-detecting devices, and alarm and fire-fighting systems are checked throughout the ship. If you spot fire or smoke, use the nearest fire alarm box, alert a member of staff, or contact the bridge.

As of 1 July 2002, all ocean-going cruise ships on international voyages will be required to carry voyage data recorders (VDRs — similar to black boxes carried by aircraft).

SAILING TIME

In each port of call, the ship's sailing and all-aboard times are posted at the gangway. The all-aboard time is usually half an hour before sailing (ships cannot wait for individual passengers who are delayed).

SEASICKNESS

The French term *mal de mer* may sound quaint, but the malady has been nauseating to seafarers since the Phoenicians. Fortunately, seasickness is rare these days, even in rough weather (less than 3 percent of all passengers become seasick). Ships have stabilizers — large underwater "fins" on each side of the hull — to counteract any rolling motion. Nevertheless, it is possible to develop some symptoms — anything from slight nausea to vomiting.

Seasickness occurs when the brain receives confusing messages from the body's sensory organs, causing an imbalance of a mechanism in the inner ear. The mind and brain are accustomed to our walking or riding on a nonmoving surface. If the surface itself moves in another direction, a signal is sent to the brain that something's wrong. Continuous mixed signals result in headaches, clammy skin, dizziness, paleness, and yawning, soon followed by nausea and vomiting. There is still no explanation for the great difference in individual susceptibility to seasickness.

Both old-time sailors and modern physicians have their own remedies, and you can take your choice or try them all (but not at the same time):

→ When you notice the first movement of a ship, go out on deck and walk back and forth. You will find that your knees, which are our own form of stabilizer, will start getting their feel of balance and counteraction. This is the sign that you are "getting your sea legs."

→ Get the fresh sea breeze into your face (arguably the best antidote of all), and if nauseated, suck an orange or a lemon.

→ When on deck, focus on a steady point, such as the horizon.

→ Eat lightly. Do not make the mistake of thinking a heavy meal will keep your stomach well anchored. It will not.

→ Dramamine (dimenhydrinate, a sedative, which was introduced just after World War II) will be available in tablet (chewable) form on board the ship.

→ Scopoderm (also known as Transderm Scop), known as "The Patch" (manufactured by Ciba-Geigy), has an ingredient known as scopolamine, which has proven effective. It was reintroduced in 1997 after being taken off the market for several years.

→ If you are really distressed, the ship's doctor can give you an injection that should cure all discomfort. It may also make you drowsy, but the last thing on your mind will be staying awake at the movie.

→ Try Travel Oil, an aromatherapy oil made by Borealis Healthcare in the UK. It is a natural alternative to drug-based medications. Applied to the temples and across the forehead, there are no side effects.

→ Another natural preventive is ginger in powder form. Mix half a teaspoon in a glass of warm water or milk, and drink it before sailing. This is said to settle any stomach for a period of up to eight hours.

→ "Sea Bands" (or "Aquastraps") are a drug-free method of controlling motion sickness. These are slim bands (in varying colors) that are wrapped around the wrist, with a circular "button" that presses against an acupressure point (nei kuan) on the lower arm. Attach them a few minutes before you step aboard and wear on both wrists throughout the cruise.

All this being said, bear in mind that in addition to stabilizers in the hull, most cruises are in warm, calm waters and most cruise ships spend much time along the coast or pull into port regularly. The odds are very much against being seasick.

SECURITY

A recognized standard of passenger ship protection exists, following the hijacking of *Achille Lauro* in 1985. Cruise lines reached this recognized standard as a result of several factors: a moral obligation which, like safety, is inherent in the industry; passenger expectation; and the firmer, more formal pressures being applied across the world by governments and coast guards. You may be required to go through metal detection devices at the gangway, and your baggage may be subject to more stringent inspection.

All cabins can be locked, and it is recommended that you keep your cabin locked at all times when you are not there. Old-style keys are made of metal and operate a mechanical lock; most will be plastic key cards that operate electronically coded locks. Cruise lines do not accept responsibility for any money or valuables left in cabins and suggest that you store them in a safety deposit box at the purser's office, or, if one is supplied, in your in-cabin personal safe.

You will be issued a personal boarding pass when you embark (the latest high-tech passes may include your photo, lifeboat station, restaurant seating, and other pertinent information). This serves as identification and must be shown at the gangway each time you board (you may also be asked for a separate photo ID, such as a driver's license). The system of boarding passes is one of many ways in which cruise lines ensure passenger safety.

SHIPBOARD ETIQUETTE

Cruise lines want you to have a good vacation, but there are some rules to be observed.

→ In public rooms, smoking and nonsmoking sections are available. In the dining room, however, cigar and pipe smoking are not permitted at all.

→ If you take a video camera with you, be aware that you are not allowed to tape any of the professional entertainment shows and cabarets due to imposed international copyright infringement regulations.

83

➙ It is all right to be casual when on vacation, but not to enter a ship's dining room in just a bathing suit. Bare feet, likewise, are not permitted. If you are uncomfortable eating with the typical ten-piece dining room cutlery setting, don't fret; some cruise lines now have etiquette classes to help you.

SHIPBOARD INJURY

Slipping, tripping, and falling are the major sources of shipboard injury. This does not mean that ships are unsafe, but there are some things you can do to minimize the chance of injury. If you *do* suffer from injury aboard ship, feel it is the cruise line's fault, and want to take some kind of legal action against the company, you should be aware of the following:

In the United States, Appendix 46, Section 183(b) of the US Civil Code requires that "the injured passenger notify the cruise line in writing within six months from the date of the injury to file a claim and suit must be filed within one year from the date of injury." So, if you file a claim after the one-year period, the cruise line will probably seek a summary judgement for dismissal.

It is imperative that you first *read your ticket*. The passenger ticket is a *legal contract* between passenger and cruise line. It will invariably state that you must file suit in the state (or country) designated in the ticket. Thus, if a resident of California buys a cruise, and the cruise line is based in Florida, then the lawsuit must be filed in Florida. If you reside in the US and you purchase a cruise in the Mediterranean and the cruise line is based in Italy, then you would have to file suit in Italy. This is known as the Forum Clause.

A clause in the ticket typically reads:

"The Carrier's legal responsibility for death, injury, illness, damage, delay, or other loss or detriment of person or property of whatever kind suffered by the Passenger will, in the first instance, be governed by the Athens Convention relating to the Carriage of Passengers and their Luggage by Sea, 1974, with protocols and amendments, together with the further provisions of the International Convention on Limitation of Liability for Maritime Claims, 1976, with revisions and amendments (hereinafter collectively referred to as the "Convention"). The Carrier shall not be liable for any such death, injury, illness, damage, delay, loss, or detriment caused by Act of God, war or warlike operations, civil commotions, labor trouble, interference by Authorities, perils of the sea, or any other cause beyond the control of the Carrier, fire, thefts or any other crime, errors in the navigation or management of the Vessel, or defect in, or unseaworthiness of hull, machinery, appurtenances, equipment, furnishings, or supplies of the Vessel, fault or neglect of pilot, tugs, agents, independent contractors, such as ship's Physician, Passengers or other persons on board not in the Carrier's employ or for any other cause of whatsoever nature except and unless it is proven that such death, injury, illness, damage, delay, loss resulting from Carrier's act or omission was committed with the intent to cause such loss or with knowledge that such loss would probably result therefrom and in that event the Carrier's liability therefore shall not exceed the specified limitations per Passenger in Special Drawing Rights (S.D.R.) as defined in the applicable conventions or in any further revision and/or amendment thereto as shall become applicable."

One area in which passengers may not be able to sue a cruise line is in the event of injury or accident when they are on a shore excursion advertised and sold aboard ship. This is because the tour operators are independent contractors. So, when you buy your shore excursion, ask if the ship's insurance fully covers you under the terms of the passenger ticket contract.

In Your Cabin

Note that aboard many ships, particularly older vessels, there are raised lips separating the bathroom from the sleeping area.

➙ Do not hang anything from the fire sprinkler heads located on most cabin ceilings.

➙ On older ships, it is wise to note how the door lock works. Some require a key on the inside in order to unlock the door. Leave the key in the lock, so that in the event of a real emergency, you do not have to hunt for the key.

On Deck

➙ Aboard older ships, watch for raised lips in doorways leading to open deck areas. Be alert and do not trip over them.

➙ Wear sensible shoes with rubber soles (not crepe) when walking on deck or going to pool and lido areas. Do not wear high heels.

→ Walk with caution when the outer decks are wet after being washed, or if they are wet after rain. This warning applies especially to metal decks. There is nothing more painful than falling onto a solid steel deck.

→ Do not throw a lighted cigarette or cigar butt, or knock out your pipe, over the ship's side. The sea might seem like a safe place to throw such items, but they can easily be sucked into an opening in the ship's side or onto an aft open deck area, only to cause a fire.

How to Survive A Shipboard Fire

Shipboard fires generate heat, smoke, and often panic. In the unlikely event that you are in one, try to remain calm and think logically and clearly.

When you board the ship and get to your cabin, check the way from there to the nearest emergency exits fore and aft. Count the number of cabin doorways and other distinguishing features to the exits in case you have to escape without the benefit of lighting, or in case the passageway is filled with smoke and you cannot see clearly. New ships will use the "low location" lighting systems more and more, which are either the electroluminescent or photoluminescent type.

Exit signs are located just above floor level, but aboard older vessels the signs may be above your head, which is virtually useless, as smoke and flames always rise. Note the nearest fire alarm location and know how to use it in case of dense smoke and/or no lighting.

In the future, it is likely that directional sound evacuation beacons will be mandated; these will direct passengers to exits, escape-ways and other safe areas and appear to be better than the present visual aids, which can be all but useless if the compartment you are in is completely surrounded by smoke.

If you are in your cabin and there is fire in the passageway outside, first put on your lifejacket and feel for the cabin door. If the door handle is hot, soak a towel in water and use it to turn the handle of the door. If there is a raging fire in the passageway, cover yourself in wet towels and go through the flames. It may be your only means of escape, unless you have a balcony.

Check the passageway. If there are no flames, or if everything looks clear, walk to the nearest emergency exit or stairway. If there is smoke in the passageway, crawl to the nearest exit. If the exit is blocked, then go to an alternate one.

It may take considerable effort to open a fire door to the exit, as they are heavy. Don't use the elevators, as they may stop at a deck that is on fire or full of smoke.

In the event of fire in your cabin, report it immediately by telephone. Then get out of your cabin if you can and close the door behind you to prevent any smoke or flames from entering the passageway. Finally, sound the alarm and alert your neighbors.

SHORE EXCURSIONS

→ Cruise lines plan and oversee shore excursions under the assumption that you have not seen a place, and aim to show you its highlights in a comfortable manner and at a reasonable price.

→ Buses, rather than taxis or private cars, are often the principal choice of transportation. This cuts costs and allows the tour operator to narrow the selection of guides to only those most competent, knowledgeable, and fluent in whatever language the majority of passengers speak, while providing some degree of security and control.

→ Brochure-Speak: Shore excursion descriptions include artistic license, often written by personnel who have not visited the port of call. All cruise lines should adopt the following definitions in their descriptive literature and for their lectures and presentations: The term "visit" should be taken to mean actually entering the place or building concerned. The term "see" should be taken to mean viewing from the outside (as from a bus, for example).

→ Shore excursions are timed to be most convenient for the greatest number of participants, taking into account the timing of meals on board (these may be altered according to excursion times). Departure times are listed in the descriptive literature and in the *Daily Program*, and may or may not be announced over the ship's public address system. There are no refunds if you miss the excursion.
Note: If you are hearing impaired, make arrangements with the shore excursion manager to assist you in departing for your excursions at the correct times.

→ The ship's representative that supervises the shore excursion program is the eyes and ears of the cruise line, and he or she can recommend to the head office that any excursion be suspended if it is not up to standard. Shore excursion staff will be dockside dispatching the excursions in each port.

*Attend lectures, poetry readings, and concerts while cruising to your next destination aboard **Europa** (Hapag-Lloyd Cruises).*

→ Most excursions give little in-depth history, and guides are often not acquainted with details beyond a superficial general knowledge.

→ City excursions are basically superficial. To get to know a city intimately, go alone or with a small group. Go by taxi or bus, or walk directly to the places that are of most interest to you.

→ Many ships operate diving excursions at a reasonable price that includes all equipment. Instruction is offered on board, and underwater cameras can often be rented, too.

→ When you buy a shore excursion from the cruise line, you are fully covered by the ship's insurance; do it on your own and you are not covered when you step off the ship.

→ Shore excursion booking forms should be forwarded with your cruise tickets and documents. In some ships, they can be booked via the interactive television system in your cabin.

→ Book early, particularly for those listed as "limited participation." This means that there are a restricted number of places available, sold on a first come-first served basis. In some ships, where shore excursions can be booked prior to the sailing date, sellouts often occur.

→ For cancellations, most ships require a minimum of 24 hours' notice before the advertised shore excursion departure time. Refunds are at the discretion of the cruise line.

→ Only take along what is necessary; leave any valuables aboard ship, together with any money and credit cards you do not plan to use. Groups of people are often targets for pickpockets in popular sightseeing destinations and major cities. Also, beware of excursion guides who give you a colored disk to wear for "identification." They may be marking you as a "rich" tourist for local shopkeepers.

→ Going solo? If you hire a taxi for sightseeing, negotiate the price in advance, and do not pay until you get back to the ship or to your final destination. If you are with friends, hiring a taxi for a full- or half-day sightseeing trip can often work out to be far cheaper than renting a car, and you also avoid the hazards of driving. Naturally, prices vary according to destination, but if you can select a driver who speaks your language, and the taxi is comfortable, even air-conditioned, you are ahead of the game.

SHOPPING

→ Many cruise lines that operate in Alaska, the Bahamas, the Caribbean, and the Mexican Riviera openly engage a company that provides the services of a "shopping lecturer." The shopping lecturer promotes selected shops, goods, and services heavily, fully authorized by the cruise line (which receives a commission from the same). This relieves the cruise director of any responsibilities, together with any question about his involvement, credibility, and financial remuneration.

→ Shopping maps, with "selected" stores highlighted, are placed in your cabin. Often, they come with a "guarantee" such as: "Shop with confidence at each of the recommended stores. Each merchant listed on this map has been carefully selected on the basis of quality, fair dealing, and value. These merchants have given Cruise Line X a guarantee of satisfaction valid for thirty (30) days after purchase, excluding passenger negligence and buyers' regret, and have paid a promotional fee for inclusion as a guaranteed store."

→ Know in advance just what you are looking for, especially if your time is limited. But if time is no problem, browsing can be fun.

→ When shopping time is included in shore excursions, be wary of stores recommended by tour guides; the guides are likely to be receiving commissions from the merchants.

→ Shop around and compare prices before you buy. Good shopping hints and recommendations are often given in the port lecture at the start of your cruise.

→ When shopping for local handicrafts, make sure they have indeed been made locally.

→ Be wary of "bargain-priced" name brands, as they may well be counterfeit and of dubious quality. For watches, check the guarantee. Some shopping information may be available in information literature about the port and this should be available at the ship's shore excursion office.

→ Remember that the ship's shops are also duty-free and, for the most part, competitive in price. The shops on board are closed while in port, however, due to international customs regulations.

SPORTS FACILITIES

The variety of sports facilities on board depends on the size of the ship. Facilities typically include: badminton, basketball practice area, golf driving cage, horseshoes, jogging track, miniature putting green, paddle tennis, ping pong, quoits, ring toss, shuffleboard, skeet shooting, squash (rarely), and volleyball.

SUN

Cruising to the sun? Note that the closer you get to the equator the more potent and penetrating are the rays. They are most harmful when the sun is directly overhead. Use a protective sun lotion (15–30 factor), and reapply it every time you go for a swim or soak in the pool or ocean. Start with just 15 minutes' exposure and gradually work your way up to an hour or so. It is better to go home with a suntan than sunburn.

SWIMMING POOLS

Most ships have outdoor or indoor swimming pools, or both. They may be closed in port owing to local health regulations and/or cleaning. Opening hours will be listed in the *Daily Program*. Diving is not allowed, since pools are shallow. Parents should note that most pools are unsupervised. Be aware that some ships use excessive chlorine or bleaching agents for cleaning; these could cause bathing suit colors to run.

TELEVISION

Television programming is obtained from a mixture of satellite feeds and onboard videos. Some ships can lock-on to live international news programs (such as CNN or BBC World News), or to text-only news services, for which cruise lines pay a subscription fee. Satellite television reception is sometimes poor, however, due to the fact that ships constantly move out of the narrow beam being downloaded from the satellite and they therefore cannot "track" the signal as accurately as a land-based facility.

TIPPING (GRATUITIES)

Many travelers feel that the ship should host its passengers, and that the passengers should not host the crew by means of tips, so the question of tipping is awkward and embarrassing. In some ships, there are subtle suggestions made regarding tips; in others, cruise directors get carried away and are simply dictatorial regarding tipping. Some ships offer hints on tipping via the in-cabin video system. Some cruise brochures state "tipping is not required." They may not be required, but will definitely be expected by the ship's staff.

The accepted cruise industry standard for gratuities follows:

→ **Dining room waiter**: $3–$4 per person per day;

↳ **Busboy**: $1.50–$2.00 per day;
↳ **Cabin steward/stewardess**: $3.00–$3.50 per person per day;
↳ **Butler**: $5 –$6 per person per day.
↳ Aboard many ships a gratuity of 10 or 15 percent is automatically added to your bar check.

Tips are normally given on the last evening of a cruise of up to 14 days' duration. For longer cruises, you would extend half of the tip halfway through your trip and the rest on your last evening. *Note*: In some Greek-flagged ships, gratuities are pooled and given to the chief steward, who gives them out at the end of each cruise ($8–$10 per person per day is the norm).

Gratuities are included in the cruise fare aboard a small number of ships (principally those in the luxury end of the market), where no extra tipping is permitted (in theory). Gratuities are increasingly being added automatically to onboard accounts by most of the major cruise lines.

Origin of the Word "Tips"

Before the introduction of postage stamps, coachmen who carried passengers were often asked to carry a letter or other package. A small recompense was given for this service, called "tips" — which stands for "to insure personal service." Hence, when in the future some special service was provided, particularly in the hospitality industry, tips became an accepted way of saying thank-you for services rendered.

VALUABLES

Many ships now have a small personal safe in each cabin. However, items of special value should be kept in a safety deposit box in the purser's office. You will then have simple and convenient access to your valuables during the cruise.

VISITORS

Passes for visitors to see you on board prior to sailing must be arranged in advance, preferably at the time you make your booking. Announcements will be made when it is time for all visitors to go ashore.

Sadly, bon voyage parties, such as those you may have seen in the movies, are virtually a thing of the past. They are no longer possible (with the exception of ships operating around-the-world cruises) owing to greatly increased security concerns and insurance regulations.

Courtesy Norwegian Coastal Voyage Inc.

Business becomes pleasure on a cruise.

WATER SPORTS

Some small ships have a watersports platform that is lowered from the ship's stern or side. These ships carry windsurfers, water-ski boats, jet skis, water skis, and SCUBA and snorkel equipment, usually at no extra charge. Some may also feature an enclosed swimming "cage" for areas of the world where unpleasant fish might be lurking.

Although such facilities look good in the cruise brochures, in many cases ships seem reluctant to use them. This is because many itineraries have too few useful anchor ports. Also, the sea must be in an almost flat calm condition, which is seldom the case. Another more prosaic reason is simply because of strict insurance regulations.

WINE AND LIQUOR

The cost of drinks on board is generally lower than on land, since ships have access to duty-free liquor. Drinks may be ordered in the dining room, at any of the ship's bars or from room service. Some lines charge "corkage," a fee to deter passengers from bringing their own wines into the dining room.

In the dining room, you can order wine with your meals from an extensive and reasonably priced wine list. For wine with your dinner, try to place your order at lunchtime, as wine waiters are always at their busiest at the evening meal.

In some ships, a duty-free sales point allows you to purchase wine and liquor for personal consumption in your cabin. You will not normally be permitted to bring these purchases into the dining room or other public rooms, nor any duty-free wine or liquor purchased in port. These regulations are made to protect bar sales, which are a substantial source of onboard revenue for the cruise line.

20 PRACTICAL TIPS FOR A GOOD CRUISE EXPERIENCE

What to Do If...

1. Your luggage does not arrive at the ship.

If you are part of the cruise line's air/sea package, the airline is wholly responsible for locating your luggage and delivering it to the next port. If you arranged your own air transportation, it is wholly *your* problem. Always have easy-to-read name and address tags both *inside* as well as *outside* your luggage. Keep track of claim documents and give the airline a detailed itinerary and list of port agents (usually included with your documents).

2. You miss the ship.

If you miss the ship's departure (due to late or non-performing flight connections, etc.), and you are traveling on an air/sea package, the airline will arrange to get you to the ship. If you are traveling "cruise-only," however, and have arranged your own air transportation, then you are responsible for onward flights, hotel stays, and transfers. Many cruise lines now have "deviation" desks, where (for a fee) you can adjust airline flights and dates to suit personal preferences. If you arrive at the port just as your ship is pulling away, see the ship's port agent immediately.

3. Your cabin is too small.

Almost all cruise ship cabins are too small! When you book a cruise, you pay for a certain category and type of cabin but have little or no control over which one you actually get. See the hotel manager as soon as possible, explaining what is wrong with the cabin (noisy, too hot, etc.). If the ship is full (and most are nowadays), it will be difficult to change. However, the hotel manager will probably try to move you from known problem cabins, although they are not required to do so.

4. Your cabin has no air-conditioning, is noisy, or there are plumbing problems.

If there is anything wrong in your cabin, or if there is something wrong with the plumbing in your bathroom, bring it to the attention of your cabin steward immediately. If nothing gets better, complain to the hotel manager. Some cabins, for example, are located above the ship's laundry, generator, or galley (hot); others may be above the disco (noisy). If the ship is full, it may be difficult to change.

5. You have noisy cabin neighbors.

First, politely tell your neighbors that you can hear them brushing their hair as the cabin walls are so thin, and would they please not bang the drawers shut at 2am! If that does not work, complain to the purser or hotel manager, and ask them to attend to the problem.

6. You have small children and the brochure implied that the ship has special programs for them, but when on board you find out it is not a year-round program.

In this instance, either the brochure was misleading, or your travel agent did not know enough about the ship or did not bother to ask the right questions. If you have genuine cause for complaint, then see your travel agent when you get home. Ships generally will try to accommodate your young ones, but may not be covered by their insurance for "looking after" them throughout the day, as the brochure seemed to promise. Again, check thoroughly with your travel agent *before* you book.

7. You do not like your dining room seating.
Most "standard" market ships operate two seatings for dinner (sometimes for all meals). When you book your cruise, you are asked whether you want the first or second seating. The line will make every attempt to please you. But if you want second seating and are given first seating, there may be little the restaurant manager can do.

8. You want a table for two and are put at a table for eight.
See the restaurant manager and explain why you are not satisfied. A little gratuity should prove helpful.

9. You cannot communicate with your dining room waiter.
Dining room waiters are probably of a nationality and tongue completely foreign to yours, and all they can do is smile. This could prove frustrating for a whole cruise, especially if you need something out of the ordinary. See the restaurant manager, and tell him you want a waiter with whom you can communicate. If he does not solve the problem, see the hotel manager.

10. The food is definitely not "gourmet" cuisine as advertised in the brochure.
If the food is not as described (for example, whole lobster in the brochure, but only cold lobster salad once during the cruise, or the "fresh squeezed" orange juice on the breakfast menu is anything but), tell the maître d.'

11. A large group has taken over the ship.
Sometimes, large groups have blocked (pre-booked) several public rooms for meetings (seemingly every hour on the hour in the rooms you want to use). This means the individual passenger (that is you) becomes a second-class citizen. Make your displeasure known to the hotel manager immediately, tell your travel agent, and write a follow-up letter to the line when you return home.

12. A port of call is deleted from the itinerary.
If you only took the cruise because the ship goes to the place you have wanted to go for years, then read the fine print in the brochure *before* you book. A cruise line is under *no* obligation to perform the stated itinerary. For whatever reason (political unrest, weather, mechanical problems, no berth space, safety, etc.), the ship's captain has the ultimate say.

13. You are unwell aboard ship.
Do not worry. There will be a qualified doctor (who generally operates as a concession, and therefore charges) and medical facilities, including a small pharmacy. You will be well taken care of. Although there are charges for medical services rendered, almost all cruise lines offer insurance packages that include medical coverage for most eventualities. It is wise to take out this insurance when you book.

14. You have a problem with a crew member.
Go to the hotel manager or chief purser and explain the problem (for single women this could be a persistent cabin steward with a master door key). No one will do anything unless you complain. Cruise ships try to hire decent staff, but, with so many crew, there are bound to be a few bad apples. Insist on a full written report of the incident, which must be entered into the ship's daily log by the staff captain (deputy captain).

15. You leave some personal belongings on a tour bus.
If you have left something on a tour bus, and you are back on board your ship, first advise the shore excursion manager or the purser's office. The shore excursion manager will contact the tour operator ashore to ascertain whether any items have been handed in to their office.

16. The cruise line's air arrangements have you flying from Los Angeles via Timbuktu to get to your cruise ship.
Fine if your cruise ship is in Timbuktu (difficult, as it is inland). Most cruise lines that have low rates also use the cheapest air routing to get you to your ship. That could mean flights from a central hub. Be warned: You get what you pay for. Ask questions *before* you book.

17. You fly internationally to take a cruise.

If your cruise is a long distance away from your home, then it makes good sense to fly to your cruise embarkation point and stay for at least a day or two before the cruise. Why? You will be better rested. You will have time to adjust to any time changes. You will step aboard your ship already relaxed.

18. The ship's laundry ruins your clothes.

If any of your clothing is ruined or discolored by the ship's laundry, tell your cabin steward(ess), and then follow up by going to the purser's office and getting it registered as a proper complaint. Get a copy of it, so you can follow up when you get home. Unfortunately, you will probably find a disclaimer on the laundry list saying something to the effect that liability is limited to about $1 per item, which is not a lot. So, although the laundry and dry cleaning facilities generally work well, things can occasionally go wrong just like ashore.

19. You have extra charges on your bill.

Check your itemized bill carefully. Then talk to the purser's office and ask them to show you the charge slips. Make sure you are given a new copy of your bill, *after* any modifications have been made.

20. You are unhappy with your cruise experience.

You (or your travel agent) ultimately choose the ship and cruise. But if your ship does not meet your specific lifestyle and interests, or the ship performs less well than the brochure promises, then let your travel agent and the cruise line know as soon as possible. If your grievance is valid, many cruise lines will offer a credit, good towards a future cruise. But do read the fine print on the ticket.

THE PASSENGER'S PRAYER

"Heavenly Father, look down on us, Your humble, obedient passengers who are doomed to travel the seas and waterways of this earth, taking photographs, mailing postcards, buying useless souvenirs, and walking around in ill-fitting swimwear.

"We beseech You, oh Lord, to see that our plane is not hijacked, our luggage is not lost, and that our oversized carry-ons go unnoticed.

"Protect us from surly and unscrupulous taxi drivers, avaricious porters, and unlicensed, English-speaking guides in foreign places.

"Give us this day Divine guidance in the selection of our cruise ships and our travel agents — so that we may find our bookings and dining room reservations honored, our cabins of generous proportions, that our luggage arrives before the first evening meal, and that our beds are made up.

"We humbly ask that our shower curtains do not provoke us into meaningless frustration and destructive thoughts.

"We pray that our cabin telephones work, the operator (human or electrical) speaks our tongue, and that there are no phone calls from our children forcing us to abandon our cruise early.

"Lead us, dear Lord, to good, inexpensive restaurants in the world ashore — where the food is superb, the waiters friendly, and the wine included in the price of a meal.

"Please grant us a cruise director who does overly celebrate the spoils of bingo or horse racing, or does not stress only those jewelry stores from which he accepts an offering.

"Grant us the strength to take shore excursions — to visit the museums, cathedrals, spice stalls, and gift shops listed in the guidebooks.

"And if on our return journey by non-air-conditioned buses we slip into slumber, have mercy on us for our flesh is weak, hot, and tired.

"Give us the wisdom to tip correctly at the end of our voyage. Forgive us for under-tipping out of ignorance, and over-tipping out of fear. Please make the chief purser and ship's staff loves us for what we are and not for what we can contribute to their worldly goods or company comment forms.

"Dear God, keep our wives from shopping sprees and protect them from bargains they do not need or cannot afford. Lead them not into temptation in St. Thomas or Hong Kong for they know not what they do.

"Almighty Father, keep our husbands from looking at foreign women and comparing them to us. Save them from making fools of themselves in cafés and nightclubs. Above all, please do not forgive them their trespasses for they know exactly what they do.

"And when our voyage is over and we return home to our loved ones, grant us the favor of finding someone who will look at our home videos and listen to our stories, so our lives as tourists will not have been in vain. This we ask you in the name of our chosen cruise line, and in the name of American Express, Visa, Mastercard, and our banks. Amen."

QUIPS AND QUOTES

Passengers cruising for the first time are the source of all the following questions to me when I worked aboard ships all those years ago:
"Do the crew sleep on board?"
"How far above sea level are we?"
"Is the island surrounded by water?"
"How does the captain know which port to go to?"
"Can we get off in the Panama Canal?"
"Does the ship generate its own electricity?"
"Does this elevator go up as well as down?"
"Will this elevator take me to my cabin?"
"Why is the sauna so hot?"
"What time's the midnight buffet?"
"Are there two seatings at the midnight buffet?"
"Can I please have some hot iced tea?"
"Do we have to stay up until midnight to change our clocks?"
"Does the chef cook himself?"
"What do they do with the ice sculptures after they melt?"
"How many fjords to the dollar?"
"What time's the 2 o'clock tour?"
"Where's the bus for the walking tour?"
"Will we have time to take the shore excursion?"
"If I don't buy a shore excursion, am I allowed off in port?"
"Are the entertainers paid?"
"Why don't we have a Late Night Comedy Spot in the afternoon?"
"Why aren't the dancers fully dressed?"
"How do we know which photos are ours?"
"Will the ship wait for the tour buses to get back?"
"Will I get wet if I go snorkeling?"
"Is the mail brought in by plane?"
"Does the ship dock in the middle of town?"
"Who's driving the ship if the captain is at the cocktail party?"
"Does the sun always rise on the left side of the ship?"
"Is the doctor qualified?"
"Is trapshooting held outside?"
"I'm married, but can I come to the Singles Party?"
"Should I put my luggage outside the cabin before or after I go to sleep?"
"Does an outside cabin mean it's outside the ship?"

In Alaska:
"Are the glaciers always here?"
In the dining room:
Me: "Do you have a decanter for this young red wine?"

Wine waiter: "Not unless it's on the wine list."
Overheard in the cigar smoking room:
"I'm looking for a no-smoking seat."
Overheard in the dining room:
"Is all the salmon smoked? I am a non-smoker."
"Waiter, this vichyssoise is cold."
"Was the fish caught this morning by the crew?"
Passenger: "Waiter, what is caviar?"
Waiter: "Fish eggs, sir."
Passenger: "In that case, I'll have two, over-easy!"
Overheard on an Antarctic cruise:
"Where is the good shopping in Antarctica?"
Overheard on a British islands cruise:
"Windsor Castle is terrific. But why did they build it so close to the airport?"
Overheard on a Greek islands cruise:
"Why did the Greeks build so many ruins?"
Overheard on a round-Japan cruise, in Kagoshima, with Mount Suribaya in the background (*QE2*):
"Can you tell me what time the volcano will erupt? I want to be sure to take a photograph."

Then there is the cruise brochure that describes the cabin layout as: "cabins with double bed, can accommodate a third passenger!" (the now defunct Premier Cruise Lines).

And what about the saying, "He let the cat out of the bag?" On board a square-rigger 150 years ago, this would have sent shudders through one's spine — for it meant that a sailor had committed an offense serious enough to have the "cat o' nine tails" extracted from its bag.

The "cat" was a whip made of nine lengths of cord (each about 18 inches long with three knots at the end), all fixed to a rope handle. It could bring serious injuries, even death upon the victim. It is no longer carried on today's tall ships, outlawed by the US Congress in 1850, and then by Britain's Royal Navy in 1879.

ENTERTAINMENT

DID YOU KNOW...?

...that Roy, of the famous Siegfried & Roy (Siegfried Fischbacher and Roy Uwe Ludwig Horn) illusion act, used to be a steward aboard the German liner *Bremen*?

...that the Cunard White Star Line's *Queen Mary* was the first ship to have a system of colored lights that varied according to music (chromosonics)?

...that Verdi wrote an opera to commemorate the opening of the Suez Canal? Its name is *Aida*.

...that the 212-passenger *Seabourn Legend* was the star of the film *Speed 2: Cruise Control*, released in July 1997 in the US? The film was shot on location in Marigot, the capital of the French side of the tiny two-nation Caribbean island of St. Martin/St. Maarten. The filming called for the building of almost a complete "town" at Marigot, into which the ship crashes.

...that *Titanic*, the stage musical, cost $10 million dollars to mount in New York in 1997? That's $2.5 million more than it cost to build the original ship that debuted in 1912. The play debuted at the Lunt-Fontanne Theater in April 1997 (the ship sank on April 14, 1912).

... that the Hollywood film that cost the most, but made the most money was based aboard a passenger liner? The film, *Titanic*, was released in 1997.

...that the cruise ship used in the movie *Juggernaut*, in which seven bombs in oil drums were placed aboard, was *Maxim Gorkiy*? The film starred Richard Harris, David Hemmings, and Anthony Hopkins.

THAT'S ENTERTAINMENT!

After food, the most subjective (and talked-about) part of any mainstream cruise experience is the entertainment. Menus always present you with a choice of several foods, whereas the same is not often possible with cruise ship entertainment, which has to be diversified and innovative but never controversial. Ask 1,000 people what they would like to see as part of any evening entertainment program, and 1,000 different answers will ensue. It is all a matter of personal taste and choice. Whatever one expects, the days are gone when you would have been entertained by waiters doubling as singers, although a few bar waiters are still known to perform tray-spinning effects to boost their tips!

Many passengers, despite having paid so little for their cruise, expect to see top-notch entertainment, "headline" marquee-name cabaret artists, the world's most "popular" singers, and the most dazzling shows with slick special effects, just as one would find in the best venues in Las Vegas, London, or Paris. There are many reasons why it is not exactly so. International star acts invariably have an entourage that accompanies them to any venue: their personal manager, their musical director (often a pianist or conductor), a rhythm section (with bass player and drummer), even their hairdresser. On land, one-night shows are possible, but with a ship, an artist cannot always disembark after just one night, especially when it involves moving equipment, costumes, and baggage. This makes the whole matter logistically and financially unattractive for all but the very largest ships on fixed itineraries, where a marquee-name act might be considered a marketing draw.

When you are at home you can literally bring the world's top talent into your home via television. Cruise ships are a different matter. Most entertainers do not like to be away from their "home base" for long periods, as they rely on telephone contact. Most do not like the long contracts that the majority of ships must offer in order to amortize the cost.

So many acts working aboard cruise ships are interchangeable with so many other acts also working aboard cruise ships. Ever wonder why? Entertainers aboard ship must also live with their audiences for several days (sometimes weeks), something unheard-of on land, as well as work on stages aboard older ships that were not designed for live performances. However, there is no question that cruise ships are the new location for vaudeville acts, where a guaranteed audience is a bonus for many former club-date acts, as well as fresh acts waiting to break in to the big time on land.

Many older (pre-1970) ships have extremely limited entertainment spaces, and very few ships provide proper dressing rooms and backstage facilities for the storage of costumes, props, or effects, not to mention the extensive sound and lighting equipment most live "name" artists demand or need. Only the latest ships provide the extensive facilities required for presenting the kind of high-tech shows one would find in Las Vegas, London, or New York, for example. Among these features are elaborate electronic backdrops, revolving stages, orchestra pits, multi-slide projection, huge stageside video screens, pyrotechnic capabilities, and the latest light-mover and laser technology. Even the latest ships often lack enough dressing room and hanging space for the 150 costumes required in a single typical ship production show.

However, more emphasis has been placed on entertainment since the mid-1970s. Entertainment on today's large mainstream ships is market-driven. In other words, it is directed toward that segment of the industry that the cruise line's marketing department is specifically targeting (discounting notwithstanding). This is predominantly a family audience, so the entertainment must appeal to as broad an age range as possible — a tall order for any cruise line's director of entertainment.

A cruise line with several ships in its fleet will normally employ an entertainment department that is made up of an entertainment director and several assistants, and most cruise lines have contracts with one or more entertainment agencies that specialize in entertainment for cruise ships.

It is no use, for example, in a company booking a juggler who needs a floor-to-ceiling height of 12 feet but finds that the ship has a show lounge with a height of just 7 feet. ("Couldn't he juggle sideways?" I have heard one cruise company executive ask!); or an acrobatic knife-throwing act (in a moving ship?); or a concert pianist when the ship only has an upright honky-tonk piano; or a singer who sings only in English when the passengers are German-speaking, and so on.

Indeed, the hardest audience to cater to is one of mixed nationalities (each of whom will expect entertainers to cater exclusively to their particular linguistic group). Given that cruise lines are now marketing to more international audiences in order to fill ships, the problem of finding the right entertainment is far more acute.

The more upscale lines offer more classical music, even some light opera, and more fine guest lecturers and world-renowned authors than the seven-day package cruises heading for warm-weather destinations.

One area of entertainment that has become part of the experience, and is expected — particularly aboard large cruise ships — is that of the glamorous "production show." This is the kind of show one would expect to see in any good Las Vegas show palace, with a team of singers and dancers, a production manager, lavish backdrops, extravagant sets, grand lighting, special effects, and stunning custom-designed costumes. Unfortunately, many cruise line executives, who know little or nothing about entertainment, regard plumes and huge peacock feathers paraded by showgirls who step, but cannot dance, as being desirable. Some cruise ships have coarse shows that are not becoming to either dancer or passenger. Such things went out of vogue about 20 years ago. Shows that offer more creative costuming and real dancing win more votes today.

Book back-to-back seven-day cruises (on alternating eastern and western Caribbean itineraries, for example), and you should note that entertainment is generally geared to seven-day cruises. Thus, you will probably find the same two or three production shows and the same acts on the second week of your cruise. The way to avoid seeing everything twice is to pace yourself. Go to some shows during the first week and save the rest for the second week.

Regular passengers will notice that they seem to see the same acts time after time on various ships. For the reasons given above (and more), the criteria narrow the field even though there are many fine land-based acts. In addition, ship entertainers need to enjoy socializing. Successful shipboard acts tend to be good mixers, are presentable when in public, do not do drugs or take excess alcohol, are not late for rehearsals, and must cooperate with the cruise director and his or her staff as well as with the band.

Sadly, with cruise lines forever looking for ways to cut costs, entertainment has of late been a major target for some companies (particularly the smaller ones). Cutting costs translates into bringing on board, for example, lower-cost singers (who often turn out to be vocally-challenged persons) and bands that cannot read charts (musician-speak for musical arrangements) brought on board by cabaret acts.

SHOW BIZ AT SEA

In today's high-tech world, the putting together of a lavish 45–50-minute production show involves the concerted efforts of a range of experienced people from the world of show business, and a cost of $500,000 to $1 million per show is not unheard of. Weekly running costs (performers' salaries, costume cleaning and repair, royalties, replacement audio and videotapes, and so on) all add up to an expensive package for what can be a largely unappreciative and critical audience. Cruise lines look hard at the costs of such an undertaking.

WHO'S WHO

Although production companies differ in their approach, the following gives some idea of the various people involved behind the scenes.

Executive Producer

Transfers the show's concept from design to reality. First, the brief from the cruise line's director of entertainment might be for a new production show (the average being two major shows per seven-day cruise). Together they must plan the show. After deciding on an initial concept, they then call in the choreographer, vocal coach, and musical arranger, so everyone agrees on the flow of the show, the story line, and linkage.

Choreographer

Responsible for auditioning the dancers and for creating, selecting, and teaching the routines.

Courtesy Douglas Ward

Musical revues and entertaining shows are included on many cruises.

Musical Director

Coordinates all musical scores and arrangements; trains the singers in voice and microphone techniques, projection, accenting, phrasing, memory, and general presentation; and oversees singers and musicians for the recording sessions, and click-track tapes.

Musical Arranger

After the music has been selected, the musical arrangements must be made. Just one song can cost as much as $2000 for a single arrangement for a 12-piece orchestra.

Costume Designer

Provides creative original designs for a minimum of seven costume changes in one show lasting 45 minutes. The costumes must also be practical, as they will be used repeatedly.

Costume Maker

Purchases all materials, and must be able to produce all of the costumes required by the costume designer, in the time frame allotted.

Graphic Designer

Provides all the set designs, whether they are physical one- two- or three-dimensional sets for the stage, or photographic images created on slide film, video, laser disk, or other electronic media. The trend is for digital computer technology to play an increasingly important part in creating the images to be transferred via an electronic medium.

Lighting Designer

Create the lighting patterns and effects for a production show. Sequences and action on stage must be carefully lit to the best advantage. The completed lighting plot is sent to a software company that will etch the plot into computer-controlled disks to be used every time the show runs.

BANDS/MUSICIANS

Before the big production shows and artists can be booked, bands and musicians must be hired, often for long contracts. Naturally, live musicians are favored for a ship's show band, as they are excellent music readers (necessary for all visiting cabaret artists, not to mention the big production shows). Big bands are often placed in some of the larger ships for special sailings, or for world cruises, on which ballroom dancing plays a large part.

Most musicians work to contracts of about six months. Entertaining lounge duos and solo pianists or singer/pianists are generally hired through an entertainment agency specializing in cruise ships. Steel bands are recruited from the Caribbean, while other specialist bands (such as popular country and western bands) may be invited aboard for special occasions or charters.

OTHER ENTERTAINMENT

Most cruise ships organize acts that, while perhaps not nationally recognized "names," can provide two or three different shows during a seven-day cruise. These will be male/female singers, illusionists, puppeteers, hypnotists, and even circus acts, with wide age-range appeal.

There are comedians, comediennes, and comedy duos who perform "clean" material and who may find employment year-round on what is now known as the "cruise ship circuit." These popular comics enjoy good accommodation, are stars while on board, and often go from ship to ship on a standard rotation every few days. There are raunchy, late-night "adults only" comedy acts in some of the ships with younger, "hip" audiences, but few seem to have enough material for several shows.

The larger a ship, the larger the entertainment program will be. In some ships, the cruise director may "double" as an act, but most companies prefer him/her to be strictly an administrative and social director, allowing more time to be with passengers. Whichever ship and cruise you choose, you will find that being entertained "live" is an experience far superior to that of sitting at home in front of a television set, watching its clinical presentation. That's show business!

IT'S ALL A GAME!

Television game shows may well be the next audience participation event aboard the large ships with the huge showlounges. Celebrity Cruises, for example, has "Dream Ticket" while Disney Cruise Line has "Who Wants to be a Mouseketeer?" These professionally produced game shows, licensed from television companies, involve all passengers seated in a ship's showlounge, with interactive buttons wired into every seat. The game shows are great fun, and provide good entertainment. While they are not inexpensive to mount, they provide something different from the costumed production show extravaganzas that cost the cruise lines millions to produce.

NAUTICAL NOTES

DID YOU KNOW...?

...that in 1903 the British liner *Lucania* became the first ship to have wireless equipment, which enabled her to keep in touch with both sides of the Atlantic Ocean at the same time?

...that the first ship-to-shore wireless telegraphy took place on the American passenger ship *St. Paul*, in 1899?

...that the first twin-screw passenger ship was the Compagnie Generale Transatlantique's 3,200-ton *Washington*, built in 1863 and converted in 1868?

...that the first floating eclipse expedition was led by US astronomer Ted Pedas in 1972, when 800 passengers sailed to a spectacular rendezvous with a total sun eclipse in the North Atlantic?

...that the first passenger ship to exceed 80,000-tons was the Compagnie Generale Transatlantique's *Normandie*, which measured at 82,799-tons in 1936?

...that the first gravity lifeboats were aboard the Compagnie Generale Transatlantique's *Ile de France* of 1928?

The world of ships is a world of its own, and associated with it is a whole language and culture that can sometimes be confusing — but fascinating — to the newcomer. Here are a few tidbits of nautical information for you, which may contribute to the pleasure of your cruise.

RULES OF THE ROAD

Ships, the largest moving objects made by man, are subject to stringent international regulations. They must keep to the right in shipping lanes, and pass on the right (with certain exceptions). When circumstances raise some doubt, or shipping lanes are crowded, ships use their whistles in the same way an automobile driver uses directional signals to show which way he will turn. When one ship passes another and gives a single blast on its whistle, this means it is turning to starboard (right). Two blasts mean a turn to port (left). The other ship acknowledges by repeating the same signal. Ships switch on navigational running lights at night — green for starboard, red for port, plus two white lights on the masts, the forward one lower than the aft one.

Flags and pennants form another part of a ship's communication facilities and are displayed for identification purposes. Each time a country is visited, its national flag is shown. While entering and leaving a port, the ship flies a blue-and-white vertically striped flag to request a pilot, while a half red, half white flag (divided vertically) indicates that a pilot is on board. Cruise lines also display their own "house" flag from the mast.

A ship's funnel (smokestack) is one other means of identification, each line has its own design and color scheme. The size, height, and number of funnels were points worth advertising at the turn of the century. Most ocean liners of the time had four funnels and were called "four-stackers."

There are numerous customs at sea, many of them older than any maritime law. Superstition has always been an important element, as in the following example quoted from the British Admiralty Manual of Seamanship: "The custom of breaking a bottle of wine over the stem of a ship when it is being launched originates from the old practice of toasting prosperity to a ship with a silver goblet of wine, which was then cast into the sea in order to prevent a toast of ill intent being drunk from the same cup. This was a practice that proved too expensive, and it was replaced in 1690 by the breaking of a bottle of wine over the stem."

WIND SPEEDS

A navigational announcement to passengers is normally made once or twice a day, giving the ship's position, temperature, and weather information.

Various winds affect the world's weather patterns. Such well-known winds as the Bora, Mistral, Northwind, and Sirocco, among others, play an important part in the makeup of weather at and above sea level. Wind velocity is measured on the Beaufort scale, a method that was devised in 1805 by Commodore Francis Beaufort, later Admiral and Knight Commander of the Bath, for measuring the force of wind at sea. Originally, it measured the effect of the wind on a fully rigged man-of-war (which was usually laden with cannons and heavy ammunition). It became the official way of recording wind velocity in 1874, when the International Meteorological Committee adopted it.

You might be confused by the numbering system for wind velocity. There are 12 velocities, known as "force" on the Beaufort scale. They are as follows:

Force	Speed (mph)	Description/Ocean Surface
0	0–1	Calm; glassy (like a mirror)
1	1–3	Light wind; rippled surface
2	4–7	Light breeze; small wavelets
3	8–12	Gentle breeze; large wavelets, scattered whitecaps
4	13–18	Moderate breeze; small waves, frequent whitecaps
5	19–24	Fresh breeze; moderate waves, numerous whitecaps
6	25–31	Strong breeze; large waves, white foam crests
7	32–38	Moderate gale; streaky white foam
8	39–46	Fresh gale; moderately high waves
9	47–54	Strong gale; high waves
10	55–63	Whole gale; very high waves, curling crests
11	64–73	Violent storm; extremely high waves, froth and foam, poor visibility
12	73+	Hurricane; huge waves, thundering white spray, visibility nil

KNOTS AND LOGS

A knot is a unit of speed measuring one nautical mile. (A nautical mile is equal to one-sixtieth of a degree of the earth's circumference and measures exactly 6,080.2 ft (1,852 km). It is about 800 ft (243 m) longer than a land mile. Thus, when a ship is traveling at a speed of 20 knots (*Note*: this is never referred to as 20 knots per hour), she is traveling at 20 nautical miles per hour.

This unit of measurement has its origin in the days prior to the advent of modern aids, when sailors used a log and a length of rope to measure the distance that their boat had covered, as well as the speed at which it was advancing. In 1574, a tract by William Bourne, entitled *A Regiment for the Sea*, records the method by which this was done. The log was weighted down at one end while the other end was affixed to a rope. The weighted end, when thrown over the stern, had the effect of making the log stand upright, thus being visible. Sailors believed that the log remained stationary at the spot where it had been cast into the water, while the rope unraveled. By measuring the length of rope used, they could ascertain how far the ship had traveled, and were thus able to calculate its speed.

Sailors first tied knots at regular intervals, eventually fixed at 47 ft, 3 inches (14.4 m) along a rope, then counted how many knots had passed through their hands in a specified time (later established as 28 seconds), and measured by the amount of sand that had run out of an hourglass. They used simple multiplication to calculate the number of knots their ship was traveling at over the period of an hour.

The data gathered from this way were put into a record, called a logbook. Today, a logbook is used to record the day-to-day details of the life and events of a ship and its crew as well as other pertinent information.

LATITUDE AND LONGITUDE

Latitude signifies the distance north or south of the equator, while longitude signifies distance east or west of the 0 degree at Greenwich Observatory, London. Both are recorded in degrees, minutes, and seconds. At the equator, one minute of longitude is equal to one nautical mile, but as the meridians converge after leaving the equator and meeting at the poles, the size of a degree becomes smaller.

PLIMSOLL MARK

The safety of ships at sea and all those aboard owes much to the 19th-century social reformer Samuel Plimsoll, a member of the British Parliament concerned about the frequent loss of ships due to overloading. In those days, some shipowners would load their vessels down to the gunwales to squeeze every ounce of revenue out of them. They gambled on good weather, good fortune, and good seamanship to bring them safely into port. Consequently, many ships went to the bottom of the sea — the result of their buoyancy being seriously impaired by overloading.

Plimsoll helped to enact legislation that came to be known as the Merchant Shipping Act of 1875. This required shipowners to mark their vessels with a circular disc 12 inches (30.5 cm) long bisected by a line 18 inches (45.7 cm) long, as a measure of their maximum draft; that is, the depth to which a ship's hull could be safely immersed at sea. The Merchant Shipping Act of 1890 went even further, and required the Plimsoll mark (or line) to be positioned on the sides of vessels in accordance with tables drawn up by competent authorities.

The Plimsoll mark is now found on the ships of every nation. The Plimsoll mark indicates three different depths: the depth to which a vessel can be loaded in fresh water, which is less buoyant than salt water; the depth in summer, when seas are generally calmer; and the depth in winter, when seas are much rougher.

SHIP TALK
Ships and the sea have their own special vocabulary. This list may be of use.

Abeam: off the side of the ship, at a right angle to its length.

Aft: near, toward, or in the rear of the ship.

Ahead: something that is ahead of the ship's bow.

Alleyway: a passageway or corridor.

Alongside: said of a ship when it is beside a pier or another vessel.

Amidships: in or toward the middle of the ship; the longitudinal center portion of the ship.

Anchor Ball: black ball hoisted above the bow to show that the vessel is anchored.

Astern: is the opposite of Ahead (i.e., something behind the ship).

Backwash: motion in the water caused by the propeller(s) moving in a reverse (astern) direction.

Bar: sandbar, usually caused by tidal or current conditions near the shore.

Beam: width of the ship between its two sides at the widest point.

Bearing: compass direction, expressed in degrees, from the ship to a particular objective or destination.

Below: anything beneath the main deck.

Berth: dock, pier, or quay. Also means bed on board ship.

Bilge: lowermost spaces of the infrastructure of a ship.

Boat Stations: allotted space for each person during lifeboat drill or any other emergency when lifeboats are lowered.

Bow: the forward most part of the vessel.

Bridge: navigational and command control center.

Bulkhead: upright partition (wall) dividing the ship into compartments.

Bunkers: the space where fuel is stored; "bunkering" means taking on fuel.

Cable Length: a measured length equaling 100 fathoms or 600 ft (182.8 m).

Chart: a nautical map used for navigating.

Colors: refers to the national flag or emblem flown by the ship.

Companionway: interior stairway.

Course: direction in which the ship is headed, in degrees.

Davit: a device for raising and lowering lifeboats.

Deadlight: a ventilated porthole cover to prevent light from entering.

Disembark (also debark): to leave a ship.

Dock: berth, pier, or quay.

Draft (or draught): measurement in feet from the ship's waterline to the lowest point of its keel.

Embark: to join a ship.

Fantail: the rear or overhang of the ship.

Fathom: distance equal to 6 ft (1.82 m).

Flagstaff: a pole at the stern of a ship where the flag of the ship's country of registry is flown.

Free Port: port or place that is free of customs duty and regulations.

Funnel: chimney from which the ship's combustion gases are propelled into the atmosphere.

Galley: the ship's kitchen.

Gangway: the stairway or ramp link between ship and shore.

Gross Registered Tons (grt): not the weight of a ship but the total navigation of all permanently enclosed spaces above and below decks, with certain exceptions, such as the bridge, radio room, galleys, washing facilities, and other specified areas. It is the basis for harbor dues. International regulations introduced in 1982 required shipowners to remeasure the grt of their vessels (1 grt = 100 cubic ft of enclosed space/2.83 cubic m). This unit of measure was invented in England centuries ago for taxation purposes, when wine shipped from France was stored in standard-size casks, called tonneaux. Thus a ship carrying twenty casks measured 20 tons, and taxes were applied accordingly.

Helm: the apparatus for steering a ship.

House Flag: the flag denoting the company to which a ship belongs.

Hull: the frame and body of the ship exclusive of masts or superstructure.

Leeward: the side that is sheltered from the wind.

Manifest: a list of the ship's passengers, crew, and cargo.

Nautical Mile: one-sixtieth of a degree of the circumference of the Earth.

Pilot: a person licensed to navigate ships into or out of a harbor or through difficult waters, and to advise the captain on handling the ship during these procedures.

Pitch: the rise and fall of a ship's bow that may occur when the ship is under way.

Port: the left side of a ship when facing forward.

Quay: berth, dock, or pier.

Rudder: a finlike device astern and below the waterline, for steering the vessel.

Screw: a ship's propeller.

Stabilizer: a gyroscopically operated retractable "fin" extending from either or both sides of the ship below the waterline to provide a more stable ride.

Starboard: the right side of the ship when facing forward.

Stern: the aftmost part of the ship that is opposite the bow.

Tender: a smaller vessel, often a lifeboat, that is used to transport passengers between the ship and shore when the vessel is at anchor.

Wake: the track of agitated water left behind a ship when in motion.

Waterline: the line along the side of a ship's hull corresponding to the water surface.

Windward: the side toward which the wind blows.

Yaw: the erratic deviation from the ship's set course, usually caused by a heavy sea.

THE BRIDGE

A ship's navigation bridge is manned at all times, both at sea and in port. Besides the captain, who is master of the vessel, other senior officers take "watch" turns for four- or eight-hour periods. In addition, junior officers are continually honing their skills as experienced navigators, waiting for the day when they will be promoted to master.

WHAT IS AN ISLAND?

An island is defined as any land mass smaller than the smallest continent, and completely surrounded by water.

THE COLOR OF SEAWATER

Seawater is colorless. We only see "color" in seawater because quantities of the water play with light. The deep blue of deep seawater is produced in part by the refraction of light particles in the water and by the reflection of the sky. Also, the color blue is absorbed least by seawater. "Green" seas are found closer to land and are the result of greater quantities of suspended matter carried in coastal waters. Thus, the color essentially results from the combination of the blue-looking ocean water and the yellow pigments that result from the decomposition of plant matter. The Red Sea was so named due to the periodic swarming of an alga that stains its surface.

WAVES

Water waves are produced when the air-sea surface interface is distorted by a force such as the wind. Waves provide one of the most important mechanisms for transporting energy from one point to another on the surface of the sea. A restoring force such as gravity, surface tension, or the Coriolis force then acts to return the surface to equilibrium.

The captain is always in command at times of high risk, such as when the ship is entering or leaving a port, when the density of traffic is particularly high, or when visibility is severely restricted by poor weather.

Navigation has come a long way since the days of the ancient mariners, who used only the sun and the stars to calculate their course across the oceans. The space-age development of sophisticated navigation devices (using satellites) has enabled us to eliminate the guesswork of early navigation (the first global mobile satellite system came into being in 1979).

A ship's navigator today can establish accurately where the ship is in any weather and at any time. There follows a description of some of the navigation instruments, which will help you understand the complexities of seamanship today.

System Control

The most sophisticated state-of-the-art machinery and navigation systems are such technical marvels that sailors of yesteryear could not even conceive of their invention. The latest navigation system, known as the "Electronic Chart Precise Integrated Navigation System" (ECPINS) combines the electronics of the latest satellite positioning methods (Global Positioning System) with automatic course plotting, video map displays of the oceans, gyrocompass, echo sounders, sonar Doppler log, wind speed, and various sensors to provide a comprehensive, at-a-glance display of the ship in relation to the rest of the world.

The Compass

This is the instrument by which a ship may be steered on a preselected course, and by which bearings of visible objects can be taken in order to fix a ship's position on a navigation chart. There are two kinds:

The magnetic compass uses the inherent magnetic forces within and around the Earth;

The gyrocompass, a relatively recent invention, uses the properties of gyroscopic inertia and precession, ideally to align itself to a true north-south position.

Steering

Two different methods can be used to steer a ship:

Electrohydraulic steering uses automatic (telemotor-type) transmission from the wheel itself to the steering gear aft. This is generally used in conditions of heavy traffic, during maneuvers into and out of ports, or when there is poor visibility.

Automatic steering (gyropilot) is used only in the open sea. This system does not require anyone at the wheel because it is controlled by computer. However, aboard all ships, a quartermaster is always at the wheel, for extra safety, and just in case a need should arise to switch from one steering system to that of another.

Satellite Navigator

Using this latest high-tech piece of equipment, ship's officers can read, on a small television screen, the ship's position in the open ocean anywhere in the world, any time, and in any weather with pinpoint accuracy.

Satellite navigation systems use the information transmitted by a constellation of orbiting satellites. Each is in a normal circular polar orbit at an altitude of 450 to 700 nautical miles, and orbits the Earth in about 108 minutes. Data from each gives the current orbital position every two minutes. Apart from telling the ship where it is, it continuously provides the distance from any given point, calculates the drift caused by currents and so on, and tells the ship when the next satellite will pass.

The basis of the satellite navigation is the US Navy Satellite System (NNSS). This first became operational in January 1964 as the precision guidance system for the Polaris submarine fleet and was made available for commercial use in 1967.

The latest (and more accurate) system is the GPS (Global Positioning System), which is now fitted to an increasing number of ships. This uses 24 satellites (18 of which are on-line at any given time) that provide accuracy in estimating a ship's position to plus or minus six feet. Another variation is the NACOS (Navigational Command System), which collects information from a variety of sources: satellites, radar, gyroscopic compass, speed log, and surface navigational systems as well as engines, thrusters, rudders, and human input. It then displays relevant computations and information on one screen, controlled by a single keyboard.

Radar

Radar is one of the most important discoveries ever made for the development of navigational aids, providing a picture of all solid objects in a range selected by the navigator, which is from a half-mile to a 72-mile (115.873 km) radius. Its greatest asset is as an aid to collision avoidance with other ships, although it is of value in finding a position at a distance when navigational marks or charted coastlines are within its range.

Engine Telegraph

These automatic signaling devices are used to communicate orders between the bridge and the engine room. There may be three, one on the bridge and one on each bridgewing.

Bow Thruster

This small two-way handle is used to control the bow thrusters, powerful engines in the bow that push the ship away from the dockside without tugs. Some new ships may also have thrusters positioned at the stern.

Rudder Angle Indicator

This device is normally positioned in front of, and above, the quartermaster. It provides both the commanding officer and the quartermaster with a constant readout of the degrees of rudder angle, either to port (left) or starboard (right).

VHF Radio

This is a radio receiver and transmitter, operating on VHF (Very High Frequency) with a "line-of-sight" range. It is used for communicating with other ships, pilots, port authorities, and so on.

Radio Direction Finder

This operates on radio waves, enabling its operator to take bearings of shore radio stations. By crossing two or more bearings, you find the ship's position.

Depth Indicator

This equipment (which is an echo-sounder) provides a ship with a constant digital monitor readout, together with a printed chart.

Sails unfurl and you are on your way aboard **Wind Surf** *(Windstar Cruises).*

Course Recorder
This records and prints all courses followed by the ship at all times.

Clearview Screen
This device makes simple but effective use of centrifugal force, where instead of an automobile-type windshield wiper, a ship has circular screens that rotate at high speed to clear rain or sea spray away, providing those on the bridge with the best possible view in even the worst weather.

Engine Speed Indicators
These provide a reading of the number of revolutions per minute being generated by the engines. Each engine has a separate indicator, giving the speed in forward or reverse.

Facsimile Recorder
This special radio device is designed to receive meteorological and oceanographic maps, satellite pictures, and other pertinent weather information transmitted by maritime broadcast stations throughout the world.

Fire Control
If anyone sounds the fire alarm, an alarm is automatically set off on the bridge. A red panel light will be illuminated on a large plan, indicating the section of the ship that has to be checked so that the crew can take immediate action.

Ships are sectioned into several zones, each of which can be tightly closed off. In addition, almost all ships have a water-fed sprinkler system that can be activated at the touch of a button, or automatically activated when sprinkler vials are broken by fire-generated heat. New electronic fire detection systems are being installed aboard ships in order to increase safety further.

Emergency Ventilation Control
This automatic fire damper system also has a manual switch that is activated to stop or control the flow of air to all areas of the ship, in this way reducing the fanning effect on flame and smoke via air-conditioning and fan systems.

Watertight Doors Control
Watertight doors throughout the ship can be closed off, in order to contain the movement of water flooding the ship. A master switch activates all the doors in a matter of seconds. All watertight doors can be operated electrically and manually, which means that nobody can be trapped in a watertight compartment.

Stabilizers Control
The ship's two stabilizing fins can be extended, housed, or controlled. They normally operate automatically under the command of a gyroscope located in the engine control room.

ALTERNATIVE CRUISES

DID YOU KNOW...?

...that the whole disc of the sun is visible for 24 hours a day at some points north of the Arctic Circle? North Cape (May 14–July 29); Hammerfest (May 16–July 27); Tromso (May 20–July 22); Harstad (May 26–July 19); Bodo (June 4–July 8).

COASTAL CRUISES

Europe

There is year-round coastal cruising along the shores of Norway to the Land of the Midnight Sun aboard the ships of Norwegian Coastal Voyages (known locally as the Hurtig-Ruten, or "Highway 1"). The fleet consists of small, comfortable, working express coastal packet steamers and contemporary cruise vessels that deliver mail, small packaged goods, and foodstuffs, and take passengers, to the communities spread along the shoreline.

This is a 2,500-mile (4023.36km) journey from Bergen, Norway to Kirkenes, close to the Russian border (half of which is north of the Arctic Circle) and takes 12 days. You can join it at any of the 34 ports of call and stay as long as you wish (the ships sail every day of the year). In 1999, the company carried almost 300,000 passengers.The service started in 1893 and is run by a combination of three companies. The ships can accommodate between 144 and 674 passengers. The newest ships in the fleet have an elevator that can accommodate a wheelchair passenger.

Archipelago hopping can be done along Sweden's eastern coast, too, by sailing in the daytime and staying overnight in one of the many small hotels. One vessel sails from Norrtalje, north of Stockholm, to Oskarshamn, near the Baltic island of Öland, right through the spectacular Swedish archipelago. You can also cruise from the Finnish city of Lappeenranta to the Estonian city of Viborg without a visa, thanks to perestroika. Point-to-point coastal transportation between neighboring countries, major cities, and commercial centers is big business in Northern Europe.

Scotland

The fishing town of Oban, two hours west of Glasgow by road, perhaps seems an unlikely point to start a cruise, but it is the base for one of the world's finest cruise experiences. *Hebridean Princess* is an absolute gem, with delicate floral interiors. This ship carries passengers around some of Scotland's most magnificent coastline and islands. Take lots of warm clothing, however (layers are ideal), as the weather can be somewhat unkind.

United States

In the US, coastal vessels flying the American flag offer a change of style from big oceangoing cruise ships. On these cruises, informality is the order of the day. Accommodating up to 226 passengers, the ships are more like private parties — there's no pretentiousness. Unlike large cruise ships, these small

NORWEGIAN COASTAL EXPRESS SHIPS

SHIP	TONNAGE	BUILT	BERTHS
Finnmarken	12,000	2002	675
Harold Jarl	2,568	1960	165
Kong Harald	11,200	1993	490
Lofoten	2,621	1964	228
Midnatsol	6,100	1982	322
Narvik	4,073	1982	314
Nordkapp	11,386	1996	490
Nordlys	11,200	1994	490
Nordnorge	11,386	1997	490
Polarlys	12,000	1996	490
Richard With	11,205	1993	490
Trollfjord	12,000	2002	674
Vesteralen	4,073	1983	314

vessels are rarely out of sight of land. Their operators seek out lesser-known areas, offering in-depth visits to destinations inaccessible to larger ships, both along the eastern coast and in Alaska.

During the last few years, there has been little growth in this segment of the cruise market, although this is now changing. If you are the sort of person who prefers a small country inn to a larger resort, this type of cruise might appeal to you. The ships, each of which measures under 2,500 tons and is classified as a "D-class" vessel, are subject neither to the bureaucratic regulations nor the union rules that sounded the death knell for large US-registered ships.

These vessels are restricted to cruising no more than 20 miles (32.18 km) off shore, at a comfortable 12 knots. Public room facilities are limited, and because the vessels are of American registry, there is no casino. For entertainment, passengers are usually left to their own devices. Most vessels are in port during the evening, so you can go ashore for the local nightlife. Getting ashore is extremely easy; passengers can be off in a matter of minutes, with no waiting at the gangway.

Accommodation is in outside-view cabins (some open directly onto the deck, not convenient when it rains), each with a picture window and small bathroom. The cabins are small but cozy, and closet space is very limited, so take only what you absolutely need. There's no room service, and you turn your own bed down at night. Cabins are closer to the engines and generators so noise can be considerable at night. The quietest cabins are at the bow, and most cruising is done during the day so passengers can sleep better at night. Tall passengers should note that the overall length of beds rarely exceeds 6 ft (1.82 m), maximum.

The principal evening event is dinner in the dining room, which accommodates all passengers at once. This can be a family-style affair, with passengers at long tables, and the food passed around. The cuisine is decidedly American, with fresh local specialties featured.

These vessels usually have three or four decks, and no elevators. Stairs can be on the steep side and are not recommended for people with walking difficulties. This kind of cruise is good for those who do enjoy a family-type cruise experience in pleasant surroundings. The maxim "You just relax, we'll move the scenery" is very appropriate in this case.

A small selection of coastal and inland cruise vessels is featured in the profiles in Part Two, since they are small and specialized and have limited facilities.

RIVER AND BARGE CRUISES

Whether you want to cruise down the Nile, along the mighty Amazon or the lesser Orinoco, the stately Volga or the primal Sepik, the magnificent Rhine or the "blue" Danube, along the mystical Irrawaddy (now renamed Ayeyarwady) or the "yellow" Yangtze — to say nothing of the Don and the Dnieper, the Elbe, or Australia's Murray — there's a river vessel and cruise to suit you.

What sort of person enjoys cruising aboard river vessels? Well, anyone who survives well without dressing up, bingo, casinos, discos, or constant entertainment, and those who want a totally unstructured lifestyle.

European River Cruising

Cruising down one of Europe's great waterways is a soothing experience — it's quite different from sailing on an open sea, where motion has to be taken into consideration (rivers are calm). These cruises provide a constant change of scenery, often passing through several countries, each with its own history and architecture, in a weeklong journey. River vessels are always close to land and provide a chance to visit cities and areas inaccessible to large ships. Indeed, watching stunning scenery slip past your floating hotel is one of the most relaxing and refreshing ways to absorb the beauty that has inspired poets and artists through the centuries. A cruise along the Danube, for example, will take you through four countries and from the Black Forest to the Black Sea.

In 1840–1841, the Marquess of Londonderry, a member of the British aristocracy, traveled across Europe along the Rhine and Danube Rivers. She then wrote about these experiences, which were published in London in 1842, in a book entitled *A Steam Voyage to Constantinople*. And who could forget the romance implied by Johann Strauss's famous waltz "The Blue Danube"? The new Rhine-Main-Danube waterway, at 2,175 miles (3,500 km), is the longest waterway in Europe. It connects 14 countries, from Rotterdam on the North Sea to Sulina and Izmail on the Black Sea, and offers river travelers some of the most fascinating sights anywhere.

River vessels are long and low in the water, and their masts fold down in order to negotiate low bridges. Although small when compared to oceangoing cruise ships, they have a unique and friendly international atmosphere. The most modern of them are air-conditioned and offer the discreet luxury of a small floating hotel, with several public rooms including a dining room, observation lounge,

Barge cruising lets you enjoy your cruise experience at a slower pace.

bar, and features such as heated swimming "dip" pool (some even have a heated indoor pool), sauna, solarium, whirlpool, gymnasium, massage, hairdresser, and shop kiosk.

Although the cabins may be small, with limited closet space (take casual clothing, as informality is the order of the day), they are functional. Most have an outside view (facing the river), with a private bathroom, and will prove very comfortable for a one-week journey. Romantics should note that twin beds are the norm (they can seldom be pushed together). Many cabins in the latest vessels feature a personal safe, a mini-bar, a television, and an alarm clock/radio. The ceilings are rather low, and the beds are short.

River cruising in Europe is popular and has reached a very sophisticated level so you can be assured of good service and meals of a consistently high European standard. Dining is a pleasant, although not always gourmet, experience (the best food is that catered by Austrian and Swiss companies). While lunch is generally a buffet affair, dinners feature a set menu consisting of three or four courses.

Typical rates for river cruises are from $800 to over $3,000 per person for a one-week cruise, including meals, cabin with private facilities, side trips, and airport/railway transfers. If you are already in Europe, many cruises can be purchased "cruise-only" for greater flexibility.

Tip: It is best to go for an outside-view cabin on a deck that does not have a promenade deck walkway outside it. Normally, cabins on the lowest deck have a four-berth configuration. It does not matter which side of the vessel you are on, as you will see a riverbank and wonderful scenery from either side of the boat.

River Cruising: Russia

Perhaps the best way to get to know Russia is on a river/inland waterway cruise. Often referred to as the "Waterways of the Tsars," the country benefits from a well-developed network of rivers, lakes, and canals. Geographically, river routes for tourists are divided into three main areas: Central European Russia, Northwestern European Russia, and Asian Russia.

Rechtflot is the Russian government's management overlord, with 21 shipping companies and a combined fleet of more than 5,000 vessels. The largest is the United Volga River Shipping Company, which has over 2,000 river vessels, carrying more than 5 million passengers and about 100 million tons of cargo each year. The Moscow River Shipping Company is the next largest, with more than 1,000 vessels; it transports up to 11 million passengers and about 60 million tons of cargo each year.

In the Central Basin, Moscow is the hub of river tourism, and the newly opened waterways between Moscow and St. Petersburg allow a seven-day cruise link between the present and former capitals.

107

COASTAL CRUISE VESSELS (OVER 10 CABINS)

SHIP	CRUISE LINE	CABINS	REGION
Ambassador I	Marco Polo Cruises	45	Galapagos
American Eagle	American Cruise lines	27	East Coast (US)
Callisto	Classical Cruises	17	Greek Isles
Cape Cod Light	Delta Queen Coastal Cruises	114	East Coast (US)
Cape May Light	Delta Queen Coastal Cruises	114	East Coast (US)
Columbia Queen	Delta Queen Steamboat Company	81	Pacific NW(US)
Coral Princess	Coral Princess Cruises	27	Australia
Coral Princess II	Coral Princess Cruises	25	Australia
Corinthian	Ecoventura/Galapagos Network	45	Galapagos
Dro Ki Cakau	Captain Cook Cruises	59	Australia
Eclipse	Abercrombie & Kent	24	Galapagos
Executive Explorer	Glacier Bay Tours & Cruises	25	Alaska
Grande Caribe	American Canadian Caribbean Line	48	Alaska
Isabela II	Metropolitan Touring	20	Galapagos
Island Explorer	Voyages Jues Verne	74	Maldives
Lycinda	Blue Lagoon Cruises	21	Fijian Islands
Mystique Princess	Blue Lagoon Cruises	36	Fijian Islands
Nantucket Clipper	Clipper Cruise Line	51	US
Nanuya Princess	Blue Lagoon Cruises	25	Fijian Islands
Niagara Prince	American Canadian Caribbean Line	42	US
Pacific Aurora	Inside Passage Cruises	35	Alaska
Reef Endeavor	Captain Cook Cruises	75	Australia
Santa Cruz	Metropolitan Touring	43	Galapagos
Sea Bird	Lindblad Expeditions	35	Alaska
Sea Lion	Lindblad Expeditions	35	Alaska
Spirit of '98	Cruise West	48	Alaska
Spirit of Alaska	Cruise West	39	Alaska
Spirit of Columbus	Cruise West	39	Alaska
Spirit of Discovery	Cruise West	25	Alaska
Spirit of Endeavor	Cruise West	51	Alaska
Spirit of Glacier Bay	Cruise West	43	Alaska
Spirit of Oceanus	Cruise West	50	Alaska/S.Pacific
Sydney 2000	Captain Cook Cruises	60	Australia
Temptress Explorer	Temptress Adventure Cruises	50	Central America
Temptress Voyager	Temptress Adventure Cruises	33	Central America
Terra Australis	Cruceros Australis	55	Patagonia
Wilderness Adventurer	Glacier Bay Tours & Cruises	38	Alaska
Wilderness Discoverer	Glacier Bay Tours & Cruises	43	Alaska
Wilderness Explorer	Glacier Bay Tours & Cruises	18	Alaska
Yasawa Princess	Blue Lagoon Cruises	33	Fijian Islands
Yorktown Clipper	Clipper Cruise Line	69	US

The best-known Russian rivers are the Don, Moskva, Neva, and Volga, but the lesser known Belaya, Dvina (and North Dvina) Irtysh, Kama, Ob (longest river in Siberia), Oka, Svir, Tura, and Vyatka connect the great system of rivers and lakes in the vast Russian hinterland.

Many Russian vessels are chartered to foreign (non-Russian) cruise wholesalers and tour packagers. The vessels do vary in quality and facilities. Some are air-conditioned and most are clean.

One unusual Russian river vessel worth mentioning, *Rossiya*, is used for state visits and is extremely elegant and fitted throughout with exceptionally fine materials. Cruises include the services of a cruise manager and lecturers. Some companies also specialize in pre- or post-cruise "home stays" as part of a cultural package.

River Cruising: The Nile

A journey along the Nile — the world's longest (and historically the greatest) river — is a journey back in time, to over 4,000 years B.C. — when the Pharaohs thought they were immortal. Even though time proved them mistaken, the people who lived along the riverbanks formed one of the greatest civilizations the world has known. The scenery has changed little in over 2,000 years. The best way to see it, of course, is by riverboat.

In all, there are over 7,000 departures every year aboard approximately 200 Nile cruise vessels, many offering standards of comfort, food, and service that vary between very good and extremely poor. Most have a swimming pool, lounge, piano bar, and disco. A specialist lecturer in ancient Egyptian history accompanies almost all sailings, which cruise the 140 miles between Aswân and Luxor in four or five days. Extended cruises, typically of seven or eight days, cover about 295 miles (475 km) and visit Dendera and Abydos. The longest cruises, of 10 to 12 days, cover 590 miles (950 km) and include visits to Sohâg, El Amarna, Tuna El Gabal, and Ashmuneim, ending in Cairo.

Most Nile cruises include sight-seeing excursions, which are accompanied by experienced, trained guides who may reside on board, or who may meet the boat at each call. Multilingual guides also accompany each cruise.

River Cruising: China

There are now several new river vessels featuring cruises along the Yangtze, the world's third-longest river, particularly through the area known as the Three Yangtze River Gorges, a 100-mile stretch between Nanjin Pass in the east and White King City in the west. The Yangtze stretches 3,900 miles (6,276 kilometers) from Shanghai through the very heartland of China. The Three Gorges include the 47-mile-long Xiling Gorge, the 25-mile-long Wu Gorge, and the 28-mile-long Qutang Gorge (known locally as "Wind Box Gorge"). The Lesser Three Gorges (or Three Small Gorges) are also an impressive sight, often part of the main cruise but also reached by small vessels from Wushan. If possible, take a cabin with a balcony. It is worth the extra money, and the view is better. Note: Standards of hygiene are generally far lower than you may be used to at home. In China, rats and rivers often go together, so you should be aware that rat poison may well be found under your bed.

Among the best operators are Regal China Cruises (*Elaine*, *Jeannie*, and *Sheena*: 258 passengers) and Victoria Cruises (*Victoria*, *Victoria Pearl*, and *Victoria III*: 154 passengers). All have Chinese- and western-style restaurants, a beauty salon, a small health club with sauna, and private mah-jongg and karaoke rooms. Fine Asian hospitality and service prevail, and cabins are kept supplied with fresh towels and hot tea. There are several other operators, but do check on the facilities, meet-and-greet service, and the newness of the vessels before booking. The best time of the year to go is May–June, and late August–October (July and early August are extremely hot and humid).

Note that the new $60 billion hydroelectric Sanxia (Three Gorges) Dam, the world's largest (first envisioned by Sun Yat-sen in 1919), is presently under construction, essentially blocking off this major tourist attraction and creating a reservoir that will be 375 miles (603.5 km) long, and 575 ft (175.26 m) deep, with an average width of 3,600 ft (1,097 m). It is scheduled for full completion in 2009, and will submerge 13 cities, 140 towns, 1,352 villages, 657 factories and 66 million acres of cultivated land (more than 1.5 million people will be relocated). Once completed, it will raise the Yangtze River 150 ft (45.7 m), and cruise vessels of up to 10,000 tons will be able to sail up the Yangtze from the Pacific Ocean.

Ayeyarwady (Irrawaddy) River (Myanmar)

How about the *Road to Mandalay*? Orient Express Hotels operates a fine river cruise vessel in Myanmar (formerly known as Burma). The river vessel *Road to Mandalay* operates weekly between Mandalay and Pagan, along the Ayeyarwady (formerly Irrawaddy) River. There's also the small *Pandaw*, a stern-wheeler built in Scotland in 1947.

109

River Murray (Australia)
The fifth-largest river in the world, the Murray, was the lifeblood of the pioneers who lived on the driest continent on earth. Today, the river flows for more than 1,250 miles (2,765 km) across a third of Australia, her banks forming protected lagoons for an astonishing variety of bird and animal life. Paddlewheel boats such as *Murray Princess* offer all the amenities found aboard America's *Mississippi Queen*. There are even six cabins for the physically disabled.

Barge Cruising: Europe
Smaller and more intimate than river vessels, and more accurately called boats, "hotel barges" ply the inland waterways and canals of Europe from spring to fall, when the weather is best. Barge cruises (usually of 3 to 13 days' duration) offer a completely informal atmosphere, and a slow pace of life, for up to a dozen passengers. They cruise along slowly in the daytime, and moor early each evening, giving you time to pay a visit to a local village and get a restful night's sleep. The inland waterways of Europe all adhere to the CEVNI regulations (Code European des Voies de la Navigation Interieur), a United Nations instrument with international authority and relevance.

Hotel barges tend to be beautifully fitted out with rich wood paneling, full carpeting, custom-built furniture, and tastefully chosen fabrics. Each barge has a dining room/lounge-bar and is equipped with passenger comfort in mind. Each barge captain takes pride in his vessel, often acquiring some rare memorabilia to be incorporated into the decor.

Locally grown fresh foods are usually purchased and prepared each day, allowing you to live well and feel like a houseguest. Most barges can also be chartered exclusively so you can just take your family and friends, for example.

The waterways of France especially offer beauty, tranquillity, and a diversity of interests, and barge cruising is an excellent way of exploring an area not previously visited. Most cruises include a visit to a famous vineyard and wine cellar, as well as side trips to places of historic, architectural, or scenic interest. Shopping opportunities are limited, and evening entertainment is always impromptu. You will be accompanied by a crew member familiar with the surrounding countryside. You can even go hot-air ballooning over the local countryside and land to a welcome glass of champagne and your flight certificate. Although ballooning is an expensive extra, the experience of floating within earshot of chateaux and villages, over pastoral landscapes, is a pleasant memory treasure.

How you dine on board a barge will depend on which barge and area you choose; dining ranges from home-style cooking to outstanding *nouvelle cuisine*. Often, the owner of the barge, or his/her spouse, could turn out to be the cook, and you can be assured that the ingredients are all very fresh.

Barging on the canals often means going through a constant succession of locks. Nowhere is this more enjoyable and entertaining than in the Burgundy region of France where, between Dijon and Mâcon, for example, a barge can negotiate as many as 54 locks during a six-day cruise. Interestingly, all lockkeepers in France are women!

Rates typically range from $600 to more than $3,000 per person for a six-day cruise. I do not recommend taking children. Rates include a cabin with private facilities, all meals, good wine with lunch and dinner, other beverages, use of bicycles, side trips, and airport/railway transfers. Some operators also provide a hotel the night before or after the cruise. Clothing, by the way, is totally casual at all times, but at the beginning and end of the season, the weather can be unreliable, so make sure you take sweaters and rain gear.

Steamboating: United States
The most famous of all river cruises in the United States are those aboard the steamboats of the mighty Mississippi River. Mark Twain, an outspoken fan of Mississippi cruising, at one time said: "When man can go 700 miles an hour, he'll want to go seven again."

The grand traditions of the steamboat era are maintained by the *American Queen*, and by the older, smaller *Delta Queen* and *Mississippi Queen* (Delta Queen Steamboat Company), all of which are powered by steam engines that drive huge wooden paddlewheels at the stern.

The smallest and oldest of the three boats, the 174-passenger *Delta Queen*, was built on Scotland's Clydeside in 1926, and was placed on the US National Register of Historic Places in 1989. She gained attention when President Carter spent a week aboard her in 1979.

Half a century younger, the $27-million, 400-passenger *Mississippi Queen* was built in Jefferson, Indiana, where nearly 5,000 steamboats were built during the 19th century. Mississippi Queen was designed by James Gardner of London (creator of Cunard Line's QE2).

The latest, a $65 million, 222-cabin, 436-passenger American-built steamboat, *American Queen*

110

(Delta Queen Steamboat Company), debuted in June 1995. Built by McDermott Shipyard, Morgan City, Louisiana, the riverboat is fitted out with vintage tandem compound horizontal reciprocating steam engines (circa 1930) that originally drove a steam dredge called Kennedy. The engines are used to drive the 45-ton stern paddle wheel, with paddles made up of individual bucket boards that are 30 ft long and 2 ft wide (9.14 by .6 m). *American Queen* is the 30th steamboat built for the Delta Queen Steamboat Company. Each of the steamboats features one of the rarest musical instruments — a calliope, or "steam piano," driven by the boat's engine.

Traveling aboard one of the steamboats makes you feel as if you are stepping back into the past, into the world of American folklore. There is a certain charm and old-world graciousness as well as delightful woods, brass, and flowing staircases. And once every year, boats challenge each other in the Great Steamboat Race — a ten-day extravaganza.

Steamboat cruises last from 2 to 12 days, and during the year there are several theme cruises, with big bands and lively entertainment. The steamboats cruise up and down the Mississippi and Ohio rivers. As for food, it is really "Americana" fare, which means steak and shrimp, Creole sauces, fried foods, and a modicum of fresh vegetables.

Traveling on the river is a great way of taking a vacation and avoiding the crush of congested roads and airports. And of course, there are no immigration or customs procedures in the heartland of America.

EXPEDITION/NATURE CRUISES

Passenger Ships Through The Northwest Passage

1984 *Lindblad Explorer*
1985 *World Discoverer*
1986 *World Discoverer*
1988 *Society Explorer*
1991 *Frontier Spirit* (ship returned at Flaxman Island — trip cancelled)
1992 *Frontier Spirit*
1994 *Kapitan Khlebnikov*
1995 *Hanseatic*
1995 *Kapitan Khlebnikov*
1996 *Hanseatic* (ship grounded for ten days — passengers taken aboard *Kapitan Dranitsyn*)
1997 *Hanseatic*
1998 *Kapitan Khlebnikov*
1998 *Hanseatic*

With so many opportunities to cruise in Alaska and in the Baltic, Caribbean, Mediterranean, and Mexican Riviera areas, you may be surprised to discover a small but growing group of enthusiasts heading out for strange and remote waters. But there are countless virtually untouched areas to be visited by the more adventurous, whose motto might be "see it before it is spoiled." Such passengers tend to be more self-reliant and more interested in learning than in being entertained.

Passengers take an active role in almost every aspect of the voyage, which is destination-, exploration-, and nature-intensive. Naturalists, historians, and lecturers (rather than entertainers) are aboard each ship to provide background information and observations about wildlife. Each participant receives a personal logbook, illustrated and written by the wildlife artists and writers who accompany each cruise. The logbook documents the entire voyage and serves as a great source of information as well as a complete memoir of your cruise. Adventure cruise companies provide expedition parkas and waterproof boots, but you will need to take waterproof trousers (for Antarctica and the Arctic).

You can walk on pack ice in the Arctic Circle, explore a gigantic penguin rookery on Antarctica or the Falkland Islands, and search for "lost" peoples in Melanesia. Or you can cruise close to the source of the Amazon, gaze at species of flora and fauna in the Galapagos Islands (Darwin's laboratory), or watch a genuine dragon on the island of Komodo (from a comfortable distance!).

Briefings and lectures bring a cultural and intellectual element to expedition cruise vessels. There is no formal entertainment as such; passengers enjoy this type of cruise more for the camaraderie and learning experience. The ships are designed and equipped to sail in ice-laden waters, and yet they have a shallow enough draft to glide over coral reefs.

Expedition cruise vessels can, nevertheless, provide comfortable and even elegant surroundings for up to 200 passengers, and offer first-class food and service. Without traditional cruise

111

ports at which to stop, a ship must be self-sufficient, capable of long-range cruising, and environmentally friendly.

Expedition cruising came about as a result of people wanting to find out more about this remarkable planet of ours and its incredible animal, bird, and marine life. Lars-Eric Lindblad pioneered it in the late 1960s. A Swedish American, he was determined to turn travel into adventure by opening up parts of the world tourists had not visited.

After chartering several vessels for cruises to Antarctica (which he started in 1966), he organized the design and construction of a ship capable of going almost anywhere in comfort and safety.

In 1969, *Lindblad Explorer* was launched. The ship earned an enviable reputation in adventure travel. Lindblad sold the ship to Salen-Lindblad Cruising in 1982. They subsequently resold her to Society Expeditions, who renamed her *Society Explorer* (the ship is presently operated by Abercrombie & Kent as *Explorer*).

Specialist adventure/expedition cruise companies provide in-depth expertise and specially constructed vessels with ice-hardened hulls that can penetrate the vast reaches of the Arctic and Antarctica.

Expedition/Nature Cruise Areas

Buddha was once asked to express verbally what life meant to him. He waited a moment — then, without speaking, held up a single rose. Several "destinations" on our planet cannot be adequately described by words. They have instead to be experienced, just as a single rose.

The principal adventure cruise areas of the world are Alaska and the Aleutians, the Amazon and the Orinoco, Antarctica, Australasia and the Great Barrier Reef, the Chilean fjords, the Galapagos Archipelago, Indonesia, Melanesia, the Northwest Passage, Polynesia, and the South Pacific. Baja California and the Sea of Cortez, Greenland, the Red Sea, East Africa, the Réunion Islands and the Seychelles, West Africa and the Ivory Coast, and the South China Seas and China Coast are other adventure cruise destinations growing in popularity.

To put together cruise expeditions, companies turn to knowledgeable sources and advisors. Scientific institutions are consulted; experienced world explorers and naturalists provide up-to-date reports on wildlife sightings, migrations, and other natural phenomena. Although some days are scheduled for relaxation or preparing for the days ahead, participants are kept physically and mentally active. Speaking of physical activity, it is unwise to consider such an adventure cruise if you are not completely ambulatory.

Passengers aboard Hapag-Lloyd's **Hanseatic** *take to Zodiacs to explore Antarctica up close.*

DID YOU KNOW...?

...that passengers once asked the operations director of a well-known expedition cruise ship where the best shops were in Antarctica? His reply: "On board, madam!"

...that in 1984, Salen Lindblad Cruising made maritime history by successfully negotiating a westbound voyage through the Northwest Passage, a 41-day epic that started from St. John's, Newfoundland, in Canada, and ended at Yokohama, Japan? The expedition cruise had taken two years of planning and was sold out just days after it was announced. The search for a Northwest Passage to the Orient attracted brave explorers for more than four centuries. Despite numerous attempts and loss of life, including Henry Hudson in 1610, a "white passage" to the East remained an elusive dream. Amundsen's 47-ton ship *Gjoa* eventually navigated the route in 1906, taking three years to do so. It was not until 1943 that a Canadian ship, *St. Roch*, became the first vessel in history to make the passage in a single season. *Lindblad Explorer* became the 34th vessel, and the first cruise vessel, to complete the Northwest Passage.

...that Quark Expeditions had the good fortune of making maritime history in July/August 1991, when its chartered Russian icebreaker, *Sovetskiy Soyuz*, made a spectacular 21-day voyage to negotiate a passage from Murmansk, Russia, to Nome, Alaska, across the North Pole? The ship followed the trail that had been set in 1909 by Admiral Peary, who crossed the North Pole with 56 Eskimos, leaving by sled from Ellesmere Island. Although the polar ice cap had been navigated by the US nuclear submarines Skate and Nautilus, as well as by dirigible and airplane, this was the first passenger ship to make the hazardous crossing (planning for it took over two years).

...that the most expensive expedition cruise excursion was a cruise/dive to visit the resting place of RMS *Titanic* aboard the two deep ocean submersibles *Mir I* and *Mir II* used in James Cameron's Hollywood blockbuster. Just 60 participants went as up-close-and-personal observers in 1998, and another 60 were taken in 1999.

Antarctica

Maybe the most intriguing destination on earth is Antarctica, first sighted only in 1820 by the American sealer Nathaniel Palmer, British naval officer Edward Bransfield, and Russian captain Fabian Bellingshausen. For most, it is nothing but a wind-swept frozen wasteland (it has been calculated that the ice mass contains almost ninety percent of the snow and ice in the world). For others, however, it represents the last pristine place on earth, empty of people, commerce, and pollution, yet offering awesome scenery and a truly wonderful abundance of marine and bird life. There are no germs and not a single tree. Over 6,000 people visited the continent in 1997 — the only smoke-free continent on earth. The first human to come here did so within a generation of man landing on the moon. There is not a single permanent inhabitant of the continent, whose ice is as much as two miles thick. Its total land mass equals more than all the rivers and lakes on earth and exceeds that of China and India combined. Indeed, icebergs can easily be the size of Belgium! The continent has a raw beauty and an ever-changing landscape.

Once part of the ancient land mass known as Gondwanaland (which also included Africa, South America, India, Australasia, and Madagascar), it is, perhaps, the closest thing on earth to another planet, and it has an incredibly fragile ecosystem that needs international protection.

Although visited by "soft" expedition cruise ships and even "normal"-sized cruise ships with ice-hardened hulls, the more remote "far side" — the Oates and Scott Coasts, McMurdo Sound, and the famous Ross Ice Shelf — can only be visited by real icebreakers such as *Kapitan Dranitsyn*, *Kapitan Khlebnikov*, *Sovetskiy Soyuz*, and *Yamal* (they carry 100 passengers or fewer), as the winds can easily reach more than 100 mph.

As there are no docks in Antarctica, venturing "ashore" is done by Zodiac rubber inflatable craft, an integral part of the Antarctica experience. Be aware that you *can* get stuck even aboard these specialized expedition ships, as did *Clipper Adventurer* in February 2000, in an ice field. It had to be rescued by an Argentine Navy icebreaker.

Arctic

The Arctic is defined best as that region north of which no trees grow, and where water is the primary feature of the landscape. The Arctic is an ocean surrounded by continents, whereas Antarctica is a continent surrounded by ocean. The Arctic Circle is located at 66 degrees, 33 minutes, and 3 seconds north, although this really designates where 24-hour days and nights begin. It is technically a desert (receiving less than 10 inches of rainfall a year) but actually teems with wildlife. It has short, cool summers; long, cold winters; and frequent high winds. Canada's Northwest Territories, which cover 1.3 million square miles, is part of the Arctic region.

Galapagos

A word of advice about the Galapagos Islands: Do not even think about taking a cruise with a "non-Ecuadorian flag" ship; the Ecuadorians jealously guard their islands and prohibit the movement of almost all non-Ecuadorian-registered cruise vessels within its boundaries. The best way to see this place that Darwin loved is to fly to Quito and cruise aboard an Ecuadorian-registered vessel.

The government of Ecuador set aside most of the islands as a wildlife sanctuary in 1934, while uninhabited areas were declared national parks in 1959. The national park now includes approximately 97 per cent of the islands' landmass together with 19,305.1 sq miles (50,000 square km) of ocean. The government created the Galapagos Marine Resources Reserve in 1986, while the Charles Darwin Research Station was established in 1964.

Note that the Galapagos National Park tax is presently about $100 per person. Smoking is prohibited on the islands of the Galapagos, and visitors are limited to 50,000 per year.

Greenland

The world's largest island, Greenland, in the Northern Hemisphere's Arctic Circle, is technically a desert that is 82 percent covered with ice (actually compressed snow) that is up to 11,000 ft (3,352.8 m) thick. Greenland's rocks are among the world's oldest (the 3.8 billion-year-old Isukasia formations), and its ecosystem is one of the newest. Forget Alaska, in comparison the glacier at Jacobshavn (also known as Ilulissat) is the fastest moving in the world and creates a new iceberg every five minutes. Greenland is said to have more dogs than people, and these provide the principal means of transport for the Greenlanders.

The Environment

Since the increase in environmental awareness, adventurers have banded together to protect the environment from further damage. In the future, only those ships that are capable of meeting new "zero discharge" standards, like those introduced in the Arctic by the Canadian Coast Guard, will be allowed to proceed through environmentally sensitive areas.

Expedition cruise companies are very concerned about the environment (none more than Hapag-Lloyd Cruises and Quark Expeditions), and they spend much time and money in educating both crews and passengers about safe environmental procedures.

An "Antarctic Traveler's Code" has been created, the rules of which are enforced by the expedition cruise companies, based on the *Antarctic Conservation Act of 1978* to protect and preserve the ecosystem, flora, and fauna of the Antarctic continent. Briefly, the Act makes it unlawful, unless authorized by regulation or permit issued under the Act, to take native animals or birds, to collect any special native plant or introduce species, to enter certain special areas (SPAs), or to discharge or dispose of any pollutants. To "take" means to remove, harass, molest, harm, pursue, hunt, shoot, kill, trap, capture, restrain, or tag any native mammal or bird, or to attempt to do so.

Under the Act, violators are subject to civil penalties, including a fine of up to $10,000 and one year imprisonment for each violation. The Act is found in the library of each adventure/expedition ship that visits the continent.

Will large cruise ships ever cruise in Antarctica? Not in the foreseeable future. Ships are limited to a maximum of 400 passengers, so the likelihood of a mega-ship zooming in on the penguins with 2,000-plus passengers is unlikely.

THE COMPANIES

Abercrombie & Kent

This well-known company operates the older, but still highly suitable *Explorer* (formerly the-*Society Explorer*).

Clipper Cruise Lines
This company operates *Clipper Adventurer*, a small ship with an ice-hardened hull.

Hapag-Lloyd Cruises
This company operates *Bremen* and *Hanseatic*, small, high-tech expedition cruise vessels. Both ships have fine, rather luxurious appointments (*Bremen* is less luxurious than *Hanseatic*) and are marketed to both English- and German-speaking passengers.

Lindblad Expeditions
This company operates *Polaris*, a small expedition vessel operating in the Galapagos Islands, which features fine appointments and full creature comforts (see page 438 for details). In addition, two small vessels, *Sea Bird* and *Sea Lion* (ex-Exploration Cruise Lines vessels) operate "soft" coastal cruises in protected coastal areas in the United States, including Alaska.

Marine Expeditions
This Canadian company charters several Russian vessels for "soft" expedition/nature cruises to several popular areas, including Antarctica. The company applies its own ship names for the duration of the charter.

Quark Expeditions
Quark Expeditions charters Russian-owned nuclear- or diesel-powered icebreakers fitted with some outstanding amenities and decent creature comforts for up to 100 passengers. The operator specializes in itineraries to the Antarctic, the Arctic, and North Polar regions. Among the vessels chartered are the superb *Kapitan Dranitsyn, Kapitan Khlebnikov, Sovetskiy Soyuz*, and *Yamal*.

SAIL-CRUISE SHIPS
Thinking of a cruise but really want to sail — to be free as the wind? Have you been cruising on a conventional large cruise ship that is more like an endurance test? Whatever happened to the romance of sailing? Think no more, for the answer is here.

Think of cruising under sail, with towering masts, the creak of taut ropes and snow-white sails to power you along? There is nothing that beats the thrill of being aboard a multi-mast tall ship, sailing under thousands of square feet of canvas through waters that mariners have sailed for centuries.

This is cruising in the traditional manner, aboard authentic sailing ships, contemporary copies of clipper ships, or aboard the latest high-tech cruise-sail ships. Even the most jaded passengers will, I am convinced, enjoy the exhilaration of being under sail.

There are no rigid schedules, and life aboard equates to an unstructured lifestyle, apart from meal times. Weather conditions may often dictate whether a scheduled port visit will be made or not, but passengers sailing on these vessels are usually unconcerned with being ashore anywhere. They would rather savor the thrill of being one with nature, albeit in a comfortable, civilized setting, and without having to do the work themselves.

Real Tall Ships
While we have all been dreaming of adventure, a pocketful of designers and yachtsmen committed pen to paper, hand in pocket, and rigging to mast, and came up with a potpourri of stunning vessels to delight the eye and refresh the spirit. Look in Part Two for these true, working tall ships: *Royal Clipper, Sea Cloud, Sea Cloud II, Star Clipper*, and *Star Flyer*. Of these, *Sea Cloud* has a history that spans over 70 years — a true veteran working sailing ship that still is at the height of luxury under sail.

In the Caribbean, Windjammer Barefoot Cruises also operates a fleet of five tall ships offering very basic fun-and-sun cruises: *Flying Cloud, Legacy, Mandalay, Polynesia*, and *Yankee Clipper*. Only shorts and T-shirts are needed. Although cabin towels are provided, you'll need to take your own beach towels. Only one vessel is certified by the US Coast Guard, the others are not, although they do comply with most international safety regulations.

Contemporary Sail-Cruise Ships
To combine sailing with push-button automation, try *Club Med 2* (Club Méditerranée) or *Wind Surf* (Windstar Cruises) — with five tall aluminum masts, they are the world's largest sail-cruise ships — and *Wind Song, Wind Spirit*, and *Wind Star* (Windstar Cruises), with four masts. Not a hand

115

touches the sails; they are computer controlled from the navigation bridge. These ships are contemporary oceangoing robots. There's little sense of sailing as the computer controls keep the ship on a steady, even keel. From a yachtsman's viewpoint, the sail-to-power ratio is poor. That's why these cruise ships with sails have engine power to get them into and out of port. (The Star Clipper ships, by contrast, do it by sail alone, except when there is no wind, which is infrequent.). You should be aware that on some itineraries, when there is little wind you could well be under motor power for most of the cruise, with only a few hours spent under sail. The four Windstar Cruises' vessels and one Club Med ship are typically under sail about 40 percent of the time.

It was a Norwegian living in New York, Karl Andren, who first turned the concept of a cruise vessel with sails into reality. "Boyhood dream stuff," he said. The shipyard (Société Nouvelle des Ateliers et Chantiers du Havre – or ACH, as it is known locally), enjoyed the challenge of building these most unusual vessels.

The shipyard had much experience in the design and construction of cable-laying ships using the hydraulic power of servomechanisms. This was a concept that was adopted for the Windstar's automatic computer-controlled sail rig. Gilbert Fournier, the shipyard president and an expert computer programmer, became fascinated with the project. Three ships (a fourth was planned but never built) were delivered to Windstar Cruises. These ships carry mainly North American passengers, whereas the Club Med vessel caters primarily to French-speaking passengers.

Another slightly smaller but very chic vessel is the sleek *Le Ponant*. This three-mast ship caters to just 64 French-speaking passengers in elegant, yet casual, high-tech surroundings, developing the original Windstar concept to an advanced state of 1990s technology.

FREIGHTER TRAVEL

More than 3,000 passengers presently travel by freighter each year, and the number is growing as passengers become further disenchanted with the large resort ships that form a major part of the cruise industry today. Traveling by freighter is also the ultimate way to travel for those seeking a totally unstructured voyage without entertainment or other diversions.

There are approximately 250 cargo ships (freighters and container vessels) offering berths, with German operators now accounting for about more than half of the ships. True freighters — the general breakbulk carrier ships and feeder container vessels — carry up to 12 passengers. Freighter schedules change constantly, depending on the whim of the owner and the cargo to be carried, whereas container ships travel on regular schedules. For the sake of simplicity, they are all termed freighters.

Today's freighters have changed dramatically over the past few years, as cost management and efficiency have become the most relevant factors for successful ship operators. Container ships today are operated as the passengers' liners used to be — running line voyages on set schedules, or name-day voyages, as they are presently termed.

Passengers opting for this type of travel typically include independent types (anyone allergic to traveling in groups), retirees, relocating executives, people with family connections in other countries, graduates returning home from an overseas educational establishment, or professors on sabbatical. Because there are no medical facilities, maximum age limits are imposed by most freighter companies and anyone over the age of 65 will have to produce a medical certificate of good health.

What do you get when you book a freighter voyage? You get a cabin with double or twin beds, a small writing table, and a private bathroom. You also get good company, cocktails with conversation, hearty food (you'll eat in one seating with the ship's officers), an interesting voyage, a lot of water, and the allure of days at sea. What don't you get? Entertainment, bingo, horse racing, and other parlor games (unless you take them with you). You will certainly have time to relax and unwind completely, read books (some freighters have a small library), or play card games or board games with the few other passengers that will be on board.

The accommodation aboard today's freighters will typically consist of a spacious and well-equipped outside-view cabin high above the water line, with a large window rather than a porthole, comfortable lounge/sitting area, and private facilities —far larger than most cruise ship cabins.

While freighter travel can be less expensive than regular cruise ship travel on a per day basis (between $75 and $150), remember that freighter voyages are of much longer duration. A typical voyage lasts about 30 days or more, so the cost of a voyage can actually add up to a considerable amount. Most voyages are sold out far in advance (often more than a year ahead), so do plan ahead, and remember to purchase trip cancellation insurance.

DID YOU KNOW...?

...that the Dollar Steamship Line featured a round-the-world cruise that started October 15, 1910 from New York, aboard the *ss Cleveland*? The cruise was advertised as "one-class, no overcrowding" voyage. The cost was "$650 and up," according to an advertisement placed by the Frank Clark Travel Agency, of the Times Building in New York.

...that a round-the-world cruise was made in 1922–1923 by Cunard's *Laconia* (19,680 grt), a three-class ship that sailed from New York? The itinerary included many of the ports of call that are still popular with world cruise travelers today. The vessel accommodated 350 persons in each of its first two classes, and 1,500 in third class, giving a total capacity of 2,200 passengers, more than many ships of today.

...about the lady who went to her travel agent, who asked if she had enjoyed her cruise around the world? The lady replied, "Yes, but next year I want to go somewhere different!"

What to take with you? Casual clothing (do check with the freighter line concerned, as some require you to dress for dinner — that means jacket and tie), all medication, cosmetics, and personal toiletry items, hair dryer, multi-voltage converter plug, laundry detergent, and other sundry items. There may be a small "shop" on board (for the crew) but only the bare essentials like toothpaste will be available. Remember to take some extra photos of yourself in case the ship makes unannounced port stops and visas are required. The only gratuities you will need to give are for the waiter and cabin steward, at about $1–$2 per day, per person.

The following lines offer *regular* passenger voyages year-round:

American President Lines, Australia New Zealand Direct Lines, Bank Line, Blue Star Line, Canada Maritime, Chilean Lines, Cho Yang Shipping, Columbus Line, Egon Oldendorff, Great Lakes Shipping, Hamburg-Sud, Hanseatic Shipping Company, Hapag-Lloyd, Ivaran Lines, Lykes Brothers Steamship Company, Mediterranean Shipping Company, Nauru Pacific Line, Safmarine Cruises, and United Baltic Corporation.

Note that freighters can, and do, sometimes cancel port calls due to various reasons. So, if it's the itinerary, or a certain port that attracts you, be aware that it doesn't always go according to plan. In other words, if you can't accept last minute changes or disappointment, don't consider freighter cruising.

Freighter Bookings and Information

Traveltips Cruise & Freighter Association
P.O. Box 580188, Flushing, NY 11358, USA
Freighter World Cruises
180 South Lake Avenue, Suite 335, Pasadena, CA 91101, USA
The Cruise People
88 York Street, London W1H 1DP, England
Strand Voyages
Charing Cross Shopping Concourse, Strand, London WC2N 4HZ, England
Sydney International Travel Centre
75 King Street, Level 8, Sydney 2000, Australia

CROSSINGS

By "crossings," I mean crossings of the North Atlantic, that is, 3,000 miles or so of it, from the Old World to the New World or vice versa, although crossings might also include any other major ocean, such as the Pacific or the Indian Ocean.

Crossing the North Atlantic by ship is an adventure, when time seems to be totally suspended. It really is the most delicious way of enjoying life aboard ship. It actually takes little more than a long weekend. After the embarkation procedures have been completed, you will be shown to the gangway. Cross the gangway from pier to ship and you are in another world. It is a world that provides

117

a complete antidote to the pressures of contemporary life ashore, and it allows you to practice the fine art of doing nothing, if you so wish. After the exhilaration of a North Atlantic crossing, the anticipation of landfall among passengers throughout any ship is nothing short of electric.

The North Atlantic

Hemmed in by the polar ice caps, the Atlantic Ocean divides Europe and Africa from the Americas. It is three times the size of North America and contains the world's longest mountain range, which extends (undersea) over 7,000 miles (11,265 kilometers) and rises over 6,000 feet (1,828 meters) above the ocean floor. The only points of this ridge that rise to the surface are at St. Helena (Ascension), St. Paul's Rocks (the Azores), and Tristan da Cunha. The ocean's average width is 2,500 miles (4,023 kilometers).

Although half the size of the Pacific Ocean, the Atlantic Ocean receives more than half of the water drainage of the world (four times that of the Pacific Ocean). Its average depth is 18,900 feet (5,760 meters) and its greatest depth, which is known as the Milwaukee Depth, goes down beyond 30,240 feet (9,217 meters).

Crossing the North Atlantic by passenger vessel should really be considered an art form. I have done it myself 150 times and still enjoy it immensely. I consider crossings as rests in musical parlance, for both are described as "passages." Indeed, musicians do often "hear" rests in between notes. So if ports of call are the musical notes of a voyage, then the rests are the days at sea — a temporary interlude, when the indulgence of the person and psyche are of paramount importance.

Experienced mariners will tell you that a ship only behaves like a ship when it is doing a crossing, for that's what a real ship is built for. Yet the days when ships were built specifically for crossings are gone. The only ship offering a regularly scheduled transatlantic service (a "crossing") is Cunard Line's *Queen Elizabeth 2*, a 70,327-grt ship designed to hold up against the worst weather the North Atlantic has to offer. Indeed, captains work harder on a crossing than on regular Atlantic cruising schedules.

The most unpredictable weather in the world, together with fog off the Grand Banks of Newfoundland, can mean that the captain will spend torturous hours on the bridge, with little time for socializing. When it is foggy, the crew of *QE2* are often pestered by passengers wanting to know if the ship has yet approached latitude 41°46' north, longitude 50°14' west — where White Star Line's *Titanic* (43,326-tonnes) struck an Arctic iceberg on that fateful April night in 1912.

There is something magical in "doing a crossing." It takes you back to the days when hordes of passengers turned up at the piers of the ports of New York, Southampton, Cherbourg, or Hamburg, accompanied by chauffeurs and steamer trunks, jewels and finery, ablaze in a show of what they thought was best in life. Movie stars of the 1920s, 1930s, and 1940s often traveled abroad on the largest liners of the day, to arrive refreshed and ready to dazzle European fans.

Excitement and anticipation precede a crossing. First there is the hubbub and bustle of check-in, then the crossing of the threshold on the gangway before being welcomed into the calmness aboard, and finally escorted to one's accommodation for the next several days. Once the umbilical cord of the gangway is severed, bow and stern mooring lines are cast off, and with three long blasts on the ship's deep whistle, the *QE2* is pried gently from her berth. She sails silently down the waterway, away from the world, as pretty as a picture, as serene as a Rolls-Royce, and as sure as the Bank of England.

Passengers on deck often observe numerous motorboats trying to keep up with the giant liner as she edges down the Hudson River, past Battery Park City, the Statue of Liberty, the restored Ellis Island, then out toward the Verrazano-Narrows Bridge, and out to the open sea.

Coming westbound, arriving in New York by ship is one of the world's thrilling travel experiences. Following a six-day crossing aboard the *QE2*, where five of the days are 25 hours long (they are 23 hours long on an eastbound crossing), *everything else* is an anticlimax.

The *QE2* can also accommodate up to 12 cars per crossing, just in case you really do not want to be parted from your wheels. Kennels are provided, so you can even take your pet, although when crossing eastbound to Southampton, they will have to be quarantined for up to six months. The *QE2* is a distillation of over 150 years of transatlantic traditions and an oasis of creature comforts offered by no other ship.

QE2 is special — part liner, part cruise ship — a legend in her own lifetime, and the only ship offering regularly scheduled crossings throughout the year. Vast amounts of money have been spent on refurbishment over time. During the ship's initial planning stages, naval architect Dan Wallace and director of engineering Tom Kameen were responsible for the ship's design — for a high-speed, twin-screw ship capable of carrying out safely a six-day transatlantic crossing. Cunard Line's chair-

118

DID YOU KNOW...?

...that the first regular steamship service across the North Atlantic was inaugurated on 28 March 1838, when the 703-ton steamer *Sirius* left London for New York via Cork, Ireland?

...that the winter of 1970–71 was the first time since 1838 that there was no regular passenger service on the North Atlantic?

...that the first scheduled transatlantic advertisement appeared in the *New York Evening Post* on 27 October 1817, for the 424-ton sailing packet J*ames Monroe* to sail from New York to Liverpool on 5 January 1818, and for *Couvier* to sail from Liverpool to New York on 1 January?

...that the following are just some of the personalities that have crossed in the *QE2*? Carl Sagan, Joan Fontaine, Larry Hagman, Ben Lyon, Joan Rivers, Elaine Stritch, and Arthur Schlesinger, Jr.

...that the *QE2* is still the fastest passenger ship in service?

...that since the ship's maiden voyage in 1969, the *QE2* has traveled more than four million nautical miles, and carried almost two million passengers?

...that the amount of paint used to cover the *QE2*'s hull would completely cover one of the towers of New York's World Trade Center?

man, Sir Basil Smallpiece, invited James Gardner and Dennis Lennon, well-known industrial designers, as general design coordinators.

Gardner concentrated on exterior aesthetics, while Lennon, in addition to designing the restaurant interiors — the basic shape of which had already been determined by structural and operational requirements — was also concerned with the introduction of a design signature that would be immediately apparent throughout the ship; for example, in the staircases and corridors. The aim was that the interior design of the *QE2* would emphasize the "classless" ship concept.

Apart from the *QE2*'s regular crossings, a number of cruise ships feature transatlantic crossings. Although they are little more than repositioning cruises — a way of moving ships that cruise the Mediterranean in summer to the Caribbean in winter, and vice versa — they offer more chances to experience the romance and adventure of a crossing, usually in the spring and in the fall. These are particularly good for those wanting uninterrupted days at sea and plenty of leisure time. Most cruise ships operating repositioning crossings actually cross the Atlantic using the "sunny southern route" — typically departing from southern ports such as Ft. Lauderdale, San Juan, or Barbados, and ending the journey in Lisbon, Genoa, or Copenhagen via the Azores or the Canary Islands off the coast of northern Africa. In this way, they avoid the more difficult weather that is often encountered in the North Atlantic. The crossings take longer, however, and last between eight and twelve days.

WORLD CRUISES AND SEGMENTS

The ultimate classic voyage for any experienced traveler is a round-the-world cruise. This is usually defined as the complete circumnavigation of the earth in a continuous one-way voyage. The ports of call are carefully planned for their interest and diversity, and the entire voyage can last as long as six months.

Ships that sail from cold to warm climates — almost always during January, February, and March, when the weather in the southern hemisphere is at its best — give you the experience of crisp, clear days, sparkling nights, delicious food, tasteful entertainment, superb accommodation, delightful company, and unforgettable memories. It is for some the cultural, social, and travel experience of a lifetime, and for the few who can afford it, an annual event!

The concept of the world sea cruise first became popular in the 1920s, although it has existed since the 1880s (the first around-the-world voyage was actually made by Ferdinand Magellan in 1519). A world cruise aboard a modern ship means experiencing stabilized, air-conditioned comfort

119

in luxury cabins, and extraordinary sight-seeing and excursions on shore and overland. In some ships, every passenger will get to dine with the captain at least once.

A world cruise gives you the opportunity to indulge yourself. Although at first the idea may sound totally extravagant, it need not be, and fares can be as low as $100 per day to more than $3000 per day. Alternately, you can book just a segment of the cruise if that fits your pocket and interest. There is a difference in what you get for your money, however. For example, aboard ships rated at four stars or more, shuttle buses from your ship to the center of town (or attraction) will probably be included; this is not so aboard ships rated three stars or less.

Special Features
Some of the special events planned for a world cruise will typically include:
→ Celebrity entertainers
→ World-renowned lecturers
→ Themed formal balls and parties
→ Equator crossing ceremony
→ International dateline crossing ceremony
→ Overnight and multiday overland shore excursions
→ Personalized stationery

Planning and Preparation
Few enterprises can match the complexity of planning and preparing for a world cruise. For example, more than 675,000 main meals will be prepared in the galleys during a typical *QE2* world cruise. Several hundred professional entertainers, lecturers, bands, and musicians must all be booked about a year in advance of the voyage. Crew changeovers during the cruise must be organized. A ship the size of the *QE2* requires two major crew changes during the three-month-long voyage.

Because a modern world cruise ship has to be totally self-contained, a warehouse-full of spare parts (electrical, plumbing, and engineering supplies, for example) must be planned for, ordered, loaded, and stored somewhere aboard ship prior to sailing. For just about every shipboard department, the same basic consideration will apply: once at sea, it will be impossible to pick up a replacement projector bulb, air-conditioning belt, table tennis ball, saxophone reed, or anything else that the ship might run out of.

Courtesy Douglas Ward

*The ships owned by Renaissance Cruises, of which **R One** is one, are totally nonsmoking.*

The cruise director will have his/her hands full planning entertainment and social events for a long voyage. It is not like the "old days" when an occasional game of bingo, horse racing, or the daily tote would satisfy passengers.

A cruise line must give advance notice of the date and time that pilots will be needed, together with requirements for tugs, docking services, customs and immigration authorities, or meetings with local dignitaries and the press. Then there is the organization of dockside labor and stevedoring services at each port of call, plus planning and contracting of bus or transportation services for shore excursions. Other preparations include reserving fuel at various ports on the itinerary.

The complexity of the preparations requires the concerted efforts of many departments and people on every continent to bring about, with precise timing, this ultimate cruising experience for travelers.

World Cruise Segments

Cruises to exotic destinations — China, the Orient, the South Pacific, around Africa, the Indian Ocean, and around South America — offer all the delights associated with a world cruise. The cruise can be shorter and hence less expensive, yet offer the same elegance and comfort, splendid food, delightful ambience, and interesting, well-traveled fellow passengers.

An exotic voyage can be a totally self-contained cruise to a specific destination, lasting anywhere from 30 days to more than 100 days. Or you can book a segment of a world cruise to begin at one of its ports of call, getting off at another port. "Segmenting" is ideal for those who wish to be a part of a world cruise but have neither the time nor the money for the prolonged extravagance of a three- to six-month vacation.

Segment cruising necessarily involves flying either to or from your cruise (or both). You can travel to join your exotic cruise at one of the principal ports such as Genoa, Rio de Janeiro, Acapulco, Honolulu, Sydney, Hong Kong, Singapore, Bangkok, Colombo, Mumbai (Bombay), Mombasa, or Athens, depending on the ship and the itinerary.

Ships that roam worldwide during the year offer the most experienced world cruises or segments. Most of these world cruise ships operate at about 75 percent capacity, thus providing considerably more space for passengers than they would normally have.

Going P.O.S.H.

This colloquialism for "grand" or "first-rate" has its origin in the days of ocean steamship travel between England and India. Wealthy passengers would, at some considerable cost, book round-trip passage as "Port Outward, Starboard Home." They would thus secure a cabin on the cooler side of the ship while crossing the unbearably hot Indian Ocean under the sun. Abbreviated as P.O.S.H., the expression soon came to be applied to first-class passengers who could afford that luxury. (*Brewers Dictionary of Phrase & Fable*, Cassell Ltd.).

However, the reality is that the monsoon winds that blow in and out of the Asian area shift between winter and summer, so that the sheltered side of a ship would change according to the season. Further, in looking at deck plans of ships of the period, most cabins were located *centrally*, with indoor promenades or corridors along each side, so the actual definition of the origin of P.O.S.H. could be said to be taken as artistic license.

121

AROUND THE WORLD CRUISES: 2002

This list includes ships presently scheduled to operate an around-the-world cruise in 2002.

SHIP	COMPANY	DAYS	DATE (Start)
Albatros	Phoenix Seereisen	110	December 22, 2001
Amsterdam	Holland America Line	99	January 20, 2002
Astor	Transocean Tours	122	December 22, 2001
Asuka	NYK Cruises	102	April 5, 2001
Aurora	P&O Cruises	90	January 4, 2002
Crystal Symphony **	Crystal Cruises	100	January 17, 2002
Delphin	Delphin Seereisen	169	November 29, 2001
Maxim Gorkiy	Phoenix Seereisen	135	December 16, 2001
Nippon Maru	Mitsui OSK Passenger Line	99	January 9, 2002
Oriana	P&O Cruises	92	January 5, 2002
Queen Elizabeth 2	Cunard Line	108	January 7, 2002
*Royal Princess**	Princess Cruises	71	February 11, 2002
Saga Rose	Saga Cruises	101	January 4, 2002
Seabourn Sun	Seabourn Cruise Line	102	January 9, 2002
Seven Seas Navigator	Radisson Seven Seas Cruises	105	January 20, 2002
Silver Wind	Silversea Cruises	106	January 5, 2002

KEY:
* = This is not a complete around-the-world cruise.
** = This is a "Grand Pacific Circle" cruise.

FROM (Finish)	DATE	TO	DIRECTION	NUMBER OF PORTS
(Start)	(Finish)			
Genoa	April 1, 2002	Genoa	Westbound	52
Los Angeles	April 29, 2002	New York	Westbound	38
Nice	April 22, 2002	Nice	Eastbound	58
Yokohama	July 16, 2001	Kobe	Westbound	29
Southampton	April 5, 2002	Southampton	Westbound	25
Los Angeles	April 27, 2002	Los Angeles	Westbound	33
Genoa	May 16, 2002	Genoa	Westbound	68
Bremerhaven	April 30, 2002	Bremerhaven	Westbound	62
Tokyo	April 21, 2002	Kobe	Eastbound	19
Southampton	April 6, 2002	Southampton	Eastbound	30
New York	April 26, 2002	Ft. Lauderdale	Westbound	33
Ft. Lauderdale	March 24, 2001	Athens	Westbound	25
Southampton	April 15, 2002	Southampton	Westbound	36
San Francisco	April 22, 2002	Ft. Lauderdale	Westbound	36
Los Angeles	May 5, 2002	Ft. Lauderdale	Westbound	49
Ft. Lauderdale	March 30, 2002	London	Westbound	24

FUN FACTS

Cruise ship design is interesting. Aesthetically, the beauty of design lies in curves, and not in straight lines. Today's large cruise ships, designed merely for cruising in warm weather regions and not for voyaging across the North Atlantic (heaven forbid, the delivery voyage was enough), are made of straight lines. They are boxy and cold in appearance, yet of course they provide much more usable space inside the ship. Take a look at *Norway* (the former liner *France*) and you won't find a straight line anywhere. Then take a look at *Imagination* and compare the two.

Norwegian Cruise Line features a "chocoholic" buffet aboard its ships once each cruise. This midnight extravaganza should appease even the most dedicated chocolate lovers.

Cruise lines and charity go hand in hand. Cunard donated some 1,500 pieces of classic furniture from the 1994 refit of *Queen Elizabeth 2* to the Salvation Army for its adult rehabilitation program. Crew aboard the same ship, when on its annual around-the-world cruise, donate money to buy guide dogs for the blind, or an ambulance for the St. John's Ambulance Brigade in the UK. Princess Cruises made a "sizeable" contribution to UNICEF following the death of Audrey Hepburn in 1993 (she named the company's *Star Princess*, presently operating as *Arcadia* for P&O Cruises). Passengers of Hapag-Lloyd's *Europa* have donated more than DM2 million to children's homes in Vietnam. Both Holland America Line and Princess Cruises have contributed heavily to the Raptor Center in Juneau, Alaska.

The sky's the limit! Now you can have a private astrological report including a horoscope analysis provided for you in two special "astroflash" booths set up aboard Norwegian Cruise Lines's, *Norwegian Sky*.

Carnival Cruise Lines carried over 500,000 seniors (those over 55 years of age) in 1999 aboard its "fun ships" fleet (this number represents about one-third of its passengers), and more than 250,000 children.

Naming a ship can be a bubbly sort of business. In fact, so bubbly that when Royal Caribbean International's *Legend of the Seas* was named by Cindy Pritzker on 16 May 1995 in Miami, the company ordered a "sovereign" of champagne (the largest in the world, equal to 34 ordinary bottles of champagne) from Moet & Chandon.

Times were different then. In the mid-1960s there were 12 "bell boys" ("piccolos" in hotelspeak) aboard the Cunard Line's RMS *Queen Elizabeth* and RMS *Queen Mary*. They manned the elevators and opened the doors to the various restaurants. Each day, before they were allowed to work, they all lined up and their fingernails were inspected.

On Valentine's Day (14 February) 1998, some 5,000 couples collectively renewed their wedding vows aboard the ships of Princess Cruises.

Tall ship lovers who are also music lovers may like to know about "*The Tall Ship Suite*," a work in three movements (The Race Begins; The Open Sea; Landfall and the Grand Parade of Sail). It was jointly composed and orchestrated by Dave Roylance and Bob Gavin. The two composers met in Liverpool in 1980 and composed the suite in 1992 in commemoration of the Grand Regatta Columbus '92. The work is played by the Royal Liverpool Philharmonic Orchestra conducted by Bill Conifer, available on CD. Also on the disc are two other works by the same composing team: "*Ocean Fantasia*," a tone poem (18 mins:19 secs), and "*Voyager*," an orchestral piece (8 mins:11 secs). With strong themes and excellent scoring, this music should be in every tall ship lover's music library.

Part Two:
THE CRUISE SHIPS AND RATINGS

Mandalay: courtesy Windjammer Barefoot Cruises

HOW SHIPS ARE EVALUATED

I have been evaluating and rating cruise ships and the onboard product professionally since 1980. In addition, I am provided with regular reports from a small team of trained "professional passengers." The ratings are conducted with total objectivity, from a set of predetermined criteria and a modus operandi designed to work globally, not just regionally, across the entire spectrum of ocean-going cruise ships today, in all segments of the marketplace.

There really is no "best cruise line in the world" or "best cruise ship"— only the ship and cruise that is right for you. Therefore, different criteria are applied to ships of different sizes, styles, and market segments throughout the world. Since so many new ships are of similar dimensions, but with different décor, more emphasis is placed on the standard of the dining experience, and the service and hospitality aspects of the cruise.

This section includes 269 oceangoing cruise ships in service when this book was completed. Almost all except the newest ships have been carefully evaluated, taking into account more than 400 separate inspection points based on personal cruises, visits and revisits to ships, as well as observations and comments from my reporting team. These are channeled into 20 major areas, each with a possible 100 points. The maximum possible score for any ship is, thus, 2,000 points.

For the sake of clarity and at-a-glance user-friendliness, however, only the overall score for each ship is provided.

Cruise lines, ship owners, and operators should note that ratings, like stocks and shares, can go down as well as up each year, due to increased competition, the introduction of newer ships with more custom-designed facilities, and other market- or passenger-driven factors.

The ratings more reflect the standards of the cruise product delivered to passengers (the software), and less the physical plant (the hardware). Thus, although a ship may be the latest, most stunning vessel in the world in terms of design and décor, if the food, service, staff, and hospitality are not so good, the scores and ratings will reflect these aspects more clearly.

The stars beside the name of the ship at the top of each page relate directly to the Overall Rating. The highest number of stars awarded is five stars (★★★★★), and the lowest is one star. This system is universally recognized throughout the hospitality industry. A plus (+) indicates that a ship deserves just that little bit more than the number of stars attained. However, *it is the number of points achieved rather than the number of stars attained* that perhaps is more meaningful to anyone comparing ships.

SCORING METHOD: THE RATINGS

Overall Score	Number of Stars	Overall Score	Number of Stars
1851–2000	★★★★★ +	1101–1250	★★★
1701–1850	★★★★★	951–1100	★★ +
1551–1700	★★★★ +	801–950	★★
1401–1550	★★★★	651–800	★+
1251–1400	★★★ +	500–650	★

WHAT THE RATINGS MEAN

1851–2000 Points ★★★★★ +
You can expect to have an outstanding luxury cruise experience— in fact, it doesn't get any better than this. It should be truly memorable, with the highest attention to detail, finesse, and highly personal service (how important you are made to feel is critically important). The décor must be elegant and tasteful, measured by restraint and not flashiness, with fresh flowers in abundance, and the layout of the public rooms might well be in accordance with the principles of *feng shui*. Any ship with this rating must be just about unsurpassable in the cruise industry, and it has to be very, very special, with service and hospitality levels to match. There must be the very highest quality surroundings, comfort and service levels, the finest and freshest quality foods, including all breads and rolls baked on board. Highly creative menus, regional cuisine, and dining alternatives that provide maximum choice and variety, and special orders will be part of the dining ritual.

Dining room meals (particularly dinners) are expected to be grand, memorable affairs, correctly served on the finest china, with a choice of wines of suitable character and vintage available, and served in the correct-sized glasses. The service staff will take pleasure in providing you with the ultimate personal, yet unobtrusive, attention with the utmost of finesse, and the word "no" should definitely not be in their vocabulary. This is the very best of the best in terms of refined, unstructured living at sea, and may cause serious damage to your bank statement.

1701–1850 Points ★★★★★

You can expect to have a truly excellent cruise experience that should be very memorable, and with the finesse and attention to detail commensurate with the amount of money paid. The service and hospitality levels will be extremely high from all levels of officers and staff, with strong emphasis on fine hospitality training (all service personnel members must make you feel important).

Food and service will be commensurate with the high level expected from what is virtually the best that is possible — attentive yet unobtrusive. The food should be quite memorable, with ample taste. Special orders should never present a problem, with a creative cuisine that will be of a very high standard. There must be a varied selection of wines, which should be properly served in the correct-sized glasses. Entertainment is expected to be of prime quality and variety. Again, the word "no" should not be in the vocabulary of any member of staff aboard a ship with this rating. A cruise aboard a ship with this high rating may well cause damage to your bank statement, particularly if you choose the most spacious grades of accommodation.

1551–1700 Points ★★★★ +

You should expect to have a high quality cruise experience that will be quite memorable, and just a little short of being excellent in all aspects. Perhaps the personal service and attention to detail could be slightly better, but, nonetheless, this should prove to be a fine all-round cruise experience, in a setting that is extremely clean and comfortable, with few lines anywhere, a caring attitude from service personnel, and a good standard of entertainment. The cuisine and service will be well rounded, with mostly fresh ingredients and varied menus that should appeal to almost anyone, served on high quality china. All in all, this should prove to be an extremely well rounded cruise experience, probably in a ship that is new or almost new.

1401–1550 Points ★★★★

You should expect to have a very good quality all-round cruise experience, most probably aboard a modern, highly comfortable ship that will provide a good range of facilities and services. The food and service will be quite decent overall, although decidedly not as "gourmet" and fanciful as the brochures with the always-smiling faces might have you believe. The service on board will be well organized, although it will perhaps be a little robotic and impersonal at times, and only as good as the cruise line's training program allows. However, you should have a good time, and only a moderate amount of damage will be done to your bank statement.

1251–1400 Points ★★★ +

You should expect to have a decent quality cruise experience, from a ship where the service levels should be good, but perhaps without the finesse that could be expected from a more upscale environment. The crew aboard any ship achieving this score should reflect a positive attitude with regard to hospitality, and a willingness to accommodate your needs, up to a point. Staff training will probably be in need of more attention to detail and flexibility. Food and service levels in the dining room(s) should be reasonably good, although special orders or anything out of the ordinary might prove more difficult.

1101–1250 Points ★★★

You can expect to have a reasonably decent, middle-of-the-road cruise experience, with a moderate amount of space and quality in furnishings, fixtures, and fittings. The cabins are likely to be a little on the small side. The food and service levels will be quite acceptable, but somewhat inflexible with regard to special orders, as almost everything is standardized. Crew attitude could certainly be improved, the level of hospitality and cleanliness will be moderate but little more, and entertainment will probably be weak. Good, however, for those looking for the reasonable comforts of home without pretentious attitudes, and little damage to one's bank statement.

951-1100   Points ★★ +

You should expect to have a cruise experience that is below average in terms of accommodation, quality, food, service, and hospitality levels, in surroundings that are completely unpretentious. In particular, the food and its service will probably prove to be most disappointing and rather typical of roadside café standards. There will be little flexibility in the levels of service, hospitality and staff training, which will be no better than poor. Thus, the overall experience will be commensurate with the small amount of money you paid for the cruise.

801-950   Points ★★

You should expect to have a cruise experience of modest quality aboard a ship that is probably in need of more attention to maintenance and service levels, not to mention hospitality. The food is likely to be quite tasteless and homogenized, and of low quality, and service will leave much to be desired in terms of attitude, which will tend to be mediocre at best. Staff training will be minimal, and turnover is likely to be high. The "end-of-pier" entertainment could well leave you wanting to read a good book.

651-800   Points ★ +

You can expect to have only the most basic cruise experience, with little or no attention to detail, from a poorly trained staff that is probably paid low wages and to whom you are just another body. The ship will, in many cases, probably be in need of much maintenance and upgrading, and will probably have few facilities. Cleanliness and hygiene may well be questionable, and there will be absolutely no finesse in personal service levels, with poor attitude from the crew, and dismal entertainment as significant factors in the low score and rating. On the other hand, the price of a cruise is probably extremely inexpensive.

500-650   Points ★

You can expect to have a cruise experience that is the absolute bottom of the barrel, with almost nothing in terms of hospitality or finesse. You can forget about attention to detail – there isn't any. This will be the kind of experience that would equal a stay in the most basic motel, with few facilities, a poorly trained, uncaring staff, most of whom will have undergone a hospitality bypass, and a ship that is in need of better maintenance and upgrading. The low cost of a cruise aboard any cruise ship with this rating should provide a clue to the complete lack of any quality. This will be particularly true in the areas of food, service, and entertainment. In other words, this could well be a totally forgettable cruise experience.

The Ratings and Evaluations cover five principal areas, each of which is almost as important as the next:

A) The Ship	D) Service
B) Accommodation	E) The Cruise Experience
C) Cuisine	

THE SHIP

This section forms 25 percent of the whole rating system.

Ship: Hardware/Maintenance/Safety

This score reflects the general profile and condition of the ship as hardware, its age and maintenance, hull condition, exterior paint, decking and caulking, swimming pool and surrounds, deck furniture, shore tenders, lifeboats, life rafts, and other safety items. Also reflects interior cleanliness (public restrooms, elevators, floor coverings, wall coverings, stairways, passageways, and doorways), food preparation areas, refrigerators, garbage handling, compacting, and incineration, and waste disposal facilities.

Ship: Outdoor Facilities/Space

This score reflects the overall space per passenger on open decks, crowding, swimming pools/whirlpools and their surrounds, lido deck areas, number and type of deck lounge chairs (with/without cushioned pads) and other deck furniture, outdoor sports facilities, shower enclosures and changing facilities, towels, and quiet areas (those without music).

Ship: Interior Facilities/Space/Flow

This score reflects the use of common interior public spaces, including enclosed promenades; passenger flow and points of congestion; ceiling height; lobby areas, stairways, and all passenger hallways; elevators; public restrooms and facilities; signage, lighting, air-conditioning and ventilation; and degree of comfort and density.

Ship: Décor/Furnishings/Artwork

This score reflects the overall interior décor and color scheme; hard and soft furnishings, wood (real, imitation, or veneer) paneling, carpeting (tuft density, color, and practicality), fit and finish (seams and edging), chairs (comfort, height, and support), ceilings and décor treatments, reflective surfaces, artwork (paintings, sculptures, and atrium centerpieces), and lighting.

Ship: Spa/Fitness Facilities

This score reflects any health spa, wellness center, and fitness facilities; location and accessibility; lighting and flooring materials; fitness and muscle-training machines and other equipment; fitness programs; sports and games facilities; indoor swimming pools; whirlpools; grand baths; aqua-spa pools; saunas and steam rooms; rasul, the various types of massage, and other treatment rooms; changing facilities; jogging and walking tracks; and promenades.

ACCOMMODATION

This section forms 15 percent of the whole rating system.

Cabins: Suites and Deluxe Grades

This score reflects the design and layout of all grades of suites and deluxe grade cabins, private balconies (whether full floor-to-ceiling partition or part partitions, balcony lighting, balcony furniture). Also beds/berths, furniture (its placement and practicality), and other fittings; closets and other hanging space, drawer space, and bedside tables; vanity unit, bathroom facilities, washbasin, cabinets, and toiletries storage; lighting, air-conditioning, and ventilation; audiovisual facilities; quality and degree of luxury; artwork; bulkhead insulation, noise, and vibration levels. Suites should not be so designated unless the sleeping room is completely separate from the living area. Note: Some large cruise ships now have whole decks devoted to superior grade accommodation, with much difference between this accommodation and that of "standard" cabins.

Also the soft furnishings and details such as the information manual (list of services); paper and postcards (including personalized stationery); telephone directory; laundry lists; tea- and coffee-making equipment; flowers (if any); fruit (if any); bathroom personal amenities kits, bathrobes, slippers, and the size, thickness, quality, and material content of towels.

Cabins: Standard Sizes

This score reflects the design and layout (whether outside or inside), beds/berths, furniture (its placement and practicality), and other fittings. Also closets and other hanging space, drawer space, bedside tables, and vanity unit; bathroom facilities, washbasin, cabinets, and toiletries storage; lighting, air-conditioning and ventilation; audiovisual facilities; quality and degree of fittings and furnishings; artwork; bulkhead insulation, noise, and vibration levels.

Also - the information manual (directory of services); paper and postcards (including stationery); telephone directory; laundry lists; tea- and coffee-making equipment; flowers (if any); fruit (if any); and bathroom amenities kits, bathrobes, slippers, and the size, thickness, quality, and material content of towels.

CUISINE

This section forms 15 percent of the whole rating system and is very important, as food is often the main feature of today's cruises. Cruise lines put maximum emphasis on telling passengers how good their food is, often to the point of being unable to deliver what is promised. Generally, the standard of food is good. The rule of thumb is: if you were to eat out in a good restaurant, what would you expect? Does the ship meet your expectations? Would you come back again for the food?

There are perhaps as many different tastes as there are passengers. The "standard" market cruise lines cater to a wide range of tastes, while the more exclusive cruise lines can offer better quality food, cooked individually to your taste. As in any good restaurant, you get what you pay for.

129

Food: Dining Room/Cuisine

This score reflects the physical structure of dining rooms; window treatments; seating (alcoves and individual chairs, with or without armrests); lighting and ambience; table set-ups; the quality and condition of linen, china, and cutlery; and table centerpieces (flowers). Also reflects menus, food quality, presentation, food combinations, culinary creativity, variety, design concepts, appeal, taste, texture, palatability, freshness, color, balance, garnishes, and decorations; appetizers, soups, pastas, flambeaus, tableside cooking; fresh fruit and cakes; the wine list (and connoisseur wine list), price range, and wine service. Alternative dining venues are checked for menu variety, food and service quality, décor and noise levels.

Food: Informal Dining/Buffets

This score reflects the hardware (including the provision of hot and cold display units, sneeze guards, tongs, ice containers and ladles, and serving utensils); buffet displays (which have become quite disappointing and institutionalized); presentation; trays and set-ups; correct food temperatures; food labeling; breakfast, luncheon, deck buffets, midnight buffets, and late-night snacks; decorative elements such as ice carvings; and staff attitude, service, and communication skills.

Food: Quality of Ingredients

This score reflects the overall quality of ingredients used, including consistency and portion size; grades of meat, fish, and fowl; and the price paid by the cruise line for its food product per passenger per day. It is the quality of ingredients that most dictates the eventual presentation and quality of the finished product as well as its taste. Also included is the quality of tea and coffee (better quality ships are expected to provide better quality tea and coffee).

Food: Tea/Coffee/Bar Snacks

This score reflects the quality and variety of teas and coffees available (including afternoon teas/coffees and their presentation); whether mugs or cups and saucers are presented/available; whether milk is served in the correct open containers or in sealed packets; whether self-service or graciously served. The quality of such items as cakes, scones, and pastries, as well as bar/lounge snacks, hot and cold canapes, and hors d'oeuvres also forms part of this section.

SERVICE

This section forms 20 percent of the whole rating system.

Service: Dining Room

This score reflects the professionalism of the restaurant staff: maître d' Hotel, dining room managers, head section waiters, waiters and assistant waiters (busboys), and sommeliers and wine waiters. It includes place settings and correct service (serving, taking from the correct side), communication skills, attitude, flair, dress sense (uniform), and finesse. Waiters should note whether passengers are right- or left-handed and, aboard ships with assigned table places, make sure that the cutlery and glasses are placed on the side of preference. Cutlery and wine glasses are also included.

Service: Bars

This score reflects the lighting and ambience; overall service in bars and lounges; noise levels; communication skills (between bartenders and bar staff and passengers); staff attitude, personality, flair and finesse; correct use of glasses (and correct size of glasses); billing and attitude when presenting the bill (aboard those ships where a charge is made).

Service: Cabins

This score reflects the cleaning and housekeeping staff, butlers (for penthouse and suite passengers), cabin stewards/stewardesses and their supervisory staff, attention to detail and cleanliness, in-cabin food service, linen and bathrobe changes, and language and communication skills.

Service: Open Decks

This score reflects steward/stewardess service for beverages and food items around the open decks; service for placement and replacement of towels on deck lounge chairs, self-help towels, and emptying of used towel bins; general tidiness of all associated deck equipment; and the availability of service at nonstandard times (in the evening or early morning, for example).

THE CRUISE EXPERIENCE
This section forms 25 percent of the whole rating system.

Cruise: Entertainment
This score reflects the overall entertainment program and content as designed and targeted to spe-cific passenger demographics. Cruise ship entertainment has to appeal to passengers of widely vary-ing ages and types. Included is the physical plant (stage/bandstand); technical support, lighting, fol-low spotlight operation and set/backdrop design; sound and light systems (including laser shows); recorded click-tracks and all special effects; variety and quality of large-scale production shows (including story, plot, content, cohesion, creativeness of costumes, relevancy, quality, choreography, and vocal content); cabaret; variety shows; game shows, visual acts; bands and solo musicians.

Cruise: Activities Program
This score reflects the variety, quality, and quantity of daytime activities and events. The rating includes the cruise director and cruise staff (including their visibility, availability, ability, and pro-fessionalism), sports programs, participation games, special interest programs, port and shopping lecturers, and mind-enrichment lecturers.

This score also reflects any water sports equipment carried (including banana boat, jet skis, scuba tanks, snorkeling equipment, waterski boat and windsurfers), instruction programs, overall staff supervision, the marina (usually located aft) or side-retractable water sports platforms, and any enclosed swimming area (if applicable).

Cruise: Movies/Television Programming
This score reflects movies screened in onboard theaters, including screen, picture and sound quali-ty; videos screened on the in-cabin television system; other televised programming, including a ship's own television station programming; content; and entertainment value. Cabin television audio channels are also included in this section.

Cruise: Hospitality Standard
This score reflects the level of hospitality of the crew and their attention to detail and personal satisfaction. It includes the professionalism of senior officers, middle management, supervisors, cruise staff, and general crew; social contact, appearance, and dress codes or uniforms; atmos-phere and ambience; motivation; communication skills (most important); the general ambience and the attention to detail.

Cruise: Overall Product Delivery
This score reflects the quality of the overall cruise as a vacation experience_—_what the brochure states and promises (real or implied), which reflects on the level of expectation versus the onboard product delivery.

THE RATING RESULTS — THE AUTHOR'S NOTES
Cruise ship evaluations and ratings have of necessity become tougher and much more complex. Although a ship may be the newest, with all the latest high-tech facilities possible, passengers reit-erate that it is the onboard food and service that often disappoints.

Cruise companies defend themselves by stating that their passengers are willing to accept lesser quality with regard to food in return for lower prices. However, this attitude only results in a down-ward spiral that affects food quality, freshness, variety, creativity, and presentation, as well as ser-vice, quality of personnel, crew training, safety, maintenance, and other related items.

Cuts (in food quality, crew wages and detail items) are often made by cruise companies in the hope that passengers will not notice. However, in the final analysis, it is the little things that add to points lost on the great scorecard.

The ratings are intended to help the cruise companies to take note of their product, listen to their income-generating passengers, and return some of the items and the finesse currently missing in the overall cruise vacation experience, while adjusting fares to better reflect long-term growth of this good value-for-money vacation.

THE SHIP PROFILES AND RATINGS

SHIP SIZE
Small Ship (up to 500 passengers)
Mid-Size Ship (500–1,000 passengers)
Large Ship (over 1,000 passengers)

LIFESTYLE
Designated as Standard, Premium, or Luxury, according to a general classification into which segment of the market the ship falls. It should thus further allow you to choose the right size ship and cruise experience to fit your lifestyle.
→ Those designated STANDARD are the least expensive.
→ Those designated PREMIUM are more expensive, have generally better food, service, and facilities.
→ Those designated LUXURY are the most expensive and provide the best facilities, food, and
   service, and the finest cruise experience possible.

CRUISE LINE
The cruise line and operator may be different if the company that owns the vessel does not market and operate it.

FIRST ENTERED SERVICE
Where two dates are given, the first is the ship's maiden passenger voyage when new, and the second is the date it began service for the present operator.

PROPULSION
The type of propulsion is given (i.e., gas turbine, diesel, diesel-electric, or steam turbine), together with the output (at 100 percent), expressed as MW (megawatts) or kW (kilowatts) generated.

PROPELLERS
Number of propellers or azimuthing pods (in which a propeller is mounted externally, replacing conventional propeller and shaft)

PASSENGER CAPACITY
The number of passengers is based on:
→ Two lower beds/berths per cabin, plus all cabins for single occupancy.
→ All available beds/berths filled (Note: This figure may not always be accurate, as cruise lines
   often make changes by adding or taking away third/fourth berths according to demand).

PASSENGER SPACE RATIO (TONNES PER PASSENGER)
Achieved by dividing the gross registered tonnage by the number of passengers.

CREW TO PASSENGER RATIO
Achieved by dividing the number of passengers by the number of crew (lower beds/all possible beds and berths filled).

CABIN SIZE RANGE
From the smallest cabin to the largest suite (including private balconies), in square feet and square meters, rounded up to the nearest number.

WHEELCHAIR ACCESIBLE CABINS
Cabins designed to accommodate passengers with mobility problems.

DEDICATED CINEMA /SEATS
A "Yes" means that there is a separate, dedicated cinema, where large-screen movies can be shown throughout the day and evening, and not a show lounge that can also screen movies during the day (afternoon) and live shows at night. The number of seats is provided where known.

Note: In the Other Comments section at the bottom of each page, all gratuities, including insurance and port taxes are usually at extra cost unless specifically included in the price.

132

THE CRUISE LINES: MARKET CLASSIFICATION

Luxury

Crystal Cruises
Hapag-Lloyd Cruises (3)
Radisson Seven Seas Cruises (3)
Seabourn Cruise Line

Cunard Line
Hebridean Island Cruises
Sea Cloud Cruises
Silversea Cruises

Premium

Abercrombie & Kent
Classical Cruises
Club Mediterranee Cruises
Fred Olsen Cruise Lines
Holland America Line
NYK Cruises
Orient Lines
Ponant Cruises
Renaissance Cruises
Saga Shipping
Swan Hellenic Cruises
Windstar Cruises

Celebrity Cruises
Clipper Cruise Line
Discoverer Reederei
Golden Sea Cruises
Lindblad Expeditions
Noble Caledonia
P&O Cruises (3)
Quark Expeditions
Radisson Seven Seas Cruises (3)
Society Expeditions
Venus Cruise (Japan Cruise Line)

Standard

Aida Cruises
Alaska's Glacier Bay Cruises
American Cruise Line
Arcalia Shipping (2)
Canodros
Clipper Cruise Line
Croatia Cruise Lines
Delta Queen Coastal Cruises
Disney Cruise Line
Festival Cruises (1)
First European Cruises (1)
Great Lakes Cruises
Hapag-Lloyd Cruises (3)
Islas Galapagos y Turismos
Jahn Reisen
Louis Cruise Lines
Mediterranean Shipping Cruises
Mitsui OSK Passenger Line
Noble Caledonia
P&O Cruises (3)
Peace Boat
Plantours & Partner
Pullmantour Cruises
Royal Caribbean International
St. Helena Shipping
Spanish Cruise Line
Star Clippers
Thomson Cruises
Transtours
Valtur Tourism
World Explorer Cruises

Airtours Sun Cruises
American Canadian Caribbean Line
American Hawaii Cruises
Carnival Cruise Lines
Classic International Cruises (2)
Costa Cruises
Cruise West
Delphin Seereisen
Dreamline Cruises
First Choice
Galapagos Cruises
Golden Sun Cruises
Island
Imperial Majesty Cruise Line
Kristina Cruises
Mano Maritime
Metropolitan Touring
New Paradise Cruises
Norwegian Cruise Line
P&O Cruises (Australia)
Phoenix Seereisen
Princess Cruises
Regal Cruises
Royal Olympic Cruises
Seetours
Star Cruises
Star Line Cruises
Transocean Tours
United States Lines
Windjammer Barefoot Cruises

Notes:
1) This company operated under two different brand names in Europe and North America.
(2) These companies are one and the same.
(3) This company has different ships for different market segments and is thus listed under more
    than one market classification.

Adventure of the Seas

Large Ship:	137,276 tons	Cabins (wheelchair accessible):	26
Lifestyle:	Standard	Cabin Current:	110-volt
Cruise Line:	Royal Caribbean International	Full-Service Dining Rooms:	1 + 3 cafés
Former Names:	-	Elevators:	14 (6 glass-enclosed)
Builder:	Kvaerner Masa-Yards (Finland)	Casino (gaming tables):	Yes
Original Cost:	$500 million	Slot Machines:	Yes
Entered Service:	November 2001	Swimming Pools (outdoors):	3
Registry:	Liberia	Swimming Pools (indoors):	0
Length (ft/m):	1,020.6/311.1	Whirlpools:	6
Beam (ft/m):	155.5/47.4	Fitness Center:	Yes
Draft (ft/m):	28.8/8.8	Sauna/Steam Room:	Yes/Yes
Propulsion/Propellers:	Diesel-electric	Massage:	Yes
	(75,600kW)/3 azimuthing pods	Self-Service Launderette:	No
Passenger Decks:	14	Dedicated Cinema:	No
Total Crew:	1,185	Library:	Yes
Passengers (lower beds/all berths): 3,114/3,840		Classification Society:	Det Norske Veritas
Pass.Space Ratio(lowerbeds/all berths):	44.0/35.7		
Crew/Pass. Ratio (lower beds/all berths):	2.6/3.2		
Navigation Officers:	Scandinavian		
Cabins (total):	1,557		
Size Range (sq ft/sq m): 151.0–1,146.0/14.0–106.5			
Cabins (outside view):	939		
Cabins (interior/no view):	618		
Cabins (for one person):	0		
Cabins (with private balcony):	765		

OVERALL SCORE: NOT YET RATED

Note that this ship had not entered service when this book was completed. However, the score is expected to be similar to *Explorer of the Seas* and *Voyager of the Seas*.

Accommodation: There is an extensive range of 22 cabin categories from which to choose, in four major groupings: Premium ocean-view suites and cabins, Promenade-view (interior-view) cabins, Ocean-view cabins, and Interior (no view) cabins. Note that many cabins are of a similar size – good for incentives and large groups, and 300 have interconnecting doors – good for families.

A total of 138 interior (no view) cabins have bay windows that look into a horizontal atrium – first used to good effect aboard the Baltic passenger ferries Silja Serenade (1990) and Silja Symphony (1991) with interior (no view) cabins that look into a central shopping plaza. Regardless of what cabin grade you choose, however, all except for the Royal Suite and Owner's Suite feature twin beds that convert to a queen-sized unit, television, radio and telephone, personal safe, vanity unit, minibar (called an Automatic Refreshment Center) hairdryer and private bathroom.

The largest accommodation includes luxuriously appointed penthouse suites (whose occupants, sadly, must share the rest of the ship with everyone else, except for their own exclusive, and private, concierge club). The grandest is the Royal Suite, which is positioned on the port side of the ship. It features a king-sized bed in a separate, large bedroom, a living room with an additional queen-sized sofa bed, baby grand piano (no pianist is included, however), refrigerator/wet bar, dining table, entertainment center, and large bathroom.

The slightly smaller, but still highly desirable Owner's Suites (there are 10 of these, all located in the center of the ship, on both port and starboard sides) and the Royal Family suites (four of them) all feature similar items. However, the four Royal Family suites, which have two bedrooms (including one with third/fourth upper Pullman berths) are located at the stern of the ship and have magnificent views over the ship's wash.

All cabins feature twin beds that convert to a queen-sized bed, a private bathroom with shower enclosure (towels are 100 percent cotton), as well as interactive, closed circuit and satellite television, and pay-per-view movies. Cabins with "private balconies" should note that they are not so private, as the partitions are only partial, leaving you exposed to your neighbor's smoke or conversation. The balcony decking is made of Bolidt – a sort of rubberized sand – and not wood, while the balcony rail is of wood.

Dining: The main dining room (total capacity 1,919) is undoubtedly large and is set on three levels, all of which are named after composers (Mozart, Strauss, Vivaldi). A dramatic staircase connects all three levels. However, all three feature exactly the same menus and food. There are also two small private wings for private groups: La Cetra and La Notte — each seats 58 persons. The dining room is totally nonsmoking, there are two seatings, and tables are for four, six, eight, ten, or twelve. The place settings, china, and cutlery are of good quality.

The cuisine in the main dining room is mass banquet catering that offers standard fare comparable to that found in American family-style restaurants ashore. While menu descriptions are tempting, the actual food may be somewhat disappointing and non-memorable. On a seven-day cruise, a typical menu rotation will include a Welcome Aboard Dinner, French Dinner, Italian Dinner, International Dinner, and Captain's Gala Dinner.

While the USDA prime beef is very good, other meats may not be (they are often disguised with gravies or heavy sauces). Most of the fish (apart from salmon) and seafood is overcooked and lacking in taste. Green vegetables are scarce, although salad items are plentiful. Rice is often used to replace potatoes and other sources of carbohydrates. Breads and pastry items are generally good (although some items, such as croissants, for example, may not be made on board). Dessert items are very standardized, and the selection of cheeses is poor (almost all come from the US — a country known for its processed, colored cheeses), as is the choice of crackers to go with the cheese.

Dining options for casual and informal meals at all hours (according to company releases) include:

Café Promenade: continental breakfast, all-day pizzas, and specialty coffees (provided in paper cups).

Windjammer Café: buffet-style breakfast, lunch, and light dinner (except for the last night of the cruise).

Island Grill (this is actually a section inside the Windjammer Café): casual dinner (no reservations necessary) featuring a grill and open kitchen.

Portofino: an "upscale" (nonsmoking) Euro-Italian restaurant, with 98 seats, for dinner (reservations are required).

Johnny Rockets: a retro 1950s all-day, all-night eatery that features hamburgers, malt shakes (at extra cost), and jukebox hits, with both indoor and outdoor seating.

Sprinkles: for round-the-clock ice cream and yogurt.

Other Comments: *Adventure of the Seas* is a stunning, large, floating leisure resort, and sister to *Explorer of the Seas* and *Voyager of the Seas*, which debute_____ 1999, respectively, and two others still to come. The exterior design is not unlike an enlarge_____ ne company's *Vision*-class ships. The ships are, at present, the largest cruise vessels in the w_____ of tonnage measurement (although, to keep things in perspective, the ships are not quite as l_____ gian Cruise Line's *Norway*).

The ship's propulsion is derived from three _____ wered by electric motors (two azimuthing, and one fixed at the centerline) instead of conve_____ rs and propellers, in the latest configuration of high-tech propulsion systems.

With her large proportions, she provides n_____ and options, and caters to more passengers than any other Royal Caribbean International_____ the past, and yet the ship manages to have a healthy passenger space ratio (the amount of _____ assenger). Being a "non-Panamax" ship, she is simply too large to go through the Panama C_____ imiting her itineraries almost exclusively to the Caribbean (where few islands can accept her_____ se as a floating island resort. Spend the first few hours exploring all the many facilities and pu_____ s aboard this vessel and it will be time well spent.

Although she is a large ship, even the acc_____ n hallways are quite attractive, with artwork cabinets and wavy lines to interject and break u_____ ony. In fact, there are plenty of decorative touches to help avoid what would otherwise be a_____ environment.

Embarkation and disembarkation take_____ h two stations/access points in a new purpose-built passenger terminal in Miami. These a_____ o minimize the inevitable lines at the start and end of the cruise (that's over 1,500 peopl_____ ccess point). Once inside the ship, you'll need good walking shoes, particularly when yo_____ from one end to the other — it really is quite a long way.

The four-decks-high Royal Promenade_____ 7 ft (120 m) long, is the main interior focal point (it's a good place to hang out, to meet sor_____ range to meet someone). The length of two football fields, it has two internal lobbies (atri_____ s many as 11 decks high. Restaurants, shops, and entertainment locations front this windin_____ erior "with-view" cabins look into it from above. It is designed loosely in the image of Lor_____ ble Burlington Arcade, although there's not a real brick in sight, and I wonder if the design_____ visited the real thing!

The atrium houses a "traditional" En_____ a, naturally, draft beer and plenty of "street-front" seating (it's funny, but North American_____ down, while British passengers stand at the bar). There is also a Champagne Bar, a Side_____ continental breakfast, all-day pizzas, specialty coffees and desserts), Sprinkles (for round-the-clock ice cream and yogurt), and Weekend Warrior (a sports bar). There are also several shops — jewelry shop, gift shop, liquor shop, and the logo souvenir shop. Altogether, the Royal promenade is a nice place to see and be seen. The Guest Reception and Shore Excursion counters are located at the aft end of the promenade, as is an ATM machine. Things to watch for: Look up to see the large moving, asteroid-like sculpture (constantly growing and contracting), parades, and street entertainers.

Arched across the promenade is a captain's balcony. Meanwhile, in the center of the promenade is a stairway that connects you to the deck below, where you'll find Schooner Bar (a piano lounge) and the colorful Casino Royale. This is, naturally, large and full of flashing lights and noises. Casino gaming includes blackjack, Caribbean stud poker, roulette, and craps.

Aft to the casino is the Aquarium Bar, while close by are some neat displays of oceanographic inter-est. Royal Caribbean International has teamed up with the University of Miami's Rosenstiel School of Marine and Atmospheric Science to study the ocean and the atmosphere. A small onboard laboratory is part of the project.

Action man and action woman can enjoy more sporting pursuits, such as a rock-climbing wall that's 32.8 ft (10 m) high. It is located outdoors at the aft end of the funnel. You'll get a great "buzz" being 200 ft (70 m) above the ocean while the ship is moving — particularly when it rolls.

There's also an in-line skating track, a dive-and-snorkel shop, a full-size basketball court, and 9-hole golf driving range. A ShipShape health spa measures 15,000 sq ft (1,393.5 sq m) and includes a large aerobics room, fitness center (with the usual stairmasters, treadmills, stationary bikes, weight machines and free weights), treatment rooms, men's and women's sauna/steam rooms, while another 10,000 sq ft (929sq m) is devoted to a solarium (with magrodome sliding glass roof) for relaxation after you've exercised too much!

There is also a regulation-size ice-skating rink (Studio B), featuring real, not fake, ice, with "bleach-er" seating for up to 900, and the latest in broadcast facilities. Ice Follies shows are also presented here. A number of slim pillars obstruct clear-view arena stage sight lines, however.

If ice-skating in the Caribbean doesn't appeal to you, perhaps you'd like the stunning two-deck library (it's the first aboard any ship, and it's open 24 hours a day). A grand $12 million has been spent on per-manent artwork. Drinking places include a neat Aquarium Bar, which comes complete with 50 tons of glass and water in four large aquariums (whose combined value is over $1 million). Other drinking places include the small and intimate Champagne Bar, Crown & Anchor Pub, and a Connoisseur Club — for cigars and cognacs. Lovers of jazz might appreciate High Notes, an intimate room for cool music, or the Schooner Bar piano lounge. Golfers might enjoy the 19th Hole — a golf bar.

Show lovers will find that the Palace Showlounge seats 1,350-seat and spans the height of five decks. It features a hydraulic orchestra pit and stage areas, and is decorated in the style of the grand European theaters from the fin-de-siecle period.

There is a TV studio, located adjacent to rooms that can be used for trade show exhibit space. Lovers can tie the knot in a wedding chapel in the sky, called the Skylight Chapel (it's located on the upper level of the Observation Lounge, and even has wheelchair access via an electric stairway lift). Outdoors, the pool and open deck areas provide a resort-like environment.

Families with children have not been forgotten, and the children's facilities are extensive. "Aquanauts" is for 3–5 year olds; "Explorers" is for 6–8 year olds; "Voyagers" is for 9–12 year olds. "Optix" is a ded-icated area for teenagers, including a daytime club (with several computers), soda bar, and dance floor. "Challenger's Arcade" features an array of the latest video games. "Paint and Clay" is an arts and crafts center for younger children. Adjacent to these indoor areas is Adventure Beach, an area for all the family to enjoy; this includes swimming pools, a water slide, and game areas outdoors.

In terms of sheer size, this ship dwarfs all other ships in the cruise industry, but in terms of personal service, it's more like the reverse. Royal Caribbean International does, however, try hard to provide a good standard of programmed service from its hotel staff. This is impersonal city life at sea, millennium-style, and a superb, well-designed alternative to a land-based resort, which is what the company wanted to build. Welcome to the real, escapist world of highly programmed resort living aboard ship. Perhaps if you dare to go outside, you might even be able to see the sea — now there's a novelty! Keep in mind that you'll need to pay for all the additional cost items.

The ship is large, so remember that if you meet someone somewhere and want to meet them again, you'll need to make an appointment (arrange to meet along the Royal Promenade). This really is a large, Las Vegas-style American floating resort-city for the lively of heart and fleet of foot. Note that this ship will probably achieve a rating score similar to that for sister ships *Explorer of the Seas* and *Voyager of the Seas*.

Weak Points: Standing in line for embarkation, disembarkation, shore tenders, and for self-serve buffet meals is an inevitable aspect of cruising aboard all large ships. If you are a non-US resident and stay at an RCI-booked hotel, all formalities can be completed there and then you'll simply walk on board to your cabin. Suites and cabins with private balcony have Bolidt floors (a substance that looks like rubberized sand) instead of wood. If you have a cabin with a door that interconnects to another cabin, be aware that you'll be able to hear everything your next-door neighbors say and do! Bathroom toilets are explosively noisy. You'll need to plan what you want to take part in wisely, as almost everything requires you to sign-up in advance (many activities take place only on sea days). The cabin bath towels are small and skimpy. There are very few quiet places to sit and read — almost everywhere there is intrusive acoustic wallpaper (background music). Food costs are well below that for Celebrity Cruises, for example, and so you should not expect the same food quality, variety, and taste.

SATELLITE NAVIGATOR

Using this latest high-tech piece of equipment, ship's officers can read, on a small television screen, the ship's position in the open ocean anywhere in the world, any time, and in any weather with pinpoint accuracy.

Satellite navigation systems use the information transmitted by a constellation of orbiting satellites. Each is in a normal circular polar orbit at an altitude of 450 to 700 nautical miles, and orbits the Earth in about 108 minutes. Data from each gives the current orbital position every two minutes. Apart from telling the ship where it is, it continuously provides the distance from any given point, calculates the drift caused by currents and so on, and tells the ship when the next satellite will pass.

The basis of the satellite navigation is the US Navy Satellite System (NNSS). This first became operational in January 1964 as the precision guidance system for the Polaris submarine fleet and was made available for commercial use in 1967.

The latest (and more accurate) system is the GPS (Global Positioning System), which is now fitted to an increasing number of ships. This uses 24 satellites (18 of which are on-line at any given time) that provide accuracy in estimating a ship's position to plus or minus six feet. Another variation is the NACOS (Navigational Command System), which collects information from a variety of sources: satellites, radar, gyroscopic compass, speed log, and surface navigational systems as well as engines, thrusters, rudders, and human input. It then displays relevant computations and information on one screen, controlled by a single keyboard.

Aegean I
★★ +

Mid-Size Ship:	11,563 tons	Cabins (for one person):	0
Lifestyle:	Standard	Cabins (with private balcony):	8
Cruise Line:	Golden Sun Cruises	Cabins (wheelchair accessible):	0
Former Names:	*Aegean Dolphin, Dolphin, Aegean*	Cabin Current:	220-volt
	Dolphin, Alkyon, Narcis	Full-Service Dining Rooms:	1
Builder:	Santierul N. Galatz (Romania)	Elevators:	2
Original Cost:	n/a	Casino (gaming tables):	Yes
Entered Service:	1974/May 1988	Slot Machines:	Yes
Registry:	Greece	Swimming Pools (outdoors):	1
Length (ft/m):	460.9/140.5	Swimming Pools (indoors):	0
Beam (ft/m):	67.2/20.5	Whirlpools:	0
Draft (ft/m):	20.3/6.2	Fitness Center:	Yes
Propulsion/Propellers:	Diesel (10,296kW)/2	Sauna/Steam Room:	Yes/No
Passenger Decks:	8	Massage:	Yes
Total Crew:	200	Self-Service Launderette:	No
Passengers (lower beds/all berths):	560/682	Dedicated Cinema/Seats:	Yes/172
Pass. Space Ratio (lower beds/all berths):	20.6/16.8	Library:	Yes
Crew/Pass. Ratio (lower beds/all berths):	2.8/3.4	Classification Society:	Lloyd's Register
Navigation Officers:	Greek		
Cabins (total):	280		
Size Range (sq ft/sq m):	134.5–290.6/12.5–27.0		
Cabins (outside view):	198		
Cabins (interior/no view):	82		

OVERALL SCORE: **972**

(OUT OF A POSSIBLE 2,000 POINTS)

Accommodation: This ship has nine different cabin grades. The cabins mostly have an outside view, and most are of the same size and configuration, although the largest cabins can be found on the Sun Deck. All feature a small refrigerator and telephone. They are reasonably spacious, considering the size of the ship, and they are quite pleasantly decorated, although closet, drawer, and luggage storage space for two is limited (it certainly is not enough for a long cruise, although it is adequate for one), and the walls and ceilings are very plain. The cabin soundproofing is extremely poor, and you can hear almost everything that's happening in the adjacent cabin(s).

The partly-tiled bathrooms are small and basic, and only just adequate, but there really is little space for personal toiletry items. Bathrobes are typically only provided for occupants of accommodation designated as suites (this also depends on anyone who may charter and operate the vessel). All toilets are of the non-vacuum type and are quiet, although the toilet seats are extremely high, at 20 inches (52 cm).

There are two suites on the Sun Deck — the largest accommodation aboard this ship. Although the lounge area is not even curtained off from the sleeping area, it is quite large. The bathroom features a full size bathtub, although the "lip" (step) into the bathroom is unnecessarily high (11 inches/28 cm).

Dining: The dining room, which is located on one of the lowest passenger decks, features restful colors, and has mostly large tables (there are no tables for two). It is a nonsmoking room, there are two seatings, and the ceilings are plain. There is a decent amount of space around each table, allowing waiters room to provide decent service, although this tends to be quite hurried at times. Features a mixture of Continental and Greek cuisine, with only a limited selection of breads, cheeses, and fruits, which tend to be very standard items.

For casual meals, small (limited choice) self-serve breakfast and lunch buffets are available on the Lido Deck aft, where a popular outdoor gyro and salad bar is available.

Other Comments: The profile of this ship looks reasonably smart — almost contemporary — although the stern is very square and angular, the result of an extensive $26 million conversion, which involved a "chop and stretch" operation between 1986 and 1988. The open deck space can be said to be moderately good, but it is certainly not enough when the ship is full, and that means it could be difficult to find good sunbathing space, and the number of deck lounge chairs is very limited.

Inside, the public rooms are quite tastefully decorated in soft, mostly pastel colors, although there is much use of mirrored surfaces. There is a reasonable show lounge, laid out in a single-level amphitheater-style, although ten pillars obstruct the sight lines from many seats. The Belvedere Lounge, which is set high atop the ship and forward, features a piano bar and good ocean views through large windows.

A dialysis station is a useful addition to medical facilities. The beauty salon and spa facilities are cramped and poor.

In general, the service, from a mainly Greek hotel staff, could be said to be selectively friendly (when they want to be), although there is certainly no finesse, and many of them can be seen smoking in public areas (this would be totally against the regulations of almost all non-Greek cruise companies).

This ship really caters primarily to European passengers. The ship is often placed under charter to various operators, and cruises are sold by a number of different organizations in many countries.

The ship will provide you with a cruise in moderately comfortable but very densely populated surroundings, but at a fair price — therefore you should not expect the spit and polish that other ships might provide in the same price range.

Weak Points: Although at first glance the ship appears to have a good range of nicely decorated public rooms, on closer inspection some of the materials used in their construction are held together by the "patch and fix" method of shipbuilding and refurbishment, which is definitely below internationally accepted standards. There are too many unnecessary announcements (often made in several languages, depending on the passenger mix and cruise). The teak decking around the swimming pool is in poor condition. The gangway is narrow and steep in some ports. There are no cushioned pads for the deck lounge chairs (lying on a towel on plastic ribbing is no fun for more than a few minutes!). The poor attitude and lack of hospitality from most officers and crew is not acceptable, and officers should learn to turn their two-way radios down.

Aegean Spirit
★★

Mid-Size Ship:	17,900 tons	Cabins (for one person):	5
Lifestyle:	Standard	Cabins (with private balcony):	0
Cruise Line:	Golden Sun Cruises	Cabins (wheelchair accessible):	0
Former Names:	*Symphony, EnricoCosta,*	Cabin Current:	220-volt
	Enrico "C", Provence	Full-Service Dining Rooms:	1
Builder:	Swan, Hunter (UK)	Elevators:	2
Original Cost:	n/a	Casino (gaming tables):	Yes
Entered Service:	March 1951/May 2000	Slot Machines:	Yes
Registry:	Greece	Swimming Pools (outdoors):	3
Length (ft/m):	579.0/176.49	Swimming Pools (indoors):	0
Beam (ft/m):	73.1/22.31	Whirlpools:	0
Draft (ft/m):	24.6/7.52	Fitness Center:	Yes
Propulsion/Propellers:	Diesel (8,096kW)/2	Sauna/Steam Room:	No/No
Passenger Decks:	7	Massage:	Yes
Total Crew:	308	Self-Service Launderette:	No
Passengers (lower beds/all berths):	665/839	Dedicated Cinema/Seats:	Yes/102
Pass. Space Ratio (lower beds/all berths):	26.9/21.3	Library:	No
Crew/Pass. Ratio (lower beds/all berths):	2.1/2.7	Classification Society:	RINA
Navigation Officers:	Greek		
Cabins (total):	335		
Size Range (sq ft/sq m):	86.1–216.3/8.0–20.1	**OVERALL SCORE:**	**906**
Cabins (outside view):	162	(OUT OF A POSSIBLE 2,000 POINTS)	
Cabins (interior/no view):	173		

Accommodation: There are a wide variety of cabin sizes and configurations from which to choose, typically in 11 different grades. Most of the cabins are compact, basic, but comfortable units, with tasteful pastel decor and soft furnishings to match. They have chrome locks and real keys — a throwback to her former life as a two-class ocean liner. The accommodation passageways have wooden handrails, but inconsistent lighting quality.

The bathrooms are really very basic units compared with those found aboard more modern ships, although in some of the larger cabins, the bathrooms are large and feature a bidet in addition to a bathtub, washbasin, and toilet.

The largest cabins (on the Promenade Deck) have ample space for two, and some include a lounge area with sofa, table and two chairs, personal safe, and small refrigerator; the bathrooms have a good size bathtub with shower, washbasin, bidet, and toilet.

You should note that many of the interior (no view) cabins have upper/lower single berths (not good for romantics).

Dining: The dining room is reasonably comfortable, although it is extremely noisy (particularly adjacent to the waiter stations, which seem to be everywhere), but it does have pleasing traditional wood portholes (you can't see out of them when you are seated, however).

The painted pegboard ceiling in many areas looks old and shabby and should be replaced. There are typically two seatings for dinner, while breakfast consists of a poor serve-yourself buffet. The cuisine is motorway café basic. The dishes lack any hint of quality and the presentation and consistency are both really poor; also the food ingredient quality (meat and fish) leaves much to be desired. The self-serve buffet breakfasts (even in the dining room) are pitiful. Dining room service lacks finesse and is provided by Greek stewards, who are selectively friendly.

A casual outdoors "café" (with plastic chairs and tables) located adjacent to one the three swimming pools, features a self-serve buffet for breakfast, lunch, and, depending on the itinerary and ports, dinner.

Other Comments: *Aegean Spirit* has very traditional ocean liner styling and a well-balanced profile, typical of ships of the 1950s. This very solidly built ship, with a strong, riveted hull — now over 50 years old — originally started life as a cargo-passenger liner, but was successfully converted into a passenger ship, and then into a full-time cruise vessel by Costa Cruises, who also gave the vessel an extensive refurbishment in 1996. Her next owners, Mediterranean Shipping Cruises, sadly neglected the ship. The ship's propulsion is derived from three pod units, powered by electric motors (two azimuthing, and one fixed at the centerline) instead of conventional rudders and propellers, in the latest configuration of high-tech propulsion systems.

In late 1999 the ship was sold to Golden Sun Cruises, who undertook some refurbishment prior to placing her in service in May 2000. She has a single, large funnel and a deep draft, so she is quite stable at sea, even in inclement weather conditions. Although there are fairly decent open deck promenade areas, there is no wraparound promenade deck.

Inside the ship, the public rooms (there really are only two lounges and a discotheque) feature what can best be described as "Belle Epoque" decor, and high ceilings. They are rather smart and welcoming, although they are certainly crowded when full. The great amount of fine old wood paneling and occasional bits of brass trim throughout the ship add warmth and an old-world, elegant feel often lacking in many of the new breed of glitzy ships. The newer facilities added during various refurbishments are fine, while other, older facilities have been upgraded somewhat.

One of the lounges (Alessio Lounge) acts as the show lounge, although the shape is less than ideal, and the sight lines are obstructed from many seats by 12 pillars. One nice feature, however, is the ship's small, but dedicated cinema. In addition, a small chapel has been installed behind the cinema screen.

This ship caters primarily to budget-minded European passengers looking for an Aegean/Mediterranean cruise without any of the finer trimmings associated with more upscale vessels. It offers an extremely basic, no-frills cruise experience for backpackers and tracksuiters — adequate for a first cruise in totally unpretentious and unstuffy surroundings aboard a classic vintage ship with comfortable public areas and cabins that are, well, basic cabins.

Aegean Spirit operates 3- and 4-day Greek Islands and Turkey cruises during the summer season each year, while longer cruises during the winter take the ship to more unusual locales. The ship may well be under charter to various tour operators during the winter season, while during the summer, many tour operator groups from various countries send their low-budget passengers. Go for the itinerary and shore excursions — the ship is really nothing more than a water-taxi to get you to the destinations.

Weak Points: The food. The ship does not have stabilizers (there are plans to add them after 2001). The ceilings are very plain and uninteresting. The entertainment is loud and of very low quality. There are far too many loud, unnecessary, and repetitious announcements (particularly on the day of embarkation). Seats in the cinema are not staggered. There are no showers or toilets adjacent to the main pool deck. Behind the façade of the public rooms, the ship is a mess of old exposed, painted-over wiring and plumbing, and poor, very cramped conditions for many of the crew.

AIDAcara
★★★★

Large Ship:	38,600 tons	Cabins (for one person):	0
Lifestyle:	Standard	Cabins (with private balcony):	4
Cruise Line:	Aida Cruises	Cabins (wheelchair accessible):	4
Former Names:	*Aida*	Cabin Current:	110/220-volt
Builder:	Kvaerner Masa-Yards (Finland)	Full-Service Dining Rooms:	3
Original Cost:	DM300 million	Elevators:	5
Entered Service:	June 1996	Casino (gaming tables):	No
Registry:	Liberia	Slot Machines:	No
Length (ft/m):	634.1/193.3	Swimming Pools (outdoors):	1
Beam (ft/m):	90.5/27.6	Swimming Pools (indoors):	0
Draft (ft/m):	20.3/6.2	Whirlpools:	3
Propulsion/Propellers:	Diesel (21,720kw)/2	Fitness Center:	Yes
Passenger Decks:	9	Sauna/Steam Room:	Yes/Yes
Total Crew:	370	Massage:	Yes
Passengers (lower beds/all berths):	1,186/1,230	Self-Service Launderette:	Yes
Pass. Space Ratio (lower beds/all berths):	32.5/31.3	Dedicated Cinema:	No
Crew/Pass. Ratio (lower beds/all berths):	3.2/3.3	Library:	Yes
Navigation Officers:	German	Classification Society:	Germanischer Lloyd
Cabins (total):	593		
Size Range (sq ft/sq m):	145.3–376.7/13.5–35.0		
Cabins (outside view):	391		
Cabins (interior/no view):	202		

OVERALL SCORE: 1,548
(OUT OF A POSSIBLE 2,000 POINTS)

Accommodation: There are five grades: A-outside (182.9 sq ft/17.0 sq m); B-outside (145.3 sq ft/13.5 sq m); C-Interior (156.0 sq ft/14.5 sq m); Junior Suite (269.1 sq ft/25.0 sq m); Suite (376.7 sq ft/35.0 sq m). The decor is bright, splashy, youthful, and contemporary. All cabins are accented with multipat-terned fabrics, wood-trimmed cabinetry (with nicely rounded edges), and rattan furniture. The twin beds have duvets, and a fabric canopy from headboard to ceiling. Windows feature full pull-down blackout blinds.

Grades A, B, and C have just a small amount of drawer space, but, as you will not need many clothes, this is not really a drawback. Some cabins in grades A, B, and C have one bed and a convert-ible daytime sofa bed. All cabin bathrooms are compact, but well designed. They feature showers and wall-mounted soap/shampoo dispensers, so there is no wastage of throwaway plastic bottles (environ-mentally friendly). Bring your own conditioner, hand lotion, or other personal toiletry items. Cotton bathrobes are also provided. Although bathrooms do not feature a hairdryer, one is located in the van-ity unit in the cabin. *Note*: there is no cabinet for personal toiletry items. For the ultimate in accom-modation, choose one of two beautifully decorated Presidential Suites, each of which measures 1,173 sq ft (109.0 m²). These are located amidships in the most desirable position. Each can be combined with the adjacent minisuite via an interconnecting door to provide a living space of 1,515 sq ft (140.7 m²). Each has a marble-floored foyer, a living room with a mahogany wood floor, and a hand-woven rug. Other fea-tures include a separate dining area with a six-seat dining table, a butler's pantry with wet bar, a wine bar with private label stock, a refrigerator, and a microwave. There is also a large private balcony with dining table for two, chaise lounge chairs with cushioned pads, hot tub and dimmer-controlled lighting; master bedroom with king-size bed, dressed with fine fabrics and draperies and Egyptian cotton bed linen, and walk-in closet with abundant storage space. The all-marble bathroom has a jet-spray shower and whirlpool bath.

Four suites have a forward-facing private balcony (all four share the same, ship-wide balcony, as there are no partitions for privacy) and more luxurious furnishings and fittings. Seating in the cabin lounge area is in contemporary rattan chairs. There is a wall unit that houses a TV that can be turned for viewing from either lounge or bedroom, and a refrigerator.

Suites and Junior Suites have a generous amount of closet, drawer, and other storage space, a stocked minibar, and a VCR. Bathrooms feature a full-size bathtub and hairdryer.

The cabins are cleaned and beds are made each morning, but not in the evening. For anyone allergic to natural fibers, down-filled duvets and pillows can be replaced with those made of synthetic materials.

Dining: There are two large self-service buffet restaurants (Caribbean and Market), open almost 24 hours a day, and the Maritime Restaurant, an à la carte restaurant, with waiter and sommelier service.

The standard of food offered at the serve-yourself buffet islands is good to very good, with creative presentation and good table-clearing service. There is no standing in long lines as is common aboard most other cruise ships. There is always a fine selection of breads, cheeses, cold cuts, fruits, and make-your-own teas (with a choice of more than 30 types of loose-leaf regular and herbal teas, as well as coffee).

At peak times, the buffet restaurants may remind you of motorway cafés (albeit elegant ones), with all their attendant noise, but a good selection of foods is provided (more than 1,200 items are provided). You can sit where you want, when you want, and with whom you want, so dining really becomes a socially interactive occasion. Because of the two large self-serve buffet rooms and dining concept, the actual crew to passenger ratio looks poor; but this is because there really are no waiters as such (except in the à la carte Maritime Restaurant), only staff for clearing tables.

The Maritime Restaurant, which has 74 mostly high-back seats, has an intimate dining atmosphere. It is open for dinner only, and features a set five- or six-course menu that is changed every two or three days. There is no extra charge, except for additional à la carte menu items (such as sevruga caviar, smoked salmon, châteaubriand, rib-eye steak), and for wines. Reservations are made at the reception desk each morning of the day you want to eat in the Maritime Restaurant.

Other Comments: *AIDAcara* (originally named *Aida*, the ship's name was changed in 2001) has a contemporary profile, is well proportioned, and has a swept-back funnel and wedge-shaped stern. There is no mistaking the red lips painted on her bows, as well as the blue eyes of Aida (from Verdi's opera of the same name, written to commemorate the opening of the Suez Canal in 1871).

AIDAcara is known as a "Club Ship," offering a seagoing version of Germany's popular Robinson Clubs. This fun ship includes a whole army of "animateurs" (like the GOs of Club Med, but better), who enjoy leading a variety of activities by day (they also act as escorts for shore excursions), and as entertainers by night, acting in the colorful, often funny shows alongside the professional entertainers. They (along with other staff) also interact with passengers throughout the ship, and can drink with them at the bars — something not allowed aboard most cruise ships.

There is a wraparound promenade deck outdoors, good for strolling, or for sitting in a deck lounge chair and just taking in the sea air. Outside on deck, the swimming pool and surrounding area have several cascading levels at the forward end for deck chairs and sun lounging, plus a basketball court, although the pool itself is small. Although she is a large ship, even the accommodation hallways are quite attractive, with cabinets containing artwork and wavy lines to interject and break up the monotony. In fact, there are plenty of decorative touches to help avoid what would otherwise be a very clinical environment.

Inside, there is no wasted space, and the public rooms are open and flow into each other instead of being contained spaces. The "you are here" (deck plan) signs are excellent, and finding your way around is a simple matter. The decor is upbeat and trendy, and will appeal to younger passengers, particularly those who may not have cruised before. A large observation lounge is set high atop the ship overlooking the bow. There is a wide array of intimate public rooms and spaces from which to choose.

The fitness, wellness, and sports programming is among the most extensive in the cruise industry. An excellent Wellness Center is located forward. It measures 11,840.6 sq ft (1,100sq m), and contains two saunas (one seats more than 20 persons and has glass ocean-view walls), massage and other treatment rooms, and a large lounging area. Forward and outside the wellness center, is an FKK (FreiKoerperKultur) nude sunbathing deck. One popular feature is the choice of more than two dozen "Hit Bikes" — mountain bikes with tough front and rear suspension units, for conducted biking excursions in each port of call — the concept and concession of Austrian Downhill Champion Skier Erwin Resch. In addition, there is a 1,312-ft- (400-m-) long jogging track.

Central to all social interactions is The Aida Lounge, which features novel "lollipop stick" decorations on the bar counter. The bar itself, at 162.4 ft (49.5 m) long, is the longest bar aboard any cruise ship. The feel is youthful, colorful, unpretentious, casual, relaxed, and sporting.

This is a family-friendly ship, with plenty of activities for younger family members (children are split into two age groups: Seepferdchen, from 4–7 years; Sharks, from 8–13 years). There is a diverse selection of children's and youth programs — good for families. Children can make their own menus for the week (together with the chef), and get to go into the galley to make cookies and other items — a novel idea that more ships could adopt.

The ship caters best to first-time passengers and youthful German-speaking couples seeking good value for the money in a fun environment. The dress code is simple: casual (no dinner jackets or ties required) at all times.

There are two alternating itineraries in the Mediterranean during the summer, and in the winter, there are two alternating itineraries in the Caribbean. Alternating 7-night itineraries can be combined for a 14-day cruise. In addition, packages created by tour operators such as Jahn Reisen and Seetours can add land stays for an even longer cruise and resort holiday experience. This presents a good amount of flexibility.

About 20 nationalities are represented among the crew, who are upbeat and cheerful, and really want passengers to have a good time in an unstuffy atmosphere. And they do, for this is definitely a young, vibrant, and fun ship, with plenty of passenger participation in all kinds of events. The brochure accurately describes the lifestyle, and only real passengers (not models) are used.

All port taxes and gratuities are included, and, with rates of approximately DM250–DM300 per day, it is almost cheaper than staying home, and better value than almost any land-based vacation. The deutschmark is the currency used on board.

Weak Points: Standing in line for embarkation, disembarkation, shore tenders, and for self-serve buffet meals is an inevitable aspect of cruising aboard all large ships. There is a charge of DM1 for use of the washing machine and DM1 for the dryer in the self-service launderette. The swimming pool is too small for the number of passengers carried — particularly during the hot winter (Caribbean) season.

AIDAvita

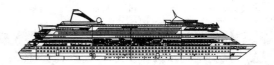

Large Ship:	42,200 tons	Cabins (wheelchair accessible):	4
Lifestyle:	Standard	Cabin Current:	220-volt
Cruise Line:	Aida Cruises	Full-Service Dining Rooms:	3
Former Names:	-	Elevators:	6
Builder:	Aker MTW (Germany)	Casino (gaming tables):	No
Original Cost:	$350 million	Slot Machines:	No
Entered Service:	March 2002	Swimming Pools (outdoors):	2
Registry:	n/a	Swimming Pools (indoors):	0
Length (ft/m):	662.7/202.0	Whirlpools:	5
Beam (ft/m):	92.2/28.1	Fitness Center:	Yes
Draft (ft/m):	20.7/6.3	Sauna/Steam Room:	Yes/Yes
Propulsion/Propellers:	Diesel-electric/2	Massage:	Yes
Passenger Decks:	10	Self-Service Launderette:	Yes
Total Crew:	418	Dedicated Cinema:	No
Passengers (lower beds/all berths):	1,266/1,582	Library:	Yes
Pass. Space Ratio (lower beds/all berths):	33.3/26.6	Classification Society:	Germanischer Lloyd
Crew/Pass. Ratio (lower beds/all berths):	3.0/3.7		
Navigation Officers:	German		
Cabins (total):	633		
Size Range (sq ft/sq m):	145.3–376.7/13.5–35.0		
Cabins (outside view):	422		
Cabins (interior/no view):	211		
Cabins (for one person):	0		
Cabins (with private balcony):	60		

OVERALL SCORE: NOT YET RATED

Note that this ship had not entered service when this book was completed. However, the score is expected to be similar to *AIDAcara*.

Accommodation: There are five grades of accommodation: Suite (376.7 sq ft/35.0 sq m); A-outside (182.9 sq ft/17.0 sq m) with balcony; A-outside (182.9 sq ft/17.0 sq m) without balcony: B-Interior (150.6 sq ft/14.0 sq m). All suites and cabins are designed for two persons; however, a total of 94 cabins also have two extra beds/berths for children.

The decor is bright, splashy, youthful, and contemporary. All cabins are accented with multipatterned fabrics, wood-trimmed cabinetry (with nicely rounded edges), and rattan furniture. The twin beds have duvets, and a fabric canopy from headboard to ceiling. Windows feature full pull-down blackout blinds. Note that some cabins in the center of the ship have views that are obstructed by lifeboats. All cabin bathrooms are compact, but well designed, and feature showers, and wall-mounted soap/shampoo dispensers, so there is no wastage of throwaway plastic bottles (environmentally friendly). You should bring your own conditioner, hand lotion, or any other personal toiletry items. Cotton bathrobes are also provided. Although the bathrooms do not feature a hairdryer, one is located in the vanity unit in the cabin.

There are two large suites, located at the front of the ship, each with its own private balcony. These offer much more space, including more drawer and storage space, and better quality furnishings, as one would expect.

Dining: There are two large self-service buffet restaurants (Caribbean and Market) — with a wide range of food (more than 1,200 items) that is available almost 24 hours a day, and an à la carte restaurant, the Maritime Restaurant, which has waiter and sommelier service. The standard of food offered at the serve yourself buffet islands is good to very good, with creative presentation and good table-clearing service. The islands cut down on the waiting time for food, as is common aboard most other cruise ships of a similar size and passenger carry. There is always a fine selection of breads, cheeses, cold cuts, fruits, and make-your-own teas (with a choice of 30 types of loose-leaf regular and herbal teas, as well as coffee).

The Maritime Restaurant features mostly high-back seats, and has an intimate dining atmosphere. It is open for dinner only, and features a set five- or six-course menu that is changed every two or three days. There is no extra charge, except for additional à la carte menu items (such as sevruga caviar, smoked salmon, châteaubriand, rib-eye steak), and for wines. Reservations are made at the reception desk each morning of the day you want to eat in the Maritime Restaurant.

Aft of the funnel, the Calypso Terraces provide a casual dining alternative, complete with a large bar and seating outdoors (as well as seating under a sailcloth canopied cover).

Other Comments: *AIDAvita* is a "Club Ship" (and a slightly larger sister to *AIDAcara*) and offers a seagoing version of Germany's popular Robinson Clubs. The ship has a contemporary profile, is well proportioned, and has a swept-back funnel and wedge-shaped stern. Her bows feature the red lips as well as the blue eyes of Aida (from Verdi's opera of the same name, written to commemorate the opening of the Suez Canal in 1871). There is a good amount of open deck and sunbathing space, including some rather nice, quiet space above the navigation bridge. There is one egg-shaped swimming pool, set in a "beach-like" environment with splash and play areas (these facilities are larger and better than aboard *AIDAcara*.

This fun ship includes a whole army of "animateurs" (like the GOs of Club Med, but better) who enjoy leading a variety of activities by day (they also act as escorts for shore excursions), and as entertainers by night, acting in the colorful, often funny, shows alongside the professional entertainers. They (along with other staff) also interact with passengers throughout the ship, and can drink with them at the bars — something not allowed aboard most cruise ships.

Inside, there is no wasted space, and the public rooms are open and flow into each other instead of being contained spaces. The "you are here" (deck plan) signs are excellent, and finding your way around is a simple matter. The decor is upbeat and trendy, and will appeal to younger passengers, particularly those who may not have cruised before. A large observation lounge is set high atop the ship overlooking the bow. There is a wide array of intimate public rooms and spaces from which to choose.

The fitness, wellness, and sports programming is among the most extensive in the cruise industry. An excellent Wellness Center is located forward. It measures approximately 11,840 sq ft (1,100sq m), and contains two saunas (one seats more than 20 persons and has glass ocean-view walls), massage and other treatment rooms, and a large lounging area. Forward and outside the wellness center, is an FKK (FreiKoerperKultur) nude sunbathing deck. The "Hit Bikes" — mountain bikes with tough front and rear suspension units — for conducted biking excursions in each port of call, the concept and concession of Austrian Downhill Champion Skier Erwin Resch — will be available.

This certainly is going to be a family-friendly ship, with plenty of activities for younger family members (children are split into two age groups: Seepferdchen, from 4 to 7 years; Sharks, from 8 to 13 years). There is a diverse selection of children's and youth programs — good for families. Children can make their own menus for the week (together with the chef), and get to go into the galley to make cookies and other items — a novel idea that more ships could adopt.

The ship caters best to first-time passengers and youthful German-speaking couples seeking good value for money in a fun environment. The dress code is simple: casual (no dinner jackets or ties) at all times.

During the summer, *AIDAvita* sails itineraries in the Mediterranean, and in the winter, she sails in the Caribbean. Alternating 7-night itineraries can be combined for a 14-day cruise. In addition, packages created by tour operators such as Jahn Reisen, Seetours, and TUI can add land stays for an even longer cruise and resort holiday experience. This presents a good amount of flexibility.

About 20 nationalities are represented among the crew, who are upbeat and cheerful, and really want passengers to have a good time in an unstuffy, unpretentious atmosphere. They will, for this will definitely be a young, vibrant, and fun ship, typically with plenty of passenger participation in all kinds of events. The brochure accurately describes the lifestyle, and only real passengers (not models) are used.

All port taxes and gratuities are included, and, with rates of approximately DM50–DM300 per day, it is almost cheaper than staying home, and better value than almost any land-based vacation. If you've cruised aboard the smaller sister ship *AIDAcara* before, I am certain you'll also like this newer, slightly larger ship. The deutschmark is the currency used on board.

Weak Points: Standing in line for embarkation, disembarkation, shore tenders, and for self-serve buffet meals is an inevitable aspect of cruising aboard all large ships.

Akademik Sergey Vavilov
★★ +

Small Ship:	6,231 tons	Cabins (for one person):	0
Lifestyle:	Standard	Cabins (with private balcony):	0
Cruise Line:	Quark Expeditions	Cabins (wheelchair accessible):	0
Former Names:	-	Cabin Current:	110/220-volt
Builder:	Hollming (Finland)	Full-Service Dining Rooms:	1
Original Cost:	n/a	Elevators:	0
Entered Service:	1988	Casino (gaming tables):	No
Registry:	Russia	Slot Machines:	No
Length (ft/m):	386.4/117.8	Swimming Pools (outdoors):	1
Beam (ft/m):	59.7/18.1	Swimming Pools (indoors):	0
Draft (ft/m):	19.3/5.9	Whirlpools:	0
Propulsion/Propellers:	Diesel/2	Fitness Center:	Yes
Passenger Decks:	4	Sauna/Steam Room:	Yes/No
Total Crew:	45	Massage:	No
Passengers (lower beds/all berths):	76/76	Self-Service Launderette:	No
Pass. Space Ratio (lower beds/all berths):	81.9/81.9	Dedicated Cinema:	No
Crew/Pass. Ratio (lower beds/all berths):	1.6/1.6	Library:	Yes
Navigation Officers:	Russian	Classification Society:	Russian Shipping Register
Cabins (total):	38		
Size Range (sq ft/sq m):	n/a	**OVERALL SCORE:**	**963**
Cabins (outside view):	38	**(OUT OF A POSSIBLE 2,000 POINTS)**	
Cabins (interior/no view):	0		

Accommodation: The accommodation is arranged over three decks. With the exception of a single "suite," which is quite large for the size of the ship, almost all other cabins are very small, utilitarian, and rather clinical, although all have a small desk and a reasonable amount of closet space. There are two-berth cabins with shower and toilet, or there are two-bed cabins on the lowest deck, whose occupants must share an adjacent bathroom and toilet.

Dining: There are two dining rooms (the galley is located between them), and all passengers are accommodated in a single seating. The meals are hearty international fare, with no frills. When under charter to various specialist operators, Western chefs oversee the food operation.

Other Comments: This vessel was originally specially constructed for the former Soviet Union's polar and oceanographic research program and was not taken as a cruise ship, although it was converted in the early 1990s to carry passengers, and then refurbished in 1996 and fitted out specifically for expedition cruising. This is the sister ship to *Akademik Ioffe* (also known as *Marine Adventurer*). This ship is typically operated under charter to various "expedition" cruise companies, such as Quark Expeditions. Has an ice-hardened steel hull, which makes the vessel ideally suited to cruising in both the Arctic and Antarctic regions. All passengers have access to the navigation bridge. There are several Zodiac landing craft for close-in shore excursions and nature observation trips.

Inside, the limited public rooms consist of a library and lounge/bar. The dining rooms also serve as a lecture room. This ship does have good medical facilities.

This is expedition-style cruising, in a very small ship with limited facilities. However, it provides a somewhat primitive, but genuine adventure experience, taking you to places others can only dream about. The bigger ships cannot get this close to Antarctica, but this little vessel will sail you close to the face of the ice continent.

Weak Points: Although there is a swimming pool, note that it is very, very small, and is best described as nothing more than a "dip" pool.

Albatros
★★★ +

Mid-Size Ship:	24,803 tons	Cabins (for one person):	0
Lifestyle:	Standard	Cabins (with private balcony):	0
Cruise Line:	Phoenix Seereisen	Cabins (wheelchair accessible):	0
Former Names:	*Dawn Princess, Sitmar Fairwind,*	Cabin Current:	110-volt
	FairWind, Sylvaniana	Full-Service Dining Rooms:	2
Builder:	John Brown & Co. (UK)	Elevators:	3
Original Cost:	n/a	Casino (gaming tables):	Yes
Entered Service:	June 1957/August 1993	Slot Machines:	Yes
Registry:	Bahamas	Swimming Pools (outdoors):	3
Length (ft/m):	608.2/185.40	Swimming Pools (indoors):	0
Beam (ft/m):	80.3/24.49	Whirlpools:	0
Draft (ft/m):	29.3/8.94	Fitness Center:	Yes
Propulsion/Propellers:	steam turbine (18,300kW)/2	Sauna/Steam Room:	Yes/No
Passenger Decks:	11	Massage:	Yes
Total Crew:	340	Self-Service Launderette:	Yes
Passengers (lower beds/all berths):	940/1,100	Dedicated Cinema/Seats:	Yes/300
Pass. Space Ratio (lower beds/all berths):	26.3/22.5	Library:	No
Crew/Pass. Ratio (lower beds/all berths):	2.7/3.2	Classification Society:	Lloyd's Register
Navigation Officers:	European		
Cabins (total):	470		
Size Range (sq ft/sq m):	89.3–240.0/8.3–22.3	**OVERALL SCORE:**	**1,253**
Cabins (outside view):	239	**(OUT OF A POSSIBLE 2,000 POINTS)**	
Cabins (interior/no view):	231		

Accommodation: There is a wide range of cabin sizes and configurations (28 categories), a throwback to the days when she was a ship operating transatlantic crossings. All of the cabins feature really heavy-duty furniture, fittings, strong doors, and good storage space (many of the larger cabins have wood-paneled walls), although closet and storage space could become limited for long voyages, particularly in the smaller, lower grade cabins.

The bathrooms are fairly large, with cabinets and shelf space for toiletries in most. Bathrobes are provided for all passengers, as are some personal toiletry amenities.

Anyone booking a suite or one of the top five grades receives Phoenix VIP service, which includes flowers for the cabin, separate check-in desk, and priority disembarkation.

Dining: There are two dining rooms, both of which are charming and comfortable (with high ceilings), but the tables are very close together; this means they are also quite noisy (although some would call this "ambience"). There is a single seating. The menu is moderately creative, the choice is rather limited, and the food is best described as "down home basic."

The service is friendly and attentive, in true European style (the staff do speak German), although there is little finesse in their style of service. Still, it is unpretentious. Because there are two seatings for meals, one cannot dine leisurely.

Other Comments: *Albatros* is a vintage all-white classic ship with a forthright profile and a single, large, centrally placed funnel painted in the turquoise/aquamarine blue of Phoenix Seereisen. She is sturdily constructed, and has a riveted hull that is virtually impossible to find today, and she has a deep draft that makes her very stable at sea, built as a two-class liner specifically for Cunard Line's transatlantic crossings in the 1950s. Since August 1993 she has been under long-term charter to Phoenix Seereisen.

Albatros is an unpretentious ship with an interesting old-world ambience and charm that somehow help to make up for the lack of finesse associated with more upscale, newer (and thus more expensive) products.

There is plenty of open deck and sunbathing space. There is a second swimming pool (fitted into what was formerly a cargo hold) for children, as Phoenix Seereisen appeals particularly well to families with children. Particularly popular are two decks of sheltered promenade decks, which are ideal for strolling or just sitting on one of the many deck lounge chairs.

Inside the ship, a great deal of dark wood paneling and trim that was used in her original interiors has been retained. There are also many solid brass accents throughout her interiors and public rooms. There is a fine, serene library, with a good selection of both hardback and paperback books, as well as some reference material.

There are, however, relatively few public rooms from which to choose, they are usually crowded, and it is hard to get away from the smell of stale cigarette smoke. There are also a number of "thresholds" (high sills) to step over at doorways, particularly to the outside decks and pool area, and so the ship cannot be recommended to anyone confined to a wheelchair under any circumstances.

The company features extensive, interesting, destination-intensive itineraries, and young, friendly Phoenix Seereisen staff members are aboard every cruise to help with shore excursions. There is a very informal atmosphere and a very relaxed, casual dress code prevails throughout.

Although the ship has been generally well maintained, remember that she is an old ship, having been designed for transatlantic service. Thus, the layout is somewhat disjointed and passageways are narrow. Because she is a steam ship, you should be aware of the possibility of black soot falling on the aft decks occasionally (in other words, do not wear white!).

This ship will prove to be good for a first cruise experience with fellow German-speaking passengers and crew. Phoenix Seereisen always has a good onboard team of social staff to look after you, and the company's cruise directors are very experienced, fun-loving people who really do go out of their way to help you enjoy your cruise experience.

Far from being a new ship, she performs and behaves extremely well, and the resulting product is both entertaining and extremely reasonably priced for the popular market seeking an ocean-going holiday in totally relaxed, unstuffy, and unpretentious surroundings. It represents an excellent value-for-money cruise vacation. The currency aboard is the Deutschmark.

Ambasador I
★

Small Ship:	2,573 tons	Cabins (for one person):	0
Lifestyle:	Standard	Cabins (with private balcony):	0
Cruise Line:	Islas Galapagos Turismos y Vapores	Cabins (wheelchair accessible):	0
FormerNames:	*Jedinstvo, Aquanaut Ambassador,*	Cabin Current:	220-volt (DC)
	Atlas Ambasador	Full-Service Dining Rooms:	1
Builder:	Brodogradiliste (Yugoslavia)	Elevators:	0
Original Cost:	n/a	Casino (gaming tables):	No
Entered Service:	1959/1993	Slot Machines:	No
Registry:	Ecuador	Swimming Pools (outdoors):	1
Length (ft/m):	296.2/90.30	Swimming Pools (indoors):	0
Beam (ft/m):	42.7/13.03	Whirlpools:	0
Draft (ft/m):	14.0/4.45	Fitness Center:	No
Propulsion/Propellers:	Diesel (7,060kw)/2	Sauna/Steam Room:	No/No
Passenger Decks:	5	Massage:	No
Total Crew:	68	Self-Service Launderette:	No
Passengers (lower beds/all berths):	124/160	Dedicated Cinema:	No
Pass. Space Ratio (lower beds/all berths):	20.7/16.0	Library:	Yes
Crew/Pass. Ratio (lower beds/all berths):	1.9/2.3	Classification Society:	Jugoslavenski Registrar
Navigation Officers:	International		Brodova
Cabins (total):	62		
Size Range (sq ft/sq m):	95.0–190.0/8.8–17.6	**OVERALL SCORE:**	**620**
Cabins (outside view):	43		
Cabins (interior/no view):	19	**(OUT OF A POSSIBLE 2,000 POINTS)**	

Accommodation: Depending on which tour operator is marketing the ship, there are, in general, five cabin grades (the higher the deck, the higher the price), with accommodation spread over three decks. Almost all cabins really are very small, with only the most minimal amount of furniture, fittings, and furnishings. The bathrooms are tiny, and the plumbing leaves much to be desired. The cabins are, thus, barely adequate and not very comfortable. Some cabins have upper/lower berths, and some also accommodate three or four persons.

Dining: The dining room is reasonably pleasant, and accommodates all passengers in a single seating, but there are no tables for two. The service is quite forgettable, as is the food.

Other Comments: She is a vintage style of ship — over 40 years old — formerly owned and operated by a Yugoslavian shipping company. She has a single, squat, blue funnel placed squarely amidships. She is not a handsome vessel, by any stretch of the imagination, and maintenance is of the "patch here, patch there" type. There is only a small amount of outdoor deck space for sunbathing, as the decks are quite cluttered.

Inside the ship there is only one main public room, the main lounge, which is used for just about every public activity.

This small cruise ship operates cruises of the Galapagos Islands, although the price is not really very modest. It's adequate only so long as you do not expect much. Although the ship can carry more passengers, there is a limit of 86 passengers for these cruises, set by the Galapagos National Park regulations.

The Galapagos National Park tax is an additional $100 per person (approximate), payable in cash when you land at your incoming airport.

Weak Points: The cruise prices are extremely high for what you get, and for such an old vessel with limited facilities. It's simply basic, basic, basic, all the way. The public passageways are quite dark, and the carpeting is well worn. The swimming pool is really tiny; it is merely a "dip" pool.

American Eagle
★★

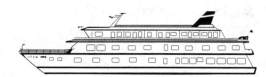

Small Ship:	1,480 tons	Cabins (with private balcony):	5
Lifestyle:	Standard	Cabins (wheelchair accessible):	1
Cruise Line:	American Cruise Lines	Cabin Current:	110-volt
Former Names:	-	Full-Service Dining Rooms:	1
Builder:	Chesapeake Shipbuilding (US)	Elevators:	1
Original Cost:	n/a	Casino (gaming tables):	No
Entered Service:	April 2000	Slot Machines:	No
Registry:	US	Swimming Pools (outdoors):	0
Length (ft/m):	174.0/53.00	Swimming Pools (indoors):	0
Beam (ft/m):	40.5/12.30	Whirlpools:	0
Draft (ft/m):	6.5/1.98	Fitness Center:	No
Propulsion/Propellers:	Diesel/2	Sauna/Steam Room:	No/No
Passenger Decks:	4	Massage:	No
Total Crew:	22	Self-Service Launderette:	No
Passengers (lower beds/all berths):	49/49	Dedicated Cinema:	No
Pass. Space Ratio (lower beds/all berths):	30.2/30.2	Library:	No
Crew/Pass. Ratio (lower beds/all berths):	2.2/2.2	Classification Society:	American Bureau
Navigation Officers:	American		of Shipping
Cabins (total):	27		
Size Range (sq ft/sq m):	176.0–382.0/16.3–35.4		
Cabins (outside view):	27	**OVERALL SCORE:**	**827**
Cabins (interior/no view):	0		
Cabins (for one person):	5	(OUT OF A POSSIBLE 2,000 POINTS)	

Accommodation: There are cabins for couples and singles, two suites, as well as dedicated cabins for the physically challenged. All of the cabins feature twin beds, a small desk with chair, and clothes-hanging space. The six most expensive cabins also have a color TV, VCR, and compact disc (audio) player. All cabins feature a private bathroom with separate shower enclosure, washbasin, and toilet (none of the cabins has a bathtub), as well as windows that open.

Dining: The dining salon, which is located in the latter third of the vessel, has large, panoramic picture windows on three of its sides. Open seating is featured, although dining times are set. The food is very much Americana fare — good and wholesome, featuring regional cuisines, and presented and served in a basic, unfussy manner. Note that there is little or no choice of entrees, and only one appetizer, one soup, etc. There is no wine list, although basic white and red low-quality American table wines are included.

Other Comments: American Cruise Lines features intra-coastal waterway cruising, as well as sailings in New England and the Hudson River Valley. *American Eagle* is a new ship that was built specifically for coastal cruising and cannot venture far into open seas away from the coastline (a sister vessel is planned, with more balcony cabins).

The ship's uppermost deck is open (good for scenery observation), and there are tables and chairs, a few deck lounge chairs, and a small putting green.

There are two public lounges. The principal one, the observation lounge, is located forward and has windows on three sides (an open bar is set up each afternoon). This becomes the principal meeting place for passengers. A second, smaller lounge is sandwiched between cabins on the same deck.

The whole point of a cruise aboard this ship is to get close to the inland areas, cities, and towns of America's intra-coastal waterways and coastline. There's no waiting in line — you can board whenever you want. The dress code is "no ties–casual."

Weak Points: It really is extremely expensive for what you get, compared even to those ships of a similar size and purpose (although this is a new ship and the cabins are of a better size and are slightly better equipped). Although there is an elevator, note that it does not go to the uppermost deck. The limited choice of food is extremely disappointing. There are no health spa facilities — not even a sauna, steam room, or massage — and there are no medical facilities.

151

Amsterdam
★★★★

Large Ship:	61,000 tons	Cabins (for one person):	0
Lifestyle:	Premium	Cabins (with private balcony):	172
Cruise Line:	Holland America Line	Cabins (wheelchair accessible):	20
Former Names:	-	Cabin Current:	110/220-volt
Builder:	Fincantieri (Italy)	Full-Service Dining Rooms:	2
Original Cost:	$400 million	Elevators:	12
Entered Service:	October 2000	Casino (gaming tables):	Yes
Registry:	The Netherlands	Slot Machines:	Yes
Length (ft/m):	780.8/238.00	Swimming Pools (outdoors):	1
Beam (ft/m):	105.8/32.25	Swimming Pools (indoors):	1 (magrodome cover)
Draft (ft/m):	25.5/7.80	Whirlpools:	2
Propulsion/Propellers: Diesel-electric(37,500kW)/2		Fitness Center:	Yes
azimuthing pods (15.5MW each)		Sauna/Steam Room:	Yes/Yes
Passenger Decks:	12	Massage:	Yes
Total Crew:	600	Self-Service Launderette:	Yes
Passengers (lower beds/all berths):	1,380/1,653	Dedicated Cinema/Seats:	Yes/235
Pass. Space Ratio (lower beds/all berths): 44.2/36.9		Library:	Yes
Crew/Pass. Ratio (lower beds/all berths):	2.3/2.7	Classification Society:	Lloyd's Register
Navigation Officers:	Dutch		
Cabins (total):	690		
Size Range (sq ft/sq m): 184.0–1,124.8/17.1–104.5			
Cabins (outside view):	557		
Cabins (interior/no view):	133		

OVERALL SCORE: 1,548

(OUT OF A POSSIBLE 2,000 POINTS)

Accommodation: The accommodation is spread over five decks (a number of cabins have full or partial-ly obstructed views), and is in 16 grades: 11 with outside views, 5 interior grades (no view). There are four penthouse suites, and 50 suites (14 more than aboard sister ship *Rotterdam*). Interestingly, no cabin is more than 130 ft (39.6 m) from a stairway, which makes it very easy to find your way from cabins to public rooms. Although 81% of cabins have outside views, only 25% of those have balconies.

All of the "standard" interior and outside cabins are tastefully furnished, and have twin beds that con-vert to a queen-size bed (the space is a little tight for walking between beds and the vanity unit, howev-er). There is a decent amount of closet and drawer space, although this will prove tight for the longer voy-ages featured. The bathrooms, which are fully tiled, are small (particularly if the ship undertakes any long cruises), the shower tubs are very small, and the cabinets for one's personal toiletries are quite basic. There is little detailing to distinguish the bathrooms from those aboard the *Statendam*-class ships. All cabin TVs feature CNN and TNT, as well as movies, and ship information and shopping channels.

There are 50 Verandah Suites and four Penthouse Suites on the Navigation Deck (more than sister ship *Rotterdam*, due to the fact that the deck has been extended aft, and a swimming pool moved one deck higher). The suites all share a private Concierge Lounge with a concierge to handle such things as special dining arrangements, shore excursions, and special requests, although strangely there are no butlers for these suites, as aboard other ships with similar facilities. The lounge, with its wood detailing and private library, is accessible only by private key-card.

The four Penthouse Suites are the ultimate in civilized living spaces aboard *Amsterdam*. Each has a separate steward's entrance, as well as a separate bedroom with king-size bed, vanity desk, large walk-in closet with excellent drawer and hanging space, living room, dining room (it can seat up to eight persons), wet bar, and pantry. The bathroom is large, and features a big oval whirlpool bathtub, separate shower enclosure, two washbasins, separate toilet, and bidet. There is also a guest bathroom with toilet and wash-basin. There is a good-size private balcony.

Suite occupants get extra-special things such as personal stationery, complimentary laundry and iron-ing, cocktail-hour hors d'oeuvres and other goodies, as well as priority embarkation and disembarkation.

Dining: The main dining room, La Fontaine, spans two-levels, and features a huge stained glass ceiling measuring almost 1,500 sq ft (140 sq m), with a floral motif. There are tables for four, six, or eight (there are also a few tables for two). Open seating is featured for breakfast and lunch, with two seatings for dinner (with both smoking and nonsmoking sections). Rosenthal china and fine cutlery are featured (although there are no fish knives).

Unfortunately, Holland America Line food isn't as nice as the china it's placed on. It may be adequate for most passengers who are not used to better food, but it does not match the standard found aboard other ships in the premium segment of the industry. While USDA beef is of a good quality, fowl tends to be battery-tough, and most fish is overcooked and has the consistency of a cricket bat. What are also definitely not luxurious are the endless packets of sugar, and packets (instead of glass jars) of breakfast jam, marmalade and honey, and poor quality teas. While these may be suitable for a family diner, they do not belong aboard a ship that claims to have "award-winning cuisine." Dessert and pastry items are of good quality (specifically for American tastes), although there is much use of canned fruits and jellies. Forget the selection of "international" cheeses as most of it didn't come from anywhere other than the US.

There is also an alternative 88-seat Odyssey Restaurant, available to all passengers on a reservation-only basis, although there's no extra charge. The whimsically surreal artwork features scenic landscapes. The cuisine is decidedly California-Italian in style, with small portions, and few vegetables.

As another alternative, the Lido Buffet is open for casual dinners on all except the last night of each cruise, in an open-seating arrangement. Tables are set with crisp linens, flatware, and stemware. A set menu is featured, and this includes a choice of four entrees. Portofino: an "upscale" (nonsmoking) Euro-Italian restaurant, with 98 seats, for dinner (reservations required).

For casual breakfasts and lunches, the Lido Buffet provides old-style, stand-in-line serve-yourself canteen food — adequate for those that are used to TV dinner-tray food, but most definitely not lavish, as the brochures claim. Salad items appear adequate, but are quite tasteless, like the iceberg lettuce that doesn't seem to go away.

Other Comments: She is a close sister ship to *Rotterdam*, and has a nicely raked bow, as well as the familiar interior flow and design style. Also retained is the twin-funnel feature well recognized by former Holland America Line passengers. *Amsterdam* is, however, the first ship in the Holland America Line fleet to feature an azimuthing pod propulsion system. Each pod houses an electric motor and propeller, replacing the traditional long shaft, propeller and rudder system of the past.

The interior public spaces also carry on the same layout and flow as found aboard *Rotterdam*. The interior café is best described as restrained and formal, with much use of medium and dark wood accenting. As a whole, the café of this ship is extremely refined, with much of the traditional ocean liner detailing so loved by frequent Holland America Line passengers. Much of the artwork features items from Holland America Line's glorious past, as well as items depicting the history of the city of Amsterdam from the 17th through the 20th centuries.

The interior focal point is a three-deck high atrium, in an oval, instead of circular, shape. A whimsical "Astrolobe" is the featured centerpiece in this atrium. Also centered around the atrium are the reception desk, shore excursion desk, photo shop, and photo gallery.

Amsterdam features three principal passenger stairways, so much better than two from the viewpoint of safety, flow, and accessibility. There is a magrodome-covered pool on the Lido Deck between the mast and the ship's twin funnels, watched over by a sculpture of a brown bear catching salmon.

There are children's and teens' play areas, although these really are token gestures by a company that traditionally does not cater well to children. Popcorn is available at the Wajang Theatre for moviegoers, while adjacent is the popular Java Café. The casino, which is located in the middle of a major passenger flow, features blackjack, roulette, poker, and dice tables alongside the requisite rows of slot machines.

She is an extremely comfortable ship in which to cruise, with some fine, elegant, and luxurious decorative features. However, these are marred by the poor quality of dining room food and service, and the lack of understanding of what it takes to make a "luxury" cruise experience, despite what is touted in the company's brochures. The company does not add an automatic 15% gratuity for beverage purchases.

The company offers free cappuccino and espresso coffees, and free ice cream during certain hours of the day aboard its ships, as well as hot hors d'oeuvres in all the bars at cocktail time — something other major lines seem to have dropped, or charge extra for.

Weak Points: Standing in line for embarkation, disembarkation, shore tenders, and for self-serve buffet meals is an inevitable aspect of cruising aboard all large ships. With one whole deck of suites (and a dedicated, private concierge lounge, with preferential passenger treatment), the company has, in effect, created a two-class ship. The charge to use the washing machines and dryers in the self-service launderette is petty and irritating, particularly for the occupants of high-priced accommodation. Communication (in English) with many of the staff, can prove extremely frustrating! The room service is poor. Nonsmokers should avoid this ship, as smokers are everywhere.

Arcadia
★ +

Small Ship:	5,200 tons	Cabins (for one person):	4
Lifestyle:	Standard	Cabins (with private balcony):	0
Cruise Line:	Golden Sun Cruises	Cabins (wheelchair accessible):	2
Former Names:	*Angelina Lauro, Vicente Puchol,*	Cabin Current:	220-volt
	Arcadia	Refrigerator:	No
Builder:	Union de Levante (Spain)	Full-Service Dining Rooms:	1
Original Cost:	n/a	Elevators:	1
Entered Service:	1969/May 1990	Casino (gaming tables):	Yes
Registry:	Greece	Slot Machines:	Yes
Length (ft/m):	360.8/110.0	Swimming Pools (outdoors):	1
Beam (ft/m):	86.2/16.30	Swimming Pools (indoors):	0
Draft (ft/m):	16.3/4.97	Whirlpools:	0
Propulsion/Propellers:	Diesel (4,589kW)/2	Fitness Center:	Yes
Passenger Decks:	6	Sauna/Steam Room:	Yes/No
Total Crew:	130	Massage:	Yes
Passengers (lower beds/all berths):	274/342	Self-Service Launderette:	No
Pass. Space Ratio (lower beds/all berths):	18.9/14.5	Dedicated Cinema:	No
Crew/Pass. Ratio (lower beds/all berths):	2.1/2.6	Library:	Yes
Navigation Officers:	Greek	Classification Society:	Hellenic Registry
Cabins (total):	139		
Size Range (sq ft/sq m):	n/a	**OVERALL SCORE:**	**724**
Cabins (outside view):	109		
Cabins (interior/no view):	30	**(OUT OF A POSSIBLE 2,000 POINTS)**	

Accommodation: Although this is a small ship, the cabins are extremely small, and come only just equipped with the bare essentials. Closet, drawer, and storage space is very limited, the ceilings are plain, and the bathrooms really are tiny. Four cabins have double beds, while all others have fixed twin beds or lower beds. Some cabins also have third/fourth person upper berths, although if you take one of these, not only do you need to be small, you need to make sure you don't have any luggage.

Note that although there are two cabins designated as wheelchair-accessible, the only thing that's accessible is the cabin door. Once inside, there is no room to maneuver, and the bathroom is totally inaccessible, with a "lip" of 11 inches (28 cm).

Dining: The (nonsmoking) dining room, although small, has large mirrors along both sides, making it appear double the size it actually is (however, there are no windows or portholes). Although noisy, it is somehow mildly charming, with its pastel pink color and warm, very casual ambience. Two seatings are featured, and the chairs, which have armrests, are very comfortable. The cuisine is very basic fare (as is the price of a cruise) and so there is little choice in food, and the bread is of poor quality and choice. Adequate basic service is provided, but it is hurried, and there's absolutely no finesse.

Other Comments: *Arcadia* is a small vessel (originally an ex-Spanish ferry) with an all-white hull, a red line dividing superstructure and hull, and twin funnels. She was, for a short time operated by the now-defunct Lauro Cruises as *Angelina Lauro*. A recent refurbishment makes the vessel smarter in her new "whites." The tiny aft swimming pool is really only a "cool dip" pool.

The interior decor is "1980s contemporary" and quite tastefully carried out, although there is too much use of reflective surfaces (mirrors), which dates it. Chairs in the public lounges (there are only two) are of the low back tub type, are not comfortable at all, and they are prone to tipping over. The main lounge has six pillars that obstruct the sight lines from many seats.

This ship has been well worn, and caters principally to an international mix of passengers seeking a small ship on which to cruise the Greek islands with minimum comfort and fuss. There is no finesse and the mixed crew displays only marginal hospitality, and poor communication.

In June 2001, the ship operated 3-, 4- and 7-day cruises in the Canada/US Great Lakes region under charter to Great Lakes Cruises, of Waukesha, Wisconsin, US.

Weak Points: There are very low ceilings throughout. Vibration, engine noise, and diesel fumes are very evident in several areas, particularly in the center and aft sections of the vessel on the lower decks. The entertainment is provided at deafening volumes, and there are too many loud, repetitive announcements.

THE COMPASS

This is the instrument by which a ship may be steered on a pre-selected course, and by which bearings of *visible* objects can be taken in order to fix a ship's position on a navigation chart. There are two kinds:

The magnetic compass uses the inherent magnetic forces within and around the Earth;

The gyrocompass, a relatively recent invention, uses the properties of gyroscopic inertia and precession, ideally to align itself to a true north-south position.

STEERING

Two different methods can be used to steer a ship:

Electrohydraulic steering uses automatic (telemotor-type) transmission from the wheel itself to the steering gear aft. This is generally used in conditions of heavy traffic, during maneuvers into and out of ports, or when there is poor visibility.

Automatic steering (gyropilot) is used only in the open sea. This system does not require anyone at the wheel because it is controlled by computer. However, aboard all ships, a quartermaster is always at the wheel, for extra safety, and just in case a need should arise to switch from one steering system to another.

Arcadia
★★★ +

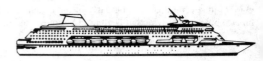

Large Ship:	63,524 tons	Cabins (for one person):	64
Lifestyle:	Standard	Cabins (with private balcony):	50
Cruise Line:	P&O Cruises	Cabins (wheelchair accessible):	8 0
Former Names:	*Star Princess, FairMajesty*	Cabin Current:	110/220-volt
Builder:	Chantiers de L'Atlantique (France)	Full-Service Dining Rooms:	1
Original Cost:	$200 million	Elevators:	9
Entered Service:	March 1989/December 1997	Casino (gaming tables):	Yes
Registry:	Great Britain	Slot Machines:	Yes
Length (ft/m):	810.3/247.00	Swimming Pools (outdoors):	3
Beam (ft/m):	105.6/32.20	Swimming Pools (indoors):	0
Draft (ft/m):	26.9/8.20	Whirlpools:	4
Propulsion/Propellers: Diesel-electric (39,000kW)/2		Fitness Center:	Yes
Passenger Decks:	12	Sauna/Steam Room:	Yes/No
Total Crew:	650	Massage:	Yes
Passengers (lower beds/all berths):	1,461/1,549	Self-Service Launderette:	Yes
Pass. Space Ratio (lower beds/all berths):	43.4/38.5	Dedicated Cinema/Seats:	Yes/205
Crew/Pass. Ratio (lower beds/all berths):	2.2/2.3	Library:	Yes
Navigation Officers:	British	Classification Society:	Lloyd's Register
Cabins (total):	748		
Size Range (sq ft/sq m):	179.7–529.6/16.7–49.2	**OVERALL SCORE:**	**1,374**
Cabins (outside view):	583	**(OUT OF A POSSIBLE 2,000 POINTS)**	
Cabins (interior/no view):	165		

Accommodation: There are 12 different cabin grades: eight outside and four interior (no view) categories. Almost all of the interior (no view) and outside-view standard-grade cabins for two are of an excellent size and layout, and are quite well equipped, with a good amount of wooden drawer and other storage space, plus some under-bed space for luggage), and walk-in (open) closets. However, you should note that the sound insulation between cabins is quite poor (TVs late at night can be particularly irritating, as can loud children). A number of cabins also feature third and fourth person berths (in which case the drawer and storage space becomes tight, and there is only one personal safe). Some cabins can also be designated for single occupancy.

The modular bathrooms are of a decent size and have good shower enclosures and retractable clothesline. None have bathtubs, except suites and mini-suites, as the ship was originally built for American passengers (who prefer showers), and personal toiletry amenity kits that typically include a shower cap, nail files, sewing kit, cotton swabs, and lint remover. Soap is provided, and a soap/shampoo dispenser is fitted into the shower enclosure (although there is no conditioner).

There are 14 suites and 36 mini-suites (each is thoughtfully named after historical P&O ships of the past), and more living space, with a separate bedroom and lounge. Each has a private balcony (although the partitions are not of the full floor-to-ceiling type, so you may hear your neighbors — or, unfortunately smell their smoke).

All of the suites and standard cabins have large walk-in closets, personal safe, refrigerator, TV, VCR, telephone, trouser press, retractable clothesline, and hairdryer. Suite bathrooms have a bathtub and separate shower enclosure, while mini-suite bathrooms have a wooden floor, and bathtubs with an integral shower. Both suite and mini-suite occupants get bathrobes and slippers.

Room service for breakfast, afternoon tea, and snacks for suite occupants is very basic, and should be upgraded. Apart from a limited continental breakfast menu, no other room service items are available in the standard (non-suite) cabins. Note that many passengers like to fall asleep with soft music playing, however, because music is only available through the TV, there is no way to obtain any of the music channels without having a TV picture on.

Dining: The Pacific Restaurant has two levels (there are two steps up to the center, raised section), but dining in it can be fairly noisy, as the sound seems to reverberate everywhere. There are tables for two, four, six, eight, or ten, mostly in small sections that help give an almost cozy feel to the room. Two seatings are featured, both of which are nonsmoking.

The food is typical of P&O, unpretentious and not at all memorable, although the choice is reasonably varied, and the quality of meat and fish is very ordinary (don't expect Scottish Black Angus beef, for example). If you like 'meat and two veg' fare, and you're into a curry a day, you'll be fine here, but if you like anything more adventurous, forget it. The presentation is straightforward, with little use of garnishes. Special orders can be arranged, but are difficult to achieve unless you are on a special diet. Vegetarian dishes are incorporated into the menu each day, although the selection is limited. The service is warm and friendly. The "Great British Breakfast" is always a popular and necessary feature of all P&O ships, and Arcadia is no exception in its delivery. A statement in the onboard cruise folder states that P&O Cruises does not knowingly purchase genetically modified foods.

The indoor-outdoor Conservatory buffet restaurant (it is open for breakfast and lunch, and for the occasional alternative, special-theme self-serve buffet dinner, such as "Gateway to India") is small and crowded (particularly when the ship is full). There is also the Al fresco Pizzeria (one standard pizza plus two different special pizzas are featured each day on a 7-day rotation, although the pizza slices are bread-based, and not made from pizza dough), an ice cream bar (sundaes), a patisserie, and a caviar bar. Note that all informal dining spots are nonsmoking.

Other Comments: This ship is the third to bear the name *Arcadia* (the name possibly being taken from a mythical region of Greece, although it also means heaven on earth — not the definition I would have chosen) for P&O. The company's first *Arcadia* was launched in 1887, the second, in 1954. This latest ship has good seagoing characteristics and provides a suitable, updated replacement for the company's much-loved *Canberra* (taken out of service in late 1997 and sent for scrap).

The ship was originally designed and built for Sitmar Cruises, which was absorbed into Princess Cruises in 1988 prior to the ship's completion (the ship's former operators prior to P&O Cruises). She was extensively refurbished in late 1997 at the Harland & Wolff shipyard in Belfast, and reconfigured specifically for British cruise passengers. The ship is well proportioned, and has a good amount of open deck space for sunbathing around her twin swimming pools (one has a sit-in bar — a first for P&O Cruises), as well as on her open decks aft of the funnel. Eight bells are sounded each day at noon, and relayed throughout the ship's public areas, in true nautical tradition.

Her interiors feature restrained styling mixed with traditional shipboard decor, including some pleasing Art Deco touches (stainless steel balustrades), so nothing jars the senses, is garish, or is out of place. A large selection of artwork (much of which was installed in 2000) provides some warmth to what would otherwise be a rather clinical, staid interior.

There is a lack of public rooms (although most have high ceilings) for the number of passengers carried; there are few little nooks and crannies, and almost nowhere that could be called a quiet room.

The focal point of a three-decks-high foyer is highlighted by a stainless steel kinetic sculpture (it resembles a Swiss Army knife) that brings one's attention to the multi-deck, horseshoe-shaped staircase. Afternoon tea dances are enjoyed here.

The largest public room is the two-deck-high Palladium Showlounge; it is horseshoe-shaped, with main and balcony levels, and there are adequate sight lines from most of the banquet-style seating, which was improved in the ship's latest refit in January 2000.

There is a domed observation lounge atop the ship (it is called the Horizon Lounge and sits atop the ship forward of the mast like a lump of Camembert cheese). A little out of the traffic flow, it is a restful spot for cocktails, although it turns into a night-spot/discotheque for night owls, with the accompanying thumping music. Several shops (one always carries chocolates and other sweets for the British, who like to snack) and a dedicated cinema complete the picture.

Out on the open deck (Deck 12), there are two swimming pools; the forward pool is for adults (new, sloping steps were installed in the latest retrofit), while the aft pool is reserved for families and children. Four whirlpools are set on a raised platform, and two shower cubicles stand adjacent to the Splash Bar.

Little vignettes of the former P&O liner *Canberra* are displayed in the small Canberra Room, while the necessary cricket memorabilia are displayed resplendently in the The Oval, a wood-paneled pub, which also has a central (wooden) dance floor.

The Monte Carlo casino offers three blackjack tables and two roulette tables, plus an array of 79 slot machines (often called fruit machines by the British). Although the library has a good selection of books, it is simply too small, has poor lighting, few comfortable chairs, and is located in the wrong place — out of the main passenger flow. There is a beauty salon, gymnasium, and sauna/steam room complex low down in the ship, although not particularly inviting.

Arcadia (priced lower than newer sister ships *Aurora* and *Oriana*) provides a traditional large ship cruise ambience for the many British repeat passengers who enjoy such facilities and some degree of anonymity, all in unpretentious surroundings. Thankfully, there are few announcements.

157

Families with children will enjoy P&O's excellent children's programs. The children's playroom, called Peter Pan, is located aft, and also features an outdoor paddling pool and games area. Children can be entertained until 10pm, which gives parents time to have dinner and go dancing. There is no extra charge for use of the Night Nursery (6pm–2am). Teenagers also have their own hangout — Decibels.

There is always a good mix of entertainment aboard the ships of P&O Cruises, and this includes the Stadium Theatre Company, which provides the production shows. There are also cabaret acts suited to British taste.

P&O Cruises has a fine program of special theme cruises, including antiques, The Archers (a long-running British radio program), art appreciation, classical music, comedy, cricket, gardening, jazz, motoring, popular fiction, Scottish dance, and sequence dancing among the themes. Check with your travel agent to see what is available at the time you want to cruise. Most of *Canberra's* crew was transferred to *Arcadia* and the ship features an interesting assortment of cruise itineraries. P&O's brochures, incidentally, are quite logical in layout and easy to follow.

A coach service for passengers who are embarking/disembarking in Southampton covers much of the UK (it is operated by Eavesway Travel); car parking is also available (one rate for undercover, one rate for open compound), and is operated by Andrews Garage.

Note that as of May 2002 this ship will become a ship for adults only—no children or teens allowed. Families with children should sail aboard *Aurora, Oriana,* and a ship to be introduced in 2002, *Oceana.*

Weak Points: Standing in line for embarkation, disembarkation, shore tenders, and for self-serve buffet meals is an inevitable aspect of cruising aboard all large ships. There is a permanent odor of stale cigarettes in many areas of the ship (nonsmokers may well be in the minority). There is no full wraparound promenade deck outdoors (open port and starboard walking areas stretch only partly along the sides). As "acoustic wallpaper" is everywhere, there is no "music-free" bar for a drink and quiet conversation. The female (digitally recorded) voice and her constant "mind the doors" reminders every time the elevator doors close are extremely irritating to passengers (most of whom would like to rip out the speaker system). The stairways and passageways are dull; the library is simply too small, has poor lighting and few chairs. The size of the cabins with third and fourth (upper) berths is far too small in this day and age. The croupiers in the casino have clearly had a hospitality by-pass. The sauna/steam room area is in need of a complete revamp — it looks like something from the 1950s.

Arion
★★

Small Ship:	6,000 tons	Cabins (for one person):	4
Lifestyle:	Standard	Cabins (with private balcony):	0
Cruise Line:	Classic International Cruises	Cabins (wheelchair accessible):	0
Former Names:	*Astra I, Istra*	Cabin Current:	220-volt
Builder:	Brodgradiliste (Yugoslavia)	Full-Service Dining Rooms:	1
Original Cost:	n/a	Elevators:	1
Entered Service:	1965/1999	Casino (gaming tables):	Yes
Registry:	Panama	Slot Machines:	Yes
Length (ft/m):	381.5/116.3	Swimming Pools (outdoors):	1
Beam (ft/m):	54.1/16.5	Swimming Pools (indoors):	0
Draft (ft/m):	18.3/5.6	Whirlpools:	0
Propulsion/Propellers:	Diesel (11,030kW)/2	Fitness Center:	No
Passenger Decks:	5	Sauna/Steam Room:	No/No
Total Crew:	120	Massage:	No
Passengers (lower beds/all berths):	334/340	Self-Service Launderette:	No
Pass. Space Ratio (lower beds/all berths):	17.7/17.6	Dedicated Cinema:	No
Crew/Pass. Ratio (lower beds/all berths):	2.7/2.8	Library:	Yes
Navigation Officers:	Portuguese	Classification Society:	Bureau Veritas & Rinave
Cabins (total):	169		
Size Range (sq ft/sq m):	n/a	**OVERALL SCORE:**	**859**
Cabins (outside view):	142		
Cabins (interior/no view):	27	**(OUT OF A POSSIBLE 2,000 POINTS)**	

Accommodation: There are 12 cabin grades — a lot for such a small ship. Except for the top two grades, the cabins are very modest in size and features, and one would not want to spend much time in them, particularly for those who have cruised aboard some of the more contemporary ships with larger living spaces. Note that cabins 1–8, which have windows, have lifeboat-obstructed views. Some cabins have windows, while others have portholes (depending on the deck — higher deck cabins have windows). Some cabins have a twin bed arrangement (side by side), while in others an "L"-shaped configuration is featured. Each cabin has a small TV, so you can watch movies if you do not want to be in the public rooms in the evening. There is little closet and storage space (so take only the minimal amount of clothing), and the bathrooms are tiny and basic, yet somehow adequate.

Dining: Although the dining room is quite warm and mildly attractive, with decent place settings, there are few tables for two, and the tables are very close together (leaving very little room for waiters to serve properly), and the chairs do not have armrests. All passengers are accommodated in one seating. The food itself is limited in choice and variety. The selection of vegetables, fresh fruits, and breads could be better. The Portuguese waiters are quite friendly, attentive, and may occasionally smile, but there is no service finesse. The wine list is quite basic, and the wine glasses are small.

Casual breakfasts and luncheons can be taken in the Lido Lounge, which is just forward of the swimming pool and open deck aft.

Other Comments: *Arion* (the name comes from a poet who, according to legend, was saved from drowning by dolphins) is a small ship, originally built for close-in cruises of the Dalmatian coast, and has a typical low-built early sixties profile that is mildly attractive. The ship was extensively (and lovingly) reconstructed by her new owners, Classic International Cruises (even the navigation bridge has been relocated forward) over several months at the end of 1999/beginning of 2000, after the company purchased the ship at auction in Haifa in March 1999.

At present the ship is being operated under charter to various tour operators, and thus attracts an international mix of passengers who enjoy cruising aboard the smaller ships that have some character, and for those for whom the big "apartment block" ships hold no interest. There is not a lot of open deck space, although the ship does have a small, enclosed teak promenade deck. The small swimming pool can really only be described correctly as a "dip" pool, but it is adequate considering the size of the ship.

There are few public rooms, but the owner has done a pleasing job of making the interiors much more attractive than before the reconstruction, although the lighting in some places could be better. There is a show lounge, although it is only one deck in height, and the sight lines are quite restricted from many seats.

Features interesting itineraries, at very lowest prices, both of which attract many of her passengers. The ship is particularly suited to the "nooks and crannies" ports of call, such as those found in the Mediterranean.

The dress code is extremely casual and there is a relaxed, unpretentious ambience. The service staff is mainly Portuguese; they are quite friendly and attentive, although some of them tend to put themselves first, and passengers second, when the reverse should be practiced.

Weak Points: Because she is a small ship, there are few public rooms and facilities, and very little open deck space, although this was improved during the reconstruction in 1999/2000. The interior passageways are narrow and not very well lit. The public rooms are always crowded and it is hard to get away from cigarette smokers. There are no cushioned pads for the deck lounge chairs. This ship should not be considered for wheelchair or other disabled passengers, as it is simply too small and confined, with narrow hallways.

Arkona
★★★★

Mid-Size Ship:	18,591 tons	Cabins (for one person):	0
Lifestyle:	Premium	Cabins (with private balcony):	0
Cruise Line:	Seetours	Cabins (wheelchair accessible):	0
Former Names:	*Astor*	Cabin Current:	220-volt
Builder:	Howaldtswerke Deutsche	Full-Service Dining Rooms:	1
	Werft (Germany)	Elevators:	3
Original Cost:	$55 million	Casino (gaming tables):	No
Entered Service:	December 1981/February 2002	Slot Machines:	No
Registry:	Liberia	Swimming Pools (outdoors):	1
Length (ft/m):	539.2/164.35	Swimming Pools (indoors):	1
Beam (ft/m):	74.1/22.60	Whirlpools:	0
Draft (ft/m):	20.0/6.11	Fitness Center:	Yes
Propulsion/Propellers:	Diesel (13,200kW)/2	Sauna/Steam Room:	Yes/No
Passenger Decks:	8	Massage:	Yes
Total Crew:	243	Self-Service Launderette:	No
Passengers (lower beds/all berths):	516.0/618.0	Dedicated Cinema:	No
Pass. Space Ratio (lower beds/all berths):	36.0/30.0	Library:	Yes
Crew/Pass. Ratio (lower beds/all berths):	2.1/2.5	Classification Society:	Germanischer Lloyd
Navigation Officers:	European		
Cabins (total):	258		
Size Range (sq ft/sq m):	150.0–725.0/13.4–65.3		
Cabins (outside view):	176		
Cabins (interior/no view):	82		

OVERALL SCORE: 1,532
(OUT OF A POSSIBLE 2,000 POINTS)

Accommodation: There are 14 categories of cabins from which to choose. Boat Deck suite rooms are simply lovely, and have just about everything one would need. Most of the other, more standard cabins are also well appointed and decorated, and all feature crisp, clean colors (some might find them plain, as are the ceilings).

The bathrooms are quite compact units, although there is a decent-sized shower enclosure. They are fully tiled, and have a decent cabinet for storing personal toiletry items.

Dining: The Restaurant, located high in the ship, has big, ocean-view picture windows and is reasonably attractive, with dark wood paneling and restful decor; two seatings are featured. The food is adequate to very good, though choice is somewhat limited, but the service, by some charming waitstaff, does help. The occasional formal candlelight dinners provide a romantic ambience.

The daily outdoor deck buffets (for breakfast and luncheon) are quite varied, although the presentation could be improved. The cabin service food menu is very limited.

Other Comments: *Arkona* is a traditional cruise ship (slightly smaller than her sister ship *Astor*), origi- nally constructed for the now defunct Astor Cruises. The ship has cruised under the Seetours banner from October 1985 and will continue until February 2002, when it will be transferred to her new owners, Transocean Tours, and renamed *Astoria*. Some minor modifications are anticipated so that *Astor* and *Astoria* will operate in tandem — two ships of a similar size and with very similar facilities, decor and ambience, operating as one product.

Arkona is a well-constructed modern vessel with a well-balanced profile. There is a very good amount of open deck and sunbathing space for her size, with some excellent teakwood decking and polished rail- ings. Cushioned pads are provided for all deck lounge chairs. For the sports-minded there is a large vol- leyball court.

Beautifully appointed interior fittings and decor, with much rosewood paneling and trim. Subdued lighting and soothing ambience, highlighted by fine artwork throughout make for a pleasant, relaxing cruise experience. There are good meeting facilities, and a fine, well-stocked library. There is an excellent pub (naturally with draught German lager) looking aft over the sun deck, which is definitely the late-night meeting place.

There is an excellent indoor spa and fitness center, with a good range of facilities that include a swimming pool, fitness center, and three sun-bed rooms for tanning sessions. In addition, sophisticated hospital facilities include oxygen multi-step therapy.

The atmosphere is a little starchy. There are many cigarette and cigar smokers. The ship features good traditional European hotel service, and a mostly German (expensive, under the German flag) staff. The reception desk is open 24 hours daily.

Astoria features good value-for-money cruising in contemporary comfort, and is best recommended for passengers who appreciate quality, fine surroundings, good food, and excellent destination-intensive itineraries, all packaged neatly in a relaxed, informal ambience. Many cruises have special themes. Transocean Tours staff is available aboard every cruise; they will go out of their way to make sure that you will have an excellent cruise experience in very comfortable surroundings. The ship has many repeat passengers, who enjoy the extremely friendly, mostly German crew (who provide a fun crew show). Port taxes are included. Gratuities are suggested at DM8–10 per person per day, and pooled.

Note that the evaluation and rating were done when the ship was in operation as *Arkona*. However, it is expected that the score would be similar under the ship's new name of *Astoria* in February 2002.

Weak Points: There is no wraparound promenade deck outdoors. The show lounge has 14 pillars obstructing the sight lines, and the stage is also the dance floor and cannot be raised for shows; entertainment, therefore, is mostly cabaret-style. Finally, nonsmokers should note that there are many cigarette and cigar smokers, and it is often hard to get away from them.

Astor
★★★★

Mid-Size Ship:	20,158 tons	Cabins (with private balcony):	0
Lifestyle:	Premium	Cabins (wheelchair accessible):	0
Cruise Line:	Transocean Tours	Cabin Current:	220-volt
Former Names:	*Fedor Dostoyevskiy, Astor (II)*	Full-Service Dining Rooms:	1
Builder:	Howaldtswerke DeutscheWerft (Germany)	Elevators:	3
Original Cost:	$65 million	Casino (gaming tables):	No
Entered Service:	February 1987/April 1997	Slot Machines:	No
Registry:	Bahamas	Swimming Pools (outdoors):	1
Length (ft/m):	579.0/176.50	Swimming Pools (indoors):	1
Beam (ft/m):	74.1/22.61	Whirlpools:	0
Draft (ft/m):	20.0/6.10	Fitness Center:	Yes
Propulsion/Propellers:	Diesel (15,400kW)/2	Sauna/Steam Room:	Yes/No
Passenger Decks:	7	Massage:	Yes
Total Crew:	300	Self-Service Launderette:	No (ironing room)
Passengers (lower beds/all berths):	590/650	Dedicated Cinema:	No
Pass. Space Ratio (lower beds/all berths):	34.1/31.0	Library:	Yes
Crew/Pass. Ratio (lower beds/all berths):	1.9/2.1	Classification Society:	Germanischer Lloyd
Navigation Officers:	Russian/Ukrainian		
Cabins (total):	295		
Size Range (sq ft/sq m):	140.0–280.0/13.0–26.0		
Cabins (outside view):	199		
Cabins (interior/no view):	96		
Cabins (for one person):	0		

OVERALL SCORE: 1,547

(OUT OF A POSSIBLE 2,000 POINTS)

Accommodation: The cabins (there are 18 categories) are all very nicely appointed and tastefully decorated in fresh pastel colors, and have dark wood accents and cabinetry, so they are very restful. There is plenty of closet and drawer space in each cabin, as well as some under-bed storage space for luggage. The bathrooms are very practical, and each has a decent size cabinet for personal toiletry items, as well as all the necessary fittings, 100% cotton towels, and a bathrobe for each passenger. In addition, the suites, which have a completely separate bedroom, living room, and bathroom, have a refrigerator as well as a minibar/refrigerator, and a large, boxed set of bathroom amenities.

However, the cabin service menu is poor and could be better (there is a charge for sandwiches, and little else is available).

Dining: The dining room is reasonably elegant, well laid out, and operates two seatings. It also has two small wings (good for private parties or groups of up to 30). The service throughout is friendly and unpretentious, and the food quality and presentation has received much attention and upgrading from the food caterer. The menus are reasonably creative, and the quality and presentation are both very good. In addition to the regular entrees (typically three entrees for dinner), there is a pasta dish and a vegetarian specialty dish.

The casual breakfast and lunch buffets are reasonably well presented, and constantly refreshed, although they are somewhat repetitive; the choice of foods is limited and could be better.

Other Comments: *Astor* was the original name for this ship, the larger of two ships bearing this same name in the 1980s (the other being the present Transocean Tours ship *Arkona*), originally built for the now-defunct Astor Cruises. Her previous owners, the now defunct AquaMarin Cruises, brought back the name *Astor* from her previous name *Fedor Dostoyevskiy*.

She is a very attractive modern ship with a raked bow, a large square-ish funnel and a nicely balanced contemporary profile. The ship was constructed in the best German tradition (slightly larger than the first *Astor* (now called *Arkona*), and was extensively refurbished in late 1995 before commencing service for AquaMarin Cruises. She was then was taken over by Transocean Tours in 1996 (she is under long-term charter to Transocean Tours until 2007 from her present owners, Russia's Sovcomflot) following the collapse of AquaMarin Cruises.

This ship represents a nice mix of traditional and contemporary styling. Built to a high standard (in a

163

German shipyard), fine teakwood decking and polished wooden rails are seen outside almost everywhere.

She has an excellent amount of open deck and sunbathing space, as well as padded cushions for the deck lounge chairs. There is a basketball court for active passengers, as well as a large deck chess game on an aft deck.

Her interior fittings are of extremely fine quality. There is a supremely comfortable and varied array of public rooms and conference facilities, most of which have high ceilings. A wood-paneled tavern (always with good German lager on draught) is a fine retreat, and extremely popular. There is a well-designed interior fitness center and large indoor swimming pool, but the charge of DM10 for use of the sauna is absurd (there should be no charge at any time).

The company features interesting and well-designed destination-intensive worldwide itineraries, and cruises are a very attractive price. The Russian/Ukrainian hotel staff is friendly without being obtrusive.

This ship, which caters exclusively to German-speaking passengers, provides style, comfort, and elegance, and a fine leisurely cruise experience in a relaxed, spacious setting (there is no crowding anywhere) that is less formal than a ship such as *Europa*. Port taxes, insurance, and gratuities are included in the cruise price. The ship can be booked at any DERPART, Transmarin, or UDR travel agency, and represents a good choice for those seeking a well-packaged cruise in fine contemporary surroundings. Transocean Tours staff can be found aboard every cruise, some of which are designated as special-theme cruises. The currency aboard is the German deutschmark and US dollar. Port taxes, insurance, and all gratuities to staff are included!

Note that *Astor* will be joined by sister ship *Astoria* and both will operate in tandem — two ships of a similar size and with very similar facilities, decor, and ambience, operating as one product.

Weak Points: The show lounge has pillars obstructing the sight lines, and the stage is also the dance floor, and cannot be raised for shows; entertainment, therefore, is mostly cabaret-style. The bathroom towels are small and should be larger.

Asuka
★★★★ +

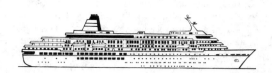

Mid-Size Ship:	28,856 tons	Cabins (with private balcony):	108
Lifestyle:	Premium	Cabins (wheelchair accessible):	2
Cruise Line:	NYK Cruises	Cabin Current:	110-volt
Former Names:	-	Full-Service Dining Rooms:	1 (+ sushi restaurant)
Builder:	Mitsubishi Heavy Industries (Japan)	Elevators:	5
Original Cost:	$150 million	Casino (gaming tables):	Yes
Entered Service:	December 1991	Slot Machines:	Yes
Registry:	Japan	Swimming Pools (outdoors):	1
Length (ft/m):	632.5/192.81	Swimming Pools (indoors):	0
Beam (ft/m):	81.0/24.70	Whirlpools:	3
Draft (ft/m):	21.6/6.6	Fitness Center:	Yes
Propulsion/Propellers:	Diesel (17,300kW)/2	Sauna/Steam Room:	Yes/Yes
Passenger Decks:	8	Massage:	Yes
Total Crew:	262	Self-Service Launderette:	Yes
Passengers (lower beds/all berths):	600/618	Dedicated Cinema/Seats:	Yes/97
Pass. Space Ratio (lower beds/all berths):	48.0/46.6	Library:	Yes
Crew/Pass. Ratio (lower beds/all berths):	2.2/2.3	Classification Society:	Nippon Kaiji Kyokai
Navigation Officers:	Japanese		
Cabins (total):	300		
Size Range (sq ft/sq m):	182.9–649.0/17.0–60.3		
Cabins (outside view):	300	**OVERALL SCORE:**	**1,658**
Cabins (interior/no view):	0	(OUT OF A POSSIBLE 2,000 POINTS)	
Cabins (for one person):	0		

Accommodation: There are seven cabin categories (Suite, and grades A, B, C, D, F, and J), although there are really only five types of suites and cabins. Three decks (8, 9, and 10) have suites and cabins with a small private balcony. There is no exterior light, however. All cabins have ocean views, although some are slightly obstructed by the ship's gangway, when in the raised position; there are no interior (no view) cabins.

In all grades, the cabinetry is of cherry wood, with rounded edges. The cabin insulation is excellent. There is a good amount of closet and drawer space, including some lockable drawers and a personal safe. Facilities include a hot water (tea-making) unit (with a selection of both Western and Japanese teas), refrigerator, bathrobe, yukata (cotton house robe), slippers, and down duvets (instead of sheets/blankets).

All grades feature bathrooms with full, deep bathtubs (while the "club" suite bathrooms are of generous proportions, the standard bathrooms are rather small) and tiled floor and bath/shower area. The range of personal toiletry items includes soap, shampoo, rinse, toothbrush/toothpaste, comb, shower cap, razor set, and vanity pack for ladies.

Two suites provide the largest accommodation (one is decorated in blue, the other in salmon); these are larger versions of the "A" grade cabins. Each has a separate bedroom, with walk-in closet that includes a luggage deck, and twin beds that convert to a queen-size bed, sofa, two chairs and coffee table, large vanity desk, plenty of drawer space, and large color TV. The marble-clad bathroom is large and has a whirlpool bathtub set alongside large ocean-view windows overlooking the private balcony, and twin washbasins. There is also a living room, and separate guest bathroom. The private balcony is quite large and has a tall tropical plant set in a glass enclosure.

"A" grade cabins are excellent living spaces, and feature twice the size and space of the standard cabins "D," "F," and "J." They are very nicely decorated and outfitted, and have twin beds (convertible to a queen-size bed), sofa, two chairs and coffee table, large vanity desk, plenty of drawer space, large color TV, and wooden ogurosaburo puzzle. Many have a private balcony (with full floor-to-ceiling partition and a green synthetic turf floor, but no outside light), with floor-to-ceiling sliding door (with door handles that are awkward). In addition to all the standard cabin amenities, a walk-in closet (with long hanging rod and plenty of drawer space) is provided. The bathrooms are of generous proportions, and include a glass-fronted (but plastic) toiletries cabinet. Four new suites were added to what was previously an unused space on Panorama Deck 10 in the ship's 1999 dry-dock.

The room service menu includes continental breakfast and light snacks throughout the day and evening. Sashimi and sushi are available while the sushi bar is open (typically 6pm–11pm), at extra cost.

Dining: The main dining room (totally nonsmoking, and no cellular phones allowed), which is laid out in two sections, with ocean-view windows along one side only, has a good amount of space around the tables, although there are very few tables for two. There are two seatings, and both Japanese and Western cuisine is featured — traditional Japanese breakfast and luncheon in the restaurant, Western cuisine in the Lido Café, and Japanese dinners, with the occasional Western dinner. There is a limited selection of wines.

Umihiko is a small à la carte sushi bar that features fresh seafood, beautifully prepared and presented (at extra cost), together with a good selection of Japanese sake. It is open also for lunch as well as dinner on some short cruises, and for dinner on longer cruises. There is a good range of hot and cold sake.The ship's propulsion is derived from three pod units, powered by electric motors (two azimuthing, and one fixed at the centerline) instead of conventional rudders and propellers, in the latest configuration of high-tech propulsion systems.

For casual breakfasts and lunches, an informal self-serve Lido Café is provided. This popular eatery was expanded in 1999 and now provides more indoor seating. Although she is a large ship, even the accommodation hallways are quite attractive, with artwork cabinets and wavy lines to interject and break up the monotony. In fact, there are plenty of decorative touches to help avoid what would otherwise be a very clinical environment.

A traditional washitsu tatami room (the whole floor is covered in tatami mats, no shoes allowed) is provided for special afternoon tea ceremonies and haiku readings.

Other Comments: When introduced, *Asuka* was the first all-new large ship specially designed for the still slow-growing Japanese cruise market, and the largest cruise ship constructed in Japan (for the Japanese market). However, she is quickly becoming outdated.

The ship has pleasing exterior styling and profile, with a large, squat funnel. There is a good amount of open deck space (although Japanese passengers do not use it much), however). There is a wraparound promenade deck outdoors, good for strolling.

The "cake-layer" stacking of the public rooms hampers passenger flow and makes it somewhat disjointed, although the ship's Japanese passengers like the separation of public rooms. There are many intimate public rooms and plenty of space so that there is never a feeling of crowding. There is an excellent, spacious, and true Japanese grand bath with large ocean-view windows. However, the massage room is located away from the grand bath area and would be better if it were to be integrated.

The interior decor is elegant but understated, with pleasing color combinations, quality fabrics and fine soft furnishings. Fascinating Japanese artwork is featured, including a four-deck-high mural located on the wall of the main foyer staircase by Noriko Tamara, called *Song of the Seasons*. The Mariner's Club, decorated in the style of an English gentleman's club, is a popular evening spot.

Cellular pay phones are located in one of the deck foyers, good for use when the ship features short cruises around Japan. Features a good mix of Western and traditional Japanese entertainment. There are good facilities for meetings and groups, with some of the latest high-tech equipment available.

There are formal and informal nights as far as the dress code goes, while during the day, the dress code is very casual. In case you want to do your own laundry, the self-service launderette has 12 washing machines. One nice touch is the fact that streamers are still used when the ship is cruising around Japan — a tradition that so many other cruise ships have stopped. Gratuities are neither expected, nor allowed. Note that children under 10 are not generally accepted, except during summer festival and holiday cruises.

A specialist courier company provides an excellent luggage service and will collect your luggage from your home before the cruise, and deliver it back to your home after the cruise (this service is available only in Japan). In the spring of 2002, *Asuka* is scheduled to go to a shipyard for substantial upgrading of public rooms and accommodation.

Weak Points: There is no butler service in the Asuka Club suites. The forward staircase is utilitarian and quite plain. The ship is in need of further refurbishment and upgrading in some areas in order to compete effectively in the international marketplace.

Atalante
★ +

Small Ship:	13,562 tons	Cabins (for one person):	2
Lifestyle:	Standard	Cabins (with private balcony):	0
Cruise Line:	New Paradise Cruises	Cabins (wheelchair accessible):	0
Former Names:	*Tahitien*	Cabin Current:	220-volt (DC)
Builder:	Direction des Construction et Armes Navales (France)	Full-Service Dining Rooms:	1
		Elevators:	0
Original Cost:	n/a	Casino (gaming tables):	Yes
Entered Service:	May 1953/December 1992	Slot Machines:	Yes
Registry:	Cyprus	Swimming Pools (outdoors):	2
Length (ft/m):	548.5/167.20	Swimming Pools (indoors):	0
Beam (ft/m):	67.9/20.70	Whirlpools:	0
Draft (ft/m):	20.7/6.30	Fitness Center:	No
Propulsion/Propellers:	Diesel (7,700kW)/2	Sauna/Steam Room:	No/No
Passenger Decks:	7	Massage:	No
Total Crew:	170	Self-Service Launderette:	No
Passengers (lower beds/all berths):	518/705	Dedicated Cinema:	No
Pass. Space Ratio (lower beds/all berths):	26.1/19.2	Library:	No
Crew/Pass. Ratio (lower beds/all berths):	3.0/4.1	Classification Society:	Bureau Veritas
Navigation Officers:	Cypriot/Greek		
Cabins (total):	260		
Size Range (sq ft/sq m):	129.1–247.5/12.0–23.0		
Cabins (outside view):	171		
Cabins (interior/no view):	89		

OVERALL SCORE: **666**

(OUT OF A POSSIBLE 2,000 POINTS)

Accommodation: The cabins, in ten grades, are all rather small and Spartan, although most have been redecorated in pastel shades. While many cabins have two lower beds, many also have third- and fourth-person upper Pullman berths. There is limited closet space, but you do not need much clothing for this casual cruise. Note that additional cabins that were installed in a 1993 retrofit are noisy and squeaky, which makes them quite difficult to sleep in. The top-grade cabins also have a refrigerator.

Dining: The Venus Dining Room is located low down in the ship and always seems to have a musty odor. Buffets are featured for most meals, and the food really is quite basic — with few choices and poor presentation. Service is provided mainly by Greek waiters, who are friendly but without finesse. There is also a small cafeteria for casual snacks.

Other Comments: Now well over 40 years of age, *Atalante*, a former passenger-car liner, is well worn. She has a small, squat funnel amidships and a really long foredeck (something that is not generally found aboard new ships). She is quite a stable ship at sea, with a deep draft, and rides well. There is a generous amount of open deck and sunbathing space, but the outdoor decking is well worn, as are the deck lounge chairs.

The number of public rooms is very limited, and the layout is quite awkward and disjointed. The main public room is the show lounge, an uncomfortable room that is immersed in high-volume, low-quality shows. Recent decor changes are for the better, although much of the interior decor is dated, yet adequate and comfortable for those who do not want the glitz of newer ships. Much emphasis is placed on duty-free shopping.

This ship is perhaps acceptable for younger, budget-minded passengers wanting to party and travel with just the basics and without the need for much service. The ship operates two- and three-night short, casual cruises from Cyprus to Egypt and Israel. Currency: Cyprus Pound. There will be a wide variety of nationalities on board, so international language skills may be useful.

Weak Points: The ceilings in the public rooms are low. The nightlife is disco-loud, as is the music. There is no finesse anywhere, although the staff is reasonably enthusiastic. Many passengers smoke so it is difficult to get away from the smell of stale smoke everywhere.

Aurora
★★★★

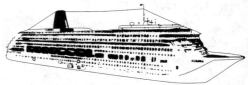

Large Ship:	76,152 tons	Cabins (with private balcony):	406
Lifestyle:	Standard	Cabins (wheelchair accessible):	22
Cruise Line:	P&O Cruises	(8 with private balcony)	
Former Names:	-	Cabin Current:	110/220-volt
Builder:	Meyer Werft (Germany)	Full-Service Dining Rooms:	2
Original Cost:	$375 million	Elevators:	10
Entered Service:	May 2000	Casino (gaming tables):	Yes
Registry:	Great Britain	Slot Machines:	Yes
Length (ft/m):	885.8/270.0	Swimming Pools (outdoors):	3 (1 with magrodome)
Beam (ft/m):	105.6/32.2	Swimming Pools (indoors):	0
Draft (ft/m):	25.9/7.9	Whirlpools:	5
Propulsion/Propellers: Diesel-electric (40,000kW)/2		Fitness Center:	Yes
Passenger Decks:	10	Sauna/Steam Room:	Yes/Yes
Total Crew:	816	Massage:	Yes
Passengers (lower beds/all berths):	1,868/1,975	Self-Service Launderette:	Yes
Pass. Space Ratio (lower beds/all berths):	40.7/38.5	Dedicated Cinema/Seats:	Yes/200
Crew/Pass. Ratio (lower beds/all berths):	2.2/2.4	Library:	Yes
Navigation Officers:	British	Classification Society:	Lloyd's Register
Cabins (total):	934		
Size Range (sq ft/sq m):	150.6–953.0/14.0–88.5		
Cabins (outside view):	655		
Cabins (interior/no view):	279		
Cabins (for one person):	0		

OVERALL SCORE: **1,548**

(OUT OF A POSSIBLE 2,000 POINTS)

Accommodation: There are five principal grades of accommodation, in 21 price categories. Included are 2 two-deck penthouses, 10 suites with balconies, 18 mini-suites with balconies, 368 cabins with balconies, 225 standard outside-view cabins, and 16 interconnecting cabins for families. All grades, from the largest to the smallest, provide the following common features: polished cherry wood laminate cabinetry, full-length mirror, tea and coffee-making facilities, as well as a personal safe, refrigerator, TV, individually-controlled air-conditioning; twin beds that convert to a queen-size double bed, sofa, and coffee table. There are four whole decks of cabins with private balconies (this is about 40% of all cabins), and these feature easy-to-open sliding glass floor-to-ceiling doors; the partitions are of the almost full floor-to-ceiling type — so they really are quite private and cannot be overlooked from above.

Note that cabin insulation could be much better (particularly poor is the noise created by the magnetic catches in drawers and on the closet doors). Also, the TVs sadly provide only monaural — not stereo — sound. Note that although most doorways are 26 inches (66 cm) wide, the measurement of actual access is 2 inches (5 cm) less because of the doorframe; however, some doorways are only 21.5 inches (55 cm) wide. A good range of high-quality personal amenities (shampoo, body lotion, shower gel) are provided for all accommodation designated as penthouse suites, suites or mini-suites. For all other accommodation, only soap is provided, together with a "sport wash" combination soap and shampoo in a dispenser in the shower (so take your favorite shampoo and conditioner), and a small pouch containing assorted personal care items. All accommodation grades get a "hair and body sport wash" dispenser mounted in all bathrooms, as well as thick, 100% cotton bathrobes, and 100% cotton towels. All accommodation designated as suites features European duvets instead of sheets/blankets, fresh flowers, a VCR, use of the AquaSpa without charge, and butler service. Electrically operated blinds and other goodies are also standard in some suites.

The largest accommodation consists of two penthouse suites (named Library Suite and Piano Suite), each measuring 953 sq ft (88.5 sq m). They have forward-facing views, and are located directly underneath the navigation bridge (the blinds must be drawn at night so as not to affect navigation). Each is spread over two decks in height, and connected by a beautiful wooden curved staircase. As their name implies, one suite features a baby grand piano (playable manually, or it can be set to play electronically), while the other features a private library. The living area is on the lower deck (Deck 10), and incorporates a dining suite (a first in a P&O ship) and a small private balcony. Upstairs (on Deck 11), the bedroom, complete with walk-in closet (and bathroom, in porcelain and polished granite, with twin basins, bathtub and separate shower enclosure), and small private balcony. Butler service is provided.

Accommodation designated as suites (there are 10 of them) measure about 445 sq ft (41.3 sq m). They feature a separate bedroom with two lower beds that convert to a queen-size bed. There is a walk-in dressing area and closet, with plenty of drawer space, trouser press, and ironing board. The lounge features a sofa, armchairs, dining table and chairs, writing desk, TV, radio, and stereo system. The marble-clad bathroom features a whirlpool bath, shower, and toilet. The private balcony has space for two deck lounge chairs, plus two chairs and two tables. Butler service is provided.

Next come the mini-suites, at about 325 sq ft (30.1 sq m). These feature a separate bedroom area with two lower beds that convert to a queen-size bed. There are one double and two single closets, a good amount of drawer space, binoculars, a trouser press, and ironing board. Each private balcony has a blue plastic deck covering, one deck lounge chair, one chair and table, and exterior light.

Accommodation designated as double cabins with private balcony measure about 175 sq ft (16.2 sq m). They have two lower beds that convert to a queen-size bed. The sitting area has a sofa and table. There's also a vanity table/writing desk, and a private balcony with blue plastic deck covering, two chairs (with only a small recline) and small table. Note that a 110-volt (American) socket is located underneath the vanity desk drawer — in a difficult-to-access position.

Outside-view or interior (with no view) cabins have two lower beds that convert to a queen-size bed, closet (but very few drawers), and measure 150 sq ft (14 sq m). The bathroom has a minibath/shower and toilet, or shower and toilet.

All bathrooms in all grades (except those designated as suites) are compact, modular units, and have mirror-fronted cabinets, although the lighting is quite soft (not strong enough for the application of make-up), and, in cabins with bathtubs, the retractable clothesline is located too high for most people to reach (you may need to stand on the side of the bathtub to use it — this could prove unsafe).

There are 22 wheelchair-accessible cabins, well outfitted for the physically challenged passenger, and almost all are located within very easy access to elevators. However, one cabin (D165 on Deck 8) is located between forward and midships stairways, and it is difficult to access the public rooms on Deck 8 without first going to the deck below, due to several steps and tight corners. All other wheelchair-accessible cabins are well positioned, and eight of them have a private balcony.

Dining: The two main dining rooms, Alexandria and Medina (each seats 525) feature tables for two, four, six, eight, and ten, and there are two seatings. Medina, the midships restaurant, features a slight Moorish theme decor, while Alexandria, with windows on three sides, features Egyptian decor. Both restaurants are nonsmoking, and both feature more tables for two aboard this ship than in the equivalent restaurants aboard close sister ship *Oriana*. The china is Wedgwood, the silverware is Elkington.

The cuisine is very British — a little adventurous at times, but always with plenty of curry dishes and other standard British items — and with good presentation (better than other ships in the P&O Cruises fleet). However, you should not expect exquisite dining. This is British hotel catering that does not pretend to offer caviar and other gourmet foods, but what it does present is attractive and tasty, with some excellent gravies and sauces to accompany meals. However, in keeping with the British-ness of P&O Cruises, the desserts are always good. A statement in the onboard cruise folder states that P&O Cruises does not knowingly purchase genetically modified foods. The service is provided by a team of friendly stewards from the island of Goa, with which P&O has had a long relationship

In addition to the two formal dining rooms, there are several other dining options. You can, for example, also have dinner in the 24-hour, 120-seat French bistro-style restaurant, Café Bordeaux, for which there is a cover charge (for dinner only). Breakfasts and lunches are also featured here, as are several types of coffees: espresso, cappuccino, latte, ristretto, as well as flavored coffees.

Casual, self-serve breakfasts and lunches can be taken in a dazzlingly colorful eatery named The Orangery. Other casual dining spots include the Sidewalk Café (for fast food items poolside), a French patisserie (for pastries and coffee), champagne bar and, in a first for a P&O cruise ship, a coffee and chocolate bar. Note that all informal dining spots are nonsmoking

Other Comments: *Aurora* (named after the goddess of the Dawn in Greek, Melanesian, and Slavonic mythologies, or perhaps the carnation Dianthus Aurora, or it could be the famous Northern and Southern Lights — Aurora borealis and Aurora australis) was built specifically for the growing British traditional cruise market. The ship is the flagship of P&O Cruises, and is based at Southampton, England. *Aurora* is a close sister ship and running mate to the company's popular *Oriana*, and was christened by HRH The Princess Royal (Princess Anne), although *Aurora* has more space per passenger.

As ships evolve, slight differences in layout occur, as is the case with *Aurora*. One big difference can be found in the addition of a large, magrodome-covered indoor/outdoor swimming pool (this is good for use in all weather conditions). The stern superstructure is nicely rounded and has several tiers that overlook the aft decks, pool, and children's outdoor facilities. There is a good amount of open deck and sunbathing space, an important plus for her outdoors-loving, mainly British passengers. There is also an extra-wide wraparound promenade deck outdoors, with plenty of (white plastic) deck lounge chairs for relaxing in.

The ship's interiors are gentle, welcoming and restrained, with good colors and combinations that do not clash. The public rooms and areas have been designed in such a way that each room is individual, and yet there appears to be an open, yet cohesive flow throughout all of the public areas — something difficult to achieve when a number of designers are involved. There is good horizontal passenger flow, and wide passageways help to avoid congestion. Very noticeable are the fine, detailed ceiling treatments.

Being a ship for all types of people, specific areas have been designed to attract different age groups and lifestyles. The focal point is a four-decks-high atrium lobby and a dramatic, calming, 35-feet (10.6 meters) high, Lalique-style sculpture (it's actually made of fiberglass) of two mythical figures behind a veil of water. At the top of the atrium is the ship's library (larger and in a different location than *Oriana*).

The carpeting throughout the ship is of excellent quality, much of it custom designed and made of long-lasting 100% wool. There are original artworks by all-British artists that include several tapestries and sculptures. However, for a weird experience, try standing on the midships staircase and look at the oil on canvas paintings, by Nicholas Hely Hutchinson. They are curved, and this has a dramatic effect on one's ability not to be seasick while cruising through the Bay of Biscayne — or any unkind sea.

Other features include a virtual reality games room, 12 lounges/bars (among the nicest are Anderson's — similar to Anderson's aboard *Oriana*, with a fireplace and mahogany paneling, and the Crows Nest, complete with a lovely one-sided model of one of P&O's former liners, *Strathnaver* of 1931 (ship buffs may know she was scrapped in Hong Kong in 1962). There is also a golf simulator (extra charge), and a dedicated cinema (so few new ships have these today) that doubles as a concert and lecture hall.

Families with children are well catered to, with special facilities and rooms for children and teenagers (even a night nursery), and a whole deck outdoors to play on (swimming pools and whirlpools included just for the youngsters). In addition, 16 cabins have interconnecting doors — good for families with children (or maid). Note that at peak holiday times (summer, Christmas, Easter) there could be 400 or more children on board. However, the ship absorbs them well, and the children's programming goes a long way to keep them out of the way of adult passengers who may or may not like cruising with lots of children.

For those interested in well-being, the Oasis Spa is located midship and almost atop the ship. It is moderately large, and provides all the standard alternative treatment therapies (note that the sauna and steam room are both co-ed, so you'll need to wear a bathing suit). There is also a gymnasium with the latest high-tech muscle-toning equipment, a beauty salon with a spiral staircase, and a relaxation area that overlooks the forward swimming pool.

The library also houses several writing desks, as well as large leather audio listening chairs (in which you can relax — or fall asleep — with a good compact disc), and three computer stations with Internet access. The library features a good range of hardback books (and a librarian), and skillfully crafted inlaid wood tables. On the second day of almost any cruise, however, the library will have been almost stripped of books by word-hungry passengers. The library also sells some nautical books.

All ballroom dance aficionados will be pleased to note that there are four good-size wooden dance floors aboard this ship. The ship always carries a professional dance couple as hosts and teachers, and there is plenty of dancing time included in the entertainment programming.

Children and teens have "Club Aurora" programs with their own rooms (Toybox, Jumping Jacks, and Decibels), as well as their own outdoor pool. Children can be entertained until 10pm, which gives parents time to have dinner and go dancing. All cabins also have a baby-listening device. A special night nursery for small children (ages 2–5) is available at no extra charge (6pm–2am). Teenagers also have their own hangout — Decibels.

There is a wide variety of mainly British entertainment aboard *Aurora*, from production shows to top British "name" and lesser artists. There is also a program of theme cruises (antiques, The Archers, art appreciation, classical music, comedy, cricket, gardening, jazz, motoring, popular fiction, Scottish dance, and sequence dancing are examples). Check with your travel agent to see what is available at the time you want to take your cruise.

In this ship, P&O Cruises has improved on the facilities of older sister ship *Oriana*, with cabins and suites that are larger, and with more dining options and choice of public areas. *Aurora* provides a decent, standardized cruise experience — and good value for the money for her mainly British passengers (of all dialects) — absolutely ideal for those who do not want to fly to join a cruise ship, as the ship sails from Southampton. Once each year, *Aurora* features an around-the-world cruise — always calling in Australia. This is excellent value for money.

However, note that in the quest for increased onboard revenue (and shareholder value), even birthday cakes are an extra cost item, as are espressos and cappuccinos (fake ones, made from instant coffee, are available in the dining rooms). Also at extra cost are ice cream and bottled water (these can add up to a considerable amount on an around-the-world cruise, for example). For gratuities, you should typically allow £3.50 per person, per day.

A fine British brass band send-off accompanies all sailings. Other touches include church bells that sound throughout the ship for the interdenominational Sunday church service. A coach service for any passengers embarking or disembarking in Southampton covers much of the UK. Car parking is also available (one rate for undercover parking, one rate for parking in an open compound).

Weak Points: The layout is a little disjointed in places, with several dead ends and some poor signage in places. The hours of opening of the Reception Desk (7am–7pm, when I last sailed) are simply too short. Except for the suites, no cabins have illuminated closets. The cabin ceilings are disappointingly plain. Standing in line for embarkation, disembarkation, shore tenders, and for self-serve buffet meals is an inevitable aspect of cruising aboard all large ships. During the school holidays, you should be aware that there will be many children aboard; this can be a cause of irritation and frustration to many older passengers. The cost of sending e-mails (from the four computers in the library) is high, at £3 for 10 minutes. "Cashless Cruising" doesn't include tips (for an around-the-world cruise this means carrying more than $750 in cash), or stamps, or condoms (available in machines in public restrooms).

Ausonia
★★ +

Mid-Size Ship:	12,609 tons	Cabins (for one person):	1
Lifestyle:	Standard	Cabins (with private balcony):	0
Cruise Line:	Louis Cruise Lines/First Choice	Cabins (wheelchair accessible):	0
Former Names:	-	Cabin Current:	220-volt
Builder:	Cantieri Riuniti dell' Adriatico (Italy)	Full-Service Dining Rooms:	1
Original Cost:	n/a	Elevators:	1
Entered Service:	September 1957/May 1998	Casino (gaming tables):	Yes
Registry:	Cyprus	Slot Machines:	Yes
Length (ft/m):	522.5/159.26	Swimming Pools (outdoors):	1
Beam (ft/m):	69.8/21.29	Swimming Pools (indoors):	0
Draft (ft/m):	21.4/6.54	Whirlpools:	1
Propulsion/Propellers: Steam turbine (12,799kW)/2		Fitness Center:	Yes
Passenger Decks:	8	Sauna/Steam Room:	Yes/No
Total Crew:	280	Massage:	Yes
Passengers (lower beds/all berths):	508/701	Self-Service Launderette:	No
Pass. Space Ratio (lower beds/all berths): 24.8/17.9		Dedicated Cinema/Seats:	Yes/125
Crew/Pass. Ratio (lower beds/all berths):	1.8/2.5	Library:	Yes
Navigation Officers:	Greek/Cypriot	Classification Society:	Registro Navale Italiano
Cabins (total):	254		
Size Range (sq ft/sq m):	69.9–269.1/6.5–25.0		
Cabins (outside view):	152		
Cabins (interior/no view):	102		

OVERALL SCORE: 1,006
(OUT OF A POSSIBLE 2,000 POINTS)

Accommodation: From suites to standard interior and outside cabins, all are small and compact, yet reasonably comfortable, in six cabin grades. They have all the basics, including a private bathroom and adequate closet space for frugal packers (drawer space is limited, however).

The uppermost cabin grades feature a full-size bathtub (two suites feature whirlpool baths), while all others have showers. There are several family cabins. Note that some interior and outside standard cabins have upper and lower berths.

Dining: The dining room (totally nonsmoking) is set high up in the vessel, has good ocean views from large picture windows, and features fine china and pleasant table settings. Tables are for four, six, or eight, in two seatings. Features friendly, efficient service with well programmed flair and attention. The cuisine is international in nature, and provides a good mix of Continental fare, with some regional Mediterranean specialties and British favorites. The selection of fruits and cheeses is limited. The wine list, while basic, provides an inexpensive range and a decent choice of wines.

Other Comments: *Ausonia* is an all-white ship that has a somewhat classic steamship profile, with a large, single funnel placed amidships. There is a decent amount of open deck and sunning space, although the swimming pool is tiny. She was purchased by Louis Cruise Lines in 1997, and underwent an extensive amount of refurbishing and upgrading in October 1998. Under her previous owners she had not been well maintained during the past few years, and is now still in need of a lot of attention to detail.

Inside, most of the public rooms are located on one deck (Corfu Deck). Most of the public areas have had upgraded decor and color changes, and are now lighter and more cheerful, with new soft furnishings.

The number of public lounges and rooms is limited. The Majorca Lounge (main show lounge) is pleasantly decorated, although the sight lines to the stage area are poor due to pillars obstructing the view; seats on the raised sections on the port and starboard sides are slightly better. There is also a small nightclub, casino, duty-free shop, and an enclosed "winter garden" lounge/reading area.

This ship is presently under a charter arrangement to the UK's First Choice Holidays, and will provide a reasonable, no-frills first cruise experience for those who choose to cruise on a limited budget (as long as your expectations are not grand). Hopefully the ship will exceed your expectations.

Weak Points: There are few public rooms. Many passengers are heavy smokers and it is difficult to avoid them. Has a narrow gangway (this can be steep in some ports). You can book the deck you want your cabin to be on, but cabins are assigned by First Choice Cruises.

Azur
★★ +

Mid-Size Ship:	14,717 tons	Cabins (for one person):	2
Lifestyle:	Standard	Cabins (with private balcony):	0
Cruise Line:	Festival Cruises	Cabins (wheelchair accessible):	2
Former Names:	*The Azur, Azur, Eagle,*	Cabin Current:	220-volt
	Aegean	Full-Service Dining Rooms:	1
Builder:	Dubigeon-Normandie (France)	Elevators:	3
Original Cost:	n/a	Casino (gaming tables):	Yes
Entered Service:	May 1971/April 1994	Slot Machines:	Yes
Registry:	Panama	Swimming Pools (outdoors):	2
Length (ft/m):	465.8/142.0	Swimming Pools (indoors):	0
Beam (ft/m):	71.8/21.9	Whirlpools:	0
Draft (ft/m):	18.7/5.73	Fitness Center:	Yes
Propulsion/Propellers:	Diesel (16,300kW)/2	Sauna/Steam Room:	Yes/No
Passenger Decks:	7	Massage:	No
Total Crew:	350	Self-Service Launderette:	No
Passengers (lower beds/all berths):	720/850	Dedicated Cinema/Seats:	Yes/175
Pass. Space Ratio (lower beds/all berths):	20.4/17.3	Library:	Yes
Crew/Pass. Ratio (lower beds/all berths):	2.0/2.4	Classification Society:	Bureau Veritas
Navigation Officers:	Greek		
Cabins (total):	361		
Size Range (sq ft/sq m):	94.7–212.0/8.8–19.7	**OVERALL SCORE:**	**1,069**
Cabins (outside view):	148	**(OUT OF A POSSIBLE 2,000 POINTS)**	
Cabins (interior/no view):	213		

Accommodation: Most of the cabins are of a decent size, but many also have upper berths, thus accommodating three or four persons. Note that there are many interior (no view) cabins (there are more interiors than outsides). These are, naturally, the least expensive, but they have a limited amount of storage space (the under-bed storage space is good, however). Although the cabins are plain, they are furnished and decorated in soft earth tones accented by brightly colored soft furnishings. All have a private bathroom, nicely refurbished with tiled floor, shower, retractable clothesline, and good storage space for personal toiletries.

A number of deluxe cabins have a full bathtub/shower combination, hairdryer, illuminated closets, minibar/refrigerator, and plenty of closet, drawer, and under-bed storage space.

There are two outside cabins for the physically challenged, but the ship really cannot be recommended for anyone in a wheelchair, as access to most of it is difficult at best.

The cabin insulation is poor throughout the ship. Housekeeping is provided by a friendly group of Goanese cabin staff.

Dining: The low-ceilinged dining room (totally nonsmoking) is reasonably charming and has large ocean-view windows on three sides, but the chairs are not really comfortable. Two seatings are featured. The food is actually good, and its presentation is attractive, as are the menus. There is a rather limited selection of breads, fruits, and cheeses. Multilingual waiters provide the service. Meal hours can vary, depending on the itinerary (and shore excursions). The wine list is decent (the wines are young, however), and prices are modest. A number of deluxe cabins have a full bathtub/shower combination, hairdryer, illuminated closets, minibar/refrigerator, and plenty of closet, drawer, and under-bed storage space.
Informal breakfast and lunch buffets are adequate but never seem to look very attractive, the result of a food concession that is used to the repetition and routine of doing things the same way all the time. There is, however, plenty of food.

Other Comments: This fairly smart, though somewhat stubby-looking ship (the first ship that this relatively new cruise line placed into service) has a very short bow and twin tall funnels and was originally constructed as a cruise-ferry. There is a modest amount of open deck space for sunbathing, and this becomes really tight when the ship is full (which is most of the time). There are no cushioned pads for the plastic deck lounge chairs. The two swimming pools (located on different decks, one atop the ship, the other aft) are very small (more like "dip" pools).

Inside, the layout is a little awkward to get used to at first, with many stairways in the aft section of the ship that have short, steep steps (this is typical of her original cruise-ferry construction). There is a reasonable selection of public rooms and several bars, with light, upbeat decor and the use of many mirrored surfaces (if you wear glasses, reflections could prove to be a problem). The show lounge has extremely poor sight lines and a low ceiling, although it is good for group meetings and lectures. A cinema (it is unusual for a ship of this size to have one) is used for movies and lectures. There is almost always lively action in the casino (which has its own bar), although the room is somewhat out of the main passenger flow. A two-deck-high indoor volleyball court is a bonus for sports fans, although it is located adjacent to the children's playroom.

The ship looks really neat and tidy in most areas, but in some others she looks unkempt and sloppy, the result of uneven refurbishments.

Festival Cruises has done a good job of creating a totally European product in a short space of time, and garnered a good name for honest, value-for-money cruising. Festival Cruises (known in the US as First European Cruises) provides destination-intensive cruises principally aimed at European passengers. The ship is a popular vessel for those seeking a friendly environment, and should appeal to the young, active set looking for a good first cruise experience to a host of destinations, at an extremely attractive price. Add the ingredients of friendly service, unpretentious, but tasty, food, and a mix of international passengers speaking many different languages, and what you get is extremely good value for money, despite the fact that the ship is tired and well worn in places.

The ship provides all announcements, daily programs, news, entertainment, and shore excursions in five languages.

Weak Points: It is difficult to find quiet spaces, as music is playing constantly in all public rooms and open spaces (for ambience? or annoyance?). The cabins really are small and cramped. Smokers are everywhere, and are difficult to avoid (in typical European fashion, ashtrays are simply moved — if used at all — to wherever smokers happen to be sitting). The constant announcements in several languages are irritating. The poolside towels are small and thin. The show lounge is really poor. The seats in the cinema are not staggered, and so sight lines can be awkward.

Black Prince
★★★

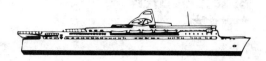

Small Ship:	11,209 tons	Cabins (for one person):	30
Lifestyle:	Standard	Cabins (with private balcony):	0
Cruise Line:	Fred Olsen Cruise Lines	Cabins (wheelchair accessible):	2
Former Names:	-	Cabin Current:	230-volt
Builder:	Fender Werft (Germany)	Full-Service Dining Rooms:	2
Original Cost:	$20 million	Elevators:	2
Entered Service:	1966	Casino (gaming tables):	Yes
Registry:	Norway	Slot Machines:	No
Length (ft/m):	470.4/143.40	Swimming Pools (outdoors):	1
Beam (ft/m):	66.6/20.30	Swimming Pools (indoors):	1
Draft (ft/m):	20.0/6.10	Whirlpools:	2
Propulsion/Propellers:	Diesel (12,310kW)/2	Fitness Center:	Yes
Passenger Decks:	7	Sauna/Steam Room:	Yes/No
Total Crew:	200	Massage:	Yes
Passengers (lower beds/all berths):	446/517	Self-Service Launderette:	No
Pass. Space Ratio (lower beds/all berths):	25.1/21.6	Dedicated Cinema:	No
Crew/Pass. Ratio (lower beds/all berths):	2.2/2.5	Library:	Yes
Navigation Officers:	European	Classification Society:	Det Norske Veritasr
Cabins (total):	238		
Size Range (sq ft/sq m):	80.7–226.0/7.5–21.0	**OVERALL SCORE:**	**1,144**
Cabins (outside view):	168	(OUT OF A POSSIBLE 2,000 POINTS)	
Cabins (interior/no view):	70		

Accommodation: There is a wide range of cabin sizes and configurations, and a good percentage of cabins are for single passengers. Many cabins have poor air-conditioning, however, and hard beds. The outside suites are reasonably decent (particularly comfortable are the Gran Canaria and Lanzarote suites, with their wood-paneled walls) and nicely appointed. Other cabins are small, but nicely equipped, and tastefully decorated for a smaller ship. Note that there is a charge for room service. The upper grade cabins have a refrigerator.

Dining: The two main dining rooms have big picture windows. There are two seatings (sometimes, first- and second-seating diners exchange seatings, a good arrangement). Features average cuisine that is attractively presented, with an emphasis on seafood. The food is generally of good quality, although the menu variety is somewhat limited, particularly at the buffet lunches. Breakfast buffets are repetitious, however. The wine list is very limited and basic (rather like supermarket wines). Filipino stewards provide the dining room service.

Other Comments: This is a solidly built ship that has been well maintained, but has a rather ungainly profile, and she does tend to pitch heavily in unkind seas.
   There is a good indoor fitness/leisure center (added in 1996), complete with an indoor swimming pool (this is unusual for such a small ship), and health spa area.
   The decor has a very homey, restrained feel and ambience, and many of the soft furnishings have been hand-tailored on board by the Filipino crew. Good wooden stairways throughout, although the steps are a little steep. An ironing room is provided — this is useful.
   This small ship has a friendly feel, an almost totally Filipino staff, and is well suited to the informal, older, British passenger, but the standards of service are slipping. Still, there are many repeat passengers who would not dream of trying another ship.

Weak Points: It is often difficult to get away from smokers, and the service has become overly casual and sloppy of late. The company lists recommended gratuities of £4.00 per passenger per day.

Black Watch
★★★★

Mid-Size Ship:	28,492 tons	Cabins (for one person):	37
Lifestyle:	Standard	Cabins (with private balcony):	9
Cruise Line:	Fred Olsen Cruise Lines	Cabins (wheelchair accessible):	4
Former Names:	*Star Odyssey, Westward,*	Cabin Current:	110/220-volt
	Royal Viking Star	Full-Service Dining Rooms:	1
Builder:	Wartsila (Finland)	Elevators:	5
Original Cost:	$22.5 million	Casino (gaming tables):	Yes
Entered Service:	June 1972/November 1996	Slot Machines:	Yes
Registry:	Bahamas	Swimming Pools (outdoors):	2
Length (ft/m):	674.1/205.47	Swimming Pools (indoors):	0
Beam (ft/m):	82.6/25.20	Whirlpools:	3
Draft (ft/m):	24.7/7.55	Fitness Center:	Yes
Propulsion/Propellers:	Diesel (13,400kW)/2	Sauna/Steam Room:	Yes/Yes
Passenger Decks:	8	Massage:	Yes
Total Crew:	330	Self-Service Launderette:	Yes
Passengers (lower beds/all berths):	807/892	Dedicated Cinema/Seats:	Yes/156
Pass. Space Ratio (lower beds/all berths):	35.3/31.9	Library:	Yes
Crew/Pass. Ratio (lower beds/all berths):	2.4/2.7	Classification Society:	Det Norske Veritasr
Navigation Officers:	European		
Cabins (total):	422		
Size Range (sq ft/sq m):	135.6–579.1/12.6–53.8		
Cabins (outside view):	375		
Cabins (interior/no view):	47		

OVERALL SCORE: 1,420
(OUT OF A POSSIBLE 2,000 POINTS)

Accommodation: A wide range of cabins provides something for everyone, from spacious suites with separate bedrooms, to small (interior) cabins. All are nicely equipped, and there is plenty of good closet, drawer, and storage space (drawers are metal and tinny, however, and in some closets they are of the wire-basket type. Nonsmoking cabins are available. Note that some cabin bathrooms have awkward access, and insulation between cabins is very poor. The towels are of substandard quality and are just too small. The room service menu could be improved.

Dining: The dining room has a high ceiling, and provides plenty of space at each table; there are two seatings. Features average cuisine that is attractively presented, with an emphasis on seafood. The food is generally of good quality, although the menu variety is somewhat limited, particularly at the buffet lunches. Breakfast buffets are repetitious, however. Communication with the Filipino waiters can prove frustrating at times. The self-service beverage station needs improvement. There is a reasonably decent range of wines. The room service (in-cabin) menu is limited and unimaginative.

Other Comments: Acquired by Fred Olsen Cruise Lines in late 1996, this handsome ship, originally built for long-distance cruising, has a sharply raked bow and a sleek appearance, "stretched" in 1981. There is an excellent amount of open deck and sunbathing space, and a good health-fitness spa high atop ship.

The interior decor is quiet and restful, although many passengers find the artwork drab. In general, good materials, fabrics (including the use of the Black Watch tartan) and soft furnishings add to a pleasant ambience and comfortable feeling experienced throughout the public rooms. The spacious public rooms have high ceilings, and the staircases are wide and well lit. There is a good cinema with a steeply tiered floor, and a pleasant library and card room. The observation lounge high atop ship has commanding views and is very comfortable.

This ship has settled in well under the Fred Olsen Cruise Lines brand, and will provide a good cruise experience, at a modest price, with a friendly staff and good service.

Weak Points: Do remember that she is now an old ship, which means little problems with plumbing and other idiosyncrasies can occur occasionally.

Bolero
★★★

Mid-Size Ship:	15,781 tons	Cabins (for one person):	0
Lifestyle:	Standard	Cabins (with private balcony):	0
Cruise Line:	Spanish Cruise Line	Cabins (wheelchair accessible):	2
Former Names:	*Starward*	Cabin Current:	110/220-volt
Builder:	A.G. Weser (Germany)	Full-Service Dining Rooms:	1
Original Cost:	n/a	Elevators:	4
Entered Service:	December 1968/May 2001	Casino (gaming tables):	Yes
Registry:	Panama	Slot Machines:	Yes
Length (ft/m):	525.9/160.30	Swimming Pools (outdoors):	2
Beam (ft/m):	74.9/22.84	Swimming Pools (indoors):	0
Draft (ft/m):	22.5/6.86	Whirlpools:	0
Propulsion/Propellers:	Diesel (12,950kW)/2	Fitness Center:	Yes
Passenger Decks:	7	Sauna/Steam Room:	Yes/No
Total Crew:	330	Massage:	Yes
Passengers (lower beds/all berths):	802/984	Self-Service Launderette:	Yes/210
Pass. Space Ratio (lower beds/all berths):	19.6/16.0	Dedicated Cinema:	No
Crew/Pass. Ratio (lower beds/all berths):	2.4/2.9	Library:	Yes
Navigation Officers:	Greek	Classification Society:	Det Norske Veritasr
Cabins (total):	401		
Size Range (sq ft/sq m):	111.9–324.0/10.4–30.1	**OVERALL SCORE:**	**1,197**
Cabins (outside view):	237	(OUT OF A POSSIBLE 2,000 POINTS)	
Cabins (interior/no view):	164		

Accommodation: Except for five decent sized suites, the cabins are very compact units that are moderately comfortable and are decorated in soft colors, accented by colorful soft furnishings. They are, however, adequate for a one-week cruise, particularly as this company specializes in destination-intensive cruises. While the closet space is limited, there are plenty of drawers, although they are metal and tinny. The bathrooms are small and tight, and the towels are not large, although they are made of 100% cotton; the toilets are of the "gentle flush" and not the "barking dog suction" variety as found aboard newer ships. The insulation between cabins could be better (each cabin has a notice asking passengers to keep the audio system to a minimum to avoid "cabin rage" complaints from neighbors).

The five suites (all, strangely, with Jamaican names) are of a good size, with a "privacy" curtain between the hallway/closet and the sleeping/lounging area. There is plenty of space to walk in these suites, which feature separate vanity desk, curtained-off closet, plenty of drawer and storage space for luggage, lounge with sofa that converts into an additional bed, drinks table, and two chairs. The bathroom features a small but deep bathtub with shower.

Dining: This ship has a dining room (nonsmoking) that is cheerful and charming, with some prime tables overlooking the stern (most are for four, six, or eight). There are two seatings (Spanish dining hours are much later than those of most other nationalities). A reasonable food selection is provided — it is totally geared to Spanish tastes. The service is cheerful, friendly, and comes with a smile (remember, this is an inexpensive, informal cruise experience, so you should not expect haute cuisine). The wine list is acceptable, but the wines, for the most part, are very young.

In addition, breakfast and lunch buffets are provided indoors at Signals Café, with seating provided outdoors at tables set around the aft swimming pool (space is tight, however, and there simply isn't enough of it). There is a good selection of bread and rolls, cold cuts of meat, fresh fruits, and cheeses at the buffets, which are presented reasonably well, given the space limitations.

Other Comments: This ship has a fairly contemporary upper profile with dual swept-back funnels, and is an ideal size for cruising in the Mediterranean region. *Bolero* was formerly a Caribbean-based ship owned and operated for many years by Norwegian Cruise Line. Festival Cruises acquired the ship in 1995. In May 2001 *Bolero* commenced operations for Spanish Cruise Line (Festival Cruises is a one-third owner of the new cruise line, together with Spanish tour operator Iberojet, and Spanish ferry operator Transmed, parent company of Spanish Cruise Line).

The open deck and sunbathing space is very limited (some of the decks are of plain steel, painted blue), and cluttered with plenty of white, plastic deck lounge chairs and blue-and-yellow sun umbrellas for shade at the aft outdoor decks. Just forward of her twin blue funnels is an enclosed basketball/volleyball court, while aft of the mast is a large solarium-style shielded housing, with multilevel lounge/bar/disco that is adjacent to one of the ship's two swimming pools.

Inside the ship, there is a good choice of public rooms for this size of vessel, and they feature clean, contemporary furnishings and upbeat, cheerful fabric colors and decor.

Bolero is a very comfortable vessel that is ideal for Mediterranean cruises, with a warm, friendly, and lively ambience. She is reasonably attractive and should prove to be a good choice for first-time passengers seeking a destination-intensive cruise at very attractive prices.

Spanish Cruise Line provides a totally Spanish shipboard life and cruise experience in rather crowded, though moderately comfortable (certainly not elegant or glitzy) surroundings, at a very modest price that translates to very good value for money. The staff is friendly and they try hard to make you feel welcome, like a member of a family.

Weak Points: This is a very high-density vessel that really does feel crowded when full (some might call it "ambience"). Has a less than handsome "duck-tailed" sponson stern (this acts rather like a stabilizer). Smokers are everywhere, and are difficult to avoid (in typical European fashion, ashtrays are simply moved — if used at all — to wherever smokers happen to be sitting). There are no cushioned pads for the deck lounge chairs. The diesel engines are somewhat noisy and tend to "throb" in some parts of the vessel (particularly when the ship is going full speed), including in many cabins on the lower decks. Cabins do not have TVs. There are simply too many loud, repetitive announcements (all in Spanish).

Bordeaux
★★ +

Small Ship:	4,000 tons	Cabins (for one person):	0
Lifestyle:	Standard	Cabins (with private balcony):	0
Cruise Line:	Dreamline Cruises	Cabins (wheelchair accessible):	0
Former Names:	*Stella Maris, Bremerhaven*	Cabin Current:	220-volt
Builder:	Alder Werft (Germany)	Full-Service Dining Rooms:	1
Original Cost:	n/a	Elevators:	0
Entered Service:	1960/1998	Casino (gaming tables):	No
Registry:	Luxembourg	Slot Machines:	No
Length (ft/m):	289.4/88.22	Swimming Pools (outdoors):	1
Beam (ft/m):	45.9/14.00	Swimming Pools (indoors):	0
Draft (ft/m):	14.4/4.40	Whirlpools:	0
Propulsion/Propellers:	Diesel (6,220kW)/2	Fitness Center:	No
Passenger Decks:	4	Sauna/Steam Room:	No /No
Total Crew:	65	Massage:	No
Passengers (lower beds/all berths):	186/186	Self-Service Launderette:	No
Pass. Space Ratio (lower beds/all berths):	21.5/21.5	Dedicated Cinema:	No
Crew/Pass. Ratio (lower beds/all berths):	2.8/2.8	Library:	Yes
Navigation Officers:	French	Classification Society:	Lloyd's Register
Cabins (total):	93		
Size Range (sq ft/sq m):	96.0–151.0/9.0–14.0		
Cabins (outside view):	80		
Cabins (interior/no view):	13		

OVERALL SCORE: **1,006**

(OUT OF A POSSIBLE 2,000 POINTS)

Accommodation: The 16 cabins designated as "deluxe" are quite roomy considering the size of the ship, but all others are small — very small. There really is very little drawer space, and the closet and other storage space is really minimal. There are two beds, although, in most cases, they cannot be placed together, as they are fixed; typically there is one bed, and one "sofa bed," which doubles as a sofa for seating during the day. The bathrooms are also very small (particularly the shower enclosures), and there is little space to put one's personal toiletry items. Only the 16 deluxe cabins have a bathtub.

Dining: The Poseidon Dining Room is intimate and quite charming, and all passengers dine at the same time (one seating). Although there is only a limited selection of fruits and cheeses, and very little choice on the menu, the food quality is surprisingly good. The catering is by a French company, and there is a small, but rather nice wine list.

Other Comments: *Bordeaux* is a charming little ship that was operated for many years by Sun Line (which merged with Epirotiki Lines to become the present-day Royal Olympic Cruises in 1995); the ship is presently owned by the Swiss company Reiseburo Mittelthurgau and operated by Dreamline Cruises. Although the hardware has been well maintained, it is a rather dated and tired ship in places, yet it remains a very comfortable vessel. She is of an ideal size for close-in destination cruising.

Apart from the dining room, there is only one other public room of note, and that is the Athenian Lounge (main lounge), which is the central meeting point for all passengers. Fresh flower arrangements throughout the ship add a splash of color. The service is quite decent from an attentive, considerate staff. The ambience is welcoming and quite intimate — almost yacht-like.

This ship will provide you with very comfortable small ship surroundings, and the line's personal attention to detail should make for a highly intimate and personable experience. Do remember that this is a very small ship, with few public rooms and facilities.

Weak Points: There are limited public rooms (only one main lounge, two bars, and a small shop) and open deck space, and the swimming pool is tiny — it's really best described only as a "dip" pool. A small ship, she does not sail well in open waters.

Bremen
★★★★

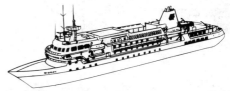

Small Ship:	6,752 tons	Cabins (with private balcony):	18
Lifestyle:	Premium	Cabins (wheelchair accessible):	2
Cruise Line:	Hapag-Lloyd Cruises	Cabin Current:	110/220-volt
Former Names:	*Frontier Spirit*	Full-Service Dining Rooms:	1
Builder:	Mitsubishi Heavy Industries (Japan)	Elevators:	2
Original Cost:	$42 million	Casino (gaming tables):	No
Entered Service:	November 1990/November 1993	Slot Machines:	No
Registry:	Bahamas	Swimming Pools (outdoors):	1
Length (ft/m):	365.8/111.51	Swimming Pools (indoors):	0
Beam (ft/m):	55.7/17.00	Whirlpools:	0
Draft (ft/m):	15.7/4.80	Fitness Center:	Yes
Propulsion/Propellers:	Diesel (4,855kW)/2	Sauna/Steam Room:	Yes/No
Passenger Decks:	6	Massage:	No
Total Crew:	94	Self-Service Launderette:	No
Passengers (lower beds/all berths):	164/184	Lecture/Film Room:	Yes (seats 164)
Pass. Space Ratio (lower beds/all berths):	41.1/36.6	Library:	Yes (open 24 hours)
Crew/Pass. Ratio (lower beds/all berths):	1.7/1.9	Zodiacs:	12
Navigation Officers:	European	Helicopter Pad:	Yes
Cabins (total):	82	Classification Society:	Lloyd's Register
Size Range (sq ft/sq m):	174.3–322.9/16.2–30.0		
Cabins (outside view):	82		
Cabins (interior/no view):	0		
Cabins (for one person):	0		

OVERALL SCORE: **1,461**

(OUT OF A POSSIBLE 2,000 POINTS)

Accommodation: The accommodation comes in only four different configurations. All cabins have an outside view (the lowest deck of cabins have portholes; all others have good-sized picture windows).

All of the cabins are well equipped for the size of the vessel; each features a color TV (small), telephone, refrigerator (soft drinks are provided and replenished daily, at no charge), vanity desk, and sitting area with small drinks table. Each has a private bathroom (of the "me first, you next" variety) with tiled floor, shower, toiletries cabinet, and good under-sink storage space (there's also an electrical outlet).

Each cabin has moderate (illuminated) closet space, although the drawer space is limited (suitcases can be stored under the beds). The beds feature European cotton duvets. Some cabins (Sun Deck and Bridge Deck) also have a small balcony (but these are tiny), a first for any expedition cruise vessel.

Two Sun Deck suites have a separate lounge area with sofa and coffee table, bedroom (with large wall clock), large walk-in closet, and bathroom with a bathtub and two sinks.

Dining: The dining room features open seating when operating for mixed German and International passenger cruises, and a single seating (with assigned seats) when operated only as German-speaking cruises. It is fairly attractive, with pleasing decor and colors; it also has big picture windows. The food is extremely good and made with high-quality ingredients. Although the portions are small, the presentation is very appealing to the eye. There is a good choice of freshly made breads and pastries, and a good selection of cheeses and fruits. The service is good, with smartly dressed bilingual (German- and English-speaking) waiters and waitresses. As an alternative to the dining room, breakfast and luncheon buffets are available in The Club, or outside on the Lido Deck (weather permitting), where The Grill is also operated for hamburgers and other grilled food items.

Other Comments: This purpose-built expedition cruise vessel (formerly *Frontier Spirit*, for the now defunct US-based Frontier Cruises) has a handsome, wide, and squat contemporary profile and fairly decent high-tech equipment. Its wide beam provides decent stability and the vessel's long cruising range and ice-hardened hull provides the ship with access to remote destinations. The ship carries the highest ice classification. In 1993 Hapag-Lloyd spent $2 million in refurbishment costs to reconfigure the restaurant and make other changes to the ship.

Zero-discharge of waste matter is practiced; this means that absolutely nothing is discharged into the ocean that does not meet with the international conventions on ocean pollution (MARPOL). All the equipment for in-depth marine and shore excursions is provided, including a boot-washing station. When the ship goes to cold weather/ice areas such as the Arctic or Antarctic, red parkas (waterproof outdoor jackets) are supplied, as are high waterproof boots (take some waterproof trousers and several pairs of thick socks, plus "thermal" underwear).

There is almost a wraparound walking deck (you must go up and down the steps at the front of the deck to complete the "wrap"). The ship has an unusual number of public rooms for her size, including a forward-facing observation lounge/lecture room, and a main lounge with high ceiling, bandstand, and bar.

Bremen features fine, well-planned destination-intensive itineraries, with good documentation and port information. The ship provides a high degree of comfort (although not as luxurious as her slightly larger sister *Hanseatic*). A 24-hour reception desk, fine array of expert lecturers, a friendly crew, and no annoying "elevator" music played in the corridors or on the open decks all add to the extremely sound cruise experience you should have aboard this ship.

Bremen is a very comfortable and practical expedition cruise vessel (she is arguably a better expedition vessel than sister *Hanseatic*). Cruises aboard the ship will provide you with a fine learning and expedition experience, and operates particularly well when on Antarctic cruises. The ship underwent an extensive upgrading of her interiors in 1993. The onboard ambience is casual, comfortable, and unstuffy (no tux needed).

Note that special sailings may be under the auspices of various tour operators, although the ship is operated by Hapag-Lloyd Cruises. Thus, your fellow passengers (I prefer to refer to expedition cruisers as participants) may well be from many different countries. Insurance, port taxes and all staff gratuities are typically included in the cruise fare, and an expedition cruise logbook is typically provided at the end of each cruise for all passengers — a superb reminder of what's been seen and done during the course of your expedition adventure cruise.

Weak Points: The swimming pool is very small, as is the open deck space around it, although there are both shaded and open areas.

Brilliance of the Seas

Large Ship:	90,090 tons	Cabins (wheelchair accessible):	24
Lifestyle:	Standard	Cabin Current:	110-volt
Cruise Line:	Royal Caribbean International	Full-Service Dining Rooms:	1 (+2 alternative)
Former Names:	-	Elevators:	9
Builder:	Meyer Werft (Germany)	Casino (gaming tables):	Yes
Original Cost:	$350 million	Slot Machines:	Yes
Entered Service:	July 2002	Swimming Pools (outdoors):	2
Registry:	Liberia	Swimming Pools (indoors):	0
Length (ft/m):	961.9/293.2	Whirlpools:	3
Beam (ft/m):	105.6/32.2	Fitness Center:	Yes
Draft (ft/m):	27.8/8.5	Sauna/Steam Room:	Yes/Yes
Propulsion/Propellers:	Gas turbine/2 pods	Massage:	Yes
	(19.5MW each)	Self-Service Launderette:	No
Passenger Decks:	13	Dedicated Cinema/Seats:	Yes/40
Total Crew:	869	Library:	Yes
Passengers (lower beds/all berths):	2,188/2,501	Classification Society:	Det Norske Veritas
Pass. Space Ratio (lower beds/all berths):	41.1/36.0		
Crew/Pass. Ratio (lower beds/all berths):	2.5/2.8		
Navigation Officers:	Norwegian	**OVERALL SCORE: NOT YET RATED**	
Cabins (total):	1,094		
Size Range (sq ft/sq m):	165.8–734.4/15.41–68.23		
Cabins (outside view):	813	Note that this ship had not entered service when this	
Cabins (interior/no view):	237	book was completed. However, the score is expect-	
Cabins (for one person):	0	ed to be very similar to sister ship *Radiance of the*	
Cabins (with private balcony):	577	*Seas*.	

Accommodation: There is a wide range of suites and standard outside-view and interior (no view) cabins to suit different tastes, requirements, and depth of wallet. Apart from the largest suites, which feature king-size beds, almost all other cabins have twin beds that convert to a queen-size bed (all sheets are of 100% Egyptian cotton, although the blankets are of nylon). All cabins feature rich (but faux) wood cabinetry, including a vanity desk (with hairdryer), faux wood drawers that close silently (hooray!), TV, personal safe, and three-sided mirrors. Some cabins have ceiling recessed, pull-down berths for third and fourth persons, although closet and drawer space would be extremely tight for four persons (even if two of them are children), and some have interconnecting doors (so families with children can cruise together, in separate, but adjacent cabins). Note that audio channels are available through the TV; however, if you want to go to sleep with soft music playing in the background, you'll need to put a towel over the screen, as it is impossible to turn the picture off.

Most bathrooms feature tiled accenting and a terrazzo-style tiled floor, and a shower enclosure in a half-moon shape (it is rather small, however, considering the size of many typical North American passengers), 100% Egyptian cotton towels, a small cabinet for personal toiletries and a small shelf. In reality, there is little space to stow personal toiletries for two (or more).

The largest accommodation consists of a family suite with two bedrooms. One bedroom has twin beds (convertible to queen-size bed), while a second has two lower beds and two upper Pullman berths, a combination that can sleep up to eight persons (this would be suitable for large families).

Occupants of accommodation designated as suites also get the use of a private Concierge Lounge (where priority dining room reservations, shore excursion bookings, and beauty salon/spa appointments can be made).

Dining: Minstrel is the name of the main dining room, which spans two decks (the upper deck level has floor-to-ceiling windows, while the lower deck level has windows). It seats 1,104, and has Middle Ages theme music and decor. There are tables for two, four, six, eight, or ten in two seatings for dinner. Two small private dining rooms (Zephyr, with 94 seats and Lute, with 30 seats) are located off the main dining room. The cuisine in the main dining room is similar in nature to that offered aboard the company's other ships. In other words, we are talking about mass banquet catering that offers very standard fare comparable to that found in American family-style restaurants ashore. You'll be waited on by "servers" (not waiters) in what is a change in terminology that ties in with RCI's vacation experience concept. I'll continue to call them waiters and assistant waiters.

For a change from the main dining room, there are two alternative dining spots: Portofino, with 112 seats, featuring Italian cuisine, and Chops Grille Steakhouse, with 95 seats and an open (show) kitchen, featuring premium meats. Both alternative dining spots feature food that is of a much higher quality than in the main dining room, with extremely good presentation. There is an additional charge of $20 per person (this includes gratuities to staff), and reservations are required for both dining spots, which are typically open between 6pm and 11pm. Be prepared to eat a lot of food (perhaps this justifies the cover charge). Unfortunately, the dress code is casual.

Also, casual meals can be eaten (for breakfast, lunch, and dinner) in the self-serve, buffet-style Windjammer Café, which can be accessed directly from the pool deck. It has islands dedicated to specific foods, and indoors and outdoors seating.

Additionally, there is the Seaview Café, open for lunch and dinner. Choose from the self-serve buffet, or from the menu for casual, fast food seafood items including fish sandwiches, popcorn shrimp, fish 'n' chips, as well as non-seafood items such as hamburgers and hot dogs. The decor, naturally, is marine and ocean related.

Other Comments: This is the second Royal Caribbean International ship to use gas turbine power instead of the more conventional diesel or diesel-electric combination. Pod propulsion power is also provided, instead of the previously conventional rudder and propeller shafts. As is common aboard all RCI vessels, the navigation bridge is of the fully enclosed type (good for cold-weather cruising areas).

Brilliance of the Seas is a streamlined, contemporary ship, and features a two-deck-high wraparound structure in the forward section of the funnel. Along the ship's starboard side, a central glass wall protrudes, giving great views (cabins with balconies occupy the space directly opposite on the port side). The gently rounded stern has nicely tiered decks, which gives the ship an extremely well balanced look.

Inside the ship, the decor is contemporary, yet elegant, bright, and cheerful, designed for active, young, hip and trendy types. The artwork is plentiful, and truly eclectic (so there should be something for all tastes). A nine-deck-high atrium lobby features glass-walled elevators (on the port side of the ship) that travel through 12 decks, face the sea, and provide a link with nature and the ocean. The Centrum (as the atrium is called), has several public rooms connected to it: the guest relations (the contemporary term for purser's office) and shore excursions desks, a Lobby Bar, Champagne Bar, the Library, Royal Caribbean Online, the Concierge Club, and a Crown & Anchor Lounge. A great view can be had of the atrium by looking down through the flat glass dome high above it.

Other facilities include a wedding chapel (located at the top of the Viking Crown Lounge); a three-decks-high show lounge (Pacifica Theatre) with 874 seats (including 24 stations for wheelchairs); a second entertainment lounge for cabaret shows; and a neat shop that combines books and coffee (it's called Books, Books and Coffee and is rather like a Seattle coffee house, with freshly made pastries and cakes). There's also a Champagne Bar, and a large Schooner Bar that houses maritime art in an integral art gallery, not to mention the necessary Casino Royale. There's also a small, deeply tiered, dedicated screening room for movies (with space for two wheelchairs), as well as a 194-seat conference center, and a business center.

The Viking Crown Lounge, set around the ship's funnel, functions as an observation lounge during the daytime. In the evening, the space features Starquest, a futuristic, high-energy dance club, and Hollywood Odyssey, a more intimate and relaxed entertainment venue for softer mood music and black box theater.

For the Internet-connect set, Royal Caribbean Online is a dedicated computer business center that features 12 IBM computers with high-speed Internet access for sending and receiving e-mail.

As aboard *Adventure of the Seas, Explorer of the Seas, Radiance of the Seas,* and *Voyager of the Seas* (the largest ships in the RCI fleet), there is a 30-ft high rock-climbing wall with five separate climbing tracks (to take part you'll need to sign-up). Other sports facilities include a jogging track, basketball court, 9-hole miniature golf course (with novel decorative ornaments), and an indoor/outdoor country club with golf simulator.

Health and fitness facilities have themed decor, and include a 10,176 sq foot (945 sq meter) solarium with whirlpool and counter current swimming under a retractable magrodome roof, gymnasium (with 44 cardiovascular machines), 50-person aerobics room, sauna and steam rooms, and therapy treatment rooms. There is also an exterior jogging track.

Youth facilities include "Adventure Ocean," an "edu-tainment" area with four separate age-appropriate sections for junior passengers: "Aquanaut Center" (for ages 3–5); "Explorer Center" (for ages 6–8); "Voyager Center" (for ages 9–12); and the "Optix Teen Center" (for ages 13–17). There is also "Adventure Beach," which includes a splash pool complete with waterslide; "Surfside," with computer lab stations with entertaining software; and "Ocean Arcade," a video games hangout.

It is clear that this second of a new generation of RCI ships (more will follow) has been constructed specifically for longer itineraries, with more space and comfortable public areas, larger cabins, and more dining options — for the young, active, hip, and trendy set.

Weak Points: Crowds. Lines. Waiting. No cushioned pads for the deck lounge chairs.

THE BRIDGE

A ship's navigation bridge is manned at all times, both at sea and in port. Besides the captain, who is master of the vessel, other senior officers take "watch" turns for four- or eight-hour periods. In addition, junior officers are continually honing their skills as experienced navigators, waiting for the day when they will be promoted to master.

The captain is always in command at times of high risk, such as when the ship is entering or leaving a port, when the density of traffic is particularly high, or when visibility is severely restricted by poor weather.

Navigation has come a long way since the days of the ancient mariners, who used only the sun and the stars to calculate their course across the oceans. The space-age development of sophisticated navigation devices (using satellites) has enabled us to eliminate the guesswork of early navigation (the first global mobile satellite system came into being in 1979).

A ship's navigator today can establish accurately where the ship is in any weather and at any time.

Calypso
★★ +

Small Ship:	11,162 tons	Cabins (for one person):	0
Lifestyle:	Standard	Cabins (with private balcony):	0
Cruise Line:	Louis Cruise Lines	Cabins (wheelchair accessible):	2
Former Names:	*Regent Jewel, Sun Fiesta, Ionian*	Cabin Current:	110-volt
	Harmony, Canguro Verde	Dining Rooms:	1
Builder:	Fincantieri (Italy)	Elevators:	2
Original Cost:	n/a	Casino (gaming tables):	Yes
Entered Service:	1968/July 2000	Slot Machines:	No
Registry:	Bahamas	Swimming Pools (outdoors):	1
Length (ft/m):	444.2/135.4	Swimming Pools (indoors):	0
Beam (ft/m):	62.9/19.2	Whirlpools:	0
Draft (ft/m):	20.6/6.3	Fitness Center:	Yes
Propulsion/Propellers:	Diesel (9,000kW)/2	Sauna/Steam Room:	Yes/No
Passenger Decks:	8	Massage:	Yes
Total Crew:	220	Self-Service Launderette:	No
Passengers (lower beds/all berths):	486/596	Dedicated Cinema:	No
Pass. Space Ratio (lower beds/all berths):	22.9/18.8	Library:	Yes
Crew/Pass. Ratio (lower beds/all berths):	2.2/2.7	Classification Society:	Lloyd's Register
Navigation Officers:	European		
Cabins (total):	243		
Size Range (sq ft/sq m):	135–244/12.5–22.6	**OVERALL SCORE:**	**1,066**
Cabins (outside view):	158		
Cabins (interior/no view):	85	(OUT OF A POSSIBLE 2,000 POINTS)	

Accommodation: The ship features mostly cabins with an outside view, which are quite attractive, with warm, pastel colors, although the fabrics and soft furnishings could be of better quality. The cabin bathrooms all have showers, but none have bathtubs.

The cabins really are quite small and barely adequate, so take only the minimum amount of clothing. Some cabins have double beds, while most others have twin beds, and many feature third and fourth berths (good for families). Has a limited cabin service menu.

Dining: The dining room is located aft. It is reasonably attractive and well decorated, although its layout is somewhat awkward, as it is positioned on two slightly different levels. There are two seatings, with tables for four, six, and eight persons. Good general cuisine and service standards are provided, and attractive buffets feature plenty of cheeses and cold cuts of meat, which are essential to German passengers.

Other Comments: This former Strintzis Line ferry (which operated Mediterranean ferry services) was extensively reconstructed in Greece (although her resulting exterior profile is certainly less than attractive) and then operated by the now-defunct Regency Cruises before being placed under a 5-year bare-boat charter to Transocean Tours. Following this the ship was laid up in Greece for two years prior to being purchased by Louis Cruise Lines.

The ship carries a predominantly German-speaking clientele who seek to travel to interesting and somewhat offbeat destinations in modest surroundings, at a very modest price.

One really practical feature is the ship's enclosed wooden promenade deck, good for strolling. There are plenty of public rooms, bars and lounges to use considering the size of the ship. The fit and finish of the vessel is disappointingly poor, as is the quality of some of the interior decoration.

A cozy, relaxed, and unpretentious ambience is what many passengers want, and get, aboard this ship. The dress code is very relaxed, and formal attire is definitely not required. So, those seeking a casual cruise experience in unstuffy surroundings should be comfortable aboard this ship, which caters well to first-time passengers.

Weak Points: This really is a high-density ship, which means that it is very crowded when full, so expect some lines to form for shore excursions and buffets. Expect a large number of smokers. There are very steep, narrow stairways on the outer decks.

Cape Cod Light

Small Ship:	1,580 tons	Cabins (wheelchair accessible):	2
Lifestyle:	Standard	Cabin Current:	110-volt
Cruise Line:	Delta Queen Coastal Cruise	Full-Service Dining Rooms:	1
Former Names:	-	Elevators:	1
Builder:	Atlantic Marine (US)	Casino (gaming tables):	No
Original Cost:	$60 million	Slot Machines:	No
Entered Service:	August 2001	Swimming Pools (outdoors):	0
Registry:	US	Swimming Pools (indoors):	0
Length (ft/m):	300.0/91.4	Whirlpools:	0
Beam (ft/m):	50.0/15.2	Fitness Center:	0
Draft (ft/m):	12.5/3.8	Sauna/Steam Room:	No/No
Propulsion/Propellers:	Diesel/2	Massage:	No
Passenger Decks:	7	Self-Service Launderette:	No
Total Crew:	77	Dedicated Cinema:	No
Passengers (lower beds/all berths):	226/226	Library:	Yes
Pass. Space Ratio (lower beds/all berths):	12.6/12.6	Classification Society	American Bureau of
Crew/Pass. Ratio (lower beds/all berths):	2.9/2.9		Shipping
Navigation Officers:	American		
Cabins (total):	114		
Size Range (sq ft/sq m)	107.0–328.0/9.9–30.4		
Cabins (outside view):	111		
Cabins (interior/no view):	13		
Cabins (for one person):	2		
Cabins (with private balcony):	0		

OVERALL SCORE: NOT YET RATED

Note that this ship had not entered service when this book was completed.

Accommodation: There are five accommodation categories, and sizes vary between 107 and 328 sq ft (9.9–30.4 sq m).

The largest accommodation can be found in the two Owner's Suites, located directly underneath the navigation bridge (called the Pilot House). With large windows forward and along one sidethese are decorated with New England Federal-style furnishings and can accommodate a third person.

Most cabins feature either full-size twin beds or a queen-size bed. Although there are no cabins with private balconies, some cabins do have doors that open onto the Observation Deck.

There are also two wheelchair-accessible cabins, measuring 188 sq ft (17.4 sq m), each of which has a "roll-in" shower in the bathroom.

No matter what grade, all cabins feature a TV, video player, audio channels, direct-dial satellite-linked telephone, hairdryer, an iron, and an ironing board.

Dining: The Beechwood Dining Room, which seats 144, evokes images of historic elegance, and operates two seatings (main and late). Regional American cuisine is featured. The wine list contains a heavy dose of American wines from California and Washington states.

The Lighthouse Keeper's Bar is a casual outdoor lounge area, with 74 seats. It is used for serve-yourself breakfast buffets, and happy hour cocktails.

Other Comments: Although in this book *Cape Cod Light* comes alphabetically before *Cape May Light*, this is actually the second ship to debut for Delta Queen Coastal Voyages — a sister company to the Delta Queen Steamboat Company (whose parent company is American Classic Voyages). The ship operates close-in cruises along the East and West coasts of the US (including Alaska) and Canada's East coast. The ship's name — *Cape Cod Light* — was chosen because it represents one of two of the most historically important lighthouses in America.

The ship evokes images of a bygone era. The design was based on ships of the Fall River Line, whose vessels sailed between 1847 and 1937. The ship, with its dark colored hull, has two funnels (the aft funnel being slightly taller than the forward funnel), and has the profile and look of a late 19th-century river steamer, rather than an ocean-going cruise vessel.

Inside, as you might expect, everything is decorated in the retro style of the river steamers of the late

1800s. The four decks have pleasantly different names: Beacon Deck, Lantern Deck, Harbor Deck, and Cove Deck. The 160-seat Penobscot Lounge is the ship's main lounge, and features a dance floor and an interesting stamped metal ceiling. During the daytime, the saloon is used for lectures and for buffets.

The Pilot's Point Pub is somewhat reminiscent of the Texas Lounge aboard *Delta Queen*, has 58 seats and features windows on both port and starboard sides with stained glass upper sections. There is a three-sided wooden bar, a baby grand piano in one corner, and bookshelves filled with books about Revolutionary and Civil War heroes, and other Americana history, as well as books about the ship's destinations.

In the Harbor Deck Foyer and Purser's Lobby, the artwork on the walls depicts vessels and scenes from the days of the Fall River Line. Pier 19 is the name of the ship's gift shop. Gratuities are also extra, at a suggested $13 per person, per day.

Weak Points: Having two seatings makes this a rather disjointed passenger mix. The cabin ceilings are very plain — they would have been better with one-piece plaster ceilings. The cruise fares are high, and passengers are expected to tip as well.

Cape May Light

Small Ship	1,580 tons	Cabins (wheelchair accessible):	2
Lifestyle:	Standard	Cabin Current:	110-volt
Cruise Line:	Delta Queen Coastal Cruises	Full-Service Dining Rooms:	1
Former Names:	-	Elevators:	1
Builder:	Atlantic Marine (US)	Casino (gaming tables):	No
Original Cost:	$30 million	Slot Machines:	No
Entered Service:	May 2001	Swimming Pools (outdoors):	0
Registry:	US	Swimming Pools (indoors):	0
Length (ft/m):	300.0/91.4	Whirlpools:	0
Beam (ft/m):	50.0/15.2	Fitness Center:	0
Draft (ft/m):	12.5/3.8	Sauna/Steam Room:	No/No
Propulsion/Propellers:	Diesel/2	Massage:	No
Passenger Decks:	5	Self-Service Launderette:	No
Total Crew:	77	Dedicated Cinema:	No
Passengers (lower beds/all berths):	226/226	Library:	Yes
Pass. Space Ratio (lower beds/all berths):	12.6/12.6	ClassificationSociety:	American Bureau
Crew/Pass. Ratio (lower beds/all berths):	2.9/2.9		of Shipping
Navigation Officers:	American		
Cabins (total):	114		
Size Range (sq ft/sq m):	107.0–328.0/9.9–30.4		
Cabins (outside view):	111		
Cabins (interior/no view):	13		
Cabins (for one person):	2		
Cabins (with private balcony):	0		

OVERALL SCORE: NOT YET RATED

Note that this ship had not entered service when this book was completed.

Accommodation: There are five accommodation categories, and sizes vary between 107 and 328 sq ft (9.9–30.4 sq m).

The largest accommodation can be found in the two Owner's Suites, located directly underneath the navigation bridge (called the Pilot House). These have large windows forward and along one side. These are decorated with New England Federal-style furnishings, and can accommodate a third person. The ceilings, however, are surprisingly plain.

Most cabins feature either full-size twin beds or a queen-size bed. Although there are no cabins with private balconies, some cabins do have doors that open onto the Observation Deck.

There are also two wheelchair-accessible cabins, measuring 188 sq ft (17.4 sq m), each of which has a "roll-in" shower in the bathroom.

No matter what grade, all cabins feature a TV, video player, audio channels, direct-dial satellite-linked telephone, hairdryer, an iron, and an ironing board.

Dining: The Rosecliffe Dining Room, which seats 144, evokes images of historic elegance, and operates two seatings (main and late). Regional American cuisine is featured. The wine list contains a heavy dose of American wines from California and Washington states.

The Lighthouse Keeper's Bar is a casual outdoor lounge area, with 74 seats. It is used for serve-your-self breakfast buffets, and happy hour cocktails.

Other Comments: This is the first ship for Delta Queen Coastal Voyages — a sister company to the Delta Queen Steamboat Company (whose parent company is American Classic Voyages) — and operates close-in cruises along the east and west coasts of the US (including Alaska) and Canada's east coast. The ship's name — *Cape May Light* — was chosen because it represents one of two of the most historically important lighthouses in America. Indeed, the Cape May Light was first lit in 1797.

The ship evokes images of a bygone era. The design was based on ships of the Fall River Line, whose vessels sailed between 1847 and 1937. The ship, with its dark colored hull, has two funnels (the aft funnel being slightly taller than the forward funnel), and has the profile and look of a late 19th-century river steamer rather than an ocean-going cruise vessel. Inside, as you might expect, everything is decorated in the retro style of the river steamers of the late 1800s. The four decks have pleasantly different names:

Beacon Deck, Lantern Deck, Harbor Deck, and Cove Deck. The 160-seat Harbor Lights Lounge is the ship's main lounge, and features a dance floor and an interesting stamped metal ceiling. During the daytime, the saloon is used for lectures and for buffets.

The Fogcutter's Pub is reminiscent of the Texas Lounge aboard *Delta Queen*, has 58 seats, and features windows on both port and starboard sides with stained glass upper sections. There is a three-sided wooden bar, a baby grand piano in one corner, and bookshelves filled with books about Revolutionary and Civil War heroes, and other Americana history, as well as books about the ship's destinations.

In the Harbor Deck Foyer and Purser's Lobby, the artwork on the walls depicts vessels and scenes from the days of the Fall River Line. Pier 19 is the name of the ship's gift shop.

Note that all regularly scheduled shore excursions are included in the price, while port charges are not. Gratuities are also extra, at a suggested $13 per person, per day.

Weak Points: Having two seatings makes this a rather disjointed passenger mix. The cabin ceilings are very plain — they would have been better with one-piece plaster ceilings. The cruise fares are high, and passengers are expected to tip as well.

Carnival Destiny
★★★★

Large Ship:	101,353 tons	Cabins (for one person):	0
Lifestyle:	Standard	Cabins (with private balcony):	418
Cruise Line:	Carnival Cruise Lines	Cabins (wheelchair accessible):	25
Former Names:	-	Cabin Current:	110-volt
Builder:	Fincantieri (Italy)	Full-Service Dining Rooms:	2
Original Cost:	$400 million	Elevators:	18
Entered Service:	November 1996	Casino (gaming tables):	Yes
Registry:	Bahamas	Slot Machines:	Yes
Length (ft/m):	892.3/272.0	Swimming Pools (outdoors):3 (+1 with magrodome)	
Beam (ft/m):	116.0/35.3	Swimming Pools (indoors):	0
Draft (ft/m):	27.0/8.2	Whirlpools:	7
Propulsion/Propellers: Diesel-electric (63,400kW)/2		Fitness Center:	Yes
Passenger Decks:	12	Sauna/Steam Room:	Yes/Yes
Total Crew:	1,000	Massage:	Yes
Passengers (lower beds/all berths):	2,642/3,400	Self-Service Launderette:	Yes
Pass. Space Ratio (lower beds/all berths): 38.3/29.8		Dedicated Cinema:	No
Crew/Pass. Ratio (lower beds/all berths):	2.6/3.4	Library:	Yes
Navigation Officers:	Italian	Classification Society:	Lloyd's Register
Cabins (total):	1,321		
Size Range (sq ft/sq m):	179.7–482.2/16.7–44.8		
Cabins (outside view):	806		
Cabins (interior/no view):	515		

OVERALL SCORE: **1,455**

(OUT OF A POSSIBLE 2,000 POINTS)

Accommodation: Over half of all cabins have an oceanview, and at 225 sq ft/21 sq m they are the largest in the standard market. They are spread over four decks and have private balconies (with glass rather than steel balustrades, for better, unobstructed ocean views), extending over the ship's side. The balconies also feature bright fluorescent lighting.

The standard cabins are of good size and come equipped with all the basics, although the furniture is rather square and angular, with no rounded edges. Three decks of cabins (eight on each deck, each with private balcony) overlook the stern (with three days at sea on each of two alternating itineraries, vibration is kept to a minimum).

Eight penthouse suites, each with a large balcony, have lavish appointments, although, at only 483 sq ft (44.8 sq m) are small when compared to the best suites in many smaller ships. There are also 40 other suites, each of which features a decent-sized bathroom, and a good amount of lounge space.

In those cabins with balconies (more cabins have balconies aboard this ship than those that do not), the partition between each balcony is open at top and bottom, so you can hear noise from neighbors (or smell their cigarettes). It is disappointing to see three categories of cabins (both outside and interior) with upper and lower bunk beds (lower beds are far more preferable, but this is how the ship accommodates an extra 600 passengers over and above the lower bed capacity).

The cabins feature soft color schemes and more soft furnishings in more attractive fabrics than any other ship in the fleet. Interactive "Fun Vision" technology lets you choose movies on demand (for a fee). Bathrooms, which have good-size showers, feature good storage space in the toiletries cabinet. A gift basket is now provided in all grades of accommodation; it includes aloe soap, shampoo, conditioner, deodorant, breath mints, candy, and pain relief tablets

Dining: The ship's two dining rooms (the Galaxy, forward, with windows on two sides, has 706 seats; the Universe, aft, with windows on three sides, has 1,090 seats); both are nonsmoking. Each spans two decks (a first for any Carnival ship), and incorporates a dozen pyramid-shaped domes and chandeliers, and a mellow, peachy color scheme. The Universe dining room features a two-deck-high wall of glass overlooking the sternwith tables for four, six, and eight (and a few tables for two that the line tries to keep for honeymoon-ers). Dining is now in four seatings, for greater flexibility: approximately 6pm, 6:45pm, 8pm, and 8:45pm. Although the menu choice looks good, the actual cuisine delivered is adequate, but quite nonmemorable.

All ships also feature a serve-yourself casual Lido Buffet — for breakfast and lunch, although at dinner this turns into the Seaview Bistro for use as a casual alternative eatery — for those that do not want to dress to go to the formal dining rooms. These include specialty stations where you can order omelets, eggs, fajitas, chicken Caesar salad, pasta, and stir-fry items. And, if you are still hungry — there's always a midnight buffet around the corner!

Carnival meals stress quantity, not quality, although the company constantly works hard to improve the cuisine. While passengers seem to accept it, few find it worth remembering. However, food and its taste are still not the company's strongest points (you get what you pay for, remember).

While the menu items sound good, their presentation and taste leave much to be desired. While meats are of a high quality, fish and seafood is not. Presentation is simple, and few garnishes are used. Many meat and fowl dishes are disguised with gravies and sauces. The selection of fresh green vegetables, breads, rolls, cheeses, and fruits is limited, and there is too much use of canned fruit and jellied desserts. However, do remember that this is banquet catering, with all its attendant standardization and production cooking (it is, therefore, difficult to ask for anything remotely unusual or off-menu).

Although there is a decent wine list, there are no wine waiters (the waiters are expected to serve both food and wine), or decent sized wine glasses. However, the waiters do sing and dance (be prepared for "Hot, Hot, Hot" and "The Macarena" — again) and there are constant waiter parades; the dining room is show business — all done in the name of gratuities at the end of your cruise. If you like pizzas, this ship typically serves an average of over 800 pizzas every day.

The dining room entrances have comfortable drinking areas for pre-dinner cocktails. There are also many options for casual dining, particularly during the daytime. Two decks high is the Sun and Sea Restaurant, the ship's informal international food court-style eatery, which is adjacent to the aft pool and can be covered by a magrodome glass cover in inclement weather. Included in this eating mall are a Trattoria (for Italian cuisine, with made-to-order pasta dishes), Happy Valley (Chinese cuisine, with wok preparation), a 24-hour pizzeria, and a patisserie (extra charge for pastries), as well as a grill (for fast foods such as hamburgers and hot dogs). At night, the Seaview Bistro (as the Lido Café is known) provides a casual alternative to eating in the main dining rooms. It serves pasta, steaks, salads, and desserts.

Other Comments: *Carnival Destiny* is Carnival's 11th new ship in the past 15 success-filled years, and the first ship that is unable to transit the Panama Canal, due to her size. The ship has the trademark large wing-tipped funnel in the company colors of red, white, and blue.

She is quite a stunning ship, built to impress at every turn, and has the most balanced profile of all the ships in the Carnival fleet, although the bow is extremely short. Amidships on the open deck is the longest water slide at sea (200 ft/61 m in length), as well as tiered sunbathing decks positioned between two swimming pools and several hot tubs. As aboard all Carnival ships, there is a "topless" sunbathing area set around the funnel base (can't be seen from the pool deck below).

Inside, Joe Farcus, the interior designer who has designed all of the ship interiors for Carnival Cruise Lines, has outdone himself, but tastefully so. The decor is superb, and a fantasy land for the senses (though nowhere near as glitzy as the *Fantasy*-class ships). The layout is logical, so finding your way around is easy.

There are three decks full of lounges, ten bars, and lots of rooms to play in. Like her smaller (though still large) predecessors, this ship features a doublewide indoor promenade, nine-deck-high, glass-domed rotunda atrium lobby, and a large (15,000 sq ft /1,393.5 sq m) Nautica Spa. The three-level (nonsmoking) Palladium Showlounge is stunning, and features a revolving stage, hydraulic orchestra pit, superb sound, and seating on three levels (the upper levels being tiered through two decks). There is a proscenium over the stage that acts as a scenery loft (there are two large-scaled Vegas-style razzle-dazzle production shows each cruise). For those that like to gamble, the Millionaire's Club Casino is certainly large and action-packed. There are also more than 320 slot machines.

An additional feature that this ship has which the *Fantasy*-class ships do not have is the Flagship Bar, located in the Rotunda (atrium), which faces forward to glass-walled elevators. Another new (for Carnival) feature is the sports bar (All Star Bar); with tables that feature sports memorabilia.

Children are provided with good facilities, including their own two-level Children's Club (including an outdoor pool), and are well cared for with "Camp Carnival," the line's extensive children's program.

From the viewpoint of safety, passengers can embark directly into the lifeboats from their secured position without having to wait for them to be lowered, thus saving time in the event of a real emergency.

However, this is a large ship, with lots of people everywhere, and that means some waiting in lines, particularly for shore excursions, buffets, embarkation, and disembarkation (although the port of Miami has greatly improved terminal facilities specifically for this ship, with some 90 check-in desks). It also means a very impersonal cruise experience. For such a large ship, there really is not much open deck space per passenger; so on any sea days you can expect some crowding.

This ship is one of the great floating playgrounds for young, active adults who enjoy constant stimulation, close contact with lots and lots of others, as well as the three Gs — glitz, glamour, and gambling that

191

together amount to Splash Vegas. It is a live board game with every move executed in typically grand, colorful, fun-filled Carnival Cruise Lines style. This is also a fine vessel for large incentive groups! Potential passengers of other nationalities should note that this is definitely an all-American experience and product, with all its attendant glitz and jazzy/rock sounds — a real "life on the ocean rave." Forget fashion — having fun is the sine qua non of a Carnival cruise. Gratuities can be prepaid. Sister ships include *Carnival Triumph* and *Carnival Victory*, with *Carnival Conquest* also set to join the fleet in late 2002.

Weak Points: The terraced pool deck is really cluttered, and there are no cushioned pads for the deck chairs. Getting away from people and noise is difficult. The Photo Gallery, adjacent to the atrium/purser's office, becomes extremely congested when photos are on display. Standing in line for embarkation, disembarkation, shore tenders, and for self-serve buffet meals is an inevitable aspect of cruising aboard all large ships. There is absolutely no escape from unnecessary and repetitive announcements (particularly for activities that bring revenue, such as art auctions, bingo, horse racing) that intrude constantly into your cruise, and a great deal of hustling for drinks, although it is sometimes done with a knowing smile.

Carnival Pride

Large Ship:	88,500 tons	Cabins (wheelchair accessible):	16
Lifestyle:	Standard	Cabin Current:	110-volt
Cruise Line:	Carnival Cruise Lines	Full-Service Dining Rooms:	1
Former Names:	-	Elevators:	12
Builder:	Kvaerner Masa-Yards	Casino (gaming tables):	Yes
Original Cost:	$375 million	Slot Machines	Yes
Entered Service:	April 2002	Swimming Pools (outdoors):	2+1 children's pool
Registry:	Panama	Swimming Pools (indoors):	1 (indoor/outdoor)
Length (ft/m):	959.6/292.5	Whirlpools:	5
Beam (ft/m):	105.6/32.2	Fitness Center:	Yes
Draft (ft/m):	25.5/7.8	Sauna/Steam Room:	Yes/Yes
Propulsion/Propellers:	Diesel-electric (34,000kW)/2	Massage:	Yes
Passenger Decks:	12	Self-Service Launderette:	Yes
Total Crew:	1,029	Dedicated Cinema:	No
Passengers (lower beds/all berths):	2,124/2,667	Library:	Yes
Pass. Space Ratio (lower beds/all berths):	41.6/33.1	Classification Society:	Registro Navale Italiano
Crew/Pass. Ratio (lower beds/all berths):	2.2/2.8		
Navigation Officers:	Italian		
Cabins (total):	1,062	**OVERALL SCORE: NOT YET RATED**	
Size Range (sq ft/sq m):	185.0–490.0/17.1–45.5		
Cabins (outside view):	849	Note that this ship had not entered service when this	
Cabins (interior/no view):	213	book was completed. However, the score is expect-	
Cabins (for one person):	0	ed to be very similar to that of *Carnival Spirit*.	
Cabins (with private balcony):	682		

Accommodation: There are 20 accommodation price categories to choose from. The range of accommo-dation includes suites (with private balcony), outside-view cabins with private balcony, 68 ocean-view cabins with French doors (pseudo-balconies that have doors that open, but no balcony to step out onto), and a healthy proportion of standard outside-view to interior (no view) cabins. A gift basket of personal amenities is now provided in all grades of accommodation; it includes aloe soap, shampoo, conditioner, deodorant, breath mints, candy, and pain relief tablets.

All of the cabins feature twin beds that can be converted into a queen-size bed, individually controlled air-conditioning, TV, and telephone. A number of cabins on the lowest accommodation deck have views that are obstructed by lifeboats.

Some of the most desirable suites and cabins are those with private balconies on five of the aft-facing decks; these feature views overlooking the stern and ship's wash. You should note, however, that even the largest suites are extremely small when compared with suites aboard other ships of a similar size (for example, Celebrity Cruises' *Infinity, Millennium, Summit*). Carnival Cruise Lines has fallen behind in the move to larger living spaces, and, with this ship, has lost an opportunity to provide more space for those seeking it.

Dining: In a departure from previous ships (of the *Destiny* and *Fantasy* class), this ship features a single large, two-decks-high main dining room called the Normandie Restaurant, (the galley is located under-neath the restaurant, accessed by escalators). There are tables for two, four, six, or eight. Dining is in four seatings, for greater flexibility: 6pm, 6:45pm, 8pm, and 8:45pm (these times are approximate).

Carnival meals stress quantity, not quality, although the company constantly works hard to improve the cuisine. While passengers seem to accept it, few find it worth remembering. However, food and its taste are still not the company's strongest points (you get what you pay for, remember).

While the menu items sound good, their presentation and taste leave much to be desired. While meats are of a high quality, fish and seafood is not. Presentation is simple, and few garnishes are used. Many meat and fowl dishes are disguised with gravies and sauces. The selection of fresh green vegetables, breads, rolls, cheeses, and fruits is limited, and there is too much use of canned fruit and jellied desserts. However, do remember that this is banquet catering, with all its attendant standardization and production cooking (it is, therefore, difficult to ask for anything remotely unusual or off-menu).

Although there is a decent wine list, there are no wine waiters (the waiters are expected to serve both food and wine). The service is quite robotic, closely timed, highly programmed, and inflexible, although the waiters are willing and reasonably friendly. However, the waiters do sing and dance (be prepared for "Hot, Hot, Hot" and "The Macarena" — again) and there are constant waiter parades; the dining room is show business — all done in the name of gratuities at the end of your cruise.

For casual eaters, there is the extensive Pizzeria and Mermaid's Grille, which form an eatery that wraps around the funnel housing and extends aft with great views over the multideck atrium.

There is also an alternative, more upscale dining spot atop the ship, with just 156 seats. It is called David's Supper Club, complete with show kitchen where chefs can be seen preparing their masterpieces, and is located on two of the uppermost decks of the ship, above the Pizzeria and Mermaid's Grille. This eatery has fine table settings, china, and silverware, as well as leather bound menus, and it features crab claws — supplied by famed Joe's Stone Crabs of South Miami Beach. Reservations are required and there is a $15 cover (service/gratuity) charge. A connoisseur's wine list is also available (typically including such nice wines as Opus One and Chateau Lafite-Rothschild).

Other Comments: *Carnival Pride* (sister ship to *Carnival Spirit*) is the 17th new ship for Carnival Cruise Lines — the giant of the cruise industry. The ship has Carnival's trademark large wing-tipped funnel in the company's American red, white, and blue colors. The first thing that regular passengers will notice is the extreme length of this ship — longer than the company's larger trio (*Carnival Destiny, Carnival Triumph, Carnival Victory*), and only a hair's-breadth shorter than Cunard Line's *Queen Elizabeth 2* (which the Carnival Corporation, Carnival Cruise Lines' parent company, owns). The new design makes the ship look much more sleek than any other in the Carnival Cruise Lines fleet (except for sister *Carnival Spirit*) — a process of continuing ship design and evolvement.

When you first walk into the ship, you'll be greeted by the immense size of a dramatic lobby space that spans eight decks. The atrium lobby presents a stunning wall decoration that is best seen from any of the multiple viewing balconies on each deck above the main lobby floor level. Take a drink from the lobby bar and look upwards — the surroundings are simply stunning.

There are two whole entertainment/public room decks, the upper of which also features an exterior promenade deck — something new for this fun cruise line. Although it doesn't go around the whole ship, it's long enough to do some serious walking. Additionally, there is also a jogging track outdoors, located around the ship's mast and the forward third of the ship.

Without doubt, the most dramatic room aboard this ship is the show lounge. It spans four decks in the forward section of the ship. The main floor level, which is called Butterflies Lounge, has a bar in its starboard aft section, while the upper three levels are called the Taj Mahal Showlounge. Spiral stairways at the back of the lounge connect all levels. Stage shows are best seen from the upper three levels, from where the sight lines are reasonably good.

A small wedding chapel is located forward of the uppermost level of the two main entertainment decks (a new feature for Carnival Cruise Lines). Other facilities include a winding shopping street with several boutique stores (including all the usual logo items), photo gallery, video games room, an observation balcony in the center of the vessel (at the top of the multideck atrium), and a large casino.

A large, two-decks-high health spa — called the Body Beautiful Spa — is located directly above the navigation bridge. Facilities include a solarium, eight treatment rooms, sauna and steam rooms for men and women, a beauty parlor, and a large gymnasium with floor-to-ceiling windows on three sides, including forward-facing ocean views.

There are two centrally located swimming pools outdoors, and one of the pools can be used in inclement weather due to its retractable magrodome (glass dome) cover. Two whirlpool tubs, located adjacent to the swimming pools, are abridged by a bar. Another smaller pool is available for children; it incorporates a winding water slide that spans two decks in height. There is also an additional whirlpool tub outdoors.

In this ship, Carnival Cruise Lines has installed its "tele-radiology" system that enables shipboard physicians to digitally transmit X-rays and other patient information to shore-side facilities — useful for peace of mind for passengers and crew.

However, this is another large ship, with lots of people everywhere, and that means some waiting in line, particularly for shore excursions, buffets, embarkation, and disembarkation (although the port of Miami now has greatly improved terminal facilities). It also means a very impersonal cruise experience. For such a large ship, there really is not much open deck space per passenger; so on any sea days you can expect some crowding.

This ship is a great floating playground for young, active adults who enjoy constant stimulation, close contact with lots and lots of others, as well as the three Gs — glitz, glamour, and gambling. It is a live board game with every move executed in typically grand, colorful, fun-filled Carnival Cruise Lines style. It could also prove to be an interesting vessel for large incentive groups. Potential passengers of other nationalities should note that this is definitely an all-American experience and product, with all its attendant glitz and jazzy/rock sounds — a real "life on the ocean rave." Forget fashion — having fun is the sine qua non of a Carnival cruise.

Carnival Pride is based in Port Canaveral for year-round seven-day cruises. This is the first ship in the Carnival Cruise Lines fleet to call at a "private" island. Note that gratuities can be prepaid, and soft-drinks packages can be purchased for adults and children.

Weak Points: The information desk in the lobby is far too small. There is simply not enough outdoors space for all those deck lounge chairs and suntan-oiled bodies. It is difficult to escape from noise and loud music, not to mention smokers, and masses of people walking around in unsuitable clothing and clutching plastic sport drinks bottles, at any time of the day or night. Many of the private balconies are not so private, and can be overlooked from various public locations.

There are far too many pillars obstructing passenger flow and sight lines throughout the ship; pillars are everywhere. Indeed, the many pillars in the dining room make it extremely difficult for the waiters and the proper service of food. Standing in line for embarkation, disembarkation, shore tenders, and for self-serve buffet meals is an inevitable aspect of cruising aboard all large ships. There is absolutely no escape from unnecessary and repetitious announcements (particularly for activities that bring revenue, such as art auctions, bingo, horse racing) that intrude constantly into your cruise, and a great deal of hustling for drinks, although it is sometimes done with a knowing smile.

Carnival Spirit
★★★★

Large Ship:	88,500 tons	Cabins (for one person):	0
Lifestyle:	Standard	Cabins (with private balcony):	682
Cruise Line:	Carnival Cruise Lines	Cabins (wheelchair accessible):	16
Former Names:	-	Cabin Current:	110-volt
Builder:	Kvaerner Masa-Yards	Full-Service Dining Rooms:	1
Original Cost:	$375 million	Elevators:	12
Entered Service:	April 2001	Casino (gaming tables):	Yes
Registry:	Panama	Slot Machines	Yes
Length (ft/m):	959.6/292.5	Swimming Pools (outdoors):	2 +1 children's pool
Beam (ft/m):	105.6/32.2	Swimming Pools (indoors)	1 (indoor/outdoor)
Draft (ft/m):	25.5/7.8	Whirlpools:	5
Propulsion/Propellers:	Diesel-electric	Fitness Center:	Yes
(34,000kW)/2/azimuthing pods (17.6MW each)		Sauna/Steam Room:	Yes/Yes
Passenger Decks:	12	Massage:	Yes
Total Crew:	930	Self-Service Launderette:	Yes
Passengers (lower beds/all berths):	2,124/2,667	Dedicated Cinema:	No
Pass. Space Ratio (lower beds/all berths):	41.6/33.1	Library:	Yes
Crew/Pass. Ratio (lower beds/all berths):	2.2/2.8	Classification Society:	Registro Navale Italiano
Navigation Officers:	Italian		
Cabins (total):	1,062		
Size Range (sq ft/sq m):	185.0–490.0/17.1–45.5	**OVERALL SCORE:**	**1,469**
Cabins (outside view):	849		
Cabins (interior/no view):	231	**(OUT OF A POSSIBLE 2,000 POINTS)**	

Accommodation: There are 20 accommodation price categories to choose from. The range of accommodation includes suites (with private balcony), outside-view cabins with private balcony, 68 ocean view cabins with French doors (pseudo-balconies that have doors which open, but no balcony to step out onto), and a healthy proportion of standard outside-view to interior (no view) cabins. A gift basket of personal amenities is now provided in all grades of accommodation; it includes aloe soap, shampoo, conditioner, deodorant, breath mints, candy, and pain relief tablets.

Regardless of the grade of accommodation chosen, all cabins feature twin beds that can be converted into a queen-sized bed, individually controlled air-conditioning, television, and telephone. A number of cabins on the lowest accommodation deck have views that are obstructed by lifeboats.

Some of the most desirable suites and cabins are those with private balconies on five of the aft-facing decks; these feature views overlooking the stern and ship's wash. You should note, however, that even the largest suites are extremely small when compared with suites aboard other ships of a similar size (for example, Celebrity Cruises' *Infinity, Millennium, Summit*). Carnival Cruise Lines has fallen behind in the move to larger living spaces, and, with this ship, has lost an opportunity to provide more space for those seeking it.

Dining: In a departure from previous ships (of the *Destiny* and *Fantasy* class), this ship features a single, large, two-decks-high main dining room called the Empire Restaurant, (the galley is located underneath the restaurant, accessed by escalators). There are tables for two, four, six or eight, and the decor is heavily Napoleonic (early 19th century French) style. Dining is now in four seatings, for greater flexibility: 6pm, 6:45pm, 8pm, and 8:45pm (these times are approximate).

Carnival meals stress quantity, not quality, although the company constantly works hard to improve the cuisine. While passengers seem to accept it, few find it worth remembering. However, food and its taste are still not the company's strongest points (you get what you pay for, remember).

Carnival meals stress quantity, not quality, although the company constantly works hard to improve the cuisine. While passengers seem to accept it, few find it worth remembering. However, food and its taste are still not the company's strongest points (you get what you pay for, remember).

While the menu items sound good, their presentation and taste leave much to be desired. While meats are of a high quality, fish and seafood is not. Presentation is simple, and few garnishes are used. Many meat and fowl dishes are disguised with gravies and sauces. The selection of fresh green vegetables, breads, rolls, cheeses and fruits is limited, and there is too much use of canned fruit and jellied desserts. However, do remember that this is banquet catering, with all its attendant standardization and production cooking (it is, therefore, difficult to ask for anything remotely unusual or off-menu). The selection of breads, rolls, cheeses and fruits is limited (there is too much use of canned fruit).

Although there is a decent wine list, there are no wine waiters (the waiters are expected to serve both food and wine). The service is quite robotic, closely timed, highly programmed, and inflexible, although the waiters are willing and reasonably friendly. However, the waiters do sing and dance (be prepared for "Hot, Hot, Hot" and "The Macarena" — again) and there are constant waiter parades. To Carnival, the dining room is pure show business — all done in the name of gratuities at the end of your cruise.

For casual eaters, while there is no lido café, there is the extensive Pizzeria and La Playa Grille, which form an eatery that wraps around the funnel housing and extends aft with great views over the multideck atrium.

There is also an alternative, more upscale dining spot atop the ship — another first for Carnival Cruise Lines. It is the 156-seat Nouveau Supper Club, complete with show kitchen where chefs can be seen preparing their masterpieces, and is located on two of the uppermost decks of the ship, above the Pizzeria and La Playa Grille. This eatery features fine table settings, china and silverware, as well as leather bound menus, and it features crab claws — supplied by famed Joe's Stone Crabs of South Miami Beach, as well as prime steaks (be prepared for huge cuts of meat). The decor features a floral pattern as well as a stained glass balcony on the upper level, and, in addition, has a stage and dance floor. Reservations are required and there is a $15 cover (service/gratuity) charge. A connoisseur's wine list is also available (typically including such nice wines as Opus One and Chateau Lafite-Rothschild).

Other Comments: *Carnival Spirit* is the 16th new ship for Carnival Cruise Lines — the giant of the cruise industry. This ship also features Carnival's trademark large wing-tipped funnel in the Miami-based company's red, white, and blue colors. The first thing that regular passengers will notice is the extreme length of this ship — longer than the company's larger trio (*Carnival Destiny, Carnival Triumph, Carnival Victory*), and only a hair's-breadth shorter than Cunard Line's *Queen Elizabeth 2* (which the Carnival Corporation, Carnival Cruise Lines' parent company, owns). The new design makes the ship look much more sleek than any other in the Carnival Cruise Lines fleet — a process of continuing ship design and evolvement. What's new for this ship is the pod propulsion system, which gives the ship more maneuverability, while reducing required machinery space and vibration at the stern.

There are two centrally located swimming pools outdoors, and one of the pools can be used in inclement weather due to its retractable magrodome (glass dome) cover. Two whirlpool tubs, located adjacent to the swimming pools, are abridged by a bar. Another smaller pool is available for children; it incorporates a winding water slide that spans two decks in height. There is also an additional whirlpool tub outdoors.

When you first walk into the ship, you'll be greeted by the immense size of the dramatic lobby space that spans eight decks. The atrium lobby, with its two grand stairways, presents a stunning wall decoration that is best seen from any of the multiple viewing balconies on each deck above the main lobby floor level. Take a drink from the lobby bar and look upwards — the surroundings are simply stunning.

There are two whole entertainment/public room decks, the upper of which also features an exterior promenade deck — something new for this fun cruise line. Although it doesn't go around the whole ship, it's long enough to do some serious walking on. Additionally, there is also a jogging track outdoors, located around the ship's mast and the forward third of the ship.

Without doubt, the most dramatic room aboard this ship is the show lounge. It spans four decks in the forward section of the ship. The main floor level, which is called Versailles Lounge, has a bar in its starboard aft section, while the upper three levels are called Pharaoh's Palace. Spiral stairways at the back of the lounge connect all levels. Stage shows are best seen from the upper three levels, from where the sight lines are reasonably good. Other facilities include a winding shopping street with several boutique stores and logo shops.

A small wedding chapel (a new feature for Carnival Cruise Lines) is located forward of the uppermost level of the two main entertainment decks, and decorated in Gothic style; it also has a bride's room with dressing area. Other facilities include a winding shopping street with several boutique stores (including all the usual logo items), photo gallery, video games room, an observation balcony in the center of the vessel (at the top of the multideck atrium), a large casino, and a piano lounge (with Chinese decor).

The casino is large (one has to walk through it to get from the restaurant to the show lounge on one of the entertainments decks), and is equipped with all the gaming paraphernalia and array of slot machines you can think of. Make no mistake about it this is Splash Vegas — and then some!

A large, two-decks-high health spa — called the Roman Spa — is located directly above the navigation bridge. Facilities include a solarium, eight treatment rooms, sauna and steam rooms for men and women, a beauty parlor, and a large gymnasium with floor-to-ceiling windows on three sides, including forward-facing ocean views.

With this ship, Carnival Cruise Lines has introduced its "tele-radiology" system that enables shipboard physicians to digitally transmit X-rays and other patient information to shore-side facilities — useful for peace of mind for passengers and crew.

However, this is another large ship, with lots of people everywhere, and that means some waiting in line, particularly for shore excursions, buffets, embarkation and disembarkation (although the port of Miami now has greatly improved terminal facilities). It also means a very impersonal cruise experience. For such a large ship, there really is not much open deck space per passenger; so on any sea days you can expect much crowding and noise.

This ship is a floating playground for young, active adults who enjoy lots of stimulation, close contact with lots and lots of others, as well as the three Gs — glitz, glamour, and gambling — in other words, Splash Vegas. It is a live board game with every move executed in typically grand, colorful, fun-filled Carnival Cruise Lines style. *Carnival Spirit* could prove to be an interesting vessel for large incentive groups. Potential passengers of other nationalities should note that this is definitely an all-American experience and product, with all its attendant glitz and jazzy/rock sounds — a real "life on the ocean rave." Forget fashion — having fun is the sine qua non of a Carnival cruise. Note that gratuities can be prepaid, and soft-drinks packages can be purchased for adults and children.

Weak Points: The information desk in the lobby is far too small. There is simply not enough outdoors space for all those deck lounge chairs and suntan-oiled bodies. It is difficult to escape from noise and loud music, not to mention smokers, and masses of people walking around in unsuitable clothing and clutching plastic sport drinks bottles, at any time of the day or night. Many of the private balconies are not so private, and can be overlooked from various public locations.

There are far too many pillars obstructing passenger flow and sight lines throughout the ship; pillars are everywhere. Indeed, the many pillars in the dining room make it extremely difficult for the waiters and the proper service of food. Standing in line for embarkation, disembarkation, shore tenders and for self-serve buffet meals is an inevitable aspect of cruising aboard all large ships. There is absolutely no escape from unnecessary and repetitious announcements (particularly for activities that bring revenue, such as art auctions, bingo, horse racing) that intrude constantly into your cruise, and a great deal of hustling for drinks, although it is sometimes done with a knowing smile.

Carnival Triumph
★★★★

Large Ship:	101,509 tons	Cabins (for one person):	0
Lifestyle:	Standard	Cabins (with private balcony):	508
Cruise Line:	Carnival Cruise Lines	Cabins (wheelchair accessible):	25
Former Names:	-	Cabin Current:	110-volt
Builder:	Fincantieri (Italy)	Full-Service Dining Rooms:	2
Original Cost:	$420 million	Elevators:	18
Entered Service:	October 1999	Casino (gaming tables):	Yes
Registry:	Bahamas	Slot Machines:	Yes
Length (ft/m):	893.0/272.2	Swimming Pools (outdoors): 3 (+1 with magrodome)	
Beam (ft/m):	116.0/35.3	Swimming Pools (indoors):	0
Draft (ft/m):	27.0/8.2	Whirlpools:	7
Propulsion/Propellers:	Diesel-electric	Fitness Center:	Yes
(34,000kW)/2/azimuthing pods (17.6MW each)		Sauna/Steam Room:	Yes/Yes
Passenger Decks:	13	Massage:	Yes
Total Crew:	1,150	Self-Service Launderette:	Yes
Passengers (lower beds/all berths):	2,758/3,473	Dedicated Cinema:	No
Pass. Space Ratio (lower beds/all berths): 36.8/29.2		Library:	Yes
Crew/Pass. Ratio (lower beds/all berths):	2.3/3.0	Classification Society:	Lloyd's Register
Navigation Officers:	Italian		
Cabins (total):	1,379		
Size Range (sq ft/sq m):	179.7–482.2/16.7–44.8	**OVERALL SCORE:**	**1,455**
Cabins (outside view):	853	(OUT OF A POSSIBLE 2,000 POINTS)	
Cabins (interior/no view):	526		

Accommodation: Over half of all cabins are outside (and at 225 sq ft/21 sq m they are the largest in the standard market). They are spread over four decks and have private balconies (with glass rather than steel balustrades, for better, unobstructed ocean views), with balconies extending from the ship's side. The balconies also feature bright fluorescent lighting.

The standard cabins are of good size and come equipped with all the basics, although the furniture is rather square and angular, with no rounded edges. Three decks of cabins (eight cabins on each deck, each with private balcony) overlook the stern.

Eight penthouse suites, each with a large balcony, are quite lavish in their appointments, although, at only 483 sq ft (44.8 sq m) are really quite small when compared to the best suites in many smaller ships. There are also 40 other suites, each of which features a decent-sized bathroom and a good amount of lounge space.

In the cabins with balconies (more cabins have balconies aboard this ship than those that do not), the partition between each balcony is open at top and bottom, so you may well hear noise from neighbors (or smell their cigarettes). It is disappointing to see three categories of cabins (both outside and interior) with upper and lower bunk beds (lower beds are far more preferable, but this is how the ship accommodates an extra 600 passengers over and above the lower bed capacity).

The cabins feature soft color schemes and more soft furnishings in more attractive fabrics than any other ship in the fleet. Interactive "Fun Vision" technology lets you choose movies on demand (and for a fee). The bathrooms, which have good-size showers, feature good storage space in the toiletries cabinet. A gift basket is now provided in all grades of accommodation; it includes aloe soap, shampoo, conditioner, deodorant, breath mints, candy, and pain relief tablets.

Dining: The ship's two dining rooms (the London, forward, with windows on two sides, has 706 seats; the Paris, aft, with windows on three sides, has 1,090 seats), and both are nonsmoking. Each dining room spans two decks, and incorporates a dozen domes and chandeliers. The Paris dining room features a two-deck-high wall of glass overlooking the stern. There are tables for four, six, and eight (and even a few tables for two that the line tries to keep for honeymooners).

Dining is now in four seatings, for greater flexibility: 6pm, 6:45pm, 8pm, and 8:45pm (these times are approximate). Although the menu choice looks good, the actual cuisine delivered is adequate, but quite nonmemorable.

All ships also feature a serve-yourself casual Lido Buffet — for breakfast and lunch, although at dinner this turns into the Seaview Bistro for use as a casual alternative eatery — for those that do not want to dress to go to the formal dining rooms. These include specialty stations where you can order omelets, eggs, fajitas, chicken Caesar salad, pasta, and stir-fry items. And, if you are still hungry — there's always a midnight buffet around the corner!

Carnival meals stress quantity, not quality, although the company constantly works hard to improve the cuisine. While passengers seem to accept it, few find it worth remembering. However, food and its taste are still not the company's strongest points (you get what you pay for, remember).

While the menu items sound good, their presentation and taste leave much to be desired. While meats are of a high quality, fish and seafood is not. Presentation is simple, and few garnishes are used. Many meat and fowl dishes are disguised with gravies and sauces. The selection of fresh green vegetables, breads, rolls, cheeses, and fruits is limited, and there is too much use of canned fruit and jellied desserts. However, do remember that this is banquet catering, with all its attendant standardization and production cooking (it is, therefore, difficult to ask for anything remotely unusual or off-menu).

Although there is a decent wine list, there are no wine waiters (the waiters are expected to serve both food and wine), or decent sized wine glasses. The service is quite robotic, closely timed, highly programmed, and inflexible, although the waiters are willing and reasonably friendly However, the waiters do sing and dance (be prepared for "Hot, Hot, Hot" and "The Macarena" — again) and there are constant waiter parades; the dining room is show business — all done in the name of gratuities at the end of your cruise. If you like pizzas, this ship typically serves an average of over 800 pizzas every day.

The dining room entrances have comfortable drinking areas for pre-dinner cocktails. There are also many options for casual dining, particularly during the daytime.

The South Beach Club is the ship's informal, international, self-serve buffet-style eatery, with seating on two levels. Included in this eatery are the New York Deli (typically open 11am to 11pm), and the Hong Kong Noodle Company (for Chinese cuisine, with wok preparation), and a 24-hour pizzeria.

There is also a grill for fast foods (such as grilled chicken, hamburgers, and hot dogs), and salad bar — all part of the poolside South Beach Club. In addition, there is a self-serve ice cream and frozen yogurt station (no extra charge).

At night, the South Beach Club turns into the Seaview Bistro and provides a casual alternative to eating in the main dining rooms. It serves pasta, steaks, salads, and desserts.

Other Comments: *Carnival Triumph* is Carnival Cruise Lines' 14th new ship in the Carnival fleet, and one of three ships in the company that is unable to transit the Panama Canal due to her size. The ship has the trademark large wing-tipped funnel in the company colors of red, white, and blue. The American talk show hostess, Rosie O'Donnell, named *Carnival Triumph*.

She is quite a stunning ship, built to impress at every turn, has the most balanced profile of all the ships in the Carnival Cruise Lines fleet, although the bow itself is extremely short. Amidships on the open deck is the longest water slide at sea (200 ft/61 m in length), as well as tiered sunbathing decks positioned between two swimming pools and several hot tubs. As aboard all Carnival ships, there is a "topless" sunbathing area set around the funnel base (can't be seen from the pool deck below). The Lido Deck space is more expansive than aboard sister ship *Carnival Destiny* (the swim-up bar has been eliminated), and the pool is larger.

Inside the ship, Joe Farcus, the interior designer who has designed all of the ship interiors for Carnival Cruise Lines, has outdone himself, but tastefully so. The ship is simply superb, and a fantasy land for the senses (though nowhere near as glitzy as the *Fantasy*-class ships). The layout is logical, so finding your way around is a fairly simple matter

There are three decks full of lounges, ten bars, and lots of rooms to play in. Like her smaller (though still large) predecessors, this ship features a doublewide indoor promenade, nine-deck-high, glass-domed rotunda atrium lobby, and a huge (15,000 sq ft /1,393.5 sq m) Nautica Spa. The three-level (nonsmoking) Rome Showlounge is stunning, and features a revolving stage, hydraulic orchestra pit, superb sound, and seating on three levels (the upper levels are tiered through two decks). There is a proscenium over the stage that acts as a scenery loft (there are two large-scaled Vegas-like razzle-dazzle production shows each cruise). For those that like to gamble, the Club Monaco is certainly a large (and noisy) casino; there are also more than 320 slot machines.

An additional feature that this ship has, which the *Fantasy*-class ships do not have, is the Flagship bar, located in the Rotunda (atrium). It faces forward to the glass-walled elevators. A sports bar (Olympic Bar) has tables that feature sports memorabilia.

Children are provided with good facilities, including their own two-level Children's Club (including an outdoor pool), and are well cared for with "Camp Carnival," the line's extensive children's program.

For safety reasons, passengers will be able to embark directly into the lifeboats in their secured position without having to wait for them to be lowered, thus saving time in the event of a real emergency. Well done.

However, this certainly is a big ship, with lots of people everywhere, and that means some waiting in line, particularly for shore excursions, buffets, embarkation and disembarkation (although the port of Miami has greatly improved terminal facilities specifically for this ship, with some 90 check-in desks). It also means a very impersonal cruise experience. For such a large ship, there really is not much open deck space per passenger; so on any sea days you can expect crowding.

This ship is one of the great floating playgrounds for young, active adults who enjoy constant stimulation, close contact with lots and lots of others, as well as the three Gs — glitz, glamour, and gambling that together amount to Splash Vegas. It is a live board game with every move executed in typically grand, colorful, fun-filled Carnival Cruise Lines style. It is a fine vessel for large incentive groups! Potential passengers of other nationalities should note that this is definitely an all-American experience and product, with all its attendant glitz and jazzy/rock sounds — a real "life on the ocean rave." Forget fashion — having fun is the sine qua non of a Carnival cruise. Gratuities can be prepaid. Sister ships include *Carnival Destiny* and *Carnival Victory*, with *Carnival Conquest* also set to join the fleet in late 2002.

Weak Points: The terraced pool deck is really cluttered, and there are no cushioned pads for the deck chairs. Although the outdoor deck space has been improved, there is still much crowding when the ship is full and at sea. Getting away from people and noise is difficult. The Photo Gallery becomes extremely congested when photos are on display. Standing in line for embarkation, disembarkation, shore tenders, and for self-serve buffet meals is an inevitable aspect of cruising aboard all large ships. There is absolutely no escape from unnecessary and repetitive announcements (particularly for activities that bring revenue, such as art auctions, bingo, horse racing) that intrude constantly into your cruise, and a great deal of hustling for drinks, although it is sometimes done with a knowing smile.

Carnival Victory
★★★★

Large Ship:	101,509 tons	Cabins (for one person):	0
Lifestyle:	Standard	Cabins (with private balcony):	508
Cruise Line:	Carnival Cruise Lines	Cabins (wheelchair accessible):	25
Former Names:	-	Cabin Current:	110-volt
Builder:	Fincantieri (Italy)	Full-Service Dining Rooms:	2
Original Cost:	$410 million	Elevators:	18
Entered Service:	August 2000	Casino (gaming tables):	Yes
Registry:	Panama	Slot Machines:	Yes
Length (ft/m):	893.0/272.2	Swimming Pools (outdoors):	3 (+1 with magrodome)
Beam (ft/m):	116.0/35.3	Swimming Pools (indoors):	0
Draft (ft/m):	27.0/8.2	Whirlpools:	7
Propulsion/Propellers:	Diesel-electric	Fitness Center:	Yes
(34,000kW)/2azimuthing pods 17.6MW each		Sauna/Steam Room:	Yes/Yes
Passenger Decks:	13	Massage:	Yes
Total Crew:	1,150	Self-Service Launderette:	Yes
Passengers (lower beds/all berths):	2,758/3,473	Dedicated Cinema:	No
Pass. Space Ratio (lower beds/all berths):	36.8/29.2	Library:	Yes
Crew/Pass. Ratio (lower beds/all berths):	2.3/3.0	Classification Society:	Lloyd's Register
Navigation Officers:	Italian		
Cabins (total):	1,379		
Size Range (sq ft/sq m):	179.7–482.2/16.7–44.8	**OVERALL SCORE:**	**1,455**
Cabins (outside view):	853		
Cabins (interior/no view):	526	**(OUT OF A POSSIBLE 2,000 POINTS)**	

Accommodation: Over half of all cabins are outside (and at 225 sq ft/21 sq m they are the largest in the standard market). They are spread over four decks and have private balconies (with glass rather than steel balustrades, for better, unobstructed ocean views), with balconies extending from the ship's side. The balconies also feature bright fluorescent lighting.

The standard cabins are of good size and come equipped with all the basics, although the furniture is rather square and angular, with no rounded edges. Three decks of cabins (eight on each deck, each with private balcony) overlook the stern (with three days at sea on each of two alternating itineraries, vibration is kept to a minimum).

Eight penthouse suites, each with a large balcony, are lavish in their appointments, although, at only 483 sq ft (44.8 sq m), they really are quite small when compared to the best suites in many smaller ships. There are also 40 other suites, each of which features a decent-sized bathroom, and a good amount of lounge space.

In cabins with balconies (more cabins have balconies aboard this ship than those that do not), the partition between each balcony is open at the top and bottom, so you may well hear noise from neighbors (or smell their cigarettes). It is disappointing to see three categories of cabins (both outside and interior) with upper and lower bunk beds (lower beds are far more preferable, but this is how the ship accommodates an extra 600 passengers over and above the lower bed capacity).

The cabins feature soft color schemes and more soft furnishings in more attractive fabrics than any other ship in the fleet. Interactive "Fun Vision" technology lets you choose movies on demand (and for a fee). The bathrooms, which have good-size showers, feature good storage space in the toiletries cabinet. A gift basket is now provided in all grades of accommodation; it includes aloe soap, shampoo, conditioner, deodorant, breath mints, candy, and pain relief tablets.

Dining: The ship's two dining rooms (the Atlantic, forward, with windows on two sides, has 706 seats; the Pacific, aft, with windows on three sides, has 1,090 seats), and both are nonsmoking. Each dining room spans two decks, and incorporates a dozen domes and chandeliers. The Pacific dining room features a two-deck-high wall of glass overlooking the stern. There are tables for four, six and eight (and even a few tables for two that the line tries to keep for honeymooners). Dining is now in four seatings, for greater flexibility: 6pm, 6:45pm, 8pm, and 8:45pm (these times are approximate). Although the menu choice looks good, the actual cuisine delivered is adequate, but quite nonmemorable.

All ships also feature serve-yourself casual buffets — for breakfast and lunch, although at dinner this turns into the Seaview Bistro for use as a casual alternative eatery — for those that do not want to dress to go to the formal dining rooms. These include specialty stations where you can order omelets, eggs, fajitas, chicken Caesar salad, pasta, and stir-fry items. And, if you are still hungry — there's always a midnight buffet around the corner!

Carnival meals stress quantity, not quality, although the company constantly works hard to improve the cuisine. While passengers seem to accept it, few find it worth remembering. However, food and its taste are still not the company's strongest points (you get what you pay for, remember).

While the menu items sound good, their presentation and taste leave much to be desired. While meats are of a high quality, fish and seafood is not. Presentation is simple, and few garnishes are used. Many meat and fowl dishes are disguised with gravies and sauces. The selection of fresh green vegetables, breads, rolls, cheeses, and fruits is limited, and there is too much use of canned fruit and jellied desserts. However, do remember that this is banquet catering, with all its attendant standardization and production cooking (it is, therefore, difficult to ask for anything remotely unusual or off-menu). If you like pizzas, this ship typically serves an average of over 800 pizzas every day.

Although there is a decent enough wine list, there are no wine waiters (the waiters are expected to serve both food and wine), or decent sized wine glasses. The service is quite robotic, closely timed, highly programmed, and inflexible, although the waiters are willing and reasonably friendly However, the waiters do sing and dance (be prepared for "Hot, Hot, Hot" and "The Macarena" — again) and there are constant waiter parades; the dining room is show business — all done in the name of gratuities at the end of your cruise.

The dining room entrances have comfortable drinking areas for pre-dinner cocktails. There are also many options for casual dining, particularly during the daytime.

The Mediterranean Restaurant is the ship's informal international self-serve buffet-style eatery, with seating on two levels. Included in this eatery are the East River Deli (a New York-style deli, open 11am to 11pm), the Yangtse Wok (for Chinese cuisine, with wok preparation), and a 24-hour pizzeria.

There is also the Mississippi Barbeque for grilled fast foods (such as grilled chicken, hamburgers, and hot dogs), and a salad bar. In addition, there is a self-serve ice cream and frozen yogurt station (no extra charge).

At night, the Mediterranean Restaurant turns into the Seaview Bistro and provides a casual alternative to eating in the main dining rooms, serving pasta, steaks, salads, and desserts.

Other Comments: This is Carnival Cruise Lines' 15th new ship, and one of three ships in the company that is unable to transit the Panama Canal due to her size. The ship has the trademark large wing-tipped funnel in the company colors of red, white, and blue.

She is quite a stunning ship, built to impress at every turn, has the most balanced profile of all the ships in the Carnival Cruise Lines fleet, although the bow itself is extremely short. Amidships on the open deck is the longest water slide at sea (200 ft/61 m in length), as well as tiered sunbathing decks positioned between two swimming pools and several hot tubs. As aboard all Carnival ships, there is a "topless" sunbathing area set around the funnel base (it cannot be seen from the pool deck below). The Lido Deck space is more expansive than aboard sister ship *Carnival Destiny* (the swim-up bar has been eliminated), and the pool is larger.

Inside the ship, Joe Farcus, who has designed all of the ship interiors for Carnival Cruise Lines, has outdone himself, but tastefully so. The ship's decor is a tribute to the oceans of the world (and nowhere near as glitzy as the *Fantasy*-class ships). Seahorses (no you can't race them), corals, and shells are found throughout the design. The layout is logical, so finding your way around is a fairly simple matter.

There are three decks full of lounges, ten bars, and lots of rooms to play in. Like her smaller (though still large) predecessors, this ship features a doublewide indoor promenade, nine-deck-high, glass-domed rotunda atrium lobby, and a huge (15,000 sq ft /1,393.5 sq m) Nautica Spa. The three-level (nonsmoking) Caribbean Showlounge is stunning, and features a revolving stage, hydraulic orchestra pit, superb sound, and seating on three levels (the upper levels being tiered through two decks). There is a proscenium over the stage that acts as a scenery loft (there are two large-scaled Vegas-style razzle-dazzle production shows each cruise). For those that like to gamble, the South China Sea Club is certainly a large (and noisy) casino; there are also more than 320 slot machines.

An additional feature that this ship has that the *Fantasy*-class ships do not have is the Capitol bar, located in the Rotunda (atrium), which faces forward to the glass-walled elevators and sits under the ten-deck-high atrium dome. A sports bar (Aegean Bar) has tables that feature sports memorabilia.

Children are provided with good facilities, including their own two-level Children's Club (including an outdoor pool), and are well cared for with "Camp Carnival," the line's extensive children's program.

From the viewpoint of safety, passengers will be able to embark directly into the lifeboats from their secured position without having to wait for them to be lowered, thus saving time in the event of a real emergency. Well done.

However, this certainly is a big ship, with lots of people everywhere, and that means some waiting in line, particularly for shore excursions, buffets, embarkation, and disembarkation (although the port of Miami has greatly improved terminal facilities specifically for this ship, with some 90 check-in desks). It also means a very impersonal cruise experience. For such a large ship, there really is not much open deck space per passenger; so on any sea days you can expect crowding.

This ship is one of the great floating playgrounds for young, active adults who enjoy constant stimulation, close contact with lots and lots of others, as well as the three Gs — glitz, glamour, and gambling that together amount to Splash Vegas. It is a live board game with every move executed in typically grand, colorful, fun-filled Carnival Cruise Lines style. It is a fine vessel for large incentive groups! Potential passengers of other nationalities should note that this is definitely an all-American experience and product, with all its attendant glitz and jazzy/rock sounds — a real "life on the ocean rave." Forget fashion — having fun is the sine qua non of a Carnival cruise. Gratuities can be prepaid. Sister ships include *Carnival Triumph* and *Carnival Spirit*, with *Carnival Conquest* also set to join the fleet in late 2002.

Weak Points: The terraced pool deck is really cluttered, and there are no cushioned pads for the deck chairs. Although the outdoor deck space has been improved, there is still much crowding when the ship is full and at sea. Getting away from people and noise is extremely difficult. The Photo Gallery becomes extremely congested when photos are on display. Standing in line for embarkation, disembarkation, shore tenders, and for self-serve buffet meals is an inevitable aspect of cruising aboard all large ships. There is absolutely no escape from unnecessary and repetitious announcements (particularly for activities that bring revenue, such as art auctions, bingo, horse racing) that intrude constantly into your cruise, and a great deal of hustling for drinks, although it is sometimes done with a knowing smile.

Caronia
★★★★ +

Mid-Size Ship:	24,492 tons	Cabins (for one person):	73
Lifestyle:	Luxury	Cabins (with private balcony):	25
Cruise Line:	Cunard Line	Cabins (wheelchair accessible):	4
Former Names:	*Vistafjord*	Cabin Current:	110-volt
Builder:	Swan, Hunter (UK)	Full-Service Dining Rooms:	1
Original Cost:	$35 million	Elevators:	6
Entered Service:	May 1973/May 1984	Casino (gaming tables):	Yes
Registry:	Great Britain	Slot Machines:	Yes
Length (ft/m):	626.9/191.09	Swimming Pools (outdoors):	1
Beam (ft/m):	82.1/25.05	Swimming Pools (indoors):	1
Draft (ft/m):	27.0/8.23	Whirlpools:	2
Propulsion/Propellers:	Diesel (17,900kW)/2	Fitness Center:	Yes
Passenger Decks:	9	Sauna/Steam Room:	Yes/No
Total Crew:	400	Massage:	Yes
Passengers (lower beds/all berths):	679/732	Self-Service Launderette:	Yes
Pass. Space Ratio (lower beds/all berths):	36.0/33.4	Dedicated Cinema/Seats:	Yes/190
Crew/Pass. Ratio (lower beds/all berths):	1.6/1.8	Library:	Yes
Navigation Officers:	British	Classification Society:	Lloyd's Register
Cabins (total):	376		
Size Range (sq ft/sq m):	66.7–871.9/6.2–81.0	**OVERALL SCORE:**	**1,649**
Cabins (outside view):	324		
Cabins (interior/no view):	52	**(OUT OF A POSSIBLE 2,000 POINTS)**	

Accommodation: According to the brochure, there are 16 cabin categories (four of which are for single travelers wanting a cabin for themselves), from duplex penthouse suites with huge private balconies, to small interior (no view) cabins, in a wide range of different configurations.

The grandest accommodation can be found in two duplex apartments (Caronia Suite and Saxonia Suite). They are really excellent living spaces and occupy two levels. The lower level features a large bedroom and marble-clad bathroom with whirlpool bathtub. The upper level features an expansive living room with floor-to-ceiling windows with expansive, unobstructed front and side views, top-of-the-line sound system, treadmill, private bar, and a large bathroom (with whirlpool bathtub) and separate private sauna. There is a huge, very private balcony outdoors on deck, complete with a two-person hot tub and great views. A private internal stairway connects the upper and lower levels.

Most other accommodation (on Bridge Deck lower level, and Sun Deck) designated as suites have private balconies, are very nicely equipped, and have ample closet and drawer space (some also have a large walk-in closet), vanity desk, large beds, and a couple of bookshelves filled with suitable destination books. The marble-clad bathrooms are large and feature a full-size whirlpool bathtub, two washbasins, toilet, and bidet.

All other cabins are extremely well appointed and tastefully redecorated (all had new bathrooms installed in a 1994 refit), and all feature a refrigerator, minibar, personal safe, European duvets (in two thicknesses), and thick 100% cotton bathrobes. All the wooden furniture has nicely rounded edges. All feature a good amount of closet and drawer space (the closets are illuminated), and a VCR. The bathrooms feature a whisper-quiet (non-vacuum) toilet.

This ship also has an excellent range of cabins for single travelers. Some Sun Deck and Promenade Deck suites have obstructed views. Note however that the smallest cabins really are quite small, with little room to move around.

Dining: The Franconia Dining Room is a grand, elegant room, and has been expanded for single-seating dining. There are tables for two, four, six or eight (there are more tables for two than almost any other cruise ship). This is because the company has recognized that a great number of its passengers are single.

Senior officers each host a table for dinner each evening. A main feature is single-waiter service in the best European tradition. The tables are a little close together, however, making it somewhat difficult for waiters to serve properly in some areas.

The ship features international cuisine offering the highest quality and variety of ingredients (there is an excellent variety of breads at every meal). A cold table is set for such things as breads and cheeses at lunchtime, and passengers can either help themselves or be served by a waiter. Salad items, many salad dressings, juices, and cheeses (a fine selection of more than 40 international cheeses) are always available. Plate service (where vegetables and entrees are set artistically on the main course plate) is provided. Extra vegetables can always be obtained on request. This is European-style service in the classic seagoing tradition. Waiters are well trained through a good onboard management structure.

Although tableside flambeaus cannot be done at individual tables, they are done in several central locations, and the waiters collect the finished product to take to their respective tables.

The chef has his favorites, but menus are not repeated, even on long voyages. Also, one of the good points about this and other ships in her class (five stars) is that, while the menus are very creative, you can order "off-menu" at any time and create your own delightful cuisine. Little touches in presentation, such as paper doilies under teacups, soup bowls, and towel-wrapped water jugs make an apparent difference in product delivery.

Apart from the regular menu (several appetizers, two or three soups, sorbet, five entrees, two salads, several desserts, and a superb selection of international cheeses at every dinner meal), there is always a Cunard Spa menu, a vegetarian menu, and diabetic desserts every day. Once each cruise a White Star Line menu is recreated in a salute to the past history of the Cunard-White Star Line.

Different colored tablecloths and napkins are featured daily for luncheon and dinner. There is an outstanding and extensive wine list, with prices typically ranging from $13 to almost $400. Cappuccino and espresso coffees are available at any time in the dining room, at no charge. There is an excellent selection of breads, tropical fruits, and cheeses.

Tivoli is the name of a delightful 40-seat Italian à la carte restaurant (an alternative nonsmoking dining spot) that is elegant and very intimate, and the cuisine (featuring Northern Italian items) is excellent, from a varied menu that features many special dishes daily. It has the feel of a small, exclusive bistro. A tea/coffee station is available 24 hours a day (a machine provides espresso and cappuccino coffees).

The Lido Deck Café is a popular informal dining area that provides a wide range of self-service buffets that have a different theme daily, for breakfast and for lunch.

Other Comments: This ship has classic liner styling and profile, and really does look like a ship. She is finely proportioned, with delightful, rounded, flowing lines, a sleek profile with a good line of sheer, and a large funnel amidships. Following an extensive refit in late 1999, she underwent a name change, from *Vistafjord* to *Caronia* (the third Cunard ship to bear the name, the first two were named in 1905 and 1947). The hull is now painted in royal blue, which shows off her strong, balanced lines even more, and these are further balanced by the ship's orange-red funnel. The ship was built with excellent quality materials throughout, has been well maintained. At sea she is stable, smooth, and quiet in operation. Each day, the ship's bell is sounded at noon in fine maritime tradition.

The open decks and sunbathing space are expansive. There is a good teak wraparound promenade deck outdoors, and the deck lounge chairs have cushioned pads.

Inside, the spacious and elegant public rooms have high ceilings and tasteful decor throughout — improved in her latest refit. There is a real ballroom (this doubles as the ship's show lounge), and it has a fine, large, wooden dance floor, as well as a big band for ballroom dancing. Conservative, sophisticated, classically oriented entertainment. The wide interior stairwells are subtly illuminated. Few international ships can compete with this ship for the relaxing ambience and service from a well-organized and happy crew. There are refreshingly few announcements and interruptions.

This ship caters especially well to discerning passengers in an elegant, refined, yet friendly style and with very comfortable surroundings for adults (children do not fit, nor are there any facilities for them). Features very good service from a European and Filipino staff. Although not shiny and new, she has been well cared for, and provides a most pleasant, gracious and civilized travel experience.

Weak Points: When the ship is full, as is often the case under Cunard Line's new owners (Carnival Corporation), some crowding is evident (the staff is less stressed at an 80–90% occupancy).

Carousel
★★★

Large Ship:	23,149 tons	Cabins (for one person):	0
Lifestyle:	Standard	Cabins (with private balcony):	0
Cruise Line:	Airtours Sun Cruises	Cabins (wheelchair accessible):	0
Former Names:	*Nordic Prince*	Cabin Current:	110-volt
Builder:	Wartsila (Finland)	Full-Service Dining Rooms:	1
Original Cost:	$13.5 million	Elevators:	4
Entered Service:	July 1971/May 1995	Casino (gaming tables):	Yes
Registry:	Bahamas	Slot Machines:	Yes
Length (ft/m):	637.5/194.32	Swimming Pools (outdoors):	1
Beam (ft/m):	78.8/24.03	Swimming Pools (indoors):	0
Draft (ft/m):	21.9/6.70	Whirlpools:	0
Propulsion/Propellers:	Diesel (13,400kW)/2	Fitness Center:	Yes
Passenger Decks:	7	Sauna/Steam Room:	Yes/No
Total Crew:	400	Massage:	Yes
Passengers (lower beds/all berths):	1,050/1,158	Self-Service Launderette:	No
Pass. Space Ratio (lower beds/all berths):	22.0/19.9	Dedicated Cinema:	No
Crew/Pass. Ratio (lower beds/all berths):	2.6/2.8	Library:	Yes
Navigation Officers:	International	Classification Society:	Det Norske Veritas
Cabins (total):	525		
Size Range (sq ft/sq m):	119.4–482.2/11.1–44.8	**OVERALL SCORE:**	**1,226**
Cabins (outside view):	340	**(OUT OF A POSSIBLE 2,000 POINTS)**	
Cabins (interior/no view):	185		

Accommodation: The cabins are provided in just four grades (Standard, Superior, Promenade, and Deluxe) and six types, making it an easy matter to select your accommodation. You can also choose and book the exact cabin you want (this came into being in the winter of 2001, but note that an extra charge of £50 per cabin applies).

Most cabins are of a similar size (dimensionally challenged comes to mind) and the insulation between them is poor. The cabins also have mediocre closets and very little storage space, yet somehow everyone seems to manage (the ship was built originally for Caribbean cruising). The best advice is therefore to take only casual clothing and only the things you really need. Cabin electricity is 110-volt. Note that, in the past, cabins were not assigned until you arrived at the ship; however, now you can book the cabin you want. Only the owner's suite features a refrigerator.

Dining: The dining room, which operates in two seatings, is large, but noisy, and the tables (for four, six, or eight) are close together. The catering operation is quite good, however, although all the food seems to taste alike. There is a limited selection of breads, cheeses, and fruits. Attentive, friendly, but rather frenzied service (particularly for those on the first seating).

The cuisine? In a nutshell, it's basic, no-frills British motorway café cuisine — adequate for those who do not expect much in the way of presentation or quality, but definitely not memorable. Indeed, it is quantity, not quality, that prevails, but it's all provided at a low cost — as is a cruise aboard this ship. Presentation is a weak point, and there are no fish knives. Remember that, like anything, you get what you pay for. If you enjoy going out to eat and like being adventurous, then you will probably be disappointed. There is an adequate, but limited, wine list, and the wines are almost all very young — typical of those found in supermarkets. Wine prices are quite modest, as are the prices for most alcoholic beverages.

Other Comments: This ship, originally built for and operated by Royal Caribbean International, has a fairly handsome, contemporary look with good lines, a nicely raked bow, and large blue funnel (complete with sunburst logo). This ship was acquired by Airtours Sun Cruises (one of the UK's "Big Three" tour companies) in 1995. Airtours is now partly owned by Carnival Corporation, who also own Carnival Cruise Lines (and others), and provides an activity-filled cruise product in comfortable, but fairly busy surroundings. The ship underwent a $7 million refit in late 1997. While most of the work was below decks, with the fitting of new, better, more powerful generators, some cosmetic work was completed in her interiors.

There is a good, polished wraparound promenade deck outdoors (it can be slippery when wet) and wooden railings. The open deck space for sunbathing is very crowded and noisy when the ship is full (which is most of the time), but makes for a good party ambience.

The interior layout and passenger flow is sound, with clean, bright decor and some good wooden paneling and trim. The dress code is very casual, good for unstuffy, unpretentious cruising. This is a very affordable cruise, particularly for families with children, and Airtours also features a wide selection of pre- and post-cruise hotel programs. Note, however, that Sun Cruises does not actively market or specialize in cruises for families with children, and the children's/youth facilities are limited (and there is no evening baby-sitting service for youngsters).

Airtours is known for packaging its products really well, and this ship represents an excellent buy for families who want to cruise, but on a limited budget. Also, if you want a little more than the basics, Airtours Sun Cruises offers special packages — good for celebrating something special. These come in four packages: bronze, silver, gold, and platinum, with each at a little extra cost. Go for gold or platinum and you get breakfast in bed with champagne, flowers, fruit basket, and dinner at the captain's table.

Airtours also has its own fleet of aircraft, and this is one reason that the company is able to offer complete cruise-air-stay packages at such low rates. Airtours Sun Cruises does a fine job in getting you and your luggage from airplane to ship without having to go through immigration (depending on itinerary) in foreign countries whenever possible, making your cruise vacation as seamless as possible.

Airtours Sun Cruises brochures tell it like it is, so you know before you go exactly what you will get for your money, with the exception of its claim to "first class food," which is a gross exaggeration. If you want just the basics, you pay the least amount. If you want all the goodies choose a wider "premium" seat with extra leg room on your Airtours aircraft; choose your own cabin; choose your dinner seating; breakfast in bed and dinner with the captain (no, not in bed) — then you'll pay for all those "privileges." Note, however, that, however you choose to cruise, all gratuities are included. Insurance is also included (but you will be charged for it) unless you decline it on the booking form.

The company will fly you to and from the ship in one of its own modern jet aircraft, and all transfers to/from the ship are included for good measure. The company really does go out of its way to provide a fine "no-nonsense" good value-for-money vacation, as long as your expectations are not too high. This is not the ship if you are looking for a quiet and relaxing vacation. If you have been on a land-based Airtours vacation, you'll know what to expect. The currency is the pound sterling. All gratuities are included. Insurance is also included (but you will be charged for it) unless declined on the booking form.

Weak Points: The cabin hallways are very narrow. There are too many repetitive announcements. There are no cushioned pads for the deck lounge chairs. Standing in line for embarkation, disembarkation, shore tenders, and for self-serve buffet meals is an inevitable aspect of cruising aboard all large ships.

Celebration
★★★ +

Large Ship:	47,262 tons	Cabins (for one person):	0
Lifestyle:	Standard	Cabins (with private balcony):	10
Cruise Line:	Carnival Cruise Lines	Cabins (wheelchair accessible):	14
Former Names:	-	Cabin Current:	110-volt
Builder:	Kockums (Sweden)	Full-Service Dining Rooms:	2
Original Cost:	$130 million	Elevators:	8
Entered Service:	March 1987	Casino (gaming tables):	Yes
Registry:	Panama	Slot Machines:	Yes
Length (ft/m):	732.6/223.30	Swimming Pools (outdoors):	3
Beam (ft/m):	92.5/28.20	Swimming Pools (indoors):	0
Draft (ft/m):	25.5/7.80	Whirlpools:	2
Propulsion/Propellers:	Diesel (23,520kW)/2	Fitness Center:	Yes
Passenger Decks:	10	Sauna/Steam Room:	Yes/No
Total Crew:	670	Massage:	Yes
Passengers (lower beds/all berths):	1,486/1,896	Self-Service Launderette:	Yes
Pass. Space Ratio (lower beds/all berths):	31.8/24.9	Dedicated Cinema:	No
Crew/Pass. Ratio (lower beds/all berths):	2.2/2.8	Library:	Yes
Navigation Officers:	Italian	Classification Society:	Lloyd's Register
Cabins (total):	734		
Size Range (sq ft/sq m):	184.0/17.1	**OVERALL SCORE:**	**1,318**
Cabins (outside view):	453	**(OUT OF A POSSIBLE 2,000 POINTS)**	
Cabins (interior/no view):	290		

Accommodation: This ship has a range of suites, outside-view and interior (no view) cabins. The cabins are quite standard and mostly identical in terms of layout and decor (which means they are good for large groups who generally like to have identical cabins for their participants), are of fairly generous proportions, except for the interior (no view) cabins, which are quite small. They are reasonably comfortable and well equipped, but are nothing special. A gift basket is now provided in all grades of accommodation; it includes aloe soap, shampoo, conditioner, deodorant, breath mints, candy, and pain relief tablets.

The best accommodation can be found in the ten suites, each of which has more space, its own private balcony, a larger bathroom, and more closet, drawer, and storage space.

Dining: There are two dining rooms (Horizon and Vista). They are quite cramped when full, and very noisy (both are nonsmoking), and they have low ceilings in the raised sections of their centers. There are tables are for four, six, or eight (no tables for two). The decor is bright and extremely colorful, to say the least. Dining is in four seatings, for greater flexibility: 6pm, 6:45pm, 8pm, and 8:45pm (approximately).

Carnival meals stress quantity, not quality, although the company constantly works hard to improve the cuisine. While passengers seem to accept it, few find it worth remembering. However, food and its taste are still not the company's strongest points (you get what you pay for, remember).

While the menu items sound good, their presentation and taste leave much to be desired. While meats are of a high quality, fish and seafood is not. Presentation is simple, and few garnishes are used. Many meat and fowl dishes are disguised with gravies and sauces. The selection of fresh green vegetables, breads, rolls, cheeses, and fruits is limited, and there is too much use of canned fruit and jellied desserts. However, do remember that this is banquet catering, with all its attendant standardization and production cooking (it is, therefore, difficult to ask for anything remotely unusual or off-menu).

Although there is a decent wine list, there are no wine waiters (the waiters are expected to serve both food and wine). The service is quite robotic, closely timed, highly programmed, and inflexible, although the waiters are willing and reasonably friendly. However, the waiters do sing and dance (be prepared for "Hot, Hot, Hot" and "The Macarena" — again) and there are constant waiter parades; the dining room is show business — all done in the name of gratuities at the end of your cruise.

Casual meals can be self-serve buffets in the Wheelhouse Bar & Grill, although the foods provided are very basic and quite disappointing, with much repetition (particularly for breakfast) and little variety. At night, the Seaview Bistro provides a casual alternative to eating in the main dining rooms. It serves pasta, steaks, salads, and desserts.

Other Comments: *Celebration* is the fourth new cruise ship for Carnival Cruise Lines. The ship's exterior is rather angular, but typical of the space-conscious designs that were introduced in the early 1980s, particularly by Carnival Cruise Lines, in an effort to maximize interior (revenue-generating) space. The swimming pools are smaller than one would expect, but the open deck space is good, provided the ship is not full, when, like most ships, the deck always seems crowded.

Inside, this ship has double-width indoor promenades and a very good selection of public rooms in which to play. The flamboyant interior decor in public rooms is stimulating instead of relaxing, as is the colorful artwork. Features New Orleans-themed decor throughout the public rooms, except for some nautical-themed decor in the Wheelhouse Bar & Grill. There is a large, very active, and very noisy casino. The party atmosphere is good for anyone wanting a stimulating cruise experience. Features a wide range of entertainment and activities.

Carnival Cruise Lines excels at providing plenty of entertainment venues and passenger participation activities to keep you occupied.

This ship is a floating playground for young, active adults who enjoy constant stimulation, close contact with lots and lots of others, as well as the three Gs — glitz, glamour, and gambling. It is a live board game with every move executed in typically grand, colorful, fun-filled Carnival Cruise Lines style. This ship should prove a good choice for families with children (there are so many places for them to explore). There are good dazzle and sizzle shows on stage, which are suitable for the whole family. This ship is good if you are taking your first cruise, providing that you like lots of people, noise, and lively action. Forget fashion — having fun is the sine qua non of a Carnival cruise. *Celebration* operates 4- and 5-day Western Caribbean cruises from Galveston, Texas. Gratuities can be prepaid.

Weak Points: There is absolutely no escape from unnecessary and repetitive announcements (particularly for activities that bring revenue, such as art auctions and bingo) that intrude constantly into your cruise, and a great deal of hustling for drinks, although it is sometimes done with a knowing smile. There really is nowhere to go for privacy, peace, and quiet, but then you should choose another ship for that. Standing in line for embarkation, disembarkation, shore tenders, and for self-serve buffet meals is an inevitable aspect of cruising aboard all large ships.

Century
★★★★ +

Galaxy
mercury

Large Ship:	70,606 tons	Cabins (for one person):	0
Lifestyle:	Premium	Cabins (with private balcony):	61
Cruise Line:	Celebrity Cruises	Cabins (wheelchair accessible):	8
Former Names:	-	Cabin Current:	110/220-volt
Builder:	Meyer Werft (Germany)	Full-Service Dining Rooms:	2
Original Cost:	$320 million	Elevators:	9
Entered Service:	December 1995	Casino (gaming tables):	Yes
Registry:	Liberia	Slot Machines:	Yes
Length (ft/m):	807.1/246.0	Swimming Pools (outdoors):	2
Beam (ft/m):	105.6/32.2	Swimming Pools (indoors):	1 hydropool
Draft (ft/m):	24.6/7.5	Whirlpools:	4
Propulsion/Propellers:	Diesel (29,250kW)/2	Fitness Center:	Yes
Passenger Decks:	10	Sauna/Steam Room:	Yes/Yes
Total Crew:	858	Massage:	Yes
Passengers (lower beds/all berths):	1,750/2,150	Self-Service Launderette:	Yes
Pass. Space Ratio (lower beds/all berths):	40.3/32.8	Dedicated Cinema/Seats:	Yes/190
Crew/Pass. Ratio (lower beds/all berths):	2.0/2.5	Library:	Yes
Navigation Officers:	Greek	Classification Society:	Lloyd's Register
Cabins (total):	875		
Size Range (sq ft/sq m):	168.9–1,514.5/15.7–140.7	**OVERALL SCORE:**	**1,696**
Cabins (outside view):	569	**(OUT OF A POSSIBLE 2,000 POINTS)**	
Cabins (interior/no view):	306		

Accommodation: A wide variety of cabin types include 18 family cabins, each with two lower beds, two foldaway beds and one upper berth. All cabins have wood cabinetry and accenting, interactive TV and entertainment systems (you can go shopping, book shore excursions, or play casino games, interactively), as well as hairdryers in the bathrooms, and 100% cotton towels. However, the standard 24-hour cabin menu is disappointing, and very limited. There are no cabins for single occupancy.

All cabins feature a personal safe, minibar/refrigerator (extra cost) and are nicely equipped and decorated, with warm wood-finish furniture, and none of the boxy feel of cabins in many ships, due to the angled placement of vanities and audio-video consoles. In addition, all suites on Deck 10 (and the Sky Deck suites on Deck 12) feature butler service and in-cabin dining facilities. Suites that have private balconies also have floor-to-ceiling windows and sliding doors to balconies (a few have outward opening doors).

For the ultimate in accommodation, choose one of two beautifully decorated Presidential Suites, each of which measures 1,173 sq ft (109.0 sq m). These are located amidships in the most desirable position (each can be combined with the adjacent mini-suite via an interconnecting door, to provide a living space of 1,515 sq ft (140.7 sq m). Each has a marble-floored foyer, and a living room with mahogany wood floor and hand-woven rug. Other features include a separate dining area with six-seat dining table; butler's pantry with wet bar; a wine bar with private label stock, refrigerator, and microwave. There is also a large private balcony with dining table for two, chaise lounge chairs with cushioned pads, hot tub, and dimmer-controlled lighting; master bedroom with king-size bed, dressed with fine fabrics and draperies, Egyptian cotton bed linen, and walk-in closet with abundant storage space. The all-marble bathroom has a jet-spray shower and whirlpool bath.

All grades of accommodation feature interactive Sony audio and video facilities for booking shore excursions, ordering room service, and purchasing goods from the ship's boutiques, so you do not have to leave your quarters if you do not wish to, especially if you do not like the ports of call. The interactive system is available in English, French, German, Italian, and Spanish.

All accommodation designated as suites feature European duvets instead of sheets/blankets, fresh flowers, VCR, use of the AquaSpa without charge, and butler service. Electrically operated blinds and other goodies are also standard in some suites.

Dining: A grand staircase connects the upper and lower levels of the splendid two-level Grand Dining Room. Huge windows overlook the stern (electrically operated blinds feature several different backdrops).

211

Each of the two levels has a separate finishing galley. There are two seatings. The design of the two galleys is excellent, and is such that food that should be hot does arrive hot at the table. Three different decorative panels, changed according to theme nights, adorn the huge aft windows. The dining room chairs, which are heavy, should, but do not, have armrests.

There is also a large indoor/outdoor Lido café ("Islands") with four separate well-designed self-service buffet lines, as well as two grill serving stations located adjacent to the swimming pools outdoors.

All meals can also be served course-by-course, including full dinners in all suites and cabins, no matter what accommodation grade you choose. For those that cannot live without them, freshly baked pizzas (boxed) can also be delivered, in an insulated pouch, to your cabin.

Celebrity Cruises has established an enviable reputation for fine dining aboard its ships, and this tradition is being continued. Michel Roux designs Celebrity Cruises' menus and exerts tight personal control over their correct cooking and delivery to assure consistency of product. All meals are made from scratch, with nothing precooked or prepackaged ashore. However, the food served as room-service is decidedly below the standard of food featured in the dining room.

Other Comments: This ship, which looks externally like a larger version of the company's popular *Horizon* and *Zenith*, is well balanced despite its squared-off stern. It has the distinctive Celebrity Cruises' "X" funnel ("X" being the Greek letter "C" which stands for Chandris, the former owning company). With a high passenger space ratio for such a large ship, there is no real sense of crowding, and passenger flow is good. A high crew/passenger ratio of 1/1.9 provides a sound basis for excellent passenger service.

The decor is quite elegant and understated. Technical and engineering excellence prevails, and there is overindulgence in fire and safety equipment. She is a contemporary ship, with fine public rooms, and an array of TV and video screens in many of them, all provided by Sony. The medical facilities are also excellent.

There is a three-quarter, two-level teakwood promenade deck, and, for joggers, a wraparound jogging track atop the ship. A stunning, two-level, 1,000-seat show lounge/theater with side balconies features a huge stage, a split orchestra pit (hydraulic), and the latest in high-tech lighting and sound equipment.

A three-deck-high main foyer (atrium) features one wall with nine large TV screens providing constantly changing scenery. The atrium is not glitzy, but its decor somehow does not closely match the rest of the ship.

There are 4.5 acres of open deck space, together with a fine array of other public rooms and enhanced passenger facilities. An outstanding AquaSpa that measures (9,340 sq ft /867.6 sq m), set forward and high, has some of the more unusual wellness treatments (including a steamy rasul room), with large panoramic windows and the latest high-tech equipment, all set in a calming environment, complete with shoji screens and Japanese-inspired rock garden.

Wide passageways provide plenty of indoor space for strolling, so there is no feeling of being crowded, and passenger flow is excellent. In fact, the ship absorbs passengers really well. A small, dedicated cinema also doubles as a conference and meeting center with all the latest audiovisual technology that includes three-language simultaneous translation and headsets for the hearing-impaired.

Cigar smokers will love Michael's Club — a cigar and cognac room of superb taste; it is a lovely triangular-shaped room that has become a favorite watering place for those who smoke, with large comfortable chairs and decor reminiscent of a real gentlemen's club. Features include a cigar humidor, and a choice of almost 20 different cigars.

Tastings is the place for those who enjoy the very best in coffee, all provided by the impeccable Cova of Milan, Italy (the original Cova Café, located near the La Scala Opera House, opened in 1756). It is set around the second level of the atrium, and several display cases show off the extensive range of Cova coffee, chocolates, and alcoholic digestives. This is the place to see and be seen.

The large casino is tightly packed with slot machines and gaming tables, and even has a satellite-linked ATM machine.

Outstanding are the 500 pieces of art that adorn the ship — a $3.8 million art collection that includes many Warhol favorites and some fascinating contemporary sculptures (look for the colored violins on Deck 7). The "*Century* Collection" includes a comprehensive survey of the most important artists and the major developments in art since the 1960s, and embraces Abstract Expressionism, Pop, Conceptualism, Minimalism, and Neo-Expressionism.

Century operates Caribbean and Mediterranean cruises (1999 was the first year that Celebrity Cruises featured cruises in Europe). Overall, *Century* is a fine vessel for a big-ship cruise vacation, although some wear and tear and sloppy maintenance show in some areas. The overall product delivered, however, is extremely good, with what can be said to be very good hospitality from a well-dressed staff that is enthusiastic and generally well trained.

Weak Points: Although this is a beautiful ship, the shore excursion operation, embarkation, and disembarkation remain weak links in the Celebrity Cruises operation, and the cruise staff is young and unpolished. Standing in line for embarkation, disembarkation, shore tenders, and for self-serve buffet meals is an inevitable aspect of cruising aboard all large ships. The room service menu is poor, and room service food items are below the standard of food featured in the dining room. The interactive TV system is frustrating to use, and the larger suites have three remotes for TV/audio equipment (one would be better).

SHIP TALK

Abeam: off the side of the ship, at a right angle to its length.

Aft: near, toward, or in the rear of the ship.

Ahead: something that is ahead of the ship's bow.

Alleyway: a passageway or corridor.

Alongside: said of a ship when it is beside a pier or another vessel.

Amidships: in or toward the middle of the ship; the longitudinal center portion of the ship.

Anchor Ball: black ball hoisted above the bow to show that the vessel is anchored.

Astern: is the opposite of Ahead (i.e., meaning something behind the ship).

Backwash: motion in the water caused by the propeller(s) moving in a reverse (astern) direction.

Bar: sandbar, usually caused by tidal or current conditions near the shore.

Beam: width of the ship between its two sides at the widest point.

Bearing: compass direction, expressed in degrees, from the ship to a particular objective or destination.

Below: anything beneath the main deck.

Berth: dock, pier, or quay. Also means bed on board ship.

Bilge: lowermost spaces of the infrastructure of a ship.

Boat Stations: allotted space for each person during lifeboat drill or any other emergency when lifeboats are lowered.

Bow: the forward most part of the vessel.

Bridge: navigational and command control center.

Bulkhead: upright partition (wall) dividing the ship into compartments.

Bunkers: the space where fuel is stored; "bunkering" means taking on fuel.

Clelia II
★★★★ +

Small Ship:	4,077 tons	Cabins (for one person):	0
Lifestyle:	Premium	Cabins (with private balcony):	4
Cruise Line:	Golden Sea Cruises	Cabins (wheelchair accessible):	0
Former Names:	*Renaissance Four*	Cabin Current:	110-volt
Builder:	Cantieri Navale Ferrari (Italy)	Full-Service Dining Rooms:	1
Original Cost:	$20 million	Elevators:	1
Entered Service:	January 1991/March 1998	Casino (gaming tables):	No
Registry:	Bahamas	Slot Machines:	No
Length (ft/m):	289.0/88.1	Swimming Pools (outdoors):	1
Beam (ft/m):	50.1/15.3	Swimming Pools (indoors):	0
Draft (ft/m):	13.4/4.1	Whirlpools:	1
Propulsion/Propellers:	Diesel (3,514kW)/2	Fitness Center:	Yes
Passenger Decks:	5	Sauna/Steam Room:	No/Yes
Total Crew:	55	Massage:	No
Passengers (lower beds/all berths):	84/84	Self-Service Launderette:	No
Pass. Space Ratio (lower beds/all berths):	48.5/48.5	Dedicated Cinema:	No
Crew/Pass. Ratio (lower beds/all berths):	1.5/1.5	Library:	Yes
Navigation Officers:	Greek	Classification Society:	Lloyd's Register
Cabins (total):	42		
Size Range (sq ft/sq m):	210.0–538.2/19.5–50.0		
Cabins (outside view):	42		
Cabins (interior/no view):	0		

OVERALL SCORE: **1,551**

(OUT OF A POSSIBLE 2,000 POINTS)

Accommodation: Fine outside-view cabins (called "suites" in the brochure) combine highly polished imitation rosewood paneling with lots of mirrors, and fine, hand-crafted Italian furniture. All suites have twin beds that can convert to a queen-size bed, a sitting area with three-person sofa, one individual chair, coffee table, minibar/refrigerator (all drinks are at extra cost), color TV and VCR, and direct-dial satellite telephone. Note that while closet space is good, space for stowing luggage is tight, and there is little drawer space (each cabin has three drawers, two of which are lockable, plus several open shelves in a separate closet). Also note that there are no music channels in the cabins, and there is no switch to turn announcements off in your cabin.

The number of cabins was reduced from 50 to 42 when the present owners acquired the vessel in 1997, thus providing more space per passenger. Outside each cabin are two brass porthole-shaped lights, which provide a stately, nautical feel to the dark wood-paneled hallways.

The marble bathrooms are compact units that have showers (no bathrooms have a bathtub) with fold-down (plastic) seat, real teakwood floor, marble vanity, large mirror, recessed towel rail (good for storing personal toiletries), and built-in hairdryer. *Note*: there is a high "lip" into the bathroom.

There are also four VIP "apartments," each consisting of two consecutive adjoining "suites," thus providing a bedroom, large lounge (with red-leather topped office desk), and two bathrooms (his and hers).

There is one Presidential Apartment (owner's suite) with an en-suite office, two full separate bedrooms and living room (each with three windows), two bathrooms, and private, though narrow, balcony.

Dining: The Golden Star Restaurant, which has an open seating policy (it can seat up to 100), is bright, elegant, and welcoming (nonsmoking). It is on the lowest deck and has portholes rather than windows, due to maritime regulations. There are tables for two, four, six, or eight, and you can sit where you like, with whom you like, when you like in this open seating arrangement. Dinners are normally sit-down affairs, although, depending on the itinerary and length of cruise, there could be an occasional buffet. Breakfast and lunch are usually buffets and can be taken at the poolside (weather permitting), in your suite, or in the restaurant.

The cuisine consists of continental dishes complemented by local (regional) delicacies. The food quality, choice, and presentation are all good. While the food is very well presented, the choice of entrees is limited to three for dinner.

Other Comments: *Clelia II*, with its royal blue hull and white superstructure, has the look and feel of a contemporary mega-yacht, with handsome styling throughout, although the exterior profile is not particularly handsome. There are two teakwood wraparound promenade decks outdoors. There is a small water sports platform at the stern, and a "Baby Clelia" water jet-propelled shore tender hangs over the stern. The ship also carries jet skis, water-ski boat and sailfish for use when cruising in warm weather areas.

The accommodation is located forward, with public rooms aft. Features pleasing colors and refined and attractive interior decor, with some accents based on Greek design. There is a small library, which also houses the video library, a lounge that can accommodate all passengers (good for use as a lecture room), and a piano bar/lounge.

Originally one of a fleet of eight similar-size ships operated by Renaissance Cruises, this ship was very nicely refurbished for service in early 1998. Greek artists are featured in many pieces of art around the ship, courtesy of the new owners. With her name change (the new name is also the name of the ship's owner), this charming little ship operates Greek Island cruises during most of the year. She is very comfortable and inviting, and is close, but not quite the equal of some of the other small premium ships (but neither is the price). This ship provides a destination-intensive, refined, quiet, and relaxed cruise for passengers who do not like crowds, dressing up, scheduled activities, or entertainment.

The ship is often placed under charter to companies such as Abercrombie&Kent, Classical Cruises, and other tour packagers for much of the year. No smoking is allowed anywhere inside the ship, only on open decks.

Weak Points: The tiny "dip" pool is not a swimming pool. The open deck and sunbathing space is very limited. The decor consists of plastic woods instead of real woods (it looks almost too perfect in places). There are many slim pillars in the public rooms in odd places. The constant music ("acoustic wallpaper") played throughout the public spaces (including accommodation hallways) is irritating and unnecessary.

Clipper Adventurer
★★★

Small Ship:	5,750 tons	Cabins (for one person):	0
Lifestyle:	Standard	Cabins (with private balcony):	0
Cruise Line:	Clipper Cruise line	Cabins (wheelchair accessible):	0
Former Names:	*Alla Tarasova*	Cabin Current:	220-volt
Builder:	Brodgradiliste Uljanik (Yugoslavia)	Full-Service Dining Rooms:	1
Original Cost:	n/a	Elevators:	0
Entered Service:	1976/April 1998	Casino (gaming tables):	No
Registry:	Bahamas	Slot Machines:	No
Length (ft/m):	328.1/100.01	Swimming Pools (outdoors):	No
Beam (ft/m):	53.2/16.24	Swimming Pools (indoors):	No
Draft (ft/m):	15.2/4.65	Whirlpools:	No
Propulsion/Propellers:	Diesel (3,884kW)/2	Fitness Center:	No
Passenger Decks:	3	Sauna/Steam Room:	Yes/No
Total Crew:	84	Massage:	No
Passengers (lower beds/all berths):	122/122	Self-Service Launderette:	No
Pass. Space Ratio (lower beds/all berths):	47.1/47.1	Dedicated Cinema:	No
Crew/Pass. Ratio (lower beds/all berths):	1.4/1.4	Library:	Yes
Navigation Officers:	European	Classification Society:	Russian Shipping Register
Cabins (total):	61		
Size Range (sq ft/sq m):	119.0–211.0/11.0–19.6		
Cabins (outside view):	61		
Cabins (interior/no view):	0		

OVERALL SCORE: 1,175

(OUT OF A POSSIBLE 2,000 POINTS)

Accommodation: All of the cabins (there are seven grades, including a dedicated price for single cabin occupancy) have outside views and twin lower beds, with a private bathroom with shower and toilet. The bathrooms are really tiny (of the "me first, you next" variety), although they are tiled, and come with all the basics. Several double-occupancy cabins can be booked by passengers who are traveling alone (although special rates apply).

All cabins feature a private lockable drawer for valuables, telephone, and individual temperature control. Some cabins have picture windows, while others have portholes, depending on the deck location. Two larger cabins (called suites in the brochure, which they really are not) are quite well equipped for the size of the vessel.

Dining: Pleasant, though with somewhat dark decor, the dining room, which has deep ocean-view windows, seats all passengers at a single seating: the room was extended aft during a 1998 refit. The food consists of a combination of American and Continental cuisine, prepared freshly by chefs trained at some of America's finest culinary institutions. There are limited menu choices, but the food is wholesome, and simply and attractively presented, but not in any way shape or form can it be considered gourmet. Young American waitresses provide the dining room service; their bubbly enthusiasm makes up for a lack of training in service finesse.

Casual, self-service breakfast and luncheon buffets are typically taken in the main lounge, as are cocktail-hour hors d'oeuvres and other snacks.

Other Comments: *Clipper Adventurer* is a small ship — originally one of a series of eight built for the Murmansk Shipping Company. It has an ice-strengthened (A-1 ice classification), royal blue hull and white funnel, bow-thruster, and stabilizers. However, even with an ice classification, the ship became stuck in an ice field in the Bellingshausen Sea in February 2000. Fortunately, the Argentine Navy icebreaker *Almirante Irizar* freed it.

Although the ship is not new, it went through a $15 million refit/conversion in the winter of 1997/1998, meets the latest international safety codes and requirements, and specializes in operating close-in expedition-style cruising. She carries ten Zodiac rubber inflatable landing craft for in-depth excursions and wet landings, and has a covered promenade deck made of Oregon pine.

Clipper Adventurer is now a tidy, neat, clean, and quite handsome ship throughout, with attractive, warm decor, lots of polished dark wood paneling and numerous real brass fixtures (like a "real" ship). She is cozy and caters to travelers rather than mere passengers. The dress code is totally casual during the day, although at night, many passengers wear jacket and tie for the more formal evenings. However, for trekking ashore it is wise to take long-sleeved garments.

The public spaces are a little limited, with just one main lounge (this was extended forward over a former cargo hold during the refit so that it now accommodates all passengers for lectures) and bar (the baked-onboard chocolate-chip cookies available in the late afternoon are delicious). There is a small library, complete with high wingback chairs, and a decent selection of books.

There is no observation lounge with forward-facing views, although there is an outdoor observation area directly below the bridge. Clipper Cruise Line provides its own cruise staff, and experienced historians and naturalist lecturers accompany all cruise expeditions.

She is now a smart looking vessel, and features cruises to unusual destinations that are not frequented by the flood of larger vessels. A nonsmoking policy throughout all interior areas is in effect, although smoking is permitted on the outside decks. Travel insurance is included in the cruise fare.

Weak Points: The passageways are narrow (it is difficult to pass housekeeping carts), and the stairs are steep on the outer decks. There is no observation lounge with forward-facing views.

Clipper Odyssey
★★★★ +

Small Ship:	5,218 tons	Cabins (for one person):		0
Lifestyle:	Premium	Cabins (with private balcony):		8
Cruise Line:	Clipper Cruise Line	Cabins (wheelchair accessible):		1
Former Names:	*Oceanic Odyssey, Oceanic Grace*	Cabin Current:		115-volt
Builder:	NKK Tsu Shipyard (Japan)	Full-Service Dining Rooms:		1
Original Cost:	$40 million	Elevators:		1
Entered Service:	April 1989/November 1999	Casino (gaming tables):		No
Registry:	Bahamas	Slot Machines:		No
Length (ft/m):	337.5/102.9	Swimming Pools (outdoors):		1
Beam (ft/m):	50.5/15.4	Swimming Pools (indoors):		0
Draft (ft/m):	14.1/4.3	Whirlpools:		1
Propulsion/Propellers:	Diesel (5,192kW)/2	Fitness Center:		Yes
Passenger Decks:	5	Sauna/Steam Room:		Yes/Yes
Total Crew:	52	Massage:		No
Passengers (lower beds/all berths):	128/128	Self-Service Launderette:		No
Pass. Space Ratio (lower beds/all berths):	43.4/43.4	Dedicated Cinema:		No
Crew/Pass. Ratio (lower beds/all berths):	2.4/2.4	Library:		Yes
Navigation Officers:	European	Classification Society:	Nippon Kaiji Kyokai	
Cabins (total):	64			
Size Range (sq ft/sq m):	195.9–258.3/18.2–24.0	**OVERALL SCORE:**		**1,678**
Cabins (outside view):	64	(OUT OF A POSSIBLE 2,000 POINTS)		
Cabins (interior/no view):	0			

Accommodation: There are six categories of accommodation. This ship has all outside-view cabins that are quite tastefully furnished and feature blond wood cabinetry, twin- or queen-size beds, living area with sofa, personal safe, minibar/refrigerator, TV and VCR, and three-sided mirror. All bathrooms feature a deep, half-size bathtub. Cabins have private balconies; however, note that these are very small, almost token-gesture balconies, and they have awkward door handles. You should note that the bathroom toilet seats are extremely high.

Dining: The dining room is very warm and inviting, and all passengers eat in a single seating. The cuisine features fresh foods from local ports, in a mix of regional and some Western cuisine, with open seating. A young, friendly American staff provides the service.

Other Comments: *Clipper Odyssey* features impressive, though square, contemporary looks and sports twin outboard funnels. She was designed in Holland and built in Japan originally as an attempt to copy the *Sea Goddess* concept specifically for the Japanese market. The ship has expansive areas outdoors considering the size of the ship — these are excellent for sunbathing or for spotting wildlife.

There is a decompression chamber for scuba divers, and water sports equipment is carried, as is a fleet of Zodiacs — inflatable landing craft for "soft" expedition use. There is an aft platform for water sports, including SCUBA, snorkeling, and a water-ski boat. There is plenty of open deck and sunbathing space, with a wide teakwood outdoor jogging track. The small swimming pool is just a "dip" pool, however.

Inside, nothing jars the senses, as the interior design concept successfully balances East-West color combinations with some Indonesian accents. The ambience is decidedly warm and intimate, and is for those who seek a small ship where entertainment and loud music is not a priority. *Clipper Odyssey* will provide a pleasing antidote to cruising aboard the large ships.

Under new owners Clipper Cruise Line, the ship operates 3- and 4-day cruises from November–April and 10-days and longer cruises from April–November (islands of the North Pacific region, New Zealand, and Australia's Great Barrier Reef).

Weak Points: There are lots of pillars in almost all public areas, which do tend to spoil the decor and the views somewhat.

Club Med 2
★★★★

Small Ship:	14,983 tons	Size Range (sq ft/sq m):	193.8–322.0/18.0–30.0
Lifestyle:	Premium	Cabins (outside view):	197
Cruise Line:	Club Med Cruises	Cabins (interior/no view):	0
Former Names:	-	Cabins (for one person):	0
Builder:	Ateliers et Chantiers du Havre(France)	Cabins (with private balcony):	0
Original Cost:	$125 million	Cabins (wheelchair accessible):	0
Entered Service:	December 1992	Cabin Current:	110/220-volt
Registry:	Wallis & Fortuna	Full-Service Dining Rooms:	2
Length (ft/m):	613.8/187.10	Elevators:	2
Beam (ft/m):	65.6/20.00	Casino (gaming tables):	No
Draft (ft/m):	16.4/5.00	Slot Machines:	No
Type of Vessel	high-tech sail-cruiser	Swimming Pools (outdoors):	2
No. of Masts:	5 (164 ft/50 m high)/7 computer-controlled sails	Whirlpools:	0
		Fitness Center:	Yes
Sail Area (sq ft/sq m):	26,910/2,500	Sauna/Steam Room:	Yes/No
Main Propulsion:	a) engines b) sails	Massage:	Yes
Propulsion/Propellers:	Diesel (9,120kW)/2	Self-Service Launderette:	No
Passenger Decks:	8	Library:	Yes
Total Crew:	200	Classification Society:	Bureau Veritas
Passengers (lower beds/all berths):	394/409		
Pass. Space Ratio (lower beds/all berths):	38.0/36.6		
Crew/Pass. Ratio (lower beds/all berths):	1.9/2.0	**OVERALL SCORE:**	**1,546**
Navigation Officers:	French	**(OUT OF A POSSIBLE 2,000 POINTS)**	
Cabins (total):	197		

Accommodation: There are five suites, and 192 standard cabins (all the same size). All cabins are very nicely equipped and very comfortable, and have an inviting decor that includes much blond wood cabinetry. They all feature a minibar/refrigerator, 24-hour room service (but you pay for food), a personal safe, color TV, plenty of storage space, bathrobes, and a hairdryer. There are six, four-person cabins, and some 35 doubles are fitted with an extra Pullman berth — good for young families, although this makes them a little more cramped when occupied.

Dining: There are two dining rooms, each with tables for one, two, or more. Open seating is featured, so you may sit with whom you wish. The Odyssey Restaurant has a delightful open terrace for informal meals. Complimentary wines and beers are available with lunch and dinner (there is also an à la carte wine list, at extra cost). Afternoon tea is a delight. The cuisine provides French, continental, and Japanese specialties, and the presentation is good.

Other Comments: *Club Med 2* is one of a pair of the world's largest high-tech sail-cruisers (her sister ship is Windstar Cruises' *Wind Surf*), part cruise ship, part yacht, like a larger version of the three earlier, smaller Windstar Cruises vessels (*Wind Song, Wind Spirit, Wind Star*).

There are extensive water sports facilities (their use, with the exception of SCUBA gear, is included in your cruise fare) and an aft marina platform. The water sports equipment includes 12 windsurfers, 3 sailboats, 2 water-ski boats, several kayaks, 20 single SCUBA tanks, snorkels, and 4 motorized water sport boats. The ship's two, small swimming pools are saltwater pools.

Inside, other facilities include a meeting room and a golf simulator (extra charge) as well as a fitness and beauty center, piano bar, and lounge.

The onboard activities come under the direction of a large team of young, energetic GOs (Gentiles Ordinaires), who, like their equals on land, have the run of the ship. Although enthusiastic, the entertainment is quite amateurish, although everyone seems to have fun.

This vessel is excellent for more upscale active singles and couples who might like casual elegance rather than the wilder vacation experience of some Club Med resorts, and for those who enjoy water sports. No gratuities are expected or accepted.

C. Columbus
★★★ +

Small Ship:	14,903 tons	Cabins (for one person):	0
Lifestyle:	Standard	Cabins (with private balcony):	2
Cruise Line:	Hapag-Lloyd Cruises	Cabins (wheelchair accessible):	0
Former Names:	-	Cabin Current:	110-volt
Builder:	MTW Schiffswerft (Germany)	Full-Service Dining Rooms:	1
Original Cost:	$69 million	Elevators:	3
Entered Service:	July 1997	Casino (gaming tables):	No
Registry:	Bahamas	Slot Machines:	No
Length (ft/m):	472.8/144.13	Swimming Pools (outdoors):	1
Beam (ft/m):	70.5/21.50	Swimming Pools (indoors):	0
Draft (ft/m):	16.8/5.15	Whirlpools:	0
Propulsion/Propellers:	Diesel (10,560kW)/2	Fitness Center:	Yes
Passenger Decks:	6	Sauna/Steam Room:	Yes/No
Total Crew:	170	Massage:	Yes
Passengers (lower beds/all berths):	410/423	Self-Service Launderette:	No
Pass. Space Ratio (lower beds/all berths):	36.3/35.2	Dedicated Cinema:	No
Crew/Pass. Ratio (lower beds/all berths):	2.4/2.4	Library:	Yes
Navigation Officers:	German	Classification Society:	Germanischer Lloyd
Cabins (total):	205		
Size Range (sq ft/sq m):	129.1–322.9/12.0–30.0	**OVERALL SCORE:**	**1,383**
Cabins (outside view):	158		
Cabins (interior/no view):	47	**(OUT OF A POSSIBLE 2,000 POINTS)**	

Accommodation: The standard cabins are really small, and many of them are interior. All but ten cabins feature lower berths, but the 16 categories established really are a lot for this size of ship. Except for two forward-facing suites, there are no balcony cabins. The cabin decor is bright and upbeat, and a good amount of closet and shelf space is provided. The bathrooms are fully tiled and have large shower stalls (none have bathtubs). All cabins feature a minibar/refrigerator (all items are at extra cost, as in hotels ashore), personal safe, and hairdryer (bathrobes are available on request, plus a small surcharge).

There are eight suites (each is at least double the size of a standard cabin), and each has a curtained partition between its lounging and sleeping areas, with a wall unit that houses a TV that can be turned 360 degrees for viewing from either the lounge or bedroom. Two of the suites located at the bow each have a narrow private veranda (with two teak lounge chairs and coffee table), bedroom (with large wall clock) and lounge area separated by a curtain, two TVs, and an excellent amount of closet, drawer, and shelf space. The cabinetry, with its walnut-finish and birds-eye pattern, makes these suites feel warm and luxurious. All the suites have a small room service menu. The bathrooms have a large shower (it is big enough for two), hairdryer, and under-sink storage space. There is 24-hour room service. Limited room service menu available for all cabins.

Dining: There is one large main dining room located at the stern, with large ocean-view windows on three sides, and seats all passengers in a single seating, with assigned tables. There are only two tables for two, but others seat up to 16 — good for family reunions. The cuisine is fairly good, although the menu selection is quite limited (choice of two or three entrees for dinner). There is an excellent selection of fresh-baked breads and rolls every day.

Breakfast and lunch can as be taken in the bright, but casual, setting of the Palm Garden, which is also the ship's very comfortable observation lounge. Light dinners also can be taken in the Palm Garden, where a small dance floor adds another dimension.

Other Comments: *C. Columbus* (known simply as *Columbus* in the German-speaking market) has a smart contemporary profile, with a single, large funnel (painted in Hapag-Lloyd's orange-and-blue colors). Hapag-Lloyd Cruises has chartered the ship from the German company Conti Reederei, the owner, until 2002.

The ship also features an ice-hardened hull, which is useful for cold-weather cruise areas. In addition, the bridge "wings" can fold inward (as do the overhang lights) flush with the ship's side so that the vessel can enter the locks in the US/Canadian Great Lakes region, including the St. Lawrence Seaway and Welland Canal, for which the ship was specifically built.

The ship has a good passenger space ratio. Each deck has a distinctly different color scheme and carpeting, making it easy to find one's way around. There is a reasonable range of public rooms to choose from, most of which are located in a "cake-layer" vertical stacking aft of the accommodation. Although the ceilings in the public rooms are plain and unimaginative (except for the Palm Garden), the decor is really bright and upbeat, and very different from all other ships in the Hapag-Lloyd fleet. The most popular room is arguably the delightful multifunction Palm Garden, which is also the ship's forward-facing observation lounge.

The fit and finish of the ship is a little utilitarian (the mottled gray walls are a little cold, but a contrast to the splashes of color found in carpeting and other decorative touches). The artwork chosen is, for the most part, minimal and uncoordinated, yet it all works together to provide cheerful surroundings. Ship buffs will be pleased to find some superb original photographs from the Hapag-Lloyd archives adorning the stairways.

She is a good ship for the standard market, German-speaking traveler, and, as such, she offers excellent value for the money in very comfortable, unpretentious surroundings. However, you should know that the level of "luxury" is well below that of Hapag-Lloyd's *Europa*, and the experience is completely different (so is the cruise price).

First-time cruise passengers in particular will find this a fresh, comfortable, casual, and unpretentious ship for a cruise vacation. You don't need to buy a new wardrobe, and you can leave your tuxedo at home; for this ship you need only informal and casual clothes.

Well-planned itineraries and destination-intensive cruises are featured. Of particular note are the Great Lakes cruises, which are only possible because of the pencil-slim design of *C. Columbus* (the last ocean-going cruise vessel to operate Great Lakes cruises was *World Discoverer* in 1974).

Weak Points: The swimming pool is small (more like a "dip" pool), as is the open deck space. The standard cabins are also very small. There is no wraparound promenade deck outdoors. The layout and sight lines (including several pillars) in the show lounge are poor.

Costa Allegra
★★★

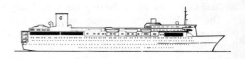

Mid-Size Ship:	28,430 tons	Cabins (for one person):	0
Lifestyle:	Standard	Cabins (with private balcony):	10
Cruise Line:	Costa Cruises	Cabins (wheelchair accessible):	8 (interior)
Former Names:	*Annie Johnson*	Cabin Current:	110/220-volt
Builder:	Mariotti Shipyards (Italy)	Full-Service Dining Rooms:	1
Original Cost:	$175 million	Elevators:	4
Entered Service:	December 1992	Casino (gaming tables):	Yes
Registry:	Italy	Slot Machines:	Yes
Length (ft/m):	616.1/187.8	Swimming Pools (outdoors):	1
Beam (ft/m):	83.9/25.6	Swimming Pools (indoors):	0
Draft (ft/m):	23.9/7.3	Whirlpools:	2
Propulsion/Propellers:	Diesel(19,200kW)/2	Fitness Center:	Yes
Passenger Decks:	8	Sauna/Steam Room:	Yes/Yes
Total Crew:	400	Massage:	Yes
Passengers (lower beds/all berths):	820/1,072	Self-Service Launderette:	No
Pass. Space Ratio (lower beds/all berths):	34.7/26.5	Dedicated Cinema:	No
Crew/Pass. Ratio (lower beds/all berths):	2.0/2.6	Library:	Yes
Navigation Officers:	Italian	Classification Society:	Registro Navale Italiano
Cabins (total):	410		
Size Range (sq ft/sq m):	105.4–265.8/9.8–24.7		
Cabins (outside view):	218		
Cabins (interior/no view):	192		

OVERALL SCORE:	**1,210**
(OUT OF A POSSIBLE 2,000 POINTS)	

Accommodation: The standard cabins are quite light and airy, with alluring splashes of fabric colors, and tasteful wood accenting, and are laid out in a practical manner. However, they are small, and there is little closet and drawer space, so take only casual clothing. There are many small interior (no view) cabins, and all cabins suffer from poor soundproofing. Many cabins also have Pullman berths for a third or fourth occupant. The bathrooms are compact, although they do feature good shower enclosures, with sliding circular door instead of the usual limp curtain. The cabin service menu is extremely limited.

On Rousseau Deck there are three forward-facing suites (the largest accommodation on board), each of which features a living room, dinette, and wet bar. A further ten slightly smaller mini-suites feature small, very narrow balconies, but they are really not private, as they can be seen from the walking track on the deck above.

Dining: The 370-seat Montmartre Restaurant is fairly spacious and has expansive glass windows that look out over the stern, while the port side and starboard side feature large portholes. It is a very noisy room, with tables for four, six, eight, or ten (there are no tables for two). Note that the time for dinner is later when the ship operates in Europe. Romantic candlelight dining is typically featured on a formal night. The cuisine is mostly continental, with many Italian dishes featured.

Although there is plenty of food, its quality and presentation often prove disappointing to those who expect better. While the quality of meats is adequate, it could be better, and is often disguised with gravies and rich sauces. Fish and seafood tend to be lacking in taste and are typically overcooked, and green vegetables are hard to come by. However, good pasta dishes are served each day (the pasta is made fresh on board daily), although quantity, not quality, is what appears from the galley. Breads and rolls are typically good, but desserts tend to be towards their "sell-by" date.

The service is basically sound, although you will probably note that there are few Italians serving in the dining room, as one might expect aboard the ship of an Italian company. There is a wine list, although there are no wine waiters (the table waiters are expected to serve both food and wine), and almost all wines are young — very young.

The Yacht Club is the informal dining spot, with two small centrally located buffet lines. Where breakfast and lunch buffets are concerned, Costa Cruises comes way down the list; they are rather plain, repetitive, and unimaginative, and fresh (ripe) fruit and cheese selections are poor. For ice cream lovers, a gelati cart provides welcome relief at least once each day.

Other Comments: *Costa Allegra* was originally a container ship built for Swedish Johnson Line that has undergone a skillful transformation into contemporary cruise vessel; this resulted in a jazzy, rather angular-looking ship with a low-slung appearance. There are three bolt-upright yellow funnels that have become a signature for almost all the ships of Costa Cruises (exception: *Costa Riviera*). Slightly longer and larger than her sister ship *Costa Marina* (following the addition of a 43 ft/13.44 m section), this ship enjoys a much better standard of interior fit and finish, with more outdoor space than her sister ship. Has an interesting glass-enclosed stern.

There is a high glass-to-steel ratio, with numerous glass domes and walls admitting light, as well as Murano glass light fixtures in some places. There is a good amount of outdoor deck and sunbathing space, although there is no observation lounge with forward-facing views over the ship's bows. Cushioned pads are provided for the deck lounge chairs outdoors.

The decks are named after famous painters. This ship features surprisingly nice interior decor, with cool, restful colors and soft furnishings, as well as domed ceilings and a big use of glass. In the Follies Bergeres Showlounge, some 14 pillars obstruct the sight lines to the semicircular stage from many seats.

Costa Allegra will provide a decent first cruise experience for young adults who enjoy European-style service and a real upbeat, almost elegant atmosphere with an Italian accent and lots of noise. However, few of the officers and crew are actually Italian, as one might expect.

Weak Points: There are few public restrooms. The children's room is too small, and the ship is simply not equipped to handle large numbers of children, which are aboard in the summer and at peak holiday periods. The many loud and extended announcements (in several languages) quickly become tiresome — there are no quiet spots to be found anywhere. The opening hours for the small library are really minimal. Tipping envelopes state the amount you are expected to give.

Costa Atlantica
★★★★

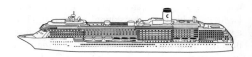

Large Ship:	85,700 tons	Cabins (with private balcony):	742
Lifestyle:	Standard	Cabins (wheelchair accessible):	8
Cruise Line:	Costa Cruises	Cabin Current:	110-volt
Former Names:	-	Full-Service Dining Rooms:	1
Builder:	Kvaerner Masa-Yards (Finland)		(+1 specialty restaurant)
Original Cost:	$335 million	Elevators:	12
Entered Service:	July 2000	Casino (gaming tables):	Yes
Registry:	Italy	Slot Machines:	Yes
Length (ft/m):	959.6/292.5	Swimming Pools (outdoors):	2 (+1 indoor/outdoor)
Beam (ft/m):	105.6/32.2	Swimming Pools (indoors):	No
Draft (ft/m):	25.5/7.8	Whirlpools:	Yes
Propulsion/Propellers: Diesel-electric (34,000kW)/2		Fitness Center:	Yes
Passenger Decks:	12	Sauna/Steam Room:	Yes/Yes
Total Crew:	902	Massage:	Yes
Passengers (lower beds/all berths):	2,112/2,680	Self-Service Launderette:	No
Pass. Space Ratio (lower beds/all berths): 40.5/31.9		Dedicated Cinema:	No
Crew/Pass. Ratio (lower beds/all berths): 2.3/2.9		Library:	Yes
Navigation Officers:	Italian	Classification Society:	Registro Navale Italiano
Cabins (total):	1,056		
Size Range (sq ft/sq m):	161.4–387.5/15.0–36.0		
Cabins (outside view):	843		
Cabins (interior/no view):	213		
Cabins (for one person):	0		

OVERALL SCORE: **1,438**

(OUT OF A POSSIBLE 2,000 POINTS)

Accommodation: There is a healthy (78%) proportion of outside-view to interior (no view) cabins. All of the cabins feature twin beds that can be converted into a queen-size bed, individually controlled air-conditioning, TV, and telephone. Note that some cabins have their views obstructed by lifeboats — on Deck 4 (Roma Deck), the lowest of the accommodation decks, as well as some cabins on Deck 5. Some cabins feature pull-down Pullman berths that are fully hidden in the ceiling when not in use.

Some of the most desirable suites and cabins are those with private balconies on the five aft-facing decks (Decks 4, 5, 6, 7, and 8) with views overlooking the stern and ship's wash. The other cabins with private balconies will find the balconies not so private — the partition between one balcony and the next is not a full partition — so you will be able to hear your neighbors (or smell their smoke). However, these balcony occupants all have good views through glass and wood-topped railings, and the deck is made of teak. The cabins are well laid out, typically with twin beds that convert to a queen-size bed, vanity desk (with built-in hairdryer), large TV, personal safe, and one closet that features moveable shelves — thus providing more space for luggage storage. However, note that the lighting is fluorescent, and much too harsh (the bedside control is for a master switch only — other individual lights cannot be controlled). The bathroom is a simple, modular unit that features shower enclosures with soap dispenser; there is a good amount of stowage space for personal toiletry items.

The largest suites are those designated as Penthouse Suites, although they are really quite small when compared with suites aboard other ships of a similar size (for example, those of Celebrity Cruises' *Century, Galaxy, Mercury, Millennium*). However, they do at least offer more space to move around in, and a slightly larger, better bathroom.

Dining: The Tiziano (main) Dining Room is large, and located on two levels, with a spiral stairway between them (the galley itself is located under the dining room, and accessed by escalators). There are two seatings, with tables for two, four, six, or eight. Themed evenings are a part of the Costa Cruises tradition, and three different window blinds help create a different feel. However, the artwork is placed at table height, so the room seems more closed in than it should.

Although there is plenty of food, its quality and presentation prove disappointing to those who expect better. The quality of meats is adequate, but could be better, and is often disguised with gravies and rich sauces. Fish and seafood tend to lack flavor and are typically overcooked, and green vegetables are hard to come by. However, good pasta dishes are served daily (the pasta made fresh every day), although quantity, not quality, rules the galley. Breads and rolls are typically good, but desserts tend to be towards their "sell-by" date.

The service is basically sound, although you will probably note that there are few Italians serving in the dining room, as one might expect aboard the ship of an Italian company. There is a wine list, although there are no wine waiters (the table waiters are expected to serve both food and wine), and almost all wines are young — very young.

A reservations-only alternative for dinner, Ristorante Magnifico by Zeffirino, is available six nights each week, with a service charge of $18.75 per person (passengers occupying suites will get a complimentary pass for one evening).

Undoubtedly the place that most people will want to see and be seen is at the Caffe Florian — a total replica of the famous indoor/outdoor café of the same name, which opened in December 1720 in St. Mark's Square, Venice. There are four separate salons (Sala delle Stagioni, Sala del Senato, Sala Liberty, and Sala degli Uomini Illustri), and the same fascinating mosaic, marble and wood floors, opulent ceiling art, and special lampshades. Even the espresso/cappuccino machine is a duplicate of that found in the real thing. This Caffe Florian is ideal for drinks (fortunately the prices aboard ship are a little lower), music, and people-watching. The only problem is with the chairs — they were obviously designed for children, not the size of passengers that might inhabit the ship during the winter (Caribbean) season.

Casual breakfast and luncheon self-serve buffet-style meals can be taken in the Botticelli Buffet Restaurant, adjacent to the swimming pools, with seating both indoors and outdoors. A grill (for hamburgers and hot dogs) and a pasta bar are conveniently located outside adjacent to the second pool, while the Napoli Pizzeria is indoors.

Other Comments: The first thing that regular passengers will notice is the extremely long length of this ship. Longer than the company's largest ship to date (*Costa Victoria*), and only a tad shorter than Cunard Line's *Queen Elizabeth 2*, the new design makes the ship look much more sleek than any other ship in the Costa Cruises fleet. She is the largest ship in the fleet, and has basically the same exterior design and internal layout as that of the second ship in the new "8000" series, *Carnival Spirit*.

Costa Atlantica sports the now familiar, and instantly recognizable, yellow upright funnels, with one large funnel and two small exhaust funnels set farther back, in a slightly different arrangement to the clusters of previous newbuilds (*Costa Classica, Costa Romantica,* and *Costa Victoria*). The propulsion is provided by two azimuthing pods which are hung under the ship's stern (rather like giant outboard motors). These replace the conventional shaft and rudder system (the pods have forward-facing propellers that can be turned through 360 degrees).

There are two centrally located swimming pools outdoors, one of which can be used in inclement weather due to its retractable magrodome cover. A bar abridges two adjacent whirlpool tubs. Another smaller pool is available for children; there is also a winding water slide that spans two decks in height (it starts on a platform bridge located between the two aft funnels). There is also an additional whirlpool tub outdoors.

Inside, the layout is somewhat of an extension of that found in previous newbuilds for Costa Cruises — particularly that of *Costa Victoria*. All the deck names are Italian (Roma Deck, Le Notte di Cabiria, La Voce della Luna, La Strada, La Luci del Varieta, for example), with one curious exception, a deck named Ginger and Fred! The interior design is, however, a bold and brash mix of classical Italy and contemporary features. Good points include the fact that the interior design allows good passenger flow from one public space to another, and there are several floor spaces for dancing, and a range of bars and lounges for socializing.

There is a three-deck-high show lounge (called the Caruso Theater), with a main floor and two balcony levels around the perimeter (spiral stairways at the back of the lounge connect all three levels). A small chapel (there is one aboard all the ships of Costa Cruises) is located forward of the uppermost level.

Other facilities include a winding shopping street with several boutique stores (Fendi, Gianni Versace, Paul & Shark Yachting, as well as a shop dedicated to selling Caffe Florian products), photo gallery, video games room, an observation balcony in the center of the vessel (at the top of the multideck atrium), a casino, and a library (with Internet access via one of several computer terminals).

Health spa facilities include a solarium, eight treatment rooms, sauna and steam rooms for men and women, beauty parlor, and gymnasium with floor-to-ceiling windows on three sides. There is also a jogging track outdoors, located around the ship's mast and the forward third of the ship.

Costa Cruises has, during the recent past, been busy updating its image and retraining its staff, in order to provide more hospitality and better personal service for its passengers. With the debut of *Costa Atlantica* came many new, better uniforms for many departments, as well as more choice in a ship that is designed to wow the hip and trendy as well as pay homage to many of Italy's great art masters. Food and service levels have been raised to a better standard than that found aboard all other Costa Cruises ships to date. This new ship operates 7-night Mediterranean cruises during the summer (from Venice) and 7-night Caribbean cruises during the winter (from Ft. Lauderdale).

Weak Points: There are too many lines; however, standing in line for embarkation, disembarkation, shore tenders, and for self-serve buffet meals is an inevitable aspect of cruising aboard all large ships. There is too much use of fluorescent lighting in the suites and cabins, and the soundproofing could be much better than it is; some bathroom fixtures — bath and shower taps in particular — are quite frustrating to use until you get the hang of them. Some tables in the Tiziano Dining Room have a less than comfortable view of the harsh lighting of the escalators between the galley and the two decks of the dining room. There are far too many pillars obstructing passenger flow and sight lines throughout the ship; the pillars are everywhere (there is even one right in the middle — actually positioned slightly off-center — of a winding "shopping street"). Indeed, the many pillars in the dining room make it extremely difficult for the waiters and the proper service of food. The fit and finish of some of the interior decoration is quite poor. The hospitality levels and service are inconsistent and very spotty, and below the standard of several other "major" cruise lines.

Costa Classica
★★★ +

Large Ship:	52,950 tons	Cabins (for one person):	0
Lifestyle:	Standard	Cabins (with private balcony):	10
Cruise Line:	Costa Cruises	Cabins (wheelchair accessible):	6 (interior)
Former Names:	-	Cabin Current:	110/220-volt
Builder:	Fincantieri (Italy)	Full-Service Dining Rooms:	1
Original Cost:	$283.3 million	Elevators:	8
Entered Service:	January 1992	Casino (gaming tables):	Yes
Registry:	Italy	Slot Machines:	Yes
Length (ft/m):	718.5/220.61	Swimming Pools (outdoors):	2
Beam (ft/m):	98.4/30.80	Swimming Pools (indoors):	0
Draft (ft/m):	25.0/7.60	Whirlpools:	4
Propulsion/Propellers:	Diesel (22,800kW)/2	Fitness Center:	Yes
Passenger Decks:	10	Sauna/Steam Room:	Yes/Yes
Total Crew:	600	Massage:	Yes
Passengers (lower beds/all berths):	1,308/1,764	Self-Service Launderette:	No
Pass. Space Ratio (lower beds/all berths):	40.4/30.0	Dedicated Cinema:	No
Crew/Pass. Ratio (lower beds/all berths):	2.1/2.9	Library:	Yes
Navigation Officers:	Italian	Classification Society:	Registro Navale Italiano
Cabins (total):	654		
Size Range (sq ft/sq m):	185.1–430.5/17.2–40.0	**OVERALL SCORE:**	**1,368**
Cabins (outside view):	438	(OUT OF A POSSIBLE 2,000 POINTS)	
Cabins (interior/no view):	216		

Accommodation: The cabins are of a fairly generous size, and are laid out in a practical manner. They have cherry wood-veneered cabinetry and include a vanity desk unit with a large mirror. There are useful sliding doors to bathroom and closets, and good soundproofing. The soft furnishings are of good quality, but the room service menu is disappointing. The suites feature more space (although they are not large), and hand-woven bedspreads.

In November 2001, *Costa Classica* was due to undergo a $10 million refurbishment program, which includes many changes in cabins and bathrooms.

Dining: The Tivoli Dining Room has a lovely indented clean white ceiling, although it is extremely noisy (there are two seatings), and there are a good number of tables for two, as well as tables for four, six, or eight. Changeable wall panels help create a European Renaissance atmosphere, albeit at the expense of blocking off windows (but during dinner, it's dark outside anyway — unless you are in the far North). Note that the dinner times for European cruises are later than when the ship operates in the Caribbean. Romantic candlelight dining is typically featured on formal nights. Features reasonable continental cuisine, with many Italian dishes that are typically quite salty, and the presentation and quality are poor.

Although there is plenty of food, its quality and presentation often prove disappointing to those who expect better. While the quality of meats is adequate, it could be better, and is often disguised with gravies and rich sauces. Fish and seafood tend to be lacking in taste and are typically overcooked, and green vegetables are hard to come by. However, good pasta dishes are served each day (the pasta is made fresh on board daily), although quantity, not quality, is what appears from the galley. Breads and rolls are typically good, but desserts tend to be towards their "sell-by" date.

The service is basically sound, although you will probably note that there are few Italians serving in the dining room, as one might expect aboard the ship of an Italian company. There is a wine list, although there are no wine waiters (the table waiters are expected to serve both food and wine), and almost all wines are young — very young.

For casual eating, the Alfresco Café, located outdoors, is moderately good, depending on what you expect. Unfortunately, breakfast and luncheon buffets are really poor and unimaginative, with little variety, and long lines are typical. The selection of bread rolls, fruits, and cheeses is disappointing.

Other Comments: *Costa Classica*, all-white with a straight slab-sided profile, topped by Costa Cruises' unmistakable trio of tall yellow funnels, has brought Costa into the mainstream of cruising, Italian-style.

Inside, the ship features contemporary, innovative Italian design and styling that is best described as befitting European tastes. There is an excellent range of public rooms, lounges, and bars from which to choose. A number of specially designed good business and meeting facilities can be found; the rooms provide multiflexible configurations.

There is some fascinating artwork, including six hermaphrodite statues in one lounge. There is a fine, if unconventional, multitiered amphitheater-style show lounge, but the seats are bolt upright and are uncomfortable for more than a few minutes. The multilevel atrium is stark and angular, and cold.

The marble-covered staircases look pleasant, but are uncarpeted and really do not work well aboard a cruise ship, and are institutional (not to mention just a little dangerous if water or drinks are spilled on them when the ship is moving).

Perhaps the interior is best described as an innovative design project that almost works. A forward observation lounge/nightclub sits atop ship like a lump of cheese, and, unfortunately, fails to work well as a nightclub. Internet access is available from one of several computer terminals in the Internet Café.

The staff is reasonably friendly, and, although the "spit and polish" of fine service is definitely missing, they will help you to have an enjoyable cruise (especially when pushing for gratuities). Sadly, the dress code has become very casual throughout, even on formal nights. Most passengers will be Italian, with a generous sprinkling of other European nationalities. One night (towards the end of each cruise) is typically reserved for a "Roman Bacchanal," which means that passengers dress up toga-style for dinner and beyond.

In November 2001 the ship is scheduled to enter dry-dock for a "chop-and-stretch" operation that will increase her tonnage to 78,000, her length to 870.7 ft (265.4 m), and her passenger capacity to 2,516. The stretch will accommodate a new section of 147 ft (44.8 m) to be added forward of the parallel midbody. Included in the stretch/refit will be a further 356 passenger cabins (some of which are proposed for single occupancy). On the technical side, her engines will be upgraded for better fuel efficiency, and more generators will be added to cope with the increased demand for electricity and air-conditioning, etc.

Weak Points: Standing in line for embarkation, disembarkation, shore tenders, and for self-serve buffet meals is an inevitable aspect of cruising aboard all large ships. There is no wraparound promenade deck outdoors. There are too many loud, repetitive and irritating announcements. Shore excursions are very expensive. Tipping envelopes provided in your cabin state the amount you are expected to give.

Costa Marina
★★★

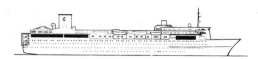

Mid-Size Ship:	25,441 tons	Cabins (for one person):	0
Lifestyle:	Standard	Cabins (with private balcony):	8
Cruise Line:	Costa Cruises	Cabins (wheelchair accessible):	0
Former Names:	*Axel Johnson*	Cabin Current:	110/220-volt
Builder:	Mariotti Shipyards (Italy)	Full-Service Dining Rooms:	1
Original Cost:	$130 million	Elevators:	8
Entered Service:	July 1990	Casino (gaming tables):	Yes
Registry:	Italy	Slot Machines:	Yes
Length (ft/m):	571.8/174.25	Swimming Pools (outdoors):	1
Beam (ft/m):	84.6/25.75	Swimming Pools (indoors):	0
Draft (ft/m):	26.1/8.20	Whirlpools:	3
Propulsion/Propellers:	Diesel(19,152kW)/2	Fitness Center:	Yes
Passenger Decks:	8	Sauna/Steam Room:	Yes/Yes
Total Crew:	400	Massage:	Yes
Passengers (lower beds/all berths):	772/1,005	Self-Service Launderette:	No
Pass. Space Ratio (lower beds/all berths):	32.9/25.3	Dedicated Cinema:	No
Crew/Pass. Ratio (lower beds/all berths):	1.9/2.5	Library:	Yes
Navigation Officers:	Italian	Classification Society:	Registro Navale Italiano
Cabins (total):	386		
Size Range (sq ft/sq m):	104.4–264.8/9.7–24.6		
Cabins (outside view):	183	**OVERALL SCORE:**	**1,209**
Cabins (interior/no view):	205	**(OUT OF A POSSIBLE 2,000 POINTS)**	

Accommodation: Both the outside-view and interior (no view) cabins are quite comfortable, but have very plain, almost clinical, decor and no warmth. Bathrooms are functional, but there is little space for personal toiletry items. The illuminated cabin numbers outside each cabin are novel. The room service menu is poor.

Dining: The 452-seat Cristal Restaurant is fairly spacious and has expansive glass windows that look out over the stern, while port and starboard sides feature large portholes. There are two seatings. The color scheme, however, is institutional. There are only two tables for two, the other tables are for four, six, or eight. Romantic candlelight dining is typically featured on a formal night.

Although there is plenty of food, its quality and presentation often prove disappointing to those who expect better. While the quality of meats is adequate, it could be better, and is often disguised with gravies and rich sauces. Fish and seafood tend to be lacking in taste and are typically overcooked, and green vegetables are hard to come by. However, good pasta dishes are served each day (the pasta is made fresh on board daily), although quantity, not quality, is what appears from the galley. Breads and rolls are typically good, but desserts tend to be towards their "sell-by" date.

The service is basically sound, although you will probably note that there are few Italians serving in the dining room, as one might expect aboard the ship of an Italian company. There is a wine list, although there are no wine waiters (the table waiters are expected to serve both food and wine), and almost all wines are young — very young.

Other Comments: *Costa Marina* is an interesting, though very angular-looking, mid-size ship, the first of two such ships (her almost identically designed, though slightly longer sister ship is *Costa Allegra*). There is a high glass-to-steel ratio, with numerous glass domes and walls, and a cutaway stern virtually replaced by a glass wall (which are in fact the dining room windows), and a stark upright cluster of three yellow funnels.

Most public rooms are located above the accommodation decks and feature several bars and lounges. This is very much an Italian ship and will provide a good first cruise experience for young European passengers. There is generally good passenger flow throughout her public room spaces, although congestion occurs when first seating passengers move from the dining room to the show lounge and other public rooms, and when second seating passengers move from the public rooms to the dining room.

As this book was completed, it was announced that *Costa Marina* would be dedicated to the German-speaking market, starting in spring 2002, and that the ship would undergo considerable interior redecoration accordingly.

Weak Points: The fit and finish of this vessel are below standard. There is a very limited amount of open deck and sunbathing space. Note that there is no observation lounge with forward-facing views. The swimming pool is really tiny. There are simply too many interior (no view) cabins. There are poor sight lines in the show lounge, with too many pillars (14). The library is really poor. Tipping envelopes provided in your cabin state the amount you are expected to give.

QUESTIONS TO ASK YOUR TRAVEL AGENT

→ Is air transportation included in the cabin rate quoted? If not, what will be the extra cost?

→ What other extra costs will be involved? These can include port charges, insurance, gratuities, shore excursions, laundry, and drinks.

→ What is the cruise line's cancellation policy?

→ If I want to make changes to my air arrangements, routing, dates, and so on, will the insurance policy cover everything in case of missed or canceled flights?

→ Does your agency deal with only one or several different insurance companies?

→ Does the cruise line offer advance booking discounts or other incentives?

→ Do you have preferred suppliers or do you book any cruise on any cruise ship?

→ Have you sailed aboard the ship I want to book or one that you are recommending?

→ Is your agency bonded and insured? If so, by whom?

→ If you book the shore excursions offered and recommended by the cruise line, is insurance coverage provided?

Costa Riviera
★★★

Mid-Size Ship:	30,340 tons	Cabins (for one person):	0
Lifestyle:	Standard	Cabins (with private balcony):	0
Cruise Line:	Costa Cruises	Cabins (wheelchair accessible):	0
Former Names: *American Adventure, CostaRiviera,*		Cabin Current:	110/220-volt
Guglielmo Marconi		Full-Service Dining Rooms:	1
Builder:	Cantieri Riuniti dell' Adriatico (Italy)	Elevators:	7
Original Cost:	$33.7 million (reconstruction)	Casino (gaming tables):	Yes
Entered Service:	October 1963/May 1995	Slot Machines:	Yes
Registry:	Italy	Swimming Pools (outdoors):	1
Length (ft/m):	700.1/213.4	Swimming Pools (indoors):	0
Beam (ft/m):	94.1/28.71	Whirlpools:	3
Draft (ft/m):	23.9/7.3	Fitness Center:	Yes
Propulsion/Propellers: Steam turbine (32,800kW)/2		Sauna/Steam Room:	Yes/Yes
Passenger Decks:	8	Massage:	Yes
Total Crew:	500	Self-Service Launderette:	No
Passengers (lower beds/all berths):	974/1,819	Dedicated Cinema/Seats:	Yes/180
Pass. Space Ratio (lower beds/all berths):	31.1/16.6	Library:	Yes
Crew/Pass. Ratio (lower beds/all berths):	1.9/3.6	Classification Society:	Registro Navale Italiano
Navigation Officers:	Italian		
Cabins (total):	487		
Size Range (sq ft/sq m):	150.6–209.9/14.0–19.5	**OVERALL SCORE:**	**1,152**
Cabins (outside view):	285	**(OUT OF A POSSIBLE 2,000 POINTS)**	
Cabins (interior/no view):	202		

Accommodation: There are a wide variety of cabin sizes, styles, and configurations from which to choose. Many cabins are large enough for families of five or six, while many others will accommodate three or four persons. The cabin insulation is not good, however (you can hear your neighbor brushing their hair), and the bathrooms are small, very compact units, with little space to place or store personal toiletry items. All cabins have a telephone.

Dining: The 770-seat Portofino Restaurant, which has portholes and not windows, is large and bubbly (noisy), although it is plain and unattractive (especially the ceiling). There are two seatings. Romantic candlelight dining is typically featured on a formal night. Reasonable continental food is provided; this includes plenty of good pasta dishes (the pasta is made fresh on board daily), pizza, and buffet variety, but the desserts are really forgettable.

Although there is plenty of food, its quality and presentation often prove disappointing to those who expect better. While the quality of meats is adequate, it could be better, and is often disguised with gravies and rich sauces. Fish and seafood tend to be lacking in taste and are typically overcooked, and green vegetables are hard to come by. However, quantity, not quality, is what appears from the galley. Breads and rolls are typically good, but desserts tend to be towards their "sell-by" date.

The service is basically sound, although you will probably note that there are few Italians serving in the dining room, as one might expect aboard the ship of an Italian company. There is a wine list, although there are no wine waiters (the table waiters are expected to serve both food and wine), and almost all wines are young — very young.

Other Comments: *Costa Riviera* is a reconstructed former two-class ocean liner from the 1960s which was completely refurbished in 1993 in theme-park style to appeal to families, refurbished again in 1994 for Italian family cruising, and updated again in 1998. She is a solidly built ship that is stable and quiet at sea, with no vibration due to the surprising fact that she is powered by steam turbines. She rides well, due to her deep draft. Built-up fore and aft decks provide a good amount of open deck and sunbathing space.

The interior decor and styling, colors, appointments, and everything else are geared principally to couples and families with children. There is a good array of public rooms (most are located on one main entertainment deck). One nice feature is the cinema, which also has a balcony level. The lobby provides more light and room, and is now two decks high.

There is a very casual, unpretentious and bubbly (noisy) ambience and a very relaxed dress code. This ship will provide you with a cruise in relatively comfortable, family-filled surroundings for a modest price, with activities designed for participation, which means lots of noise. Think of her as a colorful, activity-filled ship, particularly catering to an Italian family clientele.

Weak Points: Standing in line for embarkation, disembarkation, shore tenders, and for self-serve buffet meals is an inevitable aspect of cruising aboard all large ships. The internal layout is a little disjointed; this is because the ship was originally built as a two-class ocean liner. There is no observation lounge with forward-facing views over the ship's bows. The many announcements quickly become tedious. There is noise everywhere, and a lot of cigarette smoke. Cleanliness could be better in some areas. The air-conditioning is quite noisy in many cabins, and there is very little adjustment. Tipping envelopes provided in your cabin and state the amount you are expected to give.

Costa Romantica
★★★ +

Large Ship:	53,049 tons	Cabins (for one person):	0
Lifestyle:	Standard	Cabins (with private balcony):	10
Cruise Line:	Costa Cruises	Cabins (wheelchair accessible):	6 (interior)
Former Names:	-	Cabin Current:	110-volt
Builder:	Fincantieri (Italy)	Full-Service Dining Rooms:	1
Original Cost:	$325 million	Elevators:	8
Entered Service:	November 1993	Casino (gaming tables):	Yes
Registry:	Italy	Slot Machines:	Yes
Length (ft/m):	718.5/220.61	Swimming Pools (outdoors):	2
Beam (ft/m):	98.4/30.89	Swimming Pools (indoors):	0
Draft (ft/m):	25.0/7.60	Whirlpools:	4
Propulsion/Propellers:	Diesel (22,800kW)/2	Fitness Center:	Yes
Passenger Decks:	10	Sauna/Steam Room:	Yes/No
Total Crew:	600	Massage:	Yes
Passengers (lower beds/all berths):	1,356/1,779	Self-Service Launderette:	No
Pass. Space Ratio (lower beds/all berths):	39.1/29.8	Dedicated Cinema:	No
Crew/Pass. Ratio (lower beds/all berths):	2.2/2.9	Library:	Yes
Navigation Officers:	Italian	Classification Society:	Registro Navale Italiano
Cabins (total):	678		
Size Range (sq ft/sq m):	185.1–430.5/17.2–40.0	**OVERALL SCORE:**	**1,369**
Cabins (outside view):	462		
Cabins (interior/no view):	216	**(OUT OF A POSSIBLE 2,000 POINTS)**	

Accommodation: The 16 suites (with floor-to-ceiling windows) and 18 mini-suites are really quite pleasant (except for the balconies of the 10 suites on Madrid Deck, where a solid steel half-wall blocks the view; a glass half-wall and polished wood rail would be better). A sliding door separates the bedroom from the living room, and bathrooms are of a decent size. Cherry wood walls and cabinetry help make these suites warm and very attractive. The six suites at the forward section of Monte Carlo Deck are the largest, and have huge glass windows with superb forward views, but no balconies.

All other cabins are of a standard, moderately generous size, and all have nicely finished cherry wood cabinetry and walls (the ceilings are plain). However, the cabin bathrooms and shower enclosures are small. There are a good number of triple and quad cabins that are ideal for families with children. The company's in-cabin food service menu is extremely basic.

Dining: The 728-seat Botticelli Restaurant is better designed and a little less noisy than in her sister ship of the same size (*Costa Classica*, before the ship was due to be "stretched" in late 2001), and there are several tables for two, four, six, or eight. There are two seatings, and there are both smoking and non-smoking sections. Romantic candlelight dining is typically featured on a formal night. Reasonable continental cuisine, but the presentation and food quality need improving. The pasta dishes and cream sauces, however, are very good.

Although there is plenty of food, its quality and presentation often prove disappointing to those who expect better. While the quality of meats is adequate, it could be better, and is often disguised with gravies and rich sauces. Fish and seafood tend to be lacking in taste and are typically overcooked, and green vegetables are hard to come by. However, good pasta dishes are served each day (the pasta is made fresh on board daily), although quantity, not quality, is what appears from the galley. Breads and rolls are typically good, but desserts tend to be towards their "sell-by" date.

The service is basically sound, although you will probably note that there are few Italians serving in the dining room, as one might expect aboard the ship of an Italian company. There is a wine list, although there are no wine waiters (the table waiters are expected to serve both food and wine), and almost all wines are young — very young.

For informal dining there is a much improved and more practical buffet layout than in her sister ship, but it is far too small, and buffets are very much standard fare, really unimaginative, with the exception of some good commercial pasta dishes. One would expect Italian waiters, but, sadly, this is not the case now, with most of the waiters coming from countries other than Italy (many are from the Philippines).

Other Comments: *Costa Romantica* is a bold, contemporary ship with an upright yellow funnel cluster of three typical of Italian styling today. Costa is well established in Europe, and its Italian-style cruising is something it does well. Sadly, there is no wraparound promenade deck outdoors, and so contact with the sea is minimal, although there is some good open space on several of the upper levels.

She has a much nicer interior design than her sister ship, *Costa Classica*, and the decor is decidedly warmer. The layout and flow are somewhat disjointed, however. She has a good number of business and conference facilities, with several flexible meeting rooms for groups of different sizes. The decor is decidedly Italian, chic and very tasteful, and should appeal to both Europeans and sophisticated North Americans.

The multilevel atrium is open and spacious, and features a revolving mobile sculpture. The amphitheater-style, two-deck-high, multitiered show lounge is good, and has interesting artwork, but the stark upright seating is really uncomfortable. Ten large pillars obstruct the sight lines to the stage from many seats. There is also a small chapel (in a different location than in her sister ship), and several intimate public rooms, lounges and bars. Internet access is available from one of several computer terminals in the Internet Café.

Costa Cruises does a good job of providing first-time cruise passengers with a well-packaged vacation that is a mix of sophistication and basic fare, albeit accompanied by rather loud music and an international staff that seem to have lost direction. During the summer, this ship cruises in the Mediterranean region, while during the winter she cruises in the Caribbean (when there are more American passengers than Europeans).

Weak Points: Standing in line for embarkation, disembarkation, shore tenders, and for self-serve buffet meals is an inevitable aspect of cruising aboard all large ships. Announcements are plentiful and loud. The reception desk staff is very poor and impersonal, like in a bad hotel, and cigarette smoke is everywhere. Tipping envelopes provided in your cabin state the amount you are expected to give.

Costa Tropicale
★★★

Large Ship:	35,190 tons	Cabins (for one person):	0
Lifestyle:	Standard	Cabins (with private balcony):	12
Cruise Line:	Costa Cruises	Cabins (wheelchair accessible):	11
Former Names:	*Tropicale*	Cabin Current:	110-volt
Builder:	Aalborg Vaerft (Denmark)	Full-Service Dining Rooms:	1
Original Cost:	$100 million	Elevators:	8
Entered Service:	January 1982/June 2001	Casino (gaming tables):	Yes
Registry:	Italy	Slot Machines:	Yes
Length (ft/m):	671.7/204.76	Swimming Pools (outdoors):	3
Beam (ft/m):	86.7/26.45	Swimming Pools (indoors):	0
Draft (ft/m):	23.3/7.11	Whirlpools:	0
Propulsion/Propellers:	Diesel (19,566kW)/2	Fitness Center:	Yes
Passenger Decks:	10	Sauna/Steam Room:	Yes/No
Total Crew:	5500	Massage:	Yes
Passengers (lower beds/all berths):	1,022/1,412	Self-Service Launderette:	Yes
Pass. Space Ratio (lower beds/all berths):	34.4/24.9	Dedicated Cinema:	No
Crew/Pass. Ratio (lower beds/all berths):	1.8/2.5	Library:	Yes
Navigation Officers:	Italian	Classification Society:	Registro Navale Italiano
Cabins (total):	511		
Size Range (sq ft/sq m):	180.0–350.0/16.7–32.5	**OVERALL SCORE:**	**1,239**
Cabins (outside view):	324	(OUT OF A POSSIBLE 2,000 POINTS)	
Cabins (interior/no view):	187		

Accommodation: There are 12 accommodation categories to choose from. Most of the "standard" interior (no view) and outside-view cabins are all of the standard cookie-cutter variety (although they are of quite a decent size), with an imaginative European-style decor, and just enough closet and drawer space for passengers to manage for a week. The bathrooms are quite plain, but adequate. A number of cabins have third and fourth person upper berths added — these are good for families with children.

The best accommodation can be found in 12 "suites" — each of which has a small (narrow) semiprivate balcony. Naturally, there is more space, with the living and sleeping areas divided. The bathroom is marginally larger, too. However, all of these suites have their views substantially blocked by the positioning of the lifeboats.

Dining: The Riviera Restaurant is located on the ship's lowest deck. It is colorful, very cheerful, brightly lit, but noisy and extremely cramped, which makes correct service quite difficult. There are tables for four, six, or eight (there are no tables for two), and dining is in two seatings.

Although there is plenty of food, its quality and presentation often prove disappointing to those who expect better. While the quality of meats is adequate, it could be better, and is often disguised with gravies and rich sauces. Fish and seafood tend to be lacking in taste and are typically overcooked, and green vegetables are hard to come by. However, good pasta dishes are served each day (the pasta is made fresh on board daily), although quantity, not quality, is what appears from the galley. Breads and rolls are typically good, but desserts are very standard, nondescript affairs.

The service is basically sound, although you will probably note that there are few Italians serving in the dining room, as one might expect aboard the ship of an Italian company. There is a wine list, although there are no wine waiters (the table waiters are expected to serve both food and wine), and almost all wines are young — very young.

The Lido Café features self-yourself buffets, which are very basic, as is the selection of breads, rolls, fruit, and cheeses. At night, the Seaview Bistro (as the Lido Café becomes known) provides a casual alternative to eating in the main dining room. It serves pasta, steaks, salads, and desserts.

Other Comments: *Costa Tropicale* (whose former name was simply *Tropicale*) was the first new ship ever ordered by the former owner, Carnival Cruise Lines, and her exterior design led the way for that company's clutch of newbuildings during the following years. The ship was acquired by Costa Cruises in January 2001, and given a $24 million dollar refit and refurbishment, including a new yellow funnel, after which

235

she has settled down well into the European itineraries and programs of Costa Cruises. The ship has a fairly distinctive, though somewhat squared-off look.

The interior design is reasonably well laid out, and the ship generally has a good passenger flow. The public rooms are decorated in European colors, which are designed to make everyone feel lively. The show lounge is only one deck high, and the sight lines to the stage are not good from many seats, due to several pillars positioned in the way. Internet access is also available from one of several computer terminals in the Internet Café.

Costa Tropicale is a good ship for families with children, as Costa Cruises goes out of its way to entertain young cruisers as well as their parents, particularly during summer and other busy school holiday periods.

Costa Tropicale now looks spiffy and more contemporary under the Costa Cruises banner, although she is one of the smallest ships in the fleet. This is not a luxury cruise product, nor does it pretend to be. But you and your family will probably have fun, and there are plenty of opportunities for gaming and partying.

Weak Points: Standing in line for embarkation, disembarkation, shore tenders, and for self-serve buffet meals is an inevitable aspect of cruising aboard all large ships. There are few balcony cabins. Unfortunately, there is no wraparound open promenade deck — or any walking space outdoors. The ship has low quality fittings and cabinetry in many areas. There is noise and loud music everywhere. The health spa is small and has only the most minimal facilities.

Costa Victoria
★★★★

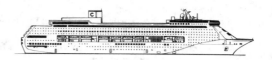

Large Ship:	75,200 tons	Cabins (for one person):	0
Lifestyle:	Standard	Cabins (with private balcony):	0
Cruise Line:	Costa Cruises	Cabins (wheelchair accessible):	0
Former Names:	-	Cabin Current:	110/220-volt
Builder:	Bremer Vulkan (Germany)	Full-Service Dining Rooms:	2
Original Cost:	$388 million	Elevators:	12
Entered Service:	July 1996	Casino (gaming tables):	Yes
Registry:	Italy	Slot Machines:	Yes
Length (ft/m):	823.0/251.00	Swimming Pools (outdoors):	2
Beam (ft/m):	105.5/32.25	Swimming Pools (indoors):	1
Draft (ft/m):	25.6/7.8	Whirlpools:	4
Propulsion/Propellers:	Diesel (30,000kW)/2	Fitness Center:	Yes
Passenger Decks:	10	Sauna/Steam Room:	Yes/Yes
Total Crew:	800	Massage:	Yes
Passengers (lower beds/all berths):	1,928/2,464	Self-Service Launderette:	Yes
Pass. Space Ratio (lower beds/all berths):	39.0/30.5	Dedicated Cinema:	No
Crew/Pass. Ratio (lower beds/all berths):	2.4/3.0	Library:	Yes
Navigation Officers:	Italian	Classification Society:	Registro Navale Italiano
Cabins (total):	964		
Size Range (sq ft/sq m):	120.0–430.5/11.1–40.0		
Cabins (outside view):	573		
Cabins (interior/no view):	391		

OVERALL SCORE: 1,406
(OUT OF A POSSIBLE 2,000 POINTS)

Accommodation: There are six large Panorama suites (each has third/fourth Pullman berths in a separate, tiny, train-like compartment) and 14 mini-suites (the six suites feature delicate floral fabrics), all with butler service; 65% of all other cabins have outside views, but they are small (for two). While the suites are not large, all other cabins are of rather mean dimensions. Some (only 16) of the interior (no view) cabins accommodate four, while all other cabins are for two or three persons.

All cabins feature wood cabinetry, with a fair amount of closet and drawer space for two for a one-week cruise, excellent air-conditioning, minibar/refrigerator, and electric blackout window blind (there are no curtains). The ocean-view cabins have large picture windows. The cabin bathrooms are small but well appointed, and (sensibly) have a sliding door. There are six cabins for the physically handicapped (each has two bathrooms); all are well located, and adjacent to elevators in the center of the ship.

Note that the personal safe is difficult to reach, and cabin stewards simply have too many cabins to clean, and no help, which means that the service is less than desirable.

Dining: The two main dining rooms, the 594-seat Minuetto Restaurant, and the 506-seat Fantasia Restaurant are separated by the main galley between the two. There are two seatings, and smoking and nonsmoking sections in both restaurants. They are expansive (there are a few tables for two, most being for four, six, or eight) and feature marble and pine walls. Romantic candlelight dining is typically featured on a formal night. The cuisine is good basic fare, and the presentation is adequate, but nothing special. Somewhat lacking is the use of garnishes to dress the plates. As you would expect, there is always plenty of pasta (the pasta is made fresh on board daily).

Although there is plenty of food, its quality and presentation often prove disappointing to those who expect better. While the quality of meats is adequate, it could be better, and is often disguised with gravies and rich sauces. Fish and seafood tend to be lacking in taste and are typically overcooked, and green vegetables are hard to come by. However, quantity, not quality, is what appears from the galley. Breads and rolls are typically good, but desserts tend to be towards their "sell-by" date.

The service is basically sound, although you will probably note that there are few Italians serving in the dining room, as one might expect aboard the ship of an Italian company. There is a wine list, although there are no wine waiters (the table waiters are expected to serve both food and wine), and almost all wines are young — very young.

A reservations-only alternative for dinner, Ristorante Magnifico by Zeffirino, is available six nights

237

each week, with a service charge of $18.75 per person (passengers occupying suites will get a complimentary pass for one evening).

The ship also features casual breakfast and lunch buffets with indoor/outdoor seating (under a canvas sailcloth canopy for the outdoor section), although the buffet displays are very disappointing. There is also a pizzeria (open in the afternoon and evening), good for casual fast-food devotees who may be used to frozen/re-heated commercial pizzas.

Other Comments: *Costa Victoria's* exterior profile is similar to that of an enlarged version of the popular and very successful *Costa Classica* and *Costa Romantica*, with huge upright yellow funnels that are instantly recognizable. A sister ship, *Costa Olympia* was scheduled for delivery in 1998, but was not completed due to the bankruptcy of the shipyard. Having replaced almost all its older tonnage in the past few years, Costa Cruises now has a good contemporary fleet, operating in the Caribbean, Mediterranean, and in South America.

This ship has a fully enclosed bridge. There is an outdoor wraparound promenade deck (but it is full of deck lounge chairs) as well as a wraparound jogging track.

Inside the ship is a lovely four-deck-high forward-facing observation lounge (Concorde Plaza) with a "beam-me-up" glass elevator; in the center is a cone-shaped waterfall (huge video screens flank the walls), while "pod" balconies overlook the room's center; it is a stunning space, and has its own bar. Sadly, thick floor-to-ceiling pillars obstruct sight lines from most seats.

The seven-deck-high "planetarium" atrium (a novel, but somewhat impractical design) has four glass elevators that travel up to a clear crystal dome (you can see the weather outside through it). The uppermost level of the atrium is the deck where two outside swimming pools are located, together with four blocks of showers, and an ice cream bar and grill. There is a large forward shopping area, adjacent to the atrium. Ship lovers should look in the Tavernetta Lounge (aft) for ten paintings of past and present Costa Cruises ships. There is also a small chapel.

Unusual for a new ship (and welcomed by European passengers) is a pleasant (but small) indoor swimming pool, sauna (it is tiny, and there are no adjacent changing or locker facilities, which makes it very user-unfriendly). Also adjacent is a steam room and gymnasium (limited assortment of equipment), as well as a covered walking/jogging track. There is also a tennis court. Sunbathers on the forward-most section of the outdoor deck close to the mast have their own showers (excellent) and no music (good).

Where this ship differs from most large ships is in her distinct European interior decor, with decidedly Italian styling. The ship is modern without being glitzy, and bold without being brash. Internet access is available from one of several computer terminals in the Teens Center.

Weak Points: Standing in line for embarkation, disembarkation, shore tenders, and for self-serve buffet meals is an inevitable aspect of cruising aboard all large ships. When inside, there is absolutely no feeling that this is a ship. There are not enough seats in the show lounge. There are no fresh flowers in evidence anywhere. The service is decidedly loud and casual (make that sloppy and inconsistent) and there is little real hospitality. The telephone numbering system is incredibly complicated (try remembering 05313 for the information desk, or 06718 to book a massage).

The live music everywhere is loud, very loud, and there are too many repetitive announcements. Tipping envelopes provided in your cabin state the amount you are expected to give. The indigo blue interior walls look pleasant enough, but in the event of a power failure they would make the vessel appear pitch black.

Crown Odyssey
★★★★

Large Ship:	34,242 tons	Cabins (for one person):	0
Lifestyle:	Standard	Cabins (with private balcony):	16
Cruise Line:	Orient Lines	Cabins (wheelchair accessible):	4
Former Names:	*Norwegian Crown, Crown Odyssey*	Cabin Current:	110-volt
Builder:	Meyer Werft (Germany)	Full-Service Dining Rooms:	1
Original Cost:	$178 million	Elevators:	4
Entered Service:	June 1988/May 2000	Casino (gaming tables):	Yes
Registry:	Bahamas	Slot Machines:	Yes
Length (ft/m):	615.9/187.75	Swimming Pools (outdoors):	1
Beam (ft/m):	92.5/28.20	Swimming Pools (indoors):	1
Draft (ft/m):	23.8/7.26	Whirlpools:	4
Propulsion/Propellers:	Diesel (21,330kW)/2	Fitness Center:	Yes
Passenger Decks:	10	Sauna/Steam Room:	Yes/No
Total Crew:	470	Massage:	Yes
Passengers (lower beds/all berths):	1,052/1,221	Self-Service Launderette:	No
Pass. Space Ratio (lower beds/all berths):	32.5/28.0	Dedicated Cinema/Seats:	Yes/215
Crew/Pass. Ratio (lower beds/all berths):	2.2/2.5	Library:	Yes
Navigation Officers:	European/Norwegian	Classification Society:	Bureau Veritas
Cabins (total):	526		
Size Range (sq ft/sq m):	153.9–613.5/14.3–57.0		
Cabins (outside view):	410		
Cabins (interior/no view):	116		

OVERALL SCORE: **1,471**

(OUT OF A POSSIBLE 2,000 POINTS)

Accommodation: There are 18 categories of accommodation to choose from; typically the higher the deck, the more expensive will be your accommodation

Most cabins (the line calls them staterooms, which they are not) are of the same size and layout, have blond wood cabinetry, an abundance of mirrors, and closet and drawer space, and are very well equipped. Although almost all cabins show some signs of wear and tear, an ongoing refurbishment program keeps them looking good. All cabins feature a color TV, hair dryer, thin 100% cotton bathrobe, music console (and a button that can be used to turn announcements on or off), personal safe, and private bathroom with shower (many upper grade cabins have a good-size bathtub). All towels are of 100% cotton, although they could be larger; soap, shampoo, body lotion, shower cap, and sewing kit are the amenities provided. The cabin soundproofing is generally good, and nonsmoking cabins are available. Some cabins have interconnecting doors, so that they connect to make a two-room suite. You should note that almost all cabins on Deck 8 have lifeboat-obstructed views. Ice machines can be found in all passageways along the accommodation.

The largest accommodation can be found in the 16 suites on Penthouse Deck 10. Each is decorated in a different style, in accordance with the name of the suite (from fore to aft they are: Edinburgh, Inverness, Balmoral, Sandringham, Shalimar, Taj Mahal, Mykonos, Portofino, Bel Air, Hollywood, Bali, Tahiti, Imperial, Shangri-La, Dynasty, Mandarin). They are very spacious, and provide a sleeping area and separate living room (including some nicely finished wood cabinetry and a huge amount of drawer space), together with a large, white marble-clad bathroom (features a full-size bathtub with integral shower), and a semiprivate balcony (note that the balcony can be overlooked from the open deck above). Passengers occupying these suites have the use of a concierge, who will arrange private parties, obtain theater tickets, and provide assistance for private shore excursion arrangements.

The next most spacious accommodation can be found in cabins with bay windows. These include a separate sleeping area with twin beds, a huge amount of drawer space in a large vanity/writing desk, and a lounge typically with two sofas, tub chairs, heavy glass table, refrigerator, and TV. Electrically-operated window blinds, together with the curtains that front them provide good blackouts for the bay windows. There are four wheelchair-accessible cabins; these provide plenty of space to maneuver, and all four include a bathroom with roll-in shower. However, please note that wheelchair accessibility in some of the ports on the many different itineraries operated by this ship (particularly in Europe) may prove to be quite frustrating and wheelchair-accessible transportation will be very limited.

Dining: The Seven Continents Dining Room, which has large picture windows on both port and starboard sides, is large. It is also, unfortunately, extremely noisy (particularly for tables that are positioned adjacent to the open waiter stations). It features a stained glass ceiling, and comfortable seating at tables for two, four, six, or eight (although the chairs do not have armrests), and two seatings. The dining room is totally nonsmoking

The cuisine, while it is not gourmet either in quality or presentation, is quite adequate for the expectations of Orient Lines' passengers. It is unfussy, yet there is plenty of taste. What is very noticeable is the extensive use of fresh vegetables (whenever they can be obtained).

As for service, the Filipino waiters are generally good, and provide friendly service that is reasonably attentive, although there is a distinct lack of polish. There is a decent, well-priced wine list, although the wines are almost all extremely young, and the Filipino wine waiters have little knowledge of wines, or how to pour them (note that a 15% gratuity is automatically added to all wine and drinks bills).

Informal, self-serve buffet-style breakfasts and luncheons (tablecloths are provided) can be taken in the Yacht Club, which also features as an alternative venue for informal dinners (reservations only, and a cover charge of $15 per person).

In addition, casual luncheons can be taken in the Café Italia, located on an open deck aft, adjacent to a sunbathing and whirlpool area, and an open-air bar. This is also used for dining outdoors on selected nights — complete with tablecloths, table umbrellas, and fine silverware (this is quite lovely when in ports such as Mykonos or Santorini).

Other Comments: *Crown Odyssey* is a well-designed and built ship, originally constructed for the now defunct Royal Cruise Line, after which Norwegian Cruise Line operated it for several years before the ship was transferred to Orient Lines in 2000. *Crown Odyssey* has been operated by Orient Lines (a subsidiary of the Star Cruises/Norwegian Cruise Line group) since spring 2000. The ship has quite a handsome exterior profile, and now looks even better and more balanced, with its royal blue hull and white superstructure. One nice feature is a full, wraparound teak promenade deck outdoors, although it does become quite narrow at the fore part of the vessel; a jogging track is also to be found on the uppermost deck outdoors. There is one swimming pool outdoors on an aft Lido Deck.

Inside, there is generally a good passenger flow, ample space, and fine-quality interiors. Generous amounts of warm woods and marble have been used in the decor, although there are many mirrored surfaces. However, these interiors (particularly the passageways) are now showing signs of wear.

The ship has a spacious layout and a good array of public rooms, including a lobby that is two decks high; a large, gold sculpture of the world (by Pomodoro) is located on the lower level, adjacent to the semicircular staircase that connects the two levels. On the upper level, there are boutiques, a piano lounge with bar, and a casino.

There is a theater-style show lounge, where production shows and cabaret are featured, with sight lines that are generally good, but could be better (four pillars obstruct the views from some seats). Off to the port, aft area of the show lounge is a bar.

At the top of the ship is a fine observation lounge (called Top of the Crown) with panoramic views, which, in the evenings, becomes a nightclub. Other facilities include a library, an Internet Center (with four computer terminals), a cinema, and a palm court area.

There is a good Roman-style indoor spa, pool, gymnasium, and several beauty treatment rooms, with services provided by Mandara Spa of Bali (note that 15% gratuity is added to all beauty treatments). Massage can also be provided in the privacy of your suite or cabin.

Crown Odyssey should prove to be an excellent choice for passengers wanting destination-intensive cruising in a ship that has some semblance of European quality, style, and charm, for what is really a very moderate cruise price. Orient Lines specializes in destination-intensive itineraries, and ties in with an extensive pre- and post-cruise program.

All in all, *Crown Odyssey* features extremely good value-for-money cruises in very comfortable, quite elegant yet unpretentious surroundings, while a friendly and accommodating Filipino crew help make a cruise aboard her a very pleasant, no-hassle experience.

Weak Points: Much of the paneling in the passageways is quite marked and badly scuffed (due, in part, to its very light color), and lets down an otherwise very pleasant ship. Shore excursion and port information could be better. While staff hospitality is generally good, there is little polish or finesse to service. Congestion occurs between first and second seating passengers on days when the captain's cocktail parties are held in the show lounge, and a line forms outside. The production shows, while colorful, are very amateurish, with much material copied from other ships and producers.

240

Crown Princess
★★★★

Large Ship:	69,845 tons	Cabins (for one person):	0
Lifestyle:	Standard	Cabins (with private balcony):	184
Cruise Line:	Princess Cruises	Cabins (wheelchair accessible):	10
Former Names:	*Crown Princess*	Cabin Current:	110/220-volt
Builder:	Fincantieri Navali (Italy)	Full-Service Dining Rooms:	1
Original Cost:	$276.8 million	Elevators:	9
Entered Service:	July 1990	Casino (gaming tables):	Yes
Registry:	Bermuda	Slot Machines:	Yes
Length (ft/m):	811.0/247.2	Swimming Pools (outdoors):	2
Beam (ft/m):	105.8/32.26	Swimming Pools (indoors):	0
Draft (ft/m):	26.5/8.10	Whirlpools:	4
Propulsion/Propellers: Diesel-electric (24,000kW)/2		Fitness Center:	Yes
Passenger Decks:	11	Sauna/Steam Room:	Yes/Yes
Total Crew:	696	Massage:	Yes
Passengers (lower beds/all berths):	1,590/1,910	Self-Service Launderette:	Yes
Pass. Space Ratio (lower beds/all berths):	43.9/36.5	Dedicated Cinema/Seats:	Yes/169
Crew/Pass. Ratio (lower beds/all berths):	2.2/2.7	Library:	Yes
Navigation Officers:	Italian	Classification Society:	Lloyd's Register
Cabins (total):	795		
Size Range (sq ft/sq m):	189.4–574.8/17.6–53.4		
Cabins (outside view):	624		
Cabins (interior/no view):	171		

OVERALL SCORE: **1,509**
(OUT OF A POSSIBLE 2,000 POINTS)

Accommodation: In general, the cabins are well designed and have large bathrooms as well as good soundproofing. Walk-in closets, refrigerator, personal safe, and an interactive video system are provided in all cabins, as are chocolates on your pillow each night. Twin beds convert to queen-size beds in standard cabins. Bathrobes and personal toiletry amenities are provided, and all cabins feature a small refrigerator and color TV. You should note that the outside-view handicapped cabins have views that are obstructed by lifeboats. Note that Princess Cruises features CNN, CNBC, ESPN, and TNT on the in-cabin color TV system (when available, depending on cruise area).

The 14 most expensive suites (each of which has a large private balcony) are very well laid out, with a practical design that positions most things in just the right place. The bedroom is separated from the living room by a heavy wooden door, and there are TVs in both rooms. The closet and drawer space is very generous, and there is enough of it even for long cruises.

Dining: The dining room, as aboard all the ships of Princess Cruises, is totally nonsmoking. It is large, but has only a few tables for two (most are for four, six, or eight). Some of the most desirable tables overlook the stern. There are two seatings. The cuisine is, for the most part, disappointing (it is stodgy, with poor creativity and presentation), although there has been more creativity of late. The general service level is quite reasonable, but it always seems hurried, particularly for those who are at the first seating. The wine list is average, with a heavy emphasis on California wines. Note that 15% is added to all beverage bills, including wines (whether you order a $15 bottle or a $120 bottle, although it's the same amount of service to open and pour the wine).

There is an excellent pizzeria, however, for informal meals; this is particularly popular at lunchtime and in the afternoons. Themed late-night buffets are provided, but afternoon teas are poor. For sweet snacks during the day, a Patisserie (items are at extra charge) is located in the spacious lobby.

Other Comments: *Crown Princess* was the first ship in the 70,000-ton range for Princess Cruises. The ship has an interesting, jumbo-airplane look to it when viewed from the front, with a dolphin-like upper structure (made of lightweight aluminum alloy), and a large upright "dustbin-like" funnel (also made from aluminum alloy) placed aft.

Inside, innovative and elegant, contemporary styling is mixed with traditional features and a spacious interior layout. The interior spaces are quite well designed, although the layout itself is somewhat disjointed. An understated decor of soft pastel shades is highlighted by some very colorful artwork.

The observation dome, set high atop the ship like the head of a dolphin, features a large casino (which unfortunately makes the space very noisy), with numerous rubber trees, a dance floor, and live music. The room, however, does not work well as a multiuse space.

A striking, elegant three-deck-high atrium features a grand staircase with fountain sculpture (real, stand-up cocktail parties are held here). Characters Bar, located adjacent to the pizzeria on the open deck forward, has wonderful drink concoctions and some unusual glasses.

This ship provides a very pleasant cruise in elegant and very comfortable surroundings, and the fine-tuned staff will make you feel welcome.

Note that in early 2002, the ship will leave the Princess Cruises fleet, and is scheduled to debut for Seetours of Germany in March 2002, following a major refurbishment that sees the ship tailored specifically for the German-speaking family market.

Weak Points: Standing in line for embarkation, disembarkation, shore tenders, and for self-serve buffet meals is an inevitable aspect of cruising aboard all large ships. The open deck space is extremely limited considering the size of the ship and the number of passengers carried (probably designed on purpose to keep passengers inside the ship for revenue purposes). Sadly, there is no forward observation viewpoint outdoors. There is also no wraparound promenade deck outdoors (the only walking space is along the port and starboard sides of the ship). In fact, there is very little contact with the outdoors at all. The sunbathing space is really limited when the ship is full (which appears to be most of the time). There are many support pillars in the public rooms that obstruct the sight lines and flow. Inside, the layout is disjointed, and takes getting used to. Galley fumes seem to waft constantly over the aft open decks. There is no indoor swimming pool.

Crystal Harmony
★★★★★

Mid-Size Ship:	49,400 tons	Cabins (with private balcony):	260
Lifestyle:	Luxury	Cabins (wheelchair accessible):	4
Cruise Line:	Crystal Cruises	Cabin Current:	115/220-volt
Former Names:	-	Full-Service Dining Rooms:	3
Builder:	Mitsubishi Heavy Industries (Japan)		(2 alternative restaurants)
Original Cost:	$240 million	Elevators:	8
Entered Service:	July 1990	Casino (gaming tables):	Yes
Registry:	Bahamas	Slot Machines:	Yes
Length (ft/m):	790.5/240.96	Swimming Pools (outdoors):	2 (1 with magrodome)
Beam (ft/m):	97.1/29.60	Swimming Pools (indoors):	0
Draft (ft/m):	24.6/7.50	Whirlpools:	2
Propulsion/Propellers:	Diesel-electric (32,800kW)/2	Fitness Center:	Yes
Passenger Decks:	8	Sauna/Steam Room:	Yes/Yes
Total Crew:	545	Massage:	Yes
Passengers (lower beds/all berths):	960/1,010	Self-Service Launderette:	Yes
Pass. Space Ratio (lower beds/all berths):	51.4/48.9	Dedicated Cinema/Seats:	Yes/270
Crew/Pass. Ratio (lower beds/all berths):	1.7/1.8	Library:	Yes
Navigation Officers:	Scandinavian/Japanese	Classification Society:	Lloyd's Register/
Cabins (total):	480		Nippon Kaiji Kyokai
Size Range (sq ft/sq m):	182.9–947.2/17.0–88.0		
Cabins (outside view):	461		
Cabins (interior/no view):	19		
Cabins (for one person):	0		

OVERALL SCORE: **1,755**

(OUT OF A POSSIBLE 2,000 POINTS)

Accommodation:

Deck 10 Penthouses:

Four delightful Crystal penthouses measure 948–982 sq ft (88.0–91.2 sq m) and feature a huge private balcony and lounge with audiovisual entertainment center, separate master bedroom with king-size bed and electric curtains, large walk-in closets, and stunning ocean-view bathrooms that come with jet bathtub, bidet, two washbasins, and plenty of storage space for one's personal toiletry items. These really are among the best in fine, private, pampered living spaces at sea, and come with all the best priority perks, including butler service, free laundry service, a wide variety of alcoholic beverages and other goodies — in fact, almost anything you require.

Other Deck 10 Suites:

All of the other suites on this deck are worth the asking price, have plenty of space (all feature a private balcony, with outside light), including a separate lounge with large sofa, coffee table and chairs, large TV/VCR, and a separate sleeping area that can be curtained off (thick drapes mean you can sleep totally in the dark if you so wish). The bathrooms are quite large, and extremely well appointed. In fact, any of the suites on this deck are equipped with everything necessary for refined, private living at sea.

Butlers provide the best in personal service in all the top category suites on this deck (with a total of 132 beds), where all room service food arrives correctly on large silver trays. Afternoon tea trolley service and evening hors d'oeuvres are standard fare in the "butler service" suites.

Deck 9/8/7/5 Cabins:

Many of the cabins feature a private balcony (in fact, 50% of all cabins have private balconies, with outside lights), and are extremely comfortable, although a little tight for space. They are very compact units, and it's one-way traffic past the bed. There is a reasonable amount of drawer and storage space (the drawers are small, however), although the closet hanging space is somewhat limited for long voyages. Some cabins in grades G and I have lifeboat-obstructed views. All cabins have a color TV, VCR, minirefrigerator, personal safe, small sofa and coffee table, and excellent soundproofing. The bathrooms, although well appointed, are of the "you first, me next" variety (and size), but they do come with generously sized personal toiletry items and amenities.

Regardless of the accommodation category you select, duvets and down pillows are provided, as are lots of other niceties, and a socket for connecting a personal laptop computer.

Dining: There are several dining choices aboard this fine ship. The dining room (totally nonsmoking) is moderately elegant, with plenty of space around each table, well-placed waiter service stations and a good number of tables for two, as well as tables for four, six, or eight. It is noisy at times (particularly in the raised, center section), making it difficult to carry on a conversation at the larger tables in the center section. The food is attractively presented and well served in a friendly but correct manner. It is of a high standard, with high-quality ingredients used throughout. Features a mixture of European specialties and North American favorites. The menus are extremely varied, and special orders are available (including caviar and other niceties). All in all, the food is most acceptable and, with the choice of the two alternative dining spots, provides consistently high marks from passengers.

Unfortunately, dinner in the main dining room is in two seatings (the early seating is simply too rushed), although with two alternative restaurants, off-menu choices, a fine hand-picked European staff and excellent service, dining is often memorable.

Pasta specialties are made each day on request to the headwaiters. For those who enjoy caviar, it is available, although it is sevruga (malossol) and not beluga. The wine list is superb, with an outstanding collection of across-the-board wines, including a mouthwatering connoisseur selection.

Afternoon tea (and coffee) in the Palm Court is good. The choice of sandwiches, cakes, and pastries is also good. Needless to say, service is generally excellent.

The two alternative dining spots — Prego (featuring fine pasta dishes), and Kyoto (featuring pseudo-Japanese and other southeast Asian specialties), are intimate, have great views, and serve fine food. There is no extra charge, other than a recommended $6 waiter gratuity per meal that should be included in the cruise fare. There should be separate entrances for these two alternative restaurants (at present a single entrance serves both). Both are nonsmoking.

In addition, The Bistro — with its popular sidewalk café ambience — provides a fine array of snacks, cakes, coffees, and teas throughout the day, with unusual, Crystal Cruises logo china that can also be purchased in one of the ship's boutiques.

Other Comments: *Crystal Harmony* is a handsome, contemporary ship with raked clipper bow and well-balanced, sleek flowing lines. She has excellent open deck and sunbathing space, and sports facilities that include a paddle tennis court. One of two outdoor swimming pools has a magrodome cover. There is almost no sense of crowding anywhere, a superb example of comfort by design. There is a wraparound teakwood deck for walking, and an abundance of open deck and sunbathing space.

Inside, the design shows that form follows function superbly well. There is a fine assortment of public entertainment lounges and small intimate rooms (except for a nightclub/lounge that is simply too large for the number of late-night passengers frequenting it), and passenger flow is excellent. Outstanding are the Vista (observation) Lounge and the supremely tranquil, elegant Palm Court, one of the nicest rooms afloat. A Business Center features laptop computers, printers, satellite faxes, and phones.

There is a decent book and video library. The theater features high-definition video projection and headsets for the hearing-impaired. There is a self-service launderette on each deck, particularly useful for long voyages. Fine-quality fabrics and soft furnishings, china, flatware, and silver are used throughout. Features an excellent array of in-cabin TV programming, as well as close-captioned videos for the hearing-impaired. Smokers will enjoy the fine range of cigars available in the Connoisseurs Club, adjacent to the Avenue Saloon. It incorporates the best in premium brands of liquor and cigars for those who can appreciate (and pay for) such things.

This ship has a very friendly, well-trained, highly professional staff and excellent teamwork (with one of the lowest turnovers of staff in the industry) that is under the direction of a solid, all-European middle management. It is the superb extra attention to detail that makes a cruise aboard this ship so worthwhile, such as almost no announcements, and no background music anywhere. The company pays attention to its fine base of repeat passengers (particularly those in Deck 10 accommodation), and makes subtle changes in operations in order to constantly fine-tune its product.

This ship has just about everything for the discerning, seasoned traveler who wants and is prepared to pay for fine style, space, and the comfort and the facilities of a large vessel capable of longer voyages. *Crystal Harmony* is a fine example of the latest style in contemporary grand hotels afloat and provides abundant choices and flexibility, and an excellent guest lecture program. The passenger mix is approximately 85% North American (typically half of these will be from California) and 15% other nationalities.

Following a refit in 1997, some of the public rooms have been expanded (most notably the casino) and refurbished. Although now over 10 years old (and showing signs of wear in both accommodation and public areas) the ship is being well maintained, and should give pleasure to passengers for many years to come. In 2000, an expanded range of spa facilities and treatments was introduced, under the aegis of Steiner Platinum Service. Also new is a Computer Learning Center, complete with more than 20 Compaq computers. Private lessons are available (although they are expensive, starting at $75 per hour).

The final word — this is announcement-free cruising in a well-tuned, very professionally run, service-oriented, ship — the approximate equivalent of a Four Seasons hotel.

Weak Points: Your evenings will be rather structured, due to the fact that there are two seatings for dinner (unless you eat in the alternative dining spots), and two shows (the show lounge cannot seat all passengers at once) — detracting from the otherwise luxurious setting of the ship and the fine professionalism of its staff. Gratuities should really be included on a ship so highly rated (they can, however, be prepaid). The carpeting in some areas is laid in such a manner that the seams show.

RULES OF THE ROAD

Ships, the largest moving objects made by man, are subject to stringent international regulations. They must keep to the right in shipping lanes, and pass on the right (with certain exceptions). When circumstances raise some doubt, or shipping lanes are crowded, ships use their whistles in the same way an automobile driver uses directional signals to show which way he will turn. When one ship passes another and gives a single blast on its whistle, this means it is turning to starboard (right). Two blasts mean a turn to port (left). The other ship acknowledges by repeating the same signal. Ships switch on navigational running lights at night [md] green for starboard, red for port, plus two white lights on the masts, the forward one lower than the aft one.

Flags and pennants form another part of a ship's communication facilities and are displayed for identification purposes. Each time a country is visited, its national flag is shown. While entering and leaving a port, the ship flies a blue-and-white vertically striped flag to request a pilot, while a half red, half white flag (divided vertically) indicates that a pilot is on board. Cruise lines also display their own "house" flag from the mast.

A ship's funnel (smokestack) is one other means of identification, each line having its own design and color scheme. The size, height, and number of funnels were points worth advertising at the turn of the century. Most ocean liners of the time had four funnels and were called "four-stackers."

There are numerous customs at sea, many of them older than any maritime law. Superstition has always been an important element, as in the following example quoted from the British Admiralty Manual of Seamanship: "The custom of breaking a bottle of wine over the stem of a ship when it is being launched originates from the old practice of toasting prosperity to a ship with a silver goblet of wine, which was then cast into the sea in order to prevent a toast of ill intent being drunk from the same cup. This was a practice that proved too expensive, and it was replaced in 1690 by the breaking of a bottle of wine over the stem."

Crystal Symphony
★★★★★

Mid-Size Ship:	51,044 tons	Cabins (for one person):	0
Lifestyle:	Luxury	Cabins (with private balcony):	276
Cruise Line:	Crystal Cruises	Cabins (wheelchair accessible):	7
Former Names:	-	Cabin Current:	110/220-volt
Builder:	Masa-Yards (Finland)	Full-Service Dining Rooms:	3
Original Cost:	$300 million	Elevators:	8
Entered Service:	March 1995	Casino (gaming tables):	Yes
Registry:	Bahamas	Slot Machines:	Yes
Length (ft/m):	777.8/237.10	Swimming Pools (outdoors):	2 (1 with magrodome)
Beam (ft/m):	98.0/30.20	Swimming Pools (indoors):	0
Draft (ft/m):	24.9/7.60	Whirlpools:	2
Propulsion/Propellers: Diesel-electric (33,880kW)/2		Fitness Center:	Yes
Passenger Decks:	8	Sauna/Steam Room:	Yes/Yes
Total Crew:	545	Massage:	Yes
Passengers (lower beds/all berths):	960/1,010	Self-Service Launderette:	Yes
Pass. Space Ratio (lower beds/all berths): 53.1/50.5		Dedicated Cinema/Seats:	Yes/143
Crew/Pass. Ratio (lower beds/all berths): 1.7/1.8		Library:	Yes
Navigation Officers:	Scandinavian	Classification Society:	Lloyd's Register
Cabins (total):	480		
Size Range (sq ft/sq m): 201.2–981.7/18.7–91.2			
Cabins (outside view):	480		
Cabins (interior/no view):	0		

OVERALL SCORE: **1,769**

(OUT OF A POSSIBLE 2,000 POINTS)

Accommodation:

Deck 10 Penthouses:

Two delightful Crystal Penthouses measure 982 sq ft (91.2x sq m) and feature a huge private balcony (with outside light) and lounge with entertainment center, separate master bedroom with king-size bed, large walk-in closets, and stunning ocean-view marble bathrooms that come with a whirlpool bathtub, bidet, two wash-basins, and plenty of storage space for one's personal toiletry items. These really are among the best in fine, private, pampered living spaces at sea, and come with all the best priority perks, including laundry service.

Other Deck 10 Suites:

All of the other suites on this deck have plenty of space (all feature a private balcony, with outside light), including a separate lounge with large sofa, coffee table and chairs, and a separate sleeping area that can be curtained off. Rich wood cabinetry provides much of the warmth of the decor. The bathrooms are quite large, and are extremely well appointed. In fact, any of the suites on this deck are equipped with everything necessary for refined, private living at sea.

Five butlers provide the best in personal service in all the top category suites on Deck 10 (with a total of 132 beds), where all room service food arrives on silver trays. Afternoon tea trolley service and evening hors d'oeuvres are standard fare in the "butler service" suites.

Decks 5/6/7/8/9:

More than 50% of all cabins have private balconies. All are well equipped, and extremely comfortable, with excellent sound insulation. The balcony partitions, however, do not go from floor to ceiling. Even in the lowest category of standard cabins, there is plenty of drawer space, but the closet hanging space may prove somewhat limited for long voyages. Has generously sized personal bathroom amenities, duvets and down pillows. European stewardesses provide excellent service and attention.

Some cabins (grades G and I) have obstructed views. Except for the suites on Deck 10, most other cabin bathrooms are very compact units.

Regardless of the accommodation category you select, duvets and down pillows are provided, as are lots of other niceties, and there is a socket for connecting a personal laptop computer.

Dining: The main dining room (totally nonsmoking) is elegant, with crisp design and plenty of space around each table, and well-placed waiter service stations. The main dining room is well laid out, and features a raised, circular central section, although it is somewhat noisy at times, and not conducive to a fine dining experience. There are tables for two (many of them near large windows), four, six, or eight.

The food is attractively presented and well served (using both plate service as well as silver service). It is of a high standard, with fine quality ingredients. European dishes are predominant. Menus are extremely varied, and feature a good selection of meat, fish, and vegetarian dishes. Special (off-menu) orders are available, as are caviar and other culinary niceties.

Overall, the food is really good for the size of ship, and, with the choice of the two alternative dining spots, receives high praise. Dinner in the main dining room is in two seatings, although with two alternative restaurants, off-menu choices, a fine staff and excellent service, dining can be memorable. Fresh pasta and dessert flambeau specialties are made tableside each day by the headwaiters.

The wine list is superb, with an outstanding collection of across-the-board wines, including a mouth-watering connoisseur selection.

Afternoon tea in the Palm Court is a delightful daily event. The Lido provides breakfast and luncheon buffets that are fairly standard fare.

Two alternative dining spots, the 75-seat Prego (featuring fine Italian cuisine), and the 84-seat Jade Garden (featuring contemporary Chinese dishes), are appreciably larger than those aboard her sister ship, and set on a lower deck (Deck 6). Each restaurant has a separate entrance and themed decor. They both provide an excellent standard of culinary fare, with food cooked to order at no extra charge (although many feel that the recommended $6 waiter gratuity per meal should be included in the cruise fare).

In addition, The Bistro — with its popular sidewalk café ambience — provides a fine array of snacks, cakes, coffees, and teas throughout the day, with unusual, Crystal Cruises logo china.

Other Comments: *Crystal Symphony* is a contemporary ship that has a nicely raked clipper bow and well-balanced lines. While some might not like the "apartment block" look of the ship's exterior, it is the look of the future, as balconies have become standard aboard almost all new cruise ships. This ship has an excellent amount of open deck, sunbathing space, and sports facilities. The aft of two outdoor swimming pools can be covered by a magrodome in inclement weather. There is no sense of crowding anywhere, a superb example of comfort by design, high-quality construction and engineering. Has a wide wraparound teakwood deck for walking, uncluttered by lounge chairs.

The interior decor is restful, with color combinations that do not jar the senses. Has a good mixture of public entertainment lounges and small intimate rooms. Outstanding is the Palm Court, an observation lounge with forward-facing views over the ship's bows. There is an excellent book, video and CD-ROM library (combined with a Business Center). The theater (smaller than aboard sister ship *Crystal Harmony*) features high-definition video projection and headsets for the hearing-impaired. Useful self-service launderettes are provided on each deck. Fine-quality fabrics and soft furnishings, china, flatware, and silver are used. Excellent in-cabin TV programming (including CNN and ESPN) is featured, as well as close-captioned videos for the hearing-impaired.

In 1999, the ship added a Connoisseurs Club, located adjacent to the Avenue Saloon. It features some fine premium brands of liquor and cigars for those who can appreciate (and pay for) such things. Also new is a Computer Learning Center, complete with more than 20 computers. Private lessons are available (although they are expensive, starting at $75 per hour).

In 2000, an expanded range of spa facilities and treatments was introduced, under the aegis of Steiner Platinum Service.

This ship has just about everything for the discerning, seasoned traveler who wants and is prepared to pay good money for fine style, abundant space, and the comfort and facilities of a large vessel capable of extended voyages, including an excellent program of guest lecturers.

Crystal Cruises takes care of its ships and its staff, and it is the staff that makes the cruise experience really special. They are a well-trained group that stress hospitality at all times. The ship achieves a high rating because of her fine facilities, service and crew. The passenger mix is approximately 85% North American (typically half of these will be from California) and 15% other nationalities.

The final word — this is announcement-free cruising in a well-tuned, very professionally run, service-oriented, ship — the approximate equivalent of a Four Seasons hotel.

Weak Points: Your evenings will be rather structured, due to the fact that there are two seatings for dinner (unless you eat in one of the alternative dining spots), and two shows (the show lounge cannot seat all passengers at once) — detracting from the otherwise luxurious setting of the ship and the fine professional staff. Gratuities should be included on a ship this highly rated ship (they can be prepaid).

Dalmacija
★★

Small Ship:	5,650 tons	Cabins (for one person):	0
Lifestyle:	Standard	Cabins (with private balcony):	0
Cruise Line:	Croatia Cruise Lines	Cabins (wheelchair accessible):	0
Former Names:	-	Cabin Current:	220-volt
Builder:	Brodogradiliste Uljanik (Yugoslavia)	Full-Service Dining Rooms:	1
Original Cost:	n/a	Elevators:	0
Entered Service:	1965	Casino (gaming tables):	No
Registry:	Croatia	Slot Machines:	No
Length (ft/m):	383.4/116.87	Swimming Pools (outdoors):	1
Beam (ft/m):	54.1/16.51	Swimming Pools (indoors):	0
Draft (ft/m):	17.3/5.28	Whirlpools:	0
Propulsion/Propellers:	Diesel (11,030kW)/2	Fitness Center:	No
Passenger Decks:	5	Sauna/Steam Room:	No/No
Total Crew:	112	Massage:	No
Passengers (lower beds/all berths):	284/300	Dedicated Cinema:	No
Pass. Space Ratio (lower beds/all berths):	19.8/18.8	Library:	Yes
Crew/Pass. Ratio (lower beds/all berths):	2.5/2.6	Classification Society:	n/a
Navigation Officers:	Croatian		
Cabins (total):	142		
Size Range (sq ft/sq m):	n/a	**OVERALL SCORE:**	**821**
Cabins (outside view):	90	**(OUT OF A POSSIBLE 2,000 POINTS)**	
Cabins (interior/no view):	52		

Accommodation: The cabins really are very small, and most have only a limited amount of drawer space, although the closet space is reasonably adequate (for short cruises). Each cabin has its own private bathroom, which is very small and utilitarian, with a tiny shower stall in which you will dance with the shower curtain.

Dining: This ship has a dining room that is pleasant, with cheerful decor and service; dining is in a single seating with assigned tables. The service staff is friendly and attentive, although the service really is just basic. The choice of meals is very limited, and the food is generally overcooked. There is little choice of fresh fruits, cheeses, and breads. The wine list is poor.

Other Comments: This ship has an all-white exterior, and presents a reasonably clean-looking small ship profile. She is a cozy, very high-density ship that does not pretend to be glamorous. She is clean and tidy throughout, however, having undergone a refurbishment in 1997. Her limited number of public rooms feature wood accenting, which helps warm the otherwise plain decor.

There is a small outdoor swimming pool (which is really a "dip" pool), an entertainment lounge, photo shop, small fitness center, and two bars.

She caters primarily to European passengers looking for a destination-intensive cruise in moderately comfortable, but not elegant, surroundings. Cruise at a modest price, without the fuss and pretentiousness of many other ships. The ship is often under charter to various tour packagers, and so the standard of product delivery, food, and service can differ.

Weak Points: There is a limited amount of open deck and sunbathing space. Passenger hallways are really dark and dreary, and lighting throughout is inconsistent.

Dawn Princess
★★★★

Large Ship:	77,499 tons	Cabins (for one person):	0
Lifestyle:	Standard	Cabins (with private balcony):	446
Cruise Line:	Princess Cruises	Cabins (wheelchair accessible):	19
Former Names:	-	Cabin Current:	110/220-volt
Builder:	Fincantieri (Italy)	Full-Service Dining Rooms:	2 main/3 others
Original Cost:	$300 million	Elevators:	11
Entered Service:	May 1997	Casino (gaming tables):	Yes
Registry:	Great Britain	Slot Machines:	Yes
Length (ft/m):	857.2/261.3	Swimming Pools (outdoors):	4
Beam (ft/m):	105.6/32.2	Swimming Pools (indoors):	0
Draft (ft/m):	26.5/8.1	Whirlpools:	5
Propulsion/Propellers:	Diesel-electric (46,080kW)/2	Fitness Center:	Yes
Passenger Decks:	10	Sauna/Steam Room:	Yes/Yes
Total Crew:	900	Massage:	Yes
Passengers (lower beds/all berths):	2,100/2,250	Self-Service Launderette:	Yes
Pass. Space Ratio (lower beds/all berths):	36.9/34.4	Dedicated Cinema:	No
Crew/Pass. Ratio (lower beds/all berths):	2.1/2.5	Library:	Yes
Navigation Officers:	British/Italian	Classification Society:	Registro Navale Italiano
Cabins (total):	975		
Size Range (sq ft/sq m):	158.2–610.3/14.7–56.7	**OVERALL SCORE:**	**1,539**
Cabins (outside view):	603	(OUT OF A POSSIBLE 2,000 POINTS)	
Cabins (interior/no view):	372		

Accommodation: The brochure shows 28 different cabin grades: 20 outside-view and 8 interior (no view) cabins. Although the standard outside-view and interior (no view) cabins are a little small, they are well designed and functional in layout, and have earth tone colors accentuated by splashes of color from the bedspreads. Proportionately, there are quite a lot of interior (no view) cabins. Many of the outside-view cabins have private balconies, and all seem to be quite well soundproofed, although the balcony partition is not floor to ceiling type, so you can hear your neighbors clearly (or smell their smoke). Note: the balconies are very narrow, only just large enough for two small chairs, and there is no dedicated lighting.

A decent amount of closet space and abundant drawer and other storage space are provided in all cabins — adequate for a 7-night cruise. Cabins have a TV and refrigerator. Each night a chocolate appears on your pillow. The cabin bathrooms are practical, and come complete with most of the things needed, although they really are tight spaces, and are best described as one-at-a-time units. They do, however, have a decent shower enclosure, a small amount of shelving for your personal toiletries, real glasses, a hair dryer, and a bathrobe.

The largest accommodation can be found in six suites, two on each of three decks located at the stern of the ship, each with large private balcony. These are well laid out, and have large bathrooms with two sinks, a whirlpool bathtub, and a separate shower enclosure. The bedroom features generous amounts of wood accenting and detailing, indented ceilings, and TV sets in both bedroom and lounge areas. The suites also have a dining room table and four chairs.

The mini-suites typically have two lower beds that convert into a queen-size bed. There is a separate bedroom/sleeping area with vanity desk, and a lounge with sofa and coffee table, indented ceilings with generous amounts of wood accenting and detailing, walk-in closet, and larger bathroom with whirlpool bathtub and separate shower enclosure.

Note that Princess Cruises features CNN, CNBC, ESPN, and TNT on the in-cabin color TV system (when available, depending on cruise area).

Dining: There are two main dining rooms, Florentine and Venetian (both are nonsmoking, as are all dining rooms aboard the ships of Princess Cruises); each of which has its own galley and each is split into multitier sections to help create a feeling of intimacy. There is a lot of noise from the waiter stations, which are adjacent to many tables. Breakfast and lunch are provided in an open seating arrangement, while dinner is in two seatings.

Despite the fact that the portions are generous, the food and its presentation are somewhat disappointing. The quality of fish is poor (often disguised by crumb or batter coatings), the selection of fresh

249

green vegetables is limited, and few garnishes are used. However, do remember that this is banquet catering, with all its attendant standardization and production cooking. Meats are of a decent quality, although often disguised by gravy-based sauces, and pasta dishes are acceptable (though voluminous), and are typically served by section headwaiters that may also make "something special just for you" — in search of gratuities and good comments.

On any given seven-day cruise, a typical menu cycle will include a Sailaway Dinner, Captain's Welcome Dinner, Chef's Dinner, Italian Dinner, French Dinner, Captain's Gala Dinner, and Landfall Dinner. The wine list is reasonable, but not good, and the company has, sadly, seen fit to eliminate all wine waiters. Note that 15% is added to all beverage bills, including wines (whether you order a $15 bottle or a $120 bottle, even though it takes the same amount of service to open and pour the wine).

With a sheltered view over the Riviera Pool, the Balcony Grill features "Sterling Steakhouse" for those that want to taste four different cuts of Angus beef from the popular Sterling Silver brand of USDA prime meats — Filet Mignon, New York Strip, Porterhouse, and Rib-Eye — all presented on a silver tray. The Balcony Grill also provides a barbecue chicken option, plus the usual baked potato or French fries as accompaniments. This is available as an alternative to the dining rooms, between 6:30pm and 9:30pm only, at an additional charge (at press time) of $8 per person.

There is also a patisserie (for cappuccino/espresso coffees and pastries), a wine/caviar bar, and a pizzeria (complete with cobblestone floors and wrought iron decorative features), with excellent pizzas (there are six to choose from).

The Horizon Buffet is open 24 hours a day, and, at night, features an informal dinner setting with sit-down waiter service; a small bistro menu is also available. The buffet displays are, for the most part, quite repetitious, but better than they have been in the last few years (however, plastic plates are used). The cabin service menu is very limited, and presentation of the food items featured is very poor.

Other Comments: Although large, this all-white ship has a decent profile, and is well balanced by a large funnel, which contains a deck tennis/basketball/volleyball court in its sheltered aft base. There is a wide, teak wraparound promenade deck outdoors, some real teak steamer-style deck chairs (complete with royal blue cushioned pads), and 93,000 sq ft (8,640 sq m) outdoors space. A great amount of glass on the upper decks provides plenty of light and connection with the outside world.

The ship, while large, absorbs passengers well, and has an almost intimate feel to her, which is what the interior designers intended. Her interiors are very pretty and warm, with attractive colors and welcoming decor that includes some very attractive wall murals and other artwork. The signs around the ship could be improved, however.

There is a wide range of public rooms to choose from, with several intimate rooms and spaces so that you don't get the feel of being overwhelmed by large spaces. Features tasteful decors, with attractive color combinations that are warm and do not clash (nothing is brash). The interior focal point is a huge four-deck-high atrium lobby with winding, double stairways, complete with two panoramic glass-walled elevators.

The main public entertainment rooms are located under three cabin decks. There is plenty of space and the traffic flow is good. There are two show lounges, one at each end of the ship; one is a superb 550-seat, theater-style show lounge (movies are also shown here) and the other is a 480-seat cabaret-style lounge, complete with bar.

A glass-walled health spa complex is located high atop ship and includes a gymnasium with high-tech machines. One swimming pool is "suspended" aft between two decks (there are two other pools, although they are not large for the size of the ship).

The library is a very warm room and has six large buttery leather chairs for listening to CDs, with ocean-view windows. There is a conference center for up to 300, as well as a business center, with computers, copy and fax machines. The collection of artwork is good, particularly on the stairways, and helps make the ship feel smaller than it is, although in places it doesn't always seem coordinated. The casino, while large, is not really in the main passenger flow and so it does not generate the "walk-through" factor found aboard so many ships.

The most traditional room aboard is the Wheelhouse Lounge/Bar, which is decorated in the tastefully rich style of a turn-of-the-century gentleman's club, complete with wood paneling and comfortable seating. The focal point is a large ship model from the P&O collection archives: aboard *Dawn Princess* it is Kenya.

At the end of the day, as is the case aboard most large ships today, if you live in the top suites, you will be well attended; if you do not, you will merely be one of a very large number of passengers. One nice feature is the captain's cocktail party — it is held in the four-deck-high main atrium, so you can come and go as you please and there's no standing in line (to have your photograph taken with the captain) if you don't want to.

Weak Points: Standing in line for embarkation, disembarkation, shore tenders, and for self-serve buffet meals is an inevitable aspect of cruising aboard all large ships. There is absolutely no escape from unnecessary and repetitive announcements (particularly for activities that bring revenue, such as art auctions and bingo) that intrude constantly into your cruise. The in-your-face art auctions are simply overbearing, and the paintings, lithographs, and faux, framed pictures that are strewn throughout the ship (and clash irritatingly with the ship's interior decor) are an annoying intrusion into what should be a vacation, not a cruise inside a floating "art" emporium.

The digital voice announcing elevator deck stops is irritating to passengers (many of whom tell me they would like to rip out the speaker system). There are a number of dead ends in the interior layout, so it's not as user-friendly as a ship this size should be. The walls of the passenger accommodation decks are very plain (some artwork here would be an improvement). The cabin numbering system is extremely illogical, with numbers going through several hundred series on the same deck.

The swimming pools are quite small for so many passengers, and the pool deck is cluttered with white, plastic deck lounge chairs, which do not have cushioned pads. Waiting for tenders in anchor ports can prove irritating, but typical of large ship operations. Charging for the machines in the self-service launderette is trifling (even though it's only $1 per wash, 50 cents per dryer cycle, and 50 cents for detergent).

Delphin
★★★ +

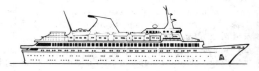

Small Ship:	16,214 tons	Cabins (for one person):	0
Lifestyle:	Standard	Cabins (with private balcony):	0
Cruise Line:	Delphin Seereisen	Cabins (wheelchair accessible):	0
Former Names:	*Kazakhstan II, Belorussiya*	Cabin Current:	220-volt
Builder:	Wartsila (Finland)	Full-Service Dining Rooms:	1
Original Cost:	$25 million	Elevators:	2
Entered Service:	January 1975/December 1993	Casino (gaming tables):	No
Registry:	Malta	Slot Machines:	No
Length (ft/m):	512.5/156.24	Swimming Pools (outdoors):	1
Beam (ft/m):	71.8/21.90	Swimming Pools (indoors):	0
Draft (ft/m):	20.3/6.20	Whirlpools:	0
Propulsion/Propellers:	Diesel(13,250kW)/2	Fitness Center:	Yes
Passenger Decks:	8	Sauna/Steam Room:	Yes/Yes
Total Crew:	234	Massage:	Yes
Passengers (lower beds/all berths):	466/556	Self-Service Launderette:	Yes
Pass. Space Ratio (lower beds/all berths):	35.6/29.8	Dedicated Cinema:	No
Crew/Pass. Ratio (lower beds/all berths):	1.9/2.3	Library:	Yes
Navigation Officers:	Ukrainian	Classification Society:	Germanischer Lloyd
Cabins (total):	233		
Size Range (sq ft/sq m):	150.0–492.0/14.0–45.7	**OVERALL SCORE:**	**1,279**
Cabins (outside view):	128	**(OUT OF A POSSIBLE 2,000 POINTS)**	
Cabins (interior/no view):	105		

Accommodation: There are ten grades of accommodation to choose from. Typically, the higher the deck, the more expensive will be the accommodation.

The Boat Deck suites (located forward) are very large and well equipped, with an absolute abundance of drawers and good closet space, and all feature blond wood furniture, and a refrigerator. The bathrooms are very spacious, and come with full-size bathtubs and large toiletries cabinet; bathrobes are also provided.

All the other outside-view and interior (no view) cabins are very compact units, yet adequate (but not for an around-the-world cruise), although there is little drawer space, and storage space is tight on the long cruises that this ship often features. All of the beds feature European duvets, and all cabins receive fresh flowers each cruise. The bathrooms are small, but there is good space for toiletry items.

Dining: There is one large main dining room — the Pacific Restaurant, with 554 seats. It has a high ceiling, large ocean-view picture windows, and pleasing, elegant decor; all passengers dine in one seating.

In general, the food is attractively presented (although inconsistent), and very reasonable. The choice is good and includes selections for vegetarians. While standard white and red table wines are included for lunch and dinner, there is also an additional wine list with a reasonably good selection at moderate prices. The gala buffet is very good. Service comes with a smile from Ukrainian waitresses, although communicating with them can prove awkward at times.

For casual meals, breakfast and lunch buffets can be taken in The Lido. The food featured is decent enough, with reasonable choice, although there is some repetition, particularly of breakfast items.

Other Comments: *Delphin* is a reasonably smart-looking cruise ship (originally built as one of a series of five vessels in the same class), topped by a square funnel. It was well refitted and refurbished throughout following a shipyard rollover incident (when she was a ferry named *Belorussiya*). Her original car decks have long been converted into useful public rooms and additional cabins, and the former car loading ramps on the vessel's stern have been fully sealed.

When she last underwent a major refurbishment, several new facilities were added. These improved almost all the public areas and added better health/fitness and spa facilities and an improved lido deck. The circular swimming pool is small, however, and is really only useful as a "dip" pool. The promenade decks outdoors are quite reasonable, although there are "lips" to step over in the forward section.

Sports participants will find volleyball, basketball, and table tennis. There is also fitness center (with sauna, solarium, and massage treatments), as well as a dialysis station for up to 26 persons.

Delphin will provide a reasonably comfortable cruise experience for German-speaking passengers who seek destination-intensive cruises in comfortable, though not luxurious, surroundings at an extremely attractive price. It is not a luxury product, nor does it pretend to be, but she is a comfortable and friendly ship in which to cruise. *Delphin* attracts many repeat passengers because of the destination-intensive itineraries and decent level of service. The company continues to spend money on little refinements throughout the ship, which are appreciated by the many loyal repeat passengers. Delphin Seereisen's own onboard cruise director and staff are very good.

Port taxes and insurance are included. The currency on board is the deutschmark.

Weak Points: There are many pillars throughout the public rooms, and these inhibit sight lines. The ceiling height is quite low in most public rooms, and the stairways are quite steep, with steps that are short and difficult to replace without major structural changes (a leftover from her build as a passenger ferry). The gangway is quite narrow. There is no wraparound promenade deck outdoors, and no observation lounge/bar with forward-facing views over the ship's bows.

PLIMSOLL MARK

The safety of ships at sea and all those aboard owes much to the 19th-century social reformer Samuel Plimsoll, a member of the British Parliament concerned about the frequent loss of ships due to overloading. In those days, some shipowners would load their vessels down to the gunwales to squeeze every ounce of revenue out of them. They gambled on good weather, good fortune, and good seamanship to bring them safely into port. Consequently, many ships went to the bottom of the sea [md] the result of their buoyancy being seriously impaired by overloading.

Plimsoll helped to enact legislation that came to be known as the Merchant Shipping Act of 1875. This required shipowners to mark their vessels with a circular disc 12 inches (30.5 cm) long bisected by a line 18 inches (45.7 cm) long, as a measure of their maximum draft; that is, the depth to which a ship's hull could be safely immersed at sea. The Merchant Shipping Act of 1890 went even further, and required the Plimsoll mark (or line) to be positioned on the sides of vessels in accordance with tables drawn up by competent authorities.

The Plimsoll mark is now found on the ships of every nation. The Plimsoll mark indicates three different depths: the depth to which a vessel can be loaded in fresh water, which is less buoyant than salt water; the depth in summer, when seas are generally calmer; and the depth in winter, when seas are much rougher.

Disney Magic
★★★★ +

Large Ship:	83,338 tons	Cabins (with private balcony):	388
Lifestyle:	Standard	Cabins (wheelchair accessible):	12
Cruise Line:	Disney Cruise Line	Cabin Current:	110-volt
Former Names:	-	Full-Service Dining Rooms:	3 main
Builder:	Fincantieri (Italy)		(+1 Alternative +1 Café)
Original Cost:	$350 million	Elevators:	12
Entered Service:	July 1998	Casino (gaming tables):	No
Registry:	Bahamas	Slot Machines:	No
Length (ft/m):	964.5/294.00	Swimming Pools (outdoors):	3
Beam (ft/m):	105.7/32.22	Swimming Pools (indoors):	0
Draft (ft/m):	26.2/8.0	Whirlpools:	6
Propulsion/Propellers:	Diesel-electric (38,000kW)/2	Fitness Center:	Yes
Passenger Decks:	11	Sauna/Steam Room:	Yes/Yes
Total Crew:	945	Massage:	Yes
Passengers (lower beds/all berths):	1,750/3,325	Self-Service Launderette:	Yes (3)
Pass. Space Ratio (lower beds/all berths):	47.6/25.0	Dedicated Cinema/Seats:	Yes /270
Crew/Pass. Ratio (lower beds/all berths):	1.8/3.5	Library:	No
Navigation Officers:	European/Scandinavian	Classification Society:	Lloyd's Register
Cabins (total):	875		
Size Range (sq ft/sq m):	180.8–968.7/16.8–90.0		
Cabins (outside view):	720		
Cabins (interior/no view):	155		
Family Cabins:	80		

OVERALL SCORE: **1,553**

(OUT OF A POSSIBLE 2,000 POINTS)

Accommodation: Spread over six decks, there are several types of suites and cabins from which to choose; all have been designed for practicality and have space-efficient layouts. Most cabins have common features such as a neat vertical steamer trunk for clothes storage, illuminated closets, a hair dryer located at a vanity desk (or in the bathroom), and bathrobes for all passengers. Many cabins have third- and fourth pull-down berths that rise and are totally hidden in the ceiling when not in use, but the standard interior and outside cabins, while acceptable for two, are extremely tight with three or four. The decor is practical, creative, and colorful, with lots of neat styling touches. Cabins with refrigerators can have them stocked with one of several packages (at extra cost).

The bathrooms, although compact (due to the fact that the toilet is separate from the rest of the bathroom), are really functional units, designed with split-use facilities so that more than one person can use them at the same time (good for families); many have bathtubs (really shower tubs).

Accommodation designated as suites offer much more space, and extra goodies such as VCRs, CD players, large screen TVs, and extra beds that are useful for larger families. Some of the suites are, however, beneath the pool deck, teen lounge, or informal café, so there could be lots of noise as the ceiling insulation is poor (but the cabin-to-cabin insulation is good).

Wheelchair-bound passengers have a variety of cabin sizes and configurations to choose from, including suites with a private balcony (unfortunately you cannot get a wheelchair through the balcony's sliding door) and extra-large bathrooms with excellent roll-in showers, and good closet and drawer space (almost all of the vessel is accessible). Note that for the sight-impaired, cabin numbers and elevator buttons are Braille-encoded.

Room service is available 24 hours (suite occupants also get concierge service); however, the room service menu is very limited, as is the cabin breakfast menu. There is a 15% service charge for all beverage deliveries (including tea and coffee).

Dining: There are three main dining rooms (all nonsmoking), each with over 400 seats, two seatings, and unique themes. Lumiere's has Beauty and the Beast; Parrot Cay has a tacky, pseudo-Caribbean theme; Animator's Palate (the most visual of the three) features food and electronic art that makes the evening decor change from black and white to full-color. You will eat in all three dining rooms in rotation (twice per 7-day cruise), and move with your assigned waiter and assistant waiter to each dining room in turn, thus providing a different dining experience (each has a different decor and different menus). As you will have the same waiter in each of the three restaurants, any gratuities go only to "your" waiter. Parrot Cay and Lumiere's have open seating for breakfast and lunch (the lunch menu is pitiful). The noise level in all three dining rooms is extremely high. Note that if the formal nights happen to fall on the evening you are due to eat in Parrot Cay, formal wear and the decor of Parrot Cay Restaurant do not go together, in any shape or form.

In addition, Palo is an elegant 140-seat reservations-only alternative restaurant (with a $5 cover/gratuity charge), featuring Italian cuisine. It has a 270-degree view, and is for adults only (no "Munchkins" allowed); the à la carte cuisine is cooked to order, and the wine list is good (although prices are high). Make your reservations as soon as you board or miss out on the only decent food aboard this ship. Afternoon High Tea is also presented here, on days at sea.

For casual eating, Topsider's is an indoor/outdoor café featuring low-quality self-serve breakfast and lunch buffets with very poor choice and presentation, and a buffet dinner for children (consisting mostly of fried foods). There is also an ice cream and frozen yogurt bar (Scoops) that opens infrequently; other fast food outlets include Pluto's (for hamburgers, hot dogs), and Pinocchio's, which is open throughout the day but not in the evening (for basic pizza and sandwiches). On one night of the cruise, there is also an outdoor, self-serve "Tropicalifragilisticexpialidocious" buffet.

Overall, the food has improved since the ship was first introduced (it needed to, it was of a very low quality) and is now more attractively presented, although there are still so few green vegetables. Vegetarians and those seeking healthy spa alternatives will be totally underwhelmed, as will those who want spa (light) cuisine. Guest chefs from Walt Disney World Resort prepare signature dishes each cruise, and also host cooking demonstrations.

Other Comments: Zip-a-Dee-Do-Dah, Zip-a-Dee-Day! *Disney Magic*'s profile has managed to combine streamlining with tradition and nostalgia, and has two large red and black funnels designed to remind you of the ocean liners of the past. *Disney Magic* is the first cruise ship built with two funnels since the 1950s. However, one of the funnels is a dummy, and contains a variety of public spaces, including a neat ESPN sports bar and a broadcast center. The ship was actually constructed in two halves, which were then joined together in the shipyard in Venice, Italy. The ship's whistle even plays "When You Wish Upon A Star" (or a sort of sickly version of it). The bow features handsome gold scrollwork that is more typically seen adorning the tall ships of yesteryear. There is a wraparound promenade deck outdoors for strolling.

Disney Cruise Line has not added ostentatious decoration to the ship's exterior. However, Mickey's ears are painted on the funnels; there is also a special 85-ft- (26-m-) long paint stripe that cleverly incorporates Disney characters into the whimsical yellow paintwork along each side of the hull at the bow. It's cute: The ship's exterior colors are also those of Mickey Mouse himself (call it a well-planned coincidence). Also of note is a 15-ft- (4.5-m-) tall Goofy, hanging upside down in a bosun's chair, painting the stern of the vessel.

Inside, the ship is quite stunning, although poorly finished in several places. The Art Deco theme of the old ocean liners has been tastefully carried out (check out the stainless steel/pewter Disney detailing on the handrails and balustrades in the three-deck-high lobby). Most public rooms have high ceilings. The decor is reminiscent of New York's Radio City Music Hall. The interior detailing is stunning, much of it whimsical — pure Disney. The lobby provides a real photo opportunity, with a 6-ft- (1.8-m-) high bronze statue of Mickey in the role of a ship's helmsman. Mickey is also visible in many other areas, albeit subtly (for Disney). If you can't sleep, try counting the number of times Mickey's logo appears — it's an impossible task!

There are two large shops and an abundance of Disney-theme clothing, soft toys, collectibles, and specialty items. Features a superb, 1,040-seat Walt Disney Theatre (spread over four decks but without a balcony), piano bar, adults-only nightclub/disco, family lounge, and a dedicated cinema (where classic Disney films are shown, as well as first-run movies).

On deck, a sports deck features a paddle tennis court, table tennis, basketball court, shuffleboard, and golf driving range. An ESPN Skybox Bar features 12 TVs of differing sizes for live (by satellite) sports events and noisy conversation (cigar smokers welcome). There are three outdoor pools: one pool for adults only (in theory), one for children, and one for families (guess which one has Mickey's ears painted into the bottom?). However, there's music everywhere (four different types), and it's impossible to find a quiet spot (in fact, you can sit in many places and get two types of music blaring at you at the same time). The children's pool features a long yellow water slide (available at specified times), held up by the giant hand of Mickey Mouse.

For fitness devotees, part of the fitness room and spa (measuring 8,500 sq ft/789.6 sq m) has ocean-view windows that overlook the navigation bridge below. There are several treatment rooms, and a "rain forest" with scented steam rooms, although the pounding from the basketball court located directly above makes relaxing spa treatments impossible, and thus a waste of money.

The children's entertainment areas measure 13,000 sq ft (1,207.7 sq m); more than 30 children's counselors run the extensive programs. There is also a separate teen club and video game arcade. A child drop-off service is available in the evenings, and private baby-sitting services are available ($11 per hour), as are character "tuck-ins" for children, and character breakfasts and lunches. Strollers are available, at no charge, and parents can be provided with beepers, so that they can also enjoy their time alone, away from the kids for much of the day.

The entertainment and activities programming for families and children are extremely good. The stage shows (in the 977-seat show lounge) feature Disney themes; "Hercules — A Muse-ical Comedy," "Disney Dreams" (a bedtime story with Peter Pan, Aladdin, the Little Mermaid, and others), and "C'est Magique" (featuring a host of fine illusions revolving around Prospero, a 19th century magician, with some of the background music provided by the Royal Philharmonic Orchestra): Sadly, all are performed without a hint of a live orchestra, although lighting and staging are excellent. A show called "Island Magic," which features only Disney characters, is the only show featuring a "live" orchestra. Other notable Disney exclusives include the game show "Who Wants to be a Mouseketeer?" (with prizes that include free cruises and onboard credits of up to $1,000) and "Tea with Wendy Darling" (from Disney's "Peter Pan").

Adults can play in Beat Street — an adult entertainment area that includes a wacky Hollywood-style street with flashing traffic lights, and three entertainment rooms. Sessions is a jazz piano lounge, complete with private headphones for listening to music of all types when no live music is scheduled; Rockin' Bar D (for high-energy rock 'n roll, country music, and cabaret acts); and Off-Beat (for improvisational comedy with audience participation). During the day, creative enrichment programs have also been added.

Ports of call include St. Maarten, St. Thomas, and the highlight for most is Disney's private island, Castaway Cay. It is an outstanding private island (perhaps the benchmark for all private islands for families with children), with its own pier so that the ship can dock alongside — a cruise industry first. There is a post office with its own special Bahamas/Disney stamp, and a whole host of dedicated, well thought-out attractions and amenities for all ages (including a large adults-only beach, complete with massage cabanas).

Disney characters are aboard for all cruises and lots of photo opportunities; they come out to play mainly when children's activities are scheduled. All the artwork throughout the ship's public areas comes from Disney films or animation features, with many original drawings dating from the early 1930s.

This ship should appeal to couples, single parents, and families alike (there are few activities for couples during the daytime, but plenty of entertainment at night). Whether cruising with 1,000 (or more) kids aboard will make for a relaxing vacation for those without kids depends on how much noise one can absorb (there will probably be even more juniors aboard at peak vacation periods. Disney points out that 25% of Walt Disney World's visitors are adults (perhaps these are the real kids). However, if you bring children, they will have so much fun that they will not want to leave at the end of the cruise. Members of Disney's Vacation Club can exchange points for cruises.

At Port Canaveral, a special terminal has been constructed (a copy of the original Ocean Terminal used by the transatlantic liners *Queen Elizabeth* and *Queen Mary* in Southampton, England). Embarkation and disembarkation is an entertainment event rather than the hassle-laden affair that it has become for many cruise lines with large ships (if all the buses do not arrive together).

Disney Magic features year-round 7-day cruises to the Eastern Caribbean (and Castaway Cay in the Bahamas) — more relaxing than the 3- or 4-day version, and passengers will find more activities, more lecturers, and additional shows that somehow make it all worthwhile. It's all tied up in one encapsulated, well-controlled, seamless, and crime-free environment that promises escape and adventure. American Express cardholders get special treatment and extra goodies.

Castaway Cay (in the Bahamas) is Disney's exclusive private (wholly owned) island, with separate beaches for children and adults. Watersports equipment (floats, paddleboats, kayaks, hobie cats, aqua fins, aqua trikes, and snorkels) can be rented.

Transfers between Walt Disney World resorts in Orlando and the ship are included. Special buses feature vintage 1930s/1940s style interior decor (30 sets of Mickey's face and ears can be found in the blue fabric of each seat). Five of the 45 custom-made buses are outfitted to carry wheelchair passengers.

Disney Magic is the cruise industry's principal floating theme park, a seagoing never never land. You should be aware, however, that this is a highly programmed, strictly timed and regimented onboard experience, with tickets, lines, and reservations necessary for almost everything. Since its introduction, the product has improved along with Disney's understanding that cruise ships operate differently from theme parks.

Take mainly casual clothing (that's Casual with a capital "C" folks), although there are two formal nights on the 7-day cruise, and wish upon a star — that's really all you'll need to do to enjoy yourself aboard this stunning ship. *Disney Wonder* is the sister ship.

Weak Points: There is no observation lounge with forward-facing views over the ship's bows. There is no dance floor with live orchestra for adults (other than Rockin Bar D in Beat Street for throbbing disco/country-style music). The elevators are very small, and so is the gymnasium (for such a large ship). It is expensive (but so is a week at any Disney resort), gratuities are extra, and 15% is added to all bar/beverage/wine and spa accounts. Don't even think about it if you are not a Disney fan, or you don't like kids, lining up and registering for things, and service with only a moderate sprinkling of hospitality. Standing in line for embarkation, disembarkation, shore tenders, and for self-serve buffet meals is an inevitable aspect of cruising aboard all large ships. Lines at various outlets can prove irritating (some creative Disney Imagineering is needed, including a large sprinkling of pixie dust), as can trying to get through to Guest Services by telephone. The food product and delivery has improved, but falls short of less expensive cruise products. There is no proper library — something that many regular cruise passengers miss.

WIND SPEEDS

A navigational announcement to passengers is normally made once or twice a day, giving the ship's position, temperature, and weather information.

Various winds affect the world's weather patterns. Such well-known winds as the Bora, Mistral, Northwind, and Sirocco, among others, play an important part in the makeup of weather at and above sea level. Wind velocity is measured on the Beaufort scale, a method that was devised in 1805 by Commodore Francis Beaufort, later Admiral and Knight Commander of the Bath, for measuring the force of wind at sea. Originally, it measured the effect of the wind on a fully rigged man-of-war (which was usually laden with cannons and heavy ammunition). It became the official way of recording wind velocity in 1874, when the International Meteorological Committee adopted it.

You might be confused by the numbering system for wind velocity. There are 12 velocities, known as "force" on the Beaufort scale. They are as follows:

Force	Speed (mph)	Description/Ocean Surface
0	0–1	Calm; glassy (like a mirror)
1	1–3	Light wind; rippled surface
2	4–7	Light breeze; small wavelets
3	8–12	Gentle breeze; large wavelets, scattered whitecaps
4	13–18	Moderate breeze; small waves, frequent whitecaps
5	19–24	Fresh breeze; moderate waves, numerous whitecaps
6	25–31	Strong breeze; large waves, white foam crests
7	32–38	Moderate gale; streaky white foam
8	39–46	Fresh gale; moderately high waves
9	47–54	Strong gale; high waves
10	55–63	Whole gale; very high waves, curling crests
11	64–73	Violent storm; extremely high waves, froth and foam, poor visibility
12	73+	Hurricane; huge waves, thundering white spray, visibility nil

Disney Wonder
★★★★ +

Large Ship:	85,000 tons	Cabins (with private balcony):	388
Lifestyle:	Standard	Cabins (wheelchair accessible):	12
Cruise Line:	Disney Cruise Line	Cabin Current:	110-volt
Former Names:	-	Full-Service Dining Rooms:	3 main
Builder:	Fincantieri (Italy)		(+1 Alternative +1 Café)
Original Cost:	$350 million	Elevators:	12
Entered Service:	August 1999	Casino (gaming tables):	No
Registry:	Bahamas	Slot Machines:	0
Length (ft/m):	964.5/294.00	Swimming Pools (outdoors):	3
Beam (ft/m):	105.7/32.22	Swimming Pools (indoors):	0
Draft (ft/m):	26.2/8.0	Whirlpools:	6
Propulsion/Propellers:	Diesel-electric (38,000kW)/2	Fitness Center:	Yes
Passenger Decks:	11	Sauna/Steam Room:	Yes/Yes
Total Crew:	945	Massage:	Yes
Passengers (lower beds/all berths):	1,750/3,325	Self-Service Launderette:	Yes (3)
Pass. Space Ratio (lower beds/all berths):	48.5/25.5	Dedicated Cinema/Seats:	Yes /270
Crew/Pass. Ratio (lower beds/all berths):	1.8/3.5	Library:	No
Navigation Officers:	European/Scandinavian	Classification Society:	Lloyd's Register
Cabins (total):	875		
Size Range (sq ft/sq m):	180.8–968.7/16.8–90.0		
Cabins (outside view):	720	**OVERALL SCORE:**	**1,553**
Cabins (interior/no view):	155	**(OUT OF A POSSIBLE 2,000 POINTS)**	
Family Cabins:	80		

Accommodation: Spread over six decks, there are several types of suites and cabins from which to choose; all have been designed for practicality and have space-efficient layouts that are well designed. Most cabins have common features such as a neat vertical steamer trunk used for clothes storage, a hair dryer located at a vanity desk (or in the bathroom), and bathrobes for all passengers. Many cabins have third- and fourth pull-down berths that rise and are totally hidden in the ceiling when not in use, but the standard interior and outside cabins, while acceptable for two, are extremely tight when occupied by three or four persons. The decor is practical, creative, and very colorful, with lots of neat styling touches. Cabins with refrigerators can have them stocked with one of three packages (at extra cost, of course).

The bathrooms, although compact (due to the fact that the toilet is separate from the rest of the bathroom), are really functional units, designed with split-use facilities so that more than one person can use them at the same time (good for families); many have bathtubs (really shower tubs).

The suites, quite naturally, offer much more space and goodies such as VCRs, CD players, large screen TVs, and extra beds that are useful for larger families. Some of the suites are, however, beneath the pool deck, teen lounge, or informal café, so there could be lots of noise as the ceiling insulation is poor (but cabin-to-cabin insulation is good).

Wheelchair-bound passengers have a variety of cabin sizes and configurations to choose from, including suites with a private balcony (unfortunately you cannot get a wheelchair through the balcony's sliding door), extra-large bathrooms with excellent roll-in showers, and good closet and drawer space (most of the vessel is quite accessible). Note that for the sight-impaired, cabin numbers and elevator buttons are Braille-encoded.

Room service is available 24 hours (suite occupants also get concierge service); the room service menu is limited, however, as is the in-cabin breakfast menu. There is a 15% service charge for beverage deliveries.

Dining: There are three main dining rooms (all nonsmoking), each with over 400 seats, two seatings, and unique theme decor. Triton's, Parrot Cay, and Animator's Palate (the most visual of the three, which features food and electronic art that make the evening decor change from black and white to full color). You will get to eat in all three dining rooms in rotation, and move with your assigned waiter and assistant waiter to each dining room in turn, thus providing a different dining experience (each has a different decor and different menus). *Note*: as you will have the same waiter in each of the three restaurants, any gratuities go only to "your" waiter. Parrot Cay and Triton's feature open seating for breakfast and lunch (the lunch menu is poor). The noise level in all three dining rooms is extremely high.

In addition, Palo is an elegant 140-seat reservations-only alternative restaurant (with a $5 cover/gratuity charge) featuring Italian cuisine. It has a 270-degree view, and is for adults only (no "Munchkins" allowed); the à la carte cuisine is cooked to order, and the wine list is good (prices are high). Make your reservations as soon as you board or miss out on the only decent food aboard this ship.

For casual eating, Topsider's is an indoor/outdoor café featuring low-quality, self-serve breakfast and lunch buffets with very poor choice and presentation, and a buffet dinner for children (consisting mostly of fried foods). There is also an ice cream and frozen yogurt bar (Scoops) that opens infrequently; other fast food outlets include Pluto's (for hamburgers, hot dogs), and Pinocchio's, which is open throughout the day but not in the evening (for basic, inedible pizza and sandwiches).

Overall, the food has improved since the ship was first introduced, and is now more attractively presented, although there are still so few green vegetables. Vegetarians and those seeking healthy spa alternatives will be underwhelmed. Guest chefs from Walt Disney World Resort prepare signature dishes each cruise, and host occasional cooking demonstrations.

Other Comments: Zip-a-Dee-Do-Dah, Zip-a-Dee-Day! *Disney Wonder*'s profile has managed to combine streamlining with tradition and nostalgia, and has two large red and black funnels designed to remind you of the ocean liners of the past. *Disney Wonder* is the first cruise ship built with two funnels since the 1950s. However, one of the funnels is a dummy, and contains a variety of public spaces, including a neat ESPN sports bar and a broadcast center. The ship was actually constructed in two halves, which were then joined together in the shipyard in Venice, Italy. The ship's whistle plays "When You Wish Upon A Star" (or a sort of sickly version of it). The bow features handsome gold scrollwork that is more typically seen adorning the tall ships of yesteryear. There is a wraparound promenade deck outdoors for strolling.

Disney Cruise Line has not added ostentatious decoration to the ship's exterior. However, Mickey's ears are painted on the funnels; there is also a special 85-ft- (25.9- m-) long paint stripe that cleverly incorporates Disney characters into the whimsical yellow paintwork along each side of the hull at the bow. It's cute: The ship's exterior colors are also those of Mickey Mouse himself (call it a well-planned coincidence). Also of note is a whimsical, 15-ft- (4.5-m-) tall Donald Duck and Huey hanging upside down in a bosun's chair, painting the stern.

Inside, the ship is visually stunning. The Art Deco theme of the old ocean liners has been tastefully carried out (check out the stainless steel/pewter Disney detailing on the handrails and balustrades in the three-deck-high lobby). Most public rooms have high ceilings. The decor and detailing are stunning, much of it whimsical — pure Disney. Mickey is visible in many areas. If you can't sleep, try counting the number of times Mickey's logo appears — it's an impossible task! The lobby provides a photo opportunity that should not be missed: a 6-foot-high bronze statue of "The Little Mermaid."

There are two large shops and an abundance of Disney-theme clothing, soft toys, collectibles, and specialty items. Features a superb, 1,040-seat Walt Disney Theatre (spread over four decks but designed cinema-style, without a balcony), piano bar, adults-only nightclub/disco, family lounge, dedicated cinema (where classic Disney films are shown, as well as first-run movies).

On deck, a sports deck features a paddle tennis court, table tennis, basketball court, shuffleboard, and golf driving range. An ESPN Skybox Bar features 12 screens featuring live sports events and noisy conversation (cigar smokers welcome). There are three outdoor pools — one pool for adults only (in theory), one for children, and one for families (guess which one has Mickey's ears painted into the bottom of the pool?). However, there's music everywhere, and it's virtually impossible to find a quiet spot. The children's pool features a long yellow waterslide (available at specified times), held up by Mickey's hand.

For fitness devotees, the fitness room, which is part of the spa (measuring 8,500 sq ft /789.6 sq m) has ocean-view windows that overlook the navigation bridge below. There are several treatment rooms, and a "rain forest" with scented steam rooms.

The children's entertainment areas measure 13,000 sq ft (1,207.7 sq m), and more than 30 counselors are aboard for any given cruise. There is also a separate teen club and video game arcade. A child drop-off service works in the evenings; private baby-sitting services are available ($11 per hour), as are character "tuck-ins" for children, and character breakfasts and lunches. Strollers are available, at no charge, and parents can be provided with beepers, so that they can also enjoy their time alone, away from the kids for much of the day.

Entertainment and the activities programming for families and children are outstanding. Stage shows feature Disney themes; "Hercules — A Muse-ical Comedy," "Voyage of the Ghost Ship" (a lighthearted look at cruising), and "Disney Dreams" (a bedtime story with Peter Pan, Aladdin, the Little Mermaid, and others). Sadly, all are performed without a hint of a live orchestra, although lighting and staging are excellent. A show called "Island Magic," which features only Disney characters, is performed the day before reaching Castaway Cay, and is the only show featuring "live" music. On the four-day cruise, an additional local Bahamian show takes place outdoors at the middle swimming pool.

For adults, there is Route 66 — an adult entertainment area that includes a wacky Hollywood-style street, and three entertainment rooms. Cadillac is a jazz piano lounge, complete with private headphones for listening to music of all types when no live music is scheduled; Wavebands (for ear-splitting rock 'n roll and country music); and Barrel of Laughs (for improvisational comedy with audience participation). During the day, creative enrichment programs have been added.

While Nassau is decidedly unappealing and not tourist-friendly, the highlight of the itinerary is Disney's private island, Castaway Cay. It is an outstanding private island (perhaps the benchmark for all private islands), with its own pier so that the ship can dock alongside — a cruise industry first. There is a post office with its own special Bahamas/Disney stamp, and a whole host of dedicated, well thought-out attractions and amenities for all ages (including a large adults-only beach, complete with massage cabanas). Water sports equipment (floats, paddleboats, kayaks, hobie cats, aqua fins, aqua trikes, and snorkels) can be rented.

Disney characters are aboard for all cruises and lots of photo opportunities; they come out to play mainly when children's activities are scheduled. All the artwork throughout the ship's public areas comes from Disney films or animation features, with many original drawings dating from the early 1930s.

This ship should appeal to couples, single parents, and families alike (there are few activities for couples during the daytime, but plenty of entertainment at night). Whether cruising with 1,000 (or more) kids aboard will make for a relaxing vacation for those without kids depends on how much noise one can absorb (there will probably be even more juniors aboard at peak vacation periods). Disney always points out that 25% of Walt Disney World's visitors are adults (these are the real kids). If you bring children, they will have so much fun that they will not want to leave at the end of the cruise. Members of Disney's Vacation Club can exchange points for cruises.

At Port Canaveral, a special terminal has been constructed; it's a copy of the original Ocean Terminal used by the transatlantic liners *Queen Elizabeth* and *Queen Mary* in Southampton, England. Embarkation and disembarkation is an entertainment event rather than the hassle-laden affair that it has become for many cruise lines with large ships (if all the buses do not arrive together).

Disney Wonder features year-round 3- and 4-day cruises to the Bahamas — part of a 7-night vacation package that includes a 3- or 4-day stay at a Walt Disney World resort hotel in Orlando. The cruise then forms the second half of the vacation. It's all tied up in one encapsulated, well-controlled, seamless, and crime-free environment that promises escape and adventure. You can also book just the cruise without the resort stay. American Express cardholders get special treatment and extra goodies. Transfers between Walt Disney World resorts in Orlando and the ship are included. Special buses feature vintage 1930s/1940s style interior decor (30 sets of Mickey's face and ears can be found in the blue fabric of each seat). Five of the 45 custom-made buses are outfitted to carry wheelchair passengers.

Disney Wonder (and sister ship *Disney Magic*) are the cruise industry's floating theme parks — seagoing never never lands that are rated on their own, in common with all other ships in this book. This rating does not include any additional 3- or 4-day stay at a Disney World resort, which forms part of the total Disney Cruise Line vacation (although it is now possible to book just the cruise).

You should be aware that this is a highly programmed, strictly timed and regimented onboard experience, with tickets, lines, and reservations necessary for almost everything. Since its introduction, the product has improved; almost to the point that Disney understands that cruise ships are different from theme parks in operation. Take only casual clothing (that's Casual with a capital "C" folks) and wish upon a star — that's really all you'll need to do to enjoy yourself aboard this stunning ship.

Weak Points: There is no dance floor with live orchestra for adults (other than Rockin Bar D in Beat Street for throbbing disco/country-style music). The elevators are very small, and so is the gymnasium (for such a large ship). It is expensive (but so is a week at any Disney resort), gratuities are extra, and 15% is added to all bar/beverage/wine and spa accounts. Don't even think about it if you are not a Disney fan, or are troubled by kids, lining up and registering for things, moderate food, and service with low-grade hospitality attitude. Standing in line for embarkation, disembarkation, shore tenders, and for self-serve buffet meals is an inevitable aspect of cruising aboard all large ships. Lines at various outlets can prove irritating (some creative Disney Imagineering is needed, including a large sprinkling of pixie dust), as can be trying to get through to Guest Services by telephone. The food product and delivery has improved, but falls short of less expensive cruise products. There is no proper library — something that many regular cruise passengers miss.

Ecstasy
★★★ +

Large Ship:	70,367 tons	Cabins (for one person):	0
Lifestyle:	Standard	Cabins (with private balcony):	54
Cruise Line:	Carnival Cruise Lines	Cabins (wheelchair accessible):	22
Former Names:	-	Cabin Current:	110-volt
Builder:	Kvaerner Masa-Yards (Finland)	Full-Service Dining Rooms:	2
Original Cost:	$275 million	Elevators:	14
Entered Service:	June 1991	Casino (gaming tables):	Yes
Registry:	Panama	Slot Machines:	Yes
Length (ft/m):	855.8/260.6	Swimming Pools (outdoors):	3
Beam (ft/m):	103.0/31.4	Swimming Pools (indoors):	0
Draft (ft/m):	25.9/7.9	Whirlpools:	6
Propulsion/Propellers:	Diesel-electric (42,240kW)/2	Fitness Center:	Yes
Passenger Decks:	10	Sauna/Steam Room:	Yes/Yes
Total Crew:	920	Massage:	Yes
Passengers (lower beds/all berths):	2,040/2,594	Self-Service Launderette:	Yes
Pass. Space Ratio (lower beds/all berths):	34.4/27.1	Dedicated Cinema:	No
Crew/Pass. Ratio (lower beds/all berths):	2.2/2.8	Library:	Yes
Navigation Officers:	Italian	Classification Society:	Lloyd's Register
Cabins (total):	1,020		
Size Range (sq ft/sq m):	173.2–409.7/16.0–38.0		
Cabins (outside view):	618		
Cabins (interior/no view):	402		

OVERALL SCORE: **1,385**

(OUT OF A POSSIBLE 2,000 POINTS)

Accommodation: As in sister ships *Elation, Fantasy, Fascination, Imagination, Inspiration, Paradise,* and *Sensation,* the standard outside-view and interior (no view) cabins have plain decor. They are marginally comfortable, yet spacious enough and practical (most are of the same size and appointments), with good storage space and well-designed bathrooms.

Those booking one of the outside suites will find more space, whirlpool bathtubs, and some fascinating, rather eclectic decor and furniture. These are mildly attractive, but nothing special, and they are much smaller than those aboard the ships of a similar size of several competing companies.

A gift basket is now provided in all grades of accommodation; it includes aloe soap, shampoo, conditioner, deodorant, breath mints, candy, and pain relief tablets.

Dining: The two dining rooms have attractive decor and colors, but are large, crowded, and very noisy. The food is adequate, although Carnival Cruise Lines has made several improvements. Dining is now in four seatings, for greater flexibility: 6pm, 6:45pm, 8pm, and 8:45pm (these times are approximate).

Carnival meals stress quantity, not quality, although the company constantly works hard to improve the cuisine. While passengers seem to accept it, few find it worth remembering. However, food and its taste are still not the company's strongest points (you get what you pay for, remember).

While the menu items sound good, their presentation and taste leave much to be desired. The meats are of a high quality, but fish and seafood are unfortunately not. Presentation is simple, and few garnishes are used. Many meat and fowl dishes are disguised with gravies and sauces. The selection of fresh green vegetables, breads, rolls, cheeses, and fruits is limited, and there is too much use of canned fruit and jellied desserts. However, do remember that this is banquet catering, with all its attendant standardization and production cooking (it is, therefore, difficult to ask for anything remotely unusual or off-menu).

Although there is a decent wine list, there are no wine waiters (the waiters are expected to serve both food and wine). The service is quite robotic, closely timed, highly programmed, and inflexible, although the waiters are willing and reasonably friendly However, the waiters do sing and dance (be prepared for "Hot, Hot, Hot" and "The Macarena" — again) and there are constant waiter parades; the dining room is show business — all done in the name of gratuities at the end of your cruise.

The Lido Café provides the usual casual serve-yourself buffet foods, although it's completely nonmemorable. At night, the Seaview Bistro (as the Lido Café becomes known) provides a casual alternative to eating in the main dining rooms. It serves pasta, steaks, salads, and desserts.

Other Comments: *Ecstasy* is the second in the successful *Fantasy*-class of eight almost identical ships for Carnival Cruise Lines, and the sixth newbuild for this giant company. Although the exterior displays a bold profile, the large funnel, with its familiar wing tips and red, white, and blue colors, offsets it.

The general passenger flow is good, and the interior design is clever, functional, and extremely colorful. The neon lighting in the interior decor takes a little getting used to at first, as the color combinations are vivid, to say the least. There is a vintage Rolls Royce car located on the principal, double-width indoor promenade. The health spa and fitness facilities are decent. A stunning, 10-ton sculpture graces the marble and glass atrium, which spans seven decks. The library has delightful decor, but there are few books. The Chinatown Lounge comes complete with Oriental decor, and features hanging lanterns and smoking dragon. The balconied show lounge is large, but some 20 pillars obstruct the views from several seats.

This ship is one of the great floating playgrounds for young, active adults who enjoy constant stimulation, close contact with lots and lots of others, as well as the three Gs — glitz, glamour, and gambling. It is a live board game with every move executed in typically grand, colorful, fun-filled Carnival Cruise Lines style. This ship will provide a great introduction to cruising for the novice passenger seeking an action-packed short cruise experience in contemporary surroundings, with a real swinging party atmosphere, and minimum fuss and finesse. You will have a fine time if you like nightlife and lots of silly participation games. Like life in the fast lane, this is cruising in theme-park fantasyland, and the dress code is extremely casual. The staff will help you have organized fun, and that is what Carnival does best. Want to party? Then this should prove to be a great ship for you. Forget fashion — having fun is the sine qua non of a Carnival cruise. Gratuities can be prepaid.

Weak Points: Standing in line for embarkation, disembarkation, shore tenders, and for self-serve buffet meals is an inevitable aspect of cruising aboard all large ships. This ship is not for those who want a quiet, relaxing cruise experience. There is absolutely no escape from unnecessary and repetitious announcements (particularly for activities that bring revenue, such as art auctions and bingo) that intrude constantly into your cruise, and a great deal of hustling for drinks, although it is sometimes done with a knowing smile.

Elation
★★★ +

Large Ship:	70,367 tons	Cabins (for one person):	0
Lifestyle:	Standard	Cabins (with private balcony):	54
Cruise Line:	Carnival Cruise Lines	Cabins (wheelchair accessible):	22
Former Names:	-	Cabin Current:	110-volt
Builder:	Kvaerner Masa-Yards (Finland)	Full-Service Dining Rooms:	2
Original Cost:	$300 million	Elevators:	14
Entered Service:	March 1998	Casino (gaming tables):	Yes
Registry:	Panama	Slot Machines:	Yes
Length (ft/m):	855.0/260.6	Swimming Pools (outdoors):	3
Beam (ft/m):	103.3/31.5	Swimming Pools (indoors):	0
Draft (ft/m):	25.9/7.9	Whirlpools:	6
Propulsion/Propellers:	Diesel-electric	Fitness Center:	Yes
(42,842kW)/2azimuthing pods (14MW each)		Sauna/Steam Room:	Yes/Yes
Passenger Decks:	10	Massage:	Yes
Total Crew:	920	Self-Service Launderette:	Yes
Passengers (lower beds/all berths):	2,040/2,594	Dedicated Cinema:	No
Pass. Space Ratio (lower beds/all berths):	34.4/26.7	Library:	Yes
Crew/Pass. Ratio (lower beds/all berths):	2.2/2.8	Classification Society:	Lloyd's Register
Navigation Officers:	Italian		
Cabins (total):	1,020		
Size Range (sq ft/sq m):	173.2–409.7/16.0–38.0		
Cabins (outside view):	618		
Cabins (interior/no view):	402		

OVERALL SCORE: **1,387**

(OUT OF A POSSIBLE 2,000 POINTS)

Accommodation: As in sister ships *Ecstasy, Fantasy, Fascination, Imagination, Inspiration, Paradise,* and *Sensation,* the standard outside-view and interior (no view) cabins have plain decor. They are marginally comfortable, yet spacious enough and practical (most are of the same size and appointments), with good storage space and well-designed bathrooms.

Those booking one of the outside suites will find more space, whirlpool bathtubs, and some fascinating, rather eclectic decor and furniture. These are mildly attractive, but nothing special, and they are much smaller than those aboard the ships of a similar size of several competing companies.

A gift basket is now provided in all grades of accommodation; it includes aloe soap, shampoo, conditioner, deodorant, breath mints, candy, and pain relief tablets.

Dining: There are two large, lively dining rooms (Imagination and Inspiration). Both are nonsmoking. Dining is now in four seatings, for greater flexibility: 6pm, 6:45pm, 8pm, and 8:45pm (these times are approximate).

Carnival meals stress quantity, not quality, although the company constantly works hard to improve the cuisine. While passengers seem to accept it, few find it worth remembering. However, food and its taste are still not the company's strongest points (you get what you pay for, remember).

While the menu items sound good, their presentation and taste leave much to be desired. While meats are of a high quality, fish and seafood is not. Presentation is simple, and few garnishes are used. Many meat and fowl dishes are disguised with gravies and sauces. The selection of fresh green vegetables, breads, rolls, cheeses, and fruits is limited, and there is too much use of canned fruit and jellied desserts. However, do remember that this is banquet catering, with all its attendant standardization and production cooking (it is, therefore, difficult to ask for anything remotely unusual or off-menu).

Although there is a decent wine list, there are no wine waiters (the waiters are expected to serve both food and wine). The service is quite robotic, closely timed, highly programmed, and inflexible, although the waiters are willing and reasonably friendly However, the waiters do sing and dance (be prepared for "Hot, Hot, Hot" and "The Macarena" — again) and there are constant waiter parades; the dining room is show business — all done in the name of gratuities at the end of your cruise.

For casual meals, there's The Lido, which, aboard this ship, has some improvements and additions worthy of note, such as: orange juice machine, where you put in oranges and out comes fresh juice (better than the concentrate stuff supplied in the dining room). There's also a sushi bar. Things are looking up, which means more choices. At night, the Seaview Bistro (as the Lido Café becomes known) provides a casual alternative to eating in the main dining rooms. It serves pasta, steaks, salads, and desserts.

Other Comments: Although externally angular and not handsome *Elation* is the seventh in a series of eight ships of the same series and identical internal configuration (but actually the 12th newbuild for Carnival Cruise Lines). It is a very successful design for this successful company that targets the mass market, and particularly the first-time passenger. The ship has a bold, forthright, angular appearance that is typical of today's space-creative designs. She is powered by a pod propulsion system, which gives the ship more maneuverability, while reducing required machinery space and vibration at the stern.

Splashy, showy, public rooms and interior colors — pure Las Vegas, and ideal for those who love it. The theme of the interior decor is composers and their compositions (most of the public rooms have musical names), and the colors, while bright, are less so than aboard previous ships in this series. As in her sister ships, there is a dramatic six-deck-high atrium, appropriately dressed to impress, topped by a large glass dome, and featuring a fascinating, entertaining artistic centerpiece. There are expansive open deck areas and a large, three-deck-high glass-enclosed health spa that is always busy; it includes a gymnasium full of the latest high-tech muscle-pumping machinery, and there is also a banked jogging track outdoors.

There are public entertainment lounges, bars, and clubs galore, with something for everyone, including a children's playroom, larger than aboard the previous ships in this series. Some busy colors and design themes abound in the handsome public rooms — these are connected by wide indoor boulevards and beg your attention. There is also a good art collection, much of it bright and vocal. The library is a fine room, as aboard most Carnival ships (but there are few books). One neat feature (not found aboard previous ships in this series) is an atrium bar, complete with live classical music — something new for this company.

Features a lavish, yet almost elegant, multitiered 1,010-seat show lounge and the line's fine, loud, high-energy razzle-dazzle shows.

This ship is one of the great floating playgrounds for young, active adults who enjoy constant stimulation, close contact with lots and lots of others, as well as the three Gs — glitz, glamour, and gambling. It is a live board game with every move executed in typically grand, colorful, fun-filled Carnival Cruise Lines style. Good for those who like big city life ashore and want it on their vacation. Operates 7-night Mexican Riviera cruises year-round from the port of Los Angeles, but the ship is arguably better than the ports of call! Forget fashion — having fun is the sine qua non of a Carnival cruise. Gratuities can be prepaid.

Weak Points: Standing in line for embarkation, disembarkation, shore tenders, and for self-serve buffet meals is an inevitable aspect of cruising aboard all large ships. This is another ship that provides a rather impersonal cruise experience, as the ship is large and there are so many other passengers. There is absolutely no escape from unnecessary and repetitive announcements (particularly for activities that bring revenue, such as art auctions and bingo) that intrude constantly into your cruise, and a great deal of hustling for drinks, although it is sometimes done with a knowing smile.

Enchantment of the Seas
★★★★

Large Ship:	74,137 tons	Cabins (with private balcony):	212
Lifestyle:	Standard	Cabins (wheelchair accessible):	14
Cruise Line:	Royal Caribbean International	Cabin Current:	110/220-volt
Former Names:	-	Full-Service Dining Rooms:	1
Builder:	Kvaerner Masa-Yards (Finland)	Elevators:	9
Original Cost:	$300 million	Casino (gaming tables):	Yes
Entered Service:	July 1997	Slot Machines:	Yes
Registry:	Norway	SwimmingPools(outdoors):	1
Length (ft/m):	915.6/279.1	Swimming Pools (indoors):	1
Beam (ft/m):	105.6/32.2	(indoor/outdoor w/sliding glass roof)	
Draft (ft/m):	25.5/7.6	Whirlpools:	6
Propulsion/Propellers:	Diesel-electric (50,400kW)/2	Fitness Center:	Yes
Passenger Decks:	11	Sauna/Steam Room:	Yes/Yes
Total Crew:	760	Massage:	Yes
Passengers (lower beds/all berths):	1,950/2,446	Self-Service Launderette:	No
Pass. Space Ratio (lower beds/all berths):	38.0/30.3	Dedicated Cinema:	No
Crew/Pass. Ratio (lower beds/all berths):	2.4/3.2	Library:	Yes
Navigation Officers:	Norwegian/International	Classification Society:	Det Norske Veritas
Cabins (total):	975		
Size Range (sq ft/sq m):	158.2–1,033.3/14.7–96.0		
Cabins (outside view):	576	**OVERALL SCORE:**	**1,521**
Cabins (interior/no view):	399	**(OUT OF A POSSIBLE 2,000 POINTS)**	
Cabins (for one person):	0		

Accommodation: All standard outside-view and interior (no view) cabins feature twin beds that convert to a queen-size bed. There is a reasonably good amount of closet space for a one-week cruise, and an adequate amount of drawer space, although under-bed storage space for luggage is limited. The bathrooms are practical, but the decor is plain. The category A and B cabins also have a VCR.

Dining: The 1,195-seat, nonsmoking dining room is spread over two decks, with both levels connected by a grand, sweeping staircase. There are two seatings.

The dining operation is well orchestrated, with emphasis on highly programmed (insensitive), extremely hurried service that many find intrusive. Most nights feature themed menus (typically French, Oriental, Italian, Caribbean, American), as they have been for years, with waiters and busboys in appropriate costumes. The food is typical of hotel banquet catering. The menu descriptions make the food sound better than it is, which is consistently average, mostly disappointing, and without much taste. However, a decent selection of light meals is provided, and a vegetarian menu is available. The selection of breads, rolls, fruit, and cheese is quite poor, however, and should be upgraded. There is no good caviar; special orders, tableside carving, and flambeau items are not offered.

The wine list is not very extensive, but the prices are moderate. The waiters, many of whom are from Caribbean countries, are perhaps overly friendly for some tastes — particularly on the last night of the cruise, when tips are expected.

Casual, self-serve breakfasts and luncheons can be taken in the 790-seat informal Windjammer Café. It features a great expanse of ocean-view glass windows, and the decor is bright and cheerful.

An intimate Champagne/Caviar Bar terrace is located forward of the lower level of the two-deck-high dining room and just off the atrium for those who might like to taste something a little out of the ordinary, in a setting that is bright and contemporary.

Other Comments: *Enchantment of the Seas* is one of two of a recent breed of ships for this popular cruise line (her sister ship is *Grandeur of the Seas*), introduced in December 1996. She looks long, with her single funnel located well aft, has a nicely rounded stern (rather like the *Sovereign of the Seas*-class ships), and a Viking Crown Lounge set amidships. This, together with the forward mast, provides three distinct focal points in her exterior profile. There is a wraparound promenade deck outdoors (there are no cushioned pads for the deck lounge chairs, however).

A large Viking Crown Lounge (a trademark of all Royal Caribbean International ships) sits between funnel and mast, and overlooks the forward section of the swimming pool deck, as aboard *Legend of the Seas* and *Splendour of the Seas*, with access provided from stairway off the central atrium.

Inside is a seven-deck-high Centrum (atrium), which provides a central focal and meeting point (the Purser's Desk and Shore Excursion Desk are located on one level). Many public entertainment rooms and facilities can be located off the atrium.

There are two show lounges; one (the principal show lounge, with 875 seats), for big production shows; the other (the secondary show lounge, with 575 seats), for smaller shows and adult cabarets. The children and teens' facilities are good, much expanded from previous ships in the fleet.

This ship is quite pretty, and will provide a good cruise vacation, particularly for first-time passengers seeking comfortable surroundings typical of what would be found in a Hyatt Hotel-style setting, with fabrics and soft furnishings that blend together to provide a contemporary resort environment. The food is typical of what one would find in a big-city brasserie — adequate in quantity and nicely presented, but made from premixed ingredients. This company provides a well-organized, but rather homogenous cruise experience, with the same old passenger participation activities and events that have been provided for the past 25 years.

Weak Points: Standing in line for embarkation, disembarkation, shore tenders, and for self-serve buffet meals is an inevitable aspect of cruising aboard all large ships. There are too many announcements, and constant contemporary pop music played around the swimming pool throughout the day and night (difficult to get away from).

Endeavour
★★★ +

Small Ship:	3,132 tons	Cabins (for one person):	11
Lifestyle:	Standard	Cabins (with private balcony):	0
Cruise Line:	Lindblad Expeditions	Cabins (wheelchair accessible):	0
Former Names:	*Caledonian Star, North Star,*	Cabin Current:	110/220-volt
	Marburg, Lindmar	Full-Service Dining Rooms:	1
Builder:	A.G. Weser Seebeckwerft (Germany)	Elevators:	0
Original Cost:	n/a	Casino (gaming tables):	No
Entered Service:	1966/1984	Slot Machines:	No
Registry:	Bahamas	Swimming Pools (outdoors):	1
Length (ft/m):	292.6/89.20	Whirlpools:	0
Beam (ft/m):	45.9/14.00	Fitness Center:	Yes
Draft (ft/m):	20.3/6.20	Sauna/Steam Room:	Yes/No
Propulsion/Propellers:	Diesel (3,236kW)/1	Massage:	No
Passenger Decks:	6	Self-Service Launderette:	No
Total Crew:	64	Lecture/Film Room:	Yes
Passengers (lower beds/all berths):	113/124	Library:	Yes
Pass. Space Ratio (lower beds/alberths):	27.7/25.2	Zodiacs:	10
Crew/Pass. Ratio (lower beds/all berths):	1.7/1.9	Helicopter Pad:	No
Navigation Officers:	Scandinavian	Classification Society:	Det Norske Veritas
Cabins (total):	62		
Size Range (sq ft/sq m):	191.6–269.1/17.8–25.0		
Cabins (outside view):	62		
Cabins (interior/no view):	0		

OVERALL SCORE: 1,263

(OUT OF A POSSIBLE 2,000 POINTS)

Accommodation: The all-outside-view cabins are very compact, but reasonably comfortable, and they are decorated in warm, muted tones. All cabins feature a minibar/refrigerator, VCR, a decent amount of closet and drawer space (but tight for long voyages), and a clock. The cabin ceilings are plain, however, and bathrooms are tight, with little space for the storage of personal toiletry items, except under the sink.

The "suites" are basically double the size of a standard cabin, and have a wood partition separating the bedroom and lounge area. The bathroom is still small, however.

Dining: The dining room is small and fairly charming, but the low-back chairs are small. Open seating is the policy (so you can sit where you wish, with whomever you wish). The cuisine is European in style with high-quality, very fresh ingredients, but not a lot of menu choice. Service is attentive and friendly.

Other Comments: She is a reasonably handsome ship that is extremely tidy and has been well cared for. She has an open bridge policy and carries Zodiac landing craft. There is also an enclosed shore tender.

This ship was formerly known as *CalStar* by her many regular passengers. Her name was changed to *Endeavour* in June 2001. She is quite comfortable and totally unpretentious, with a warm, intimate ambience, and a casual dress code that helps make her passengers feel quite at home.

For such a small ship there is a good range of public rooms and facilities (all were nicely refurbished in mid-1998) that includes a good lecture lounge/bar/library, where a selection of videos is stocked for in-cabin use. An excellent set of lecturers that are placed aboard for each cruise make this a real life-enrichment and learning experience for an intellectual (mainly North American and British) clientele wanting to travel and learn, while enveloped in comfortable, unpretentious surroundings (you won't need a tuxedo or any dressy clothes).

This very likeable, homey little ship provides a well-tuned destination-intensive, soft expedition-style cruise experience, at a very reasonable price. She attracts a lot of loyal repeat passengers. Her itineraries now include Antarctica, where she started operating in December 1998.

Weak Points: The interior stairways are a little steep. The exterior stairway to the zodiac embarkation points is also steep. There is noise from the diesel engines (generators) that can prove quite irksome at times, particularly on the lower decks. Communication with staff can sometimes prove frustrating.

Europa
★★★★★ +

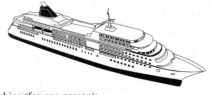

Small Ship::	28,437 tons	Cabins (for one person):	0
Lifestyle:	Luxury	Cabins (with private balcony):	168
Cruise Line:	Hapag-Lloyd Cruises	Cabins (wheelchair accessible):	2
Former Names:	-	Cabin Current:	110/220-volt
Builder:	Kvaerner Masa-Yards (Finland)	Full-Service Dining Rooms:	3
Original Cost:	DM260 million	Elevators:	4
Entered Service:	September 1999	Casino (gaming tables):	No
Registry:	Bahamas	Slot Machines:	No
Length (ft/m):	651.5/198.6	Swimming Pools (outdoors):	1
Beam (ft/m):	78.7/24.0	Swimming Pools (indoors):	1
Draft (ft/m):	20.0/6.1	(indoor/outdoor with magrodome)	
Propulsion/Propellers: Diesel-electric (21,600 kW)/2		Whirlpools:	1
azimuthing pods (13.3MW each)		Fitness Center:	Yes
Passenger Decks:	7	Sauna/Steam Room:	Yes/Yes
Total Crew:	264	Massage:	Yes
Passengers (lower beds/all berths):	408/450	Self-Service Launderette:	Yes (2)
Pass. Space Ratio (lower beds/all berths):	69.6/63.1	Dedicated Cinema/Seats:	Yes/60
Crew/Pass. Ratio (lower beds/all berths):	1.5/1.7	Library:	Yes
Navigation Officers:	German	Classification Society:	Germanischer Lloyd
Cabins (total):	204		
Size Range (sq ft/sq m):	355.2–914.9/33.0–85.0	**OVERALL SCORE:**	**1,857**
Cabins (outside view):	204	**(OUT OF A POSSIBLE 2,000 POINTS)**	
Cabins (interior/no view):	0		

Accommodation: The accommodation is provided in four configurations and 12 price categories, and consists of all outside-view suites: two Penthouse Grand Suites (Hapag and Lloyd) and ten Penthouse Deluxe Suites (Bach, Beethoven, Brahms, Handel, Lehar, Haydn, Mozart, Schubert, Strauss, Wagner); 156 suites with private balcony; and 36 standard suites. There are two suites (with private balcony) for the physically challenged and eight suites with interconnecting doors (good for families). Almost all suites have a private balcony (with wide teakwood deck and good lighting), complete with see-through glass topped by a teakwood rail. Among the most sought after accommodation are 12 suites (six on each of two decks) that overlook the stern (they each have private balconies with canvas "ceilings" for shade and privacy).

All Suites:

Each suite features a sleeping area with twin beds that can convert to a queen-size bed, and two bedside tables with lamps and two drawers. There is a separate lounge area (with curtain divider) and birdseye maple wood cabinetry and accenting (with rounded edges). Facilities include a refrigerator/minibar (beer and soft drinks are supplied at no extra charge), a vanity writing desk, and a sofa with large table in a separate lounge area. An illuminated walk-in closet provides ample hanging-rail space, six drawers, personal safe (this can be opened with your suite keycard or a credit card), umbrella, shoehorn, and clothes brush. European duvets are provided, and, in another cruise industry first, so is a full-color daily newspaper, *Die Welt* (*Welt am Sonntag* on Sundays), or, in fact, any one of about ten different newspapers from various regions. Almost all suites have totally unobstructed views and excellent soundproofing, both between suites as well as above and below.

In what is a cruise industry first, a superb integrated color TV/computer monitor and "infotainment" system — 24 hours per day video- and audio-on-demand (at no charge) is featured, so you choose when you want to watch a movie, or when you want to listen to a specific audio CD. The infotainment system is provided by a full-size computer located in a cabinet that also houses the refrigerator and the TV, while the keyboard is located in a drawer in the adjacent vanity unit. Restaurant seating plans, menus, shore excursion video clips, plus other informational video clips are featured. The keyboard also allows you to access e-mail sent to you aboard ship. Your own private e-mail address is provided with your tickets and other documentation (there is no charge for incoming or outgoing e-mails, only for attachments). A modem (data) socket is also provided should you decide to bring your own laptop computer (the ship can also provide a laptop for your use). Online connectivity is available 24 hours a day, anywhere in the world.

All suites have 24-hour room service. Illuminated walk-in closets provide a generous amount of hanging and storage space even for long voyages. Each features a 100% air-circulation system. Western European butlers and cabin stewardesses are featured (butlers for the 12 premium suites on Deck 10, cabin stewardesses for all other suites).

The white/gray/sea green marble-tiled bathrooms are very well designed, have light decor, and include two good-size cabinets for personal toiletry items. All bathrooms feature a full bathtub (plus an integral shower and a retractable clothesline) as well as a large, separate glass-fronted shower enclosure. Thick, 100% cotton bathrobes are provided, as are slippers and an array of personal toiletry amenities.

Penthouse Deck 10:

For those desiring even more exclusivity and larger living space, Deck 10 features two Penthouse Grand suites and 10 Penthouse Deluxe suites. These feature a teak entrance hall, spacious living room with full-size dining table and four chairs, fully stocked drinks cabinet with refrigerator, butler service, complimentary bar set-up (replenished with whatever you need), laundry and ironing service included, priority spa reservations, caviar (always available on request), hand-made chocolates, canapés, petit-fours, and other niceties at no extra charge. In addition, the two Penthouse Grand suites also feature larger bathrooms, with a private sauna, extensive forward views from their prime, supremely quiet location one deck above the navigation bridge, a very large wraparound private balcony, and large flat-screen TVs.

Suites for the Disabled:

The suites for the wheelchair-bound passengers are spacious, and feature electronically-operated beds with hydraulic lift. The bathroom has a roll-in shower area. All fittings are at the correct height, and there are several grab handles, as well as an emergency call-for-help button. Note that wheelchair-accessible public toilets are also provided on the main restaurant/entertainment deck.

Dining: The Europa Restaurant is a beautiful dining room that is two decks high, and can accommodate all passengers in one seating, with tables assigned for dinner only (breakfast and lunch are open seating). Passengers thus keep their favorite waiter throughout each cruise (for dinner). There are two sections, forward and aft, with the aft section being slightly higher than the forward section (gently sloping carpeted wheelchair ramps are provided). In common with most German-oriented ships, both smoking and non-smoking sections are provided. There are tables for two (quite a few), four, six, or eight. For superb service, a waiter and chef de rang (assistant waiter) are provided, so that the waiter is always at the station, with the chef de rang acting as runner. Plated presentation of food is provided for entrees, with silver service for additional vegetables, as well as tableside flambeaus. The size of portions is sensible, and never overwhelming. Just two words can be used to describe the cuisine — simply superb.

Table settings include Dibbern china, 150-gm weight Robbe & Berking silverware, and Riedel wine glasses. The cuisine is very international, with many German favorites featured, as well as regional dishes from around the world. The quality of food items is extremely high. Although top-grade caviar is found on dinner menus at least once each week, caviar is always available on request (at extra cost). An extensive wine list is provided, and this includes a good selection of fine French wines, as well as an extremely fine and well-balanced selection of Austrian, German, and Swiss wines.

Dining options include two intimate alternative dining spots: the Oriental Restaurant, for Euro-Asian cuisine that is both extremely creative and beautifully presented; and Venezia, for Italian cuisine (and an excellent choice of olive oils and grappa). Both are adjacent to and forward of the main restaurant, and provide the setting for a more intimate dining experience, in nicely appointed surroundings. These are available by reservation, and there is no extra charge. The Oriental Restaurant features custom-made Bauscher china, while in Venezia Rosenthal china is featured.

For more casual dining, there is a Lido Café for serve-yourself breakfasts, lunches, and dinners, with both indoor and outdoor seating and a long indoor/outdoor bar. Rosenthal china and themed evening dining are featured, when tableside service is the norm. Constant variety is provided, and many special lunch buffets feature a number of popular themes and regional specialties.

In addition, *Europa* is also famous for its delicious German sausages, available late each night in the Clipper Bar.

Other Comments: This new ship's sleek appearance should please even the most critical of passengers, with her sweeping lines, graceful profile, and the well known Hapag-Lloyd orange-and-blue funnel. Stand at the aft Lido Deck fantail and look down and you will see the vast sweeping curving lines of a graceful stern, unlike the box-like rears of so many contemporary ships.

Europa is the first Hapag-Lloyd ship to feature the pod propulsion system, designed to improve efficiency and handling, by pulling, rather than pushing, the ship through the water, virtually eliminating vibration.

Pods, which resemble huge outboard motors, replace internal electric propulsion motors, shaft lines, rudders, and their machinery, and are compact, self-contained units. When going ahead, pod units face with the propeller forward (the ship can go astern either by rotating the pods 180 degrees or by reversing the thrust).

She is a very stable ship in open sea conditions, and there is absolutely no vibration or noise. The ship also carries seven Zodiac landing craft for use during close-up shore excursions. Port and starboard bootwashing/changing rooms are also provided. There is a jogging track for the sporting, as well as an FKK (FreiKoerperKultur) deck for those who enjoy nude sunbathing, and a full teakwood wraparound outside promenade deck. The deck lounge chairs are aluminum with teak armrests, and have thick cushioned pads (with the name of the ship embroidered on them). The swimming pool is long and rectangular in shape (it was modified from its original "bottle"-shaped design in December 2000), and, while not the widest, it is certainly longer than the pools aboard most other cruise ships today (it measures 57 ft x 17 ft/17 x 5 m).

Europa is simply the most spacious purpose-built cruise ship in the world, and the company's replacement for the previous (larger) *Europa*, which, during her 17-year history, amassed a fine clutch of loyal devotees and high ratings for her service standards (except during the former *Europa*'s last two years in service, when the standards were decidedly lower — the result of inflexible union members).

With this new ship, Hapag-Lloyd has been able to reach and maintain the high standards which the ship's passengers expect and demand. The ship's principal measurements (length and beam) are very close to that of the former *Europa*, and yet the ship carries about 200 fewer passengers. So, the space per passenger is incredibly high, and there is never a hint of a line anywhere, and both restaurant and show lounge seat a full complement of passengers.

Europa is also beautifully appointed. Only the finest quality soft furnishings have been chosen for her interiors, and these blend traditional with modern designs and materials in a subtle manner. *Europa* has several public rooms and hallways with extremely high ceilings, and these provide an incredible sense of space and grandeur. The colors used in the ship's interior decor are light and provide a more contemporary "designer-speak" than one might expect.

As in the former *Europa*, public rooms include a Club Belvedere (where afternoon tea and intimate classical recitals are regular features), a Grand Lounge (the ship's main show lounge), which has a U-shaped seating configuration and a proper stage, although there are several pillars. Much artwork was taken from the former *Europa*, so regular passengers may be familiar with much of it.

In addition, there is a Clipper Lounge/Bar (with high ceilings), an Atrium Piano Bar (set opposite the reception and shore excursion desks), with Steinway baby grand piano. When the ship first debuted there was a casino, although this proved to be so little used that Hapag-Lloyd Cruises dispensed with it. It is expected that it will be replaced by an enlarged Oriental Restaurant, which has proven to be highly popular.

There is also a superb sidewalk Havana Bar cigar lounge set off to one side of a winding indoor promenade. This is equipped with three large glass-fronted, fully temperature-controlled and conditioned humidor cabinets, and carries an extensive range of cigars from Cuba and other countries. Cigars carried include a range of sizes of the following well-known makes: Avo Uvezian, Cohiba, Cohiba Linea 1492, Davidoff, Griffin's, Montechristo, Partagas, Romeo y Julia, and Sancho Pansa, from 102mm to 232mm. The bar also serves a fine range of armagnacs, calvados and cognacs, all poured tableside, as well as Cuban beer.

Other facilities include a fully stocked library (open 24 hours) with real-time Internet access provided via two computers with flat screen monitors, and per minute billing to your onboard account. There is also a small cinema/meeting/function room, an electronic golf simulator room (there are also golf driving ranges and a deck tennis court on the open deck, as well as shuffleboard). Other features include a business center, and special rooms for children (complete with video games) and hobbies (arts and crafts).

A delightful seven-deck-high central atrium is featured, together with two glass-walled elevators (operated by "piccolos" on embarkation day), and a lobby on the lower level that features a Steinway grand piano and lobby bar, reception desk, concierge desk, shore excursion desk and future cruise sales desk. An experienced concierge is available to all passengers, for any special arrangements both aboard and ashore.

Europa excels in its fine, intellectual entertainment program, which includes a constant supply of high-quality classical and contemporary music artists, as well as a fine program of expert lecturers, poetry readings, and so on, together with an occasional colorful production show, and local shows from destinations throughout the world.

The Lancaster Health Spa features the whole range of beauty services and treatments, including hot stone massage, and an array of other rejuvenating treatments (including full-day spa packages). Lancaster, the well-known German cosmetics firm, operates the spa and provides the staff. The facilities include a steam room and sauna (co-ed), two shower enclosures and two foot-washing stations, relaxation room, and two changing/dressing rooms. There is also a separate gymnasium (enlarged and relocated during a modification in December 2000) and a beauty salon. A special Japanese Spa is featured (including a cream massage, gentle steam room, and a two-tatami mat relaxation area), which is booked individually for a special 90-minute treatment that will have you floating on air when you leave.

Wheelchair passengers should note that a special ramp is provided from the swimming pool/outdoors deck down to where the lifeboats are located. When the ship was delivered there were several small lips at door thresholds (particularly at fire zone doors) throughout the ship. Some of these have now been ramped or replaced with airtight-sealing rubber strips, so that wheelchair access is now good throughout. When this rating was completed, only one toilet in the public areas (outdoors on Lido Deck 8) was wheelchair-accessible, although others may have been modified.

This ship will appeal to all those who desire to be aboard what is arguably the most luxurious and finest of all the new (small) cruise ships today. For the German-speaking market, little else comes close. Combined with a mostly young, enthusiastic, and well-trained crew, whose aim is to serve and please passengers in the most sumptuous manner and in fine surroundings, the tradition of luxury cruising, in a contemporary setting, is carried to the highest expression. Although a children's playroom is provided, *Europa* really is a ship for adults to cruise in a quiet, refined setting that mixes formality and informality well.

You may ask why the rating for this ship is so high. Well, it's in all the little details and the extra attention to personal comfort and service that this line excels. For example, if you relax at the swimming pool in a hot climate, the deck steward will not only set your deck lounge chair and cover the mattress pad with a towel, he will also serve you drinks, give you a cold towel, and spray you with Evian water to keep you cool while you take the sun. Only real glasses are used at the swimming pool and on the open decks — no plastic glasses would ever be considered, thank goodness. Flowers, pot-pourri and cloth towels (paper towels are not permissible at this rating level) are provided in the public restrooms. Fresh flowers are everywhere. Details, details, details — that's what *Europa* is all about.

In addition, excellent port information is provided (both in written form and via the TV infotainment system), as are lots of extra touches not found aboard most other cruise ships today. All port taxes and gratuities are also included, although further tipping is not prohibited. The currency used is the Euro. A souvenir logbook of every cruise is provided for each passenger. When taking all things into account — the unhurried lifestyle of single seating dining, lots of balcony accommodation, superb classical artists and lecturers, absolutely no vibration anywhere, and the outstanding cuisine and attentive, friendly service from a staff dedicated to being the world's best — it all adds up to the most luxurious cruise ship and cruise experience in the world today. While there are plenty of imitators, there are no equals.

In 2003, *Europa* will operate an around-the-world cruise of 239 days, featuring a staggering 125 port calls — the most extensive world cruise in the cruise industry.

Weak Points: There are very few weak points, although perhaps an indoor swimming pool (which was located adjacent to the health spa) may be missed by the many regular passengers that cruised aboard the former *Europa*. The balcony partitions are partial partitions, but would be more private if they were of the full (floor-to-ceiling) type.

European Stars

Large Ship:	58,600 tons	Cabins (with private balcony):	132
Lifestyle:	Standard	Cabins (wheelchair accessible):	2
Cruise Line:	Festival Cruises	Cabin Current:	110/220-volt
Former Names:	-	Full-Service Dining Rooms:	2
Builder:	Chantiers de l'Atlantique (France)	Elevators:	6
Original Cost:	$245 million	Casino (gaming tables):	Yes
Entered Service:	April 2002	Slot Machines:	Yes
Registry:	France	Swimming Pools (outdoors):	1
Length (ft/m):	823.4/251.0	Swimming Pools (indoors):	0
Beam (ft/m):	94.4/28.8	Whirlpools:	1 (thalassotherapy)
Draft (ft/m):	22.4/6.85	Fitness Center:	Yes
Propulsion/Propellers:	Diesel (31,680kW)/2 pods	Sauna/Steam Room:	Yes/Yes
Passenger Decks:	10	Massage:	Yes
Total Crew:	450	Self-Service Launderette:	No
Passengers (lower beds/all berths):	1,566/2,223	Dedicated Cinema:	No
Pass. Space Ratio (lower beds/all berths):	37.4/27.6	Classification Society:	Bureau Veritas
Crew/Pass. Ratio (lower beds/all berths):	2.2/3.1		
Navigation Officers:	European		
Cabins (total):	783		
Size Range (sq ft/sq m):	139.9–236.8/13.0–22.0		
Cabins (outside view):	302		
Cabins (interior/no view):	223		
Cabins (for one person):	0		

OVERALL SCORE: NOT YET RATED

Note that this ship had not entered service when this book was completed. However, the score is expected to be very similar to that of *Mistral*.

Accommodation: There are 11 accommodation price categories to choose from. These include 132 suites with private balcony, outside-view cabins, and interior (no view) cabins.

No matter which accommodation grade you choose, all suites and cabins are equipped with a TV, hair dryer, minibar/refrigerator, bathroom with shower and toilet. Suite grade accommodation also has more room, a larger bathroom with bathtub, shower and toilet, and private balcony.

Dining: There are four dining spots aboard this ship (all are designated as nonsmoking areas). The principal dining room is the 610-seat Marco Polo Restaurant, with two seatings for meals. The cuisine featured by Festival Cruises is, in general, quite sound, and, with varied menus and good presentation, should prove a highlight for most passengers. The wine list features a wide variety of wines at fairly reasonable prices, although almost all wines are very young.

La Pergola is the second, and most formal, restaurant aboard this ship, and features stylish Italian cuisine. This is the restaurant assigned to all passengers occupying accommodation designated as suites, and other passengers can dine in it too, although reservations must be made.

Chez Claude, located on the starboard side aft, adjacent to the ship's funnel, is a grill area for fast-food items.

La Brasserie is the name of the casual, self-serve buffet eatery, which is open 24 hours a day. The selections are very standardized, however, and could be better.

Additionally, Caffe Quadri, which is located on the upper, second level of the main lobby, is for coffees and pastry items — as well as for people-watching throughout the day.

Other Comments: Although this ship is slightly larger, it is a close "cousin" to *Mistral* (the first new ship to be built for Festival Cruises), and sister to *European Vision*, although there is an added deck around the forward mast (this allowed for the addition of more suites with private balconies in a premium area of real estate) which also happens to provide a better balance to the ship's overall profile. A 114.8 ft- (35-m-) long midsection was added to increase the ship's length, thus providing more space per passenger than *Mistral*. From the technical viewpoint, the ship is quite different from *Mistral*, and is fitted with an azimuthing pod propulsion system, instead of conventional rudders and propellers, in the latest configuration of high-tech propulsion systems

The Lido deck surrounding the outdoor swimming pool also features whirlpool tubs, and a large bandstand is set in raised canvas-covered pods. All the deck lounge chairs have cushioned pads.

Inside, the layout and passenger flow is good, as are the "you are here" deck signs. The decor is decidedly "European Moderne" — whatever that means — and it includes clean lines, minimalism in furniture designs (including some chairs that look interesting but are totally impractical without incurring reconstructive surgery for occupants).

Facilities include: Amadeus, the ship's show lounge, and La Gondola Theatre — for plays and other theatrical presentations; a cigar smoking room (called Ambassador), which has all the hallmarks of a gentleman's club of former times; as well as a piano bar. The Goethe Library/Card Room has real writing desks (something many ships seem to omit today), and this ship has an Internet Café, as well an English pub called the White Lion. Gamblers will find solace in The Lido Casino, with blackjack, poker, and roulette games, plus the slot machines.

For the sports minded participant, there is a simulated climbing wall outdoors, while other sports and fitness facilities include a volleyball/basketball court, and mini-golf. For personal pampering, the Atlantica Spa features some body-pampering treatments, as well as a gymnasium with the usual high-tech, muscle-pumping machinery and gadgets.

All prices aboard ship are quoted in Euros. *European Stars* was built for a European company, and designed and constructed by Europeans, with European decor and colors, for European passengers, with European food, service, and entertainment. In other words, as the company so strongly states, this is a ship for Europeans (however, the ship is also marketed in the US, but under the company name of First European Cruises). Note that the names of the public rooms were not known at press time, so those of sister ship *European Vision* (which debuted in June 2001) have been used provisionally.

Weak Points: Standing in line for embarkation, disembarkation, shore tenders, and for self-serve buffet meals is an inevitable aspect of cruising aboard all large ships. Smokers will typically be everywhere, as they are aboard the company's other ships, and are virtually impossible to avoid (in typical European fashion, ashtrays are simply moved — if used at all — to wherever smokers happen to be sitting). There are simply too many announcements — each conducted in several languages.

European Vision

Large Ship:	58,600 tons	Cabins (wheelchair accessible):	2
Lifestyle:	Standard	Cabin Current:	110/220-volt
Cruise Line:	Festival Cruises	Full-Service Dining Rooms:	2
Former Names:	-	Elevators:	6
Builder:	Chantiers de l'Atlantique (France)	Casino (gaming tables):	Yes
Original Cost:	$245 million	Slot Machines:	Yes
Entered Service:	June 2001	Swimming Pools (outdoors):	2
Registry:	Italy	Swimming Pools (indoors):	0
Length (ft/m):	823.4/251.0	Whirlpools:	1 (thalassotherapy)
Beam (ft/m):	94.4/28.8	Fitness Center:	Yes
Draft (ft/m):	22.4/6.85	Sauna/Steam Room:	Yes/Yes
Propulsion/Propellers:	Diesel-electric	Massage:	Yes
	(31,680kW)/2 pods	Self-Service Launderette:	No
Passenger Decks:	10	Dedicated Cinema:	No
Total Crew:	710	Library:	Yes
Passengers (lower beds/all berths):	1,566/2,223	Classification Society:	Bureau Veritas
Pass. Space Ratio (lower beds/all berths):	37.4/27.6		
Crew/Pass. Ratio (lower beds/all berths):	2.2/3.1		
Navigation Officers:	European		
Cabins (total):	783		
Size Range (sq ft/sq m):	139.9–236.8/13.0–22.0		
Cabins (outside view):	302		
Cabins (interior/no view):	223		
Cabins (for one person):	0		
Cabins (with private balcony):	132		

OVERALL SCORE: NOT YET RATED

Note that this ship had not entered service when this book was completed. However, the score is expected to be very similar to that of *Mistral*.

Accommodation: There are 11 accommodation price categories to choose from. These include 132 suites with private balcony, outside-view cabins, and interior (no view) cabins.

No matter which accommodation grade you choose, all suites and cabins are equipped with a TV, hair dryer, minibar/refrigerator, bathroom with shower and toilet. Suite grade accommodation also has more room, a larger bathroom with bathtub, shower and toilet, and private balcony.

Dining: There are four dining spots aboard this ship (all are designated as nonsmoking areas). The principal dining room is the 610-seat Marco Polo Restaurant, with two seatings for meals. The cuisine featured by Festival Cruises is, in general, quite sound, and, with varied menus and good presentation, should prove a highlight for most passengers. The wine list features a wide variety of wines at fairly reasonable prices, although almost all wines are very young.

La Pergola is the most formal restaurant aboard this ship, and features stylish Italian cuisine. This is the restaurant assigned to all passengers occupying accommodation designated as suites, and other passengers can dine in it too, although reservations must be made.

Chez Claude, located on the starboard side aft, adjacent to the ship's funnel, is a grill area for fast-food items.

La Brasserie is the name of the casual, self-serve buffet eatery, which is open 24 hours a day. The selections are very standardized, however, and could be better.

Additionally, Caffe Quadri, which is located on the upper, second level of the main lobby, is for coffees and pastry items — as well as for people-watching throughout the day.

Other Comments: Although this ship is slightly larger, it is a close "cousin" to *Mistral* (the first new ship to be built for Festival Cruises), although there is an added deck around the forward mast (this allowed for the addition of more suites with private balconies in a premium area of real estate) which also happens to provide a better balance to the ship's overall profile. A 114.8 ft- (35-m-) long midsection has also been added to increase the ship's length, thus providing more space per passenger than *Mistral*. From the technical viewpoint, the ship is quite different from *Mistral*, and is fitted with an azimuthing pod propulsion system, instead of conventional rudders and propellers, in the latest configuration of high-tech propulsion systems.

European Vision started its working life on an auspicious note, having been selected to be a floating hotel to accommodate the leaders and staff of the G8 summit in 2001.

The Lido Deck surrounding the outdoor swimming pool also features whirlpool tubs, and a large band-stand is set in raised canvas-covered pods. All the deck lounge chairs have cushioned pads.

Inside, the layout and passenger flow is good, as are the "you are here" deck signs. The decks are named after European cities such as: Oxford Deck (with British public room names), Venice Deck (with Italian public room names), and Biarritz Deck (with French public room names). The decor is decidedly "European Moderne" — whatever that means — and it includes clean lines, minimalism in furniture designs (including some chairs that look interesting but are totally impractical without incurring recon-structive surgery for occupants).

Facilities include: Amadeus, the ship's show lounge, and La Gondola Theatre — for plays and other theatrical presentations; a cigar smoking room (called Ambassador), which has all the hallmarks of a gen-tleman's club of former times; as well as a piano bar. The Goethe Library/Card Room has real writing desks (something many ships seem to omit today), and this ship has an Internet Café, as well as an English pub called the White Lion. Gamblers will find solace in The Lido Casino, with blackjack, poker, and roulette games, plus the slot machines.

For the sports minded participant, there is a simulated climbing wall outdoors, while other sports and fitness facilities include volleyball/basketball court, and mini-golf. For personal pampering, the Atlantica Spa features some body-pampering treatments, as well as a gymnasium with the usual high-tech, muscle-pumping machinery and gadgets.

All prices aboard ship are quoted in Euros. *European Vision* was built for a European company, and designed and constructed by Europeans, with European decor and colors, for European passengers, with European food, service, and entertainment. In other words, as the company so strongly states, this is a ship for Europeans (however, the ship is also marketed in the US, but under the company name of First European Cruises).

Weak Points: Standing in line for embarkation, disembarkation, shore tenders, and for self-serve buf-fet meals is an inevitable aspect of cruising aboard all large ships. The reception desk is named Piccadilly — perhaps Piccadilly Circus would be more appropriate! Smokers are everywhere, and are virtually impossible to avoid (in typical European fashion, ashtrays are simply moved — if used at all — to wherever smokers happen to be sitting). There are simply too many announcements — each made in several languages.

Explorer
★★ +

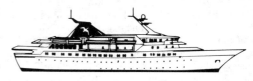

Small Ship:	2,398 tons	Cabins (for one person):	8
Lifestyle:	Standard	Cabins (with private balcony):	0
Cruise Line:	Abercrombie & Kent	Cabins (wheelchair accessible):	0
Former Names:	*Society Explorer, Lindblad*	Cabin Current:	220-volt
	Explorer, World Explorer	Full-Service Dining Rooms:	1
Builder:	Nystad Varv Shipyard (Finland)	Elevators:	0
Original Cost:	$2.5 million	Casino (gaming tables):	No
Entered Service:	1969/March 1993	Slot Machines:	No
Registry:	Liberia	Swimming Pools (outdoors):	1
Length (ft/m):	239.1/72.88	Whirlpools:	0
Beam (ft/m):	46.0/14.03	Exercise Room:	Yes
Draft (ft/m):	13.7/4.20	Sauna/Steam Room:	Yes/No
Propulsion/Propellers:	Diesel(2,795kW)/1	Massage:	Yes
Passenger Decks:	6	Self-Service Launderette:	No
Total Crew:	71	Lecture/Film Room:	Yes
Passengers (lower beds/all berths):	100/114	Library:	Yes
Pass. Space Ratio (lower beds/all berths):	23.9/21.0	Zodiacs:	Yes
Crew/Pass. Ratio (lower beds/all berths):	1.4/1.6	Helicopter Pad:	No
Navigation Officers:	European	Classification Society:	Det Norske Veritas
Cabins (total):	50		
Size Range (sq ft/sq m):	81.8–161.4/7.6–15.0	**OVERALL SCORE:**	**1,095**
Cabins (outside view):	50	(OUT OF A POSSIBLE 2,000 POINTS)	
Cabins (interior/no view):	0		

Accommodation: The cabins are extremely small and utilitarian, and there is very little closet, drawer, and storage space. They are just about adequate for this type of cruising, where you need only very casual clothing. The bathrooms (and the towels) are really tiny, and there is little room for your personal toiletry items.

Dining: The dining room is cheerful and intimate, although somewhat noisy, but it does seat all passengers in one seating, with assigned tables. Features creatively presented food, although the choice is quite limited, as is the wine list. Smiling, attentive, and genuinely friendly service, although it is quite casual.

Other Comments: *Explorer* is the original expedition cruise vessel, and started expedition cruising with passengers (participants) in 1969 under the guidance of the father of expedition cruising, Lars-Eric Lindblad. She is a surprisingly strong ship, having experienced a couple of groundings. Abercrombie & Kent acquired *Explorer* in 1992 and carries on the excellent tradition of providing adventure/discovery cruises to lesser-traveled regions such as the Amazon and Antarctic.

Although she is a small vessel, she is fitted with all the necessary equipment for successful in-depth exploration cruising, including a fleet of Zodiac landing craft. She is now showing many signs of wear and tear, and cannot compete effectively with the newer expedition-style ships, despite recent refurbishment. Has an ice-hardened hull and a well-balanced profile, and is extremely maneuverable.

There are few public rooms, but the interior decor is tasteful and cheerful, and the ambience is intimate. There is a large reference library of books associated with nature and wildlife. Good lecturers and nature specialists are on board for each cruise, provided by Abercrombie & Kent.

When cruising in the Antarctic region, she often carries fresh fruits and other produce, and medication to the research stations.

This is cruising for the serious "in-your-face" adventurer who wants to explore specialized areas of the world yet have some of the most basic creature comforts of home within reach. All shore excursions and gratuities are included.

Weak Points: The original modern-day expedition cruise vessel is now old and quirky, so you simply must not try to compare her with other small ships.

Explorer of the Seas
★★★★

same as adventure

Large Ship:	137,308 tons	Cabins (for one person):	0
Lifestyle:	Standard	Cabins (with private balcony):	757
Cruise Line:	Royal Caribbean International	Cabins (wheelchair accessible):	26
Former Names:	-	Cabin Current:	110-volt
Builder:	Kvaerner Masa-Yards (Finland)	Full-Service Dining Rooms:	1 + 3 cafés
Original Cost:	$500 million	Elevators:	14 (6 glass-enclosed)
Entered Service:	October 2000	Casino (gaming tables):	Yes
Registry:	Liberia	Slot Machines:	Yes
Length (ft/m):	1,020.6/311.1	Swimming Pools (outdoors):	3
Beam (ft/m):	155.5/47.4	Swimming Pools (indoors):	0
Draft (ft/m):	28.8/8.8	Whirlpools:	6
Propulsion/Propellers:	Diesel-electric (75,600kW)/3 azimuthing pods	Fitness Center:	Yes
		Sauna/Steam Room:	Yes/Yes
Passenger Decks:	14	Massage:	Yes
Total Crew:	1,181	Self-Service Launderette:	No
Passengers (lower beds/all berths):	3,114/3,840	Dedicated Cinema:	No
Pass. Space Ratio (lower beds/all berths):	44.0/35.7	Library:	Yes
Crew/Pass. Ratio (lower beds/all berths):	2.6/3.2	Classification Society:	Det Norske Veritas
Navigation Officers:	Scandinavian		
Cabins (total):	1,557		
Size Range (sq ft/sq m):	151.0–1,146.0/14.0–106.5		
Cabins (outside view):	939		
Cabins (interior/no view):	618		

OVERALL SCORE: 1,545
(OUT OF A POSSIBLE 2,000 POINTS)

Accommodation: There is an extensive range of 22 cabin categories from which to choose, in four major groupings: Premium ocean-view suites and cabins, Promenade-view (interior-view) cabins, Ocean-view cabins, and Interior (no view) cabins. Note that many cabins are of a similar size — good for incentives and large groups, and 300 have interconnecting doors — good for families.

A total of 138 interior (no view) cabins have bay windows that look into a horizontal atrium — first used to good effect aboard the Baltic passenger ferries *Silja Serenade* (1990) and *Silja Symphony* (1991) with interior (no view) cabins that look into a central shopping plaza. Regardless of what cabin grade you choose, however, all except for the Royal Suite and Owner's Suite feature twin beds that convert to a queen-size unit, TV, radio and telephone, personal safe, vanity unit, minibar (called an Automatic Refreshment Center), hair dryer, and private bathroom.

The largest accommodation includes luxuriously appointed penthouse suites (whose occupants, sadly, must share the rest of the ship with everyone else, except for their own exclusive, and private, concierge club). The grandest is the Royal Suite, which is positioned on the port side of the ship. It features a king-size bed in a separate, large bedroom, a living room with an additional queen-size sofa bed, baby grand piano (no pianist is included, however), refrigerator/wet bar, dining table, entertainment center, and large bathroom.

The slightly smaller, but still highly desirable Owner's Suites (there are ten of these, all located in the center of the ship, on both port and starboard sides) and the Royal Family suites (four of them) all feature similar items. However, the four Royal Family suites, which have two bedrooms (including one with third/fourth upper Pullman berths) are located at the stern of the ship and have magnificent views over the ship's wash.

All cabins feature a private bathroom with shower enclosure (towels are 100% cotton), as well as interactive TV and pay-per-view movies.

Dining: The main dining room is large and is set on three levels, all of which are named after explorers (Christopher Columbus, Da Gama, and Magellan). A dramatic staircase connects all three levels. However, all three feature exactly the same menus and food. The dining room is totally nonsmoking, there are two seatings, and tables are for four, six, eight, ten, or twelve.

The cuisine in the main dining room(s) is similar in nature to that offered aboard the company's other ships. In other words, we are talking about mass banquet catering that offers standard fare comparable to that found in American family-style restaurants ashore. Such items as caviar (once a standard menu item) incur a hefty extra charge, while rice with many dinner entrees seems to have replaced potatoes and other carbohydrate sources.

Alternative dining options for casual and informal meals at all hours of the day (according to company releases) include:

Café Promenade: continental breakfast, all-day pizzas, and specialty coffees (sadly provided in paper cups).

Windjammer Café: casual buffet-style breakfast, lunch, and light dinner (except for the last night of the cruise).

Island Grill (this is actually a section inside the Windjammer Café): casual dinner (no reservations necessary) featuring a grill and open kitchen.

Portofino: an "upscale" (nonsmoking) Euro-Italian restaurant, for dinner (reservations required).

Johnny Rockets: a retro 1950s all-day, all-night eatery that features hamburgers, malt shakes (at extra cost), and jukebox hits, with both indoor and outdoor seating.

Sprinkles: round-the-clock ice cream and yogurt.

Other Comments: *Explorer of the Seas* is a stunning, large, floating leisure resort, and sister to *Voyager of the Seas* and *Adventure of the Seas*, which debuted in 1999 and 2001 respectively, and two others still to come. The exterior design is not unlike an enlarged version of the company's *Vision*-class ships. The ships are, at present, the largest cruise vessels in the world in terms of tonnage measurement (although, to keep things in perspective, the ships are not quite as long as Norwegian Cruise Line's *Norway*).

The ship's propulsion is derived from three pod units, powered by electric motors (two azimuthing, and one fixed at the centerline) instead of conventional rudders and propellers, in the latest configuration of high-tech propulsion systems.

With her large proportions, she provides more facilities and options, and caters to more passengers than any other Royal Caribbean International ship has in the past, and yet the ship manages to have a healthy passenger space ratio (the amount of space per passenger). Being a "non-Panamax" ship, she is simply too large to go through the Panama Canal, thus limiting her itineraries almost exclusively to the Caribbean (where few islands can accept her), or for use as a floating island resort. Spend the first few hours exploring all the many facilities and public spaces aboard this vessel and it will be time well spent.

Although she is a large ship, even the accommodation hallways are quite attractive, with artwork cabinets and wavy lines to interject and break up the monotony. In fact, there are plenty of decorative touches to help you avoid what would otherwise be a very clinical environment.

Embarkation and disembarkation take place through two stations/access points in a new purpose-built passenger terminal in Miami. These are designed to minimize the inevitable lines at the start and end of the cruise (that's over 1,500 people for each access point). Once inside the ship, you'll need good walking shoes, particularly when you need to go from one end to the other — it really is quite a long way

The four-decks-high Royal Promenade, which is 393.7 ft (120 m) long, is the main interior focal point (it's a good place to hang out, to meet someone, or to arrange to meet someone). The length of two football fields, it has two internal lobbies (atria) that rise to as many as 11 decks high. Restaurants, shops, and entertainment locations front this winding street, and interior "with-view" cabins look into it from above. It is designed loosely in the image of London's fashionable Burlington Arcade, although there's not a real brick in sight, and I wonder if the designers have ever visited the real thing!

The atrium houses a "traditional" English pub, with, naturally, draft beer and plenty of "street-front" seating (it's funny, but North American passengers sit down, while British passengers stand at the bar). There is also a Champagne Bar, a Sidewalk Café (for continental breakfast, all-day pizzas, specialty coffees, and desserts), Sprinkles (for round-the-clock ice cream and yogurt), and Weekend Warrior (a sports bar). There are also several shops — jewelry shop, gift shop, liquor shop, and the logo souvenir shop. Altogether, the Royal promenade is a nice place to see and be seen. The Guest Reception and Shore Excursion counters are located at the aft end of the promenade, as is an ATM machine. Things to watch for: Look up to see the large moving, asteroid-like sculpture (constantly growing and contracting); parades; and street entertainers.

Arched across the promenade is a captain's balcony. Meanwhile, in the center of the promenade is a stairway that connects you to the deck below, where you'll find Schooner Bar (a piano lounge) and the colorful Casino Royale. This, is, naturally, large and full of flashing lights and noises. Casino gaming includes blackjack, Caribbean stud poker, roulette, and craps.

Aft to the casino is the Aquarium Bar, while close by are some neat displays of oceanographic interest. Royal Caribbean International has teamed up with the University of Miami's Rosenstiel School of Marine and Atmospheric Science to study the ocean and the atmosphere. To this end, a small onboard laboratory is part of the project.

278

Action man and action woman can enjoy more sporting pursuits, such as a rock-climbing wall that's 32.8 ft (10 m) high. It is located outdoors at the aft end of the funnel. You'll get a great "buzz" being 200 ft (61 m) above the ocean while the ship is moving — particularly when it rolls.

There's also an in-line skating track, a dive-and-snorkel shop, a full-size basketball court, and 9-hole golf driving-range. A ShipShape health spa measures 15,000 sq ft (1,393.5 sq m) and includes a large aerobics room, fitness center (with the usual stairmasters, treadmills, stationary bikes, weight machines and free weights), treatment rooms, men's and women's sauna/steam rooms, while another 10,000 sq ft (929 sq m) are devoted to a Solarium (with magrodome sliding glass roof) for relaxation after you've exercised too much!

There is also a regulation-size ice-skating rink (Studio B), featuring real, not fake, ice, with stadium-style seating for up to 900, and the latest in broadcast facilities. Ice Follies shows are also presented here. A number of slim pillars obstruct clear-view arena stage sight lines, however.

If ice-skating in the Caribbean doesn't appeal to you, perhaps you'd like the stunning two-deck library (open 24 hours a day). A grand $12 million has been spent on permanent artwork. Drinking places include a neat Aquarium Bar, which comes complete with 50 tons of glass and water in four large aquariums (whose combined value is over $1 million). Other drinking places include the small and intimate Champagne Bar, Crown & Anchor Pub, and a Connoisseur Club, for cigars and cognacs. Lovers of jazz might appreciate High Notes, an intimate room for cool music, or the Schooner Bar piano lounge. Golfers might enjoy the 19th Hole — a golf bar.

Show lovers will find that the Palace Showlounge seats 1,350 and spans the height of five decks. It features a hydraulic orchestra pit and stage areas, and is decorated in the style of the grand European theaters from the fin-de-siecle period.

There is a TV studio, located adjacent to rooms that can be used for trade show exhibit space. Lovers can tie the knot in a wedding chapel in the sky, called the Skylight Chapel (it's located on the upper level of the Observation Lounge, and even has wheelchair access via an electric stairway lift). Meanwhile, outdoors, the pool and open deck areas provide a resort-like environment.

Families with children have not been forgotten, and the children's facilities are extensive. "Aquanauts" is for 3–5 year olds; "Explorers" is for 6–8 year olds; "Voyagers" is for 9–12 year olds. "Optix" is a dedicated area for teenagers, including a daytime club (with several computers), soda bar, disc jockey, and dance floor. "Challenger's Arcade" features an array of the latest video games. "Paint and Clay" is an arts and crafts center for younger children. Adjacent to these indoor areas is Adventure Beach, an area for all the family to enjoy. It includes swimming pools, a waterslide and game areas outdoors.

In terms of sheer size, this ship dwarfs all other ships in the cruise industry, but in terms of personal service, it's more like the reverse. Royal Caribbean International does, however, try hard to provide a good standard of programmed service from its hotel staff. This is impersonal city life at sea, millennium-style, and a superb, well-designed alternative to a land-based resort, which is what the company wanted to build. Welcome to the real, escapist world of highly programmed resort living aboard ship. Perhaps if you dare to go outside, you might even be able to see the sea — now there's a novelty! Keep in mind that you'll need to pay for all the additional cost items.

The ship is large, so remember that if you meet someone somewhere, and want to meet them again you'll need to make an appointment — for this really is a large, Las Vegas-style American floating resort-city for the lively of heart and fleet of foot. Good advice is to arrange to meet somewhere along the Royal Promenade.

Weak Points: Expect lines for check-in, embarkation, and disembarkation (it's better if you are a non-US resident and stay at an RCI-booked hotel, as you will complete all formalities there and then simply walk on board to your cabin). Suites and cabins with private balcony have Bolidt floors (a substance that looks like rubberized sand) instead of wood. If you have a cabin with an interconnecting door to another cabin, be aware that you'll be able to hear everything your next-door neighbors say and do! Bathroom toilets are explosively noisy.

You'll need to plan what you want to take part in wisely, as almost everything requires you to sign-up in advance (many activities take place only on sea days). The cabin bath towels are small and skimpy. There are very few quiet places to sit and read — almost everywhere there is intrusive acoustic wallpaper (background music). Although the menus and food variety offered have been upgraded since the introduction, remember that you get what you pay for. Food costs are well below that for Celebrity Cruises, for example, and so you should not expect the same food quality.

Fantasy
★★★ +

Large Ship:	70,367 tons	Cabins (for one person):	0
Lifestyle:	Standard	Cabins (with private balcony):	54
Cruise Line:	Carnival Cruise Lines	Cabins (wheelchair accessible):	22
Former Names:	-	Cabin Current:	110-volt
Builder:	Kvaerner Masa-Yards (Finland)	Full-Service Dining Rooms:	2
Original Cost:	$225 million	Elevators:	14
Entered Service:	March 1990	Casino (gaming tables):	Yes
Registry:	Panama	Slot Machines:	Yes
Length (ft/m):	855.8/263.6	Swimming Pools (outdoors):	3
Beam (ft/m):	103.0/31.4	Swimming Pools (indoors):	0
Draft (ft/m):	25.9/7.9	Whirlpools:	6
Propulsion/Propellers:	Diesel-electric (42,240kW)/2	Fitness Center:	Yes
Passenger Decks:	10	Sauna/Steam Room:	Yes/Yes
Total Crew:	920	Massage:	Yes
Passengers (lower beds/all berths):	2,044/2,634	Self-Service Launderette:	Yes
Pass. Space Ratio (lower beds/all berths):	34.4/26.7	Dedicated Cinema:	No
Crew/Pass. Ratio (lower beds/all berths):	2.2/2.8	Library:	Yes
Navigation Officers:	Italian	Classification Society:	Lloyd's Register
Cabins (total):	1,022		
Size Range (sq ft/sq m):	173.2–409.7/16.0–38.0	**OVERALL SCORE:**	**1,385**
Cabins (outside view):	620	**(OUT OF A POSSIBLE 2,000 POINTS)**	
Cabins (interior/no view):	402		

Accommodation: As in sister ships *Ecstasy*, *Elation*, *Fascination*, *Imagination*, *Inspiration*, *Paradise*, and *Sensation*, the standard outside-view and interior (no view) cabins have plain decor. They are marginally comfortable, yet spacious enough and practical (most are of the same size and appointments), with good storage space and well-designed bathrooms.

Those booking one of the outside suites will find more space, whirlpool bathtubs, and some fascinating, rather eclectic decor and furniture. These are mildly attractive, but nothing special, and they are much smaller than those aboard the ships of a similar size of several competing companies.

A gift basket is now provided in all grades of accommodation; it includes aloe soap, shampoo, conditioner, deodorant, breath mints, candy, and pain relief tablets.

Dining: The two large dining rooms, both with ocean-view windows (both nonsmoking), are noisy, but the decor is attractive, although it is rather vivid. Dining is now in four seatings, for greater flexibility: 6pm, 6:45pm, 8pm, and 8:45pm (these times are approximate).

Carnival meals stress quantity, not quality, although the company constantly works hard to improve the cuisine. While passengers seem to accept it, few find it worth remembering. However, food and its taste are still not the company's strongest points (you get what you pay for, remember).

While the menu items sound good, their presentation and taste tend to leave much to be desired. While meats are of a high quality, fish and seafood is not. Presentation is simple, and few garnishes are used. Many meat and fowl dishes are disguised with gravies and sauces. The selection of fresh green vegetables, breads, rolls, cheeses, and fruits is limited, and there is too much use of canned fruit and jellied desserts. However, do remember that this is banquet catering, with all its attendant standardization and production cooking (it is, therefore, difficult to ask for anything remotely unusual or off-menu).

Although there is a decent wine list, there are no wine waiters (the waiters are expected to serve both food and wine). The service is quite robotic, closely timed, highly programmed, and inflexible, although the waiters are willing and reasonably friendly However, the waiters do sing and dance (be prepared for "Hot, Hot, Hot" and "The Macarena" — again) and there are constant waiter parades; the dining room is show business — all done in the name of gratuities at the end of your cruise.

At night, the Seaview Bistro (as the Windows on the Sea is known) provides a casual alternative to eating in the main dining rooms. It serves pasta, steaks, salads, and desserts.

In addition, there is a patisserie offering specialty coffees and sweets (at extra charge).

Other Comments: Although externally angular and not handsome, *Fantasy* was the first in a series of eight almost identical, very successful ships built for Carnival Cruise Lines (and the company's fifth new ship). Almost vibration-free service is provided by the diesel-electric propulsion system.

Decorative features include vibrant colors and an extensive use of neon lighting for total sensory stimulation. Has a six-deck-high atrium, topped by a large glass dome, featuring a spectacular artistic centerpiece. Has expansive open deck areas, but they quickly become inadequate when the ship is full and everyone wants to be out on deck.

Inside, this ship has public entertainment lounges, bars, and clubs galore, with something for everyone (except quiet space). There is a fine library and reading room, but few books. Her handsome public rooms, connected by a wide indoor boulevard called "Via Marina," with decor inspired by the ancient Roman city of Pompeii, beat a colorful mix of classic and contemporary design elements that beg your indulgence.

The multitiered show lounge is quite lavish, although 20 pillars obstruct the views from several seats. The dramatic three-deck-high glass-enclosed health spa has a banked jogging track. The large casino has almost non-stop action, as one would expect aboard any Carnival Cruise Lines ship.

What should be of great interest to families, however, is a special partnership with Universal Studios' travel company, which packages a cruise together with a land stay and choice of three different theme parks: Universal Studios, Wet 'n Wild, and Sea World. The pricing is competitive with that of the Disney land-cruise product. Aboard the ship, kids will enjoy "Children's World," a 2,500 sq ft (232 sq m) play-area with games and fun stuff for kids of all ages, including Apple computers loaded with educational software, and an arts and crafts area with spin-and-sand art machines.

The cuisine is just so-so but the real fun begins at sundown, when Carnival really excels in action, lights, razzle-dazzle shows, and late-night high-decibel sounds. From the futuristic Electricity Disco to the ancient Cleopatra's Bar, this ship will entertain you well.

Forget fashion — having fun is the sine qua non of a Carnival cruise. Gratuities can be prepaid.

Weak Points: Standing in line for embarkation, disembarkation, shore tenders, and for self-serve buffet meals is an inevitable aspect of cruising aboard all large ships. There is absolutely no escape from unnecessary and repetitious announcements (particularly for activities that bring revenue, such as art auctions and bingo) that intrude constantly into your cruise, and a great deal of hustling for drinks, although it is sometimes done with a knowing smile.

Fascination
★★★ +

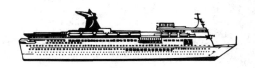

Large Ship:	70,367 tons	Cabins (for one person):	0
Lifestyle:	Standard	Cabins (with private balcony):	54
Cruise Line:	Carnival Cruise Lines	Cabins (wheelchair accessible):	22
Former Names:	-	Cabin Current:	110-volt
Builder:	Kvaerner Masa-Yards (Finland)	Full-Service Dining Rooms:	2
Original Cost:	$315 million	Elevators:	14
Entered Service:	July 1994	Casino (gaming tables):	Yes
Registry:	Bahamas	Slot Machines:	Yes
Length (ft/m):	855.0/260.60	Swimming Pools (outdoors):	3
Beam (ft/m):	103.0/31.40	Swimming Pools (indoors):	0
Draft (ft/m):	25.7/7.86	Whirlpools:	6
Propulsion/Propellers:	Diesel-electric (42,240kW)/2	Fitness Center:	Yes
Passenger Decks:	10	Sauna/Steam Room:	Yes/Yes
Total Crew:	920	Massage:	Yes
Passengers (lower beds/all berths):	2,040/2,594	Self-Service Launderette:	Yes
Pass. Space Ratio (lower beds/all berths):	34.4/26.7	Dedicated Cinema:	No
Crew/Pass. Ratio (lower beds/all berths):	2.2/2.8	Library:	Yes
Navigation Officers:	Italian	Classification Society:	Lloyd's Register
Cabins (total):	1,020		
Size Range (sq ft/sq m):	173.2–409.7/16.0–38.0		
Cabins (outside view):	618		
Cabins (interior/no view):	402		

OVERALL SCORE: 1,385
(OUT OF A POSSIBLE 2,000 POINTS)

Accommodation: As in sister ships *Ecstasy*, *Elation*, *Fantasy*, *Imagination*, *Inspiration*, *Paradise*, and *Sensation*, the standard outside-view and interior (no view) cabins have plain decor. They are marginally comfortable, yet spacious enough and practical (most are of the same size and appointments), with good storage space and well-designed bathrooms.

Those booking one of the outside suites will find more space, whirlpool bathtubs, and some fascinating, rather eclectic decor and furniture. These are mildly attractive, but nothing special, and they are much smaller than those aboard the ships of a similar size of several competing companies.

A gift basket is now provided in all grades of accommodation; it includes aloe soap, shampoo, conditioner, deodorant, breath mints, candy, and pain relief tablets.

Dining: There are two large, noisy dining rooms (both are nonsmoking) that come with Carnival's typically usual efficient, assertive, fast service. The buffets are rather run-of-the-mill, with little creativity. Dining is now in four seatings, for greater flexibility: 6pm, 6:45pm, 8pm and 8:45pm (these times are approximate).

Carnival meals stress quantity, not quality, although the company constantly works hard to improve the cuisine. While passengers seem to accept it, few find it worth remembering. However, food and its taste are still not the company's strongest points (you get what you pay for, remember).

While the menu items sound good, their presentation and taste leave much to be desired. While meats are of a high quality, fish and seafood is not. Presentation is simple, and few garnishes are used. Many meat and fowl dishes are disguised with gravies and sauces. The selection of fresh green vegetables, breads, rolls, cheeses, and fruits is limited, and there is too much use of canned fruit and jellied desserts. However, do remember that this is banquet catering, with all its attendant standardization and production cooking (it is, therefore, difficult to ask for anything remotely unusual or off-menu).

Although there is a decent wine list, there are no wine waiters (the waiters are expected to serve both food and wine). The service is quite robotic, closely timed, highly programmed, and inflexible, although the waiters are willing and reasonably friendly However, the waiters do sing and dance (be prepared for "Hot, Hot, Hot" and "The Macarena" — again) and there are constant waiter parades; the dining room is show business — all done in the name of gratuities at the end of your cruise.

At night, the Seaview Bistro (as the Lido Café becomes known) provides a casual alternative to eating in the main dining rooms. It serves pasta, steaks, salads, and desserts.

Other Comments: Although externally angular and not handsome, *Fascination* is the fourth in a series of eight almost identical, very successful ships built for Carnival Cruise Lines (and the company's eighth new ship). Almost vibration-free service is provided by the diesel-electric propulsion system.

The open deck areas are quite expansive, although they quickly become inadequate when the ship is full and everyone wants to be out on deck (the aft decks tend to be less noisy, whereas all the activities are focused around the main swimming pool and whirlpools). A well-defined "topless" sunbathing area can be found around the funnel base on Verandah Deck.

This is another ship that reflects the fine creative interior design work of Joe Farcus. It features a some-what ungainly external profile, but the interior spaces created by the design have been well utilized. A dra-matic atrium lobby spans six decks, and features cool marble and hot neon topped by a large glass dome and a spectacular artistic centerpiece called *Nucleus*, which illustrates the klieg lights of a Hollywood premiere, according to the ship's designer.

The ship offers public entertainment lounges, bars, and clubs galore, with something for everyone. The interior decor aboard all Carnival ships is themed; this one sports a sophisticated Hollywood theme that begs your indulgence. The principal public rooms are connected by a double-width indoor promenade. Excellent photo opportunities exist with some 24 superb life-like figures from the movies. Look for Marilyn Monroe and James Dean outside the casino at Stars Bar, while Humphrey Bogart and Ingrid Bergman are seated at the piano at Bogart's Café; Sophia Loren and Paul Newman are close by, and Vivien Leigh and Clark Gable can be found in Tara's Library. Meanwhile, John Wayne is at the entrance to the Passage to India Lounge, while Edward J. Robinson is inside; outside the Diamonds Are Forever dis-cotheque are none other than Elizabeth Taylor and Elvis Presley. Lena Horne and Sydney Poitier can be found outside the Beverly Hills Bar, while inside are Katharine Hepburn and Spencer Tracy. Oh, and just in case you want to gamble, you'll find Lucille Ball outside the casino. Incidentally, all the slot machines aboard all Carnival ships are linked into a big prize, called Megacash.

The multitiered show lounge is lavish, and features good, though raucous, razzle-dazzle shows (sight lines are obscured from seats behind or adjacent to 20 pillars). Has a dramatic, well-segmented three-deck-high glass-enclosed health spa and gymnasium with the latest muscle-pumping equipment. There is a large shop, but it is stuffed to the gills with low quality merchandise.

However, the real fun begins at sundown, when Carnival excels in lights, razzle-dazzle shows, and late-night high-decibel sounds. This ship will entertain you in timely fashion. With such an enormous ship to play on, you will never be bored and even may forget to get off in port! There's no doubt that Carnival does "fun" better than anyone else, and if you want to party and live it up, then this ship should do it. Forget fashion — having fun is the sine qua non of a Carnival cruise.

This ship is one of the great floating playgrounds for young, active adults who enjoy constant stimu-lation, close contact with lots and lots of others, as well as the three Gs — glitz, glamour, and gambling. It is a live board game with every move executed in typically grand, colorful, fun-filled Carnival Cruise Lines style. Gratuities can be prepaid.

Weak Points: Standing in line for embarkation, disembarkation, shore tenders, and for self-serve buffet meals is an inevitable aspect of cruising aboard all large ships. There are fewer announcements in a mil-itary training camp. There is absolutely no escape from unnecessary and repetitious announcements (par-ticularly for activities that bring revenue, such as art auctions and bingo) that intrude constantly into your cruise, and a great deal of hustling for drinks, although it is sometimes done with a knowing smile.

Finnmarken

Mid-Size Ship:	15,000 tons	Cabins (with private balcony):	14
Lifestyle:	Standard	Cabins (wheelchair accessible):	4
Cruise Line:	Norwegian Coastal Voyages (OVDS)	Cabin Current:	220-volt
Former Names:	-	Full-Service Dining Rooms:	1
Builder:	Kleven Werft (Norway)	Elevators:	2
Original Cost:	$105 million	Casino (gaming tables):	No
Entered Service:	April 2002	Slot Machines:	No
Registry:	Norway	Swimming Pools (outdoors):	1
Length (ft/m):	444.5/135.5	Swimming Pools (indoors):	0
Beam (ft/m):	70.5/21.5	Whirlpools:	2
Draft (ft/m):	15.7/4.8	Fitness Center:	Yes
Propulsion/Propellers:	Diesel/2	Sauna/Steam Room:	Yes/No
Passenger Decks:	8	Massage:	Yes
Total Crew:	150	Self-Service Launderette:	Yes
Passengers (lower beds/all berths):	634/1,000	Dedicated Cinema:	No
Pass. Space Ratio (lower beds/all berths):	23.6/15.0	Library:	Yes
Crew/Pass. Ratio (lower beds/all berths):	4.2/6.6	Classification Society:	Det Norske Veritas
Navigation Officers:	Norwegian		
Cabins (total):	286		
Size Range (sq ft/sq m):	118.4–349.8/11.0–32.5		
Cabins (outside view):	249		
Cabins (interior/no view):	37		
Cabins (for one person):	0		

OVERALL SCORE: NOT YET RATED

Note that this ship had not entered service when this book was completed.

Accommodation: There are five categories of accommodation. These include two grand suites with private balcony, 12 suites with private balcony, 18 mini-suites, and 249 deluxe and standard outside-view and interior (no view) cabins. Note that all cabins have a 220-volt outlet, so take adapters and converters if you need to.

Dining: The main dining room (no smoking allowed) has 340 seats, and dining is in two seatings. Tables are assigned when you embark. Three meals each day are included in the cruise fare: breakfast and lunch (featuring the famous Norwegian "cold table") are self-serve buffet-style meals, while dinner is a sit-down affair, with three courses.

In addition, the Morestuen Wine Bar features light meals in its bistro-like setting.

Other Comments: The Norwegian Coastal Voyage is a service that was started in 1863 (it is jointly operated by two companies: Ofotens og Vesteraalen Dampskibsselskab (OVDS) and Troms Fylkes Dampskibsselskab (TFDS). The complete journey, of 1,250 nautical miles, takes in 34 ports of call in a 12-day roundtrip voyage between Bergen and Kirkenes (on the border with Russia), above the Arctic Circle (where a special "Crossing the Arctic Circle" ceremony welcomes newcomers). The journey can also be done in a one-way voyage that takes seven days (northbound) or six days (southbound). The ships carry passengers as well as mail and other cargo.

Perhaps you will be able to peek at the midnight sun (mid-May to late June, north of the Arctic Circle), experience the Northern Lights (Aurora Borealis, mostly seen during winter months, and only when the atmospheric conditions are right), and be part of the daily life of the hardy Norwegians. Approximately 60% of the passengers will be Norwegian/Scandinavian/European, while the rest will be a mix of North American and other nationalities. Although the passenger bed capacity is quoted, note that many additional passengers may be on board as day passengers, sailing between two coastal ports — the ship is the equivalent of a seagoing bus for the coastal commuters. As for the weather, the West coast of Norway is warmed by the Gulf Stream, and temperatures will be similar to those found in New England.

Larger and more luxurious in appointments than the ships introduced in the 1990s, *Finnmarken* is the way of the future for the Norwegian Coastal Voyage. The ship, the third to carry the name *Finnmarken* (the first was in 1912, the second in 1956), carries a maximum of 1,000 passengers, although, with berths for 675, this means that 325 can also be accommodated as day passengers; in addition, there is room for 50 cars.

The ship's interior decor was provided by 11 different Norwegian artists, and recalls the elegance of the first coastal ships of the 1890s. In other words, retro is in. There are four conference rooms, the largest of which has a capacity of 150. A laundry room with washing machines, tumble dryers, and irons is provided (useful for those for whom the cruise is only part of a more extensive vacation).

Best suited to adult couples, single travelers, and families with children wanting to cruise along the coast of Norway and experience the area's natural beauty. It's ideal for anyone who doesn't need entertainment or mindless parlor games, but wants to relax and unwind, enjoys being close to nature, and is probably a bit of an adventurer. This is an excellent way to experience the beautiful coastline of Norway and its fascinating and coastal towns. There will be a fascinating mix of passengers — it's a good way to meet new people and make new friends from different countries. The dress code is casual and comfortable — layered clothing is best. The currency is the Norwegian Krone.

Weak Points: Drinks prices are extremely high — the same as ashore in Norway.

Flamenco
★★★

Mid-Size Ship:	17,042 tons	Cabins (for one person):	4
Lifestyle:	Standard	Cabins (with private balcony):	0
Cruise Line:	Festival Cruises	Cabins (wheelchair accessible):	2
Former Names: *Southern Cross, Star/Ship Majestic,*		Cabin Current:	110/220-volt
SunPrincess, Spirit of London		Full-Service Dining Rooms:	1
Builder: Cantieri Navale Del Tirreno & Riuniti		Elevators:	4
(Italy)		Casino (gaming tables):	Yes
Original Cost:	n/a	Slot Machines:	Yes
Entered Service: November 1972/December 1997		Swimming Pools (outdoors):	1
Registry:	Bahamas	(+children's wading pool)	
Length (ft/m):	535.7/163.30	Swimming Pools (indoors):	0
Beam (ft/m):	73.4/22.40	Whirlpools:	0
Draft (ft/m):	22.4/6.85	Fitness Center:	Yes
Propulsion/Propellers: Diesel (13,450kW)/2		Sauna/Steam Room:	No/No
Passenger Decks:	7	Massage:	Yes
Total Crew:	350	Self-Service Launderette:	No
Passengers (lower beds/all berths):	798/987	Dedicated Cinema/Seats:	Yes/186
Pass. Space Ratio (lower beds/all berths):	21.3/17.2	Library:	Yes
Crew/Pass. Ratio (lower beds/all berths):	2.2/2.8	Classification Society:	Lloyd's Register
Navigation Officers:	Greek		
Cabins (total):	401		
Size Range (sq ft/sq m): 996.8–236.8/9.0–22.0		**OVERALL SCORE:**	**1,203**
Cabins (outside view):	272	(OUT OF A POSSIBLE 2,000 POINTS)	
Cabins (interior/no view):	129		

Accommodation: There are 12 cabin grades. Those described as deluxe suites are reasonably spacious, with separate sleeping and living areas. All other interior and outside-view cabins are on the small side, but quite well equipped, and with colorful soft furnishings. However, the cabin walls are really thin, which means you will be able to hear your next-door neighbors brushing their teeth. There is little drawer space. The cabin telephone system is rather antiquated and should be updated. The bathrooms are compact units, but adequate, and feature 100% cotton towels; the toilets are of the "gentle flush" and not the "barking dog suction" variety as found aboard newer ships.

Dining: The Galaxy Restaurant (nonsmoking), has two seatings and is quite attractive, and with its high ceiling and ocean-view porthole-shaped windows, provides a light and airy space. However, it can be extremely noisy as the tables are very close together (as aboard Festival Cruises' other ships), as well as close to the waiter stations. The service standards are good, and are being fine-tuned constantly. The quality of food and its presentation are reasonably good. There is a limited choice of breads, rolls, cheeses, and fruits, which all tend to be quite standard. Informal self-service buffets for breakfast and lunch are quite decent, however, and well presented in the Satellite Café.

Other Comments: This ship has a fairly handsome 1970s profile, with a rakish superstructure, an all-white hull, and a single large blue funnel. Originally ordered by Klosters Rederi for Norwegian Caribbean Lines, the order was subsequently cancelled, and then taken over by P&O, who took over the contract to complete the ship, in 1971. After being operated by P&O, then Premier Cruises, followed by CTC Cruise Lines, the ship underwent a $9 million refurbishment in late 1997, after being acquired by Festival Cruises from her former owners, the now-defunct CTC Cruise Lines.

There is a reasonable open deck and sunbathing space for a ship of this size, although it is tight when full, and there are no cushioned pads for the deck lounge chairs.

Inside the ship, the layout is practical, making it easy to find your way around. The public rooms received a facelift during the 1997 refurbishment by her new owners. All of the public rooms are quite comfortable, with attractive decor and soft furnishings, while tasteful colors mixed with the extensive use of reflective surfaces provide an upbeat, contemporary, yet comfortable feel. Particularly nice is the Piano Bar/Casino lounge area, with its warm wood room dividers and long bar. Do remember, however, this is not a new ship, and cannot compare with the latest vessels. Where this company does score highly, however, is in the friendliness of the crew, which is very international.

This ship provides very good value for the money, and a comfortable cruise experience in relaxed surroundings. Festival Cruises (called First European Cruises in the US) specializes in "cruising for Europeans". The languages (and therefore announcements) used throughout ship are typically English, French, German, Italian, and Spanish. The itineraries are well designed and include several sea days on longer voyages.

Weak Points: She is a high-density vessel, and so there will be some crowding during embarkation and disembarkation, as well as for tenders and buffets. There is no wraparound promenade deck outdoors, although you can walk around the front sections of one of the open decks. Smokers are everywhere, and are difficult to avoid (in typical European fashion, ashtrays are simply moved — if used at all — to wherever smokers happen to be sitting). There are too many loud announcements, in several languages.

SHIP TALK

Cable Length: a measured length equaling 100 fathoms or 600 feet.

Chart: a nautical map used for navigating.

Colors: refers to the national flag or emblem flown by the ship.

Companionway: interior stairway.

Course: direction in which the ship is headed, in degrees.

Davit: a device for raising and lowering lifeboats.

Deadlight: a ventilated porthole cover to prevent light from entering.

Disembark (also debark): to leave a ship.

Dock: berth, pier, or quay.

Draft (or draught): measurement in feet from the ship's waterline to the lowest point of its keel.

Embark: to join a ship.

Fantail: the rear or overhang of the ship.

Fathom: distance equal to six feet.

Flagstaff: a pole at the stern of a ship where the flag of the ship's country of registry is flown.

Free Port: port or place that is free of customs duty and regulations.

Funnel: chimney from which the ship's combustion gases are propelled into the atmosphere.

Galley: the ship's kitchen.

Gangway: the stairway or ramp link between ship and shore.

Flying Cloud
★★

Small Ship	400 tons	Cabins (outside view):	18
Lifestyle:	Standard	Cabins (interior/no view):	15
Cruise Line:	Windjammer Barefoot Cruises	Cabins (for one person):	0
Former Names:	*Oisseau des Isles*	Cabins (with private balcony):	0
Builder:	Ancione Chantiers Dibignon (France)	Cabins (wheelchair accessible):	0
Entered Service:	1935/1968	Cabin Current:	110-volt
Registry:	Equatorial Guinea	Full-Service Dining Rooms:	1
Length (ft/m):	208.0/63.3	Elevators:	0
Beam (ft/m):	32.0/9.7	Casino (gaming tables):	No
Draft (ft/m):	16.0/4.8	Slot Machines:	No
Type of Vessel:	Barkentine	Swimming Pools (outdoors):	0
No. of Masts:	3	Whirlpools:	0
Sail Area (sq ft/sq m):	10,500.5/975.5:	Fitness Center:	No
Main Propulsion:	Sail power	Sauna/Steam Room:	No/No
Propulsion/Propellers:	Diesel/1 Passenger	Massage:	No
Decks:	3	Self-Service Launderette:	No
Total Crew:	28	Library:	Yes
Passengers (lower beds/all berths):	66/66	Classification Society:	None
Pass. Space Ratio (lower beds/all berths):	5.8/5.8		
Crew/Pass. Ratio (lower beds/all berths):	2.3/2.3		
Navigation Officers:	International		
Cabins (total):	33		
Size Range (sq ft/sq m):	60.2–148.0/5.6–13.7		

OVERALL SCORE: 902

(OUT OF A POSSIBLE 2,000 POINTS)

Accommodation: There are four grades of accommodation. All are dimensionally challenged, particularly when compared to standard cruise ships, but this is a casual cruise experience and you will need so few clothes anyway. All are equipped with upper and lower berths, and most of them are quite narrow.

Dining: There is one dining room, and meals are all casual in style and service. Breakfast is served on board, as is dinner, while lunch could be either on board or at a beach, picnic-style.

Other Comments: This ship was built in 1935 for the French Navy and originally was operated as a cadet sail-training vessel.

Her interior decor includes stained glass windows, a spiral staircase, and lots of lovely wood.

Aboard one of the Windjammer Barefoot Cruises' fleet you can let the crew do all the work, or you can lend a hand at the helm yourself, if you feel so inclined. One neat thing to do is just to sit or lie in the nets at the bows of the vessel, without a care in the world — it's a great feeling.

The mood is free and easy, the ships are equipped very simply, and only the most casual clothes are required (T-shirts and shorts), and shoes are optional on board. Quite possibly the most used item will be your bathing suit. Smoking is allowed only on the open decks.

Entertainment in the evenings consists of you and the crew. You can put on a toga, or create a pirate outfit and join in the fun. None of that programmed big-ship production show stuff here.

Jammin' aboard a Windjammer (first-time passengers are called "crewmates" while repeat passengers are called "jammers") is no-frills cruising (it could be called an "anti-cruise") in a no-nonsense, friendly environment, for the young at heart and those who don't need programmed activities. It's all about going to sea and the romance of being at sea under sail. Those who enjoy beaches, SCUBA diving, and snorkeling around the Caribbean will be best suited to a Windjammer Barefoot Cruises cruise.

Although itineraries (islands) are provided in the brochure, the captain actually decides which islands to go to in any given area, depending on sea and weather conditions. *Flying Cloud* features year-round cruises in the British and US Virgin Islands. Brochure rates might seem inexpensive, but you'll need to add on the airfare in order to get the true cost. Tips to the crew are suggested — at $50 per week!

Complies with all international safety regulations, with the exception of the 1966 fire safety standards. Sails from Tortola (British Virgin Islands). Other ships of the fleet in this book: *Legacy*, *Mandalay*, *Polynesia*, and *Yankee Clipper*.

Fuji Maru
★★★ +

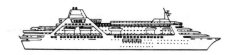

Small Ship:	23,340 tons	Cabins (with private balcony):	0
Lifestyle:	Standard	Cabins (wheelchair accessible):	2
Cruise Line:	Mitsui OSK Passenger Line	Cabin Current:	100-volt
Former Names:	-	Full-Service Dining Rooms:	1
Builder:	Mitsubishi (Japan)	Elevators:	5
Original Cost:	$63.5 million	Casino (gaming tables):	Yes (no cash can be won, only gifts)
Entered Service:	April 1989		
Registry:	Japan	Slot Machines:	No
Length (ft/m):	547.9/167.00	Swimming Pools (outdoors):	1
Beam (ft/m):	78.7/24.00	Swimming Pools (indoors):	0
Draft (ft/m):	21.4/6.55	Whirlpools:	0 (4 Japanese Baths)
Propulsion/Propellers:	Diesel (15,740kW)/2	Fitness Center:	Yes
Passenger Decks:	8	Sauna/Steam Room:	Yes/No
Total Crew:	190	Massage:	Yes
Passengers (lower beds/all berths):	328/603	Self-Service Launderette:	Yes
Pass. Space Ratio (lower beds/all berths):	71.1/38.7	Dedicated Cinema/Seats:	Yes/142
Crew/Pass. Ratio (lower beds/all berths):	1.7/3.1	Library:	Yes
Navigation Officers:	Japanese	Classification Society:	Nippon Kaiji Kyokai
Cabins (total):	164		
Size Range (sq ft/sq m):	182.9–376.7/17.0–35.0		
Cabins (outside view):	164		
Cabins (interior/no view):	0		
Cabins (for one person):	0		

OVERALL SCORE: **1,371**

(OUT OF A POSSIBLE 2,000 POINTS)

Accommodation: There are two suites that are quite lovely, with separate bedroom and living room. The deluxe cabins are also of a good standard, and come with a vanity/writing desk, minibar/refrigerator, and full-size, deep bathtub. Almost all of the other (standard) cabins are furnished very simply, but they are good for seminar and school cruises (they are much too small for any long voyages), with many accommodating three or four persons. The cabin insulation is reasonable, but could be better. The bathrooms are small and utilitarian, with old-style fixtures and some exposed plumbing. The folded blankets, a MOPAS (Mitsui OSK Passenger Line) tradition, are lovely.

Dining: The single, large dining room is quite attractive and has a high ceiling, but rather bright lighting, which makes it look more like a cafeteria or school dining hall. Both Japanese and Western cuisines are featured for all meals, in a single seating. The food itself is of a good standard, with simple, but colorful, presentation, and a good variety. There are several beverage machines around the ship for those who are used to them ashore (again, these are much appreciated by those attending seminars and training session cruises).

Other Comments: *Fuji Maru* has a well thought-out, and flexible, design for multifunctional uses, but its principal use is for incentives, conventions, as a seminar and training ship, and only occasionally for individual passengers. The outdoor decks are quite utilitarian and very little used.

Her interiors are plain and a little clinical, although there is some good artwork throughout to brighten things up. There are extensive lecture and conference facilities. The largest and most flexible lecture hall is two decks high, seats 600, and converts into a sports stadium or exhibition hall for industrial product introductions. The lobby is quite elegant and open and is part of a two-level atrium.

The ship features a classic, wood-paneled library. Other features include two Japanese-style grand baths and a traditional Washitsu tatami mat room. A Hanaguruma owner's room is reasonably elegant for small formal functions. The Sakura Salon is soothing, with a blend of Western and traditional Japanese design. The media and TV systems throughout the ship include much high-tech equipment (bilingual multiplex TVs are located in all crew cabins).

This is a fascinating exhibition, training, and educational charter cruise ship that has reasonably up-to-date facilities, although it is not ideally designed for individual passengers. As in any ship for Japanese passengers, tipping is not allowed. There are many more modern ships in the international marketplace (also serving Japanese passengers), with better facilities, more dining choices, and a less utilitarian feel and ambience, and so the score for this ship has been adjusted slightly downwards accordingly.

A specialist courier company provides an excellent luggage service and will collect your luggage from your home before the cruise, and deliver it back to your home after the cruise (this service available only in Japan).

Weak Points: There is a real waste of open deck space, and poor maintenance of what is available. The deck furniture is plastic and utilitarian. The lighting is too bright, and the noise level allows for little ambience.

KNOTS AND LOGS

A knot is a unit of speed measuring one nautical mile. (A nautical mile is equal to one-sixtieth of a degree of the earth's circumference and measures exactly 6,080.2 ft (1,852 km). It is about 800 ft (243 m) longer than a land mile. Thus, when a ship is traveling at a speed of 20 knots (*note*: this is never referred to as 20 knots per hour), she is traveling at 20 nautical miles per hour.

This unit of measurement has its origin in the days prior to the advent of modern aids, when sailors used a log and a length of rope to measure the distance that their boat had covered, as well as the speed at which it was advancing. In 1574, a tract by William Bourne, entitled *A Regiment for the Sea*, records the method by which this was done. The log was weighted down at one end while the other end was affixed to a rope. The weighted end, when thrown over the stern, had the effect of making the log stand upright, thus being visible. Sailors believed that the log remained stationary at the spot where it had been cast into the water, while the rope unraveled. By measuring the length of rope used, they could ascertain how far the ship had traveled, and were thus able to calculate its speed.

Sailors first tied knots at regular intervals, eventually fixed at 47 feet 3 inches (14.4 meters) along a rope, then counted how many knots had passed through their hands in a specified time (later established as 28 seconds), and measured by the amount of sand that had run out of an hourglass. They then used simple multiplication to calculate the number of knots their ship was traveling at over the period of an hour.

The data gathered in this way were put into a record, called a logbook. Today, a logbook is used to record the day-to-day details of the life of a ship and its crew as well as other pertinent information.

Funchal
★★ +

Small Ship:	9,563 tons	Cabins (for one person):	14
Lifestyle:	Standard	Cabins (with private balcony):	0
Cruise Line:	Classic International Cruises	Cabins (wheelchair accessible):	0
Former Names:	-	Cabin Current:	220-volt
Builder:	Helsingor Skibsvog (Denmark)	Full-Service Dining Rooms:	2
Original Cost:	n/a	Elevators:	3
Entered Service:	October 1961/May 1986	Casino (gaming tables):	Yes
Registry:	Panama	Slot Machines:	Yes
Length (ft/m):	503.6/153.51	Swimming Pools (outdoors):	1
Beam (ft/m):	62.5/19.08	Swimming Pools (indoors):	0
Draft (ft/m):	20.3/6.20	Whirlpools:	0
Propulsion/Propellers:	Diesel (7,356kW)/2	Fitness Center:	Yes
Passenger Decks:	6	Sauna/Steam Room:	Yes/No
Total Crew:	155	Massage:	No
Passengers (lower beds/all berths):	430/524	Self-Service Launderette:	No
Pass. Space Ratio (lower beds/all berths):	22.2/18.2	Dedicated Cinema:	No
Crew/Pass. Ratio (lower beds/all berths):	2.7/3.3	Library:	Yes
Navigation Officers:	Greek/Portuguese	Classification Society:	Rinave Portuguesa
Cabins (total):	222		
Size Range (sq ft/sq m):	102.2–252.9/9.5–23.5	**OVERALL SCORE:**	**1,097**
Cabins (outside view):	151	(OUT OF A POSSIBLE 2,000 POINTS)	
Cabins (interior/no view):	71		

Accommodation: The cabins are extremely compact (some would say dimensionally challenged), yet tastefully appointed units, and come in both twin and double-bedded configurations. Each now has a private bathroom (all were refurbished in1997/1998), and there is just enough closet and drawer space, providing you don't pack too many clothes. The cabins are decorated in very plain colors, accented with colorful soft furnishings. All cabin bathrooms have soap, shampoo, shower cap, shoeshine and sewing kits, and bathrobe.

Dining: There are two dining rooms, Coimbra (which also doubles as a video screening room after dinner) and Lisboa, both of which have large ocean-view picture windows on port and starboard sides. They are tastefully decorated dining rooms, and have a very homey and cozy old-world atmosphere, although the ceilings are quite low. There is one seating, so everyone eats at the same time. The food is European in style (and includes plenty of fresh fish) and is surprisingly good, as is the service from friendly Portuguese waiters. There is a decent selection of breads, cheeses, and fruits, and the wine list, while not extensive, includes a good selection of Portuguese wines at very modest prices.

Other Comments: *Funchal* has a real classic 1960s small ship profile with well-balanced, rounded lines, and pleasing real wooden decks (not a hint of synthetic turf anywhere), including one outdoor deck with two sheltered promenades, although they do not completely encircle the ship.

Her interiors feature an abundance of fine woodwork and heavy-duty fittings. One deck houses all the main public rooms, the most appealing of which is the Porto Bar, which is reminiscent of a late 19th-century drinking club with its wood-paneled walls, furniture, and lovely bar. A highly polished wooden spiral stairway is a beautiful, classic piece of decoration not found in today's ships, and is reminiscent of the days of the transatlantic steamers of the early 20th century.

The mostly Portuguese staff is friendly, caring, and quite attentive, although a little reserved at first. This ship is popular with Europeans and Scandinavians during the summer and Brazilians during the winter (anyone used to new cruise ships would probably find the ship too eclectic). She features destination-intensive cruises in a comfortable, old-world atmosphere, ideally suited to couples and solo passengers seeking good value for money and a good balance of sea days and port days.

She attracts a great number of loyal repeat passengers, who sail again and again (particularly in the summer) because of the charming, mostly Portuguese crew. *Funchal* is like an old, well-worn shoe — comfortable, but in need of a little spit and polish, and so she hovers just a tad under the three-star level (a two-and-a-half star vessel with a three-star heart). The ship and overall product is actually quite good if you enjoy small, vintage vessels with all their accompanying eccentricities. While the ship cannot be compared to the latest brand of new, larger ships, *Funchal* has delightful old-world character and charm. The feeling of camaraderie and friendliness from her loyal crew (many of whom have been aboard the ship for many years) offsets some of the hardware negatives. The ship often operates under charter to various tour packagers and operators.

Weak Points: Much of the ship's exterior paintwork is sloppy. The show lounge is extremely poor. A lack of proper maintenance in her early life has resulted in some of the exterior plating being well worn and thin.

Courtesy Douglas Ward

The battle for upkeep is constantly waged.

Galapagos Explorer II
★★★ +

Small Ship:	3,990 tons	Cabins (for one person):	0
Lifestyle:	Premium	Cabins (with private balcony):	4
Cruise Line:	Kleintours	Cabins (wheelchair accessible):	0
Former Names:	*Renaissance Three*	Cabin Current:	110-volt
Builder:	Cantieri Navale Ferrari (Italy)	Full-Service Dining Rooms:	1
Original Cost:	$20 million	Elevators:	1
Entered Service:	August 1990/January 1998	Casino (gaming tables):	Yes
Registry:	Liberia	Slot Machines:	Yes
Length (ft/m):	289.6/88.30	Swimming Pools (outdoors):	1
Beam (ft/m):	50.1/15.30	Swimming Pools (indoors):	0
Draft (ft/m):	11.9/3.65	Whirlpools:	1
Propulsion/Propellers:	Diesel (3,514kW)/2	Fitness Center:	No
Passenger Decks:	5	Sauna/Steam Room:	Yes/No
Total Crew:	72	Massage:	No
Passengers (lower beds/all berths):	100/111	Self-Service Launderette:	No
Pass. Space Ratio (lower beds/all berths):	39.9/35.9	Dedicated Cinema:	No
Crew/Pass. Ratio (lower beds/all berths):	1.3/1.5	Library:	No
Navigation Officers:	International	Classification Society:	Registro Navale Italiano
Cabins (total):	50		
Size Range (sq ft/sq m):	231.4–282.0/21.5–26.2		
Cabins (outside view):	50		
Cabins (interior/no view):	0		

OVERALL SCORE: 1,365
(OUT OF A POSSIBLE 2,000 POINTS)

Accommodation: The accommodation is located forward, with public rooms aft. Pleasant, all-outside cabins feature a large picture window and combine gorgeous, highly polished imitation rosewood paneling with lots of mirrors, hand-crafted Italian furniture, wet bar (prestocked when you book, and all items are at extra cost). All cabins feature a queen-size bed, a sitting area, and most things you need, including a minibar/refrigerator, TV, VCR, and hair dryer. The cabins have small closets, however; space for luggage is quite tight, and there is very little drawer space (there are, however, two lockable drawers).

The bathrooms, which are small, have showers (none have bathtubs) with a fold-down seat, real teakwood floors, and marble vanities.

Dining: The dining room features open seating, so you can sit where and with whom you wish. It is small and elegant, and is in three sections. It is on lowest deck and has portholes (construction regulations requirement), although it is quite cozy and welcoming, and there are tables for two, four, six, and even eight. Sit where you like, with whom you like, and at what time you like on the first night, after which you sit at the same table for the duration of the cruise.

The meals are self-service, buffet-style cold foods for breakfast and lunch (sometimes lunch will be on deck), with local delicacies featured. Food quality, choice, and presentation are all fairly decent, but not that memorable There is limited choice, particularly with regard to the entrees.

Other Comments: *Galapagos Explorer II* was originally constructed as one of a fleet of four small, identical and intimate cruise vessels for Renaissance Cruises (out of a total fleet of eight ships — the second four were slightly larger and had more powerful propulsion). This vessel is comfortable and inviting, although it has not been particularly well maintained. Water sports facilities include an aft platform, sailfish, snorkel equipment, and several zodiacs.

The ship has contemporary mega-yacht looks and handsome styling, and there is a wooden promenade deck outdoors. Inside, the limited number of public rooms feature decor that is quite smart and restful. The main lounge also doubles as a lecture room, but the piano bar is perhaps the best place to relax in the evening.

This ship will provide a destination-intensive, refined, quiet and relaxed cruise for passengers who do not like crowds, dressing up, scheduled activities, or entertainment. Naturalist guides that have been trained at the Darwin Station lead the guided shore excursions, which are included in the fare.

This ship operates 3-, 4-, and 7-night Galapagos cruises year-round from San Cristobal, sold through various tour operators. Liquor, beer, cocktails, and soft drinks are included in the fare, but wine and champagne are not. Also included are guided visits to the islands. The brochure rates may or may not include the Galapagos Islands visitor tax (about $100 depending on which country you book from). If the cruise rates do not include the visitor tax, note that under present rules it must be paid in cash at Guayaquil or Quito airports or in the islands. Shore visits take place in "pangas" (local lingo for "dinghies"). Gratuities for shipboard staff are excessive, at a recommended $80 per person, per seven-night cruise. Onboard currency: US$ or Ecuadorian Sucre.

Weak Points: The tiny "dip" pool is not a swimming pool. The open deck and sunbathing space is quite cramped. Plastic wood instead of real wood is used everywhere (although it looks good). While the service is without finesse, the crew is quite willing. The small library is attractive, but book selection is poor. The ship does not sail well in inclement weather.

Galaxy
★★★★ +

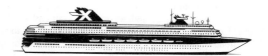

Large Ship:	77,713 tons	Cabins (with private balcony):	220
Lifestyle:	Standard	Cabins (wheelchair accessible):	8
Cruise Line:	Celebrity Cruises	Cabin Current:	110/220-volt
Former Names:	-	Full-Service Dining Rooms:	2
Builder:	Meyer Werft (Germany)	Elevators:	10
Original Cost:	$320 million	Casino (gaming tables):	Yes
Entered Service:	December 1996	Slot Machines:	Yes
Registry:	Liberia	Swimming Pools (outdoors):	2
Length (ft/m):	865.8/263.9	Swimming Pool (indoors):	1
Beam (ft/m):	105.6/32.20		indoor/outdoor (w/ magrodome)
Draft (ft/m):	25.2/7.70	Whirlpools:	4
Propulsion/Propellers:	Diesel (31,500kW)/2	Fitness Center:	Yes
Passenger Decks:	10	Sauna/Steam Room:	Yes/Yes
Total Crew:	909	Massage:	Yes
Passengers (lower beds/all berths):	1,870/2,681	Self-Service Launderette:	No
Pass. Space Ratio (lower beds/all berths):	41.5/28.9	Dedicated Cinema/Seats:	Yes/200
Crew/Pass. Ratio (lower beds/all berths):	2.0/2.9	Library:	Yes
Navigation Officers:	Greek	Classification Society:	Lloyd's Register
Cabins (total):	935		
Size Range (sq ft/sq m):	168.9–1,514.5/15.7–140.7		
Cabins (outside view):	639		
Cabins (interior/no view):	296		
Cabins (for one person):	0		

OVERALL SCORE: 1,697
(OUT OF A POSSIBLE 2,000 POINTS)

Accommodation: The largest suites are the two Presidential Suites, located amidships. Each is a pent-house measuring 1,173 sq ft (108.9 sq m), with its own butler's pantry and has an interconnecting door (when joined with the next-door suite it becomes an impressive 1,515 sq ft (140.7 sq m) apartment.

Most of the Deck 10 suites and cabins are of generous proportions, are beautifully equipped, and have balconies with full floor-to-ceiling partitions, as well as VCRs. The Sky Deck suites are also excellent, with huge balconies (the partitions are not quite of the floor-to-ceiling type), wall clock, large floor-to-ceiling mirrors, marble-topped vanity/writing desk, excellent closet and drawer space, and even dimmer-controlled ceiling lights.

All of the standard interior and outside cabins are of a good size and come nicely furnished with twin beds that can convert to a queen-size unit. The bathrooms, in particular, are spacious and come well equipped (with generous-size showers, hair dryers, and space for personal toiletry items). Unfortunately, there are no cabins for singles. Baby-monitoring telephones are also in all cabins.

All cabins feature interactive TV (available in English, French, German, Italian, and Spanish) for book-ing shore excursions, ordering room service, playing electronic casino games and purchasing goods from the ship's boutiques. So, you do not have to leave your quarters if you do not wish to, especially if you do not like the ports of call.

Most of the suites with private balconies have floor-to-ceiling windows and sliding doors to balconies (a few have outward-opening doors). All accommodation designated as suites feature duvets on the beds instead of sheets/blankets. In-suite massage service is available (with the right balcony, such as those in the Sky Suites, this is an excellent service). Some suites at the stern have balconies, although they can be overlooked, and are not so private.

Dining: There is a huge two-level dining room (with two seatings for dinner), and tables for two, four, six, or eight. It is reminiscent of the dining halls aboard the ocean liners of the 1930s, with a grand stair-case between both levels and perimeter alcoves that provide more intimate dining spaces. Each level of the dining room has its own separate galley, and the noise level in the two sections is quite acceptable (more noise is noticeable on the larger, lower level, however). The cuisine is based on menus created by Michel Roux, and executed by the chefs and cooks on board. The food has lots of taste (in particular the sauces that accompany many of the main dishes), has fine color balance, and is nicely presented.

Just outside the lower-level entrance, a champagne and caviar bar features ossetra and sevruga caviar, nicely presented with all the trimmings, and, of course, champagne and vodka to go with it.

For informal breakfasts and lunches, there is the two-level Lido Café, with several serving lines (features warm wood-accented decor), and eight bay windows provide some really prime seating spots. There are also two poolside grills; one located adjacent to the midships pools, the other wedged into the aft pool.

In addition, Tastings is a coffee lounge and bar for specialty coffees and pastries. For passengers in the two Presidential and 48 other suites, in-cabin dining is an option. However, the food served for room service is decidedly below the standard of food featured in the dining room. For those that cannot live without them, freshly baked pizzas (in a box) can be delivered, in an insulated pouch, to your cabin.

Celebrity Cruises is known for its excellent cuisine and presentation, and, although it is more difficult to deliver aboard the new, larger ships, Celebrity Cruises seems to have got it just right.

Other Comments: Slightly longer than sister ship *Century* (by 45.9 ft/14.0 m), *Galaxy*'s extra length provides room for a third swimming pool, which is covered by a large glass magrodome. Although there are over 4.5 acres of space on the open decks, it does seem a little small and crowded when the ship is full.

Inside, there are two foyers (atriums); one is a four-deck-high main foyer, and the second is a three-decks-high atrium. There is a 1,000-seat show lounge with large side balconies and good sight lines from just about every seat. There is also a small, dedicated cinema, which doubles as a conference and meeting center with all the latest audiovisual technology that includes three-language simultaneous translation and headsets for the hearing-impaired.

The AquaSpa, which has proved extremely popular aboard *Century*, contains 9,040 sq ft (839.8 sq m) of space dedicated to well-being and body treatments, and includes a large fitness/exercise area, complete with all the latest high-tech muscle machines and video cycles.

The ship has a superb, somewhat whimsical collection of artwork, which casts an eclectic look at life in some of its many forms. The collection is the result of the personal work of Christina Chandris. A "zero announcement" policy is much appreciated by passengers.

Apart from the "front-of-house" aspects of this ship, it is the "back-of-house" facilities, the design and flow of the main galley (2,200 sq m), where the ship really shines. The consideration for safety is second to none. Also has excellent tender-loading platforms.

Stratosphere, the ship's large combination observation lounge (with forward-facing as well as wrap-around views) and discotheque, provides what is probably the best viewing room when the ship operates Alaska cruises.

For a big-ship cruise experience, this one has it all. *Galaxy* delivers an outstanding product that is worth much more than the cruise fare charged.

Weak Points: Standing in line for embarkation, disembarkation, shore tenders, and for self-serve buffet meals is an inevitable aspect of cruising aboard all large ships. The one area of congestion is the Photo Gallery, when passenger flow at peak evening times is poor. Although improved, shore excursions are still a weak point of this operation.

Golden Princess
★★★★

Large Ship:	108,806 tons	Cabins (with private balcony):	710
Lifestyle:	Standard	Cabins (wheelchair accessible):	28
Cruise Line:	Princess Cruises	(18 outside/10 interior)	
Former Names:	-	Cabin Current:	110/220-volt
Builder:	Fincantieri (Italy)	Full-Service Dining Rooms:	3 main, 2 others
Original Cost:	$450 million	Elevators:	14
Entered Service:	March 2001	Casino (gaming tables):	Yes
Registry:	Bermuda	Slot Machines:	Yes
Length (ft/m):	951.4/290.0	Swimming Pools (outdoors):	4
Beam (ft/m):	118.1/36.0	Swimming Pools (indoors):	0
Draft (ft/m):	26.2/8.0	Whirlpools:	9
Propulsion/Propellers:	Diesel-electric (42,000kW)/2	Fitness Center:	Yes
Passenger Decks:	13	Sauna/Steam Room:	Yes/Yes
Total Crew:	1,100	Massage:	Yes
Passengers (lower beds/all berths):	2,600/3,100	Self-Service Launderette:	Yes
Pass. Space Ratio (lower beds/all berths):	41.8/35.0	Dedicated Cinema:	No
Crew/Pass. Ratio (lower beds/all berths):	2.3/2.8	Library:	Yes
Navigation Officers:	British/Italian	Classification Society:	Registro Navale Italiano
Cabins (total):	1,300		
Size Range (sq ft/sq m):	161.4–764.2/15.0–71.0		
Cabins (outside view):	928		
Cabins (interior/no view):	372		
Cabins (for one person):	0		

OVERALL SCORE: **1,549**

(OUT OF A POSSIBLE 2,000 POINTS)

Accommodation: There are six principal types of cabins and configurations: grand suite, suite, mini-suite, outside double with balcony, outside double, and interior (no view) double. There are, however, 35 different brochure price categories; the choice is bewildering for both travel agents and passengers. Pricing depends on two things, size and location.

The largest, most lavish suite is the Grand Suite (B748, which is located at the ship's stern — a different position to the two Grand Suites aboard *Grand Princess*). It features a large bedroom with queen-size bed, huge walk-in (illuminated) closets, two bathrooms, a lounge (with fireplace, sofa bed, wet bar, and refrigerator), and a large private balcony (with hot tub that can be accessed from both balcony and bedroom).

Suites (with a semiprivate balcony) have a separate living room (with sofa bed) and bedroom (with a TV in each). The bathroom is quite large and features both a bathtub and shower stall. The mini-suites also have a private balcony, and feature a separate living and sleeping area (with a TV in each). The bathroom is also quite spacious and features both a bathtub and shower stall. The differences between the suites and mini-suites are basically in the size and appointments, the suite being more of a square shape while mini-suites are more rectangular, and have fewer drawers. Both feature butler service (known in Princess Cruises' language as "Grand Class Gold"), very plush bathrobes, and fully tiled bathrooms with ample open shelf storage space. Grand Class Gold passengers receive greater attention, including priority embarkation and disembarkation privileges. What is not good is that the most expensive accommodation aboard this ship has only semiprivate balconies that can be seen from above and so there is absolutely no privacy whatsoever (Suites C401 / 402 / 409 / 410 / 414 / 415 / 420 / 421 / 422 / 423 / 424 / 425 on Caribe Deck in particular). Also, the suites D105 and D106 (Dolphin Deck), which are extremely large, have balconies that can be seen from above.

Both interior and outside-view (the outsides come either with or without private balcony) cabins are of a functional, practical, design, although almost no drawers are provided. They are very attractive, with warm, pleasing decor and fine soft furnishing fabrics. The tiled bathrooms have a good amount of open shelf storage space for personal toiletries.

Additionally, two family suites consist of two suites with an interconnecting door, plus a large balcony. These can sleep up to ten (if at least four are children, or up to eight people if all are adults).

All accommodation occupants receive turndown service and chocolates on pillows each night, as well as bathrobes and toiletry amenity kits (larger, naturally, for suite/mini-suite occupants). You should note

297

that the majority of the outside cabins on Emerald Deck have views obstructed by the lifeboats. Sadly, there are no cabins for singles.

Note that Princess Cruises features CNN, CNBC, ESPN, and TNT on the in-cabin color TV system (when available, depending on cruise area).

Dining: As befits the size of the ship, there are a wide variety of informal dining options, more than aboard any other Princess Cruises ship to date (except sister ship *Grand Princess*). For formal meals there are three principal dining rooms (Botticelli, Da Vinci, and Michaelangelo), and seating is assigned according to the location of your cabin. There are two seatings in one restaurant, while open seating is featured in the other two. All three are nonsmoking and split into multitier sections in a nonsymmetrical design similar to those seen in *Grand Princess*, breaking what are quite large spaces into many smaller sections, for better ambience. Each dining room has its own galley.

Despite the fact that the portions are generous, the food and its presentation are somewhat disappointing. The quality of fish is poor (often disguised by crumb or batter coatings), the selection of fresh green vegetables is limited, and few garnishes are used. However, do remember that this is banquet catering, with all its attendant standardization and production cooking. Meats are of a decent quality, although often disguised by gravy-based sauces, and pasta dishes are acceptable (though voluminous), and are typically served by section headwaiters that may also make "something special just for you" — in search of gratuities and good comments.

On any given seven-day cruise, a typical menu cycle will include a Sailaway Dinner, Captain's Welcome Dinner, Chef's Dinner, Italian Dinner, French Dinner, Captain's Gala Dinner, and Landfall Dinner.

Several other dining areas are provided: Sabatini's Trattoria (for pizzas and other Italian fare), with flair and entertainment from the staff (by reservation only, with a cover charge of $15 per person), as well as Desert Rose (southwestern American food; by reservation only; cover charge). A coffee bar/patisserie (extra charge), wine/caviar bar (extra charge), a poolside hamburger grill and pizza bar (no extra charge) are additional dining spots for casual bites.

Specially designed dinnerware and high-quality linens and silverware are featured; Dudson of England dinnerware, Frette Egyptian cotton table linens, and silverware by Hepp of Germany. Note that 15% is added to all beverage bills, including wines (whether you order a $15 bottle or a $120 bottle, although it's the same amount of service to open and pour the wine).

Other Comments: Princess Cruises clearly has grand designs on its share of the cruise market, as *Golden Princess* presents a bold, forthright profile, with a racy "spoiler" effect at her galleon-like transom stern that I personally do not consider at all handsome (this acts as an observation lounge with aft-facing views by day, and a stunning discotheque by night). She is quite a ship — too wide to transit the Panama Canal (she is more than 43 ft (13 m) wider than the canal), with many balcony cabins overhanging the hull.

There is a good sheltered teakwood promenade deck, which almost wraps around (three times round is equal to one mile) and a walkway which goes right to the (enclosed, protected) bow of the ship. The outdoor pools have various beach-like surroundings. One lap pool has a pumped "current" to swim against.

Unlike the outside decks, there is plenty of space inside the ship (but there are also plenty of passengers), and a wide array of public rooms to choose from, with many intimate (this being a relative word) spaces and places to play. The passenger flow has been well thought out, and works with little congestion. The decor is very attractive, with lots of earth tones (well suited to both American and European tastes). In fact, she is the culmination of the best of all that Princess Cruises has to offer from its many years of operating what is now a well-tuned, good quality product.

Four areas center on swimming pools, one of which is two decks high and is covered by a magrodome, itself an extension of the funnel housing. A large health spa complex surrounds one of the swimming pools (you can have a massage or other spa treatment in an ocean-view treatment room). High atop the stern of the ship is a ship-wide glass-walled disco pod (I have nicknamed it the ETR — energy transfer room). It looks like an aerodynamic "spoiler" and is positioned high above the water, with spectacular views from the extreme port and starboard side windows.

An extensive collection of artworks has been chosen, and this complements the interior design and colors well. If you see something you like, you will be able to purchase it on board — it's almost all for sale.

Like sister ship *Grand Princess*, this ship also features a Wedding Chapel (a live web-cam can relay ceremonies via the Internet). The ship's captain can legally marry (American) couples, due to the ship's Bermuda registry and a special dispensation (which should be verified when in the planning stage, according to where you reside). So, what better way is there to be married and have your honeymoon in a location that actually moves with you? Princess Cruises offers three wedding packages — Pearl, Emerald, Diamond; the fee includes registration and official marriage certificate. However, to get married and take your close family members and entourage with you on your honeymoon is going to cost a lot of money (do you really want your family with you on your honeymoon?). The Hearts & Minds chapel is also useful for "renewal of vows" ceremonies.

Another neat feature is the motion-based virtual reality room with its enclosed motion-based rides, and a blue screen studio, where passengers can star in their own videos. Features an excellent library/CD-Rom computer room, and a separate card room. For children there is a two-deck-high playroom, teen room, and a host of specially trained counselors.

For entertainment, Princess Cruises prides itself on its glamorous all-American production shows, and the shows aboard this ship will not disappoint. Neither will the comfortable show lounges (the largest of which features $3 million in sound and light equipment, as well as a nine-piece orchestra, and a scenery loading bay that connects directly from stage to a hull door for direct transfer to the dockside). Two other entertainment lounges help spread things around. Casino lovers should enjoy what is presently one of the largest casinos at sea, with more than 260 slot machines (all with dolphin-shaped handles); there are blackjack, craps, and roulette tables, plus newer games such as Let It Ride Bonus, Spanish 21, and Caribbean Draw Progressive. But the highlight could well be Neptune's Lair, a multimedia gaming extravaganza.

Ship lovers should enjoy the wood-paneled Wheelhouse Bar, finely decorated with memorabilia and ship models tracing part of parent company P&O's history.

Princess Cays — Princess Cruises' own "private island" in the Caribbean — is "yours" (along with a couple of thousand other passengers) for a day; however, you will need to take a shore tender to get to and from it, and this can take some time. A high-tech hospital is provided, with live SeaMed telemedicine linkups with specialists at the Cedars-Sinai Medical Center in Los Angeles available for emergency help; it's the first such seagoing system in the world.

The ship operates 7-night Caribbean and Mediterranean cruises, and provides you with a stunning, grand playground in which to roam when you are not ashore. Princess Cruises delivers a fine, well-packaged vacation product, with a good sense of style, at an attractive, highly competitive price, and this ship will appeal to those that really enjoy a big city to play in, with all the trimmings and lots of fellow passengers. The ship is full of revenue centers, however, which are designed to help you part with even more money than what is paid for in the price of your cruise ticket.

Whether this really can be considered a relaxing vacation is a moot point, but with so many choices and "small" rooms to enjoy, the ship has been extremely well designed, and the odds are that you'll have a fine cruise vacation.

Weak Points: Standing in line for embarkation, disembarkation, shore tenders, and for self-serve buffet meals is an inevitable aspect of cruising aboard all large ships. If you are not used to large ships, it will take you some time to find your way around (take good walking shoes), despite the company's claim that this vessel offers passengers a "small ship feel, big ship choice." The cabin bath towels are small, and drawer space is very limited.

The automated telephone system is frustrating, and luggage delivery is inefficient. Lines form for many things, but particularly for the purser's office, and for open seating breakfast and lunch in the three main dining rooms. Long lines for shore excursions and shore tenders are also a fact of life aboard large ships such as this, as is waiting for elevators at peak times.

You'll have to live with the many extra charge items (such as ice cream) and activities (such as yoga and kick boxing classes at $10 per session, not to mention $4 per hour for group baby-sitting services— at the time this book was completed). Some of the spa (massage) treatment rooms are located directly underneath the basketball court, which makes it utterly frustrating trying to relax while the ceiling above your head is being pounded by bouncing balls!

Passengers are also forced to endure countless pieces of (highly questionable) art found in almost every foyer and public room—an annoying reminder that today, cruising aboard large ships such as *Golden Princess* and *Grand Princess* is really like living in a bazaar of paintings surrounded by a ship. Now, what am I to bid for this piece of art that is really worth only $10—let's hear it—$1,200, do I hear $1,400, or will someone actually think it's worth more?

Grand Princess
★★★★

Large Ship:	108,806 tons	Cabins (with private balcony):		710
Lifestyle:	Standard	Cabins (wheelchair accessible):		28
Cruise Line:	Princess Cruises	(18 outside /10 interior)		
Former Names:	-	Cabin Current:		110/220-volt
Builder:	Fincantieri (Italy)	Full-Service Dining Rooms:		3 main, 2 others
Original Cost:	$450 million	Elevators:		14
Entered Service:	May 1998	Casino (gaming tables):		Yes
Registry:	Bermuda	Slot Machines:		Yes
Length (ft/m):	951.4/290.0	Swimming Pools (outdoors):		4
Beam (ft/m):	118.1/36.0	Swimming Pools (indoors):		0
Draft (ft/m):	26.2/8.0	Whirlpools:		9
Propulsion/Propellers:	Diesel-electric (42,000kW)/2	Fitness Center:		Yes
Passenger Decks:	13	Sauna/Steam Room:		Yes/Yes
Total Crew:	1,100	Massage:		Yes
Passengers (lower beds/all berths):	2,600/3,100	Self-Service Launderette:		Yes
Pass. Space Ratio (lower beds/all berths):	41.8/35.0	Dedicated Cinema:		No
Crew/Pass. Ratio (lower beds/all berths):	2.3/2.8	Library:		Yes
Navigation Officers:	British/Italian	Classification Society:		Registro Navale Italiano
Cabins (total):	1,300			
Size Range (sq ft/sq m):	161.4–764.2/15.0–71.0			
Cabins (outside view):	928			
Cabins (interior/no view):	372			
Cabins (for one person):	0			

OVERALL SCORE: 1,549
(OUT OF A POSSIBLE 2,000 POINTS)

Accommodation: There are six types of cabins and configurations: grand suite, suite, mini-suite, outside double with balcony, outside double, and interior (no view) double. There are, however, 35 different brochure price categories; the choice is bewildering for both travel agents and passengers. Pricing depends on two things, size and location.

The plushest suite is the Grand Suite, which has a hot tub accessible from both the private balcony and from the bedroom, two bedrooms, a lounge, two bathrooms, a huge walk-in closet, and plenty of drawer and storage space.

Suites (with a semiprivate balcony) have a separate living room (with sofa bed) and bedroom (with a TV in each). The bathroom is quite large and features both a bathtub and shower stall. The mini-suites also have a private balcony, and feature a separate living and sleeping area (with a TV in each). The bathroom is also quite spacious and features both a bathtub and shower stall. The differences between the suites and mini-suites are basically in the size and appointments, the suite being more of a square shape, while mini-suites are more rectangular, and have few drawers. Both suites and mini-suites feature butler service (known in Princess Cruises' language as "Grand Class Gold"), really plush bathrobes,and fully tiled bathrooms with ample open shelf storage space. Grand Class Gold passengers receive priority attention, including speedy embarkation and disembarkation privileges. What is really unacceptable is that the most expensive accommodation aboard this ship has only semi-private balconies that can be seen from above and so there is absolutely no privacy whatsoever (Suites C401 / 402 / 409 / 410 / 414 / 415 / 420 / 421 / 422 / 423 / 424 / 425 on Caribe Deck). Also, the suites D105 and D106 (Dolphin Deck) are extremely large, but their balconies can be seen from above.

Both interior and outside-view (the outsides come either with or without private balcony) cabins are of a functional, practical, design, although almost no drawers are provided. They are very attractive, with warm, pleasing decor and fine soft furnishing fabrics; 80% of the outside cabins have a private balcony. The tiled bathrooms have a good amount of open shelf storage space for personal toiletries.

Additionally, two family suites consist of two suites with an interconnecting door, plus a large balcony), and can sleep up to ten (if at least four are children, or up to eight people if all are adults).

All accommodation occupants receive turndown service and chocolates on pillows each night, as well as bathrobes and toiletry amenity kits (larger, naturally, for suite/mini-suite occupants). You should note that the majority of the outside cabins on Emerald Deck have views obstructed by the lifeboats. Unfortunately, there are no cabins for singles.

Note that Princess Cruises features CNN, CNBC, ESPN, and TNT on the in-cabin color TV system (when available, depending on cruise area).

Dining: As befits the size of the ship, there is a wide variety of informal dining options, more than aboard any other Princess Cruises ship to date (except *Golden Princess*). For formal meals there are three principal dining rooms, Botticelli (504 seats), Da Vinci (486 seats), and Michelangelo (486 seats), assigned according to the location of your cabin. There are two seatings in one restaurant, while the other two feature open seating — so you can go when you want, and be seated with whom you wish. All three are non-smoking and split into multitier sections in a nonsymmetrical design similar to those seen in *Dawn Princess* and *Sun Princess*, breaking what are quite large spaces into many smaller sections, for better ambience. Each dining room has its own galley.

Despite the fact that the portions are generous, the food and its presentation are somewhat disappointing. The quality of fish is poor (often disguised by crumb or batter coatings), the selection of fresh green vegetables is limited, and few garnishes are used. However, do remember that this is banquet catering, with all its attendant standardization and production cooking. Meats are of a decent quality, although often disguised by gravy-based sauces, and pasta dishes are acceptable (though voluminous), and are typically served by section headwaiters that may also make "something special just for you" — in search of gratuities and good comments.

On any given seven-day cruise, a typical menu cycle will typically include a Sailaway Dinner, Captain's Welcome Dinner, Chef's Dinner, Italian Dinner, French Dinner, Captain's Gala Dinner, and Landfall Dinner.

Specially designed dinnerware and high-quality linens and silverware are featured; Dudson of England dinnerware, Frette Egyptian cotton table linens, and silverware by Hepp of Germany. Note that 15% is added to all beverage bills, including wines (whether you order a $15 bottle or a $120 bottle, although it's the same amount of service to open and pour the wine).

Several other dining areas are provided: Sabatini's — a Trattoria (for pizzas and other Italian fare, with entertaining flair (by reservation only, cover charge $15 per person), as well as the Painted Desert (Southwestern American food, by reservation only, also with a cover charge, of $8). A poolside hamburger grill and pizza bar are additional dining spots for casual bites, while extra charges will apply if you order items to eat at either the coffee bar/patisserie, or the caviar/champagne bar.

Other Comments: Princess Cruises clearly has grand designs on its share of the cruise market, as *Grand Princess* presents a bold, forthright profile, with a racy "spoiler" effect at her galleon-like transom stern that I personally do not consider at all handsome (this acts as an observation lounge with aft-facing views by day, and a stunning discotheque by night). She is quite a ship — too wide to transit the Panama Canal (she is more than 43 ft (13 m) wider than the canal), with many balcony cabins overhanging the hull.

There is a good sheltered teakwood promenade deck, which almost wraps around (three times round is equal to one mile) and a walkway which goes right to the (enclosed, protected) bow of the ship. The outdoor pools have various beach-like surroundings. One lap pool has a pumped "current" to swim against.

Unlike the outside decks, there is plenty of space inside the ship (but there are also plenty of passengers), and a wide array of public rooms to choose from, with many intimate (this being a relative word) spaces and places to play. The passenger flow has been well thought out, and works with little congestion. The decor is very attractive, with lots of earth tones (well suited to both American and European tastes). In fact, she is the culmination of the best of all that Princess Cruises has to offer from its many years of operating a fine quality product.

Four areas center on swimming pools, one of which is two decks high and is covered by a magrodome, itself an extension of the funnel housing. A large health spa complex surrounds one of the swimming pools (you can have a massage or other spa treatment in an ocean-view treatment room). High atop the stern of the ship is a ship-wide glass-walled disco pod (I have nicknamed it the ETR — energy transfer room). It looks like an aerodynamic "spoiler" and is positioned some 150.1 ft (45.75 m) above the waterline, with spectacular views from the extreme port and starboard side windows (you can look along the ship's side and onto lots of "private" balconies).

An extensive collection of art works has been chosen, and this complements the interior design and colors well. If you see something you like, you will be able to purchase it on board — it's almost all for sale.

This ship features the first oceangoing Wedding Chapel (a live web-cam can relay ceremonies via the internet). The ship's captain can legally marry (American) couples, due to the ship's Bermuda registry and a special dispensation (which should be verified when in the planning stage, according to where you reside). So, what better way is there to be married and have your honeymoon in one location that moves with you? Princess Cruises offers three wedding packages — Pearl, Emerald, Diamond; the fee includes registration and official marriage certificate. However, to get married and take your close family mem-

301

bers and entourage with you on your honeymoon is going to cost a lot of money (do you really want your family with you on your honeymoon?). The Hearts & Minds chapel is also useful for "renewal of vows" ceremonies.

Another neat feature is the motion-based virtual reality room with its enclosed motion-based rides, and a blue screen studio, where passengers can star in their own videos. Features an excellent library/CD-ROM computer room, and a separate card room. For children there is a two-decks-high playroom, teen room, and a host of specially trained counselors.

For entertainment, Princess Cruises prides itself on its glamorous all-American production shows, and the shows aboard this ship ("Gotta Sing, Gotta Dance," "Glamour," and "Swing Time") will not disappoint. Neither will the comfortable show lounges (the largest of which features $3 million in sound and light equipment, as well as a nine-piece orchestra, and a scenery loading bay that connects directly from stage to a hull door for direct transfer to the dockside). Two other entertainment lounges help spread things around. Casino lovers should enjoy what is presently one of the largest casinos at sea, with more than 260 slot machines (all with dolphin-shaped handles); there are blackjack, craps and roulette tables, plus newer games such as Let It Ride Bonus, Spanish 21, and Caribbean Draw Progressive. But the highlight could well be Neptune's Lair, a multimedia gaming extravaganza.

Ship lovers should enjoy the wood-paneled Wheelhouse Bar, finely decorated with memorabilia and ship models tracing part of parent company P&O's history (British India Line's Kenya is a focal point model).

Princess Cays — Princess Cruises' own "private island" in the Caribbean — is "yours" (along with a couple of thousand other passengers) for a day; however, you will need to take a shore tender to get to and from it, and this can take some time. A high-tech hospital is provided, with live SeaMed telemedicine linkups with specialists at the Cedars-Sinai Medical Center in Los Angeles available for emergency help (hardly useful for international passengers that do not reside in the USA).

The ship operates 7-night Caribbean cruises year-round, and provides you with a stunning, grand playground in which to roam when you are not ashore. Princess Cruises delivers a fine, well-packaged vacation product, with a good sense of style, at an attractive, highly competitive price. This ship will appeal to those that really enjoy a big city to play in, with all the trimmings and lots of fellow passengers. The ship is full of revenue centers, however, which are designed to help you part with even more money than what you think you paid for in the price of your cruise ticket.

The dress code has been simplified — reduced to formal or smart casual (whatever that means). Gratuities of $6.50 per person, per day are added to your account for dining (no matter where or in which outlet you eat), and you can also charge gratuities for your cabin steward to your account. If you don't get the service you should, you can ask for this gratuity to be reduced.

Whether this really can be considered a relaxing vacation is a moot point, but with so many choices and "small" rooms to enjoy, the ship has been extremely well designed; the odds are that you'll have a fine cruise vacation.

Weak Points: Standing in line for embarkation, disembarkation, shore tenders and for self-serve buffet meals is an inevitable aspect of cruising aboard all large ships. If you are not used to large ships, it will probably take you some time to find your way around (take good walking shoes), despite the company's claim that this vessel offers passengers a "small ship feel, big ship choice." The cabin bath towels are small, and drawer space is very limited.

The automated telephone system is very frustrating, and luggage delivery needs to be more efficient. Lines form for many things, but particularly for the purser's office, and for open seating breakfast and lunch in the three main dining rooms. Long lines for shore excursions and shore tenders are also a fact of life aboard large ships such as this, as is waiting for elevators at peak times.

You'll have to live with the many extra charge items (such as ice cream) and activities (such as yoga and kick boxing classes at $10 per session, not to mention $4 per hour for group baby-sitting services—at the time this book was completed). Some of the spa (massage) treatment rooms are located directly underneath the basketball court, which makes it utterly frustrating trying to relax while the ceiling above your head is being pounded by bouncing balls!

Passengers are also forced to endure countless pieces of (highly questionable) art found in almost every foyer and public room—an annoying reminder that today, cruising aboard large ships such as *Golden Princess* and *Grand Princess* is really like living in a bazaar of paintings surrounded by a ship. Now, what am I to bid for this piece of art that is really worth only $10—let's hear it—$1,200, do I hear $1,400, or will someone actually think it's worth more?

Grande Caribe
★★ +

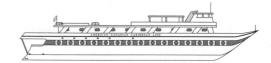

Small Ship:	99 tons	Cabins (with private balcony):	0
Lifestyle:	Standard	Cabins (wheelchair accessible):	0
Cruise Line:	American Canadian Caribbean Line	Cabin Current:	110-volt
Former Names:	-	Full-Service Dining Rooms:	1
Builder:	Blount industries (US)	Elevators:	0
Original Cost:	$8 million	Casino (gaming tables):	No
Entered Service:	June 1997	Slot Machines:	No
Registry:	US	Swimming Pools (outdoors):	0
Length (ft/m):	183.0/55.7	Swimming Pools (indoors):	0
Beam (ft/m):	40.0/12.1	Whirlpools:	0
Draft (ft/m):	6.5/1.9	Fitness Center:	0
Propulsion/Propellers:	Diesel (1,044kW)/2	Sauna/Steam Room:	No/No
Passenger Decks:	3	Massage:	0
Total Crew:	17	Self-Service Launderette:	No
Passengers (lower beds/all berths):	100/100	Dedicated Cinema:	No
Pass. Space Ratio (lower beds/all berths):	0.99/0.99	Library:	Yes
Crew/Pass. Ratio (lower beds/all berths):	5.8/5.8	Classification Society:	American Bureau of
Navigation Officers:	American		Shipping
Cabins (total):	50		
Size Range (sq ft/sq m):	72.0–96.0/6.6–8.9		
Cabins (outside view):	41	**OVERALL SCORE:**	**1,095**
Cabins (interior/no view):	9		
Cabins (for one person):	0	**(OUT OF A POSSIBLE 2,000 POINTS)**	

Accommodation: The cabins are all extremely small, relatively utilitarian units, with very little closet space (but just enough drawers) and very small bathrooms. The twin beds convert to queen-size beds (there is good storage space under the beds). There is no room service menu, and only soap is supplied (bring your own shampoo and other toiletries). Each cabin has its own air-conditioner, so passengers do not have to share air with the rest of the ship (and other passengers). Refreshingly, there are no cabin keys.

Dining: The dining room seats all passengers in one open seating; you dine with whomever you wish, so you can make new friends and enjoy different conversation each day (it is also good for small groups). The tables convert to card tables for use between meals. Passengers are welcome to bring their own alcohol, as the company does not sell it aboard ship. Effervescent, young American waitresses provide the service, although there is no finesse.

Other Comments: *Grande Caribe* is the largest and the most contemporary of the Blount-built vessels. During passenger emergency drill, passengers are taught how to use fire extinguishers — a useful piece of training.

This vessel's shallow draft enables it to cruise into off-the-beaten-path destinations well out of reach of larger ships, and also features a retractable navigation bridge — practical for those low bridges along inland waterways. *Grande Caribe*, together with sister vessel *Grande Mariner* (but not *Niagara Prince*) has stabilizers. An underwater video camera allows passengers to see what a SCUBA diver might see underneath the ship, while seated in (dry) comfort in the lounge, on large-screen TV monitors. Underwater lights, which attract fish and other marine life, are also fitted.

The style is unpretentious and casual (no jackets or ties) by day and night. There are two 24-passenger launches (one of which is a glass-bottom boat), and some snorkeling equipment.

There is one lounge/bar, located on a different deck from the dining room. Water sports facilities include a glass-bottom boat and sunfish sailboat.

This vessel will be good for anyone who does not want crowds, or entertainment of any kind, or a high standard of service. All gratuities given by passengers are pooled and shared by all the staff (although you should note that the suggested daily rate is very high).

Grande Mariner
★★ +

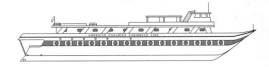

Small Ship:	99 tons	Cabins (with private balcony):	0
Lifestyle:	Standard	Cabins (wheelchair accessible):	0
Cruise Line:	American Canadian Caribbean Line	Cabin Current:	110-volt
Former Names:	-	Full-Service Dining Rooms:	1
Builder:	Blount industries (US)	Elevators:	0
Original Cost:	$8 million	Casino (gaming tables):	No
Entered Service:	June 1998	Slot Machines:	No
Registry:	US	Swimming Pools (outdoors):	0
Length (ft/m):	183.0/55.7	Swimming Pools (indoors):	0
Beam (ft/m):	40.0/12.1	Whirlpools:	0
Draft (ft/m):	6.5/1.9	Fitness Center:	0
Propulsion/Propellers:	Diesel (1,044kW)/2	Sauna/Steam Room:	No/No
Passenger Decks:	3	Massage:	0
Total Crew:	17	Self-Service Launderette:	No
Passengers (lower beds/all berths):	100/100	Dedicated Cinema:	No
Pass. Space Ratio (lower beds/all berths):	0.99/0.99	Library:	Yes
Crew/Pass. Ratio (lower beds/all berths):	5.8/5.8	Classification Society:	American
Navigation Officers:	American		Bureau of Shipping
Cabins (total):	50		
Size Range (sq ft/sq m):	72.0–96.0/6.6–8.9		
Cabins (outside view):	41		

Cabins (interior/no view):	9
Cabins (for one person):	0

OVERALL SCORE: 1,095
(OUT OF A POSSIBLE 2,000 POINTS)

Accommodation: The cabins are all extremely small, relatively utilitarian units, with very little closet space (but just enough drawers) and very small bathrooms. There are 50 cabins, each with twin beds convertible to queen-size beds (there is good storage space under the beds). There is no room service menu, and only soap is supplied (bring your own shampoo and other toiletries). Each cabin has its own air-conditioner, so passengers do not have to share air with the rest of the ship (and other passengers). Refreshingly, there are no cabin keys.

Dining: The dining room seats all passengers in a single, open seating, so you dine with whomever you wish. The advantage of this is that you can make new friends and enjoy different conversation each day (it is also good for small groups). The dining tables convert to card tables for use between meals. Passengers are welcome to bring their own alcohol, as the company does not sell it aboard ship. Effervescent, young American waitresses provide the service, although there is no finesse.

Other Comments: This is another example of a contemporary Blount-built vessel. During passenger emergency drill, passengers are taught how to use fire extinguishers — a very useful piece of training.

This vessel has a shallow draft, which enables it to cruise into off-the-beaten-path destinations well out of reach of larger ships, and also features a retractable navigation bridge — practical for those low bridges along the inland waterways. *Grande Mariner*, together with sister vessel *Grande Caribe* (but not *Niagara Prince*) has stabilizers. An underwater video camera allows passengers to see what a SCUBA diver might see underneath the ship, while seated in (dry) comfort in the lounge, on large-screen TV monitors. Underwater lights, which should attract fish and other marine life, are also fitted.

The style is unpretentious and extremely casual (definitely no jackets or ties) both day and night. There are two 24-passenger launches (one of which is a glass-bottom boat), and some snorkeling equipment.

There is one lounge/bar, located on a different deck from the dining room — a departure for ACCL from the company's former vessels. Water sports facilities include a glass-bottom boat and sunfish sailboat.

This vessel will be good for anyone who does not want crowds, or entertainment of any kind, or a high standard of service. All of the gratuities given by passengers are pooled and shared by all the staff (although you should note that the suggested daily rate is very high for the product delivered).

Grandeur of the Seas
★★★★

Large Ship:	74,137 tons	Cabins (with private balcony):	212
Lifestyle:	Standard	Cabins (wheelchair accessible):	14
Cruise Line:	Royal Caribbean International	Cabin Current:	110/220-volt
Former Names:	-	Full-Service Dining Rooms:	1
Builder:	Kvaerner Masa-Yards (Finland)	Elevators:	9
Original Cost:	$300 million	Casino (gaming tables):	Yes
Entered Service:	December 1996	Slot Machines:	Yes
Registry:	Liberia	Swimming Pools (outdoors):	1
Length (ft/m):	916.0/279.6	Swimming Pools (indoors):	1
Beam (ft/m):	105.6/32.2	(indoor/outdoor w/sliding glass roof)	
Draft (ft/m):	25.5/7.6	Whirlpools:	6
Propulsion/Propellers:	Diesel-electric (50,400kW)/2	Fitness Center:	Yes
Passenger Decks:	11	Sauna/Steam Room:	Yes/Yes
Total Crew:	760	Massage:	Yes
Passengers (lower beds/all berths):	1,950/2,446	Self-Service Launderette:	No
Pass. Space Ratio (lower beds/all berths):	38.0/30.3	Dedicated Cinema:	No
Crew/Pass. Ratio (lower beds/all berths):	2.5/3.2	Library:	Yes
Navigation Officers:	International	Classification Society:	Det Norske Veritas
Cabins (total):	975		
Size Range (sq ft/sq m):	158.2–1,033.3/14.7–96.0		
Cabins (outside view):	576		
Cabins (interior/no view):	399		
Cabins (for one person):	0		

OVERALL SCORE: **1,521**

(OUT OF A POSSIBLE 2,000 POINTS)

Accommodation: The suites are very well appointed and have very pleasing decor, with good wood and color accenting (the largest suite even has a baby grand piano). Category A and B cabins also have VCRs. All standard cabins have twin beds that convert to a queen-size bed, ample closet space for a one-week cruise, and a good amount of drawer space, although under-bed storage space is not good for large suitcases. The bathrooms have nine mirrors. The plastic buckets for champagne/wine are really shoddy.

Dining: The 1,195-seat, nonsmoking dining room is spread over two decks, with both levels connected by a grand, sweeping staircase. There are two seatings.

The dining operation is well orchestrated, with emphasis on highly programmed (insensitive), extremely hurried service that many find intrusive. Most nights feature themed menus (typically French, Oriental, Italian, Caribbean, American), as they have been for years, with waiters and busboys in appropriate costumes. The food is typical of hotel banquet catering. The menu descriptions make the food sound better than it is, which is consistently average, mostly disappointing and without much taste. However, a decent selection of light meals is provided, and a vegetarian menu is available. The selection of breads, rolls, fruit, and cheese is quite poor, however, and should be upgraded. There is no good caviar; special orders, tableside carving, and flambeau items are not offered.

The wine list is not very extensive, but the prices are moderate. The waiters, many of whom are from Caribbean countries, are perhaps overly friendly for some tastes — particularly on the last night of the cruise, when tips are expected.

A cavernous, 790-seat informal Windjammer Café, which features a great expanse of ocean-view glass windows, is where breakfast and lunch buffets are available as an alternative to the dining room.

An intimate terrace Champagne Bar is located forward of the lower level of the two-deck-high dining room and just off the atrium for those who might like to taste something a little out of the ordinary, in a setting that is bright and contemporary.

Other Comments: The ships in the Royal Caribbean International fleet are always evolving, and *Grandeur of the Seas* is no exception. She presents a nice long profile, with a funnel placed well aft (almost a throwback to some ship designs used in the 1950s). She has a well-rounded stern (as have the three *Sovereign of the Seas*-class ships) and a Viking Crown Lounge in the center, just forward of the funnel. This lounge, together with the forward mast and aft funnel, provides three distinct focal points in her exterior profile.

305

The Viking Crown Lounge sits between funnel and mast and overlooks the forward section of the swimming pool deck, as aboard *Legend of the Seas* and *Splendour of the Seas*, with access provided by a multideck atrium. No cushioned pads are provided for the plastic-webbed deck lounge chairs.

There is a wraparound promenade deck outdoors, with a seven-deck-high atrium inside. A delightful champagne terrace bar sits forward of the lower level of the two-deck-high dining room. There is a good use of tropical plants throughout the public rooms, which helps to counteract the clinical pastel wall colors, while huge murals of opera scenes adorn several stairways.

There are two show lounges. One is the principal show lounge, for the big production shows, and has excellent sight lines from 98% of the 875 seats; the other is the secondary lounge, for smaller shows and adult cabaret, with 575 seats. There are good children's and teens' facilities, which are larger than those of previous ships in the fleet.

This is another new ship design for Royal Caribbean International (her sister ship is *Enchantment of the Seas*), with what, inside, has proven to be a good passenger flow. The vessel has a good, varied collection of artworks (including several sculptures), principally by British artists, with classical music, ballet, and theater themes. The casino has a fascinating, somewhat theatrical, glass-covered, under-floor exhibit.

This ship will be good for first-time cruise passengers who want fine, very comfortable surroundings, and all the very latest in facilities, entertainment lounges, and high-tech sophistication in one neat, well-packaged, and fine-tuned cruise vacation, with plenty of music and entertainment.

Weak Points: Standing in line for embarkation, disembarkation, shore tenders, and for self-serve buffet meals is an inevitable aspect of cruising aboard all large ships.

Hanseatic
★★★★★

Small Ship:	8,378 tons	Cabins (for one person):	0
Lifestyle:	Luxury	Cabins (with private balcony):	0
Cruise Line:	Hapag-Lloyd Cruises	Cabins (wheelchair accessible):	2
Former Names:	*Society Adventurer*	Cabin Current:	220-volt
Builder:	Rauma Yards (Finland)	Full-Service Dining Rooms:	1
Original Cost:	$68 million	Elevators:	2
Entered Service:	March 1993	Swimming Pools (outdoors):	1
Registry:	Bahamas	Whirlpools:	1
Length (ft/m):	402.9/122.80	Exercise Room:	Yes
Beam (ft/m):	59.1/18.00	Sauna/Steam Room:	Yes/No
Draft (ft/m):	15.5/4.71	Massage:	Yes
Propulsion/Propellers:	Diesel (5,880kW)/2	Self-Service Launderette:	No
Passenger Decks:	7	Lecture/Film Room:	Yes (seats 160)
Total Crew:	122	Library:	Yes
Passengers (lower beds/all berths):	184/194	Zodiacs:	14
Pass. Space Ratio (lower beds/all berths):	45.5/43.1	Helicopter Pad:	Yes
Crew/Pass. Ratio (lower beds/all berths):	1.5/1.5	Classification Society:	Det Norske Veritas
Navigation Officers:	German		
Cabins (total):	92		
Size Range (sq ft/sq m):	231.4–470.3/21.5–43.7	**OVERALL SCORE:**	**1,740**
Cabins (outside view):	92		
Cabins (interior/no view):	0	**(OUT OF A POSSIBLE 2,000 POINTS)**	

Accommodation: The all-outside cabins, located in the forward section of the ship, are large and very well equipped, and include a separate lounge area next to a large picture window (which has a pull-down blackout blind as well as curtains) and refrigerator. All furniture is in warm woods such as beech, and everything has rounded edges. Wood trim accents the ceiling perimeter, and acts as a divider between bed and lounge areas. Each cabin has a minibar, TV, VCR, two locking drawers, and plenty of closet and drawer space, as well as two separate cupboards and hooks for all-weather outerwear.

All cabin bathrooms have a large bathtub, two toiletries cabinets, wall-mounted hair dryer, and bathrobe. There are only two types of cabins; 34 have double beds, others have twin beds. Towels, bed linens, and pillowcases are of 100% cotton, and individual cotton-filled duvet covers are provided.

The luxurious suites and cabins on Bridge Deck have impeccable butler service and full in-cabin dining privileges, as well as personalized stationery. Soft drinks are supplied in the cabin refrigerator, and replenished daily, at no charge (all liquor is at extra cost, however). A very relaxed ambience prevails on board.

Dining: The dining room is elegant, warm, and welcoming, and features large picture windows on two sides as well as aft, and table settings are graced with fine Rosenthal china and silverware. There is a single seating. The cuisine and service are absolutely first rate, but are more informal than, for example, aboard the larger *Europa* (which is at or close to the same price level). Top quality ingredients are always used, and most items are purchased fresh when available.

The meals are very creative and nicely presented, and each is appealing to the eye as well as to the palate. There is always an excellent selection of breads, cheeses, desserts, and pastry items. Note that when operating in the Arctic or Antarctic, table setups are often minimal, due to the possible movement of the ship (stabilizers cannot be used in much of the Antarctic region), so cutlery is provided and changed for each course.

In March 1996, the ship added an alternative dining room. The Columbus Lounge, which is an informal, open seating, self-serve (or waiter service) buffet-style eatery by day that changes into an Oriental dining room at night. Reservations are required (you make them in the morning of the day you want to dine there), but there is no extra charge, and there is no tipping at any time. Also, on each cruise a full Viennese teatime is featured, as well as a regular daily teatime.

Other Comments: Originally ordered for Society Cruises as *Society Adventurer* (although she never sailed under that name, due to the fact that the company declared bankruptcy and never took possession of the vessel), *Hanseatic* was designed and constructed specifically to provide worldwide exploration-style cruises in luxurious contemporary surroundings. As such, she looks like the practical vessel she was designed to be. The ship is extremely environmentally friendly and features the latest "zero-discharge," nonpolluting waste disposal system including pollution-filtered incinerator, full biological sewage treatment plant and large storage capacity. This is one of the few ships that will allow you to sign up for an engine room tour.

She is an outstanding ship for the best in destination-intensive exploration voyages, and is under long-term charter to Hapag-Lloyd Cruises. Features a fully enclosed bridge (with an open bridge policy, so that passengers can visit the bridge at almost any time) and an ice-hardened hull with the highest passenger vessel classification of 1A1 Super. The ship also features the very latest in high-tech navigation equipment.

A fleet of 14 Zodiac inflatable craft, each named after a famous explorer is used for in-depth shore landings. These craft provide the ship with tremendous flexibility in itineraries, and provide excellent possibilities for up-close wildlife viewing in natural habitats, with small numbers of passengers. Rubber boots, parkas, a boot-washing station, and storage room are provided for passengers, particularly useful for Arctic and Antarctic cruises.

Inside, the ship is equipped with fine quality luxury fittings and soft furnishings. There is a choice of several public rooms, all of them well furnished and decorated, and all of them have high ceilings, which helps to provide an impression of space; the result is that the ship feels much larger than her actual size. The library/observation lounge provides a good selection of hardback books and videos in both the English and German languages.

Hanseatic provides destination-intensive, nature, and life-enrichment cruises and expeditions in elegant, but unstuffy surroundings, to some of the world's most fascinating destinations, at a suitably handsome price. The passenger maximum is generally kept to about 150, which means plenty of comfort and lots of space for everyone — and no lines, no hassle.

The ship really is at her best when operating in Arctic and Antarctic regions (infirm passengers are advised not to consider these areas). Safety is paramount, particularly when operating in the Antarctic, and in this the ship excels with professionalism, pride, and skilled seamanship. The ship always operates in two languages, English and German (many staff speak several languages) and caters well to all passengers. All port taxes, insurance, gratuities, Zodiac trips, and most shore excursions (except when the ship operates in Europe) are included.

Hapag-Lloyd Cruises specializes in providing outstanding, well-planned itineraries. Where this ship really scores, however, is in her Antarctic sailings, where the experience of her captain and cruise director and the crew really shine. The lectures, briefings, and the amount of information provided about the itinerary and ports of call are outstanding. Outstanding lecturers and naturalists accompany each cruise, and an expedition cruise logbook is typically provided at the end of each cruise for all passengers — a superb reminder of what's been seen and done during the course of your expedition adventure cruise.

Weak Points: There are few negative things about this ship. She is principally marketed to German-speaking and English-speaking passengers, so other nationalities may find it hard to integrate. There are no marine-quality telescopes mounted outdoors (there should be). There is, at present, no privacy curtain between cabin door and the sleeping area (there should be).

Harald Jarl
★★

Small Ship:	2,568 tons	Cabins (with private balcony):	0
Lifestyle:	Standard	Cabins (wheelchair accessible):	0
Cruise Line:	Norwegian Coastal Voyages (TFDS)	Cabin Current:	220-volt
Former Names:	-	Full-Service Dining Rooms:	1
Builder:	Trondheims Mek (Norway)	Elevators:	0
Original Cost:	n/a	Casino(gamingtables):	No
Entered Service:	1960	Slot Machines:	No
Registry:	Norway	Swimming Pools (outdoors):	0
Length (ft/m):	286.7/87.4	Swimming Pools (inside):	0
Beam (ft/m):	43.3/13.2	Whirlpools:	0
Draft (ft/m):	15.0/4.5	Fitness Center:	No
Total Crew:	40	Sauna/Steam Room:	No/No
Passengers (lower beds/all berths):	178/178	Massage:	No
Pass. Space Ratio (lower beds/all berths):	14.4/14.4	Self-Service Launderette:	No
Crew/Pass. Ratio (lower beds/all berths):	4.4/4.4	Dedictated Cinema:	No
Navigation Officers:	Norwegian	Library:	No
Cabins (total):	89	Classification Society:	Det Norske Veritas
Size Range (sq ft/sq m):	n/a		
Cabins (outside view):	38	**OVERALL SCORE:**	**940**
Cabins (interior/no view):	51	(OUT OF A POSSIBLE 2,000 POINTS)	
Cabins (for one person):	0		

Accommodation: All cabins feature a mix of lower beds, lower berths, and upper berths (there are no cabins with double bed). The cabins are cozy, which translates to very, very small; the bathrooms, likewise, are tiny, although they do have a shower and toilet. All cabins have a 220-volt outlet, so take adapters and converters if you need to.

Dining: There is one dining room (no smoking allowed), and tables are assigned when you embark. Three meals each day are included in the cruise fare: breakfast and lunch (featuring the famous Norwegian 'cold table') are self-serve buffet-style meals, while dinner is a sit-down affair, with three courses. Additionally, there is a cafeteria, which is open 24 hours, where snacks and light meals can be purchased.

Other Comments: The Norwegian Coastal Voyage is a service that was started in 1863 (it is jointly operated by two companies: Ofotens og Vesteraalen Dampskibsselskab (OVDS) and Troms Fylkes Dampskibsselskab (TFDS). The complete journey, of 1,250 nautical miles, takes in 34 ports of call in a 12-day roundtrip voyage between Bergen and Kirkenes (on the border with Russia), above the Arctic Circle (where a special "Crossing the Arctic Circle" ceremony welcomes newcomers). The journey can also be done in a one-way voyage that takes seven days (northbound) or six days (southbound). The ships carry passengers as well as mail and other cargo.

Perhaps you will be able to peek at the midnight sun (mid-May to late June, north of the Arctic Circle), experience the Northern Lights (Aurora Borealis, mostly seen during winter months, and only when the atmospheric conditions are right), and be part of the daily life of the hardy Norwegians. Approximately 60% of the passengers will be Norwegian/Scandinavian/European, while the rest will be a mix of North American and other nationalities. Although the passenger bed capacity is quoted, note that many additional passengers may be on board as day passengers, sailing between two coastal ports — the ship is the equivalent of a seagoing bus for the coastal commuters. As for the weather, the West coast of Norway is warmed by the Gulf Stream, and temperatures will be similar to those found in New England.

The ship is best suited to adult couples, single travelers, and families with children wanting to cruise along the coast of Norway and experience the area's natural beauty. It's ideal for anyone who doesn't need entertainment or mindless parlor games, but wants to relax and unwind, enjoys being close to nature, and is probably a bit of an adventurer. This is an excellent way to experience the beautiful coastline of Norway and its fascinating coastal towns. There will be an interesting mix of passengers — it's a good way to meet new people and make new friends from different countries.

The rates vary by season, cabin location, and whether the ship is of the "new generation" (*Kong Harald, Nordkapp, Nordlys, Nordnorge, Polarlys, Richard With*), the "mid-generation" (*Narvik, Midnatsol,*

Vesteralen), or the "traditional" (*Harald Jarl, Lofoten*) type ships. Senior citizens (those aged 67 and over) qualify for a special discount.

The dress code is casual and comfortable — layered clothing is recommended. The currency is the Norwegian Krone.

Operates Norwegian coast and fjords cruises (year-round): 7-day (northbound) voyage between Bergen and Kirkenes, Norway; a 6-day (southbound) voyage between Kirkenes and Bergen, Norway; or a 12-day roundtrip voyage.

Weak Points: The ship does not have stabilizers, so you should expect some movement when the weather is inclement or unkind. Drinks prices are extremely high — the same as ashore in Norway. The cabins are small, and the bathrooms are really tiny. Although not needed during the winter, there is little outdoors deck space considering the number of passengers carried.

CABIN AMENITIES

Cabins provide some, or all, of the following:

→ Private bathroom (generally small and compact) fitted with shower, wash basin, and toilet. Higher-grade cabins and suites may have full-size bathtubs. Some even have a whirlpool bath and/or bidet, a hair dryer, and more space.

→ Electrical outlets for personal appliances, usually 110 and/or 220 volts.

→ Multichannel radio, television (regular satellite channels or closed circuit), and VCR.

→ Two beds or a lower and upper berth (possibly, another one or two upper berths) or a double-, queen-, or king-size bed. In some ships, twin beds can be pushed together to form a double.

→ Telephone, for intercabin or ship-to-shore communication.

→ Depending on cabin size, a chair, or chair and table, or sofa and table, or even a separate lounge/sitting area (higher accommodation grades).

→ Refrigerator and bar (higher accommodation grades).

→ Vanity/desk unit with chair or stool.

→ Personal safe.

→ Closet space, some drawer space, plus storage room under beds for suitcases.

→ Bedside night stand/table unit.

→ Towels, soap, shampoo, and conditioner.

Hebridean Princess
★★★★★

Small Ship:	2,112 tons	Cabins (for one person):	11
Lifestyle:	Luxury	Cabins (with private balcony):	4
Cruise Line:	Hebridean Island Cruises	Cabins (wheelchair accessible):	0
Former Names:	*Columba*	Cabin Current:	240-volt
Builder:	Hall Russell (Scotland)	Full-Service Dining Rooms:	1
Original Cost:	n/a	Elevators:	0
Entered Service:	1964/April 1989	Casino (gaming tables):	No
Registry:	Great Britain	Slot Machines:	No
Length (ft/m):	235.0/71.6	Swimming Pools (outdoors):	0
Beam (ft/m):	46.0/14.0	Swimming Pools (indoors):	0
Draft (ft/m):	10.0/3.0	Whirlpools:	0
Propulsion/Propellers:	Diesel (1,790kW)/2	Fitness Center:	Yes
Passenger Decks:	5	Sauna/Steam Room:	No/No
Total Crew:	37	Massage:	No
Passengers (lower beds/all berths):	49/49	Self-Service Launderette:	No
Pass. Space Ratio (lower beds/all berths):	43.1/43.1	Dedicated Cinema:	No
Crew/Pass. Ratio (lower beds/all berths):	1.3/1.3	Library:	Yes
Navigation Officers:	British	Classification Society:	Lloyd's Register
Cabins (total):	30		
Size Range (sq ft/sq m):	144.0–340.0/13.4–31.6	**OVERALL SCORE:**	**1,701**
Cabins (outside view):	24	**(OUT OF A POSSIBLE 2,000 POINTS)**	
Cabins (interior/no view):	6		

Accommodation: All cabins have different color schemes and names (there are no numbers, and, refreshingly, no door locks, so don't ask for the door key). All are individually designed and created (no two cabins are identical), with sweeping chintz curtains and drapes over the beds. They really are quite delightful and come in a wide range of configurations (some with single, some with double, some with twin beds). Four have a private balcony (lovely). All except two cabins have a private bathroom with bath or shower; all feature a refrigerator, ironing board with iron, trouser press, and tea/coffee making set. Naturally, all towels and bathrobe are of 100% cotton, as is the bed linen.

All cabins come with real Victorian-style bathroom fittings (some are even gold-plated), and some have brass cabin portholes that actually open. Three of the newest cabins added are outfitted in Scottish Baronial style. Some cabins also have a VCR. No cabins have keys, although they can be locked from the inside.

Dining: The ship features a totally nonsmoking dining room with ocean-view windows, and tables that are laid with crisp white linen, and sometimes with lace overlays. There is one seating, at assigned tables. Some chairs have armrests while some do not. The cuisine is extremely creative, and at times outstanding — about the same quality and presentation as *Seabourn Goddess I* and *Seabourn Goddess II*. Fresh ingredients are purchased locally — a welcome change from the mass catering of most ships. Although there are no flambeau items (the galley has electric, not gas, cookers), what is created is beautifully presented and of the very highest standard. The desserts are definitely worth saving space for!

The breakfast menu is standard each day, although you can always ask for any favorites you may have, and each day a specialty item is featured. Try the porridge and a "wee dram" — it's lovely when its cold outside, and it sets you up for the whole day! Although there is waiter service for most things, there is also a good buffet table display for breakfast and lunch. This little ship features a very decent wine list, with extremely moderate prices (an additional connoisseur's list is also available for those seeking fine vintage wines). There are also many wonderful whiskeys and vintage cognacs available. Highly personal and attentive service from an attentive British/Scottish crew completes the picture

Other Comments: Small is beautiful! Originally built as a Scottish ferry, she was skillfully converted into a gem of a cruise ship in order to operate island-hopping itineraries in Scotland, together with the occasional jaunt to Ireland and Norway. She was re-christened in 1989 by the Duchess of York. There is an outdoor deck for occasional sunbathing and al fresco meals, as well as a bar (occasionally, formal cocktail parties are held here when the weather conditions are right). There is no wraparound deck, although inside the ship there is a mini-gym for those seeking to pedal or row themselves to the next destination. The ship carries a Zodiac inflatable runabout, as well as a rowing boat (for passenger use).

Use of the ship's small boats, speedboat, bicycles, and fishing gear are included in the price, as are entrance fees to gardens, castles, other attractions, and the occasional coach tour (depending on itinerary). The destination-intensive cruises have very creative itineraries and there really is plenty to do, despite the lack of big-ship features. Specialist guides, who give nightly talks about the destinations to be visited and some fascinating history and local folklore, accompany all cruises.

The principal inside room is the Tiree Lounge, which features a real brick-walled fireplace, as well as a very cozy bar with a wide variety of whiskeys (the selection of single malts is excellent) and cognacs for connoisseurs.

This utterly charming little ship has stately home service and a warm, totally cosseted, traditional country house ambience that is unobtrusive but always at hand when you need it. Inspector Hercules Poirot would be very much at home here. Who needs megaships when you can take a retro-cruise aboard this absolute gem of a ship. Sheer pleasure is a week (or more) aboard *Hebridean Princess* — a superb Scottish Island Fling. Direct bookings are accepted.

What is so appreciated by passengers is the fact that the ship does not have photographers or some of the trappings found aboard larger ships. Passengers also love the fact that there is no bingo, horse racing, art auctions, or mindless parlor games.

Hebridean Princess has an all-UK crew, and remains one of the world's most well-kept travel secrets. A polished gem, she is especially popular with single passengers, and typically more than 50% of her passengers are repeaters (note that children under the age of nine are not accepted). If you cruise from Oban, you will be met at Glasgow station (or airport) and taken to/from the ship by private coach (motor, not horse-drawn). All gratuities and all soft drinks are included in the fare (the company earnestly requests that no additional gratuities be given).

Hebridean Island Cruises also has a sister ship, acquired in 2001, called *Hebridean Spirit*.

Weak Points: Although this vessel is strong, she does have structural limitations and noisy engines that cause some vibration (however, the engines do not run at night, and the ship anchors before bedtime, providing soul-renewing peace and tranquility). Drinks are not, but should, at this price, be included (soft drinks are, however, included). It is often cold (and very wet) in the Scottish islands, so take plenty of warm clothing for layering.

Hebridean Spirit

Small Ship:	4,200 tons	Cabin Current:	110/220-volt
Lifestyle:	Luxury	Full-Service Dining Rooms:	1
Cruise Line:	Hebridean Island Cruises	Elevators:	1
Former Names:	*MegaStar Capricorn, Sun Viva II,*	Casino (gaming tables):	No
	Renaissance Six	Slot Machines:	No
Builder:	Nuovi Cantieri Apuania (Italy)	Swimming Pools (outdoors):	1
Entered Service:	March 1991/July 2001	Swimming Pools (indoors):	0
Registry:	Great Britain	Whirlpools:	1
Length (ft/m):	297.2/90.60	Fitness Center:	Yes
Beam (ft/m):	50.1/15.30	Sauna/Steam Room:	No/Yes
Draft (ft/m):	13.7/4.20	Massage:	Yes
Propulsion/Propellers:	Diesel (5,000kW)/2	Self-Service Launderette:	No
Passenger Decks:	5	Dedicated Cinema:	No
Total Crew:	72	Library:	Yes
Passengers (lower beds/all berths):	81/97	Classification Society:	Lloyd's Register
Pass. Space Ratio (lower beds/alberths):	51.8/43.2		
Crew/Pass. Ratio (lower beds/all berths):	1.1/1.3		
Navigation Officers:	British		
Cabins (total):	50		
Size Range (sq ft/sq m):	215.0–365.9/20.0–34.0		
Cabins (outside view):	50		
Cabins (interior/no view):	0		
Cabins (for one person):	19		
Cabins (with private balcony):	12		
Cabins (wheelchair accessible):	0		

OVERALL SCORE: NOT YET RATED

Note that this ship had not entered service when this book was completed. However, the score is expected to be very similar to that of sister ship *Hebridean Princess*.

Accommodation: The cabins (with names like Glens, Isles, Castles, and Clans) are quite spacious units, measuring between 215 sq ft and 365 sq ft (20–34 m). All have outside views, and all feature wallpapered walls, dressing table with three-sided vanity mirrors, tea/coffee-making equipment, combination color TV and DVD player, refrigerator/minibar (always stocked with fresh milk and mineral water), personal safe, ironing board, and trouser press. The two suites and 14 other cabins have an additional sofa bed. Naturally, all towels and bathrobe are of 100% cotton, as is the bed linen.

The bathrooms are quite small, but all are marble clad; they have real teakwood floors and marble vanities, and shower enclosures (except for "Suite," "Glen," and "Isle" grade cabins, which have a bathtub/shower combination).

Dining: The Argyll Restaurant is a nonsmoking dining room with ocean-view portholes, and operates with table assignments for all meals, in one seating. It is small and elegant, with fine furnishings and subtle lighting. There are many tables for two, although there are also tables for four, six, and eight. Tables are laid with crisp white linen, and sometimes with lace overlays.

The cuisine is extremely creative — at times outstanding — and about the same quality and presentation as can be found aboard *Seabourn Goddess I* and *Seabourn Goddess II*. Fresh ingredients are often purchased locally — a welcome change from the mass catering of most ships. And the desserts are definitely worth saving space for!

Breakfasts and lunches are typically taken outdoors at the alfresco brasserie.

Other Comments: The ship has a contemporary look and handsome styling with twin, flared funnels. The navigation bridge is a well-rounded half-moon design. She was one of four identical vessels originally built for Renaissance Cruises, and acquired by Hebridean Island Cruises in November 2000. After being chartered to Star Cruises until March 2001, the ship underwent an extensive redesign and refurbishment program. Her exterior design has been altered somewhat with the addition of an enclosed lounge deck forward of the single funnel, which has been made to look similar to that of sister ship *Hebridean Princess*. An open bridge policy means that passengers can go to the bridge at any time (except during maneuvers or in inclement weather conditions), and may also visit the engine room.

There are two teak promenade decks outdoors, and a reasonable amount of open deck and sunbathing space. All of the deck furniture — the tables and chairs — are made of teak and the deck lounge chairs have thick cushioned pads. There is also a teak water sports platform at the stern of the ship. The ship also carries a number of lightweight bicycles (helmets are also provided, and required), for those that like to be independent explorers in ports of call.

Inside the ship, you will find elegant interior design and the touches reminiscent of a small, lavish country house hotel (most of her original furnishings and fittings were removed in a multimillion pound refurbishment program when the ship was delivered to Hebridean Island Cruises in 2001). The Skye Lounge (the ship's main lounge with the feel of a traditional drawing room), has a large white fireplace, and is the focal point for all social activities and cocktail parties. There is also a travel library/reading room.

Smokers can enjoy their very own Lookout Lounge, adjacent to the Panorama Lounge (where you'll find Internet-connect computer stations), located forward of the funnel, atop the ship.

The ship's itineraries take participants mostly to quiet, off-the-beaten-track ports not often visited by larger cruise ships. So, what is so good about a cruise aboard this ship? It's the faultless, friendly, but unobtrusive service, and the attention to detail so lacking in most large ships today. This utterly charming little ship has a warm, totally cosseted, traditional country house ambience that is unobtrusive but always at hand when you need it. Inspector Hercules Poirot would be very much at home here. The fact that the ship does not have photographers and some of the trappings found aboard larger ships does not matter one bit. Passengers also love the fact that there is no formal entertainment, game shows, bingo, horse racing, art auctions, or mindless parlor games — just good company and gentle conversation. The dress code is casual and comfortable; although there are typically two formal evenings each cruise when passengers do enjoy dressing up.

Hebridean Island Cruises also operates a much smaller, even more intimate sister ship, mainly in the western islands off the coast of Scotland, *Hebridean Princess*. The company's brochure uses only real passengers in its photographs. Note that children under the age of nine are not accepted on board.

All gratuities and all soft drinks are included in the fare (the company earnestly requests that no additional gratuities be given to staff).

Holiday
★★★ +

Large Ship:	46,052 tons	Cabins (for one person):	0
Lifestyle:	Standard	Cabins (with private balcony):	10
Cruise Line:	Carnival Cruise Lines	Cabins (wheelchair accessible):	15
Former Names:	-	Cabin Current:	110-volt
Builder:	Aalborg Vaerft (Denmark)	Full-Service Dining Rooms:	2
Original Cost:	$170 million	Elevators:	8
Entered Service:	July 1985	Casino (gaming tables):	Yes
Registry:	Bahamas	Slot Machines:	Yes
Length (ft/m):	726.9/221.57	Swimming Pools (outdoors):	3
Beam (ft/m):	92.4/28.17	Swimming Pools (indoors):	0
Draft (ft/m):	25.5/7.77	Whirlpools:	2
Propulsion/Propellers:	Diesel (22,360kW)/2	Fitness Center:	Yes
Passenger Decks:	9	Sauna/Steam Room:	Yes/No
Total Crew:	660	Massage:	Yes
Passengers (lower beds/all berths):	1,452/1,800	Self-Service Launderette:	Yes
Pass. Space Ratio (lower beds/all berths):	31.7/25.5	Dedicated Cinema:	No
Crew/Pass. Ratio (lower beds/all berths):	2.2/2.7	Library:	Yes
Navigation Officers:	Italian	Classification Society:	Lloyd's Register
Cabins (total):	726		
Size Range (sq ft/sq m):	182.9–189.4/17.0–17.6		
Cabins (outside view):	447		
Cabins (interior/no view):	279		

OVERALL SCORE: 1,318

(OUT OF A POSSIBLE 2,000 POINTS)

Accommodation: Carnival Cruise Lines has always tried to provide an adequate amount of space in passenger cabins, and the cabins aboard *Holiday* are no exception. They are quite functional and provide all the basics; bathrooms are practical units, with decent-size shower stalls. A gift basket is now provided in all grades of accommodation; it includes aloe soap, shampoo, conditioner, deodorant, breath mints, candy, and pain relief tablets.

Dining: There are two dining rooms (Four Winds and Seven Seas); both are large and have low ceilings, making the raised center sections seem crowded, and noisy because they are always full. Dining is now in four seatings, for greater flexibility: 6pm, 6:45pm, 8pm, and 8:45pm (these times are approximate).

Carnival meals stress quantity, not quality, although the company constantly works hard to improve the cuisine. While passengers seem to accept it, few find it worth remembering. However, food and its taste are still not the company's strongest points (you get what you pay for, remember).

While the menu items sound good, their presentation and taste leave much to be desired. While meats are of a high quality, fish and seafood is not. Presentation is simple, and few garnishes are used. Many meat and fowl dishes are disguised with gravies and sauces. The selection of fresh green vegetables, breads, rolls, cheeses, and fruits is limited, and there is too much use of canned fruit and jellied desserts. However, do remember that this is banquet catering, with all its attendant standardization and production cooking (it is, therefore, difficult to ask for anything remotely unusual or off-menu).

Although there is a decent wine list, there are no wine waiters (the waiters are expected to serve both food and wine). The service is quite robotic, closely timed, highly programmed, and inflexible, although the waiters are willing and reasonably friendly However, the waiters do sing and dance (be prepared for "Hot, Hot, Hot" and "The Macarena" — again) and there are constant waiter parades; the dining room is show business — all done in the name of gratuities at the end of your cruise.

The Lido Café self-serve buffets are very basic, as is the selection of breads, rolls, fruit, and cheeses. At night, the Seaview Bistro (as the Lido Café becomes known) provides a casual alternative to eating in the main dining rooms. It serves pasta, steaks, salads, and desserts.

Other Comments: The second new ship for Carnival Cruise Lines, *Holiday* is a bold, high-sided, all-white contemporary ship with short, rakish bow and stubby stern typical of so many recently built ships. Has a distinctive, large, swept-back wing-tipped funnel in Carnival Cruise Lines colors of red, white, and blue.

Inside, the passenger flow is quite good. There are numerous public rooms on two entertainment decks to choose from and play in, and these flow from a double-width indoor promenade. A real red and cream bus is located right in the middle of one of the two promenades, and this is used as a snack café.

There is a stunning, multitiered show lounge, although the sight lines are restricted from some seats that are located behind the several pillars.

The bright (very bright) interior decor has a distinct Broadway theme. The Carnegie Library (which has very few books) is the only public room that is not bright. The casino is good, and there is around-the-clock action. There is plenty of dazzle and sizzle entertainment, while "Camp Carnival" takes care of the junior cruisers (facilities include virtual-reality machines).

This ship, now over 10 years old, is ideal for a first cruise experience in glitzy, very lively surroundings, and for the active set who enjoy constant stimulation, loud music, and a fun-filled atmosphere, at an attractive price. The line does not provide finesse, nor does it claim to. But forget fashion — having fun is the *sine qua non* of a Carnival cruise. There is no doubt that Carnival does a great job of providing a fun venue, but many passengers say that once is enough, and after you will want to move to a more upscale experience. Gratuities can be prepaid.

Weak Points: Standing in line for embarkation, disembarkation, shore tenders, and for self-serve buffet meals is an inevitable aspect of cruising aboard all large ships. A cruise aboard this ship is a noisy affair, and not relaxing at all (good if you want big-city nightlife). There is absolutely no escape from unnecessary and repetitious announcements (particularly for activities that bring revenue, such as art auctions and bingo) that intrude constantly into your cruise, and a great deal of hustling for drinks, although it is sometimes done with a knowing smile.

Horizon
★★★★ +

Large Ship:	46,811 tons	Cabins (for one person):	0
Lifestyle:	Premium	Cabins (with private balcony):	0
Cruise Line:	Celebrity Cruises	Cabins (wheelchair accessible):	4
Former Names:	-	Cabin Current:	110-volt
Builder:	Meyer Werft (Germany)	Full-Service Dining Rooms:	1
Original Cost:	$185 million	Elevators:	7
Entered Service:	May 1990	Casino (gaming tables):	Yes
Registry:	Liberia	Slot Machines:	Yes
Length (ft/m):	681.1/207.6	Swimming Pools (outdoors):	2
Beam (ft/m):	95.1/29.0	Swimming Pools (indoors):	0
Draft (ft/m):	23.6/7.2	Whirlpools:	0
Propulsion/Propellers:	Diesel (19,960kW)/2	Fitness Center:	Yes
Passenger Decks:	9	Sauna/Steam Room:	Yes/No
Total Crew:	642	Massage:	Yes
Passengers (lower beds/all berths):	1,354/1,660	Self-Service Launderette:	No
Pass. Space Ratio (lower beds/all berths):	34.5/28.1	Dedicated Cinema:	No
Crew/Pass. Ratio (lower beds/all berths):	2.1/2.5	Library:	Yes
Navigation Officers:	Greek	Classification Society:	Lloyd's Register
Cabins (total):	677		
Size Range (sq ft/sq m):	172.0–340.0/17.0–31.0	**OVERALL SCORE:**	**1,618**
Cabins (outside view):	529	**(OUT OF A POSSIBLE 2,000 POINTS)**	
Cabins (interior/no view):	148		

Accommodation: There are 12 grades of accommodation, including outside-view suites and cabins, and interior (no view) cabins, but even the smallest cabin is considerably larger than most of the standard outside and interior (no view) cabins aboard the ships of sister company Royal Caribbean International. All of the standard interior (no view) and outside-view cabins have good quality fittings with lots of wood accenting, are tastefully decorated and of an above-average size, with an excellent amount of closet and drawer space, and reasonable insulation between cabins. The bathrooms have a very generous shower area, and a small range of toiletries is provided (the bathroom towels are a little small, however), as is storage space for personal toiletry items. The lowest-grade outside-view cabins have a porthole, but all others have picture windows.

The largest cabins are the suites on Deck 10; these feature butler service, and have a separate bedroom and lounge, and larger bathroom complete with whirlpool bathtub. All accommodation designated as suites feature European duvets on the beds instead of sheets/blankets. However, no cabins have private balconies (they were not yet in vogue when this ship was constructed).

Dining: Celebrity Cruises has achieved an enviable reputation for providing outstanding quality food, fine presentation, and service. The Starlight Restaurant, which also has two wings (good for small groups) is set on a single level with a raised central section, is large, yet it feels almost intimate. It is quite elegant, and there are several tables for two. There are two seatings. The chairs do not have armrests, however, due to space limitations. There are separate menus for vegetarians and children. The wine list is quite extensive, and the prices are quite reasonable.

An informal Coral Seas Café features decent buffets for breakfast (including an omelet station) and lunch (including a pasta station and vegetarian salad bar); waiters take your trays of food and escort you to tables. At night, the informal café changes into an alternative dining venue for those who want good food, but in a more casual setting than the main restaurant, with items such as grilled salmon, steaks, and rotisserie chicken, as well as specialties that change frequently (ideal for families with children).

An outdoor grill serves fast-food items such as hamburgers and hot dogs. Caviar, at extra cost, is available in the America's Cup Club. For those that cannot live without them, freshly baked pizzas (in a box) can be delivered, in an insulated pouch, to your cabin.

Other Comments: *Horizon* is quite a handsome, contemporary ship (it was the first new ship for Celebrity Cruises), with any sharp angles softened by clever exterior styling (blue striping along the ship's hull breaks up the monotonous, all-white exterior typical of so many of today's ships). There is a good amount of open deck space, and cushioned pads are provided for poolside deck lounge chairs.

Inside, the public rooms are quite spacious, feature high ceilings, and provide very good passenger flow throughout. Elegant furnishings and appointments are the norm, with fine quality fabrics used throughout. Soothing pastel colors are relaxing, but not boring. The wood-paneled casino has a stately look (outside is a satellite-linked BankAtlantic ATM machine, with a $5 access charge).

The two-level show lounge has excellent sight lines from most seats, including the balcony level. There is nothing brash or glitzy about this ship anywhere, although the decor is a little plain and clinical in places. The two-deck-high lobby has a peachy Miami Beach Art-Deco hotel look. A self-service laun-derette would have proven useful for longer cruises. Much appreciated by many passengers is the "zero announcement" policy.

An extensive refurbishment in October 1998 saw the addition (on Deck 8) of the grand Michael's Club, a cigar-smoking lounge in what was formerly the underused discotheque (it includes a bar, fireplace, and extremely comfortable chairs and leather sofas). A new library was added, complete with audio CD listen-ing seats, card room, and small business area with two computers/printers for passenger use. Also new, on Deck 7, is a small, delightful Art-Deco-style martini bar (with 26 martinis to choose from). A room dedi-cated to the display of artwork (for art auctions) was added. The health spa has also been expanded. This now includes a seraglio (rasul) treatment room, relocated beauty salon, enlarged fitness/exercise areas, and five massage and other treatment rooms. The new Cova Café has replaced what was formerly the Plaza Bar (Cova is the name of the Milan-based coffee house that also makes exclusive chocolates and liqueurs — the original Cova Café, located near La Scala Opera House, opened in 1756. Celebrity Cruises has an exclu-sive agreement with Pasticceria Confetteria Cova.). This ship delivers a well-defined North American cruise experience at a very modest price.

Weak Points: Unlike the company's larger ships *Century, Galaxy, Mercury, and Millennium,* no suites or cabins have private balconies. Trying to get Cabin Service or the Guest Relations Desk to answer the phone (to order breakfast, for example, if you don't want to do so via the interactive TV) is a matter of luck, timing, and patience (a sad reminder of the automated age and the lack of personal contact). The room service menu foods (and presentation) are well below the standard of cuisine featured in the din-ing room. The doors to the public restrooms and the outdoor decks are heavy. The public restrooms are clinical and need warmer decor. There are cushioned pads for poolside deck lounge chairs only, but not for chairs on other outside decks. There is a charge for using the AquaSpa/sauna/steam room complex unless you are purchasing a spa treatment. Passenger participation activities are amateurish and should be upgraded.

Imagination
★★★ +

Large Ship:	70,367 tons	Cabins (for one person):	0
Lifestyle:	Standard	Cabins (with private balcony):	54
Cruise Line:	Carnival Cruise Lines	Cabins (wheelchair accessible):	22
Former Names:	-	Cabin Current:	110-volt
Builder:	Kvaerner Masa-Yards (Finland)	Full-Service Dining Rooms:	2
Original Cost:	$330 million	Elevators:	14
Entered Service:	July 1995	Casino (gaming tables):	Yes
Registry:	Bahamas	Slot Machines:	Yes
Length (ft/m):	855.0/260.6	Swimming Pools (outdoors):	3
Beam (ft/m):	103.0/31.4	Swimming Pools (indoors):	0
Draft (ft/m):	25.9/7.9	Whirlpools:	6
Propulsion/Propellers: Diesel-electric (42,240kW)/2		Fitness Center:	Yes
Passenger Decks:	10	Sauna/Steam Room:	Yes/Yes
Total Crew:	920	Massage:	Yes
Passengers (lower beds/all berths):	2,040/2,594	Self-Service Launderette:	Yes
Pass. Space Ratio (lower beds/all berths):	34.4/26.7	Dedicated Cinema:	No
Crew/Pass. Ratio (lower beds/all berths):	2.2/2.8	Library:	Yes
Navigation Officers:	Italian	Classification Society:	Lloyd's Register
Cabins (total):	1,020		
Size Range (sq ft/sq m):	173.2–409.7/16.0–38.0	**OVERALL SCORE:**	**1,387**
Cabins (outside view):	618	(OUT OF A POSSIBLE 2,000 POINTS)	
Cabins (interior/no view):	402		

Accommodation: As in sister ships *Ecstasy*, *Elation*, *Fantasy*, *Fascination*, *Inspiration*, *Paradise*, and *Sensation*, the standard outside-view and interior (no view) cabins have plain decor. They are marginally comfortable, yet spacious enough and practical (most are of the same size and appointments), with good storage space and well-designed bathrooms.

Those booking one of the outside suites will find more space, whirlpool bathtubs, and some fascinating, rather eclectic decor and furniture. These are mildly attractive, but nothing special, and they are much smaller than those aboard the ships of a similar size of several competing companies.

A gift basket is now provided in all grades of accommodation; it includes aloe soap, shampoo, conditioner, deodorant, breath mints, candy, and pain relief tablets.

Dining: There are two large, colorful, noisy dining rooms (Pride and Spirit), and both are nonsmoking. Shorts are permitted in the dining room for one dinner each cruise. Dining is now in four seatings, for greater flexibility: 6pm, 6:45pm, 8pm, and 8:45pm (these times are approximate). This should give you some idea of what to expect from your dining experience.

Carnival meals stress quantity, not quality, although the company constantly works hard to improve the cuisine. While passengers seem to accept it, few find it worth remembering. However, food and its taste are still not the company's strongest points (you get what you pay for, remember).

While the menu items sound good, their presentation and taste leave much to be desired. While meats are of a high quality, fish and seafood is not. Presentation is simple, and few garnishes are used. Many meat and fowl dishes are disguised with gravies and sauces. The selection of fresh green vegetables, breads, rolls, cheeses, and fruits is limited, and there is too much use of canned fruit and jellied desserts. However, do remember that this is banquet catering, with all its attendant standardization and production cooking (it is, therefore, difficult to ask for anything remotely unusual or off-menu).

Although there is a decent wine list, there are no wine waiters (the waiters are expected to serve both food and wine), and no decent-size wine glasses. The service is quite robotic, closely timed, highly programmed, and inflexible, although the waiters are willing and reasonably friendly However, the waiters do sing and dance (be prepared for "Hot, Hot, Hot" and "The Macarena" — again) and there are constant waiter parades. The dining room is show business — all done in the name of gratuities at the end of your cruise.

The Lido Café self-serve buffets are very basic, as is the selection of breads, rolls, fruit, and cheeses. At night, the Seaview Bistro (as the Lido Café becomes known) provides a casual alternative to eating in the main dining rooms. It serves pasta, steaks, salads, and desserts. There's also a Pizzeria (this is open 24 hours a day and typically serves over 500 pizzas every single day)!

Other Comments: The ship has a forthright, angular appearance typical of today's space-creative designs. This is the fifth in a series of eight identically-sized Carnival ships that reflects the talents of interior designer Joe Farcus, whose philosophy is that the cruise ship environment should provide fantasy and an escape from routine.

Like all Carnival ships, this one has themed decor for her interiors; classical mythology and ethereal decor can be found throughout the public rooms, which are connected by a double-width indoor boulevard. The ship has expansive open deck areas and a good, well-segmented health spa, and there is also a $1 million art collection, with many items in public areas featuring some timeless mosaics.

Ship buffs will enjoy six Stephen Card paintings of clipper ships, positioned in the Grand Bar. The Victorian-era-style library is a curious room, with intentionally mismatched furnishings (reminding one of Alice in Wonderland), fine oriental rugs, and even a few books. The lavish, yet somehow elegant multi-tiered show lounge (despite 20 pillars obstructing sight lines), presents colorful, frenetic, razzle-dazzle shows. An ATM machine is located outside the large casino (all the slot machines aboard all Carnival ships are linked into a Megacash giveaway).

This ship is one of the great floating playgrounds for young, active adults who enjoy constant stimulation, close contact with lots and lots of others, as well as the three Gs — glitz, glamour, and gambling. It is a live board game with every move executed in typically grand, colorful, fun-filled Carnival Cruise Lines style. This ship will provide a great introduction to cruising for the novice passenger seeking an action-packed short cruise experience in contemporary surroundings, with a real swinging party atmosphere, and minimum fuss and finesse. You will have a fine time if you like nightlife and lots of silly participation games. Like life in the fast lane, this is cruising in a theme-park fantasyland, and the dress code is extremely casual. The staff will help you have organized fun, and that is what Carnival does best. Want to party? Then this should prove to be a great ship for you. Forget fashion — having fun is the sine qua non of a Carnival cruise. Gratuities can be prepaid.

Weak Points: Standing in line for embarkation, disembarkation, shore tenders, and for self-serve buffet meals is an inevitable aspect of cruising aboard all large ships. This ship is not for those who want a quiet, relaxing cruise experience. There is absolutely no escape from unnecessary and repetitious announcements (particularly for activities that bring revenue, such as art auctions and bingo) that intrude constantly into your cruise, and a great deal of hustling for drinks, although it is sometimes done with a knowing smile.

Independence
★★ +

Mid-Size Ship:	30,090 tons	Cabins (for one person):	26
Lifestyle:	Standard	Cabins (with private balcony):	0
Cruise Line:	American Hawaii Cruises	Cabins (wheelchair accessible):	3
Former Names:	*Oceanic Independence, Sea Luck I*	Cabin Current:	110-volt
Builder:	Bethlehem Shipbuilders (US)	Full-Service Dining Rooms:	1
Original Cost:	$25 million	Elevators:	4
Entered Service:	February 1951/June 1980	Casino (gaming tables):	No
Registry:	US	Slot Machines:	No
Length (ft/m):	682.4/208.01	Swimming Pools (outdoors):	2
Beam (ft/m):	89.1/27.18	Swimming Pools (indoors):	0
Draft (ft/m):	30.1/9.19	Whirlpools:	0
Propulsion/Propellers:	Steam turbine (40,456kW)/2	Fitness Center:	Yes
Passenger Decks:	9	Sauna/Steam Room:	Yes/No
Total Crew:	317	Massage:	Yes
Passengers (lower beds/all berths):	866/1,066	Self-Service Launderette:	Yes
Pass. Space Ratio (lower beds/all berths):	34.7/28.2	Dedicated Cinema/Seats:	Yes/144
Crew/Pass. Ratio (lower beds/all berths):	2.7/3.2	Library:	Yes
Navigation Officers:	American	Classification Society: American Bureau of Shipping	
Cabins (total):	446		
Size Range (sq ft/sq m):	75.3–575.0/7.0–53.5		
Cabins (outside view):	206		
Cabins (interior/no view):	240		

OVERALL SCORE: 1,092
(OUT OF A POSSIBLE 2,000 POINTS)

Accommodation: There is a wide range of cabin types, with more than 50 different configurations to choose from (a carry-over from her nights as a three-class liner), all of which offer ample room to move in. There is adequate closet and drawer space and fairly bright decor, with Hawaiian-themed soft furnishings. However, all the cabinetry is made of steel, and is absolutely lacking in warmth (the metal drawers are particularly tinny). Also, the cabin bathrooms are very small and utilitarian. Overall, the cabins are adequate, but they do reflect the age of the vessel.

Six large "solarium suites," with skylights, are located without access from inside the ship, which means you must go up the forward stairs and out on deck to get to them (fine if it's not raining or windy).

Dining: The dining room is set low down, and without the benefit of an ocean view (the bilevel forward section is more elegant), but it is fairly cheerful, and has tables for two, four, six, eight or ten. There are two seatings. The cuisine is decidedly Americana fare, with the norm being quantity, not quality. The first evening's dinner is buffet-style. The informal buffet area is good, but buffets are predictable, not creative. Fresh local fruits are plentiful, as are snacks and hors d'oeuvres.

Other Comments: American-built (with two engine rooms), registered and crewed, she, together with her former sister ship *Constitution* (which sank while under tow in November 1997 after being laid-up for some time), were among the first passenger ships to have air-conditioning installed. *Independence* was originally constructed for the transatlantic trade between New York and the Mediterranean in the 1950s, and became famous in 1956 when it carried Grace Kelly to Monaco for her wedding to Prince Ranier III. The ship has also played host to many other well known dignitaries and film stars in the past, including Rita Hayworth, Alfred Hitchcock, Ronald and Nancy Reagan, Harry Truman, and John Wayne.

This all-white ship has expansive open deck space for sun-worshippers, particularly on her aft, tiered sections, and features a wrap-around teakwood promenade deck outdoors.

Originally designed as a three-class ship (but now operated as a one-class vessel) her interior layout is rather awkward and disjointed, and staggered elevators, hidden stairwells, and dead-end corridors all add to the confusing layout. The ship's original interior design was coordinated by Henry Dreyfuss, the man who designed the rotary telephone.

The public rooms are spacious and have high ceilings (although those of sister ship *Constitution* were considered far more attractive). There are reasonably good facilities for meetings. The decor, with its Hawaiian theme, is a natural for the ship's operating area. Local Hawaiian artists have their artwork featured on board. The heavy-duty, "neo-Art Deco" furniture and fittings were designed for the unkind oceans of the world. Hardwood floors, ceiling fans, and large plants add up to a tropical 1950s look and feel.

The ambience and dress code are decidedly casual, and the entertainment is understandably regional. Fortunately, such things as bingo and horseracing are low-key, and not daily. Those intending to marry should look into the company's Nani Kai (Bountiful Seas) wedding package.

Because a laid-back atmosphere prevails, Aloha smiles come poring from the friendly staff, although the lack of service finesse does show through. This is a destination-intensive operation aboard a ship that is very tired and worn, despite a $30 million renovation in 1994. On top of the cruise fare, a Hawaii State Tax of 4.166% is applied in addition to port charges and, for singles, there is a single supplement (plus gratuities). Airfare is also an additional cost, and 15% is added to all drinks and wine purchases.

Having said all the above, there is something utterly magical about seeing the islands of Hawaii by ship (the ship's home port is now Maui), and this ship provides the means to do so in a modicum of comfort. Complimentary shuttles to nearby shopping areas are provided at each port of call — a welcome touch.

Weak Points: The ship is now over 40 years old, and although she has been through some refurbishment, she is looking decidedly sad and tired in many places. The show lounge is not large enough and is always crowded. The price of drinks is extremely high. There are no stabilizers, so the ship can certainly roll in inclement weather.

Infinity
★★★★★

Large Ship:	90,228 tons	Cabins (for one person):	0
Lifestyle:	Premium	Cabins (with private balcony):	590
Cruise Line:	Celebrity Cruises	Cabins (wheelchair accessible):	26
Former Names:	-		(17 with private balcony)
Builder:	Chantiers de l'Atlantique (France)	Cabin Current:	110/220-volt
Original Cost:	$350 million	Full-Service Dining Rooms:	1 main, 1 specialty
Entered Service:	March 2001	Elevators:	10
Registry:	Liberia	Casino (gaming tables):	Yes
Length (ft/m):	964.5/294.0	Slot Machines:	Yes
Beam (ft/m):	105.6/32.2	Swimming Pools (outdoors):	2
Draft (ft/m):	26.2/8.0	Swimming Pools (indoors):	1 (with magrodome)
Propulsion/Propellers:	Gas turbine/2 azimuthing pods (39,000kW)	Whirlpools:	4
Passenger Decks:	11	Fitness Center:	Yes
Total Crew:	999	Sauna/Steam Room:	Yes/Yes
Passengers (lower beds/all berths):	1,950/2,450	Massage:	Yes
Pass. Space Ratio (lower beds/all berths):	46.6/37.1	Self-Service Launderette:	No
Crew/Pass. Ratio (lower beds/all berths):	1.9/2.4	Dedicated Cinema/Seats:	Yes/368
Navigation Officers:	Greek	Library:	Yes
Cabins (total):	975	Classification Society:	Lloyd's Register
Size Range (sq ft/sq m):	165.1–2,350.0/15.34–218.3		
Cabins (outside view):	780		
Cabins (interior/no view):	195		

OVERALL SCORE: **1,707**
(OUT OF A POSSIBLE 2,000 POINTS)

Accommodation: There are eight different accommodation types, ranging from Penthouse Suites to interior (no view) cabins, in 20 different price grades. There are several categories of suites, but those at the stern of the ship are in a prime location and have huge balconies that are really private and not overlooked from above.

Two Penthouse Suites (on Penthouse Deck) comprise the largest accommodation aboard this ship and are really beautiful apartments. Each measures a huge 2,530 sq ft (235 sq m): 1,432 sq ft (133 sq m) of living space, plus a huge wraparound balcony measuring 1,098 sq ft (102 sq m) with 180-degree views, which occupies one half of the beam (width) of the ship, overlooking the ship's stern. It includes a wet bar, hot tub, and whirlpool tub, and features include a marble foyer, a separate living room (complete with ebony baby grand piano — bring your own pianist if you don't play yourself) and a formal dining room. The master bedroom has a large walk-in closet, personal exercise equipment, dressing room with vanity desk, marble master bathroom with twin sinks, deep whirlpool bathtub, separate shower, toilet, and bidet. There are also flat-screen TVs (one in the bedroom and one in the lounge) and electronically controlled drapes. Butler service is standard, and a butler's pantry, with separate entry door, features a full-size refrigerator, temperature-controlled wine cabinet, microwave oven, and good-size food preparation and storage areas.

Eight wood-panelled Royal Suites (733 sq ft/68 sq m) feature separate a living room with dining and lounge areas, and decor in different ethnic styles (African, Chinese, Mexican, French, Indian, Italian, Moroccan, and Portuguese). There are two entertainment centers with flat-screen TVs (one each in the lounge and bedroom), and a large walk-in closet with vanity desk. The bathroom features a whirlpool bathtub and a separate shower enclosure. The balcony also features a whirlpool hot tub. Butler service is standard.

Eight Celebrity Suites (467.0 sq ft/43.3 sq m) each feature floor-to-ceiling windows; separate living room with dining and lounge areas; two entertainment centers with flat-screen TVs; walk-in closet with vanity desk; bathroom with whirlpool bathtub. Interconnecting doors allow two suites to be used as a family unit. These suites overhang the starboard side of the ship (they are located opposite a group of glass-walled elevators) and provide stunning ocean views from the glass-walled sitting/dining area, which extends out from the ship's side (hence these suites do not have a private balcony). Butler service is standard.

All other outside-view and interior (no view) cabins (those not designated as suites) feature a lounge area with sofa or convertible sofa bed, sleeping area with twin beds that can convert to a double bed, a good amount of closet and drawer space, personal safe, minibar/refrigerator (all items are at extra cost), interactive TV, and private bathroom. The cabins are nicely decorated with warm wood-finish furniture, and there is none of the boxy feel of cabins in so many ships, due to the angled placement of vanity and audio-video consoles. Even the smallest interior (no view) cabin has a good-size bathroom and shower enclosure.

Wheelchair-accessible accommodation is available in six Sky Suites, three premium outside-view cabins, eight deluxe ocean-view cabins, four standard ocean-view and five interior (no view) cabins. All these cabins measure 347 sq ft to 362 sq ft (32.2 sq m to 33.6 sq m) and are located in the most practical parts of the ship and close to elevators for good accessibility (all have doorways and showers that are wheelchair accessible).

Butler Service: Butler service (in all accommodation designated as suites) includes full breakfast, en-suite lunch and dinner service, afternoon tea service, evening hors d'oeuvres, complimentary espresso and cappuccino, daily news delivery, shoeshine service, and other personal touches.

Suite occupants in Penthouse, Royal, and Celebrity suites also get welcome champagne; a full personal computer in each suite, including a printer and Internet access (on request in the Sky Suites); choice of films from a video library; personalized stationery; tote bag; priority dining room seating preferences; private portrait sitting; and en-suite massage service.

Dining: The Thellis Restaurant is the ship's 1,170-seat formal dining room. Two decks high including its atrium gallery, it has a grand staircase connecting the two levels, a huge glass wall overlooking the sea at the stern of the ship (electrically operated blinds provide several different backdrops), and a musician's gallery on the upper level (typically for a string quartet/quintet). There are two seatings, and the dining room is a totally nonsmoking area. Besides the principal dining room, there are several dining options, particularly for those seeking more casual dining spots. Full-service in-cabin dining is also available for all meals (including dinner).

The United States Restaurant is the ship's alternative dining room, located adjacent to the conference center (aboard sister ship *Millennium* the restaurant is called The Olympic). A dining lounge (rather like an anteroom) contains actual glass paneling from the former United States Lines liner *United States*, which, in 1952, gained renown for the fastest transatlantic crossing by a passenger ship and took the famed "Blue Riband" from the Cunard liner *Queen Mary*.

Superb tableside preparation is the feature of this alternative dining room, whose classic French cuisine (plus some menu items from the famous liner United States) and service are absolutely outstanding (masterminded by Michel Roux, owner of a three-star Michelin restaurant near Windsor in England). This is haute cuisine at the peak of professionalism, for this is, indeed, a room for a full degustation, and not merely a dinner. However, with just 134 seats, not all passengers will be able to experience it even once during a one-week cruise (reservations are necessary, and a cover charge of $25 per person applies). A dine-in wine cellar is also a feature, as is a demonstration galley, and tableside preparation is a feature of this unique dining spot.

For casual eating, the Oceanview Café & Grill is a self-serve buffet area, with six principal serving lines and 754 seats; there is also a grill and pizza bar.

For champagne and caviar lovers, the Platinum Club has a platinum and silver Art Deco decor that is reminiscent of a 1930s gentlemen's club. It includes a diamond-pane reflective mirror wall. There's also a Martini Bar.

Other Comments: *Infinity* is a sister ship to *Millennium*. Jon Bannenberg (famous as a mega-yacht designer) designed the exterior that features a royal-blue-and-white hull and racy lines. This is the second Celebrity Cruises ship to be fitted with a "pod" propulsion system (and controllable pitch propellers) coupled with an energy-efficient, smokeless, gas turbine power plant. She is powered by a gas turbine (two GE gas turbines provide engine power while a single GE steam turbine drives the electricity generators).

Inside, the ship features the same high-class decor and materials, and public rooms that have made the existing ships in the fleet so popular and user-friendly. But in a first for Celebrity Cruises, the atrium spans 11 decks. It is capped with a glass dome, and four glass elevators travel through the port side of the atrium. Michael's Club (a cigar and cognac specialty lounge that features almost 20 varieties of cigars) is located on Promenade Deck.

Facilities include a combination cinema/conference center, an expansive shopping arcade with more than 14,000 sq ft (1,300 sq m) of retail store space (including H. Stern, Donna Karan, Fossil, and the exclusive Michel Roux culinary store), a lavish four-decks-high show lounge with the latest in staging and lighting equipment, two-level library (one level for English-language books; a second level for books in other languages), card room, CD listening room, art auction center (with seating that looks rather more like a small chapel), "Cosmos" — a combination observation lounge/discotheque, and an Internet Center with 18 computer stations.

One unique feature is a conservatory that includes seating, set in a botanical environment of flowers, plants, tress, mini-gardens, and fountains, designed by the award-winning floral designer Emilio Robba of Paris. It is located directly in front of the main funnel and has glass walls that overlook the ship's side.

Outdoor facilities include two outdoor pools, one indoor/outdoor pool, and six whirlpools. There is also a large AquaSpa (with large thalassotherapy pool under a huge solarium dome), complete with health bar for light breakfast and lunch items, and freshly squeezed fruit and vegetable juices. Spa facilities (measuring 25,000 sq ft/2323 sq m) include 16 treatment rooms; plus eight treatment rooms with showers and one treatment room specifically designed for wheelchair passengers; aerobics room; gymnasium (complete with all the latest high-tech muscle machines); large male and female saunas (with large ocean-view porthole window); a co-ed thermal suite (containing several steam and shower mist rooms with different fragrances such as chamomile, eucalyptus, and mint, plus a glacial ice fountain); and a beauty salon. Among the different types of massage available is a delightful hot and cold stone massage therapy that lasts almost an hour and a half.

Sports facilities include a full-size basketball court, compact football, paddle tennis, volleyball, golf simulator, shuffleboard (on two different decks), and a jogging track. A 70-person capacity sports bar called Extreme (a first for a Celebrity Cruises ship, although it just doesn't, somehow, belong) is located directly in front of the main funnel and has glass walls that overlook the ship's side. Gaming includes Fortunes Casino, with blackjack, roulette, and numerous slot machines.

Families with children will appreciate the Fun Factory (for children) and The Tower (for teenagers).

With such extensive facilities, this ship has an extremely comfortable environment for a large ship, with good food and dining facilities, and a well-run shipboard operation that will provide all the things necessary for you to have a fine vacation at sea, for a very fair price. My advice is to book a suite-category cabin for all the extra benefits it brings — it really is worth it.

Weak Points: Standing in line for embarkation, disembarkation, shore tenders, and self-serve buffet meals is an inevitable aspect of cruising aboard all large ships. There is, sadly, no wraparound wooden promenade deck outdoors. There are cushioned pads for poolside deck lounge chairs only, but not for chairs on other outside decks.

Inspiration
★★★ +

Large Ship:	70,367 tons	Cabins (for one person):	0
Lifestyle:	Standard	Cabins (with private balcony):	54
Cruise Line:	Carnival Cruise Lines	Cabins (wheelchair accessible):	22
Former Names:	-	Cabin Current:	110-volt
Builder:	Kvaerner Masa-Yards (Finland)	Full-Service Dining Rooms:	2
Original Cost:	$270 million	Elevators:	14
Entered Service:	April 1996	Casino (gaming tables):	Yes
Registry:	Bahamas	Slot Machines:	Yes
Length (ft/m):	855.0/260.6	Swimming Pools (outdoors):	3
Beam (ft/m):	103.0/31.4	Swimming Pools (indoors):	0
Draft (ft/m):	25.9/7.9	Whirlpools:	6
Propulsion/Propellers:	Diesel-electric	Fitness Center:	Yes
	(42,240kW)/2	Sauna/Steam Room:	Yes/Yes
Passenger Decks:	10	Massage:	Yes
Total Crew:	920	Self-Service Launderette:	Yes
Passengers (lower beds/all berths):	2,040/2,594	Dedicated Cinema:	No
Pass. Space Ratio (lower beds/all berths):	34.4/26.7	Library:	Yes
Crew/Pass. Ratio (lower beds/all berths):	2.2/2.8	Classification Society:	Lloyd's Register
Navigation Officers:	Italian		
Cabins (total):	1,020		
Size Range (sq ft/sq m):	173.2–409.7/16.0–38.0	**OVERALL SCORE:**	**1,385**
Cabins (outside view):	618	**(OUT OF A POSSIBLE 2,000 POINTS)**	
Cabins (interior/no view):	402		

Accommodation: As in sister ships *Ecstasy, Elation, Fantasy, Fascination, Imagination, Paradise,* and *Sensation,* the standard outside-view and interior (no view) cabins have plain decor. They are marginally comfortable, yet spacious enough and practical (most are of the same size and appointments), with good storage space and well-designed bathrooms.

Those booking one of the outside suites will find more space, whirlpool bathtubs, and some fascinating, rather eclectic decor and furniture. These are mildly attractive, but nothing special, and they are much smaller than those aboard the ships of a similar size of several competing companies.

A gift basket is now provided in all grades of accommodation; it includes aloe soap, shampoo, conditioner, deodorant, breath mints, candy, and pain relief tablets.

Dining: There are two large, rather noisy — or perhaps that should be better translated as "lively" — dining rooms (Carnivale and Mardi Gras), and both are nonsmoking. The service is attentive, but far too fast and assertive, and lacks any kind of finesse. Dining is now in four seatings, for greater flexibility: 6pm, 6:45pm, 8pm, and 8:45pm (these times are approximate).

Carnival meals stress quantity, not quality, although the company constantly works hard to improve the cuisine. While passengers seem to accept it, few find it worth remembering. However, food and its taste are still not the company's strongest points (you get what you pay for, remember).

While the menu items sound good, their presentation and taste leave much to be desired. While meats are of a high quality, fish and seafood are not. Presentation is simple, and few garnishes are used. Many meat and fowl dishes are disguised with gravies and sauces. The selection of fresh green vegetables, breads, rolls, cheeses, and fruits is limited, and there is too much use of canned fruit and jellied desserts. However, do remember that this is banquet catering, with all its attendant standardization and production cooking (it is, therefore, difficult to ask for anything remotely unusual or off-menu).

Although there is a decent wine list, there are no wine waiters (the waiters are expected to serve both food and wine). The service is quite robotic, closely timed, highly programmed, and inflexible, although the waiters are willing and reasonably friendly. However, the waiters do sing and dance (be prepared for "Hot, Hot, Hot" and "The Macarena" — again) and there are constant waiter parades. The dining room is show business — all done in the name of gratuities at the end of your cruise.

What has improved, however, is the quality of food available at the informal food outlets such as the Brasserie Bar and Grill, which also includes a pizzeria (open 24 hours a day — it typically serves more than 500 pizzas every single day!). At night, the "Seaview Bistro" (as the Lido Café becomes known) provides a casual alternative to eating in the main dining rooms. It serves pasta, steaks, salads, and desserts.

Other Comments: Bold and forthright all-white ship has a large wing-tipped funnel in red, white, and blue; at its base is a "topless" area for sunbathing.

Like her seven sister ships of the same size, this ship also features a seven-decks-high atrium topped by a glass dome. The atrium features scrolled shapes resembling the necks and heads of violins, and a marble staircase. There are expansive open-deck areas and an excellent, three-decks-high glass-enclosed health spa. There are public entertainment lounges, bars, and clubs galore, with something for just about everyone. The public rooms connect to wide indoor boulevards.

Various colors and design themes have been used throughout, although the ship does feature somewhat softer decor than on some of Carnival's ships. Includes a $1 million art collection. Particularly fascinating is the avant-garde rendition of the famed Mona Lisa, in Pablo's Lounge. The decor itself is themed after the arts (in an art nouveau style) and literature.

The Shakespeare Library is a stunning, stately room (25 of his quotations adorn the oak veneer). Another dazzling room is the Rock and Roll Discotheque, with its guitar-shaped dance floor and dozens of video monitors around the room. The ship also features a lavish, multitiered show lounge (although some 20 pillars cause some seats to have obstructed sight lines) and high-energy razzle-dazzle shows. The casino is large and always humming with hopeful action.

This ship is one of the great floating playgrounds for young, active adults who enjoy constant stimulation, close contact with lots and lots of others, as well as the three Gs — glitz, glamour, and gambling. It is a live board game with every move executed in typically grand, colorful, fun-filled Carnival Cruise Lines style.

Finally, the company's brochure tells it exactly like it is, by providing a good look at the unpretentious lifestyle of its passengers. This ship provides a fine adult playground for those that like to party. It will entertain you well, but do not go for the food — go for the fun, the almost nonstop, all-too-predictable action and participation activities, and for a way to visit the Caribbean in a well-packaged manner that would best be described as a compact Las Vegas afloat. Forget fashion — having fun is the sine qua non of a Carnival cruise. Gratuities can be prepaid.

Weak Points: Standing in line for embarkation, disembarkation, shore tenders, and for self-serve buffet meals is an inevitable aspect of cruising aboard all large ships. There are no cushioned pads for the deck lounge chairs, which are plastic and hard to sit on with just a towel for any length of time. There is absolutely no escape from unnecessary and repetitive announcements (particularly for activities that bring revenue, such as art auctions and bingo) that intrude constantly into your cruise, and a great deal of hustling for drinks, although it is sometimes done with a knowing smile. There is too much use of plastic on board, particularly in the informal food service areas.

Jubilee
★★★ +

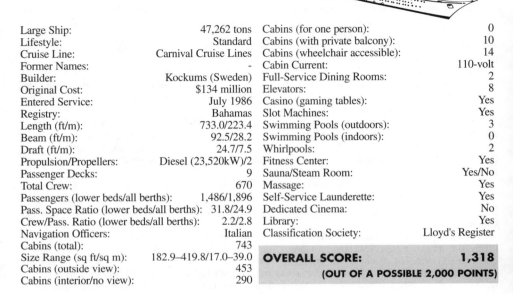

Large Ship:	47,262 tons	Cabins (for one person):	0
Lifestyle:	Standard	Cabins (with private balcony):	10
Cruise Line:	Carnival Cruise Lines	Cabins (wheelchair accessible):	14
Former Names:	-	Cabin Current:	110-volt
Builder:	Kockums (Sweden)	Full-Service Dining Rooms:	2
Original Cost:	$134 million	Elevators:	8
Entered Service:	July 1986	Casino (gaming tables):	Yes
Registry:	Bahamas	Slot Machines:	Yes
Length (ft/m):	733.0/223.4	Swimming Pools (outdoors):	3
Beam (ft/m):	92.5/28.2	Swimming Pools (indoors):	0
Draft (ft/m):	24.7/7.5	Whirlpools:	2
Propulsion/Propellers:	Diesel (23,520kW)/2	Fitness Center:	Yes
Passenger Decks:	9	Sauna/Steam Room:	Yes/No
Total Crew:	670	Massage:	Yes
Passengers (lower beds/all berths):	1,486/1,896	Self-Service Launderette:	Yes
Pass. Space Ratio (lower beds/all berths):	31.8/24.9	Dedicated Cinema:	No
Crew/Pass. Ratio (lower beds/all berths):	2.2/2.8	Library:	Yes
Navigation Officers:	Italian	Classification Society:	Lloyd's Register
Cabins (total):	743		
Size Range (sq ft/sq m):	182.9–419.8/17.0–39.0	**OVERALL SCORE:**	**1,318**
Cabins (outside view):	453		
Cabins (interior/no view):	290	**(OUT OF A POSSIBLE 2,000 POINTS)**	

Accommodation: The cabins are quite spacious, neatly appointed, and have attractive, though spartan, decor. Especially nice are the ten large suites on Verandah Deck. The outside cabins feature large picture windows. A gift basket is now provided in all grades of accommodation; it includes aloe soap, shampoo, conditioner, deodorant, breath mints, candy, and pain relief tablets.

Dining: There are two dining rooms (Bordeaux and Burgundy). They are quite cramped when full, and extremely noisy (both are nonsmoking, however), and they have low ceilings in the raised sections of their centers. There are tables for four, six, or eight (there are no tables for two). The decor is bright and extremely colorful, to say the least. Dining is now in four seatings, for greater flexibility: 6pm, 6:45pm, 8pm, and 8:45pm (these times are approximate).

Carnival meals stress quantity, not quality, although the company constantly works hard to improve the cuisine. While passengers seem to accept it, few find it worth remembering. However, food and its taste are still not the company's strongest points (you get what you pay for, remember).

While the menu items sound good, their presentation and taste leave much to be desired. While meats are of a high quality, fish and seafood are not. Presentation is simple, and few garnishes are used. Many meat and fowl dishes are disguised with gravies and sauces. The selection of fresh green vegetables, breads, rolls, cheeses, and fruits is limited, and there is too much use of canned fruit and jellied desserts. However, do remember that this is banquet catering, with all its attendant standardization and production cooking (it is, therefore, difficult to ask for anything remotely unusual or off-menu).

Although there is a decent wine list, there are no wine waiters (the waiters are expected to serve both food and wine). The service is quite robotic, closely timed, highly programmed, and inflexible, although the waiters are willing and reasonably friendly. However, the waiters do sing and dance (be prepared for "Hot, Hot, Hot" and "The Macarena" — again) and there are constant waiter parades. The dining room is show business — all done in the name of gratuities at the end of your cruise.

For casual meals, these can be taken as self-serve buffets in the Wheelhouse Bar & Grill, although the foods provided are very basic, and quite disappointing, with much repetition (particularly for breakfast) and little variety. At night, the "Seaview Bistro" (as the Lido Café is known) provides a casual alternative to eating in the main dining rooms. It serves pasta, steaks, salads, and desserts.

Other Comments: *Jubilee* has a bold, forthright all-white profile, but a very short, rakish bow. She sports Carnival's distinctive swept-back wing-tipped, red-white-and-blue funnel.

Inside, there are flamboyant, vivid colors in all the public rooms except for the somewhat elegant Churchill's Library, which, sadly, is almost devoid of books. A large casino has almost round-the-clock action. The numerous public rooms are spread throughout two whole decks full of entertainment rooms, bars, and lounges. A fine, double-width promenade deck features a white gazebo. The multitiered Atlantis Lounge has a large theater stage, and bold, stimulating colors. This ship provides constant entertainment and activities designed for passenger participation in a party-like setting.

This ship is a floating playground for young, active adults who enjoy constant stimulation, close contact with lots and lots of others, as well as the three Gs — glitz, glamour, and gambling. It is a live board game with every move executed in typically grand, colorful, fun-filled Carnival Cruise Lines style. The ship, now more than ten years old, provides novice cruisers with a good first cruise experience in comfortable but visually busy surroundings. Fun-filled, noisy, almost nonstop action equates to a stimulating vacation, targeted particularly to those that like to party and have fun. Good for families with children, and especially good for singles who want constant action (sleep before you cruise). Provides very good value, with plenty of dazzle-and-sizzle entertainment and constant activities, which Carnival does so well, particularly for first-time cruise passengers. Forget fashion — having fun is the sine qua non of a Carnival cruise. Gratuities can be prepaid.

Weak Points: Standing in line for embarkation, disembarkation, shore tenders, and for self-serve buffet meals is an inevitable aspect of cruising aboard all large ships. There are many annoying and unnecessarily loud, repetitive announcements. There is absolutely no escape from unnecessary and repetitious announcements (particularly for activities that bring revenue, such as art auctions, bingo, horse racing) that intrude constantly into your cruise, and a great deal of hustling for drinks, although it is sometimes done with a knowing smile. There are no cushioned pads for the deck lounge chairs. There are virtually no quiet spaces aboard to get away from crowds or noise.

Kapitan Dranitsyn
★★★ +

Small Ship:	12,288 tons	Cabins (with private balcony):	0
Lifestyle:	Standard	Cabins (wheelchair accessible):	0
Cruise Line:Murmansk Shipping/Quark Expeditions		Cabin Current:	220-volt
Former Names:	-	Full-Service Dining Rooms:	1
Builder:	Wartsila (Finland)	Elevators:	0
Original Cost:	n/a	Casino (gaming tables):	No
Entered Service:	December 1980	Slot Machines:	No
Registry:	Russia	Swimming Pools (outdoors):	0
Length (ft/m):	434.6/132.49	Swimming Pools (indoors):	1
Beam (ft/m):	86.9/26.50	Whirlpools:	0
Draft (ft/m):	27.8/8.50	Fitness Center:	Yes
Propulsion/Propellers:	Diesel-electric (18,270kW)/3	Sauna/Steam Room:	Yes-2/No
Passenger Decks:	4	Massage:	No
Total Crew:	90	Lecture/Film Room:	No
Passengers (lower beds/all berths):	106/113	Library:	Yes
Pass. Space Ratio (lower beds/all berths):115.9/108.7		Zodiacs:	4
Crew/Pass. Ratio (lower beds/all berths):	1.1/1.2	Helicopter Pad:	Yes (1 helicopter)
Navigation Officers:	Russian	Classification Society:	RS
Cabins (total):	53		
Size Range (sq ft/sq m):	150.6–269.0/14.0–25.0		
Cabins (outside view):	53	**OVERALL SCORE:**	**1,287**
Cabins (interior/no view):	0	(OUT OF A POSSIBLE 2,000 POINTS)	
Cabins (for one person):	0		

Accommodation: The cabins, in four price categories, are spread over four decks, and all have private facilities and plenty of storage space. Although nothing special, they are quite comfortable, with two lower berths, large closets, a small desk, and portholes that actually open. The bathrooms are practical and utilitarian.

Dining: The dining room is plain and unpretentious. It is totally nonsmoking; there is a single seating, with assigned tables. Features real hearty food in generous portions (with an emphasis on fish), served by waitresses in a dining room that is comfortable and practical. European chefs oversee the cuisine and its presentation, and Western foods are brought in specifically for these chartered voyages.

Other Comments: *Kapitan Dranitsyn* is a real, working icebreaker, one of a fleet of ten that were built in Finland to exacting Russian specifications for arctic and polar work, and now available for various charters. The ship has an incredibly thick hull, forthright profile, and a bow like an inverted whale head. The funnel is placed just about amidships, and the accommodation block is located forward of it. An open bridge policy allows passengers to visit the bridge at almost any time. Strong diesel-electric engines (delivering 24,000 horsepower) allow her to plow through ice several feet thick. There is plenty of open deck and observation space. Has a heated (but very small) indoor swimming pool.

There is always a team of excellent naturalists and lecturers aboard. Light but warm parkas are provided for passengers, who really become participants in this kind of hands-on expedition cruising. A helicopter is usually carried and can be used by all passengers (as well as a fleet of Zodiac landing craft) for sightseeing forays.

If you are someone who feels the call of the wild, this vessel is particularly good for tough expedition cruising and will provide thoroughly practical surroundings, a friendly, experienced, and dedicated crew, and excellent value for the money in true expeditionary style. An expedition cruise logbook is typically provided at the end of each cruise for all passengers — a superb keepsake that acts as a reminder of what's been seen and done during the course of your expedition adventure cruise.

Weak Points: The ship offers only basic cruise amenities and very spartan, no-frills decor. Also, you should be prepared for some tremendous roaring noise when the ship breaks through pack ice.

Kapitan Khlebnikov
★★★ +

Small Ship:	12,288 tons	Cabins (with private balcony):	0
Lifestyle:	Standard	Cabins (wheelchair accessible):	0
Cruise Line: Murmansk Shipping/Quark Expeditions		Cabin Current:	220-volt
Former Names:	-	Full-Service Dining Rooms:	1
Builder:	Wartsila (Finland)	Elevators:	1
Original Cost:	n/a	Casino (gaming tables):	No
Entered Service:	1981	Slot Machines:	No
Registry:	Russia	Swimming Pools (outdoors):	0
Length (ft/m):	434.6/132.49	Swimming Pools (indoors):	1
Beam (ft/m):	87.7/26.75	Whirlpools:	0
Draft (ft/m):	27.8/8.50	Fitness Center:	Yes
Propulsion/Propellers: Diesel-electric (18,270kW)/3		Sauna/Steam Room:	Yes-2/No
Passenger Decks:	4	Massage:	No
Total Crew:	60	Lecture/Film Room:	No
Passengers (lower beds/all berths):	108/114	Library:	Yes
Pass. Space Ratio(lower beds/all berths):113.7/107.7		Zodiacs:	4
Crew/Pass. Ratio (lower beds/all berths):	1.8/1.9	Helicopter Pad:	Yes (1 helicopter)
Navigation Officers:	Russian	Classification Society:	RS
Cabins (total):	54		
Size Range (sq ft/sq m):	150.6–269.0/14.0–25.0		
Cabins (outside view):	54		
Cabins (interior/no view):	0		
Cabins (for one person):	0		

OVERALL SCORE: **1,287**

(OUT OF A POSSIBLE 2,000 POINTS)

Accommodation: The cabins, in four price categories, are spread over four decks, and all have private facilities and plenty of storage space. Although nothing special, they are quite comfortable, with two lower berths, large closets, a small desk, and portholes that actually open. The bathrooms are practical and utilitarian.

Dining: The dining room is plain and unpretentious. It is totally nonsmoking; there is a single seating, with assigned tables. Features real hearty food in generous portions (with an emphasis on fish), served by waitresses in a dining room that is comfortable and practical. European chefs oversee the cuisine and its presentation, and Western foods are brought in specifically for these chartered voyages.

Other Comments: *Kapitan Khlebnikov* is a real, working icebreaker, one of a fleet of ten that were built in Finland to exacting Russian specifications for arctic and polar work, and now available for various charters. The ship has an incredible 45-mm-thick hull, a forthright profile, and a bow that looks like an inverted whale head. The funnel is placed amidships, and the accommodation block is placed forward. An open bridge policy allows passengers to visit the bridge at almost any time. Strong diesel-electric engines (delivering 24,000 horsepower) allow her to plow through ice several feet thick. There is plenty of open deck and observation space. Has a heated (but very small) indoor swimming pool.

There is always a team of excellent naturalists and lecturers aboard, something in which Quark Expeditions excels. Light but warm parkas are provided for passengers, who really become participants in this kind of hands-on expedition cruising. A helicopter is usually carried and can be used (as well as a fleet of Zodiac landing craft) by all passengers for sightseeing forays.

If you are someone who feels the call of the wild, this vessel is particularly good for tough expedition cruising and will provide thoroughly practical surroundings, a friendly, experienced, and dedicated crew, and excellent value for the money in true expeditionary style. An expedition cruise logbook is typically provided at the end of each cruise for all passengers — a superb keepsake that acts as a reminder of what's been seen and done during the course of your expedition adventure cruise.

Weak Points: The ship offers only basic cruise amenities and very spartan, no-frills decor. Also, you should be prepared for some tremendous roaring noise when the ship breaks through pack ice.

331

Kong Harald
★★★ +

Small Ship:	11,200 tons	Cabins (wheelchair accessible):	0
Lifestyle:	Standard	Cabin Current:	220-volt
Cruise Line:	Norwegian Coastal Voyages (TFDS)	Full-Service Dining Rooms:	1
Former Names:	-	Elevators:	2
Builder:	Stralsund Wolkverft (Norway)	Casino (gaming tables):	No
Original Cost:	n/a	Slot Machines:	No
Entered Service:	1993	Swimming Pools (outdoors):	0
Registry:	Norway	Swimming Pools (inside):	0
Length(ft/m):	399.6/121.8	Whirlpools:	0
Beam (ft/m):	62.9/19.2	Fitness Center:	Yes
Draft (ft/m):	16.0/4.9	Sauna/Steam Room:	Yes/No
Navigation officers:	Norwegian	Massage:	No
Total Crew:	70	Self-Service Launderette:	Yes
Passengers (lower beds/all berths):	446/490	Dedictated Cinema:	No
Pass. Space Ratio (lower beds/all berths):	25.1/22.8	Library:	Yes
Crew/Pass. Ratio (lower beds/all berths):	6.3/7.0	Classification Society:	Det Norske Veritas
Cabins (total):	223		
Size Range:	n/a		
Cabins (outside view):	179		
Cabins (interior/no view):	44	**OVERALL SCORE:**	**1,285**
Cabins (for one person):	0		
Cabins (with private balcony):	0	**(OUT OF A POSSIBLE 2,000 POINTS)**	

Accommodation: There are nine grades of cabin, including three wheelchair-accessible cabins (one of the ship's two elevators accommodates a wheelchair). Double beds are only available in the two suites; all other cabins have beds and berths that cannot be moved. Some cabins also have an additional third (upper) berth, and a number of cabins are available for single occupancy, albeit with a price premium. All cabins have a 220-volt outlet, so take adapters and converters if you need to.

Dining: There is one main dining room (the Martha-Salen Restaurant — no smoking allowed), and tables are assigned when you embark. Three meals each day are included in the cruise fare: Breakfast and lunch (featuring the famous Norwegian "cold table") are self-serve buffet-style meals, while dinner is a sit-down affair, with three courses. Additionally, there is the Roald Amundsen Café, which is open 24 hours, where snacks and light meals can be purchased.

Other Comments: The Norwegian Coastal Voyage is a service that was started in 1863. It is jointly operated by two companies: Ofotens og Vesteraalen Dampskibsselskab (OVDS) and Troms Fylkes Dampskibsselskab (TFDS). The complete journey, of 1,250 nautical miles, takes in 34 ports of call in a 12-day roundtrip voyage between Bergen and Kirkenes (on the border with Russia), above the Arctic Circle (where a special "Crossing the Arctic Circle" ceremony welcomes newcomers). The journey can also be done in a one-way voyage that takes seven days (northbound) or six days (southbound). The ships carry passengers as well as mail and other cargo.

Perhaps you will be able to peek at the midnight sun (mid-May to late June, north of the Arctic Circle), experience the northern lights (aurora borealis, mostly seen during winter months, and only when the atmospheric conditions are right), and be part of the daily life of the hardy Norwegians. Approximately 60% of the passengers will be Norwegian/Scandinavian/European, while the rest will be a mix of North American and other nationalities. Although the passenger bed capacity is quoted, note that many additional passengers be on board as day passengers, sailing between two coastal ports — the ship is the equivalent of a seagoing bus for the coastal commuters. As for the weather, the west coast of Norway is warmed by the Gulf Stream, and temperatures will be similar to those found in New England.

The rates vary by season, cabin location, and whether the ship is of the "new generation" (*Kong Harald, Nordkapp, Nordlys, Nordnorge, Polarlys, Richard With*), the "mid-generation" (*Narvik, Midnatsol, Vesteralen*), or the "traditional" (*Harald Jarl, Lofoten*) type ships, the scenery is what the voyage is all about. Senior citizens (those age 67 and over) qualify for a special discount.

Adult couples, single travelers, and families with children wanting to sail along the coast of Norway and experience the area's natural beauty are best suited to this scenic cruise. It's ideal for anyone who doesn't need entertainment or mindless parlor games but wants to relax and unwind, enjoys being close to nature, and is probably a bit of an adventurer. There will be an interesting mix of passengers — it's a good way to meet new people and make new friends from different countries.

The dress code is casual and comfortable — layered clothing is the best and wisest choice. The currency is the Norwegian Krone.

Norwegian coast and fjords cruises typically consist of a 7-day (northbound) voyage between Bergen and Kirkenes, Norway; or a 6-day (southbound) voyage between Kirkenes and Bergen, Norway; or a 12-day roundtrip voyage.

Weak Points: The ship does not have stabilizers, so you should expect some movement when the weather is inclement or unkind. Drink prices are extremely high — the same as ashore in Norway. The cabins are small, and the bathrooms are really tiny. Although not needed during the winter, there is little outdoor deck space considering the number of passengers carried.

Kristina Regina
★★ +

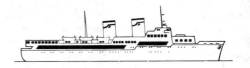

Small Ship:	4,295 tons	Cabins (with private balcony):	0
Lifestyle:	Standard	Cabins (wheelchair accessible):	0
Cruise Line:	Kristina Cruises	Cabin Current:	220-volt
Former Names:	*Borea, Bore*	Full-Service Dining Rooms:	2 (1 for buffets/
Builder:	Oskarshamn Shipyard (Sweden)	/	1 à la carte)
Original Cost:	n/a	Elevators:	0
Entered Service:	1960/1987	Casino (gaming tables):	No
Registry:	Finland	Slot Machines:	No
Length (ft/m):	327.4/99.80	Swimming Pools (outdoors):	0
Beam (ft/m):	50.1/15.30	Swimming Pools (indoors):	0
Draft (ft/m):	17.3/5.30	Whirlpools:	0
Propulsion/Propellers:	Diesel (3,233kW)/2	Fitness Center:	No
Passenger Decks:	6	Sauna/Steam Room:	Yes/No
Total Crew:	55	Massage:	No
Passengers (lower beds/all berths):	290/370	Self-Service Launderette:	No
Pass. Space Ratio (lower beds/all berths):	14.8/11.6	Dedicated Cinema:	No
Crew/Pass. Ratio (lower beds/all berths):	5.2/6.7	Library:	Yes
Navigation Officers:	Finnish	Classification Society:	Lloyd's Register
Cabins (total):	145		
Size Range (sq ft/sq m):	64.5–124.8/6.0–11.6		
Cabins (outside view):	112		
Cabins (interior/no view):	33		
Cabins (for one person):	0		

OVERALL SCORE: 1,052
(OUT OF A POSSIBLE 2,000 POINTS)

Accommodation: There is a wide assortment of cabin sizes and configurations. Some cabins have a queen-size bed; others have two beds, while some have upper and lower berths. All cabins have shower and toilet, radio, telephone, but not much else, and they are really tiny, as are the bathrooms. As the cabins have very little closet and drawer space, do take only what's really necessary. There are also five allergy-free cabins, as well as several interconnecting cabins.

Dining: The dining room is charming and features continental (European) cuisine, with a distinct accent on fish, seafood, and fresh berries. The breads and cheeses are also good. There is single seating at assigned tables, and fine, hearty, and friendly service comes with a smile.

Other Comments: This lovely old-world ship was built specifically for close-in northern European coastal and archipelago cruises and was extensively refurbished in 1990 and 2001. She is one of the few ships left today that has two funnels, and is owned by a single family.

Exterior features include a wraparound wooden promenade deck outdoors. There are few public rooms (there is, however, a small conference room), but she does have some beautiful hardwoods and lots of brass features throughout her interior decor. The Scandinavian artwork is also quite fascinating. The ship exudes old-world charm. It has a well-designed auditorium that doubles as a cinema.

In the ship's latest refit and refurbishment (undertaken in 2000), a more expansive health center was installed, replacing many cabins that formerly occupied this now larger space.

The onboard currency is both the US dollar and the Finnish mark. All nonalcoholic beverages are complementary during cruises.

Her itineraries take her to the Baltic States and Russia, into White Sea ports, and she also occasionally cruises to Scotland.

Le Levant
★★★★ +

Small Ship:	3,504 tons	Cabins (for one person):	0
Lifestyle:	Premium	Cabins (with private balcony):	0
Cruise Line:	Ponant Cruises/Classical Cruises	Cabins (wheelchair accessible):	0
Former Names:	-	Cabin Current:	110/220-volt
Builder:	Leroux & Lotz (France)	Full-Service Dining Rooms:	2
Original Cost:	$35 million	Elevators:	1
Entered Service:	January 1999	Casino (gaming tables):	No
Registry:	Wallis and Fortuna	Slot Machines:	No
Length (ft/m):	328.0/100.00	Swimming Pools (outdoors):	1
Beam (ft/m):	45.9/14.00	Swimming Pools (indoors):	0
Draft (ft/m):	11.4/3.50	Whirlpools:	0
Propulsion/Propellers:	Diesel (3,000 kW)/2	Fitness Center:	Yes
Passenger Decks:	5	Sauna/Steam Room:	No/Yes
Total Crew:	50	Massage:	No
Passengers (lower beds/all berths):	90/90	Self-Service Launderette:	No
Pass. Space Ratio (lower beds/all berths):	38.9/38.9	Dedicated Cinema:	No
Crew/Pass. Ratio (lower beds/all berths):	1.8/1.8	Library:	Yes
Navigation Officers:	French	Classification Society:	Bureau Veritas
Cabins (total):	45		
Size Range (sq ft/sq m):	199.1/18.5	**OVERALL SCORE:**	**1,609**
Cabins (outside view):	45		
Cabins (interior/no view):	0	(OUT OF A POSSIBLE 2,000 POINTS)	

Accommodation: There are 45 ocean-view cabins (the brochure says "suites") and all are located mid-ships and forward, in five different price categories. Each cabin features a large ocean-view window, inlaid wood furniture and accenting, designer fabrics, two beds that will convert to a queen-size bed, a TV, VCR, refrigerator, personal safe, and personal amenity kits in the marble-appointed bathrooms, all of which feature a shower (there are no cabins with bathtubs).

Dining: There are two dining rooms. The main one is a wood paneled Dining Room (one seating only), which has round and oval tables; the second is the more informal Verandah Restaurant, with a panoramic view overlooking the stern. Dining is in open seating, with unassigned seats, so you can dine with whomever you wish. Complimentary wines are included for lunch and dinner, and the cuisine is, naturally, classic French.

Other Comments: *Le Levant* is a new high-class vessel that looks like a streamlined private mega-yacht and has quite a stunning low profile appearance with its royal blue (ice-hardened) hull and blue-and-white superstructure. She has two slim funnels that extend over port and starboard sides to carry any soot away from the vessel (somewhat like the design of the first four former Renaissance Cruises vessels). Built in a yacht shipyard in St. Malo, France. An "open bridge" policy is featured, so that passengers may visit the bridge whenever they wish (except when maneuvering in difficult conditions).

She sports a stern "marina" platform for SCUBA diving, snorkeling, or swimming. Two special landing craft are carried for shore visits, hidden in the stern, as well as six inflatable Zodiacs runabouts for landings in "soft" expedition areas such as the Amazon.

Inside, the vessel features contemporary, clean, and uncluttered decor, and all the facilities of a private yacht. The public rooms are elegant and refined, with much use of wood trim and accenting throughout. Particularly pleasing and inviting is the wood-paneled library, a feature so often lacking aboard many ships today. There is also one grand salon, which accommodates all passengers, and is used by day as a lecture room and by night as the main lounge/bar. A resident SCUBA dive master is aboard for all Caribbean sailings. In addition, Classical Cruises features life-enrichment lecturers aboard each cruise, as well as tour leaders.

This ship is presently under charter to the New York-based Classical Cruises, who operate her in some offbeat destinations and cruise regions. During the summer of 2001 she was in the Great Lakes, sailing between Toronto and Chicago, (her pencil-slim beam allows her to navigate the locks). During the fall she heads to Canada/New England, and even as far north as Hudson Bay and the Northern Territories of Canada. During the winter months she heads to the Caribbean and South America.

The company also owns and operates *Le Ponant*, a chic ultra-sleek sailing vessel. This is all-inclusive cruising, with all port charges, gratuities, shore excursions, and port charges included in the cruise fare. The crew is almost entirely French.

Weak Points: Although you can walk around the uppermost accommodation deck, there really is no wraparound promenade deck. Sadly, none of the cabins has a private balcony.

DID YOU KNOW...?

...that the first "en suite" rooms (with private bathroom in cabin) were on board Cunard Line's *Campania* of 1893?

...that the first single-berth cabins built as such were aboard Cunard Line's *Campania* of 1893?

...that the first liner to offer private terraces with their first-class suites was *Normandie* in 1935 (the Trouville Suite had four bedrooms as well as a private terrace)?

...that the first ships to feature private balconies were the *Saturnia* and *Vulcania* in the early 1900s?

...that the first ship to be fitted with interior plumbing was the 6,283-tonne *Normandie* of 1883?

...that the first ship to be fitted with an internal electric lighting system was aboard the Inman liner *City of Berlin* in 1879?

...that cruising today is not the same as it was in the nineteenth century? On the first cruise ships there was little entertainment, and passengers had to clean their own cabins! Orders enforced on all ships sailing from Great Britain in 1849, for example, instructed all passengers to be in their beds by 10pm!

Le Ponant
★★★★

Small Ship:	1,489 tons	Size Range (sq ft/sq m):	139.9/13.0
Lifestyle:	Premium	Cabins (outside view):	32
Cruise Line:	Ponant Cruises	Cabins (interior/no view):	0
Former Names:	-	Cabins (for one person):	0
Builder:	SFCN (France)	Cabins (with private balcony):	0
Original Cost:	n/a	Cabins (wheelchair accessible):	0
Entered Service:	1991	Cabin Current:	220-volt
Registry:	France	Full-Service Dining Rooms:	1
Length (ft/m):	288.7/88.00	Elevators:	No
Beam (ft/m):	39.3/12.00	Casino (gaming tables):	No
Draft (ft/m):	13.1/4.00	Slot Machines:	No
Type of Vessel:	High tech sail-cruiser	Swimming Pools (outdoors):	0
No. of Masts:	3	Whirlpools:	0
Sail Area (sq.ft/sq.m):	16,150/1,500	Fitness Center:	Yes
Main Propulsion:	a) engine/b) sails	Sauna/Steam Room:	No/No
Propulsion/Propellers:	Diesel/sail power/1	Massage:	No
Passenger Decks:	3	Self-Service Launderette:	No
Total Crew:	30	Library:	Yes
Passengers (lower beds/all berths):	64/67	Classification Society:	Lloyd's Register
Pass. Space Ratio (lower beds/all berths):	23.2/22.2		
Crew/Pass. Ratio (lower beds/all berths):	2.1/2.2	**OVERALL SCORE:**	**1,540**
Navigation Officers:	French		
Cabins (total):	32	**(OUT OF A POSSIBLE 2,000 POINTS)**	

Accommodation: Crisp, clean, blond woods and pristine white cabins feature double or twin beds, mini-bar, personal safe, and private bathroom. All cabins feature portholes, artwork, and a refrigerator. There is a limited amount of storage space, however, and few drawers. The cabin bathrooms are quite small, but efficiently designed.

Dining: The lovely Karukera dining room (open seating) features complimentary wines and good food. There is fresh fish every day, and meals are true "affaires gastonomiques." There is also a charming outdoor café under canvas sailcloth awning.

Other Comments: Ultra sleek, very efficient, this latest generation of sail-cruise ship has three masts that rise 54.7 feet (16.7 meters) above the water line. This captivating ship has plenty of room on her open decks for sunbathing. Water sports facilities include an aft marina platform, windsurfers, water-ski boat, and SCUBA and snorkel equipment.

Very elegant, no glitz interior design is clean, stylish, and functional, and ultra-high-tech throughout. Three public lounges have pastel decor, soft colors, and great European flair.

One price fits all. Marketed mainly to young, sophisticated French-speaking passengers who love yachting and the sea. *Tres* French, and *tres* chic. The company also has a stunning mega-yacht cruise vessel, *Le Levant*. Gratuities are not "required," but they are expected.

Legacy
★★ +

Small Ship:	1,740 tons	Cabins (outside view):	46
Lifestyle:	Standard	Cabins (interior/no view):	15
Cruise Line:	Windjammer Barefoot Cruises	Cabins (for one person):	0
Former Names:	*France II*	Cabins (with private balcony):	0
Builder:	Forges et al Mediterranée du Havre	Cabins (wheelchair accessible):	0
	(France)	Cabin Current:	110-volt
Original Cost:	n/a	Full-Service Dining Rooms:	1
Entered Service:	1959/1997	Elevators:	0
Registry:	Equatorial Guinea	Casino (gaming tables):	No
Length (ft/m):	294.0/89.6	Slot Machines:	No
Beam (ft/m):	40.0/12.1	Swimming Pools (outdoors):	0
Draft (ft/m):	23.0/7.0	Whirlpools:	0
Type of Vessel:	Barkentine	Fitness Center:	0
No. of Masts:	4	Sauna/Steam Room:	No/No
Sail Area (sq ft/sq m):	19,900/1,848.7	Massage:	No
Main Propulsion:	sail power	Self-Service Launderette:	No
Propulsion/Propellers:	Diesel/1	Library:	Yes
Passenger Decks:	4	Classification Society:	American Bureau of
Total Crew:	43		Shipping
Passengers (lower beds/all berths):	122/122		
Pass. Space Ratio (lower beds/all berths):	14.2/14.2		
Crew/Pass. Ratio (lower beds/all berths):	2.8/2.8		
Navigation Officers:	International	**OVERALL SCORE:**	**1,029**
Cabins (total):	61		
Size Range (sq ft/m):	75.0–159.0/6.9–14.7	**(OUT OF A POSSIBLE 2,000 POINTS)**	

Accommodation: There are eight grades of accommodation (Burke's Berth, Admiral DeLuxe, Admiral Suite, Commodore Double, Commodore Triple, Ensign Cabin, Standard Cabin, and Standard Single). Except for the top three grades, all other cabins are dimensionally challenged, particularly when compared to regular cruise ships. Remember, however, that this is a very casual cruise experience and you will need so few clothes anyway. All are equipped with upper and lower berths, and most of them are quite narrow.

Dining: There is one dining room, and the meals are all very simple in style and service, with little choice and only the most basic presentation. Breakfast is served on board, as is dinner, while lunch could be either on board or at a beach, picnic-style. Wine is included with dinner.

Other Comments: When built, this barkentine with four masts served as a meteorological research and exploration vessel for the French government before being converted into a traditional tall ship by Windjammer Barefoot Cruises in 1998/1999.

Aboard one of the Windjammer Barefoot Cruises' fleet you can let the crew do all the work, or you can lend a hand at the helm yourself, if you feel so inclined. One neat thing to do is just to sit or lie in the nets at the bows of the vessel, without a care in the world — it's a great feeling.

The mood is free and easy, the ships are equipped very simply, and only the most casual clothes are required (T-shirts and shorts), and shoes are optional, although you may need them if you go off in one of the ports. Quite possibly the most used item will be your bathing suit — better take more than one! Smoking is allowed only on the open decks.

Entertainment in the evenings consists of you and the crew. You can put on a toga, or create a pirate outfit and join in the fun. This is cruising free 'n' easy style — none of that programmed big-ship production show stuff here.

Jammin' aboard a Windjammer (first-time passengers are called "crewmates" while repeat passengers are called "jammers") is no-frills cruising (it could be called an "anti-cruise") in a no-nonsense, friendly environment, for the young at heart and those who don't need programmed activities. It's best suited to young couples and (many) singles that seek sun, sea, sand, and other things, including rum swizzles, and lovers of old sailing ships.

It's all about the romance of being at sea under sail. You can even lend a hand with the sails if you wish. Those that enjoy beaches, SCUBA diving, and snorkeling around the Caribbean will be best suited to a Windjammer Barefoot Cruises journey. This ship can anchor in neat little Caribbean hideaways that larger (regular) cruise ships can't get near.

Although itineraries (islands) are provided in the brochure, the captain actually decides which islands to go to on any given cruise, depending on sea and weather conditions. Legacy features year-round cruises in the British and US Virgin Islands. Brochure rates might seem inexpensive, but you'll need to add on the airfare in order to get the true cost.

Legacy operates Caribbean cruises (from Fajardo, Puerto Rico). Other tall ships in the fleet include *Flying Cloud, Mandalay, Polynesia,* and *Yankee Clipper.*

Weak Points: It's extremely casual. There's very little room per passenger. Everything is basic, basic, basic. Tips to the crew are suggested — at $50 per week!

Legend of the Seas
★★★★

Large Ship:	69,130 tons	Cabins (for one person):	0
Lifestyle:	Standard	Cabins (with private balcony):	231
Cruise Line:	Royal Caribbean International	Cabins (wheelchair accessible):	17
Former Names:	-	Cabin Current:	110/220-volt
Builder:	Chantiers de l'Atlantique (France)	Full-Service Dining Rooms:	1
Original Cost:	$325 million	Elevators:	11
Entered Service:	May 1995	Casino (gaming tables):	Yes
Registry:	Liberia	Slot Machines:	Yes
Length (ft/m):	867.0/264.2	Swimming Pools (outdoors):	2 (1 with sliding roof)
Beam (ft/m):	105.0/32.0	Swimming Pools (indoors):	0
Draft (ft/m):	23.9/7.3	Whirlpools:	4
Propulsion/Propellers:	Diesel (40,200kW)/2	Fitness Center:	Yes
Passenger Decks:	11	Sauna/Steam Room:	Yes/Yes
Total Crew:	720	Massage:	Yes
Passengers (lower beds/all berths):	1,800/2,076	Self-Service Launderette:	No
Pass. Space Ratio (lower beds/all berths):	38.3/33.2	Dedicated Cinema:	No
Crew/Pass. Ratio (lower beds/all berths):	2.5/2.8	Library:	Yes
Navigation Officers:	Norwegian	Classification Society:	Det Norske Veritas
Cabins (total):	900		
Size Range (sq ft/sq m):	137.7–1,147.4/12.8–106.6	**OVERALL SCORE:**	**1,511**
Cabins (outside view):	575		
Cabins (interior/no view):	325	**(OUT OF A POSSIBLE 2,000 POINTS)**	

Accommodation: Royal Caribbean International has realized that small cabins do not make passengers happy. The company, therefore, set about designing a ship with much larger standard cabins than in any of the company's previous vessels (except sister ship *Splendour of the Seas*). Some cabins on Deck 8 also have a larger door for wheelchair access in addition to the 17 cabins for the physically challenged, and the ship is very accessible, with ample ramped areas and sloping decks. All cabins have a sitting area and beds that convert to double configuration, and there is ample closet and drawer space, although there is not much space around the bed (and the showers could have been better).

Cabins with balconies have glass railings rather than steel/wood to provide less intrusive sight lines. The largest accommodation, named the Royal Suite, is a superb living space for those that can afford the best. It is beautifully designed, finely decorated, and features a baby grand piano, whirlpool bathtub, and other fine amenities. Several quiet sitting areas are located adjacent to the best cabins amidships. Seventeen cabin categories is really too many. Unfortunately, there are no cabins for singles.

Dining: The two-decks-high dining room has dramatic glass side walls, so many passengers both upstairs and downstairs can see both the ocean and each other in reflection (it would, perhaps, have been even better located at the stern), but it is quite noisy when full (call it atmosphere). There are two seatings. The dining operation is well orchestrated, with emphasis on highly programmed (insensitive), extremely hurried service that many find intrusive.

Most nights are themed (typically French, Oriental, Italian, Caribbean, American), as they have been for years, with waiters and busboys in appropriate costumes. The food is typical of hotel banquet catering. The menu descriptions make the food sound better than it is, which is consistently average, mostly disappointing and without much taste. However, a decent selection of light meals is provided, and a vegetarian menu is available. The selection of breads, rolls, fruits, and cheeses is quite poor, however, and should be upgraded. There is no good caviar; special orders, tableside carving, and flambeau items are not offered. One thing this company does once each cruise is to feature the "Galley Buffet," whereby passengers go through a section of the galley picking up food for a midnight buffet.

The wine list is not very extensive, but the prices are moderate. The waiters, many of whom are from Caribbean countries, are perhaps overly friendly for some tastes — particularly on the last night of the cruise, when tips are expected.

There is also a cavernous indoor-outdoor café, located towards the bow and above the bridge, as well as a good-size snack area, which provide more informal dining choices.

Other Comments: This ship's contemporary profile looks somewhat unbalanced (but it soon grows on you), and she does have a nicely tiered stern. The pool deck amidships overhangs the hull to provide an extremely wide deck, while still allowing the ship to navigate the Panama Canal. With engines placed amidships, there is little noise and no noticeable vibration, and the ship has an operating speed of up to 24 knots.

The interior decor is quite colorful, but too glitzy for European tastes. The outside light is brought inside in many places, with an extensive amount of glass area that provides contact with sea and air (there is, in fact, over two acres of glass). Features an innovative single-level sliding glass roof (not a magrodome) over the more formal setting of one of two swimming pools, thus providing a multi-activity, all-weather, indoor-outdoor area, called the Solarium. The glass roof provides shelter for the Roman-style pool and adjacent health and fitness facilities (which are superb), and slides aft to cover the miniature golf course when required (both cannot be covered at the same time, however).

Golfers might enjoy the 18-hole, 6,000 sq ft (558 sq m), miniature golf course. It has the topography of a real golf course, complete with trees, foliage, grass, bridges, water hazards, and lighting for play at night. The holes themselves are 155–230 sq ft (14–21 sq m).

Inside, two full entertainment decks are sandwiched between five decks full of cabins. The tiered and balconied show lounge, which covers two decks, is expansive and has excellent sight lines and very comfortable seats. Several large-scale production shows are provided here, and the orchestra pit can be raised or lowered as required. A multi-tiered seven-decks-high atrium lobby, complete with a huge stainless steel sculpture, connects with the impressive Viking Crown Lounge via glass-walled elevators. The casino is really expansive, overly glitzy and absolutely packed. The library, outside of which is a bust of Shakespeare, is a fine facility, with over 2,000 books.

There is, unfortunately, no separate cinema. The casino could be somewhat disorienting, with its mirrored walls and lights flashing everywhere, although it is no different from those found in Las Vegas fantasy gaming halls. As with any large ship, you can expect to find yourself standing in lines for embarkation, disembarkation, buffets, and shore excursions, although the company does its best to minimize such lines.

Representing natural evolution, this ship is an outstanding new cruise vessel for the many repeat passengers who enjoy Royal Caribbean International's consistent delivery of a well-integrated, fine-tuned, very comfortable, and well-liked product. With larger cabins, excellent decor, and contemporary style, *Legend of the Seas* has taken Royal Caribbean International passengers, most of whom are typically from middle-America, into a much upgraded cruise experience from that of the company's other ships. The ship provides a very cost-effective cruise for all ages.

Weak Points: Standing in line for embarkation, disembarkation, shore tenders, and self-serve buffet meals is an inevitable aspect of cruising aboard all large ships.

Lofoten
★★

Small Ship:	2,621 tons	Cabins (with private balcony):	0
Lifestyle:	Standard	Cabins (wheelchair accessible):	0
Cruise Line:	Norwegian Coastal Voyages (OVDS)	Cabin Current:	220-volt
Former Names:	-	Full-Service Dining Rooms:	1
Builder:	Akers Mek (Norway)	Elevators:	0
Original Cost:	n/a	Casino (gaming tables):	No
Entered Service:	1964	Slot Machines:	No
Registry:	Norway	Swimming Pools (outdoors):	0
Length (ft/m):	286.7/87.4	Swimming Pools (inside):	0
Beam (ft/m):	44.2/13.5	Whirlpools:	0
Draft (ft/m):	15.0/4.5	Fitness Center:	No
Total Crew:	40	Sauna/Steam Room:	No/No
Passengers (lower beds/all berths):	180/180	Massage:	No
Pass. Space Ratio (lower beds/all berths):	14.5/14.5	Self-Service Launderette:	No
Crew/Pass. Ratio (lower beds/all berths):	4.5/4.5	Dedicated Cinema:	No
Navigation Officers:	Norwegian	Library:	No
Cabins (total):	90	Classification Society:	Det Norske Veritas
Size Range (sq ft/sq m):	n/a		
Cabins (outside view):	25		

OVERALL SCORE: 940
(OUT OF A POSSIBLE 2,000 POINTS)

Cabins (interior/no view): 65
Cabins (for one person): 0

Accommodation: All cabins feature a mix of lower beds, lower berths, and upper berths (there are no cabins with double bed). Bathrooms have a shower and toilet (note that some interior cabins on the lowest deck do not have private facilities and share a shower room). All cabins have a 220-volt outlet, so take adapters and converters if you need to.

Dining: There is one dining room (no smoking allowed), and tables are assigned when you embark. Three meals each day are included in the cruise fare: Breakfast and lunch (featuring the famous Norwegian "cold table") are self-serve buffet-style meals, while dinner is a sit-down affair, with three courses. Additionally, there is a cafeteria, open 24 hours, where snacks and light meals can be purchased.

Other Comments: The Norwegian Coastal Voyage is a service that was started in 1863. It is jointly operated by two companies: Ofotens og Vesteraalen Dampskibsselskab (OVDS) and Troms Fylkes Dampskibsselskab (TFDS). The complete journey, of 1,250 nautical miles, takes in 34 ports of call in a 12-day roundtrip voyage between Bergen and Kirkenes (on the border with Russia), above the Arctic Circle (where a special "Crossing the Arctic Circle" ceremony welcomes newcomers). The journey can also be done in a one-way voyage that takes seven days (northbound) or six days (southbound). The ships carry passengers as well as mail and other cargo.

Perhaps you will be able to peek at the midnight sun (mid-May to late June, north of the Arctic Circle), experience the Northern Lights (Aurora Borealis, mostly seen during winter months, and only when the atmospheric conditions are right), and be part of the daily life of the hardy Norwegians. Approximately 60% of the passengers will be Norwegian/Scandinavian/European, while the rest will be a mix of North American and other nationalities. Although the passenger bed capacity is quoted, note that many additional passengers may be on board as day passengers, sailing between two coastal ports — the ship is the equivalent of a seagoing bus for the coastal commuters. As for the weather, the west coast of Norway is warmed by the Gulf Stream, and temperatures will be similar to those found in New England.

Best suited to adult couples, single travelers, and families with children wanting to cruise along the coast of Norway and experience the area's natural beauty. It's ideal for anyone who doesn't need entertainment or mindless parlor games, but wants to relax and unwind, enjoys being close to nature, and is probably a bit of an adventurer. This is an excellent way to experience the beautiful coastline of Norway and its fascinating coastal towns. There will be an interesting mix of passengers — it's a good way to meet new people and make new friends from different countries.

The rates vary by season, cabin location, and whether the ship is of the "new generation" (*Kong Harald, Nordkapp, Nordlys, Nordnorge, Polarlys, Richard With*), the "mid-generation" (*Narvik, Midnatsol, Vesteralen*), or the "traditional" (*Harald Jarl, Lofoten*) type ships. Senior citizens (those age 67 and over) qualify for a special discount.

The dress code is casual and comfortable—layered clothing is recommended. The currency is the Norwegian krone.

Operates Norwegian coast and fjords cruises (year-round): 7-day (northbound) voyage between Bergen and Kirkenes, Norway; or a 6-day (southbound) voyage between Kirkenes and Bergen, Norway; or a 12-day roundtrip voyage. The ship also has space for four cars.

Weak Points: The ship does not have stabilizers, so you should expect some movement when the weather is inclement or unkind. Drinks prices are extremely high—the same as ashore in Norway. The cabins are small, and the bathrooms are really tiny. Although not needed during the winter, there is little outdoor deck space considering the number of passengers carried.

Maasdam
★★★★

Large Ship:	55,451 tons	Cabins (for one person):	0
Lifestyle:	Premium	Cabins (with private balcony):	150
Cruise Line:	Holland America Line	Cabins (wheelchair accessible):	6
Former Names:	-	Cabin Current:	110/220-volt
Builder:	Fincantieri (Italy)	Full-Service Dining Rooms:	1
Original Cost:	$215 million	Elevators:	12
Entered Service:	December 1993	Casino (gaming tables):	Yes
Registry:	The Netherlands	Slot Machines:	Yes
Length (ft/m):	719.3/219.30	Swimming Pools (outdoors):	1
Beam (ft/m):	101.0/30.80	Swimming Pools (indoors):	1 (magrodome)
Draft (ft/m):	24.6/7.50	Whirlpools:	2
Propulsion/Propellers:	Diesel-electric (34,560kW)/2	Fitness Center:	Yes
Passenger Decks:	10	Sauna/Steam Room:	Yes/No
Total Crew:	557	Massage:	Yes
Passengers (lower beds/all berths):	1,266/1,627	Self-Service Launderette:	Yes
Pass. Space Ratio (lower beds/all berths):	43.8/34.0	Dedicated Cinema/Seats:	Yes/249
Crew/Pass. Ratio (lower beds/all berths):	2.2/2.9	Library:	Yes
Navigation Officers:	Dutch	Classification Society:	Lloyd's Register
Cabins (total):	632		
Size Range (sq ft/sq m):	186.2–1,124.8/17.3–104.5	**OVERALL SCORE:**	**1,533**
Cabins (outside view):	502	(OUT OF A POSSIBLE 2,000 POINTS)	
Cabins (interior/no view):	131		

Accommodation: The accommodation ranges from small interior (no view) cabins to a large penthouse suite, in 17 different categories. All cabin TVs feature CNN and TNT.

The 148 interior (no view) and 336 outside (with a view) standard cabins feature twin beds that convert to a queen-size bed, and there is a separate living space with sofa and coffee table. However, although the drawer space is generally good, the closet space is actually very tight, particularly for long cruises (although more than adequate for a seven-night cruise). The bathrooms are tiled, and compact but practical — they come with a good range of personal toiletry amenities. Bathrobes are also provided, as are hair dryers. The bathrooms are quite well laid out, but the bathtubs are small units better described as shower tubs. Note that no cabins have interconnecting doors (unlike *Ryndam, Veendam*).

On Navigation Deck, 28 suites have accommodation for up to four. These suites also feature in-suite dining as an alternative to the dining room, for private, reclusive meals. These are very spacious, tastefully decorated and well laid-out, and feature a separate living room, bedroom with two lower beds (convertible to a king-size bed), a good-size living area, dressing room, plenty of closet and drawer space, and a marble bathroom with Jacuzzi tub.

The largest accommodation of all is a penthouse suite; there is only one, located on the starboard side of Navigation Deck. It features a king-size bed, walk-in closet with superb drawer space, oversize whirlpool bath and separate shower enclosure, living room, dressing room, large private balcony, pantry, minibar/refrigerator, a guest toilet, and floor-to-ceiling windows.

Dining: The two-level dining room, located at the stern, is quite dramatic and has a grand staircase (although few seem to use it), panoramic views on three sides, and a music balcony. Fine china and cutlery are featured (although there are no fish knives). Features open seating for breakfast and lunch, and two seatings for dinner. The waiter stations in the dining room are very noisy for anyone seated adjacent to them.

Unfortunately, Holland America Line food isn't as nice as the china it's placed on. It may be adequate for most passengers who are not used to better food, but it does not match the standard found aboard other ships in the premium segment of the industry. While USDA beef is of a good quality, fowl tends to be battery-tough, and most fish is overcooked and has the consistency of a baseball bat. What are also definitely not luxurious are the endless packets of sugar, and packets (instead of glass jars) of breakfast jam, marmalade, and honey, and the poor quality teas. While these may be suitable for a family diner, they do not belong aboard a ship that claims to have "award-winning cuisine." Dessert and pastry items are of good quality (specifically for American tastes), although there is much use of canned fruits and jellies. Forget the selection of "international" cheeses.

Instead of the more formal dining room, the Lido Buffet is open for casual dinners, typically on all except the last night of each cruise, in an open-seating arrangement. Tables are set with crisp linens, flatware, and stemware. A set menu is featured, and this includes a choice of four entrees. The extensive, dual-line, self-serve Lido Buffet (one side is for smokers, the other side for nonsmokers) is also open for casual breakfasts and lunches (and dinners on most nights). There is much use of canned fruits (good for older passengers with no teeth!) and packeted items, although there are several commercial low-calorie salad dressings. The choice of cheeses (and accompanying crackers) is very poor. The beverage station is no better than those found in family outlets ashore in the US. In addition, a poolside grill provides basic American hamburgers and hot dogs.

Other Comments: This is one of a series of four almost identical ships in the same series — the others are *Statendam*, *Ryndam*, and *Veendam*. The exterior styling is rather angular (some would say boxy — the funnel certainly is), although it is softened and balanced somewhat by the fact that the hull is painted black. There is a full wraparound teakwood promenade deck outdoors, excellent for strolling. Thankfully, there is no sign of synthetic turf anywhere. The deck lounge chairs are wood and come with comfortable cushioned pads.

Inside, an asymmetrical layout breaks up the interiors and helps to reduce bottlenecks and congestion. The decor is softer, more sophisticated, and far less eclectic than in sister ship *Statendam* (the first in this series of what the company terms Statendam-class ships). In general, however, a restrained approach to interior styling is taken using a mixture of contemporary materials combined with traditional woods and ceramics. There is, fortunately, little "glitz" anywhere.

What is outstanding is the array of artworks throughout the ship (costing about $2 million), assembled and nicely displayed to represent the fine Dutch heritage of Holland America Line and to present a balance between standard itineraries and onboard creature comforts. Also noticeable are the fine flower arrangements throughout the public areas and foyers — used with good effect to brighten up what to some is dull decor.

Atop the ship, with forward facing views that wrap around the sides is the Crow's Nest Lounge. By day it makes a fine observation lounge (particularly in Alaska), while by night it turns into a nightclub with extremely variable lighting.

A three-decks-high atrium foyer is quite stunning, although its sculpted centerpiece makes it look a little crowded and leaves little room in front of the purser's office. A hydraulic magrodome (glass) roof covers the reasonably sized swimming pool/whirlpools and central lido area (whose focal point is a large dolphin sculpture) so that this can be used in either fine or inclement weather.

The two-decks-high show lounge is basically well designed, but the ceiling is low and the sight lines from the balcony level are poor. Has a large and quite lovely, relaxing reference library. The company keeps its ships very clean and tidy, and there is good passenger flow throughout.

Maasdam is a well-built ship and has fairly decent interior fit and finish. Holland America Line is constantly fine-tuning its performance as a cruise operator and its regular passengers (almost all of whom are North American — there are few international passengers) find the company's ships very comfortable and well run. The company continues its strong maritime traditions, although the present food and service components still let the rest of the cruise experience down. *Note:* The line does not add an automatic 15% gratuity for beverage purchases, unlike many other cruise lines.

Holland America Line's many repeat passengers always seem to enjoy the fact that social dancing is always on the menu. The company also offers cappuccino and espresso coffees, and free ice cream during certain hours of the day aboard its ships, as well as hot hors d'oeuvres in all bars — something other major lines seem to have dropped, or charge extra for. In the final analysis, however, the score for this ship (and her sisters *Ryndam*, *Statendam*, and *Veendam*) ends up just a tad disappointing, considering what it could be if the food and food service staff were better (more professional training might help). This ship is now deployed year-round in the Caribbean, where her rather dark interior decor contrasts with the strong sunlight of the subtropical region.

Weak Points: Standing in line for embarkation, disembarkation, shore tenders, and self-serve buffet meals is an inevitable aspect of cruising aboard all large ships. The service staff is Indonesian and, although quite charming (for the most part), communication with them often proves frustrating for many passengers, and service is spotty and inconsistent. Note that passengers are forced to eat at the Lido Café on days when the dining room is closed for lunch (this is typically once or twice per cruise, depending on ship and itinerary). The single escalator is virtually useless. There is no door bell outside the suites. The room service is poor. The charge to use the washing machines and dryers in the self-service launderette is really petty and irritating, particularly for the occupants of suites, as they pay high prices for their cruises.

Majesty of the Seas
★★★ +

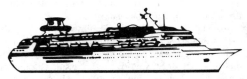

Large Ship:	73,941 tons	Cabins (for one person):	0
Lifestyle:	Standard	Cabins (with private balcony):	62
Cruise Line:	Royal Caribbean International	Cabins (wheelchair accessible):	4
Former Names:	-	Cabin Current:	110-volt
Builder:	Chantiers de l'Atlantique	Full-Service Dining Rooms:	2
Original Cost:	$300 million	Elevators:	11
Entered Service:	April 1992	Casino (gaming tables):	Yes
Registry:	Norway	Slot Machines:	Yes
Length (ft/m):	879.9/268.2	Swimming Pools (outdoors):	2
Beam (ft/m):	105.9/32.3	Swimming Pools (indoors):	0
Draft (ft/m):	24.9/7.6	Whirlpools:	2
Propulsion/Propellers:	Diesel (21,844kW)/2	Fitness Center:	Yes
Passenger Decks:	14	Sauna/Steam Room:	Yes/No
Total Crew:	822	Massage:	Yes
Passengers (lower beds/all berths):	2,350/2,744	Self-Service Launderette:	No
Pass. Space Ratio (lower beds/all berths):	31.4/26.9	Dedicated Cinema/Seats:	Yes/200
Crew/Pass. Ratio (lower beds/all berths):	2.8/3.3	Library:	Yes
Navigation Officers:	Norwegian	Classification Society:	Det Norske Veritas
Cabins (total):	1,175		
Size Range (sq ft/m):	118.4–446.7/11.0–41.5	**OVERALL SCORE:**	**1,394**
Cabins (outside view):	732		
Cabins (interior/no view):	443	**(OUT OF A POSSIBLE 2,000 POINTS)**	

Accommodation: Except for a few suites, all other cabins are very small and confined (particularly by today's standards), simply because the company's policy has always been one of getting passengers out into the public areas. They are quite attractively decorated in a basic way, but the bathrooms are small and utilitarian. There is no doubt that the cabin space is the weak point of a cruise aboard this ship. Special "family suites," located amidships, sleep four.

Dining: The two large dining rooms (both are nonsmoking) have Hollywood musical themes. There are tables for four, six, or eight, but no tables for two, and there are two seatings. The dining operation is well orchestrated, with emphasis on highly programmed (insensitive), extremely hurried service that many find intrusive.

  Most nights are themed (typically French, Oriental, Italian, Caribbean, American), as they have been for years, with waiters and busboys in appropriate costumes. The food is typical of hotel banquet catering. The menu descriptions make the food sound better than it is, which is consistently average, mostly disappointing and without much taste. However, a decent selection of light meals is provided, and a vegetarian menu is available. The selection of breads, rolls, fruits, and cheeses is quite poor, however, and should be upgraded. One thing this company does once each cruise is to feature the "Galley Buffet," whereby passengers go through a section of the galley picking up food for a midnight buffet.

  The wine list is not very extensive, but the prices are moderate. The waiters, many of whom are from Caribbean countries, are perhaps overly friendly for some tastes — particularly on the last night of the cruise, when tips are expected.

  For casual breakfasts and lunches, the Windjammer Café is the place to go, although there are often long lines at peak times, and the selection is very average.

Other Comments: When first introduced, she was an innovative vessel. Royal Caribbean International's trademark Viking Crown lounge and bar surrounds the funnel and provides a stunning view. The open deck space is very cramped when full, as aboard any large ship, although there seems to be plenty of it. There is a basketball court for sports lovers.

  This ship has a spacious, well-designed interior, with excellent deck plans and signs. A beautiful, well-stocked library adds a touch of class. The five-decks-high Centrum is the focal point of a large atrium lobby, and there are two glass-walled elevators. The entertainment program is very good, and includes good children's/teens' programs and cheerful youth counselors.

In the final analysis, you will probably be overwhelmed by the public spaces, and underwhelmed by the size of the cabins. However, this is basically a well run, fine-tuned, highly programmed cruise product geared particularly to those seeking an action-packed cruise vacation in seven days, at a moderately good price, with around 2,500 fellow passengers.

Weak Points: Standing in line for embarkation, disembarkation, shore tenders, and self-serve buffet meals is an inevitable aspect of cruising aboard all large ships. There are too many loud, intrusive, repetitive announcements. The officers, junior officers, and staff often forget that hospitality is the key to happy passengers.

WHAT IS AN ISLAND?

An island is defined as any land mass smaller than the smallest continent, and completely surrounded by water.

THE COLOR OF SEAWATER

Seawater is colorless. We only see "color" in seawater because quantities of the water play with light. The deep blue of deep seawater is produced in part by the refraction of light particles in the water and by the reflection of the sky. Also, the color blue is absorbed least by seawater. "Green" seas are found closer to land and are the result of greater quantities of suspended matter carried in coastal waters. Thus, the color essentially results from the combination of the blue-looking ocean water and the yellow pigments that result from the decomposition of plant matter. The Red Sea was so named due to the periodic swarming of an alga that stains its surface.

WAVES

Water waves are produced when the air-sea surface interface is distorted by a force such as the wind. Waves provide one of the most important mechanisms for transporting energy from one point to another on the surface of the sea. A restoring force such as gravity, surface tension, or the Coriolis force then acts to return the surface to equilibrium. The average ocean wave is between 150 and 300 feet in length and moves at a fair speed. Note that a wave breaks whereas a swell does not. When winds blow at a rate faster than the waves, the waves soak up the energy of the wind and continue to grow in size. Thus, the waves of the Pacific Ocean are generally larger than those of the Atlantic Ocean as they have greater distances over which they can build up.

Mandalay
★★

Small Ship:	420 tons	Size Range (sq ft/sq m):	65.0–100.1/6.0–9.3
Lifestyle:	Standard	Cabins (outside view):	30
Cruise Line:	Windjammer Barefoot Cruises	Cabins (interior/no view):	6
Former Names:	*Vema, Hussar*	Cabins (for one person):	0
Builder:	Cox & Stevens (UK)	Cabins (with private balcony):	2
Original Cost:	n/a	Cabins (wheelchair accessible):	0
Entered Service:	1923/1982	Cabin Current:	110-volt
Registry:	Equatorial Guinea	Full-Service Dining Rooms:	1
Length (ft/m):	236.0/71.9	Elevators:	0
Beam (ft/m):	33.0/10.0	Casino (gaming tables):	No
Draft (ft/m):	15.0/4.5	Slot Machines:	No
Type of Vessel:	Barkentine	Swimming Pools (outdoors):	0
No. of Masts:	3	Whirlpools:	0
Sail Area (sq.ft/sq.m):	12,002.1/1,115.0	Fitness Center:	No
Main Propulsion:	Sail power	Sauna/Steam Room:	No/No
Propulsion/Propellers:	Diesel/1	Massage:	No
Passenger Decks:	3	Self-Service Launderette:	No
Total Crew:	28	Library:	Yes
Passengers (lower beds/all berths):	72/72	Classification Society:	none
Pass. Space Ratio (lower beds/all berths):	5.8/5.8		
Crew/Pass. Ratio (lower beds/all berths):	2.5/2.5	**OVERALL SCORE:**	**902**
Navigation Officers:	International	**(OUT OF A POSSIBLE 2,000 POINTS)**	
Cabins (total):	36		

Accommodation: There are four grades of accommodation (Admiral's Suite, Deck Cabin, Captain's Cabin, and Standard Cabin). The cabins are dimensionally challenged, however, particularly when compared to regular cruise ships. Remember that this is a very casual cruise experience and you will need few clothes anyway. All are equipped with upper and lower berths, and most of them are narrow.

Dining: There is one dining room, and meals are all very simple in style and service, with little choice and only the most basic presentation. Breakfast is served on board, as is dinner, while lunch could be either on board or at a beach, picnic-style. Wine is included with dinner.

Other Comments: *Mandalay* was originally built for the American financier E.F. Hutton; it was sold to shipping magnate George Vettelman. Windjammer Barefoot Cruises acquired the ship in 1982. Aboard one of the Windjammer Barefoot Cruises' fleet you can let the crew do all the work, or you can lend a hand at the helm yourself, if you feel so inclined. One neat thing to do is just to sit or lie in the nets at the bows of the vessel, without a care in the world — it's a great feeling.

The mood is free and easy, the ships are equipped simply, and only the most casual clothes are required (T-shirts and shorts), shoes are optional on board. Quite possibly the most used item will be your bathing suit.

Entertainment in the evenings consists of you and the crew. You can put on a toga, or create a pirate outfit and join in the fun. No programmed big-ship production shows here.

Jammin' aboard a Windjammer is no-frills cruising in a no-nonsense, friendly environment, for the young at heart and those who don't need programmed activities. It's all about the romance and experience of being at sea under sail. Anyone that enjoys beaches, SCUBA diving, and snorkeling, and anyone seeking sun, sea, and sand will be best suited to a Windjammer Barefoot Cruises cruise, as well as lovers of old sailing ships.

This ship can anchor in neat little Caribbean hideaways that larger cruise ships can't get near. Although itineraries are provided in the brochure, the captain actually decides which islands to go, depending on the sea and weather conditions. *Mandalay* features year-round cruises in the Caribbean, and sails from Antigua and Grenada. Although the brochure rates might seem inexpensive, you'll need to add on the airfare in order to get the true cost. Other ships in the fleet include *Flying Cloud, Legacy, Polynesia,* and *Yankee Clipper.*

Weak Points: There's very little space per passenger. Tips are suggested — at $50 per week!

Marco Polo
★★★★

Mid-Size Ship:	22,080 tons	Cabins (wheelchair accessible):	2
Lifestyle:	Premium	Cabins (for one person):	(many doubles sold for
Cruise Line:	Orient Lines		single occupancy)
Former Names:	*Aleksandr Pushkin*	Cabin Current:	110/220-volt
Builder:	VEB Mathias Thesen Werft (Germany)	Full-Service Dining Rooms:	2
Original Cost:	n/a	Elevators:	4
Entered Service:	April 1966/November 1993	Casino (gaming tables):	Yes
Registry:	Bahamas	Slot Machines:	Yes
Length (ft/m):	578.4/176.28	Swimming Pools (outdoors):	1
Beam (ft/m):	77.4/23.60	Swimming Pools (indoors):	0
Draft (ft/m):	26.8/8.17	Whirlpools:	3
Propulsion/Propellers:	Diesel (14,444kW)/2	Fitness Center:	Yes
Passenger Decks:	8	Sauna/Steam Room:	Yes/No
Total Crew:	356	Massage:	Yes
Passengers (lower beds/all berths):	848/915	Self-Service Launderette:	No
Pass. Space Ratio (lower beds/all berths):	26/24.1	Dedicated Cinema:	No
Crew/Pass. Ratio (lower beds/all berths):	2.3/2.5	Library:	Yes
Navigation Officers:	Scandinavian	Classification Society:	Bureau Veritas
Cabins (total):	425		
Size Range (sq ft/sq m):	93.0–484.0/8.6–44.9		
Cabins (outside view):	292		
Cabins (interior/no view):	133		
Cabins (with private balcony):	0		

OVERALL SCORE: 1,406
(OUT OF A POSSIBLE 2,000 POINTS)

Accommodation: The cabins, which come in 13 different grades, are a profusion of different sizes and configurations. All are quite pleasingly decorated and feature rich wood cabinetry, wood and mirror-fronted closets, adequate drawer and storage space, TV, thin cotton bathrobe, hair dryer (in the bathroom), and non-vacuum (non-noisy) toilets. Carpets, curtains, and bedspreads are all nicely color coordinated. Weak points include extremely poor sound insulation between cabins (you can hear your neighbors brushing their hair), and the fact that the bathrooms are small, with little storage space for toiletries (particularly for long cruises).

The largest accommodation can be found in two deluxe suites and two junior suites. The deluxe suites (Dynasty and Mandarin), feature a queen-size bed, separate living room, and marble bathroom with bathtub/shower, walk-in closet, refrigerator, TV, and VCR. The Junior Suites feature two lower beds, lounge area, and marble bathroom with bathtub/shower, walk-in closet, and refrigerator.

Also very comfortable are the Superior Deluxe ocean-view cabins that feature two lower beds (some can be converted to a queen-size bed), marble bathroom with bathtub/shower, and refrigerator.

Note that some cabins on Upper Deck and Sky Deck have lifeboat-obstructed views. Unfortunately there is no 24-hour room service, particularly because many passengers are of senior years.

Dining: The Seven Seas Restaurant is nicely decorated in soft pastel colors, practical in design, and functions well, but it has a low ceiling, is noisy, and the tables are very close together. There are two seatings. There are tables for two to ten, and fine place settings and china. The food itself is of a good standard, with good presentation. The wine list is quite extensive, and the prices are very reasonable, although most wines are quite young.

Raffles is the place for informal self-serve breakfasts and lunches (there is seating inside as well as outdoors around the ship's swimming pool). On assorted evenings each cruise it also becomes an alternative dining spot, for about 75 persons. Reservations are required, but there is no extra charge.

Note that a 15% gratuity is added to all bar and wine accounts.

Other Comments: This ship was constructed as one of five almost identical sister ships for the Russian/Ukrainian fleet (originally built to reopen the Leningrad to Montreal transatlantic route in 1966, after a long absence since 1949). The ship has a fine "real-ship" profile, an extremely strong ice-strengthened hull and huge storage spaces for long voyages. After being completely refitted (from the hull and engines up) and refurbished, the ship now features well-designed destination-intensive cruises, at very realistic prices.

Orient Lines, and its single ship *Marco Polo*, was purchased by Norwegian Cruise Line in May 1998 (and subsequently by Star Cruises in 2000) but continues to operate under the growing Orient Lines brand name. A second ship (*Crown Odyssey*) was added to the fleet in 2000.

Marco Polo is fitted with the latest navigational aids and biological waste treatment center, and carries ten Zodiac landing craft for in-depth shore trips in eco-sensitive areas.

This is a very comfortable vessel throughout and, because it has a deep draft, rides well in unkind sea conditions. There are two large, forward-facing, open-deck viewing areas. There is also a helicopter-landing pad atop the ship. The wood-decked aft swimming pool and Lido Deck area is kept in good condition. Joggers and walkers can circle around the ship — not on the promenade deck, but one deck above, although this goes past vast air intakes that are noisy, and the walkway is very narrow.

As soon as you walk aboard, you feel a warm, welcoming, homey ambience that is instantly comforting. There is a wide range of public rooms, most of which are arranged on one deck. A sense of spaciousness pervades, as most have high ceilings. There is very tasteful interior decor, with careful use of mirrored surfaces, and colors that do not clash but are relaxing without being boring, and subdued lighting helps maintain an air of calmness and relaxation.

Although this ship is more than 35 years old, it is in remarkably fine shape — a tribute to the management and crew who work to keep the ship in good order. Indeed, *Marco Polo* is in better shape than many ships that are ten years old, and the ship's interiors are constantly being refurbished and refreshed.

All in all, *Marco Polo* features well-planned destination-intensive cruises and offers extremely fine value for money in very comfortable, elegant but unpretentious surroundings, while a friendly and accommodating Filipino crew help make a cruise aboard her a very pleasant, no-hassle experience.

Weak Points: Avoid Cabins 310/312, as these are located close to the engine room doorway and the noise level is considerable. There is no observation lounge with forward-facing views over the ship's bows. There is a little too much use of plastic and Styrofoam cups when glass would be much better for presentation. There are many "lips" or raised thresholds in this ship, so you need to be on your guard when walking through the ship, and particularly when walking up or down the exterior stairways. This could prove difficult for wheelchair-bound passengers.

Maxim Gorkiy
★★★ +

Mid-Size Ship:	24,981 tons	Cabins (for one person):	2
Lifestyle:	Standard	Cabins (with private balcony):	0
Cruise Line:	Phoenix Seereisen	Cabins (wheelchair accessible):	0
Former Names:	*Hanseatic, Hamburg*	Cabin Current:	220-volt
Builder:	Howaldtswerke Deutsche Werft	Full-Service Dining Rooms:	3
	(Germany)	Elevators:	4
Original Cost:	£5.6 million	Casino (gaming tables):	No
Entered Service:	March 1969/January 1974	Slot Machines:	No
Registry:	Bahamas	Swimming Pools (outdoors):	1
Length (ft/m):	638.8/194.72	Swimming Pools (indoors):	1
Beam (ft/m):	87.3/26.62	Whirlpools:	0
Draft (ft/m):	27.0/8.25	Fitness Center:	Yes
Propulsion/Propellers:	Steam turbine (16,900kW)/2	Sauna/Steam Room:	Yes/No
Passenger Decks:	10	Massage:	Yes
Total Crew:	340	Self-Service Launderette:	Yes
Passengers (lower beds/all berths):	650/88	Dedicated Cinema/Seats:	Yes/290
Pass. Space Ratio (lower beds/all berths):	38.4/31.7	Library:	Yes
Crew/Pass. Ratio (lower beds/all berths):	1.9/2.3	Classification Society:	Det Norske Veritas
Navigation Officers:	Russian/Ukrainian		
Cabins (total):	326		
Size Range (sq ft/sq m):	145.3–296.0/13.5–27.0	**OVERALL SCORE:**	**1,385**
Cabins (outside view):	210	(OUT OF A POSSIBLE 2,000 POINTS)	
Cabins (interior/no view):	116		

Accommodation: The brochure shows outside view and interior (no view) cabins in 18 grades. Most cabins are actually quite spacious, and many of them have wood paneling, accenting, and trim, while the decor is comfortable and quite restful. The bathrooms are quite large and feature full-size bathtubs in all except 20 cabins. There is a decent amount of space for the storage of one's personal toiletry items.

Cabins designated as deluxe are of a good size, come fully equipped with almost everything one would need, and have huge picture windows (most others have portholes). The in-cabin TV system features both German and Russian satellite TV programming.

Anyone booking a suite or one of the top five grades receives Phoenix VIP service, which includes flowers for the cabin, a separate check-in desk, and priority disembarkation.

Dining: There are three restaurants (all feature one seating, with assigned tables, so you have the same waiter throughout your cruise). All three restaurants are located low down in the ship, but they are cheerfully decorated. Draft lager is always available, and the wine list features many wines from different regions of Germany, Switzerland, and Austria, as well as a modest selection from France and other countries. Moderately decent food is served, and wine with lunch and dinner is included in the cruise fare, but more choice and better presentation would be welcome.

The service is quite attentive and courteous from the well-meaning staff, although it is somewhat hurried even though there is only one seating for all meals. Cushions would be a welcome addition to some of the banquette seating.

Other Comments: This all-white ship was originally built as *Hamburg* for the transatlantic service of the now defunct Deutsche Atlantik Linie. The ship has long, pleasing lines and outer styling, and is easily identified by its platform-topped funnel, which was designed to disperse smoke away from the aft, tiered, open decks. In January 1974 she was sold to the Black Sea Shipping Company and renamed *Maxim Gorkiy*. She was modernized in 1988, but on June 20, 1989 she gained notoriety when she rammed the cruise ship *Vasco da Gama* (presently named *Seawind Crown*) in the ice near Spitzbergen. Also in 1989, *Maxim Gorkiy* gained more fame when she played host to an international summit between George Bush and Mikail Gorbachev, in Malta. Since December 1992 she has been placed under long-term charter to Phoenix Seereisen from present owners, Russia's Sovcomflot.

She has been generally well maintained, and more facilities were added during the ship's last refurbishment. There is a generous amount of open deck and sunbathing space, and the deck lounge chairs have cushioned pads. Open deck sports include a large basketball court aft of the funnel.

Inside, there are some handsome, well-designed (although now slightly dated) public rooms; the passenger flow is good, with few congested areas. A generous amount of wood paneling was used in her construction — most of it still looks good, although some refinishing is needed in some areas. The decor is dark and somewhat dull, although it is quite relaxing and soporific. The show lounge is decent enough, although it simply does not have enough seating; the stage and lighting facilities could also be improved. The gymnasium is small, and much of the equipment needs updating. There are two relaxing winter gardens with large ocean-view windows. An added bonus is an indoor swimming pool — always good for those times when there is inclement weather.

Maxim Gorkiy will provide a very good general cruise experience in comfortable, quite elegant, but very traditional surroundings, at a modest price, although you should remember that this is an older ship that does not have the latest in facilities. Particularly targeted to German-speaking passengers who appreciate good value and well-planned, destination-intensive itineraries. The mostly Russian and Ukrainian service staff provides friendly, attentive service. Port taxes, insurance, and gratuities are included.

Phoenix Seereisen has, over the years, attained almost a cult status among her passengers, in that the company provides a consistently fine, very popular product for those seeking a casual cruise experience and lifestyle among friendly passengers that seek good value for money. Where passengers are required to fly to join their cruises, the airline most used by Phoenix Seereisen is LTU. The currency on board is the deutschmark.

Melody
★★★ +

Large Ship:	36,500 tons	Cabins (with private balcony):	0
Lifestyle:	Standard	Cabins (wheelchair accessible):	Yes
Cruise Line:	Mediterranean Shipping Cruises	Cabin Current:	110-volt
Former Names:	*Star/Ship Atlantic, Atlantic*	Full-Service Dining Rooms:	1
Builder:	C.N.I.M. (France)	Elevators:	4
Original Cost:	$100 million	Casino (gaming tables):	Yes
Entered Service:	April 1982/June 1997	Slot Machines:	Yes
Registry:	Panama	Swimming Pools (outdoors):	1
Length (ft/m):	671.9/204.81	Swimming Pools (indoors):	1
Beam (ft/m):	89.7/27.36	Whirlpools:	3
Draft (ft/m):	25.5/7.80	Fitness Center:	Yes
Propulsion/Propellers:	Diesel (22,070kW)/2	Sauna/Steam Room:	Yes/No
Passenger Decks:	9	Massage:	Yes
Total Crew:	535	Self-Service Launderette:	No
Passengers (lower beds/all berths):	1,098/1,600	Dedicated Cinema/Seats:	Yes/227
Pass. Space Ratio (lower beds/all berths):	33.2/22.8	Library:	Yes (2 book racks)
Crew/Pass. Ratio (lower beds/all berths):	2/2.9	Classification Society:	American Bureau
Navigation Officers:	Italian		of Shipping
Cabins (total):	549		
Size Range (sq ft/sq m):	137.0–427.0/12.7–39.5		
Cabins (outside view):	392	**OVERALL SCORE:**	**1,259**
Cabins (interior/no view):	157		
Cabins (for one person):	0	**(OUT OF A POSSIBLE 2,000 POINTS)**	

Accommodation: Six suites have plenty of space for families of four, and feature a decent walk-in closet. The bathroom is large and has a full-size bathtub, oversize sink (large enough to bathe twins in), and an uncomfortable square toilet.

Other outside view and interior (no view) cabins are of a decent size, and have ample closet and drawer space. Many cabins have upper berths — good for families, although with four adults there is very little space for anything else, such as luggage. The cabin insulation is extremely poor (you can hear your neighbors brushing their hair), and the room service menu is quite basic. Bathrooms are of a decent size and are quite practical in appointments.

Dining: The dining room, located on a lower deck, is large and quite attractive, but the tables are much too close together, and it is difficult for waiters to serve properly. Also, the chairs do not have armrests, and the noise level is extremely high. There are two seatings, and the cuisine is Italian-continental. The food quality generally is adequate for the price paid, but dishes, when presented, are not as good as the menu description would have you believe. There is a limited wine list. An attentive, multinational staff provides the service, although it needs polishing. The buffets are quite poor when compared to many other ships in this standard category.

Other Comments: This ship (originally built for the now defunct Home Lines, then operated for many years by the now defunct Premier Cruise Lines) has a short, stubby bow and squat funnel. Her hull is all white.

There is a good amount of outdoor deck space, but noise levels can be high when the ship is full, and there are many families with children (particularly during the summer season).

The interior is quite spacious, with plenty of public rooms, most of which have high ceilings. The decor is somewhat somber in places, and lighting is very subdued. There is a generous amount of stainless steel and teak wood trim. A large observation lounge is wasted as an informal eating area. There is a good indoor-outdoor pool area (covered by a magrodome in inclement weather).

For families, there is a fairly good children's program during the peak periods, and several children's (and teen) counselors. In any event, this ship (the largest in the MSC fleet so far) will provide a good basic cruise experience for families, at a fair price, in comfortable, modern surroundings, in typical MSC style, and that means lots of extra charges. Typically about 60% of passengers will be Italian, while the rest may be a mix of other Europeans.

Weak Points: Standing in line for embarkation, disembarkation, shore tenders, and self-serve buffet meals is an inevitable aspect of cruising aboard all large ships. The almost constant, loud, and repetitive announcements are annoying and intrusive, particularly when the ship is in port. There is no wraparound promenade deck outdoors, nor are cushioned pads provided for the deck lounge chairs. The ship has only four elevators — not enough for this number of passengers.

COMMUNICATIONS

Most ships now have a direct-dial satellite telephone system. In addition, all ships are given an internationally recognized call sign, made up of a combination of several letters and digits. When the ship is at sea, you can call from your cabin (or the ship's radio room) to anywhere in the world:

→ via radiotelephone (a slight/moderate background noise might be noticed).

→ via satellite (which will be as clear as your own home phone).

Direct dial satellite calls (this service started in 1986) are more expensive, but are completed instantly. Some ships also have credit card telephones located in public areas; these also connect instantly, via satellite. Satellite calls can also be made when the ship is in port (radiotelephone calls cannot). Satellite telephone calls cost between $5 and $15 per minute, depending on the type of communications equipment the ship carries (the latest systems are digital). Calls are charged to your onboard account.

Your relatives and friends can reach you by calling the High Seas Operator in most countries (in the United States, dial 1-800-SEA-CALL). The operator will need the name of the ship, together with the ocean code (Atlantic is 871; Pacific is 872; and the Indian Ocean is 873).

Mercury
★★★★ +

Large Ship:	77,713 tons	Cabins (with private balcony):	220
Lifestyle:	Premium	Cabins (wheelchair accessible):	8
Cruise Line:	Celebrity Cruises	Cabin Current:	110/220-volt
Former Names:	-	Full-Service Dining Rooms:	2
Builder:	Meyer Werft (Germany)	Elevators:	10
Original Cost:	$320 million	Casino (gaming tables):	Yes
Entered Service:	November 1997	Slot Machines:	Yes
Registry:	Liberia	Swimming Pools (outdoors):	2
Length (ft/m):	865.8/263.90	Swimming Pools (indoors):	1 indoor/outdoor
Beam (ft/m):	105.6/32.20		(magrodome)
Draft (ft/m):	25.2/7.70	Whirlpools:	4
Propulsion/Propellers:	Diesel (31,500kW)/2	Fitness Center:	Yes
Passenger Decks:	10	Sauna/Steam Room:	Yes
Total Crew:	909	Massage:	Yes
Passengers (lower beds/all berths):	1,870/2,681	Self-Service Launderette:	No
Pass. Space Ratio (lower beds/all berths):	41.5/28.9	Dedicated Cinema/Seats:	Yes/183
Crew/Pass. Ratio (lower beds/all berths):	2/2.9	Library:	Yes
Navigation Officers:	Greek	Classification Society:	Lloyd's Register
Cabins (total):	935		
Size Range (sq ft/sq m):	171.0–1,514.5/15.8–140.7		
Cabins (outside view):	639		
Cabins (interior/no view):	296		
Cabins (for one person):	0		

OVERALL SCORE: **1,697**

(OUT OF A POSSIBLE 2,000 POINTS)

Accommodation: The accommodation is extremely comfortable throughout this ship, regardless of which cabin grade you choose. Naturally, if you choose a suite you will find more space, butler service (whether you want it or not), more amenities, and more personal service than if you choose any of the standard cabin grades.

Occupants of all accommodation designated as suites (Deck 12, Deck 10) get gold cards to open their doors (and priority service throughout the ship, free cappuccino/espresso coffees served by a butler, welcome champagne, flowers, VCR, and use of the AquaSpa thalassotherapy pool). All occupants of standard (interior and outside) cabins have white cards. Suites that have private balconies also have floor-to-ceiling windows and sliding doors to balconies (a few suites have outward opening doors).

Two Presidential Suites are located amidships. These provide spectacular living spaces, perhaps even better than those in Century and Galaxy, depending on your personal taste. There is a separate bedroom (with high-tech multimedia entertainment center), large lounge (complete with dining table), huge walk-in closet with mountains of drawers, and king-size marble-tiled bathroom with every appointment necessary.

There is in-suite dining for the two Presidential and 12 Century Suites, as well as for the 24 Sky Suites (1202/1203/1236/1237) have enormous, fully private balconies, while the others are only semiprivate). All suites feature full butler service, personalized stationery, and business cards. If you choose one of the forward-most Sky Deck suites, however, be warned that you may well be subject to constant music and noise from the pool deck (one deck below) between 8am and 6pm (not good if you want to relax). The closet and drawer space provided in these suites is superb. In the bathrooms of the Sky Suites, the shaving mirror is positioned too high, and in the bedroom, the TV cannot be viewed from the bed. Push-button bell and privacy curtains should be, but are not, provided. In-suite massage is available (this really is pleasant when provided on the balcony of the Sky Suites).

The standard (interior and outside) cabins are quite spacious and nicely decorated with cheerful fabrics and a marble-topped vanity unit. The bathrooms are generous with space, tiled from floor to ceiling, and the power showers are extremely practical units.

All cabins feature interactive TV for booking shore excursions, ordering cabin service items, and purchasing goods from the ship's boutiques, so you do not have to leave your quarters if you do not wish to, especially if you do not like the ports of call. The system works in English, French, German, Italian, and Spanish. There are five channels of music — all available from the TV (therefore you cannot have music without having a picture). All cabins are also equipped with a "baby monitoring telephone system" that allows you to telephone your cabin from elsewhere aboard ship, and to have a two-way intercom to "listen in." Automatic "wake-up" calls can be dialed in. All accommodation designated as suites have duvets on the beds instead of sheets and blankets.

Dining: The two-level formal Manhattan Restaurant, located at the ship's stern, is really grand and elegant (each level has its own full galley); a grand staircase connects the two levels. Large picture windows provide sea views on three sides; at night, large blinds (with scenes of Manhattan) roll down electronically to cover the stern-facing windows. There are two seatings. Three-star Michelin chef, Michel Roux, directs the same excellent cuisine that has made Celebrity Cruises the shining star of the contemporary cruise industry. The menus are creative, and the food is very attractively presented. There is also an excellent wine list, and real wine waiters (unlike so many other large ship companies), although prices are high (particularly for good champagne), and the wine vintages are young — very young.

There are also several informal dining spots as an alternative to the main dining room: a Lido Café, with four main serving lines; a poolside grill, and another indoor/outdoor grill located behind the aft swimming pool. The Lido Café has fine wood paneling and is much more elegant than the informal dining areas found aboard most ships today. It has some seating in bay window areas with great ocean views.

In the center of the ship is Tastings, a delightful coffee/tea lounge; in one corner is a presentation of goodies made by COVA, the chocolatier from Milan — an exclusive to Celebrity Cruises (the original Cova Café, located near the La Scala Opera house, in Milan, opened in 1756).

Finally, for those that cannot live without them, freshly baked pizzas can be ordered and delivered, in a box, inside an insulated pouch, to your cabin.

Other Comments: She is quite a stunning ship, both inside and outside. As aboard her identical sister *Galaxy*, there is a 1,000-seat show lounge, with side balconies and no pillars to obstruct views (there are three high-tech "dazzle and sizzle" production shows per seven-night cruise, although they consist mainly of running, jumping, smoke, colored laser lighting, and little story line intelligence). Other facilities include a three-decks-high main foyer with marble-floored lobby and waterfall; over 4.5 acres (1.8 hectares) of open deck space (poolside lounge chairs have cushioned pads, those on other decks do not); a magrodome-covered indoor-outdoor pool; AquaSpa thalassotherapy pool (with several "active" water jet stations); and assorted treatment rooms including a rasul mud treatment room. Other facilities include "Michael's Club" — a cigar and cognac room on Promenade Deck that overlooks the atrium, a small but luxurious cinema, a large casino (this is extremely glitzy, with confusing and congested layout). The children's facilities are good (open until 10pm, it is called the "Fun Factory"). There is also an outdoor play area and paddling pool.

The decor includes plenty of wood (or faux wood) paneling and accenting throughout, and many refinements have been made during the three-ship "Century Series" that Celebrity Cruises has introduced in the past few years. The ship also houses a $3.5 million living art collection with true, museum-quality pieces. The health and fitness facilities are among the nicest aboard any ship, and have been well thought out and designed for quiet, efficient operation, with everything in just the right place.

This ship will provide you with a finely packaged cruise vacation in elegant surroundings. The ship is efficiently run. There are many more staff per passengers than would be found aboard other ships of the same size in the premium category, so service in general is very good.

Weak Points: Standing in line for embarkation, disembarkation, shore tenders, and self-serve buffet meals is an inevitable aspect of cruising aboard all large ships. Obtaining Cabin Service, or the Guest Relations Desk to answer the phone (to order breakfast, for example, if you don't want to do so via the interactive TV) is a matter of luck, timing, and patience (a sad reminder of the automated age, and lack of personal contact). The library is disappointingly small and poorly located away from the main flow of passengers. There is a charge for using the Aquaspa/sauna/steam room complex. The room-service menu is poor, and food items are decidedly below the standard of food featured in the dining room.

While under the direction of its former owner John Chandris, Celebrity Cruises managed to create a superb quality cruise vacation product virtually unbeatable at the prices charged in the Alaska and Caribbean markets, representing outstanding value for money. However, given the subtle changes that have occurred since Celebrity Cruises was integrated into the Royal Caribbean International family in late 1997, it has become evident that slippage of product delivery standards and staff has occurred, and the latest score reflects these changes.

Midnatsol
★★ +

Small Ship:	6,100 tons	Cabins (with private balcony):	0
Lifestyle:	Standard	Cabins (wheelchair accessible):	1
Cruise Line:	Norwegian Coastal Voyages (TFDS)	Cabin Current:	220-volt
Former Names:	-	Full-Service Dining Rooms:	1
Builder:	Ulstein Hatlo (Norway)	Elevators:	1
Original Cost:	n/a	Casino (gaming tables):	No
Entered Service:	1982	Slot Machines:	No
Registry:	Norway	Swimming Pools (outdoors):	0
Length (ft/m):	356.2/108.6	Swimming Pools (inside):	0
Beam (ft/m):	54.1/16.5	Whirlpools:	0
Draft (ft/m):	15.0/4.5	Fitness Center:	No
Total Crew:	55	Sauna/Steam Room:	No/No
Passengers (lower beds/all berths):	306/325	Massage:	No
Pass. Space Ratio (lower beds/all berths):	19.9/18.7	Self-Service Launderette:	No
Crew/Pass. Ratio (lower beds/all berths):	5.5/5.9	Dedictated Cinema:	No
Navigation Officers:	Norwegian	Library:	No
Cabins (total):	153	Classification Society:	Det Norske Veritas
Size Range (sq ft/sq m):	n/a		
Cabins (outside view):	91		
Cabins (interior/no view):	62		
Cabins (for one person):	0		

OVERALL SCORE: 1,093
(OUT OF A POSSIBLE 2,000 POINTS)

Accommodation: There are eight cabin grades. Except for one mini-suite, which has two beds (no, they cannot be moved together), all other cabins feature a mix of lower beds, lower berths, and upper berths. The cabins are cozy—which translates to very, very small; the bathrooms, likewise, are tiny, although they do have a shower and toilet. All cabins have a 220-volt outlet, so take adapters and converters if you need to.

Dining: There is one cafeteria/dining room (no smoking allowed), and tables are assigned when you embark. Three meals each day are included in the cruise fare: Breakfast and lunch (featuring the famous Norwegian "cold table") are self-serve, buffet-style meals, while dinner is a sit-down affair, with three courses. Additionally, there is a cafeteria, open 24 hours, where snacks and light meals can be purchased.

Other Comments: The Norwegian Coastal Voyage is a service that was started in 1863. It is jointly operated by two companies: Ofotens og Vesteraalen Dampskibsselskab (OVDS) and Troms Fylkes Dampskibsselskab (TFDS). The complete journey, of 1,250 nautical miles, takes in 34 ports of call in a 12-day roundtrip voyage between Bergen and Kirkenes (on the border with Russia), above the Arctic Circle (where a special "Crossing the Arctic Circle" ceremony welcomes newcomers). The journey can also be done in a one-way voyage that takes seven days (northbound) or six days (southbound). The ships carry passengers as well as mail and other cargo.

Perhaps you will be able to peek at the midnight sun (mid-May to late June, north of the Arctic Circle), experience the northern lights (aurora borealis, mostly seen during winter months, and only when the atmospheric conditions are right), and be part of the daily life of the hardy Norwegians. Approximately 60% of the passengers will be Norwegian/Scandinavian/European, while the rest will be a mix of North American and other nationalities. Although the passenger bed capacity is quoted, note that many additional passengers may be on board as day passengers, sailing between two coastal ports—the ship is the equivalent of a seagoing bus for the coastal commuters. As for the weather, the west coast of Norway is warmed by the Gulf Stream, and temperatures will be similar to those found in New England.

Best suited to adult couples, single travelers, and families with children wanting to cruise along the coast of Norway and experience the area's natural beauty. It's ideal for anyone who doesn't need entertainment or mindless parlor games, but wants to relax and unwind, enjoys being close to nature, and is probably a bit of an adventurer. This is an excellent way to experience the beautiful coastline of Norway and its fascinating coastal towns. There will be an interesting mix of passengers — it's a good way to meet new people and make new friends from different countries.

The rates vary by season, cabin location, and whether the ship is of the "new generation" (*Kong Harald, Nordkapp, Nordlys, Nordnorge, Polarlys, Richard With*), the "mid-generation" (*Narvik, Midnatsol, Vesteralen*), or the "traditional" (*Harald Jarl, Lofoten*) type ships. Senior citizens (those age 67 and over) qualify for a special discount.

The dress code is casual and comfortable — layered clothing is recommended. The currency is the Norwegian krone.

Operates Norwegian coast and fjords cruises (year-round): 7-day (northbound) voyage between Bergen and Kirkenes, Norway; or a 6-day (southbound) voyage between Kirkenes and Bergen, Norway; or a 12-day roundtrip voyage. The ship also has space for up to 60 cars.

Weak Points: The ship does not have stabilizers, so you should expect some movement when the weather is inclement or unkind. Drinks prices are extremely high—the same as ashore in Norway. The cabins are small, and the bathrooms are really tiny. Although not needed during the winter, there is little outdoor deck space considering the number of passengers carried.

Millennium
★★★★★

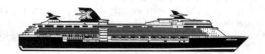

Large Ship:	90,228 tons	Cabins (for one person):	0
Lifestyle:	Premium	Cabins (with private balcony):	590
Cruise Line:	Celebrity Cruises	Cabins (wheelchair accessible):	26 (17 with private
Former Names:	-		balcony)
Builder:	Chantiers de l'Atlantique (France)	Cabin Current:	110/220-volt
Original Cost:	$350 million	Full-Service Dining Rooms:	1 main, 1 specialty
Entered Service:	June 2000	Elevators:	10
Registry:	Liberia	Casino (gaming tables):	Yes
Length (ft/m):	964.5/294.0	Slot Machines:	Yes
Beam (ft/m):	105.6/32.2	Swimming Pools (outdoors):	2
Draft (ft/m):	26.2/8.0	Swimming Pools (indoors):	1 (with magrodome)
Propulsion/Propellers:	Gas turbine/	Whirlpools:	4
	2 azimuthing pods (39,000kW)	Fitness Center:	Yes
Passenger Decks:	11	Sauna/Steam Room:	Yes/Yes
Total Crew:	999	Massage:	Yes
Passengers (lower beds/all berths):	1,950/2,450	Self-Service Launderette:	No
Pass. Space Ratio (lower beds/all berths):	46.2/36.8	Dedicated Cinema/Seats:	Yes/368
Crew/Pass. Ratio (lower beds/all berths):	1.9/2.4	Library:	Yes
Navigation Officers:	Greek	Classification Society:	Lloyd's Register
Cabins (total):	975		
Size Range (sq ft/sq m):	170.0–2,350.0/15.7–235.0		
Cabins (outside view):	780		
Cabins (interior/no view):	195		

OVERALL SCORE: **1,707**

(OUT OF A POSSIBLE 2,000 POINTS)

Accommodation: There are eight different accommodation types, ranging from Penthouse Suites to interior (no view) cabins, in 20 different price grades. There are several categories of suites, but those at the stern of the ship are in a prime location and have huge balconies that are really private and not overlooked from above.

Two Penthouse Suites (on Penthouse Deck) comprise the largest accommodation aboard this ship and are really beautiful apartments. Each measures a huge 2,530 sq ft (235 sq m): This is divided into 1,432 sq ft (133 sq m) of living space, plus a huge wraparound balcony measuring 1,098 sq ft (102 sq m) with 180-degree views, which occupies one half of the beam (width) of the ship, overlooking the ship's stern. It includes a wet bar, hot tub, and whirlpool tub. Suites feature a marble foyer, a separate living room (complete with ebony baby grand piano — bring your own pianist if you don't play yourself), and a formal dining room. The master bedroom has a large walk-in closet; personal exercise equipment; dressing room with vanity desk; exercise equipment; marble master bathroom with twin sinks; deep whirlpool bathtub; separate shower; toilet and bidet areas; flat-screen TVs (one in the bedroom and one in the lounge); and electronically controlled drapes. Butler service is standard, and a butler's pantry, with separate entry door, features a full-size refrigerator, temperature-controlled wine cabinet, microwave oven, and good-size food preparation and storage areas.

Eight wood-panelled Royal Suites (733 sq ft/68 sq m) feature a separate living room with dining and lounge areas, and decor in the style of a country (Africa, China, Mexico, France, India, Italy, Morocco, and Portugal). There are two entertainment centers with flat-screen TVs (one each in the lounge and bedroom), and a large walk-in closet with vanity desk. The bathroom features a whirlpool bathtub, and a separate shower enclosure. The balcony also features a whirlpool hot tub. Butler service is standard.

Eight Celebrity Suites (467.0 sq ft/43.3 sq m) each feature floor-to-ceiling windows; separate living room with dining and lounge areas; two entertainment centers with flat-screen TVs; walk-in closet with vanity desk; bathroom with whirlpool bathtub. Interconnecting doors allow two suites to be used as a family unit. These suites, located amidships on the starboard side of the ship (they are located opposite a group of glass-walled elevators), provide stunning ocean views from the glass-walled sitting/dining area, which extends out from the ship's side (hence these suites do not have a private balcony). Butler service is standard.

All other outside-view and interior (no view) cabins (those not designated as suites) feature a lounge area with sofa or convertible sofa bed, sleeping area with twin beds that can convert to a double bed, a

359

good amount of closet and drawer space, personal safe, minibar/refrigerator (all items are at extra cost), interactive TV, and private bathroom. The cabins are nicely decorated with warm wood-finish furniture, and there is none of the boxy feel of cabins in so many ships, due to the angled placement of the vanity and audio-video consoles. Even the smallest interior (no view) cabin has a good-size bathroom and shower enclosure.

Wheelchair-accessible accommodation is available in six Sky Suites, three premium outside-view cabins, eight deluxe ocean-view cabins, four standard ocean-view and five interior (no view) cabins measure 347– 362 sq ft (32.2–33.6sq m) and are located in the most practical parts of the ship and close to elevators for good accessibility (all have doorways and bathroom doorways and showers are wheelchair-accessible).

Butler Service: Butler service (in all accommodation designated as suites) includes full breakfast, in-suite lunch and dinner service, afternoon tea service, evening hors d'oeuvres, complimentary espresso and cappuccino, daily news delivery, shoeshine service, and other personal touches.

Suite occupants in Penthouse, Royal, and Celebrity Suites also get welcome champagne; a full personal computer in each suite, including a printer and Internet access (on request in the Sky Suites); choice of films from a video library; personalized stationery; tote bag; priority dining room seating preferences; private portrait sitting; and in-suite massage service.

Dining: The Metropolitan Dining Room (nonsmoking), which seats 1,224 passengers, is a really grand, two-decks high room that includes its own atrium gallery. A grand staircase connects the two levels (the focal point on the upper level being an orchestra gallery), and a huge glass wall overlooks the sea at the stern of the ship (electrically operated blinds feature several different backdrops). There are two seatings, and tables for two, four, six, eight, or ten.

In *Millennium*, Celebrity Cruises has created its first true alternative restaurant — and what a restaurant it is! The Olympic Restaurant is named after White Star Line's transatlantic ocean liner of the same name, *Olympic* (sister ship to the ill-fated *Titanic*). It is located adjacent to the conference and reception areas, and its dining lounge (rather like an anteroom) contains figured French walnut wood paneling from the à la carte dining room of the 1911 ship, which was decorated in Louis XVI splendor, complete with ornate gold accenting. Ship buffs should be delighted with this rare find. The paneling was found in a house in the north of England and purchased at auction in 1999.

Superb tableside preparation is the feature of this alternative dining room, whose classic French cuisine and service (masterminded by Michel Roux) are absolutely outstanding and at the height of professionalism. This is, indeed, a room for a full degustation, and not merely a dinner. Throughout each dinner, a piano and violin duo plays music appropriate to the period, in costumes that have been reproduced from the designs used by the musicians aboard the trio of sister ships *Britannic*, *Olympic*, and *Titanic*.

A wine cellar, in which it is possible to dine, is also a feature, as is a demonstration galley. The wine list is extremely extensive. But the real treat for rare wine lovers is the additional list of rare vintage wines, including (when I was last aboard): a magnum of 1949 Chateau Petrus (at $12,400), a 1907 Heidsieck Monopole Champagne (a mere $7,000 — brought to the surface from a sunken German ship), and a Chateau Lafite-Rothschild Pouillac from 1890 (a real snip at $2,160).

To undertake dinner in this exquisite setting — it's rather like dining in a living museum — takes a minimum of three hours of culinary excellence and faultless service and is, without any shadow of doubt, the very finest dining experience at sea today. However, with just 134 seats, not all passengers will be able to experience it even once during a one-week cruise (reservations are necessary, and a cover charge of $25 per person applies).

For casual meals, the self-serve Ocean Buffet is an extensive area that features six principal serving lines and can seat 754. At the aft end of the Ocean Buffet, a separate grill/rotisserie and pizza service provides freshly created items. Note that all pizzas are made aboard from pizza dough and do not come ready-made for reheating, as with many cruise lines. On selected evenings, alternative dinners can be taken here (reservations are necessary).

There is also an outdoor grill, for hamburgers and hot dogs, roast chicken, and other fast food items, located adjacent to the swimming pool.

As with Celebrity Cruises' other ships, there are several dining options, particularly for those seeking more casual dining spots. Full service in-cabin dining is also available for all meals (including dinner).

For champagne and caviar lovers, the Platinum Club has a platinum and silver art deco decor that is reminiscent of a 1930s gentlemen's club. It includes a diamond-pane reflective mirror wall. It has a Champagne Bar and a Martini Bar, each of which features a cut-crystal chandelier.

A Cova Café di Milano (this one has 92 seats) is a signature feature aboard all the ships of Celebrity Cruises. It is a delightful setting for those who appreciate fine Italian coffees (espresso, espresso macchiato, cappuccino, latte) and pastries. An enclosed Tea Room is also featured, with ocean-view windows.

Other Comments: *Millennium* is a slightly enlarged and elongated version of the company's successful trio, *Century*, *Galaxy*, and *Mercury*, and was constructed in the same building dock where the famous former ocean liner *France* (now *Norway*) was built. Jon Bannenberg designed the exterior that features a royal-blue-and-white hull, and racy lines in red, white, and gold. This is the first Celebrity Cruises ship to be fitted with a "pod" propulsion system (and controllable pitch propellers) coupled with a gas turbine powerplant. Indeed, she is the first cruise ship in the world to be powered by a gas turbine (two GE gas turbines provide engine power while a single GE steam turbine drives the electricity generators). Sadly, the ship was dogged by several technical problems in her early days.

Inside, the ship features the same high-class decor and materials (including lots of wood, glass, and marble) and public rooms that have made the existing ships in the fleet so popular and user-friendly. The atrium (with separately enclosed room for booking shore excursions) is a friendly four decks high and houses the reception desk, tour operator's desk, and bank. Four dramatic glass-walled elevators travel through the ship's exterior (port) side, connecting the atrium with another seven decks (thus traveling through 11 passenger decks), including the tender station — a nice ride.

Cigar smokers will appreciate Michael's Club — the superb cigar and cognac specialty lounge that features almost 20 varieties of cigars, as well as travel humidor packs and cigar cutters, all for sale. It is approximately twice the size of the one aboard *Century*, and is decorated in an 18th-century Georgian style, with sofas, high-back chairs, and writing tables.

Facilities include a combination cinema/conference center, an expansive shopping arcade with over 14,000 sq ft (1,300 sq m) of retail store space (including H. Stern, Donna Karan, Fossil, and the exclusive Michel Roux culinary store), a lavish four-decks-high show lounge with the latest in staging and lighting equipment, two-level library (one level for English-language books; a second level for books in other languages); card room; CD listening room; art auction center (with seating that makes it look more like a small chapel); "Cosmos," a combination observation lounge/discotheque; and an Internet Center with 19 computer stations.

In addition, a flower shop is enclosed in a two-decks-high glass circular tower and features fresh flowers for any occasion, and a selection of Emilio Robbe glass and flower creations, as well as pot pourri and other flora and fauna items.

Outdoor facilities include two outdoor pools, one indoor/outdoor pool, and six whirlpools. There is also a large AquaSpa (with large thalassotherapy pool under a huge solarium dome), complete with health bar for light breakfast and lunch items, and fresh squeezed fruit and vegetable juices. Spa facilities (measuring 25,000 sq ft/ 2323 sq m) include 16 treatment rooms; plus eight treatment rooms with showers and one treatment room specifically designed for wheelchair passengers, aerobics room, gymnasium (complete with all the latest high-tech muscle machines), large male and female saunas (with large ocean-view porthole window), a co-ed thermal suite (containing several steam and shower mist rooms with different fragrances such as chamomile, or eucalyptus and mint, plus a glacial ice fountain), and a beauty salon. Among the different types of massage available is a superb hot and cold stone massage therapy that lasts almost 1 1/2 hours.

Sports facilities include a full-size basketball court, compact football, paddle tennis, volleyball, golf simulator, shuffleboard (on two different decks), and a jogging track. A 70-person capacity sports bar called Extreme (a first for a Celebrity Cruises' ship, although it just doesn't, somehow, belong) is located directly in front of the main funnel and has glass walls that overlook the ship's side. Gaming sports include Fortunes Casino, with blackjack, roulette, and numerous slot machines.

Families with children will appreciate the "Fun Factory" (for children) and "The Tower" (for teenagers).

With such extensive facilities, this ship has an extremely comfortable environment for a large ship, with excellent food and dining facilities, and a well-run shipboard operation that will provide all the things necessary for you to have an outstanding vacation for a very modest price. My advice is to book a suite-category cabin for all the extra benefits it brings — it really is worth it.

Weak Points: There is, sadly, no wraparound wooden promenade deck outdoors. Standing in line for embarkation, disembarkation, shore tenders, and self-serve buffet meals is an inevitable aspect of cruising aboard all large ships. There are cushioned pads for poolside deck lounge chairs only, but not for chairs on other outside decks.

Minerva
★★★★

Small Ship:	12,500 tons	Cabins (for one person):	4
Lifestyle:	Premium	Cabins (with private balcony):	12
Cruise Line:	Swan Hellenic Cruises	Cabins (wheelchair accessible):	4
Former Names:	*Okean*	Cabin Current:	220-volt
Builder:	Marriotti (Italy)	Full-Service Dining Rooms:	1
Original Cost:	n/a	Elevators:	2
Entered Service:	April 1996	Casino (gaming tables):	No
Registry:	Bahamas	Slot Machines:	No
Length (ft/m):	436.3/133.0	Swimming Pools (outdoors):	1
Beam (ft/m):	65.6/20.0	Swimming Pools (indoors):	0
Draft (ft/m):	19.6/6.0	Whirlpools:	0
Propulsion/Propellers:	2 x Diesels (3,480kW)/2	Fitness Center:	Yes
Passenger Decks:	6	Sauna/Steam Room:	Yes/No
Total Crew:	157	Massage:	Yes
Passengers (lower beds/all berths):	352/474	Self-Service Launderette:	Yes
Pass. Space Ratio (lower beds/all berths):	35.5/26.3	Dedicated Cinema/Seats:	Yes/96
Crew/Pass. Ratio (lower beds/all berths):	2.1/3.0	Library:	Yes
Navigation Officers:	European	Classification Society:	Registro Navale Italiano
Cabins (total):	178		
Size Range (sq ft/sq m):	140.1–277.0/13.02–25.74	**OVERALL SCORE:**	**1,476**
Cabins (outside view):	126		
Cabins (interior/no view):	52	**(OUT OF A POSSIBLE 2,000 POINTS)**	

Accommodation: There is a decent range of accommodation; however, most are extremely small. All suites and cabins have a decent amount of closet and storage space, TV, and VCR; those designated as suites and deluxe cabins also have a refrigerator (however, there is no "privacy curtain" between the entry-way and sleeping area).

The cabin bathrooms are totally white and have very small showers (except for the suites, which have bathtubs and green-and-black marble floors), and plumbing fixtures were poorly installed. The cabin electrical sockets are of the British square, three-pin type.

No matter what grade of accommodation you book, all grades feature a pair of binoculars, hair dryer, bathrobe, TV with music channels, and telephone.

Dining: Open-seating dining is featured (this means that you can dine with whomever you wish) in both the main restaurant and the informal indoor/outdoor café. The menus are quite simple, but the food is attractively presented and has good taste. A staff that is a mix of Eastern Europeans and Filipinos provides the dining room service. Some "quiet tables" are provided for breakfast for those who like to eat without talking — a very welcome touch that I feel more ships would be wise to adopt.

Coffee and tea are available 24 hours a day from a beverage station in the serve-yourself Bridge Café, which also features casual breakfasts and lunches.

Other Comments: Originally intended to be a spy ship (named *Okean*) for the Soviet navy, the 1989-built hull was constructed at Nikolajev on the River Ingul in Ukraine. The hull originally had a stern ramp for launching submersibles for submarine tracking. It was then purchased by V-Ships (the ship's present owners), who towed it to Italy, where she was converted into a ship specifically tailored to the requirements of Swan Hellenic Cruises as the ship's charterer. She replaced *Orpheus*, which Swan Hellenic had chartered for the previous 21 years. She has a well-balanced, squat profile, with a single, central funnel, and a stern that is slightly rounded. The navigation bridge, however, always looks as if it should have been located one deck higher than it is. There is ample open and shaded deck space for this size ship (particularly in the aft section), and there is also a teakwood wraparound promenade deck.

Inside, there is an excellent selection of public rooms that includes a vast, well-stocked library, with classical decor. In general, the decor throughout the ship is best described as contemporary, yet restrained (for European passengers with good taste). Cigar smokers will appreciate the special smoking room and humidor service, and the high-back leather chairs provide a feeling of exclusivity.

The ship has fine wool carpets throughout, with an Oriental motif running through the passageways and public rooms. Perhaps the most used public room in the ship is the library, with its fine range of reference books (many of university standard). Passengers take delight in the multitude of puzzles and games — there are jigsaw puzzles galore. The reception desk is manned 24 hours a day.

Perhaps the most striking detail of interior decoration is the outstanding array of artwork aboard this ship. It is everywhere, in all passageways, on stairwells, in all public rooms, and cabins (most of it provided by Swan Hellenic passengers, and more is being added all the time). The one disappointment is in the plain white ceilings in the public rooms.

A cruise aboard *Minerva* really is cruising for the intelligent passenger (most of whom are — or were — professional people ashore) who yearns to learn more about life and times in civilizations past and present, albeit in a refined, comfortable setting. Intelligent conversation is a major part of Swan Hellenic cruises. The company features well planned, in-depth itineraries and shore excursions (the majority of which are included in the cruise fare) accompanied by some fine lecturers. All gratuities and shore excursions are included (these are carried out with almost military precision). Note that this ship is not recommended for children.

Weak Points: The cabins are very small.

Mistral
★★★★

Large Ship:	47,276 tons	Cabins (for one person):	0
Lifestyle:	Standard	Cabins (with private balcony):	80
Cruise Line:	Festival Cruises	Cabins (wheelchair accessible):	2
Former Names:	-	Cabin Current:	110/220-volt
Builder:	Chantiers de l'Atlantique (France)	Full-Service Dining Rooms:	2
Original Cost:	$245 million	Elevators:	6
Entered Service:	July 1999	Casino (gaming tables):	Yes
Registry:	Wallis & Fortuna (France)	Slot Machines:	Yes
Length (ft/m):	708.6/216.00	Swimming Pools (outdoors):	1
Beam (ft/m):	94.6/28.84	Swimming Pools (indoors):	0
Draft (ft/m):	22.4/6.85	Whirlpools:	1 (thalassotherapy)
Propulsion/Propellers:	Diesel-electric (31,680kW)/2	Fitness Center:	Yes
Passenger Decks:	8	Sauna/Steam Room:	No/Yes
Total Crew:	480	Massage:	Yes
Passengers (lower beds/all berths):	1,196/1,715	Self-Service Launderette:	No
Pass. Space Ratio (lower beds/all berths):	39.5/27.5	Dedicated Cinema:	No
Crew/Pass. Ratio (lower beds/all berths):	2.4/3.5	Library:	Yes
Navigation Officers:	European	Classification Society:	Bureau Veritas
Cabins (total):	598		
Size Range (sq ft/sq m):	139.9–236.8/13.0–22.0	**OVERALL SCORE:**	**1,529**
Cabins (outside view):	275		
Cabins (interior/no view):	223	**(OUT OF A POSSIBLE 2,000 POINTS)**	

Accommodation: There are three basic cabin types, in 11 different grades: suites (each of which has a private balcony, although the partitions are only of the partial, and not the full type); ocean-view standard cabins; and interior (no view) standard cabins. In addition, there are two interior (no view) wheelchair-accessible cabins for the handicapped. Good planning and layout means that no outside-view cabins have obstructed views of lifeboats, as aboard many ships today. The cabin numbering system goes against maritime tradition, where even-numbered cabins are located on the port side and odd-numbered cabins are located on the starboard side; in *Mistral*, the opposite is in effect.

All of the cabins feature twin beds that convert to a queen-size unit; bold, colorful bedspreads; a personal safe; a combination color TV/VCR; telephone; and a good amount of closet and drawer space for a one-week cruise. The bathrooms, although not large, do have a good-size shower enclosure, and there is a decent amount of stowage space for personal toiletry items.

Accommodation designated as suites (these are really only larger cabins and not suites, as there is no separation of lounge and sleeping space) quite naturally feature more space, larger (walk-in) closets, more drawers, and better storage space, plus a two-person sofa, coffee table and additional armchair, vanity desk, floor-to-ceiling mirrors, and hair dryer. The bathrooms feature a bathtub/shower combination.

Dining: There are two dining rooms (and two seatings for meals), which can be configured in any of several different ways. Both have ocean-view windows. The principal dining room (L'Etoile, which seats 600) has round tables for two, four, six, or eight, and a small podium complete with baby grand piano. A second dining room (Rialto, which seats 380 and is located on a different deck) is used for suite passengers and anyone wishing to "upgrade" to a smaller, more intimate restaurant. It has tables for two, four, or six. Both dining rooms are nonsmoking.

The food featured by Festival Cruises is quite sound and, with varied menus and good presentation, should prove a highlight for most passengers. The wine list features a wide variety of wines at fairly reasonable prices, although almost all wines are very young.

In addition, there is a casual cafeteria for informal buffet-style breakfasts and lunches, with ocean-view windows, as well as a pleasant little coffee bar, also with ocean-view windows.

Other Comments: *Mistral* is an all-white ship, with a single blue funnel, and blue and yellow bands to separate hull from superstructure. She is the first brand new ship for this growing European cruise line, which caters almost exclusively to European passengers, and two more ships of the same type (but marginally enlarged) soon followed (*European Vision* in 2001 and *European Dream* in 2002). *Mistral* is the name of a famous desert wind; it's also the name of a violin concerto. The company's older and smaller *Azur* and *Flamenco* will, more than likely, be positioned for full charters in the future, in order to differentiate the old from the new tonnage.

Mistral is owned by a consortium of French investors and is being operated under long-term charter to Festival Cruises, a vibrant young company that is growing rapidly. She is the largest ship sailing under the French flag (it is actually Wallis & Fortuna, a French possession). The ship's profile is similar to that of most new cruise ships, although her built-up stern makes the ship look a trifle bulky and unhandsome.

The ship is comparable in size to Celebrity Cruises' *Horizon* and *Zenith*, has slightly fewer cabins and therefore a better space ratio, which means the ship absorbs passengers quite well.

The Lido Deck surrounding the outdoor swimming pool also features whirlpool tubs and a large bandstand is set in raised canvas-covered pods. All the deck lounge chairs have cushioned pads.

Inside, the layout and passenger flow is very good, as are the "you are here" deck signs. The deck names are those of European capitals, the public rooms are located on Paris Deck and Rome Deck. The interior decor is light and cheerful without being glitzy in any way (with not even a hint of colored neon) and there is much use of blond wood paneling and rich, textured soft furnishings. The names of public rooms, bars, and lounges are named after European places or establishments.

There is a smoking room, which has all the hallmarks of a gentlemen's club of former times, as well as a piano bar. The library has real writing desks (something many ships seem to omit today).

The main show lounge is tiered and has good sight lines from most seats (banquette-style seating is featured), and there is a small balcony level at the rear. There's also a bar/lounge on the lower (main) level at the entrance to the show lounge. High atop the ship is an observation lounge with a twist — it faces aft, instead of forward — a nice change. The room also doubles as a discotheque for the late-night set. A conference center adds facilities that are good for meetings.

There is also a good-size spa/beauty complex, set forward of the mast. This includes a fitness center with lots of muscle-toning equipment and life-cycles/life-rowing machines and a view over the bow of the ship through large floor-to-ceiling windows. There are six rooms for massage and other body treatments, as well as a sauna each for men and women, plus an aerobics exercise room. Adjacent is a video game room for teens, and a children's center. Dialysis equipment is available in the hospital, as well as trained technicians.

The ship operates seven-night Mediterranean cruises from Italy during the summer and fall, and sevennight Caribbean cruises during the winter. As the ship operates in several languages (remember that this means all announcements will be in several languages), a good number of multilingual cruise staff and reception desk staff are featured at all key points. All prices aboard ship are quoted only in euros. *Mistral* was built for a European company, and designed and constructed by Europeans, with European decor and colors, for European passengers. She features European food, service, and entertainment. In other words, as the company so strongly states, this is a ship *for Europeans*.

Weak Points: Standing in line for embarkation, disembarkation, shore tenders, and self-serve buffet meals is an inevitable aspect of cruising aboard all large ships. There is no full wraparound promenade deck outdoors, although there is a partial walking deck on both port and starboard sides (under the lifeboats), as well as an oval jogging track atop ship. Smokers are everywhere and are difficult to avoid (in typical European fashion, ashtrays are simply moved — if used at all — to wherever smokers happen to be sitting). The towels are small. The square chairs in the Caffé Greco are both uncomfortable and impractical. The cabins on Deck 10 are subject to noise from the Lido Deck above. The Lido Deck is virtually unusable in windy conditions.

Monarch of the Seas
★★★ +

Large Ship:	73,941 tons	Cabins (for one person):	0
Lifestyle:	Standard	Cabins (with private balcony):	62
Cruise Line:	Royal Caribbean International	Cabins (wheelchair accessible):	4
Former Names:	-	Cabin Current:	110-volt
Builder:	Chantiers de l'Atlantique	Full-Service Dining Rooms:	2
Original Cost:	$300 million	Elevators:	11
Entered Service:	November 1991	Casino (gaming tables):	Yes
Registry:	Norway	Slot Machines:	Yes
Length (ft/m):	879.9/268.2	Swimming Pools (outdoors):	2
Beam (ft/m):	105.9/32.3	Swimming Pools (indoors):	0
Draft (ft/m):	24.9/7.6	Whirlpools:	2
Propulsion/Propellers:	Diesel (21,844kW)/2	Fitness Center:	Yes
Passenger Decks:	14	Sauna/Steam Room:	Yes/No
Total Crew:	822	Massage:	Yes
Passengers (lower beds/all berths):	2,354/2,744	Self-Service Launderette:	No
Pass. Space Ratio (lower beds/all berths):	31/26.9	Dedicated Cinema/Seats:	Yes-2/146 each
Crew/Pass. Ratio (lower beds/all berths):	2.8/3.3	Library:	Yes
Navigation Officers:	Norwegian	Classification Society:	Det Norske Veritas
Cabins (total):	1,177		
Size Range (sq ft/sq m):	119.4–446.7/11.1–41.5		
Cabins (outside view):	732		
Cabins (interior/no view):	445		

OVERALL SCORE: **1,394**

(OUT OF A POSSIBLE 2,000 POINTS)

Accommodation: This ship has small cabins, but the company's philosophy is that you will not spend much time in your cabin. The suites are quite spacious, but most cabins are small, comfortable, and attractively decorated, except for the very plain ceilings. Special "family suites," located amidships, sleep four. The in-cabin food service menu is quite poor (too much standardization).

Dining: The two large dining rooms (both are nonsmoking) have Hollywood musical themes. There are tables for four, six, or eight, but no tables for two, and there are two seatings. The dining operation is well orchestrated, with emphasis on highly programmed (insensitive), extremely hurried service that many find intrusive.

    Most nights are themed (typically French, Oriental, Italian, Caribbean, American), as they have been for years, with waiters and busboys in appropriate costumes. The food is typical of hotel banquet catering. The menu descriptions make the food sound better than it is, which is consistently average, mostly disappointing and without much taste. However, a decent selection of light meals is provided, and a vegetarian menu is available. The selection of breads, rolls, fruits, and cheeses is quite poor, however, and should be upgraded. One thing this company does once each cruise is to feature the "Galley Buffet," where passengers go through a section of the galley picking up food for a midnight buffet.

    The wine list is not very extensive, but the prices are moderate. The waiters, many of whom are from Caribbean countries, are perhaps overly friendly for some tastes — particularly on the last night of the cruise, when tips are expected.

    For casual breakfasts and lunches, the Windjammer Café is the place to go, although there are often long lines at peak times, and the selection is very average.

Other Comments: Almost identical in size and appearance to her sister ship *Sovereign of the Seas* (the first of a trio), but with improved internal layout, public room features, passenger flow, and signs. A basketball court is provided for sports fans.

    RCI's trademark Viking Crown lounge and bar surrounds the funnel and provides a stunning view. Following grounding (just prior to Christmas 1998), the ship underwent the replacement of 460 tons of bottom shell plating. At the same time, a new facility for toddlers was created. The children's and teens' programs are good, overseen by enthusiastic youth counselors, and a busy but sound entertainment program.

There are many public rooms and spaces to play in, including a five-decks-high atrium, which really is the interior focal point of the ship and has glass elevators. There is a fine library.

Monarch of the Seas provides a wide range of facilities, with consistently sound but highly programmed service from a reasonably attentive, though rather insensitive young staff.

Weak Points: Standing in line for embarkation, disembarkation, shore tenders, and self-serve buffet meals is an inevitable aspect of cruising aboard all large ships. There are too many announcements. Because the public rooms are mostly located aft, there is often a long wait for elevators, particularly at peak times (after dinner, shows, talks). The ship looks tired.

Traveling the River Thames in London is a unique experience.

Monterey
★★ +

Mid-Size Ship:	20,040 tons	Cabins (with private balcony):	0
Lifestyle:	Standard	Cabins (wheelchair accessible):	0
Cruise Line:	Mediterranean Shipping Cruises	Cabin Current:	110-volt
Former Names:	*Free State Mariner*	Full-Service Dining Rooms:	1
Builder:	Bethlehem Steel Corp. (US)	Elevators:	2
Original Cost:	n/a	Casino (gaming tables):	Yes
Entered Service:	December 1952/August 1988	Slot Machines:	Yes
Registry:	Panama	Swimming Pools (outdoors):	1
Length (ft/m):	563.6/171.81	Swimming Pools (indoors):	0
Beam (ft/m):	80.3/24.50	Whirlpools:	2
Draft (ft/m):	29.3/8.95	Fitness Center:	Yes
Propulsion/Propellers:	Steam turbine (14,400kW)/1	Sauna/Steam Room:	Yes/No
Passenger Decks:	4	Massage:	Yes
Total Crew:	280	Self-Service Launderette:	No
Passengers (lower beds/all berths):	588/638	Dedicated Cinema/Seats:	Yes/107
Pass. Space Ratio (lower beds/all berths):	34/31.4	Library:	Yes
Crew/Pass. Ratio (lower beds/all berths):	2/2.2	Classification Society:	American Bureau of
Navigation Officers:	Italian		Shipping
Cabins (total):	294		
Size Range (sq ft/sq m):	64.5–344.4/6.5–32.0		
Cabins (outside view):	167		
Cabins (interior/no view):	127		
Cabins (for one person):	0		

OVERALL SCORE: **1,087**

(OUT OF A POSSIBLE 2,000 POINTS)

Accommodation: There is a wide choice of cabin sizes and configurations, but only the top three categories have full bathtubs, while all other cabins have shower enclosures. The suites are extremely spacious; other outside-view and interior (no view) cabins are quite roomy, well-appointed units, but most have tinny metal drawers (a carryover from her former years as a Matson Line ship).

The cabins located forward on Boat Deck have lifeboat-obstructed views, but other cabins on this deck are quite large; all have a window, plenty of closet and drawer space, a vanity desk, coffee table, sofa, and chair. Bathrobes are provided for all passengers.

Dining: The two-level dining room is set low down and is quite charmingly decorated in soft earth tones, so the ambience is quite cozy, although it is noisy when full. There are two seatings. Features continental cuisine, with some excellent pasta dishes. There is only the most basic selection of breads, cheeses, and fruits. The service is friendly and attentive, in typical Italian style, but it is somewhat hurried and lacks finesse.

For casual self-serve breakfasts and luncheons, there is also a casual café, with good views over the aft pool deck and stern.

Other Comments: This ship has a traditional but now dated 1950s ocean liner profile. She was built originally for the United States Maritime Commission as a C-4 cargo vessel before becoming a Matson Lines ship in 1956, when her name was changed to *Monterey*. She is very stable at sea, with an almost vertical bow and an overhanging aircraft-carrier-like stern that is not at all handsome when viewed from ashore, but provides a good amount of open deck space around the white-tiled swimming pool and Jacuzzis. There are also partly enclosed port and starboard walking promenades, although, sadly, they do not wrap around the vessel. On the navigation bridge is an interesting relic from her former days, a spirit level!

The ship was refurbished in a moderate Art Deco style, and a new sports deck was added several years ago. There is a reasonable amount of sheltered and open deck space, and some forward open observation deck space atop some suites that were added in the late 1980s.

Inside, there are a reasonable number of public rooms to play in. All of them have high ceilings, although there is little elegance. There is too much cold steel and not enough warmth in the interior decoration, although this has been addressed somewhat when decor changes have been made. Rising through three decks is a large, slim totem pole, a carryover from her limited days as a ship operating under the banner of Aloha Pacific Cruises.

The crew features a number of Italians, and they provide a friendly atmosphere, but there is really little finesse in service.

This ship offers cruises in reasonable style and surroundings, with mainly European and particularly Italian-speaking passengers (about 60%). Currency used aboard is the lire. Port taxes are included.

Weak Points: There is no observation lounge with forward-facing views over the ship's bows. There are far too many loud, repetitive, and unnecessary announcements — often in up to five languages. There is a charge for the sauna, which is located inside the beauty salon and operated by the concession.

SHIP TALK

Helm: the apparatus for steering a ship.

House Flag: the flag denoting the company to which a ship belongs.

Hull: the frame and body of the ship exclusive of masts or superstructure.

Leeward: the side that is sheltered from the wind.

Manifest: a list of the ship's passengers, crew, and cargo.

Nautical Mile: one-sixtieth of a degree of the circumference of the Earth.

Pilot: a person licensed to navigate ships into or out of a harbor or through difficult waters, and to advise the captain on handling the ship during these procedures.

Pitch: the rise and fall of a ship's bow that may occur when the ship is under way.

Port: the left side of a ship when facing forward.

Quay: berth, dock, or pier.

Rudder: a finlike device astern and below the waterline, for steering the vessel.

Screw: a ship's propeller.

Stabilizer: a gyroscopically operated retractable "fin" extending from either or both sides of the ship below the waterline to provide a more stable ride.

Starboard: the right side of the ship when facing forward.

Stern: the aftmost part of the ship that is opposite the bow.

Tender: a smaller vessel, often a lifeboat, that is used to transport passengers between the ship and shore when the vessel is at anchor.

Wake: the track of agitated water left behind a ship when in motion.

Waterline: the line along the side of a ship's hull corresponding to the water surface.

Windward: the side toward which the wind blows.

Yaw: the erratic deviation from the ship's set course, usually caused by a heavy sea.

Nantucket Clipper
★★★ +

Small Ship:	1,471 tons	Cabins (with private balcony):	0
Lifestyle:	Standard	Cabins (wheelchair accessible):	0
Cruise Line:	Clipper Cruise Line	Cabin Current:	110-volt
Former Names:	-	Full-Service Dining Rooms:	1
Builder:	Jeffboat (US)	Elevators:	0
Original Cost:	$9 million	Casino (gaming tables):	No
Entered Service:	December 1984	Slot Machines:	No
Registry:	US	Swimming Pools (outdoors):	0
Length (ft/m):	207.0/63.00	Swimming Pools (indoors):	0
Beam (ft/m):	37.0/11.20	Whirlpools:	0
Draft (ft/m):	8.0/2.40	Fitness Center:	No
Propulsion/Propellers:	Diesel (700kW)/2	Sauna/Steam Room:	No/No
Passenger Decks:	4	Massage:	No
Total Crew:	32	Self-Service Launderette:	No
Passengers (lower beds/all berths):	102/102	Dedicated Cinema:	No
Pass. Space Ratio (lower beds/all berths):	14.4/14.4	Library:	Yes
Crew/Pass. Ratio (lower beds/all berths):	3.1/3.1	Classification Society:	American Bureau of
Navigation Officers:	American		Shipping
Cabins (total):	51		
Size Range (sq ft/sq m):	120.5–137.7/11.2–12.8		
Cabins (outside view):	51		
Cabins (interior/no view):	0		
Cabins (for one person):	0		

OVERALL SCORE: 1,265
(OUT OF A POSSIBLE 2,000 POINTS)

Accommodation: There are four grades of all-outside cabins. All are extremely small and basic. They are relatively tastefully furnished, with wood-accented trim and good sound insulation. Honeymooners and lovers should note that beds are of the twin variety, however, and are bolted to the deck and wall. Bathrooms are tight and there's little space for toiletries. Thoughtfully, a night-light is provided.

Dining: The dining room is warm and inviting and has large picture windows. There is one seating, and you can sit with whomever you wish. There are no tables for two. Features simple and plain American cuisine that is quite tasty, although the menu choice is limited, and the portions are small. The chefs are from the Culinary Institute of America, and all ingredients are fresh. The chocolate chip cookies are popular and are served at various times, typically in the lounge.

Other Comments: This small, shallow draft vessel is specially built for coastal and inland cruises and is very maneuverable. She has been well maintained although is now showing signs of aging. This extremely high-density ship has only two public rooms — the dining room and an observation lounge, where most passengers congregate in the evening. Passengers can visit the bridge at any time. There is a wraparound teakwood deck for strolling. Not recommended for night owls. Passengers are typically over 60.

The service is by young, friendly, all-American college-age types. This is most definitely an "Americana" experience for those seeking to learn more about the coastal ports around the US. The ship features a casual, unstructured lifestyle, rather like a small (but certainly not luxurious) country club afloat, with some attention to detail. This should not be compared with big ship ocean cruising. Thankfully, there are no mindless activities or corny parlor games.

Specialist lecturers are part of every cruise. These highlight the learning experience that is an essential part of cruising with Clipper Cruise Lines. As the ship is often in coastal destinations, a few bicycles would be a welcome addition! A nonsmoking policy throughout all interior areas was put into effect in December 1996.

Weak Points: She really is a high-density ship, with only two public rooms. The engine noise level is high when the ship is under way (okay for the hard of hearing). The per diem price is high for what you get, and airfare is extra.

Narvik
★★ +

Small Ship:	6,257 tons	Cabins (with private balcony):	0
Lifestyle:	Standard	Cabins (wheelchair accessible):	2
Cruise Line:	Norwegian Coastal Voyages (OVDS)	Cabin Current:	220-volt
Former Names:	-	Full-Service Dining Rooms:	1
Builder:	Aker Trondelag (Norway)	Elevators:	1
Original Cost:	n/a	Casino (gaming tables):	No
Entered Service:	1982	Slot Machines:	No
Registry:	Norway	Swimming Pools (outdoors):	0
Length (ft/m):	356.2/108.6	Swimming Pools (inside):	0
Beam (ft/m):	54.1/16.5	Whirlpools:	0
Draft (ft/m):	16.0/4.9	Fitness Center:	No
Total Crew:	55	Sauna/Steam Room:	No/No
Passengers (lower beds/all berths):	286/312	Massage:	No
Pass. Space Ratio (lower beds/all berths):	21.8/19.9	Self-Service Launderette:	No
Crew/Pass. Ratio (lower beds/all berths):	5.2/5.6	Dedictated Cinema:	No
Navigation Officers:	Norwegian	Library:	No
Cabins (total):	143	Classification Society:	Det Norske Veritas
Size Range (sq ft/sq m):	n/a		
Cabins (outside view):	94	**OVERALL SCORE:**	**1,093**
Cabins (interior/no view):	49		
Cabins (for one person):	0	**(OUT OF A POSSIBLE 2,000 POINTS)**	

Accommodation: There are six cabin grades. All cabins feature a mix of lower beds, lower berths, and upper berths (there are no double-bedded cabins). The cabins are cozy, which translates to very, very small; the bathrooms, likewise, are tiny, although they do have a shower and toilet. All cabins have a 220-volt outlet, so take adapters and converters if you need to.

Dining: There is one dining room (no smoking allowed), and tables are assigned when you embark. Three meals each day are included in the cruise fare: Breakfast and lunch (featuring the famous Norwegian "cold table") are self-serve, buffet-style meals, while dinner is a sit-down affair, with three courses. Additionally, there is a cafeteria, open 24 hours, where snacks and light meals can be purchased.

Other Comments: The Norwegian Coastal Voyage is a service that was started in 1863. It is jointly operated by two companies: Ofotens og Vesteraalen Dampskibsselskab (OVDS) and Troms Fylkes Dampskibsselskab (TFDS). The complete journey, of 1,250 nautical miles, takes in 34 ports of call in a 12-day roundtrip voyage between Bergen and Kirkenes (on the border with Russia), above the Arctic Circle (where a special "Crossing the Arctic Circle" ceremony welcomes newcomers). The journey can also be done in a one-way voyage that takes seven days (northbound) or six days (southbound). The ships carry passengers as well as mail and other cargo.

Perhaps you will be able to peek at the midnight sun (mid-May to late June, north of the Arctic Circle), experience the northern lights (aurora borealis, mostly seen during winter months, and only when the atmospheric conditions are right), and be part of the daily life of the hardy Norwegians. Approximately 60% of the passengers will be Norwegian/Scandinavian/European, while the rest will be a mix of North American and other nationalities. Although the passenger bed capacity is quoted, note that many additional passengers may be on board as day passengers, sailing between two coastal ports — the ship is the equivalent of a seagoing bus for the coastal commuters. As for the weather, the west coast of Norway is warmed by the Gulf Stream, and temperatures will be similar to those found in New England.

Best suited to adult couples, single travelers, and families with children wanting to cruise along the coast of Norway and experience the area's natural beauty. It's ideal for anyone who doesn't need entertainment or mindless parlor games, but wants to relax and unwind, enjoys being close to nature, and is probably a bit of an adventurer. This is an excellent way to experience the beautiful coastline of Norway and its fascinating coastal towns. There will be an interesting mix of passengers — it's a good way to meet new people and make new friends from different countries.

The rates vary by season, cabin location, and whether the ship is of the "new generation" (*Kong Harald, Nordkapp, Nordlys, Nordnorge, Polarlys, Richard With*), the "mid-generation" (*Narvik, Midnatsol, Vesteralen*), or the "traditional" (*Harald Jarl, Lofoten*) type ships. Senior citizens (those age 67 and over) qualify for a special discount.

The dress code is casual and comfortable — layered clothing is recommended. The currency is the Norwegian krone.

Operates Norwegian coast and fjords cruises (year-round): 7-day (northbound) voyage between Bergen and Kirkenes, Norway; or a 6-day (southbound) voyage between Kirkenes and Bergen, Norway; or a 12-day roundtrip voyage. The ship also has space for up to 40 cars.

Weak Points: The ship does not have stabilizers, so you should expect some movement when the weather is inclement or unkind. Drinks prices are extremely high — the same as ashore in Norway. The cabins are small, and the bathrooms are really tiny. Although not needed during the winter, there is little outdoor deck space considering the number of passengers carried.

Niagara Prince
★★ +

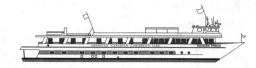

Small Ship:	99 tons	Cabins (with private balcony):	0
Lifestyle:	Standard	Cabins (wheelchair accessible):	0
Cruise Line:	American Canadian Caribbean Line	Cabin Current:	110-volt
Former Names:	-	Full-Service Dining Rooms:	1
Builder:	Blount Industries (US)	Elevators:	0
Original Cost:	$7.5 million	Casino (gaming tables):	No
Entered Service:	November 1994	Slot Machines:	No
Registry:	US	Swimming Pools (outdoors):	0
Length (ft/m):	177.0/53.9	Swimming Pools (indoors):	0
Beam (ft/m):	40.0/12.1	Whirlpools:	0
Draft (ft/m):	6.7/2.0	Fitness Center:	0
Propulsion/Propellers:	Diesel (1044kW)/2	Sauna/Steam Room:	0/0
Passenger Decks:	3	Massage:	0
Total Crew:	17	Self-Service Launderette:	No
Passengers (lower beds/all berths):	84/94	Dedicated Cinema:	No
Pass. Space Ratio (lower beds/alberths):	1.1/1.0	Library:	Yes
Crew/Pass. Ratio (lower beds/all berths):	4.9/5.5	Classification Society:	American Bureau
Navigation Officers:	American		of Shipping
Cabins (total):	48		
Size Range (sq ft/sq m):	72.0–96.0/6.6–8.9		
Cabins (outside view):	40		
Cabins (interior/no view):	2		
Cabins (for one person):	6		

OVERALL SCORE: 1,087

(OUT OF A POSSIBLE 2,000 POINTS)

Accommodation: The cabins are small, basic, and plain. Only a metal cabinet is provided for hanging your clothes, and there are a few small metal drawers. No smoking is allowed in any cabin. The air-conditioning consists of recirculated air. Beds in 75% of the cabins can be made up as two singles or a queen-size bed (ten cabins have a third berth). The bathrooms are the size of a telephone booth (tiny) and very frustrating.

Dining: The dining room is operated in one open seating (no assigned tables), with tables for four, six, eight, or ten. Meals are served "family-style." The cuisine features good, wholesome Americana fare, with fresh-baked breads, muffins, and regional dishes. There are, perhaps, too many high-cholesterol, fatty foods for the older passengers carried. A "bring your own bottle" policy exists for those who want wine with dinner, or any alcoholic beverages (however, mixers are available).

Other Comments: The vessel is equipped with a unique, retractable wheelhouse for passage under low bridges on island waterway itineraries, and there is also a small platform for those who want to swim off the stern. There is also a glass-bottom boat and a sunfish sailboat. See other comments for the company's *Grande Prince*.

An underwater video camera allows passengers to see what a SCUBA diver might see underneath the ship, while seated in (dry) comfort in the lounge, on large-screen TV monitors. Underwater lights, which attract fish and other marine life, are also fitted.

Cruising aboard this ship is for those who do not want or need pampering, or much of the service, entertainment, or facilities provided aboard regular cruise ships. This vessel is enjoyed by high percentages of repeat passengers, however, who seek a simple, unpretentious lifestyle. Take only casual clothing and the odd sweater or jacket. Although there is no elevator, there is a stair lift for those who need a little help. All gratuities are pooled by the entire staff.

Weak Points: Small, utilitarian cabins. No alcoholic beverages are available. There's no laundry aboard, so bed linen, towels and other items are all taken ashore for cleaning.

Nippon Maru
★★★ +

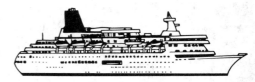

Small Ship:	21,903 tons	Cabins (with private balcony):	0
Lifestyle:	Standard	Cabins (wheelchair accessible):	2
Cruise Line:	Mitsui OSK Passenger Line	Cabin Current:	100-volt
Former Names:	-	Full-Service Dining Rooms:	1
Builder:	Mitsubishi Heavy Industries (Japan)	Elevators:	5
Original Cost:	$59.4 million	Casino (gaming tables):	Yes
Entered Service:	September 1990		(no cash can be won, only gifts)
Registry:	Japan	Slot Machines:	No
Length (ft/m):	546.7/166.65	Swimming Pools (outdoors):	1
Beam (ft/m):	78.7/24.00	Swimming Pools (indoors):	0
Draft (ft/m):	21.4/6.55	Whirlpools:	4 (Japanese baths)
Propulsion/Propellers:	Diesel (15,740kW)/2	Fitness Center:	Yes
Passenger Decks:	7	Sauna/Steam Room:	Yes/No
Total Crew:	160	Massage:	Yes
Passengers (lower beds/all berths):	408/607	Self-Service Launderette:	Yes
Pass. Space Ratio (lower beds/alberths):	53.6/36.0	Dedicated Cinema/Seats:	Yes/135
Crew/Pass. Ratio (lower beds/all berths):	2.5/3.7	Library:	Yes
Navigation Officers:	Japanese	Classification Society:	Nippon Kaiji Kyokai
Cabins (total):	204		
Size Range (sq ft/sq m):	150.6–430.5/14.0–40.0		
Cabins (outside view):	189		
Cabins (interior/no view):	15		
Cabins (for one person):	0		

OVERALL SCORE: 1,397
(OUT OF A POSSIBLE 2,000 POINTS)

Accommodation: Most of the cabins are located forward, with public rooms positioned aft. The suites are quite large (larger than aboard sister ship *Fuji Maru*) and feature a separate bedroom and living room with a solid wall divider except for the doorway (where there is a curtain but no door). A large sofa, four chairs, and coffee table occupy one section of the lounge; there is also a vanity/writing desk. The bedroom has a good amount of closet and drawer space as well as two beds. The bathroom is very small, however, although there is a small vanity desk with make-up mirror. Both slippers and bathrobes are provided.

The deluxe cabins are quite nicely decorated, and the living area has a table and two chairs, and two beds that cannot be pushed together.

The standard cabins are utilitarian and clinical (adequate for convention and seminar cruise passengers, however, and those that don't mind just the basics). Many of these have a third (or third and fourth) pull-down upper Pullman berth. The lighting is minimal and quite utilitarian.

Dining: The dining room is quite basic and features both traditional Japanese cuisine and some Western dishes. Features one seating for leisure cruises and two seatings for ship charter cruises. The food presentation is quite decent, but rather plain, and menu choice is limited, although quite welcome by most passengers.

Other Comments: Has a single, large, orange, swept-back funnel aft of amidships, with an exterior styling that is very traditional and not at all contemporary. There is a decent amount of open outdoors space, and the teak decking outdoors is good. The ship was specifically built and outfitted for Japanese passengers and the Japanese seminar/lecture marketplace.

Inside, the well-designed public rooms have very high ceilings, quality furnishings, and soothing color combinations. The interior decor throughout much of the ship is plain and unexciting.

There is an elegant, quite dramatic six-decks-high atrium. Features true Japanese baths, and a washitsu tatami room. Children's activities personnel are placed onboard only for leisure cruises.

This ship is principally for older Japanese passengers (those of "silver" years) who want to cruise at moderate rates in pleasant, but not luxurious, surrroundings, with Japanese food that is varied, colorful, and plentiful. Tipping is not allowed.

A specialist courier company provides an excellent luggage service and will collect your luggage from your home before the cruise and deliver it back to your home after the cruise (this service available only in Japan).

Weak Points: The cheap plastic deck furniture is difficult to keep clean and looks really poor and unkempt. The seats in the theater are very plain and utilitarian, and not particularly comfortable. Hospitality toward passengers could be improved (particularly by the officers).

BAGGAGE

→ There is generally no limit to the amount of personal baggage you can take on your cruise (towels, soap, shampoo, and shower caps are provided aboard most cruise ships). Do allow extra space for purchases on the cruise.

→ Tag your luggage with your name, ship, cabin number, sailing date, and port of embarkation (tags are provided by the cruise line with your tickets). Baggage transfers from airport to ship are generally smooth and problem-free when handled by the cruise line.

→ Liability for loss or damage to baggage is contained in the passenger contract (part of your ticket). Do take out insurance (the policy should extend from the date of departure until two or three days after your return home).

Noordam
★★★ +

Large Ship:	33,930 tons	Cabins (for one person):	0
Lifestyle:	Standard	Cabins (with private balcony):	0
Cruise Line:	Holland America Line	Cabins (wheelchair accessible):	4
Former Names:	-	Cabin Current:	110/220-volt
Builder:	Chantiers de l'Atlantique (France)	Full-Service Dining Rooms:	1
Original Cost:	$160 million	Elevators:	7
Entered Service:	April 1984	Casino (gaming tables):	Yes
Registry:	The Netherlands	Slot Machines:	Yes
Length (ft/m):	704.2/214.66	Swimming Pools (outdoors):	2
Beam (ft/m):	89.4/27.26	Swimming Pools (indoors):	0
Draft (ft/m):	24.2/7.40	Whirlpools:	1
Propulsion/Propellers:	Diesel (21,600kW)/2	Fitness Center:	Yes
Passenger Decks:	10	Sauna/Steam Room:	Yes/No
Total Crew:	530	Massage:	Yes
Passengers (lower beds/all berths):	1,214/1,350	Self-Service Launderette:	Yes
Pass. Space Ratio (lower beds/alberths):	28.0/25.1	Dedicated Cinema/Seats:	Yes/230
Crew/Pass. Ratio (lower beds/all berths):	2.2/2.5	Library:	Yes
Navigation Officers:	Dutch	Classification Society:	Lloyd's Register
Cabins (total):	607		
Size Range (sq ft/sq m):	150.6–296.0/14.0–27.5		
Cabins (outside view):	413		
Cabins (interior/no view):	194		

OVERALL SCORE: **1,350**

(OUT OF A POSSIBLE 2,000 POINTS)

Accommodation: There are 15 accommodation categories (9 with outside view, 6 interior with no view). In general, most of the cabins have a reasonable amount of space, although they are small when compared with those of many other ships. In general, they are adequately appointed and practically laid out, with some wood furniture and fittings, wood paneling, good counter and storage space (although there is very little drawer space), a large mirror, and a private bathroom that is very modest in size.

The top three categories of cabins (which are only marginally larger and should not really be called suites or mini-suites) have bathtubs while all others have shower enclosures only. Several cabins have king- or queen-size beds, although most have twin beds. Note that in many cabins, particularly those that are interior (no view), the bed configuration is L-shaped, and the beds cannot be pushed together.

A number of cabins also have additional berths for a third/fourth person. Room service is provided 24 hours a day. All cabin televisions feature CNN and TNT. The cabin insulation, however, is extremely poor, and bathroom towels are small. In addition, some cabins on Boat and Navigation Decks have obstructed views.

Dining: The dining room is reasonably large and quite attractive, with warm decor and ample space. Breakfast and lunch are served in an open seating (so you may get a different table and different waiters for each meal), and in two seatings for dinner (where you do have the same table and waiters, each evening). Tables are for two (although there are very few of them), four, six, or eight. The service is robotic and quite basic. The Indonesian waiters appear to try hard, but communication with them is often extremely frustrating. The wine waiters are quite useless (with a very poor understanding of good wines), as are the wine glasses. Fine china and cutlery are featured (although there are no fish knives).

Unfortunately, Holland America Line food isn't as nice as the china it's placed on. It may be adequate for most passengers who are not used to better food, but it does not match the standard found aboard other ships in the premium segment of the industry. While USDA beef is of a good quality, fowl tends to be battery-tough, and most fish is overcooked and has the consistency of a baseball bat. What are also definitely not luxurious are the endless packets of sugar and packets (instead of glass jars) of breakfast jam, marmalade, and honey, plus the poor quality teas. While these may be suitable for a family diner, they do not belong aboard a ship that claims to have "award-winning cuisine." Desserts and pastry items are of good quality (specifically for American tastes), although there is much use of canned fruits and jellies. Forget the selection of "international" cheeses.

Instead of the more formal dining room, the Lido Buffet is open for casual dinners on all except the last night of each cruise, in an open-seating arrangement. Tables are set with crisp linens, flatware, and stemware. A set menu is featured, and this includes a choice of four entrees.

Other Comments: There is a nicely raked bow, although the angular exterior design makes the ship look squat and somewhat boxy. There is a good amount of open deck space, and the traditional teak decks outdoors include a wraparound promenade deck. The ship, however, has a poor build quality and suffers from excessive vibration.

The ship has quite a spacious interior design and layout, and the soothing color combinations do not jar the senses, although they are rather dark and somber. There is much polished teak and rosewood paneling throughout. Features a fine, well-displayed collection of 17th- and 18th-century artwork and Dutch artifacts. The Crow's Nest observation lounge, located atop the ship, is a good retreat for many. The Explorers' Lounge is relaxing for after-meal coffee and live chamber music. The main lounge, which has a small balcony level, is reminiscent of those found on former ocean liners and is really good only for cabaret entertainment, and not full production shows. The flower bouquets throughout the ship add warmth to the ambience.

This ship is good for older passengers wanting pleasant surroundings and fairly bland food. *Note*: The line does not add an automatic 15% for beverage purchases, unlike many others. The company provides cappuccino and espresso coffees, and free ice cream during certain hours of the day aboard its ships, as well as hot hors d'oeuvres in all bars — something other major lines seem to have dropped, or charge extra for.

However, the latest batch of ships has more space, better facilities, and more options, which leaves this ship losing a few points in relation to the increased competition in the international marketplace. Her sister ship (formerly *Nieuw Amsterdam*) has been sold to United States Lines and is renamed *Patriot*.

Weak Points: Standing in line for embarkation, disembarkation, shore tenders, and self-serve buffet meals is an inevitable aspect of cruising aboard all large ships. This ship tries to be a Holland America Line ship but really doesn't fit in with the other (more standardized) ships in the fleet. There are simply too many interior (no view) cabins. There is a considerable amount of vibration throughout the ship, but particularly at the stern, and it's at its worst during slow maneuvering. The charge to use the washing machines and dryers in the self-service launderette is really petty and irritating, particularly for the occupants of suites, as they pay high prices for their cruises. The room service is poor. There are many pillars that obstruct the sight lines in the show lounge.

Nordic Empress
★★★ +

Large Ship:	48,563 tons	Cabins (for one person):	0
Lifestyle:	Standard	Cabins (with private balcony):	69
Cruise Line:	Royal Caribbean International	Cabins (wheelchair accessible):	4
Former Names:	-	Cabin Current:	110-volt
Builder:	Chantiers de l'Atlantique (France)	Full-Service Dining Rooms:	1
Original Cost:	$170 million	Elevators:	7
Entered Service:	June 1990	Casino (gaming tables):	Yes
Registry:	Liberia	Slot Machines:	220
Length (ft/m):	692.2/211.00	Swimming Pools (outdoors):	1 (+1 wading pool)
Beam (ft/m):	100.7/30.70	Swimming Pools (indoors):	0
Draft (ft/m):	24.9/7.60	Whirlpools:	4
Propulsion/Propellers:	Diesel (16,200kW)/2	Fitness Center:	Yes
Passenger Decks:	9	Sauna/Steam Room:	Yes/No
Total Crew:	685	Massage:	Yes
Passengers (lower beds/all berths):	1,600/2,020	Self-Service Launderette:	No
Pass. Space Ratio (lower beds/all berths):	30.2/24.0	Dedicated Cinema:	No
Crew/Pass. Ratio (lower beds/all berths):	2.3/2.9	Library:	No
Navigation Officers:	Scandinavian	Classification Society:	Det Norske Veritas
Cabins (total):	800		
Size Range (sq ft/sq m):	1176.2–269.1/10.8–25.0	**OVERALL SCORE:**	**1,355**
Cabins (outside view):	471		
Cabins (interior/no view):	329	**(OUT OF A POSSIBLE 2,000 POINTS)**	

Accommodation: Nine cabins have private balconies overlooking the stern (these consist of two owner's suites and two seven "superior" ocean-view cabins). The other cabins with private balconies also have a decent amount of living space, and a small sofa, coffee table and chair, and vanity desk.

Almost all of the other cabins are dimensionally challenged, although reasonably comfortable, particularly for the short cruises this ship operates during the winter season. All cabins (no matter what grade) have twin beds that convert to a queen-size configuration. The bathrooms are nicely laid out and have a decent amount of space for personal toiletry items

Dining: The two-level, Hollywood musical-theme dining room is noisy and has huge windows overlooking the stern. There are two seatings. The dining operation is well orchestrated, with emphasis on highly programmed (insensitive), extremely hurried service that many find intrusive.

Most evening meals are themed (typically French, Oriental, Italian, Caribbean, American), as they have been for years, with waiters and busboys in appropriate costumes. The food is typical of hotel banquet catering. The menu descriptions make the food sound better than it is, which is consistently average, mostly disappointing and without much taste. However, a decent selection of light meals is provided, and a vegetarian menu is available. The selection of breads, rolls, fruits, and cheeses is quite poor, however, and should be upgraded. One thing this company does once each cruise is to feature the "Galley Buffet," whereby passengers go through a section of the galley picking up food for a midnight buffet.

The wine list is not very extensive, but the prices are moderate. The waiters, many of whom are from Caribbean countries, are perhaps overly friendly for some tastes — particularly on the last night of the cruise, when tips are expected.

For casual breakfasts and lunches, the Windjammer Café is the place to go, although there are often long lines at peak times, and the selection is very average.

Other Comments: She is a fine contemporary ship with a short bow and squared-off stern that looks quite stunning. Nordic Empress was designed specifically for the short-cruise market, for which the ship is well suited. The ship was actually designed for Admiral Cruises, which Royal Caribbean Cruise Line (as it was then called) with the name of *Future Seas* (this was not finally adopted). There is a polished wraparound wood promenade deck outdoors, and there is a dramatic use of glass-enclosed viewing spaces that provide good contact from the upper, open decks to the sea.

Inside, a stunning nine-decks-high atrium is the focal point. Passenger flow is generally good, although at show time some congestion is inevitable adjacent to the entrance foyer. Lots of crystal and brass are used to good effect to reflect light. An ingenious use of lighting effects provides illuminating interiors that make you feel warm. The three-level casino has a sailcloth ceiling. There is a superb outdoor pool deck designed for evenings under the stars. The Viking Crown Lounge, aft of the funnel, is a two-level nightclub-disco for the late night set.

Nordic Empress is a fairly smart contemporary ship with a high passenger density. The ship features an adequate array of activities for all ages. The ship operated New York–Bermuda cruises in the summer of 2000, then repositioned to San Juan for three-and four-night cruises during the winter season.

Weak Points: Standing in line for embarkation, disembarkation, shore tenders, and self-serve buffet meals is an inevitable aspect of cruising aboard all large ships. The two-level show lounge has poor sight lines in the upper lateral balconies. The constant, loud announcements are irritating.

PHOTOGRAPHY

It is hard to find any situation more ideal for photography than a cruise. Your photographs enable you to share your memories with others at home. Here are some tips:

→ Use low-speed film in tropical areas such as the Caribbean or South Pacific (high-speed film is easily damaged by heat). Take plenty of film with you; standard sizes are available in the ship's shop, but the selection is limited. If you purchase film during a port visit, try to buy from an air-conditioned store, and check the expiration date.

→ Keep film cool, as the latent image on exposed film is fragile and easily affected by heat. There will be professional photographers on board who may develop film for you, for a fee (print film only).

→ When taking photographs in ports of call, respect the wishes of local inhabitants. Ask permission to photograph someone close-up. Most will smile and tell you to go ahead. But some people are superstitious or afraid of having their picture taken and will shy away from you. Do not press the point.

Nordkapp
★★★ +

Small Ship:	11,386 tons	Cabins (with private balcony):	0
Lifestyle:	Standard	Cabins (wheelchair accessible):	3
Cruise Line: Norwegian Coastal Voyages (OVDS)		Cabin Current:	220-volt
Former Names:	-	Full-Service Dining Rooms:	1
Builder:	Kvaerner Kleven (Norway)	Elevators:	2
Original Cost:	n/a	Casino (gaming tables):	No
Entered Service:	1996	Slot Machines:	No
Registry:	Norway	Swimming Pools (outdoors):	0
Length (ft/m):	399.6/121.8	Swimming Pools (indoors):	0
Beam (ft/m):	62.9/19.2	Whirlpools:	0
Draft (ft/m):	16.0/4.9	Fitness Center:	Yes
Total Crew:	70	Sauna/Steam Room:	Yes/No
Passengers (lower beds/all berths):	446/490	Massage:	No
Pass. Space Ratio (lower beds/all berths):	25.5/23.2	Self-Service Launderette:	Yes
Crew/Pass. Ratio (lower beds/all berths):	6.3/7.0	Dedicated Cinema:	No
Navigation Officers:	Norwegian	Library:	Yes
Cabins (total):	223	Classification Society:	Det Norske Veritas
Size Range (sq ft/sq m):	n/a		
Cabins (outside view):	179		
Cabins (interior/no view):	44		
Cabins (for one person):	0		

OVERALL SCORE: 1,285

(OUT OF A POSSIBLE 2,000 POINTS)

Accommodation: There are nine grades of cabin, including three wheelchair-accessible cabins (one of the ship's two elevators accommodates a wheelchair). Double beds are only available in the two suites; all other cabins have beds and berths that cannot be moved. Some cabins also have an additional third (upper) berth, and a number of cabins are available for single occupancy, albeit with a price premium. All cabins have a 220-volt outlet, so take adapters and converters if you need to.

Dining: There is one main dining room (the Nessekongen Restaurant — no smoking allowed), and tables are assigned when you embark. Three meals each day are included in the cruise fare: Breakfast and lunch (featuring the famous Norwegian "cold table") are self-serve, buffet-style meals, while dinner is a sit-down affair, with three courses.

Additionally, there is the Ut-Rost Café, which is open 24 hours, where snacks and light meals can be purchased.

Other Comments: The Norwegian Coastal Voyage is a service that was started in 1863. It is jointly operated by two companies: Ofotens og Vesteraalen Dampskibsselskab (OVDS) and Troms Fylkes Dampskibsselskab (TFDS). The complete journey, of 1,250 nautical miles, takes in 34 ports of call in a 12-day roundtrip voyage between Bergen and Kirkenes (on the border with Russia), above the Arctic Circle (where a special "Crossing the Arctic Circle" ceremony welcomes newcomers). The journey can also be done in a one-way voyage that takes seven days (northbound) or six days (southbound). The ships carry passengers as well as mail and other cargo.

Perhaps you will be able to peek at the midnight sun (mid-May to late June, north of the Arctic Circle), experience the northern lights (aurora borealis, mostly seen during winter months, and only when the atmospheric conditions are right), and be part of the daily life of the hardy Norwegians. Approximately 60% of the passengers will be Norwegian/Scandinavian/European, while the rest will be a mix of North American and other nationalities. Although the passenger bed capacity is quoted, note that many additional passengers may be on board as day passengers, sailing between two coastal ports — the ship is the equivalent of a seagoing bus for the coastal commuters. As for the weather, the west coast of Norway is warmed by the Gulf Stream, and temperatures will be similar to those found in New England.

This ship is one of the "new generation" of coastal voyage ships (built in the 1990s) that is rather like a mini-cruise vessel, with a better array of public rooms and facilities than the older, smaller ships in the fleet. This is an excellent way to experience the beautiful coastline of Norway and its fascinating coastal towns. There will be an interesting mix of passengers – it's a good way to meet new people and make new friends from different countries. A laundry room with washing machines, tumble dryers, and irons is provided (useful for those for whom the cruise is only part of a more extensive vacation).

The rates vary by season, cabin location, and whether the ship is of the "new generation" (Kong Harald, Nordkapp, Nordlys, Nordnorge, Polarlys, Richard With), the "mid-generation" (Narvik, Midnatsol, Vesteralen), or the "traditional" (Harald Jarl, Lofoten) type ships, the scenery is what the voyage is all about. Senior citizens (those age 67 and over) qualify for a special discount.

Adult couples, single travelers, and families with children wanting to sail along the coast of Norway and experience the area's natural beauty are best suited to this scenic cruise. It's ideal for anyone who doesn't need entertainment or mindless parlor games, but wants to relax and unwind, enjoys being close to nature, and is probably a bit of an adventurer. The dress code is casual and comfortable — layered clothing is best. The currency is the Norwegian krone.

Norwegian coast and fjords cruises consist of a 7-day (northbound) voyage between Bergen and Kirkenes, Norway; or a 6-day (southbound) voyage between Kirkenes and Bergen, Norway; or a 12-day roundtrip voyage.

Weak Points: The ship does not have stabilizers, so you should expect some movement when the weather is inclement or unkind. Drinks prices are extremely high — the same as ashore in Norway. The cabins are small, and the bathrooms are really tiny. Although not needed during the winter, there is little outdoor deck space considering the number of passengers carried.

Shore excursions can provide peaceful moments.

Nordlys
★★★ +

Small Ship:	11,200 tons	Cabins (with private balcony):	0
Lifestyle:	Standard	Cabins (wheelchair accessible):	3
Cruise Line:	Norwegian Coastal Voyages (TFDS)	Cabin Current:	220-volt
Former Names:	-	Full-Service Dining Rooms:	1
Builder:	Stralsund Wolkswerft (Norway)	Elevators:	2
Original Cost:	n/a	Casino (gaming tables):	No
Entered Service:	1994	Slot Machines:	No
Registry:	Norway	Swimming Pools (outdoors):	0
Length (ft/m):	399.6/121.8	Swimming Pools (indoors):	0
Beam (ft/m):	62.9/19.2	Whirlpools:	0
Draft (ft/m):	16.0/4.9	Fitness Center:	Yes
Total Crew:	70	Sauna/Steam Room:	Yes/No
Passengers (lower beds/all berths):	458/482	Massage:	No
Pass. Space Ratio (lower beds/all berths):	24.4/23.2	Self-Service Launderette:	Yes
Crew/Pass. Ratio (lower beds/all berths):	6.5/6.8	Dedictated Cinema:	No
Navigation Officers:	Norwegian	Library:	Yes
Cabins (total):	229	Classification Society:	Det Norske Veritas
Size Range (sq ft/sq m):	n/a		
Cabins (outside view):	180	**OVERALL SCORE:**	**1,285**
Cabins (interior/no view):	49	(OUT OF A POSSIBLE 2,000 POINTS)	
Cabins (for one person):	0		

Accommodation: There are nine grades of cabin, including three wheelchair-accessible cabins (one of the ship's two elevators accommodates a wheelchair). Double beds are only available in the two suites; all other cabins have beds and berths that cannot be moved. Some cabins also have an additional third (upper) berth, and a number of cabins are available for single occupancy, albeit with a price premium. All cabins have a 220-volt outlet, so take adapters and converters if you need to.

Dining: There is one main dining room (the St. Jernesalen Restaurant — no smoking allowed), and tables are assigned when you embark. Three meals each day are included in the cruise fare: Breakfast and lunch (featuring the famous Norwegian "cold table") are self-serve, buffet-style meals, while dinner is a sit-down affair, with three courses. Additionally, there is the Aurora Café, which is open 24 hours, where snacks and light meals can be purchased

Other Comments: The Norwegian Coastal Voyage is a service that was started in 1863. It is jointly operated by two companies: Ofotens og Vesteraalen Dampskibsselskab (OVDS) and Troms Fylkes Dampskibsselskab (TFDS). The complete journey, of 1,250 nautical miles, takes in 34 ports of call in a 12-day roundtrip voyage between Bergen and Kirkenes (on the border with Russia), above the Arctic Circle (where a special "Crossing the Arctic Circle" ceremony welcomes newcomers). The journey can also be done in a one-way voyage that takes seven days (northbound) or six days (southbound). The ships carry passengers as well as mail and other cargo.

Perhaps you will be able to peek at the midnight sun (mid-May to late June, north of the Arctic Circle), experience the northern lights (aurora borealis, mostly seen during winter months, and only when the atmospheric conditions are right), and be part of the daily life of the hardy Norwegians. Approximately 60% of the passengers will be Norwegian/Scandinavian/European, while the rest will be a mix of North American and other nationalities. Although the passenger bed capacity is quoted, note that many additional passengers may be on board as day passengers, sailing between two coastal ports — the ship is the equivalent of a seagoing bus for the coastal commuters. As for the weather, the west coast of Norway is warmed by the Gulf Stream, and temperatures will be similar to those found in New England.

This ship is one of the "new generation" of coastal voyage ships (built in the 1990s) that is rather like a mini-cruise vessel, with a better array of public rooms and facilities than the older, smaller ships in the fleet. This is an excellent way to experience the beautiful coastline of Norway and its fascinating coastal towns. There will be an interesting mix of passengers — it's a good way to meet new people and make new friends from different countries. A laundry room with washing machines, tumble dryers, and irons is provided (useful for those for whom the cruise is only part of a more extensive vacation).

The rates vary by season, cabin location, and whether the ship is of the "new generation" (*Kong Harald, Nordkapp, Nordlys, Nordnorge, Polarlys, Richard With*), the "mid-generation" (*Narvik, Midnatsol, Vesteralen*), or the "traditional" (*Harald Jarl, Lofoten*) type ships, the scenery is what the voyage is all about. Senior citizens (those age 67 and over) qualify for a special discount.

Adult couples, single travelers, and families with children wanting to sail along the coast of Norway and experience the area's natural beauty are best suited to this scenic cruise. It's ideal for anyone who doesn't need entertainment or mindless parlor games but wants to relax and unwind, enjoys being close to nature, and is probably a bit of an adventurer. The dress code is casual and comfortable — layered clothing is best. The currency is the Norwegian krone.

Norwegian coast and fjords cruises consist of a 7-day (northbound) voyage between Bergen and Kirkenes, Norway; or a 6-day (southbound) voyage between Kirkenes and Bergen, Norway; or a 12-day roundtrip voyage. The ship also has space for up to 50 cars.

Weak Points: The ship does not have stabilizers, so you should expect some movement when the weather is inclement or unkind. Drinks prices are extremely high—the same as ashore in Norway. The cabins are small, and the bathrooms are really tiny. Although not needed during the winter, there is little outdoor deck space considering the number of passengers carried.

Nordnorge
★★★ +

Small Ship:	11,386 tons	Cabins (with private balcony):	0
Lifestyle:	Standard	Cabins (wheelchair accessible):	3
Cruise Line: Norwegian Coastal Voyages (OVDS)		Cabin Current:	220-volt
Former Names:	-	Full-Service Dining Rooms:	1
Builder:	Kvaerner Kleven (Norway)	Elevators:	2
Original Cost:	n/a	Casino (gaming tables):	No
Entered Service:	1997	Slot Machines:	No
Registry:	Norway	Swimming Pools (outdoors):	0
Length (ft/m):	399.6/121.8	Swimming Pools (indoors):	0
Beam (ft/m):	62.9/19.2	Whirlpools:	0
Draft (ft/m):	16.0/4.9	Fitness Center:	Yes
Total Crew:	70	Sauna/Steam Room:	Yes/Yes
Passengers (lower beds/all berths):	428/564	Massage:	No
Pass. Space Ratio (lower beds/all berths):	26.6/20.1	Self-Service Launderette:	Yes
Crew/Pass. Ratio (lower beds/all berths):	6.1/8.0	Dedictated Cinema:	No
Navigation Officers:	Norwegian	Library:	Yes
Cabins (total):	214	Classification Society:	Det Norske Veritas
Size Range (sq ft/sq m):	n/a		
Cabins (outside view):	171		
Cabins (interior/no view):	43		
Cabins (for one person):	0		

OVERALL SCORE: 1,285

(OUT OF A POSSIBLE 2,000 POINTS)

Accommodation: There are nine grades of cabin, including three wheelchair-accessible cabins (one of the ship's two elevators accommodates a wheelchair). Double beds are only available in the two suites; all other cabins have beds and berths that cannot be moved. Some cabins also have an additional third (upper) berth, and a number of cabins are available for single occupancy, albeit with a price premium. All cabins have a 220-volt outlet, so take adapters and converters if you need to.

Dining: There is one main dining room (the Halogaland Restaurant — no smoking), and tables are assigned when you embark. Three meals each day are included in the cruise fare: Breakfast and lunch (featuring the famous Norwegian "cold table") are self-serve, buffet-style meals, while dinner is a sit-down affair, with three courses. Additionally, there is the Vagar Café, open 24 hours, where snacks and light meals can be purchased.

Other Comments: The Norwegian Coastal Voyage is a service that was started in 1863. It is jointly operated by two companies: Ofotens og Vesteraalen Dampskibsselskab (OVDS) and Troms Fylkes Dampskibsselskab (TFDS). The complete journey, of 1,250 nautical miles, takes in 34 ports of call in a 12-day roundtrip voyage between Bergen and Kirkenes (on the border with Russia), above the Arctic Circle (where a special "Crossing the Arctic Circle" ceremony welcomes newcomers). The journey can also be done in a one-way voyage that takes seven days (northbound) or six days (southbound). The ships carry passengers as well as mail and other cargo.

Perhaps you will be able to peek at the midnight sun (mid-May to late June, north of the Arctic Circle), experience the northern lights (aurora borealis, mostly seen during winter months, and only when the atmospheric conditions are right), and be part of the daily life of the hardy Norwegians. Approximately 60% of the passengers will be Norwegian/Scandinavian/European, while the rest will be a mix of North American and other nationalities. Although the passenger bed capacity is quoted, note that many additional passengers may be on board as day passengers, sailing between two coastal ports — the ship is the equivalent of a seagoing bus for the coastal commuters. As for the weather, the west coast of Norway is warmed by the Gulf Stream, and temperatures will be similar to those found in New England.

This ship is one of the "new generation" of coastal voyage ships (built in the 1990s) that is rather like a mini-cruise vessel, with a better array of public rooms and facilities than the older, smaller ships in the fleet. This is an excellent way to experience the beautiful coastline of Norway and its fascinating coastal towns. There will be an interesting mix of passengers — it's a good way to meet new people and make new friends from different countries. A laundry room with washing machines, tumble dryers, and irons is provided (useful for those for whom the cruise is only part of a more extensive vacation).

The rates vary by season, cabin location, and whether the ship is of the "new generation" (*Kong Harald, Nordkapp, Nordlys, Nordnorge, Polarlys, Richard With*), the "mid-generation" (*Narvik, Midnatsol, Vesteralen*), or the "traditional" (*Harald Jarl, Lofoten*) type ships, the scenery is what the voyage is all about. Senior citizens (those age 67 and over) qualify for a special discount.

Adult couples, single travelers, and families with children wanting to sail along the coast of Norway and experience the area's natural beauty are best suited to this scenic cruise. It's ideal for anyone who doesn't need entertainment or mindless parlor games, but wants to relax and unwind, enjoys being close to nature, and is probably a bit of an adventurer. The dress code is casual and comfortable — layered clothing is best. The currency is the Norwegian krone.

Norwegian coast and fjords cruises consist of a 7-day (northbound) voyage between Bergen and Kirkenes, Norway; or a 6-day (southbound) voyage between Kirkenes and Bergen, Norway; or a 12-day roundtrip voyage. The ship also has space for up to 50 cars.

Weak Points: The ship does not have stabilizers, so you should expect some movement when the weather is inclement or unkind. Drinks prices are extremely high — the same as ashore in Norway. The cabins are small, and the bathrooms are really tiny. Although not needed during the winter, there is little outdoor deck space considering the number of passengers carried.

Norway
★★★ +

Large Ship:	76,049 tons	Cabins (for one person):	20
Lifestyle:	Standard	Cabins (with private balcony):	56
Cruise Line:	Star Cruises	Cabins (wheelchair accessible):	11
Former Names:	*France*	Cabin Current:	110-volt
Builder:	Chantiers de l'Atlantique (France)	Full-Service Dining Rooms:	2 (+ 1 Bistro)
Original Cost:	$80 million	Elevators:	11
Entered Service:	February 1962/October 2001	Casino (gaming tables):	Yes
Registry:	Bahamas	Slot Machines:	Yes
Length (ft/m):	1035.1/315.50	Swimming Pools (outdoors):	2
Beam (ft/m):	109.9/33.50	Swimming Pools (indoors):	1 (+ Aquacize Pool)
Draft (ft/m):	35.4/10.80	Whirlpools:	2
Propulsion/Propellers:	Steam turbine (29,850kW)/4	Fitness Center:	Yes
Passenger Decks:	12	Sauna/Steam Room:	Yes/No
Total Crew:	920	Massage:	Yes
Passengers (lower beds/all berths):	2,026/2,370	Self-Service Launderette:	No
Pass. Space Ratio (lower beds/all berths):	37.5/32.8	Dedicated Cinema/Seats:	Yes/813
Crew/Pass. Ratio (lower beds/all berths):	2.2/2.5	Library:	Yes
Navigation Officers:	Scandinavian	Classification Society:	Bureau Veritas
Cabins (total):	1,013		
Size Range (sq ft/sq m):	99.0–958.0/9.2–89.0		
Cabins (outside view):	642		
Cabins (interior/no view):	371		

OVERALL SCORE: 1,393
(OUT OF A POSSIBLE 2,000 POINTS)

Accommodation: There is an extremely wide range of suites and cabins in many different grades and configurations — from luxurious, spacious outside suites that can accommodate up to six, to tiny interior (no view) cabins. All of the cabins have nice, high ceilings, long beds, good closet and drawer space and a decent range of amenities. Many cabin bathrooms feature full-size bathtubs, while others have only shower enclosures. Bottled water is placed in each cabin (but a charge will be made to your account if you open the bottle).

The owner's suites are extremely lavish, and the newest suites added to two decks atop the ship are very comfortable (however, all suite occupants should have had a private dining room). There are many cabins suitable for families of four, five, and even six.

Dining: There are two large dining rooms (both are nonsmoking) and two seatings in each. The nicer one is the Windward, with its fine domed ceiling and wall murals retained from her former days as the first-class dining room, while the Leeward (the former tourist-class restaurant) has a fine balcony level. There are few tables for two, however, and the tables are extremely close together (the result of additional suites and cabins added over the past few years).

Le Bistro is an informal alternative dining spot that provides for a change from the two restaurants (and the attendant noise). It offers a taste of Italy in a contemporary setting.

The casual, outdoor buffet area is useful for those out on deck, but it is always crowded, with long lines to get to what can best be described as "food as it shouldn't be presented." It never looks good, despite staff efforts to restock the displays.

Overall, the food provided is rather unmemorable fare that lacks taste and presentation quality; the menus, too, are uninspiring. There is a reasonably decent selection of breads, rolls, cheeses, and fruits, however. The wine list is quite decent and well put together, with moderate prices, although you won't find any good vintage wines. The cutlery is very ordinary (there are no fish knives). There is no formal afternoon tea, although you can make your own from various beverage stations. The service is, on the whole, adequate, nothing more, and proves that a good staff that can communicate well is quite difficult to find.

Other Comments: Originally built as the ocean liner *France* for the Compagnie Générale Transatlantique, she was once known for her food and service when operating transatlantic crossings from France to New York in the 1960s. She is still quite a majestic-looking ship, with two large funnels, a long foredeck and a real, distinguishable "sheer" (this is the sagging centerline of the ship, which was built by laying a keel, unlike the newest ships of today, which are built in locks).

The ship's interiors, food, and service, however, have almost no resemblance to her former days as an ocean liner. She was converted to become a Caribbean cruise vessel in 1979, at a cost of $130 million. Several years ago, some major structural alterations added two complete new glass-enclosed decks atop the ship; the new decks provide an additional 135 outside suites and junior suites, and lower the profile of the two wing-tip funnels considerably, but the balconies are not very private. Two large landing craft provide fast, efficient transportation ashore.

Recent refurbishments have also kept her interiors refreshed. Some public rooms feature Art Deco touches reminiscent of the former ocean liner she once was. There are two different color schemes in the forward and aft sections, which help first-time passengers to find their way around.

The public rooms are, for the most part, quite pleasing, and many have high ceilings. Soft furnishings and marble have kept the interiors fresh. The outdoor decks are well varnished, but the synthetic turf on the ship's top deck is just not right. Features a good indoor Roman Spa, set low down in the ship, with a good range of spa programs and 16 treatment rooms. There is an extensive jogging track, although it cannot be used before 8am (it is located above some of the most expensive cabins). The Club Internationale is an elegant carry-over from her former days (when it was the first-class lounge) and is still the perfect meeting place for cocktails and sophisticated evenings. There is an excellent proscenium Saga Theatre, complete with large balcony level, for the dazzle-and-sizzle style of production shows. A large active casino invites you to spend your money, and it is very noisy.

Take the family, as children and teens will have a fine time aboard this ship, with lots of activities and children's staff. She is large enough that there are plenty of places to play, and children will have the time of their lives exploring the ship.

This ship was for many years the world's largest cruise ship (she is still the longest). *Norway* is now a floating contemporary resort with some connections to the past in her make-up. As of November 2001, the ship will be repositioned to Southeast Asia following a three-week dry-docking in Europe.

Note that a 15% gratuity is added to all bar and spa treatment accounts.

This legendary former liner should prove fascinating for adults and children alike.

Weak Points: Standing in line for embarkation, disembarkation, shore tenders, and self-serve buffet meals is an inevitable aspect of cruising aboard all large ships. The open deck and sunbathing space is quite poor, particularly when the ship is full, which, in Southeast Asia, may not happen as often as it did in the Caribbean. *Norway* does not dock anywhere because of its size and deep draft (a problem for the nonambulatory) and passengers must go ashore by tender boats (this can take a considerable amount of time). There are just too many loud announcements, making for too much of a summer camp atmosphere.

Norwegian Dream
★★★ +

Large Ship:	50,760 tons	Cabins (with private balcony):	48
Lifestyle:	Standard	Cabins (wheelchair accessible):	6
Cruise Line:	Norwegian Cruise Line	(+ 30 for hearing-impaired)	
Former Names:	*Dreamward*	Cabin Current:	110-volt
Builder:	Chantiers de l'Atlantique (France)	Full-Service Dining Rooms:	4
Original Cost:	$240 million	Elevators:	11
Entered Service:	December 1992	Casino (gaming tables):	Yes
Registry:	Bahamas	Slot Machines:	Yes
Length (ft/m):	754.0/229.80	Swimming Pools (outdoors):	2
Beam (ft/m):	93.5/28.50	Swimming Pools (indoors):	0
Draft (ft/m):	22.3/6.80	Whirlpools:	4
Propulsion/Propellers:	Diesel (18,480kW)/2	Fitness Center:	Yes
Passenger Decks:	10	Sauna/Steam Room:	Yes/No
Total Crew:	690	Massage:	Yes
Passengers (lower beds/all berths):	1,732/2,156	Self-Service Launderette:	No
Pass. Space Ratio (lower beds/all berths):	29.3/23.5	Dedicated Cinema:	No
Crew/Pass. Ratio (lower beds/all berths):	2.5/3.1	Library:	Yes
Navigation Officers:	Norwegian	Classification Society:	Det Norske Veritas
Cabins (total):	865		
Size Range (sq ft/sq m):	139.9–349.8/13.0–32.5		
Cabins (outside view):	695	**OVERALL SCORE:**	**1,381**
Cabins (interior/no view):	170	(OUT OF A POSSIBLE 2,000 POINTS)	
Cabins (for one person):	0		

Accommodation: There are 15 grades of cabins. The majority of cabins have outside views and feature wood-trimmed cabinetry and warm decor, with multicolored soft furnishings, but there is almost no drawer space (the closets have open shelves, however), so take minimal clothing. All cabins have a sitting area, but this takes away any free space, making movement pretty tight. The bathrooms are small but practical, although there is little space for storage of personal toiletry items. Bottled water is placed in each cabin (but a charge will be made to your account if you open the bottle).

There are 18 suites (12 of which have a private entrance and a small, private balcony), each with separate living room and bedroom, fine quality cabinetry, and lots of closet and drawer space. Occupants of suites receive "concierge" service, which provides extra personal attention. In addition, 16 suites and 70 cabins have interconnecting doors — good for families cruising together, or perhaps for those that want separate "his and hers" living spaces. There are several cabins specially equipped for the hearing-impaired. Note that all cabins on the port side of the ship are designated nonsmoking.

Dining: With what NCL calls "Freestyle Dining," you can choose which restaurant you would like to eat in, at what time, and with whom. Although there are two principal dining rooms, there are also a number of other themed eating establishments, giving a wide range of choice, although it would be wise to plan in advance, particularly for dinner. All restaurants and eateries are nonsmoking.

There are two main full-service dining rooms: The Terraces (arguably the nicest, with windows that look out over the ship's tiered aft decks), and the Four Seasons (with approximately 450 seats) located amidships. All are nonsmoking and feature the same menu and food. Seating is open, so come when you want arrangement (NCL calls it "Freestyle Dining"). The Four Seasons is the largest and has some prime tables at ocean-view window seats in a section that extends from the ship's port and starboard sides in half-moon shapes (nice for lunch, but it's either dark or the curtains are drawn for dinner).

Italian fare is served in the Trattoria (formerly named the Sun Terraces), which overlooks the aft swimming pool. The Bistro features informal evening dining at no extra charge in more intimate surroundings. A 200-seat Sports Bar (typically open between 6am and 1am) features breakfast, lunch, dinner, and snacks throughout the day. There's also a poolside pizzeria and a small coffee lounge.

Overall, the food provided is rather unmemorable fare that lacks taste and presentation quality; the menus, too, are uninspiring. There is a reasonably decent selection of breads, rolls, cheeses, and fruits, however. The wine list is quite decent and well put together, with moderate prices, although you won't find any good vintage wines. There are many types of beer (including some on draft in the popular Sports Bar & Grill) to choose from. The cutlery is very ordinary (there are no fish knives). There is no formal afternoon tea, although you can make your own from various beverage stations. The service is, on the whole, adequate, nothing more, and proves that a good staff that can communicate well is quite difficult to find.

You can eat breakfast or lunch in any of the dining rooms when it's "open seating." A lavish "choco-holics" buffet is featured once each cruise — established as a firm favorite among Norwegian Cruise Line's repeat passengers.

Other Comments: Built first (her sister ship is *Norwegian Wind)*, this ship has a fairly handsome profile (despite a large, square funnel) that was better balanced before she underwent a "chop and stretch" operation in spring 1998. Following the "stretch" her exterior shape is now not as handsome. The lifeboats are inboard. There is a blue rubber-covered wraparound promenade deck outdoors. The tiered pool deck is neat, as are the multideck aft sun terraces and all her fore and aft connecting exterior stairways.

In the "chop and stretch" operation, a completely new midsection was added, and the funnel was adapted so that it could be "folded" over to allow the ship to transit the Kiel Canal in Germany. Included in the 131 ft (40 m) section: 251 new passengers cabins and 50 crew cabins, together with several new or enlarged public rooms (although there simply are not enough), including a 60-seat conference center. Some innovative features were incorporated in the original design, and these have been kept and enhanced. The passenger flow is generally good — indeed, the ship seems to absorb passengers quite well for much of the time, except at peak traffic times between dinner seatings.

The overall exterior design emphasizes a clever and extensive use of large windows that create a sense of open spaces, although the interior design provides many smaller public rooms rather than the large hangers found aboard so many other ships. However, there is no big atrium lobby, as one might expect. The pastel interior colors used are quite soothing, and she is considered by many to be a pretty ship inside. The entrance lobby is not at all attractive and feels rather confined for a ship of this size.

This ship has proven highly successful for Norwegian Cruise Line's younger, active sports-minded passengers, and provides a good alternative to the larger ships and their larger passenger numbers, although there are plenty of other passengers to keep you company. Note that a 15% gratuity is added to all bar and spa treatment accounts. Standard gratuities for staff (cabin attendants, dining room waiters, etc.) are automatically added to your onboard account (you can, however, reduce these if necessary before you disembark).

Weak Points: Standing in line for embarkation, disembarkation, shore tenders, and self-serve buffet meals is an inevitable aspect of cruising aboard all large ships. The room service menu is still poor and could be improved. The outdoor stairways are numerous and confusing. The carpeted steel interior stairwell steps are quite tinny. When the ship was "stretched" it reduced the amount of outdoor space per passenger, and this is reflected in increased density around the pools. There simply are not enough public rooms to absorb the increase in passengers well.

Norwegian Majesty
★★★ +

Large Ship:	40,876 tons	Cabins (for one person):	0
Lifestyle:	Standard	Cabins (with private balcony):	0
Cruise Line:	Norwegian Cruise Line	Cabins (wheelchair accessible):	7
Former Names:	*Royal Majesty*	Cabin Current:	110/220-volt
Builder:	Kvaerner Masa-Yards (Finland)	Full-Service Dining Rooms:	2 (+ 1 Bistro)
Original Cost:	$229 million	Elevators:	6
Entered Service:	September 1992/November 1997	Casino (gaming tables):	Yes
Registry:	Bahamas	Slot Machines:	Yes
Length (ft/m):	680.0/207.20	Swimming Pools (outdoors):	2
Beam (ft/m):	90.5/27.60	Swimming Pools (indoors):	0
Draft (ft/m):	20.3/6.20	Whirlpools:	3
Propulsion/Propellers:	Diesel (21,120kW)/2	Fitness Center:	Yes
Passenger Decks:	9	Sauna/Steam Room:	Yes/No
Total Crew:	702	Massage:	Yes
Passengers (lower beds/all berths):	1,460/1,790	Self-Service Launderette:	No
Pass. Space Ratio (lower beds/all berths):	27.9/22.8	Dedicated Cinema/Seats:	Yes/100
Crew/Pass. Ratio (lower beds/all berths):	2/2.5	Library:	Yes
Navigation Officers:	Norwegian	Classification Society:	Lloyd's Register
Cabins (total):	730		
Size Range (sq ft/sq m):	118.4–374.5/11.0–34.8		
Cabins (outside view):	481		
Cabins (interior/no view):	249		

OVERALL SCORE:	**1,386**
(OUT OF A POSSIBLE 2,000 POINTS)	

Accommodation: The suites feature concierge service and extra goodies such as late afternoon snacks and hors d'oeuvre items. Although they cannot be considered large, they are quite well equipped and come with VCRs as well as TVs. Bottled water is placed in each cabin (but a charge will be made to your account if you open the bottle).

Almost all other outside-view and interior (no view) cabins are on the small side but quite comfortable. The closets are really small, so suitcases will need to be stored under the bed to keep them out of the way (this is also the best place for shoes). The bathrooms are a little tight, although there is a generous amount of room in the shower enclosures. A number of cabins are designated for nonsmokers. Some of the cabins have obstructed views; so do check the deck plans carefully.

Dining: With what NCL calls "Freestyle Dining," you can choose which restaurant you would like to eat in, at what time, and with whom. Although there are two principal dining rooms, there are also a number of other themed eating establishments, giving a wide range of choice — although it would be wise to plan in advance, particularly for dinner. All restaurants and eateries are nonsmoking.

There are two main dining rooms: Seven Seas, with 636 seats, and the more intimate Four Seasons (added when the ship was "stretched" in 1999) with 266 seats. However, they are quite noisy and the tables are close together, which means that correct service is difficult. The food, menu, creativity, and service are basically quite sound, with a good selection of breads, but the choice of cheeses and fruits is limited (almost all cheeses are American). Some dinners are "themed" in the evening, a feature that has been popular with NCL passengers for years.

There is also a 56-seat Le Bistro Restaurant, which serves Italian- and continental-style cuisine for alternative dinners in an intimate environment (no reservations are needed).

For casual, self-serve meals, the Café Royale is a small buffet dining spot with 112 seats (not nearly enough for the number of passengers now carried). It is open for breakfast, lunch, and snacks. An outdoor grill (oddly named the Piazza San Marco) serves fast food items, including pizza (this can also be delivered to your cabin). A small coffee bar/lounge in an open passageway (street café) serves a variety of coffees, coffee-flavored drinks, "flaming" specialty drinks, and teas.

Overall, the food provided is rather unmemorable fare that lacks taste and presentation quality; the menus, too, are uninspiring. There is a reasonably decent selection of breads, rolls, cheeses, and fruits, however. The wine list is quite decent and well put together, with moderate prices, although you won't find any good vintage wines. The cutlery is very ordinary (there are no fish knives). There is no formal afternoon tea, although you can make your own from various beverage stations. The service is, on the whole, adequate, nothing more, and proves that a good staff that can communicate well is quite difficult to find.

Other Comments: This smart, stylish, contemporary cruise ship, originally constructed for the now-defunct Majesty Cruise Line, now has an improved profile and is generally a well-designed vessel (her original lines were those of a Baltic ferry with a rounded bow, however, and not at all handsome). The ship underwent a $53.3 million, 110 ft (34 m) "chop and stretch" and refurbishment operation in the spring of 1999, which added more cabins, new public rooms, much more open deck space and two new elevators, while all other existing public spaces were refreshed. For a real "wind-in-the-hair" experience, passengers can actually stand at the very bow of this ship (weather permitting) as all the mooring ropes and winches are on the deck below.

The open deck and sunbathing space has been improved (there are now two swimming pools, plus a splash pool for children). The ship's exterior profile is now sleeker and more aerodynamic. Cutting the ship in half, however, required some ingenuity, for, unlike *Norwegian Dream* and *Norwegian Wind*, it was never designed for such a splicing operation.

Inside, she is quite a pretty ship and is tastefully appointed, with lots of wood paneling and chrome and copper accents, reasonably discreet lighting, soothing colors, no glitz, and almost no neon lighting. Wide passageways provide a feeling of inner spaciousness. The ship has a nice touch of elegance and open walking areas provide a fine feel. The circular lobby is bright and classical in appearance.

There are several public rooms, bars, and lounges to choose from. The Royal Observatory lounge has fine views but is sometimes used as a karaoke lounge. The show lounge, while comfortable, is poorly designed, with 14 pillars obstructing the sight lines. Families with children will find "Kid's Korner" a useful place to deposit young ones for a full program of activities.

This ship will provide you with a comfortable cruise experience in warm, fairly elegant surroundings, with generally good food (and plenty of it) and a modicum of hospitality from a reasonably friendly crew, although there is little service finesse. The ship is based in Boston during the summer season for seven-night cruises to Bermuda, while during the winter she is based in Miami for seven-night Caribbean cruises. Note that all on-board gratuities are included, as are port taxes. Note that a 15% gratuity is added to all bar and spa treatment accounts. Standard gratuities for staff (cabin attendants, dining room waiters, etc.) are automatically added to your on-board account (you can review these before you disembark).

Weak Points: There are several repetitive announcements for revenue-producing activities, and the increased amount of squeezing for on-board revenue makes a cruise aboard her less enjoyable than it should be. The spa facilities are very poor and basic. There are no cushioned pads for the plastic deck chairs. The buffet area is simply too small for the extra number of passengers carried (while the ship was expanded, the buffet and seating areas were not). While adequate for three- and four-day cruises, the ship is only moderately comfortable for seven-day cruises. Standing in line for embarkation, disembarkation, shore tenders, and self-serve buffet meals is an inevitable aspect of cruising aboard all large ships.

Norwegian Sea
★★★ +

Large Ship:	42,276 tons	Cabins (for one person):	0
Lifestyle:	Standard	Cabins (with private balcony):	0
Cruise Line:	Norwegian Cruise Line	Cabins (wheelchair accessible):	4
Former Names:	*Seaward*	Cabin Current:	110-volt
Builder:	Wartsila (Finland)	Full-Service Dining Rooms:	2
Original Cost:	$120 million	Elevators:	6
Entered Service:	June 1988	Casino (gaming tables):	Yes
Registry:	Bahamas	Slot Machines:	Yes
Length (ft/m):	708.6/216.0	Swimming Pools (outdoors):	2
Beam (ft/m):	95.1/29.0	Swimming Pools (indoors):	0
Draft (ft/m):	22.9/7.0	Whirlpools:	2
Propulsion/Propellers:	Diesel (21,120kW)/2	Fitness Center:	Yes
Passenger Decks:	9	Sauna/Steam Room:	Yes/No
Total Crew:	630	Massage:	Yes
Passengers (lower beds/all berths):	1,510/1,798	Self-Service Launderette:	No
Pass. Space Ratio (lower beds/all berths):	28/23.5	Dedicated Cinema:	No
Crew/Pass. Ratio (lower beds/all berths):	2.3/2.8	Library:	No
Navigation Officers:	Norwegian	Classification Society:	Det Norske Veritas
Cabins (total):	755		
Size Range (sq ft/sq m):	109.7–269.1/10.2–25.0	**OVERALL SCORE:**	**1,392**
Cabins (outside view):	512	**(OUT OF A POSSIBLE 2,000 POINTS)**	
Cabins (interior/no view):	243		

Accommodation: There are 16 cabin categories, although balcony cabin is not one of them, since the ship was built before they came into vogue. The cabins are of average size for a standard cruise ship (which translates to "somewhat cramped for two") although they are quite tastefully appointed and comfortable, with warm, pastel colors, bright soft furnishings, and a touch of Art Deco styling. The walls and ceilings, however, are quite plain and simple. Audio channels are available via the TV, although the picture cannot be turned off separately. The bathrooms are efficient units that are very well designed, although quite basic; hair dryers (weak ones) are included in all bathrooms. Bottled water is placed in each cabin (but a charge will be made to your account if you open the bottle).

If you book a suite or one of two upper-grade cabins, you'll get a little more space, a lounge area with table and sofa that converts into another bed (good for families), European duvets, and a refrigerator (top three categories only). The bathrooms also feature a bathtub, shower, and retractable clothesline.

Dining: With what NCL calls "Freestyle Dining," you can choose which restaurant you would like to eat in, at what time, and with whom. Although there are two principal dining rooms, there are also a number of other themed eating establishments, giving a wide range of choice — although it would be wise to plan in advance, particularly for dinner. All restaurants and eateries are nonsmoking.

There are two principal dining rooms: Four Seasons, with 372 seats, and Seven Seas, with 476 seats. They are both comfortable and feature pastel decor. The cuisine, for a mass-market ship, ranges from adequate to reasonably good. Vegetables (few green ones are used) tend to be overcooked. Fish and poultry items are good. Meat is disappointing. The emphasis is on Tex-Mex cuisine, with a wide choice of hot and spicy sauces.

In addition to the two dining rooms, there are other alternative dining spots. For casual breakfast and lunch there's the Big Apple Café (436 seats), which has indoor and outdoor seating. There is also the intimate 82-seat Le Bistro, open for informal dinners, and Gatsby's is a popular wine bar that features a good wine and champagne list. Le Bistro and Gatsby's are both located high in the ship and have large ocean-view picture windows. The selection of wines is good, but the glasses are small. The breakfast and luncheon buffets are quite poor and should have more variety and better ingredients.

Overall, the food provided is rather unmemorable fare that lacks taste and presentation quality; the menus, too, are uninspiring. There is a reasonably decent selection of breads, rolls, cheeses, and fruits, however. The wine list is quite decent and well put together, with moderate prices, although you won't find any good vintage wines. The cutlery is very ordinary (there are no fish knives). There is no formal afternoon tea, although you can make your own from various beverage stations. The service is, on the whole, adequate, nothing more, and proves that a good staff that can communicate well is quite difficult to find.

Other Comments: This angular, yet reasonably attractive vessel has a contemporary European cruise-ferry profile with a sharply raked bow and sleek mast and funnel. There is a full wraparound promenade deck outdoors (although it is a plain steel deck, painted nautical blue).

This ship is quite well designed, with generally sound passenger flow and no major areas of congestion, and an abundance of public rooms and open interior spaces, many with high ceilings. The interior decor stresses the colors of coral, blue, and mauve. Although the hallways and stairways are quite plain, two glass-walled stairways provide good connection with sea and sky. There is a good gymnasium/fitness center for those that want to work their muscles; it is located around the mast and is accessible only from the outside deck (clearly not good when it rains).

The Crystal Court lobby is two decks high and is pleasing without being overwhelming, although at times it appears to be quite cluttered. It has a tubed crystal and water sculpture with seating around its perimeter.

The 770-seat theater/show lounge (called "Cabaret") provides large-scale dazzle-and-sizzle shows with lots of energy and volume, including a shortened version of the musical "Grease." Watch out, however, for the 12 thick pillars that obstruct the sight lines from many seats. There is also a large nightclub (again there are several pillars obstructing sight lines), and a disco ("Boomers"). For those seeking a more intimate lounge, the mahogany-paneled Oscar's Lounge is the place to go.

This ship will provide a cruise in good taste for first-time cruise passengers who want to have fun in comfortable surroundings, at a sensible, competitive price. If you like sports bars, country 'n western music, hoedowns, and amateurish participation games, this ship will prove a lot of fun. Note that a 15% gratuity is added to all bar and spa treatment accounts. Standard gratuities for staff (cabin attendants, dining room waiters, etc.) are automatically added to your on-board account (you can, however, reduce these if necessary before you disembark).

Weak Spots: Standing in line for embarkation, disembarkation, shore tenders, and self-serve buffet meals is an inevitable aspect of cruising aboard all large ships. The open decks are cluttered and largely unclean. Food buffets have very poor presentation and a low quality of ingredients. Food service and supervision need work. Badly dented and scuffed panels in the accommodation hallways are unattractive. The steps on the stairways are tinny. There is no library. The constant background music in the hallways is irritating. There is too much use of synthetic turf on the upper outdoor decks (this gets very soggy when wet). There are no cushioned pads for the deck lounge chairs. The cruise staff is very young and rather amateurish.

Norwegian Sky
★★★★

Large Ship:	77,104 tons	Cabins (for one person):	0
Lifestyle:	Standard	Cabins (with private balcony):	252
Cruise Line:	Norwegian Cruise Line	Cabins (wheelchair accessible):	6
Former Names:	-	Cabin Current:	110-volt
Builder:	Lloyd Werft (Germany)	Full-Service Dining Rooms:	2 main, 3 alternative
Original Cost:	$332 million	Elevators:	12
Entered Service:	August 1999	Casino (gaming tables):	Yes
Registry:	Bahamas	Slot Machines:	Yes
Length (ft/m):	853.0/260.00	Swimming Pools (outdoors):	2
Beam (ft/m):	105.8/32.25	Swimming Pools (indoors):	0
Draft (ft/m):	26.2/8.00	Whirlpools:	5
Propulsion/Propellers:	Diesel-electric (50,000kW)/2	Fitness Center:	Yes
Passenger Decks:	12	Sauna/Steam Room:	Yes/Yes
Total Crew:	750	Massage:	Yes
Passengers (lower beds/all berths):	2,002/2,450	Self-Service Launderette:	No
Pass. Space Ratio (lower beds/all berths):	38.5/31.4	Dedicated Cinema:	No
Crew/Pass. Ratio (lower beds/all berths):	2.6/3.2	Library:	Yes
Navigation Officers:	Norwegian	Classification Society:	Germanischer Lloyd
Cabins (total):	1,001		
Size Range (sq ft/sq m):	120.5–488.6/11.2–45.4		
Cabins (outside view):	574		
Cabins (interior/no view):	427		

OVERALL SCORE: **1,507**

(OUT OF A POSSIBLE 2,000 POINTS)

Accommodation: There are 26 accommodation categories: 17 for outside view suites and cabins, and nine for interior (no view) cabins.All of the standard outside-view and interior (no view) cabins feature two lower beds that can convert to a queen-size bed, a small lounge area with sofa and table, and a decent amount of closet space, but very little drawer space, and the cabins themselves are disappointingly small. Over 200 outside-view cabins each have their own private balcony. Each cabin has a small vanity/writing desk, color TV (typically CNN, ESPN, and TNT are carried), personal safe, climate control, and a laptop computer connection socket. Note that audio can only be obtained through the TV. Bottled water is placed in each cabin (but a charge will be made to your account if you open the bottle).

The largest accommodation can be found in four owner's suites — each of which features a hot tub, large teak table, two chairs, and two deck lounge chairs, all located outside on a huge, very private, forward-facing teakwood balcony just under the ship's navigation bridge. Each suite has a separate lounge and bedroom. The lounge features a large dining table and four chairs, two 2-person sofas, large TV, DVD/CD player, coffee table, queen-size pull-down Murphy bed, guest closet, writing desk, wet bar with two bar stools, refrigerator and sink, several cupboards for glasses, and several drawers and other cupboards for storage. The bedroom, which has sliding wood half-doors that look into the lounge, features a queen-size (with European duvet) bed under a leaf-glass chandelier, vanity desk, TV, walk-in closet with plenty of hanging rail space, five open shelves, and large personal safe. The white-tiled bathroom, although not large, features a full-size bathtub with retractable clothesline above, separate shower enclosure with glass doors, deep washbasin, and toiletries cabinets.

There are also 10 Junior Suites, each of which features a private teakwood balcony; these suites face aft in a secluded position and overlook the ship's wash. They feature almost the same facilities as found in the owner's suites, with the exception of the outdoor hot tub, and the fact that there is less space.

Dining: With what NCL calls "Freestyle Dining," you can choose which restaurant you would like to eat in, at what time, and with whom. Although there are two principal dining rooms, there are also a number of other themed eating establishments, giving a wide range of choice — although it would be wise to plan in advance, particularly for dinner. All restaurants and eateries are nonsmoking. The two main dining rooms, Four Seasons (564 seats) and Seven Seas (604 seats), both have tables for four, six, or eight and feature an open seating, "come when you want" arrangement.

Sandwiched between the two is a third, smaller dining room featuring Italian cuisine. Horizons Restaurant, with 84 seats, is available as an à la carte dining option (it has pleasant half-moon alcoves and several tables for two), for which there is an extra charge of $10 per person (including gratuity).

Other dining options include an 84-seat "Le Bistro" for some very fine meals (including such desserts as flaming cherries jubilee and chocolate fondue), and "Ciao Chow" — a casual Italian/Southeast Asian eatery. Both are by reservation, and both incur a $10 per person cover charge (including gratuity).

There is also a sports bar and grill (complete with a wall of TV screens and live satellite-televised sports action), a pizzeria, Gatsby's wine bar (with complimentary tapas), a champagne and caviar bar, and an ice cream bar.

Overall, the food provided is rather unmemorable fare that lacks taste and presentation quality; the menus, too, are uninspiring. There is a reasonably decent selection of breads, rolls, cheeses, and fruits, however. The wine list is quite decent and well put together, with moderate prices, although you won't find any good vintage wines. The cutlery is very ordinary (there are no fish knives). There is no formal afternoon tea, although you can make your own from various beverage stations. The service is, on the whole, adequate, nothing more, and proves that a good staff that can communicate well is quite difficult to find.

Other Comments: This ship was created from the hull of what was to be *Costa Olympia* (a sister to *Costa Victoria*), which was purchased for $40 million but not completed when the shipyard went into bankruptcy. Norwegian Cruise Line was thus able to build this ship in about 20 months, or about two-thirds of the time it would normally have taken. Some parts of the ship differ from the original; for example, the navigation bridge is located one deck lower than aboard *Costa Victoria*.

The amount of outdoor space is very good, and the extra-wide pool deck (the extra width created from port and starboard "overhangs" that resulted from balconies added to cabins on two decks below), with its two swimming pools and four Jacuzzi tubs. On the "catwalk" deck above the pools, an electric "skymobile" beverage cart is featured.

There is a two-level, 1,001-seat show lounge, with large proscenium stage for the high-energy dazzle-and-sizzle shows that NCL passengers enjoy. The ship features the first seagoing production of one of London's Cameron Mackintosh musicals. However, the sight lines are obstructed from many seats by several slim pillars, and the sight lines in the balcony are blocked almost completely due to the fact that the safety rail is so poorly positioned.

A separate cabaret lounge, the black-and-white theme Checkers Lounge is equipped with what NCL states is the longest bar at sea, at 98 ft (30 m) long. At present, however, this honor truly goes to Aida. Other features include a large casino, shopping arcade, children's playroom (there is also a splash pool in a prime open deck area forward atop ship), a video arcade, large health/fitness spa (including an aerobics room and separate gymnasium; open 24 hours a day), and several treatment rooms.

Other facilities include a small conference room with an "Out of Africa" decor theme, library, beauty salon, Churchill's cigar smoking lounge (adjoining the Windjammer Bar) for cigars and cognac, and an Internet Café, with 14 computer terminals and coffee available from an adjacent bar. Those with a black belt in shopping might appreciate the fact that all the shops on board are run by Colombian Emeralds, and showcase a wide range of goods, from inexpensive to very expensive.

Sports fans will appreciate the large basketball/volleyball court, baseball batting cage, golf driving range, platform tennis, shuffleboard and table tennis facilities, and sports bar with 24-hour live satellite TV coverage of major sports events. Joggers will also find a wraparound indoor/outdoor jogging track.

With this ship, Norwegian Cruise Line has made an effort to provide more public rooms and entertainment facilities and options than previously — so you get a lot of ship for your money. Norwegian Sky tries to be all things to all people and is the company's latest resort at sea (with staff hand-picked from the company's other ships). The ship certainly has more choices and options for eating than any other NCL ship. *Norwegian Sky* is based in Seattle (and not Vancouver as are most other ships) for her summer Alaska season. During the winter season, seven-night Caribbean cruises are featured, with the ship based on Miami. Note that a 15% gratuity is added to all bar and spa treatment accounts. Standard gratuities for staff (cabin attendants, dining room waiters, etc.) are automatically added to your on-board account (you can, however, reduce these if necessary before you disembark).

Weak Points: Standing in line for embarkation, disembarkation, shore tenders, and self-serve buffet meals is an inevitable aspect of cruising aboard all large ships. There are too many announcements — particularly annoying are those that state what is already written in the daily program. Anyone in the Four Seasons dining room wanting to use the restroom must exit the dining room and go across the atrium to locate the nearest one. There is little connection to the sea from many public rooms. The ceilings in the cabins are very plain and uninteresting. The passenger hallways are extremely plain, boring, and void of artwork — in other words, they are very institutional, as are some of the stairwells. "Freestyle" disembarkation isn't!

Norwegian Star
★★★ +

Mid-Size Ship:	28,078 tons	Cabins (for one person):	0
Lifestyle:	Standard	Cabins (with private balcony):	9
Cruise Line:	Star Cruises	Cabins (wheelchair accessible):	0
Former Names:	*Royal Odyssey, Royal Viking Sea*	Cabin Current:	110/220-volt
Builder:	Wartsila (Finland)	Full-Service Dining Rooms:	1 (+ 1 Bistro)
Original Cost:	$22.5 million	Elevators:	5
Entered Service:	November 1973/December 1998	Casino (gaming tables):	Yes
Registry:	Bahamas	Slot Machines:	Yes
Length (ft/m):	674.2/205.50	Swimming Pools (outdoors):	1
Beam (ft/m):	83.6/25.50	Swimming Pools (indoors):	0
Draft (ft/m):	23.9/7.30	Whirlpools:	3
Propulsion/Propellers:	Diesel (13,400kW)/2	Fitness Center:	Yes
Passenger Decks:	8	Sauna/Steam Room:	Yes/No
Total Crew:	380	Massage:	Yes
Passengers (lower beds/all berths):	800/1,150	Self-Service Launderette:	No
Pass. Space Ratio (lower beds/all berths):	35/24.4	Dedicated Cinema/Seats:	Yes/156
Crew/Pass. Ratio (lower beds/all berths):	2.2/3.0	Library:	No
Navigation Officers:	Finnish/Scandinavian	Classification Society:	Det Norske Veritas
Cabins (total):	400		
Size Range (sq ft/sq m):	119.4–612.4/11.1–56.9		
Cabins (outside view):	354		
Cabins (interior/no view):	46		

OVERALL SCORE: **1,355**

(OUT OF A POSSIBLE 2,000 POINTS)

Accommodation: According to the brochure, there are 12 grades of accommodation, ranging from expansive owner's suites with private balcony to standard outside-view cabins and down to small interior (no view) cabins.

There are four owner's suites (one has a view of the bow — located just under the navigation bridge) with twin or queen-size bed. The other three (located on the port side of Promenade Deck) have a queen-size bed, separate lounge with refrigerator, private balcony, large windows, bathrooms with full-size bathtub and shower.

All other cabins (most of which are outside) are well appointed, with good closet, drawer and storage space, although some bathrooms in the lower categories do have awkward access. Some of the newer cabins have whirlpool bathtubs. Some nonsmoking cabins are available. Note that tinny metal drawers in the cabins remain from her former days as a Royal Viking Line ship. Bathrobes are provided for suite passengers only.

Dining: The dining room has a high ceiling and is quite spacious. Dining is in two seatings, with assigned tables for two, four, six, or eight. Breakfast and luncheon can also be taken outdoors by the swimming pool. Regional foods are featured, including a decent choice of breads and tropical fruits.

There is also an informal dining spot called Le Bistro, where casual dining makes for an alternative to the dining room for those who do not wish to dress for dinner. In addition, there is a sports bar and outdoors grill.

Other Comments: Originally built for one of Royal Viking Line's three shipping partners (A.F. Klaveness & Co.), *Norwegian Star* has a smart, almost contemporary profile, with well-balanced lines and a delightful, sharply raked bow, something not found on the newest cruise ships today. She also has a decent draft, which makes her eminently suitable for the occasionally unkind waters around Australia and New Zealand, the ship's principal cruising regions. The ship has been quite well maintained and has a wide expanse of open deck, sunbathing space, and several sports areas, including a large paddle tennis court. The ship was transferred from the Norwegian Cruise Line fleet to the Star Cruises fleet in 2000 and sails in Southeast Asia.

Inside, the public rooms are quite elegant and have high ceilings. The spa and fitness facilities are generally good. The casino has tasteful decor.

This ship was "stretched" almost 20 years ago in 1983, and a further, extensive multimillion dollar reconstruction took place in 1997, when more cabins were added (sadly, the library was taken away). Also added were a playroom and a video arcade (although there really are few other facilities for children, as the ship is better suited to older adults). Families with children are catered to with an extensive program. According to age, children are called Nippers (3–6 years old), Navigators (7–12 years old), and Legends (13–17 years old). The ship provides a well-programmed cruise experience for those passengers who do not want to cruise aboard the larger ships.

Weak Points: Although she is still a smart-looking vessel, the ship is getting old and more trendy ships in other markets have superceded the design. The plumbing has presented problems for years and continues to be somewhat problematic at times.

SHIPBOARD ETIQUETTE

Cruise lines want you to have a good vacation, but there are some rules to be observed.

↪ In public rooms, smoking and nonsmoking sections are available. In the dining room, however, cigar and pipe smoking are not permitted at all.

↪ If you take a video camera with you, be aware that you are not allowed to tape any of the professional entertainment shows and cabarets due to international copyright infringement regulations.

↪ It is all right to be casual when on vacation, but not to enter a ship's dining room in just a bathing suit. Bare feet, likewise, are not permitted. If you are uncomfortable eating with the typical ten-piece dining room cutlery setting, don't fret; some cruise lines now have etiquette classes to help you.

Norwegian Star 2

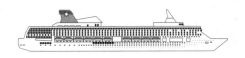

Large Ship:	91,000 tons	Cabins (with private balcony):	372
Lifestyle:	Standard	Cabins (wheelchair accessible):	20
Cruise Line:	Norwegian Cruise Line	Cabin Current:	110-volt
Former Names:	-	Full-Service Dining Rooms:	6
Builder:	Meyer Werft (Germany)	Elevators:	n/a
Original Cost:	$400 million	Casino (gaming tables):	No
Entered Service:	December 2001	Slot Machines:	No
Registry:	Panama	Swimming Pools (outdoors):	2
Length (ft/m):	964.9/294.13	Swimming Pools (indoors):	1
Beam (ft/m):	105.6/32.2	Whirlpools:	4 (+ 1 children's whirlpool)
Draft (ft/m):	26.9/8.2	Fitness Center:	Yes
Propulsion/Propellers:	Diesel-electric/	Sauna/Steam Room:	Yes/Yes
	2 azimuthing pods (19.5MW each)	Massage:	Yes
Passenger Decks:	12	Self-Service Launderette:	No
Total Crew:	1,100	Dedicated Cinema:	No
Passengers (lower beds/all berths):	2,244/4,080	Library:	Yes
Pass. Space Ratio (lower beds/all berths):	40.5/23.0	Classification Society:	Det Norske Veritas
Crew/Pass. Ratio (lower beds/all berths):	2/3.7		
Navigation Officers:	Scandinavian		
Cabins (total):	1,122	**OVERALL SCORE: NOT YET RATED**	
Size Range (sq ft/sq m):	142.0–3,030.0/13.2–281.5		
Cabins (outside view):	787	Note that this ship had not entered service when this	
Cabins (interior/no view):	363	book was completed.	
Cabins (for one person):	0		

Accommodation: The accommodation is a mix of the following grades: 36 suites, 372 standard cabins with balconies, and 107 mini-suites with balconies. Regardless of the accommodation you choose, all will feature tea- and coffee-making sets, rich cherrywood cabinetry, and bathroom with sliding door and separate toilet, shower enclosure, and washbasin compartments.

The largest accommodation can be found in six Garden Villas, located high atop the ship in a pod that is located forward of the ship's funnel, overlooking the main swimming pool. These villas feature huge glass walls and landscaped private roof gardens (Japanese-style or Thai-style) for outdoor dining (with whirlpool tubs, naturally), and private sunbathing areas. Each has several bedrooms and bathrooms and a large living room overlooking the lido/pool deck. These units have their own private elevator and private stairway and can be combined to create a large, 3,030 sq ft (281 sq m) "house."

There are many suites (the smallest of which measures 291 sq ft/ 27 sq m) in several different configurations; two are housed in a pod atop ship, some overlook the stern, while others are in the forward part of the ship. All are lavishly furnished, although closet space in some of the smaller units is tight.

Although they are nicely furnished and quite well equipped, the standard outside-view and interior (no view) cabins are quite small, particularly when occupied by three or four persons. Some have interconnecting doors, and many cabins have third and fourth person pull-down berths or trundle beds.

A small room service menu is available (all items are at extra cost, and a 15% service charge and a gratuity are automatically added to your account). Bottled water is placed in each cabin (but a charge will be made to your account if you open the bottle).

Dining: With what NCL calls "Freestyle Dining," you can choose which restaurant you would like to eat in, at what time, and with whom. Although there are two principal dining rooms, there are also a number of other themed eating establishments, giving a wide range of choice — although it would be wise to plan in advance, particularly for dinner. All restaurants and eateries are nonsmoking. There are two entire decks of restaurants to choose from, including: an ornate 375-seat first main dining room offering the traditional six-course dining experience (open 5:30pm–midnight); a contemporary-style 374-seat second main dining room, offering lighter cuisine (open 5:30pm–midnight); a Japanese Restaurant, with 193 seats, featuring sit-up sushi bar, tempura bar, show galley, and separate room with a teppanyaki grill; a French restaurant, with 66 seats, featuring Le Bistro nouvelle cuisine; "Blue Lagoon" — a food court–style eatery with 88 seats, featuring hamburgers, fish & chips, pot pies, and fast wok dishes; an indoor/outdoor self-serve buffet eatery including "action stations" featuring made-to-order omelets, waffles, fruit, soups, ethnic specialties, and pasta dishes; a Spanish tapas eatery and bar with a selection of hot and cold tapas dishes and authentic entertainment; an Italian trattoria (located inside the indoor/outdoor buffet), featuring pasta, pizza, and other popular Italian fare; and a Hawaiian theme restaurant, arranged around the second level of the central atrium and incorporating a performance stage and a large movie screen.

Other eating and drinking spots include the Red Lion (an English pub for draft beer and a game of darts), Havanas (cigar and cognac lounge), Cascades, (an atrium lobby café and bar for hot and frozen coffees, teas and pastries), a Beer Garden (for grilled foods), a Gelato Bar (for ice cream) and a Gym and Spa Bar (for health food snacks and drinks).

Other Comments: *Norwegian Star 2* is the latest state-of-the-art vessel for Norwegian Cruise Line and features a "pod" propulsion system — the first of a pair of sister ships (the second is *Norwegian Dawn*, due to debut in 2002). The pod propulsion system gives the ship more maneuverability, while reducing required machinery space and vibration at the stern. A large structure, located forward of the funnel houses a children's center and, one deck above, the six "villa" suites.

Sports facilities include a jogging track, golf driving range, basketball and volleyball courts, as well as four levels of sunbathing decks.

Facilities include a large casino gaming area (with separate VIP/Club rooms); a Cyber Café (with 18 computer stations and Internet connection); a 1,150-seat show lounge with main floor and two balcony levels; 3,000-book library; card room; writing and study room; business center; karaoke lounge (built on a traditional circus theme); Internet café; conference and meeting rooms; and a retail shopping complex measuring 20,000 sq ft (1,858 sq m).

Health devotees should enjoy the two-decks-high health spa complex (operated by the Hawaii-based Mandara Spa), located at the stern of the ship (with large ocean-view windows on three sides). There are many facilities and services to pamper you (almost all at extra charge), including Thai massage (in the spa, outdoors on deck, in your cabin, or on your private balcony). In addition, there is an indoor lap pool (measuring 45 ft/14 m), hydrotherapy pool, aromatherapy and wellness centers, and mud treatment room.

Families with children should note that teens have their own huge video arcade, while children get to play in a wet 'n' wild aft pool (complete with pirate ship and caves) and two whirlpool tubs. Plus there's all the fun and facilities of a large childcare center (open 24 hours a day). There's even a room full of cots for toddlers to use for sleepovers, and even the toilets are at a special low height. Much space is devoted to children's facilities — all tucked well away from adult recreation areas.

More choices and more dining options add up to a very attractive vacation package, particularly suitable for families with children, in a very contemporary floating leisure center. The dress code is very casual (no jacket and tie needed), and the ship operates under a "no-tipping" policy. While the initial cruise fare seems very reasonable, the extra costs and charges soon mount up if you want to indulge in more than the basics. Although service levels and finesse remain inconsistent, the level of hospitality is very good.

With so many dining choices (some of which cost extra) to accommodate the tastes of an eclectic mix of nationalities, it really depends on how much you are prepared to spend as to what your final cruise and dining experience will be like. You will need to plan where you want to eat well in advance and make the necessary reservations, or you may be disappointed. *Norwegian Star* is the largest ship to serve the Hawaii cruise region. Note that a 15% gratuity is added to all bar and spa treatment accounts. Standard gratuities for staff (cabin attendants, dining room waiters, etc.) are automatically added to your on-board account (you can review these before you disembark).

Weak Points: Although the suites and junior suites are quite spacious, the standard outside-view and interior (no view) cabins are very small — particularly when occupied by three or four persons.

Norwegian Sun

Large Ship:	77,104 tons	Cabins (with private balcony):	252
Lifestyle:	Standard	Cabins (wheelchair accessible):	6
Cruise Line:	Norwegian Cruise Line	Cabin Current:	110-volt
Former Names:	-	Full-Service Dining Rooms:	2 main, 5 alternative
Builder:	Lloyd Werft (Germany)	Elevators:	12
Original Cost:	$332 million	Casino (gaming tables):	Yes
Entered Service:	September 2001	Slot Machines:	Yes
Registry:	Bahamas	Swimming Pools (outdoors):	2
Length (ft/m):	853.0/260.00	Swimming Pools (indoors):	0
Beam (ft/m):	105.8/32.25	Whirlpools:	4
Draft (ft/m):	26.2/8.00	Fitness Center:	Yes
Propulsion/Propellers:	Diesel-electric	Sauna/Steam Room:	Yes/Yes
	(50,000kW)/2	Massage:	Yes
Passenger Decks:	12	Self-Service Launderette:	No
Total Crew:	800	Dedicated Cinema:	No
Passengers (lower beds/all berths):	2,002/2,400	Library:	Yes
Pass. Space Ratio (lower beds/all berths):	38.5/32.1	Classification Society:	Germanischer Lloyd
Crew/Pass. Ratio (lower beds/all berths):	2/2.4		
Navigation Officers:	Norwegian		
Cabins (total):	1,001		
Size Range (sq ft/sq m):	120.5–488.6/11.2–45.4		
Cabins (outside view):	574		
Cabins (interior/no view):	427		
Cabins (for one person):	0		

OVERALL SCORE: NOT YET RATED

Note that this ship had not entered service when this book was completed.

Accommodation: There are 30 different price categories of accommodation, including 6 grades of suites, 15 grades of outside-view cabins, and 9 grades of interior (no view) cabins, so choosing the right accommodation for your needs requires some thought.

All of the standard outside-view and interior (no view) cabins feature common facilities, such as: two lower beds that can convert to a queen-size bed, a small lounge area with sofa and table, and a decent amount of closet and drawer space, although the cabins themselves are disappointingly small. Over 200 outside-view cabins each have their own private balcony. Each cabin has a small vanity/writing desk, color TV, personal safe, refrigerator, climate control, and laptop computer connection socket. Bottled water is placed in each cabin (but a charge will be made to your account if you open the bottle).

There are two Honeymoon/Anniversary Suites, located at the front of the ship, with forward-facing and side views. Each suite has a separate lounge and bedroom. The lounge features a large dining table and chairs, two sofas, large TV, DVD/CD player, coffee table, queen-size pull-down Murphy bed, guest closet, writing desk, wet bar with two bar stools, refrigerator and sink, several cupboards for glasses, and several drawers and other cupboards for storage. The sleeping area features twin beds that convert to a queen-size bed and walk-in closet with a good amount of hanging space. The tiled bathroom, although not large, features a full-size whirlpool bathtub and shower, retractable clothesline, deep washbasin, and personal toiletries cabinets.

The largest accommodation can be found in two Owner's Suites, each of which features a hot tub, large teak table, two chairs, and two deck lounge chairs outside on a huge, private, all located on a forward-facing teakwood floor balcony just under the ship's navigation bridge. Each suite has a separate lounge and bedroom. The lounge features a large dining table and chairs, two sofas, large TV, DVD/CD player, coffee table, queen-size pull-down Murphy bed, guest closet, writing desk, wet bar with two bar stools, refrigerator and sink, several cupboards for glasses, and several drawers and other cupboards for storage. The bedroom, which has sliding wood half-doors that look into the lounge, features a queen-size (with European duvet) bed under a leaf-glass chandelier, vanity desk, TV, walk-in closet with plenty of hanging rail space, several open shelves, and large personal safe. The tiled bathroom, although not large, features a full-size bathtub with retractable clothesline above, separate shower enclosure with glass doors, deep washbasin, and personal toiletries cabinets.

There are also a number of other suites — each of which features a private teakwood balcony; these suites face aft in a secluded position and overlook the ship's wash. They feature some of the same facilities as found in the owner's suites, with the exception of the outdoor hot tub, and the fact that there is less space.

Dining: With what NCL calls "Freestyle Dining," you can choose which restaurant you would like to eat in, at what time, and with whom. Although there are two principal dining rooms, there are also a number of other themed eating establishments, giving a wide range of choice — although it would be wise to plan in advance, particularly for dinner. All restaurants and eateries are nonsmoking.

There are two main dining rooms: the 564-seat Four Seasons Dining Room, and the 604-seat Seven Seas Dining Room, with tables for four, six, or eight (there are no tables for two).

Sandwiched between the two (rather like a train carriage) is a third, 84-seat Italian Restaurant, available as an à la carte dining option (for which there is an extra charge), with tables for two or four persons. Reservations are necessary.

There are also several other dining options, most of which are located on one of the uppermost decks of the ship, with great views from large picture windows. These include: "Le Bistro," a 90-seat alternative dining spot for some fine French-style meals, including tableside cooking (dinner is by reservation); a Japanese Restaurant, featuring a sushi bar and a teppanyaki grill; a Pacific Rim Fusion Restaurant, featuring à la carte Californian/Hawaiian/Asian cuisine, with dining by reservation; "Healthy Living Restaurant" (with 80 seats), featuring spa cuisine and Cooking Light menus; and a 24-hour self-serve, buffet-style eatery that features fast foods and salad items, with several "food islands."

Overall, the food provided is rather unmemorable fare that lacks taste and presentation quality; the menus, too, are uninspiring. There is a reasonably decent selection of breads, rolls, cheeses, and fruits, however. The wine list is quite decent and well put together, with moderate prices, although you won't find any good vintage wines. The cutlery is very ordinary (there are no fish knives). There is no formal afternoon tea, although you can make your own from various beverage stations. The service is, on the whole, adequate, nothing more, and proves that a good staff that can communicate well is quite difficult to find.

Other Comments: This is a close sister ship to *Norwegian Sky*, although there is one additional deck of balcony cabins, and crew cabins have been added to accommodate an additional 200 crew. The amount of outdoor space is very good, and the extra wide pool deck (the extra width created from port and starboard "overhangs" that resulted from balconies added to cabins on two decks below), with its two swimming pools and four Jacuzzi tubs.

There is a two-level show lounge with over 1,000 seats, and this incorporates a large proscenium stage for the high-energy dazzle-and-sizzle shows that NCL passengers enjoy. However, the sight lines are obstructed in a number of seats by several slim pillars, although there is not as much obstruction as aboard sister ship *Norwegian Sky*.

A separate cabaret lounge, Checkers Lounge, is equipped with an extremely long bar. Other features include a large casino (this will operate 24 hours a day, and have special facilities and rooms for high-rollers and "club" members), shopping arcade, children's playroom (there is also a splash pool in a prime open deck area forward atop ship), and a video arcade

There is also a large health/fitness spa (including an aerobics room and separate gymnasium), and several treatment rooms.

Other facilities include a small conference room, library, beauty salon, a smoking lounge for cigars and cognac, and an Internet Café, located on the Promenade Deck within the ship's atrium lobby, with 20 computer stations.

Those with a black belt in shopping might appreciate the fact that there are numerous shops on board, showcasing a wide range of goods, from inexpensive to very expensive. Columbian Emeralds is the joint venture operator.

Sports fans will appreciate the large basketball/volleyball court, baseball batting cage, golf driving range, platform tennis, shuffleboard and table tennis facilities, and sports bar with 24-hour live satellite TV coverage of sports events and major games. Joggers will also find a wraparound indoor-outdoor jogging track.

Young passengers will find an array of facilities for a range of ages, which include a children's playroom called Kid's Korner for "junior sailors" (ages 3–5); First Mates (ages 6–9); Navigators (ages 10–12); and Teens (ages 13–17).

With this latest ship, Norwegian Cruise Line has made an effort to provide better public rooms and more entertainment facilities than aboard its other ships, so you get a lot of ship for your money. *Norwegian Sun* tries hard to be all things to all people, and it is the company's latest and perhaps its best resort at sea (with staff hand-picked from the company's other ships). The ship certainly has more choices and options for eating than any other NCL ship (perhaps with the exception of the larger *Norwegian Star II*, another new ship that NCL acquired from parent company Star Cruises in 2001). Note that a 15% gratuity is added to all bar and spa treatment accounts. Standard gratuities for staff (cabin attendants, dining room waiters, etc.) are automatically added to your on-board account (you can review these if necessary before you disembark).

Weak Points: Standing in line for embarkation, disembarkation, shore tenders, and self-serve buffet meals is an inevitable aspect of cruising aboard all large ships. The standard interior (no view) and outside-view cabins are very small when compared to those of other major cruise lines such as Carnival or Celebrity. The food in the large dining rooms is a weak point.

Just watching the scenery go by can be a great cruising experience.

Norwegian Wind
★★★ +

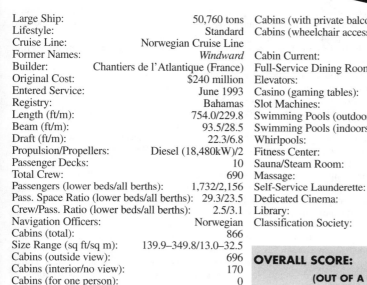

Large Ship:	50,760 tons	Cabins (with private balcony):	48
Lifestyle:	Standard	Cabins (wheelchair accessible):	6 (+ 30 for
Cruise Line:	Norwegian Cruise Line		hearing impaired)
Former Names:	*Windward*	Cabin Current:	110-volt
Builder:	Chantiers de l'Atlantique (France)	Full-Service Dining Rooms:	4
Original Cost:	$240 million	Elevators:	10
Entered Service:	June 1993	Casino (gaming tables):	Yes
Registry:	Bahamas	Slot Machines:	Yes
Length (ft/m):	754.0/229.8	Swimming Pools (outdoors):	2
Beam (ft/m):	93.5/28.5	Swimming Pools (indoors):	0
Draft (ft/m):	22.3/6.8	Whirlpools:	2
Propulsion/Propellers:	Diesel (18,480kW)/2	Fitness Center:	Yes
Passenger Decks:	10	Sauna/Steam Room:	Yes/No
Total Crew:	690	Massage:	Yes
Passengers (lower beds/all berths):	1,732/2,156	Self-Service Launderette:	No
Pass. Space Ratio (lower beds/all berths):	29.3/23.5	Dedicated Cinema:	No
Crew/Pass. Ratio (lower beds/all berths):	2.5/3.1	Library:	Yes
Navigation Officers:	Norwegian	Classification Society:	Det Norske Veritas
Cabins (total):	866		
Size Range (sq ft/sq m):	139.9–349.8/13.0–32.5		
Cabins (outside view):	696	**OVERALL SCORE:**	**1,381**
Cabins (interior/no view):	170	(OUT OF A POSSIBLE 2,000 POINTS)	
Cabins (for one person):	0		

Accommodation: There are 15 grades of cabins. The majority of cabins have outside views and feature wood-trimmed cabinetry and warm decor, with multicolored soft furnishings, but there is almost no drawer space (the closets have open shelves, however), so take minimal clothing. All cabins have a sitting area, but this takes away any free space, making movement pretty tight. The bathrooms are small but practical, although there is little space for storage of personal toiletry items.

There are 18 suites (12 of which have a private entrance and a small, private balcony), each with separate living room and bedroom, fine quality cabinetry, and lots of closet and drawer space. Occupants of suites receive "concierge" service, which provides extra personal attention. In addition, 16 suites and 70 cabins have interconnecting doors — good for families cruising together, or perhaps for those who want separate "his and hers" living spaces. There are several cabins specially equipped for the hearing-impaired. Note that all cabins on the port side of the ship are designated nonsmoking. Bottled water is placed in each cabin (but a charge will be made to your account if you open the bottle).

Dining: There are two main full-service dining rooms: The Terraces (arguably the nicest, with windows that look out over the ship's tiered aft decks), and the Four Seasons (with approximately 450 seats), located amidships. All are nonsmoking and feature the same menu and food, in an open-seating, come-when-you-want arrangement (NCL calls it "Freestyle Dining"). The Four Seasons is now the largest and has some prime tables at ocean-view window seats in a section that extends from the ship's port and starboard sides in half-moon shapes (nice for lunch, but it's either dark or the curtains are drawn for dinner).
Italian fare is served in the Trattoria, which overlooks the aft swimming pool.

Then there is The Bistro, which features informal evening dining at no extra charge in more intimate surroundings. A 200-seat Sports Bar (typically open between 6am and 1am) features breakfast, lunch, dinner, and snacks throughout the day. There's also a poolside pizzeria and a small coffee lounge.

Overall, the food provided is rather unmemorable fare that lacks taste and presentation quality; the menus, too, are uninspiring. There is a reasonably decent selection of breads, rolls, cheeses, and fruits, however. The wine list is quite decent and well put together, with moderate prices, although you won't find any good vintage wines. There are many types of beer (including some on draft in the popular Sports Bar & Grill) to choose from. The cutlery is very ordinary (there are no fish knives). There is no formal afternoon tea, although you can make your own from various beverage stations. The service is, on the whole, adequate, nothing more, and proves that a good staff that can communicate well is quite difficult to find.

You can eat breakfast or lunch in any of the dining rooms when it's "open seating." A lavish "choco-holics" buffet is featured once each cruise — established as a firm favorite among Norwegian Cruise Line's repeat passengers.

Other Comments: *Norwegian Wind* is the sister ship to *Norwegian Dream* and, as such, has a moderate-ly handsome profile (despite a large, square blue funnel) that was actually more balanced before the ship underwent a "chop and stretch" operation in the spring of 1998. There is a blue rubber-covered wraparound promenade deck outdoors. The tiered pool deck is neat, as are the multideck aft sun terraces and all her fore and aft connecting exterior stairways.

The 1998 "chop and stretch" added a completely new midsection, and the funnel was adapted so that it could be "folded" over to allow the ship to transit the Kiel Canal in Germany. It was done to both *Norwegian Wind* and sister *Norwegian Dream* at a cost of $138 million. Included in the 131 ft (40 m) sec-tion were 251 new passengers cabins and 50 crew cabins, together with several new or enlarged public rooms (although there are still not enough) including a 60-seat conference center. Some innovative features were incorporated in the original design, and these have been kept and enhanced. The passenger flow is generally good — the ship seems to absorb passengers quite well for much of the time, except at peak traf-fic times between dinner seatings.

The overall exterior design emphasizes a clever and extensive use of large windows that create a sense of open spaces, although the interior design provides many smaller public rooms rather than the large hang-ers found aboard so many other ships. However, there is no big atrium lobby, as one might expect. The pas-tel interior colors used are quite soothing, and she is considered by many to be a pretty ship inside. The entrance lobby is not at all attractive and feels rather confined for a ship of this size.

This ship has proven highly successful for Norwegian Cruise Line's younger, active sports-minded pas-sengers, and provides a good alternative to the larger ships with their greater passenger capacity — although there will be plenty of other passengers to keep you company. The dress code is casual, and there are no formal nights when you have to dress up. Note that a 15% gratuity is added to all bar accounts, as well as for spa treatments. Standard gratuities for staff (cabin attendants, dining room waiters, etc.) are automatically added to your on-board account (you can review these charges before you disembark).

Weak Points: Standing in line for embarkation, disembarkation, shore tenders, and self-serve buffet meals is an inevitable aspect of cruising aboard all large ships. The room service menu is still poor and could be improved. The outdoor stairways are numerous and confusing. The carpeted steel interior stair-well steps are quite tinny. When the ship was "stretched" it reduced the amount of outdoor space per pas-senger, and this is reflected in increased density around the pools. There simply are not enough public rooms to absorb the increase in passengers well.

OceanBreeze
★★+

Mid-Size Ship:	21,486 tons	Cabins (for one person):	0
Lifestyle:	Standard	Cabins (with private balcony):	0
Cruise Line:	Imperial Majesty Cruise Line	Cabins (wheelchair accessible):	0
Former Names:	*Azure Seas, Calypso, Monarch Star, Southern Cross*	Cabin Current:	110-volt
Builder:	Harland & Wolff (UK)	Full-Service Dining Rooms:	1
Original Cost:	n/a	Elevators:	1
Entered Service:	March 1955/May 1992	Casino (gaming tables):	Yes
Registry:	Bahamas	Slot Machines:	Yes
Length (ft/m):	603.8/184.06	Swimming Pools (outdoors):	1
Beam (ft/m):	80.0/24.41	Swimming Pools (indoors):	0
Draft (ft/m):	26.1/7.97	Whirlpools:	1
Propulsion/Propellers:	Steam turbine (14,900kW)/2	Fitness Center:	Yes
Passenger Decks:	9	Sauna/Steam Room:	No/No
Total Crew:	370	Massage:	Yes
Passengers (lower beds/all berths):	780/1,012	Self-Service Launderette:	No
Pass. Space Ratio (lower beds/all berths):	27.5/21.2	Dedicated Cinema/Seats:	Yes/55
Crew/Pass. Ratio (lower beds/all berths):	2.1/2.7	Library:	Yes
Navigation Officers:	International	Classification Society:	Lloyds Register
Cabins (total):	390		
Size Range (sq ft/sq m):	96.8–398.2/9.0–37.0		
Cabins (outside view):	236		
Cabins (interior/no view):	154		

OVERALL SCORE: 1,095

(OUT OF A POSSIBLE 2,000 POINTS)

Accommodation: There are a wide variety of cabin shapes, sizes, and configurations to choose from, in 11 price categories. Most of them are moderately comfortable and nicely decorated in earth tones and pastel colors. Although they are not large and have only basic appointments, all have one or two lower beds and heavy-duty fittings. Note that many interior (no view) cabins are actually larger than some of the outside-view cabins. Most cabins have very plain walls. The lighting is minimal; there is little drawer space, although the closet space is sufficient for two (particularly for two-night cruises). The bathrooms are very basic; most have a shower enclosure, and soap and shampoo are provided.

On Boat Deck there are 12 larger suites, three of which have forward views over the ship's long foredeck; these come with a separate bedroom and living area (including TV). They are very comfortable, and could sleep five or six — good for families with children. All suites have a minibar and refrigerator.

Room service is available 24 hours daily, although the menu is very limited.

Dining: The 500-seat Caravelle Restaurant, which is located on a lower deck, has a warm, cheerful ambience. There are two seatings, at tables for two, four, six, or ten; the chairs, however, do not have armrests. The cuisine is generally basic but sound, and there is plenty of it, but it certainly is not gourmet food, despite what the brochure claims, and the presentation is minimal. However, having said that, there is enough of a variety to please just about everyone. Lunch and dinner menus include a vegetarian appetizer and entree. The service is reasonable and attentive, but extremely hurried (particularly for first seating). There is only the most basic choice of cheeses and fresh fruits.

For the short cruise product that this ship provides, the wine list is actually quite extensive (it focuses on wines from the US and the Americas), and the prices reflect extremely good value for the money in a short cruise.

Casual, self-serve food is available buffet-style for breakfast, lunch, and midnight snacks in the self-serve Café Miramar. The room also acts as a cabaret room/nightclub. You can, if you like, also sit outside under a canvas-style awning for midnight snacks.

Other Comments: *OceanBreeze* is a real vintage ship, originally built to operate line voyages from England to Australia in the 1950s for the now-defunct Shaw Savill line. The ship, which was originally christened in a naming ceremony by England's Queen Elizabeth II, has a long, low profile, and is easily identified by its single funnel set almost at the very stern in what was, when built, a radical departure from all other passenger vessels of the period. The ship's new owners have thoughtfully provided a display of the ship's history (including a letter from England's Queen Elizabeth II) found in three wooden showcases close to the ship's main lounge.

The ship, which has a dark blue hull and white superstructure, has been maintained quite well, although she is now showing her age in several areas — she is, after all, well over 40 years old! Her large areas of wooden open decks (complete with wooden deck lounge chairs and thick blue cushioned pads) are still in a very reasonable condition. One bonus feature is the fact that the ship has steam turbine propulsion; this translates to little or no vibration, unlike many of today's newer ships that are powered by diesel or diesel-electric engines.

A refurbishment of the ship in 2000 revitalized the ship's interiors, although some of the interesting Art Deco features and wood and etched glass doors (a carryover from her former days as an ocean liner) have been kept. The Monte Carlo casino is on two levels (in what used to be the cinema, with a bar on the upper level) and is nicely decorated in an Art Deco style. Other features include a health and fitness/spa area, gift shop, and video arcade. There is a cardroom/library, although there are no books (there really is no time to relax and read on a two-night cruise with one day in port).

There is also a main lounge (for evening shows, shore excursion lectures), although, with its single-deck height, it quickly becomes crowded, and the sight lines are quite poor.

All in all, *OceanBreeze* is an old but very reasonable ship for those wanting a pleasant short cruise get-away for a modest price, in casual, no-frills surroundings. You should note that the program is a busy one and, because the cruise is only two days long, there will be little time to relax. The ship will provide you with a taste of the pleasures of cruising, all in a package that relieves you of some of the decision-making normally necessary for a typical land-based two-night vacation break. *OceanBreeze* was purchased by Imperial Majesty Cruise Line in May 2000 and operates two-night cruises from Ft. Lauderdale to the Bahamas. Note that (when this book was completed) $19.50 (per person; per two-night cruise) is added to your on-board account for gratuities. You can, however, decline or change this amount by visiting the Purser's Desk. Note also that a 15% gratuity is added to all bar accounts.

Weak Points: Do expect to wait in line for embarkation, disembarkation, shore excursions, and the self-serve buffets. There are many smokers among the passengers, and the entertainment is of the low-budget variety.

Oceanic
★★★+

Large Ship:	38,772 tons	Cabins (with private balcony):	21
Lifestyle:	Standard	Cabins (wheelchair accessible):	1
Cruise Line:	Pullmantur Cruises	Cabin Current:	110 volts
Former Names:	*Big Red Boat I, Oceanic*	Full-Service Dining Rooms:	1
Builder:	Cantieri Riuniti dell' Adriatico (Italy)	Elevators:	5
Original Cost:	$40 million	Casino (gaming tables):	Yes
Entered Service:	April 1965/May 2001	Slot Machines:	Yes
Registry:	Spain	Swimming Pools (outdoors):	2
Length (ft/m):	782.1/238.40	Swimming Pools (inside):	0
Beam (ft/m):	96.5/29.44	Whirlpools:	3
Draft (ft/m):	28.2/8.60	Fitness Center:	Yes
Propulsion/Propellers:	Steam turbine (45,100kW)/2	Sauna/Steam Room:	No/No
Passenger Decks:	10	Massage:	Yes
Total Crew:	565	Self-Service Launderette:	No
Passengers (lower beds/all berths):	1,124/1,800	Dedicated Cinema:	No
Pass. Space Ratio (basis 2):	34.7/21.54	Library:	Yes
Pass. Space Ratio (all berths):	21.5/3.1	Classification Society:	Bureau Veritas
Navigation Officers:	Spanish		
Cabins (total):	562		
Size Range (sq ft/m):	139.9–454.2/13.0–42.2		
Cabins (outside view):	252		
Cabins (interior/no view):	310		
Cabins (for one person):	0		

OVERALL SCORE: 1,093
(OUT OF A POSSIBLE 2,000 POINTS)

Accommodation: *Oceanic* has a wide range of suites and standard outside-view and interior (no view) cabins. Note that there are far more interior (no view) cabins than outside-view cabins. There are eight deluxe suites, each of which has a private balcony; 65 suites (13 of which have a private balcony), the rest being a mixture of inside (no view) and outside (sea-view) cabins. Note that many of the suites have their views obstructed by lifeboats.

The ceiling height is good, which helps give an impression of space. All cabins have heavy-duty furniture and are quite well equipped, although many are now in need of refurbishment. Many cabins feature double beds. All cabins have a television, telephone, and climate control.

Dining: The dining room, which operates two seatings, is large and cheerful, but extremely noisy when full. The tables are very close together, and chairs do not have armrests (there's no room for them). The cuisine is adequate, no more, and dining room service is of only a very basic standard—there is absolutely no finesse in service. Although food is plentiful, there is a limited selection of breads, cheeses and fruits. The wine list is reasonably decent (with many Spanish wines featured), and prices are reasonable.

Other Comments: Built originally as an ocean liner for Home Lines, *Oceanic* (which was the ship's first name) underwent a successful conversion to provide cheap and cheerful family cruises following her purchase by Premier Cruise Lines in 1985. When Premier Cruise Lines went into bankruptcy in 2000, the ship was purchased at auction—and is now owned and operated by the Spanish tour operator Pullmantur Cruises.

There is a reasonable amount of open teak-covered deck space for sunbathing, but it becomes cramped and noisy when the ship is full, and there are no cushioned pads for the deck lounge chairs. The twin swimming pools atop the ship have a sliding magrodome roof that can be used in inclement weather.

Her interiors feature upbeat decor and cheerful soft furnishing colors and fabrics. One neat feature is the enclosed promenades (they were popular on ocean liners of yesteryear for crossing the North Atlantic in all weather conditions) for strolling around the ship, or for just sitting. During a refurbishment in May 2000, a new kid's room and teen room were built, and an Internet Café was installed. This ship will provide a decent first cruise experience for families with children, with many youth activity counselors.

Although the ship got off to a rather chaotic start under the new operators, Pullmantur Cruises, it will provide a family with children with a fun-filled cruise aboard a classic ship setting, but it certainly does remind me of a summer camp at sea, particularly when school vacations mean lots (and I mean lots) of children have the run of the ship.

Weak Points: There are lines everywhere. There is much congestion at the self-service buffets for breakfast and lunch. The noise pollution is high throughout the ship, with constant repetitive announcements that are really irritating. The interiors need more attention to detail, and cleanliness could be better. Many public rooms have numerous support pillars to obstruct sight lines. Smokers are everywhere—there is no escape.

DID YOU KNOW...?

...that the first vessel built exclusively for cruising was Hamburg-Amerika Line's two-funnel yacht, the 4,409-tonne *Princessin Victoria Luise*? This luxury ship even included a private suite for the German Kaiser.

...that the first ship to be fitted with real stabilizers (not an autogyro device) was the Peninsular & Oriental Steam Navigation Company's 1949-built 24,215-tonne *Chusan*?

...that the first consecrated oceangoing Roman Catholic chapel aboard a passenger ship was in Compagnie Generale Transatlantique's *Ile de France* of 1928?

Ocean Majesty
★★★ +

Mid-Size Ship:	10,417 tons	Cabins (for one person):	11
Lifestyle:	Standard	Cabins (with private balcony):	8
Cruise Line:	Majestic International Cruises	Cabins (wheelchair accessible):	2
Former Names: *Homeric, Olympic, Ocean Majesty,*		Cabin Current:	110/220-volt
Kypros Star, Sol Christina, Juan March		Full-Service Dining Rooms:	1
Builder:	Union Navale de Levante (Spain)	Elevators:	3
Original Cost:	$65 million	Casino (gaming tables):	Yes
Entered Service:	1966/April 1994	Slot Machines	Yes
Registry:	Greece	Swimming Pools (outdoors):	1
Length (ft/m):	443.8/135.30	Swimming Pools (indoors):	0
Beam (ft/m):	62.9/19.20	Whirlpools:	1
Draft (ft/m):	19.5/5.95	Fitness Center:	Yes
Size Range (sq ft/m):	96.8–182.9/9.0–17.0	Sauna/Steam Room:	Yes/No
Propulsion/Propellers:	Diesel (12,200kW)/2	Massage:	Yes
Passenger Decks:	8	Self-Service Launderette:	No
Total Crew:	235	Dedicated Cinema:	No
Passengers (lower beds/all berths):	535/621	Library:	Yes
Pass. Space Ratio (lower beds/all berths):	19.4/16.7	Classification Society:	American Bureau of
Crew/Pass. Ratio (lower beds/all berths):	2.2/2.6		Shipping
Navigation Officers:	Greek		
Cabins (total):	273		
Size Range (sq ft/sq m):	97–183/917	**OVERALL SCORE:**	**1,274**
Cabins (outside view):	186	**(OUT OF A POSSIBLE 2,000 POINTS)**	
Cabins (interior/no view):	87		

Accommodation: Too many cabin categories for a ship of this size. Cabins are small but functional, with a decent amount of closet and drawer space. Ceilings are plain, soundproofing could be better, but overall they are neat and tidy. All have twin lower beds or double beds; some also have additional upper (Pullman) berths.

The tiled bathrooms all have a shower; none have a bathtub. They are bright and functional, with good lighting, but do lack space for the storage of personal toiletry items.

Although there are two wheelchair accessible cabins, you should be aware that wheelchair access throughout much of the ship will prove difficult and is not recommended.

Dining: The dining room, set low down in the ship, features two seatings. It is reasonably attractive but extremely noisy. Few tables for two; most passengers dine at large tables that seat eight. The cuisine is continental, with a decent enough selection, highlighted by Greek specialties and signature dishes. There is a small selection of breads, fruits, and cheeses, and the buffets are generally simple, unimaginative, and repetitive affairs that have been improved somewhat since being catered by an Italian maritime catering company.

Other Comments: This ship has a balanced, somewhat handsome profile, with an aft funnel. She underwent an extensive transformation in 1994, with the exception of hull, shaft, and propellers. She has a unique "walk-through" funnel. There is a good amount of open deck space, although the plastic deck furniture is tacky.

There are several good public rooms, bars, and lounges, furnished with good quality materials and soft furnishing fabrics. The decor includes an abundance of highly polished mirrored surfaces.

Cruising aboard this ship will provide a busy, destination-oriented experience in surroundings that are very casual, yet comfortable; you will not need to take any dressy clothes. The ship is of an ideal size for cruising in the Aegean and Mediterranean areas, and can get into many ports that larger ships cannot.

This ship is often chartered to various tour operators and packagers. This means the standards of product delivery can vary on board. During each summer, the ship is under charter to the UK's Page & Moy for cruises to Northern Europe and the Baltics (during these charters, the food and its presentation are improved).

Weak Points: This is a high-density vessel, so expect lines for shore excursions and buffets. No cabins have bathtubs. She has a somewhat awkward interior layout and steep interior stairways with short steps.

Ocean Princess
★★★★

Large Ship:	77,499 tons	Cabins (for one person):	0
Lifestyle:	Standard	Cabins (with private balcony):	410
Cruise Line:	Princess Cruises	Cabins (wheelchair accessible):	19
Former Names:	-	Cabin Current:	110/220-volt
Builder:	Fincantieri (Italy)	Full-Service Dining Rooms:	2 main/3 others
Original Cost:	$300 million	Elevators:	11
Entered Service:	February 2000	Casino (gaming tables):	Yes
Registry:	Great Britain	Slot Machines:	Yes
Length (ft/m):	857.2/261.3	Swimming Pools (outdoors):	4
Beam (ft/m):	105.6/32.2	Swimming Pools (indoors):	0
Draft (ft/m):	26.5/8.1	Whirlpools:	5
Propulsion/Propellers:	Diesel-electric (28,000kW)/2	Fitness Center:	Yes
Passenger Decks:	10	Sauna/Steam Room:	Yes/Yes
Total Crew:	900	Massage:	Yes
Passengers (lower beds/all berths):	1,950/2,250	Self-Service Launderette:	Yes
Pass. Space Ratio (lower beds/all berths):	39.7/34.4	Dedicated Cinema:	No
Crew/Pass. Ratio (lower beds/all berths):	2.1/2.5	Library:	Yes
Navigation Officers:	British/Italian	Classification Society:	Registro Navale Italiano
Cabins (total):	975		
Size Range (sq ft/m):	158.2–610.3/14.7–56.7		
Cabins (outside view):	603		
Cabins (interior/no view):	372		

OVERALL SCORE: 1,539

(OUT OF A POSSIBLE 2,000 POINTS)

Accommodation: There are 28 different cabin grades: 20 outside-view and 8 interior (no view) cabin grades. Although the standard outside-view and interior (no view) cabins are a little small, they are well designed and functional in layout, and have earth tone colors accentuated by splashes of color from the bedspreads. Proportionately, there are quite a lot of interior (no view) cabins. Many of the outside-view cabins have private balconies, and all seem to be quite well soundproofed, although the balcony partition is not the floor-to-ceiling type, so you can hear your neighbors clearly (or smell their smoke). Note: The balconies are very narrow, just large enough for two small chairs, and there is no dedicated lighting.

A reasonable amount of closet space as well as abundant drawer and other storage space is provided in all cabins, which is adequate for a seven-night cruise. Cabins have TV and refrigerator. Each night a chocolate will appear on your pillow. Cabin bathrooms are practical and come with all the details one needs, although they really are tight spaces, best as one-person-at-a-time units. They have a decent shower enclosure, a small amount of shelving for personal toiletries, real glasses, hair dryer, and bathrobe.

The largest accommodation can be found in six suites, two on each of three decks located at the stern. These are well laid out and have large bathrooms with two sinks, a Jacuzzi bathtub, a separate shower enclosure, and a large private balcony. The bedroom features generous amounts of wood accenting and detailing, indented ceilings, and TV sets in both bedroom and lounge areas, which have a dining room table and four chairs.

The mini-suites typically have two lower beds that convert to a queen-size bed. There is a separate bedroom/sleeping area with vanity desk, and a lounge with sofa and coffee table, indented ceilings with generous amounts of wood accenting and detailing, walk-in closet, and larger bathroom with Jacuzzi bathtub and separate shower enclosure.

Note that Princess Cruises features CNN, CNBC, ESPN, and TNT on the in-cabin color TV system (when available, depending on cruise area).

Dining: There are two main dining rooms. Both Sardinian and Tuscan are nonsmoking, as are dining rooms aboard all the ships of P&O Cruises. Each has its own galley and is split into multitier sections, which help create a feeling of intimacy, although there is a lot of noise from the waiter stations, adjacent to many tables. Breakfast and lunch are provided in an open-seating arrangement, while dinner is in two seatings.

Despite the fact that the portions are generous, the food and its presentation are somewhat disappointing. The quality of fish is poor (often disguised by crumb or batter coatings), the selection of fresh green vegetables is limited, and few garnishes are used. However, do remember that this is banquet catering, with all its attendant standardization and production cooking. Meats are of a decent quality, although often disguised by gravy-based sauces, and pasta dishes are acceptable (though voluminous), and are typically served by section headwaiters that may also make "something special just for you" — in search of gratuities and good comments.

On any given seven-day cruise, a typical menu cycle will include a Sailaway Dinner, Captain's Welcome Dinner, Chef's Dinner, Italian Dinner, French Dinner, Captain's Gala Dinner, and Landfall Dinner. The wine list is reasonable, but the company has, sadly, eliminated all wine waiters. Note that 15% is added to all beverage bills, including wines (whether you order a $15 bottle or a $120 bottle, even though it takes the same amount of service to open and pour the wine).

With a sheltered view over the Riviera Pool, the Riviera Grill features the "Sterling Steakhouse" for those that want to taste four different cuts of Angus beef from the popular "Sterling Silver" brand of USDA prime meats — filet mignon, New York strip, porterhouse, and rib-eye — all presented on a silver tray. The Riviera Grill also provides a barbecue chicken option, plus the usual baked potato or French fries as accompaniments. This is available as an alternative to the dining rooms, between 6:30pm and 9:30pm only, at an additional charge (at press time) of $8 per person.

There is also a patisserie (for cappuccino, espresso, and pastries), a wine and caviar bar, and a pizzeria (complete with cobblestone floors and wrought iron decorative features), that has six excellent pizzas to choose from.

The Horizon Buffet is open 24 hours a day and features an informal dinner setting with sit-down waiter service and a small bistro menu. The buffet displays are, for the most part, repetitious, but better than they have been in the last few years (however, plastic plates are used). The cabin service menu is limited, and presentation of the food items featured is basic.

Other Comments: Although large, this all-white ship has a good profile and is well balanced by its large funnel, which contains a deck tennis/basketball/volleyball court in its sheltered aft base. There is a wide, teak wraparound promenade deck outdoors, and real teak steamer-style deck chairs (complete with royal blue cushioned pads), and 93,000 sq ft (8,640 sq m) of outdoor space. A great amount of glass area on the upper decks provides plenty of light and connection with the outside world.

The ship, while large, absorbs passengers well and has an almost intimate feel, which is what the interior designers intended. Her interiors are very pretty and warm, with attractive colors and welcoming decor that includes some very attractive wall murals and other artwork.

There is a wide range of public rooms to choose from, with several intimate rooms so that you do get the feel of being overwhelmed by large spaces. Features tasteful decor, with attractive color combinations that are warm and do not clash (nothing is brash). The interior focal point is a huge four-decks-high atrium lobby with winding double stairways, complete with two panoramic glass-walled elevators.

The main public entertainment rooms are located under three cabin decks. There is plenty of space, and the traffic flow is good. There are two show lounges, one at each end of the ship; one is a superb 550-seat, theater-style show lounge (movies are also shown here) and the other is a 480-seat cabaret-style lounge, complete with bar.

A glass-walled health spa complex is located high atop ship and includes a gymnasium with high-tech machines. One swimming pool is "suspended" aft between two decks (there are two other pools, although they are not large for the size of the ship).

The library is a warm room and has six large buttery leather chairs for listening to CDs while looking out ocean-view windows. There is a conference center for up to 300, as well as a business center, with computers, copy machines, and fax machines. The collection of artwork is good, particularly on the stairways, and helps make the ship feel smaller than it is, although in places it doesn't always seem coordinated. The casino, while large, is not really in the main passenger flow and so it does not generate the "walk-through" factor found aboard so many ships.

The most traditional room aboard is the Wheelhouse Lounge and Bar, which is decorated in the style of a turn-of-the-century gentlemen's club, with wood paneling and comfortable seating.

At the end of the day, as is the case aboard most large ships, if you live in the top suites, you will be well attended; if you do not, you will merely be one of a very large number of passengers. One nice feature is the captain's cocktail party — it is held in the four-decks-high main atrium, so you can come and go as you please. No standing in line to have your photograph taken with the captain if you don't want to.

Note that this ship will be transferred from Princess Cruises to the P&O Cruises division in October 2002. As such, the ship's new name will be *Oceana*.

Weak Points: Standing in line for embarkation, disembarkation, shore tenders, and self-serve buffet meals is an inevitable aspect of cruising aboard all large ships. There is absolutely no escape from unnecessary and repetitious announcements (particularly for activities that bring revenue, such as art auctions and bingo) that intrude constantly into your cruise. In-your-face art auctions are overbearing, and the paintings, lithographs, and faux, framed pictures strewn throughout the ship (clashing with the ship's interior decor) are an annoying intrusion into what should be a vacation, not a cruise inside a floating art emporium.

The digital voice announcing elevator deck stops is irritating to passengers (many of whom tell me they would like to rip out the speaker system). There are a number of dead ends in the interior layout, so it's not as user-friendly as it should be. The cabin numbering system is illogical, with numbers going through several hundred series' on the same deck. The walls of the passenger accommodation decks are very plain (some artwork here would be an improvement).

The swimming pools are quite small for so many passengers, and the pool deck is cluttered with white plastic deck lounge chairs that do not have cushioned pads. Waiting for tenders in anchor ports can prove irritating but is typical of large ship operations. Charging for the machines in the self-service launderette is trifling (even though it's only $1 per wash, $0.50 per dryer cycle, $0.50 for detergent).

Odysseus
★★ +

Small Ship:	9,821 tons	Cabins (interior/no view):	43
Lifestyle:	Standard	Cabins (for one person):	0
Cruise Line:	Royal Olympic Cruises	Cabins (with private balcony):	0
Former Names:	*Aquamarine, Marco Polo, Princesa*	Cabins (wheelchair accessible):	0
	Isabel	Cabin Current:	110-volt
Builder:	Astilleros Espanoles (Spain)	Full-Service Dining Rooms:	1
Original Cost:	n/a	Elevators:	1
Entered Service:	1962/2000	Casino (gaming tables):	Yes
Registry:	Greece	Slot Machines:	Yes
Length (ft/m):	483.1/147.30	Swimming Pools (outdoors):	1
Beam (ft/m):	61.2/18.67	Swimming Pools (indoors):	0
Draft (ft/m):	24.1/7.35	Whirlpools:	4
Size Range (sq ft/m):	102.2–279.8/9.5–26.0	Fitness Center:	Yes
Propulsion/Propellers:	Diesel (6,766kW)/2	Sauna/Steam Room:	Yes/No
Passenger Decks:	7	Massage:	Yes
Total Crew:	194	Self-Service Launderette:	No
Passengers (lower beds/all berths):	452/484	Dedicated Cinema:	No
Pass. Space Ratio (lower beds/all berths):	21.7/20.2	Library:	Yes
Crew/Pass. Ratio (lower beds/all berths):	2.3/2.4	Classification Society:	Lloyd's Register
Navigation Officers:	Greek		
Cabins (total):	226		
Size Range (sq ft/sq m):	102–280/10–26		
Cabins (outside view):	183		

OVERALL SCORE: 1,071
(OUT OF A POSSIBLE 2,000 POINTS)

Accommodation: The attractive, spacious, mostly outside-view cabins have either convertible sofa beds or twin beds (few cabins have genuine double beds). There is a reasonable amount of closet and drawer space, and tasteful gray wood cabinetry that, in most cabins, includes a writing/vanity desk. Some cabins have third/fourth upper Pullman berths. The cabin bathrooms are really quite small (particularly the shower stalls) and very basic, with little storage space and harsh fluorescent lighting. Soap, shampoo/bath foam, perfumed hand lotion, shower cap, and sewing kit are provided. The towels are of 100% cotton. Note that some cabins in the center of the ship on Poseidon Deck and Venus Deck are subject to throbbing diesel generator noise.

There is a 24-hour room service menu, but any in-cabin food/beverage service tends to be very basic, without the finesse found aboard more expensive vessels.

The largest accommodation is in the four suites; each has a separate lounge and sleeping area (with double bed), plenty of closet, drawer, and other storage space, and a reasonably large bathroom.

Dining: The dining room is quite basic in furnishings and setting, and because it is small, it does tend to be extremely noisy, due to the low ceiling height and the location of waiter stations. Because it is small, there are two seatings (both of which are nonsmoking). The chairs do not have armrests and are quite small and low. The food is typically continental and includes many well-known Greek dishes. Reasonably warm attentive service is provided in typical Greek fashion, but the menu choice is rather limited and presentation is inconsistent. The quality and selection of breads, cheeses, and fruits could be better. You should note that dining room seating and table assignments are typically provided by the maître d' upon embarkation, although this may or may not be so when the ship is under charter and an open seating is operated.

An informal eatery is available poolside for casual buffet-style breakfasts and lunches, although the selection is quite limited. Seating is at plastic deck chairs, which, without cushions, are uncomfortable. A very basic beverage station is provided, with plastic cups.

Other Comments: This moderately attractive traditional vessel has a balanced, somewhat low profile, with a royal blue, riveted hull and white superstructure. She was acquired and completely reconstructed by Epirotiki Cruise Line (now part of Royal Olympic Cruises) in 1987. There is ample open deck and sun-bathing space. There are twin teak-decked sheltered promenade walking areas.

There is a reasonable range of public rooms for the size of the vessel. Almost all of them feature dated Mediterranean decor, very plain colors, and very little artwork. Almost all of the public rooms are located on one principal deck, so finding them is easy. The show lounge, located forward, is quite poor, as four large pillars obstruct sight lines from many seats. A small nightclub/disco is popular with the late night set.

This ship is really best suited to those who want to cruise at a modest cost, in adequate though dated surroundings, aboard a comfortable smaller vessel. She features interesting and popular destination-intensive itineraries principally in the Aegean and Mediterranean areas.

The ship is often placed under charter to various tour operators, and packages are sold by a number of cruise-tour companies in various countries. This means that passengers are likely to consist of a wide mix of nationalities, and daily programs and announcements, therefore, could well be in several languages.

Under Greek Seaman's Union rules, all gratuities (suggested at $9 per person/per day) are pooled among the crew (you give them to the chief steward). The exception to this is when the ship is operating under charter and the charterer/operator includes gratuities in the fare.

Weak Points: The dining room is small and extremely noisy. There is no wraparound outdoor promenade deck. Some of the interior stairways are very steep and have very short steps. There are only two bars. The company provides little port information for passengers wishing to go ashore individually but heavily sells its own shore excursion programs. The staff hospitality factor is adequate, but more training is needed. In fact, there is little consistency across the company's range of ships with regard to standards of food, service, and hospitality.

Olvia
★★

Small Ship:	15,791 tons	Cabins (with private balcony):	0
Lifestyle:	Standard	Cabins (wheelchair accessible):	0
Cruise Line:	K&O Cruises	Cabin Current:	220 volts
Former Names:	*Kareliya, Leonid Brezhnev*	Refrigerator:	Boat Deck cabins only
Builder:	Wartsila (Finland)	Full-Service Dining Rooms:	2
Original Cost:	$25 million	Elevators:	2
Entered Service:	December 1976/October 1998	Casino (gaming tables):	Yes
Registry:	Liberia	Slot Machines:	Yes
Length (ft/m):	512.6/156.27	Swimming Pools (outdoors):	1 (+ child pool)
Beam (ft/m):	71.8/21.90	Swimming Pools (indoors):	0
Draft (ft/m):	19.4/5.92	Whirlpools:	0
Propulsion/Propellers:	Diesel (13,430kW)/2	Fitness Center:	Yes
Passenger Decks:	8	Sauna/Steam Room:	Yes/No
Total Crew:	250	Massage:	Yes
Passengers (lower beds/all berths):	468/660	Self-Service Laundry:	No
Pass. Space Ratio (lower beds/all berths):	33.7/23.9	Dedicated Cinema/Seats:	Yes/140
Crew/Pass. Ratio (lower beds/all berths):	1.8/2.6	Library:	Yes
Navigation Officers:	Ukrainian	Classification Society: Ukraine Register of Shipping	
Cabins (total):	234		
Size Range (sq ft/m):	90.4–409.0/8.4–38.0		
Cabins (outside view):	110	**OVERALL SCORE:**	**842**
Cabins (interior/no view):	124	**(OUT OF A POSSIBLE 2,000 POINTS)**	
Cabins (for one person):	0		

Accommodation: Two forward Boat Deck suites are large and well appointed. They have large beds with good under-bed storage drawers, plenty of closet and drawer space, sofa, chairs, and glass-topped coffee table, as well as a large bathroom with full-size bathtub and bidet. Another ten Boat Deck suites also have plenty of space and a bathroom that includes a full-size bathtub and bidet. All Boat Deck suites and cabins have windows that actually open—a nice change from the forced air-conditioning system. Bathrobes should be, but are not, provided for the suite occupants (neither are personal toiletries such as shampoo or body lotion).

All of the other cabins are on the small side, but adequate for short cruises, though very cramped for any form of long voyage. All have a telephone and three-channel radio, although there really is very little closet and drawer space (definitely not enough for cruises longer than seven days). The cabin bathrooms are small and utilitarian, with little space for toiletries. Note that there is no cabin service menu. Towels, however, are changed twice daily and bed linen twice weekly.

Dining: There are two dining rooms (in general, both are nonsmoking, although this really depends on the charterer and cruise itinerary of the vessel) and two seatings. They are basic rooms, not very attractive, although they are noisy. Ukrainian waitresses who try hard, although there is no finesse whatsoever, provide service, and much more training is needed. The menus are very limited, and presentation, garnishes, food quality, and presentation all could be improved greatly. There is a very limited selection of breads, fruits, cheeses, and salad dressings. Forget the wine list.

Other Comments: This small (by today's standards) but reasonably smart-looking vessel sports a large, square funnel. She is one of a series of five ships of the same size and class originally built to carry both vehicles and passengers, but later converted for cruise-ship use several years ago. Her original car decks were converted into useful public rooms long ago and additional cabins and the former car-loading ramps on the stern have been fully sealed. Perhaps more noticeable than anything else are the completely outdated old style of operations.

Has a moderately comfortable interior, although the decor is rather plain, uncoordinated, and decidedly dated. Her newer facilities (added during various refits) provide more public rooms and choices for passengers. The library is small and the choice of books is poor.

There are several small public rooms, most of which are cozy bars. The Music Salon is the equivalent of a show lounge and has raised seating along the port and starboard sides; however, ten slim pillars obstruct views to the stage area. The Dneipr Bar and Sadko Lounge are the two main bars, while the Kiji Bar also acts as the ship's discotheque. Direct-dial satellite credit-card telephones are positioned in several of the foyer areas, although there is no privacy.

There is a separate cinema, located low down in the ship (it occupies space on what was a former car deck), and, although it is tiered, the seating is not staggered, so the sight lines are not as good as they could be. A good-size basketball court is positioned between mast and funnel – essential for the Ukrainian staff but seldom used by passengers. There is a large sauna and relaxation facility.

This ship has fairly comfortable, reasonably cosy surroundings (for a vessel of this vintage), although you should not expect any degree of finesse in service levels. The training of the Ukrainian service staff needs much attention, particularly in the dining rooms, where Western standards simply have not been reached. Even though some of the staff seems to be willing, the management and supervision really is by outdated methods and needs to be brought more up-to-date.

Much of this ship's cruising life is spent under charter to various operators or organizations, which really means that the standard of product delivery can and does vary according to the type of cruises featured by the charterer (and thus the price paid by passengers).

Weak Points: The condition and cleanliness of exterior open decks, stairways, and railings are poor and need attention. There are too many crew announcements, all of which are put through into the cabins at all hours. There are more interior than outside-view cabins. There is a long, steep gangway in many ports. Noticeably lacking in the ship's interiors are fresh flowers.

Olympia Countess
★★★

Mid-Size Ship:	17,593 tons	Cabins (for one person):	0
Lifestyle:	Standard	Cabins (with private balcony):	0
Cruise Line:	Royal Olympic Cruises	Cabins (wheelchair accessible):	0
Former Names:	*Awani Dream I, Cunard Countess*	Cabin Current:	110/220-volt
Builder:	Burmeister & Wein (Denmark)	Full-Service Dining Rooms:	1
Original Cost:	£12 million	Elevators:	2
Entered Service:	August 1976/1998	Casino (gaming tables):	Yes
Registry:	Panama	Slot Machines:	Yes
Length (ft/m):	536.6/163.56	Swimming Pools (outdoors):	1
Beam (ft/m):	74.9/22.84	Swimming Pools (indoors):	0
Draft (ft/m):	19.0/5.82	Whirlpools:	2
Size Range (sq ft/m):	87.1–264.8/8.1–24.6	Fitness Center:	Yes
Propulsion/Propellers:	Diesel (15,670kW)/2	Sauna/Steam Room:	Yes/No
Passenger Decks:	8	Massage:	No
Total Crew:	350	Self-Service Launderette:	No
Passengers (lower beds/all berths):	846/959	Dedicated Cinema/Seats:	Yes/126
Pass. Space Ratio (lower beds/all berths):	20.7/18.3	Library:	Yes
Crew/Pass. Ratio (lower beds/all berths):	2.4/2.7	Classification Society:	Lloyd's Register
Navigation Officers:	Greek		
Cabins (total):	423		
Size Range (sq ft/sq m):	87–265/8–25	**OVERALL SCORE:**	**1,240**
Cabins (outside view):	281	**(OUT OF A POSSIBLE 2,000 POINTS)**	
Cabins (interior/no view):	142		

Accommodation: The cabins are mostly of a standard (very compact) size, and come in light colors and plain but pleasant decor. They are best described as space-efficient units with metal fixtures and poor insulation — you can talk to your neighbors without having to use the telephone! Cabins on the lowest deck (Poseidon Deck) suffer from vibration and the odor of diesel fuel. The cabin bathrooms are small modular units, good for one, but just about impossible for two.

Dining: The single dining room has large ocean-view picture windows on two sides, and seating is mostly at tables for four, six, or eight. There are two seatings. Reasonable banquet food is standard, tailored for American and European passengers. Out-of-the-ordinary requests are difficult. Limited fresh fruit and cheese selection. Good, cheerful service from an attentive Greek staff.

Additionally, a casual self-serve, open-air area is available at the stern of the ship for breakfast, lunches, and occasional buffet dinners.

Other Comments: Originally built for Cunard Line as an informal Caribbean cruise vessel, she was purchased by the now defunct Awani Dream Cruises, of Indonesia, and then by Royal Olympic Cruises in 1997. *Olympia Countess* still displays a contemporary profile, with crisp, clean lines and a distinctive swept-back funnel (her almost identical sister presently operates as *Rhapsody* for Mediterranean Shipping Cruises).

Inside, there is a good selection of public rooms to choose from, most with attractive, light colors and cheerful decor. Aft of the show lounge, which is a single-level room with raised seating on its port and starboard sides (eight pillars obstruct the sight lines, however, and the ceiling is low), is a good indoor-outdoor entertainment lounge/nightclub that incorporates a large aft open deck area.

Passengers seeking a casual, destination-intensive cruise will probably like this comfortable vessel, which is a change from the newer, larger ships of today and is well suited to cruising in the Aegean/Mediterranean region. Gratuities (suggested at $9 per person per day) are pooled among the crew.

Weak Points: This is a very high-density ship. The outside decks need attention. Too many loud and unnecessary announcements do not allow for a relaxing cruise.

Olympia Explorer
★★★★

Mid-Size Ship:	24,500 tons	Cabins (for one person):	0
Lifestyle:	Standard	Cabins (with private balcony):	24
Cruise Line:	Royal Olympic Cruises	Cabins (wheelchair accessible):	4
Former Names:	-	Cabin Current:	110/230-volt
Builder:	Blohm & Voss (Germany)	Full-Service Dining Rooms:	1
Original Cost:	$175 million	Elevators:	4
Entered Service:	May 2001	Casino (gaming tables):	Yes
Registry:	Gibraltar	Slot Machines:	Yes
Length (ft/m):	590.5/180.0	Swimming Pools (outdoors):	1
Beam (ft/m):	83.6/25.5	Swimming Pools (indoors):	0
Draft (ft/m):	23.2/7.1	Whirlpools:	0
Propulsion/Propellers:	Diesel (37,800kW)/2	Fitness Center:	Yes
Passenger Decks:	8	Sauna/Steam Room:	Yes/No
Total Crew:	360	Massage:	Yes
Passengers (lower beds/all berths):	840/920	Self-Service Launderette:	No
Pass. Space Ratio (lower beds/all berths):	29.1/26.6	Dedicated Cinema:	No
Crew/Pass. Ratio (lower beds/all berths):	2.3/2.5	Library:	Yes
Navigation Officers:	Greek	Classification Society:	Germanischer Lloyd
Cabins (total):	420		
Size Range (sq ft/sq m):	140.0–258.0/13.0–23.9	**OVERALL SCORE:**	**1,434**
Cabins (outside view):	296	(OUT OF A POSSIBLE 2,000 POINTS)	
Cabins (interior/no view):	124		

Accommodation: The accommodation, in 11 price grades, consists of 12 Sky Suites (with balcony), 12 Balcony Cabins (with a covered ceiling and full partitions — so you can't hear your neighbor or smell their smoke), 20 Junior Suites, 292 cabins (double occupancy), 72 cabins with two lower beds and a third, upper berth, four cabins with two lower beds and two upper berths, and four wheelchair-accessible cabins with spacious bathrooms and roll-in showers.

Standard Cabins

The standard interior (no view) and outside-view cabins are quite compact (some interior cabins are larger than others) but practically laid-out, and the decor includes warm blond wood cabinetry, accents, and facings, and pleasing soft furnishings. The bathrooms are small but have a decent-size shower enclosure, and storage facilities for personal toiletry items. All cabins include TV (with pay-per-view movies), hair dryer, minibar/refrigerator, and personal safe. The Junior Suites have a little more room than the standard cabins.

Sky Suites

The largest accommodation can be found in the Sky Suites located high atop the ship and in the forward-most section. They have large private balconies, floor-to-ceiling windows, limited butler service, and 24-hour dining service (although the glass-topped table is far too low for use as a dining table for anything other than snacks). Some suites have walk-in closets, while others have closets facing the entranceway; all, however, feature an abundance of drawer and hanging space, and chrome pullout shoe rack and tie rack. The bathroom features a combination bathtub/shower (although the bathtub is extremely small and is really only for sitting in) and a retractable clothesline. A thick 100% cotton bathrobe is provided. All suites feature wood-paneled walls with vanity desk, stocked minibar/refrigerator, sofa, coffee table, and sleeping area that is partly separated from the lounge area by a wood-and-glass divider. Four of the suites have huge structures above their balconies that constitute port side and starboard side gangway lowering mechanisms; they are noisy in ports of call and anchor ports, and thus the balconies cannot be considered very private. Also, you should note that when the ship is traveling at speed, wind sweeps across the balcony — rendering it all but useless.

Deluxe (Balcony) Suites

The 12 cabins with private balconies have superb electric sliding doors to the balconies that operate by compressed air filling a "skirt" around the door frame to keep them absolutely airtight and soundproof. Facilities include wood-paneled walls with vanity desk, stocked minibar/refrigerator, sofa, a drinks table (this is fixed and cannot be raised for dining). There is a separate sleeping area (with twin or queen-size bed), and a vanity/make-up desk with a good amount of drawer space. There is a decent amount of closet space and an abundance of drawer and hanging space, chrome pullout shoe-rack baskets, and tie rack. The bathroom features a combination bathtub/shower (although the bathtub is extremely small and is really only for sitting) and a retractable clothesline. A thick 100% cotton bathrobe is provided.

Dining: The 470-seat Dining Room is located aft and has picture windows on three sides. There are two seatings, and there are tables for two, four, six, or eight. It has a semicircular walkway, with minimalist decor, at its entrance. The decor in the dining room itself is warm and welcoming, and quite tasteful, characterized by what is best described as a "Greek Moderne" style.

For casual breakfast and lunch self-service buffets, the Garden Restaurant is a pleasant but very basic room, with large picture windows and an open feel. There is seating for 210 indoors and 199 outdoors, where there is also a bar with a sailcloth cover. The layout of the buffet line is atrocious; it is too small and causes congestion — a testament to poor, inflexible shipbuilding in the 21st century.

Additional munching outlets include a pizzeria/salad bar and an ice cream bar.

Other Comments: This is the second new ship (sister ship *Olympia Voyager* was the first) ordered by Royal Olympic Cruises. It takes the company into the contemporary cruise market. The ship features a compact outer design, complete with a royal-blue hull and streamlined funnel. She is a medium-size but high-density ship.

The exterior hull design is similar to that found in naval frigates, with a slender fore-body and two engine rooms (forward and amidships) capable of providing a 27-knot speed (and even some additional power in reserve). The ship is thus designed for destination-intensive (port-hopping) itineraries that can be covered in a shorter time, which allows passengers more time in each port.

There is a reasonable amount of open deck space, provided the ship isn't full, although there are not many deck lounge chairs. All exterior railings are made of stainless steel. The seawater swimming pool is located aft and is quite small; adjacent are two shower enclosures.

The interior design combines contemporary conveniences with quiet, restrained decor intended to remind one of the Mediterranean region the ship is specifically designed for, with warm colors and an abundance of blond woods and opaque glass paneling.

Perhaps the most striking features in terms of design and decoration can be found in the artwork. Of particular note are the two flowing poems that are etched in illuminated opaque glass panels that are backlit on the stairways.

Most of the public rooms are located on one principal deck in a horizontal-flow layout that makes it easy to find your way around quickly, with a slightly winding open passageway that links several leisure lounges in one neat "street scene" (the artwork consists of valuable rocks and gems from Greece and the islands). A cigar smoking room for cigar and cognac devotees is located just aft of the main show lounge, complete with fireplace. There's also a library, a separate card room, and a piano lounge with bar.

A casino (with its own bar) features blackjack, roulette, and aces poker tables, while another section houses 44 slot machines (tokens only). Note that any winnings can only be paid out in Greek drachmae under Greek law (when the ship operates its Mediterranean itineraries, based on Piraeus).

One of the nicest and most useful facilities aboard this ship can be found in the spa. This is well run by a Greek concession and provides Ayurvedic massage as well as Swedish remedial/aromatherapy massage, a hydrotherapy bath, mosaic tiled steam room and sauna (both are co-ed, so you will need to wear a bathing suit), and several treatment rooms, all in an area that is secluded from the main passenger flow.

The program of special interest guest lecturers that accompanies each cruise is very good; these may be destination, cultural, lifestyle, or former-government lecturers.

The crew typically consists of a Greek and international mix, with Greek officers. There is a good degree of warmth and friendliness throughout the ship — a factor that so many cruise lines seem to have dismissed. While service is not perfect, it comes with a smile. Gratuities are given directly to dining room stewards and cabin stewardesses and are not pooled as they are aboard most Greek-flag ships.

Weak Points: There is no full wraparound promenade deck outdoors, although you can walk around parts of the vessel outdoors. There are no dedicated facilities or rooms for the large numbers of children and teens that are typically carried during the July–August summer holidays. There is no public toilet that is accessible by wheelchair. There are not enough deck lounge chairs for the number of passengers carried, and not enough open deck space. Overall, the cabins are very small for anything longer than seven-day cruises. The sight lines in the show lounge are appalling — from about 40% of the seats.

Olympia Voyager
★★★★

Mid-Size Ship:	24,391 tons	Cabins (for one person):	0
Lifestyle:	Standard	Cabins (with private balcony):	12
Cruise Line:	Royal Olympic Cruises	Cabins (wheelchair accessible):	4
Former Names:	-	Cabin Current:	110/230 volts
Builder:	Blohm & Voss (Germany)	Full-Service Dining Rooms:	1
Original Cost:	$150.8 million	Elevators:	4
Entered Service:	July 2000	Casino (gaming tables):	Yes
Registry:	Greece	Slot Machines:	Yes
Length (ft/m):	590.5/180.0	Swimming Pools (outdoors):	1
Beam (ft/m):	83.6/25.5	Swimming Pools (indoors):	0
Draft (ft/m):	23.2/7.1	Whirlpools:	0
Propulsion/Propellers:	Diesel (37,800kW)/2	Fitness Center:	Yes
Passenger Decks:	8	Sauna/Steam Room:	Yes/No
Total Crew:	360	Massage:	Yes
Passengers (lower beds/all berths):	840/920	Self-Service Launderette:	No
Pass. Space Ratio (lower beds/all berths):	29.0/26.5	Dedicated Cinema:	No
Crew/Pass. Ratio (lower beds/all berths):	2.3/2.5	Library:	Yes
Navigation Officers:	Greek	Classification Society:	Germanischer Lloyd
Cabins (total):	420		
Size Range (sq ft/m):	140.0–258.0/13.0–23.9		
Cabins (outside view):	294		
Cabins (interior/no view):	126		

OVERALL SCORE: **1409**

(OUT OF A POSSIBLE 2,000 POINTS)

Accommodation: The accommodation, in 11 price grades, consists of 12 Sky Suites, 16 Bay Window Suites, 20 Junior Suites, 292 cabins (double occupancy), 72 cabins (two lower beds, one upper berth), 4 four-person cabins (two lower beds, two upper berths) and 4 wheelchair-accessible cabins (with spacious bathrooms and roll-in showers).

Standard Cabins

The standard interior (no view) and outside-view cabins are quite compact, but practically laid-out, and the decor includes warm blond wood cabinetry, accents, and facings, and pleasing soft furnishings. The bathrooms are small but have a decent-size shower enclosure and good storage facilities for personal toiletry items. All cabins include television (with pay-per-view movies), hair dryer, minibar/refrigerator and a personal safe. You should note that only one personal safe is provided in each cabin, although there could be as many as four persons sharing the same cabin.

Junior Suites

The accommodation designated as Junior Suites simply have a little more room than the standard interior (no view) and outside-view cabins. The bathrooms are small but have a decent-size shower enclosure and good storage facilities for personal toiletry items.

Bay Window Suites

There are 16 bay window cabins (Corinthos, Delphi, Dodoni, Knossos, Lindos, Marathon, Mycenae, Nemea, Olympia, Parthenon, Phaistos, Sounion, Sparti, Thivae, Tylissos, Vergina) in the forward section of the ship; each features a large window that extends over the side of the ship, and a lounge area and sleeping area.

Sky Suites

The largest accommodation can be found in 12 Sky Suites (Andromeda, Arcas, Ariadne, Bolina, Cadmos, Cassiope, Harmonia, Hersilia, Myrtilos, Parthenos, Perseas, Theseas) located high atop the ship and in the forwardmost section. They have large private balconies (some are more like large terraces), floor-to-ceiling windows, limited butler service, and 24-hour dining service (although the glass-topped table is far too low for use as a dining table for anything other than snacks). Some of the suites have walk-in closets, while others have closets facing the entranceway; all, however, feature an abundance of drawer and hanging space, and chrome pullout shoe rack and tie rack. The bathroom features a combination bathtub/shower (although the bathtub is extremely small and is really only for sitting in) and a retractable clothesline; a thick 100% cotton bathrobe is also provided. All suites feature wood-paneled walls with vanity desk, stocked minibar/refrigerator, sofa, coffee table (this is fixed and cannot be raised for dining), and sleeping area that is partly separated from the lounge area by a wood/glass divider. Note that Arcas, Ariadne, Myrtilos, and Parthenos have huge structures above their balconies that constitute port side and starboard side gangway lowering mechanisms; they are noisy in ports of call and anchor ports, and thus the balconies cannot be considered very private. Also, you should note that when the ship is traveling at speed, considerable wind sweeps, across the balcony rendering it all but useless.

Note: Outside-view and interior (no view) cabins located aft on Deck 3 (Neptune Deck: Numbers 3120–3138/3121–3151) are subject to a substantial amount of throbbing noise from the diesel engines and should be avoided if at all possible (unless you like throbbing engine noise, that is).

Dining: The 470-seat Selenes Dining Room is located aft and has picture windows on three sides. There are two seatings, and there are tables for two, four, six or eight. It has a semicircular walkway, with minimalist decor, as its entrance. The decor in the dining room itself is warm and welcoming, and quite tasteful, carried out as it is in what is best described as a "Greek Moderne" style.

For casual breakfast and lunch self-service buffets, the Horizon Garden Restaurant is a pleasant but very basic room, with large picture windows and an open feel to the room. There is seating for 210 indoors and 199 outdoors, where there is also a bar. The layout of the buffet line is atrocious; it is too small and causes congestion—a testament to poor, inflexible shipbuilding in the 21st century.

Additional munching outlets include a pizza serving area/salad bar and an ice cream bar.

Other Comments: This is the first new ship ever ordered by this company (which is a combination of two former cruise companies: Epirotiki Lines and Sun Line Cruises) and is intended to take the company into the contemporary cruise market with new ships, like many other companies today. The ship features a compact outer design, complete with a royal-blue hull, for this medium-size but high-density ship. There is a streamlined funnel, and her fast speed (up to 27 knots) enables her to operate busy (destination-intensive) itineraries.

The exterior hull design (called a Fast Monohull) is very close to that found in naval frigates, with a slender fore-body, and two engine rooms (forward and midships) capable of providing a 27-knot speed (and even some additional power in reserve). The ship is thus designed for destination-intensive (port-hopping) itineraries that can be covered in a shorter time, which allow passengers more time in each port.

There is a reasonable amount of open deck space (provided the ship isn't full), although there are not many deck lounge chairs; all exterior railings are made—unusually so—of stainless steel. The seawater swimming pool is located aft and is quite small (most passengers will be enjoying the destinations featured by this cruise line); adjacent are two shower enclosures.

The interior design combines contemporary conveniences with quiet, restrained decor intended to remind one of the Mediterranean region the ship is specifically designed for, with warm colors and an abundance of wood and opaque glass paneling.

Perhaps the most striking, yet subtle, features in terms of design and decoration can be found in the artwork. Of particular note are the two flowing poems that are etched in illuminated opaque glass panels on the stairways (these are, ironically, by poets from Greece and Cyprus—the two countries where the owning companies of Royal Olympic Cruises are located). One of the poems, from 1911 (called "Ithaca") by the Alexander the Greek poet Constantinos Petrou Kavafis, complements the poem, "Let's Say," by the Cypriot poet Yannis Papadopoulos. Also, two large canvasses (which, in turn, are composed of four smaller ones) that cleverly separate the dining room are quite entertaining.

Most of the public rooms are located on one principal deck in a horizontal-flow layout that makes it easy to find your way around quickly, with a slightly winding open passageway that links several leisure lounges in one neat "street scene." A smoking room is also featured, adjacent to the main show lounge, for cigar and cognac devotees (with a black fireplace that is from the 1890s). There's also a library and a separate card room. In the popular Silenes Piano Bar, three ship models are cleverly displayed behind large glass wall panels; their names are *Ella Woermann*, *Washington*, and *Oceanic*.

A casino (with its own bar) features blackjack, roulette, and aces poker tables, while another section houses 44 slot machines (tokens only). Note that any winnings can only be paid out in Greek drachmae under Greek law (when the ship operates its Mediterranean itineraries, based on Piraeus).

Other facilities include a show lounge (with 420 seats and too many pillars to obstruct the sight lines from many seats), a nightclub, piano bar, library, and card room.

One of the nicest and most useful facilities aboard this ship can be found in the Jade Spa. This is well run by a Greek concession and provides Ayervedic massage as well as Swedish

Remedial/Aromatherapy massage, a hydrotherapy bath, mosaic-tiled steam room and sauna (both are co-ed—so you will need to wear a bathing suit), and several treatment rooms, all in an area that is secluded from the main passenger flow.

The program of special interest guest lecturers that accompanies each cruise is very good; these may be destination, cultural, lifestyle, or ex-government lecturers.

The crew typically consists of a Greek and international mix, with Greek officers. There is a good degree of warmth and friendliness throughout the ship—a factor that so many cruise lines seem to have dismissed. While service is not perfect, it comes with a smile. Gratuities are given directly to dining room stewards and cabin stewardesses, and are not pooled as they are aboard most ships belonging to Greek companies.

Weak Points: There is no full wraparound promenade deck outdoors, although you can walk around parts of the vessel outdoors. There is considerable vibration when the ship is under way at high speed and during maneuvering at slow speeds. There are no dedicated facilities or rooms for the large numbers of children or teens that are typically carried during the July–August summer holidays. There is no public toilet that is accessible by wheelchair. The self-service buffet line is awful. There simply are not enough deck lounge chairs considering the number of passengers carried, and not enough open deck space. Overall, the cabins are very small for anything longer than seven-day cruises. The sight lines in the show lounge are appalling—from about 40%of the seats.

Oriana
★★★★

Large Ship:	69,153 tons	Cabins (for one person):	112
Lifestyle:	Premium	Cabins (with private balcony):	118
Cruise Line:	P&O Cruises	Cabins (wheelchair accessible):	8
Former Names:	-	Cabin Current:	110/220-volt
Builder:	Meyer Werft (Germany)	Full-Service Dining Rooms:	2
Original Cost:	£200 million	Elevators:	10
Entered Service:	April 1995	Casino (gaming tables):	Yes
Registry:	Great Britain	Slot Machines:	Yes
Length (ft/m):	853.0/260.0	Swimming Pools (outdoors):	3
Beam (ft/m):	105.6/32.2	Swimming Pools (indoors):	0
Draft (ft/m):	25.9/7.9	Whirlpools:	5
Propulsion/Propellers:	Diesel (47,750kW)/2	Fitness Center:	Yes
Passenger Decks:	10	Sauna/Steam Room:	Yes/Yes
Total Crew:	760	Massage:	Yes
Passengers (lower beds/all berths):	1,828/1,975	Self-Service Launderette:	Yes
Pass. Space Ratio (lower beds/all berths):	37.8/35.0	Dedicated Cinema/Seats:	Yes/189
Crew/Pass. Ratio (lower beds/all berths):	2.4/2.5	Library:	Yes
Navigation Officers:	British	Classification Society:	Lloyd's Register
Cabins (total):	914		
Size Range (sq ft/sq m):	150.6–500.5/14.0–46.5		
Cabins (outside view):	594		
Cabins (interior/no view):	320		

OVERALL SCORE: **1,530**

(OUT OF A POSSIBLE 2,000 POINTS)

Accommodation: There is a wide range of cabin configurations and categories (in 18 grades), including family cabins with extra beds. More than 100 cabins can accommodate up to four persons. The standard interior (no view) cabins and outside-view cabins are well equipped, although they are disappointingly small. There is much use of rich, warm oak or cherry wood in all cabins, which makes even the least expensive four-berth cabin seem inviting. All cabins feature a decent amount of closet and drawer space, small refrigerator, TV, full-length mirror, and blackout curtains (essential for North Cape cruises). Satellite television provided typically would include BBC World, although reception may not be good in all areas.

A good number of cabins have been provided for passengers traveling singly. Any single traveler who is sharing a cabin should note that only one personal safe is provided in most twin-bed cabins. Although the cabins for four persons (family cabins) do have four small personal safes, there are no privacy curtains.

The standard cabin bathrooms are very compact units and have mirror-fronted cabinets, although the lighting is quite soft (not strong enough for the application of make-up). All bathrooms feature a wall-mounted hair dryer (it would be better placed at the vanity desk in the living area). A shampoo and body sport wash dispenser is mounted in all bathrooms. Note that it is difficult to use the dispenser while in the bathtub (in those cabins that have bathtubs), and neither shampoo nor conditioner is provided.

There are eight suites, each measuring 501 sq ft (47 sq m). All feature butler service (there are two butlers). Features include a separate bedroom with two lower beds convertible to a queen-size bed, walk-in dressing area, two double closets, and plenty of drawer space. The lounge area features a sofa, armchairs and table, writing desk, binoculars, umbrella, trouser press, iron and ironing board, two TVs, VCR, personal safe, hair dryer, and refrigerator. The bathroom features a whirlpool bath, shower, and toilet, and there is also a guest bathroom. The whirlpool bathtubs are reasonable, although they have high sides to step over, and most are of the dimensionally challenged type where you sit in them rather than lie in them. All in all, the suites are very disappointing when compared with similar-size suites in other ships. The private balcony is suitably large enough and has two deck lounge chairs, tables, and chairs.

Other balcony cabins (called Outside Deluxe) measure 210 sq ft (19.5 sq m), and although the balconies are small, they do have good partitions, rubber matting on the deck, and a thick wooden railing. Inside, there is a curtain to separate the sleeping and living areas. There is plenty of closet and drawer space. The bathrooms are somewhat disappointing, however, and have a very small, plain sink (one would expect marble or granite units in these grades).

Some suites and cabins with balconies have an interconnecting door and include a trouser press, ironing board and iron (neatly tucked into a cupboard), binoculars, umbrella, a large atlas, and a second TV, as well as a sliding glazed panel between bedroom and sitting room.

Dining: There are two restaurants, allocated according to the cabin grade and location you choose. The Peninsular Restaurant is located amidships, while the Oriental Restaurant is located aft. Both are moderately handsome (each has tables for two, four, six, or eight). Both have interesting ceilings, chandeliers, and decor. The Oriental Restaurant has windows on three sides, including those overlooking the wash at the stern. Two seatings are featured in each restaurant, both of which are nonsmoking. For those who are interested, a statement in the cruise folder in your cabin states that P&O Cruises does not knowingly purchase genetically modified foods.

The meals are mostly of the unmemorable, unpretentious variety, and the presentation lacks creativity. The cuisine does improve on the around-the-world cruise, however. Curries are heavily featured, particularly on the luncheon menus. Afternoon tea is disappointing, with a poor selection of teas and sandwiches.

The Conservatory offers self-serve breakfast and luncheon buffets, and 24-hour self-serve beverage stands (although the selection of teas is poor and it's often hard to find teaspoons — only plastic stirrers are provided). On selected evenings, it becomes a reservation-only alternative restaurant — Le Bistro — with sit-down service. It typically features French Bistro, Indian, or Southeast Asian cuisine — popular with the ship's mainly British clientele.

A former aerobics room (which was not used very much) has been turned into the popular Al Fresco Pizzeria. Unfortunately, the pizza slices are bread-based, not made from real pizza dough).

Other Comments: The ship is quite conventional: evolutionary rather than revolutionary, but the first new ship for P&O Cruises for over 25 years. She is a ship that takes *Canberra*'s traditional appointments and public rooms and adds more up-to-date touches, together with better facilities and passenger flow, and a feeling of timeless elegance.

For a little diversion, early references to the name *Oriana* are contained in 16th-century English romances. Various musical anthologies were composed to celebrate Elizabeth I as *Oriana*, culminating in a collection of 26 madrigals published by Thomas Morley in 1601 under the title "The Triumphs of Oriana." Although attributed to 23 different composers, each madrigal ends with the words "Long Live Fair Oriana."

Back to the ship: The interiors are gentle, welcoming, and restrained. A splendid amount of open deck and sunbathing space is an important plus for her outdoors-loving British passengers. She has an extra-wide wraparound promenade deck outdoors. The stern superstructure is nicely rounded and has several tiers that overlook the aft decks, pool, and children's outdoor facilities.

Inside, the well laid-out design provides good horizontal passenger flow and wide passageways. Very noticeable are the fine, detailed ceiling treatments. To please all types of people, specific areas have been designed to attract different age groups and lifestyles.

There is a four-decks-high atrium with a soft waterfall. It is elegant but not glitzy, and is topped by a dome of Tiffany glass. The large number of public entertainment rooms provides plenty of choice, with lots of nooks and crannies in which to sit and read.

The Theatre Royal, designed by John Wyckham, is the ship's main show lounge. Decorated in rich reds, it was created specifically for drama and light theatrical presentations. It has individually air-conditioned seats, an orchestra pit, revolving stage, and excellent acoustics. The theater seats would provide better stage sight lines if they were staggered.

The Pacific Lounge is a nightclub that doubles as a second show lounge for cabaret acts and comedy acts, although its many pillars obstruct the stage view.

The L-shaped Anderson's Lounge (named after the founder of the Peninsular Steam Navigation Company in the 1830s) features a series of 19th-century marine paintings and is decorated in the manner of a fine British gentlemen's club. Although there is no fireplace (there is one in the equivalent room aboard *Aurora*), it is a popular lounge.

Atop the ship and forward is the Crow's Nest, a U-shaped room that has two small wings that can be closed off for small groups. There is a long bar, giving the barmen a great view of the bow, while passengers sitting at the bar have a view of a ship model (a former P&O ship, *Ranpura*) in a glass case. Two small stages are set into the forward port and starboard sections, and there is also a wooden dance floor. The lounge has both smoking and nonsmoking sections, although smoke lingers everywhere.

The library is a fine room and features a good range of hardback books, a librarian, beautiful inlaid wood tables, and some comfortable chairs. On the second day of almost any cruise, however, the library will have been almost stripped of books by word-hungry passengers. Adjacent is Thackeray's, the writing room (known as the sleeping room in the afternoons); it is named after William Makepeace Thackeray, a P&O passenger in 1844. Without a doubt, the most restful room is the Curzon Room, used occasionally for piano recitals.

Meanwhile, Lord's Tavern is the most sporting place to have a beverage or two, or take part in a sing-along (rather like group karaoke). It is decorated with cricket memorabilia.

The carpeting throughout the ship is of excellent quality, much of it custom designed and made of 100% wool. There are some fine pieces of sculpture that add the feeling of a floating museum, and original artworks by British artists including several tapestries and sculptures.

The Oasis Spa is located forward and almost atop the ship. It is quite large and provides all the latest alternative treatment therapies, and there is a gymnasium with the latest high-tech muscle toning equipment. The co-ed sauna is a large facility and there is a steam room.

Children and teens have "Club Oriana" programs with their own rooms ("Peter Pan" and "Decibels"), as well as their own outdoor pool. Children can be entertained until 10pm, which gives parents time to have dinner and go dancing. The cabins have a baby-listening device. A special night nursery for small children (ages 2–5) is available at no extra charge (6pm–2am).

There is a wide variety of mainly British entertainment aboard the ships of P&O Cruises. There is also a program of theme cruises (antiques, The Archers, art appreciation, classical music, comedy, cricket, gardening, jazz, motoring, popular fiction, Scottish dance, and sequence dancing are examples). Check with your travel agent to see what is available at the time you want to take your cruise.

Oriana provides a decent, standardized cruise experience for her mainly British passengers (of all dialects) who do not want to fly to join a cruise ship. However, in the quest for increased on-board revenue, even birthday cakes are an extra-cost item, as are real espressos and cappuccinos (fake ones, made from instant coffee, are available in the dining rooms). Also at extra cost are ice cream and bottled water. These can add up to a considerable amount on an around-the-world cruise.

A fine British brass band send-off accompanies all sailings. Other touches include church bells sounded throughout the ship for the interdenominational Sunday church service. For gratuities (optional), you should allow £3 per person, per day.

Weak Points: Standing in line for embarkation, disembarkation, shore tenders, and self-serve buffet meals is an inevitable aspect of cruising aboard all large ships. Smokers seem to be everywhere, as is the smell of stale smoke. Cabin soundproofing is quite poor. During school holidays, you should be aware that there will be many children aboard; this can be a cause of irritation and frustration to many older passengers.

Orient Venus
★★★ +

Small Ship:	21,884 tons	Cabins (for one person):	0
Lifestyle:	Standard	Cabins (with private balcony):	2
Cruise Line:	Venus Cruise	Cabins (wheelchair accessible):	0
Former Names:	-	Cabin Current:	110-volt
Builder:	Ishikawajima Heavy Industries (Japan)	Full-Service Dining Rooms:	2
Original Cost:	$150 million	Elevators:	3
Entered Service:	July 1990	Casino (gaming tables):	No
Registry:	Japan	Slot Machines:	No
Length (ft/m):	570.8/174.00	Swimming Pools (outdoors):	1
Beam (ft/m):	78.7/24.00	Swimming Pools (indoors):	0
Draft (ft/m):	21.3/6.52	Whirlpools:	0
Propulsion/Propellers:	Diesel (13,830kW)/2	Fitness Center:	Yes
Passenger Decks:	6	Sauna/Steam Room:	No/No
Total Crew:	120	Massage:	No
Passengers (lower beds/all berths):	390/606	Self-Service Launderette:	Yes
Pass. Space Ratio (lower beds/all berths):	56.1/36.1	Dedicated Cinema/Seats:	Yes/606
Crew/Pass. Ratio (lower beds/all berths):	3.2/5.0	Library:	Yes
Navigation Officers:	Japanese	Classification Society:	Nippon Kaiji Kyokai
Cabins (total):	195		
Size Range (sq ft/sq m):	182.9–592.0/17.0–55.0	**OVERALL SCORE:**	**1,382**
Cabins (outside view):	195	(OUT OF A POSSIBLE 2,000 POINTS)	
Cabins (interior/no view):	0		

Accommodation: There are four cabin grades (royal, deluxe, state, and standard). The all-outside standard cabins, many of which have upper berths for third and fourth passengers, have decor that is best described as plain, with a reasonable amount of closet space and little drawer space.

The largest suites (of which there are two) have an expansive lounge area with large, plush armchairs, coffee table, window-side chairs and drinks table, floor-to-ceiling windows, and a large private balcony. There is a separate sleeping room (curtained off from the living room) with twin- or queen-size bed, vanity/office desk, and large bathroom.

All grades of accommodation feature a tea drinking set (with electric hot water kettle), color TV, telephone, and stocked refrigerator.

Dining: The main dining room, which operates a single seating with assigned tables, is quite attractive, and there is plenty of space around the dining tables. In addition, an alternative Romanesque Grill is unusual, with its period Roman decor and a high, elegant ceiling. It exclusively features reasonably good, but rather commercial, Japanese washoku cuisine.

Other Comments: *Orient Venus* was the first cruise ship built for her owners, Venus Cruise, which is part of Japan Cruise Line, itself part of SHK Line Group. This is a conventional-shaped ship with a reasonably graceful profile. There is a decent amount of open deck and sunbathing space.

Inside the ship, the Night and Day Lounge looks forward over the swimming pool. Windows of the Orient is a small, attractive, peaceful forward observation lounge. The conference facilities are excellent and consist of both main and small conference rooms with 620 movable seats. There is an array of public rooms with tasteful and inviting decor. The horseshoe-shaped main lounge has very good sight lines to the platform stage.

This cruise ship, with its Western-style decor, will provide its mostly Japanese corporate passengers with extremely comfortable surroundings, and provides a superb cruise and seminar/learning environment and experience. *Orient Venus* was joined by a new, slightly larger sister ship, *Pacific Venus,* in spring 1998.

A specialist courier company provides an excellent luggage service and will collect your bags from your home before the cruise and deliver it back to your home after the cruise (this service available only in Japan).

Weak Points: The ship does not really cater to individual passengers well. The decor is rather plain in many public rooms. The crew-to-passenger ratio is quite poor, but typical of seminar-intensive ships.

Pacific Princess
★★★ +

Mid-Size Ship:	20,636 tons	Cabins (for one person):	2
Lifestyle:	Standard	Cabins (with private balcony):	0
Cruise Line:	Princess Cruises	Cabins (wheelchair accessible):	2
Former Names:	*Sea Venture*	Cabin Current:	110/220-volt
Builder:	Rheinstahl Nordseewerke (Germany)	Full-Service Dining Rooms:	1
Original Cost:	$25 million	Elevators:	4
Entered Service:	May 1971/April 1975	Casino (gaming tables):	Yes
Registry:	Great Britain	Slot Machines:	Yes
Length (ft/m):	553.6/168.74	Swimming Pools (outdoors):	2
Beam (ft/m):	80.8/24.64	Swimming Pools (indoors):	0
Draft (ft/m):	25.2/7.70	Whirlpools:	0
Propulsion/Propellers:	Diesel (13,240kW)/2	Fitness Center:	Yes
Passenger Decks:	7	Sauna/Steam Room:	Yes/No
Total Crew:	350	Massage:	Yes
Passengers (lower beds/all berths):	640/717	Self-Service Launderette:	No
Pass. Space Ratio (lower beds/all berths):	33.8/28.7	Dedicated Cinema/Seats:	Yes/250
Crew/Pass. Ratio (lower beds/all berths):	1.8/2.0	Library:	Yes
Navigation Officers:	British	Classification Society:	Lloyd's Register
Cabins (total):	320		
Size Range (sq ft/sq m):	125.9–441.3/11.7–41.0		
Cabins (outside view):	250		
Cabins (interior/no view):	70		

OVERALL SCORE: **1,370**

(OUT OF A POSSIBLE 2,000 POINTS)

Accommodation: All cabins are quite spacious and well appointed, functional and comfortable without being overdone. The decor, however, now seems a little dated and rather plain, and could do with brightening. The bathrooms are practical, and bathrobes are provided for all passengers. Note that Princess Cruises features CNN, CNBC, ESPN, and TNT on the in-cabin color TV system (when available).

Dining: The Coral Dining Room (all dining rooms aboard Princess Cruises' ships are nonsmoking) is located on a lower deck but has nice, light decor and feels comfortable and spacious. There are assigned tables and two seatings, with tables for four, six, or eight. Good service is provided, although standards have been slowly slipping for some time.

Despite the fact that the portions are generous, the food and its presentation are somewhat disappointing. The quality of fish is poor, the selection of fresh green vegetables is limited, and few garnishes are used. However, do remember that this is banquet catering, with all its attendant standardization and production cooking. Meats are of a decent quality, although often disguised by gravy-based sauces, and pasta dishes are acceptable (and voluminous) and are typically served by section headwaiters may also make "something special just for you" — in search of gratuities and good comments.

On any given seven-day cruise, a typical menu cycle will include a Sailaway Dinner, Captain's Welcome Dinner, Chef's Dinner, Italian Dinner, French Dinner, Captain's Gala Dinner, and Landfall Dinner.

Casual, self-serve, buffet-style meals (served on plastic plates) can be taken at poolside. This ship typically serves an average of over 800 pizzas every day.

Other Comments: She is a well-proportioned, handsome, medium-size ship with a relatively high superstructure and graceful lines. Princess Cruises has spent a considerable sum of money in her upkeep, and she has been quite well maintained. There is plenty of open deck space and several sunbathing areas, although there is no wraparound promenade deck outdoors. One swimming pool has a magrodome roof.

Inside, the spacious public areas have wide passageways and high ceilings. She has tasteful earth-toned decor throughout. There is a decent cinema. The production shows and general entertainment are adequate. Smartly dressed officers and crew help to add a feeling of passenger care.

This ship is definitely for the older passenger. Fairly elegant, and moderately expensive, the ship offers moderately comfortable, but dated, surroundings.

Pacific Sky
★★★ +

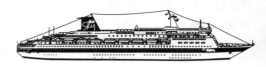

Large Ship:	46,392 tons	Cabins (for one person):	0
Lifestyle:	Standard	Cabins (with private balcony):	10
Cruise Line:	P&O Cruises (Australia)	Cabins (wheelchair accessible):	10
Former Names:	*Sky Princess*, *Fairsky*	Cabin Current:	110/220-volt
Builder:	C.N.I.M. (France)	Full-Service Dining Rooms:	2
Original Cost:	$156 million	Elevators:	6
Entered Service:	March 1984/November 2000	Casino (gaming tables):	Yes
Registry:	Great Britain	Slot Machines:	Yes
Length (ft/m):	788.6/240.39	Swimming Pools (outdoors):	3
Beam (ft/m):	91.3/27.84	Swimming Pools (indoors):	0
Draft (ft/m):	26.7/8.15	Whirlpools:	1
Propulsion/Propellers:	Steam turbine (21,700kW)/2	Fitness Center:	Yes
Passenger Decks:	11	Sauna/Steam Room:	Yes/No
Total Crew:	550	Massage:	Yes
Passengers (lower beds/all berths):	1,200/1,550	Self-Service Launderette:	Yes
Pass. Space Ratio (lower beds/all berths):	38.6/34.3	Dedicated Cinema/Seats:	Yes/283
Crew/Pass. Ratio (lower beds/all berths):	2.1/2.8	Library:	Yes
Navigation Officers:	British	Classification Society:	Lloyd's Register
Cabins (total):	600		
Size Range (sq ft/sq m):	1698.9–519.9/15.7–48.3	**OVERALL SCORE:**	**1,372**
Cabins (outside view):	385	(OUT OF A POSSIBLE 2,000 POINTS)	
Cabins (interior/no view):	215		

Accommodation: There are 19 grades of accommodation: two suite categories, eight outside-view cabin grades, and nine interior (no view) cabin grades. The cabins are, for the most part, fairly spacious, comfortable, and well appointed, with all the essentials and good-size rectangular showers. There are, however, too many interior (no view) cabins. The cabin walls and ceilings are plain and unappealing, and could do with some splashes of color to brighten them.

The largest accommodation can be found in the ten Lido Deck suites, all are named after famous places (Capri, Portofino, Estoril, Monaco, and Malaga on the port side, and Antibes, Minorca, St. Tropez, San Remo, and Amalfi on the starboard side). These are very fine living spaces and provide extra comforts such as a minibar/refrigerator, walk-in closet, a large bathroom (with bathtub and shower), and a private balcony. All have a queen-size bed, with the exception of Amalfi and Malaga, which have fixed twin beds.

There are 28 mini-suites, which each feature separate sleeping and living areas, with dressing table, sofa, coffee table and chairs, and minibar/refrigerator.

Many cabins have one or two additional upper berths, which make them extremely cramped when occupied (storage of luggage can be a problem), but they are useful for families with children. All cabins suffer from inadequate soundproofing, but all have a color TV and two lower beds. A room service menu is available 24 hours a day. Note that cabins at the aft end of Aloha Deck may be subject to noise from the adjacent Children's Playroom.

Dining: There are two dining rooms (Regency and Savoy), assigned according to the accommodation you choose. Both are nonsmoking, are brightly lit, and have decor that is pleasant. There are two seatings, and tables are for four, six, or eight (romantics should note that there are no tables for two). The food is largely standard fare and a little repetitive, and quality, flair, and presentation could be better. Friendly male Filipino waiters provide the dining room service.

For casual daytime snacking, there is the Al Fresco self-serve buffet on deck, featuring New Zealand ice cream, milkshakes, and pastries (all at extra cost).

Other casual dining alternatives include the Pizzeria, open 24 hours every day; and Harry's Café de Waves (based on the Sydney icon and famous for its world renowned "Pie and Peas") for snacks, including hot dogs. Neither the Pizzeria nor Harry's Café de Waves is included in the cruise price.

Other Comments: This well-designed vessel has a short, sharply raked bow and a large, swept-back funnel. She is the first cruise ship to have steam turbine machinery since Cunard Line's *Queen Elizabeth 2* debuted in 1969, which means that there is almost no vibration (she was originally ordered by Sitmar Cruises, which was itself acquired by Princess Cruises in 1988). Pacific Sky is a much more contemporary and spacious ship, with many more facilities than the ship she replaces — *Fair Princess*.

Inside the ship, the layout is quite comfortable and it is easy to find one's way around — good signs also help. The clean, clinical, yet oddly tasteful minimalist interior decor lacks warmth — some flowers and greenery are needed. There is a decent enough array of public rooms, including some expansive shopping space. There are nine bars and lounges to choose from, including a new Sports Bar.

Of the major public entertainment rooms, the Pacific Sky Show Lounge has decent visibility from most seats following improvements that were made by the ship's previous owners, Princess Cruises. It is only a single-level room (most new cruise ships have at least two levels for their show lounges).

The Horizon Lounge, set atop the ship, is restful at night. The casino has a split configuration. Features decent health spa/fitness facilities, although there are not enough treatment rooms.

The newly added Verandah Lounge (formerly a café) includes a dance floor and live music, while the Starlight Lounge is also for dancing and lively late-night cabaret. The ship has its own dedicated cinema (something that few new ships seem to provide), complete with balcony level.

Children have their own area aft on Aloha Deck, complete with an outdoor splash pool and a whole brightly-colored roomful of activities and fun things. Note that no children under 18 months old are accepted as passengers by P&O Holidays.

This ship provides a well-balanced, pleasing cruise experience for the mature passenger, with plenty of space and little crowding. British officers and Filipino dining staff help to create a friendly ambience aboard this ship, which commenced operations in November 2000, when she was renamed *Pacific Sky*, with her new home base in Sydney, Australia.

Weak Points: Standing in line for embarkation, disembarkation, shore tenders, and self-serve buffet meals is an inevitable aspect of cruising aboard all large ships. Unfortunately, there is no wraparound promenade deck outdoors, although there is a decent enclosed promenade deck. There are too many interior (no view) cabins.

Pacific Venus
★★★★ +

Mid-Size Ship:	26,518 tons	Cabins (for one person):	0
Lifestyle:	Standard	Cabins (with private balcony):	20
Cruise Line:	Venus Cruise	Cabins (wheelchair accessible):	1
Former Names:	-	Cabin Current:	110-volt
Builder:	Ishikawajima Heavy Industries (Japan)	Full-Service Dining Rooms:	2
Original Cost:	$114 million (Yen13 billion)	Elevators:	4
Entered Service:	April 1998	Casino (gaming tables):	Yes
Registry:	Japan	Slot Machines:	No
Length (ft/m):	601.7/183.4	Swimming Pools (outdoors):	1 (+ 1 for children)
Beam (ft/m):	82.0/25.0	Swimming Pools (indoors):	0
Draft (ft/m):	21.3/6.5	Whirlpools:	1
Propulsion/Propellers:	Diesel (13,636 kW)/2	Fitness Center:	Yes
Passenger Decks:	7	Sauna/Steam Room:	No/Yes
Total Crew:	180	Massage:	Yes
Passengers (lower beds/all berths):	532/720	Self-Service Launderette:	Yes (2)
Pass. Space Ratio (lower beds/all berths):	49.8/36.8	Dedicated Cinema/Seats:	Yes/94
Crew/Pass. Ratio (lower beds/all berths):	2.9/4.0	Library:	Yes
Navigation Officers:	Japanese	Classification Society:	Nippon Kaiji Kyokai
Cabins (total):	266		
Size Range (sq ft/sq m)	164.6–699.6/15.3–65.0	**OVERALL SCORE:**	**1,647**
Cabins (outside view):	250	**(OUT OF A POSSIBLE 2,000 POINTS)**	
Cabins (interior/no view):	16		

Accommodation: There are six different types of accommodation: royal suites, suites, deluxe cabins, state cabins (in four different price grades), and standard cabins, all located from the uppermost to lowermost decks, respectively.

The four Royal suites are decorated in two different styles — one contemporary, one in more traditional Japanese style. Each of them features a private balcony, with sliding door (teak table and two chairs), an expansive lounge area with large sofa and plush armchairs, coffee table, window-side chairs and drinks table, floor-to-ceiling windows, and a VCR. There is a separate bedroom, with twin- or queen-size bed, vanity/writing desk, large walk-in closet with personal safe, and a large bathroom with a tiny Jacuzzi bathtub. The bathroom has ocean-view windows, separate shower, and his/hers sinks.

Sixteen suites also feature a private balcony (with teak table and two chairs), a good-size living area with vanity/writing desk, dining table, chair and curved sofa, separate sleeping area, and bathroom with deep bathtub that is slightly larger than those in the Royal suites and a single large sink. There is ample lighted closet and drawer space (two locking drawers instead of a personal safe) and a VCR.

The 20 Deluxe cabins have large picture windows fronted by a large, curtained arch, sleeping area with twin (or queen-size) beds, plus a daytime sofa that converts into a third bed.

The 210 state cabins (172 of which have upper berths for third passengers) have decor that is best described as basic, with a reasonable closet but little drawer space.

The 16 standard cabins are really plain but accommodate three persons, although drawer and storage space is tight.

All cabin grades feature: a tea drinking set (with electric hot water kettle), color television, telephone, and stocked minibar/refrigerator (all items are included in the cruise price). Bathrooms feature a hair dryer and an extensive array of high quality personal toiletry items (particularly in the suites, which include after-shave, hair tonic, body lotion, shampoo, rinse, razor, toothbrush, toothpaste, sewing kit, shower cap, hairbrush, clothes brush, and shoe horn). All room service menu items are available at extra charge. All passengers receive a yukata (Japanese-style light cotton robe); in addition, suite occupants get a plush bathrobe.

Dining: The main dining room (Primavera) is located aft and has ocean views on three sides. Passengers dine in one seating, and tables are for six, ten, or twelve. The food consists of both Japanese and Western items; the menu is varied and the food is attractively presented.

A second, intimate, yet moderately stately 42-seat alternative restaurant, called Grand Siècle, features an à la carte menu. The restaurant incurs an extra charge for everything; it is decorated in Regency style, with much fine wood paneling and a detailed, indented ceiling.

Other Comments: Venus Cruise is part of Japan Cruise Line, which is itself part of SHK Line Group, a joint venture between Shin Nohonkai, Hankyu, and Kanpu ferry companies (operating more than 20 ferries). The company also owns and operates the slightly smaller and more basic *Orient Venus*, which is used principally for the charter and incentive group market. *Pacific Venus*, which is being operated for individual cruises (no charters) is one deck higher than her sister ship and also is slightly longer and beamier, the second largest cruise vessel built by a Japanese shipyard.

There is a good amount of open deck space aft of the funnel, good for deck sports, while protected sunbathing space is provided around the small swimming pool (all deck lounge chairs have cushioned pads). The base of the funnel itself is the site of a day/night lounge, which overlooks the swimming pool. There is a wraparound (rubber coated) promenade deck outdoors.

Inside the ship, the high passenger space ratio means that there is plenty of space per passenger. The decor is clean and fresh, with much use of pastel colors and blond woods. Deck 7 features a double-width indoor promenade off of which the dining rooms are located. The three-decks-high atrium has a crystal chandelier as its focal point.

Facilities include male and female Grand Baths, which include bathing pool and health/cleansing facilities. There are special rooms for meetings and conference organizers, used when the ship is chartered. There is a piano salon with colorful low-back chairs, a large main hall (with a finely sculptured high ceiling and 720 movable seats — production shows are performed here), a 350-seat main lounge for cabaret shows, a small theater, a library and card room, a casino, two private karaoke rooms, a Japanese chashitsu room for tea ceremonies (a tatami-matted room), and a beauty salon. There is also a 24-hour vending machine corner (juice, beer, camera film, and other items), self-service launderette (no charge), and several (credit card/coin) public telephone booths.

Overall, this company provides a well-packaged cruise in a ship that presents a very comfortable, serene environment. The dress code is relaxed and no tipping is allowed.

Weak Points: There are few cabins with private balconies. The open walking promenade decks are rubber-coated steel — teak would be more desirable.

Paradise
★★★ +

Large Ship:	70,367 tons	Cabins (for one person):	0
Lifestyle:	Standard	Cabins (with private balcony):	26
Cruise Line:	Carnival Cruise Lines	Cabins (wheelchair accessible):	22
Former Names:	-	Cabin Current:	110-volt
Builder:	Kvaerner Masa-Yards (Finland)	Full-Service Dining Rooms:	2
Original Cost:	$300 million	Elevators:	14
Entered Service:	November 1998	Casino (gaming tables):	Yes
Registry:	Panama	Slot Machines:	Yes
Length (ft/m):	855.0/260.6	Swimming Pools (outdoors):	3
Beam (ft/m):	103.3/31.5	Swimming Pools (indoors):	0
Draft (ft/m):	25.9/7.9	Whirlpools:	6
Propulsion/Propellers:	Diesel-electric (42,842kW)/2 azimuthing pods	Fitness Center:	Yes
		Sauna/Steam Room:	Yes/Yes
Passenger Decks:	10	Massage:	Yes
Total Crew:	920	Self-Service Launderette:	Yes
Passengers (lower beds/all berths):	2,040/2,594	Dedicated Cinema:	No
Pass. Space Ratio (lower beds/all berths):	34.4/26.7	Library:	Yes
Crew/Pass. Ratio (lower beds/all berths):	2.2/2.8	Classification Society:	Lloyd's Register
Navigation Officers:	Italian		
Cabins (total):	1,02		
Size Range (sq ft/sq m):	173.2–409.7/16.0–38.0		
Cabins (outside view):	618		
Cabins (interior/no view):	402		

OVERALL SCORE: **1,390**
(OUT OF A POSSIBLE 2,000 POINTS)

Accommodation: As in sister ships *Ecstasy, Elation, Fantasy, Fascination, Imagination, Inspiration,* and *Sensation,* the standard outside-view and interior (no view) cabins have plain decor. They are marginally comfortable, yet spacious enough and practical (most are of the same size and appointments), with good storage space and well-designed bathrooms.

Those booking one of the outside suites will find more space, whirlpool bathtubs, and some fascinating, rather eclectic decor and furniture. These are mildly attractive, but nothing special, and they are much smaller than those aboard the ships of a similar size of several competing companies.

A gift basket is now provided in all grades of accommodation; it includes aloe soap, shampoo, conditioner, deodorant, breath mints, candy, and pain relief tablets.

Dining: There are two dining rooms (Destiny and Paradise); both are nonsmoking. They have splashy, colorful decor, and are large, very crowded, and very noisy. While the menu descriptions sound inviting, the food, when it arrives, is not. It is only adequate, but the company (which provides its own catering) has made improvements. Dining is now in four seatings, for greater flexibility: 6pm, 6:45pm, 8pm, and 8:45pm (these times are approximate).

Carnival meals stress quantity, not quality, although the company constantly works hard to improve the cuisine. While passengers seem to accept it, few find it worth remembering. However, food and its taste are still not the company's strongest points (you get what you pay for, remember).

While the menu items might sound good, their presentation and taste leave much to be desired. While meats are of a high quality, fish and seafood are not. Presentation is simple, and few garnishes are used. Many meat and fowl dishes are disguised with gravies and sauces. The selection of fresh green vegetables, breads, rolls, cheeses, and fruits is limited, and there is too much use of canned fruit and jellied desserts. However, do remember that this is banquet catering, with all its attendant standardization and production cooking (it is, therefore, difficult to ask for anything remotely unusual or off-menu).

Although there is a decent wine list, there are no wine waiters (the waiters are expected to serve both food and wine) and no decent-size wine glasses. The service is quite robotic, closely timed, highly programmed, and inflexible, although the waiters are willing and reasonably friendly. However, the waiters do sing and dance (be prepared for "Hot, Hot, Hot" and "The Macarena" — again) and there are constant waiter parades. The dining room is show business — all done to attract gratuities.

For casual meals, there's the Lido Café, which, aboard this ship, has some improvements and additions worthy of note, such as a fresh orange juice machine. The Pizzeria is open 24 hours a day and typically serves over 500 pizzas every single day! There's also a sushi bar. Things are looking up, which means more choices. At night, the "Seaview Bistro" (as the Lido Café becomes known) provides a casual alternative to eating in the main dining rooms. It serves pasta, steaks, salads, and desserts.

Other Comments: *Paradise* is the eighth in a series of eight mega-ships of the same series and identical internal configuration. It is a very successful design for this successful company that targets the mass market, and particularly the first-time passenger. The ship's appearance is bold, forthright, and angular, and is typical of today's space-creative designs. What is new, however, is the pod propulsion system, which gives the ship more maneuverability, while reducing required machinery space and vibration at the stern. Although the exterior displays a bold profile, the large funnel, with its familiar wing tips and red, white, and blue colors, offsets it.

Like a breath of fresh air, this is a totally nonsmoking ship (and that includes the crew), including all open decks. There is a fine of $250 for anyone caught smoking, and you will be put off at the next port. Passengers must sign a document agreeing to this policy prior to embarkation.

All of the principal public rooms are set off to one side of a double-width boulevard. The ship has a three-decks-high glass-enclosed health spa and gymnasium with the latest muscle-pumping equipment, and a banked outdoor jogging track. A large shop is stuffed to the gills with low-quality merchandise. The large casino features gaming tables for blackjack, craps, roulette, and Caribbean stud poker, as well as slot machines. All slot machines aboard all Carnival ships are linked into a big prize, called Megacash.

The decor includes splashy, showy public rooms and interior colors — pure Las Vegas, and ideal for those who love it.

There are public entertainment lounges, bars, and clubs galore, with something for everyone, including a children's playroom, larger than aboard the other ships in this series. Some busy colors and design themes abound in the handsome public rooms are connected by wide indoor boulevards and beg your attention and indulgence. There is also a good art collection, much of it bright and vocal. The Blue Riband library is a fine room, as aboard most Carnival ships; although there are few books, there are models of ocean liners. One neat feature is an atrium bar, complete with live classical music — something new for this company.

It's a real "life on the ocean rave" for the young at heart, if you enjoy people and noise. Children are provided with good facilities, including their own two-level Children's Club (with an outdoor pool), and are well cared for with "Camp Carnival," the line's extensive children's program. The general passenger flow is good, and the interior design is clever, functional, wacky, and outrageously colorful. The ship is arguably better than the ports of call!

The company has grown dramatically over the last few years and has improved its product substantially. In 1996, the company introduced a "Vacation Guarantee" program (the first of its kind in the industry) to great success — particularly for first-time passengers who do not know whether they will enjoy cruising (few passengers ever consider leaving the cruise).

Carnival does not try to sell itself as a luxury cruise line and consistently delivers exactly what it says in its brochures (nothing more, nothing less), for which there is a huge, growing, first-time cruise audience. Carnival Cruise Lines provides a well-packaged cruise vacation, with smart new ships that have the latest high-tech entertainment facilities and features.

This ship is one of the great floating playgrounds for young, active adults who enjoy constant stimulation, close contact with lots and lots of others, as well as the three Gs — glitz, glamour, and gambling. It is a live board game with every move executed in typically grand, colorful, fun-filled Carnival Cruise Lines style. Ideally suited to those who like big city life ashore and want it on their vacation, and for those who like lively action, constant entertainment, and nightlife at any hour. Forget fashion — having fun is the sine qua non of a Carnival cruise. Gratuities can be prepaid.

Weak Points: This ship is not for those who want a quiet, relaxing cruise experience. There are simply too many annoying announcements and a great deal of hustling for drinks, although it is sometimes done with a knowing smile. The balconied show lounge is large, but 20 pillars obstruct the views from several seats. Shore excursions are booked via the in-cabin ("Fun Vision") TV system (there is no longer a shore excursion desk and, thus, no one to answer questions). In fact, getting anyone to answer your questions can prove utterly frustrating. Standing in line for embarkation, disembarkation, shore tenders, and self-serve buffet meals is an inevitable aspect of cruising aboard all large ships. The service is very, very basic and completely without a hint of finesse. There is absolutely no escape from unnecessary and repetitious announcements (particularly for activities that bring revenue, such as art auctions, bingo, or horse racing) that intrude constantly into your cruise.

Patriot
★★★ +

Large Ship:	33,930 tons	Cabins (with private balcony):	0
Lifestyle:	Standard	Cabins (wheelchair accessible):	4
Cruise Line:	United States Lines	Cabin Current:	110/220-volt
Former Names:	*Nieuw Amsterdam*	Full-Service Dining Rooms:	1
Builder:	Chantiers de l'Atlantique (France)	Elevators:	7
Original Cost:	$150 million	Casino (gaming tables):	No
Entered Service:	July 1983/December 2000	Slot Machines:	No
Registry:	US	Swimming Pools (outdoors):	2
Length (ft/m):	704.2/214.66	Swimming Pools (indoors):	0
Beam (ft/m):	89.4/27.26	Whirlpools:	1
Draft (ft/m):	24.6/7.52	Fitness Center:	Yes
Propulsion/Propellers:	Diesel (21,600kW)/2	Sauna/Steam Room:	Yes/No
Passenger Decks:	10	Massage:	Yes
Total Crew:	510	Self-Service Launderette:	Yes (3)
Passengers (lower beds/all berths):	1,214/1,350	Dedicated Cinema/Seats:	Yes/230
Pass. Space Ratio (lower beds/all berths):	28.0/25.1	Library:	Yes
Crew/Pass. Ratio (lower beds/all berths):	2.3/2.6	Classification Society:	American Bureau of
Navigation Officers:	American		Shipping
Cabins (total):	607		
Size Range (sq ft/sq m):	150.6–296.0/14.0–27.5		
Cabins (outside view):	413	**OVERALL SCORE:**	**1,340**
Cabins (interior/no view):	194	(OUT OF A POSSIBLE 2,000 POINTS)	
Cabins (for one person):	0		

Accommodation: With the exception of one "Presidential Suite," all other cabins come in just four types: Parlor Suite, Superior Ocean-view Stateroom, Ocean-view Stateroom, and Interior (no view) Stateroom, and 15 grades: 10 outside-view and five interior (no view) grades. In general, most of the cabins are quite small (below the industry standard, which is 170 sq ft/16 sq m). They are, however, reasonably well appointed and practically laid out. Some have wood furniture, fittings, or accenting, good counter and storage space (although there is very little drawer space), a large dressing mirror, and private bathrooms that are adequate, but no more.

The top categories of cabins (which are only marginally larger and should not be called suites or mini-suites) have full-size bathtubs while all others have showers. Several cabins have king- or queen-size beds, although most have twin beds.

The largest accommodation can be found in the Presidential Suite (on Eagle Deck), a new suite created when United States Lines purchased the ship. Small by comparison to suites aboard many other ships, it measures 464 sq ft (43.1 sq m) and is decorated in the style of a "Pacific White House," featuring American Federal decor, with cherry wood cabinetry, and Murano (Italian) glass light fixtures. There is a king-size bed, walk-in closet, wet bar, study and dining areas, TV, VCR, and stereo system. The bathroom includes a whirlpool tub, double sink unit, and a separate powder room.

A number of cabins also have additional berths for a third and fourth person. Room service is provided 24 hours a day. All cabin televisions feature CNN. The cabin insulation, unfortunately, is extremely poor, and bathroom towels are small. In addition, some cabins on Bridge Deck and Mariner Deck have obstructed views.

Dining: The single-level Manhattan Dining Room is quite large and reasonably attractive, with its dark wood decor, although the ceiling is quite plain. Breakfast and lunch are served in an open-seating arrangement (so you may get a different table and different waiters for each meal), and in two seatings for dinner (where you have the same table and waiter each evening). The chinaware suppliers of the original liner United States has also provided the custom-made chinaware for *Patriot*'s dining room.

The food is decidedly American/Pacific Rim fare, with different themes each evening (Aloha Dinner, Blue Riband Dinner, White Orchid Dinner, Big Apple Dinner, Stars and Stripes Dinner). The waiters are all-American, too. The wine list features — you guessed it — mostly American wines.

Instead of the more formal dining room, the Outrigger Café is available as a casual (come as you are, come when you want) self-serve, buffet-style eatery for breakfast, lunch, and dinner.

Other Comments: The ship has a bow with a nice rake to it, although the angular exterior design makes the ship look squat and extremely boxy. The ship now sports a deep blue hull, while an American eagle adorns the funnel. There is a good amount of open deck space (particularly at the aft section of the ship), and the traditional outdoors teak decks include a wraparound promenade deck. The ship, however, has a poor build quality and has always suffered from excessive vibration since she was new.

The ship has been operated by former owners Holland America Line since new and was delivered to American Classic Voyages, parent company of United States Lines (a name from the which the company purchased), in 2000. The ship's first voyage for United States Lines took place in December 2000, when her name changed from Nieuw Amsterdam to *Patriot* following a $21 million refit and refurbishment.

The ship has quite a spacious interior design and layout (although most of the public rooms are located on a single deck), and the soothing color combinations do not jar the senses (most are actually pretty nondescript). There is much polished teak and rosewood paneling throughout. The Eagle's Watch observation lounge, located atop the ship, is a good retreat — excellent for island and whale spotting — and there's also a wooden dance floor. The Mid-Ship Lounge is relaxing for after-meal coffee with live music. The main lounge, which has a small balcony level, is reminiscent of the former ocean liners' era. Newly added are a "kumu" (Hawaiian) Destination Learning Center and a Families Activity Center. Flowers throughout the ship add warmth to the ambience.

For younger passengers, Graffiti's is a teen center that includes Internet-access computer terminals; Kaleidoscope is for children ages 5–12 (including a movie viewing room).

This ship is acceptable for passengers wanting pleasant surroundings and an all-American ambiance. However, many newer ships have more space, better facilities, and more options, and these cause this ship to lose a few points in relation to the increased competition in the international marketplace. Perhaps the best part of cruising aboard *Patriot* is in the destinations, and not the ship. Take your Aloha shirt, as the dress code is casual, although you'll need something more formal for the two formal nights of the cruise.

In December 2000, the ship started operating year-round seven-night cruises of the Hawaiian Islands (four islands, five ports: Nawiliwili, Kawaii; Kahului, Maui; Hilo, Hawaii; Kona, Hawaii), from its new homeport of Honolulu (expect to be greeted by welcoming leis as you embark). The ship docks at all ports with the exception of the small fishing port cove at Kona (Hawaii), where tenders are used.

Weak Points: Standing in line for embarkation, disembarkation, shore tenders, and self-serve buffet meals is an inevitable aspect of cruising aboard all large ships. There are simply too many interior (no view) cabins. There is a considerable amount of vibration throughout the ship, particularly at the stern, that is particularly noticeable during slow maneuvering. There are no cabins with private balconies. The service is adequate and there is little finesse. The cabins really are small when compared to the newer ships in the cruise industry. The spa and gymnasium are also quite small, and the beauty salon/barber shop is located in a completely different area from the health and fitness facilities. There's a fee for the Wedding Vow Renewal service.

Paul Gauguin
★★★★ +

Small Ship:	18,800 tons	Cabins (for one person):	0
Lifestyle:	Luxury	Cabins (with private balcony):	80
Cruise Line:	Radisson Seven Seas Cruises	Cabins (wheelchair accessible):	1
Former Names:	-	Cabin Current:	110-volt
Builder:	Chantiers de l'Atlantique (France)	Full-Service Dining Rooms:	2
Original Cost:	$150 million	Elevators:	4
Entered Service:	January 1998	Casino (gaming tables):	Yes
Registry:	Wallis & Fortuna	Slot Machines:	Yes
Length (ft/m):	513.4/156.50	Swimming Pools (outdoors):	1
Beam (ft/m):	72.1/22.00	Swimming Pools (indoors):	0
Draft (ft/m):	16.8/5.15	Whirlpools:	0
Propulsion/Propellers:	Diesel-electric (9,000kW/2	Fitness Center:	Yes
Passenger Decks:	7	Sauna/Steam Room:	No/Yes
Total Crew:	206	Massage:	Yes
Passengers (lower beds/all berths):	320/320	Self-Service Launderette:	No
Pass. Space Ratio (lower beds/all berths):	58.7/58.7	Dedicated Cinema:	No
Crew/Pass. Ratio (lower beds/all berths):	1.5/1.5	Library:	Yes
Navigation Officers:	European	Classification Society:	Bureau Veritas
Cabins (total):	160		
Size Range (sq ft/sq m):	200.0–534.0/18.5–49.6	**OVERALL SCORE:**	**1,645**
Cabins (outside view):	160	**(OUT OF A POSSIBLE 2,000 POINTS)**	
Cabins (interior/no view):	0		

Accommodation: The outside-view cabins, half of which boast private balconies, are very nicely equipped, although they are strictly rectangular. Most have large windows, except those on the lowest accommodation deck, which have portholes. Each has queen- or twin-size beds (convertible to queen), and wood-accented cabinetry with rounded edges. A minibar/refrigerator, VCR, personal safe, hair dryer, and umbrella are standard. The marble-look bathrooms are nice and large and feature a bathtub as well as a separate shower enclosure. Bathrobes are provided for all passengers, and soft drinks and mineral water are complimentary.

The two largest suites have a private balcony at the front and side of the vessel. Although there is a decent amount of in-cabin space, with a beautiful long vanity unit (and plenty of drawer space), the bathrooms are disappointingly small and plain, and too similar to all other standard cabin bathrooms.

Dining: The main dining room ("L'Etoile") features lunch and dinner, while La Veranda, an alternative dining spot, is open for breakfast, lunch, and dinner. Both dining rooms provide "open seating," which means that passengers can choose when they want to dine and with whom. This provides a good opportunity to meet new people for dinner each evening. La Veranda provides dinner by reservation, with alternating French and Italian menus; the French menus are provided by Chef Jean-Pierre Vigato, a two-star Michelin chef with his own restaurant ("Apicius") in Paris.

The dining operation is well orchestrated, with cuisine and service of a high standard. Complimentary standard table wines are served with dinner, although a connoisseur selection is available, at extra cost, for real wine lovers. Mineral water, fruit juices, and soft drinks are complimentary throughout the ship — a nice touch.

In addition, an outdoor bistro provides informal café fare on deck aft of the pool, while the Connoisseur Club offers a luxurious retreat for cigars, cognacs, and wine tasting.

Other Comments: Built by a French company, managed and operated by the US-based Radisson Seven Seas Cruises, this ship is extremely spacious. While she could carry more passengers, under French law operating in the Polynesian islands, she is unable to do so. The ship has a look that is quite well balanced, and all in gleaming white, with a single funnel.

This smart looking vessel also has a retractable aft marina platform and carries two water skiing boats and two inflatable craft for water sports. Windsurfers and kayaks, as well as SCUBA and snorkeling gear, are all available for your use (all except SCUBA gear are included in the cruise fare).

Inside, there is a pleasant array of public rooms, and both the artwork and the decor have a real French Polynesian look and feel. The interior colors are quite restful, although a trifle bland.

Expert lecturers on Tahiti and Gauguin accompany each cruise, and a Fare (pronounced "foray") Tahiti Gallery offers books, videos, and other materials on the unique art, history, and culture of the islands; three original Gauguin sketches are displayed under glass. There is a good health spa program with treatment services provided by Carita of Paris, although the changing facilities are very limited, there is no sauna, and use of the steam room incurs an extra charge (it should be free).

The library is pleasant enough, although it really could be larger. This ship (a more deluxe version of the company's popular *Song of Flower*) presents Radisson Seven Seas Cruises with the opportunity to score very high marks with her passengers, as the company is known for its attention to detail and passenger care.

A no-tie policy means that the dress code is very relaxed — every day. The standard itinerary means that the ship only docks in Papeete, and shore tenders are used in all other ports. There is little entertainment, as the ship stays overnight in several ports. The ship's high crew-to-passenger ratio translates to highly personalized service, and, overall, this is a very pleasing product. Where the ship really shines is in the provision of a lot of water sports equipment, and the ship's shallow draft allows it to navigate and anchor in lovely little places that larger ships could not possibly get to. All in all, it's a delightful cruise and product, and all gratuities to staff are included.

Weak Points: Although it sounds exotic, the itinerary is only marginally interesting to the well traveled; the best island experience is in Bora Bora. The ship's shallow draft means there could be some movement, as she is high-sided for her size. A minimum purchase rule in the ship's boutique is irritating (however, this is due to local government rules); the same is true of the casino, where there is a $10 minimum. The spa is very small, and the fitness room is windowless.

Polaris
★★★

Small Ship:	2,214 tons	Cabins (with private balcony):	0
Lifestyle:	Standard	Cabins (wheelchair accessible):	0
Cruise Line:	Lindblad Expeditions	Cabin Current:	220-volt
Former Names:	*Lindblad Polaris, Oresund*	Full-Service Dining Rooms:	1
Builder:	Aalborg Vaerft (Denmark)	Elevators:	0
Original Cost:	n/a	Casino (gaming tables):	No
Entered Service:	1960/May 1987	Slot Machines:	No
Registry:	Ecuador	Swimming Pools (outdoors):	0
Length (ft/m):	236.6/72.12	Whirlpools:	0
Beam (ft/m):	42.7/13.03	Exercise Room:	No
Draft (ft/m):	13.7/4.30	Sauna/Steam Room:	Yes/No
Propulsion/Propellers:	Diesel (2,354kW)/2	Massage:	No
Passenger Decks:	4	Self-Service Launderette:	No
Total Crew:	44	Lecture/Film Room:	No
Passengers (lower beds/all berths):	82/84	Library:	Yes
Pass. Space Ratio (lower beds/all berths):	27.0/26.3	Zodiacs:	8
Crew/Pass. Ratio (lower beds/all berths):	1.8/1.8	Helicopter Pad:	No
Navigation Officers:	Ecuadorian	Classification Society:	Bureau Veritas
Cabins (total):	41		
Size Range (sq ft/sq m):	99.0–229.2/9.2–21.3		
Cabins (outside view):	41		
Cabins (interior/no view):	0	**OVERALL SCORE:**	**1,210**
Cabins (for one person):	0	**(OUT OF A POSSIBLE 2,000 POINTS)**	

Accommodation: The cabins, all of which are above the waterline, are fairly roomy and nicely appointed, but there is little drawer space. Some have been refurbished and feature large (lower) beds. Each has a hair dryer; refreshingly, cabin keys are not used. The cabin bathrooms are really tiny, however, so take only what you need. Note that there is no cabin service menu.

Dining: The dining room has big picture windows and a wraparound view. Seating is now at individual tables (formerly family style) in a leisurely single seating. Good food, with a major emphasis on local fish and seafood dishes. There is also a fine wine list. Breakfast and lunch are buffet-style. Service is friendly from an attentive staff.

Other Comments: This "soft" expedition cruise vessel, of modest proportions, sports a dark blue hull and white superstructure. She has been well maintained and operated, skillfully converted from a former Scandinavian ferry. She sports a fantail and improved aft outdoor lounge area. There are several Zodiac inflatable rubber landing craft, as well as a glass-bottom boat.

Inside, although there are few public rooms, the Scandinavian-style interior furnishings and decor are very tidy and welcoming, accented by lots of wood trim. There's a friendly, very intimate atmosphere on board, with Filipino service staff. A good team of lecturers and nature observers are featured, whose daily recaps are a vital part of the experience. A restful, well-stocked library helps passengers learn more about the region and the natural world.

This is a good small vessel, which now operates year-round nature-intensive "soft" expedition cruises around the Galapagos Islands. This is an area to which the ship is well suited (only 90 passengers from any one ship are allowed at any one time in the Galapagos Islands, where tourism is managed well by the Ecuadorean government). In fact, this ship is among the best suited to this region. All port charges are included in this product, which is marketed by Lindblad Expeditions and Noble Caledonia, together with other specialist packagers.

Polarlys
★★★ +

Small Ship:	12,000 tons	Cabins (wheelchair accessible):	3
Cruise Line:	Norwegian Coastal Voyages (TFDS)	Cabin Current:	220-volt
Former Names:	-	Full-Service Dining Rooms:	1
Builder:	Ulstein Verft (Norway)	Elevators:	2
Original Cost:	n/a	Casino (gaming tables):	No
Entered Service:	1997	Slot Machines:	No
Registry:	Norway	Swimming Pools (outdoors):	0
Length (ft/m):	399.6/121.8	Swimming Pools (indoors):	0
Beam (ft/m):	62.9/19.2	Whirlpools:	0
Draft (ft/m):	16.0/4.9	Fitness Center:	Yes
Total Crew:	70	Sauna/Steam Room:	Yes/No
Passengers (lower beds/all berths):	450/482	Massage:	No
Pass. Space Ratio (lower beds/all berths):	26.6/24.8	Self-Service Launderette:	Yes
Crew/Pass. Ratio (lower beds/all berths):	6.4/6.8	Dedictated Cinema:	No
Navigation Officers:	Norwegian	Library:	Yes
Cabins (total):	225	Classification Society:	
Size Range (sq ft/sq m):	n/a		
Cabins (outside view):	181		
Cabins (interior/no view):	44		
Cabins (for one person):	0		
Cabins (with private balcony):	0		

OVERALL SCORE: **1,285**
(OUT OF A POSSIBLE 2,000 POINTS)

Accommodation: There are nine grades of cabin, including three wheelchair-accessible cabins (one of the ship's two elevators accommodates a wheelchair). Double beds are only available in the two suites; all other cabins have beds and berths that cannot be moved. Some cabins also have an additional third (upper) berth, and a number of cabins are available for single occupancy, albeit with a price premium. All cabins have a 220-volt outlet, so take adapters and converters if you need to.

Dining: There is one main dining room (the Polaryset Restaurant — no smoking allowed), and tables are assigned when you embark. Three meals each day are included in the cruise fare: Breakfast and lunch (featuring the famous Norwegian "cold table") are self-serve, buffet-style meals, while dinner is a sit-down affair, with three courses. Additionally, there is the Fjorden Café, open 24 hours, where snacks and light meals can be purchased.

Other Comments: The Norwegian Coastal Voyage is a service that was started in 1863. It is jointly operated by two companies: Ofotens og Vesteraalen Dampskibsselskab (OVDS) and Troms Fylkes Dampskibsselskab (TFDS). The complete journey, of 1,250 nautical miles, takes in 34 ports of call in a 12-day roundtrip voyage between Bergen and Kirkenes (on the border with Russia), above the Arctic Circle (where a special "Crossing the Arctic Circle" ceremony welcomes newcomers). The journey can also be done in a one-way voyage that takes seven days (northbound) or six days (southbound). The ships carry passengers as well as mail and other cargo.

Perhaps you will be able to peek at the midnight sun (mid-May to late June, north of the Arctic Circle), experience the northern lights (aurora borealis, mostly seen during winter months, and only when the atmospheric conditions are right), and be part of the daily life of the hardy Norwegians. Approximately 60% of the passengers will be Norwegian/Scandinavian/European, while the rest will be a mix of North American and other nationalities. Although the passenger bed capacity is quoted, note that many additional passengers may be on board as day passengers, sailing between two coastal ports — the ship is the equivalent of a seagoing bus for the coastal commuters. As for the weather, the West coast of Norway is warmed by the Gulf Stream, and temperatures tend to be be similar to those found in New England.

This ship is one of the "new generations" of coastal voyage ships (built in the 1990s) that is rather like a mini-cruise vessel, with a better array of public rooms and facilities than the older, smaller ships in the fleet. This is an excellent way to experience the beautiful coastline of Norway and its fascinating coastal towns. There will be an interesting mix of passengers — it's a good way to meet new people and make new friends from different countries. A laundry room with washing machines, tumble dryers, and irons is provided (useful for those for whom the cruise is only part of a more extensive vacation).

The rates vary by season, cabin location, and whether the ship is of the "new generation" (*Kong Harald, Nordkapp, Nordlys, Nordnorge, Polarlys, Richard With*), the "mid-generation" (*Narvik, Midnatsol, Vesteralen*), or the "traditional" (*Harald Jarl, Lofoten*) type ships, the scenery is what the voyage is all about. Senior citizens (those age 67 and over) qualify for a special discount. Adult couples, single travelers, and families with children wanting to sail along the coast of Norway and experience the area's natural beauty are best suited to this scenic cruise. It's ideal for anyone who doesn't need entertainment or mindless parlor games, but wants to relax and unwind, enjoys being close to nature, and is probably a bit of an adventurer. The dress code is casual and comfortable — layered clothing is best. The currency is the Norwegian krone.

Norwegian coast and fjords cruises consist of a 7-day (northbound) voyage between Bergen and Kirkenes, Norway; or a 6-day (southbound) voyage between Kirkenes and Bergen, Norway; or a 12-day roundtrip voyage. This ship also carries up to 50 cars.

Weak Points: The ship does not have stabilizers, so you should expect some movement when the weather is inclement or unkind. Drink prices are extremely high — the same as ashore in Norway. The cabins are small, and the bathrooms are really tiny. Although not needed during the winter, there is little outdoors deck space considering the number of passengers carried.

Polynesia
★★

Small Ship:	430 tons	Size Range (sq ft/sq m):	68.0–104.0/6.3–9.6
Lifestyle:	Standard	Cabins (outside view):	14
Cruise Line:	Windjammer Barefoot Cruises	Cabins (interior/no view):	41
Former Names:	*Argu*	Cabins (for one person):	0
Builder:	Haan & Oerlemans (Holland)	Cabins (with private balcony):	0
Original Cost:	n/a	Cabins (wheelchair accessible):	0
Entered Service:	1938/1975	Cabin Current:	110-volt
Registry:	Equatorial Guinea	Full-Service Dining Rooms:	1
Length (ft/m):	248.0/75.5	Elevators:	0
Beam (ft/m):	36.0/10.9	Casino (gaming tables):	No
Draft (ft/m):	18.0/5.4	Slot Machines:	No
Type of Vessel:	Topsail schooner	Swimming Pools (outdoors):	0
No. of Masts:	4	Whirlpools:	0
Sail Area (sq.ft/sq.m):	18,000/1,672.2	Fitness Center:	No
Main Propulsion:	Sail power	Sauna/Steam Room:	No/No
Propulsion/Propellers:	Diesel/1	Massage:	No
Passenger Decks:	4	Self-Service Launderette:	No
Total Crew:	45	Library:	Yes
Passengers (lower beds/all berths):	110/122	Classification Society:	none
Pass. Space Ratio (lower beds/all berths):	3.9/3.5		
Crew/Pass. Ratio (lower beds/all berths):	2.4/2.7		
Navigation Officers:	International		
Cabins (total):	55		

OVERALL SCORE: 902
(OUT OF A POSSIBLE 2,000 POINTS)

Accommodation: There are four grades of accommodation (designated as Admiral Suite, Deck Cabin, Standard Cabin, and Bachelor/ette Cabin). The cabins really are dimensionally challenged, however, particularly when compared to regular cruise ships. Remember, however, that this is a very casual cruise experience and you will need so few clothes anyway. All are equipped with upper and lower berths, and most of them are quite narrow.

Dining: There is one dining room, with views to the outside through real portholes, and meals are all very simple in style and service, with little choice and only the most basic presentation. Breakfast is served on board, as is dinner, while lunch could be either on board or at a beach, picnic-style. Wine is included with dinner.

Other Comments: *Polynesia* was originally built to be part of the great Portuguese Grand Banks fleet. She was featured in the May 1952 edition of *National Geographic* magazine and in the late maritime writer, Allen Villers's book "*The Quest of the Schooner Argus.*" Windjammer Barefoot Cruises acquired *Polynesia* in 1975.

Aboard one of the Windjammer Barefoot Cruises' fleet you can let the crew do all the work, or you can lend a hand at the helm yourself, if you feel so inclined. One neat thing to do is just to sit or lie in the nets at the bow of the vessel, without a care in the world — it's a good feeling.

The mood is free and easy, the ships are equipped very simply, and only the most casual clothes are required (T-shirts and shorts), and shoes are optional, although you may need them if you go off in one of the ports. Quite possibly the most used item will be your bathing suit — better take more than one! Smoking is allowed only on the open decks.

Entertainment in the evenings consists of you and the crew. You can put on a toga or create a pirate outfit and join in the fun. This is cruising free 'n' easy style — none of that programmed big-ship production show stuff here.

Jammin' aboard a Windjammer (first-time passengers are called "crewmates" while repeat passengers are called "jammers") is no-frills cruising (it could be called an "anti-cruise") in a no-nonsense, friendly environment, for the young at heart and those who don't need programmed activities. It's all about the romance of being at sea under sail. You can even lend a hand with the sails if you wish. Those that enjoy beaches, SCUBA diving, and snorkeling around the Caribbean will be best suited to a Windjammer

Barefoot Cruises cruise. This ship can anchor in neat little sheltered Caribbean hideaways that larger (regular) cruise ships can't get near.

Although itineraries (islands) are provided in the brochure, the captain actually decides which islands to go to in any given area, depending on sea and weather conditions. *Polynesia* features year-round cruises in the Caribbean. The brochure rates might seem inexpensive, but remember that you will need to add on the airfare in order to arrive at the true cost.

Other tall ships in the fleet include *Flying Cloud, Legacy, Mandalay, and Yankee Clipper.*

Weak Points: There's very little room per passenger. Everything is basic, basic, basic. Tips to the crew are strongly suggested — at $50 per week!

DID YOU KNOW...?

...that in 1903 the British liner *Lucania* became the first ship to have wireless equipment, which enabled her to keep in touch with both sides of the Atlantic Ocean at the same time?

...that the first ship-to-shore wireless telegraphy took place on the American passenger ship *St. Paul*, in 1899?

...that the first twin-screw passenger ship was the Compagnie Generale Transatlantique's 3,200-tonne *Washington*, built in 1863 and converted in 1868?

...that the first floating eclipse expedition was led by US astronomer Ted Pedas in 1972, when 800 passengers sailed to a spectacular rendezvous with a total sun eclipse in the North Atlantic?

...that the first passenger ship to exceed 80,000-tonnes was the Compagnie Generale Transatlantique's *Normandie*, which measured at 82,799-tonnes in 1936?

...that the first gravity lifeboats were aboard the Compagnie Generale Transatlantique's *Ile de France* of 1928?

Princesa Amorosa
★★ +

Small Ship:	5,026 tons	Cabins (for one person):	0
Lifestyle:	Standard	Cabins (with private balcony):	0
Cruise Line:	Louis Cruise Lines	Cabins (wheelchair accessible):	0
Former Names:	*Galaxias, Galaxy, Scottish Coast*	Cabin Current:	220-volt
Builder:	Harland & Wolff (UK)	Full-Service Dining Rooms:	1
Original Cost:	n/a	Elevators:	0
Entered Service:	1957/July 1990	Casino (gaming tables):	Yes
Registry:	Cyprus	Slot Machines:	Yes
Length (ft/m):	342.2/104.32	Swimming Pools (outdoors):	1
Beam (ft/m):	52.6/16.06	Swimming Pools (indoors):	0
Draft (ft/m):	15.0/4.60	Whirlpools:	0
Propulsion/Propellers:	Diesel 4,781kW)/2	Fitness Center:	No
Passenger Decks:	6	Sauna/Steam Room:	No/No
Total Crew:	130	Massage:	No
Passengers (lower beds/all berths):	284/354	Self-Service Launderette:	No
Pass. Space Ratio (lower beds/all berths):	17.6/14.1	Dedicated Cinema:	No
Crew/Pass. Ratio (lower beds/all berths):	2.1/2.7	Library:	Yes
Navigation Officers:	Cypriot/Greek	Classification Society:	Lloyd's Register
Cabins (total):	142		
Size Range (sq ft/sq m):	107.6–172.2/10.0–16.0		

OVERALL SCORE:	970
(OUT OF A POSSIBLE 2,000 POINTS)	

Cabins (outside view):	115
Cabins (interior/no view):	27

Accommodation: Most cabins are outside and comfortable, with crisp Mediterranean colors and some wood trim, but they are small, and bathrooms do show their age. The bathrooms are also very small. Note that cabins located above the disco are very noisy late at night.

Dining: The Curium Restaurant has portholes and is reasonably attractive. The restaurant can accommodate all passengers in one seating (there are 354 seats). The food is decidedly Mediterranean, with some reasonable choice and surprisingly good presentation. In addition, a full vegetarian menu is available. The service is cheerful, and the staff does try hard to make this aspect of a cruise the best part. Both à la carte and buffet meals are featured.

Other Comments: This is an older vessel that has fairly spacious open decks for her size. Seeing the bridge is like stepping back in time, with many shiny brass instruments. The swimming pool is really only a "dip" pool, nothing more.

　　Inside the ship, the limited number of public rooms have been nicely refurbished. There is an interesting maroon wrought iron staircase whose balustrades show the ship's former British heritage. Earth-tone colors have been used to good effect in the interior decor, creating a mild sense of spaciousness. There is a pleasant lounge and bar for socializing, with comfortable seating and warm decor. The ambience aboard is delightfully warm and friendly.

　　Purchased by Louis Cruise Lines in 1989, she offers good "no frills" seven-night Greek Isles/Mediterranean cruises for those without any hint of high expectations, and is particularly well suited to the local Cypriot market, where the ship has a loyal following.

Weak Points: There is a steep, narrow gangway in some ports. There are too many announcements.

Princesa Cypria
★ +

Mid-Size-Ship:	9,984 tons	Cabins (for one person):	0
Lifestyle:	Standard	Cabins (with private balcony):	0
Cruise Line:	Louis Cruise Lines	Cabins (wheelchair accessible):	0
Former Names:	*Asia Angel/Lu Jiang/Princesse Margrethe*	Cabin Current:	110-volt
		Full-Service Dining Rooms:	2
Builder:	Cantieri del Terreno (Italy)	Elevators:	2
Original Cost:	n/a	Casino (gaming tables):	Yes
Entered Service:	1968/July 1989	Slot Machines:	Yes
Registry:	Cyprus (P3CQ3)	Swimming Pools (outdoors):	0
Length (ft/m):	409.9/124.95	Swimming Pools (indoors):	0
Beam (ft/m):	63.1/19.25	Whirlpools:	0
Draft (ft/m):	20.9/5.40	Fitness Center:	No
Propulsion/Propellers:	Diesel (12,000bhp)/2	Sauna/Steam Room:	No/No
Passenger Decks:	6	Massage:	No
Total Crew:	180	Self-Service Launderette:	No
Passengers (lower beds/all berths):	548/633	Dedicated Cinema:	No
Pass. Space Ratio (lower beds/all berths):	18.2/15.7	Library:	No
Crew/Pass. Ratio (lower beds/all berths):	3.0/3.5	Classification Society:	Det Norske Veritas
Navigation Officers:	Cypriot/Greek		
Cabins (total):	274		
Size Range (sq ft/sq m):	n/a		
Cabins (outside view):	144		
Cabins (interior/no view):	129		

OVERALL SCORE: **691**

(OUT OF A POSSIBLE 2,000 POINTS)

Accommodation: Cabins are very small and spartan with virtually no closet and drawer space, and some 171 are without private facilities. The bathrooms are tiny.

Dining: The Curium Restaurant, with 338 seats, is located forward and high up in the ship and has large picture windows, while a second dining room, the Tamassos Restaurant, with 160 seats, is set amidships. Typically, an open seating policy prevails. The food is adequate and basic, but no more, and service comes without finesse. The wine list is poor.

Other Comments: The low foredeck and short, stubby bow are typical of this former ferry, whose profile is stunted and poorly balanced, particularly at the stern, where some new cabins were added during a reconstruction of the ship in 1989/1990. The open deck and sunning space is very limited. The exterior maintenance of the ship and open deck areas need more work. She is an extremely high-density ship, which means public rooms are always crowded.

The ship carries both cars and passengers on short voyages (typically of two or three days). This vessel is for passengers looking for really low fares (ideal for backpackers) and completely unpretentious surroundings, in a cruise that goes to the Holy Land.

Offers a low-cost way to visit several ports. The public rooms are basically attractive. *Princesa Cypria* has a fairly friendly atmosphere, and lovers of old ships will find the ship quite pleasant, although it certainly cannot compare with more modern and contemporary tonnage.

Weak Points: The space per passenger ratio is very low, which translates to a very densely populated ship, and that means that it is hard to find any quiet spaces at all. Low ceilings and too many support pillars add to the rather confined feeling. There is little separation of smokers and nonsmokers.

Princesa Marissa
★★

Mid-Size Ship:	10,487 tons	Cabins (for one person):	0
Lifestyle:	Standard	Cabins (with private balcony):	0
Cruise Line:	Louis Cruise Lines	Cabins (wheelchair accessible):	0
Former Names:	*Princessan, Finnhansa*	Cabin Current:	220-volt
Builder:	Wartsila (Finland)	Dining Rooms:	2
Original Cost:	n/a	Elevators:	1
Entered Service:	1966/June 1987	Casino (gaming tables):	Yes
Registry:	Cyprus	Slot Machines:	Yes
Length (ft/m):	440.6/134.30	Swimming Pools (outdoors):	0
Beam (ft/m):	65.2/19.90	Swimming Pools (indoors):	0
Draft (ft/m):	18.7/5.70	Whirlpools:	0
Propulsion/Propellers:	Diesel (10,300kW)/2 (CP)	Fitness Center:	No
Passenger Decks:	9	Sauna/Steam Room:	Yes/No
Total Crew:	185	Massage:	No
Passengers (lower beds/all berths):	628/839	Self-Service Launderette:	No
Pass. Space Ratio (lower beds/all berths):	16.6/12.4	Dedicated Cinema:	No
Crew/Pass. Ratio (lower beds/all berths):	3.3/4.5	Library:	No
Navigation Officers:	Cypriot/Greek	Classification Society:	Det Norske Veritas
Cabins (total):	314		
Size Range (sq ft/sq m):	75.3–226.0/7.0–21.0		
Cabins (outside view):	148		
Cabins (interior/no view):	166		

OVERALL SCORE: 901
(OUT OF A POSSIBLE 2,000 POINTS)

Accommodation: The standard cabins are fairly smart and functional, although the bathrooms are very small. A whole section of new cabins, added in 1995, are of a good size and feature large picture windows. The decor is bright and cheerful, and they also have good, practical bathrooms.

Dining: There are two dining rooms. Both are quite attractive (the forward one is a little more intimate) and have comfortable chairs. There are two seatings. Both à la carte and buffet-style meals are featured, and the menu choice includes three entrees. There is also a full vegetarian menu. There is a good selection of breads and ice cream sundaes. In fact, the food is perhaps the best part of a cruise aboard this vessel.

Other Comments: This former ferry has a square stern, twin funnels, and a short, stubby bow. There is very little open deck and sunbathing space, however.

Her interiors are quite smart and tidy, and the ship has been well maintained. The public room decor is attractive, with warm, fairly bright contemporary colors, well-designed fabrics, and soft furnishings. There are some limited facilities for meetings and small conferences.

The ship provides low fare transportation in unstuffy surroundings and typically operates year-round short cruises to Egypt and Israel (principally for residents of Cyprus and for British passengers vacationing there) that include shore excursions.

Weak Points: Passenger density is high. Also, the ceilings are low and typical of ferry construction. There are few crew members for so many passengers. Passengers must board through the aft car deck, but it is no real hardship. There is little separation of smokers and nonsmokers.

Princesa Victoria
★★

Mid-Size Ship:	14,583 tons	Cabins (for one person):	8
Lifestyle:	Standard	Cabins (with private balcony):	0
Cruise Line:	Louis Cruise Lines	Cabins (wheelchair accessible):	0
Former Names:	*The Victoria, Victoria, Dunottar Castle*	Cabin Current:	115-volt
Builder:	Harland & Wolff (UK)	Full-Service Dining Rooms:	1
Original Cost:	n/a	Elevators:	3
Entered Service:	July 1936/January 1993	Casino (gaming tables):	Yes
Registry:	Cyprus	Slot Machines:	Yes
Length (ft/m):	572.8/174.60	Swimming Pools (outdoors):	2
Beam (ft/m):	71.9/21.92	Swimming Pools (indoors):	0
Draft (ft/m):	27.8/8.50	Whirlpools:	0
Propulsion/Propellers:	Diesel (10,450kW)/2	Fitness Center:	Yes
Passenger Decks:	7	Sauna/Steam Room:	Yes/No
Total Crew:	230	Massage:	Yes
Passengers (lower beds/all berths):	568/750	Self-Service Launderette:	No
Pass. Space Ratio (lower beds/all berths):	25.6/19.4	Dedicated Cinema/Seats:	Yes/250
Crew/Pass. Ratio (lower beds/all berths):	2.4/3.2	Library:	Yes
Navigation Officers:	Cypriot/Greek	Classification Society:	Lloyd's Register
Cabins (total):	287		
Size Range (sq ft/sq m):	156.0–258.3/14.5–24.0	**OVERALL SCORE:**	**895**
Cabins (outside view):	216	**(OUT OF A POSSIBLE 2,000 POINTS)**	
Cabins (interior/no view):	71		

Accommodation: The standard cabins are fairly spacious and feature heavy-duty furniture and fittings. The suite rooms are cavernous, and the large bathrooms come with deep, full bathtubs, something not seen on today's cruise vessels.

Dining: The dining room is set low down but is comfortable and has a fine two-decks-high center section with barrel-shaped ceiling, music balcony, and lots of wood paneling. There are two seatings. The standard of cuisine is good, particularly bearing in mind the price you pay. There are three entrees, as well as a complete vegetarian menu. Salads, bakery items, and fruits are reasonable.

Other Comments: This ship has a very long history. Originally built for the Union Castle Line (for voyages from England to South Africa), the ship was operated for many years by Chandris Cruises prior to her purchase by Louis Cruise Lines. She has been extremely well maintained, despite her age. There is a generous amount of open deck space and twin outdoor swimming pools (although there are no showers on deck).

Inside, the center stairway is built in true Art Deco style. There is a friendly, old-world ambience on board. The Riviera Club is a contemporary room that is totally out of keeping with the rest of ship.

Princesa Victoria provides a good cruise experience for first-time cruisers and particularly for anyone seeking to optimize their hotel vacation in Cyprus. She really is an old ship, however, and so she does not have the kind of ultra-contemporary facilities that most modern ships feature.

Weak Points: The repetitive announcements are annoying. There is little separation of smokers and non-smokers, and the ship is old and worn in many places.

Princess Danae
★★★

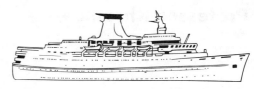

Mid-Size Ship:	17,074 tons	Cabins (for one person):	0
Lifestyle:	Standard	Cabins (with private balcony):	6
Cruise Line:	Classic International Cruises	Cabins (wheelchair accessible):	0
Former Names:	*Baltica, Starlight Express, Danae*	Cabin Current:	220-volt
	Therisos Express, Port Melbourne	Full-Service Dining Rooms:	1
Builder:	Swan, Hunter (UK)	Elevators:	2
Original Cost:	n/a	Casino (gaming tables):	Yes
Entered Service:	July 1955/1997	Slot Machines:	Yes
Registry:	Panama	Swimming Pools (outdoors):	1
Length (ft/m):	532.7/162.39	Swimming Pools (indoors):	0
Beam (ft/m):	70.0/21.34	Whirlpools:	2
Draft (ft/m):	41.9/12.80	Fitness Center:	Yes
Propulsion/Propellers:	Diesel (9,850kW)/2	Sauna/Steam Room:	Yes/No
Passenger Decks:	7	Massage:	Yes
Total Crew:	240	Self-Service Launderette:	No
Passengers (lower beds/all berths):	560/670	Dedicated Cinema/Seats:	Yes/275
Pass. Space Ratio (lower beds/all berths):	30.4/25.4	Library:	Yes
Crew/Pass. Ratio (lower beds/all berths):	2.3/2.7	Classification Society:	American Bureau of
Navigation Officers:	European		Shipping
Cabins (total):	280		
Size Range (sq ft/sq m):	200.0–270.0/18.5–25.0	**OVERALL SCORE:**	**1,101**
Cabins (outside view):	215		
Cabins (interior/no view):	65	**(OUT OF A POSSIBLE 2,000 POINTS)**	

Accommodation: Most cabins are of good size (in eight categories) and feature heavy-duty furniture and fittings with ample closet and drawer space. Note that the cabins located under the disco can suffer from thumping noise late at night. The lower-grade cabins are really plain. While 210 cabin bathrooms have a bathtub and shower, 70 have a shower only. Cabin insulation is poor.

Dining: The dining room is decorated quite nicely and has a high ceiling; it features open-seating dining, continental/European cuisine, and service that is fairly attentive, although the noise level is high from the open waiter stations.

Other Comments: *Princess Danae* is a solidly built ship, with good lines and a reasonably balanced profile, originally built for a now-defunct Greek operator, Carras Cruises. Costa Cruises then operated the ship for many years before being purchased by Classic International Cruises, her present owners. There is a decent amount of open deck space for sunbathing.

There is a pleasing traditional shipboard ambience, combined with a mixture of both traditional and contemporary features including many original interior appointments of decent quality. There are a number of spacious public rooms, although the decor is conservative. A new bar amidships was recently added. There is a roomy, traditional cinema.

This ship underwent a refurbishment early in 1996, but the fit and finish of the areas that were changed is extremely poor. She provides a moderately comfortable cruise experience. Features Caribbean cruises from Santo Domingo in winter, from Brazil during the summer, and Mediterranean cruises during some summer months. The ship is often placed under charter to various tour operators (of various nationalities), and so the character of the ship changes, as does the level of food and service provided (the principal parts of the cruise experience). In other words, use the rating only as a guide, as the actual product can be inconsistent.

Weak Points: There is no observation lounge with forward-facing views over the ship's bow. There is little finesse in the hospitality department, and service is perfunctory at best.

Professor Khromov
★★

Small Ship:	1,753 tons	Cabins (for one person):	6
Lifestyle:	Standard	Cabins (with private balcony):	0
Cruise Line:	Murmansk Shipping	Cabins (wheelchair accessible):	0
Former Names:	-	Cabin Current:	220-volt
Builder:	Wartsila (Finland)	Full-Service Dining Rooms:	2
Original Cost:	n/a	Elevators:	0
Entered Service:	1983	Casino (gaming tables):	No
Registry:	Russia	Slot Machines:	No
Length (ft/m):	234.9/71.6	Swimming Pools (outdoors):	0
Beam (ft/m):	42.0/12.8	Swimming Pools (indoors):	0
Draft (ft/m):	15.0/4.6	Whirlpools:	0
Propulsion/Propellers:	Diesel (2,327kW)/2	Fitness Center:	No
Passenger Decks:	3	Sauna/Steam Room:	Yes/No
Total Crew:	20	Massage:	No
Passengers (lower beds/all berths):	52/52	Self-Service Launderette:	No
Pass. Space Ratio (lower beds/all berths):	33.7/33.7	Dedicated Cinema:	No
Crew/Pass. Ratio (lower beds/all berths):	2.6/2.6	Library:	Yes
Navigation Officers:	Russian	Classification Society:	Russian KMLI
Cabins (total):	29		
Size Range (sq ft/sq m):	n/a	**OVERALL SCORE:**	**947**
Cabins (outside view):	29	**(OUT OF A POSSIBLE 2,000 POINTS)**	
Cabins (interior/no view):	0		

Accommodation: The accommodation is spread over three decks. Cabins on Deck 3 have portholes, but they do not have private facilities (they each have a washbasin, however), and so occupants of the eleven cabins must share common bathroom facilities (located close to the cabins). The eight cabins on Deck 4 have upper and lower berths, and their own private facilities. The seven cabins (including one suite) on Deck 5 have their own private facilities (the suite and two superior cabins also have a refrigerator).

Dining: There are two dining rooms, and all passengers are accommodated in a single seating. The meals are hearty international fare, with no frills. When under charter to Quark Expedition/Noble Caledonia, Western chefs oversee the food operation.

Other Comments: This vessel was originally specially constructed for the former Soviet Union's polar and oceanographic research program and should not be taken as a cruise ship, although it was converted in 1992 to carry passengers, refurbished, and then fitted out for expedition cruising. Other ships in the same series: *Akademik Boris Petrov, Akademik Golitsyn, Akademik M.A. Laurentiev, Akademik Nikolaj Strakhov, Akademik Shokalskiy, Livonia, Professor Molchanov, Professor Multanovskiy.* She has an ice-hardened steel hull, which is good for Arctic and Antarctic cruising. All passengers have access to the navigation bridge. There are several Zodiac landing craft for close-in shore excursions and nature observation trips.

Inside, the limited public rooms consist of a library and lounge/bar. The dining rooms also serve as lecture rooms. This ship does have good medical facilities.

This is expedition-style cruising, in a very small ship with limited facilities. However, it provides a somewhat primitive but genuine adventure experience to places others only dream about. The bigger ships cannot get this close to Antarctica, but this little vessel will sail you close to the face of the ice continent.

Professor Molchanov
★★

Small Ship:	1,753 tons	Cabins (for one person):	6
Lifestyle:	Standard	Cabins (with private balcony):	0
Cruise Line:	Murmansk Shipping	Cabins (wheelchair accessible):	0
Former Names:	-	Cabin Current:	220-volt
Builder:	Wartsila (Finland)	Full-Service Dining Rooms:	1
Original Cost:	n/a	Elevators:	0
Entered Service:	1983	Casino (gaming tables):	No
Registry:	Russia	Slot Machines:	No
Length (ft/m):	234.9/71.6	Swimming Pools (outdoors):	0
Beam (ft/m):	42.0/12.8	Swimming Pools (indoors):	0
Draft (ft/m):	15.0/4.6	Whirlpools:	0
Propulsion/Propellers:	Diesel (2,327kW)/2	Fitness Center:	No
Passenger Decks:	3	Sauna/Steam Room:	Yes/No
Total Crew:	20	Massage:	No
Passengers (lower beds/all berths):	52/52	Self-Service Launderette:	No
Pass. Space Ratio (lower beds/alberths):	33.7/33.7	Dedicated Cinema:	No
Crew/Pass. Ratio (lower beds/all berths):	2.6/2.6	Library:	Yes
Navigation Officers:	Russian	Classification Society:	Russian KMLI
Cabins (total):	29		
Size Range (sq ft/sq m):	n/a	**OVERALL SCORE:**	**947**
Cabins (outside view):	29	**(OUT OF A POSSIBLE 2,000 POINTS)**	
Cabins (interior/no view):	0		

Accommodation: With the exception of a single "suite," almost all cabins are very small and rather clinical. There are two-berth cabins with shower and toilet, or there are two-bed cabins on the lowest deck, whose occupants must share a bathroom.

Dining: There are two dining rooms (the galley is located between them), and all passengers are served in a single seating. The meals are hearty international fare with no frills. When under charter to various specialist operators such as Quark Expeditions, European chefs oversee the food operation.

Other Comments: This vessel was originally specially constructed for the former Soviet Union's polar and oceanographic research program and should not be taken as a cruise ship, although it was converted in the early 1990s to carry passengers, and then refurbished in 1996 and fitted out specifically for expedition cruising. Other ships in the same series: *Akademik Boris Petrov, Akademik Golitsyn, Akademik M.A. Laurentiev, Akademik Nikolaj Strakhov, Akademik Shokalskiy, Livonia, Professor Khromov, Professor Multanovskiy*. She has an ice-hardened steel hull, which is good for cruising in both the Arctic and Antarctic regions. All passengers have access to the navigation bridge. There are several Zodiac landing craft for close-in shore excursions and nature observation trips.

Inside, the limited public rooms consist of a library and lounge/bar. The dining rooms also serve as lecture rooms. This ship does have good medical facilities.

This is expedition-style cruising, in a very small ship with limited facilities. However, it provides a somewhat primitive but genuine adventure experience, taking you to places others only dream about. The bigger ships cannot get this close to Antarctica, but this little vessel will sail you close to the face of the ice continent.

Professor Multanovskiy
★★

Small Ship:	1,753 tons	Cabins (for one person):	9
Lifestyle:	Standard	Cabins (with private balcony):	0
Cruise Line:	Murmansk Shipping	Cabins (wheelchair accessible):	0
Former Names:	-	Cabin Current:	220-volt
Builder:	Wartsila (Finland)	Full-Service Dining Rooms:	1
Original Cost:	n/a	Elevators:	0
Entered Service:	1983	Casino (gaming tables):	No
Registry:	Russia	Slot Machines:	No
Length (ft/m):	234.9/71.6	Swimming Pools (outdoors):	0
Beam (ft/m):	42.0/12.8	Swimming Pools (indoors):	0
Draft (ft/m):	15.0/4.6	Whirlpools:	0
Propulsion/Propellers:	Diesel (2,327kW)/2	Fitness Center:	No
Passenger Decks:	3	Sauna/Steam Room:	Yes/No
Total Crew:	25	Massage:	No
Passengers (lower beds/all berths):	49/49	Self-Service Launderette:	No
Pass. Space Ratio (lower beds/all berths):	35.7/35.7	Dedicated Cinema:	No
Crew/Pass. Ratio (lower beds/all berths):	1.9/1.9	Library:	Yes
Navigation Officers:	Russian	Classification Society:	Russian Shipping Register
Cabins (total):	29		
Size Range (sq ft/sq m):	n/a		
Cabins (outside view):	29		
Cabins (interior/no view):	0		

OVERALL SCORE: 947

(OUT OF A POSSIBLE 2,000 POINTS)

Accommodation: With the exception of a single "suite," almost all cabins are very small and rather clinical. There are two-berth cabins with shower and toilet, or there are two-bed cabins on the lowest deck, whose occupants must share a bathroom.

Dining: There are two dining rooms (the galley is located between them), and all passengers are served in a single seating. The meals are hearty international fare, with no frills. When under charter to various specialist operators such as Quark Expeditions, European chef oversee the food operation

Other Comments: This vessel was originally specially constructed for the former Soviet Union's polar and oceanographic research program and should not be taken as a cruise ship, although it was converted in the early 1990s to carry passengers, and then refurbished in 1996 and fitted out specifically for expedition cruising. Other ships in the same series: *Akademik Boris Petrov, Akademik Golitsyn, Akademik M.A. Laurentiev, Akademik Nikolaj Strakhov, Akademik Shokalskiy, Livonia, Professor Khromov, Professor Molchanov.* This ship is typically operated under charter to various "expedition" cruise companies. She has an ice-hardened steel hull, which is good for cruising in both the Arctic and Antarctic regions. All passengers have access to the navigation bridge. There are several Zodiac landing craft for close-in shore excursions and nature observation trips.

Inside, the limited public rooms consist of a library and lounge/bar. The dining rooms also serve as lecture rooms. This ship does have good medical facilities.

This is expedition-style cruising, in a very small ship with limited facilities. However, it provides a somewhat primitive but genuine adventure experience, taking you to places others only dream about. The bigger ships cannot get this close to Antarctica, but this little vessel will sail you close to the face of the ice continent.

Queen Elizabeth 2
★★★★★ to ★★★ +

Large Ship:	70,327 tons	Cabins (wheelchair accessible):	4
Lifestyle:	Luxury/Premium	Cabin Current:	110/220-volt
Cruise Line:	Cunard Line	Full-Service Dining Rooms:	5
Former Names:	-	Elevators:	13
Builder:	Upper Clyde Shipbuilders (UK)	Casino (gaming tables):	Yes
Original Cost:	£29 million	Slot Machines:	Yes
Entered Service:	May 1969	Swimming Pools (outdoors):	1
Registry:	Great Britain	Swimming Pools (indoors):	1 (+ AquaSpa pool)
Length (ft/m):	962.93/293.50	Whirlpools:	4
Beam (ft/m):	105.1/32.03	Fitness Center:	Yes
Draft (ft/m):	32.4/9.87	Sauna/Steam Room:	Yes/Yes
Propulsion/Propellers: Diesel-electric (99,900kW)/2		Massage:	Yes
Passenger Decks:	13	Self-Service Launderette:	No
Total Crew:	1,015	Dedicated Cinema/Seats:	Yes/530
Passengers (lower beds/all berths):	1,782/1,906	Library:	Yes
Pass. Space Ratio (lower beds/all berths): 39.4/36.8		Classification Society:	Lloyd's Register
Crew/Pass. Ratio (lower beds/all berths):	1.7/1.8		
Navigation Officers:	British		
Cabins (total):	950	**OVERALL SCORE (GRILL CLASS):**	**1,763**
Size Range (sq ft/sq m): 107.0–1,184.0/10.0–110.0		**OVERALL SCORE (CARONIA CLASS):**	**1,625**
Cabins (outside view):	657	**OVERALL SCORE (MAURETANIA CLASS):**	**1,383**
Cabins (interior/no view):	293		
Cabins (for one person):	151	**(OUT OF A POSSIBLE 2,000 POINTS)**	
Cabins (with private balcony):	32		

Accommodation: There is a vast range of accommodation grades and cabin configurations from which to choose. The most exclusive (and, therefore, the most expensive) accommodation can be found in the Queen Elizabeth and Queen Mary split-level penthouses on Signal Deck. Next come another 30 suites on Signal Deck and Sun Deck (several on Sun Deck have private balconies, although some have lifeboat-obstructed views) and ten suites on Boat Deck. Then come the large cabins on Decks 1, 2, and 3, while the smallest outside-view cabins are to be found lower down on Decks 4 and 5 (these have portholes, which tend to make the cabins seem smaller than they are, with little natural light available), and interior (no-view) cabins. Note that when encountering unkind weather conditions on crossings of the North Atlantic, the portholes of Deck 5 cabins may have to be closed. Whichever grade you choose, bathroom cabinets have a lot of storage space — important for anyone choosing this ship for long voyages. Almost all bathrooms were replaced in a 1997 refit, although some that were not replaced are quite tacky in places.

Many of the suites and cabins on Deck 3, 2, 1, Boat Deck, Sports Deck, and Signal Deck feature fine wood-paneled walls, generous closet and drawer space, thick, real wood furniture and large marble bathrooms. Accommodation ranges from sumptuous, understated two-level suites with private balconies, walk-in closets, stocked refrigerators and minibars, and bathrooms large enough for four; to modest interior (no-view) cabins that are compact but quite well equipped. You pay for the amount of space and grade you want, and, more important, the location. Additionally, the accommodation you choose will determine in which of the ship's five restaurants you will dine.

The Penthouse Suites (on Signal Deck and Sun Deck) are truly superb, quiet, and are among the most refined, quiet living spaces at sea. During the ship's 1999 refit, three new suites were added to the list of exclusive living spaces: the Aquitania and Carinthia suites on 2 Deck, and the wheelchair-accessible Caledonia suite on Boat Deck. Occupants of these most exclusive suites have room service food items supplied by chefs from the Queens Grill (during dining hours).

Dining: There are five principal full-service restaurants (all of which include many tables for two, and two informal dining spots: The Lido (breakfast, lunch, and dinner) and The Grill (for lunchtime fast food items only). In order of excellence they are Queens Grill, Britannia Grill, Princess Grill, Caronia Restaurant (very nicely refurbished in 1999) and Mauretania Restaurant. One-seating dining is featured in all except the Mauretania Restaurant, which operates two seatings. There are both smoking and non-smoking sections in all restaurants. The menus are varied, creative, and well balanced, and include spa/light/healthy items.

Casual dinners can be taken in The Lido, a casual dining spot open during the entire day (casual dress code), which has its own galley, bar, and beverage station. The luncheon and midnight buffets provide a good range of foods, although at peak times there are lines at this popular eatery.

Fine dining (with everything cooked to order à la minute) is offered in the most formal restaurant: Queens Grill. This is comparable to some of the best shoreside gourmet restaurants anywhere, with table-side carvings, flambeaus, and outstanding presentation by dedicated British traditional restaurant managers and headwaiters, and individual chairs (no banquette seats) and many tables for two. The cuisine features many traditional British favorites, together with extensive French dishes and regional specialties from around the world.

Some frequent travelers might, however, prefer the smaller and more intimate Britannia Grill or Princess Grill (a room that remains much as it was when the ship debuted more than 30 years ago), which offer almost the same kind of tableside service and fine cuisine. During 2000, the food budget for the ship was cut severely, so you can expect to find some decrease in the quality and variety of foods available.

Other Comments: *Queen Elizabeth 2* is a true ocean liner, with a dark blue hull and single, large funnel, and performs a regular schedule of transatlantic crossings as well as several cruises each year, plus an annual around-the-world cruise (typically from January to April). She is still the fastest, as well as the most integrated, ocean liner in the world (I stress that it is important to think of this ship as an ocean liner rather than as a cruise ship in the more contemporary sense of the word). An excellent range of joint travel programs and tour configurations is integrated into the marketing of this ship. Note that the dress code is mostly formal (but becoming less so since the company's new American owners market to a more casual population that insists on dressing down), in contrast to so many ships where formal dress has all but disappeared.

Originally constructed as a steam turbine ship, she underwent a $160 million refit in Bremen, Germany, in 1986. Her original steam turbines were extracted and exchanged for a Diesel-electric propulsion system, resulting in greater speed, better economy, and more reliability. A new, fatter funnel was constructed, designed better to keep any soot off her expansive open decks. She sports a long foredeck (rather like the long snout of a 4.5-liter vintage Bentley), unsurpassed by any other cruise ship today. That foredeck makes her look powerful, yet at the same time sleek and so graceful.

Over the years, the ship has undergone a number of extensive multimillion dollar interior refurbishments that have included numerous structural changes designed to facilitate better passenger flow and provide greater dining space. Fine wood paneling and more traditional furnishings have replaced many of her original laminates that were all the rage in the 1960s. The decor is now more reminiscent of the ocean liners of yesteryear — which is what her passengers expect.

At the end of 1999, the ship underwent a further $33 million refurbishment (including $19 million on technical items). Following the 1999 refit, bathrooms in all accommodation grades have been entirely replaced. Now all feature marble fixtures and jazzy Art Deco–style toiletry cabinets. Several new suites were added. Other facilities include a large library with over 6,000 books and an integrated Cunard memorabilia shop; there is also a dedicated florist.

Other Comments: Transatlantic Crossings

She is still the fastest passenger ship presently in service, and even at a speed of close to 30 knots there is almost no vibration at the stern. Interestingly, this ship can go backwards faster (19 knots has been recorded — backwards!) than most cruise ships can go forwards (if ever it were necessary to do so). She features a wide range of facilities and public rooms with high ceilings, including garage space for up to 12 cars.

She is a city at sea, and, like any city, there are several parts of town. There are three distinct classes: Grill Class, Caronia Class, and Mauretania Class. Grill Class accommodation consists of outstanding penthouse suites (with butler service only in the Sun Deck and Sports Deck suites and room service food items provided by Queens Grill chefs, a stocked minibar refrigerator, daily fresh fruit, and personalized stationery) and large outside-view cabins (with standard cabin service in One Deck and Two Deck cabins that is quite ordinary). Caronia Class accommodation consists of outside-view double cabins, and interior (no view) and outside-view single cabins, with dining in the beautifully paneled Caronia Restaurant (decorated in an Italian style). Mauretania Class accommodation features the lowest-priced cabin grades, but dining is in two seatings in the Mauretania Restaurant (a large but very comfortable restaurant that has tables for two, four, six, eight, or ten, and many nest dining alcoves). *Note*: the Mauretania Restaurant may operate as a one-seating dining room when the ship is not full.

All passengers enjoy the use of all public rooms, except for the Queens Grill Lounge (reserved exclusively for Grill Class passengers). The Queens Grill has its own separate galley, the best waiters and service, a fine, formal atmosphere for dinner, and food that can be best described as memorable (you can also order from the à la carte menu, as well as "off-menu"). The Britannia Grill, Princess Grill, and Mauretania Restaurant share the same galley, but the service and setting in the intimate Britannia Grill and Princess Grill is far superior. The Caronia and Mauretania Restaurants have good, creative, and varied menus, with service provided by the least experienced waiters.

How nice that *QE2* now has those lovely real wood "steamer" deckchairs. Those on Sun Deck (also known as the "helicopter deck") can be reserved for a small fee when crossing the Atlantic. Grill Class is the most desirable and sophisticated way to cross the Atlantic; Caronia Class (formerly known as first class) is good but definitely not what it used to be, while Mauretania Class (formerly known as transatlantic class) provides comfortable travel in a price-sensitive setting.

In the final analysis, *Queen Elizabeth 2* is a fine transatlantic liner that provides a very civilized experience. It is ideal for those who do not like to fly, as well as for those who enjoy a quintessentially British style of life — and the grace and pace of days at sea without ports of call. The large amount of personal luggage allowed is also especially useful for anyone relocating between continents, or for extended vacations. Arriving in either New York or Southampton after six days of not having to lift a finger often proves to be a bittersweet anticlimax for most passengers — a disquieting reminder that life ashore has to be faced after the calming effects of *QE2* on one's inner being. Indeed, there is probably nothing more pleasing to the soul than a transatlantic crossing, being cosseted in the finery of dining in either of the three grill restaurants with their fine cuisine, presentation, and overall dining experience. Although gratuities are not included in the cruise fare, they are automatically charged to your on-board account. In addition, 15% is added to all bar, wine, and health spa/salon bills.

Other Comments: Cruises
The latest extensive refit in December 1999 resulted in the most cohesive interior decor the ship has had in years. The public rooms and passenger hallways were refreshed and color-coordinated for the better. The Penthouse Suites are truly superb and quiet — and are among the most refined living spaces at sea (all bathrooms were replaced in 1996).

Ship buffs can enjoy the Heritage Trail, a shipwide display consisting of more than two dozen exhibits of Cunard ocean liner history and ship models, as well as some superb paintings of former Cunard liners, spread around the ship. It includes a stunning 16-ft-long illuminated model of the company's 1907 Mauretania (strangely located outside the Caronia Restaurant, while a model of the former Caronia is located in the Mauretania Restaurant). There is a great abundance of memorabilia items (some further items are available for sale in the memorabilia bookshop/library).

There is a substantial amount of fine artwork, sculptures, and paintings. Two beautiful paintings hang in the "D" Deck foyer between Boat Deck and Upper Deck. They are the 1948 painting of H. M. Queen Elizabeth, the Queen Mother, by Sir Oswald Birley (this used to be aboard RMS *Queen Elizabeth*); and the 1949 painting of Princess Elizabeth and Prince Philip, which used to be aboard RMS *Caronia*.

Facilities include a Grand Lounge (a dedicated show lounge with thrust stage, three seating tiers, and a good sound system); Tour and Travel Center (for shore excursions, theater tickets, and concierge services); Business Center; Shopping Concourse, which features decent brand-name merchandise at high European prices (including a new Harrods shop); and a Cunard Collection shop featuring clothing and special Cunard logo items. The Yacht Club is a delightfully nautical, practical, and popular aft-facing room that becomes a nightclub (afternoon recorded classical concerts here are a bonus). An extensive indoor spa includes a ten-station AquaSpa, and several comfortable treatment rooms (treatments are at extra cost); fitness center; and beauty salons for men and women. There is also a safety deposit center, passenger accounts office, and an automated telephone system.

The Queens Room is a real ballroom, with a large dance floor, for society dancing to a big band (during the day it is a quiet, stately room with very comfortable chairs). The Midships Lobby, the ship's embarkation point, has a distinctive, ocean liner image, with fine birds-eye maple woodwork and wraparound murals of the former and present Cunard Queens. A large computer center (with daily lectures and 22 Micron computer workstations) is a real bonus. There is also a dedicated florist and a large self-service launderette (no charge). The Lido, a large, informal bistro dining spot with 24-hour hot beverage stations, is also a bonus on cruises, and all espresso and cappuccino coffees are free. The elegant Chart Room Bar is a charming, quiet drinking spot (it contains a piano from the liner *Queen Mary*).

There is a large cinema/concert hall (with 530 seats), complete with balcony level and nine-foot-long Bosendorfer piano. The Golden Lion Pub features Victorian decor and selection of over 20 beers (both bottled and draft). There is also a superb library, much loved by passengers (without doubt one of the best at sea, with over 7,000 books, in about a dozen languages), which, combined with a memorabilia bookshop, features professional librarians. The Player's Club Casino features fitting Art Deco and blond wood decor.

QE2 has British officers, although the hotel staff is a very international mix, fairly attentive and service-oriented, though many do not speak English well, as is the case aboard so many ships today. Entertainment comes in a good mix, with an extensive array of lecture programs. The ship has an excellent laundry, good dry-cleaning facilities, and self-service (no charge) launderettes. There are fine English nannies and good facilities for children. This ship offers refined living at sea for those in upper-grade accommodation — otherwise she is just a large ship, albeit with superb facilities. Tender ports should be avoided whenever possible, however; although the ship's double-deck shore tenders are fine, practical units.

MORE ABOUT *QE2*

Physically challenged passengers will appreciate four cabins specially equipped for wheelchair-bound passengers, created using the guidelines of the American Disabled Association (ADA). The cabin door is wide enough for a wheelchair (no "lip"); the bathroom door slides open electronically at the touch of a button (located at wheelchair height), and the floor is flat. The full-length bathtub has special assist handles, and the toilet has grab bars. Closets have hanging rails with hydraulically balanced lever to lower them towards the outside of the closet, to the right height. There is an intercom, alarm, and remote controls for lighting, curtains, and doors. These cabins are also good for the hearing-impaired, with three brightly colored, lighted signs on the cabin bulkhead, as well as a telephone system for the deaf. While these cabins are specially designed for the physically challenged, their ingenious design would not upset any passenger.

The Orient Express Boat Train is chartered by Cunard Line — it runs between London's Waterloo Station and Southampton Docks, and pulls up right alongside the Ocean Terminal to connect with all transatlantic voyages of the ship. This special train consists exclusively of Pullman carriages, richly paneled and fitted with individual deep-upholstery seats, and serving complimentary hot canapés and champagne. Passengers traveling from London to Southampton can complete all formalities and ship check-in procedures on the train, then simply walk directly on board *QE2* upon arrival. Baggage loaded onto the train's baggage carriage in Waterloo is delivered directly to your cabin.

The Cunard/British Airways' Concorde program is also really worth experiencing. Combining a *QE2* transatlantic crossing with a one-way British Airways Concorde flight is, without doubt, the ultimate way to go. Six days one way, and 3 hours, 15 minutes the other way is one of the great travel experiences available today. And, with special, Cunard-subsidized fares, there is no excuse for not indulging.

In 1997 *QE2* became the first cruise ship to have an e-mail address. She has traveled more than 4 million nautical miles and features the best of high-tech facilities blended with traditional ocean liner facilities. She is much like a well-worn shoe — comfortable, but a little tired and frayed around the edges in places, which makes her a difficult ship to evaluate. However, she has a wonderful, loyal following, and provides the civilized way to cross the North Atlantic Ocean with the space, pace, and grace of a real Cunard liner.

If you occupy one of the top-level (Grill Class) suites, with butler service and all the fine trimmings, your experience should be nothing short of superb: highly civilized, quiet living at sea. However, for the many that occupy lower-grade accommodations (Caronia Class and Mauretania Class), you may find that the ship does not quite come up to the high expectations that most passengers have. Will she survive the onslaught of the mega-ships? I believe she will, simply because she isn't one of them, and she does have a lifestyle that somehow will still be in vogue when all around her have become floating night clubs.

Weak Points: The ship is now over 30 years old, and it is difficult to compare her with the latest contemporary ships that have more light, multiple balconies (not practical on crossings of the North Atlantic), and more high-tech facilities. Although the interior passageways are wide, there is a feeling of being enclosed, and cabins with portholes simply seem dated (remember, however, that she is an ocean liner and not a cruise ship). Unfortunately, there is no forward observation lounge — as there was when the ship was first constructed. Missing are a few grand, flowing staircases, the air of romance, and the high standard of maintenance and food service personnel of the ocean liners of former years. The show lounge is poor when compared with those aboard newer ships, and the sight lines and seating should be better than they are. The cabins on Deck 5 (the lowest of the accommodation decks) are adequate, but no more. Some 96 bathrooms remain to be completed (from the 1996 refit when all bathrooms were scheduled to be completely remodeled). Following recent refurbishments, small, intimate hideaway bars are fewer in number. You cannot have just a sauna or use of the steam room without paying a charge for a "Spa Experience" package. As a "classless" cruise ship, the layout is rather disjointed, but as a transatlantic liner, the layout is beautifully designed to keep you in your place.

R One
★★★★

Mid-Size Ship:	30,277 tons	Cabins (for one person):	0
Lifestyle:	Premium	Cabins (with private balcony):	232
Cruise Line:	Renaissance Cruises	Cabins (wheelchair accessible):	3
Former Names:	-	Cabin Current:	110/220-volt
Builder:	Chantiers de l'Atlantique (France)	Full-Service Dining Rooms:	4
Original Cost:	$150 million	Elevators:	4
Entered Service:	July 1998	Casino (gaming tables):	Yes
Registry:	Liberia	Slot Machines:	Yes
Length (ft/m):	593.7/181.0	Swimming Pools (outdoors):	1
Beam (ft/m):	83.5/25.5	Swimming Pools (indoors):	0
Draft (ft/m):	19.5/6.0	Whirlpools:	2 (+ 1 thalassotherapy)
Propulsion/Propellers:	Diesel (18,600kW)/2	Fitness Center:	Yes
Passenger Decks:	9	Sauna/Steam Room:	No/Yes
Total Crew:	373	Massage:	Yes
Passengers (lower beds/all berths):	684/824	Self-Service Launderette:	Yes
Pass. Space Ratio (lower beds/all berths):	44.2/36.7	Dedicated Cinema:	No
Crew/Pass. Ratio (lower beds/all berths):	1.8/2.2	Library:	Yes
Navigation Officers:	European	Classification Society:	Bureau Veritas
Cabins (total):	342		
Size Range (sq ft/sq m):	145.3–962.0/13.5–293.2		
Cabins (outside view):	317		
Cabins (interior/no view):	25		

OVERALL SCORE: 1,548

(OUT OF A POSSIBLE 2,000 POINTS)

Accommodation: There are eight cabin categories. All of the standard interior (no view) and outside-view cabins (the lowest four grades) are extremely compact units, and extremely tight for two persons (particularly for cruises longer than five days). They feature twin beds (or queen-size bed), with good under-bed storage areas, personal safe, vanity desk with large mirror, good closet and drawer space (in rich, dark woods), and bathrobe. Color TVs carry a major news channel (where obtainable), plus a sports channel, and several round-the-clock movie channels.

The cabins with private balconies (66% of all cabins) have partial, and not full, balcony partitions, sliding glass doors, and, due to good design and layout, only 14 cabins on Deck 6 have lifeboat-obstructed views. The bathrooms, which have tiled floors and plain walls, are compact, standard units, and include a shower stall with a strong, removable hand held shower unit, hair dryer, 100% cotton towels, toiletries storage shelves, and retractable clothesline. Personal toiletry items include soap, shampoo, body lotion, shower cap, and shoeshine mitt.

There are 52 mini-suites, which in reality are large cabins, since the sleeping and lounge areas are not divided. While not overly large, the bathrooms feature a good-size bathtub and ample space for storing personal toiletry items. The living area features a refrigerated minibar, lounge area with breakfast table, and a balcony with two plastic chairs and a table.

The ten Owner's Suites provide the most spacious of accommodation, and are fine, large living spaces located in the forward most and aft most sections of the accommodation decks. Those that overlook the stern, on Decks 6, 7, and 8, are particularly nice, although they are subject to more movement and some vibration. Owner's Suites have more extensive private balconies that really are private and cannot be overlooked by anyone from the decks above. There is an entrance foyer, living room, bedroom, CD player (with selection of audio discs), fully tiled bathroom with Jacuzzi bathtub (no bath foam is provided, however), and a small guest bathroom.

Dining: Flexibility and choice are what the R-class ships' dining facilities are all about. There are four different restaurants: The Club Restaurant, which is the equivalent of a main dining room, has 338 seats and a raised central section. There are large ocean-view windows on three sides, several prime tables overlooking the stern, and a small bandstand for occasional live dinner music. The menu changes daily for both lunch and dinner. The Italian Restaurant has 96 seats, windows along two sides, and a set menu (together with added daily chef's specials). The Grill Room is an "American steak house" and has 98 seats, windows along two sides, and a set menu (together with added daily chef's specials). The Panorama has

455

seats for 154 indoors — not enough during cruises to cold areas or in the winter months — and 186 outdoors (it's too cold to sit outside in the winter months). It is open for breakfast, lunch, and casual dinners. It is the ship's self-serve buffet restaurant and incorporates a small pizzeria and grill. Basic salads, meat carving station, and a reasonable selection of cheeses are featured daily.

All restaurants feature open-seating dining, so you dine when you want, with whom you wish, although reservations are necessary in the Italian Restaurant and The Grill, where there are mostly tables for four or six (there are few tables for two). Service in all the restaurants is generally very good and attentive. In addition, there is a Poolside Grill Bar. Note that all cappuccino and espresso coffees cost extra.

Other Comments: Renaissance Cruises is the cruise industry's first totally nonsmoking cruise line. The R-class ships are a series of eight such ships. The exterior design manages to balance the ship's high sides by combining a deep blue hull with the white superstructure and large, square blue funnel.

Lido Deck features a swimming pool, and good sunbathing space, while one of the aft decks has a thalassaotherapy pool (it's part of a spa package and incurs an extra charge). A jogging track circles the swimming pool deck (but one deck above). The uppermost outdoors deck includes a golf driving net and shuffleboard court.

The interior decor is quite stunning and elegant, a throwback to ship decor of the ocean liners of the 'twenties and 'thirties. This includes detailed ceiling cornices, both real and faux wrought iron staircase railings, leather-paneled walls, trompe l'oeil ceilings, rich carpeting in hallways with an Oriental rug–look center section, and many other interesting (and expensive-looking) decorative touches.

The staircase in the main, two-decks-high foyer will remind you of something similar in a blockbuster hit about a certain ship, where the stars, Kate Winslet and Leonardo DiCaprio, met. Regular Renaissance Cruises passengers will probably be pleased with the fine taste with which her interiors have been designed and executed. The company's brochure is definitely understated.

The public rooms are basically spread over three decks. This is totally a nonsmoking ship (there is no smoking anywhere, including cabins, dining room, public rooms, or on the open decks, although the crew have their own smoking room).

The reception hall (lobby) features a staircase with intricate wrought iron railings. A large observation lounge called the Horizon Bar is located high atop ship. This features a long bar with forward views (for the barmen, that is) and a stack of distracting large-screen TVs; there's also an array of slot machines and bar counter-top electronic gaming machines.

There are plenty of bars, including one in each of the restaurant entrances. Perhaps the nicest of all bars and lounges is the casino bar/lounge, a beautiful room reminiscent of London's grand hotels. It features an inviting marble fireplace (in fact there are three such fireplaces aboard) and comfortable sofas and individual chairs.

The Library is a beautiful, grand room, designed in the Regency style, and features a fireplace, a high, indented, trompe l'oeil ceiling, and an excellent selection of books, as well as some very comfortable wingback chairs with footstools and sofas you could sleep on.

Renaissance Cruises provides a seamless cruise and tour package, geared specifically to North American passengers, at a price that is very hard to beat, considering the destination-rich itineraries, together with pre- and post-cruise land stays at high-quality hotels and including all transfers. You should experience a fine, hassle-free cruise vacation package aboard this or other R-class ships. Renaissance Cruises also provides a "vacation guarantee" that is automatically included with your cruise purchase.

Prices are kept low because the company packages its product well and saves money in other ways. There may not be marble bathroom fittings, or caviar and other (more expensive) niceties, but the value for money is really excellent. There are no captain's cocktail parties or interdenominational church services, but there is plenty of entertainment if you want it. High-quality hotels before and after your cruise, and all transfers, are included.

Dining staff gratuities are extremely high, however, at $15 per day per person. They are pooled, due to the fact that several different waiters in each of the four dining spots will serve you during the cruise (this means, however, that waiters don't get to know your likes, dislikes, and preferences). Also, 15% is added to all bar accounts, and the company suggests another $5 per day for the cabin stewardess. Thus, for a five-day cruise, you should allow $100 per person, and for a ten-day cruise, $200 per person.

Weak Points: There is no wraparound promenade deck outdoors, although there is a small jogging track around the perimeter of the swimming pool, and port and starboard side decks. There are no wooden decks outdoors; instead, they are covered by a sand-colored rubberized material. The charge of $20 to use the thalassotherapy pool is excessive. There is no sauna. The room service menu is extremely limited. Suggested gratuities are high. Stairways, although carpeted, are tinny. In order to keep the prices low, the air routing to get to/from your ship is often not the most direct.

R Two
★★★★

Mid-Size Ship:	30,277 tons	Cabins (for one person):	0
Lifestyle:	Premium	Cabins (with private balcony):	232
Cruise Line:	Renaissance Cruises	Cabins (wheelchair accessible):	3
Former Names:	-	Cabin Current:	110/220-volt
Builder:	Chantiers de l'Atlantique (France)	Full-Service Dining Rooms:	4
Original Cost:	$150 million	Elevators:	4
Entered Service:	July 1998	Casino (gaming tables):	Yes
Registry:	Liberia	Slot Machines:	Yes
Length (ft/m):	593.7/181.0	Swimming Pools (outdoors):	1
Beam (ft/m):	83.5/25.5	Swimming Pools (indoors):	0
Draft (ft/m):	19.5/6.0	Whirlpools:	2 (+ 1 thalassotherapy)
Propulsion/Propellers:	Diesel (18,600kW)/2	Fitness Center:	Yes
Passenger Decks:	9	Sauna/Steam Room:	No/Yes
Total Crew:	373	Massage:	Yes
Passengers (lower beds/all berths):	684/824	Self-Service Launderette:	Yes
Pass. Space Ratio (lower beds/all berths):	44.2/36.7	Dedicated Cinema:	No
Crew/Pass. Ratio (lower beds/all berths):	1.8/2.2	Library:	Yes
Navigation Officers:	European	Classification Society:	Bureau Veritas
Cabins (total):	342		
Size Range (sq ft/sq m):	145.3–962.0/13.5–293.2		
Cabins (outside view):	317	**OVERALL SCORE:**	**1,548**
Cabins (interior/no view):	25	**(OUT OF A POSSIBLE 2,000 POINTS)**	

Accommodation: There are eight cabin categories. All of the standard interior (no view) and outside-view cabins (the lowest four grades) are extremely compact units, and extremely tight for two persons (particularly for cruises longer than five days). They feature twin beds (or queen-size bed), with good under-bed storage areas, personal safe, vanity desk with large mirror, good closet and drawer space (in rich, dark woods), and bathrobe. Color TVs carry a major news channel (where obtainable), plus a sports channel, and several round-the-clock movie channels.

The cabins with private balconies (66% of all cabins) have partial, and not full, balcony partitions, sliding glass doors, and, due to good design and layout, only 14 cabins on Deck 6 have lifeboat-obstructed views. The bathrooms, which have tiled floors and plain walls, are compact, standard units, and include a shower stall with a strong, removable hand held shower unit, hair dryer, 100% cotton towels, toiletries storage shelves, and retractable clothesline. Personal toiletry items include soap, shampoo, body lotion, shower cap, and shoeshine mitt.

There are 52 mini-suites, which in reality are large cabins, since the sleeping and lounge areas are not divided. While not overly large, the bathrooms feature a good-size bathtub and ample space for storing personal toiletry items. The living area features a refrigerated minibar, lounge area with breakfast table, and a balcony with two plastic chairs and a table.

The ten Owner's Suites provide the most spacious of accommodation, and are fine, large living spaces located in the forward most and aft most sections of the accommodation decks. Those that overlook the stern, on Decks 6, 7, and 8, are particularly nice, although they are subject to more movement and some vibration. Owner's Suites have more extensive private balconies that really are private and cannot be overlooked by anyone from the decks above. There is an entrance foyer, living room, bedroom, CD player (with selection of audio discs), fully tiled bathroom with Jacuzzi bathtub (no bath foam is provided, however), and a small guest bathroom.

Dining: Flexibility and choice are what the R-class ships' dining facilities are all about. There are four different restaurants: The Club Restaurant, which is the equivalent of a main dining room, has 338 seats and a raised central section. There are large ocean-view windows on three sides, several prime tables overlooking the stern, and a small bandstand for occasional live dinner music. The menu changes daily for both lunch and dinner. The Italian Restaurant has 96 seats, windows along two sides, and a set menu (together with added daily chef's specials). The Grill Room is an "American steak house" and has 98 seats, windows along two sides, and a set menu (together with added daily chef's specials). The Panorama has

seats for 154 indoors — not enough during cruises to cold areas or in the winter months — and 186 out-doors (it's too cold to sit outside in the winter months). It is open for breakfast, lunch, and casual dinners. It is the ship's self-serve buffet restaurant and incorporates a small pizzeria and grill. Basic salads, meat carving station, and a reasonable selection of cheeses are featured daily.

All restaurants feature open-seating dining, so you dine when you want, with whom you wish, although reservations are necessary in the Italian Restaurant and The Grill, where there are mostly tables for four or six (there are few tables for two). Service in all the restaurants is generally very good and atten-tive. In addition, there is a Poolside Grill Bar. Note that all cappuccino and espresso coffees cost extra.

Other Comments: Renaissance Cruises is the cruise industry's first totally nonsmoking cruise line. The R-class ships are a series of eight such ships. The exterior design manages to balance the ship's high sides by combining a deep blue hull with the white superstructure and large, square blue funnel.

Lido Deck features a swimming pool and good sunbathing space, while one of the aft decks has a thalassaotherapy pool (it's part of a spa package and incurs an extra charge). A jogging track circles the swimming pool deck (but one deck above). The uppermost outdoor deck includes a golf driving net and shuffleboard court.

The interior decor is quite stunning and elegant, a throwback to ship decor of the ocean liners of the 'twenties and 'thirties. This includes detailed ceiling cornices, both real and faux wrought iron staircase railings, leather-paneled walls, trompe l'oeil ceilings, rich carpeting in hallways with an Oriental rug–like center section, and many other interesting (and expensive-looking) decorative touches.

The staircase in the main, two-decks-high foyer will remind you of something similar in a block-buster hit about a certain ship, where the stars, Kate Winslet and Leonardo DiCaprio, met. Regular Renaissance Cruises passengers will probably be pleased with the fine taste with which her interiors have been designed and executed. The company's brochure is definitely understated.

The public rooms are basically spread over three decks. This is totally a nonsmoking ship (there is no smoking anywhere, including cabins, dining room, public rooms, or on the open decks, although the crew have their own smoking room).

The reception hall (lobby) features a staircase with intricate wrought iron railings. A large observa-tion lounge called the Horizon Bar is located high atop ship. This features a long bar with forward views (for the barmen, that is) and a stack of distracting large-screen TVs; there's also an array of slot machines and bar counter-top electronic gaming machines.

There are plenty of bars, including one in each of the restaurant entrances. Perhaps the nicest of all bars and lounges is the casino bar/lounge, a beautiful room reminiscent of London's grand hotels. It fea-tures an inviting marble fireplace (in fact there are three such fireplaces aboard) and comfortable sofas and individual chairs.

The Library is a beautiful, grand room, designed in the Regency style, and features a fireplace, a high, indented, trompe l'oeil ceiling, and an excellent selection of books, as well as some very comfort-able wingback chairs with footstools and sofas you could sleep on.

Renaissance Cruises provides a seamless cruise and tour package, geared specifically to North American passengers, at a price that is very hard to beat, considering the destination-rich itineraries, together with pre- and post-cruise land stays at high-quality hotels and including all transfers. You should experience a fine, hassle-free cruise vacation package aboard this or other R-class ships. Renaissance Cruises also provides a "vacation guarantee" that is automatically included with your cruise purchase.

Prices are kept low because the company packages its product well and saves money in other ways. There may not be marble bathroom fittings, or caviar and other (more expensive) niceties, but the value for money is really excellent. There are no captain's cocktail parties or interdenominational church serv-ices, but there is plenty of entertainment if you want it. High-quality hotels before and after your cruise, and all transfers, are included.

Dining staff gratuities are extremely high, however, at $15 per day per person. They are pooled, due to the fact that several different waiters in each of the four dining spots will serve you during the cruise (this means, however, that waiters don't get to know your likes, dislikes, and preferences). Also, 15% is added to all bar accounts, and the company suggests another $5 per day for the cabin stewardess. Thus, for a five-day cruise, you should allow $100 per person, and for a ten-day cruise, $200 per person.

Weak Points: There is no wraparound promenade deck outdoors, although there is a small jogging track around the perimeter of the swimming pool, and port and starboard side decks. There are no wooden decks outdoors; instead, they are covered by a sand-colored rubberized material. The charge of $20 to use the thalassotherapy pool is excessive. There is no sauna. The room service menu is extremely limited. Suggested gratuities are high. Stairways, although carpeted, are tinny. In order to keep the prices low, the air routing to get to/from your ship is often not the most direct.

R Three
★★★★

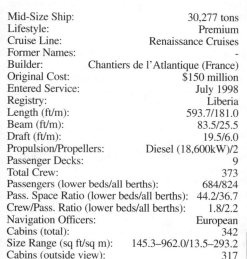

Mid-Size Ship:	30,277 tons	Cabins (for one person):	0
Lifestyle:	Premium	Cabins (with private balcony):	232
Cruise Line:	Renaissance Cruises	Cabins (wheelchair accessible):	3
Former Names:	-	Cabin Current:	110/220-volt
Builder:	Chantiers de l'Atlantique (France)	Full-Service Dining Rooms:	4
Original Cost:	$150 million	Elevators:	4
Entered Service:	July 1998	Casino (gaming tables):	Yes
Registry:	Liberia	Slot Machines:	Yes
Length (ft/m):	593.7/181.0	Swimming Pools (outdoors):	1
Beam (ft/m):	83.5/25.5	Swimming Pools (indoors):	0
Draft (ft/m):	19.5/6.0	Whirlpools:	2 (+ 1 thalassotherapy)
Propulsion/Propellers:	Diesel (18,600kW)/2	Fitness Center:	Yes
Passenger Decks:	9	Sauna/Steam Room:	No/Yes
Total Crew:	373	Massage:	Yes
Passengers (lower beds/all berths):	684/824	Self-Service Launderette:	Yes
Pass. Space Ratio (lower beds/all berths):	44.2/36.7	Dedicated Cinema:	No
Crew/Pass. Ratio (lower beds/all berths):	1.8/2.2	Library:	Yes
Navigation Officers:	European	Classification Society:	Bureau Veritas
Cabins (total):	342		
Size Range (sq ft/sq m):	145.3–962.0/13.5–293.2		
Cabins (outside view):	317		
Cabins (interior/no view):	25		

OVERALL SCORE: 1,548
(OUT OF A POSSIBLE 2,000 POINTS)

Accommodation: There are eight cabin categories. All of the standard interior (no view) and outside-view cabins (the lowest four grades) are extremely compact units, and extremely tight for two persons (particularly for cruises longer than five days). They feature twin beds (or queen-size bed), with good under-bed storage areas, personal safe, vanity desk with large mirror, good closet and drawer space (in rich, dark woods), and bathrobe. Color TVs carry a major news channel (where obtainable), plus a sports channel, and several round-the-clock movie channels.

The cabins with private balconies (66% of all cabins) have partial, and not full, balcony partitions, sliding glass doors, and, due to good design and layout, only 14 cabins on Deck 6 have lifeboat-obstructed views. The bathrooms, which have tiled floors and plain walls, are compact, standard units, and include a shower stall with a strong, removable hand held shower unit, hair dryer, 100% cotton towels, toiletries storage shelves, and retractable clothesline. Personal toiletry items include soap, shampoo, body lotion, shower cap, and shoeshine mitt.

There are 52 mini-suites, which in reality are large cabins, since the sleeping and lounge areas are not divided. While not overly large, the bathrooms feature a good-size bathtub and ample space for storing personal toiletry items. The living area features a refrigerated minibar, lounge area with breakfast table, and a balcony with two plastic chairs and a table.

The ten Owner's Suites provide the most spacious of accommodation, and are fine, large living spaces located in the forward most and aft most sections of the accommodation decks. Those that overlook the stern, on Decks 6, 7, and 8, are particularly nice, although they are subject to more movement and some vibration. Owner's Suites have more extensive private balconies that really are private and cannot be overlooked by anyone from the decks above. There is an entrance foyer, living room, bedroom, CD player (with selection of audio discs), fully tiled bathroom with Jacuzzi bathtub (no bath foam is provided, however), and a small guest bathroom.

Dining: Flexibility and choice are what the R-class ships' dining facilities are all about. There are four different restaurants: The Club Restaurant, which is the equivalent of a main dining room, has 338 seats and a raised central section. There are large ocean-view windows on three sides, several prime tables overlooking the stern, and a small bandstand for occasional live dinner music. The menu changes daily for both lunch and dinner. The Italian Restaurant has 96 seats, windows along two sides, and a set menu (together with added daily chef's specials). The Grill Room is an "American steak house" and has 98 seats, windows along two sides, and a set menu (together with added daily chef's specials). The Panorama has

459

seats for 154 indoors — not enough during cruises to cold areas or in the winter months — and 186 out-doors (it's too cold to sit outside in the winter months). It is open for breakfast, lunch, and casual dinners. It is the ship's self-serve buffet restaurant and incorporates a small pizzeria and grill. Basic salads, meat carving station, and a reasonable selection of cheeses are featured daily.

All restaurants feature open-seating dining, so you dine when you want, with whom you wish, although reservations are necessary in the Italian Restaurant and The Grill, where there are mostly tables for four or six (there are few tables for two). Service in all the restaurants is generally very good and atten-tive. In addition, there is a Poolside Grill Bar. Note that all cappuccino and espresso coffees cost extra.

Other Comments: Renaissance Cruises is the cruise industry's first totally nonsmoking cruise line. The R-class ships are a series of eight such ships. The exterior design manages to balance the ship's high sides by combining a deep blue hull with the white superstructure and large, square blue funnel.

Lido Deck features a swimming pool and good sunbathing space, while one of the aft decks has a thalassaotherapy pool (it's part of a spa package and incurs an extra charge). A jogging track circles the swimming pool deck (but one deck above). The uppermost outdoor deck includes a golf driving net and shuffleboard court.

The interior decor is quite stunning and elegant, a throwback to ship decor of the ocean liners of the 'twenties and 'thirties. This includes detailed ceiling cornices, both real and faux wrought iron staircase railings, leather-paneled walls, trompe l'oeil ceilings, rich carpeting in hallways with an Oriental rug–like center section, and many other interesting (and expensive-looking) decorative touches.

The staircase in the main, two-decks-high foyer will remind you of something similar in a block-buster hit about a certain ship, where the stars, Kate Winslet and Leonardo DiCaprio, met. Regular Renaissance Cruises passengers will probably be pleased with the fine taste with which her interiors have been designed and executed. The company's brochure is definitely understated.

The public rooms are basically spread over three decks. This is totally a nonsmoking ship (there is no smoking anywhere, including cabins, dining room, public rooms, or on the open decks, although the crew have their own smoking room).

The reception hall (lobby) features a staircase with intricate wrought iron railings. A large observa-tion lounge called the Horizon Bar is located high atop ship. This features a long bar with forward views (for the barmen, that is) and a stack of distracting large-screen TVs; there's also an array of slot machines and bar counter-top electronic gaming machines.

There are plenty of bars, including one in each of the restaurant entrances. Perhaps the nicest of all bars and lounges is the casino bar/lounge, a beautiful room reminiscent of London's grand hotels. It fea-tures an inviting marble fireplace (in fact there are three such fireplaces aboard) and comfortable sofas and individual chairs.

The Library is a beautiful, grand room, designed in the Regency style, and features a fireplace, a high, indented, trompe l'oeil ceiling, and an excellent selection of books, as well as some very comfort-able wingback chairs with footstools and sofas you could sleep on.

Renaissance Cruises provides a seamless cruise and tour package, geared specifically to North American passengers, at a price that is very hard to beat, considering the destination-rich itineraries, together with pre- and post-cruise land stays at high-quality hotels and including all transfers. You should experience a fine, hassle-free cruise vacation package aboard this or other R-class ships. Renaissance Cruises also provides a "vacation guarantee" that is automatically included with your cruise purchase.

Prices are kept low because the company packages its product well and saves money in other ways. There may not be marble bathroom fittings, or caviar and other (more expensive) niceties, but the value for money is really excellent. There are no captain's cocktail parties or interdenominational church serv-ices, but there is plenty of entertainment if you want it. High-quality hotels before and after your cruise, and all transfers, are included.

Dining staff gratuities are extremely high, however, at $15 per day per person. They are pooled, due to the fact that several different waiters in each of the four dining spots will serve you during the cruise (this means, however, that waiters don't get to know your likes, dislikes, and preferences). Also, 15% is added to all bar accounts, and the company suggests another $5 per day for the cabin stewardess. Thus, for a five-day cruise, you should allow $100 per person, and for a ten-day cruise, $200 per person.

Weak Points: There is no wraparound promenade deck outdoors, although there is a small jogging track around the perimeter of the swimming pool, and port and starboard side decks. There are no wooden decks outdoors; instead, they are covered by a sand-colored rubberized material. The charge of $20 to use the thalassotherapy pool is excessive. There is no sauna. The room service menu is extremely limited. Suggested gratuities are high. Stairways, although carpeted, are tinny. In order to keep the prices low, the air routing to get to/from your ship is often not the most direct.

R Four
★★★★

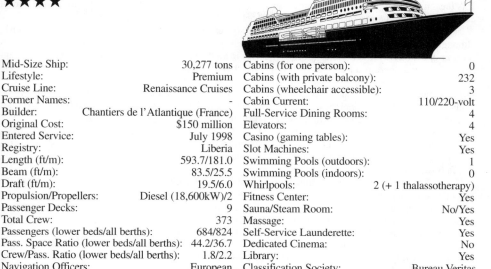

Mid-Size Ship:	30,277 tons	Cabins (for one person):	0
Lifestyle:	Premium	Cabins (with private balcony):	232
Cruise Line:	Renaissance Cruises	Cabins (wheelchair accessible):	3
Former Names:	-	Cabin Current:	110/220-volt
Builder:	Chantiers de l'Atlantique (France)	Full-Service Dining Rooms:	4
Original Cost:	$150 million	Elevators:	4
Entered Service:	July 1998	Casino (gaming tables):	Yes
Registry:	Liberia	Slot Machines:	Yes
Length (ft/m):	593.7/181.0	Swimming Pools (outdoors):	1
Beam (ft/m):	83.5/25.5	Swimming Pools (indoors):	0
Draft (ft/m):	19.5/6.0	Whirlpools:	2 (+ 1 thalassotherapy)
Propulsion/Propellers:	Diesel (18,600kW)/2	Fitness Center:	Yes
Passenger Decks:	9	Sauna/Steam Room:	No/Yes
Total Crew:	373	Massage:	Yes
Passengers (lower beds/all berths):	684/824	Self-Service Launderette:	Yes
Pass. Space Ratio (lower beds/all berths):	44.2/36.7	Dedicated Cinema:	No
Crew/Pass. Ratio (lower beds/all berths):	1.8/2.2	Library:	Yes
Navigation Officers:	European	Classification Society:	Bureau Veritas
Cabins (total):	342		
Size Range (sq ft/sq m):	145.3–962.0/13.5–293.2		
Cabins (outside view):	317		
Cabins (interior/no view):	25		

OVERALL SCORE: 1,548
(OUT OF A POSSIBLE 2,000 POINTS)

Accommodation: There are eight cabin categories. All of the standard interior (no view) and outside-view cabins (the lowest four grades) are extremely compact units, and extremely tight for two persons (particularly for cruises longer than five days). They feature twin beds (or queen-size bed), with good under-bed storage areas, personal safe, vanity desk with large mirror, good closet and drawer space (in rich, dark woods), and bathrobe. Color TVs carry a major news channel (where obtainable), plus a sports channel, and several round-the-clock movie channels.

The cabins with private balconies (66% of all cabins) have partial, and not full, balcony partitions, sliding glass doors, and, due to good design and layout, only 14 cabins on Deck 6 have lifeboat-obstructed views. The bathrooms, which have tiled floors and plain walls, are compact, standard units and include a shower stall with a strong, removable hand held shower unit, hair dryer, 100% cotton towels, toiletries storage shelves, and retractable clothesline. Personal toiletry items include soap, shampoo, body lotion, shower cap, and shoeshine mitt.

There are 52 mini-suites, which in reality are large cabins, since the sleeping and lounge areas are not divided. While not overly large, the bathrooms feature a good-size bathtub and ample space for storing personal toiletry items. The living area features a refrigerated minibar, lounge area with breakfast table, and a balcony with two plastic chairs and a table.

The ten Owner's Suites provide the most spacious of accommodation, and are fine, large living spaces located in the forward most and aft most sections of the accommodation decks. Those that overlook the stern, on Decks 6, 7, and 8, are particularly nice, although they are subject to more movement and some vibration. Owner's Suites have more extensive private balconies that really are private and cannot be overlooked by anyone from the decks above. There is an entrance foyer, living room, bedroom, CD player (with selection of audio discs), fully tiled bathroom with Jacuzzi bathtub (no bath foam is provided, however), and a small guest bathroom.

Dining: Flexibility and choice are what the R-class ships' dining facilities are all about. There are four different restaurants: The Club Restaurant, which is the equivalent of a main dining room, has 338 seats and a raised central section. There are large ocean-view windows on three sides, several prime tables overlooking the stern, and a small bandstand for occasional live dinner music. The menu changes daily for both lunch and dinner. The Italian Restaurant has 96 seats, windows along two sides, and a set menu (together with added daily chef's specials). The Grill Room is an "American steak house" and has 98 seats, windows along two sides, and a set menu (together with added daily chef's specials). The Panorama has

461

seats for 154 indoors — not enough during cruises to cold areas or in the winter months — and 186 outdoors (it's too cold to sit outside in the winter months). It is open for breakfast, lunch, and casual dinners. It is the ship's self-serve buffet restaurant and incorporates a small pizzeria and grill. Basic salads, meat carving station, and a reasonable selection of cheeses are featured daily.

All restaurants feature open-seating dining, so you dine when you want, with whom you wish, although reservations are necessary in the Italian Restaurant and The Grill, where there are mostly tables for four or six (there are few tables for two). Service in all the restaurants is generally very good and attentive. In addition, there is a Poolside Grill Bar. Note that all cappuccino and espresso coffees cost extra.

Other Comments: Renaissance Cruises is the cruise industry's first totally nonsmoking cruise line. The R-class ships are a series of eight such ships. The exterior design manages to balance the ship's high sides by combining a deep blue hull with the white superstructure and large, square blue funnel.

Lido Deck features a swimming pool and good sunbathing space, while one of the aft decks has a thalassaotherapy pool (it's part of a spa package and incurs an extra charge). A jogging track circles the swimming pool deck (but one deck above). The uppermost outdoor deck includes a golf driving net and shuffleboard court.

The interior decor is quite stunning and elegant, a throwback to ship decor of the ocean liners of the 'twenties and 'thirties. This includes detailed ceiling cornices, both real and faux wrought iron staircase railings, leather-paneled walls, trompe l'oeil ceilings, rich carpeting in hallways with an Oriental rug–like center section, and many other interesting (and expensive-looking) decorative touches.

The staircase in the main, two-decks-high foyer will remind you of something similar in a blockbuster hit about a certain ship, where the stars, Kate Winslet and Leonardo DiCaprio, met. Regular Renaissance Cruises passengers will probably be pleased with the fine taste with which her interiors have been designed and executed. The company's brochure is definitely understated.

The public rooms are basically spread over three decks. This is totally a nonsmoking ship (there is no smoking anywhere, including cabins, dining room, public rooms, or on the open decks, although the crew have their own smoking room).

The reception hall (lobby) features a staircase with intricate wrought iron railings. A large observation lounge called the Horizon Bar is located high atop ship. This features a long bar with forward views (for the barmen, that is) and a stack of distracting large-screen TVs; there's also an array of slot machines and bar counter-top electronic gaming machines.

There are plenty of bars, including one in each of the restaurant entrances. Perhaps the nicest of all bars and lounges is the casino bar/lounge, a beautiful room reminiscent of London's grand hotels. It features an inviting marble fireplace (in fact there are three such fireplaces aboard) and comfortable sofas and individual chairs.

The Library is a beautiful, grand room, designed in the Regency style, and features a fireplace, a high, indented, trompe l'oeil ceiling, and an excellent selection of books, as well as some very comfortable wingback chairs with footstools and sofas you could sleep on.

Renaissance Cruises provides a seamless cruise and tour package, geared specifically to North American passengers, at a price that is very hard to beat, considering the destination-rich itineraries, together with pre- and post-cruise land stays at high-quality hotels and including all transfers. You should experience a fine, hassle-free cruise vacation package aboard this or other R-class ships. Renaissance Cruises also provides a "vacation guarantee" that is automatically included with your cruise purchase.

Prices are kept low because the company packages its product well and saves money in other ways. There may not be marble bathroom fittings, or caviar and other (more expensive) niceties, but the value for money is really excellent. There are no captain's cocktail parties or interdenominational church services, but there is plenty of entertainment if you want it. High-quality hotels before and after your cruise, and all transfers, are included.

Dining staff gratuities are extremely high, however, at $15 per day per person. They are pooled, due to the fact that several different waiters in each of the four dining spots will serve you during the cruise (this means, however, that waiters don't get to know your likes, dislikes, and preferences). Also, 15% is added to all bar accounts, and the company suggests another $5 per day for the cabin stewardess. Thus, for a five-day cruise, you should allow $100 per person, and for a ten-day cruise, $200 per person.

Weak Points: There is no wraparound promenade deck outdoors, although there is a small jogging track around the perimeter of the swimming pool, and port and starboard side decks. There are no wooden decks outdoors; instead, they are covered by a sand-colored rubberized material. The charge of $20 to use the thalassotherapy pool is excessive. There is no sauna. The room service menu is extremely limited. Suggested gratuities are high. Stairways, although carpeted, are tinny. In order to keep the prices low, the air routing to get to/from your ship is often not the most direct.

R Five
★★★★

Mid-Size Ship:	30,277 tons	Cabins (for one person):	0
Lifestyle:	Premium	Cabins (with private balcony):	232
Cruise Line:	Renaissance Cruises	Cabins (wheelchair accessible):	3
Former Names:	-	Cabin Current:	110/220-volt
Builder:	Chantiers de l'Atlantique (France)	Full-Service Dining Rooms:	4
Original Cost:	$150 million	Elevators:	4
Entered Service:	July 1998	Casino (gaming tables):	Yes
Registry:	Liberia	Slot Machines:	Yes
Length (ft/m):	593.7/181.0	Swimming Pools (outdoors):	1
Beam (ft/m):	83.5/25.5	Swimming Pools (indoors):	0
Draft (ft/m):	19.5/6.0	Whirlpools:	2 (+ 1 thalassotherapy)
Propulsion/Propellers:	Diesel (18,600kW)/2	Fitness Center:	Yes
Passenger Decks:	9	Sauna/Steam Room:	No/Yes
Total Crew:	373	Massage:	Yes
Passengers (lower beds/all berths):	684/824	Self-Service Launderette:	Yes
Pass. Space Ratio (lower beds/all berths):	44.2/36.7	Dedicated Cinema:	No
Crew/Pass. Ratio (lower beds/all berths):	1.8/2.2	Library:	Yes
Navigation Officers:	European	Classification Society:	Bureau Veritas
Cabins (total):	342		
Size Range (sq ft/sq m):	145.3–962.0/13.5–293.2		
Cabins (outside view):	317		
Cabins (interior/no view):	25		

OVERALL SCORE: 1,548
(OUT OF A POSSIBLE 2,000 POINTS)

Accommodation: There are eight cabin categories. All of the standard interior (no view) and outside-view cabins (the lowest four grades) are extremely compact units, and extremely tight for two persons (particularly for cruises longer than five days). They feature twin beds (or queen-size bed), with good under-bed storage areas, personal safe, vanity desk with large mirror, good closet and drawer space (in rich, dark woods), and bathrobe. Color TVs carry a major news channel (where obtainable), plus a sports channel, and several round-the-clock movie channels.

The cabins with private balconies (66% of all cabins) have partial, and not full, balcony partitions, sliding glass doors, and, due to good design and layout, only 14 cabins on Deck 6 have lifeboat-obstructed views. The bathrooms, which have tiled floors and plain walls, are compact, standard units, and include a shower stall with a strong, removable hand held shower unit, hair dryer, 100% cotton towels, toiletries storage shelves, and retractable clothesline. Personal toiletry items include soap, shampoo, body lotion, shower cap, and shoeshine mitt.

There are 52 mini-suites, which in reality are large cabins, since the sleeping and lounge areas are not divided. While not overly large, the bathrooms feature a good-size bathtub and ample space for storing personal toiletry items. The living area features a refrigerated minibar, lounge area with breakfast table, and a balcony with two plastic chairs and a table.

The ten Owner's Suites provide the most spacious of accommodation, and are fine, large living spaces located in the forward most and aft most sections of the accommodation decks. Those that overlook the stern, on Decks 6, 7, and 8, are particularly nice, although they are subject to more movement and some vibration. Owner's Suites have more extensive private balconies that really are private and cannot be overlooked by anyone from the decks above. There is an entrance foyer, living room, bedroom, CD player (with selection of audio discs), fully tiled bathroom with Jacuzzi bathtub (no bath foam is provided, however), and a small guest bathroom.

Dining: Flexibility and choice are what the R-class ships' dining facilities are all about. There are four different restaurants: The Club Restaurant, which is the equivalent of a main dining room, has 338 seats and a raised central section. There are large ocean-view windows on three sides, several prime tables overlooking the stern, and a small bandstand for occasional live dinner music. The menu changes daily for both lunch and dinner. The Italian Restaurant has 96 seats, windows along two sides, and a set menu (together with added daily chef's specials). The Grill Room is an "American steak house" and has 98 seats, windows along two sides, and a set menu (together with added daily chef's specials). The Panorama has

seats for 154 indoors — not enough during cruises to cold areas or in the winter months — and 186 out-doors (it's too cold to sit outside in the winter months). It is open for breakfast, lunch, and casual dinners. It is the ship's self-serve buffet restaurant and incorporates a small pizzeria and grill. Basic salads, meat carving station, and a reasonable selection of cheeses are featured daily.

All restaurants feature open-seating dining, so you dine when you want, with whom you wish, although reservations are necessary in the Italian Restaurant and The Grill, where there are mostly tables for four or six (there are few tables for two). Service in all the restaurants is generally very good and atten-tive. In addition, there is a Poolside Grill Bar. Note that all cappuccino and espresso coffees cost extra.

Other Comments: Renaissance Cruises is the cruise industry's first totally nonsmoking cruise line. The R-class ships are a series of eight such ships. The exterior design manages to balance the ship's high sides by combining a deep blue hull with the white superstructure and large, square blue funnel.

Lido Deck features a swimming pool and good sunbathing space, while one of the aft decks has a thalassaotherapy pool (it's part of a spa package and incurs an extra charge). A jogging track circles the swimming pool deck (but one deck above). The uppermost outdoor deck includes a golf driving net and shuffleboard court.

The interior decor is quite stunning and elegant, a throwback to ship decor of the ocean liners of the 'twenties and 'thirties. This includes detailed ceiling cornices, both real and faux wrought iron staircase railings, leather-paneled walls, trompe l'oeil ceilings, rich carpeting in hallways with an Oriental rug–like center section, and many other interesting (and expensive-looking) decorative touches.

The staircase in the main, two-decks-high foyer will remind you of something similar in a block-buster hit about a certain ship, where the stars, Kate Winslet and Leonardo DiCaprio, met. Regular Renaissance Cruises passengers will probably be pleased with the fine taste with which her interiors have been designed and executed. The company's brochure is definitely understated.

The public rooms are basically spread over three decks. This is totally a nonsmoking ship (there is no smoking anywhere, including cabins, dining room, public rooms, or on the open decks, although the crew have their own smoking room).

The reception hall (lobby) features a staircase with intricate wrought iron railings. A large observa-tion lounge called the Horizon Bar is located high atop ship. This features a long bar with forward views (for the barmen, that is) and a stack of distracting large-screen TVs; there's also an array of slot machines and bar counter-top electronic gaming machines.

There are plenty of bars, including one in each of the restaurant entrances. Perhaps the nicest of all bars and lounges is the casino bar/lounge, a beautiful room reminiscent of London's grand hotels. It fea-tures an inviting marble fireplace (in fact there are three such fireplaces aboard) and comfortable sofas and individual chairs.

The Library is a beautiful, grand room, designed in the Regency style, and features a fireplace, a high, indented, trompe l'oeil ceiling, and an excellent selection of books, as well as some very comfort-able wingback chairs with footstools and sofas you could sleep on.

Renaissance Cruises provides a seamless cruise and tour package, geared specifically to North American passengers, at a price that is very hard to beat, considering the destination-rich itineraries, together with pre- and post-cruise land stays at high-quality hotels and including all transfers. You should experience a fine, hassle-free cruise vacation package aboard this or other R-class ships. Renaissance Cruises also provides a "vacation guarantee" that is automatically included with your cruise purchase.

Prices are kept low because the company packages its product well and saves money in other ways. There may not be marble bathroom fittings, or caviar and other (more expensive) niceties, but the value for money is really excellent. There are no captain's cocktail parties or interdenominational church serv-ices, but there is plenty of entertainment if you want it. High-quality hotels before and after your cruise, and all transfers, are included.

Dining staff gratuities are extremely high, however, at $15 per day per person. They are pooled, due to the fact that several different waiters in each of the four dining spots will serve you during the cruise (this means, however, that waiters don't get to know your likes, dislikes, and preferences). Also, 15% is added to all bar accounts, and the company suggests another $5 per day for the cabin stewardess. Thus, for a five-day cruise, you should allow $100 per person, and for a ten-day cruise, $200 per person.

Weak Points: There is no wraparound promenade deck outdoors, although there is a small jogging track around the perimeter of the swimming pool, and port and starboard side decks. There are no wooden decks outdoors; instead, they are covered by a sand-colored rubberized material. The charge of $20 to use the thalassotherapy pool is excessive. There is no sauna. The room service menu is extremely limited. Suggested gratuities are high. Stairways, although carpeted, are tinny. In order to keep the prices low, the air routing to get to/from your ship is often not the most direct.

464

R Six
★★★★

Mid-Size Ship:	30,277 tons	Cabins (for one person):	0
Lifestyle:	Premium	Cabins (with private balcony):	232
Cruise Line:	Renaissance Cruises	Cabins (wheelchair accessible):	3
Former Names:	-	Cabin Current:	110/220-volt
Builder:	Chantiers de l'Atlantique (France)	Full-Service Dining Rooms:	4
Original Cost:	$150 million	Elevators:	4
Entered Service:	July 1998	Casino (gaming tables):	Yes
Registry:	Liberia	Slot Machines:	Yes
Length (ft/m):	593.7/181.0	Swimming Pools (outdoors):	1
Beam (ft/m):	83.5/25.5	Swimming Pools (indoors):	0
Draft (ft/m):	19.5/6.0	Whirlpools:	2 (+ 1 thalassotherapy)
Propulsion/Propellers:	Diesel (18,600kW)/2	Fitness Center:	Yes
Passenger Decks:	9	Sauna/Steam Room:	No/Yes
Total Crew:	373	Massage:	Yes
Passengers (lower beds/all berths):	684/824	Self-Service Launderette:	Yes
Pass. Space Ratio (lower beds/all berths):	44.2/36.7	Dedicated Cinema:	No
Crew/Pass. Ratio (lower beds/all berths):	1.8/2.2	Library:	Yes
Navigation Officers:	European	Classification Society:	Bureau Veritas
Cabins (total):	342		
Size Range (sq ft/sq m):	145.3–962.0/13.5–293.2	**OVERALL SCORE:**	**1,548**
Cabins (outside view):	317	**(OUT OF A POSSIBLE 2,000 POINTS)**	
Cabins (interior/no view):	25		

Accommodation: There are eight cabin categories. All of the standard interior (no view) and outside-view cabins (the lowest four grades) are extremely compact units, and extremely tight for two persons (particularly for cruises longer than five days). They feature twin beds (or queen-size bed), with good under-bed storage areas, personal safe, vanity desk with large mirror, good closet and drawer space (in rich, dark woods), and bathrobe. Color TVs carry a major news channel (where obtainable), plus a sports channel, and several round-the-clock movie channels.

The cabins with private balconies (66% of all cabins) have partial, and not full, balcony partitions, sliding glass doors, and, due to good design and layout, only 14 cabins on Deck 6 have lifeboat-obstructed views. The bathrooms, which have tiled floors and plain walls, are compact, standard units, and include a shower stall with a strong, removable hand held shower unit, hair dryer, 100% cotton towels, toiletries storage shelves, and retractable clothesline. Personal toiletry items include soap, shampoo, body lotion, shower cap, and shoeshine mitt.

There are 52 mini-suites, which in reality are large cabins, since the sleeping and lounge areas are not divided. While not overly large, the bathrooms feature a good-size bathtub and ample space for storing personal toiletry items. The living area features a refrigerated minibar, lounge area with breakfast table, and a balcony with two plastic chairs and a table.

The ten Owner's Suites provide the most spacious of accommodation, and are fine, large living spaces located in the forward most and aft most sections of the accommodation decks. Those that overlook the stern, on Decks 6, 7, and 8, are particularly nice, although they are subject to more movement and some vibration. Owner's Suites have more extensive private balconies that really are private and cannot be overlooked by anyone from the decks above. There is an entrance foyer, living room, bedroom, CD player (with selection of audio discs), fully tiled bathroom with Jacuzzi bathtub (no bath foam is provided, however), and a small guest bathroom.

Dining: Flexibility and choice are what the R-class ships' dining facilities are all about. There are four different restaurants: The Club Restaurant, which is the equivalent of a main dining room, has 338 seats and a raised central section. There are large ocean-view windows on three sides, several prime tables overlooking the stern, and a small bandstand for occasional live dinner music. The menu changes daily for both lunch and dinner. The Italian Restaurant has 96 seats, windows along two sides, and a set menu (together with added daily chef's specials). The Grill Room is an "American steak house" and has 98 seats, windows along two sides, and a set menu (together with added daily chef's specials). The Panorama has

465

seats for 154 indoors — not enough during cruises to cold areas or in the winter months — and 186 out-doors (it's too cold to sit outside in the winter months). It is open for breakfast, lunch, and casual dinners. It is the ship's self-serve buffet restaurant and incorporates a small pizzeria and grill. Basic salads, meat carving station, and a reasonable selection of cheeses are featured daily.

All restaurants feature open-seating dining, so you dine when you want, with whom you wish, although reservations are necessary in the Italian Restaurant and The Grill, where there are mostly tables for four or six (there are few tables for two). Service in all the restaurants is generally very good and atten-tive. In addition, there is a Poolside Grill Bar. Note that all cappuccino and espresso coffees cost extra.

Other Comments: Renaissance Cruises is the cruise industry's first totally nonsmoking cruise line. The R-class ships are a series of eight such ships. The exterior design manages to balance the ship's high sides by combining a deep blue hull with the white superstructure and large, square blue funnel.

Lido Deck features a swimming pool and good sunbathing space, while one of the aft decks has a thalassaotherapy pool (it's part of a spa package and incurs an extra charge). A jogging track circles the swimming pool deck (but one deck above). The uppermost outdoor deck includes a golf driving net and shuffleboard court.

The interior decor is quite stunning and elegant, a throwback to ship decor of the ocean liners of the 'twenties and 'thirties. This includes detailed ceiling cornices, both real and faux wrought iron staircase railings, leather-paneled walls, trompe l'oeil ceilings, rich carpeting in hallways with an Oriental rug–like center section, and many other interesting (and expensive-looking) decorative touches.

The staircase in the main, two-decks-high foyer will remind you of something similar in a block-buster hit about a certain ship, where the stars, Kate Winslet and Leonardo DiCaprio, met. Regular Renaissance Cruises passengers will probably be pleased with the fine taste with which her interiors have been designed and executed. The company's brochure is definitely understated.

The public rooms are basically spread over three decks. This is totally a nonsmoking ship (there is no smoking anywhere, including cabins, dining room, public rooms, or on the open decks, although the crew have their own smoking room).

The reception hall (lobby) features a staircase with intricate wrought iron railings. A large observa-tion lounge called the Horizon Bar is located high atop ship. This features a long bar with forward views (for the barmen, that is) and a stack of distracting large-screen TVs; there's also an array of slot machines and bar counter-top electronic gaming machines.

There are plenty of bars, including one in each of the restaurant entrances. Perhaps the nicest of all bars and lounges is the casino bar/lounge, a beautiful room reminiscent of London's grand hotels. It fea-tures an inviting marble fireplace (in fact there are three such fireplaces aboard) and comfortable sofas and individual chairs.

The Library is a beautiful, grand room, designed in the Regency style, and features a fireplace, a high, indented, trompe l'oeil ceiling, and an excellent selection of books, as well as some very comfort-able wingback chairs with footstools and sofas you could sleep on.

Renaissance Cruises provides a seamless cruise and tour package, geared specifically to North American passengers, at a price that is very hard to beat, considering the destination-rich itineraries, together with pre- and post-cruise land stays at high-quality hotels and including all transfers. You should experience a fine, hassle-free cruise vacation package aboard this or other R-class ships. Renaissance Cruises also provides a "vacation guarantee" that is automatically included with your cruise purchase.

Prices are kept low because the company packages its product well and saves money in other ways. There may not be marble bathroom fittings, or caviar and other (more expensive) niceties, but the value for money is really excellent. There are no captain's cocktail parties or interdenominational church serv-ices, but there is plenty of entertainment if you want it. High-quality hotels before and after your cruise, and all transfers, are included.

Dining staff gratuities are extremely high, however, at $15 per day per person. They are pooled, due to the fact that several different waiters in each of the four dining spots will serve you during the cruise (this means, however, that waiters don't get to know your likes, dislikes, and preferences). Also, 15% is added to all bar accounts, and the company suggests another $5 per day for the cabin stewardess. Thus, for a five-day cruise, you should allow $100 per person, and for a ten-day cruise, $200 per person.

Weak Points: There is no wraparound promenade deck outdoors, although there is a small jogging track around the perimeter of the swimming pool, and port and starboard side decks. There are no wooden decks outdoors; instead, they are covered by a sand-colored rubberized material. The charge of $20 to use the thalassotherapy pool is excessive. There is no sauna. The room service menu is extremely limited. Suggested gratuities are high. Stairways, although carpeted, are tinny. In order to keep the prices low, the air routing to get to/from your ship is often not the most direct.

466

R Seven
★★★★

Mid-Size Ship:	30,277 tons	Cabins (for one person):	0
Lifestyle:	Premium	Cabins (with private balcony):	232
Cruise Line:	Renaissance Cruises	Cabins (wheelchair accessible):	3
Former Names:	-	Cabin Current:	110/220-volt
Builder:	Chantiers de l'Atlantique (France)	Full-Service Dining Rooms:	4
Original Cost:	$150 million	Elevators:	4
Entered Service:	July 1998	Casino (gaming tables):	Yes
Registry:	Liberia	Slot Machines:	Yes
Length (ft/m):	593.7/181.0	Swimming Pools (outdoors):	1
Beam (ft/m):	83.5/25.5	Swimming Pools (indoors):	0
Draft (ft/m):	19.5/6.0	Whirlpools:	2 (+ 1 thalassotherapy)
Propulsion/Propellers:	Diesel (18,600kW)/2	Fitness Center:	Yes
Passenger Decks:	9	Sauna/Steam Room:	No/Yes
Total Crew:	373	Massage:	Yes
Passengers (lower beds/all berths):	684/824	Self-Service Launderette:	Yes
Pass. Space Ratio (lower beds/all berths):	44.2/36.7	Dedicated Cinema:	No
Crew/Pass. Ratio (lower beds/all berths):	1.8/2.2	Library:	Yes
Navigation Officers:	European	Classification Society:	Bureau Veritas
Cabins (total):	342		
Size Range (sq ft/sq m):	145.3–962.0/13.5–293.2		
Cabins (outside view):	317		
Cabins (interior/no view):	25		

OVERALL SCORE: 1,548
(OUT OF A POSSIBLE 2,000 POINTS)

Accommodation: There are eight cabin categories. All of the standard interior (no view) and outside-view cabins (the lowest four grades) are extremely compact units, and extremely tight for two persons (particularly for cruises longer than five days). They feature twin beds (or queen-size bed), with good under-bed storage areas, personal safe, vanity desk with large mirror, good closet and drawer space (in rich, dark woods), and bathrobe. Color TVs carry a major news channel (where obtainable), plus a sports channel, and several round-the-clock movie channels.

The cabins with private balconies (66% of all cabins) have partial, and not full, balcony partitions, sliding glass doors, and, due to good design and layout, only 14 cabins on Deck 6 have lifeboat-obstructed views. The bathrooms, which have tiled floors and plain walls, are compact, standard units, and include a shower stall with a strong, removable hand held shower unit, hair dryer, 100% cotton towels, toiletries storage shelves, and retractable clothesline. Personal toiletry items include soap, shampoo, body lotion, shower cap, and shoeshine mitt.

There are 52 mini-suites, which in reality are large cabins, since the sleeping and lounge areas are not divided. While not overly large, the bathrooms feature a good-size bathtub and ample space for storing personal toiletry items. The living area features a refrigerated minibar, lounge area with breakfast table, and a balcony with two plastic chairs and a table.

The ten Owner's Suites provide the most spacious of accommodation, and are fine, large living spaces located in the forward most and aft most sections of the accommodation decks. Those that overlook the stern, on Decks 6, 7, and 8, are particularly nice, although they are subject to more movement and some vibration. Owner's Suites have more extensive private balconies that really are private and cannot be overlooked by anyone from the decks above. There is an entrance foyer, living room, bedroom, CD player (with selection of audio discs), fully tiled bathroom with Jacuzzi bathtub (no bath foam is provided, however), and a small guest bathroom.

Dining: Flexibility and choice are what the R-class ships' dining facilities are all about. There are four different restaurants: The Club Restaurant, which is the equivalent of a main dining room, has 338 seats and a raised central section. There are large ocean-view windows on three sides, several prime tables overlooking the stern, and a small bandstand for occasional live dinner music. The menu changes daily for both lunch and dinner. The Italian Restaurant has 96 seats, windows along two sides, and a set menu (together with added daily chef's specials). The Grill Room is an "American steak house" and has 98 seats, windows along two sides, and a set menu (together with added daily chef's specials). The Panorama has

seats for 154 indoors — not enough during cruises to cold areas or in the winter months — and 186 outdoors (it's too cold to sit outside in the winter months). It is open for breakfast, lunch, and casual dinners. It is the ship's self-serve buffet restaurant and incorporates a small pizzeria and grill. Basic salads, meat carving station, and a reasonable selection of cheeses are featured daily.

All restaurants feature open-seating dining, so you dine when you want, with whom you wish, although reservations are necessary in the Italian Restaurant and The Grill, where there are mostly tables for four or six (there are few tables for two). Service in all the restaurants is generally very good and attentive. In addition, there is a Poolside Grill Bar. Note that all cappuccino and espresso coffees cost extra.

Other Comments: Renaissance Cruises is the cruise industry's first totally nonsmoking cruise line. The R-class ships are a series of eight such ships. The exterior design manages to balance the ship's high sides by combining a deep blue hull with the white superstructure and large, square blue funnel.

Lido Deck features a swimming pool and good sunbathing space, while one of the aft decks has a thalassaotherapy pool (it's part of a spa package and incurs an extra charge). A jogging track circles the swimming pool deck (but one deck above). The uppermost outdoor deck includes a golf driving net and shuffleboard court.

The interior decor is quite stunning and elegant, a throwback to ship decor of the ocean liners of the 'twenties and 'thirties. This includes detailed ceiling cornices, both real and faux wrought iron staircase railings, leather-paneled walls, trompe l'oeil ceilings, rich carpeting in hallways with an Oriental rug–like center section, and many other interesting (and expensive-looking) decorative touches.

The staircase in the main, two-decks-high foyer will remind you of something similar in a blockbuster hit about a certain ship, where the stars, Kate Winslet and Leonardo DiCaprio, met. Regular Renaissance Cruises passengers will probably be pleased with the fine taste with which her interiors have been designed and executed. The company's brochure is definitely understated.

The public rooms are basically spread over three decks. This is totally a nonsmoking ship (there is no smoking anywhere, including cabins, dining room, public rooms, or on the open decks, although the crew have their own smoking room).

The reception hall (lobby) features a staircase with intricate wrought iron railings. A large observation lounge called the Horizon Bar is located high atop ship. This features a long bar with forward views (for the barmen, that is) and a stack of distracting large-screen TVs; there's also an array of slot machines and bar counter-top electronic gaming machines.

There are plenty of bars, including one in each of the restaurant entrances. Perhaps the nicest of all bars and lounges is the casino bar/lounge, a beautiful room reminiscent of London's grand hotels. It features an inviting marble fireplace (in fact there are three such fireplaces aboard) and comfortable sofas and individual chairs.

The Library is a beautiful, grand room, designed in the Regency style, and features a fireplace, a high, indented, trompe l'oeil ceiling, and an excellent selection of books, as well as some very comfortable wingback chairs with footstools and sofas you could sleep on.

Renaissance Cruises provides a seamless cruise and tour package, geared specifically to North American passengers, at a price that is very hard to beat, considering the destination-rich itineraries, together with pre- and post-cruise land stays at high-quality hotels and including all transfers. You should experience a fine, hassle-free cruise vacation package aboard this or other R-class ships. Renaissance Cruises also provides a "vacation guarantee" that is automatically included with your cruise purchase.

Prices are kept low because the company packages its product well and saves money in other ways. There may not be marble bathroom fittings, or caviar and other (more expensive) niceties, but the value for money is really excellent. There are no captain's cocktail parties or interdenominational church services, but there is plenty of entertainment if you want it. High-quality hotels before and after your cruise, and all transfers, are included.

Dining staff gratuities are extremely high, however, at $15 per day per person. They are pooled, due to the fact that several different waiters in each of the four dining spots will serve you during the cruise (this means, however, that waiters don't get to know your likes, dislikes, and preferences). Also, 15% is added to all bar accounts, and the company suggests another $5 per day for the cabin stewardess. Thus, for a five-day cruise, you should allow $100 per person, and for a ten-day cruise, $200 per person.

Weak Points: There is no wraparound promenade deck outdoors, although there is a small jogging track around the perimeter of the swimming pool, and port and starboard side decks. There are no wooden decks outdoors; instead, they are covered by a sand-colored rubberized material. The charge of $20 to use the thalassotherapy pool is excessive. There is no sauna. The room service menu is extremely limited. Suggested gratuities are high. Stairways, although carpeted, are tinny. In order to keep the prices low, the air routing to get to/from your ship is often not the most direct.

468

R Eight
★★★★

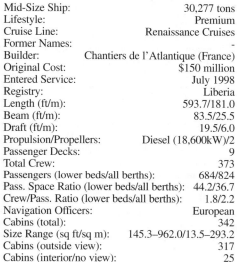

Mid-Size Ship:	30,277 tons	Cabins (for one person):	0
Lifestyle:	Premium	Cabins (with private balcony):	232
Cruise Line:	Renaissance Cruises	Cabins (wheelchair accessible):	3
Former Names:	-	Cabin Current:	110/220-volt
Builder:	Chantiers de l'Atlantique (France)	Full-Service Dining Rooms:	4
Original Cost:	$150 million	Elevators:	4
Entered Service:	July 1998	Casino (gaming tables):	Yes
Registry:	Liberia	Slot Machines:	Yes
Length (ft/m):	593.7/181.0	Swimming Pools (outdoors):	1
Beam (ft/m):	83.5/25.5	Swimming Pools (indoors):	0
Draft (ft/m):	19.5/6.0	Whirlpools:	2 (+ 1 thalassotherapy)
Propulsion/Propellers:	Diesel (18,600kW)/2	Fitness Center:	Yes
Passenger Decks:	9	Sauna/Steam Room:	No/Yes
Total Crew:	373	Massage:	Yes
Passengers (lower beds/all berths):	684/824	Self-Service Launderette:	Yes
Pass. Space Ratio (lower beds/all berths):	44.2/36.7	Dedicated Cinema:	No
Crew/Pass. Ratio (lower beds/all berths):	1.8/2.2	Library:	Yes
Navigation Officers:	European	Classification Society:	Bureau Veritas
Cabins (total):	342		
Size Range (sq ft/sq m):	145.3–962.0/13.5–293.2	**OVERALL SCORE:**	**1,548**
Cabins (outside view):	317	(OUT OF A POSSIBLE 2,000 POINTS)	
Cabins (interior/no view):	25		

Accommodation: There are eight cabin categories. All of the standard interior (no view) and outside-view cabins (the lowest four grades) are extremely compact units, and extremely tight for two persons (particularly for cruises longer than five days). They feature twin beds (or queen-size bed), with good under-bed storage areas, personal safe, vanity desk with large mirror, good closet and drawer space (in rich, dark woods), and bathrobe. Color TVs carry a major news channel (where obtainable), plus a sports channel, and several round-the-clock movie channels.

The cabins with private balconies (66% of all cabins) have partial, and not full, balcony partitions, sliding glass doors, and, due to good design and layout, only 14 cabins on Deck 6 have lifeboat-obstructed views. The bathrooms, which have tiled floors and plain walls, are compact, standard units, and include a shower stall with a strong, removable hand held shower unit, hair dryer, 100% cotton towels, toiletries storage shelves, and retractable clothesline. Personal toiletry items include soap, shampoo, body lotion, shower cap, and shoeshine mitt.

There are 52 mini-suites, which in reality are large cabins, since the sleeping and lounge areas are not divided. While not overly large, the bathrooms feature a good-size bathtub and ample space for storing personal toiletry items. The living area features a refrigerated minibar, lounge area with breakfast table, and a balcony with two plastic chairs and a table.

The ten Owner's Suites provide the most spacious of accommodation, and are fine, large living spaces located in the forward most and aft most sections of the accommodation decks. Those that overlook the stern, on Decks 6, 7, and 8, are particularly nice, although they are subject to more movement and some vibration. Owner's Suites have more extensive private balconies that really are private and cannot be overlooked by anyone from the decks above. There is an entrance foyer, living room, bedroom, CD player (with selection of audio discs), fully tiled bathroom with Jacuzzi bathtub (no bath foam is provided, however), and a small guest bathroom.

Dining: Flexibility and choice are what the R-class ships' dining facilities are all about. There are four different restaurants: The Club Restaurant, which is the equivalent of a main dining room, has 338 seats and a raised central section. There are large ocean-view windows on three sides, several prime tables overlooking the stern, and a small bandstand for occasional live dinner music. The menu changes daily for both lunch and dinner. The Italian Restaurant has 96 seats, windows along two sides, and a set menu (together with added daily chef's specials). The Grill Room is an "American steak house" and has 98 seats, windows along two sides, and a set menu (together with added daily chef's specials). The Panorama has

seats for 154 indoors — not enough during cruises to cold areas or in the winter months — and 186 outdoors (it's too cold to sit outside in the winter months). It is open for breakfast, lunch, and casual dinners. It is the ship's self-serve buffet restaurant and incorporates a small pizzeria and grill. Basic salads, meat carving station, and a reasonable selection of cheeses are featured daily.

All restaurants feature open-seating dining, so you dine when you want, with whom you wish, although reservations are necessary in the Italian Restaurant and The Grill, where there are mostly tables for four or six (there are few tables for two). Service in all the restaurants is generally very good and attentive. In addition, there is a Poolside Grill Bar. Note that all cappuccino and espresso coffees cost extra.

Other Comments: Renaissance Cruises is the cruise industry's first totally nonsmoking cruise line. The R-class ships are a series of eight such ships. The exterior design manages to balance the ship's high sides by combining a deep blue hull with the white superstructure and large, square blue funnel.

Lido Deck features a swimming pool, and good sunbathing space, while one of the aft decks has a thalassaotherapy pool (it's part of a spa package and incurs an extra charge). A jogging track circles the swimming pool deck (but one deck above). The uppermost outdoor deck includes a golf driving net and shuffleboard court.

The interior decor is quite stunning and elegant, a throwback to ship decor of the ocean liners of the 'twenties and 'thirties. This includes detailed ceiling cornices, both real and faux wrought iron staircase railings, leather-paneled walls, trompe l'oeil ceilings, rich carpeting in hallways with an Oriental rug–like center section, and many other interesting (and expensive-looking) decorative touches.

The staircase in the main, two-decks-high foyer will remind you of something similar in a blockbuster hit about a certain ship, where the stars, Kate Winslet and Leonardo DiCaprio, met. Regular Renaissance Cruises passengers will probably be pleased with the fine taste with which her interiors have been designed and executed. The company's brochure is definitely understated.

The public rooms are basically spread over three decks. This is totally a nonsmoking ship (there is no smoking anywhere, including cabins, dining room, public rooms, or on the open decks, although the crew have their own smoking room).

The reception hall (lobby) features a staircase with intricate wrought iron railings. A large observation lounge called the Horizon Bar is located high atop ship. This features a long bar with forward views (for the barmen, that is) and a stack of distracting large-screen TVs; there's also an array of slot machines and bar counter-top electronic gaming machines.

There are plenty of bars, including one in each of the restaurant entrances. Perhaps the nicest of all bars and lounges is the casino bar/lounge, a beautiful room reminiscent of London's grand hotels. It features an inviting marble fireplace (in fact there are three such fireplaces aboard) and comfortable sofas and individual chairs.

The Library is a beautiful, grand room, designed in the Regency style, and features a fireplace, a high, indented, trompe l'oeil ceiling, and an excellent selection of books, as well as some very comfortable wingback chairs with footstools and sofas you could sleep on.

Renaissance Cruises provides a seamless cruise and tour package, geared specifically to North American passengers, at a price that is very hard to beat, considering the destination-rich itineraries, together with pre- and post-cruise land stays at high-quality hotels and including all transfers. You should experience a fine, hassle-free cruise vacation package aboard this or other R-class ships. Renaissance Cruises also provides a "vacation guarantee" that is automatically included with your cruise purchase.

Prices are kept low because the company packages its product well and saves money in other ways. There may not be marble bathroom fittings, or caviar and other (more expensive) niceties, but the value for money is really excellent. There are no captain's cocktail parties or interdenominational church services, but there is plenty of entertainment if you want it. High-quality hotels before and after your cruise, and all transfers, are included.

Dining staff gratuities are extremely high, however, at $15 per day per person. They are pooled, due to the fact that several different waiters in each of the four dining spots will serve you during the cruise (this means, however, that waiters don't get to know your likes, dislikes, and preferences). Also, 15% is added to all bar accounts, and the company suggests another $5 per day for the cabin stewardess. Thus, for a five-day cruise, you should allow $100 per person, and for a ten-day cruise, $200 per person.

Weak Points: There is no wraparound promenade deck outdoors, although there is a small jogging track around the perimeter of the swimming pool, and port and starboard side decks. There are no wooden decks outdoors; instead, they are covered by a sand-colored rubberized material. The charge of $20 to use the thalassotherapy pool is excessive. There is no sauna. The room service menu is extremely limited. Suggested gratuities are high. Stairways, although carpeted, are tinny. In order to keep the prices low, the air routing to get to/from your ship is often not the most direct.

Radiance of the Seas
★★★★

Large Ship:	90,090 tons	Cabins (for one person):	0
Lifestyle:	Standard	Cabins (with private balcony):	577
Cruise Line:	Royal Caribbean International	Cabins (wheelchair accessible):	14 (8 with
Former Names:	-		private balcony)
Builder:	Meyer Werft (Germany)	Cabin Current:	110-volt
Original Cost:	$350 million	Full-Service Dining Rooms:	1 (+2 alternative)
Entered Service:	April 2001	Elevators:	9
Registry:	Liberia	Casino (gaming tables):	Yes
Length (ft/m):	961.9/293.2	Slot Machines:	Yes
Beam (ft/m):	105.6/32.2	Swimming Pools (outdoors):	2
Draft (ft/m):	27.8/8.5	Swimming Pools (indoors):	0
Propulsion/Propellers:	Gas turbine/2 azimuthing	Whirlpools:	3
	pods (20 MW each)	Fitness Center:	Yes
Passenger Decks:	13	Sauna/Steam Room:	Yes/Yes
Total Crew:	858	Massage:	Yes
Passengers (lower beds/all berths):	2,100/2,501	Self-Service Launderette:	No
Pass. Space Ratio (lower beds/all berths):	42.9/36.0	Dedicated Cinema/Seats:	Yes/40
Crew/Pass. Ratio (lower beds/all berths):	2.4/2.9	Library:	Yes
Navigation Officers:	Norwegian	Classification Society:	Det Norske Veritas
Cabins (total):	1,050		
Size Range (sq ft/sq m):	165.8–734.4/15.41–68.23	**OVERALL SCORE:**	**1,546**
Cabins (outside view):	813		
Cabins (interior/no view):	237	**(OUT OF A POSSIBLE 2,000 POINTS)**	

Accommodation: There is a wide range of suites and standard outside-view and interior (no view) cabins to suit different tastes, requirements, and depth of wallet.

Apart from the largest suites (the six Owner's Suites), which feature king-size beds, almost all other cabins have twin beds that convert to a queen-size bed (all sheets are of 100% Egyptian cotton, although the blankets are of nylon). All cabins feature rich (but faux) wood cabinetry, including a vanity desk (with hair dryer), faux wood drawers that close silently (hooray!), TV, personal safe, and three-sided mirrors. Some cabins have ceiling recessed, pull-down berths for third and fourth persons, although closet and drawer space would be extremely tight for four persons (even if two of them are children), and some have interconnecting doors, so families with children can cruise together, in separate but adjacent cabins. Note that audio channels are available through the TV; however, if you want to go to sleep with soft music playing in the background you'll need to put a towel over the TV screen, since it is impossible to turn the picture off.

Most bathrooms feature tiled accenting and a terrazzo-style tiled floor, and a small shower enclosure in a half-moon shape (which North American passengers may find cramped), 100% Egyptian cotton towels, a small cabinet for personal toiletries, and a small shelf. In reality, there is little space to stow personal toiletries for two (or more).

The largest accommodation consists of a Family Suite with two bedrooms. One bedroom has twin beds (convertible to queen-size bed), while a second has two lower beds and two upper Pullman berths, a combination that can sleep up to eight persons — suitable for large families.

Occupants of accommodation designated as suites also get access to a private Concierge Lounge (where priority dining room reservations, shore excursion bookings and beauty salon/spa appointments can be made).

Dining: "Cascades" is the name of the main dining room; it spans two decks (the upper deck level has floor-to-ceiling windows, while the lower deck level has picture windows and is a beautiful, but noisy, dining hall, reminiscent of those aboard the transatlantic liners in their heyday. It seats 1,104 and has cascading-water themed decor. There are tables for two, four, six, eight or ten in two seatings. Two small private dining rooms (Breakers, with 94 seats and Tides, with 30 seats) are located off the main dining room. The cuisine in the main dining room is similar in nature to that offered aboard the company's other ships. In other words, we are talking about mass banquet catering that offers very standard fare comparable to that found in American family-style restaurants ashore. You'll be waited on by "servers" (not wait-ers) in what is a change in terminology that ties in with RCI's vacation experience concept. I'll continue to call them waiters and assistant waiters.

For a change from the main dining room, there are two alternative dining spots: "Portofino," with 112 seats (and a magnificent "cloud" ceiling), featuring Italian cuisine, and "Chops Grille Steakhouse," with 95 seats and an open (show) kitchen, featuring premium meats in the form of chops and steaks. Both alter-native dining spots feature food that is of a much higher quality than in the main dining room, with extremely good presentation. There is an additional charge of $20 per person (this includes gratuities to staff), and reservations are required for both dining spots, which are typically open between 6:00pm and 11pm. Be prepared to eat a lot of food (perhaps this justifies the cover charge). Unfortunately, the dress code is casual.

Also, casual meals can be taken (for breakfast, lunch, and dinner) in the self-serve, buffet-style Windjammer Café, which can be accessed directly from the pool deck. It has islands dedicated to specif-ic foods, and indoor and outdoor seating.

Additionally, there is the Seaview Café, open for lunch and dinner. Choose from the self-serve buffet, or from the menu for casual, fast-food seafood items including fish sandwiches, popcorn shrimp, fish 'n' chips, as well as nonseafood items such as hamburgers and hot dogs. The decor, naturally, is marine and ocean related.

Other Comments: This is the first Royal Caribbean International ship to use gas- and steam-turbine power instead of the more conventional diesel or diesel-electric combination (two gas turbines, one steam turbine). It also utilizes podded propulsion power, instead of the more conventional rudder and propeller shafts. As is common aboard all RCI vessels, the navigation bridge is of the fully enclosed type (good for cruising in cold-weather areas such as Alaska).

Radiance of the Seas is a streamlined-looking contemporary ship and features a two-decks-high wrap-around structure in the forward section of the funnel. Along the ship's starboard side, a central glass wall protrudes, giving great views (cabins with balconies occupy the space directly opposite on the port side). The gently rounded stern has nicely tiered decks, which give the ship an extremely well-balanced look.

Inside the ship, the decor is contemporary, yet elegant, bright and cheerful, designed for active, young hip and trendy types. A nine-decks-high atrium lobby features glass-walled elevators (on the port side of the ship) that travel through 12 decks, face the sea, and provide a link with nature and the ocean. The Centrum (as the atrium is called) has several public rooms connected to it: the guest relations desk (an updated term for purser's office) and shore excursions desk, a Lobby Bar, Champagne Bar, the Library, Royal Caribbean Online, the Concierge Club, and a Crown & Anchor Lounge. A great view of the Centrum can be had by looking down through the flat glass dome high above it.

Other facilities include a three-level show lounge (Aurora Theatre) with 874 seats (including 24 stations for wheelchairs) and good sight lines from most seats; a second entertainment lounge for more casual cabaret shows (called the Colony Club); and a delightful, but very small library. A shop called "Books, Books and Coffee" features books for purchase, as well as chocolates, various coffees, pastries, and cakes — it's rather like a small Seattle coffeehouse, and located in an extensive area of shops. There's also a Champagne Bar and a large Schooner Bar (a popular favorite aboard RCI ships) that houses maritime art in a self-contained art gallery. The entrance to the Schooner Bar, with its fine, detailed ceiling, features cannons, cannon balls, and a distinct, strong aroma of smoked wood. Gambling devotees should enjoy Casino Royale, which features a French Art Nouveau decorative theme and includes 11 crystal chande-liers (although it's difficult to see them for all the slot machines and gaming tables). There's also a small dedicated screening room for movies (with space for two wheelchairs), as well as a 194-seat conference center and a business center.

The Viking Crown Lounge (a Royal Caribbean International trademark) is a large structure that is set around the base of the ship's funnel. It functions as an observation lounge during the daytime (with views forward over the swimming pool). In the evening, the space features Starquest—a futuristic, high-energy dance club; and Hollywood Odyssey — a more intimate and relaxed entertainment venue for softer mood music and "black box" theater.

For the Internet-connect set, Royal Caribbean Online is a dedicated computer center that features 12 IBM computers with high-speed Internet access for sending and receiving e-mail, located in a semi-private setting (in addition, data ports are provided in all cabins). Four more Internet-accessible computer terminals are located in Books, Books and Coffee.

Here as aboard *Adventure of the Seas*, *Explorer of the Seas,* and *Voyager of the Seas* (the largest ships in the RCI fleet), there is a 30-foot-high rock-climbing wall with five separate climbing tracks (there's no charge, but once you've done it, the typical passenger reaction is: "been there, done that, what's next?"). Other sports facilities include a nine-hole miniature golf course (with novel 17th-century decorative ornaments) and an indoor/outdoor country club with a golf simulator, a jogging track, and a basketball court. Want to play pool? Well, you can, thanks to two special tables, called Stables, whose technology was engineered for keeping North Sea oil platforms stable during rough seas.

A climate-controlled 10,176 square foot (945 square meter) indoor/outdoor Solarium (with magrodome sliding glass roof that can be closed in cool or inclement weather conditions) provides facilities for relaxation and has a fascinating African-themed decor. The Solarium features counter-current swimming and a whirlpool under a retractable magrodome roof. There's even a bronze statue of a lion cub lounging on a bench dipping its left front paw and hind leg into the pool, as well as three huge 16-foot-high (4.8 meter) carved stone elephants, with cascading waterfalls. Fitness/spa facilities, which are located on two decks, include a gymnasium (with 44 cardiovascular machines), a 50-person aerobics room, ladies' and gents' sauna and steam rooms, and therapy treatment rooms. There is also an exterior jogging track.

Youth facilities include Adventure Ocean, an "edu-tainment" area with four separate age-appropriate sections for junior passengers: the Aquanaut Center (for ages 3–5); the Explorer Center (for ages 6–8); the Voyager Center (for ages 9–12); and the Optix Teen Center (for ages 13–17). There is also Adventure Beach, which includes a splash pool complete with waterslide; Surfside, with computer lab stations with entertaining software; and Ocean Arcade, a video-game hangout.

The artwork aboard this ship is really eclectic, so there should be something for all tastes, and it provides a broad selection of color works. It ranges from Jenny M. Hansen's "A Vulnerable Moment" glass sculpture, to David Buckland's "Industrial and Russian Constructionism 1920s" in photographic images on glass and painted canvas, to a huge multi-deck high contemporary bicycle-cum-paddlewheel sculpture design suspended in the atrium.

With this new ship, Royal Caribbean International introduced a new, more upgraded ship (somewhat approaching Celebrity Cruises' *Millennium*), while the product delivery is much more casual and unstructured than RCI has been delivering previously. *Radiance of the Seas* provides more space and more comfortable public areas (and several more intimate spaces), slightly larger cabins, and more dining options — especially for the younger, active, hip and trendy set — than most other RCI ships. There is also a grand amount of glass that provides more contact with the ocean around you; of course, more glass means more cleaning of glass. However, at the end of the day, the overall product is similar to that delivered aboard other ships in the fleet. In the final analysis, while the ship is quite delightful in many ways, the on-board operation is less spectacular and suffers from a lack of service staff.

Weak Points: Many of the "private" balcony cabins are not very private, as they can be overlooked by anyone standing in the port and starboard wings of the Solarium and from other locations. Standing in lines for embarkation, the reception desk, disembarkation, port visits, shore tenders and the self-serve buffet stations in the Windjammer Café is an inevitable aspect of cruising aboard this large ship. There are no cushioned pads for the deck lounge chairs. Spa treatments are extravagantly expensive.

Radisson Diamond
★★★★ +

Small Ship:	20,295 tons	Cabins (for one person):	0
Lifestyle:	Premium	Cabins (with private balcony):	123
Cruise Line:	Radisson Seven Seas Cruises	Cabins (wheelchair accessible):	2
Former Names:	-	Cabin Current:	110/220-volt
Builder:	Rauma Yards (Finland)	Full-Service Dining Rooms: 1 (+1 Grill Restaurant)	
Original Cost:	$125 million	Elevators:	3
Entered Service:	May 1992	Casino (gaming tables):	Yes
Registry:	Bahamas	Slot Machines:	Yes
Length (ft/m):	430.4/131.2	Swimming Pools (outdoors):	1
Beam (ft/m):	104.9/32.0	Swimming Pools (indoors):	0
Draft (ft/m):	26.2/8.0	Whirlpools:	1
Propulsion/Propellers: Diesel (11,340kW)/2 nozzles		Fitness Center:	Yes
Passenger Decks:	6	Sauna/Steam Room:	Yes/Yes
Total Crew:	200	Massage:	Yes
Passengers (lower beds/all berths):	354/354	Self-Service Launderette:	No
Pass.Space Ratio (lower beds/all berths):	57.3/57.3	Dedicated Cinema:	No
Crew/Pass. Ratio (lower beds/all berths):	1.7/1.7	Library:	Yes
Navigation Officers:	Scandinavian/European	Classification Society:	Det Norske Veritas
Cabins (total):	177		
Size Range (sq ft/sq m):	220.6/20.5	**OVERALL SCORE:**	**1,591**
Cabins (outside view):	177	(OUT OF A POSSIBLE 2,000 POINTS)	
Cabins (interior/no view):	0		

Accommodation: This ship has nicely designed, spacious, and well-equipped all outside-view cabins, most of which have private balconies with outdoor lights (those without balconies have large windows instead). All are furnished in blond woods, with marble bathroom vanities and a tiny bathtub. There are bay windows in 47 units designated as suites.

All cabins are of the same dimensions, with the exception of two "VIP" master suites with private balconies (and Henri Rousseau-inspired wall murals). Each cabin has an oversized window or floor-to-ceiling balcony windows/door. Each has a spacious sitting area with sofa, chairs, dressing table with hair dryer, minibar and refrigerator, telephone, color remote-control TV with integrated VCR, twin beds that convert to a queen-size unit, two bright adjustable reading lamps, a personal safe (somewhat hidden and awkward for older passengers to reach and operate), full-length mirror, and excellent drawer space. The closet space, however, is really minimal — adequate for short cruises, but tight for two on a seven-night cruise, worse for longer cruises. Each cabin has a minibar that is stocked with beer and soft drinks; half-liter bottles of four liquors are provided. Bottled mineral water is provided. The cabin bathrooms have really small tubs (they are really shower-tubs).

Two wheelchair-accessible cabins, formerly located about as far from the elevators as one could get, have sensibly been relocated so that they are adjacent to the elevators. These feature wheel-in bathrooms and shower areas, and all fittings are sensibly provided at an accessible height.

Dining: The two-decks-high dining room is spacious and quite elegant and has a 270-degree view over the stern. Open seating is featured, so you can dine with whomever you wish, when you wish (within dining room hours, of course). The cuisine quality and food presentation is European in style and outstanding in quality, choice, and presentation. Health foods and dietary specials are always available. The waitresses (there are no waiters) are really charming and superbly supervised by experienced headwaiters. As far as wines go, although fairly decent whites and reds are included for lunch and dinner, a separate wine list is available for those who appreciate better wines (at extra cost).

"Don Vito" is the name of a 50-seat alternative Italian casual indoor/outdoor dining spot (no extra charge). Run like a real restaurant ashore (make your reservations early each day you want to eat there), this informal dining spot features excellent homemade pasta dishes and has a fine menu, including cream sauces and exotic garnishes. There is a different menu each day, and the food is presented in small portions, course by course. It is lovingly prepared and exquisite to taste, tending to richness. Seating is at sturdy, practical glass-topped wooden tables for two, four, or six. Tableside dessert flambeaus are often featured — oh, and the waiters serenade you!

"The Grill" is the place for casual breakfasts and lunches, with seating in various nooks and crannies. The self-serve buffets are of high-quality, with good choice and variety.

You can also be very private if you wish and dine, course by course, in your cabin, or on the balcony (in the right setting, and if weather conditions permit). Dining is definitely the vessel's strong point.

Other Comments: This ship features a very innovative design, based on SWATH (Small Waterplane Area Twin Hull) technology. She is thus very stable when at sea (except, of course, in rough seas), with four stabilizing fins (two on the inner side of each pontoon), so that motion is really minimized when compared with conventional (monohull) vessels. The wide beam of this design also provides outstanding passenger space, although the public rooms are stacked vertically and are contained mostly on the inside of the ship's structure, which is like a seagoing version of a Radisson hotel. The design was novel when first introduced, but, sensibly, has not been repeated in any ship order since, due to the slow speed of its propulsion system. Long voyages in open water — such as transatlantic crossings — are quite time-consuming.

At the stern of the vessel, there is a retractable, free-floating water sports marina platform, but it is really only useful in dead calm seas. There are jet-skis and a water-ski boat. There is also a little-used underwater viewing area (it actually consists of just two portholes). There is a good outdoor jogging track, although fitness fanatics will find the gymnasium quite small.

Inside, the central focal point is a five-decks-high atrium, which has glass-enclosed elevators (together with the staircase, however, they take up most of the space). There is a well-stocked library and video center, and a sophisticated business center with facilities that are ideal for small groups and conventions. These include high-tech audio- and video- conferencing facilities, and a high-tech security system that uses approximately 50 cameras to monitor just about everywhere, providing a good feeling of security and exclusivity. For regular (nongroup) passengers, however, it is somewhat annoying when the public rooms are taken over by private functions and parties. Get your travel agent to check your sailing.

Other facilities include a casino, with gaming tables on one side of a passageway that connects to the show lounge; it has slot machines on the opposite side from the gaming tables — a sensible arrangement for serious game players who do not want the sound of slot machines to intrude.

This semisubmersible, twin-hulled cruise vessel, which some say looks like a white-caped "Batman" from the stern, certainly has the most unusual and distinctive appearance of any cruise ship, although its design has not proven as successful as hoped. It should appeal to those seeking a high standard of personalized service in fairly sophisticated and personable, somewhat "hotel-style" surroundings, with mainly unstructured daytime activities and a dress code that is casual by day and a little more dressy at night. The food and standard of on-board service are very good, which compensate somewhat for the design and structural shortcomings of the vessel; flowers and greenery also help. One nice plus is the fact that all gratuities are included.

Weak Points: The design means that many public rooms are inside, with little or no connection with the sea. The ship has a maximum speed of 12.5 knots, which means it is fine for leisurely island cruising but is slow going on longer trajectories. The spaciousness of the ship, while providing flexibility among the several individual public rooms, actually detracts from the overall flow; and the awkward one-way (contra-flow) interior staircase around the atrium can prove to be quite frustrating. Also awkward is the multilevel entertainment room (show lounge). While the health spa facilities are good, the elevator does not reach them. The meet-and-greet service is inconsistent and remains the subject of passenger complaints.

Regal Empress
★★+

Mid-Size Ship:	21,909 tons	Cabins (for one person):	9
Lifestyle:	Standard	Cabins (with private balcony):	8
Cruise Line:	Regal Cruises	Cabins (wheelchair accessible):	1
Former Names:	*Caribe I, Olympia*	Cabin Current:	110/220-volt
Builder:	Alex Stephen & Son (UK)	Full-Service Dining Rooms:	1
Original Cost:	n/a	Elevators:	3
Entered Service:	October 1953/May 1993	Casino (gaming tables):	Yes
Registry:	Bahamas	Slot Machines:	Yes
Length (ft/m):	611.8/186.5	Swimming Pools (outdoors):	1
Beam (ft/m):	79.0/24.1	Swimming Pools (indoors):	0
Draft (ft/m):	28.2/8.6	Whirlpools:	2
Propulsion/Propellers:	Diesel (10,742kW)/2	Fitness Center:	Yes
Passenger Decks:	8	Sauna/Steam Room:	No/No
Total Crew:	396	Massage:	Yes
Passengers (lower beds/all berths):	905/1,068	Self-Service Launderette:	No
Pass. Space Ratio (lower beds/all berths):	24.2/20.5	Dedicated Cinema/Seats:	Yes/90
Crew/Pass. Ratio (lower beds/all berths):	2.2/2.6	Library:	Yes
Navigation Officers:	European	Classification Society:	Lloyd's Register
Cabins (total):	457		
Size Range (sq ft/sq m):	104.4–296.0/9.7–27.5	**OVERALL SCORE:**	**962**
Cabins (outside view):	230	**(OUT OF A POSSIBLE 2,000 POINTS)**	
Cabins (interior/no view):	227		

Accommodation: There is a wide range of cabin sizes and configurations, in 12 suite/cabin–price grades. Most are small, yet spacious enough, with good closet and reasonable drawer space, and heavy-duty fittings, although the decor is generally dark and dull. The largest accommodation can be found in the four "Admiral Suites," which have views over the ship's bow (when you stand up, that is), and in eight suites with private (covered and enclosed) verandas that were added in 1999, as were TVs in all cabins. Many cabins have additional upper berths, while some cabins can accommodate five persons. Otis Spunkmeyer cookies can be found on your pillow each night (this makes a change from those mint chocolates most cruise lines use).

Dining: The lovely old-world Caribbean Dining Room is a step back in time to a more gracious era, with its original oil paintings on burnished wood paneling, ornate lighting fixtures and etched glass panels, and original murals depicting New York and Rio. There are two seatings, and the whole dining room is non-smoking. Most tables are for groups of six or more, with a few tables for four.

The food is plentiful and of a reasonably decent standard considering the price (although there is much use of rice instead of potatoes and other starch-rich alternatives), with the exception of the self-serve buffets, which are really very basic and unimaginative. While the freshly baked breads (and different flavored butters daily) are good (passengers like the garlic bread), the selection of cheeses and fresh fruits is not.

La Trattoria is the place for casual self-serve buffet breakfasts, lunches, and dinners. This eatery features Italian and other European-style cuisines.

Other Comments: This ship — now almost 50 years old — has a traditional, balanced ocean-liner profile, and for many years sailed as a transatlantic liner between Greece and the United States. There is a good amount of open deck space for sun worshippers, although this can become very crowded when the ship is full. Traditional liner features include polished teak decking and handrails. There is an enclosed (air-conditioned) promenade deck that is popular with strollers, and for those that like to sit and read. Although the ship is old, Regal Cruises is spending a lot of time and effort to maintain it.

Inside the ship you'll find plenty of real woods, heavy brass, and Art Deco detailing throughout many of her public rooms, with fine satin woods and brass featured on the ship's interior staircases. Considering that the ship carries approximately 1,000 passengers, there really are very few public rooms other than a casino, a single-level show lounge (with slightly raised port and starboard sections), a nightclub/disco, and a piano lounge.

There is, however, a fine, old-fashioned library with untouched, original wood paneling and wood-beam ceiling. However, the book selection is poor and out of date; the dog-eared paperbacks just do not look right (hardback books are better); and no magazines are provided. There is also an Internet Café (it's actually a bar), for those that simply must connect while at sea.

Junior passengers are divided in to two groups: Juniors (ages 6 to 11 years) and Teens (ages 12 to 18 years).

This ship provides a basic cruise experience in reasonably adequate surroundings, but remember that, although she underwent some much-needed refurbishment in 1997, she is an old ship. The service is perfunctory, at best.

Weak Points: This is a high-density ship that feels very crowded and makes it difficult to find quiet places to relax. There are no cushioned pads for the deck lounge chairs outside on the open decks. Expect to be in a line for embarkation, disembarkation, and buffets. The ship is extremely cramped, with little space to move around when full, particularly on the short party cruises. The ship has an awkward layout, and many passageways do not extend for the length of the ship. Many ceilings in public rooms are low. Finally, the tip glasses stationed around the ship to solicit gratuities are particularly insulting.

Regal Princess
★★★★

Large Ship:	69,845 tons	Cabins (for one person):	0
Lifestyle:	Standard	Cabins (with private balcony):	184
Cruise Line:	Princess Cruises	Cabins (wheelchair accessible):	10
Former Names:	-	Cabin Current:	110/220-volt
Builder:	Fincantieri Navali (Italy)	Full-Service Dining Rooms:	1
Original Cost:	$276.8 million	Elevators:	9
Entered Service:	August 1991	Casino (gaming tables):	Yes
Registry:	Great Britain	Slot Machines:	Yes
Length (ft/m):	811.0/247.2	Swimming Pools (outdoors):	2
Beam (ft/m):	105.6/32.2	Swimming Pools (indoors):	0
Draft (ft/m):	25.5/7.8	Whirlpools:	4
Propulsion/Propellers:	Diesel (24,000kW)/2	Fitness Center:	Yes
Passenger Decks:	12	Sauna/Steam Room:	Yes/Yes
Total Crew:	696	Massage:	Yes
Passengers (lower beds/all berths):	1,590/1,910	Self-Service Launderette:	Yes
Pass. Space Ratio (lower beds/all berths):	43.9/36.5	Dedicated Cinema/Seats:	Yes/169
Crew/Pass. Ratio (lower beds/all berths):	2.2/2.7	Library:	Yes
Navigation Officers:	Italian	Classification Society:	Registro Navale Italiano
Cabins (total):	795		
Size Range (sq ft/sq m):	189.4–586.6/17.6 –54.5		
Cabins (outside view):	624		
Cabins (interior/no view):	171		

OVERALL SCORE: 1,509

(OUT OF A POSSIBLE 2,000 POINTS)

Accommodation: In general, the cabins are well designed and have large bathrooms as well as good soundproofing. Walk-in closets, refrigerator, personal safe, and an interactive video system are provided in all cabins, as are chocolates on your pillow each night. Twin beds convert to queen-size beds in standard cabins. Bathrobes and personal toiletry amenities are provided, and all cabins feature a small refrigerator and color TV. Note that Princess Cruises features CNN, CNBC, ESPN, and TNT on the in-cabin color TV system (when available, depending on cruise area). You should note that the outside-view cabins for the physically challenged have their views obstructed by lifeboats.

The 14 most expensive suites (each of which has a large private balcony) are very well laid out, with a practical design that positions most things in just the right place. The bedroom is separated from the living room by a heavy wooden door, and there are TVs in both rooms. The closet and drawer space is very generous, and there is enough of it even for long cruises.

Dining: The Palm Court dining room (nonsmoking) is large (although the galley divides it into a U-shape) but lacks tables for two, although the line's marketing tag line states that this is "The Love Boat" line. Some of the most desirable tables overlook the stern. There are two seatings.

Despite the fact that the portions are generous, the food and its presentation are somewhat disappointing. The quality of fish is poor (often disguised by crumb or batter coatings), the selection of fresh green vegetables is limited, and few garnishes are used. However, do remember that this is banquet catering, with all its attendant standardization and production cooking. Meats are of a decent quality, although often disguised by gravy-based sauces, and pasta dishes are acceptable (though voluminous) and are typically served by section headwaiters that may also make "something special just for you" — in search of gratuities and good comments.

On any given seven-day cruise, a typical menu cycle will include a Sailaway Dinner, Captain's Welcome Dinner, Chef's Dinner, Italian Dinner, French Dinner, Captain's Gala Dinner, and Landfall Dinner. The general service level is quite reasonable, but it always seems hurried, particularly for those who are at the first dinner seating. The wine list is average, with a heavy emphasis on California wines. Note that 15% is added to all beverage bills, including wines (whether you order a $15 bottle or a $120 bottle, although it's the same amount of service to open and pour the wine).

There is an excellent pizzeria, however, for informal meals; this is particularly popular at lunchtime and in the afternoons. Themed late-night buffets are provided, but afternoon teas are poor. For sweet snacks during the day, a Patisserie (items are at extra charge) is located in the spacious lobby.

Other Comments: This was the second ship in the 70,000-ton range for Princess Cruises and as such foreshadowed the even larger ships this successful company went on to build. The ship has an interesting, jumbo-airplane look to it when viewed from the front, with a dolphin-like upper structure (made of light-weight aluminum alloy) and a large upright "dustbin-like" funnel (also made from aluminum alloy) placed aft.

Inside, innovative and elegant styling of the period is mixed with traditional features and a spacious interior layout. The interior spaces are well designed, although the layout itself is somewhat disjointed. An understated decor of soft pastel shades is highlighted by some very colorful artwork.

An observation dome, set high atop the ship like the head of a dolphin, features a large casino, numerous rubber trees, a dance floor, and live music. The ship has decent health and fitness facilities. A striking, elegant three-decks-high atrium features grand staircase with fountain sculpture (real, stand-up cocktail parties are held here). Characters Bar, located adjacent to the pizzeria on the open deck forward, has wonderful drink concoctions and some unusual glasses.

This ship provides a very pleasant cruise in elegant and very comfortable surroundings, and fine-tuned staff will make you feel welcome. Princess Cruises provides white-gloved stewards to take you to your cabin when you embark, another nice touch. Crown Princess has undergone an extensive refit (remodeled atrium and dining room, new 24-hour Lido restaurant and evening bistro, and new children's center).

Weak Points: The open deck space is very limited for the size of the ship and the number of passengers carried, and, unfortunately, there is no forward observation viewpoint outdoors. There is no wraparound promenade deck outdoors (the only walking space being along the sides of the ship). In fact, there is little contact with the outdoors at all. The sunbathing space is really limited when the ship is full, although with most passengers often 50 years old and over, perhaps this is not quite so crucial. There are too many support pillars in the public rooms that obstruct the sight lines and flow. Inside, the layout is disjointed and takes getting used to. Galley fumes seem to waft constantly over the aft open decks.

Renaissance Seven
★★★★

Small Ship:	4,280 tons	Cabins (for one person):	0
Lifestyle:	Premium	Cabins (with private balcony):	4
Cruise Line:	Renaissance Cruises	Cabins (wheelchair accessible):	0
Former Names:	*Regina Renaissance*	Cabin Current:	110-volt
Builder:	Nuovi Cantieri Apuania (Italy)	Full-Service Dining Rooms:	1
Original Cost:	$25 million	Elevators:	1
Entered Service:	December 1991	Casino (gaming tables):	Yes
Registry:	Liberia	Slot Machines:	Yes
Length (ft/m):	297.2/90.60	Swimming Pools (outdoors):	1
Beam (ft/m):	50.1/15.30	Swimming Pools (indoors):	0
Draft (ft/m):	12.9/3.95	Whirlpools:	1
Propulsion/Propellers:	Diesel (5,000kW)/2	Fitness Center:	No
Passenger Decks:	5	Sauna/Steam Room:	Yes/No
Total Crew:	72	Massage:	Yes
Passengers (lower beds/all berths):	114/114	Self-Service Launderette:	No
Pass. Space Ratio (lower beds/all berths):	37.5/37.5	Dedicated Cinema/Seats:	No
Crew/Pass. Ratio (lower beds/all berths):	1.5/1.5	Library:	Yes
Navigation Officers:	Italian	Classification Society:	Registro Navale Italiano
Cabins (total):	57		
Size Range (sq ft/sq m):	215.0–312.0/20.0—29.0		
Cabins (outside view):	57		
Cabins (interior/no view):	0		

OVERALL SCORE: 1,506

(OUT OF A POSSIBLE 2,000 POINTS)

Accommodation: The spacious cabins combine highly polished imitation rosewood paneling with lots of mirrors and hand-crafted Italian furniture, lighted walk-in closets, three-sided vanity mirrors, and just about everything you need, including a TV and VCR, refrigerator (prestocked when you book, but at extra cost). The bathrooms, however, are small; they have real teakwood floors and marble vanities, but no bathtubs.

Dining: The dining room (operates with open seating for all meals) is small and elegant, with tables for two, four, six, and eight. You simply sit where you like, with whom you like, and at what time you like. The meals are self-service, buffet-style cold foods for breakfast and lunch, with hot foods chosen from a table menu and served properly. The dining room operation works well. The food quality, choice, and presentation are all fairly decent, and close to California "lean cuisine," although there is little flair.

Other Comments: The ship sports contemporary mega-yacht looks and handsome styling, with twin flared funnels. Originally a series of eight ships, Renaissance Cruises now operates only two of them.

There is one teak promenade deck outdoors and a reasonable amount of open deck and sunbathing space. The water sports facilities include an aft platform, sailfish, snorkeling equipment, and Zodiacs.

Inside the ship, one finds an elegant interior design, with polished wood-finish everywhere. The main lounge, the focal point for all social activities, has six pillars that destroy sight lines to the small stage area. There is also a very small book and video library.

This vessel is very comfortable and totally inviting, and features destination-intensive cruising for the privileged passenger who appreciates the finer things in life and is prepared to pay accordingly. Although neither ship nor product delivery is anywhere near the standard of a Seabourn Cruise Line vessel, for example, this intimate ship can still provide a good cruise experience for a moderate sum of money.

Renaissance Eight
★★★★

Small Ship:	4,280 tons	Cabins (for one person):	0
Lifestyle:	Premium	Cabins (with private balcony):	4
Cruise Line:	Renaissance Cruises	Cabins (wheelchair accessible):	0
Former Names:	-	Cabin Current:	110-volt
Builder:	Nuovi Cantieri Apuania (Italy)	Full-Service Dining Rooms:	1
Original Cost:	$25 million	Elevators:	1
Entered Service:	May 1992	Casino (gaming tables):	Yes
Registry:	Liberia	Slot Machines:	Yes
Length (ft/m):	297.2/90.60	Swimming Pools (outdoors):	1
Beam (ft/m):	50.1/15.30	Swimming Pools (indoors):	0
Draft (ft/m):	12.9/3.95	Whirlpools:	1
Propulsion/Propellers:	Diesel (5,000kW)/2	Fitness Center:	No
Passenger Decks:	5	Sauna/Steam Room:	Yes/No
Total Crew:	72	Massage:	Yes
Passengers (lower beds/all berths):	114/114	Self-Service Launderette:	No
Pass. Space Ratio (lower beds/all berths):	37.5/37.5	Dedicated Cinema:	No
Crew/Pass. Ratio (lower beds/all berths):	1.5/1.5	Library:	Yes
Navigation Officers:	Italian	Classification Society:	Registro Navale Italiano
Cabins (total):	57		
Size Range (sq ft/sq m):	215.0–312.0/20.0–29.0	**OVERALL SCORE:**	**1,506**
Cabins (outside view):	57	**(OUT OF A POSSIBLE 2,000 POINTS)**	
Cabins (interior/no view):	0		

Accommodation: The spacious cabins combine highly polished imitation rosewood paneling with lots of mirrors and hand-crafted Italian furniture, lighted walk-in closets, three-sided vanity mirrors, and just about everything you need, including a TV and VCR, refrigerator (prestocked when you book, but at extra cost). The bathrooms, however, are small; they have real teakwood floors and marble vanities, but no bathtubs.

Dining: The dining room (operates with open seating for all meals) is small and elegant, with tables for two, four, six, and eight. You simply sit where you like, with whom you like, and at what time you like. The meals are self-service, buffet-style cold foods for breakfast and lunch, with hot foods chosen from a table menu and served properly. The dining room operation works well. The food quality, choice, and presentation are all fairly decent, and close to California "lean cuisine," although there is little flair.

Other Comments: The ship sports contemporary mega-yacht looks and handsome styling, with twin flared funnels. Originally a series of eight ships, Renaissance Cruises now operates only two of them.

There is one teak promenade deck outdoors and a reasonable amount of open deck and sunbathing space. The water sports facilities include an aft platform, sailfish, snorkeling equipment, and Zodiacs.

Inside the ship, one finds an elegant interior design, with polished wood-finish everywhere. The main lounge, the focal point for all social activities, has six pillars that destroy sight lines to the small stage area. There is also a very small book and video library.

This vessel is very comfortable and totally inviting, and features destination-intensive cruising for the privileged passenger who appreciates the finer things in life and is prepared to pay accordingly. Although neither ship nor product delivery is anywhere near the standard of a Seabourn Cruise Line vessel, for example, this intimate ship can still provide a good cruise experience for a moderate sum of money.

Rhapsody
★★★

Mid-Size Ship:	17,495 tons	Cabins (for one person):	0
Lifestyle:	Standard	Cabins (with private balcony):	0
Cruise Line:	Mediterranean Shipping Cruises	Cabins (wheelchair accessible):	0
Former Names:	*Cunard Princess, Cunard Conquest*	Cabin Current:	220-volt
Builder:	Burmeister & Wein (Denmark)	Full-Service Dining Rooms:	1
Original Cost:	$17 million	Elevators:	2
Entered Service:	March 1977/May 1995	Casino (gaming tables):	Yes
Flag:	Panama	Slot Machines:	Yes
Length (ft/m):	541.0/164.9	Swimming Pools (outdoors):	1
Beam (ft/m):	76.1/23.2	Swimming Pools (indoors):	0
Draft (ft/m):	19.0/5.82	Whirlpools:	2
Propulsion/Propellers:	Diesel (15,670kW)/2	Fitness Center:	Yes
Passenger Decks:	8	Sauna/Steam Room:	Yes/No
Total Crew:	350	Massage:	No
Passengers (lower beds/all berths):	788/959	Self-Service Launderette:	No
Pass. Space Ratio (lower beds/all berths):	22.2/18.1	Dedicated Cinema/Seats:	Yes/135
Crew/Pass. Ratio (lower beds/all berths):	2.2/2.7	Library:	Yes
Navigation Officers:	Italian	Classification Society:	Lloyd's Register
Cabins (total):	394		
Size Range (sq ft/sq m):	87.1–264.8/8.1–24.6		
Cabins (outside view):	267		
Cabins (interior/no view):	127		

OVERALL SCORE: **1,194**

(OUT OF A POSSIBLE 2,000 POINTS)

Accommodation: Although the cabins are small and compact, with somewhat tinny (noisy) metal fixtures and very thin walls that provide extremely poor cabin insulation, they are adequate for short cruises. The soft furnishings are pleasing, and the closet and drawer space is reasonable. The bathrooms are adequate, if a little tight, with little storage space for toiletries.

Dining: Features a pleasant, bubbly dining room that has sea views from large picture windows, but it is fairly noisy due to its open design. There are two seatings. The standard "banquet" food is reasonable and tailored mainly to Italian passengers, with typical Italian dishes including plenty of pasta (but sadly there is no tableside cooking). The service is bubbly, cheerful, attentive, and comes with a smile, but lacks finesse. There is a limited selection of breads and fruits. The cabin service menu is very limited.

Additionally, a casual self-serve open-air area is available for breakfast, lunches, and (sometimes, depending on the itinerary) buffet dinners.

Other Comments: This ship is almost identical to her sister, the former *Cunard Countess*, with the same contemporary profile and good looks. She was acquired in 1995 by StarLauro Cruises, which in turn was renamed Mediterranean Shipping Cruises, as a replacement for its *Achille Lauro*, which caught fire and sank in 1995. There is a good amount of open deck space for sun-worshippers.

There is a good selection of public rooms with attractive decor, in light, bright colors, including an observation lounge above the bridge, overlooking the bow. Aft of the show lounge, which is a single-level room with raised seating on its port and starboard sides (eight pillars obstruct sight lines, and the ceiling height is very low). There is also an excellent indoor-outdoor entertainment nightclub and bar, which incorporates the occasional use of an aft open-deck area.

Rhapsody will provide a very comfortable first cruise experience, featuring destination-intensive itineraries, in a pleasing, casual, but very high-density environment.

This ship is now marketed mostly to Europeans, and to Italian passengers in particular (who form about 60% of the passengers). While the ship still looks sharp following an extensive refit and refurbishment in 1997, the standard of food and service offered are disappointingly commonplace.

Weak Points: There is no outdoor wraparound promenade deck outdoors. The cabins really are very small.

Rhapsody of the Seas
★★★★

Large Ship:	78,491 tons	Cabins (for one person):	0
Lifestyle:	Standard	Cabins (with private balcony):	229
Cruise Line:	Royal Caribbean International	Cabins (wheelchair accessible):	14
Former Names:	-	Cabin Current:	110/220-volt
Builder:	Chantiers de l'Atlantique (France)	Full-Service Dining Rooms:	1
Original Cost:	$275 million	Elevators:	9
Entered Service:	May 1997	Casino (gaming tables):	Yes
Registry:	Norway	Slot Machines:	Yes
Length (ft/m):	915.3/279.0	Swimming Pools (outdoors):	1
Beam (ft/m):	105.6/32.2	Swimming Pools (indoors):	1 (inside/outside)
Draft (ft/m):	24.9/7.6	Whirlpools:	6
Propulsion/Propellers:	Diesel-electric (50,400kW)/2	Fitness Center:	Yes
Passenger Decks:	11	Sauna/Steam Room:	Yes/Yes
Total Crew:	765	Massage:	Yes
Passengers (lower beds/all berths):	2,000/2,435	Self-Service Launderette:	No
Pass. Space Ratio (lower beds/all berths):	39.2/32.2	Cinema/Seats:	No
Crew/Pass. Ratio (lower beds/all berths):	2.6/3.1	Library:	Yes
Navigation Officers:	International	Classification Society:	Det Norske Veritas
Cabins (total):	1,000		
Size Range (sq ft/sq m):	148.5–1,059.2/13.8–98.4		
Cabins (outside view):	593		
Cabins (interior/no view):	407		

OVERALL SCORE: **1,519**

(OUT OF A POSSIBLE 2,000 POINTS)

Accommodation: The standard cabins are of an adequate size, and have just enough functional facilities to make them comfortable for a one-week cruise, but longer might prove confining. The decor is bright and cheerful, although the ceilings are plain. Twin lower beds convert to queen-size beds, and there is a reasonable amount of closet and drawer space (there is little room to maneuver between the bed and desk/TV unit). The bathrooms are functional, although the shower units themselves are small. The towels could be larger and thicker. In the passageways, upbeat artwork depicts musical themes, from classical to jazz and popular.

The ultimate accommodation aboard this ship is the Royal Suite, which resembles a Palm Beach apartment, complete with white baby grand (player) piano. The decor is simple and elegant, with pastel colors, and wood accented ceiling treatments.

Dining: The two-level main dining room (called Edelweiss) is attractive and works well, although the noise level can be high. There are two seatings. The quality and serving of meals aboard Royal Caribbean International ships has become very mechanized over the past few years. It can best be described as good, but rather basic, hotel banquet food, but, as is typical aboard so many ships today, there is little taste. While meats are of reasonable quality, the fish is not, and most vegetables taste the same. In other words, the meals are basically sound, but certainly not memorable. There is also a limited selection of breads and cheeses. There is a decent but fairly basic wine list, but the prices are high. The dining room features an open seating arrangement for breakfast and lunch, while dinner is typically at 6am for the main seating and 8:30am for the second seating.

The informal dining spots are well designed, with contemporary decor and colors, but the food is really basic fare and disappointing, the four-sided self-service buffet area is small for the number of passengers that use it. More money needs to be spent for better-quality ingredients. Each evening, buffets feature a different theme, something this company has been doing for more than 25 years — perhaps it's time for more creativity. One thing this company does once each cruise is to feature a "Galley Buffet," whereby passengers go through a section of the galley picking up food for a midnight buffet.

Other Comments: This striking ship shares design features that make many (but not all) of the Royal Caribbean International ships identifiable, including a Viking Crown Lounge, which is a terrific multi-level night spot (the music can be loud and overbearing, as can the cigarette smoke around the bar). The Viking Crown Lounge (which is also the ship's disco) aboard this and sister ship *Vision of the Seas* is positioned just forward of the center of the ship. The funnel is located well aft — a departure from all other Royal Caribbean International ships to date, which have the lounge positioned around, or at the base of, the funnel. The ship's stern is beautifully rounded. There is a reasonable amount of open-air walking space, although this can become cluttered with deck lounge chairs.

There is a wide range of interesting public rooms, lounges and bars to play in, and the interiors have been cleverly designed to avoid congestion and to aid passenger flow into revenue areas. Apropos of these, for those who enjoy gambling, the astrologically-themed casino is large and glitzy (although not as bold as aboard some of the company's other ships), again typical of most of the new large ships; a couple of pieces of "electrostatic" art in globe form provide fascinating relief.

There is, as one might expect, a large shopping area, although the merchandise is consistently tacky, and identical to that found in most American malls. The artwork throughout the ship is really upbeat and colorful, with music as its theme: classical, jazz, popular, and rock 'n' roll. Much improved over previous new ships in the fleet is the theater, with more entrances and fewer bottlenecks; there are still pillars obstructing sight lines from many seats, however. Also improved are the facilities for children and teens.

This ship has good health spa facilities, set in a spacious environment on one of the uppermost decks. The decor here has an Egyptian theme, with pharaohs lining the pool.

Ship lovers will enjoy the chair fabric in the Shall We Dance lounge, with its large aft-facing windows, and the glass-case-enclosed mechanical sculptures.

Royal Caribbean International provides a consistently good, highly programmed cruise vacation for those seeking to travel in a large ship, with a large number of other lively passengers. What, in particular, makes this ship feel warm and cozy is the use of fine, light wood surfaces throughout her public rooms, as well as the large array of potted plants everywhere.

Weak Points: Standing in line for embarkation, disembarkation, shore tenders and self-serve buffet meals is an inevitable aspect of cruising aboard all large ships. The daily program is so full of the day's events, in small-type size, that it is extremely difficult to read. The light-colored carpeting used on the stairwells is impractical.

Richard With
★★★ +

Small Ship:	11,205 tons	Cabins (with private balcony):	0
Lifestyle:	Standard	Cabins (wheelchair accessible):	3
Cruise Line:	Norwegian Coastal Voyages (OVDS)	Cabin Current:	220 volts
Former Names:	-	Full-Service Dining Rooms:	1
Builder:	Stralsund Wolkswerft (Norway)	Elevators:	2
Original Cost:	n/a	Casino (gaming tables):	No
Entered Service:	1993	Slot Machines:	No
Registry:	Norway	Swimming Pools (outdoors):	0
Length (ft/m):	399.6/121.8	Swimming Pools (inside):	0
Beam (ft/m):	62.9/19.2	Whirlpools:	0
Draft (ft/m):	16.0/4.9	Fitness Center:	Yes
Total Crew:	70	Sauna/Steam Room:	Yes/No
Passengers (lower beds/all berths):	448/490	Massage:	No
Pass. Space Ratio (lower beds/all berths):	25.0/22.8	Self-Service Launderette:	Yes
Crew/Pass. Ratio (lower beds/all berths):	6.4/7.0	Cinema/Seats:	No
Navigation Officers:	Norwegian	Library:	Yes
Cabins (total):	224	Classification Society:	Det Norske Veritas
Size Range (sq ft/sq m):	n/a		
Cabins (outside view):	173	**OVERALL SCORE:**	**1,285**
Cabins (interior — no view):	51	**(OUT OF A POSSIBLE 2,000 POINTS)**	
Cabins (for one person):	0		

Accommodation: There are nine grades of cabin, including three wheelchair-accessible cabins (one of the ship's two elevators accommodates a wheelchair). Double beds are only available in the two suites; all other cabins have beds and berths that cannot be moved. Some cabins also have an third (upper) berth, and a number of cabins are available for single occupancy, albeit with a price premium. All cabins have a 220-volt outlet, so take adapters and converters if you need to.

Dining: There is one main dining room (the Polar Restaurant — no smoking allowed), and tables are assigned when you embark. Three meals each day are included in the cruise fare: breakfast and lunch (featuring the famous Norwegian 'cold table') are self-serve buffet-style meals, while dinner is a sit-down affair, with three courses. Additionally, there is the Los Holtes Café, which is open 24 hours, where snacks and light meals can be purchased.

Other Comments: The Norwegian Coastal Voyage is a service that was started in 1863. It is jointly operated by two companies: Ofotens og Vesteraalen Dampskibsselskab (OVDS) and Troms Fylkes Dampskibsselskab (TFDS). The complete journey, of 1,250 nautical miles, takes in 34 ports of call in a 12-day roundtrip voyage between Bergen and Kirkenes (on the border with Russia), above the Arctic Circle (where a special "Crossing the Arctic Circle" ceremony welcomes newcomers). The journey can also be done in a one-way voyage that takes seven days (northbound) or six days (southbound). The ships carry passengers as well as mail and other cargo.

Perhaps you will be able to peek at the midnight sun (mid-May to late June north of the Arctic Circle), experience the northern lights (aurora borealis, mostly seen during winter months, and only when the atmospheric conditions are right), and be part of the daily life of the hardy Norwegians. Approximately 60% of the passengers will be Norwegian/Scandinavian/European, while the rest will be a mix of North American and other nationalities. Although the passenger bed capacity is quoted, note that many additional passengers may be on board as day passengers, sailing between two coastal ports — the ship being the equivalent of a seagoing bus for the coastal commuters. As for the weather, the west coast of Norway is warmed by the Gulf Stream, and temperatures will be similar to those found in New England.

This ship is one of the "new generations" of coastal voyage ships (built in the 1990s) that is rather like a mini-cruise vessel, with a better array of public rooms and facilities than the older, smaller ships in the fleet. This is an excellent way to experience the beautiful coastline of Norway with its fascinating coastal towns. There will be a engaging mix of passengers — it's a good way to meet new people and make new friends from different countries. A laundry room with washing machines, tumble dryers and irons is provided (useful for those for whom the cruise is only part of a more extensive vacation).

The rates vary by season, cabin location, and whether the ship is of the "new generation" (*Kong Harald, Nordkapp, Nordlys, Nordnorge, Polarlys, Richard With*) the "mid-generation" (*Narvik, Midnatsol, Vesteralen*) or the "traditional" (*Harald Jarl, Lofoten*) type ships, the scenery is what the voyage is all about. Senior citizens (those age 67 and over) qualify for a special discount.

Adult couples, single travelers and families with children wanting to sail along the coast of Norway and experience the area's natural beauty are best suited to this scenic cruise. It's ideal for anyone who doesn't need entertainment or mindless parlor games, but wants to relax and unwind, enjoys being close to nature, and is probably a bit of an adventurer. The dress code is casual and comfortable — layered clothing is best. The currency is the Norwegian krone.

Norwegian coast and fjords cruises consist of a 7-day (northbound) voyage between Bergen and Kirkenes, Norway; or a 6-day (southbound) voyage between Kirkenes and Bergen, Norway; or a 12-day roundtrip voyage. This ship also carries up to 50 cars.

Weak Points: The ship does not have stabilizers, so you should expect some movement when the weather is inclement or unkind. Drink prices are extremely high — the same as ashore in Norway. The cabins are small, and the bathrooms are really tiny. Although not needed during the winter, there is little outdoors deck space considering the number of passengers carried.

Rotterdam
★★★★

Large Ship:	59,652 tons	Cabins (for one person):	0
Lifestyle:	Premium	Cabins (with private balcony):	160
Cruise Line:	Holland America Line	Cabins (wheelchair accessible):	20
Former Names:	-	Cabin Current:	110/220-volt
Builder:	Fincantieri (Italy)	Full-Service Dining Rooms:	2
Original Cost:	$250 million	Elevators:	12
Entered Service:	December 1997	Casino (gaming tables):	Yes
Registry:	The Netherlands	Slot Machines:	Yes
Length (ft/m):	777.5/237.00	Swimming Pools (outdoors):	1
Beam (ft/m):	105.8/32.25	Swimming Pools (indoors):	1 (magrodome cover)
Draft (ft/m):	25.5/7.80	Whirlpools:	2
Propulsion/Propellers:	Diesel-electric (37,500kW)/2	Fitness Center:	Yes
Passenger Decks:	12	Sauna/Steam Room:	Yes/Yes
Total Crew:	593	Massage:	Yes
Passengers (lower beds/all berths):	1,320/1,668	Self-Service Launderette:	Yes
Pass. Space Ratio (lower beds/all berths):	45.1/35.7	Cinema/Seats:	Yes/235
Crew/Pass. Ratio (lower beds/all berths):	2.2/2.8	Library:	Yes
Navigation Officers:	Dutch	Classification Society:	Lloyd's Register
Cabins (total):	660		
Size Range (sq ft/sq m):	184.0–1,124.8/17.1–104.5		
Cabins (outside view):	542		
Cabins (interior/no view):	118		

OVERALL SCORE: 1,548

(OUT OF A POSSIBLE 2,000 POINTS)

Accommodation: The accommodation is spread over five decks (a number of cabins have full or partially obstructed views). Interestingly, no cabin is more than 144 ft. (44 m) from a stairway, which makes it easier to get from cabins to public rooms. All cabin doors feature a bird's-eye maple look, and hallways feature framed fabric panels to make them warmer and less clinical. All cabin TVs feature CNN and TNT.

All standard inside and outside cabins are tastefully furnished, and have twin beds that convert to a queen-size bed (space is tight for walking between beds and vanity unit). There is a decent amount of closet and drawer space, although this will prove tight for the longer voyages featured. The bathrooms, which are fully tiled, are disappointingly small (particularly for long cruises) and have small shower tubs, utilitarian personal toiletries cupboards, and exposed under-sink plumbing. There is no detailing to distinguish them from bathrooms aboard the Statendam-class ships, given that this ship is claimed by Holland America Line to be the "flagship" of the fleet.

There are 36 full Verandah Suites (Navigation Deck), including four Penthouse Suites, which share a private Concierge Lounge with a concierge to handle such things as special dining arrangements, shore excursions and special requests, although strangely there are no butlers for these suites, as aboard ships with similar facilities. Each suite has a separate steward's entrance and separate bedroom, dressing and living areas. Suite passengers get personal stationery, complimentary laundry and ironing, cocktail hour hors d'oeuvres and other goodies, as well as priority embarkation and disembarkation. The concierge lounge, with its latticework teak detailing and private library is accessible only by private key-card.

Physically challenged passengers have 20 cabins to choose from, including two of the large Penthouse suites (which include concierge services). However, there are different cabin configurations, and it is wise to check with your booking agent.

Dining: There is one principal, large two-level dining room (La Fontaine), with tables for four, six, or eight, similar to the *Statendam*-class ships (there are just nine tables for two). Open seating is featured for breakfast and lunch, with two seatings for dinner (with both smoking and no-smoking sections on both upper and lower levels). Fine Rosenthal china and good cutlery are featured (although there are no fish knives).

Unfortunately, Holland America Line food isn't as nice as the china it's placed on. It may be adequate for most passengers who are not used to better food, but it does not match the standard found aboard other ships in the premium segment of the industry. While USDA beef is of a good quality, fowl tends to be battery-tough, and most fish is overcooked and has the consistency of a baseball bat. What are also definitely not luxurious are the endless packets of sugar and packets (instead of glass jars) of breakfast jam, mar-

487

malade and honey, and poor quality teas. While these may be suitable for a family diner, they do not belong aboard a ship that claims to have "award-winning cuisine." Dessert and pastry items are of good quality (specifically for American tastes), although there is much use of canned fruits and jellies. Forget the selection of "international" cheeses, however, as most of it didn't come from anywhere other than the US, a country that is known for its processed, highly colored slices, and not fine cheese-making.

As an alternative to the more formal dining room, the Lido Buffet is open for casual dinners on all except for the last night of each cruise, in an open-seating arrangement. Tables are set with crisp linens, flatware, and stemware. A set menu is featured, and this includes a choice of four entrees.

The food is marginally better than that presently served aboard other Holland America Line ships, with better buffets and more attention to detail, although it does not come up to the standard of other ships in the premium segment of the industry. What is definitely not luxurious is the long lines.

There is also an 88-seat Odyssey Italian alternative restaurant, decorated in the manner of an opulent baroque Italian villa, and available to all passengers on a reservation basis. This alternative restaurant is a first on any Holland America Line ship (there's no extra charge). The room, whose basic color is black with gold accenting, is divided into three sections. The cuisines from the Perugia, Tuscany, and Umbria regions of Italy are featured, although portions are very small.

Other Comments: The current *Rotterdam* has been constructed to look like a slightly larger (longer and beamier), but certainly a much sleeker version of the *Statendam*-class ships, while retaining the graceful lines of the former *Rotterdam*, including a nicely-raked bow, as well as the familiar interior flow and design style. Also retained is the twin-funnel feature well recognized by former Holland America Line passengers, though now somewhat more streamlined. The new *Rotterdam* (the sixth Holland America Line ship to bear the name) is capable of 25 knots, which is useful for the longer distance itineraries that she features.

The interior focal point is a three-decks high atrium, in an oval, instead of circular, shape. The atrium's focal point is a huge "one-of-a-kind" clock, which includes an astrolabe, an astrological clock, and 14 other clocks. Instead of the just two staircases aboard the *Statendam*-class ships, *Rotterdam* features three (better from the viewpoint of safety and passenger accessibility). There is a magrodome-covered pool on the Lido Deck between the mast and the ship's twin funnels, as compared to the company's *Statendam*-class ships, which have only one large, very square funnel.

The interior public spaces also carry on the same layout and flow as found aboard the *Statendam*-class ships. The interior decor is best described as restrained, with much use of wood accenting. One room features a glass ceiling similar to that found aboard a former *Statendam*. As a whole, the decor of this ship is extremely refined, with much of the traditional ocean liner detailing so loved by frequent Holland America Line passengers. Additions are children's and teens' play areas, although these really are token gestures by a company that traditionally does not cater well to young people. Popcorn is available at the Wajang Theatre for moviegoers, while adjacent is the popular Java café. The casino, which is located in the middle of a major passenger flow, now features blackjack, roulette, poker and dice tables alongside the requisite rows of slot machines.

The artwork consists of a collection of 17th-century Dutch and Japanese artifacts together with contemporary works specially created for the ship, although there seems little linkage between some of the items.

Holland America Line's new flagship replaced the former ship of the same name when she was retired in September 1997 — just in time for the start of the company's 125th anniversary in 1998. She is the most contemporary ship for Holland America Line, with lighter, brighter decor. She is an extremely comfortable ship in which to cruise, with some fine, elegant and luxurious decorative features. However, these are marred by the poor quality of dining room food and service and the lack of understanding of what it takes to make a "luxury" cruise experience, despite what is touted in the company's brochures. Refreshingly, the company does not add an automatic 15% gratuity for beverage purchases.

The company does offer free cappuccino and espresso coffees, and free ice cream during certain hours of the day aboard its ships, as well as hot hors d'oeuvres in all bars — something other major lines seem to have dropped, or charge extra for.

Weak Points: Standing in line for embarkation, disembarkation, shore tenders and self-serve buffet meals is an inevitable aspect of cruising aboard all large ships. With one whole deck of suites (and a dedicated, private concierge lounge, and preferential passenger treatment), the company has in effect created a two-class ship. The charge to use the washing machines and dryers in the self-service launderette is really petty and irritating, particularly for the occupants of suites, as they pay high prices for their cruises. Communication (in English) with many of the staff, particularly in the dining room and buffet areas, can prove very frustrating! Room service is poor. Nonsmokers should avoid this ship, as smokers are everywhere.

Royal Clipper
★★★★

Small Ship:	5,061 tons	Size Range (sq ft/sq m):	100.0–320.0/9.3–29.7
Lifestyle:	Premium	Cabins (outside view):	108
Cruise Line:	Star Clippers	Cabins (interior/no view):	6
Former Names:	-	Cabins (for one person):	0
Builder:	De Merwede (Holland)	Cabins (with private balcony):	14
Original Cost:	$75 million	Cabins (wheelchair accessible):	0
Entered Service:	October 2000	Cabin Current:	110/220-volt
Registry:	Luxembourg	Full-Service Dining Rooms:	1
Length (ft/m):	439.6/134.0	Elevators:	0
Beam (ft/m):	54.1/16.5	Casino (gaming tables):	No
Draft (ft/m):	18.5/5.6	Slot Machines:	No
Type of Vessel:	sail-cruise (square rigger)	Swimming Pools (outdoors):	3
No. of Masts:	5	Whirlpools:	0
Sail Area (sq ft/sq m):	56,000/5,205	Fitness Center:	Yes
Main Propulsion:	42 sails	Sauna/Steam Room:	No/Yes
Propulsion/Propellers:	Diesel (3,700kW)/1	Massage:	Yes
Passenger Decks:	5	Self-Service Launderette:	No
Total Crew:	100	Library:	Yes
Passengers (lower beds/all berths):	228/255	Classification Society:	Lloyd's Register
Pass. Space Ratio (lower beds/all berths):	22.1/19.8		
Crew/Pass. Ratio (lower beds/all berths):	2.2/2.5	**OVERALL SCORE:**	**1,540**
Navigation Officers:	International		
Cabins (total):	114	**(OUT OF A POSSIBLE 2,000 POINTS)**	

Accommodation: There are eight grades of accommodation: Owner's Suite (2), Deluxe Suite (14), and Categories 1-6. No matter what grade of accommodation you choose, all feature polished wood-trimmed cabinetry and wall-to-wall carpeting, personal safe, full-length mirror, small TV with audio channels and 24-hour text-based news, and private bathroom. Most feature twin beds, 86 of which convert into a queen-size bed, while 28 are fixed queen-size beds that cannot be separated; and all have hair dryer and satellite-linked telephone. The six interior (no view) cabins, and a handful of other cabins have a permanently fixed double bed. Most cabins feature a privacy curtain, so that you cannot be seen from the hallway when the cabin attendant opens the door (useful if you are not wearing any clothes). In addition, 27 cabins sleep three persons.

The two Owner's Suites, located at the very aft of the ship, provide the most lavish accommodation, and feature one queen-size bed and one double bed, a separate living area with semi-circular sofa, large vanity desk, wet bar/refrigerator, marble-clad bathroom with whirlpool bathtub, plus one guest bathroom, and butler service. The two suites have an interconnecting door, so that the combined super-suite can sleep eight persons. However, there is no private balcony.

The 14 "Deck Suites" have interesting names: Ariel, Cutty Sark, Doriana, Eagle Wing, Flying Cloud, France, Golden Gate, Gloria, Great Republic, Passat, Pommern, Preussen, and Thermopylae. However, they are not actually suites, since the sleeping area cannot be separated from the lounge—they are simply larger cabins with a more luxurious interior, more storage space and a larger bathroom. Each features two lower beds convertible to a queen-size, small lounge area, minibar/refrigerator, writing desk, small private balcony, and marble-clad bathroom with combination whirlpool bathtub/shower, washbasin and toilet, and butler service. The door to the balcony can be opened so that fresh air floods the room (note that there is a 12-inch (30 cm) threshold to step over). There are no curtains, only roll-down blinds for the windows and balcony door. The balcony itself typically has two white plastic chairs and drinks table; however, teak chairs and table would be more in keeping with the nature of the ship. The 14 balconies are not particularly private, and most have ship's tenders or zodiacs overhanging them, or some rigging obscuring the views. Two other "name" cabins (Lord Nelson and Marco Polo — designated as Category 1 cabins) are located aft, but do not have private balconies, although the facilities are similar.

Note that the interior (no view) cabins and the lowest grades of outside view cabins are extremely small and tight, with very little room to move around the beds. Therefore, take only the minimum amount of clothing and luggage, as there will simply not be enough room for it. Note that when in cabins where beds

489

are linked together to form a double bed, you will have to clamber up over the front of the bed, since both sides have built-in storm barriers (this applies in inclement weather conditions only).

There is a small room-service menu (all items cost extra).

Dining: The dining room is constructed on several connecting levels (getting used to the steps is not easy), and seats all passengers at one seating under a three-deck-high atrium dome. You can sit with whom you wish at tables for four, six, eight, or ten. However, it is a noisy dining room, due to the positioning of the many waiter stations and the poor staff training, so mealtimes are not as enjoyable as one would wish them to be. Some tables are so badly positioned that correct waiter service is impossible, and much reaching over has to be done in order to serve everyone.

One corner can be closed off for private parties. Breakfasts and lunches are self-serve buffets, while dinner is a sit-down affair with table service, although the ambience is always friendly and lighthearted. The wine list consists of very young wines, and prices are quite high.

The cuisine is certainly nothing to write home about. Although perfectly acceptable, it certainly cannot be considered in the same class as that found aboard ships such as *Sea Cloud* or *Sea Cloud II*.

Other Comments: The culmination of an owner's childhood dream, *Royal Clipper* is truly a stunning sight under sail. Being marketed as the largest true fully rigged sailing ship in the world, this is a logical extension of the company's two other smaller ships, the 4-masted tall ships *Star Clipper* and *Star Flyer*. *Royal Clipper's* 5-masted design is based on the only other 5-masted sailing ship to be built, the 1902-built *Preussen*, and has approximately the same dimensions, albeit 45.9 feet (14 meters) shorter (she is much larger than the famous *Cutty Sark*, for example). She is almost 40 ft (12.1 meters) longer than the next largest sailing ship presently in commission — the four-mast Russian barkentine *Sedov*. However, to keep things in perspective, *Royal Clipper* is the same overall length as *Wind Song, Wind Spirit,* and *Wind Star* — the computer-controlled cruise-sail vessels of Windstar Cruises.

The construction time for this ship was remarkably short, due to the fact that her hull had been almost completed (at Gdansk shipyard, Poland) for another owner but became available to Star Clippers for completion and fitting out. The ship is instantly recognizable due to her geometric blue and white hull markings. Power winches, as well as hand winches, are employed in her deck fittings, as well as a mix of horizontal furling for the square sails and hydraulic power assist to roll the square sails along the yardarm. The sail handling system, which was designed by the ship's owner, Mikael Krafft, is such that she can be converted from a full rigger to a schooner in an incredibly short amount of time.

Her masts reach as high as 197 feet (60 meters) above the waterline, and the top 19 ft (5.8 meters) can be hinged over 90 degrees to clear bridges, cable lines and other port-based obstacles. Up to 42 sails can be used: 26 square sails (fore upper topgallant, fore lower topgallant, fore upper topsail, fore lower topsail, foresail, main royal, main upper topgallant, main lower topgallant, main upper topsail, main lower topsail, mainsail, middle royal, middle upper topgallant, middle lower topgallant, middle upper topsail, middle lower topsail, middle course, mizzen upper topgallant, mizzen lower topgallant, mizzen upper topsail, mizzen lower topsail, mizzen course, jigger topgallant, jigger upper topsail, jigger lower topsail, crossjack), 11 staysails (main royal staysail, main topgallant staysail, main topmast staysail, middle royal staysail, middle topgallant staysail, middle topmast staysail, mizzen royal staysail, mizzen topgallant staysail, mizzen topmast staysail, jigger topgallant staysail, jigger topmast staysail); 4 jibs (flying jib, outer jib, inner jib, fore topmast staysail) and 1 gaff-rigged spanker, she looks quite magnificent when under full sail — an area of some 54,360 sq ft (5,050 sq m). Also, watching the sailors manipulate ropes, rigging and sails is like watching a ballet — the precision and cohesion of a group of men who make it all look so simple.

As a passenger, you are allowed to climb to special lookout points aloft — maybe even for a glass of champagne! Passengers are also allowed on the bridge at any time (but not in the galley or engine room).

There is a large amount of open deck space and sunning space aboard this ship — something most tall ships lack, although, naturally, this is laid with ropes for the rigging. A marina platform can be lowered at the stern of the vessel, from where you can use the surfboards, sailing dinghies, take a ride on the ship's own banana boat, or go water-skiing or swimming. Snorkeling gear is available at no cost, while scuba diving is available at an extra charge. Note that you will be asked to sign a waiver if you wish to use the water sports equipment.

Inside, a midships atrium that is three decks high sits under one of the ship's three swimming pools, and sunlight streams down through a piano lounge on the uppermost level inside the ship and down into the dining room, which is on the lower level. A forward observation lounge is a real plus, and this is connected to the piano lounge via a central corridor. An Edwardian library/card room is decorated with a *belle epoque* fireplace.

A lounge called the Captain Nemo Club is where passengers can observe fish and sea life when the ship is at anchor, through thick glass portholes (floodlit from underneath at night — to attract the fish).

It is also adjacent to the ship's health spa, which incorporates a beauty salon, Moroccan steam room (extra charge) and gymnasium. Thai massage as well as traditional massage, and other beauty treatments, are available.

This delightful, quite spectacular tall ship for tourists operates seven-night and 14-day cruises in the Grenadines and Lower Windward Islands of the Caribbean during the winter and seven-night and 14-night cruises in the Mediterranean during the summer. It is good to note that her officers navigate using both traditional (sextant) and contemporary methods (advanced electronic positioning system).

Being a tall ship with true sailing traditions, there is, naturally, a parrot (sometimes kept in a large, gilded cage, but often seen around the ship on someone's shoulder), which is part of the crew (as aboard all Star Clippers' ships). The general ambience on board is extremely relaxed, friendly and casual — completely unpretentious. The passenger mix is international (often consisting of a good cross-section of yachting types) and the dress code is casual at all times (shorts and casual tops are the order of the day — yachting wear), with no ties needed at any time.

There is no doubt that *Royal Clipper* is a superb vessel for the actual experience of sailing — a tall ship probably without equal, since much more time is spent actually under sail than aboard almost any other tall ship (including the smaller *Sea Cloud* and *Sea Cloud II*). However, apart from the sailing experience, it is in the cuisine and service that the lack of professionalism and poor standards of delivery show. Much of this is the result of insufficient training and supervision, which the company is slowly addressing. The result is a score that could be higher if the cuisine and service were better.

The suites and cabins are larger than those aboard the tall ships of the Windjammer Barefoot Cruises fleet, while generally smaller than aboard *Sea Cloud* and *Sea Cloud II*. While the food and service are far superior to the Windjammers, both are well below the standard found aboard *Sea Cloud* and *Sea Cloud II*. I do not include the Windstar Cruises' ships (*Wind Song, Wind Spirit, Wind Star, Wind Surf*), because they cannot, in any sense of the word, be considered tall ships. *Royal Clipper*, however, is exactly that — a real, working, wind-and-sails-in-your-face tall ship with a highly personable captain and crew that welcome you as if you were part of the team. What also gives the ship a little extra in the scoring department is the fact that many water sports are included in the price of your cruise.

Weak Points: The food — its quality, variety, presentation, and service — is still the weakest point of a cruise aboard this tall ship, although it is better than that provided aboard the company's smaller vessels, *Star Clipper* and *Star Flyer*. This ship is not for the physically impaired, or for children. The steps of the internal stairs are steep, as in most sailing vessels. The tipping system, where all tips are pooled (the suggested amount is $8 per passenger, per day), causes concern for many passengers.

Royal Princess
★★★★

Large Ship:	44,348 tons	Cabins (for one person):	0
Lifestyle:	Standard	Cabins (with private balcony):	152
Cruise Line:	Princess Cruises	Cabins (wheelchair accessible):	4
Former Names:	-	Cabin Current:	110/220-volt
Builder:	Wartsila (Finland)	Full-Service Dining Rooms:	1
Original Cost:	$165 million	Elevators:	6
Entered Service:	November 1984	Casino (gaming tables):	Yes
Registry:	Great Britain	Slot Machines:	Yes
Length (ft/m):	754.5/230.0	Swimming Pools (outdoors):	2 (plus 2 splash pools)
Beam (ft/m):	95.8/29.2	Swimming Pools (indoors):	0
Draft (ft/m):	25.5/7.8	Whirlpools:	2
Propulsion/Propellers:	Diesel (29,160kW)/2	Fitness Center:	Yes
Passenger Decks:	9	Sauna/Steam Room:	Yes/No
Total Crew:	520	Massage:	Yes
Passengers (lower beds/all berths):	1,200/1,275	Self-Service Launderette:	Yes
Pass. Space Ratio (lower beds/all berths):	36.9/34.7	Dedicated Cinema/Seats:	Yes/150
Crew/Pass. Ratio (lower beds/all berths):	2.3/2.4	Library:	Yes
Navigation Officers:	British	Classification Society:	Lloyd's Register
Cabins (total):	600		
Size Range (sq ft/sq m):	67.8–805.1/6.3–74.8	**OVERALL SCORE:**	**1,536**
Cabins (outside view):	600	(OUT OF A POSSIBLE 2,000 POINTS)	
Cabins (interior/no view):	0		

Accommodation: The all-outside cabins (152 of which have private balconies) are featured in only four accommodation grades (including suites). All are quite well thought out, very comfortable and well appointed. The suites are extremely attractive, and feature good personal toiletry amenity kits.

All cabins have a full bathtub and shower, three-sided mirrors, and color TV. Note that Princess Cruises feature CNN, CNBC, ESPN, and TNT (when available, depending on cruise area) on the in-cabin color TV system. Bathrobes are provided for all passengers, as are chocolates on your pillow each night. Prompt, attentive room service is available 24 hours a day. Note that some cabins located on both Baja Deck and Caribe Deck have lifeboat-obstructed views. The cabin numbering system is extremely illogical, with numbers going through several hundred series on the same deck.

Dining: The elegant Continental Dining Room is set low down, adjacent to the lobby. There are two seatings for dinner. The service is reasonably friendly, and sound. All dining rooms aboard Princess Cruises ships are nonsmoking.

Despite the fact that the portions are generous, the food and its presentation are somewhat disappointing. The quality of fish is poor (often disguised by crumb or batter coatings), the selection of fresh green vegetables is limited, and few garnishes are used. However, remember that this is banquet catering, with all its attendant standardization and production cooking. Meats are of a decent quality, although often disguised by gravy-based sauces, and pasta dishes are acceptable (though voluminous), typically served by section headwaiters that may also make "something special just for you" — in search of gratuities and good comments.

On any given seven-day cruise, a typical menu cycle will include a Sailaway Dinner, Captain's Welcome Dinner, Chef's Dinner, Italian Dinner, French Dinner, Captain's Gala Dinner, and Landfall Dinner. The wine list is average, with a heavy emphasis on California wines. Note that 15% is added to all beverage bills, including wines (whether you order a $15 bottle or a $120 bottle, although it's the same amount of service to open and pour the wine).

The in-cabin service menu is basic and could include more items. The indoor-outdoor Lido Café was expanded dramatically in a refit not long ago and now features 24-hour food service for casual dining (plastic plates are provided, however), and better beverage stations that translates to less standing in lines.

Other Comments: This ship has handsome, contemporary outer styling, with a short, well-raked bow. Quality construction and materials were used throughout. There is an excellent amount of outdoor deck and sunbathing space, and traditional wraparound teak deck.

Well-designed, though slightly unconventional interior layout and passenger flow provides passenger cabins that are located above the public room decks. Features include large, beautifully appointed and spacious public rooms rather than the smaller, more intimate public rooms and lounges found aboard many ships today. There are spacious passageways and delightful, imposing staircases. Contemporary without being the least bit garish, the decor reflects the feeling of space, openness, and light.

The Horizon Lounge, set around the funnel base, has fine views, and makes for a peaceful environment during the day. This ship will provide a fine cruise experience in spacious, elegant surroundings, at the appropriate price, although attention to the small details of service finesse is often missing.

When this ship first debuted, she was a state-of-the-art vessel. It is amazing to see that now she is lagging behind the latest ships in several ways. Although still a very fine ship (particularly well-liked by both her American and British passengers), there is increasing competition in the marketplace.

Weak Points: Standing in line for embarkation, disembarkation, shore tender and self-serve buffet meals is an inevitable aspect of cruising aboard all large ships. The signs throughout the ship are adequate at best, and some of them are difficult to read.

Royal Star
★★ +

Small Ship:	5,360 tons	Cabins (for one person):	0
Lifestyle:	Standard	Cabins (with private balcony):	1
Cruise Line:	African Safari Cruises/	Cabins (wheelchair accessible):	0
	Star Line Cruises	Cabin Current:	110/220-volt
Former Names:	*Ocean Islander, San Giorgio,*	Full-Service Dining Rooms:	1
	City of Andros	Elevators:	1
Builder:	Cantieri Riuniti dell' Adriatico (Italy)	Casino (gaming tables):	Yes
Original Cost:	n/a	Slot Machines:	Yes
Entered Service:	1956/December 1990	Swimming Pools (outdoors):	1
Registry:	Bahamas	Swimming Pools (indoors):	0
Length (ft/m):	367.4/112.00	Whirlpools:	0
Beam (ft/m):	51.0/15.55	Fitness Center:	Yes
Draft (ft/m):	18.2/5.56	Sauna/Steam Room:	Yes/No
Propulsion/Propellers:	Diesel (29,160kW)/2	Massage:	Yes
Passenger Decks:	5	Self-Service Launderette:	No
Total Crew:	130	Dedicated Cinema:	No
Passengers (lower beds/all berths):	222/255	Library:	Yes
Pass. Space Ratio (lower beds/all berths):	24.1/21.0	Classification Society:	American Bureau of
Crew/Pass. Ratio (lower beds/all berths):	1.7/1.9		Shipping
Navigation Officers:	Greek		
Cabins (total):	111		
Size Range (sq ft/sq m):	107.0–398.0/10.0–37.0		
Cabins (outside view):	97		
Cabins (interior/no view):	14		

OVERALL SCORE: 1,080
(OUT OF A POSSIBLE 2,000 POINTS)

Accommodation: There are eight grades of accommodation. Except for one President Suite, the cabins are not large, although they are pleasantly decorated with good-quality furnishings and ample closet and drawer space. The cabin bathrooms, however, are really tiny, although the suites have two bathrooms, with hair dryer. There is a limited cabin service menu.

Dining: The Belvedere Restaurant is a charming dining room, with reasonably good service and an international cuisine, although standards are variable. There are two seatings. There is a limited selection of breads, cheeses, and fruits, and the choice of teas is poor. The dining room service is provided by Filipino and Indonesian waiters.

Other Comments: The African Safari Club is a Swiss hotel and tour operator that has been specializing in land-based safaris and East African resort stays for over 30 years. The company, which has six hotels in Mombasa, has been operating this ship for several years in conjunction with these land-based safaris. *Royal Star* is a charming little vessel (she was formerly operated by the now defunct Ocean Cruise Lines), with a well-balanced profile. There is an open bridge policy for all passengers while the ship is at sea (weather permitting). She has reasonable open deck space for sunbathing (but remember this operates for much of the year close to the equator, so the sun is incredibly strong).

Royal Star is suited to cruising in sheltered areas. Moderately clean and tidy, she provides a reasonably warm, friendly, relaxed, and personable ambience, though service finesse is lacking. Although the ship is now quite old, the interior decor is reasonably attractive, accented by brass railings and solid wood doors. The ship has a newly improved fitness center (though small). There is very little entertainment; it is very low-key (and low budget), and the crew provides much of it.

Well-packaged and operated, with interesting itineraries, this little ship will provide an enjoyable cruise/safari experience in very comfortable, small-ship surroundings, at a realistic price. The African Safari Club has its own aircraft to transport you from Frankfurt (or Basle) to Mombasa. Check with your travel agent in case a visa is needed. The official currency on board is the U.S. dollar.

Weak Points: The cleanliness of the vessel leaves much to be desired, particularly in the "back of house" areas.

Ryndam
★★★★

Large Ship:	55,451 tons	Cabins (for one person):	0
Lifestyle:	Premium	Cabins (with private balcony):	150
Cruise Line:	Holland America Line	Cabins (wheelchair accessible):	6
Former Names:		Cabin Current:	110/220-volt
Builder:	Fincantieri (Italy)	Full-Service Dining Rooms:	1
Original Cost:	$215 million	Elevators:	12
Entered Service:	November 1994	Casino (gaming tables):	Yes
Registry:	The Netherlands	Slot Machines:	Yes
Length (ft/m):	719.3/219.3	Swimming Pools (outdoors):	1
Beam (ft/m):	101.0/30.8	Swimming Pools (indoors):	1 (magrodome)
Draft (ft/m):	24.6/7.5	Whirlpools:	2
Propulsion/Propellers:	Diesel-electric (34,560kW)/2	Fitness Center:	Yes
		Sauna/Steam Room:	Yes/No
Passenger Decks:	10	Massage:	Yes
Total Crew:	557	Self-Service Launderette:	Yes
Passengers (lower beds/all berths):	1,266/1,627	Dedicated Cinema/Seats:	Yes/249
Pass. Space Ratio (lower beds/all berths):	43.8/34.0	Library:	Yes
Crew/Pass. Ratio (lower beds/all berths):	2.2/2.9	Classification Society:	Lloyd's Register
Navigation Officers:	British/Dutch		
Cabins (total):	633		
Size Range (sq ft/sq m):	186.2--1,124.8/17.3–104.5		
Cabins (outside view):	502		
Cabins (interior/no view):	131		

OVERALL SCORE: 1,533
(OUT OF A POSSIBLE 2,000 POINTS)

Accommodation: The accommodation ranges from small interior (no view) cabins to a large penthouse suite, in 17 categories. All cabins TVs feature CNN and TNT. The 148 interior (no view) and 336 outside (with a view) standard cabins feature twin beds that convert to a queen-size bed, and there is a separate living space with sofa and coffee table. However, although the drawer space is generally good, the closet space is actually very tight, particularly for long cruises (although more than adequate for a seven-night cruise). The bathrooms are tiled, and compact but practical — they come with a good range of personal toiletry amenities. Bathrobes are also provided, as are hair dryers. The bathrooms are quite well laid out, but the bathtubs are small units better described as shower tubs. Some cabins have interconnecting doors — good for families with children — or older couples with their own butler/maid or nurse.

On Navigation Deck 28, suites have accommodation for up to four. These suites also feature en-suite dining as an alternative to the dining room, for private, reclusive meals. These are very spacious, tastefully decorated and well laid-out, and feature a separate living room, bedroom with two lower beds (convertible to a king-size bed), a good size living area, dressing room, plenty of closet and drawer space and marble bathroom with Jacuzzi tub.

The largest accommodation of all is a Penthouse Suite; there is only one, located on the starboard side of the Navigation Deck. It features a king-size bed, walk-in closet with superb drawer space, oversized whirlpool bath and separate shower enclosure, living room, dressing room, large private balcony, pantry, minibar/refrigerator, a guest toilet and floor to ceiling windows.

Dining: The two-level Rotterdam Dining Room, located at the stern is quite dramatic, and has a grand staircase, panoramic views on three sides, and a music balcony. It features open seating for breakfast and lunch, and two seatings for dinner. The waiter stations in the dining room are very noisy for anyone seated adjacent to them. Fine Rosenthal china and cutlery are featured (although there are no fish knives).

Unfortunately, Holland America Line food isn't as nice as the china it's placed on. It may be adequate for most passengers who are not used to better food, but it does not match the standard found aboard other ships in the premium segment of the industry. While USDA beef is of a good quality, fowl tends to be battery-tough, and most fish is overcooked and has the consistency of a baseball bat. What are also definitely not luxurious are the endless packets of sugar and packets (instead of glass jars) of breakfast jam, marmalade and honey, and poor quality teas. While these may be suitable for a family diner, they do not belong aboard a ship that claims to have "award-winning cuisine." Dessert and pastry items are of good quality (specifically for American tastes), although there is much use of canned fruits and jellies. Forget the selection of "international" cheeses, however, as most of it didn't come from anywhere other than the US, a country that is known for its processed, highly colored slices, and not fine cheese-making.

As an alternative to the more formal dining room, the Lido Buffet is open for casual dinners on all except for the last night of each cruise, in an open-seating arrangement. Tables are set with crisp linens, flatware and stemware. A set menu is featured, and this includes a choice of four entrees.

The Lido Buffet also serves casual breakfasts and lunches, offering a wide choice and dual-line access, one side for smokers, the other for non-smokers. Unfortunately, there is much use of canned fruits (good for older passengers with no teeth!) and packeted items, although there are several commercial low-calorie salad dressings. The choice of cheeses (and accompanying crackers) is very poor. The beverage station is also a let-down, for it is no better than those found in family outlets ashore in the United States. In addition, a poolside grill provides basic American hamburgers and hot dogs.

Other Comments: This is one of a series of four almost identical ships in the same series — the others being *Maasdam, Statendam,* and *Veendam*. The exterior styling is rather angular (some would say boxy — the funnel certainly is), although it is softened and balanced somewhat by the fact that the hull is painted black. There is a full wraparound teakwood promenade deck outdoors. The deck lounge chairs are wood and come with comfortable cushioned pads.

Inside, an asymmetrical layout breaks up the interiors and helps to reduce bottlenecks and congestion. The decor is softer, more sophisticated, and far less eclectic than sister ship *Statendam*, while the interiors of *Ryndam* seem to improve further on the theme. In general, however, a restrained approach to interior styling is taken using a mixture of contemporary materials combined with traditional woods and ceramics. There is, fortunately, little "glitz" anywhere.

What is outstanding is the array of artworks throughout the ship (costing about $2 million), assembled and nicely displayed to represent the fine Dutch heritage of Holland America Line and to present a balance between standard itineraries and on-board creature comforts. Also noticeable are the fine flower arrangements throughout the public areas and foyers.

Atop the ship, with forward facing views that wrap around the sides is the Crow's Nest Lounge. By day it makes a fine observation lounge (particularly in Alaska), while by night it turns into a nightclub with extremely variable lighting.

The three-decks-high atrium foyer is quite stunning, although its sculptured centerpiece makes it look a little crowded, and leaves little room in front of the purser's office. A hydraulic magrodome (glass) roof covers the reasonably sized swimming pool/whirlpools and central Lido area (whose focal point is a large dolphin sculpture) so that this can be used in either fine or inclement weather.

The two-deck-high show lounge is basically well designed, but the ceiling is low and the sight lines from the balcony level are poor. The ship has a large and quite lovely and relaxing reference library. The company keeps its ships very clean and tidy, and there is good passenger flow throughout.

Ryndam is a well-built ship, and has fairly decent interior fit and finish. Holland America Line is constantly fine-tuning its performance as a cruise operator and its regular passengers (almost all of whom are North American — there are few international passengers) find the company's ships very comfortable and well run. The company continues its strong maritime traditions, although the present food and service components still let the rest of the cruise experience down. *Note*: The line does not add an automatic 15% gratuity for beverage purchases, unlike many other cruise lines.

Holland America Line's many repeat passengers always seem to enjoy the fact that social dancing is always on the menu. The company also offers complimentary cappuccino and espresso coffees, and free ice cream during certain hours of the day aboard its ships, as well as hot hors d'oeuvres in all bars, something other major lines seem to have dropped, or charge extra for. In the final analysis, however, the score for this ship (and her sisters *Maasdam, Statendam* and *Veendam*) ends up just a disappointing tad under what it could be if the food and food service staff were better (more professional training might help). This ship is now deployed year-round in the Caribbean, where her rather dark interior decor contrasts with the strong sunlight of the sub-tropical region.

Weak Points: Standing in line for embarkation, disembarkation, shore tender, and self-serve buffet meals is an inevitable aspect of cruising aboard all large ships. Although the Indonesian service staff is quite charming (for the most part), communication with them often proves frustrating for many passengers, and service is spotty and inconsistent. Note that passengers are forced to eat at the Lido Café on days when the dining room is closed for lunch (this is typically once or twice per cruise, depending on ship and itinerary). The single escalator is virtually useless. There is no bell push outside the suites. The charge to use the washing machines and dryers in the self-service launderette is really petty and irritating, particularly for the occupants of suites, as they pay high prices for their cruises. Room service is poor.

Saga Rose
★★★★

Mid-Size Ship:	24,474 tons	Cabins (for one person):	60
Lifestyle:	Premium	Cabins (with private balcony):	26
Cruise Line:	Saga Shipping	Cabins (wheelchair accessible):	8
Former Names:	*Gripsholm, Sagafjord*	Cabin Current:	110-volt
Builder:	Forges et Chantiers de la	Full-Service Dining Rooms:	1
	Méditeranée (France)	Elevators:	4
Original Cost:	$30 million	Casino (gaming tables):	No
Entered Service:	October 1965/May 1997	Slot Machines:	No
Registry:	Bahamas	Swimming Pools (outdoors):	1
Length (ft/m):	619.6/188.88	Swimming Pools (indoors):	1
Beam (ft/m):	80.3/24.49	Whirlpools:	0
Draft (ft/m):	27.0/8.25	Fitness Center:	Yes
Propulsion/Propellers:	Diesel (20,150kW)/2	Sauna/Steam Room:	Yes/No
Passenger Decks:	7	Massage:	Yes
Total Crew:	350	Self-Service Launderette:	Yes
Passengers (lower beds/all berths):	584/620	Dedicated Cinema/Seats:	Yes/181
Pass. Space Ratio (lower beds/all berths):	40.8/39.4	Library:	Yes
Crew/Pass. Ratio (lower beds/all berths):	1.6/1.7	Classification Society:	Det Norske Veritas
Navigation Officers:	British		
Cabins (total):	322		
Size Range (sq ft/sq m):	96.8–387.5/9.0–36.0	**OVERALL SCORE:**	**1,460**
Cabins (outside view):	290	**(OUT OF A POSSIBLE 2,000 POINTS)**	
Cabins (interior/no view):	32		

Accommodation: There are 18 grades of accommodation: three designated as suites, ten outside-view grades and two interior (no view) cabins (six grades are designated for single occupancy, including one with a private balcony). Several cabins have interconnecting doors, and some have obstructed views.

All grades feature fine quality fittings and appointments. All cabins have excellent insulation, and all were refurbished in 1997. There is also a large number of single cabins (useful for the over-50 traveler who enjoys privacy). There is a generous amount of drawer, under-bed storage, and illuminated closet space, and all cabins have European duvets and a personal lockbox. All bathrooms feature a combination bathtub/shower.

The service provided by the cabin stewards and stewardesses is good. Soft, 100% cotton bathrobes and towels are provided, as well as several personal toiletry items: shampoo/conditioner, body lotion, bath gel, shower cap, and soap.

Those who choose a cabin with a private balcony will find a teak balcony, with see-through railings, enough space for two deck lounge chairs and table, and an outside light.

Note that the cabin voltage is 110-volt, so take an adapter if you have a 220-volt electrical appliance (such as a hair dryer).

Dining: The dining room is superb in the classic sense, and has a central ceiling that is two decks high, with large ocean-view picture windows on the port and starboard sides and a horseshoe-shaped grand staircase at the forward end. One-seating dining is featured at assigned tables, with tables for two (there are lots of these), four, six, eight, or ten. The chinaware is Royal Doulton, while the flatware is also of a good quality.

The cuisine is quite creative, with a good variety of menu choices, and good-quality ingredients are used. The entrees are generally well presented, pastries and dessert items are of a good standard, and there is a reasonable choice of cheeses and fruits. There is a fairly comprehensive wine list, and the prices are very modest. Generally, the service is good, in the style of a grand hotel, from thoughtful and attentive waiters.

For casual meals, the Lido Café is available as a serve-yourself venue for breakfast and lunch. Several special theme buffets are provided each cruise.

Other Comments: *Saga Rose* is still a finely proportioned vessel, one of the more traditional cruise ships afloat today, and presents a sweeping profile with classic liner styling: clean, delightfully rounded lines, royal blue hull and well-placed buff-colored funnel amidships. Like an aging Bentley, she will hopefully not go out of style. In fine maritime tradition, the ship's bell and whistle are sounded at noon each day. There is a wraparound teak promenade deck outdoors, and thick pads for all deck lounge chairs. The ship has expansive open deck and sunbathing areas, and lots of nooks and crannies for privacy.

This classic ship, built in the mid-1960s for long-distance cruising, provides a traditional ship experience for discriminating over-50 passengers (*Note*: those under 50 are not accepted as passengers). Constructed to a high standard (the French shipyard that built her even went bankrupt because of the losses incurred), this ship has been quite well maintained and is operated with pride by her present owners, who have spent considerable sums of money in restoring her to fine condition.

The interiors are spacious, with high-ceilinged public rooms and tasteful decor (although there are too many low-back chairs). There are fine quality furnishings and fittings, including hardwoods, brass and stainless steel. In fact, it is quite difficult to find any plastic in her interior fittings, except for the laminates used to line the walls of the accommodation areas.

Public room facilities include a real ballroom/main lounge — among the nicest afloat for proper cocktail parties (where you stand and mingle, rather than sit), with furniture that can be moved for almost any configuration, and a large wood dance floor. Other facilities include an indoor swimming pool (and adjacent fitness center) as well as an outdoor pool, lots of recreational space, and delightful little nooks and crannies outdoors. The Britannia Lounge (observation lounge) is a fine room for social activities (or a spot of quiet reading), while the adjacent North Cape Bar provides a good bar and hangout for the cocktail crowd. The ship also sports a delightful piano bar/lounge (Shakespeare's), a real, large cinema, a nightclub, and computer-learning center (in what used to be the upper level of the nightclub).

Saga Rose is suffused with an air of comfortable familiarity, based on its intelligent design and high-quality appointments. Now in her mid-thirties, she has become a gracious old lady of the sea, and the few places she looks worn or tired only endear her the more. She attracts passengers who appreciate fine surroundings, decent service, and low drink prices, and they return to her again and again, assuring her a place in the crowded cruise market. Designed for long-distance cruising, the ship excels in offering quiet, refined living in surroundings of good comfort, with friendly, unobtrusive service. Entertainment has now improved, featuring popular chamber music (especially string quartet) concerts. Especially delicious are the themed afternoon tea concerts: Chocolate, English, and Viennese.

This is classic cruising for her mainly British passengers (the ship is based at Dover and Southampton), under the banner of Saga Cruises. Port taxes, insurance and gratuities are included, and if you pay for your on-board expenses with a Saga Visa Card and you get a 5% discount.

Weak Points: The interiors are quite dark (restful) and somber in places (particularly the accommodation hallways). While the food has improved, it is still a little disappointing. There are few balcony cabins. Access to some of the upper grade cabins is a little disjointed. The elevator does not go down as far as the indoor pool deck (C Deck).

St. Helena
★★★

Small Ship:	6,767 tons	Cabins (for one person):	0
Lifestyle:	Standard	Cabins (with private balcony):	0
Cruise Line:	St. Helena Shipping	Cabins (wheelchair accessible):	1
Former Names:	-	Cabin Current:	220-volt
Builder:	A&P Appledore (Scotland)	Full-Service Dining Rooms:	1
Original Cost:	$46 million	Elevators:	1
Entered Service:	October 1990	Casino (gaming tables):	No
Registry:	England	Slot Machines:	Yes (3)
Length (ft/m):	344.4/105.0	Swimming Pools (outdoors):	1
Beam (ft/m):	62.9/19.2	Swimming Pools (indoors):	0
Draft (ft/m):	19.6/6.0	Whirlpools:	0
Propulsion/Propellers:	Diesel (6,534kW)/2	Fitness Center:	No
Passenger Decks:	4	Sauna/Steam Room:	No/No
Total Crew:	53	Massage:	No
Passengers (lower beds/all berths):	98/128	Self-Service Launderette:	Yes
Pass. Space Ratio (lower beds/all berths):	69.0/52.8	Dedicated Cinema:	No
Crew/Pass. Ratio (lower beds/all berths):	1.8/2.4	Library:	Yes
Navigation Officers:	British/St. Helenian	Classification Society:	Lloyd's Register
Cabins (total):	49		
Size Range (sq ft/sq m):	51.0–202.0/4.8–18.7	**OVERALL SCORE:**	**1,219**
Cabins (outside view):	37		
Cabins (interior/no view):	12	**(OUT OF A POSSIBLE 2,000 POINTS)**	

Accommodation: The accommodation is in two-, three-, or four-berth cabins (there are 11 grades— which is a lot for such a small vessel), which are quite simply furnished, yet comfortable. The bathrooms are quite small, and of the "me first, you next" variety. There are nine cabins that do not have private facilities.

Dining: The dining room is totally nonsmoking. It has two seatings, which, on such a small ship, is rather disruptive. The food is very British, with hearty breakfasts and a relatively simple menu, attractively presented on fine china. Afternoon tea, complete with freshly baked cakes, is a must. If you want tea or coffee at any time, you can make it yourself in the steward's pantry — even in the middle of the night.

Other Comments: This is a fine little combination of contemporary working cargo-passenger ship that has all modern conveniences, including stabilizers and air-conditioning. Passengers can even take their pets. It operates just like a full-size cruise vessel, and has an "open bridge" policy. The swimming pool, however, is really a "dip" pool only, and is tiny.

Inside, the decor is tasteful and homey. There is a pleasant library/reading lounge (audio recordings and videos are also available). There is a complimentary self-service laundry facility.

The brochure states that landing at Ascension is at times "a hazardous process" due to slippery and steep wharf steps — now that's telling it like it is. The staff is warm, welcoming, eager to see you enjoying the journey, and delightful to sail with.

The ship operates a regular Cardiff–Tenerife–St. Helena (this was the final place of exile for Napoleon Bonaparte, and the island can only be reached by sea)–Ascension Island–Tristan Da Cunha–Capetown line service, which is like a mini-cruise, or long voyage, with lots of days at sea. There are, at present, six round-trip sailings a year. Occasionally, a special theme sailing is featured, such as one for ornithologists. And for those who have yet to meet Father Neptune when crossing the Equator, rest assured that you get to meet him.

Weak Points: The plastic deck furniture spoils the outdoors (teak tables and chairs would not only look much better, but they would be able to withstand the inclement weather sometimes incurred while crossing this vast expanse of open ocean).

Sapphire
★★★

Small Ship:	12,183 tons	Cabins (interior/no view):	139
Lifestyle:	Standard	Cabins (for one person):	0
Cruise Line:	Louis Cruise Lines	Cabins (with private balcony):	0
Former Names:	*Princesa Oceanica, Sea Prince V,*	Cabins (wheelchair accessible):	0
	Sea Prince, Ocean Princess,	Cabin Current:	110-volt
	Princess Italia, Italia	Full-Service Dining Rooms:	1
Builder:	Cantieri Navale Felszegi (Italy)	Elevators:	5
Original Cost:	n/a	Casino (gaming tables):	Yes
Entered Service:	August 1967/April 1996	Slot Machines:	Yes
Registry:	Cyprus	Swimming Pools (outdoors):	1
Length (ft/m):	491.7/149.8	Swimming Pools (indoors):	0
Beam (ft/m):	70.9/21.5	Whirlpools:	0
Draft (ft/m):	21.6/6.6	Fitness Center:	No
Propulsion/Propellers:	Diesel (11,050kW)/2	Sauna/Steam Room:	No/No
Passenger Decks:	8	Massage:	Yes
Total Crew:	250	Self-Service Launderette:	No
Passengers (lower beds/all berths):	576/650	Dedicated Cinema/Seats:	Yes/170
Pass. Space Ratio (lower beds/all berths):	21.1/18.7	Library:	Yes
Crew/Pass. Ratio (lower beds/all berths):	2.3/2.6	Classification Society:	Registro Navale Italiano
Navigation Officers:	Greek		
Cabins (total):	288	**OVERALL SCORE:**	**1,220**
Size Range (sq ft/sq m):	75.3–226.0/7.0–21.0		
Cabins (outside view):	149	**(OUT OF A POSSIBLE 2,000 POINTS)**	

Accommodation: Outside (view) and interior (no view) cabins are in several cabin grades, and the price depends on the location and deck. Reasonable-sized cabins have pleasing, though plain, decor, furnishings, and fittings. In almost all cases, the cabin closet and drawer space is very limited. All have tiled bathrooms, but they are small. There is a 24-hour cabin service menu, although there is only a limited choice of items.

Dining: The dining room is charming and has an Art Deco feel, a raised center ceiling, and lovely etched glass dividers, but the noise level is high from the waiter stations. There are two seatings. Service is reasonably attentive from a willing, friendly staff. The menu features international cuisine, although do remember that this is a low-cost cruise, and so you should not expect high-class food.

For casual breakfast and luncheon, the Café de Paris (located indoors but looking out onto the pool deck) is the place (it also has a bar).

Other Comments: *Sapphire* has had an interesting life, including a time, when, in 1993, she sank in the Amazon River before being purchased by her present owners and refitted. She has long, low-slung, handsome lines and a swept-back aft-placed funnel, all of which combine to provide a very attractive profile for this small ship. There is a good amount of open deck and sunbathing space, but the heated pool is very small, and is really only a "dip" pool.

Inside, fairly smart, contemporary interior decor is featured. There is a mix of attractive colors, together with much use of mirrored surfaces, which help to add warmth in the public rooms. Some public rooms have a low ceiling height. Harry's Bar is perhaps the most popular gathering place, although there are few seats (the gaming tables are adjacent). There is also a cinema with comfortable seating.

Louis Cruise Lines purchased the ship in August 1995, and, following an extensive refurbishment, placed her into service in April 1996. This ship will take you to some decent destinations in good, contemporary surroundings, and in a relaxed, casual, yet comfortable style. The realistic, inexpensive price of this product is a bonus for first-time passengers.

Seabourn Goddess I
★★★★★

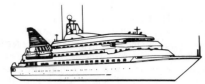

Small Ship:	4,260 tons	Cabins (with private balcony):	0
Lifestyle:	Luxury	Cabins (wheelchair accessible):	0
Cruise Line:	Seabourn Cruise Line	Cabin Current:	110/220-volt
Former Names:	*Sea Goddess I*	Full-Service Dining Rooms:	1
Builder:	Wartsila (Finland)	Elevators:	1
Entered Service:	April 1984	Casino (gaming tables):	Yes
Registry:	Norway	Slot Machines:	Yes
Length (ft/m):	343.8/104.81	Swimming Pools (outdoors):	1
Beam (ft/m):	47.9/14.60	Swimming Pools (indoors):	0
Draft (ft/m):	13.6/4.17	Whirlpools:	1
Propulsion/Propellers:	Diesel (3,540kW)/2	Fitness Center:	Yes
Passenger Decks:	5	Sauna/Steam Room:	Yes/No
Total Crew:	90	Massage:	Yes
Passengers (lower beds/all berths):	116/116	Self-Service Launderette:	No
Pass. Space Ratio (lower beds/all berths):	36.7/36.7	Dedicated Cinema:	No
Crew/Pass. Ratio (lower beds/all berths):	1.2/1.2	Library:	Yes
Navigation Officers:	Norwegian/Scandinavian	Classification Society:	Lloyd's Register
Cabins (total):	58		
Size Range (sq ft/sq m):	179.0–410.0/16.7–38.0		
Cabins (outside view):	58		
Cabins (interior/no view):	0		
Cabins (for one person):	0		

OVERALL SCORE: 1,790

(OUT OF A POSSIBLE 2,000 POINTS)

Accommodation: The cabins are fully equipped suites with an outside view through windows (or portholes, depending on the deck chosen). The beds are positioned next to the window so that you can entertain in the living area without going past the sleeping area (as one must aboard the other small Seabourn Cruise Line ships, for example). All cabinetry and furniture is of thick blond wood, with beautifully rounded edges. A long vanity desk in the sleeping area has a large mirror above it (but no three-sided mirrors), and two small drawers for cosmetic items; there is also a brass clock located on one wall. A long desk in the lounge area has six drawers, plus a vertical cupboard unit that houses a sensible safe, refrigerator and drink cabinet. There is also a VCR. Beds have thick cotton duvets, and non-allergenic pillows (and duvets) are also available.

The bathrooms are quite small (particularly for those who are of larger than average build), and doors open inward, so space inside really is at a premium. There is a glass shelf for personal toiletry items, while an under-sink drawer and cupboard provides space for larger items. Plush, thick 100% cotton bathrobes and towels are supplied.

For the best in accommodation aboard this ship, choose a double suite (there are eight of them), each with interconnecting doors and two bathrooms (his and hers), with one suite acting as a lounge/dining room, the other as a bedroom.

One accommodation drawback is the fact that the insulation between cabins is not as good as it could be, although rarely does this present a problem, as most passengers aboard the *Seabourn Goddesses* ships are generally extremely quiet, considerate types who are allergic to noise.

Dining: The dining salon is bright, warm, and inviting in its new primrose yellow decor. It is cozy, yet with plenty of space around each table for fine service, and the ship provides a floating culinary celebration in an open seating arrangement, so you can dine whenever, and with whomever you want.

Tables for two, four, six, or eight are immaculately laid with settings of real silver-base plates, pristine white table linen, and fresh flowers (there are also fresh flowers in several wall sconces). Hutschenreuther, Villeroy and Boch, and Tiffany are the appointments, and candlelight dinners are part of the setting. There is even a box of spare eye-glasses for menu reading in case you forget your own. You get leather-bound menus, and supremely attentive, close to impeccable personalized European service.

The *Seabourn Goddess* experience really is all about dining, and is the height of culinary excellence at sea. The service is relaxed and European, with everything prepared individually to order. The ship features exquisite, creative cuisine, utilizing only the very freshest and finest quality ingredients. Special orders are welcomed, and flaming desserts are cooked at your table. You can also dine, course by course in your suite for any meals, at any time (you can also eat à la carte 24 hours a day if you wish). There is plenty of fine quality caviar, at any time of the day or night. And, thankfully, never a hint of baked Alaska!

Table wines are included in the cruise fare for lunch and dinner. Real wine connoisseurs will appreciate the availability of an extra wine list, consisting of a selection of really special vintages and *premier crus* (at extra cost). If you want to do something different with a loved one, you can also arrange to dine one evening on the open (but covered) deck, overlooking the swimming pool and stern — it is a magical and very romantic setting.

There is also an informal outdoor Café, where excellent buffets are provided for breakfast and lunch, and you never have to fetch or carry your food — the waiters will do that for you. Recently added teak-wood tables and chairs add an additional (but essential and expected) touch of finery.

Other Comments: This small ship has an ultra-sleek profile and the ambience of a private club. She has been well-maintained, although there are signs of wear and tear. The ship was refurbished in late 1997, when new teakwood deck furniture was added. At her stern is a small water sports platform. Water-ski boats, windsurfers, jet skis, scuba, and snorkeling equipment are provided at no extra charge. However, the sea conditions have to be just right (minimal swell) for these items to be used, which, on average is once or twice in a seven-night cruise. You may also be allowed to swim off the stern platform.

Inside, there is a delightful feeling of unabashed but discreet sophistication. Elegant, chic public rooms feature flowers and pot-pourris everywhere. There is even a cute (meaning very small) gymnasium and sauna, hidden around the funnel base. Oriental rugs can be found in the lobby. Fine quality furnishings and fabrics are used throughout, with marble and blond wood accents.

The *Seabourn Goddesses* are really the ultimate boutique ships — like having your own private island where hospitality and anticipation are high art forms. The staff is delightful and accommodating ("no" is not in the staff's vocabulary); if there is anything special you want, you have only to ask, and the staff will be only too happy to oblige — in the style of the best European hotels. The dress code is resort casual by day (one could almost live in one's bathrobe), informal by night (no tuxedos allowed).

So, what type of persons will enjoy the *Seabourn Goddess* experience? Answer: those who enjoy life without dressing up, bingo, casinos, discos, or evening entertainment, and those seeking a totally unstruc-tured lifestyle. The *Seabourn Goddesses* provide indulgent, refined, unstructured and relaxed private liv-ing at sea, in a casual setting. One delightful feature of each cruise in warm weather areas is a "caviar in the surf" beach barbecue. This fine boutique cruise vessel is for experienced, independent travelers who do not like regular cruise ships, large ships, glitzy lounges, platoons of people, or kids running around, or dressing up. No one under the age of 16 is allowed aboard, without exception — a new rule put into effect in 1998, to the cheers of many repeat passengers.

All drinks (with the exception of premium brands and connoisseur wines) and gratuities are included, while port charges and insurance are not included. Life could hardly be better at sea — so, as many reg-ular *Seabourn Goddess* passengers say, why bother with ports of call at all? Embarkation starts at 3:00 am, never before, in case you are eager to get aboard.

Weak Points: Although these were the first of the mega-yacht-style ships when they were built, none of the cabins have private balconies (these arrived just a couple of years later aboard other, newer ships). The com-pany has sadly seen fit to decrease the standard of personal amenities supplied in the bathrooms, and some other little special touches and details have disappeared lately. These matters are reflected in the scores.

Seabourn Goddess II
★★★★★

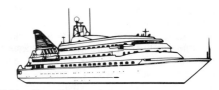

Small Ship:	4,260 tons	Cabins (for one person):	0
Lifestyle:	Luxury	Cabins (with private balcony):	0
Cruise Line:	Seabourn Cruise Line	Cabins (wheelchair accessible):	0
Former Names:	*Sea Goddess II*	Cabin Current:	110/220-volt
Builder:	Wartsila (Finland)	Full-Service Dining Rooms:	1
Original Cost:	$34 million	Elevators:	1
Entered Service:	May 1985	Casino (gaming tables):	Yes
Registry:	Norway	Slot Machines:	Yes
Length (ft/m):	343.8/104.81	Swimming Pools (outdoors):	1
Beam (ft/m):	47.9/14.60	Swimming Pools (indoors):	0
Draft (ft/m):	13.6/4.17	Whirlpools:	1
Propulsion/Propellers:	Diesel (3,540kW)/2	Fitness Center:	Yes
Passenger Decks:	5	Sauna/Steam Room:	Yes/No
Total Crew:	90	Massage:	Yes
Passengers (lower beds/all berths):	116/116	Self-Service Launderette:	No
Pass. Space Ratio (lower beds/all berths):	36.7/36.7	Dedicated Cinema:	No
Crew/Pass. Ratio (lower beds/all berths):	1.2/1.2	Library:	Yes
Navigation Officers:	Norwegian/Scandinavian	Classification Society:	Lloyd's Register
Cabins (total):	58		
Size Range (sq ft/sq m):	179.0–410.0/16.7–38.0	**OVERALL SCORE:**	**1,792**
Cabins (outside view):	58	(OUT OF A POSSIBLE 2,000 POINTS)	
Cabins (interior/no view):	0		

Accommodation: The cabins are fully equipped suites with an outside view through windows (or portholes, depending on the deck chosen). The beds are positioned next to the window so that you can entertain in the living area without going past the sleeping area (as one must aboard the other small Seabourn Cruise Line ships, for example). All cabinetry and furniture is of thick blond wood, with beautifully rounded edges. A long vanity desk in the sleeping area has a large mirror above it (but no three-sided mirrors for women to see the back of their hair) and two small drawers for cosmetic items; there is also a brass clock located on one wall. A long desk in the lounge area has six drawers, plus a vertical cupboard unit that houses a sensible safe, refrigerator and drinks cabinet. There is also a VCR. Beds have thick cotton duvets, and non-allergenic pillows (and duvets) are also available.

The bathrooms are quite small (particularly for those who are of larger than average build), and doors open inward, so space inside really is at a premium. There is a glass shelf for personal toiletry items while an under-sink drawer and cupboard provides space for larger items. Plush, thick 100% cotton bathrobes and towels are supplied.

For the best in accommodation aboard this ship, choose a double suite (there are eight of them), each with interconnecting doors and two bathrooms (his and hers), with one suite acting as a lounge/dining room, the other as a bedroom.

One accommodation drawback is the fact that the insulation between cabins is not as good as it could be, although rarely does this present a problem, as most passengers aboard the *Seabourn Goddesses* are generally extremely quiet, considerate types who are allergic to noise.

Dining: The dining salon is bright, warm, and inviting in its new primrose yellow decor. It is cozy, yet with plenty of space around each table for fine service, and the ship provides a floating culinary celebration in an open seating arrangement, so you can dine whenever, and with whomever you want. A grand piano is located at one end, for quiet dinner music.

Tables for two, four, six, or eight are immaculately laid with settings of real silver-base plates, pristine white table linen, and fresh flowers (there are also fresh flowers in several wall sconces). Hutschenreuther, Villeroy and Boch, and Tiffany are the appointments, and candlelight dinners are part of the setting. There is even a box of spare eye-glasses for menu reading in case you forget your own. You get leather-bound menus, and supremely attentive, close to impeccable personalized European service.

The *Seabourn Goddess* experience really is all about dining, and is the height of culinary excellence at sea. The service is relaxed and European, with everything prepared individually to order. The ship features exquisite, creative cuisine, utilizing only the very freshest and finest quality ingredients. Special orders are welcomed, and flaming desserts are cooked at your table. You can also dine, course by course in your suite for any meals, at any time (you can also eat à la carte 24 hours a day if you wish). There is plenty of fine quality caviar, at any time of the day or night. And, thankfully, never a hint of baked Alaska!

Table wines are included in the cruise fare for lunch and dinner. Real wine connoisseurs will appreciate the availability of an extra wine list, consisting of a selection of really special vintages and *premier crus* (at extra cost). If you want to do something different with a loved one, you can also arrange to dine one evening on the open (but covered) deck, overlooking the swimming pool and stern — it is a magical and very romantic setting.

There is also an informal outdoor Café, where excellent buffets are provided for breakfast and lunch, and you never have to fetch or carry your food — the waiters will do that for you. Recently added teak-wood tables and chairs add an additional (but essential and expected) touch of finery.

Other Comments: This small ship has an ultra-sleek profile and the ambience of a private club. She has been well-maintained, although there are signs of wear and tear. The ship was refurbished in late 1997, when new teakwood deck furniture was added. At her stern is a small water sports platform. Water-ski boats, windsurfers, jet skis, scuba, and snorkeling equipment are provided at no extra charge. However, the sea conditions have to be just right (minimal swell) for these items to be used, which, on average is once or twice in a seven-night cruise. You may also be allowed to swim off the stern platform.

Inside, there is a delightful feeling of unabashed but discreet sophistication. Elegant, chic public rooms feature flowers and pot pourris everywhere. There is even a cute (meaning very small) gymnasium and sauna, hidden around the funnel base. Oriental rugs can be found in the lobby. Fine quality furnishings and fabrics are used throughout, with marble and blond wood accents.

The *Seabourn Goddesses* are really the ultimate boutique ships — like having your own private island where hospitality and anticipation are high art forms. The staff is delightful and accommodating ("no" is not in the staff's vocabulary); if there is anything special you want, you have only to ask, and the staff will be only too happy to oblige — in the style of the best European hotels. The dress code is resort casual by day (one could almost live in one's bathrobe), informal by night (no tuxedos allowed).

So, what type of persons will enjoy the *Seabourn Goddess* experience? Answer: those who enjoy life without dressing up, bingo, casinos, discos, or evening entertainment, and those seeking a totally unstructured lifestyle. The *Seabourn Goddesses* provide indulgent, refined, unstructured and relaxed private living at sea, in a casual setting. One delightful feature of each cruise in warm weather areas is a "caviar in the surf" beach barbecue. This fine boutique cruise vessel is for experienced, independent travelers who do not like regular cruise ships, large ships, glitzy lounges, platoons of people, or kids running around, or dressing up. No one under the age of 16 is allowed aboard, without exception — a new rule put into effect in 1998, to the cheers of many repeat passengers.

All drinks (with the exception of premium brands and connoisseur wines) and gratuities are included, while port charges and insurance are not included. Life could hardly be better at sea — so, as many regular *Seabourn Goddess* passengers say, why bother with ports of call at all? Embarkation starts at 3:00 am, never before, in case you are eager to get aboard.

Weak Points: Although these were the first of the mega-yacht-style ships when they were built, none of the cabins have private balconies (these arrived just a couple of years later aboard other, newer ships). The company has sadly seen fit to decrease the standard of personal amenities supplied in the bathrooms, and some other little special touches and details have disappeared lately. These matters are reflected in the scores.

Seabourn Legend
★★★★★

Small Ship:	9,975 tons	Cabins (for one person):	0
Lifestyle:	Luxury	Cabins (with private balcony):	6
Cruise Line:	Seabourn Cruise Line	Cabins (wheelchair accessible):	4
Former Names:	*Queen Odyssey,*	Cabin Current:	110/220-volt
	Royal Viking Queen	Full-Service Dining Rooms:	1
Builder:	Schichau Seebeckwerft (Germany)	Elevators:	3
Original Cost:	$87 million	Casino (gaming tables):	Yes
Entered Service:	March 1992/July 1996	Slot Machines:	Yes
Registry:	Norway	Swimming Pools (outdoors):	1
Length (ft/m):	439.9/134.10	Swimming Pools (indoors):	0
Beam (ft/m):	62.9/19.20	Whirlpools:	3
Draft (ft/m):	16.7/5.10	Fitness Center:	Yes
Propulsion/Propellers:	Diesel (7,280kW)/2	Sauna/Steam Room:	Yes/Yes
Passenger Decks:	6	Massage:	Yes
Total Crew:	150	Self-Service Launderette:	Yes
Passengers (lower beds/all berths):	200/200	Dedicated Cinema:	No
Pass. Space Ratio (lower beds/all berths):	49.8/49.8	Library:	Yes
Crew/Pass. Ratio (lower beds/all berths):	1.3/1.3	Classification Society:	Det Norske Veritas
Navigation Officers:	Norwegian		
Cabins (total):	100		
Size Range (sq ft/sq m):	277.0–590.0/25.7–54.8	**OVERALL SCORE:**	**1,791**
Cabins (outside view):	100	**(OUT OF A POSSIBLE 2,000 POINTS)**	
Cabins (interior/no view):	0		

Accommodation: All the suites are comfortably large and beautifully equipped with everything one could need (they are larger than those aboard the company's smaller *Seabourn Goddesses*, but the ship is also larger, and carries almost double the number of passengers). All suites feature a sleeping area and separate living area, large walk-in closet (illuminated automatically when you open the door), 100% thick cotton towels and plush terrycloth bathrobes, designer soaps, VCR, personalized stationery, and leather ticket wallet (this arrives suitably boxed and nicely packaged before your cruise). Nonsmoking cabins are also available, as are course-by-course dinners (during restaurant dinner hours), and 24-hour room service. Menus for each dinner are delivered to your suite during the day.

Four Owner's Suites (Ibsen/Grieg, each measuring 530 sq ft/49 sq m and Eriksson/Heyerdahl, each measuring 575 sq ft/53 sq m), and two Classic Suites (Queen Maud/Queen Sonja, each measuring 400 sq ft/37 sq m) offer superb, private living spaces. Each has a walk-in closet, second closet, full bathroom plus a guest toilet with washbasin. There is a fully secluded forward- or side-facing balcony, with sun lounge chairs and wooden drinks table (Ibsen/Grieg do not have a balconies). The living area has ample bookshelf space (including a complete edition of *Encyclopedia Britannica*), large refrigerator/drinks cabinet, TV and VCR (plus a second TV in the bedroom). All windows, as well as the door to the balcony, have manually operated blackout blinds, and a complete blackout is possible in both bedroom and living room.

Dining: Elegant decor prevails in the formal dining room, which has a mixture of marble and carpeted floor. Seabourn Cruise Line's fine, creative cuisine is artfully presented, with almost all items cooked to order. Open seating dining means you can dine when you want, with whomever you wish. The 150-gram weight silverware is by Robbe & Berling.

The menus are nicely balanced, and special orders are available. While caviar is available on request, it is now sadly an extra cost item. Tableside flambeaus are presented, as are flaming desserts cooked at your table. There is always a good selection of exotic fruits and cheeses.

Each day, basic table wine is included for lunch and dinner, but all others (the decent ones) are at extra cost. The wine list is quite extensive, with prices ranging from moderate to high; many of the wines come from smaller, more exclusive vineyards. The European dining room staff is hand-picked and provides excellent, unhurried service.

In addition, relaxed breakfasts (available until at least 11am — civilized enough for late-risers) and lunch buffets and informal alternative, casual candlelight dinners (except on formal nights) can be taken in the popular Veranda Café adjacent to the swimming pool, instead of in the dining room. En-suite, course-by-course dining is available at any time.

Other Comments: This is a strikingly sleek ship with a handsome profile, almost identical in looks to *Seabourn Pride* and *Seabourn Spirit*, but built to a higher standard, with streamline "decorator" bars located along the side of the upper superstructure. The ship features two fine mahogany water taxis for use as shore tenders. There is also an aft water-sports platform and marina, which can be used in suitably calm warm-water areas. Water sports facilities include a small, enclosed "dip" pool, sea kayaks, snorkel equipment, windsurfers, water ski boat, and Zodiac inflatable boats.

Inside, there is a wide central passageway throughout the accommodation areas. The finest quality interior fixtures, fittings, and fabrics have been combined in her sumptuous public areas to present an outstanding, elegant decor, with warm color combinations (there is no glitz anywhere) and some fine artwork. A 360-degree mural in the reception lobby includes the ship's interior designer painted in. Relaxed by day, a more formal dress code applies at night.

A small, but well equipped health spa/fitness center has sauna and steam rooms (separate facilities for men and women), and an exercise room, with videotapes for private, individual aerobics workouts.

This ship provides discerning passengers with an outstanding level of personal service and a superb, utterly civilized cruise experience. For a grand, small ship cruise experience in the finest surroundings, with only just over 100 other couples as neighbors, this ship is very difficult to beat. All drinks (with the exception of premium brands and connoisseur wines) and gratuities are included, while port charges and insurance are not included.

Weak Points: The plastic chairs on the open decks really are unacceptable for this type of ship and should be changed to teakwood. Sadly, caviar is no longer free. There is no wraparound promenade deck outdoors, however, and there is little shade adjacent to the swimming pool.

Seabourn Pride
★★★★★

Small Ship:	9,975 tons	Cabins (with private balcony):	6
Lifestyle:	Luxury	Cabins (wheelchair accessible):	4
Cruise Line:	Seabourn Cruise Line	Cabin Current:	110/220-volt
Former Names:	-	Full-Service Dining Rooms:	1
Builder:	Seebeckwerft (Germany)	Elevators:	3
Original Cost:	$50 million	Casino (gaming tables):	Yes
Entered Service:	December 1988	Slot Machines:	Yes
Registry:	Norway	Swimming Pools (outdoors):	1 (+ 1 aft
Length (ft/m):	439.9/134.10		marina-pool)
Beam (ft/m):	62.9/19.20	Swimming Pools (indoors):	0
Draft (ft/m):	16.8/5.15	Whirlpools:	3
Propulsion/Propellers:	Diesel (5,355kW)/2	Fitness Center:	Yes
Passenger Decks:	6	Sauna/Steam Room:	Yes/Yes
Total Crew:	150	Massage:	Yes
Passengers (lower beds/all berths):	200/200	Self-Service Launderette:	Yes
Pass. Space Ratio (lower beds/all berths):	49.8/49.8	Dedicated Cinema:	No
Crew/Pass. Ratio (lower beds/all berths):	1.3/1.3	Library:	Yes
Navigation Officers:	Norwegian	Classification Society:	Det Norske Veritas
Cabins (total):	100		
Size Range (sq ft/sq m):	277.0–575.0/25.7—53.4		
Cabins (outside view):	100	**OVERALL SCORE:**	**1,790**
Cabins (interior/no view):	0		
Cabins (for one person):	0	**(OUT OF A POSSIBLE 2,000 POINTS)**	

Accommodation: The all-outside cabins (called suites in brochure-speak) are comfortably large and beautifully equipped with everything, including refrigerator, personal safe, VCR, personalized stationery, and large walk-in illuminated closet with wooden hangers. Electric blackout blinds are provided for the large windows in addition to curtains. All cabinetry is made of blond woods, with softly rounded edges, and cabin doors are neatly angled away from passageway (each pair of cabins also has a further door fronting on the passageway outside). The cabin ceilings are, however, quite plain.

The marble bathrooms feature two washbasins, a decent sized bathtub, plenty of storage areas, 100% thick cotton towels, plush terrycloth bathrobe, designer soaps, and a full range of personal bathroom amenities. Course-by-course in-cabin dining is available during dinner hours; there is also 24-hour room service.

Four Owner's suites (King Haakon/King Magnus, each measuring 530 sq ft/49 sq m and Amundsen/Nansen, each measuring 575 sq ft/53 sq m), and two Classic Suites (King Harald/King Olav, each measuring 400 sq ft/37 sq m) offer superb, private living spaces. Each has a walk-in closet, second closet, full bathroom; plus a guest toilet with washbasin. There is a fully secluded forward- or side-facing balcony, with sun lounge chairs and wooden drinks table. The living area has ample bookshelf space (including a complete edition of *Encyclopedia Britannica*), large refrigerator/drinks cabinet, TV and VCR (plus a second TV in the bedroom). All windows, as well as the door to the balcony, have manually operated blackout blinds, and a complete blackout is possible in both bedroom and living room.

Dining: The part-marble, part-carpeted dining room features portholes and elegant decor but is not as warm and intimate as that found aboard the *Seabourn Goddesses*. The silverware (150 gram weight — the best available) is by Robbe & Berling. Open seating dining means that you can dine when you want, with whom you wish. Course-by-course meals can also be served in your cabin.

The menus are nicely balanced, and special orders are available. While caviar is available on request, it is now sadly an extra cost item. Tableside flambeaus are presented, as are flaming desserts cooked at your table. There is always a good selection of exotic fruits and cheeses.

Each day, basic table wine is included for lunch and dinner, but all others (the decent ones) cost extra. The wine list is quite extensive, with prices ranging from moderate to high; many of the wines come from the smaller, more exclusive vineyards. The European dining room staff is hand-picked and provides excellent, unhurried service.

In addition, relaxed breakfasts (available until at least 11am — civilized enough for late-risers), lunch buffets, and informal alternative, casual candlelight dinners (except on formal nights) can be taken in the popular Veranda Café adjacent to the swimming pool, instead of in the dining room. En-suite, course-by-course dining is available at any time.

Other Comments: This luxuriously appointed cruise vessel has sleek exterior styling; a handsome profile with swept-back, rounded lines; and is an identical sister vessel to the *Seabourn Spirit*. She also has two superb mahogany water taxis for shore visits.

There is an aft water sports platform and marina, which is used in suitably calm, warm-water areas. Water sports facilities include an aft platform, enclosed marina pool, banana boat, pedalos, scuba, sea kayaks, snorkel, windsurfers, and water-ski boat.

There is a wide central passageway throughout the accommodation areas. Inviting, sumptuous public areas have warm colors. Fine quality interior fixtures, fittings, and fabric combine to present an outstanding, elegant decor, with tasteful color combinations and artwork. For a small ship, there is wide range of public rooms from which to choose. These include a main lounge (featuring light cabaret shows); nightclub (expanded in 1999); an observation lounge with bar, large, deep armchairs; and a cigar-smoking area complete with cabinet, cigar humidor, and respectable selection of good cigars (added in 1999). There is also a small business center and meeting room, and even a modest casino with roulette and blackjack tables, and a cubbyhole with a few slot machines.

A concise, well-equipped health spa/fitness center has sauna and steam rooms (separate facilities for men and women), and an exercise room, with videotapes for private, individual aerobics workouts.

Not for the budget-minded, this ship is for those desiring the utmost in supremely elegant, stylish, small-ship surroundings, but she is perhaps too small for long voyages in open waters. All drinks (with the exception of premium brands and connoisseur wines) and gratuities are included, while port charges and insurance are not included.

Weak Points: The deck lounge chairs are plastic (although light and easy to store, they are second class, and should be made of wood or stainless steel). Caviar is no longer free. There is no wraparound promenade deck outdoors. There are no seat cushions on the wooden chairs at the indoor/outdoor café. There is only one dryer in the self-service launderette.

Seabourn Spirit
★★★★★

Small Ship:	9,975 tons	Cabins (with private balcony):	6
Lifestyle:	Luxury	Cabins (wheelchair accessible):	4
Cruise Line:	Seabourn Cruise Line	Cabin Current:	110/220-volt
Former Names:	-	Full-Service Dining Rooms:	1
Builder:	Seebeckwerft (Germany)	Elevators:	3
Original Cost:	$50 million	Casino (gaming tables):	Yes
Entered Service:	November 1989	Slot Machines:	Yes
Registry:	Norway	Swimming Pools (outdoors):	1 (+ aft
Length (ft/m):	439.9/134.10		marina-pool)
Beam (ft/m):	62.9/19.20	Swimming Pools (indoors):	0
Draft (ft/m):	16.8/5.15	Whirlpools:	3
Propulsion/Propellers:	Diesel (5,355kW)/2	Fitness Center:	Yes
Passenger Decks:	6	Sauna/Steam Room:	Yes/Yes
Total Crew:	150	Massage:	Yes
Passengers (lower beds/all berths):	200/200	Self-Service Launderette:	Yes
Pass. Space Ratio (lower beds/all berths):	49.8/49.8	Dedicated Cinema:	No
Crew/Pass. Ratio (lower beds/all berths):	1.3/1.3	Library:	Yes
Navigation Officers:	Norwegian	Classification Society:	Det Norske Veritas
Cabins (total):	100		
Size Range (sq ft/sq m):	277.0–575.0/25.7–53.4		
Cabins (outside view):	100	**OVERALL SCORE:**	**1,790**
Cabins (interior/no view):	0	(OUT OF A POSSIBLE 2,000 POINTS)	
Cabins (for one person):	0		

Accommodation: The all-outside cabins (called suites in brochure-speak) are comfortably large and beautifully equipped with everything, including refrigerator, personal safe, VCR, personalized stationery, and large walk-in illuminated closet with wooden hangers. Electric blackout blinds are provided for the large windows in addition to curtains. All cabinetry is made of blond woods, with softly rounded edges, and cabin doors are neatly angled away from passageway (each pair of cabins also has a further door fronting on the passageway outside). The cabin ceilings are, however, quite plain.

The marble bathrooms feature two washbasins, a decent sized bathtub, plenty of storage areas, 100% thick cotton towels, plush terrycloth bathrobe, designer soaps and a full range of personal bathroom amenities. Course-by-course in-cabin dining is available during dinner hours; there is also 24-hour room service.

Four Owner's suites (Bergen/Oslo, each measuring 530 sq ft/49 sq m and Copenhagen/Stockholm, each measuring 575 sq ft/53 sq m), and two Classic Suites (Helsinki/Reykjavik, each measuring 400 sq ft/37 sq m) offer superb, private living spaces. Each has a walk-in closet, second closet, full bathroom plus a guest toilet with washbasin. There is a fully secluded forward- or side-facing balcony, with sun lounge chairs and wooden drinks table. The living area has ample bookshelf space (including a complete edition of *Encyclopedia Britannica*), large refrigerator/drinks cabinet, TV and VCR (plus a second TV in the bedroom). All windows, as well as the door to the balcony, have manually operated blackout blinds, and a complete blackout is possible in both bedroom and living room.

Dining: The part marble, part carpeted dining room features portholes and elegant decor but is not as warm and intimate as that found aboard the *Seabourn Goddesses*. The silverware (150 gram weight — the best available) is by Robbe & Berling. Open seating dining means that you can dine when you want, with whom you wish. Course-by-course meals can also be served in your cabin.

The menus are nicely balanced, and special orders are available. While caviar is available on request, it is now sadly an extra cost item. Tableside flambeaus are presented, as are flaming desserts cooked at your table. There is always a good selection of exotic fruits and cheeses.

Each day, basic table wine is included for lunch and dinner, but all others (the decent ones) are at extra cost. The wine list is quite extensive, with prices ranging from moderate to high; many of the wines come from the smaller, more exclusive vineyards. The European dining room staff is hand-picked and provides excellent, unhurried service.

In addition, relaxed breakfasts (available until at least 11am — civilized enough for late-risers), lunch buffets and informal alternative, casual candlelight dinners (except on formal nights) can be taken in the popular Veranda Café adjacent to the swimming pool, instead of in the dining room. En-suite, course-by-course dining is available at any time.

Other Comments: This luxuriously appointed cruise vessel has sleek exterior styling handsome profile with swept-back, rounded lines, and is an identical sister vessel to *Seabourn Pride*. She also has two superb mahogany water taxis for shore visits.

There is an aft water sports platform and marina, which is used in suitably calm, warm-water areas. Water sports facilities include an aft platform, enclosed marina pool, banana boat, pedalos, scuba, sea kayaks, snorkel, windsurfers, and water-ski boat.

There is a wide central passageway throughout the accommodation areas. Inviting, sumptuous public areas have warm colors. Fine quality interior fixtures, fittings, and fabric combine to present an outstanding, elegant decor with tasteful color combinations and artwork. For a small ship, there is wide range of public rooms from which to choose. These include a main lounge (featuring light cabaret shows); night-club (expanded in 1999); an observation lounge with bar, large, deep armchairs; and a cigar-smoking area complete with cabinet, cigar humidor, and respectable selection of good cigars (added in 1999). There is also a small business center and meeting room, and even a modest casino with roulette and blackjack tables, and a cubbyhole with a few slot machines.

A concise, well-equipped health spa/fitness center has sauna and steam rooms (separate facilities for men and women), and an exercise room, with videotapes for private, individual aerobics workouts.

Not for the budget-minded, this ship is for those desiring the utmost in supremely elegant, stylish, small-ship surroundings, but she is perhaps too small for long voyages in open waters. All drinks (with the exception of premium brands and connoisseur wines) and gratuities are included, while port charges and insurance are not included.

Weak Points: The deck lounge chairs are plastic (although light and easy to store, they are second class, and should be made of wood or stainless steel). Caviar is no longer free. There is no wraparound promenade deck outdoors. There are no seat cushions on the wooden chairs at the indoor/outdoor café. There is only one dryer in the self-service launderette.

Seabourn Sun
★★★★★

Mid-Size Ship:	37,845 tons	Cabins (for one person):	2
Lifestyle:	Luxury	Cabins (with private balcony):	145
Cruise Line:	Seabourn Cruise Line	Cabins (wheelchair accessible):	4
Former Names:	*Royal Viking Sun*	Cabin Current:	110-volt
Builder:	Wartsila (Finland)	Full-Service Dining Rooms:	1
Original Cost:	$125 million	Elevators:	4
Entered Service:	December 1988/November 1999	Casino (gaming tables):	Yes
Registry:	Bahamas	Slot Machines:	Yes
Length (ft/m):	674.2/205.5	Swimming Pools (outdoors):	2
Beam (ft/m):	91.8/28.0	Swimming Pools (indoors):	0
Draft (ft/m):	23.6/7.2	Whirlpools:	2
Propulsion/Propellers:	Diesel (21,120kW)/2	Fitness Center:	Yes
Passenger Decks:	8	Sauna/Steam Room:	Yes/Yes
Total Crew:	460	Massage:	Yes
Passengers (lower beds/all berths):	758/814	Self-Service Launderette:	Yes
Pass. Space Ratio (lower beds/all berths):	49.9/46.4	Dedicated Cinema/Seats:	Yes/101
Crew/Pass. Ratio (lower beds/all berths):	1.6/1.7	Library:	Yes
Navigation Officers:	European/Norwegian	Classification Society:	Det Norske Veritas
Cabins (total):	380		
Size Range (sq ft/sq m):	137.7–723.3/12.8–67.2		
Cabins (outside view):	355		
Cabins (interior/no view):	25		

OVERALL SCORE: **1,725**

(OUT OF A POSSIBLE 2,000 POINTS)

Accommodation: There are ten grades of accommodation, ranging from Penthouse Suites to standard outside-view cabins.

The Owner's Suite (723 sq ft/67.2 sq m), is a most desirable living space, although not as large as other penthouse suites aboard some other ships. It is light and airy, and features two bathrooms, one of which has a large whirlpool bathtub with ocean views, and anodized gold bathroom fittings. The living room contains a large dining table and chairs, large sofas, and plenty of space to spread out. There is also a substantial private balcony, and butler service, naturally.

Eighteen Penthouse Suites have large balconies and gracious butler service, two sofas, large bar/entertainment center, (minibar/refrigerator, color television, VCR, and CD player); bathrooms have separate toilet, sink and toiletries cabinets, connecting sliding door into the bedroom, large mirror, two toiletries cabinets, plenty of storage space, full bathtub, and anodized gold fittings. Each evening the butler brings different goodies. Liquor and wines are included in the cruise fare.

If you choose one of the Penthouses on Sky Deck, it might be best on the starboard side where they are located in a private hallway, while those on the port side (including the Owner's Suite) are positioned along a public hallway. All of the Penthouse Suites on Bridge Deck are positioned along private hallways.

Most of the other cabins (spread over five other decks) are of generous proportions and are well appointed with just about everything you would need (including a VCR). Some 38% of all cabins have a private balcony. All cabins feature walk-in closets, lockable drawers (the line calls them "safe drawers"), full-length mirrors, hair dryers, large fluffy cotton bathrobes and ample cotton towels. A good mix of Scandinavian and Filipino stewardesses provides excellent unobtrusive service.

A few cabins have third berths, while some cabins have interconnecting doors.

Four well-equipped, L-shaped cabins for the physically challenged are quite well-designed, fairly large, and feature special wheel-in bathrooms with shower facilities and closets.

The principal disappointment is with the rather plain cabin ceilings. All cabins underwent a complete refurbishment in 1997.

Dining: Fine quality cuisine and service are provided in an unhurried environment, with one-seating dining and menus that are not repeated, no matter how long the voyage. Crystal glasses, and fine quality plate ware and cutlery are provided. The food is creative and well presented, with good use of color combinations and garnishes. Selected red and white wines are included in the cruise fare and provided each day for lunch and dinner. In addition, there is a well-chosen wine list from distinguished vintners from around the world, although the prices are extremely high. Mineral water should be served for all meals in the dining room, instead of the standard chlorinated ship water provided.

For alternative dining, Venezia is a fine; separate à la carte Italian restaurant that is an elegant spot, with fine views from one of the ship's uppermost decks. Reservations are required.

There is also a decent indoor-outdoor Lido Buffet area (Garden Café), with a good variety and creative presentation (particularly with the special themed buffets that are provided). For those wanting a light dinner alternative in a casual setting, The Bistro is also available at night. Finally, if you want total privacy, you can also dine, course by course, in your suite or cabin.

Other Comments: This contemporary, well-designed ship has sleek, flowing lines, a sharply raked bow and a well-rounded profile, with lots of floor-to-ceiling glass. Seabourn Cruise Line acquired the ship in 1998, and, following an extensive refit and refurbishment program (which unfortunately did not go far enough), renamed her *Seabourn Sun* in November 1999. She is the largest ship in the Seabourn Cruise Line fleet. The ship's tenders are thoughtfully air-conditioned and even have radar and a toilet.

Wide teakwood decks provide excellent walking areas, including a wraparound promenade deck outdoors. The swimming pool (outdoors on Lido Deck) is not large, but adequate, while on the deck above, a croquet court and golf driving range are featured.

Inside, there are two glass-walled elevators at the aft elevator bank. Separate baggage elevators mean passengers do not have to wait for luggage. The interior layout is very spacious (it is even more ideal when a maximum of 600 passengers are aboard). Impressive public rooms and tasteful decor now reign. Two handrails — one of wood, one of chrome — are thoughtfully provided on all stairways, a thoughtful touch.

The Stella Polaris Lounge, the ship's forward observation lounge, is simply one of the most elegant, but contemporary (at least in decor), lounges at sea. Pebble Beach is the name of the electronic golf simulator room, complete with wet bar, with play possible on 11 virtual courses. The Ibsen Library is well organized, although it is simply not large enough for long-distance cruising.

The Oak Room is the ship's cigar/pipe smoker's lounge; it features a marble fireplace, which unfortunately cannot be used due to United States Coast Guard regulations. I have always thought it would make a fine library, although it is also excellent as a cigar-smoking room.

Following the 1999 refit, a new, much expanded (and much needed) heath spa was installed across the beam at the aft of the ship. This now includes six treatment rooms (with integral showers), a *rasul* chamber, a gymnasium with views over the stern (it is located where the aft swimming pool used to be), and separate sauna, steam room, and changing rooms for ladies and gents.

There is a computer-learning center, with ten workstations (although there is little privacy when getting one's e-mail). An excellent lecture program presents subjects of cultural interest, while gentlemen "dance hosts" provide partners for ladies traveling alone.

Whether by intention or not, the ship has a definite two-class feeling, with passengers in "upstairs" penthouse suites and "A" grade staterooms gravitating to the somewhat quieter Stella Polaris lounge (particularly at night), while other passengers (the participants) go to the main entertainment deck.

This ship has a wide range of facilities, including a concierge, self-service launderettes (useful when on long voyages), an excellent guest lecture program, 24-hour information office, and true 24-hour cabin service, and good food and service, regardless of price. This ship operates mainly long-distance cruises in great comfort (free shuttle buses are provided in almost all ports of call).

Committed to the pursuit of fine living at sea, she is a fine floating hotel. *Seabourn Sun's* direct competitors are *Crystal Harmony* and *Crystal Symphony* (arguably slightly newer and more elegant ships, with larger suites, but with two seatings for dinner).

While *Seabourn Sun* is not perfect, the few design flaws that are evident are minor points. Even though the hardware is not perfect, the software (personnel and service) is generally sound, although there has been some corner cutting since the ship was taken over by Seabourn Cruise Line.

A cruise aboard this ship should prove to be an extremely civilized travel experience (although, as with any ship, the larger the cabin the better and more exclusive the experience), with plenty of space per passenger, uncluttered surroundings, and no lines anywhere. Gratuities are extra, and they are added to your shipboard account at $10-$13 per day, according to the accommodation grade chosen. Perhaps the ship's best asset is her friendly and personable, mostly European crew.

In Spring 2002 *Seabourn Sun* will be transferred to Holland America Line after the ship's 2002 around-the-world cruise. The ship will then undergo some refurbishment, and public rooms will be renamed before entering service in June 2002 in Europe.

Weak Points: The cabin ceilings are plain. She is a very spacious ship, but is showing signs of wear and tear in some areas (particularly in the accommodation passageways), despite recent refurbishments. The library is much too small (particularly for some of the long cruises operated by this ship).

Sea Bird
★ ★

Small Ship:	99.7 tons	Cabins (for one person):	2
Lifestyle:	Standard	Cabins (with private balcony):	0
Cruise Line:	Lindblad Expeditions	Cabins (wheelchair accessible):	0
Former Names:	*Majestic Explorer*	Cabin Current:	110-volt
Builder:	Whidbey Island (USA)	Full-Service Dining Rooms:	1
Original Cost:	n/a	Elevators:	0
Entered Service:	1981	Casino (gaming tables):	No
Registry:	Bahamas	Slot Machines:	No
Length (ft/m):	151.9/46.3	Swimming Pools (outdoors):	0
Beam (ft/m):	30.8/9.4	Swimming Pools (indoors):	0
Draft (ft/m):	8.0/2.4	Whirlpools:	0
Propulsion/Propellers:	Diesel/2	Fitness Center:	No
Passenger Decks:	4	Sauna/Steam Room:	No/No
Total Crew:	22	Massage:	No
Passengers (lower beds/all berths):	70/70	Self-Service Launderette:	No
Pass. Space Ratio (lower beds/all berths):	1.4/1.4	Dedicated Cinema:	No
Crew/Pass. Ratio (lower beds/all berths):	3.1/3.1	Library:	No
Navigation Officers:	Scandinavian	Classification Society: American Bureau of Shipping	
Cabins (total):	36		
Size Range (sq ft/sq m):	73.0–202.0/6.7–18.7	**OVERALL SCORE:**	**943**
Cabins (outside view):	36		
Cabins (interior/no view):	0	**(OUT OF A POSSIBLE 2,000 POINTS)**	

Accommodation: All the cabins aboard this little ship have an outside view through picture windows, except for those on the lowest deck, which have portholes. Some cabins have double beds, some have twin beds, which can be pushed together to form a queen-size bed, and some are for singles (at a surcharge of 150%). There is plenty of room to stow your luggage. All cabins have a private bathroom, although it really is tiny. There is no room service for food or beverages.

Dining: The dining room (nonsmoking), which has ocean-view picture windows, is large enough to accommodate all passengers in a single seating. The tables are not assigned, so you can sit with whom you like. The food is unpretentious, good, and wholesome, and features regional specialties, although its presentation is very plain, with no frills. The wine list is very limited and is comprised mostly of wines from California.

Other Comments: The vessel carries a fleet of motorized Zodiac landing crafts for use as shore tenders and for up-close shore exploration. A number of sea kayaks are also carried.

The vessel is small enough to operate in ports and narrow inlets inaccessible to larger ships. Lecturers and recap sessions are part of each day. An "open bridge" policy means that you can visit the ship's navigation bridge at almost any time.

This small craft (together with sister ship *Sea Lion*) is adequate for looking at nature and wildlife close-up, in modest but comfortable surroundings that provide an alternative to big-ship cruising. A cruise on the *Sea Bird* best suits couples and single travelers who enjoy learning about nature, geography, history and other life sciences, in casual, non-dressy surroundings without a hint of pretension. Cruises operate in Alaska; Baja, California; and the Sea of Cortes. Tipping is suggested at about $7 per person per day.

Weak Points: In the cabins, the mattresses are enclosed in a wood frame with sharp corners, which you can bang into constantly.

Sea Cloud
★★★★★

Small Ship:	2,532 tons	Size Range (sq ft/sq m):	102.2–409.0/9.5–38.0
Lifestyle:	Luxury	Cabins (outside view):	34
Cruise Line:	Sea Cloud Cruises	Cabins (interior/no view):	0
Former Names:	*Sea Cloud of Grand Cayman,*	Cabins (for one person):	0
	IX-99, Antama, Patria, Angelita,	Cabins (with private balcony):	0
	Sea Cloud, Hussar	Cabins (wheelchair accessible):	0
Builder:	Krupp Werft (Germany)	Cabin Current:	220-volt
Entered Service:	August 1931/1979 (restored)	Full-Service Dining Rooms:	1
Registry:	Malta	Elevators:	0
Length (ft/m):	359.2/109.5	Casino (gaming tables):	No
Beam (ft/m):	48.28/14.9	Slot Machines:	No
Draft (ft/m):	16.8/5.13	Swimming Pools (outdoors):	0
Type of Vessel:	Barkentine	Whirlpools:	2
No. of Masts:	4 (17.7 meters)/30 sails	Fitness Center:	No
Sail Area (sq.ft/sq.m):	32,292/3,000	Sauna/Steam Room:	No/No
Main Propulsion:	sail power	Massage:	No
Propulsion/Propellers:	Diesel (4,476kW)/2	Self-Service Launderette:	No
Passenger Decks:	3	Library:	Yes
Total Crew:	60	Classification Society:	Germanischer Lloyd
Passengers (lower beds/all berths):	68/69		
Pass. Space Ratio (lower beds/all berths):	37.2/36.6		
Crew/Pass. Ratio (lower beds/all berths):	1.1/1.1	**OVERALL SCORE:**	**1,704**
Navigation Officers:	European	**(OUT OF A POSSIBLE 2,000 POINTS)**	
Cabins (total):	34		

Accommodation: Because *Sea Cloud* was built as a private yacht, there is a wide variation in cabin sizes and configurations. Some cabins have double beds, while some have twin beds (side by side or in an L-shaped configuration) that are fixed and cannot be placed together. Many of the original cabins have a fireplace (now with an electric fire).

All of the accommodation is very comfortable, but those on Main Deck (Cabins 1-8) were part of the original accommodation aboard this ship. Of these, the two Owner's Suites (Cabins 1 and 2) are really opulent, and feature real, original Chippendale furniture, fine gilt detailing, a real fireplace, French canopy bed, and large Italian Carrara marble bathrooms with gold fittings. The Owner's Cabin Number 1 is decorated in white throughout, and has a fireplace and Louis Phillippe chairs. Owner's Cabin Number 2 is completely paneled in rich woods, and retains the mahogany secretary used 60 years ago by Mr. Edward F. Hutton (Marjorie Post's husband).

Other cabins are all beautifully furnished (all were refurbished in 1993) and are surprisingly large for the size of the ship. There is good closet and drawer space and all cabins feature a personal safe and telephone. The cabin bathrooms, too, are quite luxurious, and equipped with really everything you will need, including bathrobes and hair dryer, and an assortment of personal toiletry items (there is also a 110 volt AC shaver socket in each bathroom). Note that the "new" cabins are small for two persons, so take minimal luggage.

There is no cabin food or beverage service. Also, if you occupy one of the original cabins on Main Deck you will probably be subjected to some noise when the motorized capstans are used to raise and lower or trim the sails. On one day each cruise, an "open-house" cocktail party is held on Main Deck, with all cabins available for any passengers to see.

Dining: The dining room, created from the original owner's living room/salon, is located in the center of the vessel. It is exquisite and elegant in every detail (it also houses the ship's library), has beautiful wood paneled walls and a wood beam ceiling. There is ample space at each table, so there is never a crowded feeling, and meals are taken in an open seating arrangement, so you can sit and dine with whom you wish, where you wish. German chefs are in charge, and the cuisine is very international, with a good balance of "nouvelle cuisine" and regional dishes featured (depending on which region the ship is sailing in). Outstanding quality food and cuisine are featured throughout. Place settings for dinner (often by candlelight) are navy blue, white, and gold Bauscher china.

European wines are typically provided for lunch and dinner (soft drinks and bottled water are included in the price, while alcoholic drinks cost extra). There is always excellent seafood and fish (this is always purchased fresh, locally, when available, as are most other ingredients). For breakfast and lunch, self-serve buffets are featured. These are really good, and beautifully presented (typically indoors for breakfast and outdoors on the Promenade Deck for lunch). Mealtimes are announced by the ship's bell. On the last day of each cruise, homemade ice cream is produced.

Other Comments: *Sea Cloud* is the oldest and most beautiful sailing ship in the world, and the largest private yacht ever built (at three times the size of Captain Cook's *Endeavour*), a beautiful, completely authentic 1930s barkentine whose three masts are almost as high as a 20-story building (the main mast is 178 feet/54.2 meters above the main deck). She was the largest private yacht ever built when constructed in 1931 by E. F. Hutton for his wife, Marjorie Merriweather Post (the American cereal heiress). Originally constructed for $1 million as *Hussar* in the Krupp shipyard in Kiel, Germany, this steel-hulled yacht is immensely impressive when in port, but absolutely exhilarating when under full sail.

During World War II, the vessel saw action as a weather observation ship, under the code name *IX-99*. You can still see five chevrons on the bridge, one for each half-year of duty, serving as a reminder of those important years.

There is plenty of deck space, even under the vast expanse of white sail, and the promenade deck outdoors still has wonderful varnished sea chests. The decks themselves are made of mahogany and teak, and wooden "steamer"-style deck lounge chairs are provided. One of the most beautiful aspects of sailing aboard this ship is her "Blue Lagoon," located at the very stern of the vessel. Weather permitting, you can lie down on the thick blue padding and gaze up at the stars and night sky — it's one of the great pleasures — particularly when the ship is under sail, with engines turned off.

The original engine room (with diesel engines) is still in operation for the rare occasions when sail power cannot be used. An open bridge policy is the norm — passengers are always allowed access there, except during times of poor weather or navigational maneuvers.

In addition to her retained and refurbished original suites and cabins, with their gorgeous wood paneling and antiques and dressers, some newer, smaller cabins were also added in 1979, when a consortium of German yachtsmen and businessmen purchased the ship. The owners spent $7.5 million refurbishing her. Many original oil paintings adorn her interior walls.

Her interiors exude warmth, and are finely hand crafted. There is much antique mahogany furniture, fine original oil paintings, gorgeous carved oak paneling, parquet flooring and burnished brass everywhere, as well as some finely detailed ceilings. There is absolutely no doubt that Marjorie Merryweather Post was accustomed only to the very finest things in life. The ship was designed by Gibbs & Cox and Cox & Stevens, then the foremost ship design firm in North America.

Sea Cloud is, without doubt, the ultimate, most romantic sailing ship afloat today. Although there are many imitations, there still is none better than this beautiful vintage vessel. She is still kept close to her original state when she was built. The ship operates under charter for much of the year, and sails in both the Caribbean and European/Mediterranean waters.

A cruise aboard *Sea Cloud* is, in three words, a truly exhilarating experience. She still exudes the warmth and feel today much as it was when she was first launched. She really is a special ship like no other, for the discerning few to relish the uncompromising comfort and elegance of a bygone era. Truly like a stately home afloat, this ship remains one of the world's finest travel experiences, and a wonderful escape from the stress and strain of contemporary life ashore. The activities are few, and so relaxation is the key, in a setting that provides fine service and style, but in an unpretentious way.

The only "dress-up" night is the Captain's Welcome Aboard Dinner, but otherwise, smart casual clothing is all that is needed (no tuxedo). The dress code is casual (note that mini-skirts would be impractical due to the steep staircases in some places — trousers are more practical). Also note that a big sailing vessel such as this can tip to one side occasionally (so bring only flat shoes, and no high heels).

The crew is made up from a number of nationalities, and the sailors that climb the rigging and set the sails include females as well as males. On the last night of the cruise, the sailor's choir sings seafaring songs for all. The U.S. Dollar is used as the on-board currency. Gratuities are suggested at $15 per person, per day, although these can be charged to your on-board account.

The owning company, Sea Cloud Cruises, which is German, also operates the new river vessel *River Cloud,* introduced in May 1996, for cruises on the Danube, Main, Mosel, and Rhine areas, and, in 2001 introduced a brand new companion sailing ship, named *Sea Cloud II.*

Sea Cloud is, for much of each year, under charter to Hapag-Lloyd Cruises. As such, white and red wines and beer are included for lunch and dinner; soft drinks, espresso and cappuccino coffees are also included at any time; shore excursions are an optional extra, as are gratuities. Other charter operators (such as Abercrombie & Kent) may include variations of the foregoing.

515

Note: Passengers are not permitted to climb the rigging, as may be possible aboard some other tall ships, but this is due to the fact that the mast rigging on this vintage sailing ship is of a very different type to the more modern sailing vessels. However, passengers may be able participate occasionally in the furling and unfurling of the sails.

Although now just over 70 years old, *Sea Cloud* is so lovingly maintained and operated that anyone who sails aboard her cannot fail to be impressed. If you seek entertainment, casinos, bingo, horse racing, and flashy resort cruising, this is not the ship for you. However, if you want to be part of one of the most exclusive communities at sea aboard a ship that is nothing other than utterly graceful, serene, and calming, you will love *Sea Cloud*. The food and service are extremely good, as is the interaction between passengers and crew, many of whom have worked aboard her for many, many years. One really important bonus is the fact that the doctor on board is available at no charge for medical emergencies or seasickness medication.

Weak Points: Some staircases are steep, as they are aboard almost all sailing vessels.

RIGGING

For the sailors among you, the sails are (in order, from fore to aft mast, top to bottom).

Fore Mast: flying jib, outer jib, inner jib, fore topmast staysail, fore royal, fore topgallant, fore upper-top sail, fore lower-top sail, foresail.
Main Mast: main royal staysail, main topgallant staysail, main topmast staysail, skysail, main royal, main topgallant, main upper topsail, main lower topsail, main sail.
Mizzen Mast: mizzen royal staysail, mizzen topgallant staysail, mizzen topmast staysail, mizzen royal topsail, mizzen topgallant, mizzen upper topsail, mizzen lower topsail, mizzen course.
Spanker Mast: spanker top mast staysail, spanker staysail, spanker-gaff topsail, B spanker.

Sea Cloud II
★★★★★

Small Ship:	3,849 tons	Cabins (total):	48
Lifestyle:	Luxury	Size Range (sq ft/sq m):	215.2–322.9/20.0–30.0
Cruise Line:	Sea Cloud Cruises	Cabins (outside view):	48
Former Names:	-	Cabins (interior/no view):	0
Builder:	Astilleros Gondan, Figueras (Spain)	Cabins (for one person):	0
Original Cost:	DM 50 million	Cabins (with private balcony):	0
Entered Service:	February 2001	Cabins (wheelchair accessible):	0
Registry:	Malta	Cabin Current:	110/220-volt
Length (ft/m):	383.8/117.0	Full-Service Dining Rooms:	1
Beam (ft/m):	52.9/16.15	Elevators:	0
Draft (ft/m):	17.7/5.4	Swimming Pools (outdoors):	0
Type of Vessel:	barkentine	Whirlpools:	0
No. of Masts:	3 (24 sails)	Exercise Room:	Yes
Sail Area (sq.ft/sq.m):	32,292/3,000	Sauna/Steam Room:	Yes/No
Main Propulsion:	sail power	Massage:	No
Propulsion/Propellers:	Diesel (2,500kW)/2	Self-Service Launderette:	No
Passenger Decks:	4	Library:	Yes
Total Crew:	60	Classification Society:	Germanischer Lloyd
Passengers (lower beds/all berths):	96/96		
Pass. Space Ratio (lower beds/all berths):	40.0/40.0		
Crew/Pass. Ratio (lower beds/all berths):	1.6/1.6		
Navigation Officers:	American/European		

OVERALL SCORE: **1,709**

(OUT OF A POSSIBLE 2,000 POINTS)

Accommodation: The decor in the cabins is very tasteful 1920s retro, with lots of bird's-eye maple wood paneling, brass accenting, and beautiful molded white ceilings. All cabins feature a vanity desk, hair dryer, refrigerator (typically stocked with soft drinks and bottled water), and a combination TV/video player. All cabins have a private bathroom with shower enclosure (or bathtub/shower combination), and plenty of storage space for your personal toiletries. Note that the cabin electrical current is 220-volt, although all bathrooms also include a 110-volt socket (but only for shavers).

There are two suites. Naturally, these have more space (but not as much space as the two owner's suites aboard sister vessel Sea Cloud), and comprise a completely separate bedroom (with four-poster bed) and living room, while the marble-clad bathroom features a full-sized bathtub.

There are 16 junior suites. These provide a living area and sleeping area with twin beds that convert to a queen-size bed. The marble-clad bathroom is quite opulent, and features a small bathtub/shower combination, with lots of little cubbyholes to store personal toiletry items.

Dining: The one-seating dining room operates an open seating policy, so you can dine with whom you wish, when you wish (within operating hours). It is decorated in a light, modern maritime style, with wood and carpeted flooring, comfortable chairs with armrests, and circular light fixtures. The gold-rimmed plateware used for the captain's dinner (which is typically a candlelit repast) has the ship's crest emblazoned in the white porcelain; it is extremely elegant (and highly collectible). The cuisine is very good, with small portions that are well presented, and accompanying sauces that are light and complementary. House wines are typically included for lunch and dinner.

Other Comments: This new, three-mast tall ship (slightly longer than the original *Sea Cloud*) has the look, ambience, and feel of a 1930s sailing vessel, but with all the latest high-tech navigational aids. The ship complements the company's beautiful, original, 1931-built *Sea Cloud* in almost every way, including her external appearance — except for a very rounded stern in place of the counterstern of sister ship *Sea Cloud*). Despite some appallingly low standards in the original fitting out of her interiors and carpeting by a shipyard that needs to learn the meaning of the word "quality," Sea Cloud Cruises quickly acted to correct all the irritating items, and has a ship for those seeking the very best in terms of luxurious comfort and surroundings inside a wonderful sailing vessel.

A small water sports platform is built into the aft quarter of the starboard side (with adjacent shower), and the ship carries four inflatable crafts for close-in shore landings, as well as snorkeling equipment.

The main lounge is elegance personified, with sofa and large individual tub chair seating around oval drinks tables. The ceiling is ornate, with an abundance of wood detailing, and an oval centerpiece is set around skylights to the open deck above. A bar is set into the aft port side of the room, which also has audio-visual aids built in for lectures and presentations.

One of the most rewarding aspects of sailing aboard this ship is the "Blue Lagoon," located at the very stern of the vessel — part of the outdoor bar and casual dining area. Weather permitting, you can lie down on thick blue padding and gaze up at the stars and warm night sky — it's one of the great pleasures — particularly when the ship is under sail, with the engines turned off.

Completely elegant in decor, but using modern materials to reproduce the period intended, the interior designers have managed to continue the same beautiful traditional look and design as that of her sister ship, *Sea Cloud*. These design details and special decorative touches will make you feel instantly at home. Whether the modern materials used will stand up to 70 years of use like those of the original *Sea Cloud* remains to be seen, although they are of a high quality. In any event, passengers who have sailed aboard the original *Sea Cloud* will no doubt compare the original with the new.

Overall, *Sea Cloud II* is the most luxurious true sailing ship in the world, although not the largest (that distinction goes to competitor Star Clippers' *Royal Clipper*). However, in terms of interior design, degree of luxury in appointments, the passenger flow, fabrics, food and service, the ceiling height of public rooms, larger cabins, great open deck space, better passenger space ratio, and crew-to-passenger ratio, there is none better than *Sea Cloud II*. If you sail both vessels (as I have), I am absolutely certain you would agree with me, and that your overall sail-cruise experience will be a truly memorable one.

Note that your personal experience will depend on which company is operating the ship under charter at the time of your sailing, and exactly what is to be included in the package. This is, however, as exclusive as it gets — sailing in the lap of luxury.

Rigging: This consists of up to 24 sails: flying jib, outer jib, inner jib; fore royal, fore topgallant, fore upper topsail, fore lower topsail, fore course; main royal staysail, main topgallant staysail, main topmast staysail; sky sail, main royal, main topgallant, main upper topsail, main lower topsail, main sail; mizzen topgallant staysail, mizzen topmast staysail; mizzen gaff topsail, mizzen upper gaff sail, mizzen lower gaff sail, middle gaff, upper gaff.

Weak Points: If you have sailed in the original cabins aboard the original *Sea Cloud* before, you will probably be disappointed with the more limited space and decoration of the equivalent cabins aboard this ship.

Sea Lion
★★

Small Ship:	99.7 tons	Cabins (for one person):	2
Lifestyle:	Standard	Cabins (with private balcony):	0
Cruise Line:	Lindblad Expeditions	Cabins (wheelchair accessible):	0
Former Names:	*Great Rivers Explorer*	Cabin Current:	110-volt
Builder:	Whidbey Island (USA)	Full-Service Dining Rooms:	1
Original Cost:	n/a	Elevators:	0
Entered Service:	1982	Casino (gaming tables):	No
Registry:	Bahamas	Slot Machines:	No
Length (ft/m):	151.9/46.3	Swimming Pools (outdoors):	0
Beam (ft/m):	30.8/9.4	Swimming Pools (indoors):	0
Draft (ft/m):	8.0/2.4	Whirlpools:	0
Propulsion/Propellers:	diesel/2	Fitness Center:	No
Passenger Decks:	4	Sauna/Steam Room:	No/No
Total Crew:	22	Massage:	No
Passengers (lower beds/all berths):	72/76	Self-Service Launderette:	No
Pass. Space Ratio (lower beds/all berths):	1.3/1.3	Dedicated Cinema:	No
Crew/Pass. Ratio (lower beds/all berths):	3.2/3.4	Library:	No
Navigation Officers:	Scandinavian	Classification Society: American Bureau of Shipping	
Cabins (total):	37		
Size Range (sq ft/sq m):	73.0–202.0/6.7–18.7	**OVERALL SCORE:**	**943**
Cabins (outside view):	37		
Cabins (interior/no view):	0	**(OUT OF A POSSIBLE 2,000 POINTS)**	

Accommodation: All the cabins aboard this little ship have an outside view through picture windows, except for those on the lowest deck, which have portholes. Some cabins have double beds, some have twin beds, which can be pushed together to form a queen-size bed, and some are for singles (at a surcharge of 150%). There is plenty of room to stow your luggage. All cabins have a private bathroom, although it really is tiny. There is no room service for food or beverages.

Dining: The dining room (nonsmoking), which has ocean-view picture windows, is large enough to accommodate all passengers in a single seating. The tables are not assigned, and so you can sit with whom you like. The food is unpretentious, good, and wholesome, and features regional specialties, although its presentation is very plain. The wine list is very limited, and is comprised mostly of wines from California.

Other Comments: The vessel carries a fleet of motorized Zodiac landing crafts for use as shore tenders and for up-close shore exploration. A number of sea kayaks are also carried.

The vessel is small enough to operate in ports and narrow inlets inaccessible to larger ships. Lecturers and recap sessions are part of each day. An open bridge policy means that you can visit the ship's navigation bridge at almost any time.

This small craft (together with sister ship *Sea Bird*) is adequate for looking at nature and wildlife close-up, in modest but comfortable surroundings that provide an alternative to big-ship cruising. A cruise on the *Sea Lion* best suits couples and single travelers who enjoy learning about nature, geography, and history in casual, non-dressy surroundings without a hint of pretension. Cruises operate in Alaska; Baja, California; and the Sea of Cortes. Tipping is suggested at about $7 per person per day.

Weak Points: In the cabins, the mattresses are enclosed in a wood frame with sharp corners, which you can bang into constantly.

Sea Princess
★★★★

Large Ship:	77,499 tons	Cabins (for one person):	0
Lifestyle:	Standard	Cabins (with private balcony):	446
Cruise Line:	Princess Cruises	Cabins (wheelchair accessible):	20
Former Names:	-	Cabin Current:	110/220-volt
Builder:	Fincantieri (Italy)	Full-Service Dining Rooms:	2 main/3 others
Original Cost:	$300 million	Elevators:	11
Entered Service:	December 1998	Casino (gaming tables):	Yes
Registry:	Great Britain	Slot Machines:	Yes
Length (ft/m):	857.2/261.3	Swimming Pools (outdoors):	3
Beam (ft/m):	105.6/32.2	Swimming Pools (indoors):	0
Draft (ft/m):	26.5/8.1	Whirlpools:	5
Propulsion/Propellers:	Diesel-electric	Fitness Center:	Yes
	(46,080kW)/2	Sauna/Steam Room:	Yes/Yes
Passenger Decks:	10	Massage:	Yes
Total Crew:	900	Self-Service Launderette:	Yes
Passengers (lower beds/all berths):	2,100/2,250	Dedicated Cinema:	No
Pass. Space Ratio (lower beds/all berths):	36.9/34.4	Library:	Yes
Crew/Pass. Ratio (lower beds/all berths):	2.1/2.5	Classification Society:	Registro Navale Italiano
Navigation Officers:	Italian		
Cabins (total):	1,050		
Size Range (sq ft/sq m):	158.2–610.3/14.7–56.7	**OVERALL SCORE:**	**1,539**
Cabins (outside view):	652		
Cabins (interior/no view):	398	(OUT OF A POSSIBLE 2,000 POINTS)	

Accommodation: There are 28 different cabin grades: 20 outside-view and 8 interior (no view) cabins. Although the standard outside (view) and interior (no view) cabins are a little small, they are well designed and functional in layout, and have earth-tone colors accentuated by splashes of color from the bedspreads. Proportionately, there are quite a lot of interior (no view) cabins. Many of the outside-view cabins have private balconies, and all seem to be quite well soundproofed, although the balcony partition is not floor-to-ceiling type, so you can hear your neighbors clearly (or smell their smoke). *Note*: The balconies are very narrow, and only large enough for just two small chairs, and there is no dedicated lighting.

A reasonable amount of closet and abundant drawer and other storage space is provided in all cabins — adequate for a seven-night cruise, as are a color TV and refrigerator. Each night a chocolate will appear on your pillow. The cabin bathrooms are practical, and come complete with all the details one needs, although they really are tight spaces, best described as one-person-at-a-time units. They do, however, have a decent shower enclosure, a small amount of shelving for your personal toiletries, real drinking glasses, a hair dryer, and a bathrobe.

The largest accommodation can be found in six suites, two on each of three decks located at the stern of the ship, with large private balcony. These are well laid out, and have large bathrooms with two sinks, a Whirlpool bathtub, and a separate shower enclosure. The bedroom features generous amounts of wood accenting and detailing, indented ceilings, and TV sets in both bedroom and lounge areas. The suites also have a dining room table and four chairs.

Mini-suites typically have two lower beds that convert into a queen-size bed. There is a separate bedroom/sleeping area with vanity desk, and a lounge with sofa and coffee table, indented ceilings with generous amounts of wood accenting and detailing, walk-in closet, and larger bathroom with Whirlpool bathtub and separate shower enclosure.

Note that Princess Cruises features CNN, CNBC, ESPN and TNT on the in-cabin color TV system (when available, depending on cruise area).

Dining: There are two principal dining rooms, Neapolitan and Sicilian. Both are nonsmoking, as are the dining rooms aboard all ships of Princess Cruises. You are assigned to one or the other depending on the location of your accommodation. Each dining room has its own galley, and each is split into multitier sections, which help create a feeling of intimacy, although there is a lot of noise from the waiter stations. Breakfast and lunch are provided in an open seating arrangement, while dinner is in two seatings.

The food, its presentation, and delivery are somewhat disappointing, and only adequate at best (this is banquet catering, after all), and let this otherwise nicely decorated ship down. On any given seven-day cruise, a typical menu cycle will include a Sailaway Dinner, Captain's Welcome Dinner, Chef's Dinner, Italian Dinner, French Dinner, Captain's Gala Dinner, and Landfall Dinner. The wine list is reasonable, but not good, and the company has unfortunately seen fit to eliminate all wine waiters. Note that 15% is added to all beverage bills, including wines.

With a sheltered view over the Riviera Pool, the Riviera Grill features Sterling Steakhouse for those that want to taste four different cuts of Angus beef from the popular "Sterling Silver" brand of USDA prime meats — Filet Mignon, New York Strip, Porterhouse, and Rib-Eye — all presented on a silver tray. The Riviera Grill also provides a barbecued chicken option. This is available as an alternative to the dining rooms, between 6:30pm and 9:30pm only, at an additional charge (at press time) of $8 per person.

There is also a patisserie (for cappuccino/espresso coffees and pastries), a wine/caviar bar, and a pizzeria (complete with cobblestone floors and wrought iron decorative features) with excellent pizzas.

The Horizon Buffet is open 24 hours a day, and, at night, features an informal dinner setting with sit-down waiter service; a small bistro menu is also available. The buffet displays are, for the most part, quite repetitious, but better than they have been in the last few years (plastic plates are provided, however). The cabin service menu is very limited, and presentation of the featured food items is very poor.

Other Comments: Although large, this all-white ship has a profile that is well balanced by a large funnel, which contains a deck tennis/basketball/volleyball court in its sheltered aft base. There is a wide, teak wraparound promenade deck outdoors, some real teak steamer-style deck chairs (with royal blue cushioned pads), and 93,000 sq ft (8,640 sq m) of outdoors space. A great amount of glass area on the upper decks provides plenty of light and connection with the outside world.

The ship, while large, absorbs passengers well, and has an almost intimate feel to her. Her interiors are pretty, with attractive colors and welcoming decor. The signs around the ship could be improved, however.

There is a wide range of public rooms to choose from, with several intimate rooms and spaces. The interior focal point is a huge four-decks-high atrium lobby with winding, double stairways, complete with two panoramic glass-walled elevators.

The main public entertainment rooms are located under three cabin decks. There are two show lounges, one at each end of the ship; one is a superb 550-seat, theater-style show lounge (movies are also shown here) and the other is a 480-seat cabaret-style lounge with bar.

A glass-walled health spa complex is located high atop ship with gymnasium and high-tech machines. One swimming pool is "suspended" aft between two decks. There are two other pools, although they are not large for the size of the ship.

The library is a very warm room and has six large buttery leather chairs for listening to CDs, with ocean-view windows. There is a conference center for up to 300, as well as a business center, with computers, copy and fax machines. The collection of artwork is good, particularly on the stairways, and helps make the ship feel smaller than it is, although in places it doesn't always seem coordinated. The casino, while large, is not really in the main passenger flow.

The most traditional room aboard is the Wheelhouse Lounge/Bar, which is decorated in the style of a turn-of-the-century gentleman's club, complete with wood paneling and comfortable seating. The focal point is a large ship model from the P&O collection archives: *Arandora Star*.

As is the case aboard most large ships today, if you live in the top suites, you will be well attended; if you do not, you will merely be one of a very large number of passengers. One nice feature is the captain's cocktail party — it is held in the four-decks-high main atrium — so you can come and go as you please — and there's no standing in line to have your photograph taken with the captain.

Weak Points: Standing in line for embarkation, disembarkation, shore tenders, and self-serve buffet meals is an inevitable aspect of cruising aboard all large ships. There is no escape from repetitious announcements that intrude (depending on itinerary). In-your-face art auctions are overbearing, and the paintings, lithographs, and faux, framed pictures are strewn throughout the ship — they are an annoying intrusion into what should be a vacation, not a cruise in a floating "art" store.

The digital voice announcing elevator deck stops is irritating to passengers. There are a number of dead ends in the interior layout, so it's not as user-friendly as it should be. The cabin numbering system is extremely illogical, with numbers going through several hundred series on the same deck. The walls of the passenger accommodation decks are very plain.

The swimming pools are quite small for so many passengers, and the pool deck is cluttered with white, plastic deck lounge chairs, without cushioned pads. Waiting for tenders in anchor ports can prove irritating, but typical of large ship operations. Charging for the machines in the self-service launderette is trifling (even though it's minimal).

Seawing
★★★

Mid-Size Ship:	16,710 tons	Cabins (interior/no view):	132
Lifestyle:	Standard	Cabins (for one person):	0
Cruise Line:	Airtours Sun Cruises/	Cabins (with private balcony):	0
	Louis Cruise Lines	Cabins (wheelchair accessible):	0
Former Names:	*Southward*	Cabin Current:	110-volt
Builder:	Cantieri Navale del Tirreno	Full-Service Dining Rooms:	1
	et Riuniti (Italy)	Elevators:	4
Original Cost:	n/a	Casino(gaming tables):	Yes
Entered Service:	November 1971/March 1995	Slot Machines:	Yes
Registry:	Bahamas	Swimming Pools (outdoors):	1
Length (ft/m):	535.7/163.30	Swimming Pools (indoors):	0
Beam (ft/m):	74.7/22.79	Whirlpools:	0
Draft (ft/m):	21.3/6.50	Fitness Center:	Yes
Propulsion/Propellers:	Diesel (13,400kW)/2	Sauna/Steam Room:	Yes/No
Passenger Decks:	7	Massage:	Yes
Total Crew:	334	Self-Service Launderette:	No
Passengers (lower beds/all berths):	784/926	Dedicated Cinema/Seats:	Yes/198
Pass. Space Ratio (lower beds/all berths):	21.3/18.0	Library:	Yes
Crew/Pass. Ratio (lower beds/all berths):	2.5/2.9	Classification Society:	Det Norske Veritas
Navigation Officers:	International		
Cabins (total):	392		
Size Range (sq ft/sq m):	89.3–255.1/8.3–23.7		
Cabins (outside view):	260		

OVERALL SCORE: **1,165**
(OUT OF A POSSIBLE 2,000 POINTS)

Accommodation: According to the Airtours Sun Cruises brochure, there are three cabin grades (Standard, Superior, and Deluxe) and five price categories. Note that, in the past, cabins were not assigned until you arrived at the ship; however, now you can book the cabin you want.

The ten Boat Deck deluxe cabins are reasonably spacious for the size of the vessel, although the two forward-facing units overlook the mooring deck; these can prove noisy, and are much smaller than the other eight suites. All the suites and deluxe cabins are quite comfortable, and have full bathtubs.

All other outside-view and interior (no view) cabins are very compact (dimensionally challenged), yet they are basically clean and tidy, with adequate closet space for a one-week cruise. Room service food items incur an extra charge.

Dining: The dining room is reasonably charming, with warm colors. There are tables for four, six, eight ,or ten, in two seatings. The food is adequate (for the price), but certainly not memorable, so do not expect gourmet fare. The bread and fruit selections are very basic. The service and ambience are both informal.

The cuisine? In a nutshell, it's basic, no-frills British motorway café cuisine: adequate for those who do not expect much in the way of presentation or quality. Indeed, it is quantity, not quality, that prevails — but it's all provided at a low cost — as is a cruise aboard this ship. Presentation is a weak point. Remember that like anything, you get what you pay for. If you enjoy going out to eat, and like being adventurous — then you will be disappointed. There is an adequate, but limited, wine list, and the wines are almost all very young — typical of those found in supermarkets. Wine prices are quite modest, as are the prices for most alcoholic beverages on board.

There is a self-serve buffet for casual breakfasts and luncheons, although the selection is quite limited, and the presentation is repetitive.

Other Comments: This ship, which was formerly operated for many years by Norwegian Cruise Line, was the first ship with which Airtours entered the cruise marketplace. However, in 2000 the ship was transferred to Louis Cruise Lines' sister company Royal Olympic Cruises as part of a deal under which Direct Cruises (a company owned by Airtours) was released from a four-year full charter of *Apollon*. Instead, *Seawing* was provided to Louis Cruise Lines (parent company of Royal Olympic Cruises) as compensation. Airtours Sun Cruises operates the ship under charter during the summer months, while Royal Olympic Cruises operates the ship during the winter months.

Seawing has a crisp, clean profile with rakish superstructure, dual funnels and inboard lifeboats. The open deck and sunbathing space is rather limited, however, and the swimming pool is small.

Inside, there is a good selection of comfortable public rooms with bright, fairly contemporary and upbeat decor. Perhaps the favorite is the nightclub, set high atop adjacent to the ship's forward mast. There is also a cinema with a balcony. The show lounge is adequate for cabaret-style shows, although there are too many pillars causing obstruction to the sight lines. Families with children will find lots to do, and Airtours has special staff to provide activities and entertainment for youngsters.

This is basic, but reasonably sound, cruising for those wanting a no-frills vacation in pleasant surroundings, at a really modest price level. Airtours provides good value for money with these cruises, designed for the young at heart. The company is known for packaging its products really well. This ship provides all the right ingredients for an active, fun-filled short cruise vacation for sunloving couples and families at the right price, but the ship shows her age in places.

If you want a little more than the basics, Airtours Sun Cruises offers special packages — good for celebrating something special. These come in four packages — bronze, silver, gold, and platinum, with each adding a little extra cost. Want to buy the captain? Go for gold, or platinum and you get breakfast in bed with champagne, flowers, fruit basket, and dinner at the captain's table.

Airtours also has its own fleet of aircraft, and this is one reason that the company is able to offer complete cruise-air-stay packages at such low rates. Airtours Sun Cruises typically does a fine job in getting you and your luggage from airplane to ship without having to go through immigration (although this will depend on the itinerary and operating area) in foreign countries whenever possible — so your cruise vacation is as seamless as possible.

Airtours Sun Cruises brochures tell it like it is — so you know before you go exactly what you will get for your money, with the exception of its claim to "first class food," which is a gross exaggeration. If you want just the basics, you pay the least amount. If you want all the goodies — choose a wider "premium" seat with extra leg room on your Airtours aircraft, choose your own cabin, choose your dinner seating, breakfast in bed and dinner with the captain (no, not in bed) — then you'll pay for all those "privileges." Note, however, that, however you choose to cruise, all gratuities are included. Insurance is also included (but you will be charged for it) unless you decline it on the booking form. On-board currency is the pound sterling.

Weak Points: Like the other ships in the fleet, the space per passenger is tight when the ship is full (which is most of the time). The cabin TVs are extremely small (except for those in the suites). Note that couples that travel without children will be surrounded by large number of children during the summer months — and, thus, increased noise levels. The food is of low quality, and the presentation is poor. There is little choice of tea and coffee. There are no cushioned pads for the deck lounge chairs.

Sensation
★★★ +

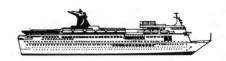

Large Ship:	70,367 tons	Cabins (for one person):	0
Lifestyle:	Standard	Cabins (with private balcony):	54
Cruise Line:	Carnival Cruise Lines	Cabins (wheelchair accessible):	20
Former Names:	-	Cabin Current:	110-volt
Builder:	Kvaerner Masa-Yards (Finland)	Full-Service Dining Rooms:	2
Original Cost:	$300 million	Elevators:	14
Entered Service:	November 1993	Casino(gaming tables):	Yes
Registry:	Bahamas	Slot Machines:	Yes
Length (ft/m):	855.0/260.6	Swimming Pools (outdoors):	3
Beam (ft/m):	104.0/31.4	Swimming Pools (indoors):	0
Draft (ft/m):	25.9/7.9	Whirlpools:	6
Propulsion/Propellers:	Diesel-electric	Fitness Center:	Yes
	(42,240kW)/2	Sauna/Steam Room:	Yes/Yes
Passenger Decks:	10	Massage:	Yes
Total Crew:	920	Self-Service Launderette:	Yes
Passengers (lower beds/all berths):	2,040/2,594	Dedicated Cinema:	No
Pass. Space Ratio (lower beds/all berths):	34.4/26.7	Library:	Yes
Crew/Pass. Ratio (lower beds/all berths):	2.2/2.8	Classification Society:	Lloyd's Register
Navigation Officers:	Italian		
Cabins (total):	1,020		
Size Range (sq ft/sq m):	173.2–409.7/16.0 –38.0	**OVERALL SCORE:**	**1,385**
Cabins (outside view):	618		
Cabins (interior/no view):	402	**(OUT OF A POSSIBLE 2,000 POINTS)**	

Accommodation: As in sister ships (*Ecstasy, Elation, Fantasy, Fascination, Imagination, Inspiration, Paradise*), the standard outside-view and interior (no view) cabins have plain decor. They are marginally comfortable, yet spacious enough and practical, with good storage space and well-designed bathrooms.

Those booking one of the outside suites will find more space, whirlpool bathtubs, and some fascinating, rather eclectic decor and furniture. These are mildly attractive, but nothing special, and they are much smaller than those aboard the ships of a similar size of several competing companies.

A gift basket is now provided in all grades of accommodation; it includes aloe soap, shampoo, conditioner, deodorant, breath mints, candy, and pain relief tablets.

Dining: There are two huge, noisy dining rooms (Ecstasy and Fantasy, both of which are nonsmoking) with the usual efficient, assertive service. Dining in each restaurant is now in four seatings, for greater flexibility: 6pm, 6:45 pm, 8pm, and 8:45pm (these times are approximate).

Carnival meals stress quantity, not quality, although the company constantly works hard to improve the cuisine. While passengers seem to accept it, few find it worth remembering. However, food and its taste are still not the company's strongest points (you get what you pay for, remember).

While the menu items sound good, their presentation and taste leave much to be desired. While meats are of a high quality, fish and seafood is not. Presentation is simple, and few garnishes are used. Many meat and fowl dishes are disguised with gravies and sauces. The selection of fresh green vegetables, breads, rolls, cheeses, and fruits is limited, and there is too much use of canned fruit and jellied desserts. However, do remember that this is banquet catering, with all its attendant standardization and production cooking (it is, therefore, difficult to ask for anything remotely unusual or off-menu).

Although there is a decent wine list, there are no wine waiters (the waiters are expected to serve both food and wine). The service is quite robotic, closely timed, highly programmed, and inflexible, although the waiters are reasonably friendly. However, the waiters do sing and dance (be prepared for "Hot, Hot, Hot" and "The Macarena" — again), and there are constant waiter parades. The dining room is show business — all done in the name of gratuities at the end of your cruise.

The Lido Café self-serve buffets are very basic, as is the selection of breads, rolls, fruit, and cheeses. At night, the Seaview Bistro (as the Lido Café becomes known) provides a casual (dress down) alternative to eating in the main dining rooms, serving pasta, steaks, salads and desserts. The Pizzeria is open 24 hours a day — and typically serves over 500 every single day!

Other Comments: *Sensation*, the seventh new build for Carnival Cruise Lines, features almost vibration-free operational service from its diesel-electric propulsion system, and the ship features its trademark large wing-tipped funnel in the company colors of red, white, and blue.

Inside, the general passenger flow is good, and the interior design is clever, functional, and extremely colorful. A dramatic six-deck-high atrium, with cool marble and hot neon, is topped by a large colored glass dome, and features a spectacular artistic centerpiece. There are expansive open-deck areas and a good health spa/fitness center, with a large gymnasium and the latest high-tech muscle machines. There are public entertainment lounges, bars, and clubs galore, with something for everyone. Dazzling colors and design themes in handsome public rooms connected by wide boulevards indoors.

There is also a $1 million art collection, much of it bright and vocal. The library is a lovely room, but there are few books (Carnival perhaps feels that its passengers do not read). The Michelangelo Lounge is a creative thinker's delight, while Fingers Lounge is sheer sensory stimulation. The lavish but elegant multi-tiered show lounge (there are 20 pillars to obstruct some sight lines) offers high-energy razzle-dazzle shows. Dramatic three-deck-high glass enclosed health spa. Banked jogging track. Gigantic casino has non-stop action.

This ship is a fine floating playground for young, active adults who enjoy constant stimulation, close contact with lots and lots of others, as well as the three Gs: glitz, glamour, and gambling. It is a live board game with every move executed in typically grand, colorful, fun-filled Carnival Cruise Lines style. This ship will entertain you well. Forget fashion — having fun is the *sine qua non* of a Carnival cruise. *Sensation* operates 7-night cruises year-round from the Port of Tampa, Florida. Gratuities can be prepaid.

Weak Points: Standing in line for embarkation, disembarkation, shore tenders, and self-serve buffet meals is an inevitable aspect of cruising aboard all large ships. This ship is not for those who want a quiet, relaxing cruise experience. As in most Carnival ships, there is a sense of overwhelming sensory indulgence, as if you are in the midst of a video game parlor. There are too many loud, repetitive announcements. The constant and aggressive hustling for drinks by bar waiters is irritating, as are drinks in plastic glasses.

Serenade
★★

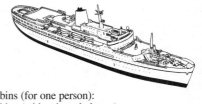

Mid-Size Ship:	14,173 tons	Cabins (for one person):	0
Lifestyle:	Standard	Cabins (with private balcony):	0
Cruise Line:	Louis Cruise Lines	Cabins (wheelchair accessible):	0
Former Names:	*Mermoz, Jean Mermoz*	Cabin Current:	110/220-volt
Builder:	Chantiers de l'Atlantique (France)	Full-Service Dining Rooms:	2
Original Cost:	n/a	Elevators:	2
Entered Service:	May 1957/September 1999	Casino(gaming tables):	Yes
Registry:	Bahamas	Slot Machines:	Yes
Length (ft/m):	531.5/162.01	Swimming Pools (outdoors):	2
Beam (ft/m):	65.0/19.82	Swimming Pools (indoors):	0
Draft (ft/m):	20.9/6.40	Whirlpools:	Yes
Propulsion/Propellers:	Diesel (8,000kW)/2	Fitness Center:	No
Passenger Decks:	9	Sauna/Steam Room:	Yes/No
Total Crew:	320	Massage:	Yes
Passengers (lower beds/all berths):	600/739	Self-Service Launderette:	No
Pass. Space Ratio (lower beds/all berths):	23.6/19.1	Dedicated Cinema/Seats:	Yes/240
Crew/Pass. Ratio (lower beds/all berths):	1.8/2.3	Library:	Yes
Navigation Officers:	Cypriot/Greek	Classification Society:	Bureau Veritas
Cabins (total):	600		
Size Range (sq ft/sq m):	n/a	**OVERALL SCORE:**	**946**
Cabins (outside view):	230		
Cabins (interior/no view):	70	**(OUT OF A POSSIBLE 2,000 POINTS)**	

Accommodation: All cabins are equipped with lower beds. The cabins are quite small and only equipped with basic facilities, but they are tastefully furnished, cozy and quite comfortable, with solid fixtures and lots of wood everywhere. There is a fair amount of closet and drawer space, but the cabin bathrooms are very small, with little room for storage of toiletry items. Although bathrobes were provided for all passengers, they may no longer be under the new operators.

Dining: In the main dining room, there are assigned tables, for two, four, six, or eight. There is also a smaller Grill Room, which has wicker furniture. In general, the food is creatively presented. The service is provided by waiters of many nationalities, most of whom are quite friendly and attentive.

Other Comments: *Serenade* has traditional 1950s lines, and now presents a very dated profile. She was operated for many years by the now-defunct Paquet Cruises. Louis Cruise Lines purchased the ship in September 1999, and now operates her in the Mediterranean. There is a reasonable amount of open deck and sunbathing space, although much of the teak decking is not in good condition.

Inside, the ship has what can be best described as a reasonably chic Art Deco-style decor that is rather eclectic, with a pastel color scheme and a "colonial" ambience. The spa and solarium are good spaces, with a main emphasis on hydrotherapy treatments. However, apart from the main lounge, there are few public rooms.

This ship has a fine, perhaps somewhat eclectic character, and is for those who enjoy being aboard an older ship, with all its quirks and idiosyncrasies, albeit for a moderate price. It would not be an exaggeration to call its style outdated, even worn out, and this may cause enough of a decrease in its popularity to affect its profitability. The dress code is casual throughout.

Weak Points: There is no observation lounge with forward-facing views over the ship's bows. *Serenade* feels tired and worn out, and should be replaced.

Seven Seas Mariner
★★★★★

Mid-Size ship:	48,015 tons	Cabins (for one person):	0
Lifestyle:	Luxury/Premium	Cabins (with private balcony):	354
Cruise Line:	Radisson Seven Seas Cruises	Cabins (wheelchair accessible):	6
Former Names:	-	Cabin Current:	110-volt
Builder:	Chantiers de l'Atlantique (France)	Full-Service Dining Rooms:	4
Original Cost:	$240 million	Elevators:	5
Entered Service:	March 2001	Casino(gaming tables):	Yes
Registry:	France	Slot Machines:	Yes
Length (ft/m):	713.0/217.3	Swimming Pools (outdoors):	1
Beam (ft/m):	95.1/29.0	Swimming Pools (indoors):	0
Draft (ft/m):	21.4/6.5	Whirlpools:	3
Propulsion/Propellers:	Diesel-electric/2 azimuthing	Fitness Center:	Yes
	pods (8.5MW each)	Sauna/Steam Room:	Yes/Yes
Passenger Decks:	9	Massage:	Yes
Total Crew:	445	Self-Service Launderette:	Yes (3)
Passengers (lower beds/all berths):	708/752	Dedicated Cinema:	No
Pass. Space Ratio (lower beds/all berths):	67.8/63.8	Library:	Yes
Crew/Pass. Ratio (lower beds/all berths):	1.6/1.7	Classification Society:	Bureau Veritas
Navigation Officers:	French		
Cabins (total):	354		
Size Range (sq ft/sq m):	301.3–1,528.4/28.0–142.0		
Cabins (outside view):	354		
Cabins (interior/no view):	0		

OVERALL SCORE: **1,703**

(OUT OF A POSSIBLE 2,000 POINTS)

Accommodation: This is the first "all-suite, all-balcony" ship in the cruise industry (terminology that marketing departments thoroughly enjoy, although not actually correct, as not all accommodation features sleeping areas that are completely separated from living areas). However, all grades of accommodation have private, marble-clad bathrooms with bathtub, and all suite entrances are neatly recessed away from the passenger hallways, to provide an extra modicum of quietness. Note that in comparison with *Seven Seas Navigator*, the bathrooms aboard this ship are not as large in the lower grade of accommodation.

Master Suite (1,580 sq ft/146.7 sq m)
    The largest accommodation can be found in the two Master Suites. These have two separate bedrooms, living room with TV/VCR and CD player, walk-in closet, dining area, large, two marble-clad bathrooms with bathtub and separate shower enclosure, and two private teak-decked balconies. These suites are located on the deck under the ship's navigation bridge, one balcony providing delightful forward-facing views, while a second balcony provides port or starboard views. Butler service is provided. To keep things in perspective, these two Master Suites are nowhere near as large as the two Penthouse Suites aboard the much larger Celebrity Cruises ships *Infinity, Millennium,* and *Summit* (which measure 2,350 sq ft/235 sq m).

Mariner Suite (739 sq ft/68.6 sq m)
    Six Mariner Suites, located on port and starboard sides of the atrium on three separate decks, feature a separate bedroom, living room with TV/VCR and CD player, walk-in closet, dining area, large, marble-clad bathroom with bathtub and separate shower enclosure, and a good sized private balcony with either port or starboard views. Butler service is provided.

Grand Suite (707 sq ft/65.6 sq m)
    Two Grand Suites are located one deck above the ship's navigation bridge, and feature a separate bedroom, living room with TV/VCR and CD player, walk-in closet, dining area, two marble-clad bathrooms (one with bathtub and separate shower enclosure, the second with a bathtub and a separate shower enclosure), and a good-sized private balcony with port or starboard views. Butler service is provided.

Seven Seas Suites (697 sq ft/64.6 sq m)
    A total of six spacious suites overlook the ship's stern (two suites are located on each of four decks) and

have an extremely generous amount of private balcony space and good wrap-around views over the ship's stern and to port or starboard. However, the balconies are only semi-private and can be partly overlooked by neighbors in Horizon Suites as well as from above. Another two Seven Seas Suites are located just aft of the ship's navigation bridge and measure a slightly smaller 602 sq ft (60 sq m), and have balconies with either port or starboard views. These suites feature a separate bedroom, living room with TV/VCR and CD player, walk-in closet, dining area, large, and marble-clad bathroom with a combination bathtub/shower.

Horizon Suites (522 sq ft/48.4 sq m)

There are twelve Horizon Suites overlooking the ship's stern (three suites are located on each of four decks, sandwiched between the Seven Seas Suites) and have a good-sized balcony (though not as large as the Seven Seas Suites) and good views. These suites feature a separate bedroom, living room with TV/VCR, walk-in closet, dining area, large, marble-clad bathroom with a combination bathtub/shower.

All Other Cabins (301 sq ft/28 sq m)

All other cabins (Categories A-H in the brochure, listed as Deluxe Suites and Penthouse Suites) feature twin beds that can convert to a queen-size bed (European duvets are standard), small walk-in closet, marble-lined bathroom with combination bathtub/shower, 100% cotton bathrobe, 100% cotton towels, vanity desk, hair dryer, TV/VCR, refrigerator (stocked with soft drinks and bar set-up on embarkation), and personal safe. Note that in these suites, the sleeping area is separated from the living area only by partial room dividers, and therefore is a cabin (albeit a good-sized one), and not a suite.

Six wheelchair-accessible suites are all located as close to an elevator as one could possibly get, and provide ample living space, together with a large roll-in shower and all bathroom fittings located at the correct height.

Dining: There are four different dining venues, all of which are operated on an open seating basis, so that you can sit with whom you want, when you wish. In reality, this means that dining aboard ship is like dining on land — you can go to a different dining spot each night. The downside of this is that waiters do not get to know and remember your preferences. Reservations are required in two of the four dining spots. In general, the cuisine is very good, with creative presentation and a wide variety of food choices.

The main dining room is the 570-seat Compass Rose Restaurant, which is located in the center of the ship. It has a light, fresh decor, and seating at tables for two, four, six, or eight. A large pre-dinner drinks bar is conveniently located adjacent on the starboard side. Fine Dudson china is featured.

Off to the port side of the Compass Rose Restaurant is Latitudes. With 80 seats, it is the smallest of the specialty restaurants for alternative dining, with tableside preparation of dishes from all parts of the world. The decor, too, is an interesting, rather eclectic international mix. There is seating for two, four, or six, and reservations are required.

A 120-seat supper club, called Signatures — which has its own dedicated galley — is located one deck above the main galley (for convenient vertical supply and staff access), and has ocean views along the room's port side. It is directed and staffed by chefs wearing the white toque and blue riband of Le Cordon Bleu in Paris, the most prestigious culinary authority in the world; hence the cuisine is classic French. Doors open onto a covered area outdoors, complete with stage and dance floor. Porsgrund china is featured, as are silver show plates and the very finest silverware. Seating is at tables of two, four, or six, and reservations are required.

For more casual meals, La Veranda is a large self-serve indoor/outdoor café with seats for 450 (the teak-decked outdoor seating is particularly pleasant), and fresh, light decor is featured. This eatery features several food islands as well as substantial counter display space. There is also an outdoor grill, adjacent to the swimming pool.

As another variation on the dining theme, you can also choose to dine in your cabin. There is a 24-hour room service menu, and, during regular dinner hours, you can choose from the full dining room menu.

Other Comments: This is presently the largest ship in the Radisson Seven Seas Cruises fleet, and the first to receive a "pod" propulsion system, replacing the traditional shaft and rudder system (the pods have forward-facing propellers that can be turned through 360 degrees). The ship was (for the technically minded) built in 32 blocks, using the same hull design as for Festival Cruises' *Mistral*, although the interior design is totally different. In the fitting-out stage, for example, many changes were made to accommodate Radisson Seven Seas Cruises' need for all-outside-view suites. Consequently, her passenger space ratio is now the highest in the cruise industry, at just a fraction above those for *Europa*. Seven Seas Mariner is operated by Radisson Seven Seas Cruises, although the ship is actually owned by a joint-venture company established with ship managers V-Ships.

There is quite a wide range of public rooms to play in, almost all of which are located below the accommodation decks. Three sets of stairways (forward, center, aft) mean it is easy to find your way around the vessel. An atrium lobby spans nine decks, with the lowest level opening directly onto the tender-landing stage.

Facilities include a delightful observation lounge, a casino, a shopping concourse (conveniently located opposite the casino) — complete with open-market area, a garden lounge/promenade arcade, a large library with internet-connected computers, business center, card room, and a conference room.

The main show lounge spans two decks and is quite stunning, and the sight lines are very good from almost all seats. There is also a nightclub (called Stars) with an oval-shaped dance floor, a cigar-smoking lounge (called the Connoisseur Club, for cigars, cognacs, and other assorted niceties), and a photo gallery.

Health and fitness facilities include an extensive health spa with gymnasium and aerobics room, beauty parlor, and separate changing, sauna and steam rooms for men and women. Specialist Judith Jackson operates the spa and beauty services, which are located not at the top of the ship, as is common with many other ships today, but just off the atrium. Sports devotees can play in the paddle tennis court, golf driving and practice cages.

Gratuities are included, as are complimentary bar set-ups on embarkation and complimentary table wines for dinner (although premium and connoisseur selections are available at extra cost).

With the introduction of *Seven Seas Mariner*, Radisson Seven Seas Cruises has clearly moved into a new breed of larger ships that are more economical to operate, and provide more choices for passengers. However, the downside of a larger ship such as this is that there is a loss of the sense of intimacy that the company's smaller ships have previously been able to maintain. Thus, some of the former personal service of the smaller ships has been absorbed into a larger structure. Another downside is the fact that this ship is simply too large to enter the small harbors and berths that the company's smaller ships can, and so loses some of the benefits of small upscale ship cruising.

Due to these consequences of its size, this ship loses a few points in scoring. At present, it scores very highly in terms of hardware and software, but operationally may lose a few points if it is deemed that the ship can only enter mid-size ship ports. By comparison, this ship is a more upscale version of the eight ships in the Renaissance Cruises fleet — with better food, more choices, and a staff that is more hospitality-conscious and generally better trained. *Seven Seas Mariner*, therefore, has ended up just a tad over the score base needed for her to join the "Five Star" Club.

Weak Points: Service and hospitality are sometimes spotty and inconsistent. The same carpeting is used throughout the public areas — with no relief or change of color or pattern on the stairwells. The decor is a little glitzy in places. The ship is too large to get into some of the smaller ports of call that the smaller ships in the fleet can get into. Also, much of the intimacy and close-knit ambience of the smaller vessels is missing.

Seven Seas Navigator
★★★★+

Small Ship:	28,550 tons	Cabins (for one person):	0
Lifestyle:	Luxury/Premium	Cabins (with private balcony):	196
Cruise Line:	Radisson Seven Seas Cruises	Cabins (wheelchair accessible):	4
Former Names:	-	Cabin Current:	110/220-volt
Builder:	T. Marriotti (Italy)	Full-Service Dining Rooms:	1 main, 1 alternative
Original Cost:	$200 million	Elevators:	5
Entered Service:	August 1999	Casino(gaming tables):	Yes
Registry:	Bahamas	Slot Machines:	Yes
Length (ft/m):	559.7/170.6	Swimming Pools (outdoors):	1
Beam (ft/m):	71.5/21.8	Swimming Pools (indoors):	0
Draft (ft/m):	21.3.0/6.5	Whirlpools:	2
Propulsion/Propellers:	Diesel (13,000kW)/2	Fitness Center:	Yes
Passenger Decks:	8	Sauna/Steam Room:	Yes/Yes
Total Crew:	325	Massage:	Yes
Passengers (lower beds/all berths):	490/530	Self-Service Launderette:	Yes
Pass. Space Ratio (lower beds/all berths):	58.2/53.8	Dedicated Cinema:	No
Crew/Pass. Ratio (lower beds/all berths):	1.5/1.6	Library:	Yes
Navigation Officers:	European/International	Classification Society:	Registro Navale Italiano
Cabins (total):	245		
Size Range (sq ft/sq m):	301.3–1,173.3/28.0–109.0	**OVERALL SCORE:**	**1,653**
Cabins (outside view):	245	(OUT OF A POSSIBLE 2,000 POINTS)	
Cabins (interior/no view):	0		

Accommodation: There are 11 grades of accommodation. The company markets this as an "all-suite" ship. Even the smallest suite is quite large, and all have outside views. Almost 90 percent of all suites feature a private balcony, with floor-to-ceiling sliding glass doors, while 10 suites are interconnecting, and 38 suites have an extra bed for a third occupant. By comparison, even the smallest suite aboard this ship is more than twice the size of the smallest cabin aboard the world's largest cruise ship, Royal Caribbean International's *Explorer of the Seas*.

All grades of accommodation feature a walk-in closet, European king-sized bed or twin beds, wooden cabinetry with nicely rounded edges, plenty of drawer space, minibar/refrigerator (stocked with complimentary soft drinks and bar set-up on embarkation), television/VCR, personal safe, and other accoutrements of fine living at sea in the latest design format. The marble-appointed bathroom has a full-size bathtub, as well as a separate shower enclosure, 100% cotton bathrobe and towels, and hair dryer.

The largest living spaces can be found in four master suites, with forward-facing views (all have double length side balconies). Each suite has a completely separate bedroom with dressing table; the living room features a full dining room table and chairs for up to six persons, wet bar, counter and bar stools, large 3-person sofa and six armchairs, and an audio-visual console/entertainment center. Each suite has a large main, marble-clad, fully tiled bathroom with full-sized bathtub and separate shower enclosure, a separate room with bidet, toilet and washbasin, with plenty of shelf and other storage space for personal toiletry items; there is also a separate guest bathroom.

Next in size are the superb Navigator Suites, which feature a completely separate bedroom, walk-in closet, large lounge with minibar/refrigerator (stocked with complimentary soft drinks and bar set-up on embarkation), television/VCR, personal safe, compact disc player, large television/VCR player, and dining area with large table and four chairs. The marble-clad, fully tiled bathroom features a full-sized bathtub with hand-held shower, plus a separate shower enclosure (the door to which is only 18 inches, however), large washbasin, toilet and bidet, and ample shelf space for personal toiletry items. It is unfortunate that the Navigator Suites are located in the center of the ship, as they are located directly underneath the swimming pool deck. They are, thus, subject to noise attacks at 6:00 a.m. daily, when deck cleaning is carried out, and chairs are dragged across the deck directly over the suites. They are further subjected to noise attacks whenever pool deck stewards drag and drop deck lounge chairs into place. Despite these comments, the Navigator Suites are delightful living spaces.

Four suites for the physically challenged have private balconies, and are ideally located adjacent to the elevators (correcting a mistake made when the company's *Radisson Diamond* was constructed, when they were located as far from any elevators as they possibly could be). However, while the suites are very practical, it is almost impossible to access the balcony, due to the "lip" or "threshold" at the bottom of the sliding glass door.

Dining: The Compass Rose Dining Room has large ocean-view picture windows and open seating dining, which means that you may be seated when and with whom you wish. Complimentary wines are served during dinner, although a connoisseur wine list is available for those who prefer to choose a vintage wine (at extra cost). The company also features "heart healthy" cuisine. Although most of the dining room is non-smoking, a small section is available for smokers.

An alternative dining spot, Portofino Grill, features informal Italian dining for dinner (reservations are required). The Grill forms part of a larger restaurant with indoor/outdoor seating. For fast food items there is also a small indoor/outdoor Grill, adjacent to the swimming pool.

You can also choose to dine in your cabin. There is a 24-hour room service menu; also, during regular dinner hours, you can choose from the full dining room menu.

Other Comments: This new ship was built using a hull that was already constructed in St. Petersburg, Russia as Akademik Nikolay Pilyugin (a the research vessel). After launching the hull, the name Blue Sea was applied for a short time. The superstructure was incorporated into the hull in an Italian shipyard - with the result being that what was (for all intents and purposes) a new ship which was delivered in record time. However, the result is less than handsome – particularly at the ship's stern. She is, however, large enough to be stable over long stretches of water, and her passenger space ratio provides an excellent amount of space per passenger.

The ship's interiors feature a mix of classical and contemporary Italian styling and decor throughout, with warm, soft colors and fine quality soft furnishings and fabrics.

The Vista Lounge is the ship's forward-view observation lounge. At the opposite end of the ship is Galileo's, a large piano lounge with good views over the ship's stern.

A Navigator's Lounge features warm mahogany and cherry wood paneling and large, comfortable, mid-back tub chairs. Meanwhile, next door, cigars and cognac (and other niceties) can be taken in the delightful Connoisseur's Club – the first, aboard a Radisson Seven Seas Cruises vessel.

There is a two-deck-high show lounge, with reasonable sight lines from most seats (several pillars obstruct the views – particularly from some of the side balcony seats). The extensive library also features several computers with direct e-mail/Internet access (for a fee).

The ship is designed for worldwide cruise itineraries, and is one of the most in the Radisson Seven Seas Cruises fleet. As with all ships in the Radisson Seven Seas Cruises fleet, all gratuities are included.

Weak Points: There is no wrap-around promenade deck outdoors, although there is a jogging track high atop the aft section of the ship around the funnel housing. Two of the upper, outer decks are laid with green Astroturf, which cheapens the look of the ship – these decks woulld be better in teak. The ceilings in several of the public rooms (including the main restaurant) are quite low, which makes the ship feel smaller and more closed in than it actually is. The ship does suffer from a considerable amount of vibration, which detracts from the comfort level when compared with other vessels of the same size. Service and hospitality are spotty and inconsistent.

Silver Cloud
★★★★★

Small Ship:	16,927 tons	Cabins (for one person):	0
Lifestyle:	Luxury	Cabins (with private balcony):	110
Cruise Line:	Silversea Cruises	Cabins (wheelchair accessible):	2
Former Names:	-	Cabin Current:	110/220-volt
Builder:	Visentini/Mariotti (Italy)	Full-Service Dining Rooms:	1 (plus1 informal café)
Original Cost:	$125 million	Elevators:	4
Entered Service:	April 1994	Casino(gaming tables):	Yes
Registry:	Bahamas	Slot Machines:	Yes
Length (ft/m):	514.4/155.8	Swimming Pools (outdoors):	1
Beam (ft/m):	70.62/21.4	Swimming Pools (indoors):	0
Draft (ft/m):	17.3/5.3	Whirlpools:	2
Propulsion/Propellers:	Diesel (11,700kW)/2	Fitness Center:	Yes
Passenger Decks:	6	Sauna/Steam Room:	Yes/Yes
Total Crew:	198	Massage:	Yes
Passengers (lower beds/all berths):	296/315	Self-Service Launderette:	Yes
Pass. Space Ratio (lower beds/all berths):	57.1/53.7	Dedicated Cinema/Seats:	Yes/306
Crew/Pass. Ratio (lower beds/all berths):	1.4/1.5	Library:	Yes
Navigation Officers:	Italian	Classification Society:	Registro Navale Italiano
Cabins (total):	148		
Size Range (sq ft/sq m):	240.0–1,314.0/22.2–122.0		
Cabins (outside view):	148		
Cabins (interior/no view):	0		

OVERALL SCORE: 1,729

(OUT OF A POSSIBLE 2,000 POINTS)

Accommodation: The all-outside suites (75% of which have fine private teakwood balconies) have convertible queen-to-twin beds and are beautifully fitted out with just about everything one needs, including huge floor-to-ceiling windows, large walk-in closets, dressing table, writing desk, stocked minibar/refrigerator (no charge), and fresh flowers. The marble floor bathrooms have bathtub, single vanity, and plenty of towels. Personalized stationery, bathrobes, and a decent amenities kit are provided in all cabins. The top grades of suites also have CD players.

All cabins have TVs and a VCR (PAL, not VHS system). However, the walk-in closets do not actually provide much hanging space (particularly for such items as full-length dresses), and it would be better for the door to open outward instead of inward (the drawers themselves are poorly positioned). Although the cabin insulation above and below each cabin is good, the insulation between cabins is not (a privacy curtain installed between entry door and sleeping area would be most useful), and light from the passageway leaks into the cabin, making it hard to achieve a dark room.

Note that the cabins with balconies on the lowest deck can suffer from sticky salt spray when the ship is moving, so the balconies require lots of cleaning. Each evening, the stewardesses bring plates of canapes to your suite — just right for a light bite with cocktails.

Dining: The contemporary dining room has an attractive arched gazebo center and a wavy ceiling design as its focal point, and is set with fine Limoges china and well-balanced Christofle flatware. Meals are served in an open seating, which means you can eat when you like (within the given dining room opening times), and with whom you like. Meals can also be served, course-by-course, in your suite, although the balcony tables are rather low for dining outdoors. The dining is good throughout the ship, with a choice of formal and informal areas, although the cuisine and presentation doesn't quite match up to that of products such as the smaller Seabourn Cruise Line ships. Standard table wines are included for lunch and dinner, but there is also a "connoisseur list" of premium wines at extra charge. Oh, and the house champagne is Moet & Chandon.

An alternative Italian restaurant, called Cucina Italiana, is very popular for evening alternative dining. By day it acts as an informal café, but by night turns into a lovely intimate dining spot, complete with candlelight and print tablecloths.

The ship also provides 24-hour in-cabin dining service (full course-by-course dinners are available).

Other Comments: *Silver Cloud* has a profile that is quite handsome, with a sloping stern reminiscent of an "Airstream" trailer. The size is just about ideal for highly personalized cruising in an elegant environment. The vertical cake-layer stacking of public rooms aft and the location of accommodation units forward ensures quiet cabins. The ship features a synthetic turf-covered wrap-around promenade deck outdoors, and a spacious swimming pool deck.

The spacious interior is well planned, with elegant decor and fine quality soft furnishings. It is accented by the gentle use of brass and fine woods and very creative ceilings throughout. The spa areas, however, need improvement, and the tiled decor is bland and uninviting.

There is a useful business center as well as a CD-ROM and hardback book library, open 24 hours a day. There is an excellent two-level show lounge with tiered seating, but the entertainment is disappointing and not as good as when the ship first debuted.

In 2000, a new concession took over the health spa and improved upon the services and range of personal treatments available. The Mandara Spa (originating in Bali) includes what are known as Ayurvedic treatments (based on traditional Indian medicine). Massages, however, are extremely expensive, at approximately $2 per minute.

There is an excellent amount of space per passenger and there is no hint of waiting in line anywhere in this unhurried environment. Excellent documentation is provided before your cruise, all of which comes in a high-quality document wallet.

An elegant onboard ambience prevails, and there is no pressure, no hype. An enthusiastic staff pampers you, with a high ratio of Europeans among them. Insurance is extra (it was included when Silversea Cruises first started). Refreshingly, all drinks, gratuities, and port taxes are included, and, also refreshingly, no further tipping anywhere on board is allowed. This ship is perhaps ideal for those who enjoy spacious surroundings, excellent food, and some entertainment. It would be difficult not to have good cruise vacation aboard this ship, albeit at a fairly high price. Silversea Cruises has come a long way since its inception, and continues to refine its product. The company's many international passengers react well to the ambience, food, service and the staff, most of whom go out of their way to please.

Few ships make it to a five-star rating today, but Silversea Cruises has earned an enviable reputation for high quality in a short space of time.

Weak Points: Some vibration is evident when bow thrusters or the anchors are used, particularly in the forward-most cabins. The self-service launderette is poor and not large enough for longer cruises, when passengers like to be able to do their own small items. unfortunately, crew facilities are minimal, and so keeping consistency is difficult, as high crew turnover is a fact of life. The artwork is quite poor.

Silver Shadow
★★★★★

Small Ship:	28,258 tons	Cabins (for one person):	0
Lifestyle:	Luxury	Cabins (with private balcony):	157
Cruise Line:	Silversea Cruises	Cabins (wheelchair accessible):	2
Former Names:	-	Cabin Current:	110/220-volt
Builder:	Visentini/Mariotti (Italy)	Full-Service Dining Rooms:	1 main, 1 grill, 1 café
Original Cost:	$150 million	Elevators:	5
Entered Service:	September 2000	Casino(gaming tables):	Yes
Registry:	Bahamas	Slot Machines:	Yes
Length (ft/m):	597.1/182.0	Swimming Pools (outdoors):	1
Beam (ft/m):	81.8/24.8	Swimming Pools (indoors):	0
Draft (ft/m):	19.6/6.0	Whirlpools:	2
Propulsion/Propellers:	Diesel/2	Fitness Center:	Yes
Passenger Decks:	7	Sauna/Steam Room:	Yes/Yes
Total Crew:	287	Massage:	Yes
Passengers (lower beds/all berths):	388/400	Self-Service Launderette:	Yes
Pass. Space Ratio (lower beds/all berths):	72.8/70.6	Dedicated Cinema:	No
Crew/Pass. Ratio (lower beds/all berths):	1.3/1.3	Library:	Yes
Navigation Officers:	Italian	Classification Society:	Registro Navale Italiano
Cabins (total):	194		
Size Range (sq ft/sq m):	287.0–1,124.0/26.6–104.5		
Cabins (outside view):	194		
Cabins (interior/no view):	0		

OVERALL SCORE: **1,765**
(OUT OF A POSSIBLE 2,000 POINTS)

Accommodation: There are two Owner's Suites, two Royal Suites, four Grand Suites, nine Silver Suites, 161 Balcony Suites, 20 Vista Suites (without balcony) and two suites for the physically challenged.

The 20 standard (Vista) suites measure 287 sq ft (26.6 sq m), and they do not have a private balcony; the 161 Veranda Suites (really a Vista Suite plus a verandah) measure 349 sq ft (32.4 sq m) and feature convertible twin-to-queen beds. They are well fitted out with just about everything you would need, including large floor-to-ceiling windows, large walk-in closet, dressing table, writing desk, stocked minibar/refrigerator (no charge), and fresh flowers. The marble floor bathrooms have a bathtub and plenty of towels.

The Silver Suites measure 705 sq ft (65.5 sq m). They feature a separate bedroom and much more living space that includes a large dining area with table and four chairs. The Owner's Suite, which measures 903 sq ft (83.8 sq m), is even larger, and includes an extra bathroom for guests, as well as more living space.

The stateliest accommodation can be found in two Royal Suites, which measure 908–1,054 sq ft (84.3–98 sq m); as well as in two Grand Suites, each of which measures between 953 and 1,124 sq ft (88–104.5 sq m). These suites feature two bedrooms, Bang & Olufsen entertainment centers, a huge living room, and large, forward-facing, very private verandah.

All suites have double vanities in the marble floor bathrooms, which also feature a bathtub and separate shower enclosure. Silversea-monogrammed Frette bed linen is provided in all cabins, as are soft down pillows, 100% cotton bathrobes, and a range of personal toiletry amenities by Bulgari, as well as personalized stationery.

The suites for the physically challenged measure a generous 398 sq ft (37 sq m).

Dining: The main dining room (called, simply, "The Restaurant") provides open seating dining in elegant surroundings, with Cristofle silverware. Three grand chandeliers provide an upward focal point, while you can dine when you want, and with whom you wish, in these refined surroundings.

A poolside Grill provides a casual alternative daytime dining spot, for grill and fast food items. Dinner can also be served course by course in your own suite.

For even more informal dining, the Terrace Café is featured. This has proved popular aboard the company's two [smaller] ships *Silver Cloud* and *Silver Wind*. In the evening this features regional Italian cuisine. Adjacent to the café is a wine bar as well as a cigar smoking room.

Other Comments: *Silver Shadow* is the second generation of vessels in the Silversea Cruises fleet, and it is slightly larger than the company's first two ships, *Silver Cloud* and *Silver Wind*, with a more stream-lined forward profile and a large, sleek single funnel. However, the stern section is not particularly hand-some. The design of this new ship (her sister ship is *Silver Whisper*) has evolved from the experience and success gained from the first pair. There is a generous amount of open deck and sunning space.

"The Humidor by Davidoff" is the ship's cigar smoking lounge. It has 25 seats and has been created in the style of an English smoking club. All the cigars for sale are provided by Davidoff, the well-known pur-veyor of fine cigars. It was Zino Davidoff, son of founder Henri Davidoff, who created the revolutionary "cigar cellar," now called a humidor.

Other new additions include a champagne bar and a computer-learning center, with four computer terminals for passenger use.

The Mandara Spa (originating in Bali) operates the health spa facilities, much expanded when com-pared to smaller sisters *Silver Cloud* and *Silver Wind*, and specializes in what are known as Ayurvedic treatments (based on traditional Indian medicine). Massages, however, are extremely expensive, at approximately $2 per minute.

Silversea Cruises features "all-inclusive" fares, including gratuities. They do not, however, include vin-tage wines, massages, or other personal services, but they do include many things that are at extra cost compared aboard the ships of many other cruise lines in the industry. Although the majority of passengers are generally North American, the passenger mix includes many nationalities, which actually makes for a more interesting experience.

Weak Points: The swimming pool is surprisingly small, as is the fitness room.

Silver Star
★★ +

Small Ship:	5,092 tons	Cabins (for one person):	0
Lifestyle:	Standard	Cabins (with private balcony):	0
Cruise Line:	Mano Maritime	Cabins (wheelchair accessible):	0
Former Names:	*Royal Dream, Odessa Song,*	Cabin Current:	220-volt
	Bashkiriya	Full-Service Dining Rooms:	1
Builder:	VEB Mathias Thesen (Germany)	Elevators:	0
Original Cost:	n/a	Casino(gaming tables):	Yes
Entered Service:	1964/1998	Slot Machines:	Yes
Registry:	Malta	Swimming Pools (outdoors):	1
Length (ft/m):	400.5/122.1	Swimming Pools (indoors):	0
Beam (ft/m):	52.4/16.0	Whirlpools:	0
Draft (ft/m):	18.3/5.59	Fitness Center:	No
Propulsion/Propellers:	Diesel/2	Sauna/Steam Room:	Yes/No
Passenger Decks:	6	Massage:	No
Total Crew:	130	Self-Service Launderette:	No
Passengers (lower beds/all berths):	314/425	Dedicated Cinema:	No
Pass. Space Ratio (lower beds/all berths):	16.2/11.9	Library:	Yes
Crew/Pass. Ratio (lower beds/all berths):	2.4/3.2	Classification Society:	Hellenic Register
Navigation Officers:	Ukrainian		
Cabins (total):	157		
Size Range (sq ft/sq m):	n/a	**OVERALL SCORE:**	**1,009**
Cabins (outside view):	134		
Cabins (interior/no view):	23	**(OUT OF A POSSIBLE 2,000 POINTS)**	

Accommodation: The Silver Iris and Silver Jasmine suites are the largest of the seven cabin grades, which is really too many for such a small ship. These have a separate living room and bedroom, plus a bathroom with full-sized bathtub.

Other cabins are small and basic, yet reasonably comfortable, and the few interior (no view) cabins are fairly large. Most cabins have beds in an "L"-shaped configuration; some cabins have third and fourth upper berths, although the closet and drawer space is extremely limited when all are occupied; all have a private bathroom with shower (soap and shampoo are provided). The cabin insulation is poor, and drawer space is very modest.

Dining: The Middle Eastern-themed dining room is set low down in the ship (it also has a low ceiling) and has portholes. There are two seatings. The food is surprisingly good, with lots of fresh salads and vegetables, as well as good meats and local fish. There is certainly plenty of variety. Kosher food can also be supplied — for a surcharge, per passenger, per cruise.

Other Comments: This former Russian vessel has a large square funnel, and is now operated under a 15-year charter to Mano Maritime of Haifa, Israel. There is very little outdoor walking space, although there is a decent amount of open deck and sunbathing space. The swimming pool is really just a "dip" pool, and the painted steel decks forward of the pool really should be covered with wood or other heat-absorbing materials.

There are just two principal public rooms. One is the main lounge/show lounge, which has a bar on the port side adjacent to the entrance. The lounge seating is arranged around a circular wooden dance floor. The second room acts as the ship's disco at night. There is also a small room for children.

Silver Star (no connection with Silversea Cruises) is an older vessel that has received extensive refit and refurbishment work, and is now operating 7-night Mediterranean cruises almost exclusively for the local Israeli market. The ship itself is very basic, but the food provides a highlight.

Weak Points: This is a very high-density ship that has little space per person. There is a charge for use of the sauna.

Silver Whisper

Small Ship:	28,258 tons	Cabins (wheelchair accessible):	2
Lifestyle:	Luxury	Cabin Current:	110/220-volt
Cruise Line:	Silversea Cruises	Full-Service Dining Rooms:	1 main, 1 grill, 1 café
Former Names:	-	Elevators:	5
Builder:	Visentini/Mariotti (Italy)	Casino(gaming tables):	Yes
Original Cost:	$150 million	Slot Machines:	Yes
Entered Service:	July 2001	Swimming Pools (outdoors):	1
Registry:	Bahamas	Swimming Pools (indoors):	0
Length (ft/m):	597.1/182.0	Whirlpools:	2
Beam (ft/m):	81.8/24.8	Fitness Center:	Yes
Draft (ft/m):	19.6/6.0	Sauna/Steam Room:	Yes/Yes
Propulsion/Propellers:	Diesel/2	Massage:	Yes
Passenger Decks:	7	Self-Service Launderette:	Yes
Total Crew:	287	Dedicated Cinema:	No
Passengers (lower beds/all berths):	388/400	Library:	Yes
Pass. Space Ratio (lower beds/all berths):	72.8/70.6	Classification Society:	Registro Navale Italiano
Crew/Pass. Ratio (lower beds/all berths):	1.3/1.3		
Navigation Officers:	Italian		
Cabins (total):	194		
Size Range (sq ft/sq m):	287.0–1,124.0/26.6–104.5		
Cabins (outside view):	194		
Cabins (interior/no view):	0		
Cabins (for one person):	0		
Cabins (with private balcony):	157		

OVERALL SCORE: NOT YET RATED

Note that this ship had not entered service when this book was completed. However, the score is expected to be similar to that of *Silver Shadow*.

Accommodation: There are two Owner's Suites, two Royal Suites, four Grand Suites, nine Silver Suites, 161 Balcony Suites, 20 Vista Suites (without balcony) and two suites for the physically challenged.

The 20 standard (Vista) suites measure 287 sq ft (26.6sq m), and they do not have a private balcony; the 161 Veranda Suites (really a Vista Suite plus a verandah) measure 349 sq ft (32.4 sq m) and feature convertible twin-to-queen beds. They are well fitted out with just about everything you would need, including large floor-to-ceiling windows, large walk-in closet, dressing table, writing desk, stocked minibar/refrigerator (no charge), and fresh flowers. The marble floor bathrooms have a bathtub and plenty of towels.

The Silver Suites measure 705 sq ft (65.5 sq m). They feature a separate bedroom and much more living space that includes a large dining area with table and four chairs. The Owner's Suite, which measures 903 sq ft (83.8 sq m), is even larger, and includes an extra bathroom for guests, as well as more living space.

The stateliest accommodation can be found in two Royal Suites, which measure 908–1,054 sq ft (84.3–98 sq m); as well as in two Grand Suites, each of which measures between 953 and 1,124 sq ft (88.5–104.5 sq m). These suites feature two bedrooms, Bang & Olufsen entertainment centers, a huge living room, and large, forward-facing, very private verandah.

All suites have double vanities in the marble floor bathrooms, which also feature a bathtub and separate shower enclosure. Silversea-monogrammed Frette bed linen is provided in all cabins, as are soft down pillows, 100% cotton bathrobes, and a range of personal toiletry amenities by Bulgari, as well as personalized stationery.

The suites for the physically challenged measure a generous 398 sq ft (37 sq m).

Dining: The main dining room (called The Restaurant) provides open seating dining in elegant surroundings, with Cristofle silverware. A poolside Grill provides a casual alternative daytime dining spot. Dinner can also be served course by course in your own suite.

For even more informal dining, the Terrace Café is featured. This has proved popular aboard the company's two [smaller] ships *Silver Cloud* and *Silver Wind*. In the evening this features regional Italian cuisine. Adjacent to the café is a wine bar as well as a cigar smoking room.

Other Comments: *Silver Whisper* is the second generation of vessels in the Silversea Cruises fleet (her sister ship is *Silver Shadow*), and is slightly larger than the company's first two ships, *Silver Cloud* and *Silver Wind*, with a more streamlined profile and large, sleek single funnel. The design of this new ship has evolved from the experience and success gained from the first pair.

"The Humidor by Davidoff" is the ship's cigar smoking lounge. It has 25 seats and has been created in the style of an English smoking club. All the cigars for sale are provided by Davidoff, the well-known purveyor of fine cigars. It was Zino Davidoff, son of founder Henri Davidoff, who created the revolutionary "cigar cellar," now called a humidor. Other facilities include a wine bar and a computer learning center.

The Mandara Spa (originating in Bali) operates the health spa facilities, much expanded when compared to smaller sisters *Silver Cloud* and *Silver Wind*, and specializes in what are known as Ayurvedic treatments (based on traditional Indian medicine). Massages, however, are extremely expensive, at approximately $2 per minute.

Silversea Cruises features "all-inclusive" fares. They do not, however, include vintage wines, or massage, or other personal services, but they do include many things that are at extra cost compared aboard the ships of many other cruise lines in the industry. Although the majority of passengers are generally North American, the passenger mix includes many nationalities, which actually makes for a more interesting experience.

Silver Wind
★★★★★

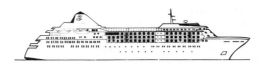

Small Ship:	16,927 tons	Cabins (for one person):	0
Lifestyle:	Luxury	Cabins (with private balcony):	110
Cruise Line:	Silversea Cruises	Cabins (wheelchair accessible):	2
Former Names:	—	Cabin Current:	110/220-volt
Builder:	Visentini/Mariotti Italy)	Full-Service Dining Rooms: 1 (plus 1 informal café)	
Original Cost:	$125 million	Elevators:	4
Entered Service:	January 1995	Casino(gaming tables):	Yes
Registry:	Italy	Slot Machines:	Yes
Length (ft/m):	514.4/155.8	Swimming Pools (outdoors):	1
Beam (ft/m):	70.62/21.4	Swimming Pools (indoors):	0
Draft (ft/m):	17.3/5.3	Whirlpools:	2
Propulsion/Propellers:	Diesel (11,700kW)/2	Fitness Center:	Yes
Passenger Decks:	6	Sauna/Steam Room:	Yes/Yes
Total Crew:	197	Massage:	Yes
Passengers (lower beds/all berths):	296/315	Self-Service Launderette:	Yes
Pass. Space Ratio (lower beds/all berths):	57.1/53.7	Dedicated Cinema/Seats:	Yes/306
Crew/Pass. Ratio (lower beds/all berths):	1.5/1.5	Library:	Yes
Navigation Officers:	Italian	Classification Society:	Registro Navale Italiano
Cabins (total):	148		
Size Range (sq ft/sq m):	240.0–1,314.0/22.2–122.0	**OVERALL SCORE:**	**1,729**
Cabins (outside view):	148	**(OUT OF A POSSIBLE 2,000 POINTS)**	
Cabins (interior/no view):	0		

Accommodation: The all-outside suites (75% of which have fine private teakwood balconies) have convertible queen-to-twin beds and are beautifully fitted out with just about everything one needs, including huge floor-to-ceiling windows, large walk-in closets, dressing table, writing desk, stocked minibar/refrigerator (no charge), and fresh flowers. The marble floor bathrooms have bathtub, single vanity, and plenty of towels. Personalized stationery, bathrobes, and a decent amenities kit are provided in all cabins. The top grades of suites also have CD players.

All cabins have TVs and a VCR (PAL, not VHS system). However, the walk-in closets do not actually provide much hanging space (particularly for such items as full-length dresses), and it would be better for the door to open outward instead of inward (the drawers themselves are poorly positioned). Although the cabin insulation above and below each cabin is good, the insulation between cabins is not (a privacy curtain installed between entry door and sleeping area would be most useful), and light from the passageway leaks into the cabin, making it hard to achieve a dark room.

Note that the cabins with balconies on the lowest deck can suffer from sticky salt spray when the ship is moving, so the balconies require lots of cleaning. Each evening, the stewardesses bring plates of canapés to your suite—just right for a light bite with cocktails.

Dining: The contemporary dining room has an attractive arched gazebo center and a wavy ceiling design as its focal point, and is set with fine Limoges china and well-balanced Christofle flatware. Meals are served in an open seating, which means you can eat when you like (within the given dining room opening times), and with whom you like. Meals can also be served, course-by-course, in your suite, although the balcony tables are rather low for dining outdoors. The dining is good throughout the ship, with a choice of formal and informal areas, although the cuisine and presentation doesn't quite match up to that found on the smaller Seabourn ships. Standard table wines are included for lunch and dinner, but there is also a "connoisseur list" of premium wines at extra charge. Oh, and the house champagne is Moet & Chandon.

An alternative Italian restaurant, called Cucina Italiana, is very popular for evening alternative dining. By day it acts as an informal café, but by night turns into a lovely intimate dining spot, complete with candlelight and print tablecloths.

The ship also provides 24-hour in-cabin dining service (full course-by-course dinners are available).

Other Comments: *Silver Wind* has a profile that is quite handsome, with a sloping stern reminiscent of an "Airstream" trailer. The size is just about ideal for highly personalized cruising in an elegant environment. The vertical cake-layer stacking of public rooms aft and the location of accommodation units forward ensures quiet cabins. The ship features a synthetic turf-covered wrap-around promenade deck outdoors, and a spacious swimming pool deck.

The spacious interior is well planned, with elegant decor and fine quality soft furnishings. It is accented by the gentle use of brass and fine woods and very creative ceilings throughout. The spa areas, however, need improvement, and the tiled decor is bland and uninviting.

There is a useful business center as well as a CD-ROM and hardback book library, open 24 hours a day. There is an excellent two-level show lounge with tiered seating, but the entertainment is disappointing and not as good as when the ship first debuted.

In 2000, a new concession took over the health spa and improved upon the services and range of personal treatments available. The Mandara Spa (originating in Bali) includes what are known as Ayurvedic treatments (based on traditional Indian medicine). Massages, however, are extremely expensive, at approximately $2 per minute.

There is an excellent amount of space per passenger and there is no hint of waiting in line anywhere in this unhurried environment. Excellent documentation is provided before your cruise, all of which comes in a high-quality document wallet.

An elegant onboard ambience prevails, and there is no pressure, no hype. An enthusiastic staff pampers you, with a high ratio of Europeans among them. Insurance is extra (it was included when Silversea Cruises first started). Refreshingly, all drinks, gratuities, and port taxes are included, and, also refreshingly, no further tipping anywhere on board is allowed. This ship is perhaps ideal for those who enjoy spacious surroundings, excellent food, and some entertainment. It would be difficult not to have good cruise vacation aboard this ship, albeit at a fairly high price. Silversea Cruises has come a long way since its inception, and continues to refine its product. The company's many international passengers react well to the ambience, food, service, and the staff, most of whom go out of their way to please.

Few ships make it to a five-star rating today, but Silversea Cruises has earned an enviable reputation for high quality in a short space of time.

Weak Points: The artwork is of very poor quality. Some vibration is evident when bow thrusters or the anchors are used, particularly in the forward-most cabins. The self-service launderette is poor and not large enough for longer cruises, when passengers like to be able to do their own small items. Unfortunately, crew facilities are minimal, and so keeping consistency is difficult, as high crew turnover is a fact of life.

Song of Flower
★★★★ +

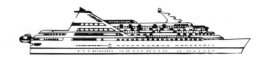

Small Ship:	8,282 tons	Cabins (for one person):	0
Lifestyle:	Luxury	Cabins (with private balcony):	10
Cruise Line:	Radisson Seven Seas Cruises	Cabins (wheelchair accessible):	0
Former Names:	*Explorer Starship*	Cabin Current:	220-volt
Builder:	KMV (Norway)/Lloyd Werft	Full-Service Dining Rooms:	1
	(Germany)	Elevators:	2
Original Cost:	n/a	Casino(gaming tables):	Yes
Entered Service:	1986/February 1990	Slot Machines:	Yes
Registry:	Bahamas	Swimming Pools (outdoors):	1
Length (ft/m):	407.4/124.2	Swimming Pools (indoors):	0
Beam (ft/m):	52.4/16.0	Whirlpools:	1
Draft (ft/m):	16.0/4.9	Fitness Center:	Yes
Propulsion/Propellers:	Diesel (5,500kW)/2	Sauna/Steam Room:	Yes/No
Passenger Decks:	6	Massage:	Yes
Total Crew:	144	Self-Service Launderette:	No
Passengers (lower beds/all berths):	198/198	Dedicated Cinema:	No
Pass. Space Ratio (lower beds/all berths):	41.8/41.8	Library:	Yes
Crew/Pass. Ratio (lower beds/all berths):	1.3/1.3	Classification Society:	Det Norske Veritas
Navigation Officers:	Norwegian		
Cabins (total):	99		
Size Range (sq ft/sq m):	183.0–398.0/17.0–37.0	**OVERALL SCORE:**	**1,651**
Cabins (outside view):	99	(OUT OF A POSSIBLE 2,000 POINTS)	
Cabins (interior/no view):	0		

Accommodation: There are 10 elegant suites; 10 cabins are nonsmoking. All are well-equipped with bathrobes and slippers, refrigerator, and VCR. All suites have excellent closet and drawer space. Many have bathtubs, but they are tiny (shower tubs would be a better description). Disabled passengers should choose a cabin with a shower instead of a bath. Unfortunately, there are no in-cabin dining facilities for dinner. When compared with the Seabourn Cruise Line and Silversea Cruises ships, the cabins are rather lackluster.

Dining: The dining room is really charming. It is decorated in warm colors and offers a welcoming ambience. There is one seating, with no assigned tables. The cuisine is very creative and presented with flare, in small, attractive, portions. All alcoholic and nonalcoholic beverages are included, with the exception of some premium wines. The staff is personable and highly attentive, resulting in excellent service. There are also several tables for two. Hand-scripted menus look like those one would find in an English country hotel. A new addition is an Italian alternative dining spot called A Taste of Italy, occupying the former casino.

Other Comments: This is an excellent small cruise ship, with tall, twin funnels that give a somewhat squat profile. If only the foredeck and bow could be a little longer it would provide a more sleek appearance. She has been well maintained and cared for and is very clean throughout, although her interiors are now looking quite tired. There is a good amount of sheltered open deck and sunbathing space. Water sports facilities include snorkeling equipment.

The interior decor is warm, with many pastel colors used in the public rooms, passageways, and on the stairways. High-quality soft furnishings and fabrics have been used throughout, making the ship very comfortable, though not luxurious. Although the health spa facility is quite compact, it is still reasonably adequate. The well-tiered show lounge is comfortable and has good sight lines from almost all seats.

The ship has a fine, warm, caring staff that really does try to anticipate your needs. Understated elegance and an informal lifestyle are the hallmarks of a cruise aboard this nice ship. It should provide a fine, destination-intensive, yet relaxing cruise experience, delivered with a decent amount of style and panache. Gratuities are included, and no further tipping is allowed; port charges are extra.

Weak Points: Announcements for the day's activities are unnecessary when everything is listed in the daily program. Vibration, particularly at the stern, and at some tables in the dining room, is a problem that continues to undermine the fine standard of hospitality experienced in the overall cruise product.

Sovereign of the Seas
★★★ +

Large Ship:	73,192 tons	Cabins (for one person):	0
Lifestyle:	Standard	Cabins (with private balcony):	0
Cruise Line:	Royal Caribbean International	Cabins (wheelchair accessible):	6
Former Names:	-	Cabin Current:	110 volts
Builder:	Chantiers de l'Atlantique (France)	Full-Service Dining Rooms:	2
Original Cost:	$183.5 million	Elevators:	13
Entered Service:	January 1988	Casino(gaming tables):	Yes
Registry:	Norway	Slot Machines:	Yes
Length (ft/m):	879.9/268.2	Swimming Pools (outdoors):	2
Beam (ft/m):	105.9/32.3	Swimming Pools (indoors):	0
Draft (ft/m):	24.9/7.6	Whirlpools:	2
Propulsion/Propellers:	Diesel	Fitness Center:	Yes
	(21,844kW)/2	Sauna/Steam Room:	Yes/No
Passenger Decks:	12	Massage:	Yes
Total Crew:	840	Self-Service Launderette:	No
Passengers (lower beds/all berths):	2,276/2,744	Dedicated Cinema/Seats:	Yes-2/144 each
Pass. Space Ratio (lower beds/all berths):	32.1/26.6	Library:	Yes
Crew/Pass. Ratio (lower beds/all berths):	2.7/3.2	Classification Society:	Det Norske Veritas
Navigation Officers:	Norwegian		
Cabins (total):	1,138		
Size Range (sq ft/sq m):	118.4–446.7/11.0–41.5	**OVERALL SCORE:**	**1,387**
Cabins (outside view):	722		
Cabins (interior/no view):	416	(OUT OF A POSSIBLE 2,000 POINTS)	

Accommodation: Twelve suites on Bridge Deck are reasonably large and nicely furnished, with separate living and sleeping spaces, and they provide more space, with better service, and more perks than the standard-grade accommodation.

The standard outside-view and interior (no view) cabins are very small, however, although an arched window treatment and colorful soft furnishings give the illusion of more space. Almost all cabins have twin beds that convert to a double bed configuration, with moveable bedside tables. All of the standard cabins have very little closet and drawer space (you will need some luggage engineering to stow your cases). You should, therefore, think of packing only minimal clothing, which is all you really need for a short cruise.

Dining: Two dining rooms provide well-presented food and service, but there are no tables for two. There are two seatings. The food varies, but doesn't seem to have much taste. Poor breads, rolls, and fruit selection, but a good selection of light meals, and a vegetarian menu is available. There is an adequate wine list and moderate prices. The staff, many of who come from countries in the Caribbean Basin, is perhaps overly friendly for some tastes.

Other Comments: This is a handsome mega-ship with a well-balanced profile, nicely rounded lines and high superstructure, but the open deck space is adequate, no more. A Viking Crown Lounge is built around the funnel and has superb views. It has a wide wrap-around outdoor polished wood deck, and there is a basketball court for sports fans.

While the interior layout is awkward (being designed in a vertical stack, with most public rooms located aft, and accommodation located forward), the ship has an impressive array of spacious and elegant public rooms. A stunning five-deck-high Centrum lobby has cascading stairways and two glass-walled elevators. There is a good two-level show lounge and a decent array of shops, albeit with lots of tacky merchandise. Casino gamers will find blackjack, craps, Caribbean stud poker, and roulette tables, plus an array of slot machines.

The line provides a good range of children's and teens' programs and counselors. The dress code is very casual.

This floating resort provides a well-tuned, yet very impersonal short cruise experience, for a lot of passengers. The ship was extensively refurbished in 1997, when some 220 new third and fourth berths were added to increase capacity to over 2,700. The shopping area was also increased as were more seats in the dining rooms. The ship features 3- and 4-night cruises to the Bahamas year-round, from Miami.

Weak Points: Standing in line for embarkation, disembarkation, shore tenders, and self-serve buffet meals is an inevitable aspect of cruising aboard all large ships. There is congested passenger flow in some areas. There are too many announcements. The ship is well used during these short cruises, and always looks tired and worn in some spots.

WHY IS A CRUISE VACATION SO POPULAR?

Well, over nine million people cannot be wrong (that's how many people took a cruise last year)! Cruising is popular today because it takes one away from the pressures and strains of contemporary life by offering an escape from reality. Cruise ships are really self-contained resorts, without the crime, which can take you to several destinations in the space of just a few days.

The sea has always been a source of adventure, excitement, romance, and wonder. It is beneficial and therapeutic, and, because you pay in advance, you know what you will spend on your vacation without any hidden surprises. There is no traffic (except when you go ashore in ports of call), and no pollution. The hassles of ordinary travel are almost eliminated in one pleasant little package. It's no wonder that 85 percent of passengers want to go again. And again. And again.

Sovetskiy Soyuz
★★★ +

Small Ship:	23,000 tons	Cabins (for one person):	3
Lifestyle:	Standard	Cabins (with private balcony):	0
Cruise Line:	Murmansk Shipping/	Cabins (wheelchair accessible):	0
	Quark Expeditions	Cabin Current:	220-volt
Former Names:	-	Full-Service Dining Rooms:	1
Builder:	Baltic Shipyard, Murmansk (Russia)	Elevators:	0
Original Cost:	$150 million	Casino(gaming tables):	No
Entered Service:	December 1989	Slot Machines:	No
Registry:	Russia	Swimming Pools (indoors):	1
Length (ft/m):	492.1/150.0	Whirlpools:	2
Beam (ft/m):	98.4/30.0	Fitness Center:	Yes
Draft (ft/m):	36.0/11.0	Sauna/Steam Room:	Yes-2/No
Propulsion/Propellers:	Nuclear-powered	Massage:	No
	turbo-electric (55,950kW)/3	Self-Service Launderette:	Yes
Passenger Decks:	4	Dedicated Cinema/Seats:	Yes/100
Total Crew:	150	Library:	Yes
Passengers (lower beds/all berths):	109/109	Zodiacs:	4
Pass. Space Ratio(lower beds/all berths):	211/211	Helicopter Pad:	2 helicopters for passenger use
Crew/Pass. Ratio (lower beds/all berths):	0.7/0.7	Classification Society:	Russian Shipping Registry
Navigation Officers:	Russian		
Cabins (total):	56		
Size Range (sq ft/sq m):	130.0–300.0/14.3–27.8	**OVERALL SCORE:**	**1,292**
Cabins (outside view):	50	(OUT OF A POSSIBLE 2,000 POINTS)	
Cabins (interior/no view):	0		

Accommodation: All of the cabins are generously sized (considering the type of specialized vessel this is), and all are outside, with private facilities, TV (for in-house viewing only), VCR (suites only), and refrigerator. There is, however, a limited amount of closet and drawer space in most cabins. The bathrooms are small and utilitarian, and you will need to take your own favorite personal toiletry items.

Dining: The ship features a nicely appointed dining room. There is one seating, and tables are not assigned, so you can dine where and with whom you please. When the ship is under charter to Quark Expeditions, the cuisine (which is surprisingly hearty) is overseen by European chefs. There are plenty of meat and potato dishes, but little choice in fruits and cheeses. Remember that these are not meant to be gourmet cruises, but the food is actually decent, and there is certainly plenty of it.

Other Comments: The ultimate in technology accompanies this special ship, one of a fleet of the world's most powerful icebreakers, with a 48 mm thick armored hull. She is, in fact, one of few surface ships ever to reach the North Pole.

Propulsion power is provided by two nuclear-powered reactors (encased in 160 tons of steel), which provide the steam for propulsion via two steam turbines. There are three powerful four-bladed propellers, each weighing about seven tons. Her icebreaking capability is assisted by an air bubbling system that delivers hot water from jets located below the surface.

Rugged, unpretentious, yet surprisingly comfortable surroundings prevail inside. There are two lounges to choose from. A tiered lecture theater with stage is the setting for a team of biologists, scientists, geologists, and other lecturers. There is a heated indoor pool. Attentive and friendly Russian service is provided. Passengers are allowed on the bridge at almost all times. Light but warm parkas are provided for all passengers. An expedition cruise logbook is typically provided at the end of each cruise for all passengers—a superb reminder of what's been seen and done during your expedition adventure cruise.

Sovetskiy Soyuz is one of a series of six formidable nuclear-powered icebreakers built between 1959 and 1993, that are often under charter to expedition cruise companies. She really is an incredible vessel, with a three-inch-thick reinforced bow for negotiating tough ice conditions (it really is noisy when ploughing through ice, of course). She carries enough fuel for four years without refueling! This is undoubtedly one of the most exciting, seat-of-your-pants expedition cruise experiences available today.

Spirit of '98
★★ +

Small Ship:	99 tons	Cabins (for one person):	0
Lifestyle:	Standard	Cabins (with private balcony):	0
Cruise Line:	Cruise West	Cabins (wheelchair accessible):	1
Former Names:	*Pilgrim Belle*, *Victorian Empress*	Cabin Current:	110-volt
Builder:	Bender Shipbuilding (USA)	Full-Service Dining Rooms:	1
Original Cost:	n/a	Elevators:	1
Entered Service:	1984/1993	Casino(gaming tables):	No
Registry:	USA	Slot Machines:	No
Length (ft/m):	192.0/58.2	Swimming Pools (outdoors):	0
Beam (ft/m):	40.0/12.1	Swimming Pools (indoors):	0
Draft (ft/m):	9.3/2.8	Whirlpools:	0
Propulsion/Propellers:	Diesel/1	Fitness Center:	0
Passenger Decks:	4	Sauna/Steam Room:	No/No
Total Crew:	30	Massage:	No
Passengers (lower beds/all berths):	96/96	Self-Service Launderette:	No
Pass. Space Ratio (lower beds/all berths):	1.0/1.0	Dedicated Cinema:	No
Crew/Pass. Ratio (lower beds/all berths):	3.2/3.2	Library:	Some bookshelves
Navigation Officers:	American	Classification Society: American Bureau of Shipping	
Cabins (total):	49		
Size Range (sq ft/sq m):	80.0–135.0/7.4–12.5	**OVERALL SCORE:**	**1,018**
Cabins (outside view):	49	**(OUT OF A POSSIBLE 2,000 POINTS)**	
Cabins (interior/no view):	0		

Accommodation: There are six grades of cabin to choose from. The Owner's Suite is the largest accommodation in the Cruise West fleet, and features large picture windows on three sides. It consists of two rooms; a lounge/living room with game table, TV and video player, refrigerator, and fully stocked/complimentary bar. There is also a separate bedroom with a king-size bed, and large bathroom with Jacuzzi bathtub.

There are also four irregular-shaped deluxe cabins at the front of the vessel, with decent closet space, a queen-size bed (or twin beds that convert to a double bed), and a bathroom with a separate shower enclosure. Two of the cabins also feature an extra sofa bed.

The other cabins are quite small when compared to most cruise ships, but they are reasonably comfortable, and feature a large picture window. While a few cabins feature queen-size or double beds, most have single beds that cannot be moved together (romantics please note). Each cabin has its own private bathroom, although these really are tiny, and feature a wall-mounted shower. There is no room service for food or snack items. You should note that the mattresses are placed within bed frames, and it's quite easy to knock your leg against the frame.

Dining: The Klondyke Dining Room is decorated in Edwardian/Gay Nineties style, and is an elegant room. The cuisine is decidedly plain and simple American fare (expect lots of seafood), as is the cutlery (no fish knifes are used, for example), although it is quite tasty. This is due to the fact that the ingredients are mostly fresh, and local. Wine and full bar services are provided.

Other Comments: This distinctive-looking vessel was built to resemble an old time coastal cruising vessels of the late 1800s. She has had a checkered past (prior to being operated by Cruise West). This vessel, which was originally built for the American Canadian Caribbean Line, is particularly suited to in-depth, in-your-face glacier spotting and for close-in cruising along the coastline of Alaska.

The interiors are designed in the style of a turn-of-century (the 19th century) Gay Nineties, and features carved cabinetry, etched glass and plush upholstery. There is only one public room inside the ship—the Grand Salon, although it is a large room.

You are much closer to nature aboard a small cruise vessel such as this one than you are on a large ship. There are no waiting lines, no loud rap or rock music blaring, no shows, no cabaret, and no casino. There is a viewing area outdoors right at the ship's bow. There is an open bridge policy, so you can visit the wheelhouse whenever you wish (except possibly during difficult maneuvers). The company has a sincere caring attitude towards protecting the natural environment.

Part Two: The Cruise Ships and Ratings

This ship and cruise are best suited to adult couples and single travelers (typically of age 60-plus), who enjoy learning about nature, geography, history, and other life sciences, in a casual, totally unpretentious setting, and who don't mind sharing confined spaces. This ship could be good for those who really do not like large cruise ships and endless lines.

The dress code is absolutely casual (not even a jacket for men is needed, and no ties, please). However, do take comfortable walking shoes, as well as photographic materials for wildlife spotting. Note that smoking is permitted only on the outside decks. The entire staff pools all the tips, using the amounts recommended in the cruise line's brochure of $10 per passenger, per day (this is high for the services offered). The cruising areas are Alaska, the Pacific Northwest, and California's wine country.

Weak Points: The ship is very small, and there are no nooks and crannies to hide away in (except for your cabin). There is an almost constant throbbing from the diesel engines/generator. Remember that there is no doctor on board (except for cruises in the Sea of Cortes), and so anyone with medical problems should really not consider this vessel. There are no cushioned pads for the deck lounge chairs.

Spirit of Alaska
★★

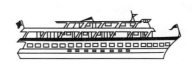

Small Ship:	97 tons	Cabins (for one person):	0
Lifestyle:	Standard	Cabins (with private balcony):	0
Cruise Line:	Cruise West	Cabins (wheelchair accessible):	0
Former Names:	*Pacific Northwest Explorer*	Cabin Current:	110-volt
Builder:	Blount Marine (USA)	Full-Service Dining Rooms:	1
Original Cost:	n/a	Elevators:	0
Entered Service:	1980/1991	Casino(gaming tables):	No
Registry:	USA	Slot Machines:	No
Length (ft/m):	143.0/43.5	Swimming Pools (outdoors):	0
Beam (ft/m):	28.5/8.6	Swimming Pools (indoors):	0
Draft (ft/m):	7.5/2.2	Whirlpools:	0
Propulsion/Propellers:	Diesel/1	Fitness Center:	0
Passenger Decks:	4	Sauna/Steam Room:	No/No
Total Crew:	20	Massage:	No
Passengers (lower beds/all berths):	78/78	Self-Service Launderette:	No
Pass. Space Ratio (lower beds/all berths):	1.2/1.2	Dedicated Cinema:	No
Crew/Pass. Ratio (lower beds/all berths):	3.9	Library:	Some bookshelves
Navigation Officers:	American	Classification Society: American Bureau of Shipping	
Cabins (total):	39		
Size Range (sq ft/sq m):	80.0–128.0/7.4–11.6	**OVERALL SCORE:**	**936**
Cabins (outside view):	27		
Cabins (interior/no view):	12	**(OUT OF A POSSIBLE 2,000 POINTS)**	

Accommodation: There are five grades of cabin to choose from. All are small but they are reasonably comfortable. A few feature double beds, but most have single beds that cannot be moved together (lovers please note). Each cabin has its own private bathroom, although these really are tiny, and feature a wall-mounted shower. Each cabin also has a small sink. There is no room service for food or snack items.

Dining: The dining room has very plain decor, but the open seating policy means that you can dine with whomever you wish, in a single seating. The cuisine is decidedly plain and simple American fare (expect lots of seafood), as is the cutlery (no fish knifes are used, for example), although it is quite tasty. This is due to the fact that the ingredients are mostly fresh and local. Wine and full bar services are provided.

Other Comments: This vessel is particularly suited to in-depth, in-your-face glacier spotting and for close-in cruising along the coastline of Alaska. There is only one public room inside the ship—the Glacier View Lounge. Smoking is permitted only on the outside decks.

You are much closer to nature aboard a small cruise vessel such as this than you are on a larger ship. There are no waiting lines, no loud rap or rock music blaring, no shows, no cabaret, and no casino. There is a viewing area outdoors right at the ship's bow. One bonus is the fact that at the bow of the vessel, a "bow gangway," comes into its own for landing passengers. There is an "open bridge" policy. The company has a sincere caring attitude towards protecting the natural environment.

This ship and cruise are best suited to adult couples and single travelers (typically of age 60-plus) who enjoy learning about nature, geography, history, and other life sciences, in a casual, totally unpretentious setting, and who don't mind sharing confined spaces.

There is only one public room inside the ship—the Riverview Lounge. The dress code is casual. However, do take comfortable walking shoes, as well as photographic materials for wildlife spotting. Smoking is permitted only on the outside decks.

All tips are pooled by all staff at $10 per passenger, per day, though this is high for the services offered. This ship navigates cruises in Alaska and the Pacific Northwest.

Weak Points: The ship is very small, and there are no nooks and crannies to hide away in (except for your cabin). There is an almost constant throbbing from the diesel engines/generator. Remember that there is no doctor on board, and so anyone with medical problems should really not consider this vessel. There are no cushioned pads for the deck lounge chairs.

Spirit of Columbia
★★

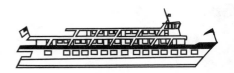

Small Ship:	98 tons	Cabins (for one person):	0
Lifestyle:	Standard	Cabins (with private balcony):	0
Cruise Line:	Cruise West	Cabins (wheelchair accessible):	0
Former Names:	*New Shoreham II*	Cabin Current:	110-volt
Builder:	Blount Marine (USA)	Full-Service Dining Rooms:	1
Original Cost:	n/a	Elevators:	0
Entered Service:	1979/1995	Casino(gaming tables):	No
Registry:	USA	Slot Machines:	No
Length (ft/m):	143.0/43.5	Swimming Pools (outdoors):	0
Beam (ft/m):	28.0/8.5	Swimming Pools (indoors):	0
Draft (ft/m):	6.5/1.9	Whirlpools:	0
Propulsion/Propellers:	Diesel/1	Fitness Center:	0
Passenger Decks:	4	Sauna/Steam Room:	No/No
Total Crew:	20	Massage:	0
Passengers (lower beds/all berths):	78/82	Self-Service Launderette:	0
Pass. Space Ratio (lower beds/all berths):	1.2/1.1	Dedicated Cinema:	No
Crew/Pass. Ratio (lower beds/all berths):	3.9/4.1	Library:	Some bookshelves
Navigation Officers:	American	Classification Society: American Bureau of Shipping	
Cabins (total):	39		
Size Range (sq ft/sq m):	80.0–121.0/7.4–11.2	**OVERALL SCORE:**	**936**
Cabins (outside view):	27	**(OUT OF A POSSIBLE 2,000 POINTS)**	
Cabins (interior/no view):	12		

Accommodation: There are five grades of cabin to choose from. All are small when compared to those on most cruise ships, but they are reasonably comfortable. A few feature double beds, but most have single beds that cannot be moved together (lovers please note). Each cabin has its own private bathroom, although these really are tiny, and feature a wall-mounted shower. Each cabin also has a small sink. There is no room service for food or snack items.

Dining: The dining room has minimal decor, but the open seating policy means that you can dine with whomever you wish, in a single seating. The cuisine is decidedly plain and simple American fare (expect good seafood), as is the cutlery (no fish knifes are used, for example), although it is quite tasty. This is due to the fact that the ingredients are mostly fresh and local. Wine and full bar services are provided.

Other Comments: This vessel is particularly suited to in-depth, in-your-face glacier spotting and for close-in cruising along the coastline of Alaska.

You are much closer to nature aboard a small cruise vessel such as this than you are on a large ship. There are no lines, no loud rap or rock music blaring, no shows, no cabaret, and no casino. There is a viewing area outdoors right at the ship's bow. One bonus is the fact that a direct-access loading ramp can be opened up from the lounge, for landing passengers. There is an open bridge policy. The company has a real caring attitude towards protecting the natural environment.

This ship and cruise are best suited to adult couples and single travelers (typically of age 60-plus) who enjoy learning about nature, geography, history, and other life sciences, in a casual, totally unpretentious setting, and who don't mind sharing confined spaces.

There is only one public room inside the ship—the Riverview Lounge. The dress code is absolutely casual. However, do take comfortable walking shoes, as well as photographic materials for wildlife spotting. Smoking is permitted only on the outside decks.

The staff pools all tips at $10 per passenger, per day (this is high for the services offered). This ship features cruises in Alaska and the Pacific Northwest.

Weak Points: The ship is very small, and there are no nooks and crannies to hide away in (except for your cabin). There is an almost constant throbbing from the diesel engines/generator. Remember that there is no doctor on board, and so anyone with medical problems should really not consider this vessel. There are no cushioned pads for the deck lounge chairs.

Spirit of Discovery
★★

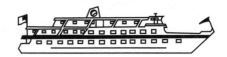

Small Ship:	94 tons	Cabins (for one person):	2
Lifestyle:	Standard	Cabins (with private balcony):	0
Cruise Line:	Cruise West	Cabins (wheelchair accessible):	0
Former Names:	*Independence, Columbia*	Cabin Current:	110-volt
Builder:	Blount Marine (USA)	Full-Service Dining Rooms:	1
Original Cost:	n/a	Elevators:	0
Entered Service:	1982/1992	Casino(gaming tables):	No
Registry:	USA	Slot Machines:	No
Length (ft/m):	166.0/50.5	Swimming Pools (outdoors):	0
Beam (ft/m):	37.0/11.2	Swimming Pools (indoors):	0
Draft (ft/m):	7.5/2.2	Whirlpools:	0
Propulsion/Propellers:	diesel/1	Fitness Center:	0
Passenger Decks:	4	Sauna/Steam Room:	No/No
Total Crew:	20	Massage:	0
Passengers (lower beds/all berths):	84/84	Self-Service Launderette:	No
Pass. Space Ratio (lower beds/all berths):	1.1/1.1	Dedicated Cinema:	No
Crew/Pass. Ratio (lower beds/all berths):	4.2/4.2	Library:	Yes
Navigation Officers:	American	Classification Society:	Lloyd's Register
Cabins (total):	43		
Size Range (sq ft/sq m):	64.0–126.0/5.9–11.7	**OVERALL SCORE:**	**946**
Cabins (outside view):	43		
Cabins (interior/no view):	0	**(OUT OF A POSSIBLE 2,000 POINTS)**	

Accommodation: There are six grades of cabin to choose from. All are small when compared to most cruise ships, but they are reasonably comfortable, and feature a large picture window and small clothes closet. A few cabins feature double beds, but most have single beds that cannot be moved together (lovers please note). Each cabin has its own private bathroom, although these really are tiny, and feature a wall-mounted shower. Each cabin also has a small sink. There is no room service for food or snack items.

Dining: The dining room has very plain decor, but the open seating policy means that you can dine with whomever you wish, in a single seating. The cuisine is decidedly plain and simple American fare (expect lots of seafood), as is the cutlery (no fish knives are used, for example), although it is quite tasty. This is due to the fact that the ingredients are mostly fresh and local. Wine and full bar services are provided.

Other Comments: This vessel is particularly suited to in-depth, in-your-face glacier spotting and for close-in cruising along the coastline of Alaska.

There is only one public room inside the ship—the Glacier View Lounge. Smoking is permitted only on the outside decks.

You are much closer to nature aboard a small cruise vessel such as this than you are aboard larger ships. There is a viewing area outdoors right at the ship's bow. There are no waiting lines, no loud rap or rock music blaring, no shows, no cabaret, and no casino. There is an open bridge policy. The company has a sincere caring attitude towards protecting the natural environment.

This ship and cruise are best suited to adult couples and single travelers (typically of age 60-plus)who enjoy learning about nature, geography, history, and other life sciences, in a casual, totally unpretentious setting, and who don't mind sharing confined spaces.

The dress code is absolutely casual. However, do take comfortable walking shoes, as well as photographic materials for wildlife spotting.

The staff pools all tips at $10 per passenger, per day (this is high for the services offered). This ship cruises in Alaska and the Pacific Northwest.

Weak Points: The ship is very small, and there are no nooks and crannies to hide away in (except for your cabin). There is an almost constant throbbing from the diesel engines/generator. Remember that there is no doctor on board, and so anyone with medical problems should really not consider this vessel. There are no cushioned pads for the deck lounge chairs.

Spirit of Endeavour
★★

Small Ship:	95 tons	Cabins (for one person):	0
Lifestyle:	Standard	Cabins (with private balcony):	0
Cruise Line:	Cruise West	Cabins (wheelchair accessible):	0
Former Names:	*Nantucket Clipper, SeaSpirit*	Cabin Current:	110-volt
Builder:	Jeffboat (USA)	Full-Service Dining Rooms:	1
Original Cost:	n/a	Elevators:	0
Entered Service:	1983/1996	Casino(gaming tables):	No
Registry:	USA	Slot Machines:	No
Length (ft/m):	217.0/66.1	Swimming Pools (outdoors):	0
Beam (ft/m):	37.0/11.3	Swimming Pools (indoors):	0
Draft (ft/m):	8.5/2.5	Whirlpools:	0
Propulsion/Propellers:	Diesel/1	Fitness Center:	0
Passenger Decks:	3	Sauna/Steam Room:	No/No
Total Crew:	28	Massage:	0
Passengers (lower beds/all berths):	102/107	Self-Service Launderette:	0
Pass. Space Ratio (lower beds/all berths):	0.9/0.8	Dedicated Cinema:	No
Crew/Pass. Ratio (lower beds/all berths):	3.6/3.8	Library:	Yes
Navigation Officers:	American	Classification Society: American Bureau of Shipping	
Cabins (total):	51		
Size Range (sq ft/sq m):	110.0–153.0/10.2–14.2	**OVERALL SCORE:**	**946**
Cabins (outside view):	51	**(OUT OF A POSSIBLE 2,000 POINTS)**	
Cabins (interior/no view):	0		

Accommodation: There are four grades of cabin to choose from. All are small when compared to those on most cruise ships, but they are reasonably comfortable for this small size vessel, and feature a large picture window (just four cabins on Main Deck have a porthole), a clothes closet, TV and VCR. A few cabins feature twin beds that can convert into a queen-size bed, but most have single beds that cannot be moved together (lovers please note). Each cabin has its own private bathroom, although these really are tiny, and features a wall-mounted shower. Several cabins have a Pullman-berth for a third occupant. Each cabin also has a small sink. There is no room service for food or snack items.

Dining: The Resolution Dining Room has plain decor, but there is an open seating policy. The cuisine is decidedly plain and simple American fare (expect lots of seafood), as is the cutlery (no fish knifes are used, for example), although it is quite tasty. This is due to the fact that the ingredients are mostly fresh, and local. Wine and full bar services are provided.

Other Comments: This vessel is the flagship of the Cruise West fleet, and is particularly suited to in-depth, in-your-face glacier spotting and for "up-close" cruising along the coastline of Alaska. There is only one public room inside the ship—the Explorer Lounge. Smoking is permitted only on the outside decks.

You are much closer to nature aboard a small cruise vessel such as this than you are aboard a giant floating resort. There is a viewing area outdoors right at the ship's bow. There are no waiting lines, no loud rap or rock music blaring, no shows, no cabaret, and no casino. There is an open bridge policy. The company has a sincere caring attitude towards protecting the natural environment.

This ship and cruise are best suited to adult couples and single travelers (typically of age 60-plus) who enjoy learning about nature, geography, history, and other life sciences, in a casual, totally unpretentious setting, and who don't mind sharing confined spaces.

The dress code is absolutely casual. However, do take comfortable walking shoes, as well as photographic materials for wildlife spotting. The staff pools all tips at $10 per passenger, per day (this is high for the services offered). The cruising areas are Alaska, the Sea of Cortes, and California's wine country.

Weak Points: The ship is very small, and there are no nooks and crannies to hide away in. There is an almost constant throbbing from the diesel engines/generator. Remember that there is no doctor on board (except for the Sea of Cortes cruises). There are no cushioned pads for the deck lounge chairs.

Spirit of Glacier Bay
★★

Small Ship:	97 tons	Cabins (for one person):	2
Lifestyle:	Standard	Cabins (with private balcony):	0
Cruise Line:	Cruise West	Cabins (wheelchair accessible):	0
Former Names:	*Glacier Bay Explorer, New*	Cabin Current:	110-volt
	Shoreham I	Full-Service Dining Rooms:	1
Builder:	Blount Marine (USA)	Elevators:	0
Original Cost:	n/a	Casino(gaming tables):	No
Entered Service:	1971/1990	Slot Machines:	No
Registry:	USA	Swimming Pools (outdoors):	0
Length (ft/m):	125.0/38.1	Swimming Pools (indoors):	0
Beam (ft/m):	28.0/8.5	Whirlpools:	0
Draft (ft/m):	6.5/1.9	Fitness Center:	0
Propulsion/Propellers:	Diesel/1	Sauna/Steam Room:	No/No
Passenger Decks:	3	Massage:	0
Total Crew:	15	Self-Service Launderette:	0
Passengers (lower beds/all berths):	52/54	Dedicated Cinema:	No
Pass. Space Ratio (lower beds/all berths):	1.8/1.7	Library:	Some bookshelves
Crew/Pass. Ratio (lower beds/all berths):	3.4/3.6	Classification Society: American Bureau of Shipping	
Navigation Officers:	American		
Cabins (total):	27		
Size Range (sq ft/sq m):	55.0–72.0/5.1–6.6	**OVERALL SCORE:**	**913**
Cabins (outside view):	14	**(OUT OF A POSSIBLE 2,000 POINTS)**	
Cabins (interior/no view):	13		

Accommodation: There are three grades of cabin to choose from. All are small when compared to most cruise ships, but they are reasonably comfortable, and most feature a large picture window and small clothes closet. A few cabins feature double beds, but most have single beds that cannot be moved together (lovers please note). Two cabins on the lowest deck, in the front of the ship have upper and lower berths. Each cabin has its own tiny private bathroom, which features a wall-mounted shower. Each cabin also has a small sink. There is no room service for food or snack items.

Dining: The dining room has really plain decor, but the open seating policy means that you can dine with whomever you wish, in a single seating. The cuisine is decidedly plain and simple American fare (expect lots of seafood), as is the cutlery (no fish knifes are used, for example), although it is quite tasty. This is due to the fact that the ingredients are mostly fresh and local. Wine and full bar services are provided.

Other Comments: This vessel is particularly suited to in-depth, in-your-face glacier spotting and for close-in cruising along the coastline of Alaska. There is only one public room inside the ship—the Glacier View Lounge. Smoking is permitted only on the outside decks.

You are much closer to nature aboard a small cruise vessel such as this than you are in a large cruise ship. There is a viewing area outdoors right at the ship's bow. There are no waiting lines, no loud rap or rock music blaring, no shows, no cabaret, and no casino. One bonus is the fact that at the bow of the vessel, a "bow gangway" comes into its own for landing passengers. There is an open bridge policy. The company has a sincere caring attitude towards protecting the natural environment.

This ship is best suited to adult couples and single travelers (typically of age 60-plus) who enjoy learning about nature, geography, history, and other life sciences, in a casual, totally unpretentious setting, and who don't mind sharing confined spaces.

The dress code is absolutely casual. However, do take comfortable walking shoes, as well as photographic materials for wildlife spotting. The staff pools all tips at $10 per passenger, per day (this is high for the services offered). The ship's cruising areas are Alaska and the Pacific Northwest.

Weak Points: The ship is very small, and there are no nooks and crannies to hide away in (except for your cabin). There is an almost constant throbbing from the diesel engines/generator. Remember that there is no doctor on board. There are no cushioned pads for the deck lounge chairs.

Spirit of Oceanus

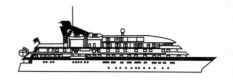

Small Ship:	4,200 tons	Cabins (with private balcony):	12
Lifestyle:	Standard	Cabins (wheelchair accessible):	0
Cruise Line:	Cruise West	Cabin Current:	110-volt
Former Names:	*MegaStar Sagittarius, Sun Viva,*	Full-Service Dining Rooms:	1
	Renaissance Five	Elevators:	1
Builder:	Nuovi Cantieri Apuania (Italy)	Casino(gaming tables):	No
Entered Service:	1991/2001	Slot Machines:	No
Registry:	Bahamas	Swimming Pools (outdoors):	1
Length (ft/m):	294.5/89.7	Swimming Pools (indoors):	0
Beam (ft/m):	50.1/15.30	Whirlpools:	1
Draft (ft/m):	13.2/4.05	Fitness Center:	Yes
Propulsion/Propellers:	Diesel (5,000kW)/2	Sauna/Steam Room:	No/No
Passenger Decks:	5	Massage:	Yes
Total Crew:	55	Self-Service Launderette:	No
Passengers (lower beds/all berths):	114/127	Dedicated Cinema:	No
Pass. Space Ratio (lower beds/all berths):	37.5/33.0	Library:	Yes
Crew/Pass. Ratio (lower beds/all berths):	2.0/4.7	Classification Society: American Bureau of Shipping	
Navigation Officers:	American		
Cabins (total):	57		
Size Range (sq ft/sq m):	215.0–353.0/20.0–32.7	**OVERALL SCORE: NOT YET RATED**	
Cabins (outside view):	57		
Cabins (interior/no view):	0	Note that this ship had not entered service when this	
Cabins (for one person):	0	book was completed.	

Accommodation: There are 6 categories of accommodation. Fine all-outside view cabins (called suites in the brochure) combine highly polished imitation rosewood paneling with lots of mirrors, and fine, handcrafted Italian furniture. All suites have twin beds that can convert to a queen-size bed, a sitting area with a three-person sofa, one individual chair, a coffee table, minibar/refrigerator (stocked with juices and bottled water), color TV and VCR, direct-dial satellite telephone, and a bowl of fresh fruit on embarkation day. Note that while closet space is good, space for stowing luggage is tight, and there is little drawer space (each cabin has three drawers, two of which are lockable, plus several open shelves in a separate closet). Also note that there are no music channels in the cabins, and there is no switch to turn off announcements off in your cabin.

The marble bathrooms are compact units that have showers (no bathrooms have a bathtub) with fold-down (plastic) seat, real teakwood floor, marble vanity, large mirror, recessed towel rail (good for storing personal toiletries), and built-in hair dryer. *Note:* there is a high "lip" into the bathroom.

Dining: The Restaurant, which has an open seating policy (it can seat all passengers at one seating), is bright, elegant, welcoming, and nonsmoking. It is on the lowest deck and has portholes rather than windows, due to maritime regulations. There are tables for two, four, six, or eight, and you can sit where you like, with whom you like, when you like in this open seating arrangement. Dinners are normally sit-down affairs, although, depending on the itinerary and length of cruise, there could be an occasional buffet. Breakfast and lunch are typically self-serve buffets and can be taken at the poolside (weather permitting), in your cabin, or in the restaurant.

Other Comments: This ship has contemporary exterior styling, a private yacht-like look and handsome styling with twin, flared funnels. The navigation bridge is a well-rounded half-moon design. This was one of four identical vessels (out of a series of eight) originally built for Renaissance Cruises, but now the ship is now being operated by its fourth owner since new.

There is a teak promenade deck outdoors, and a reasonable amount of open deck and sunbathing space. All of the deck furniture—the tables and chairs—are made of teak and the deck lounge chairs have thick cushioned pads. There is a teak water sports platform at the stern of the ship (not used in Alaska), as well as a number of Zodiac inflatable rubber landing craft. Snorkeling gear is also provided (not used in Alaska).

Inside the ship, you will find elegant interior design. The main lounge, the focal point for all social activities, has six pillars that interrupt sight lines to the small stage area. There is also a very small book and video library.

The ship was acquired by Cruise West in May 2001. It is the largest, and the only ocean-going vessel in the present fleet. *Spirit of Oceanus* cruises Alaska and British Columbia during the summer months, and in the winter sails to Tahiti, the Fiji Islands, and other Pacific Ocean destinations. What's really nice is that there are no waiting lines, no loud rap or rock music blaring, no shows, no cabaret, and no casino—just you, the ship, and nature.

CRUISING FOR HONEYMOONERS

Cruising is popular as a honeymoon vacation. The advantages are obvious: you pack and unpack only once; it is a hassle-free and crime-free environment; and you get special attention, if you want it. It is also easy to budget in advance, as one price often includes airfare, cruise, food, entertainment, several destinations, shore excursions, and pre- and post-cruise hotel stays. Once you are married, some cruise lines often offer discounts to entice you to book a future (anniversary) cruise. Just think, no cooking meals, everything will be done for you. You can think of the crew as your very own service and kitchen staff.

Cruise lines offer a variety of honeymoon packages, just as hotels and resorts on land do. Although not all cruise lines provide all services, typically they might include:

→ Private captain's cocktail party for honeymooners.

→ Tables for two in the dining room.

→ Set of crystal champagne or wine glasses.

→ Honeymoon photograph with the captain, and photo album.

→ Complimentary champagne (imported or domestic) or wine.

→ Honeymoon cruise certificate.

→ Champagne and caviar for breakfast.

→ Flowers in your suite or cabin.

→ Complimentary cake.

→ Special T-shirts.

Splendour of the Seas
★★★★

Large Ship:	69,130 tons	Cabins (for one person):	0
Lifestyle:	Standard	Cabins (with private balcony):	231
Cruise Line:	Royal Caribbean International	Cabins (wheelchair accessible):	17
Former Names:	-	Cabin Current:	110/220-volt
Builder:	Chantiers de l'Atlantique (France)	Full-Service Dining Rooms:	1
Original Cost:	$325 million	Elevators:	11
Entered Service:	March 1996	Casino(gaming tables):	Yes
Registry:	Norway	Slot Machines:	Yes
Length (ft/m):	867.0/264.2	Swimming Pools (outdoors):	2 (1 with sliding roof)
Beam (ft/m):	105.0/32.0	Swimming Pools (indoors):	0
Draft (ft/m):	24.5/7.3	Whirlpools:	4
Propulsion/Propellers:	Diesel (40,200kW)/2	Fitness Center:	Yes
Passenger Decks:	11	Sauna/Steam Room:	Yes/Yes
Total Crew:	720	Massage:	Yes
Passengers (lower beds/all berths):	1,804/2,064	Self-Service Launderette:	No
Pass. Space Ratio (lower beds/all berths):	38.3/33.4	Dedicated Cinema:	No
Crew/Pass. Ratio (lower beds/all berths):	2.5/2.8	Library:	Yes
Navigation Officers:	Norwegian	Classification Society:	Det Norske Veritas
Cabins (total):	902		
Size Range (sq ft/sq m):	137.7–1,147.4/12.8–106.6	**OVERALL SCORE:**	**1,511**
Cabins (outside view):	575	**(OUT OF A POSSIBLE 2,000 POINTS)**	
Cabins (interior/no view):	327		

Accommodation: Royal Caribbean International has realized that small cabins do not happy passengers make. The company therefore set about designing a ship with much larger standard cabins than in any of the company's previous vessels (except sister ship *Legend of the Seas*). Some cabins on Deck 8 also have a larger door for wheelchair access in addition to the 17 cabins for the physically challenged, and the ship is very accessible, with ample ramped areas and sloping decks. All cabins have a sitting area and beds that convert to double configuration, and there is ample closet and drawer space, although there is not much space around the bed (and the showers could have been better designed).

Cabins with balconies have glass railings rather than steel/wood to provide less intrusive sight lines of the ocean view. The largest accommodation, named the Royal Suite, is a superb living space for those that can afford the best. It is beautifully designed, finely decorated, and features a baby grand piano, whirlpool bathtub, and other fine amenities. Several quite pleasant sitting areas are located adjacent to the best cabins amidships. Seventeen cabin categories are really too many. Unfortunately, there are no cabins for singles.

Dining: The two-deck-high dining room has dramatic two-deck-high glass side walls, enabling many passengers both upstairs and downstairs to see both the ocean and each other in reflection (it would, perhaps, have been even better located at the stern), but it is quite noisy when full (call it "atmosphere"). There are two seatings.

The dining operation is well orchestrated, with emphasis on highly programmed (insensitive), extremely hurried service that many find intrusive.

Most nights are themed (typically French, Oriental, Italian, Caribbean, American), as they have been for years, with waiters and busboys in appropriate costumes. The food is typical of hotel banquet catering. The menu descriptions make the food sound better than it is, which is consistently average, mostly disappointing and without much taste. However, a decent selection of light meals is provided, and a vegetarian menu is available. The selection of breads, rolls, fruit, and cheese is quite poor, however, and should be upgraded. There is no good caviar; neither are there special orders, tableside carving nor flambeau items. One thing this company does once each cruise is to feature "Galley Buffet" whereby passengers go through a section of the galley picking up food for a midnight buffet.

The wine list is not very extensive, but the prices are moderate. The waiters, many of whom are from Caribbean countries, are perhaps overly friendly for some tastes—particularly on the last night of the cruise, when tips are expected.

There is also a cavernous indoor-outdoor café, located towards the bow and above the bridge, as well as a good-sized snack area, which provide more informal dining choices.

Other Comments: This ship's contemporary profile looks somewhat unbalanced (but it soon grows on you), and she does have a nicely tiered stern. The pool deck amidships overhangs the hull to provide an extremely wide deck, while still allowing the ship to navigate the Panama Canal. With engines placed amidships, there is little noise and no noticeable vibration, and the ship has an operating speed of up to 24 knots.

The interior decor is quite colorful, but too glitzy for European tastes. Daylight is brought inside in many places, with an extensive amount of glass area that provides contact with sea and air (there is, in fact, over two acres of glass). The ship features an innovative single-level sliding glass roof (not a magrodome) over the more formal setting of one of two swimming pools, providing a large, multi-activity, all-weather indoor-outdoor area, called the Solarium. The glass roof provides shelter for the Roman-style pool and adjacent health and fitness facilities (which are superb), and slides aft when required to cover the miniature golf course (both cannot be covered at the same time, however).

Golfers might enjoy the 18-hole, 6,000 sq ft (557.5 sq m) miniature golf course, with the topography of a real golf course, complete with trees, foliage, grass, bridges, water hazards, and lighting for play at night. The holes themselves are 155–230 sq ft (14.3-21.3 sq m).

Inside, two full entertainment decks are sandwiched between five decks full of cabins. The tiered and balconied show lounge, which covers two decks, is expansive, has excellent sight lines, and very comfortable seats. Several large scale production shows are provided here, and the orchestra pit can be raised or lowered as required. A multi-tiered seven-deck-high atrium lobby, complete with a huge stainless steel sculpture, connects with the impressive Viking Crown Lounge via glass-walled elevators. The casino is quite extensive, overly glitzy, and absolutely packed. The library, outside of which is a bust of Shakespeare, is a fine facility, with over 2,000 volumes.

There is, unfortunately, no separate cinema. The casino can be somewhat disorienting, with its mirrored walls and lights flashing everywhere, although it is no different to those found in Las Vegas-style gaming halls. As with any large ship, you can expect to find yourself standing in lines for embarkation, disembarkation, buffets, and shore excursions, although the company does its best to minimize such lines.

Representing a natural evolution, this ship is an outstanding new cruise vessel for the many repeat passengers who enjoy Royal Caribbean International's consistent delivery of a well-integrated, fine-tuned, very comfortable, and popular product.

Weak Points: Standing in line for embarkation, disembarkation, shore tenders, and self-serve buffet meals is an inevitable aspect of cruising aboard all large ships.

Star Clipper
★★★ +

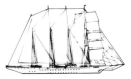

Small Ship:	3,025 tons	Cabins (total):	85
Lifestyle:	Standard	Size Range (sq ft/sq m):	95.0–150.0/8.8–14.0
Cruise Line:	Star Clippers	Cabins (outside view):	79
Former Names:	-	Cabins (interior/no view):	6
Builder:	Scheepswerven van Langerbrugge	Cabins (for one person):	0
	(Belgium)	Cabins (with private balcony):	0
Original Cost:	$30 million	Cabins (wheelchair accessible):	0
Entered Service:	May 1992	Cabin Current:	110-volt
Registry:	Luxembourg	Full-Service Dining Rooms:	1
Length (ft/m):	366.1/111.6	Elevators:	0
Beam (ft/m):	49.2/15.0	Casino(gaming tables):	No
Draft (ft/m):	17.7/5.6	Slot Machines:	No
Type of Vessel:	Barkentine schooner	Swimming Pools (outdoors):	2
No. of Masts:	4 (208 ft)	Whirlpools:	2
Sail Area (sq ft/sq m):	36,221/3,365/16 manual	Fitness Center:	No
	furled sails	Sauna/Steam Room:	No/No
Main Propulsion:	Sail power	Massage:	No
Propulsion/Propellers:	Diesel (1,030kW)/1	Self-Service Launderette:	No
Passenger Decks:	4	Library:	Yes
Total Crew:	72	Classification Society:	Lloyd's Register
Passengers (lower beds/all berths):	170/180		
Pass. Space Ratio (lower beds/all berths):	17.7/16.8	**OVERALL SCORE:**	**1,390**
Crew/Pass. Ratio (lower beds/all berths):	2.3/2.5	**(OUT OF A POSSIBLE 2,000 POINTS)**	
Navigation Officers:	European		

Accommodation: There are six price grades for accommodation; generally the higher the deck, the more expensive will your cabin be. The cabins are quite well equipped and comfortable; they feature wood-trimmed cabinetry and wall-to-wall carpeting, two-channel audio, color TV, lockable personal safe, and full-length mirrors. The bathrooms are very compact, but practical units, and feature gray marble tiling, a toiletries cabinet, some under-shelf storage space, washbasin, small shower stall, and toilet. There is no "lip" to prevent water from the shower from moving over the bathroom floor. The bed linen is of a mix of 50% cotton and 50% polyester.

The deluxe cabins are larger, and additional features include a full-sized bathtub and minibar/refrigerator. Note that there is no cabin food or beverage service.

Note that the cabins in the lowest price grade are interior cabins with upper and lower berths, and not two lower beds—so someone will need to be agile enough to climb up to the upper berth (a ladder is provided, of course). A handful of cabins have a third, upper Pullman-style berth (note that closet and drawer space will be at a premium with three persons in a cabin, so do take only the minimal amount of clothing you can).

Dining: The dining room is quite attractive, and features lots of wood accenting and nautical decor. Buffet breakfasts and lunches are featured, together with a mix of buffet and à la carte dinners (generally a choice of two entrees). There is a limited choice of bread rolls, pastry items, and fruits.

There is one (open) seating. The seating arrangement (mostly with tables of six) makes it difficult for waiters to serve properly. However, since it is in an open seating arrangement, so you can dine with whomever you wish, and this is supposed to be a casual experience. While cuisine aboard the *Star Clipper* is perhaps less than the advertised "gourmet" excellence (as far as presentation and choice are concerned), it is nevertheless fairly creative, and one has to take into account the tiny galley it comes from.

Perhaps fewer passenger cabins and more room in the galley would have enabled the chefs to provide a better dining experience than the present arrangement.

Tea and coffee should be, but are not, available 24 hours a day, particularly in view of the fact that there is no cabin food service at all. When they are available, paper cups are provided (real china would be better).

Other Comments: This is one of a pair of almost identical tall ships (her sister ship is *Star Flyer*). It is a sailing vessel with cruise accommodation that evokes memories of the 19th century clipper sailing ships.

This is an accurate four-mast, barkentine-rigged vessel with graceful lines, a finely shaped hull and masts that are 19.3 meters tall. Breathtaking when under full sail, she displays excellent sea manners. This working clipper ship relies on the wind about 80% of the time. A diesel engine is used as backup in emergencies, for generating electrical power and for desalinating the approximately 40 tons of seawater each day for shipboard needs. The crew performs almost every task, including hoisting, trimming, winching, and repairing the sails.

Water sports facilities include a water ski boat, sunfish, scuba and snorkeling equipment, and eight Zodiac inflatable crafts. Sports directors provide basic dive instruction (for a fee).

The whole cruise experience evokes the feeling of sailing aboard some famous private yacht at the turn of the last century. *Star Flyer* (sister to *Star Clipper*), the first clipper sailing ship to be built for 140 years, became the first commercial sailing vessel to cross the North Atlantic in 90 years.

Some of the amenities of large modern cruise vessels are provided, such as air-conditioning, cashless cruising, occasional live music, a small shop, and a pool to swim in (actually "dip" would be a better description). Inside the vessel, classic Edwardian nautical decor throughout is clean, warm, intimate, and inviting. The paneled library has a fireplace, with chairs that are supremely comfortable. A cruise aboard her means no waiting lines, no hassle, and classes on "Sailing a Square Rigger" are a part of every cruise.

Each morning, passengers gather for "captain's story-time"—normally held on an open deck area adjacent to the bar—which, incidentally, has a fine collection of single malt whiskies. The captain also explains sailing maneuvers when changing the rigging or directing the ship as it sails into port, and notes the important events of the day. Passengers are encouraged to lend a hand, pulling on thick ropes to haul up the main sail. And they love it.

The vessel promotes total informality and provides a carefree sailing cruise experience in a totally unstructured setting at a modest price. Take minimal clothing: short-sleeved shirts and shorts for the men, shorts and tops for the ladies are the order of the day (and night). No jackets, ties, high-heeled shoes, cocktail dresses, or the slightest hint of formal wear is needed. The deck crew consists of real sailors, brought up with yachts and tall ships—and most would not set foot aboard a cruise ship.

It is no exaggeration to say that to be sailing aboard either *Star Clipper* or *Star Flyer* is to seem to have died and gone to yachtsman's heaven, since there is plenty of sailing during the course of a typical one-week cruise. Even the most jaded passenger should enjoy the feel of the wind and sea close at hand—just don't expect good food to go with what is decidedly a fine sailing experience—which is what *Star Clipper* is all about. Note that 12.5% is added to all beverage purchases.

Weak Points: The food, its quality, variety, presentation, and service, is still the weakest point of a cruise aboard this tall ship—and it is not as good as what is provided aboard the company's larger flagship, *Royal Clipper*. This ship is not for the physically impaired, or for children. The steps of the internal stairs are steep, as in most sailing vessels. The tipping system, where all tips are pooled (the suggested amount is $8 per passenger, per day), causes concern for many passengers.

Star Flyer
★★★ +

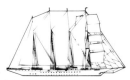

Small Ship:	3,025 tons	Cabins (total):	85
Lifestyle:	Standard	Size Range (sq ft/sq m):	95.0–150.0/8.8–14.0
Cruise Line:	Star Clippers	Cabins (outside view):	79
Former Names:	-	Cabins (interior/no view):	6
Builder:	Scheepswerven van Langerbrugge	Cabins (for one person):	0
	(Belgium)	Cabins (with private balcony):	0
Original Cost:	$25 million	Cabins (wheelchair accessible):	0
Entered Service:	July 1991	Cabin Current:	110-volt
Registry:	Luxembourg	Full-Service Dining Rooms:	1
Length (ft/m):	366.1/111.6	Elevators:	0
Beam (ft/m):	49.2/15.0	Casino(gaming tables):	No
Draft (ft/m):	17.7/5.6	Slot Machines:	No
Type of Vessel:	Barkentine schooner	Swimming Pools (outdoors):	2
No. of Masts:	4 (208 ft)	Whirlpools:	0
Sail Area (sq ft/sq m):	36,221/3,365/16 manual	Fitness Center:	No
	furled sails	Sauna/Steam Room:	No/No
Main Propulsion:	Sail power	Massage:	No
Propulsion/Propellers:	Diesel (1,030kW)/1	Self-Service Launderette:	No
Passenger Decks:	4	Library:	Yes
Total Crew:	72	Classification Society:	Lloyd's Register
Passengers (lower beds/all berths):	170/180		
Pass. Space Ratio (lower beds/all berths):	17.7/16.8	**OVERALL SCORE:**	**1,390**
Crew/Pass. Ratio (lower beds/all berths):	2.3/2.5		
Navigation Officers:	European	**(OUT OF A POSSIBLE 2,000 POINTS)**	

Accommodation: There are six price grades for accommodation; generally the higher the deck, the more expensive will your cabin be. The cabins are quite well-equipped and comfortable; they feature wood-trimmed cabinetry and wall-to-wall carpeting, two-channel audio, color TV, lockable personal safe, and full-length mirrors. The bathrooms are very compact, but practical units, and feature gray marble tiling, a toiletries cabinet, some under-shelf storage space, washbasin, small shower stall, and toilet. There is no "lip" to prevent water from the shower from moving over the bathroom floor. The bed linen is a mix of 50% cotton and 50% polyester.

The deluxe cabins are larger, and additional features include a full-sized bathtub and minibar/refrigerator. Note that there is no cabin food or beverage service.

Note that the cabins in the lowest price grade are interior cabins with upper and lower berths, and not two lower beds—so someone will need to be agile to climb up to the upper berth (a ladder is provided). A handful of cabins have a third, upper Pullman-style berth (closet and drawer space will be at a premium with three persons in a cabin, so do take only a minimal amount of clothing).

Dining: The dining room is quite attractive, and features lots of wood accenting and nautical decor. Buffet breakfasts and lunches are featured, together with a mix of buffet and à la carte dinners (generally a choice of two entrees). There is a limited choice of bread rolls, pastry items, and fruits.

There is one (open) seating. The seating arrangement (mostly with tables of six) makes it difficult for waiters to serve properly. However, it is in an open seating arrangement, so you can dine with whomever you wish, and this is supposed to be a casual experience. While cuisine aboard the *Star Flyer* is perhaps less than the advertised "gourmet" excellence (as far as presentation and choice are concerned), it is nevertheless fairly creative, and one has to take into account the tiny galley it comes from.

Perhaps fewer passenger cabins and more room in the galley would have enabled the chefs to provide a better dining experience than the present arrangement.

Tea and coffee should be, but are not, available 24 hours a day, particularly in view of the fact that there is no cabin food service at all. When they are available, paper cups are provided (real china would be better).

Other Comments: *Star Flyer* is one of a pair of almost identical tall ships (her sister ship is *Star Clipper*). It is a sailing vessel with cruise accommodation that evokes memories of the 19th-century clipper sailing ships. This is an accurate four-mast, barkentine-rigged vessel with graceful lines, a finely shaped hull and masts that are 19.3 meters tall. Breathtaking when under full sail, she displays excellent sea manners. This working clipper ship relies on the wind about 80% of the time. A diesel engine is used as backup in emergencies, for generating electrical power and for desalinating the approximately 40 tons of seawater each day for shipboard needs. The crew performs almost every task, including hoisting, trimming, winching, and repairing the sails.

Water sports facilities include a water ski boat, sunfish, scuba and snorkeling equipment, and eight Zodiac inflatable crafts. Sports directors provide basic dive instruction (for a fee).

The whole cruise experience evokes the feeling of sailing aboard some famous private yacht at the turn of the century. *Star Flyer*, the first clipper sailing ship to be built for 140 years, became the first commercial sailing vessel to cross the North Atlantic in 90 years.

Some of the amenities of large modern cruise vessels are provided, such as air-conditioning, cashless cruising, occasional live music, a small shop, and a pool to swim in (actually "dip" would be a better description). Inside the vessel, classic Edwardian nautical decor throughout is clean, warm, intimate, and inviting. The paneled library has a fireplace, with chairs that are supremely comfortable. A cruise aboard her means no lines, no hassle, and classes on "Sailing a Square Rigger" are a part of every cruise.

Each morning, passengers gather for "captain's story-time"—normally held on an open deck area adjacent to the bar—which, incidentally, has a fine collection of single malt whiskies. The captain also explains sailing maneuvers when changing the rigging or directing the ship as it sails into port, and notes the important events of the day. Passengers are encouraged to lend a hand, pulling on thick ropes to haul up the main sail. And they love it.

The vessel promotes total informality and provides a carefree sailing cruise experience in a totally unstructured setting at a modest price. Take minimal clothing: short-sleeved shirts and shorts for the men, shorts and tops for the ladies are the order of the day (and night). No jackets, ties, high-heeled shoes, cocktail dresses, or the slightest hint of formal wear is needed. The deck crew consists of real sailors, brought up with yachts and tall ships—and most would not set foot aboard a cruise ship.

It is no exaggeration to say that to be sailing aboard either *Star Flyer* or *Star Clipper* is to seem to have died and gone to yachtsman's heaven, as there is plenty of sailing during the course of a typical one-week cruise. Even the most jaded passenger should enjoy the feel of the wind and sea close at hand—just don't expect good food to go with what is decidedly a fine sailing experience—which is what *Star Flyer* is all about. Note that 12.5% is added to all beverage purchases.

Weak Points: The food, its quality, variety, presentation, and service, is still the weakest point of a cruise aboard this tall ship—and is not as good as what is provided aboard the company's larger flagship, *Royal Clipper*. This ship is not for the physically impaired, or for children. The steps of the internal stairs are steep, as in most sailing vessels. The tipping system, where all tips are pooled (the suggested amount is $8 per passenger, per day), causes concern for many passengers.

Star Pisces
★★★ +

Large Ship:	40,012 tons	Cabins (for one person):	42
Lifestyle:	Standard	Cabins (with private balcony):	0
Cruise Line:	Star Cruises	Cabins (wheelchair accessible):	6
Former Names:	*Kalypso*	Cabin Current:	220-volt
Builder:	Wartsila (Finland)	Full-Service Dining Rooms:	3 (plus2 cafés)
Original Cost:	SEK650 million	Elevators:	5
Entered Service:	1990	Casino(gaming tables):	Yes
Registry:	Panama	Slot Machines:	Yes
Length (ft/m):	579.3/176.6	Swimming Pools (outdoors):	1
Beam (ft/m):	97.1/29.6	Swimming Pools (indoors):	1
Draft (ft/m):	20.3/6.2	Whirlpools:	3
Propulsion/Propellers:	Diesel (23,760kW)/2	Fitness Center:	Yes
Passenger Decks:	12	Sauna/Steam Room:	Yes/Yes
Total Crew:	750	Massage:	Yes
Passengers (lower beds/all berths):	1,394/1,900	Self-Service Launderette:	No
Pass. Space Ratio (lower beds/all berths):	28.7/21.0	Dedicated Cinema:	No
Crew/Pass. Ratio (lower beds/all berths):	1.8/2.5	Library:	Yes
Navigation Officers:	Scandinavian	Classification Society:	Det Norske Veritas
Cabins (total):	718		
Size Range (sq ft/sq m):	67.8–145.3/6.3–13.5	**OVERALL SCORE:**	**1,247**
Cabins (outside view):	303	**(OUT OF A POSSIBLE 2,000 POINTS)**	
Cabins (interior/no view):	415		

Accommodation: There are six grades of accommodation. Except for some large "imperial" suites, almost all cabins are extremely small, and come with just the basic facilities, and very little closet and drawer space. Many cabins have third- and fourth-person upper berths—which are good for families who don't mind tight quarters. The cabin insulation is quite poor, and the bathrooms are really tiny.

The largest suites are very spacious, and are decorated in luxurious, richly lacquered materials. They feature two bathrooms, butler service, a private club meeting room, private sun deck, and spa.

Dining: There are seven restaurants that together provide a wide choice of cuisine and dining styles. A Chinese restaurant has live fish tanks from which to select your fish and seafood. A Japanese restaurant includes a sushi bar, waitresses in kimonos, and private *tatami* mat rooms. An Italian restaurant features candlelight dining. A Spice Island buffet restaurant features items such as *laksa*, *satay,* and *hawker* delights. In addition, there are three other snack cafés. Your cruise fare includes only the basic buffet restaurants—all other restaurants are à la carte, and expensive.

Other Comments: This ship is wide and squat looking in the water, and has Scandinavian design combined with a touch of the Orient. The outdoor deck and sunbathing space is limited.

There is a helipad, a huge duty-free shopping center, and a supermarket. The Regal Casino (essentially for VIPs) is large and has a high, detailed ceiling. There is also a second casino for general use. Has a fine health club for men (with many "extra" services). There are many meeting rooms, conference auditoriums, and a business center. The facilities for children are extensive and include computers and educational rooms, play areas, and a huge video machine section. There is free ice cream for kids.

Star Pisces has been skillfully converted into a cruise vessel for the Asian family market. The ship offers short cruises, with lots of Asian hospitality, choice of dining venues, karaoke, and gambling opportunities, all in a modern ship with colorful surroundings. The initial ticket price is extremely low, but almost everything on board costs extra. The ship operates short cruises from Osaka, Japan, to Korea. All gratuities are included.

Weak Points: Standing in line for embarkation, disembarkation, shore tenders, and self-serve buffet meals is an inevitable aspect of cruising aboard all large or high-passenger volume ships. This is a very high-density ship, and that means that many of the public rooms will always be crowded. The open deck space is poor, although this is mostly unused by Asian passengers. The cabins (and bathrooms) really are very small—particularly when occupied by three or four persons.

Star Princess

Large Ship:	108,000 tons		10 interior)
Lifestyle:	Premium	Cabin Current:	110/220-volt
Cruise Line:	Princess Cruises	Full-Service Dining Rooms:	3 main, 2 others
Former Names:	-	Elevators:	14
Builder:	Fincantieri (Italy)	Casino(gaming tables):	Yes
Original Cost:	$460 million	Slot Machines:	Yes
Entered Service:	February 2002	Swimming Pools (outdoors):	4
Registry:	Bermuda	Swimming Pools (indoors):	0
Length (ft/m):	951.4/290.0	Whirlpools:	9
Beam (ft/m):	118.1/36.0	Fitness Center:	Yes
Draft (ft/m):	26.2/8.0	Sauna/Steam Room:	Yes/Yes
Propulsion/Propellers: Diesel-electric (42,000kW)/2		Massage:	Yes
Passenger Decks:	13	Self-Service Launderette:	Yes
Total Crew:	1,100	Dedicated Cinema:	No
Passengers (lower beds/all berths):	2,600/3,100	Library:	Yes
Pass. Space Ratio (lower beds/all berths): 41.8/35.0		Classification Society:	Registro Navale Italiano
Crew/Pass. Ratio (lower beds/all berths):	2.3/2.8		
Navigation Officers:	British/Italian		
Cabins (total):	1,300	**OVERALL SCORE: NOT YET RATED**	
Size Range (sq ft/sq m):	161.4–764.2/15.0–71.0		
Cabins (outside view):	928		
Cabins (interior/no view):	372	Note that this ship had not entered service when this	
Cabins (for one person):	0	book was completed. However, the score is expect-	
Cabins (with private balcony):	710	ed to be similar to that of *Golden Princess* and	
Cabins (wheelchair accessible):	28 (18 outside/	*Grand Princess*.	

Accommodation: There are six principal types of cabins and configurations: (a) grand suite, (b) suite, (c) mini-suite, (d) outside double with balcony, (e) outside double, and (f) interior (no view) double. There are, however, 35 different brochure price categories; the choice is bewildering for both travel agents and passengers. Pricing depends on two things size and location.

(a) The largest, most lavish suite is the Grand Suite (B748, which is located at the ship's stern — a different position from the two Grand Suites aboard *Grand Princess*). It features a large bedroom with queen-size bed, huge walk-in (illuminated) closets, two bathrooms, a lounge (with fireplace and sofa bed) with wet bar and refrigerator, and a large private balcony (with hot tub that can be accessed from both balcony and bedroom).

(b/c) Suites (with a semi-private balcony) have a separate living room (with sofa bed) and bedroom (with a TV in each). The bathroom is quite large and features both a bathtub and shower stall. The mini-suites also have a private balcony, and feature a separate living and sleeping area (with a TV in each). The bathroom is also quite spacious and features both a bathtub and shower stall. The differences between the suites and mini-suites are basically in the size and appointments, the suite being more of a square shape while mini-suites are more rectangular, and have few drawers. Both suites and mini-suites feature butler service (known in Princess Cruises' language as "Grand Class Gold"), and very plush bathrobes, and fully tiled bathrooms with ample open-shelf storage space. Grand Class Gold passengers receive greater attention, including priority embarkation and disembarkation privileges. What is not good is that the most expensive accommodation aboard this ship has only semi-private balconies that can be seen from above and so there is absolutely no privacy whatsoever (Suites C 401 / 402 / 409 / 410 / 414 / 415 / 420 / 421 / 422 / 423 / 424 / 425 on Caribe Deck in particular). Also, the suites D105 and D106 (Dolphin Deck), which are extremely large, have balconies that can be seen from above.

(d/e/f) Both interior and outside-view (the outsides come either with or without private balcony) cabins are of a functional, practical design, although almost no drawers are provided. They are very attractive, with warm, pleasing decor and fine soft furnishing fabrics; 80% of the outside cabins have a private balcony. The tiled bathrooms have a good amount of open shelf storage space for personal toiletries.

Additionally, two family suites consist of two suites with an interconnecting door, plus a large balcony. These can sleep up to 10 (if at least four are children, or up to eight people if all are adults).

561

All accommodation occupants receive turndown service and chocolates on pillows each night, as well as bathrobes and toiletry amenity kits (larger, naturally, for suite/mini-suite occupants). You should note that the majority of the outside cabins on Emerald Deck have views obstructed by the lifeboats. Unfortunately, there are no cabins for singles.

Note that Princess Cruises features CNN, CNBC, ESPN, and TNT on the in-cabin color TV system (when available, depending on cruise area).

Dining: As befits the size of the ship, there is a wide variety of informal dining options, more than aboard any other Princess Cruises ship to date (except sister ship *Grand Princess*). For formal meals there are three principal dining rooms (Amalfi, Capri, and Portofino), and seating is assigned according to the location of your cabin. There are two seatings in one restaurant, while open seating is featured in the other two. All three are nonsmoking and split into multi-tier sections in a non-symmetrical design similar to those seen in sister ships *Golden Princess* and *Grand Princess*, breaking what are quite large spaces into many smaller sections, for better ambience. Each dining room has its own galley.

Several other dining areas are provided: Sabatini's Trattoria for pizzas and other Italian fare, with flair and entertainment from the staff (by reservation only, with a cover charge of $15.00 per person) as well as Desert Rose (Southwestern American food; by reservation only, also with a cover charge of $8 per person). A coffee bar/patisserie (extra charge), wine/caviar bar (extra charge), a poolside hamburger grill and pizza bar (no extra charge) are additional dining spots for casual bites.

Casual meals can be taken in the Horizon Court—open 24 hours a day, with large ocean-view on port and starboard sides and direct access to the two principal swimming pools and Lido Deck.

Specially designed dinnerware and high-quality linens and silverware are featured. Dinnerware is by Dudson of England; Egyptian cotton table linens are by Frette; and silverware is by Hepp of Germany. Note that 15% is added to all beverage bills, including wines (whether you order a $15 bottle or a $120 bottle, although it's the same amount of service to open and pour the wine).

Other Comments: The design for this large cruise ship, whose sister ships are *Grand Princess* and *Golden Princess*, presents a surprisingly bold, forthright profile, with a racy "spoiler" effect at her galleon-like transom stern that is simply not at all handsome (this acts as a stern observation lounge by day, and a stunning discotheque by night). She is quite a ship—too wide to transit the Panama Canal (she is more than 43 feet wider than the canal), with many balcony cabins overhanging the hull.

There is a good sheltered teakwood promenade deck, which almost wraps around (three times round is equal to one mile) and a walkway which goes right to the (enclosed, protected) bow of the ship. The outdoor pools have various beach-like surroundings. One lap pool has a pumped current to swim against.

Unlike the outside decks, there is plenty of space inside the ship (but there are also plenty of passengers), and a wide array of public rooms to choose from, with many intimate (relatively speaking) spaces and places to play. The passenger flow has been well planned and works with little congestion. The decor is very attractive, with lots of earth tones (well suited to both American and European tastes). In fact, she is the culmination of the best of all that Princess Cruises has to offer from its many years of operating what is now a well-tuned, good quality product.

Four areas center on swimming pools, one of which is two decks high and is covered by a magrodome, itself an extension of the funnel housing. A large health spa complex surrounds one of the swimming pools (you can have a massage or other spa treatment in an ocean-view treatment room). High atop the stern of the ship is a ship-wide glass-walled disco pod (I have nicknamed it the ETR—energy transfer room). It looks like an aerodynamic "spoiler" and is positioned high above the water, with spectacular views from the extreme port and starboard side windows.

An extensive collection of artworks has been chosen, and this complements the interior design and colors well. If you see something you like, you will be able to purchase it on board—it's almost all for sale.

Like sister ships *Golden Princess* and *Grand Princess*, this ship also features a Wedding Chapel (a live web-cam can relay ceremonies via the Internet). The ship's captain can legally marry (American) couples, due to the ship's Bermuda registry and a special dispensation (which should be verified when in the planning stage, according to where you reside). So, what better way to be married and have your honeymoon in a location that actually moves with you. Princess Cruises offers three wedding packages: Pearl, Emerald, Diamond; the fee includes registration and official marriage certificate. However, to get married and take your close family members and entourage with you on your honeymoon is going to cost a lot of money. (Do you really want your family with you on your honeymoon?) The "Hearts & Minds" chapel is also useful for renewal of vows ceremonies.

Another neat feature is the motion-based virtual reality room with its enclosed motion-based rides, and a "blue screen" studio, where passengers can star in their own videos. There is also an excellent library/CD-ROM computer room, and a separate card-playing room. For children there is a two-deck-high playroom, a teen room, and a host of specially trained counselors.

For entertainment, Princess Cruises prides itself on its glamorous all-American production shows, and the shows aboard this ship will not disappoint. Neither will the comfortable show lounges (the largest of which features $3 million in sound and light equipment, as well as a 9-piece orchestra, and a scenery-loading bay that connects directly from stage to a hull door for direct transfer to the dockside). Two other entertainment lounges help spread things around. Casino lovers should enjoy what is presently one of the largest casinos at sea, with more than 260 slot machines (all with dolphin-shaped handles); there are blackjack, craps, and roulette tables, plus newer games such as Let It Ride Bonus, Spanish 21, and Caribbean Draw Progressive. But the highlight could well be Neptune's Lair, a multimedia gaming extravaganza.

Ship lovers should enjoy the wood-paneled Wheelhouse Bar, finely decorated with memorabilia and ship models tracing part of parent company P&O's history.

Princess Cays—Princess Cruises' own private island in the Caribbean—is "yours" (along with a couple of thousand other passengers) for a day (but you need to take a shore tender to get to and from it, and this can take some time). A high-tech hospital is provided, with live SeaMed telemedicine link-ups with specialists at the Cedars-Sinai Medical Center in Los Angeles available for emergency help; it's the first such seagoing system in the world.

The ship operates 7-night Alaska and Mexican Riviera cruises, and provides you with a stunning, grand playground in which to roam when you are not ashore. Princess Cruises delivers a fine, well-packaged vacation product, with a good sense of style, at an attractive, highly competitive price, and this ship will appeal to those that really enjoy a big city to play in, with all the trimmings and lots of fellow passengers. The ship is full of money-making centers, however, which are designed to help you part with even more money than your cruise ticket cost you.

Whether this really can be considered a relaxing vacation is a moot point, but with so many choices and small rooms to enjoy, the ship has been extremely well-designed, and the odds are that you'll have a fine cruise vacation.

Weak Points: If you are not used to large ships, it will take you some time to find your way around (take good walking shoes), despite the company's claim that this vessel offers passengers a "small ship feel, big ship choice." The cabin bath towels are small and drawer space is very limited. The butlers simply have too many suites to look after (typically 20), which cannot possibly translate to the fine personal service experience it should be.

The automated telephone system is frustrating and luggage delivery is inefficient. Lines form for many things, but particularly for the purser's office, and for open seating breakfast and lunch in the three main dining rooms. Long lines for shore excursions and shore tenders are also a fact of life aboard large ships such as this, as is waiting for elevators at peak times.

You'll have to live with the many extra charge items (such as ice cream) and activities (such as yoga and kick boxing classes at $10 per session, not to mention $4 per hour for group babysitting services—at the time this book was completed). Some of the spa (massage) treatment rooms are located directly underneath the basketball court, which makes it utterly frustrating trying to relax while the ceiling above your head is being pounded by bouncing balls!

Passengers are also forced to endure countless pieces of (highly questionable) art found in almost every foyer and public room—an annoying reminder that today, cruising aboard large ships such as *Golden Princess* and *Grand Princess* is really like living in a bazaar of paintings surrounded by a ship. Now, what do I bid for this piece of art that is really worth only $10—let's hear it—$1,200, do I hear $1,400, or will someone actually think it's worth more?

Statendam
★★★★

Large Ship:	55,451 tons	Cabins (for one person):	0
Lifestyle:	Premium	Cabins (with private balcony):	150
Cruise Line:	Holland America Line	Cabins (wheelchair accessible):	6
Former Names:	-	Cabin Current:	110/220-volt
Builder:	Fincantieri (Italy)	Full-Service Dining Rooms:	1
Original Cost:	$215 million	Elevators:	12
Entered Service:	Jan 1993	Casino(gaming tables):	Yes
Registry:	The Netherlands	Slot Machines:	Yes
Length (ft/m):	719.4/219.3	Swimming Pools (outdoors):	1
Beam (ft/m):	101.0/30.8	Swimming Pools (indoors):	1 (magrodome)
Draft (ft/m):	24.6/7.5	Whirlpools:	2
Propulsion/Propellers:	Diesel-electric	Fitness Center:	Yes
	(34,560kW)/22	Sauna/Steam Room:	Yes/No
Passenger Decks:	10	Massage:	Yes
Total Crew:	557	Self-Service Launderette:	Yes
Passengers (lower beds/all berths):	1,266/1,627	Dedicated Cinema/Seats:	Yes/249
Pass. Space Ratio (lower beds/all berths):	43.8/34.0	Library:	Yes
Crew/Pass. Ratio (lower beds/all berths):	2.2/2.9	Classification Society:	Lloyd's Register
Navigation Officers:	Dutch		
Cabins (total):	633		
Size Range (sq ft/sq m):	186.2–1,124.8/17.3–104.5		
Cabins (outside view):	502		
Cabins (interior/no view):	131		

OVERALL SCORE: **1,533**

(OUT OF A POSSIBLE 2,000 POINTS)

Accommodation: The accommodation ranges from small interior (no view) cabins to a large penthouse suite (with ocean views), in 17 categories. All cabin TVs feature CNN and TNT.

The interior (no view) and outside-view standard cabins feature twin beds that convert to a queen-size bed, and there is a separate living space with sofa and coffee table. However, although the drawer space is generally good, the closet space is actually very tight, particularly for long cruises (although more than adequate for a 7-night cruise). The bathrooms are tiled, and compact but practical; they come with a good range of personal toiletry amenities. Bathrobes are also provided, as are hair dryers. The bathrooms are quite well laid out, but the bathtubs are small units better described as shower tubs. *Ryndam* and *Veendam* cabins have interconnecting doors.

On Navigation Deck, 28 suites have accommodation for up to four persons. These also feature en-suite dining as an alternative to the dining room, for private, reclusive meals. These are very spacious, tastefully decorated and well laid-out, and feature a separate living room, bedroom with two lower beds (convertible to a king-size bed), a good size living area, dressing room, plenty of closet and drawer space, and marble bathroom with Jacuzzi tub.

The largest accommodation of all can be found in the Penthouse Suite, located on the starboard side of the Navigation Deck. It features a king-size bed, walk-in closet with superb drawer space, oversize whirlpool bath and separate shower enclosure, living room, dressing room, large private balcony, pantry, minibar/refrigerator, a guest toilet, and floor to ceiling windows.

There is a small room-service menu (all items cost extra).

Dining: The two-level Rotterdam Dining Room, located at the stern is quite dramatic. It features a grand staircase (although few seem to use it), panoramic views on three sides, and a music balcony. There is open seating for breakfast and lunch, and two seatings for dinner. The waiter stations in the dining room are very noisy for anyone seated adjacent to them. Fine Rosenthal china and cutlery are used (although there are no fish knives).

Unfortunately, Holland America Line food isn't as nice as the china it's placed on. It may be adequate for most passengers who are not used to better food, but it does not match the standard found aboard other ships in the premium segment of the industry. While USDA beef is of a good quality, fowl tends to be battery-tough, and most fish is overcooked and has the consistency of a baseball bat. What are also definitely not luxurious are the endless packets of sugar and packets (instead of glass jars) of breakfast jam, marmalade, and honey, and poor quality teas. While these may be suitable for a family diner, they do not belong aboard a ship that claims to have "award-winning cuisine." Dessert and pastry items are of good quality (specifically for American tastes), although there is much use of canned fruits and jellies. Forget the selection of "international" cheeses, however, as most of it didn't come from anywhere other than the US, a country that is known for its processed, highly colored slices, and not fine cheese-making.

As an alternative to the more formal dining room, the Lido Buffet is open for casual dinners on all except for the last night of each cruise, in an open-seating arrangement. Tables are set with crisp linens, flatware, and stemware. A set menu is featured, and this includes a choice of four entrees.

The Lido Buffet also serves casual breakfasts and lunches, offering a wide choice and dual-line access, one side for smokers, the other for non-smokers. Unfortunately, there is much use of canned fruits (good for older passengers with no teeth!) and packeted items, although there are several commercial low-calorie salad dressings. The choice of cheeses (and accompanying crackers) is very poor. The beverage station is also a let-down, for it is no better than those found in family outlets ashore in the United States. In addition, a poolside grill provides basic American hamburgers and hot dogs.

Other Comments: *Statendam* is the first of a series of four almost identical ships in the same series, the others being *Maasdam, Ryndam,* and *Veendam.* The exterior styling is rather angular (some would say boxy—the funnel certainly is), although it is softened and balanced somewhat by the fact that the hull is painted black. There is a full wrap-around teakwood promenade deck outdoors—excellent for strolling, and, thankfully, no sign of synthetic turf anywhere. The deck lounge chairs are wood and come with comfortable cushioned pads.

Inside, an asymmetrical layout breaks up the interiors and helps to reduce bottlenecks and congestion. The decor is a little harsh and eclectic. In general, however, a mixture of contemporary materials is combined with traditional woods and ceramics. There is, fortunately, not too much "glitz" anywhere.

What is outstanding is the array of artworks throughout the ship (costing about $2 million), assembled and nicely displayed to represent the fine Dutch heritage of Holland America Line and to present a balance between standard itineraries and onboard creature comforts. Also noticeable are the fine flower arrangements throughout the public areas and foyers.

Atop the ship, with forward facing views that wrap around the sides is the Crow's Nest Lounge. By day it makes a fine observation lounge (particularly in Alaska); by night it turns into a nightclub with extremely variable lighting.

The three-deck-high atrium foyer is quite stunning, although its sculptured centerpiece makes it look a little crowded and leaves little room in front of the purser's office. A hydraulic magrodome (glass) roof covers the reasonably sized swimming pool/whirlpools and central Lido area (whose focal point is a large dolphin sculpture) so that this can be used in either fine or inclement weather.

The two-deck-high show lounge is basically well designed, but the ceiling is low and the sight lines from the balcony level are poor. There is a large, relaxing, and quite lovely reference library. The company keeps its ships very clean and tidy, and there is good passenger flow throughout.

Statendam is basically a well-built ship and has fairly decent interior fit and finish. Holland America Line is constantly fine-tuning its performance as a cruise operator and its regular passengers (almost all of whom are North American—there are few international passengers) find the company's ships very comfortable and well run. The company continues its strong maritime traditions, although the present food and service components still let the rest of the cruise experience down. Note: The line does not add an automatic 15% gratuity for beverage purchases, unlike many other cruise lines.

Holland America Line's many repeat passengers always seem to enjoy the fact that social dancing is always on the agenda. The company also offers free cappuccino and espresso coffees, and free ice cream during certain hours of the day aboard its ships, as well as hot hors d'oeuvres in all bars—something other major lines seem to have dropped, or charge extra for. In the final analysis, however, the score for this ship (and her sisters *Maasdam, Ryndam, Veendam*) ends up just a disappointing tad under what it could be if the food and food service staff were better (more professional training might help).

Weak Points: Standing in line for embarkation, disembarkation, shore tenders, and self-serve buffet meals is an inevitable aspect of cruising aboard all large ships. The service staff is Indonesian, and, although quite charming (for the most part), communication with them often proves frustrating for many passengers. Service is spotty and inconsistent. Note that passengers are forced to eat at the Lido Café on days when the dining room is closed for lunch (this is typically once or twice per cruise, depending on ship and itinerary). The single escalator is virtually useless. There is no doorbell outside the suites. The charge to use the washing machines and dryers in the self-service launderette is really petty and irritating, particularly for the occupants of suites, since they pay high prices for their cruises. Room service is poor.

Stella Oceanis
★★ +

Small Ship:	6,000 tons	Cabins (for one person):	0
Lifestyle:	Standard	Cabins (with private balcony):	0
Cruise Line:	Royal Olympic Cruises	Cabins (wheelchair accessible):	0
Former Names:	*Aphrodite*	Cabin Current:	220-volt
Builder:	Cantieri Riuniti dell' Adriatico (Italy)	Full-Service Dining Rooms:	1
Original Cost:	n/a	Elevators:	1
Entered Service:	1965/1967	Casino(gaming tables):	No
Registry:	Greece	Slot Machines:	No
Length (ft/m):	344.9/105.14	Swimming Pools (outdoors):	1
Beam (ft/m):	55.5/16.92	Swimming Pools (indoors):	0
Draft (ft/m):	14.9/4.56	Whirlpools:	0
Propulsion/Propellers:	Diesel (8,090kW)/1	Fitness Center:	No
Passenger Decks:	6	Sauna/Steam Room:	No/No
Total Crew:	140	Massage:	No
Passengers (lower beds/all berths):	318/369	Self-Service Launderette:	No
Pass. Space Ratio (lower beds/all berths):	18.8/16.2	Dedicated Cinema:	No
Crew/Pass. Ratio (lower beds/all berths):	2.1/2.6	Library:	Yes
Navigation Officers:	Greek	Classification Society:	Lloyd's Register
Cabins (total):	159		
Size Range (sq ft/sq m):	96.0–208.0/9.0–19.3	**OVERALL SCORE:**	**1,079**
Cabins (outside view):	113	**(OUT OF A POSSIBLE 2,000 POINTS)**	
Cabins (interior/no view):	46		

Accommodation: The outside-view and interior (no view) cabins come in eight price grades. They are all small and rather plain, and have limited closet and drawer space. Those on Lido and Stella decks have interconnecting doors. All cabins have private bathrooms, but there is little space for personal toiletries. Some feature a full bathtub, while others have a shower enclosure only.

Dining: The dining room is tastefully decorated and reasonably charming, although the ceiling is plain. It is small, and therefore has two seatings. The food is good, but there is really little choice, although the salads are good. Dining room seating and table assignments are done by the maitre d' upon embarkation.

Other Comments: *Stella Oceanis* is a tidy-looking, well-maintained ship with clean, rounded lines. Her original car decks (she was originally built as a ferry) were refashioned long ago into passenger facilities. Outside on deck, there is only a limited amount of open deck and sunbathing space.

The number of public rooms is limited, but this is a small ship, and the rooms are all nicely decorated, although in dated seventies style. Perhaps the most popular room is the Plaka Taverna, which is paneled in rich woods. An intimate, casual, and friendly atmosphere prevails. The gangway is narrow and steep in some ports of call, as is the case with many older ships.

This ship lacks the sophistication of some of the other ships in the fleet, but it is nonetheless charming. Royal Olympic Cruises (a combination of the Greek companies Epirotiki Lines and Sun Line Cruises) provides a good destination-intensive cruise experience, made better by the charming, friendly officers and crew.

The dress code is casual throughout (no formal nights). Gratuities (suggested at $9 per person per day) are pooled among the crew.

Stella Solaris
★★★

Mid-Size Ship:	17,832 tons	Cabins (for one person):	0
Lifestyle:	Standard	Cabins (with private balcony):	0
Cruise Line:	Royal Olympic Cruises	Cabins (wheelchair accessible):	0
Former Names:	*Stella V, Camboge*	Cabin Current:	110/220-volt
Builder:	Ateliers et Chantiers de France (France)	Full-Service Dining Rooms:	1
Original Cost:	n/an	Elevators:	3
Entered Service:	July 1953/June 1973	Casino(gaming tables):	Yes
Registry:	Greece	Slot Machines:	Yes (in separate room)
Length (ft/m):	545.1/166.15	Swimming Pools (outdoors):	1
Beam (ft/m):	72.4/22.08	Swimming Pools (indoors):	0
Draft (ft/m):	25.8/7.88	Whirlpools:	0
Propulsion/Propellers:	Diesel (17,900kW)/2	Fitness Center:	Yes
Passenger Decks:	8	Sauna/Steam Room:	No/Yes
Total Crew:	320	Massage:	Yes
Passengers (lower beds/all berths):	658/700	Self-Service Launderette:	No
Pass. Space Ratio (lower beds/all berths):	27.1/25.4	Dedicated Cinema/Seats:	Yes/275
Crew/Pass. Ratio (lower beds/all berths):	1.9/2.1	Library:	Yes
Navigation Officers:	Greek	Classification Society:	Lloyd's Register
Cabins (total):	329		
Size Range (sq ft/sq m):	96.8–226.0/9.0–21.0		
Cabins (outside view):	250		
Cabins (interior/no view):	79		

OVERALL SCORE: **1,193**
(OUT OF A POSSIBLE 2,000 POINTS)

Accommodation: There are 11 grades of accommodation divided into 166 suites and deluxe cabins with ocean views and 163 standard interior (no view) and outside-view cabins. The outside-view cabins can best be described as adequate (particularly those on Sapphire, Ruby, and Emerald decks), and many of them have what amounts to almost a full bathtub; while the interior (no-view) cabins have very small bathrooms. All bathrooms have lovely mosaic-tiled floors, but the plumbing is exposed.

The cabin decor has only been slightly changed over the years Its fabrics and colors are now brighter than they used to be, although the old pegboard ceilings remain as a reminder that the ship was built in the 1950s, when such things were in vogue. Note that the insulation between cabins and between decks is extremely poor. The accommodation passageways are reasonably wide, however. The telephone system is archaic, but at least there is real human operator to connect you and not some automated system with voice mail.

The suites on Boat Deck all have names of Greek islands such as Milos and Samos, and look out onto the promenade deck outdoors, a feature not found aboard many ships today. Some cabins even have windows that can be opened. However, those located in the aft third of the ship are subject to the irritating noise of deck lounge chairs being moved on the pool deck above, at most inconvenient times.

The floor-to-ceiling height of 6.75 ft (2.0 m) is typical of older ships, but rarely found aboard today's newbuilds, and provides an even better sense of spaciousness. There is an abundance of closet and drawer space, a vanity unit, TV (cannot be seen from the bed, only in the lounge area, which is separated from the bedroom by a lattice-work panel), and telephone. The bathrooms come with a decent-sized bathtub, small toiletries cabinet, and hair dryer. Bathrobes may be obtained upon request (suite passengers only).

Note that many cabins located on aft on Sapphire Deck and amidships on Emerald Deck are subject to throbbing engine noise. The towels are thin, although they are of 100% cotton. Personal amenities provided are soap, shampoo (doubles as bath foam), and body lotion.

A room service menu with limited items such as sandwiches, cookies, and beverages is available 24 hours a day (better selection available 7am-11pm).

Dining: The large, high-ceilinged dining room (totally nonsmoking) has tables for four or six (although when the ship is not full, tables for two can be arranged). The room's focal point is a huge mural in shades of bronze, copper, and gold that depicts scenes from Greek mythology. There are two seatings and a wide variety of food, with spa and vegetarian dishes on each lunch and dinner menu. The food, however, has

567

very little taste. Open seating for breakfast and lunch (a breakfast buffet is also set up in the dining room, but a regular à la carte breakfast menu is also available). The dining room seating and table assignments are done by the maitre d' upon embarkation.

The old-world service from Greek dining room stewards adds to the experience, although it is not nearly as good as it was in former years, and is far too hurried. The wine list is a mixture of a couple of good wines (but poor vintages) and a selection of reasonably priced wines, including many from Greece.

Informal breakfast and lunch buffets are available in the Lido Café (inside) adjacent to the pool, although the room is very small. The selection really is very limited, as is the food display. Breakfast features too many tinned fruits and packaged items.

The ship makes its own potato chips, revered by repeat passengers, and available in all bars, on most days.

Other Comments: This ship has a traditional profile, with a royal blue hull and a large, attractive funnel amidships. She was originally built to carry cargo and passengers to Indonesia during the war the French waged in that area in the 1950s, and was then successfully converted into a cruise vessel in the early seventies, when she was operated by Sun Line (merged with Epirotiki Lines into Royal Olympic Cruises in 1995). Because the ship has a deep draft she is very stable at sea.

Although she is now one of the oldest cruise ships still in active service, she is reasonably clean and tidy, although maintenance is fighting a losing battle. There is an expansive amount of open deck space, and this includes a wrap-around promenade deck (part enclosed, part outdoors). Much of the teakwood decking and caulking are now well worn, but the well-polished railings are in excellent condition. There is an attractive figure-eight-shaped pool and sunbathing area, although open deck space is tight. The mostly Greek staff is selectively friendly (more so towards females than males), and some of them have been with the company for many years. Communication with many of the non-Greek staff (from Eastern Europe and Asian countries) is limited and can prove somewhat frustrating.

Inside, the public rooms have good quality, solid furniture and fixtures, although everything has that well-worn look (sagging seats, broken springs). Unfortunately, there is no forward observation lounge, although there is a feeling of space and old-world grace. The elevators are large, and can even accommodate wheelchairs (although wheelchair access to most of the ship is awful).

There are also plenty of public restrooms, although, for some reason, many seem to be permanently locked. The fresh flowers that were formerly everywhere, are now mostly missing. The show lounge, which is combined with a bar (which itself is home to three blackjack tables and one roulette table) is large, with old-style chairs and banquette seating; all the shows feature cabaret-style entertainers, but sight lines are obstructed from many seats by eight pillars. A health spa added a few years ago provides some much-needed facilities, although the $10 per person charge to use the steam room (incorrectly called a "Turkish Bath") is irritating.

This ship is ideal for the older passenger who seeks a relaxed, unhurried, Old World cruise experience in decent, though rather worn, surroundings, at reasonable cost, with reasonably friendly service, but without the hype of the more contemporary ships. One nice feature is that toilets are quiet (not like the "barking dog" vacuum toilets aboard more modern ships).

Itineraries are well-planned and interesting. There are always a number of lecturers aboard for each cruise, as well as one or two gentlemen dance "hosts" (at least on the longer winter cruises). Gratuities ("suggested" at $9 per person, per day) are given to the Chief Steward, then pooled and shared among the crew.

Weak Points: There is no observation lounge with forward-facing views over the ship's bows. This ship and onboard cruise product really is very tired and worn, as are many of the crew, who seem to have lost the art of hospitality (unless they know you well). Considerable financial investment is needed to improve her interiors, which are dark and somber. Completely gone is the grace of yesteryear. The seats in the cinema are not staggered, hence sight lines are poor. Likewise, there are obstructed views from many seats in the show lounge. Port information literature is very limited for those who want to go ashore independently. The in-cabin audio channels are not available at night. There is absolutely no enforcement of smoking and no-smoking areas. The vibration at the stern is irritating.

Summit

Biggrr than millenium

Large Ship:	91,000 tons	Cabins (wheelchair accessible):	26 (17 with
Lifestyle:	Premium		private balcony)
Cruise Line:	Celebrity Cruises	Cabin Current:	110/220-volt
Former Names:	-	Full-Service Dining Rooms:	1 main, 1 specialty
Builder:	Chantiers de l'Atlantique (France)	Elevators:	10
Original Cost:	$350 million	Casino(gaming tables):	Yes
Entered Service:	April 2002	Slot Machines:	Yes
Registry:	Liberia	Swimming Pools (outdoors):	2
Length (ft/m):	964.5/294.0	Swimming Pools (indoors):	1 (with magrodome)
Beam (ft/m):	105.6/32.2	Whirlpools:	4
Draft (ft/m):	26.2/8.0	Fitness Center:	Yes
Propulsion/Propellers:	Gas turbine/2 azimuthing	Sauna/Steam Room:	Yes/Yes
	pods (39,000kW)2	Massage:	Yes
Passenger Decks:	11	Self-Service Launderette:	No
Total Crew:	999	Dedicated Cinema/Seats:	Yes/368
Passengers (lower beds/all berths):	1,950/2,450	Library:	Yes
Pass. Space Ratio (lower beds/all berths):	46.6/37.1	Classification Society:	Lloyd's Register
Crew/Pass. Ratio (lower beds/all berths):	1.9/2.4		
Navigation Officers:	Greek		
Cabins (total):	975		

OVERALL SCORE: NOT YET RATED

Size Range (sq ft/sq m):	165.1–2,530.0/15.34–235.0
Cabins (outside view):	780
Cabins (interior/no view):	195
Cabins (for one person):	0
Cabins (with private balcony):	590

Note that this ship was not in service when this book was completed. However, the score is expected to be very similar to that of *Infinity* and *Millennium*.

Accommodation: There are 20 grades of accommodation. Almost half of the ship's cabins have a private balcony; approximately 80% are outside-view suites and cabins, and 20% are interior (no view) cabins. There are several categories of suites, but those at the stern of the ship are in a prime location and have huge balconies that are really private and not overlooked from above.

Two Penthouse Suites (on Penthouse Deck) are the largest accommodation aboard. Each occupies one half of the beam (width) of the ship, overlooking the ship's stern. The suites, which measure 2,350 sq ft/218.3 sq m (including a large private balcony with 180-degree views), feature a marble foyer, a separate living room (complete with baby grand piano—bring your own pianist if you don't play yourself) and dining room (replete with a butler's pantry). The master bedroom has a large walk-in closet; personal exercise equipment; dressing room with vanity desk; marble master bathroom with twin sinks; deep whirlpool bathtub; separate shower; toilet and bidet areas; two large flat-screen TVs (one in the bedroom, one in the lounge), fax machine, private balcony with whirlpool hot tub and wet bar, and lounge area. All drapes are electronically controlled.

Eight Royal Suites, each measuring 733 sq ft/68 sq m, feature separate living room with dining and lounge areas, and decor in the style of a country (Africa, China, Mexico, France, India, Italy, Morocco, and Portugal). There are two entertainment centers with flat-screen TVs, a large walk-in closet. The bathroom has a whirlpool bathtub, and separate shower enclosure. The balcony also has a whirlpool hot tub.

Eight Celebrity Suites, each measuring 467 sq ft (43.3 sq m), feature floor-to-ceiling windows, a separate living room with dining and lounge areas, two entertainment centers with flat-screen TVs, walk-in closet with vanity desk, and a bathroom with a whirlpool bathtub. Interconnecting doors allow two suites to be used as a family unit. These suites overhang the starboard side of the ship (they are located opposite a group of glass-walled elevators), and provide stunning ocean views from the glass-walled sitting/dining area.

All other outside-view and interior (no view) cabins feature a lounge area with sofa or convertible sofa bed, sleeping area with twin beds that can convert to a double bed, a good amount of closet and drawer space, personal safe, minibar/refrigerator (extra cost), interactive TV, and private bathroom. The cabins are nicely decorated with warm wood-finish furniture, and there is none of the boxy feel of cabins in so many ships, due to the angled placement of vanity and audio-video consoles. Even the smallest cabin has a good-sized bathroom and shower enclosure.

Wheelchair-accessible accommodation is available in the following: six Sky Suites, three premium outside view cabins, eight deluxe ocean view cabins, four standard ocean-view cabins and five interior (no view) cabins. Space ranges from 347 sq ft to 362 sq ft (32.2 to 33.6 sq m), and all are located in the most practical parts of the ship — close to elevators for good accessibility. All have outside doorways and bathroom doorways and showers that are wheelchair-accessible. Some cabins have extra berths for a third or fourth occupant (note, however, that there is only one safe for personal belongings, which must be shared).

Dining: The 1,170-seat Trellis Restaurant (the ship's formal, nonsmoking dining room), is two decks high including its atrium gallery. It has a grand staircase connecting the two levels and a huge glass wall overlooking the sea at the stern of the ship. Electrically operated blinds provide several different backdrops. There are two seatings.

Besides the principal dining room, there are several dining options, particularly for those seeking more casual dining spots. Full service in-cabin dining is also available for all meals (including dinner).

The United States Restaurant is an alternative dining room, located adjacent to the conference center. However, with just 134 seats, not all passengers will be able to experience it even once during a one-week cruise (reservations are necessary). A dine-in wine cellar is also a feature, as is a demonstration galley. Tableside preparation is featured at this alternative dining spot.

For casual eating, the Oceanview Café & Grill is a self-serve buffet area, with six principal serving lines, and 754 seats. There is also a grill and pizza bar.

The Platinum Club, for champagne and caviar lovers, has a platinum-and-silver Art Deco motif that is reminiscent of a 1930s gentleman's club. It sports a diamond-pane reflective mirror wall. There's also a Martini Bar.

Other Comments: *Summit* is a sister ship to *Infinity* and *Millennium*. Jon Bannenberg (famous as a mega-yacht designer) designed the exterior that features a royal blue and white hull, and racy lines. This is the second Celebrity Cruises ship to be fitted with a "pod" propulsion system (and controllable pitch propellers) coupled with a gas turbine powerplant. She is powered by a gas turbine (two GE gas turbines provide engine power while a single GE steam turbine drives the electricity generators).

Inside, the ship features the same high-class decor and well-appointed public rooms that have made the existing ships in the fleet so welcoming and popular. But in a first for Celebrity Cruises, the Atrium spans 11 decks. It is capped with a glass dome, and four glass elevators travel up and down its port side. Michael's Club (a cigar-and-cognac specialty lounge that features nearly 20 varieties of cigars) is located on the Promenade Deck.

Facilities include a combination Cinema/Conference Center, an expansive shopping arcade with 14,447.4 sq ft (1,343 sq m) of retail store space, a lavish four-deck-high show lounge with the latest in staging and lighting equipment, a two-level library (one level for English-language books; a second level for books in other languages), a card room, a music room, and a combination observation lounge/discotheque.

One unique feature is a conservatory which includes 70 seats set in a botanical environment of flowers, plants, tress, mini-gardens, and fountains, designed by the award-winning floral designer Emilio Robba of Paris. It is located directly in front of the main funnel and has glass walls that overlook the ship's side.

Outdoor facilities include two outdoor pools, one indoor/outdoor pool, and six whirlpools. Spa facilities include an AquaSpa (a multi-station thalassotherapy pool), a feature in all Celebrity Cruises ships, 16 treatment rooms, plus eight treatment rooms with showers and one treatment room specifically designed for wheelchair passengers, an aerobics room, a gymnasium (complete with all the latest high-tech muscle machines), saunas and steam rooms, and a beauty salon.

Sports facilities include a full-size basketball court, compact football, paddle tennis and volleyball, golf simulator, shuffleboard (on two different decks), and a jogging track. Gaming sports include a large casino, with blackjack, roulette, and numerous slot machines. Families with children will appreciate the Fun Factory (for children) and The Tower (for teenagers).

Such extensive facilities make this ship an extremely comfortable environment for its size, with good food and dining facilities, and a well-run shipboard operation that provide everything necessary for a fine vacation at sea — at a very fair price.

Weak Points: There is, sadly, no wrap–around wooden promenade deck outdoors. Standing in line for embarkation, disembarkation, shore tenders, and for self–serve buffet meals is an inevitable aspect of cruising aboard all large ships. There are cushioned pads for poolside deck lounge chairs only, but not for chairs on other outside decks.

Sunbird
★★★ +

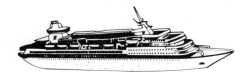

Large Ship:	37,584 tons	Cabins (for one person):	0
Lifestyle:	Standard	Cabins (with private balcony):	9
Cruise Line:	Airtours Sun Cruises	Cabins (wheelchair accessible):	0
Former Names:	*Song of America*	Cabin Current:	110-volt
Builder:	Wartsila (Finland)	Full-Service Dining Rooms:	1
Original Cost:	$140 million	Elevators:	7
Entered Service:	December 1982/May 1999	Casino(gaming tables):	Yes
Registry:	Bahamas	Slot Machines:	Yes
Length (ft/m):	705.0/214.88	Swimming Pools (outdoors):	2
Beam (ft/m):	93.1/28.40	Swimming Pools (indoors):	0
Draft (ft/m):	22.3/6.80	Whirlpools:	0
Propulsion/Propellers:	Diesel (16,480kW)/2	Fitness Center:	Yes
Passenger Decks:	11	Sauna/Steam Room:	Yes/No
Total Crew:	540	Massage:	Yes
Passengers (lower beds/all berths):	1,450/1,611	Self-Service Launderette:	No
Pass. Space Ratio (lower beds/all berths):	25.9/23.3	Dedicated Cinema:	No
Crew/Pass. Ratio (lower beds/all berths):	2.6/2.9	Library:	Yes
Navigation Officers:	International	Classification Society:	Det Norske Veritas
Cabins (total):	725		
Size Range (sq ft/sq m):	118.4–425.1/11.0–39.5	**OVERALL SCORE:**	**1,275**
Cabins (outside view):	425	(OUT OF A POSSIBLE 2,000 POINTS)	
Cabins (interior/no view):	300		

Accommodation: Accommodation is provided in five grades (L-Shaped Twin, Parallel Twin, Deluxe, Penthouse Suite, and Grand Penthouse Suite), making it an easy matter to select your cabin. You can now also choose and book the exact cabin and location you want — if you pay an extra charge of $72 (£50) per cabin (or equivalent), which also grants you the right to choose whether you want to dine at the early or late seating for dinner.

Most cabins are of a similar size (which is actually very small when compared to today's newer ships) and the insulation between them is quite poor. The cabins also have mediocre closets and very little storage space, yet somehow everyone seems to manage. The ship was built originally for one-week Caribbean cruises. They are just about adequate for a one-week cruise, since you will need only a small selection of mainly casual clothes (you'll probably have to put your shoes — and luggage — under the bed).

Most bathrooms typically contain a washbasin, toilet, and shower, with very little space for your personal toiletry items. The shower enclosure is small but reasonably cheerful and has a curtain that you will probably end up dancing with. Towels are of 100% cotton.

In some cabins, twin beds are fixed in a parallel mode (some are moveable and can be made into a queen-size bed), while others may be in an "L" shape. Note that in almost all cabins there is a "lip" or threshold (of about nine inches) at the bathroom door to step over.

For a little more money than a standard two bed cabin, you can get more space and a larger cabin if you book one of the 21 deluxe grade cabins on Promenade Deck. These typically have twin beds that convert to a queen-size bed, set diagonally into a sleeping area adjacent to outside view windows. There is more drawer space, more closet space, and the bathroom features a half-size bathtub and shower combination — bathrobes are also provided. Note that the largest of these deluxe grade cabins is Cabin 7000.

For even more exclusivity, you can book one of the nine Penthouse Suites (Owner's Suite, Commodore's Suite, Amerigo Verspucci, Christoforo Columbus, Henry the Navigator, James Cook, Leif Ericson, Sir Francis Drake, Vasco da Gama). All are located in a private area, have fine wood paneling and trim, and come with additional space and better, more personalized service. The additional space includes a lounge area with sofa (this converts to a double bed — making it ideal for families with children), coffee table and two chairs, a vanity desk, combination TV/VCR, an abundance of drawers, illuminated closets (with both hanging space and several shelves), excellent storage space, king-size bed, and bathrobes. The bathroom is fully tiled, and features a full-sized enamel bathtub (few ships have enamel tubs today) with shower, pink granite-look washbasin, and plenty of storage space for personal toiletry items. Suite occupants also get a semi-private balcony (the door of which is extremely heavy and difficult to open)

571

with a drinks table and two teakwood chairs. Private butler service is standard. You will also be able to eat in your suite from the full dining room menu for breakfast, lunch, and dinner — although there is no dining table in the suite. Book either the Owner's Suite or Commodore's Suite (called Grand Penthouse Suites in the brochure), and you'll get even more room — plus views over the ship's bows (through windows with electric blinds) and a larger balcony (these can, however, be overlooked from the open deck above), more floor space, and a walk-in closet — otherwise they feature the same facilities as the other suites mentioned above. Missing are a bedside telephone and a bathroom telephone.

Do note that, no matter what suite or cabin grade you book, the cabin voltage is 110-volt, so British passengers (the majority aboard the ships of Airtours Sun Cruises) will need to take a US-style adapter for any electrical appliances such as a hair dryer. Note that in the past, cabins were not assigned until you arrived at the ship; however, now you can book the cabin you want (for a fee, see above). The accommodation deck hallways are also very narrow on some decks. There is a room service menu, but all items (including breakfast) cost extra, unless you are in one of the suites.

Dining: The Seven Seas Restaurant is a large room, and consists of a central main section, and two long, narrow wings called the Magellan Room and Galileo Room on port and starboard sides, respectively. Each have large, ocean-view windows. However, the low ceiling creates a high level of ambient noise. There are two seatings — both are nonsmoking. There are tables for two (but only 14 of them), four, six, or eight (window tables are for two or six). The service is average in this efficiently run dining room operation. The food is of a generally decent quality and the portions are quite substantial, although the menus are standard and deviation from it is difficult. Bottled water is offered, although there is an extra charge for it; the ship's drinking water (no charge) is adequate.

The cuisine? In a nutshell — it's basic, no-frills British motorway café cuisine — acceptable for those who do not expect much in the way of presentation or quality, but certainly not memorable. Indeed, it is quantity, not quality, that prevails — but it's all provided at a low cost — as is a cruise aboard this ship. Presentation is a weak point, and there are no fish knives. Remember that, like anything, you get what you pay for. If you enjoy going out to eat and like being adventurous — then you will probably be disappointed. There is an adequate, but limited, wine list, and the wines are almost all very young — typical of those found in supermarkets. Wine prices are quite modest, as are the prices for most alcoholic beverages. The same small glasses are used for both red and white wines.

For casual, self-serve breakfasts and lunches, the Veranda Café, is the alternative choice, although the tables and seats outdoors are of metal and plastic, and the buffets are extremely basic — the kind one would expect to find in a school from the 1950s. However, remember that the price is low — and then you'll understand why you get plastic cups and plastic stirrers (teaspoons are unheard of!). At night you can "dine" under the steel and canvas canopy, where the café becomes a pleasant, outdoor alternative to the dining room, and includes waiter service and food that's cooked to order. Additionally, during lunchtime, baguettes are available at the bar forward of the forwardmost swimming pool.

Other Comments: This is the largest ship in the Airtours Sun Cruises fleet. She is a smart-looking, contemporary ship with nicely rounded lines, a sharply raked bow, and a single funnel with a cantilevered, wrap-around lounge. When the ship first debuted (for previous owners Royal Caribbean International), it was named by famous opera singer Beverly Sills. *Carousel* and *Sundream* were also purchased from the same company, although in the case of *Sunbird*, the lounge that wraps around the funnel housing was not removed. The lounge (called the "Chart Room") is a fine place from which to observe the world around and below you.

Sunbird was acquired by the UK-based Airtours in 1999. There is a decent amount of open deck and sunbathing space (but it certainly will be crowded when the ship is full, which is most of the time), and nicely polished wooden decks and rails. There are two swimming pools — the aft pool being designated for children, the forward pool for adults.

Inside, there is a good array of public rooms. The principal public rooms all have high ceilings, and are located one deck up from the dining room, in a convenient horizontal layout. These include the principal show lounge (Can Can Lounge), casino (Casino Royale), and nightclub (Oklahoma Lounge). There is also a small conference center for meetings and group business, as well as an Internet Café (with six computer terminals — but no café).

When Airtours Sun Cruises first started in cruising, its ships were effectively under the control of an outside management company. Now, however, all the ships and personnel are under direct Airtours Sun Cruises ownership and management, which has resulted a more consistent product.

Of the ships in the Airtours Sun Cruises fleet, *Sunbird* is the largest and provides more facilities and choice — particularly for the many repeat passengers that the company has acquired. This ship should prove to be a good choice if you are a first-time passenger seeking a well-rounded, destination-intensive cruise at a very modest price (book between January and March and you get half-price cabin upgrades). The pre- and post-cruise land stays are also well organized.

Airtours Sun Cruises provides a consistent, well-tuned and well-packaged, fun product, in comfortable surroundings. It offers a good vacation particularly suited to couples and families with children. Note, however, that Sun Cruises does not actively market or specialize in cruises for families with children, and the children's/youth facilities are limited (and there is no evening babysitting service for youngsters).

Airtours is known for packaging its products really well, and this ship represents an excellent buy for families who want to cruise, but on a limited budget. Also, if you want a little more than the basics, Airtours Sun Cruises offers special packages — good for celebrating something special. These come in four packages: bronze, silver, gold, and platinum, each one a little more expensive. Want to buy the captain? Go for gold or platinum and you get breakfast in bed with champagne, flowers, fruit basket, and dinner at the captain's table.

Airtours also has its own fleet of aircraft, and this is one reason that the company is able to offer complete cruise-air-stay packages at such low rates. Airtours Sun Cruises does a fine job in getting you and your luggage from airplane to ship without having to go through immigration (depending on itinerary) in foreign countries whenever possible, so your cruise vacation is as seemless as possible.

Airtours Sun Cruises brochures tell it like it is, so you know before you go exactly what you will get for your money — with the exception of its claim to "first class food," which is a gross exaggeration. However, Airtours Sun Cruises provides cruises for the "working man," at very modest prices. If you want just the basics, you pay the least amount. If you want all the goodies, choose a wider "premium" seat with extra leg room on your Airtours aircraft; choose your own cabin; choose your dinner seating, breakfast in bed and dinner with the captain (no, not in bed) — then you'll pay for all those privileges. Note that however you choose to cruise, all gratuities are included. Insurance is also included — although you will be charged for it unless you decline it on the booking form.

Weak Points: Standing in line for embarkation, disembarkation, shore tenders, and self-serve buffet meals is an inevitable aspect of cruising aboard all large ships. Like the other ships in the fleet, the space per passenger (particularly on the open decks) is very tight when the ship is full (which is most of the time). Nonsmokers will find it extremely difficult to escape from smokers who walk through public rooms. The cabin TVs are very small (except for those in the suites). Note that couples who travel without children will be surrounded by large numbers of children during the summer months and thus increased noise levels. The food is of low-budget quality, and the presentation is quite poor. There is little choice of tea and coffee. There are no cushioned pads for the deck lounge chairs.

Sundream
★★★

Large Ship:	22,945 tons	Cabins (for one person):	0
Lifestyle:	Standard	Cabins (with private balcony):	0
Cruise Line:	Airtours Sun Cruises	Cabins (wheelchair accessible):	0
Former Names:	*Song of Norway*	Cabin Current:	110-volt
Builder:	Wartsila (Finland)	Full-Service Dining Rooms:	1
Original Cost:	$13.5 million	Elevators:	4
Entered Service:	November 1970/May 1997	Casino(gaming tables):	Yes
Registry:	Bahamas	Slot Machines:	Yes
Length (ft/m):	637.5/194.32	Swimming Pools (outdoors):	1
Beam (ft/m):	78.8/24.03	Swimming Pools (indoors):	0
Draft (ft/m):	21.9/6.70	Whirlpools:	0
Propulsion/Propellers:	Diesel (13,400kW)/2	Fitness Center:	Yes
Passenger Decks:	8	Sauna/Steam Room:	No/No
Total Crew:	423	Massage:	No
Passengers (lower beds/all berths):	1,076/1,257	Self-Service Launderette:	No
Pass. Space Ratio (lower beds/all berths):	21.3/18.2	Dedicated Cinema:	No
Crew/Pass. Ratio (lower beds/all berths):	2.5/2.9	Library:	Yes
Navigation Officers:	International	Classification Society:	Det Norske Veritas
Cabins (total):	538		
Size Range (sq ft/sq m):	118.4–265.8/11.0–24.7		
Cabins (outside view):	346		
Cabins (interior/no view):	192		

OVERALL SCORE: **1,226**

(OUT OF A POSSIBLE 2,000 POINTS)

Accommodation: The cabins are provided in just four grades (Standard, Superior, Promenade, and Deluxe) and six types, making it an easy matter to select your accommodation. As of winter 2001, you can also prebook the exact cabin you want — if you pay an extra charge of $72 (£50) per cabin, which also grants you the right to choose whether you want to dine at the early or late seating for dinner.

Most cabins are of a similar size (small by today's standards) and the insulation between them is rather poor. The cabins also have mediocre closets and very little storage space, yet somehow everyone seems to manage (the ship was built originally for Caribbean cruising). However, they really are adequate for a one-week cruise, since you will need only casual clothes, and, with these destination-intensive cruises, you really will not need many clothes anyway (shoes can always go under the bed). The largest cabins are named after famous explorers of the world.

The best advice is therefore to take only casual clothing and only the things you really need. Do note that cabin voltage is 110-volt so British passengers will need to take adapters for electrical appliances such as a hair dryer. The accommodation deck hallways are also very narrow.

Dining: The large "King and I" Dining Room is reasonably attractive but noisy. There are two seatings. It is a good operation, but the food, while consistent in quality and presentation, is not memorable. The service, by friendly Filipino waiters and wine waiters, is generally adequate.

The cuisine? In a nutshell — it's basic, no-frills British motorway café cuisine — adequate for those who do not expect much in the way of presentation or quality, but definitely not memorable. Indeed, it is quantity, not quality, that prevails — but its all provided at a low cost — as is a cruise aboard this ship. Presentation is a weak point, and there are no fish knives. Remember that, like anything, you get what you pay for. If you enjoy going out to eat, and like being adventurous — then you will probably be disappointed. There is an adequate, but limited, wine list, and the wines are almost all very young — typical of those found in supermarkets. Wine prices are quite modest, as are the prices for most alcoholic beverages.

Other Comments: This smart ship, built originally for many years by Royal Caribbean International (then Royal Caribbean Cruise Line), has sleek modern lines, with a sharply raked bow, and a single blue funnel, aft of which is a large amount of open deck space for sports. It has a polished wrap-around wooden deck outdoors. There is a reasonable amount of open deck space, but it does get crowded when the ship is full (which is almost always), particularly around the small swimming pool.

Inside the ship, the layout is quite logical, which makes it easy to find one's way around. The decor is based on Broadway musicals, with fairly bright, crisp, clean colors. The passageways are not wide, but they do contain lots of artwork and wood trim. In fact, there is an abundance of artwork throughout this ship. There are several lounges and bars to choose from, most of which are located on one deck.

Sundream is the sister ship to *Carousel*, and was "stretched" in 1978, when she was operated by Royal Caribbean International. Airtours is now partly owned by Carnival Corporation, who also own Carnival Cruise Lines (and others). *Sundream*, which commenced operations for Airtours Sun Cruises (one of Britain's big three tour companies) in May 1997, caters to novice passengers efficiently and with well-programmed flair, and provides an activity-filled cruise product in comfortable, but fairly busy surroundings, at very modest cruise rates for its mainly British and Canadian passengers. Itineraries include 7-night Caribbean (winter) and 7-night Mediterranean (summer) cruises.

Airtours is known for packaging its products really well, and this ship represents an excellent buy for families who want to cruise on a limited budget. Also, if you want a little more than the basics, Airtours Sun Cruises offers special packages — good for celebrating something special. These come in four packages: bronze, silver, gold, and platinum, each one a little more expensive. Want to buy the captain? Go for gold or platinum and you get breakfast in bed with champagne, flowers, fruit basket, and dinner at the captain's table.

Note that Sun Cruises does not actively market or specialize in cruises for families with children, and the children's/youth facilities are limited (and there is no evening babysitting service for youngsters).

Airtours also has its own fleet of aircraft, and this is one reason that the company is able to offer complete cruise-air-stay packages at such low rates. Airtours Sun Cruises does a fine job in getting you and your luggage from airplane to ship without having to go through immigration (depending on itinerary) in foreign countries whenever possible, so your cruise vacation is as seemless as possible.

Airtours Sun Cruises brochures tell it like it is — so you know before you go exactly what you will get for your money, with the exception of its claim to "first class food," which is a gross exaggeration. If you want just the basics, you pay the least amount. If you want all the goodies — choose a wider "premium" seat with extra leg room on your Airtours aircraft, choose your own cabin, choose your dinner seating, breakfast in bed and dinner with the captain (no, not in bed) — then you'll pay for all those priviledges. Note that however you choose to cruise, all gratuities are included. Insurance is also included (but you will be charged for it) unless you decline it on the booking form.

Weak Points: Standing in line for embarkation, disembarkation, shore tenders, and self-serve buffet meals is an inevitable aspect of cruising aboard all large ships. There are many announcements. Many seats in the My Fair Lady show lounge have poor sight lines, obstructed by several pillars. Like the other ships in the fleet, the space per passenger (particularly on the open decks) is very tight when the ship is full (which is most of the time). The cabin TVs are extremely small (except for those in the suites). Note that couples that travel without children will be surrounded by large numbers of children during the summer months, and thus increased noise levels. The food is of low quality, and the presentation is quite poor. There is little choice of tea and coffee. There are no cushioned pads for the deck lounge chairs.

Sun Bay

Small Ship:	3,000 tons	Cabins (with private balcony):	9
Lifestyle:	Premium	Cabins (wheelchair accessible):	0
Cruise Line:	Sun Bay Cruises	Cabin Current:	220-volt
Former Names:	-	Full-Service Dining Rooms:	1
Builder:	Cassens-Werft (Holland)	Elevators:	0
Original Cost:	n/a	Casino(gaming tables):	No
Entered Service:	June 2001	Slot Machines:	No
Registry:	Bahamas	Swimming Pools (outdoors):	No
Length (ft/m):	290.3/88.5	Swimming Pools (indoors):	No
Beam (ft/m):	45.9/14.0	Whirlpools:	2
Draft (ft/m):	11.4/3.5	Fitness Center:	Yes
Propulsion/Propellers:	Diesel (3,000kW)/2	Sauna/Steam Room:	Yes/No
Passenger Decks:	4	Massage:	Yes
Total Crew:	50	Self-Service Launderette:	No
Passengers (lower beds/all berths):	92/92	Dedicated Cinema:	No
Pass. Space Ratio (lower beds/all berths):	32.6/32.6	Library:	No
Crew/Pass. Ratio (lower beds/all berths):	1.9/1.9	Classification Society:	Germanischer Lloyd
Navigation Officers:	German		
Cabins (total):	46		
Size Range (sq ft/sq m):	156.0–247.5/14.5–23.0		
Cabins (outside view):	46		
Cabins (interior/no view):	0		
Cabins (for one person):	0		

OVERALL SCORE: NOT YET RATED

Note that this ship was not in service when this book was completed.

Accommodation: There are four different accommodation price categories in two cabin types: nine suites, measuring 247.5 sq ft (23 sq m), each with its own private bacony; 34 Comfort Cabins, measuring 172.2 sq ft (16 sq m), and 3 Comfort cabins, measuring 156 sq ft (14.5 sq m).

Regardless of the category you choose, all suites and cabins have twin beds (four comfort cabins have a double bed), TV, sofa, drinks table, vanity desk with minibar, and personal safe, while bathrooms all feature a shower (no suites/cabins have bathtubs).

Dining: The Dining Room has ocean-view windows along one side, and there is a self-serve buffet area for salads, cold cuts, and cheeses. The service is provided by Ukrainian waiters/waitresses. Hanseatic Catering of Hamburg provides the food.

A casual self-serve buffet is provided on one of the open decks aft, with teak tables and chairs.

Other Comments: This is a cute little ship — more like a private yacht than a cruise vessel. For comparison, the ship is approximately the same size as the four of the original Renaissance Cruises ships. At the stern there is a platform for swimming directly from the ship.

Facilities include a main lounge, with bar and small dance floor, a boutique, fitness room, and the ship's information desk doubles as a business center.

This is the first really small yacht-like ship for German-speaking passengers. It's like a small private club — ideal for passengers that do not want to cruise aboard the larger ships. The ambience is unpretentious, unhurried, but subtly elegant at the same time. What's really good? With such a small number of passengers, there's never a line for anything.

Sun Princess
★★★★

Large Ship:	77,499 tons	Cabins (for one person):	0
Lifestyle:	Standard	Cabins (with private balcony):	410
Cruise Line:	Princess Cruises	Cabins (wheelchair accessible):	19
Former Names:	-	Cabin Current:	110/220-volt
Builder:	Fincantieri (Italy)	Full-Service Dining Rooms:	2 main/3 others
Original Cost:	$300 million	Elevators:	11
Entered Service:	December 1995	Casino(gaming tables):	Yes
Registry:	Great Britain	Slot Machines:	Yes
Length (ft/m):	857.2/261.3	Swimming Pools (outdoors):	4
Beam (ft/m):	105.6/32.2	Swimming Pools (indoors):	0
Draft (ft/m):	26.5/8.1	Whirlpools:	5
Propulsion/Propellers:	Diesel-electric	Fitness Center:	Yes
	(28,000kW)/2	Sauna/Steam Room:	Yes/Yes
Passenger Decks:	10	Massage:	Yes
Total Crew:	900	Self-Service Launderette:	Yes
Passengers (lower beds/all berths):	1,950/2,250	Dedicated Cinema:	No
Pass. Space Ratio (lower beds/all berths):	39.7/34.4	Library:	Yes
Crew/Pass. Ratio (lower beds/all berths):	2.0/2.5	Classification Society:	Registro Navale Italiano
Navigation Officers:	Italian		
Cabins (total):	975		
Size Range (sq ft/sq m):	134.5–753.4/12.5–70.0		
Cabins (outside view):	603		
Cabins (interior/no view):	372		

OVERALL SCORE: **1,539**

(OUT OF A POSSIBLE 2,000 POINTS)

Accommodation: The brochure shows 28 different cabin grades: 20 outside view and 8 interior (no view) cabins. Although the standard outside-view and interior (no view) cabins are a little small, they are well designed and functional in layout, and have earth tone colors accentuated by splashes of color from the bedspreads. Proportionately, there are quite a lot of interior (no view) cabins. Many of the outside view cabins have private balconies, and all seem to be quite well soundproofed, although the balcony partition is not floor-to-ceiling type, so you can hear your neighbors clearly (or smell their smoke). *Note:* The balconies are very narrow, and only large enough for two small chairs, and there is no dedicated lighting.

A TV and refrigerator and a reasonable amount of closet and abundant drawer and other storage space is provided in all cabins — adequate for a 7-night cruise. Each night a chocolate will appear on your pillow. The cabin bathrooms are practical and come complete with all the details one needs, although they really are tight spaces, best described as one person at-a-time units. They do, however, have a decent shower enclosure, a small amount of shelving for your personal toiletries, real drinking glasses, a hair dryer and a bathrobe.

The largest accommodation can be found in six suites, two on each of three decks located at the stern of the ship, with large private balcony. These are well laid out, and have large bathrooms with two sinks, a Jacuzzi bathtub, and a separate shower enclosure. The bedroom features generous amounts of wood accenting and detailing, indented ceilings, and TV sets in both bedroom and lounge areas. The suites also have a dining room table and four chairs.

The mini-suites typically have two lower beds that convert into a queen-size bed. There is a separate bedroom/sleeping area with vanity desk, and a lounge with sofa and coffee table, indented ceilings with generous amounts of wood accenting and detailing, walk-in closet, and larger bathroom with Jacuzzi bathtub, and separate shower enclosure.

Note that Princess Cruises features CNN, CNBC, ESPN, and TNT on the in-cabin color TV system (when available, depending on cruise area).

Dining: There are two principal dining rooms, Marquis and Regency (both are nonsmoking, as are the dining rooms aboard all the ships of Princess Cruises); which one you are assigned to depends on the location of your accommodation. Each has its own galley and each is split into multi-tier sections, which help create a feeling of intimacy, although there is a lot of noise from the waiter stations, which are adjacent to many tables. Breakfast and lunch are provided in an open seating arrangement, while dinner is typically in two seatings.

Despite the fact that the portions are generous, the food and its presentation are somewhat disappointing. The quality of fish is poor (often disguised by crumb or batter coatings); the selection of fresh green vegetables is limited; and few garnishes are used. However, do remember that this is banquet catering, with all its attendant standardization and production cooking. Meats are of a decent quality, although often disguised by gravy-based sauces, and pasta dishes are acceptable (though voluminous), and are typically served by section headwaiters, who may also make "something special just for you" — in search of gratuities and good comments.

On any given 7-day cruise, a typical menu cycle will include a Sailaway Dinner, Captain's Welcome Dinner, Chef's Dinner, Italian Dinner, French Dinner, Captain's Gala Dinner, and Landfall Dinner. The wine list is reasonable, but not good, and the company has, unfortunately, seen fit to eliminate all wine waiters. Note that 15% is added to all beverage bills, including wines (whether you order a $15 bottle or a $120 bottle, even though it takes the same amount of service to open and pour the wine).

With a sheltered view over the Riviera Pool, the Terrace Grill features "Sterling Steakhouse" for those that want to taste four different cuts of Angus beef from the popular "Sterling Silver" brand of USDA prime meats — filet mignon, New York strip, porterhouse, and rib-eye — all presented on a silver tray. The Terrace Grill also provides a barbecue chicken option, plus the usual baked potato or French fries as accompaniments. This is available as an alternative to the dining rooms, between 6:30pm and 9:30pm only, at an additional charge (at press time) of $8 per person.

There is also a patisserie (for cappuccino/espresso coffees and pastries), a wine/caviar bar, and a pizzeria (complete with cobblestone floors and wrought-iron decorative features), and excellent pizzas (there are six to choose from).

The Horizon Buffet is open 24 hours a day, and at night features an informal dinner setting with sit-down waiter service; a small bistro menu is also available. The buffet displays are, for the most part, quite repetitious, but better than they have been in the last few years (plastic plates are provided, however). The cabin service menu is very limited, and presentation of the food items featured is very poor.

Other Comments: Although large, this all-white ship has a good profile, and is well balanced by its large funnel, which shelters a deck tennis/basketball/volleyball court in its aft base. There is a wide, teak wrap-around promenade deck outdoors, some real teak steamer-style deck chairs (complete with royal blue cushioned pads), and 93,000 sq ft (8,640 sq m) of outdoor space. A great amount of glass area on the upper decks provides plenty of light and connection with the outside world.

The ship, while large, absorbs passengers well, and has an almost intimate feel to her, which is what the interior designers intended. Her interiors are very pretty and warm, with attractive colors and welcoming decor that includes some very attractive wall murals and other artwork. The signs around the ship could be improved, however.

There is a wide range of public rooms to choose from, with several intimate rooms and spaces so that you don't get the feel of being overwhelmed by large spaces. The interior focal point is a huge four-deck-high atrium lobby with winding, double stairways, complete with two panoramic glass-walled elevators.

The main public entertainment rooms are located under three cabin decks. There is plenty of space, the traffic flow is good, and the ship absorbs people well. There are two show lounges, one at each end of the ship. One is a superb 550-seat, theater-style show lounge (movies are also shown here) and the other is a 480-seat cabaret-style lounge, complete with bar.

A glass-walled health spa complex is located high atop ship and includes a gymnasium with high-tech machines. One swimming pool is "suspended" aft between two decks (there are two other pools, although they are not large for the size of the ship).

The library is a very warm room and has six large buttery leather chairs for listening to compact discs, with ocean-view windows. There is a conference center for up to 300, as well as a business center, with computers, copy and fax machines. The collection of artwork is good, particularly on the stairways, and helps make the ship feel smaller than it is, although in places it doesn't always seem coordinated. The casino, while large, is not really in the main passenger flow and so it does not generate the "walk-through" factor found aboard so many ships.

The most traditional room aboard is the Wheelhouse Lounge/Bar, which is decorated in the style of a turn-of-the-century gentleman's club, complete with wood paneling and comfortable seating. The focal point is a large ship model from the P&O archives.

If you live in the top suites, at the end of the day you will be well attended; if you do not, you will merely be one of a very large number of passengers. One nice feature is the captain's cocktail party — it is held in the four-deck-high main atrium — so you can come and go as you please — and there's no standing in line (to have your photograph taken with the captain) if you don't want to.

Weak Points: Standing in line for embarkation, disembarkation, shore tenders and self-serve buffet meals is an inevitable aspect of cruising aboard all large ships. There is absolutely no escape from unnecessary and repetitive announcements (particularly for activities that bring revenue, such as art auctions, bingo, horse racing) that intrude constantly into your cruise. In-your-face art auctions are simply overbearing, and the paintings, lithographs, and faux, framed pictures that are strewn throughout the ship (and clash irritatingly with the ship's interior decor) are an annoying intrusion into what should be a vacation, not a cruise inside a floating "art" emporium.

The digital voice announcing elevator deck stops is irritating to passengers (many of whom tell me they would like to rip out the speaker system). There are a number of dead ends in the interior layout, so it's not as user-friendly as a ship this size should be. The cabin numbering system is extremely illogical, with numbers going through several hundred series on the same deck. The walls of the passenger accommodation decks are very plain (some artwork would be an improvement).

The swimming pools are quite small for so many passengers, and the pool deck is cluttered with white, plastic deck lounge chairs, which do not have cushioned pads. Waiting for tenders in anchor ports can prove irritating, but it is typical of large ship operations. Charging for the machines in the self-service launderette is trifling (even though it's only $1 per wash, $0.50 per dryer cycle, $0.50 for detergent).

SuperStar Aries
★★★ +

Mid-Size Ship:	37,301 tons	Cabins (with private balcony):	6
Lifestyle:	Premium	Cabins (wheelchair accessible):	1
Cruise Line:	Star Cruises	Cabin Current:	110/220-volt
Former Names:	*SuperStar Europe, Europa*	Full-Service Dining Rooms:	1
Builder:	Bremer Vulkan (Germany)	Elevators:	4
Original Cost:	$120 million	Casino(gaming tables):	Yes
Entered Service:	January 1982/2002	Slot Machines:	Yes
Registry:	Bahamas	Swimming Pools (outdoors):	2 (1 magrodome)
Length (ft/m):	654.9/199.63	Swimming Pools (indoors):	1 (fresh water)
Beam (ft/m):	93.8/28.60	Whirlpools:	0
Draft (ft/m):	27.6/8.42	Fitness Center:	Yes
Propulsion/Propellers:	Diesel (21,270kW)/2	Sauna/Steam Room:	Yes/No
Passenger Decks:	10	Massage:	Yes
Total Crew:	560	Self-Service Launderette:	Yes
Passengers (lower beds/all berths):	678/1,006	Dedicated Cinema:	No
Pass. Space Ratio (lower beds/all berths):	55.0/37.0	Library:	Yes
Crew/Pass. Ratio (lower beds/all berths):	1.2/1.7	Classification Society:	Det Norske Veritas
Navigation Officers:	European/Scandinavian		
Cabins (total):	339		
Size Range (sq ft/sq m):	150.6–656.6/14.0–61.0		
Cabins (outside view):	283		
Cabins (interior/no view):	56		
Cabins (for one person):	0		

OVERALL SCORE: 1,396

(OUT OF A POSSIBLE 2,000 POINTS)

Accommodation: All of the original cabins are quite spacious, and all were refurbished in 1995 and refreshed again in 1999, when Star Cruises acquired the ship. All feature illuminated closets, dark wood cabinetry with rounded edges, several full-length mirrors, color TV and VCR, minibar/refrigerator, and personal safe, hair dryer, and excellent cabin insulation. There is a small room service menu (for such things as omelettes, fried noodles, chicken wings, etc.), and all items are at extra cost. Most cabins can now accommodate one or two additional persons, which means her original spacious feel has been greatly eroded in order to cater more to families with children. However, the cabins are, in general, much larger than those found in almost all other ships in the Star Cruises fleet.

The bathrooms have deep bathtubs (cabins without bathtubs have a large shower enclosure), a three-head shower unit, two deep sinks (not all cabins), large toiletries cabinet, and handsome personal toiletry amenities. The bath towels, although made of 100% cotton, are a little small.

The largest accommodation can be found in suites added during a refit in 1999, when Star Cruises acquired the ship. However, because of their location (they were created from what were formerly officers' cabins) they have lifeboat-obstructed views. Six other suites had private balconies added (Beethoven, Handel, Haydn, Mozart, Schubert, Wagner). There is a separate bedroom (with either queen-size or twin beds), illuminated closets, and vanity desk. The lounge includes a wet bar with refrigerator and glass cabinets, and large audio-visual center complete with large-screen TV/VCR and compact disc player. The marble-clad bathroom features a large shower enclosure, with retractable clothesline.

Burberry personal toiletry amenities are provided, as are a bathrobe, weight scale, and good-sized towels. Occupants of suites are in Admiral Class, and can order from the "breakfast in bed" menu, as well as enjoy free access to the indoor spa, priority embarkation and disembarkation, and other extras.

Dining: The Grand Restaurant is large, with ocean-view windows on two sides, and a good amount of space around each table. One side has been converted into Taipan, an à la carte, extra-charge, Chinese dining spot, with its own Chinese galley.

There are two seatings for meals, and classic white Schoenwald chinaware (from Germany) is featured. There is also a large, extremely varied self-serve cold table for all meals, with colorful displays of a wide variety of foods, located in the center of the restaurant.

For casual meals, self-serve Asian and Western breakfast, lunch and supper buffets are provided at the Clipper Terrace, and outdoor area adjacent to one of the swimming pools (and Star Club Casino).

Other Comments: Originally constructed for Hapag-Lloyd, *SuperStar Aries* was the flagship of the German cruise industry for many years before the company ordered a replacement that came into service in September 1999. The ship' s new owners, Star Cruises, purchased the ship in April 1998, and leased her back to Hapag Lloyd until July 1999, when she went into drydock for a $15 million refit and renovation.

Exterior changes include a new sponson stern, added in order to comply with the latest stability regulations, although *SuperStar Aries* still retains a moderately handsome, well-balanced profile. There is an excellent amount of outdoor deck and sunbathing space, although the former FKK (nude sunbathing) deck is now a crew recreation deck.

The ship was originally constructed with a wide range of good-sized public rooms, most of them with high ceilings that promoted an even greater sense of spaciousness. Dark, restful colors were applied to many public rooms and cabins, and subtle, hidden lighting was used throughout, particularly on the stairways. Two casinos were added during a 1999 refit: one for general use, and one serving as a private club for VIP members only.

The indoor swimming pool aboard this ship is larger than most outdoor pools aboard new, much larger ships; adjacent facilities include a sauna, fitness/exercise center, coin-operated solarium, hydrotherapy bath, spa bar, and beauty salon.

Star Cruises has made some changes to some public rooms and open areas, while leaving others alone. Unfortunately, a large casino has been added, located in what was formerly the cinema, with a spiral stairway that connects to a slot machine room on the deck below. Additionally, two private gambling clubs were installed, and, for the Asian market, a karaoke room. A children's playroom has replaced the former flower shop.

When operated by her former owners (Hapag-Loyd Cruises), it was the food, service, and quiet, refined ambience that her many repeat passengers enjoyed, together with the excellent passenger space ratio. Under Star Cruises, however, while the hospitality, and the range and variety of food were changed to cater to different ethnic tastes, the whole feeling of the ship also changed — and not for the better. Star Cruises also changed some public rooms to casino gaming areas — too many, in fact — which also changed the character of the ship. A decent level of Asian hospitality is presently provided in what is a very informal, relaxed setting, with an extremely casual dress code (in reality, there is no dress code, particularly for Asian-nation passengers). There is no question that the ship's personality has changed as Star Cruises has provided for its specialized local markets. However, this has also taken away many of the niceties and facilities which were in place previously. In 2000 and 2001 *SuperStar Aries* operated in two different markets — Japan and Thailand, and thus the ship's character changed accordingly, as did all the directional signs. At present, the ship is disjointed, and the push for additional onboard revenue has had a negative impact on what was formerly a very nice ship and product. Furthermore, the poor training and supervision of staff has led to a much lower level of service and product delivery than required to keep the ship's previous high rating.

Note that in summer 2002, *SuperStar Aries* will be moved to Orient Lines, a company it owns, and will be renamed *Ocean Voyager*. As such, after much reconfiguration and upgrading of decor (as well as changing the main casino back to a cinema, and taking out many of the third/fourth berths that Star Cruises installed), the ship will operate long-distance itineraries throughout the world, including an annual around the world cruise — under the land and cruise specialists Orient Lines. I expect that Orient Lines will also replace the present dark color schemes with decor, carpeting, and soft furnishings to reflect the lighter spirit of the company's other ships.

Weak Points: There is no wrap-around promenade deck outdoors (there are, however, half-length port and starboard promenades). The sight lines in the show lounge are quite poor from many of the seats (the room was originally built more for use as a single level concert salon than a room for shows). At present, the ship's decor is too dark, and several public rooms have been completely spoiled.

SuperStar Gemini
★★★ +

Mid-Size Ship:	19,046 tons	Cabins (for one person):	0
Lifestyle:	Standard	Cabins (with private balcony):	10
Cruise Line:	Star Cruises	Cabins (wheelchair accessible):	4
Former Names:	*Crown Jewel*	Cabin Current:	110/220-volt
Builder:	Union Navale de Levante (Spain)	Full-Service Dining Rooms:	1
Original Cost:	$100 million	Elevators:	4
Entered Service:	August 1992/July 1995	Casino(gaming tables):	Yes
Registry:	Panama	Slot Machines:	Yes
Length (ft/m):	537.4/163.81	Swimming Pools (outdoors):	1
Beam (ft/m):	73.8/22.50	Swimming Pools (indoors):	0
Draft (ft/m):	17.7/5.40	Whirlpools:	3 (2 outside/1 inside)
Propulsion/Propellers:	Diesel (13,200kW)/2	Fitness Center:	Yes
Passenger Decks:	9	Sauna/Steam Room:	Yes/Yes
Total Crew:	470	Massage:	Yes
Passengers (lower beds/all berths):	808/900	Self-Service Launderette:	No
Pass. Space Ratio (lower beds/all berths):	23.5/21.1	Dedicated Cinema:	No
Crew/Pass. Ratio (lower beds/all berths):	1.7/1.9	Library:	Yes
Navigation Officers:	Scandinavian	Classification Society:	Det Norske Veritas
Cabins (total):	404		
Size Range (sq ft/sq m):	139.9–349.8/13.0–32.5	**OVERALL SCORE:**	**1,385**
Cabins (outside view):	281	(OUT OF A POSSIBLE 2,000 POINTS)	
Cabins (interior/no view):	123		

Accommodation: The standard outside view and interior (no view) cabins and deluxe grade cabins are small but nicely furnished, and most feature broad picture windows (some deluxe cabins on Deck 6 have lifeboat-obstructed views). They are practical and comfortable, with wood-trimmed accents and multi-colored soft furnishings, but there is almost no drawer space, and the closet space is extremely small. Bathrooms are reasonably decent considering the size of the ship, and each features two small toiletries cabinets, although the shower cubicle is small. However, note that the cabin soundproofing is very poor; the 100% cotton towels are thin; there is little room for luggage, so take only what is really necessary (casual clothing only, no formal attire needed — even the captain's gala dinner night asks for "smart casual" attire).

The Executive Suites (eight have a private balcony, although the partitions are not of the floor-to-ceiling type — so you can hear your neighbors clearly — or smell their smoke) and Junior Suites (these are really little larger than standard and deluxe cabins, but with more closet space) are nicely furnished. The sleeping area can be curtained off from the living area. A tea/coffee making set, and laser disc player are provided (only in the Executive Suites).

Bathrobes, slippers, and toiletry amenities are provided in all cabins, as well as a small color TV, telephone, and bottled water.

Note: No cabins have a bathtub. Hair dryers are not supplied for any cabin category, so take your own if you need to use one. Also, there is no room service for such items as coffee or tea, nor is there a menu for snacks. The cabin numbering system and signage are confusing.

Dining: The attractive Ocean Palace dining room is located aft and has large picture windows on three sides (although the accenting in the center of the ceiling makes the room appear round). There are two seatings. The itinerary determines whether or not the dining room is open.

The ambience is good, but there are few tables for two (most tables are for four, six, or eight). International cuisine with an Oriental touch is featured, and there is open seating for all meals, except for dinner on the single "formal" night. On the six day cruise, one night includes a barbecue outside on the pool deck (the main dining room is closed on this night). The wine list itself is reasonable, but the wines are all young and prices are high (the cost of wines and spirits in Southeast Asia is high due to high import duties) and champagne is incredibly expensive.

There is also an informal café, called Mariner's Buffet (a pork-free eatery). Breakfast here always includes some Southeast Asian dishes such as *Nasi Lemak*, and fried noodles, as well as western favorites. Lunch and dinner are also provided in this eatery. Australian passengers will appreciate the ample supply of vegemite. There is a good selection of beer, including some regional varieties, and some draft lager.

Other Comments: *SuperStar Gemini* is a handsome mid-sized cruise ship with smart exterior styling (the largest cruise vessel ever built in Spain). There is a wrap-around promenade deck outdoors.

Although the fit and finish was originally poor, Star Cruises has made the ship's interiors much warmer and more colorful. Inside, the ship has a traditional layout that provides reasonable horizontal passenger flow, although the passageways are narrow. There are picture windows in almost all of the public rooms that connect passengers with the sea and the outside light. There is a fair amount of open deck and sun-bathing space, including a neat area high atop the ship in front of a glass windbreak area — perfect for enjoying those balmy evenings outdoors away from the crowds inside. Cushioned pads are provided for the deck lounge chairs.

Other features include a five-deck-high, glass-walled atrium, and there is a karaoke/disco lounge. The decor is attractive, with upbeat Art Deco color combinations and splashy, colorful soft furnishings. The artwork is fairly plain and simple and could be improved. The fitness center/spa area is decent but quite cramped.

This very informal ship caters specifically to Australian, European (mainly British and German), as well as local Singaporean passengers (all announcements are in English). The ship presently operates seven-day cruises, from Singapore. The dress code is — well, there really isn't any: it's totally casual.

All in all, the company provides really good value for money — cruising in a homey ship that is bright, contemporary, and very informal, despite the fact that the staff is young, and needs more training, experience, and supervision in the art of hospitality, service, and flexibility. Gratuities are included, and no further tipping is allowed. You should have an enjoyable, fun voyage for a destination-intensive week, with acceptable, but not memorable food and service.

Weak Points: The staff could be better trained, and there is a high turnover. There are too many announcements. Music plays constantly in public spaces, hallways, and on open decks, making a relaxing cruise experience impossible.

SuperStar Leo
★★★★

Large Ship:	75,338 tons	Cabins (for one person):	0
Lifestyle:	Standard	Cabins (with private balcony):	391
Cruise Line:	Star Cruises	Cabins (wheelchair accessible):	4
Former Names:	-	Cabin Current:	240-volt
Builder:	Meyer Werft (Germany)	Full-Service Dining Rooms:	6
Original Cost:	$350 million	Elevators:	9
Entered Service:	October 1998	Casino(gaming tables):	Yes
Registry:	Panama	Slot Machines:	Yes
Length (ft/m):	879.2/268.0	Swimming Pools (outdoors):	2
Beam (ft/m):	105.6/32.2	Swimming Pools (indoors):	0
Draft (ft/m):	25.9/7.9	Whirlpools:	4
Propulsion/Propellers:	2 diesels (50,400kW)/2	Fitness Center:	Yes
Passenger Decks:	10	Sauna/Steam Room:	Yes/Yes
Total Crew:	1,300	Massage:	Yes
Passengers (lower beds/all berths):	1,974/2,800	Self-Service Launderette:	No
Pass. Space Ratio (lower beds/all berths):	38.1/26.9	Dedicated Cinema:	No
Crew/Pass. Ratio (lower beds/all berths):	1.5/2.1	Library:	Yes
Navigation Officers:	Scandinavian	Classification Society:	Det Norske Veritas
Cabins (total):	987		
Size Range (sq ft/sq m):	150.6–638.3/14.0–59.3	**OVERALL SCORE:**	**1,498**
Cabins (outside view):	608	**(OUT OF A POSSIBLE 2,000 POINTS)**	
Cabins (interior/no view):	379		

Accommodation: Three whole decks of cabins feature private balconies, while two-thirds of all cabins have an outside view. Both the standard outside-view and interior (no view) cabins really are very small (particularly in light of the fact that all cabins have extra berths for a third/fourth person), although the bathrooms have a good-sized shower enclosure. In other words, take only the very smallest amount of clothing you can (there's almost no storage space for luggage). All cabins feature a personal safe, 100% cotton towels and 100% cotton duvets or sheets.

Choose one of the six largest suites (named Hong Kong, Malaysia, Shanghai, Singapore, Thailand, and Tokyo) and you'll have an excellent amount of private living space, with separate lounge and bedroom. Each has a large en-suite bathroom that is part of the bedroom and open to it — as is the trend in high-cost, interior architect-designed bathrooms ashore. It features a gorgeous mosaic tiled floor, kidney bean-shaped whirlpool bathtub, two sinks, separate shower enclosure, and separate toilet (with glass door). There are TVs in the lounge, bedroom, and bathroom. The Singapore and Hong Kong suites and the Malaysia and Thai suites can be combined to form a double suite (good for families with children and maid).

Choose one of the 12 Zodiac suites (each is named for a sign of the zodiac) and you will get the second largest accommodation aboard the ship. Each suite has a separate lounge, bedroom, and bathroom, and an interconnecting door to an ocean-view cabin with private balcony (good for families). All cabinetry features richly lacquered woods, large (stocked) wet bar with refrigerator, dining table and four chairs, sofa, drinks table, and trouser press. The bedroom is small, but features a queen-size bed. There is a decent amount of drawer space, although the closet space, containing two personal safes, is rather tight.

A small room service menu is available. All items cost extra, and both a 15% service charge as well as a gratuity are added to your account.

Dining: Eight eating places offer plenty of choice in fine dining and informal trans-ethnic eating spots. All are nonsmoking. You will, therefore, need to plan where you want to eat well in advance, or you may be disappointed. The following are included in the price of the cruise:

Windows on the World — the equivalent of the main dining room. It seats 632 in two seatings, is two decks high at the aft-most section, and has huge cathedral-style windows set in three sections overlooking the ship's stern and wake.

Raffles Café — a large self-serve buffet restaurant with indoor/outdoor seating for 400, and, as you might expect, pseudo-Raffles Hotel-like decor, with rattan chairs, overhead fans, and wood paneling.

Garden Room Restaurant — with 268 seats features Chinese cuisine.

The following are the à la carte (extra cost) restaurants:

Taipan — a Chinese Restaurant, with traditional Hong Kong-themed decor and items like dim sum made from fresh, not frozen, ingredients. (There are also two small private dining rooms).

Shogun — a Japanese restaurant and sushi bar, for sashimi, sushi, and tempura. A section can be closed off to make the Samurai Room, with 22 seats, while a traditional Tatami Room has seats for eight. There's also a *teppanyaki* grill, with ten seats, where the chef cooks in front of you.

Maxim's — a small à la carte restaurant with ocean-view windows, features fine dining in the classic French style.

Blue Lagoon — a small, casual street café with about 24 seats, featuring noodle dishes, fried rice, and other Southeast Asian cuisine (adjacent is a karaoke street bar called The Bund).

In the atrium lobby there is a casual patisserie serving several types of coffees, teas, cakes, and pastries.

Other Comments: *SuperStar Leo* was the first brand new ship ordered by Star Cruises specifically for the Southeast Asian market. There is a wrap-around promenade deck outdoors, good for strolling.

Inside, there are two indoor boulevards, and a stunning, six-deck-high central atrium lobby, with three glass-walled elevators and ample space to review the shops and cafés that line its inner sanctum. The lobby itself is modeled after the lobby of the Hyatt Hotel in Hong Kong, with little clutter from the usual run of desks found aboard other cruise ships; instead, there is only the reception desk — no desk for shore excursions or for banking.

The interior design theme revolves around art, architecture, history, and literature. The ship sports a mix of both Eastern and Western design and decor details, and public room names have been chosen to appeal to a mixture of Australian, European, and Asian passengers. Three stairways are each carpeted in a different color, which helps new cruise passengers find their way around easily.

The main show lounge (Moulin Rouge with 973 seats) is two decks high (a separate balcony level is reserved for "club" members only), with almost no support columns to obstruct the sight lines, and a revolving stage for Broadway-style productions and other shows (typically to recorded music — no live showband). The show lounge can also be used as a large-screen cinema, with superb surround sound.

A 450-seat room atop the ship functions as an observation lounge during the day and a nightclub at night, with live music. From it, a spiral stairway takes you down to a navigation bridge viewing area, where you can see the captain and bridge officers at work.

There is a business center (complete with conference center — good for small groups) and writing room, as well as private mahjong and karaoke rooms, and a smoking room, for those who enjoy cigars and cognac. A shopping concourse is set around the second level of the lobby.

Sports facilities include a jogging track, golf driving range, basketball and tennis courts, as well as four levels of sunbathing decks. Health devotees should enjoy Caesar's (Cleopatra's for women) and the Nero Fitness Center, with facilities and services to pamper you (all at extra charge — even for use of the sauna and steam rooms), including Thai massage outdoors on deck.

Families with children should note that teens have their own huge video arcade, while children get to play in a wet 'n' wild aft pool (complete with pirate ship and caves) and two whirlpool tubs. Plus there's all the fun and facilities of Charlie's childcare center (open 24 hours a day), which includes a painting room, computer learning center, and small cinema. There's even a room full of cots for toddlers to use for sleepovers, and even the toilets are at a special low height. Over 15,069 sq ft (1,400 sq m) are devoted to children's facilities — all tucked well away from adult recreation areas.

Ideally suited to families with children, the dress code is extremely casual (no jacket or tie needed). Watch out for the extra costs and charges mounting up if you want to indulge in more than the basics. With many dining choices (some of which cost extra) to accommodate different tastes and styles, your final cruise and dining experience will really depend on how much you are prepared to spend.

For priority check-in, disembarkation, and generally better service, book "Balcony Class" rather than "Non-Balcony Class" accommodation. *SuperStar Leo* is based in Singapore.

Weak Points: Standing in line for embarkation, disembarkation, shore tenders, and self-serve buffet meals is an inevitable aspect of cruising aboard all large ships. The cabins with balconies have extremely narrow balconies, and the cabins themselves are very small (the ship was originally constructed for three- and four-day cruises). While the ship is quite stunning and offers a wide choice of dining venues, keeping consistency of product delivery depends on the quality of the service and supervisory staff. There are many extra cost items (in addition to the à la carte dining spots), such as for morning tea, afternoon tea, and childcare. There are some inevitable entertainment and activity announcements.

SuperStar Taurus
★★★ +

Mid-Sized Ship:	25,000 tons	Cabins (for one person):	0
Lifestyle:	Standard	Cabins (with private balcony):	10
Cruise Line:	Star Cruises	Cabins (wheelchair accessible):	6
Former Names:	*Leeward, Sally Albatros,*	Cabin Current:	110/220-volt
	Viking Saga	Full-Service Dining Rooms:	2
Builder:	Wartsila (Finland)	Elevators:	4
Original Cost:	n/a	Casino(gaming tables):	Yes
Entered Service:	1980/March 2000	Slot Machines:	Yes
Registry:	Liberia	Swimming Pools (outdoors):	1
Length (ft/m):	492.1/150.0	Swimming Pools (indoors):	0
Beam (ft/m):	82.6/25.2	Whirlpools:	1
Draft (ft/m):	18.0/5.5	Fitness Center:	Yes
Propulsion/Propellers:	Diesel (19,120kW)/2	Sauna/Steam Room:	Yes/No
Passenger Decks:	7	Massage:	Yes
Total Crew:	400	Self-Service Launderette:	No
Passengers (lower beds/all berths):	950/1,150	Dedicated Cinema:	No
Pass. Space Ratio (lower beds/all berths):	26.3/21.7	Library:	No
Crew/Pass. Ratio (lower beds/all berths):	2.3/2.8	Classification Society:	Bureau Veritas
Navigation Officers:	Scandinavian		
Cabins (total):	475		
Size Range (sq ft/sq m):	53.0–387.0/5.0–36.0	**OVERALL SCORE:**	**1,278**
Cabins (outside view):	219	**(OUT OF A POSSIBLE 2,000 POINTS)**	
Cabins (interior/no view):	256		

Accommodation: Some of the top-grade cabins have private balconies that are neatly angled. Six cabins are specially designed for allergy sufferers. However, most of the standard cabins are dimensionally challenged: The bathrooms are tiny (you can certainly expect to dance with the shower curtain), and there is little room for one's personal toiletry items. Note that many outside cabins on Deck 6 have obstructed views.

A small room service menu is available. All items cost extra, and both a 15% service charge and a $3 gratuity will be added to your account.

Dining: There are two principal dining rooms, located aft. Both are nonsmoking and have two seatings. The service is generally sound, but rather hurried, particularly for those at the first seating. The menu choice is good, and presentation is reasonable, but there is no finesse. There is also Le Bistro, an attractive and popular 80-seat informal (alternative) dining spot for pasta and other lighter fare.

Other Comments: This ship has undergone a number of changes during her lifetime, from passenger ferry to cruise ship. She now has a sleek, swept-back, wedge-shaped design with steeply tiered aft decks, although there is hardly any bow. A 1995 refit cost $60 million when the ship was operated under the Norwegian Cruise Line banner. Star Cruises has spent additional monies to make her decor more suitable to Japanese/Southeast Asian tastes. The bridge is of the fully enclosed type. There is a teak wrap-around promenade deck outdoors, and a reasonably sized spa and recreation center.

The ambience aboard is warm and friendly, with typical Southeast Asian flair. The lobby is a little glitzy, but it is quite pleasant and features contemporary, bright decor, with modern artworks and splashes of color everywhere.

There is a good show lounge, which has tiered seating, and fairly good sight lines. Sports fans will like the Sports Bar and Grill, an informal TV-filled long bar and adjacent fast food joint. This is, however, a high-density ship with many low ceilings.

Weak Points: The pool deck is awful and very cramped. What this ship really needs is a forward observation lounge. The ship is presently under charter to Star Cruises for cruises from Japan, for which she is well-suited.

SuperStar Virgo
★★★★

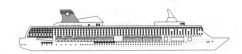

Large Ship:	75,338 tons	Cabins (for one person):	0
Lifestyle:	Standard	Cabins (with private balcony):	391
Cruise Line:	Star Cruises	Cabins (wheelchair accessible):	4
Former Names:	-	Cabin Current:	240-volt
Builder:	Meyer Werft (Germany)	Full-Service Dining Rooms:	6
Original Cost:	$350 million	Elevators:	9
Entered Service:	August 1999	Casino(gaming tables):	Yes
Registry:	Panama	Slot Machines:	Yes
Length (ft/m):	879.2/268.0	Swimming Pools (outdoors):	2
Beam (ft/m):	105.6/32.2	Swimming Pools (indoors):	0
Draft (ft/m):	25.9/7.9	Whirlpools:	4
Propulsion/Propellers:	Diesel (50,400kW)/2	Fitness Center:	Yes
Passenger Decks:	10	Sauna/Steam Room:	Yes/Yes
Total Crew:	1,300	Massage:	Yes
Passengers (lower beds/all berths):	1,974/2,800	Self-Service Launderette:	No
Pass. Space Ratio (lower beds/all berths):	38.1/26.9	Dedicated Cinema:	No
Crew/Pass. Ratio (lower beds/all berths):	1.5/2.1	Library:	Yes
Navigation Officers:	Scandinavian	Classification Society:	Det Norske Veritas
Cabins (total):	987		
Size Range (sq ft/sq m):	150.6–638.3/14.0–59.3	**OVERALL SCORE:**	**1,522**
Cabins (outside view):	608	(OUT OF A POSSIBLE 2,000 POINTS)	
Cabins (interior/no view):	379		

Accommodation: Three entire decks of cabins feature private balconies, while two-thirds of all cabins have an outside-view. Both the standard outside-view and interior (no view) cabins really are very small (particularly in light of the fact that all cabins have extra berths for a third/fourth person), so take only the very smallest amount of clothing you can (there's almost no storage space for luggage). All cabins feature a personal safe, 100% cotton towels, and 100% cotton duvets or sheets. Bathrooms have a good-sized shower enclosure, and include personal toiletry items such as Burberry soap, conditioning shampoo, and body lotion.

For more space choose one of 13 suites. Each suite has a separate lounge/dining room, bedroom, and bathroom, and an interconnecting door to an ocean-view cabin with private balcony (with light). All cabinetry features richly lacquered woods, large (stocked) wet bar with refrigerator, dining table (with a top that flips over to reveal a card table) and four chairs, sofa and drinks table, and trouser press. The bedroom is small, completely filled by its queen-size bed. There is a reasonable amount of drawer space (but the drawers are very small), and the closet space is rather tight (it contains two personal safes). A large en-suite bathroom is part of the bedroom and open to it — as is the trend in high-cost, interior architect-designed bathrooms ashore. It features a gorgeous mosaic tiled floor, kidney bean-shaped whirlpool bathtub, two sinks, separate shower enclosure (with floor-to-ceiling ocean-view window), and separate toilet (with glass door). There are TVs in the lounge, bedroom, and bathroom.

For even more space, choose one of the six largest of the 13 suites (Boracay, Nicobar, Langkawi, Majorca, Phuket, and Sentosa), and you'll have a generous amount of private living space, with a separate lounge, dining area, bedroom, large bathroom, and private balcony (with light). The Boracay and Sentosa suites and the Phuket and Langkawi suites can be combined to form a double suite (good for families with children and maid). There are TVs in the lounge, bedroom, and bathroom.

A small room service menu is available. All items cost extra, and both a 15% service charge as well as a gratuity will be added to your account.

Dining: There is certainly plenty of choice in fine dining and informal trans-ethnic eating spots, with a total of eight places to eat (all are nonsmoking). You will, therefore, need to plan where you want to eat well in advance, or you may be disappointed.

The following are included in the price of the cruise:

Bella Vista — the equivalent of a main dining room. It seats over 600 in an open seating arrangement, although, in effect, the restaurant operates two seatings. The aft section is two decks high, and huge cathedral-style windows are set in three sections overlooking the ship's stern. There are no waiter stations adjacent to the tables — instead they are tucked neatly away in side wings, thus avoiding the high noise levels normally found in large dining rooms.

Mediterranean Buffet — a large self-serve buffet restaurant with indoor/outdoor seating for 400.

The Pavilion Room — features Chinese cuisine, including dim sum.

A la carte (extra charge) dining spots:

Noble House — a Chinese Restaurant, with traditional Hong Kong-themed decor and items like dim sum. (There are also two small private dining rooms.)

Palazzo — a beautiful, if slightly ostentatious Italian restaurant. It boasts fine food, and something very unusual — a genuine Renoir painting displayed in a strategic focal point (well protected by cameras and alarms).

Samurai — a Japanese restaurant and sushi bar (for sashimi and sushi). There are two *teppanyaki* grills, each with 10 seats, where the chef cooks in front of you. The menu is extensive.

The Taj — an Indian/vegetarian dining spot that features a range of food in a self-serve buffet setup.

Blue Lagoon — a casual street café, open 24 hours, featuring noodle dishes, fried rice and other Southeast Asian cuisine.

Out of Africa — a casual karaoke café and bar, where coffees, tea, and pastries are available.

Other Comments: *SuperStar Virgo* is the second new ship ordered specifically for the Asian market. The all-white ship has a distinctive red/blue funnel with gold star logo. There is a wrap-around promenade deck outdoors, good for strolling.

Inside, there are two indoor boulevards, and a stunning, six-deck-high central atrium lobby, with three glass-walled elevators and ample space to review the shops and cafés that line its inner sanctum. There is no clutter from the usual run of desks found aboard other cruise ships; instead, there is only a reception desk, tour booking desk, and concierge.

The decor aboard *SuperStar Virgo* is much more European in design, taste, and color combinations than sister ship *SuperStar Leo*, and the layout has been modified and improved slightly (for a slightly different market). The lobby, for example, has become an Italian Piazza, with a stunning *trompe l'oeil* and a multicolored stained glass ceiling. The decor mixes east and west, and public room names have been chosen to appeal to a mixture of Australian, European, and Asian passengers. Three stairways are each carpeted in a different color, which helps new cruise passengers find their way around easily.

The main show lounge (The Lido with 973 seats) is two decks high (a separate balcony level is reserved for "club" members only), with almost no support columns to obstruct the sight lines, and a revolving stage for Broadway-style reviews. Shows that have included live tigers have given way to lavish production shows (one of which is an extra cost topless dancer show). The show lounge also turns into a large-screen cinema, with excellent surround sound.

The 450-seat Galaxy of the Stars Lounge is set atop the ship. It is an observation lounge during the day and a nightclub at night, with live music. From it, a spiral stairway takes you down to a navigation bridge viewing area, where you can see the captain and bridge officers at work.

There is a business center (complete with six meeting rooms), large library and writing room, as well as private mahjong and karaoke rooms, and a smoking room, for those who enjoy cigars and cognac. A shopping concourse is set around the second level of the lobby, and includes a wine shop.

Sports facilities include a jogging track, golf driving range, basketball and tennis courts, as well as four levels of sunbathing decks. Health devotees should enjoy the Apollo Health Spa, with facilities and services to pamper you (all at extra charge — even for use of the sauna and steam rooms), including Thai massage outdoors on deck.

Families with children should note that teens have their own huge video arcade, while children get to play in a wet 'n' wild aft pool (complete with pirate ship and caves) and two whirlpool tubs. Plus there's all the fun and facilities of Charlie's childcare center (open 24 hours a day), which includes a painting room, computer learning center, and small cinema. There's even a room full of cots for toddlers to use for sleepovers, and even the toilets are at a special low height. Some 15,069 sq ft (1,400 sq m) is devoted to children's facilities — all tucked well away from adult recreation areas.

Star Cruises has established a Southeast Asian regional cruise audience for its diverse fleet of ships. *SuperStar Virgo* is a fine ship for the active local market, and is certainly the most stunning and luxurious of any of the ships sailing year-round from this busy popular Southeast Asian spot.

SuperStar Virgo is based in Hong Kong. The passenger mix is international, although the local (regional) market has now been developed, so you can expect to find lots of families with children (who are allowed to roam around the ship uncontrolled), particularly on the weekend (Friday-Sunday) cruise. There are lots of activities and entertainment (some are extra cost items), and a lot of young passengers.

More choices, more dining options, and Asian hospitality all add up to a very attractive vacation package that is particularly suitable for families with children, in a very contemporary floating leisure center that operates from Singapore. The dress code is casual — very casual (no jacket or tie needed), and the ship operates under a "no-tipping" policy. While the initial cruise fare seems very reasonable, the extra costs and charges soon mount up if you want to indulge in more than the basics.

Although service levels and finesse remain inconsistent, hospitality is very good. With so many dining choices (some of which cost extra) to accommodate the tastes of an eclectic mix of nationalities, it really depends on how much you are prepared to spend which will determine what your final cruise and dining experience will be like. For priority check-in, disembarkation, generally better service, and priority booking of the à la carte dining spots, choose "Balcony Class" and not "Non-Balcony Class" accommodation.

Weak Points: Standing in line for embarkation, disembarkation, shore tenders, and self-serve buffet meals is an inevitable aspect of cruising aboard all large ships. The "balcony class" cabins have extremely narrow balconies. While the ship is quite stunning and offers a wide choice of dining venues, keeping consistency of product delivery depends on the quality of the service and supervisory staff, and more training is needed. There are many extra-cost items (in addition to the à la carte dining spots), such as morning tea, afternoon tea, most cabaret shows (except a crew show), and childcare. There are some inevitable entertainment and activity announcements (in English and Mandarin). Finding your way around the many areas blocked by portable "crowd containment" ribbon barriers can prove frustrating at times.

Switzerland
★★★

Small Ship:	15,739 tons	Cabins (for one person):	0
Lifestyle:	Standard	Cabins (with private balcony):	6
Cruise Line:	Dreamline Cruises	Cabins (wheelchair accessible):	0
Former Names:	*Daphne, Therisos Express,*	Cabin Current:	220-volt
	Port Sydney	Full-Service Dining Rooms:	1
Builder:	Swan, Hunter (UK)	Elevators:	2
Original Cost:	n/a	Casino (gaming tables):	Yes
Entered Service:	July 1955/September 1999	Slot Machines:	Yes
Registry:	Liberia	Swimming Pools (outdoors):	1
Length (ft/m):	532.7/162.39	Swimming Pools (indoors):	0
Beam (ft/m):	70.2/21.42	Whirlpools:	4
Draft (ft/m):	28.4/8.66	Fitness Center:	Yes
Propulsion/Propellers:	Diesel (9,850kW)/2	Sauna/Steam Room:	Yes/Yes
Passenger Decks:	7	Massage:	Yes
Total Crew:	210	Self-Service Launderette:	No
Passengers (lower beds/all berths):	422/486	Dedicated Cinema:	No
Pass. Space Ratio (lower beds/all berths):	37.1/32.3	Library:	Yes
Crew/Pass. Ratio (lower beds/all berths):	2.0/2.3	Classification Society:	Registro Navale Italiano
Navigation Officers:	International		
Cabins (total):	211		
Size Range (sq ft/sq m):	150.0–398.2/14.0–37.0	**OVERALL SCORE:**	**1,245**
Cabins (outside view):	189	(OUT OF A POSSIBLE 2,000 POINTS)	
Cabins (interior/no view):	22		

Accommodation: This ship has some very spacious forward-facing suites (incorrectly called penthouses) as well as the more standard outside-view and interior (no view) cabins. All have good solid fittings and heavy-duty doors. There really is plenty of closet and drawer space. Unfortunately, the cabin insulation is not very good. The cabin bathrooms are of a generous size and fitted out well, but there is no retractable clothesline (really useful for longer cruises), and the walls are plain. Note that there is no room service.

The largest accommodation can be found in the Penthouse Suites. These have a completely separate bedroom and living room, plus a balcony (passengers are brought complimentary cocktails on days at sea, and have a butler service). A minibar/refrigerator is provided, but all items are at extra cost. The bathroom has a full-sized bathtub and glazed tile floor, but there is no retractable clothesline. A good range of personal toiletry amenities is provided, as is a bathrobe of 100% cotton.

Dining: The dining room is reasonably warm and charming, and has an uncluttered seating arrangement, with several tables for two located by large picture windows (other tables are for four, six, or eight). There is a single, unhurried seating with assigned tables.

Service is friendly and attentive by the Russian and Ukrainian staff. The food is not very creatively presented, but is of a reasonably decent general standard, and is provided by a respected Swiss maritime catering company. Dinners consist of a selection of only one or two appetizers and entrees, but there is normally a good choice of cheeses. At all meals (except formal days) a salad buffet table, complete with cheese selection, is provided for lunch and dinner, although the salad selection is similar every day. Breakfast buffet is also provided in the dining room. There is also a separate informal café (Neptune Bar) for breakfast and lunch buffets. There is also a neat wine bar (Piazzo Vino) with a decent selection.

Other Comments: This ship (originally built for Port Line and converted into a cruise ship at a cost of $37 million in 1975) has expansive outdoor decks and plenty of sunbathing space. She was refitted and completely refurbished in early 1997 for her present owners.

Inside, the contemporary decor in the public rooms is bright and airy. There is a large, fine show lounge, which is also useful for meetings and groups. Most of the public rooms have fairly high ceilings, which help create a sense of space. There is much emphasis on health and fitness, with a wellness program that includes Ayurvedic treatments in the Aqua Vitalis spa and yoga and *tai chi* as part of the exercise program.

The ship is almost identical in outward appearance to sister ship *Princess Danae*. Originally constructed as a general cargo vessel, she was rebuilt as a cruise ship, and operated for many years for Carras Cruises as *Daphne*, then by Costa Cruises, also as *Daphne*. Now owned and operated by Dreamline Cruises on behalf of the Swiss-based travel company Mittelthurgau and marketed through a number of agencies in several countries: Chiariva (Italy), Noble Caledonia (UK), Tapis Rouge (France), and Uniworld (US). Thus, you can expect to find an international mix of passengers on each cruise.

This ship maintains an air of intimacy, has a decent array of public rooms, lounges and bars, and should represent good value when cruising on her destination-intensive itineraries. The currency on board is the Swiss Franc.

The use of mobile phones aboard ship is not permitted — this is much appreciated by passengers. *Switzerland* maintains an air of intimacy, has a fine range of public rooms, and should represent good value when cruising on her itineraries. Note that a 15% gratuity is added to all bar bills.

Weak Points: There is no forward-looking observation lounge, and no wrap-around promenade deck.

The Emerald
★★★

Mid-Size Ship:	26,431 tons	Cabins (for one person):	10
Lifestyle:	Standard	Cabins (with private balcony):	0
Cruise Line:	Louis Cruise Lines	Cabins (wheelchair accessible):	2
Former Names:	*Regent Rainbow, Diamond Island,*	Cabin Current:	110/220-volt
	Santa Rosa	Full-Service Dining Rooms:	1
Builder:	Newport News Shipbuilding (US)	Elevators:	3
Original Cost:	$25 million	Casino(gaming tables):	Yes
Entered Service:	June 1958/April 1997	Slot Machines:	Yes
Registry:	Cyprus	Swimming Pools (outdoors):	1
Length (ft/m):	599.0/182.57	Swimming Pools (indoors):	0
Beam (ft/m):	84.0/25.60	Whirlpools:	2
Draft (ft/m):	27.5/8.38	Fitness Center:	Yes
Propulsion/Propellers:	steam turbine (16,400kW)/2	Sauna/Steam Room:	Yes/No
Passenger Decks:	10	Massage:	Yes
Total Crew:	412	Self-Service Launderette:	No
Passengers (lower beds/all berths):	990/1,198	Dedicated Cinema:	No
Pass. Space Ratio (lower beds/all berths):	26.6/22.0	Library:	Yes
Crew/Pass. Ratio (lower beds/all berths):	2.4/2.9	Classification Society: American Bureau of Shipping	
Navigation Officers:	Greek/European		
Cabins (total):	500		
Size Range (sq ft/sq m):	124.8–304.6/11.6–28.3	**OVERALL SCORE:**	**1,177**
Cabins (outside view):	338	**(OUT OF A POSSIBLE 2,000 POINTS)**	
Cabins (interior/no view):	162		

Accommodation: This ship has a varied mix of cabins both old and new that offer a wide range of configurations from which to choose, presented in just three main categories: premier, superior, and standard (although there are, in effect, seven price levels). You should note that cabins are not assigned until you are at the embarkation port for check-in unless you pay a supplement in order to pre-book. This ad-hoc method of assigning cabins means that those who arrive first probably will get the best cabins.

Many of the original cabins are quite spacious, with good closet and drawer space, while newer ones are a little more compact, and have poor insulation. Continental breakfast in your cabin will cost about $7.50 (£4.50) per person (each time). There is also a 24-hour cabin service menu for snacks, all at extra cost.

Dining: The dining room has large ocean view windows and an interesting, neat orchestra balcony. There are two seatings. The food quality and presentation are good for the cost of a cruise. The service is friendly and quite attentive, although you should not expect grand hotel-style service.

Other Comments: After being laid up for over 10 years, this solid, American-built, former ocean liner underwent a great amount of reconstruction in Greece in 1992. Louis Cruise Lines spent more on another refit in 1997. With new upper decks, her profile is not exactly handsome. The open deck and sunbathing space is limited when the ship is full. There is a good wrap-around promenade deck.

Her interiors are pleasant and comfortable, with a warm decor that is contemporary without being brash. Many public rooms have high ceilings, and some fine wrought iron railings. The artwork is low budget.

For short cruises, this ship provides a range of public spaces and bars that promote a good party ambience. The casino is quite large, and has a high ceiling.

During the summer, *The Emerald*, under charter to Thomson Cruises, takes Mediterranean cruises from its base on Palma Majorca. During the winter, the ship is based on Barbados, and operates two alternating Caribbean itineraries. Thomson's wholly owned airline (Britannia Airways) will probably fly you to your port of embarkation. Despite the minor drawbacks, this ship manages to provide a decent cruise experience, and therefore achieves a very respectable rating. Note that the gratuities are included.

Weak Points: The high density of this vessel means that there is little room to move about when full, often translated to "ambience." The sight lines in the show lounge really are very poor, and the entertainment is typical of the low budget type.

The Iris

Small Ship:	12,688 tons	Cabins (with private balcony):	0
Lifestyle:	Standard	Cabins (wheelchair accessible):	1
Cruise Line:	Mano Maritime	Cabin Current:	220-volt
Former Names:	*Francesca, Konstantin Simonov*	Full-Service Dining Rooms:	1
Builder:	A. Warski (Poland)	Elevators:	2
Original Cost:	n/a	Casino (gaming tables):	Yes
Entered Service:	April 1982/March 2001	Slot Machines:	Yes
Registry:	Malta	Swimming Pools (outdoors):	1
Length (ft/m):	449.8/137.10	Swimming Pools (indoors):	0
Beam (ft/m):	68.8/21.0	Whirlpools:	1
Draft (ft/m):	19.0/5.8	Fitness Center:	Yes
Propulsion/Propellers:	Diesel (12,800kW)/2	Sauna/Steam Room:	Yes/No
Passenger Decks:	7	Massage:	Yes
Total Crew:	160	Self-Service Launderette:	Yes
Passengers (lower beds/all berths):	487/750	Dedicated Cinema:	No
Pass. Space Ratio (lower beds/all berths):	26.0/16.9	Library:	Yes
Crew/Pass. Ratio (lower beds/all berths):	3.0/4.6	Classification Society:	Russian Shipping Register
Navigation Officers:	European		
Cabins (total):	245		
Size Range (sq ft/sq m):	n/a		
Cabins (outside view):	159		
Cabins (interior/no view):	86		
Cabins (for one person):	3		

OVERALL SCORE: NOT YET RATED

Note that this ship was not in service when this book was completed.

Accommodation: There are 13 large suites and 30 large outside-view cabins among the total of 157 outside-view cabins; and 74 interior (no-view) cabins.

Except for the 13 large cabins classed as suites, all are small and somewhat utilitarian in their fittings and furnishings. There is very little drawer space, and the under-bed storage space for luggage is tight. Many cabins are fitted with upper Pullman berths. All have a private bathroom, with shower, and a small cabinet for personal toiletry items (only soap is supplied).

The suites have a much larger bathroom, with bathtub and shower combination, and each has a TV and video player. The two largest of the "luxe" cabins have a separate bedroom with plenty of closet and drawer space, and a large bathroom with bathtub and shower combination.

Dining: The dining room which has a low ceiling, has two seatings. The food is surprisingly good, with lots of fresh salads and vegetables, as well as good meats and local fish. There is certainly plenty of variety. Kosher food can also be supplied — for a surcharge, per passenger, per cruise.

Other Comments: *The Iris* has a square, angular profile with a boxy stern (complete with fold-down car ramps), stubby bow and a fat funnel placed amidships — otherwise it's a moderately handsome vessel. She has a fully enclosed bridge for all-weather operation. There is also a small helicopter landing deck.

This vessel was originally built in Poland as one of a series of five sister ships (the original names of the other four being: *Dimitry Shostakovich, Lev Tolstoi, Mikhail Sholokhov,* and *Petr Pervyy*). It was designed for carrying both cars and passengers on line voyages, this ship is now used solely as a cruise ship, having been placed under charter to Israel's Mano Cruises in 2001, and extensively reconstructed for pleasure cruising activities.

Weak Points: There is no observation lounge with forward-facing views over the ship's bows. It has a limited amount of open deck and sunning space (particularly if the ship is full) and a tiny swimming pool that is really merely a "dip" pool. The port and starboard open promenade decks are of painted steel.

The World of ResidenSea

Small Ship:	40,000 tons	Suites (for one person):	0
Lifestyle:	Luxury	Suites (with private balcony):	198
Cruise Line:	ResidenSea	Suites (wheelchair accessible):	2 (plus 2 for
Former Names:	-		hearing impared)
Builder:	Fosen MEK Versteder (Norway)	Cabin Current:	110/220-volt
Original Cost:	$380 million	Full-Service Dining Rooms:	2
Entered Service:	January 2002	Elevators:	4
Registry:	Bahamas	Casino (gaming tables):	Yes
Length (ft/m):	644.1/196.35	Slot Machines:	Yes
Beam (ft/m):	97.7/29.8	Swimming Pools (outdoors):	1
Draft (ft/m):	21.9/6.7	Swimming Pools (indoors):	1
Propulsion/Propellers:	Diesel/2	Whirlpools:	1
Passenger Decks:	12	Fitness Center:	Yes
Total Crew:	252	Sauna/Steam Room:	Yes/Yes
Passengers (lower beds/all berths):	396/1,090	Massage:	Yes
Pass. Space Ratio (lower beds/all berths):	101/36.6	Self-Service Launderette:	Yes
Crew/Pass. Ratio (lower beds/all berths):	1.1/3.1	Dedicated Cinema:	No
Navigation Officers:	Scandinavian	Library:	Yes
Private Apartments (total):	110	Classification Society:	Det Norske Veritas
Size Range (sq ft/sq m):	1,106.5–3,243.2/		
	102.8–301.3		
Guest Suites:	88	**OVERALL SCORE: NOT YET RATED**	
Size Range (sq ft/sq m):	259–648/24.0–60.1		
Suites (outside view):	198	Note that this ship was not in service when this	
Suites (interior/no view):	0	book was completed.	

Accommodation: Residents' Apartments

There are 110 elegant residences in five different sizes and price ranges, costing between $2 million and $6.8 million per apartment, plus maintenance charges of approximately 5% annually, and ranging in size from 1,106 to 3,242 sq ft (102.7 to 301.1 sq m). Owners can choose between four different design styles (the designers are Nina Campbell, Juan Pablo Molyneux, Luciano Di Pilla, and Yran & Storbraaten.) All feature a fully equipped kitchen (with top-of-the-line refrigerator, oven, microwave, and dishwasher), two to three bedrooms (each with its own bathroom, naturally), living and dining room area, and private terrace. All have built-in modern access. Chefs are available for private meals in the apartments.

Guest Accommodation: An additional 88 guest suites, in five size and configuration categories (all with musical names: Adagio, Libretto, Sonata, and Rhapsody) are available for family, friends, and general cruise passenger use, and these are marketed by Silversea Cruises.

There are eight Adagio Suites (six of which have lifeboat-obstructed views, the other two, which are for the handicapped, do not). They measure 259–325 sq ft (24.0–30.1 sq m), and have a large picture window (no private balcony), two beds that can convert to a queen-sized bed, sitting area, cocktail cabinet with refrigerator, dressing table with built-in hair dryer, writing desk, personal safe, TV, and VCR. The marble-clad bathroom features a bathtub (except the two handicapped suites) and separate shower enclosure.

There are Six Libretto Suites. They are square in shape and measure 271–309 sq ft (25.1–28.7 sq m), and feature two beds that can convert to a queen-size bed, sitting area, cocktail cabinet with refrigerator, dressing table with built-in hair dryer, writing desk, personal safe, TV, and VCR. The marble-clad bathroom features a bathtub (except the two handicapped suites) and separate shower enclosure.

There are 18 Concerto Suites, each with a private balcony. They measure 294–319 sq ft (27.3–29.6 sq m), and feature two beds that can convert to a queen-size bed, sitting area, cocktail cabinet with refrigerator, dressing table with built-in hair dryer, writing desk, personal safe, TV, and VCR. The marble-clad bathroom features a bathtub (except the two handicapped suites) and separate shower enclosure.

There are 52 Sonata Suites, each with a private balcony. They measure 328–348 sq ft (30.4–32.3 sq m), and feature two beds that can convert to a queen-size bed, sitting area, cocktail cabinet with refrigerator, dressing table with built-in hair dryer, writing desk, personal safe, TV, and VCR. The marble-clad bath-

594

room features a bathtub (except the two handicapped suites) and separate shower enclosure. Three of the suites have an interconnecting door to another Sonata Suite, providing ideal "his 'n' hers" facilities for couples, or lavish accommodation for families with children.

There are four large Rhapsody Suites (two at the stern facing aft) created by the Signature Designers of the apartments; each with a large private balcony. They measure 598–648 sq ft (55.5–60.1 sq m), and feature a large living room that includes a dining table, cocktail cabinet with refrigerator, dressing table with built-in hair dryer, writing desk, TV, and VCR. There is a completely separate bedroom with its own dressing table with built-in hair dryer, two beds that can convert to a queen-sized bed, and a large walk-in closet.

If you want to be assured of space for future cruises, you can also book "tailored time" in blocks of 100, 200, or 300 days in Adagio, Libretto, Concerto, or Sonata suites, and use the time purchased over a 24-month period. This is a little like owning an apartment, without buying one or paying an annual maintenance charge. It's ideal for those who would like an apartment, but want to keep their main residence ashore, where they can keep their cars and pets and do things they could not do aboard ship. All apartments have kitchens that are enclosed in steel, and are thus self-contained fire zones that automatically seal themselves shut (just in case you burn the toast or something more serious).

There are two suites for the hearing-impaired and two that are designed to be wheelchair accesible.

Dining: There are several restaurants and cafés, including a gourmet market/delicatessen that doubles as a street café (24-hour delivery service to all suites). Naturally, kosher, vegetarian, and diabetic meals will be available.

Portraits is the most upscale restaurant aboard the ship, for contemporary French cuisine. It is located on a low deck, on the starboard side of the ship. Smoking is not permitted.

The Marina Restaurant, for seafood, steak, and rotisserie items, is located on a lower deck at the ship's stern. It features an open "show" kitchen, and smoking is permitted.

Tides restaurant is for casual, self-serve buffet meals in a Mediterranean style, with an Italian flair. It is located on a high deck at the stern, with tables overlooking the stern, and port and starboard sides, as well as some tables indoors. Smoking is permitted only at the outdoor tables.

East is an Asian restaurant and sushi bar. It is located on a high deck, on the starboard side of the ship. The restaurant aims to serve authentic sashimi, sushi, and tempura items. Tables will be fitted with removable turntables for Asian-style (not including Japanese) dining. Smoking is not permitted.

The Outdoor Grill is for casual meals by the pool (weather permitting). Smoking is permitted

Other Comments: Now you can travel the world without leaving home — the ultimate virtual travel reality in what is the first residential community at sea (not including naval submarines). High-wealth owners like to make their own decisions, so democracy afloat could prove to be difficult, as the apartment owners get to choose (sort of) the ship's itineraries. Each apartment buyer will own a piece of the captain. In any event, the ship's occupants will create their own set of social settings, and the chance of romantic adventures afloat within a semi-permanent community could make for a fascinating study in human behavior. The mix of apartment owners is projected to be 40% American and 60% other nationalities.

Hopefully, apartment owners will like their neighbors. But what if not? And you couldn't pretend you're not in, could you? So how about the dress, or undress, code? Well, once you've purchased your apartment, it's up to you. But it could prove to be a fashion model's nightmare — fancy being seen in the same clothes twice in a year! The questions surrounding the occupants and operation of ResidenSea remain countless. And yet, the apartments have sold extremely well. If only they included a garage!

So now to the ship itself! The exterior design suggests apartments at sea, with rows and rows of private balconies extending throughout the ship's superstructure. A marina at the ship's stern folds out to provide a platform for water sports equipment and swimming; the marina is adjacent to an indoor pool.

Inside, the entrance lobby is just a restrained two decks high, but features a domed atrium.

Pleasure facilities include a cigar lounge, show lounge/theatre, a large library, an Internet Café, a Hobby Room, and a chapel.

Business facilities include computers and fax machines, and a conference center, meeting rooms, and secretarial services. Twenty-four-hour services include a concierge staff, housekeeping service, security and medical services, catering, hair and beauty salon, travel agency, and laundry and dry cleaning.

Health, Beauty, and Fitness facilities include the health spa, being operated by Clinique La Prairie, the renowned Swiss private hospital spa, health, and beauty clinic. Whether they will provide the injections of "CLP extract" a concentrated solution of biologically active substances refined at the institute (created from sheep foetuses engendered at the clinic's own farm, laminary flux, liquid nitrogen centrifugation and pasteurization, as in the real clinic) remains to be seen.

Sports facilities include a full-size tennis court, paddle tennis court, volleyball court, golf facilities with simulators, driving and putting ranges, jogging track, and a wrap-around promenade deck outdoors. There is also a retractable marina for water sports.

Children's facilities include a play center (called the Junior Lounge), located on the Sports Deck.

ResidenSea Members have reciprocal privileges in private clubs around the world. The ResidenSea Club itself occupies 51,345 sq ft (4,770 sq m) of fine dining, entertainment, activities, recreation, and shopping space.

The ship's operational plans call for the vessel to be in port for approximately 250 days in each year, and will maintain a continuous circumnavigation of the world, ostensibly in pursuit of fair weather and special international events. Itineraries in 2002, range from 5 to 19 days, including many overnight calls and more than 60 multiple-day calls.

Doctors and medical staff are on call 24 hours a day, and there is a helipad in case medical evacuations become necessary.

So, what's it going to be like? I expect that some of the facilities and accommodation provided will set the benchmark for all other (normal) cruise ships. In other words, this ship will provide the most luxurious setting in which to travel. Style upon style! World in personal oyster stuff! Whether an ambiance can be created year-round will depend entirely on several variables, namely the number of apartment occupants and cruise guests sailing at any one time, and the class and behavior of all aboard, including, of course, the personnel, who are expected to be impeccable, with a mix of European waiters and international hotel, housekeeping, and social staff.

All gratuities are included in your cruise fare, and none are expected (although they are not prohibited).

Weak Points: Apartment occupants (or anyone else) cannot take their pets, or their cars, with them.

Topaz
★★ +

Large Ship:	31,500 tons	Cabins (for one person):	6
Lifestyle:	Standard	Cabins (with private balcony):	0
Cruise Line:	Topaz International Cruises	Cabins (wheelchair accessible):	0
Former Names:	*Olympic, FiestaMarina, Carnivale,*	Cabin Current:	110-volt
	Empress of Britain, Queen Anna Maria	Full-Service Dining Rooms:	3
Builder:	Fairfield Shipbuilding (UK)	Elevators:	4
Original Cost:	£7.5 million	Casino(gaming tables):	Yes
Entered Service:	April 1956/1994	Slot Machines:	Yes
Registry:	Panama	Swimming Pools (outdoors):	2
Length (ft/m):	640.0/195.08	Swimming Pools (indoors):	0
Beam (ft/m):	87.0/26.51	Whirlpools:	1
Draft (ft/m):	29.0/8.84	Fitness Center:	Yes
Propulsion/Propellers:	Steam turbine (22,400kW)/2	Sauna/Steam Room:	No/No
Passenger Decks:	9	Massage:	Yes
Total Crew:	550	Self-Service Launderette:	No (has ironing room)
Passengers (lower beds/all berths):	1,056/1,386	Dedicated Cinema:	No
Pass. Space Ratio (lower beds/all berths):	30.0/22.7	Library:	Yes
Crew/Pass. Ratio (lower beds/all berths):	1.9/2.5	Classification Society:	Lloyd's Register
Navigation Officers:	Greek		
Cabins (total):	528		
Size Range (sq ft/sq m):	100.7–301.3/9.36–28.0		
Cabins (outside view):	228		
Cabins (interior/no view):	300		

OVERALL SCORE: 1,096
(OUT OF A POSSIBLE 2,000 POINTS)

Accommodation: There is a wide range of cabins and many different configurations, although they are assigned in only three categories: superior outside, standard outside, and standard interior. Most of them are small, although many come with rich wood furniture, and all of them have been redecorated at some stage. Many of the cabins have third and fourth berths — good for families with children.

She is an old ship, however, and the cabin bathrooms are small, even in the five suites. The cabins are not assigned until the day of embarkation, so you cannot choose when you book, except for the grade of cabin you pay for, unless you pay a supplement in order to pre-book.

Dining: The dining room is large, crowded, and noisy, although it has been pleasingly redecorated. There are two seatings, assigned upon embarkation. The food is not for gourmets, emphasizing quantity over quality. The 24-hour informal eatery (Yacht Club) is a fine piece of design, but it is a very poor operation.

Other Comments: This solidly built former ocean liner has a large funnel amidships, and the "sheer" of a classic 1950s ship that has had many lives. The ship has also been through a number of refurbishments over the years. All of the lifeboats are of the open-air type and could well be updated. Teak outdoor and glass-enclosed indoor promenade decks encircle the ship.

Inside the ship, the colors are bright and stimulating, and the public rooms have jazzy decor, and it's so nice to see several public rooms with high ceilings. The casino is large for a ship that is catering principally to Europeans. Some delightful original woods and polished brass can be found throughout her public spaces, a large whirlpool has been added, and there is a colorful tiled outdoor deck.

This ship is presently under charter to Thomson Cruises, a British company that provides a good, basic cruise vacation at very attractive prices, in a very casual setting. This could be the right ship for a first cruise, at a very modest price, to some fascinating destinations. Do remember, however, that she is an old lady, and does not have the latest high-tech facilities and features.

Topaz also features Thomson's first foray into all-inclusive pricing, whereby all drinks, including beer and basic wines (and gratuities) are included in the cruise fare. You'll pay extra for drinks from the "premium brands" list, as well as champagne. Shore excursions, laundry/cleaning, purchases from the ship's shops are not included in the all inclusive price. Neither are alcoholic drinks after 2am!

Weak Points: The announcements and constant background music are irritating. Expect some lines (queues in British English) for embarkation, disembarkation, buffets, and shore excursions.

Triton
★★ +

Mid-Size Ship:	14,155 tons	Cabins (for one person):	0
Lifestyle:	Standard	Cabins (with private balcony):	0
Cruise Line:	Royal Olympic Cruises	Cabins (wheelchair accessible):	0
Former Names:	*Cunard Adventurer, Sunward II*	Cabin Current:	110/220-volt
Builder:	Rotterdamsche Dry Dock (Holland)	Full-Service Dining Rooms:	1
Original Cost:	n/a	Elevators:	2
Entered Service:	October 1971/May 1992	Casino(gaming tables):	Yes
Registry:	Greece	Slot Machines:	Yes
Length (ft/m):	491.1/149.70	Swimming Pools (outdoors):	1
Beam (ft/m):	70.5/21.50	Swimming Pools (indoors):	0
Draft (ft/m):	19.22/5.86	Whirlpools:	0
Propulsion/Propellers:	Diesel (19,860kW)/2	Fitness Center:	Yes
Passenger Decks:	7	Sauna/Steam Room:	Yes/No
Total Crew:	265	Massage:	Yes
Passengers (lower beds/all berths):	756/945	Self-Service Launderette:	No
Pass. Space Ratio (lower beds/all berths):	18.7/14.9	Dedicated Cinema/Seats:	Yes/96
Crew/Pass. Ratio (lower beds/all berths):	2.8/3.5	Library:	No
Navigation Officers:	Greek	Classification Society:	Lloyd's Register
Cabins (total):	378		
Size Range (sq ft/sq m):	118.4–131.3/11.0–12.2	**OVERALL SCORE:**	**1,047**
Cabins (outside view):	236	**(OUT OF A POSSIBLE 2,000 POINTS)**	
Cabins (interior/no view):	142		

Accommodation: *Triton* features cabins in eight grades, most of which are small (narrow) and basic. The closet and drawer space (the drawers are rather tiny) is minimal, and cabin soundproofing is very poor. There are 32 cabins (in the two highest grades) with a bathtub/shower, otherwise the cabin bathrooms have very small shower units, and little space for personal toiletry items. However, since the ship operates short cruises, you won't need to take much.

Dining: While the dining room is reasonably attractive and has contemporary colors and ambience, it is also very noisy. There are two seatings for dinner on most nights (open seating for the first night of the cruise), and open seating for breakfast and lunch. The cuisine is continental, which means much use of oils and salt. The choice is reasonable, but the presentation is spotty and inconsistent with limited choice of bread, rolls, and fruits. The Greek dining room staff provides service that can be best described as selectively friendly, and it is hurried. Dining room seating and table assignments for the cruise (except for the first night), are done by the maître d' upon embarkation.

Casual breakfast and lunch (with limited choices) can also be taken outside on the deck adjacent to the swimming pool, or in the main lounge when the weather is inclement.

Other Comments: *Triton*, together with a sister ship, was originally built for Overseas National Airways but was then purchased by Cunard Line when ONA went bankrupt. She was later purchased by Royal Olympic Cruises for informal cruises.

The ship has a reasonably handsome profile, a deep clipper bow, and twin funnels. She has been fairly well maintained, although she is now showing her age. There is a wrap-around painted-steel outdoor promenade deck of sorts, as well as a decent amount of open deck space for sunbathing, and a small "kidney-shaped" swimming pool, although space is extremely tight when the ship is full, which is most of the time. Much of the open space outdoors is covered by canvas awnings, much appreciated by many passengers as a shelter from the intensity of the summer sun.

Inside, a good general layout and passenger flow make it easy to find your way around in a short time. There is a good choice of public rooms, most of which are decorated in cheerful, warm colors. However, the decor and artwork is eclectic, some of it left over from the ship's former days with Norwegian Cruise Line and Cunard. The deck names are Greek. There is a good nightclub with forward observation views. The show lounge is a single level room, with sight lines obstructed by six pillars. Also the floor does not slope; there are better sight lines from the rear.

There is no library other than a token gesture of two unkempt bookcases with a few old paperbacks.

On one of the upper decks is an outdoor dance floor with a bar named Jailhouse Rock — good for lively nights under the summer stars, but not used early and late in the season when the weather is cooler.

Triton is a decent, down-home ship for short cruises around the Greek islands and Mediterranean. These destination-intensive itineraries, generally running from April to November, are excellent for those who want to see many places in a short time (there are two ports of call on most days), but be warned: they are extremely busy, particularly on the first day (there are no days at sea). In other words, these three-and four-night cruises are not for relaxing, but are for sightseeing.

The dress code is very casual throughout, with no formal nights, so leave your coats and ties and long dresses at home. Suggested gratuities at $8 per person per day are pooled among the crew on the last day.

Forget about such things as chocolates on your pillow, and the other niceties associated with other cruise lines. This one will get you around the Greek islands in low budget surroundings, with food that is more quantity than quality, with mostly indifferent service. After all, with two sets of passengers each week it is hard to provide friendly contact.

Weak Points: This really is a high-density ship with crowded public areas. Expect lines for buffets and shore excursions. There are too many announcements for tours, in many languages, when in ports of call. The nature of the Greek island cruises means that crew contracts are seasonal, and, at the end of the season (end of October/beginning of November) most crew are tired and clearly want to go home — and it shows — to the detriment of the product.

Trollfjord

Mid-Size Ship:	15,000 tons	Cabins (with private balcony):	21
Lifestyle:	Standard	Cabins (wheelchair accessible):	4
Cruise Line:	Norwegian Coastal Voyages (TVDS)	Cabin Current:	220-volt
Former Names:	-	Full-Service Dining Rooms:	1
Builder:	Fosen Werft (Norway)	Elevators:	3
Original Cost:	$15 million	Casino(gaming tables):	No
Entered Service:	March 2002	Slot Machines:	No
Registry:	Norway	Swimming Pools (outdoors):	1
Length (ft/m):	445.3/135.75	Swimming Pools (indoors):	0
Beam (ft/m):	70.5/21.5	Whirlpools:	2
Draft (ft/m):	15.7/4.8	Fitness Center:	Yes
Propulsion/Propellers:	Diesel/2	Sauna/Steam Room:	Yes/No
Passenger Decks:	8	Massage:	Yes
Total Crew:	150	Self-Service Launderette:	Yes
Passengers (lower beds/all berths):	674/900	Dedicated Cinema:	No
Pass. Space Ratio (lower beds/all berths):	22.2/16.6	Library:	Yes
Crew/Pass. Ratio (lower beds/all berths):	4.4/6.0	Classification Society:	Det Norske Veritas
Navigation Officers:	Norwegian		
Cabins (total):	308		

OVERALL SCORE: NOT YET RATED

Size Range (sq ft/sq m):	118.4–349.8/11.0 –32.5
Cabins (outside view):	222
Cabins (interior/no view):	86
Cabins (for one person):	8

Note that this ship had not entered service when this book was completed.

Accommodation: The range of accommodation consists of suites, mini-suites, deluxe and standard outside-view and interior (no view) cabins. Note that all cabins have a 220-volt outlet, so take adapters and converters if you need to.

Dining: The main dining room (no smoking allowed) has 340 seats, and dining is in two seatings. Tables are assigned when you embark. Three meals each day are included in the cruise fare. Breakfast and lunch (featuring the famous Norwegian "cold table") are self-serve buffet-style meals, while dinner is a sit-down affair, with three courses.There is also an additional bistro-style dining spot for lighter fare.

Other Comments: The Norwegian Coastal Voyage is a service that was started in 1863 (it is jointly operated by two companies: Ofotens og Vesteraalen Dampskibsselskab (OVDS) and Troms Fylkes Dampskibsselskab (TFDS). The complete journey, of 1,250 nautical miles, takes in 34 ports of call in a 12-day roundtrip voyage between Bergen and Kirkenes (on the border with Russia), above the Arctic Circle, where a special "Crossing the Arctic Circle" ceremony welcomes newcomers. The journey can also be done in a one-way voyage that takes seven days northbound or six days southbound. The ships carry passengers as well as mail and other cargo.

From mid-May to late June north of the Arctic Circle you may be able to peek at the midnight sun. You may also see the Northern Lights or Aurora Borealis, mostly visible during winter months when the atmospheric conditions are right. You will certainly experience the daily life of the hardy Norwegians. Approximately 60% of the passengers will be Norwegian/Scandinavian/European, while the rest will be a mix of North American and other nationalities. Although the passenger bed capacity is quoted, note that many additional passengers may be on board as day passengers, sailing between two coastal ports, since the ship functions as a seagoing bus for the coastal commuters. As for the weather, the west coast of Norway is warmed by the Gulf Stream, and temperatures will be similar to those found in New England.

Trollfjord has a slightly different exterior design than sister ship *Finnmarken*, and this includes an upright funnel cluster, not unlike that found on the ships of Costa Cruises. In addition to the maximum 674 passengers that can be accommodated in beds/berths, the ship carries a number of day passengers, which can swell the ship's total to 900. In addition, there is room for 50 cars.

Inside, the decor is decidedly contemporary, with much use of Norwegian wood, stone, and art. There are also large expanses of glass to bring light into the ship, including glass elevators on the side of the ship. Art by Norway's renowned Kaare Espolin-Johnson decorates the ship's library. There are conference facilities for up to 150 persons, as well as several small meeting rooms. A laundry room with washing machines, tumble dryers, and irons is provided, which proves useful for those for whom the cruise is only part of a more extensive vacation.

This cruise experience is best suited to adult couples, single travelers, and families with children who want to experience the natural beauty of the coast of Norway and its fascinating and coastal towns. It's ideal for anyone who doesn't need entertainment or parlor games, but who wants to relax and unwind; who enjoys being close to nature, and is probably a bit of an adventurer. It's also a good way to meet new people and make new friends among the fascinating mix of passengers from different countries. The dress code is casual and comfortable — layered clothing is best. The currency is the Norwegian krone.

Weak Points: Drink prices are extremely high, the same as ashore in Norway.

Universe Explorer
★★★

Mid-Size Ship:	22,162 tons	Cabins (interior/no view):	80
Lifestyle:	Standard	Cabins (for one person):	5
Cruise Line:	World Explorer Cruises	Cabins (with private balcony):	0
Former Names:	*Enchanted Seas, Queen of*	Cabins (wheelchair accessible):	0
	Bermuda, Canada Star, Liberté,	Cabin Current:	110-volt
	Island Sun, Volendam,	Full-Service Dining Rooms:	1
	Monarch Sun, Brasil	Elevators:	3
Builder:	Ingalls Shipbuilding (US)	Casino(gaming tables):	No
Original Cost:	$26 million	Slot Machines:	No
Entered Service:	September 1958/November 1990	Swimming Pools (outdoors):	1
Registry:	Panama	Swimming Pools (indoors):	0
Length (ft/m):	617.4/188.2	Whirlpools:	0
Beam (ft/m):	84.3/25.7	Fitness Center:	Yes
Draft (ft/m):	27.2/8.3	Sauna/Steam Room:	No/No
Propulsion/Propellers:	Steam turbine (19,000kW)/2	Massage:	Yes
Passenger Decks:	8	Self-Service Launderette:	No
Total Crew:	365	Dedicated Cinema/Seats:	Yes/167
Passengers (lower beds/all berths):	737/846	Library:	Yes
Pass. Space Ratio (lower beds/all berths):	30.0/24.7	Classification Society: American Bureau of Shipping	
Crew/Pass. Ratio (lower beds/all berths):	2.0/2.3		
Navigation Officers:	European/Scandinavian		
Cabins (total):	371	**OVERALL SCORE:**	**1,159**
Size Range (sq ft/sq m):	103.3–292.7/9.6–27.2	**(OUT OF A POSSIBLE 2,000 POINTS)**	
Cabins (outside view):	291		

Accommodation: The cabins, of which there are many different sizes and configurations, are priced in eight grades. They are mostly of quite generous proportions for a ship of this size, with heavy duty furniture and fittings, and a good amount of closet and drawer space. The bathrooms are, however, quite old fashioned, and a bit utilitarian, as are their fittings, although they are still quite practical.

Dining: The Hamilton Dining Room is located on the starboard side of the ship. It is charming and warm and has large windows that provide plenty of light and a nice ambience. There are two seatings. The menu choice is somewhat limited and basic, but service is attentive and comes with a smile, even if it is without finesse. There is only a moderate selection of bread, rolls, cheeses (mostly processed), and fruits.

Other Comments: This ship has a classic 1960s traditional oceanliner profile that is quite low and rather squat, with an all white hull and a royal blue funnel. She has undergone extensive refurbishment and has nice teak decks. There are spacious promenade areas for walking outdoors, as well as plenty of sunbathing space.

Inside, the public rooms are moderately spacious and well appointed. Almost all have high ceilings, pleasing, but dated decor and colors that do not jar the senses. The Mid-Ocean Lounge (the ship's show lounge) is adequate, but it cannot compare with those on larger, more modern ships, and the sight lines are poor. World Explorer Cruises has turned the casino into a large library and computer center.

This ship will provide you with a reasonably enjoyable cruise experience in comfortable surroundings reminiscent of old-world style. Cruise itineraries are relaxed and not as hurried as you would find with some other cruise lines operating in the same areas.

Where the ship scores well is in her exceptional program of lecturers and educational features for passengers who want to learn more about their cruise surroundings. There is also no loud music. Instead, there are classical concerts and dance music after dinner. If you don't want the glitz of larger ships, and you don't need large scale production shows for entertainment, this may well be a good choice.

Universe Explorer offers a mixture of 14-night Alaska cruises in the summer, with cruises to the Western Caribbean and Yucatan Peninsula in the winter, as well as an annual around-the-world cruise under the "Semester at Sea" banner for schoolchildren.

Weak Points: Being an older ship, there are no cabins with private balconies.

Valtur Prima
★★★

Mid-Size Ship:	15,000 tons	Cabins (for one person):	0
Lifestyle:	Standard	Cabins (with private balcony):	8
Cruise Line:	Valtur Tourism	Cabins (wheelchair accessible):	0
Former Names:	*Italia Prima, Italia I, Surriento,*	Cabin Current:	110/220-volt
	Fridtjof Nansen, Volker,	Full-Service Dining Rooms:	1
	Volkerfreundschaft, Stockholm	Elevators:	2
Builder:	Varco Chiapella (Italy)	Casino(gaming tables):	Yes
Original Cost:	$150 million (reconstruction)	Slot Machines:	Yes
Entered Service:	February 1948/May 1994	Swimming Pools (outdoors):	1
Registry:	Italy	Swimming Pools (indoors):	0
Length (ft/m):	525.2/160.10	Whirlpools:	1
Beam (ft/m):	68.8/21.04	Fitness Center:	Yes
Draft (ft/m):	24.6/7.5	Sauna/Steam Room:	Yes/Yes (Turkish Bath)
Propulsion/Propellers:	Diesel (14,500kW)/2	Massage:	Yes
Passenger Decks:	7	Self-Service Launderette:	No
Total Crew:	280	Dedicated Cinema:	No
Passengers (lower beds/all berths):	520/600	Library:	Yes
Pass. Space Ratio (lower beds/all berths):	28.8/25.0	Classification Society:	Registro Navale Italiano
Crew/Pass. Ratio (lower beds/all berths):	1.8/2.1		
Navigation Officers:	Italian		
Cabins (total):	260		
Size Range (sq ft/sq m):	129.2–376.7/12.0–35.0	**OVERALL SCORE:**	**1,102**
Cabins (outside view):	221	(OUT OF A POSSIBLE 2,000 POINTS)	
Cabins (interior/no view):	39		

Accommodation: There are six grades of accommodation. All of the cabins have a minibar, TV, and personal safe. Each cabin has a large Italian fresco above the bed, although the ceilings are very plain. All cabin bathrooms feature a bathtub, as well as a good amount of indented space for one's personal toiletries. Single occupancy of cabins incurs a 50% surcharge.

Eight suites each feature a small private balcony, although the sight lines are not good. Each suite has a separate lounge/living area, with table and chairs; the bedroom features twin beds that convert to a queen-size bed. The bathrooms in the suites and junior suites feature Jacuzzi bathtubs with showers.

You should note that the cabins on Sole Deck forward have lifeboat obstructed views, and those on Portofino Deck may, late at night, be subject to noise from the public rooms located on the deck above.

Dining: The single, large dining room is set low down in the center of the vessel. It is quite attractive, and has tables for two, four, six, and eight. There is one seating for dinner. As you might expect, Italian cuisine is featured, with decent pasta dishes. Standard house wines are typically included for lunch and dinner. There is a limited selection of breads, fruits, and cheeses, too much use of canned fruits, and a poor cabin service menu.

For casual meals, there is also a self-serve buffet for breakfast and lunch in Il Giardino, although the selection is really quite basic.

Other Comments: This ex-ocean liner made history when, as *Stockholm*, she rammed and sank the *Andrea Doria* in July 1956. She was reconstructed as a cruise ship in 1994 using her old, riveted hull; then with a completely new superstructure, and a somewhat ungainly profile, she took on a new lease of life as *Italia Prima*. In 1999, the ship was renamed *Valtur Prima*. The ship's maneuverability at slow speeds remains quite poor, and her stability is questionable, despite the addition of a large sponson stern apron.

There is a wrap-around teak promenade deck outdoors, and heavy, real wood "steamer" deck chairs are provided, although there are no cushioned pads for them. The sunbathing space outdoors is limited, and definitely not sufficient when the ship is full. *Valtur Prima* really is a high-density ship.

Her interiors are decorated in contemporary Italian style. There is a good selection of public rooms to choose from, including a 400-seat auditorium for meetings, and a number of smart boutiques. The contemporary decor is quite upbeat and fresh and is complemented by a good selection of colorful artwork. The Afrodite Spa also sports a Turkish bath, which is quite an unusual feature aboard cruise vessels today, as is the small chapel.

Although the ship has attractive interiors, your cruise experience will depend on what you spend on the food and the service staff, whose attitude and communication skills lack any kind of finesse. The ship is operated by Valtur Tourism (Italy), and cruises are sold through a number of outlets in several countries in Europe. She sails from Havana, Cuba, on 7-night cruises within the Caribbean (a Cuban visa is necessary). Golfers can choose from several golf packages, including play at one course in Havana, Cuba. The currency used aboard ship is the US dollar.

Weak Points: The "you are here" deck plans are not easy to read. The small swimming pool is really only a "dip" pool. There is no observation lounge with forward-facing views over the ship's bows. The hallways on the accommodation decks are quite narrow. Sight lines in the single-level show lounge are poor. In the cinema, the seats are not staggered and so the sight lines are poor. The steep gangway is designed for European, not Caribbean, ports.

Van Gogh
★★★

Mid-Size Ship:	15,402 tons	Cabins (with private balcony):		0
Lifestyle:	Standard	Cabins (wheelchair accessible):		0
Cruise Line:	Nouvelles Frontières	Cabin Current:		220-volt
Former Names:	*Club 1, Odessa Sky, Gruziya*	Refrigerator:		No
Builder:	Wartsila (Finland)	Full-Service Dining Rooms:		1
Original Cost:	$25 million	Elevators:		1
Entered Service:	June 1975/May 1999	Casino(gaming tables):		Yes
Registry:	St. Vincent & the Grenadines	Slot Machines:		Yes
Length (ft/m):	512.6/156.27	Swimming Pools (outdoors):		1
Beam (ft/m):	72.3/22.05	Swimming Pools (indoors):		0
Draft (ft/m):	19.4/5.92	Whirlpools:		0
Propulsion/Propellers:	Diesel (13,430kW)/2	Fitness Center:		Yes
Passenger Decks:	7	Sauna/Steam Room:		Yes/No
Total Crew:	250	Massage:		Yes
Passengers (lower beds/all berths):	506/795	Self-Service Launderette:		Yes
Pass. Space Ratio (lower beds/all berths):	30.4/19.3	Dedicated Cinema/Seats:		Yes/140
Crew/Pass. Ratio (lower beds/all berths):	2.0/3.1	Library:		Yes
Navigation Officers:	Ukrainian	Classification Society:		Det Norske Veritas
Cabins (total):	253			
Size Range (sq ft/sq m):	90.0–492.0/8.4–45.7			
Cabins (outside view):	148	**OVERALL SCORE:**		**1,111**
Cabins (interior/no view):	105	(OUT OF A POSSIBLE 2,000 POINTS)		
Cabins (for one person):	0			

Accommodation: Four suites on Boat Deck provide the largest accommodation, with sweeping forward views. These provide very spacious accommodation for the size of the ship, have full-sized bathtubs, good closet and drawer space and reasonably decent artwork. Another six suites are almost as large but don't have the fine forward-facing views.

All other cabins are very small and sparingly furnished, but quite adequate for short cruises. Most cabins have very little drawer space, particularly those that accommodate three or four persons, and the insulation between cabins is thin.

One cabin has been "adapted" for the physically challenged, although it would be difficult to get even a junior collapsible wheelchair through the cabin door.

Dining: There is one (non-smoking) dining room, which is rather plain, but has nicely decorated soft furnishings, and is moderately comfortable. There are tables for four, six, or eight (no tables for two), assigned for the duration of the cruise. Dinner is in two seatings, typically at 7pm and 9pm.

Casual, self-serve breakfast and lunch buffets are available on the port side of the swimming pool, although the choice is quite limited.

Other Comments: One of a series of five sister ships (although today their interiors vary greatly), this is a fairly smart looking vessel with a squarish 1970s profile and smart, square funnel (with the Nouvelles Frontières logo emblazoned in red). She has a good outdoor promenade area. A past refit added a cinema, new nightclub, foyer, bar, and more cabins, while a 1999 refit refreshed her interior decor. She now provides comfortable, unpretentious cruises for French-speaking passengers, under charter to Nouvelle Frontières.

Inside, most of the public rooms (which are few) are located on one horizontal deck, There is a Captain's Bar (neatly decorated in maritime paraphernalia, brass portholes, etc.), a casino with tables and slot machines (tokens only), and boutique. Other facilities include the circular Sky Bar atop the ship, behind which, and outside, is a topless sunbathing area. There are also a small cinema and discotheque.

The ship sails in the Caribbean (including Cuba), the Baltic (Northern capitals), and Mediterranean. The language on board is French, and the currency on board is the French franc.

Weak Points: Communication with many of the staff can prove frustrating even though the staff is reasonably friendly. There are no cushioned pads for the deck lounge chairs. The gangway is narrow.

Veendam
★★★★

Large Ship:	55,451 tons	Cabins (for one person):	0
Lifestyle:	Premium	Cabins (with private balcony):	150
Cruise Line:	Holland America Line	Cabins (wheelchair accessible):	6
Former Names:	-	Cabin Current:	110/220-volt
Builder:	Fincantieri (Italy)	Full-Service Dining Rooms:	1
Original Cost:	$215 million	Elevators:	12
Entered Service:	May 1996	Casino(gaming tables):	Yes
Registry:	Bahamas	Slot Machines:	Yes
Length (ft/m):	719.3/219.3	Swimming Pools (outdoors):	1
Beam (ft/m):	101.0/30.8	Swimming Pools (indoors):	1 (magrodome)
Draft (ft/m):	24.6/7.5	Whirlpools:	2
Propulsion/Propellers:	Diesel-electric	Fitness Center:	Yes
	(34,560kW)/2	Sauna/Steam Room:	Yes/No
Passenger Decks:	10	Massage:	Yes
Total Crew:	561	Self-Service Launderette:	Yes
Passengers (lower beds/all berths):	1,266/1,627	Dedicated Cinema/Seats:	Yes/249
Pass. Space Ratio (lower beds/all berths):	43.8/34.0	Library:	Yes
Crew/Pass. Ratio (lower beds/all berths):	2.2/2.9	Classification Society:	Lloyd's Register
Navigation Officers:	British/Dutch		
Cabins (total):	633		
Size Range (sq ft/sq m):	186.2–1,124.8/17.3–104.5	**OVERALL SCORE:**	**1,533**
Cabins (outside view):	502	**(OUT OF A POSSIBLE 2,000 POINTS)**	
Cabins (interior/no view):	0		

Accommodation: The accommodation ranges from small interior (no view) cabins to a large Penthouse Suite, in 17 categories. All cabin TVs feature CNN and TNT.

The 148 interior (no view) and 336 outside (with a view) standard cabins feature twin beds that convert to a queen-size bed, and there is a separate living space with sofa and coffee table. However, although the drawer space is generally good, the closet space is actually very tight, particularly for long cruises (although more than adequate for a 7-night cruise). The bathrooms are tiled and compact but practical, and they come with a good range of personal toiletry amenities. Bathrobes are also provided, as are hair dryers. The bathrooms are quite well laid out, but the bathtubs are small units better described as shower tubs. Some cabins have interconnecting doors — good for families with children or older couples with their own butler/maid or nurse (*Maasdam, Ryndam, Veendam* only, not *Statendam*).

On the Navigation Deck, 28 suites have accommodation for up to four. These suites also feature en-suite dining as an alternative to the dining room, for private, reclusive meals. These are very spacious, tastefully decorated and well laid out, and feature a separate living room, bedroom with two lower beds (convertible to a king-size bed), a good size living area, dressing room, plenty of closet and drawer space, marble bathroom with Whirlpool tub.

The largest accommodation of all is a Penthouse Suite; there is only one, located on the starboard side of the Navigation Deck. It features a king-size bed, walk-in closet with superb drawer space, oversize whirlpool bath and separate shower enclosure, living room, dressing room, large private balcony, pantry, minibar/refrigerator, a guest toilet and floor-to-ceiling windows.

Dining: The two-level Rotterdam Dining Room, located at the stern, is quite dramatic. It features a music balcony, panoramic views on three sides and grand staircase, which few seem to use. Seating is open during breakfast and lunch, while there are two seatings for dinner. The waiter stations in the dining room are very noisy for anyone seated adjacent to them. Fine Rosenthal china and cutlery are featured.

Unfortunately, Holland America Line food isn't as nice as the china it's placed on. It may be adequate for most passengers who are not used to better food, but it does not match the standard found aboard other ships in the premium segment of the industry. While USDA beef is of a good quality, fowl tends to be battery-tough, and most fish is overcooked. What are also definitely not luxurious are the endless packets of sugar and packets (instead of glass jars) of breakfast jam, marmalade and honey, and poor quality teas. While these may be suitable for a family diner, they do not belong aboard a ship that claims to have "award-winning cuisine." Dessert and pastry items are of good quality (specifically for American tastes), although there is much use of canned fruits and jellies. Forget the selection of "international" cheeses, however, as most of it didn't come from anywhere other than the US.

As an alternative to the more formal dining room, the Lido Buffet is open for casual dinners on all except for the last night of each cruise, in an open-seating arrangement. Tables are set with crisp linens, flatware and stemware. A set menu is featured, and this includes a choice of four entrees.

The Lido Buffet also serves casual breakfasts and lunches, offering a wide choice and dual-line access, one side for smokers, the other for non-smokers. There are several commercial low-calorie salad dressings. The choice of cheeses (and accompanying crackers) is very poor. The beverage station is also a letdown. In addition, a poolside grill provides basic American hamburgers and hot dogs.

Other Comments: This is one of a series of four almost identical ships in the same series, including *Maasdam, Statendam,* and *Ryndam.* The exterior styling is rather angular (some would say boxy — the funnel certainly is), although it is softened and balanced somewhat by the fact that the hull is painted black. There is a full wrap-around teakwood promenade deck outdoors. The deck lounge chairs are wood, and come with comfortable cushioned pads.

Inside, an asymmetrical layout breaks up the interiors and helps to reduce bottlenecks and congestion. The decor is softer, more sophisticated, and far less eclectic than in sister ship *Statendam*, while the interiors of the latest in the series seem to improve further on the theme. In general, however, a restrained approach to interior styling is taken using a mixture of contemporary materials combined with traditional woods and ceramics. There is, fortunately, little "glitz" anywhere.

What is outstanding is the array of artworks throughout the ship (costing about $2 million), assembled and nicely displayed to represent the fine Dutch heritage of Holland America Line and to present a balance between standard itineraries and onboard creature comforts. Also noticeable are the fine flower arrangements throughout the public areas and foyers, which brighten up the dullish decor.

Atop the ship, with forward facing views that wrap around the sides is the Crow's Nest Lounge. By day it makes a fine observation lounge (particularly in Alaska), while by night it turns into a nightclub with extremely variable lighting.

The ship's three-decks-high atrium foyer is quite stunning, although it leaves little room in front of the purser's office, and its sculpted centerpiece makes it look a bit crowded. A hydraulic magrodome (glass) roof covers the reasonably sized swimming pool/whirlpools and central Lido area (whose focal point is a large dolphin sculpture), so that this can be used in either fine or inclement weather.

The two-decks-high show lounge is basically well designed, but the ceiling is low and the sight lines from the balcony level are poor. The ship has a large, and quite lovely, and relaxing reference library. This company keeps its ships very clean and tidy, and there is good passenger flow throughout.

Veendam is a well-built ship, and has fairly decent interior fit and finish. Holland America Line is constantly fine-tuning its performance as a cruise operator and its regular passengers (almost all of whom are North American) find the company's ships very comfortable and well run. The company continues its strong maritime traditions, although the present food and service components still let the rest of the cruise experience down. Note: The line does not add an automatic 15% gratuity for beverage purchases, unlike many other cruise lines.

Holland America Line's many repeat passengers always seem to enjoy the fact that social dancing is always on the menu. The company also offers complimentary cappuccino and espresso coffees, and free ice cream during certain hours of the day aboard its ships, as well as hot hors d'oeuvres in all bars, something other major lines seem to have dropped, or charge extra for.

In the final analysis, however, the score for this ship (and her sisters *Maasdam, Ryndam, Statendam*) ends up just a disappointing tad under what it could be if the food and food service staff were better (more professional training might help). This ship is now deployed year-round in the Caribbean, where her rather dark interior decor contrasts with the strong sunlight of the sub-tropical region.

Weak Points: Standing in line for embarkation, disembarkation, shore tenders, and self-serve buffet meals is an inevitable aspect of cruising aboard all large ships. The service staff is Indonesian, and, although quite charming (for the most part) communication with them often proves frustrating for many passengers. Service is spotty and inconsistent. Note that passengers are forced to eat at the Lido Café on days when the dining room is closed for lunch (this is typically once or twice per cruise, depending on ship and itinerary). The single escalator is virtually useless. There is no bell push outside the suites. The charge to use the washing machines and dryers in the self-service launderette is really petty and irritating, particularly for the occupants of suites, as they pay high prices for their cruises. Room service is poor.

Vesteralen
★★ +

Small Ship:	6,261 tons	Cabins (with private balcony):	0
Lifestyle:	Standard	Cabins (wheelchair accessible):	1
Cruise Line:	Norwegian Coastal Voyages	Cabin Current:	220-volt
	(OVDS)	Full-Service Dining Rooms:	1
Former Names:	-	Elevators:	1
Builder:	Kaarboe (Norway)	Casino(gaming tables):	No
Original Cost:	n/a	Slot Machines:	No
Entered Service:	1983	Swimming Pools (outdoors):	0
Registry:	Norway	Swimming Pools (indoors):	0
Length (ft/m):	356.2/108.6	Whirlpools:	0
Beam (ft/m):	54.1/16.5	Fitness Center:	No
Draft (ft/m):	15.0/4.5	Sauna/Steam Room:	No/No
Total Crew:	55	Massage:	No
Passengers (lower beds/all berths):	304/318	Self-Service Launderette:	No
Pass. Space Ratio (lower beds/all berths):	20.5/19.6	Dedicated Cinema:	No
Crew/Pass. Ratio (lower beds/all berths):	5.5/5.7	Library:	No
Navigation Officers:	Norwegian	Classification Society:	Det Norske Veritas
Cabins (total):	152		
Size Range (sq ft/sq m):	n/a		
Cabins (outside view):	97	**OVERALL SCORE:**	**1,093**
Cabins (interior/no view):	55	(OUT OF A POSSIBLE 2,000 POINTS)	
Cabins (for one person):	0		

Accommodation: The cabins are cozy, which translates to very, very small; the bathrooms, likewise, are tiny, although they do have a shower and toilet. All cabins have a 220-volt outlet, so take adapters and converters if you need to.

Dining: There is one dining room (no smoking allowed), and tables are assigned when you embark. Three meals each day are included in the cruise fare: breakfast and lunch (featuring the famous Norwegian "cold table") are self-serve buffet-style meals, while dinner is a sit-down affair, with three courses. Additionally, there is a cafeteria, which is open 24 hours, where snacks and light meals can be purchased.

Other Comments: The Norwegian Coastal Voyage is a service that was started in 1863. It is jointly operated by two companies: Ofotens og Vesteraalen Dampskibsselskab (OVDS) and Troms Fylkes Dampskibsselskab (TFDS). The complete journey of 1,250 nautical miles takes in 34 ports of call in a 12-day roundtrip voyage between Bergen and Kirkenes (on the border with Russia), above the Arctic Circle, where a special "Crossing the Arctic Circle" ceremony welcomes newcomers. The journey can also be done in a one way voyage that takes seven days northbound or six days southbound. The ships carry passengers as well as mail and other cargo.

From mid-May to late June north of the Arctic Circle you may be able to peek at the midnight sun. You may also see the Northern Lights or Aurora Borealis, mostly visible during winter months when the atmospheric conditions are right. You will certainly experience the daily life of the hardy Norwegians. Approximately 60% of the passengers will be Norwegian/Scandinavian/European, while the rest will be a mix of North American and other nationalities. Although the passenger bed capacity is quoted, note that many additional passengers may be on board as day passengers, sailing between two coastal ports, since the ship functions as a seagoing bus for the coastal commuters. As for the weather, the west coast of Norway is warmed by the Gulf Stream, and temperatures will be similar to those found in New England.

This cruise experience is best suited to adult couples, single travelers, and families with children who want to experience the natural beauty of the coast of Norway and its fascinating coastal towns. It's ideal for anyone who doesn't need entertainment or parlor games, but who wants to relax and unwind; who enjoys being close to nature, and is probably a bit of an adventurer. It's also a good way to meet new people and make new friends among the fascinating mix of passengers from different countries. The dress code is casual and comfortable — layered clothing is best. The currency is the Norwegian krone.

The rates vary by season, cabin location, and whether the ship is of the "new generation" (*Kong Harald, Nordkapp, Nordlys, Nordnorge, Polarlys, Richard With*), the "mid-generation" (*Narvik, Midnatsol, Vesteralen*), or the "traditional" (*Harald Jarl, Lofoten*) type ships. Senior citizens (those age 67 and over) qualify for a special discount.

Vesteralen operates Norwegian coast and fjords cruises year-round: 7-day (northbound) voyage between Bergen and Kirkenes, Norway; a 6-day (southbound) voyage between Kirkenes and Bergen, Norway; or a combined 12-day roundtrip voyage. This ship also carries up to 40 cars.

Weak Points: The ship does not have stabilizers, so you should expect some movement when the weather is inclement. Drink prices are extremely high—the same as ashore in Norway. The cabins are small, and the bathrooms are really tiny. Although not needed during the winter, there is little outdoor deck space considering the number of passengers carried.

Courtesy Norwegian Coastal Voyage Inc.

Victoria
★★★ +

Mid-Size Ship:	27,670 tons	Cabins (for one person):	14
Lifestyle:	Premium	Cabins (with private balcony):	0
Cruise Line:	P&O Cruises	Cabins (wheelchair accessible):	10
Former Names:	*Sea Princess, Kungsholm*	Cabin Current:	220-volt
Builder:	John Brown & Co. (UK)	Full-Service Dining Rooms:	1
Original Cost:	$22 million	Elevators:	4
Entered Service:	April 1966/February 1979	Casino(gaming tables):	Yes
Registry:	Great Britain	Slot Machines:	Yes
Length (ft/m):	660.2/201.23	Swimming Pools (outdoors):	2
Beam (ft/m):	87.1/26.57	Swimming Pools (indoors):	1
Draft (ft/m):	28.0/8.56	Whirlpools:	1
Propulsion/Propellers:	Diesel (18,800kW)/2	Fitness Center:	Yes
Passenger Decks:	8	Sauna/Steam Room:	Yes/No
Total Crew:	417	Massage:	Yes
Passengers (lower beds/all berths):	744/778	Self-Service Launderette:	Yes
Pass. Space Ratio (lower beds/all berths):	38.8/37.1	Dedicated Cinema/Seats:	Yes/289
Crew/Pass. Ratio (lower beds/all berths):	1.7/1.8	Library:	Yes
Navigation Officers:	British	Classification Society:	Lloyd's Register
Cabins (total):	379		
Size Range (sq ft/sq m):	137.7–466.0/12.8–43.3	**OVERALL SCORE:**	**1,323**
Cabins (outside view):	291		
Cabins (interior/no view):	88	**(OUT OF A POSSIBLE 2,000 POINTS)**	

Accommodation: There is a wide range of cabins to choose from, including six suites. Most cabins have a decent amount of space, and many of them feature fine wood-paneled walls. Most have been nicely refurbished over the years. In the latest refurbishment, all new soft furnishings were changed, TVs replaced, and bathrooms revamped.

Most cabins have excellent closet and drawer space, and fine wood-paneled walls. Generous-sized bathrooms have solid fixtures and storage space for toiletries. Some cabins have upper and lower berths. The bathroom towels are small, however.

Dining: The tiered European-style dining room is fairly elegant, with old-world traditions and charm, including a display of Eighteenth century Chinese porcelain, and some fine etched glass panels with nautical themes). There are tables for two, four, six, and eight (more tables for two were added during the 1997 refurbishment). There are two seatings, and smoking is not allowed at any time.

If you like meat and two-veg fare, and you're into a curry a day, you'll be fine here, but if you like anything more adventurous, forget it. The food and selection is tailored for British High Street tastes, with decent enough service from the Goanese staff. The buffets are very basic—disappointing in both display and food quality, as is the selection of breads and fruits. The wine list, alas, is very limited. A statement in the onboard cruise folder states that P&O Cruises does not knowingly purchase genetically modified foods.

The casual outdoor Lido Buffet was remodeled in the last refit, and now is less congested owing to a redesign of the area, more temperature controlled display space and better serving lines. However, the plastic chairs at the Lido buffet should at least have cushions.

Other Comments: This is a solidly built ex-ocean liner (originally built for the now-defunct Swedish America Line) that has flowing, rounded lines and a well-balanced profile, with that "sheer" that makes her look like a "real" ship. She has been nicely refurbished and well maintained (and arguably improved) since becoming a P&O Cruises ship in the late 1970s. The open deck and sunbathing space is good.

Inside, there are numerous spacious public rooms trimmed with fine woods, and with fine furnishings and fabrics. One nice feature is an indoor (sea-water) swimming pool, together with the usual associated saunas and gymnasium.

There is a decent variety of entertainment aboard the ships of P&O Cruises, as well as a good program of special themed cruises. Antiques, The Archers, art appreciation, classical music, comedy, baseball, gardening, jazz, motoring, popular fiction, Scottish dance, and sequence dancing were among the themes in 1999. Check with your travel agent to see what is available at the time you want to take your cruise.

This ship will provide an enjoyable, very traditional and conservative British cruise experience. Despite a $9 million refurbishment in late 1997 she still looks a little worn in places, with her 30 years afloat. Port taxes and insurance are included for British passengers.

Note that *Victoria* has been sold and will be taken out of the P&O Cruises fleet in November 2002.

Viking Serenade
★★★ +

Large Ship:	40,132 tons	Cabins (for one person):	0
Lifestyle:	Standard	Cabins (with private balcony):	5
Cruise Line:	Royal Caribbean International	Cabins (wheelchair accessible):	4
Former Names:	*Stardancer, Scandinavia*	Cabin Current:	110-volt
Builder:	Dubigeon-Normandie (France)	Full-Service Dining Rooms:	2
Original Cost:	$100 million	Elevators:	5
Entered Service:	October 1982/June 1991	Casino(gaming tables):	Yes
Registry:	Liberia	Slot Machines:	Yes
Length (ft/m):	623.0/189.89	Swimming Pools (outdoors):	1 (magrodome)
Beam (ft/m):	88.6/27.01	Swimming Pools (indoors):	0
Draft (ft/m):	23.9/7.30	Whirlpools:	0
Propulsion/Propellers:	Diesel (19,800kW)/2	Fitness Center:	Yes
Passenger Decks:	9	Sauna/Steam Room:	Yes/No
Total Crew:	612	Massage:	Yes
Passengers (lower beds/all berths):	1,512/1,863	Self-Service Launderette:	No
Pass. Space Ratio (lower beds/all berths):	26.5/21.5	Dedicated Cinema:	No
Crew/Pass. Ratio (lower beds/all berths):	2.4/3.0	Library:	No
Navigation Officers:	International	Classification Society:	Det Norske Veritas
Cabins (total):	756		
Size Range (sq ft/sq m):	143.1–398.2/13.3–37.0	**OVERALL SCORE:**	**1,320**
Cabins (outside view):	478	(OUT OF A POSSIBLE 2,000 POINTS)	
Cabins (interior/no view):	278		

Accommodation: The tiny, seriously dimensionally-challenged cabins are reasonably well appointed and have a moderate amount of closet space for short cruises. There are, however, far too many interior (no view) cabins. The drawer and other storage space is extremely limited, so take only a minimum of clothing. The cabin bathrooms are also tiny, so you should expect to dance with the shower curtain, particularly if you have a larger than average sized body.

Dining: There are two dining rooms (Aïda and Magic Flute). They are moderately attractive and well laid out (romantic passengers should note that there are no tables for two, however, and the ceilings are low). There are two seatings. The menu descriptions make the food sound better than it is, which is consistently average, mostly disappointing, and without much taste. However, a decent selection of light meals is provided, and vegetarian selections are also available. The selection of breads, rolls, fruit, and cheese is quite poor, and should be upgraded. Special orders, tableside carving, and flambeau items are not offered.

Other Comments: This ship, which has been extensively reconstructed from what was originally a passenger-car ferry, has a fairly decent amount of open deck and sunbathing space, and there is a magrodome-covered pool for use in inclement weather. The ship underwent a $75 million reconstruction in 1991, when Royal Caribbean International (then Royal Caribbean Cruise Line) took the ship over. She has remained the ugly duckling of the fleet ever since—not at all handsome. Operated from Los Angeles to Mexico for several years, she became known as something of a party ship, particularly for her weekend cruises. However, a new development has meant that the ship is now operated under the UK's First Choice banner, in a joint venture between First Choice and Royal Caribbean International.

Inside the ship, there is a decent enough array of public rooms and facilities, including a conference center and a Viking Crown Lounge that is cantilevered around the funnel, offering excellent ocean views. The public rooms have contemporary decor, tasteful colors and decent quality, though tired, furnishings. Good health spa facilities include a large gymnasium with some of the latest high-tech muscle-pumping equipment. The service is reasonably attentive from the largely Caribbean-basin crew. This ship should provide a decent enough one-week cruise experience for families with children with well-programmed activities in upbeat surroundings.

In November 2001, the ship will be renamed *Island Escape* and transferred to Island, a new cruise line, the result of a joint venture between First Choice Holidays and Royal Caribbean International and will operate 7-day Caribbean cruises in the winter and 7-day Mediterranean cruises in the summer. Onboard concessionaires will be UK brands Costa Coffee, Holmes Places (health & beauty spa), and Oddbins (wine merchants). The ship will commence cruising in March 2002.

Weak Points: Standing in line for embarkation, disembarkation, shore tenders, and self-serve buffet meals is an inevitable aspect of cruising aboard all large ships (those carrying more than 1,000 passengers). The ceilings in many public areas and hallways are low (the ship was originally constructed as a cruise-ferry). There are too many loud, irritating announcements and background music almost everywhere. Passenger participation events tend to be pretty amateurish. The cabins are tiny and the ship always feels crowded.

FAMILY REUNIONS

A cruise can provide the ideal place for a family reunion (either with or without children). Here are some tips to take into account when planning one.

→ Let your travel agent do the planning and make all the arrangements (ask for a group discount if the total in your group adds up to more than 15). Make sure that together you choose the right cruise line, for the right reasons.

→ Book 12 months in advance if possible, so that you can arrange cabins close to each other (remember to arrange for everyone to be at the same dinner seating, if the ship operates two seatings).

→ If anyone in the group has a birthday or anniversary, tell your travel agent to arrange a special cake (most cruise lines do not charge extra for this). Special private parties can also be arranged, although there will be an additional cost. If the group is not too large, you may be able to request to dine at the captain's table.

→ Arrange shore excursions as a group (in some ports, private arrangements may prove unbeatable).

→ Finally, get everything in writing (particularly cabin assignments and locations).

Vision of the Seas
★★★★

Large Ship:	78,491 tons	Cabins (for one person):	0
Lifestyle:	Standard	Cabins (with private balcony):	229
Cruise Line:	Royal Caribbean International	Cabins (wheelchair accessible):	14
Former Names:	-	Cabin Current:	110/220-volt
Builder:	Chantiers de l'Atlantique (France)	Full-Service Dining Rooms:	1
Original Cost:	$275 million	Elevators:	9
Entered Service:	May 1998	Casino(gaming tables):	Yes
Registry:	Liberia	Slot Machines:	Yes
Length (ft/m):	915.3/279.0	Swimming Pools (outdoors):	1
Beam (ft/m):	105.6/32.2	Swimming Pools (indoors):	1 (inside/outside)
Draft (ft/m):	24.9/7.6	Whirlpools:	6
Propulsion/Propellers:	Diesel-electric (50,400kW)2	Fitness Center:	Yes
Passenger Decks:	11	Sauna/Steam Room:	Yes/Yes
Total Crew:	660	Massage:	Yes
Passengers (lower beds/all berths):	2,000/2,435	Self-Service Launderette:	No
Pass. Space Ratio (lower beds/all berths):	39.2/32.2	Dedicated Cinema:	No
Crew/Pass. Ratio (lower beds/all berths):	3.0/3.6	Library:	Yes
Navigation Officers:	International	Classification Society:	Det Norske Veritas
Cabins (total):	1,000		
Size Range (sq ft/sq m):	148.5–1,059.2/13.8–98.4	**OVERALL SCORE:**	**1,519**
Cabins (outside view):	593		
Cabins (interior/no view):	407	**(OUT OF A POSSIBLE 2,000 POINTS)**	

Accommodation: The accommodation ranges from large suites, each of which has its own private balcony, to standard interior and outside cabins. All are reasonably tastefully furnished and come equipped with the necessary amenities for a one-week cruise. The company provides colorful soft furnishings that make one's home away from home look like the inside of a modern Scandinavian hotel: minimalist, yet colorful.

Choose a "C" grade suite if you want spacious accommodation that includes a separate (curtained-off) sleeping area, a good-sized outside balcony (with part, not full, partition), lounge with sofa, two chairs and coffee table, three closets, plenty of drawer and storage space, TV, and VCR. The bathroom is large and features a full-size bathtub, integral shower, and two washbasins/two toiletries cabinets.

All of the other standard interior and outside cabins have colorful soft furnishings, twin beds that convert to queen-size, a sofa, coffee table, and a vanity desk unit with drawers and cupboards. A color TV sits on swivel base so that it can be seen from both bed and sitting area (sofa). The bathroom is very small, and has a toilet, and shower cubicle and sink, but there is no cabinet for personal toiletries.

Dining: The dining room is set on two levels with large ocean-view picture windows on two sides (rectangular windows on the upper level, large circular windows on the lower level) and a large connecting stairway, and it is non-smoking. There are two seatings. RCI's standard of dining room food and service has always been consistent in presentation, although the food generally has little taste, the result of controlling food costs as well as the use of many mixes and pre-prepared items. While most passengers seem to enjoy it, it has become very standard, unmemorable fare, and really needs more attention and creativity. Vegetarian dishes are available for lunch and dinner. The wine list features only standard wines— none of any decent vintage.

The Windjammer Café is the ship's informal dining spot, and offers more choice for those who enjoy casual meals. The setting is contemporary, with attractive colors and decor, and large ocean-view windows that provide plenty of light. However, only the basics are available at the beverage stations.

Other Comments: This striking ship, sixth in the Vision-class of vessels, shares design features that make all Royal Caribbean International ships identifiable, including a Viking Crown Lounge (which is also the ship's disco). Aboard this ship (and sister ship *Rhapsody of the Seas*, which debuted in 1998) the Viking Crown Lounge is located just forward of the center of the ship, with the funnel located well aft—a departure from all other RCI ships to date. The ship's stern is beautifully rounded. There is a reasonable amount of open-air walking space, although this can become cluttered with deck lounge chairs (which do not have cushioned pads).

Inside, the ship provides the latest incarnation of RCI's interpretation of a floating contemporary hotel, and presents the nicest mix of colors and decor of any of the Vision-class ships, with lots of warm beige and pink tones (particularly in the expansive atrium).

The artwork (which cost $6 million) is plentiful, colorful, and very creative. Much of it seems to have been inspired by that aboard *Galaxy*, which belongs to sister company, Celebrity Cruises. Most noticeable is the extensive use of glass. Two beautiful glass sculptures stand out: one in the atrium at the entrance to a Champagne Bar, and one on the upper level of the Viking Crown Lounge. There are plenty of public rooms, bars, and lounges to play in, as well as a large, well-lit casino.

The spa, with its solarium and indoor/outdoor dome-covered pool, Inca and Mayan-theme decor, sauna/steam rooms and gymnasium, provides a haven for the health-conscious fitness buff (although there is a pizza bar forward of the pool area); there is a lovely "Mayan Serpent" sculpture in the solarium.

The Viking Crown Lounge is a multi-level nightspot. The music can be loud and overbearing, however, and so can cigarette smoke around the bar. It is one of few places where smokers can light up. Perhaps the best atmosphere can be found in the nautical-themed Schooner Bar. The Library features an excellent array of hardback books, as well as a neat wooden sculpture of something that looks like the Tin Man from *The Wizard of Oz*.

The entertainment throughout the ship is upbeat (in fact, it is difficult to get away from music and noise), and is typical of the kind of resort hotel found ashore in Las Vegas. There is even background music in all corridors and elevators, and constant music outdoors on the pool deck. If you want a quiet relaxing vacation, this is the wrong ship. If you enjoy big city life, with a fine array of sounds and entertainment around you, this could be just right.

Weak Points: Standing in line for embarkation, disembarkation, shore tenders, and self-serve buffet meals is an inevitable aspect of cruising aboard all large ships. The staff is only mildly accommodating, and only a small percentage say hello when passing you in the corridors (this includes the officers). In other words, the hospitality factor is below average. The elevators repeatedly remind you verbally whether you are "going up" or "going down." The illuminated picture displays of decks are good.

Vistamar
★★★ +

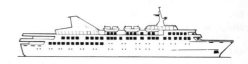

Small Ship:	7,478 tons	Cabins (for one person):	5
Lifestyle:	Standard	Cabins (with private balcony):	11
Cruise Line:	Plantours & Partners	Cabins (wheelchair accessible):	0
Former Names:	-	Cabin Current:	220-volt
Builder:	Union Navale de Levante (Spain)	Full-Service Dining Rooms:	1
Original Cost:	$45 million	Elevators:	1
Entered Service:	September 1989	Casino(gaming tables):	No
Registry:	Panama	Slot Machines:	No
Length (ft/m):	396.9/121.00	Swimming Pools (outdoors):	1
Beam (ft/m):	55.1/16.82	Swimming Pools (indoors):	0
Draft (ft/m):	14.9/4.55	Whirlpools:	0
Propulsion/Propellers:	Diesel (3,900kW)/2	Fitness Center:	Yes
Passenger Decks:	6	Sauna/Steam Room:	Yes/No
Total Crew:	110	Massage:	Yes
Passengers (lower beds/all berths):	299/320	Self-Service Launderette:	No
Pass. Space Ratio (lower beds/all berths):	25.3/23.3	Dedicated Cinema:	No
Crew/Pass. Ratio (lower beds/all berths):	2.7/2.9	Library:	Yes
Navigation Officers:	Spanish	Classification Society:	Det Norske Veritas
Cabins (total):	152		
Size Range (sq ft/sq m):	129.1–150.6/12.0–14.0	**OVERALL SCORE:**	**1,262**
Cabins (outside view):	126	**(OUT OF A POSSIBLE 2,000 POINTS)**	
Cabins (interior/no view):	26		

Accommodation: The passenger accommodation areas are located forward, while public rooms are positioned aft, which means there is a minimal amount of noise in the cabins. There are 11 cabin grades, but in just two different sizes: (a) suites with private (covered) balcony and queen-size bed; (b) outside-view or interior (no view) cabins for two, three, or four persons, all with fixed, wide single beds. All of the cabins are reasonably comfortable, although the bathrooms are *extremely* small and tight (there is a considerable "lip" to step over to access the bathroom), and both closet and drawer space is limited. Cabins have twin beds with wooden headboard, small vanity/writing desk, color television, climate control, telephone, and hair dryer. Most of the cabinetry is made with a wood finish.

There are 11 suites, each of which has a small, narrow, private, covered balcony outdoors. The suites are: Alboran, Algarve, Almeria, Armador, Cadiz, Cordoba, Granada, Huelva, Jaen, Malaga, Seville—all of which are regions of Andalucia. They also have a more spacious bathroom, with a large bathtub and integral shower. The living areas also large, and comes with a sofa, coffee table, vanity/writing desk, and a larger color television. Note that Armador is the owner's suite, and comes with a circular bathtub with integral shower, set against large picture windows (wonderful for the Arctic and Antarctic cruises that this company typically operates in the appropriate season).

No matter what accommodation grade or location you choose, all passengers get personal amenities that include soap, shampoo, body lotion, bath/shower gel, and shoeshine mitt. Accommodation hallways are provided either in hospital green, powder blue, or hot pink.

Dining: The Andalucia Restaurant is quite warm and inviting, with contemporary colors and decor, and large picture windows, although the six pillars detract from the otherwise attractive room. The room's focal point is a model of a sailing vessel with an emerald green hull (about the same color as the fabrics on the dining room chairs. There is one seating for all passengers (so meals are leisurely), with assigned tables for four, six or eight (there are no tables for two). Window-side tables are for six, and all chairs have armrests.

The food is reasonably adequate, and quite sound, and dinners typically come with a choice of three entrees (plus a vegetarian selection). The selection of cooked green vegetables, breads, cheeses, and fruits is limited, and the overall cuisine really is of quite a low standard. I find it quite similar to that found aboard other ships operated for German-speaking passengers, such as *Berlin*, and *Delphin*—which have two seatings for dinner. The service is adequate, no more, as is the wine list. *Note:* Sekt (sweet sparkling wine) is provided for breakfast, while white and red table wines are provided for lunch and dinner.

Other Comments: *Vistamar* has a moderately smart, reasonably contemporary, but rather squat small ship profile. The ship, which has an ice-hardened hull, also carries several inflatable rubber landing crafts for close up landings during certain itineraries that include the Arctic and Antarctic.

There is an open bridge policy, so you can join the captain and other navigation officers at almost any time. There is a good open observation deck at the forward-most part of the ship—atop the navigation bridge, although the other open deck and sunbathing space is a little limited—particularly on the aft open deck around the small outdoor pool. This is really only a "dip" pool, although it has a large splash surround.

As stated, the interior layout has all the public rooms located aft, in a "cake-layer" stacking, with a single, central staircase that takes up most of the space in an atrium lobby that spans three decks (with a glass elevator that is shaped like half a cable car). Features include wood trimmed interior decor, which is jazzy, attractive and warm, although the mirrored metallic ceilings are somewhat irritating.

A four-deck-high atrium with a "sky dome" has a glass-walled elevator and a wrap-around staircase, and is the focal point of the ship's interior. The library has comfortable high wingback chairs, but there are not very many books. There is also a card room, and board games are available.

The ship's main lounge, Don Fernando, is named after Senor Don Fernando Abril Martorell, the president of the Union Navale de Levante shipyard that constructed *Vistamar* in 444 days (perhaps if more time had been taken, the ship would have been constructed better!). Additionally, there is a rather jazzy nightclub/disco, with acres of glass, set around the base of the funnel, with a long bar, and dance floor, for the late night set.

This ship has been under charter to Plantours & Partners, specifically for German-speaking passengers, since 1991, and the product is aimed at the inexpensive standard market. The dress code is ultra-casual (no tuxedos, no ties required). While the ship is not in the best condition, and maintenance is spotty, there is a warm, friendly ambience, which attracts many, many repeat passengers.

There is an abundance of greenery throughout the ship, which helps to make it feel warm, more comfortable, and less clinical. The ship is quite small, so passengers can enjoy interesting destination-intensive cruises, with many port calls that larger ships simply cannot get into. Tipping is recommended at DM10-12 per person, per day (the onboard currency is the Euro).

Weak Points: The tiny "dip" swimming pool is virtually useless. There is a distinct odor of diesel fuel at the upper level of the lobby, where there is also a complete lack of air-conditioning. The ship's hotel operation is rather sloppy and needs streamlining. There is no walking track or wrap-around promenade deck outdoors. The fit, finish and maintenance of this ship are all quite poor, and well below the standard expected. The sight lines in the single-level show lounge are very poor, and there is a lack of good stage lighting.

Volendam
★★★★

Large Ship:	63,000 tons	Cabins (for one person):	0
Lifestyle:	Premium	Cabins (with private balcony):	197
Cruise Line:	Holland America Line	Cabins (wheelchair accessible):	23
Former Names:	-	Cabin Current:	110-volt
Builder:	Fincantieri (Italy)	Full-Service Dining Rooms:	1 main
Original Cost:	$300 million		(plus 1 alternative)
Entered Service:	November 1999	Elevators:	12
Registry:	The Netherlands	Casino(gaming tables):	Yes
Length (ft/m):	781.0/238.00	Slot Machines:	Yes
Beam (ft/m):	105.8/32.25	Swimming Pools (outdoors):	2
Draft (ft/m):	25.5/7.80	Swimming Pools (indoors):	1 (magrodome cover)
Propulsion/Propellers:	Diesel-electric	Whirlpools:	2
	(37,500kW)/2	Fitness Center:	Yes
Passenger Decks:	10	Sauna/Steam Room:	Yes/Yes
Total Crew:	561	Massage:	Yes
Passengers (lower beds/all berths):	1,440/1,850	Self-Service Launderette:	Yes (2)
Pass. Space Ratio (lower beds/all berths):	43.7/34.0	Dedicated Cinema/Seats:	Yes/205
Crew/Pass. Ratio (lower beds/all berths):	2.5/2.5	Library:	Yes
Navigation Officers:	Dutch	Classification Society:	Lloyd's Register
Cabins (total):	720		
Size Range (sq ft/sq m):	113.0–946.0/10.5–87.8	**OVERALL SCORE:**	**1,548**
Cabins (outside view):	581	(OUT OF A POSSIBLE 2,000 POINTS)	
Cabins (interior/no view):	139		

Accommodation: The range of accommodation is similar to that found aboard the similarly sized *Rotterdam*, and comprises 17 different categories. There is one penthouse suite, and 28 suites, with the rest of the accommodation comprised of a mix of outside-view and interior (no view) cabins, and many more balcony cabins (called "mini-suites") aboard this ship than aboard the slightly smaller *Statendam*-class ships (*Maasdam, Ryndam, Statendam, Veendam*).

All standard interior and outside cabins are tastefully furnished and have twin beds that convert to a queen-size bed. Space is very narrow for walking between beds and vanity unit. There is a decent amount of closet and drawer space, although this may prove tight for the longer voyages featured. All cabin TVs feature CNN and TNT. The bathrooms, which are fully tiled, are disappointingly small (particularly for long cruises) and have small shower tubs, utilitarian personal toiletries cupboards, and exposed under-sink plumbing. There is no detailing to distinguish them from bathrooms aboard the *Statendam*-class ships.

There are 28 full Verandah Suites (Navigation Deck), and one Penthouse Suite. All suite occupants share a private concierge lounge (the concierge handles such things as special dining arrangements, shore excursions, private parties, and special requests). Strangely there are no butlers for these suites, as aboard ships with similar facilities. Each Verandah Suite has a separate bedroom, and dressing and living areas. Suite passengers get personal stationery, complimentary laundry and ironing, cocktail hour hors d'oeuvres and other goodies, as well as priority embarkation and disembarkation. The concierge lounge, with its latticework teak detailing and private library is accessible only by private key-card.

For the ultimate in accommodation and living space aboard this ship, choose the Penthouse Suite. It has a separate steward's entrance, and features a large bedroom with king-size bed, separate living room (with baby grand piano) and a dining room, dressing room, walk-in closet, butler's pantry, and private balcony (the balcony is no larger than the balcony of any of the other suites). Other facilities include an audio-visual center with TV and VCR, wet bar with refrigerator, large bathroom with Jacuzzi bathtub, separate toilet with bidet, and a guest bathroom (with toilet and washbasin).

With the exception of the Penthouse Suite, located forward on the starboard side, the bathrooms in the other suites and "mini-suites" are a little disappointing—neither as spacious nor as opulent as one would expect. All outside-view suite and cabin bathrooms feature a bathtub/shower while interior (no view) cabins have a shower only. Also, note that the 23 cabins for the physically challenged feature a roll-in shower enclosure for wheelchair users (none have bathtubs, no mater what the category).

Dining: There is one main dining room, and one alternative dining spot, open for dinner only. The 747-seat Rotterdam Dining Room is quite a grand room, and is spread over two decks, with ocean views on three sides with a grand staircase to connect the upper and lower levels. There are two seatings for dinner, open seating for breakfast and lunch, and both smoking and non-smoking sections are provided. Fine Rosenthal china and cutlery are featured (although there are no fish knives).

Unfortunately, Holland America Line food isn't as nice as the china it's placed on. It may be adequate for most passengers who are not used to better food, but it does not match the standard found aboard other ships in the premium segment of the industry. While USDA beef is of a good quality, fowl tends to be battery-tough, and most fish is overcooked and has the consistency of a baseball bat. What are also definitely not luxurious are the endless packets of sugar, and packets (instead of glass jars) of breakfast jam, marmalade, and honey, and poor quality teas. While these may be suitable for a family diner, they do not belong aboard a ship that claims to have "award-winning cuisine." Dessert and pastry items are of good quality (specifically for American tastes), although there is much use of canned fruits and jellies. Forget the selection of "international" cheeses, however, as most of it didn't come from anywhere other than the US, a country known for its processed, highly colored slices, and not fine cheese-making.

The alternative, casual dress Marco Polo Restaurant seats 88, and there is no charge, although reservations are required. It has been created in the style of a California artists' bistro and serves Italian cuisine from a set menu together with nightly specials. Passengers thus can have more choice and an occasional change of venue. Anyone booking suite-grade accommodation gets priority reservations.

In addition, there is the Lido Buffet, a self-serve café that has proved popular aboard all Holland America Line ships for casual breakfasts and luncheons. There is also an outdoor grill serving hamburgers, hot dogs, and other grilled fast-food items. The Lido Buffet is also open for casual dinners on each night except for the last one, in an open-seating arrangement. Tables are set with crisp linens, flatware, and stemware. A set menu is featured, and this includes a choice of four entrees.

Other Comments: This is the third ship of the same name for Holland America Line and the first of the evolving generation after the Statendam-class ships. Her sister ship is *Zaandam*. The ship's name is derived from the fishing village of the same name, and is located north of Amsterdam, Holland. Her hull is dark blue, in keeping with all Holland America Line ships. Although similar in size to the line's flagship *Rotterdam*, this ship has a single funnel, not unlike that found aboard the company's much smaller *Noordam*.

Having been built to approximately the same size as the company's newest Rotterdam, the same layout and public rooms have been incorporated into her interiors. This carries on the same flow and comfortable feeling so passengers will immediately feel at home aboard almost any ship in the Holland America Line fleet.

Volendam features three principal passenger stairways, which is so much better than two stairways, particularly with regard to safety, accessibility, and passenger flow. There is a magrodome covered pool on the Lido Deck between the mast and the ship's funnel. The health spa facilities are quite extensive, and include gymnasium, separate saunas and steam rooms for men and women, and more treatment rooms, each with shower and toilet. Practice tennis courts can be found outdoors, as well as the traditional shuffleboard courts, and a jogging track, as well as a full wrap-around teak promenade deck.

The principal interior design theme is flowers, from the seventhth to the twentyfirst centuries. The interior focal point is a huge crystal sculpture called "Caleido," located in the three-decks-high atrium, by one of Italy's leading contemporary glass artists, Luciano Vistosi.

In the Casino Bar (also known as the ship's sports bar) the theme is Hollywood. Here you'll see a collection of costumes, props, photos, and posters of movies and the stars who made them.

At the Lido Deck swimming pool, leaping dolphins are the focal point, but they are of a different design from that seen aboard the *Statendam*-class ships. The pool is one deck higher than the S-class ships, offering convenient direct access between the aft and midships pools unavailable aboard the S-class ships.

This ship is perhaps best for older passengers who seek conventional, pleasant surroundings and food. Holland America Line provides complimentary cappuccino and espresso coffees, and free ice cream during certain hours of the day aboard its ships, as well as hot hors d'oeuvres in all bars, a nicety other major lines seem to have dropped, or charge extra for. Also, the line does not add an automatic 15% for beverage purchases, as many others do.

Weak Points: Standing in line for embarkation, disembarkation, shore tenders, and self-serve buffet meals is an inevitable aspect of cruising aboard all large ships. The entertainment is still a weak point. Communication with staff is not easy. Room service is poor. The charge to use the washing machines and dryers in the self-service launderette is really petty and irritating, particularly for the occupants of suites, since they pay high prices for their cruises.

Voyager of the Seas
★★★★

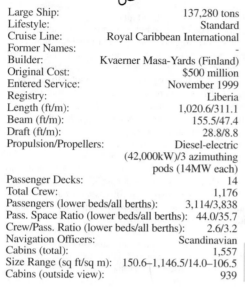

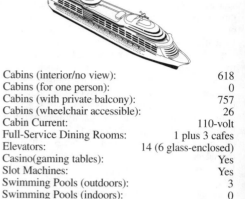

Large Ship:	137,280 tons	Cabins (interior/no view):	618
Lifestyle:	Standard	Cabins (for one person):	0
Cruise Line:	Royal Caribbean International	Cabins (with private balcony):	757
Former Names:	-	Cabins (wheelchair accessible):	26
Builder:	Kvaerner Masa-Yards (Finland)	Cabin Current:	110-volt
Original Cost:	$500 million	Full-Service Dining Rooms:	1 plus 3 cafes
Entered Service:	November 1999	Elevators:	14 (6 glass-enclosed)
Registry:	Liberia	Casino(gaming tables):	Yes
Length (ft/m):	1,020.6/311.1	Slot Machines:	Yes
Beam (ft/m):	155.5/47.4	Swimming Pools (outdoors):	3
Draft (ft/m):	28.8/8.8	Swimming Pools (indoors):	0
Propulsion/Propellers:	Diesel-electric	Whirlpools:	6
	(42,000kW)/3 azimuthing	Fitness Center:	Yes
	pods (14MW each)	Sauna/Steam Room:	Yes/Yes
Passenger Decks:	14	Massage:	Yes
Total Crew:	1,176	Self-Service Launderette:	No
Passengers (lower beds/all berths):	3,114/3,838	Dedicated Cinema:	No
Pass. Space Ratio (lower beds/all berths):	44.0/35.7	Library:	Yes
Crew/Pass. Ratio (lower beds/all berths):	2.6/3.2	Classification Society:	Det Norske Veritas
Navigation Officers:	Scandinavian		
Cabins (total):	1,557		
Size Range (sq ft/sq m):	150.6–1,146.5/14.0–106.5		
Cabins (outside view):	939		

OVERALL SCORE: **1,545**

(OUT OF A POSSIBLE 2,000 POINTS)

Accommodation: There is a wide range of 22 cabin categories from which to choose, in four major groupings: Premium ocean-view suites and cabins, interior (atrium-view) cabins, ocean-view cabins, and interior (no view) cabins. Note that many cabins are of a similar size—good for incentives and large groups, and 300 have interconnecting doors—good for families.

A total of 138 interior (no view) cabins have bay windows that look into an interior horizontal shopping atrium—a cruise industry first when the ship debuted. This atrium copies the horizontal atrium aboard the Baltic passenger ferries *Silja Serenade* (1990) and *Silja Symphony* (1991). Regardless of what cabin grade you choose, all except for the Royal Suite and Owner's Suite feature twin beds that convert to a queen-size unit, TV, radio, telephone, personal safe, vanity unit, hair dryer, and private bathroom.

The largest accommodation includes luxuriously appointed penthouse suites, whose occupants have their own exclusive, and private, concierge club. The grandest is the Royal Suite, which is positioned on the port side of the ship. It features a king-size bed in a separate, large bedroom, a living room with an additional queen-size sofa bed, baby grand piano (no pianist is included, however), refrigerator/wet bar, dining table, entertainment center, and large bathroom.

The slightly smaller, but still highly desirable Owner's Suites (there are 10 of them, all located in the center of the ship, on both port and starboard sides) and the Royal Family suites (four of them) are all similarly outfitted. The four Royal Family suites, which have two bedrooms (including one with third/fourth upper Pullman berths) are located at the stern of the ship and have magnificent views over the ship's wash.

All cabins feature a private bathroom, as well as interactive TV and pay-per-view movies, including an X-rated channel, where you must enter a "pin" code to prevent children from watching. Some grades feature a refrigerator/minibar, although there is no space left in the refrigerator, because it is stocked with "take-and-pay" items. Note: if you take anything from the minibar/refrigerator on the day of embarkation in Miami, Florida sales tax will be added to your bill.

Dining: The main dining room is extremely large and is set on three levels. Each has an operatic name and theme: Carmen, La Bohème, and Magic Flute, all of which are connected by a dramatic three-deck high staircase. All three levels feature the same menus and food. The dining room is totally non-smoking and there are two seatings.

The cuisine in the main dining room is similar in nature to that offered aboard the company's present ships. In other words, we are talking about mass banquet catering that offers standard fare comparable to that found in American family-style restaurants ashore. Such items as caviar (once a standard menu item) incur a hefty extra charge.

Alternative dining options for casual and informal meals at all hours (according to company releases) include:

Cafe Promenade, for continental breakfast, all-day pizzas, and specialty coffees (unfortunately provided in paper cups).

Windjammer Café, for casual buffet-style breakfast, lunch, and light dinner (except for the last night of the cruise).

Island Grill (this is actually a section inside the Windjammer Café), for casual dinner (no reservations necessary) featuring a grill and open kitchen.

Portofino, an upscale (non-smoking) Euro-Italian restaurant for dinner only. Reservations are required, and a $6 gratuity per person is charged. The food is of a higher quality, and with better presentation than the food in the dining room, although the restaurant is not large enough for all passengers to try even once during a cruise.

Johnny Rockets, a retro 1950s, 24-hour eatery that features hamburgers, malt shakes, and jukebox hits, with both indoor and outdoor seating, and all-singing, all-dancing waitresses that'll knock your socks off, if you can stand the noise.

Sprinkles, for round-the-clock ice cream and yogurt.

Other Comments: *Voyager of the Seas* is a stunning, large, immensely impressive floating resort (one of five such ships, the others being *Explorer of the Seas* and *Adventure of the Seas*, which debuted in 2000 and 2001 respectively, and two more to follow). The exterior design is not unlike an enlarged version of the company's Vision-class ships. She is the largest cruise vessel in the world in terms of tonnage measurement (although, to keep things in perspective, she is not quite as long as the *SS Norway*).

The ship's propulsion is derived from three pod units, powered by electric motors (two azimuthing, and one fixed at the centerline) instead of conventional rudders and propellers, in the latest configuration of high-tech propulsion systems.

With her large proportions, she provides more facilities and options, and caters to more passengers than any other Royal Caribbean International ship has in the past, and yet the ship manages to have a healthy passenger space ratio (the amount of space per passenger). Being a "non-Panamax" ship, she is simply too large to go through the Panama Canal, thus limiting her itineraries almost exclusively to the Caribbean (where few islands can accept her), or for use as a floating island resort. Spend the first few hours wandering exploring all the many facilities and public spaces aboard this vessel, and it will be time well spent.

Although she is a large ship, even the accommodation hallways are attractive, with artwork cabinets and wavy corridors to break the monotony.

At certain times, passengers are allowed to stand right at the bow of the ship at the observation point, perhaps with arms spread in an "eagle-like" position, just like the stars in the film *Titanic*. What a photo opportunity! However, for the best shots, as in the film, you'll need to hire a helicopter! Those seeking a view of the navigation bridge can see what's happening from a special spot above the bridge.

Embarkation and disembarkation take place through two separate access points from a new specially built passenger terminal in Miami. These are designed to minimize the inevitable lines at the start and end of the cruise (that's over 1,500 people for each access point). Once inside the ship, you'll need good walking shoes, particularly when you need to go from one end to the other—it really is quite a long way.

The four-decks-high Royal Promenade is the main interior focal point of the ship, and a good place to meet someone. It is 393.7 ft (120 m) long and has two internal lobbies (atria) that rise to as many as 11 decks high, one at each end. There are 16 elevators in four banks of four.

The entrance to one of the three levels of the main restaurant, together with shops and entertainment locations, are spun off from this winding street, while interior "with-view" cabins (with rather useless bay windows) look into it from above.

The ship also houses a traditional English pub ("Pig 'n' Whistle), the Champagne Bar, Scoreboard (a sports bar), Spinners (a revolving gaming arcade), and a captain's balcony, arched across the promenade. There are also several shops: jewelry shop, gift shop, liquor shop, and a logo souvenir shop, as well as a bright red telephone kiosk that houses an ATM cash machine. Altogether, it's a nice place to see and be seen, and street performers complete the scene.

The Royal Promenade is supposedly designed in the image of London's fashionable Burlington Arcade, although I doubt very much that the designers have actually been there; but unlike the real thing, there is not a red brick in sight! Actually, by far the best view of the whole promenade is from one of the 138 premium-price cabins that look into it, or from a captain's bridge that crosses above it.

The Casino Royale is naturally large. Casino gaming includes blackjack, Caribbean stud poker, craps, and roulette, featuring the world's largest interactive roulette wheel.

For the more sporting, youthful passengers, there are activities galore, including a rock-climbing wall that's 32.8 ft high (10 m), with five separate climbing tracks. It is located outdoors at the aft end of the funnel. There is a 30-minute instruction period before anyone is allowed to climb, and this is done in pairs. It's free, and all safety gear is included.

Other sports facilities include a roller-skating track, a dive-and-snorkel shop, a full-size basketball court, and a 9-hole, par-26 golf course. A 15,000 sq ft (1,393.5 sq m) health spa includes a large aerobics room, fitness center, treatment rooms, men's and women's sauna/steam rooms, while another 10,000 sq ft (929 sq m) of space is devoted to a relaxing Solarium.

The 1,350-seat show lounge is five decks high. It features hydraulic pit and stage areas, and is decorated in the style of the La Scala opera house in Milan. A second show lounge (Studio B – a regulation-size ice-skating rink that features real, not fake, ice) comes complete with arena seating for up to 900, and the latest in broadcast facilities. A number of slim pillars obstruct the clear-view arena stage sight lines, however. An Ice Follies show is presented by a professional ice-skating show team each cruise.

If ice-skating in the Caribbean doesn't appeal to you, perhaps you'd like the stunning two-deck library. It's the first aboard any ship, and it's open 24 hours a day. A whopping $12 million has been spent on permanent artwork. Drinking places include a neat Aquarium Bar, complete with 50 tons of glass and water in four large aquariums (whose combined value is over $1 million). Other drinking places include the small and intimate Champagne Bar, Crown & Anchor Pub, and a Connoisseur Club, for cigars and cognacs. Lovers of jazz might appreciate High Notes, an intimate room for cool music, or the Schooner Bar piano lounge. Golfers might enjoy the 19th Hole — a golf bar.

There is a large TV studio, located adjacent to rooms that can be used for trade show exhibit space. Lovers can tie the knot in a wedding chapel in the sky, called the Skylight Chapel, located on the upper level of the Viking Crown Lounge.

Families with children have not been forgotten, and the children's facilities are extensive. "Aquanauts" is for 3-5 year olds. "Explorers" is for 6-8 year olds. "Voyagers" is for 9-12 year olds. "Optix" is a dedicated area for teenagers, including a daytime club (with computers), soda bar, disk jockey, and dance floor. "Challenger's Arcade" features an array of the latest video games. "Virtual Submarine" is a virtual reality underwater center for all ages. "Computer Lab" features 14 computer stations loaded with fun and games. "Paint and Clay" is an arts-and-crafts center for younger children. Adjacent to these indoor areas is "Adventure Beach," an area for all the family to enjoy: it includes swimming pools, a water slide, and game areas outdoors.

Royal Caribbean International has, since its inception, always been an innovator in the cruise industry and will probably remain so with this new vessel, the first of three such ships to be placed into service by the company. *Voyager of the Seas* operates 7-night western Caribbean cruises year-round from Miami.

In terms of sheer size, this ship dwarfs every other ship in the cruise industry, but in terms of personal service, it tends towards the reverse. The company tries hard to provide a good standard of highly programmed service from its hotel staff. This is impersonal city life at sea in a floating leisure center, and a superb, well-designed alternative to a land-based resort, which is what the company wanted to achieve. Perhaps if you dare to go outside, you might even be able to see the sea — now there's a novelty! Remember to take lots of extra cash — you'll need them to pay for all the additional cost items.

This really is a large, Las Vegas-style American floating resort city for the lively of heart and fleet of foot. Good advice is to arrange to meet somewhere along the Royal Promenade.

Weak Points: Standing in line for embarkation, disembarkation, shore tenders, and self-serve buffet meals is an inevitable aspect of cruising aboard all large ships. Check-in, embarkation (better if you are a non-US resident and stay at an RCI-booked hotel, as you will complete all formalities there and simply walk on board to your cabin) and disembarkation (non-US citizens can be held up for over an hour by slow US Immigration processing in the terminal after leaving the ship). Suites and cabins with private balcony have Bolidt floors (a substance that looks like rubberized sand) instead of wood. If you have a cabin with a door that is an interconnecting door to another cabin, be aware that you'll be able to hear everything your next door neighbors say and do! Bathroom toilets are explosively noisy.

You'll need to plan what you want to take part in wisely, as almost everything requires you to sign-up in advance (many activities take place only on sea days). The cabin bath towels are small and skimpy. There are very few quiet places to sit and read (almost everywhere there is intrusive acoustic wallpaper (background music). Although the menus and variety of food offered have been upgraded since the introduction, remember that you get what you pay for. Food costs are well below that for Celebrity Cruises, for example, and so you should not expect the same food quality.

Westerdam
★★★ +

Large Ship:	53,872 tons	Cabins (for one person):	0
Lifestyle:	Premium	Cabins (with private balcony):	0
Cruise Line:	Holland America Line	Cabins (wheelchair accessible):	4
Former Names:	*Homeric*	Cabin Current:	110-volt
Builder:	Meyer Werft (Germany)	Full-Service Dining Rooms:	1
Original Cost:	$150 million	Elevators:	7
Entered Service:	May 1986/November 1988	Casino(gaming tables):	Yes
Registry:	The Netherlands	Slot Machines:	Yes
Length (ft/m):	797.9/243.23	Swimming Pools (outdoors):	2 (1 with magrodome)
Beam (ft/m):	95.1/29.00	Swimming Pools (indoors):	0
Draft (ft/m):	23.6/7.20	Whirlpools:	2
Propulsion/Propellers:	Diesel (23,830kW)/2	Fitness Center:	Yes
Passenger Decks:	9	Sauna/Steam Room:	Yes/No
Total Crew:	612	Massage:	Yes
Passengers (lower beds/all berths):	1,494/1,773	Self-Service Launderette:	Yes/5
Pass. Space Ratio (lower beds/all berths):	36.0/30.3	Dedicated Cinema/Seats:	Yes/237
Crew/Pass. Ratio (lower beds/all berths):	2.4/2.8	Library:	Yes
Navigation Officers:	Dutch	Classification Society:	Lloyd's Register
Cabins (total):	747		
Size Range (sq ft/sq m):	129.1–425.1/12.0–39.5		
Cabins (outside view):	495		
Cabins (interior/no view):	252		

OVERALL SCORE: **1,394**

(OUT OF A POSSIBLE 2,000 POINTS)

Accommodation: The cabins are generously proportioned, well appointed, and equipped with almost everything, including ample closet, drawer and storage space, and good-sized bathrooms (towels are scratchy and small). There are, however, far too many interior (no view) cabins, and the cabin insulation is rather poor. All cabin TVs feature CNN and TNT.

Dining: The traditional dining room has a raised central dome, and the portholes are highlighted at night by lighting. There are two seatings for dinner, and a single seating for breakfast and lunch. The service is reasonable, but communication can prove frustrating sometimes, and smiles from the Indonesian waiters and assistants can only do so much. Fine Rosenthal china and cutlery are featured (although there are no fish knives).

Unfortunately, Holland America Line food isn't as nice as the china it's placed on. It may be adequate for most passengers who are not used to better food, but it does not match the standard found aboard other ships in the premium segment of the industry. While USDA beef is of a good quality, fowl tends to be bat-tery-tough, and most fish is overcooked and has the consistency of a baseball bat. What are also definite-ly not luxurious are the endless packets of sugar, and packets (instead of glass jars) of breakfast jam, mar-malade and honey, and poor quality teas. While these may be suitable for a family diner, they do not belong aboard a ship that claims to have "award-winning cuisine." Dessert and pastry items are of good quality (specifically for American tastes), although there is much use of canned fruits and jellies. Forget the selection of "international" cheeses, however, as most of it didn't come from anywhere other than the US, a country known for its processed, highly colored slices, and not fine cheese-making.

The Verandah Cafe and Lido Cafe serve breakfast and lunch in self-serve buffet style, but the long lines and crowded environment are not pleasant.

Other Comments: This was formerly a Home Lines cruise ship that underwent an $84 million "chop and stretch" operation in 1990 after being purchased by Holland America Line. Indeed, you can tell where the mid-section was inserted due to the fact that the windows are larger than the fore and aft sections. The ship has good teak outside decks and a wrap-around promenade deck with real wooden deck lounge chairs. There is also a good amount of open deck space for sunbathing. The magrodome-covered swimming pool deck is, however, too small for the number of passengers. There is noticeable vibration in some areas.

The ship has elegant, functional, and restful interior decor. The public rooms are decorated in pastel tones, although some decor looks dated. She absorbs passengers well, and has good passenger flow, but the layout is awkward to learn at first. Good quality furnishings and fabrics are used throughout. The expanded health and fitness center is an improvement.

She is a well-run, modern ship that provides a satisfactory cruise experience, generally for the older passenger, but increasingly for families with kids. There is a no tipping required policy but staff do expect them, and a friendly Filipino and Indonesian crew. The product has some nice extras, like chocolates and classical music at night in the Explorer's Lounge, hot hors d'oeuvres at cocktail times, and good dance music. The line does not add an automatic 15% for beverage purchases, unlike many other cruise lines.

Note: In spring 2002, *Westerdam* will leave the Holland America Line fleet and be transferred to Costa Cruises, to start operations in June 2002 as *Prinsendam*.

Weak Points: Standing in line for embarkation, disembarkation, shore tenders, and self-serve buffet meals is an inevitable aspect of cruising aboard all large ships. This ship tries to be a Holland America Line ship, but really doesn't fit in with the other (more standardized) ships in the fleet. The entertainment is still mediocre, even though better production shows are now presented. Communication with staff is not easy. Room service is particularly poor. The charge to use the washing machines and dryers in the self-service launderette is really petty and irritating, particularly for the occupants of suites, as they pay high prices for their cruises.

Wilderness Adventurer
★★

Small Ship:	89.5 tons	Cabins (for one person):	0
Lifestyle:	Standard	Cabins (with private balcony):	0
Cruise Line:	Alaska's Glacier Bay Tours	Cabins (wheelchair accessible):	0
	and Cruises	Cabin Current:	110-volt
Former Names:	*Caribbean Prince*	Full-Service Dining Rooms:	1
Builder:	Blount Shipyards (US)	Elevators:	0
Original Cost:	$6 million	Casino(gaming tables):	No
Entered Service:	1983/1997	Slot Machines:	No
Registry:	US	Swimming Pools (outdoors):	0
Length (ft/m):	156.6/47.7	Swimming Pools (indoors):	0
Beam (ft/m):	38.0/11.0	Whirlpools:	0
Draft (ft/m):	6.5/1.8	Fitness Center:	No
Propulsion/Propellers:	Diesel (1,472kW)/1	Sauna/Steam Room:	No/No
Passenger Decks:	3	Massage:	No
Total Crew:	20	Self-Service Launderette:	No
Passengers (lower beds/all berths):	68/76	Dedicated Cinema:	No
Pass. Space Ratio (lower beds/all berths):	1.1/1.0	Library:	Yes
Crew/Pass. Ratio (lower beds/all berths):	3.4/3.8	Classification Society: American Bureau of Shipping	
Navigation Officers:	American		
Cabins (total):	34		
Size Range (sq ft/sq m):	n/a	**OVERALL SCORE:**	**939**
Cabins (outside view):	30	(OUT OF A POSSIBLE 2,000 POINTS)	
Cabins (interior/no view):	4		

Accommodation: The cabins (there are only three types to choose from, one on each of three decks) really are utilitarian, ultra-tiny, no-frills units that are just about adequate if you are not used to or do not want anything better. While 14 cabins have a double bed, all others have two lower beds, and eight also have an upper (Pullman) berth. Each cabin has its own private bathroom, although these really are miniscule. There is no room service for food or snack items.

Dining: The dining room is a room that has minimal decor, but the open seating policy means that you can dine with whomever you wish, in a single seating. The cuisine is decidedly plain and simple American fare, as is the cutlery (no fish knifes are used, for example), but it is rather tasty since the ingredients are all fresh. Wines and other alcoholic beverages are obtainable from a full-service bar.

Other Comments: This vessel, originally built for the American Canadian Caribbean Line, is good for real in-depth, up-close cruising along the coastline of Alaska. One bonus is the fact that at the bow of the vessel, a "bow gangway" comes into its own for landing passengers.

The ship is also equipped with a unique, retractable wheelhouse for passage under low bridges on inland waterways, and there is also a platform for those who want to swim off the stern. A fleet of two-person kayaks is carried, for up-close, in-your-face personal exploration of the Alaska shoreline. Water sports facilities include a glass-bottom boat/sunfish sailboat (not used on Alaska itineraries). Snorkling is possible during Mexico's Sea of Cortez itineraries only, from January through March. There is an ample supply of snorkeling gear aboard the vessel, so there is really no need to take your own.

The dress code is absolutely casual. Make sure you take comfortable walking shoes, as well as photographic materials for wildlife spotting, particularly in Alaska.

Alaska's Glacier Bay Tours and Cruises has since 1996, been owned by Goldbelt, an Alaska Tlingit Indian company. The cruises are very expensive (particularly when compared with other ships operating in the same areas), and are for those who want to venture up close to nature and wildlife, in small groups. Note that all shore excursions are included. All tips are pooled and shared among all the staff at $8-12 per passenger, per day, which is high for the services offered.

Weak Points: There is an almost constant throbbing from the diesel engines/generator. Remember that there is no doctor on board, and so anyone with medical problems should really not consider this vessel.

Wilderness Discoverer
★ ★

Small Ship:	89.5 tons	Cabins (for one person):	0
Lifestyle:	Standard	Cabins (with private balcony):	0
Cruise Line:	Alaska's Glacier Bay	Cabins (wheelchair accessible):	0
	Tours and Cruises	Cabin Current:	110-volt
Former Names:	*Mayan Prince*	Full-Service Dining Rooms:	1
Builder:	Blount Industries (US)	Elevators:	0
Original Cost:	$7.5 million	Casino(gaming tables):	No
Entered Service:	June 1992/1998	Slot Machines:	No
Registry:	US	Swimming Pools (outdoors):	0
Length (ft/m):	169.0/51.5	Swimming Pools (indoors):	0
Beam (ft/m):	38.0/11.5	Whirlpools:	0
Draft (ft/m):	6.7/2.0	Fitness Center:	No
Propulsion/Propellers:	Diesel (1,472kW)/1	Sauna/Steam Room:	No/No
Passenger Decks:	3	Massage:	No
Total Crew:	22	Self-Service Launderette:	No
Passengers (lower beds/all berths):	84/88	Dedicated Cinema:	No
Pass. Space Ratio (lower beds/all berths):	1.1/1.0	Library:	Yes
Crew/Pass. Ratio (lower beds/all berths):	4.2/4.4	Classification Society: American Bureau of Shipping	
Navigation Officers:	American		
Cabins (total):	42		
Size Range (sq ft/sq m):	70.0–80.0/6.5–7.4	**OVERALL SCORE:**	**939**
Cabins (outside view):	37	**(OUT OF A POSSIBLE 2,000 POINTS)**	
Cabins (interior/no view):	5		

Accommodation: There are four cabin grades spread over three decks, and all are dimensionally challenged, so take only the most minimal amount of clothing and personal effects you possible can. There are six cabins on the lowest deck that do not have a window, and they are really tiny. While seven cabins have a double bed, all others have two lower beds, and several also have an upper (Pullman) berth. There is no room service for food or snack items or beverages. The air-conditioning consists of re-circulated air, much like that found aboard an aircraft, and is, therefore, not very fresh. Each cabin has its own private bathroom, although these really are miniscule.

Dining: The dining room is mildly attractive and has a single, open seating policy (so you can dine with whomever you wish). The food is reasonably sound American fare, with good presentation and decent creativity. Wines and other alcoholic drinks are obtainable from a full-service bar.

Other Comments: This vessel, originally built for the upper East Coast-based American Canadian Caribbean Line, is small and squat, has a shallow draft, and is designed specifically for intensive coastal cruising. The ship is also equipped with a unique, retractable wheelhouse, although this is no longer used. A floating dock was added in 2001, as well as a small fleet of kayaks and Zodiac landing crafts.

A cruise aboard *Wilderness Discoverer* is for those who really enjoy the camaraderie of others. There is very little service and no entertainment. Indeed, unless you go to your cabin, there is no getting away from other passengers. Take only very casual clothing, since the attire is strictly non-dressy.

Alaska's Glacier Bay Tours and Cruises has since 1996, been owned by Goldbelt, an Alaska Tlingit Indian company. *Wilderness Discoverer* presently operates five-night roundtrip cruises from Juneau to Haines, Skagway, Sitka, Glacier Bay, and Tracy Arm, Alaska during the summer. The cruises are very expensive (particularly when compared with other ships operating in the same areas), and are for those who want to venture up close to nature and wildlife, in small groups. Note that all shore excursions are included. Gratuities are expected, at about $8 per person, per day.

Wind Song
★★★★

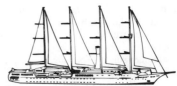

Small Ship:	5,350 tons	Cabins (total):	74
Lifestyle:	Premium	Size Range (sq ft/sq m):	182.9–220.6/17.0–20.5
Cruise Line:	Windstar Cruises	Cabins (outside view):	74
Former Names:	-	Cabins (interior/no view):	0
Builder:	Ateliers et Chantiers du	Cabins (for one person):	0
	Havre (France)	Cabins (with private balcony):	0
Original Cost:	$34.2 million	Cabins (wheelchair accessible):	0
Entered Service:	July 1987	Cabin Current:	110-volt
Registry:	Bahamas	Full-Service Dining Rooms: 1 (plus 1 informal Café)	
Length (ft/m):	439.6/134.0	Casino(gaming tables):	Yes
Beam (ft/m):	51.8/15.8	Slot Machines:	Yes
Draft (ft/m):	13.4/4.1	Swimming Pools (outdoors):	1 (dip pool)
Type of Vessel:	Computer-controlled sail-cruiser	Whirlpools:	1
No. of Masts:	4/6 self-furling sails	Fitness Center:	Yes
Sail Area (sq ft/sq m):	21,489/1,996	Sauna/Steam Room:	Yes/No
Main Propulsion:	Engines/Sails	Massage:	Yes
Propulsion/Propellers:	Diesel-electric (1,400kW)/1	Self-Service Launderette:	No
Passenger Decks:	5	Library:	Yes
Total Crew:	88	Classification Society:	Bureau Veritas
Passengers (lower beds/all berths):	148/159		
Pass. Space Ratio (lower beds/all berths):	36.1/33.6		
Crew/Pass. Ratio (lower beds/all berths):	1.6/1.8		
Navigation Officers:	European		

OVERALL SCORE: 1,518

(OUT OF A POSSIBLE 2,000 POINTS)

Accommodation: Regardless of the category of accommodation you choose, all cabins are very nicely equipped, with crisp, inviting decor, and featuring a minibar/refrigerator (stocked when you embark, but all drinks cost extra), 24-hour room service, personal safe, TV (with CNN service for news, when available) that rotates so that it is viewable from the bed or the bathroom, video player, CD player, plenty of storage space, and two portholes. The two portholes all have outside views and deadlights (steel covers that provide a complete blackout at night and can be closed in inclement weather conditions). The decor is a pleasant mix of rich woods, natural fabrics and colorful soft furnishings with high-tech yacht-style amenities. However, note that some of the cabinetry is looking a little tired, and has that "I've been varnished many times look." A basket of fruit is provided and replenished daily.

The bathrooms are compact units, designed in a figure-eight, with a teak floor in the central section. There is a good amount of storage space for personal toiletry items in two cabinets, as well as under-sink cupboard space; a wall-mounted hair dryer is also provided. The shower enclosure (no cabins have bathtubs) is circular, and features both a hand-held and a fixed shower head, so you can wash your hair without getting the rest of your body wet. Soap, shampoo,and après-sun soothing lotion are provided, as are a vanity kit and shower cap. Note, however, that the lighting is not strong enough for women to apply makeup; this is better done at the vanity desk in the cabin, which has stronger overhead (halogen) lighting. Bathrobes and towels are of 100% cotton.

Dining: There is one rather chic and elegant dining room (called The Restaurant), with ocean views from large, picture windows, a lovely wood ceiling, and wood paneling on the walls. California-style nouvelle cuisine is featured, with dishes that are attractively presented. Additionally, "signature" dishes, created by master chefs Joachim Splichal and Jeanne Jones, are featured daily. Open seating means you dine when you want and with whomever you wish to.

When the company first started, European waiters provided service with practiced finesse. However, those waiters have been replaced by Indonesians, whose communication skills at times can prove frustrating, although the service is pleasant enough. The selection of breads, cheeses, and fruits could be better.

There is a big push to sell wines, although the prices are extremely high, as they are for most alcoholic drinks. Bottled water is the highest in the industry, at $7 per liter bottle.

In addition, there is often casual dinner on the open deck under the stars, with grilled seafood and steaks. At the bars, hot and cold hors d'oeuvres appear at cocktail times.

Other Comments: *Wind Song* is one of three identical vessels (a fourth, *Wind Saga*, was never built). This is a long, sleek-looking craft that is part yacht/ part cruise ship, with four giant masts that tower 169.5 feet (51.66 meters) above the deck (they are actually 204 feet, or 62.1 meters) high, and fitted with computer-controlled sails; the masts, sails and rigging alone cost $5 million. The computer keeps the ship on an even keel (via the movement of a water-hydraulic ballast system of 142,653 gallons), so there is no heeling (rolling) over six degrees.

There is little open deck space when the ship is full, due to the amount of complex sail machinery. There is a tiny dip pool. At the stern is a small water sports platform for use when at anchor, and under really calm sea conditions. Water sports facilities include banana boat kayaks, sunfish sailboats, wind surf boards, a water ski boat, scuba and snorkel equipment, and four Zodiacs. You will be asked to sign a waiver if you wish to use the water sports equipment.

Wind Song features a finely crafted interior with pleasing, blond woods, together with soft, complementary colors and decor that is chic, even elegant, but a little cold.

The absence of scheduled activities help to make this a really relaxing, unregimented "get away from it all" vacation. The Windstar ships will cruise you in extremely comfortable surroundings that border on contemporary luxury, in an unstructured, stress-free environment. The experience is just right for seven idyllic nights in sheltered areas, but it can be disturbing when a Windstar vessel is in small ports with several huge cruise ships. It is ideal for couples who do not like large ships. The dress code is casual (no jackets and ties required), even for dinner (the brochure states casual elegance). There are no formal nights or theme nights.

You will probably be under sail for under 40% of the time (conditions and cruise area winds permitting). Gratuities are "not required" by the friendly, smiling staff, according to the brochure, but passengers find they are always accepted! Finally, this is cruising with no worries, no hassles, and no wanna go back home!

Weak Points: There is very little open deck space, and the swimming pool is really only a tiny "dip" pool. Be prepared for the whine of the vessel's generators, which are needed to run the air-conditioning and lighting systems 24 hours a day. That means you will also hear it at night in your cabin (any cabin). It takes most passengers a day or two to get used to. Beverage prices are high. The library is small, and needs more hardback fiction. Although the staff is friendly, they are casual and a little sloppy in the finer points of service at times.

Wind Spirit
★★★★

Small Ship:	5,350 tons	Cabins (total):	74
Lifestyle:	Premium	Size Range (sq ft/sq m):	185.0–220.0/17.0–22.5
Cruise Line:	Windstar Cruises	Cabins (outside view):	74
Former Names:	-	Cabins (interior/no view):	0
Builder:	Ateliers et Chantiers du	Cabins (for one person):	0
	Havre (France)	Cabins (with private balcony):	0
Original Cost:	$34.2 million	Cabins (wheelchair accessible):	0
Entered Service:	April 1988	Cabin Current:	110-volt
Registry:	Bahamas	Full-Service Dining Rooms: 1 (plus 1 informal Café)	
Length (ft/m):	439.6/134.0	Casino(gaming tables):	Yes
Beam (ft/m):	51.8/15.8	Slot Machines:	Yes
Draft (ft/m):	13.4/4.1	Swimming Pools (outdoors):	1 (dip pool)
Type of Vessel:	Computer-controlled sail-cruiser	Whirlpools:	1
No. of Masts:	4/6 self-furling sails	Fitness Center:	Yes
Sail Area (sq.ft/sq.m):	21,489/1,996.4	Sauna/Steam Room:	Yes/No
Main Propulsion:	Engines/Sails	Massage:	Yes
Propulsion/Propellers:	Diesel-electric (1,400kW)/1	Self-Service Launderette:	No
Passenger Decks:	5	Library:	Yes
Total Crew:	88	Classification Society:	Bureau Veritas
Passengers (lower beds/all berths):	148/159		
Pass. Space Ratio (lower beds/all berths):	36.1/33.6	**OVERALL SCORE:**	**1,518**
Crew/Pass. Ratio (lower beds/all berths):	1.6/1.8	**(OUT OF A POSSIBLE 2,000 POINTS)**	
Navigation Officers:	European		

Accommodation: Regardless of the category of accommodation you choose, all cabins are very nicely equipped, with crisp, inviting decor, and featuring a minibar/refrigerator (stocked when you embark, but all drinks cost extra), 24-hour room service, personal safe, TV (with CNN service for news, when available) that rotates so that it is viewable from the bed or the bathroom, video player, CD player, plenty of storage space, and two portholes. The two portholes all have outside views and deadlights (steel covers that provide a complete blackout at night and can be closed in inclement weather conditions). The decor is a pleasant mix of rich woods, natural fabrics, and colorful, soft furnishings with high-tech yacht-style amenities. However, note that some of the cabinetry is looking a little tired, and has that "I've been varnished many times look." A basket of fruit is provided and replenished daily.

The bathrooms are compact units, designed in a figure-eight, with a teak floor in the central section. There is a good amount of storage space for personal toiletry items in two cabinets, as well as under-sink cupboard space; a wall-mounted hair dryer is also provided. The shower enclosure (no cabins have bathtubs) is circular, and features both a hand-held and a fixed shower head, so you can wash your hair without getting the rest of your body wet. Soap, shampoo ,and après-sun soothing lotion are provided, as are a vanity kit and shower cap. Note, however, that the lighting is not strong enough for women to apply make-up; this is better done at the vanity desk in the cabin, which has stronger overhead (halogen) lighting. Bathrobes and towels are of 100% cotton.

Dining: There is one rather chic and elegant dining room (called The Restaurant), with ocean views from large, picture windows, a lovely wood ceiling, and wood paneling on the walls. California-style nouvelle cuisine is featured, with dishes that are attractively presented. Additionally, signature dishes, created by master chefs Joachim Splichal and Jeanne Jones, are featured daily. Open seating means you dine when you want and with whomever you wish to.

When the company first started, European waiters provided service with practiced finesse. However, those waiters have been replaced by Indonesians, whose communication skills at times can prove frustrating, although the service is pleasant enough. The selection of breads, cheeses, and fruits could be better.

There is a big push to sell wines, although the prices are extremely high, as they are for most alcoholic drinks. Bottled water is the highest in the industry, at $7 per liter bottle.

In addition, there is often casual dinner on the open deck under the stars, with grilled seafood and steaks. At the bars, hot and cold hors d'oeuvres appear at cocktail times.

Other Comments: *Wind Spirit* is one of three identical vessels (a fourth, *Wind Saga*, was never built). This is a long, sleek-looking craft that is part yacht/ part cruise ship, with four giant masts that tower 169.5 feet (51.66 meters) above the deck (they are actually 204 feet, or 62.1 meters) high, and fitted with computer-controlled sails; the masts, sails and rigging alone cost $5 million. The computer keeps the ship on an even keel (via the movement of a water-hydraulic ballast system of 142,653 gallons), so there is no heeling (rolling) over six degrees.

There is little open deck space when the ship is full, due to the amount of complex sail machinery. There is a tiny dip pool. At the stern is a small water sports platform for use when at anchor, and under really calm sea conditions. Water sports facilities include banana boat kayaks, sunfish sailboats, wind surf boards, a water ski boat, scuba and snorkel equipment, and four Zodiacs. You will be asked to sign a waiver if you wish to use the water sports equipment.

Wind Spirit features a finely crafted interior with pleasing, blond woods, together with soft, complementary colors, and decor that is chic, even elegant, but a little cold.

The absence of scheduled activities help to make this a really relaxing, unregimented "get away from it all" vacation. The Windstar ships will cruise you in extremely comfortable surroundings that border on contemporary luxury, in an unstructured, stress-free environment. The experience is just right for seven idyllic nights in sheltered areas, but it can be disturbing when a Windstar vessel is in small ports with several huge cruise ships. It is ideal for couples who do not like large ships. The dress code is casual (no jackets and ties required), even for dinner (the brochure states casual elegance). There are no formal nights or theme nights.

You will probably be under sail for under 40% of the time (conditions and cruise area winds permitting). Gratuities are "not required" by the friendly, smiling staff, according to the brochure, but passengers find they are always accepted! Finally, this is cruising with no worries, no hassles, and no wanna go back home!

Weak Points: There is very little open deck space, and the swimming pool is really only a tiny "dip" pool. Be prepared for the whine of the vessel's generators, which are needed to run the air-conditioning and lighting systems 24 hours a day. That means you will also hear it at night in your cabin (any cabin). It takes most passengers a day or two to get used to. Beverage prices are high. The library is small, and needs more hardback fiction. Although the staff is friendly, they are casual and a little sloppy in the finer points of service at times.

Wind Star
★★★★

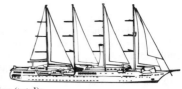

Small Ship:	5,350 tons	Cabins (total):	74
Lifestyle:	Premium	Size Range (sq ft/sq m):	185.0–220.0/17.0–22.5
Cruise Line:	Windstar Cruises	Cabins (outside view):	74
Former Names:	-	Cabins (interior/no view):	0
Builder:	Ateliers et Chantiers du Havre (France)	Cabins (for one person):	0
		Cabins (with private balcony):	0
Original Cost:	$34.2 million	Cabins (wheelchair accessible):	0
Entered Service:	December 1986	Cabin Current:	110-volt
Registry:	Bahamas	Full-Service Dining Rooms: 1 (plus 1 informal Café)	
Length (ft/m):	439.6/134.0	Casino(gaming tables):	Yes
Beam (ft/m):	51.8/15.8	Slot Machines:	Yes
Draft (ft/m):	13.4/4.1	Swimming Pools (outdoors):	1 (dip pool)
Type of Vessel:	Computer-controlled sail-cruiser	Whirlpools:	1
No. of Masts:	4/6 self-furling sails	Fitness Center:	Yes
Sail Area (sq.ft/sq.m):	21,489/1,996	Sauna/Steam Room:	Yes/No
Main Propulsion:	Engines/Sails	Massage:	Yes
Propulsion/Propellers:	Diesel-electric (1,400kW)/1	Self-Service Launderette:	No
Passenger Decks:	5	Library:	Yes
Total Crew:	88	Classification Society:	Bureau Veritas
Passengers (lower beds/all berths):	148/168		

Pass. Space Ratio (lower beds/all berths):	36.1/33.6
Crew/Pass. Ratio (lower beds/all berths):	1.6/1.8
Navigation Officers:	European

OVERALL SCORE: **1,518**

(OUT OF A POSSIBLE 2,000 POINTS)

Accommodation: Regardless of the category of accommodation you choose, all cabins are very nicely equipped, with crisp, inviting decor, and featuring a minibar/refrigerator (stocked when you embark, but all drinks cost extra), 24-hour room service, personal safe, TV (with CNN service for news, when available) that rotates so that it is viewable from the bed or the bathroom, video player, CD player, plenty of storage space, and two portholes. The two portholes all have outside views and deadlights (steel covers that provide a complete blackout at night and can be closed in inclement weather conditions). The decor is a pleasant mix of rich woods, natural fabrics, and colorful, soft furnishings with high-tech yacht-style amenities. However, note that some of the cabinetry is looking a little tired, and has that "I've been varnished many times look." A basket of fruit is provided and replenished daily.

The bathrooms are compact units, designed in a figure-eight, with a teak floor in the central section. There is a good amount of storage space for personal toiletry items in two cabinets, as well as under-sink cupboard space; a wall-mounted hair dryer is also provided. The shower enclosure (no cabins have bathtubs) is circular, and features both a hand-held and a fixed shower head, so you can wash your hair without getting the rest of your body wet. Soap, shampoo, and après-sun soothing lotion are provided, as are a vanity kit and shower cap. Note, however, that the lighting is not strong enough for women to apply make-up; this is better done at the vanity desk in the cabin, which has stronger overhead (halogen) lighting. Bathrobes and towels are of 100% cotton.

Dining: There is one rather chic and elegant dining room (called The Restaurant), with ocean views from large, picture windows, a lovely wood ceiling, and wood paneling on the walls. California-style nouvelle cuisine is featured, with dishes that are attractively presented. Additionally, signature dishes, created by master chefs Joachim Splichal and Jeanne Jones, are featured daily. Open seating means you dine when you want and with whomever you wish to.

When the company first started, European waiters provided service with practiced finesse. However, those waiters have been replaced by Indonesians, whose communication skills at times can prove frustrating, although the service is pleasant enough. The selection of breads, cheeses, and fruits could be better.

There is a big push to sell wines, although the prices are extremely high, as they are for most alcoholic drinks. Bottled water is the highest in the industry, at $7 per liter bottle.

In addition, there is often casual dinner on the open deck under the stars, with grilled seafood and steaks. At the bars, hot and cold hors d'oeuvres appear at cocktail times.

Other Comments: *Wind Spirit* is one of three identical vessels (a fourth, *Wind Saga*, was never built). This is a long, sleek-looking craft that is part yacht/ part cruise ship, with four giant masts that tower 169.5 feet (51.66 meters) above the deck (they are actually 204 feet, or 62.1 meters) high, and fitted with computer-controlled sails; the masts, sails and rigging alone cost $5 million. The computer keeps the ship on an even keel (via the movement of a water-hydraulic ballast system of 142,653 gallons), so there is no heeling (rolling) over six degrees.

There is little open deck space when the ship is full, due to the amount of complex sail machinery. There is a tiny dip pool. At the stern is a small water sports platform for use when at anchor, and under really calm sea conditions. Water sports facilities include banana boat kayaks, sunfish sailboats, wind surf boards, a water ski boat, scuba and snorkel equipment, and four Zodiacs. You will be asked to sign a waiver if you wish to use the water sports equipment.

Wind Spirit features a finely crafted interior with pleasing, blond woods, together with soft, complementary colors, and decor that is chic, even elegant, but a little cold.

The absence of scheduled activities help to make this a really relaxing, unregimented "get away from it all" vacation. The Windstar ships will cruise you in extremely comfortable surroundings that border on contemporary luxury, in an unstructured, stress-free environment. The experience is just right for seven idyllic nights in sheltered areas, but it can be disturbing when a Windstar vessel is in small ports with several huge cruise ships. It is ideal for couples who do not like large ships. The dress code is casual (no jackets and ties required), even for dinner (the brochure states casual elegance). There are no formal nights or theme nights.

You will probably be under sail for under 40% of the time (conditions and cruise area winds permitting). Gratuities are "not required" by the friendly, smiling staff, according to the brochure, but passengers find they are always accepted! Finally, this is cruising with no worries, no hassles, and no wanna go back home!

Weak Points: There is very little open deck space, and the swimming pool is really only a tiny "dip" pool. Be prepared for the whine of the vessel's generators, which are needed to run the air-conditioning and lighting systems 24 hours a day. That means you will also hear it at night in your cabin (any cabin). It takes most passengers a day or two to get used to. Beverage prices are high. The library is small, and needs more hardback fiction. Although the staff is friendly, they are casual and a little sloppy in the finer points of service at times.

Wind Surf
★★★★ +

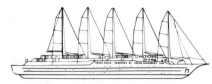

Small Ship:	14,745 tons	Size Range (sq ft/sq m):	188.0–375.6/57.3–114.5
Lifestyle:	Premium	Cabins (outside view):	154
Cruise Line:	Windstar Cruises	Cabins (interior/no view):	0
Former Names:	*Club Med I*	Cabins (for one person):	0
Builder:	Ateliers et Chantiers du	Cabins (with private balcony):	0
	Havre (France)	Cabins (wheelchair accessible):	0
Original Cost:	$140 million	Cabin Current:	220-volt
Entered Service:	February 1990/May 1998	Full-Service Dining Rooms:	2
Registry:	Bahamas	Elevators:	2
Length (ft/m):	613.5/187.0	Casino(gaming tables):	Yes
Beam (ft/m):	65.6/20.0	Slot Machines:	Yes
Draft (ft/m):	16.4/5.0	Swimming Pools (outdoors):	2
Type of Vessel:	High-tech sail-cruiser	Whirlpools:	2
No. of Masts:	5/7 Computer-controlled sails	Fitness Center:	Yes
Sail Area (sq.ft/sq.m):	26,910/2,500	Sauna/Steam Room:	Yes/No
Main Propulsion:	Engines/Sails	Massage:	Yes
Propulsion/Propellers:	Diesel (9,120kW)/2	Self-Service Launderette:	No
Passenger Decks:	8	Library:	Yes
Total Crew:	163	Classification Society:	Bureau Veritas
Passengers (lower beds/all berths):	308/308		
Pass. Space Ratio (lower beds/all berths):	47.8/47.8		
Crew/Pass. Ratio (lower beds/all berths):	1.8/1.8	**OVERALL SCORE:**	**1,567**
Navigation Officers:	European	(OUT OF A POSSIBLE 2,000 POINTS)	
Cabins (total):	154		

Accommodation: There are just three price categories, making your choice of accommodation a simple one. Regardless of the category of accommodation you choose, all cabins are very nicely equipped, with crisp, inviting decor, and featuring a minibar/refrigerator (stocked when you embark, but all drinks cost extra), 24-hour room service, personal safe, TV (with CNN service for news, when available) that rotates so that it is viewable from the bed or the bathroom, video player, CD player, plenty of storage space, and two portholes. Videos and compact discs are available from the ship's library. There are six four-person cabins; 35 doubles are fitted with an extra Pullman berth, and several cabins have an interconnecting door (good for families). However, note that some of the cabinetry is looking a little tired, and has that "I've been varnished many times look." A basket of fruit is provided and replenished daily.

The bathrooms are compact units, designed in a figure-eight, with a teak floor in the central section. There is a good amount of storage space for personal toiletry items in two cabinets, as well as under-sink cupboard space; a wall-mounted hair dryer is also provided. The shower enclosure (no cabins have bathtubs) is circular, and features both a hand-held and a fixed shower (so you can wash your hair without getting the rest of your body wet). Soap, shampoo, and après-sun soothing lotion are provided, as are a vanity kit and shower cap. Note, however, that the lighting is not strong enough for women to apply makeup. It is better done at the vanity desk in the cabin, which has stronger overhead (halogen) lighting. Bathrobes and towels are of 100% cotton, while bed linen is of a mix of 50% cotton/50% polyester (with 100% cotton sheets available on request).

In 1998, 31 new suites were added to Deck 3 during an extensive refit (one Owner's Suite, plus 30 suites that were created by using two former standard cabins for one suite). Adding these resulted in a decrease of passenger capacity from that of the ship's former owners (Club Méditerranée). All except one of the new suites feature two bathrooms (so that a couple can have one bathroom each), a separate living/dining area, sleeping area (this can be curtained off from the lounge), two writing desks (there is even enough room for you to have an en-suite massage), and four portholes instead of two. There are also two TVs (one in the lounge, on in the sleeping area), VCR and CD player. However, note that movies cannot be watched from the bed, only from the sofa in the lounge area. Popcorn (for movie viewing) is available by calling room service.

Dining: The Restaurant (which has 272 seats) has tables for two, four, or six, and open seating (with no pre-assigned tables) is featured, so you can sit with whom you wish, when you like. It is open only for dinner, which is typically between 7:30pm and 9:30pm. Both smoking and non-smoking sections are provided. California-style nouvelle cuisine is featured, with dishes that are attractively presented. Additionally, "signature" dishes, created by master chefs Joachim Splichal and Jeanne Jones, are featured daily.

A 124-seat Bistro provides an alternative venue to the main restaurant (for dinner). The menus are basically the same as in the dining room, and the Bistro really provides an overflow to the dining room, particularly when the ship is full. The Bistro is, thus, not a bistro at all. It is located high atop the ship (on Star Deck) and features picture windows on port and starboard sides, an open kitchen, and tables for two, four, or six. This is a non-smoking dining spot. Reservations are required for dinner, and passengers are restricted to two visits per 7-day cruise.

The Verandah, located amidships (on Star Deck) has its own open terrace for informal, self-serve breakfast and lunch buffets. It really is very pleasant to be outside, eating an informal meal on a balmy night. Do try the bread pudding—the ship is famous for it (available after lunch each day). Additionally, a permanent barbecue is also set up aft of the Verandah, for fresh grilled items for breakfast and lunch.

The Compass Rose, an indoor/outdoor bar, also provides snack items as well as some pastries and coffee for breakfast.

Note that the Windstar Cruises food is generally very good, although it is highly geared toward American tastes (with its California-style cuisine and presentation). Thus, Europeans and other nationals should note that items such as bacon are fried to death, the choice of cheeses is poor, as is the selection of teas. The service is also fast—geared towards Americans, who typically like to see food in front of them. Consequently, leisurely dining is quite difficult.

Other Comments: One of a pair of the world's largest sail-cruisers, *Wind Surf* is part cruise ship, part yacht (her sister ship operates as *Club Med II*). She is a larger, grander sister to the original three Windstar Cruises vessels. Five huge masts of 164 feet, or 50 meters (these actually rise 221 feett, or 67.5 meters above sea level) carry seven triangular, self-furling sails (made of Dacron) with a total surface area of 26,881 sq ft (2,497 sq m). No human hands touch the sails, as everything is handled electronically by computer control from the bridge. The computer keeps the ship on an even keel (via the movement of a water-hydraulic ballast system of 266,814 gallons), so there is no heeling (rolling) over six degrees. When the ship is not using the sails, four diesel-electric motors propel the ship at up to approximately 12 knots.

Windstar Cruises purchased this ship, in March 1998. Since then, the ship's passenger capacity has been reduced from 386 to 308, and 31 new larger suites have been created from what were formerly smaller (standard) cabins.

There is a large, hydraulic water sports platform at the stern (swimming from it is not allowed, however), and extensive water sports facilities include 12 windsurfers, three sailboats, two water-ski boats, 20 single scuba tanks, snorkels, fins and masks, and four inflatable Zodiac motorized boats (for water-skiing, etc), and all at no extra charge (except for the scuba tanks). Note that you will be asked to sign a waiver if you wish to use the water sports equipment.

There are two (saltwater) swimming pools (actually they are little more than dip pools). One is located amidships on the uppermost deck of the ship, while the other is located aft, together with two hot tubs, and an adjacent bar.

In December 2000, the ship underwent further internal redesign, with enhancement of some features and the addition of new ones. A new gangway was installed, which has improved embarkation/disembarkation. A business center has been added; this incorporates a computer center (with 10 Internet-access computer terminals so passengers can "Windsurf" the net), and a meeting room for between 30 and 60 persons. In the ship's casino/main lounge, which has an unusually high ceiling for the size of the ship, the dance floor has fortunately been relocated for better access and flow.

The health spa (with a staff of 10) features a co-ed sauna (bathing suits are required), beauty salon, several treatment rooms for massage, facials, and body wraps; there is also a decent gymnasium (on a separate deck, with ocean views), and an aerobics workout room. Unfortunately, the spa facilities are split on three separate decks, making them rather disjointed. Special spa packages can be pre-booked through your travel agent before you arrive at the ship.

Other facilities include an integrated main lounge and enlarged casino (with four blackjack tables, and one roulette table, and 21 slot machines).

Wind Surf should prove to be a good choice for couples that seek the "California Casual" dress code (no jackets or ties required) and the informality found aboard this vessel, yet don't want the inconvenience of the workings of a real tall ship. The high quality of food and its presentation is a definite plus, as is the policy of no music in passenger hallways or elevators — in other words, it's a delightful, peaceful environment — ideal if you want to de-stress and turn off from the world.

Wind Surf features cruises from Barbados (November through March) and from Nice (May through October). However, note that the European itineraries are really port-intensive, which means you sail each night and are in port each day. With such itineraries, there seems little point to having the sails.

This ship has become a somewhat larger sister ship (with more space per passenger) for the three original Windstar Cruises vessels presently operating (*Wind Song, Wind Spirit, Wind Star*). All gratuities and port taxes are included in the brochure price (no additional gratuities are expected), which itself is considerably higher than those of the three smaller vessels in the fleet.

Weak Points: There are no showers at either of the two swimming pools (actually they really are just dip pools for cooling off). At present, passengers simply get into pool or hot tubs, while covered in oil or lotion — an unhygienic arrangement. Art Auctions simply do not belong aboard this sail-cruise vessel (hopefully they will have disappeared by the time you read this). Don't even think about purchasing a cigar from the ship's shop: the air temperature in the shop is high, so any cigars purchased will be dry and absolutely worthless.(They should, of course, be sold from a properly kept humidor.)

World Renaissance
★★ +

Small Ship:	11,724 tons	Cabins (for one person):	1
Lifestyle:	Standard	Cabins (with private balcony):	0
Cruise Line:	Royal Olympic Cruises	Cabins (wheelchair accessible):	0
Former Names:	*Awani Dream, World Renaissance,*	Cabin Current:	110-volt
	Renaissance, Homeric Renaissance	Full-Service Dining Rooms:	1
Builder:	Chantiers de l'Atlantique (France)	Elevators:	1
Original Cost:	n/a	Casino(gaming tables):	Yes
Entered Service:	May 1966/January 1996	Slot Machines:	Yes
Registry:	Greece	Swimming Pools (outdoors):	2
Length (ft/m):	492.1/150.02	Swimming Pools (indoors):	0
Beam (ft/m):	69.0/21.06	Whirlpools:	0
Draft (ft/m):	22.9/7.00	Fitness Center:	Yes
Propulsion/Propellers:	Diesel (10,060kW)/2	Sauna/Steam Room:	Yes/No
Passenger Decks:	8	Massage:	Yes
Total Crew:	204	Self-Service Launderette:	No
Passengers (lower beds/all berths):	481/599	Dedicated Cinema/Seats:	Yes/110
Pass. Space Ratio (lower beds/all berths):	24.3/19.5	Library:	Yes
Crew/Pass. Ratio (lower beds/all berths):	2.2/2.9	Classification Society:	Lloyd's Register
Navigation Officers:	Greek		
Cabins (total):	241		
Size Range (sq ft/sq m):	110.0–270.0/10.2–25.0	**OVERALL SCORE:**	**1,096**
Cabins (outside view):	178	(OUT OF A POSSIBLE 2,000 POINTS)	
Cabins (interior/no view):	63		

Accommodation: Some of the cabins have some fine wood paneling. They are homey and reasonably spacious, though certainly not luxurious. The cabin bathrooms are tiled, but are very small, and there is little space for toiletries.

Dining: The dining room is reasonably pleasant, although there are no tables for two. The tables are close together, and there are two seatings. The cuisine is now predominantly Indonesian, with plenty of spicy foods. There is thus a limited selection of breads, pastry, fruit, and cheeses. The service is very basic and there is really no finesse.

Other Comments: This ship has traditional 1960s styling and profile topped by a slender funnel. She was operated for many years by Epirotiki Lines (now part of Royal Olympic Cruises), and had a short sojourn in Indonesia with Awani Dream Cruises, which ceased operations in late 1997. She has a pencil-slim funnel and white superstructure atop a royal blue hull.

The ship has a generous amount of open deck and sunbathing space for its size. The interior layout, however, is disjointed and awkward, and signage could be better.

Inside the ship, the decor can be said to be both colonial and eclectic, with some touches that still remind one of her original days as a French ship. Although the main lounge is comfortable, there are few other public rooms, and therefore the ship always feels busy (crowded). The library is a restful place to relax. She has a friendly Greek staff and good basic service, although there is little refinement.

Weak Points: The ship has a steep passenger gangway in most ports of call. There is no wrap-around promenade deck outdoors, and there are no cushioned pads for the deck lounge chairs.

Yamal
★★★ +

Small Ship:	23,000 tons	Cabins (for one person):	3
Lifestyle:	Standard	Cabins (with private balcony):	0
Cruise Line:	Murmansk Shipping	Cabins (wheelchair accessible):	0
Former Names:	-	Cabin Current:	220-volt
Builder:	Baltic Shipyard & Engineering	Full-Service Dining Rooms:	1
	(Russia)	Elevators:	0
Original Cost:	$150 million	Casino(gaming tables):	No
Entered Service:	November 1992	Slot Machines:	No
Registry:	Russia	Swimming Pools (indoors):	1
Length (ft/m):	492.1/150.0	Whirlpools:	0
Beam (ft/m):	98.4/30.0	Fitness Center:	Yes
Draft (ft/m):	36.0/11.0	Sauna/Steam Room:	Yes-2/No
Propulsion/Propellers:	Nuclear-powered	Massage:	No
	turbo-electric (55,950kW)/3	Self-Service Launderette:	Yes
Passenger Decks:	4	Lecture/Film Room:	Yes (seats 100)
Total Crew:	130	Library:	Yes
Passengers (lower beds/all berths):	109/109	Zodiacs:	4
Pass. Space Ratio (lower beds/all berths):	211/211	Helicopter Pad:	2 helicopters for passenger use
Crew/Pass. Ratio (lower beds/all berths):	0.8/0.8	Classification Society:	Russian Shipping Registry
Navigation Officers:	Russian/Ukrainian		
Cabins (total):	56		
Size Range (sq ft/sq m):	130.0–300.0/14.3–27.8		
Cabins (outside view):	56		
Cabins (interior/no view):	0		

OVERALL SCORE: **1,292**

(OUT OF A POSSIBLE 2,000 POINTS)

Accommodation: All of the cabins are generously sized (considering the type of specialized vessel this is), and all are outside, with private facilities, TV (for in-house viewing), VCR (suites only), and refrigerator. There is, however, a limited amount of closet and drawer space in most cabins. The bathrooms are small and utilitarian, and you will need to take your own favorite toiletry items.

Dining: *Yamal* has a nicely appointed dining room. When the ship is under charter to Quark Expeditions, the catering is provided by European chefs, and the cuisine is surprisingly hearty, with plenty of meat and potato dishes, but little fruit and cheese. Remember that these are not meant to be gourmet cruises, but the food is actually quite decent, and there is certainly plenty of it.

Other Comments: The ultimate in technology accompanies this special ship, one of a fleet of the world's most powerful icebreakers, with a 48mm thick armored hull. She is, in fact, one of few surface ships ever to reach the North Pole.

Propulsion power is provided by two nuclear-powered reactors (encased in 160 tons of steel), which provide the steam for propulsion via two steam turbines. There are three powerful four-bladed propellers, each weighing about seven tons. Her icebreaking capability is assisted by an air bubbling system that delivers hot water from jets located below the surface.

Two helicopters are carried for reconnaissance and passenger sightseeing use (their use is included in the expedition cruise fare).

Rugged, unpretentious, yet surprisingly comfortable surroundings prevail inside. There are two lounges to choose from. A tiered lecture theater with stage is the setting for a team of biologists, scientists, geologists, and other lecturers. There is also a heated indoor pool. Attentive and friendly Russian service is provided. Passengers are also allowed on the bridge at almost all times. Light but warm parkas are provided for all passengers. An expedition cruise logbook is typically provided at the end of each cruise for all passengers.

Yamal is one ship (out of a series of six built between 1959 and 1993) that is often under charter to various operators. This really is an incredible vessel, with a three-inch-thick reinforced bow for negotiating tough ice conditions (although the vessel really is noisy when plowing through ice). She carries enough fuel for four years without refueling! This is undoubtedly one of the most exciting, seat-of-your-pants expedition cruise experiences available today.

Yankee Clipper
★★

Small Ship:	327 tons	Cabins (outside view):	32
Lifestyle:	Standard	Cabins (interior/no view):	0
Cruise Line:	Windjammer Barefoot Cruises	Cabins (for one person):	0
Former Names:	*Pioneer, Cressida*	Cabins (with private balcony):	0
Builder:	Krupp (Germany)	Cabins (wheelchair accessible):	0
Entered Service:	1927/1965	Cabin Current:	110-volt
Registry:	Equitorial Guinea	Full-Service Dining Rooms:	1
Length (ft/m):	197.0/60.0	Elevators:	0
Beam (ft/m):	30.0/9.1	Casino(gaming tables):	No
Draft (ft/m):	17.0/5.1	Slot Machines:	No
Type of Vessel:	Schooner	Swimming Pools (outdoors):	0
No. of Masts:	3	Whirlpools:	2
Sail Area (sq ft/sq m):	8,000/743.2	Fitness Center:	No
Main Propulsion:	Sail power	Sauna/Steam Room:	No/No
Propulsion/Propellers:	Diesel/1	Massage:	No
Passenger Decks:	3	Self-Service Launderette:	No
Total Crew:	24	Library:	Yes
Passengers (lower beds/all berths):	64/64	Classification Society:	none
Pass. Space Ratio (lower beds/all berths):	5.1/5.1		
Crew/Pass. Ratio (lower beds/all berths):	2.6/2.6		
Navigation Officers:	International	**OVERALL SCORE:**	**902**
Cabins (total):	32		
Size Range (sq ft/sq m):	65.0–86.0/6.0–7.9	(OUT OF A POSSIBLE 2,000 POINTS)	

Accommodation: There are four grades of accommodation (Deck Cabin, Captain's Cabin, Captain's Double, and Standard Cabin). The cabins are dimensionally challenged, however, particularly when compared to regular cruise ships. Remember, however, that this is a very casual cruise experience and you will need few clothes anyway. All of the cabins are equipped with upper and lower berths, and most of them are quite narrow.

Dining: There is one dining room, and meals are all very simple in style and service, with little choice and only the most basic presentation. Breakfast is served on board, as is dinner, while lunch could be available either on board or at a beach, picnic-style. Wine (don't expect it to be very good) is included for dinner.

Other Comments: The ship was originally built as one of the only armor-plated private yachts in the world, for the German industrialist Alfred Krupp. She was confiscated during World War II as a war prize, later acquired by the Vanderbilts, and then purchased from the Vandertbilt Estate to join the Windjammer Barefoot Cruises fleet in 1965.

Aboard one of the Windjammer Barefoot Cruises' ships you can let the crew do all the work, or you can lend a hand at the helm yourself, if you feel so inclined. One neat thing to do is just to sit or lie in the nets at the bows of the vessel, without a care in the world—it's a great feeling.

The mood is free and easy; the ships are equipped very simply, and only the most casual clothes are required (T-shirts and shorts), and shoes are optional, although you may need them if you go off into one of the ports. Quite possibly the most used item will be your bathing suit—better take more than one! Smoking is allowed only on the open decks.

Jammin' aboard a Windjammer ship (first-time passengers are called "crewmates" while repeat passengers are called "jammers") is no-frills cruising (it could be called an "anti-cruise") in a no-nonsense, friendly environment, for the young at heart and those who don't need programmed activities. It's all about going to sea and the romance of being at sea under sail. You can even lend a hand with the sails if you wish. Those who enjoy beaches, scuba diving, and snorkeling around the Caribbean will be best suited to a Windjammer Barefoot Cruises. This ship can anchor in neat little Caribbean hideaways that larger (regular) cruise ships can't get near.

Entertainment in the evenings consists of you and the crew. You can put on a toga, take or create a pirate outfit, and join in the fun. This is cruising free 'n' easy style—none of that programmed big-ship production show stuff here.

Although itineraries (well, islands) are outlined in the brochure, the captain actually decides which islands to go to in any given area, depending on sea and weather conditions. *Yankee Clipper* makes year-round cruises in the British and US.Virgin Islands, based in Grenada. Other tall ships in the fleet include *Flying Cloud, Legacy, Mandalay*, and *Polynesia*. Brochure rates might seem inexpensive, but you'll need to add on the airfare in order to get the true cost.

Weak Points: It's extremely basic. There's very little space per passenger. Everything is basic, basic, basic. Tips to the crew are suggested—at a whopping $50 per week per person!

PLIMSOLL MARK

The safety of ships at sea and all those aboard owes much to the 19th-century social reformer Samuel Plimsoll, a member of the British Parliament concerned about the frequent loss of ships due to overloading. In those days, some shipowners would load their vessels down to the gunwales to squeeze every ounce of revenue out of them. They gambled on good weather, good fortune, and good seamanship to bring them safely into port. Consequently, many ships went to the bottom of the sea—the result of their buoyancy being seriously impaired by overloading.

Plimsoll helped to enact legislation that came to be known as the Merchant Shipping Act of 1875. This required shipowners to mark their vessels with a circular disc 12 inches (30.5 cm) long bisected by a line 18 inches (45.7 cm) long, as a measure of their maximum draft; that is, the depth to which a ship's hull could be safely immersed at sea. The Merchant Shipping Act of 1890 went even further, and required the Plimsoll mark (or line) to be positioned on the sides of vessels in accordance with tables drawn up by competent authorities.

The Plimsoll mark is now found on the ships of every nation. The Plimsoll mark indicates three different depths: the depth to which a vessel can be loaded in fresh water, which is less buoyant than salt water; the depth in summer, when seas are generally calmer; and the depth in winter, when seas are much rougher.

Yorktown Clipper
★★★ +

Small Ship:	2,354 tons	Cabins (for one person):	0
Lifestyle:	Standard	Cabins (with private balcony):	0
Cruise Line:	Clipper Cruise Line	Cabins (wheelchair accessible):	0
Former Names:	-	Cabin Current:	110-volt
Builder:	First Coast Shipbuilding (US)	Full-Service Dining Rooms:	1
Original Cost:	$12 million	Elevators:	0
Entered Service:	April 1988	Casino(gaming tables):	No
Registry:	US	Slot Machines:	No
Length (ft/m):	257.0/78.30	Swimming Pools (outdoors):	0
Beam (ft/m):	43.0/13.10	Swimming Pools (indoors):	0
Draft (ft/m):	8.0/2.43	Whirlpools:	0
Propulsion/Propellers:	Diesel (1,044kW)/2	Fitness Center:	No
Passenger Decks:	4	Sauna/Steam Room:	No/No
Total Crew:	40	Massage:	No
Passengers (lower beds/all berths):	138/138	Self-Service Launderette:	No
Pass. Space Ratio (lower beds/all berths):	17.0/17.0	Dedicated Cinema:	No
Crew/Pass. Ratio (lower beds/all berths):	3.4/3.4	Library:	Yes
Navigation Officers:	American	Classification Society: American Bureau of Shipping	
Cabins (total):	69		
Size Range (sq ft/sq m):	121.0–138.0/11.2–12.8	**OVERALL SCORE:**	**1,267**
Cabins (outside view):	69	(OUT OF A POSSIBLE 2,000 POINTS)	
Cabins (interior/no view):	0		

Accommodation: The all-outside cabins are really quite small, but, with lots of wood-accented trim and restful colors, they are reasonably comfortable and tastefully furnished. The bathrooms, likewise, are small, with little space for toiletry items (but a night-light is provided, so you don't have to turn on bright lights in the middle of the night—a thoughtful touch). There is no room service for food and beverage items, as found aboard larger ships.

Dining: The dining room is warm and fairly inviting and has large picture windows, although there are no tables for two. There is one open seating. The service is provided by a young, all-American, mid-western team who smile a lot and are quite friendly, though they lack the finesse associated with European service. The presentation is tasteful, though menu choice is limited. The food is of a good quality, and made from fresh locally purchased ingredients. There is an adequate, but very limited selection of breads and fruits.

Other Comments: This small vessel was built specifically to operate coastal and inland waterway cruises. She has a shallow draft and good maneuverability, and has been well maintained since new. There is a teak wood outdoor sun deck. Inflatable rubber Zodiac crafts are used for close-in shore excursions.

Inside, there is a glass-walled observation lounge. This ship offers a decidedly "Americana" experience for those seeking to learn more about the coastal ports around the US during the summer months. Caribbean cruises are featured during the winter months.

A casual, completely unstructured lifestyle prevails aboard, and this can best be compared to a small, congenial country club without any of the pretentiousness. It is a good antidote to cruising aboard large ships. There are no mindless activities or corny games, and no entertainment as such, except for an occasional movie after dinner (the dining room converts to a movie screening room). There are, however, always one or two lecturers aboard each sailing.

This really should not be compared with big ship ocean cruising. The price, however, is high for what you get when compared to many other ships, and airfare is extra. A no smoking policy throughout all interior areas was put into effect in December 1996.

Weak Points: She really is a high-density ship, and there are only two public rooms: a dining room and a lounge. The engine noise level is high when the ship is underway (not so noticeable for those who may be hard of hearing). The per diem price is high for what you get, and airfare is extra. Although there is a wrap-around teakwood walking deck outdoors, it is quite narrow.

Zaandam
★★★★

Large Ship:	63,000 tons	Cabins (for one person):	0
Lifestyle:	Premium	Cabins (with private balcony):	197
Cruise Line:	Holland America Line	Cabins (wheelchair accessible):	23
Former Names:		Cabin Current:	110-volt
Builder:	Fincantieri (Italy)	Full-Service Dining Rooms: 1 main (plus 1 alternative)	
Original Cost:	$300 million	Elevators:	12
Entered Service:	May 2000	Casino (gaming tables):	Yes
Registry:	The Netherlands	Slot Machines:	Yes
Length (ft/m):	777.5/237.00	Swimming Pools (outdoors):	2
Beam (ft/m):	105.8/32.25	Swimming Pools (indoors):	1 (magrodome cover)
Draft (ft/m):	25.5/7.80	Whirlpools:	2
Propulsion/Propellers:	Diesel-electric	Fitness Center:	Yes
	(37,500kW)/2	Sauna/Steam Room:	Yes/Yes
Passenger Decks:	12	Massage:	Yes
Total Crew:	561	Self-Service Launderette:	Yes
Passengers (lower beds/all berths):	1,440/1,850	Dedicated Cinema/Seats:	Yes/205
Pass. Space Ratio (lower beds/all berths):	43.7/34.0	Library:	Yes
Crew/Pass. Ratio (lower beds/all berths):	2.5/2.5	Classification Society:	Lloyd's Register
Navigation Officers:	Dutch		
Cabins (total):	720		
Size Range (sq ft/sq m):	113.0–339.2/10.5–34.3	**OVERALL SCORE:**	**1,548**
Cabins (outside view):	581	(OUT OF A POSSIBLE 2,000 POINTS)	
Cabins (interior/no view):	139		

Accommodation: The range of accommodation is similar to that found aboard the similarly sized *Rotterdam*, and comprises 17 different categories. There is one penthouse suite, and 28 suites, with the rest of the accommodation comprised of a mix of outside-view and interior (no view) cabins, and many more balcony cabins (called "mini-suites") aboard this ship than aboard the slightly smaller *Statendam*-class ships (*Maasdam, Ryndam, Statendam, Veendam*).

All standard interior and outside cabins are tastefully furnished and have twin beds that convert to a queen-size bed. Space is very narrow for walking between beds and vanity unit. There is a decent amount of closet and drawer space, although this may prove tight for the longer voyages featured. All cabin TVs feature CNN and TNT. The bathrooms, which are fully tiled, are disappointingly small (particularly for long cruises) and have small shower tubs, utilitarian personal toiletries cupboards, and exposed under-sink plumbing. There is no detailing to distinguish them from bathrooms aboard the *Statendam*-class ships.

There are 28 full Verandah Suites (Navigation Deck), and one Penthouse Suite. All suite occupants share a private concierge lounge (the concierge handles such things as special dining arrangements, shore excursions, private parties, and special requests). Strangely there are no butlers for these suites, as aboard ships with similar facilities. Each Verandahh Suite has a separate bedroom, dressing and living areas. Suite passengers get personal stationery, complimentary laundry and ironing, cocktail hour hors d'oeuvres and other goodies, as well as priority embarkation and disembarkation. The concierge lounge, with its teak-latticework detailing and private library is accessible only by private key-card.

For the ultimate in accommodation and living space aboard this ship, choose the Penthouse Suite. It has a separate steward's entrance, and features a large bedroom with king-size bed, separate living room (with baby grand piano) and a dining room, dressing room, walk-in closet, butler's pantry, and private balcony (the balcony is no larger than the balcony of any of the other suites). Other facilities include an audio-visual center with TV and VCR, wet bar with refrigerator, large bathroom with Whirlpool bathtub, separate toilet with bidet, and a guest bathroom (with toilet and washbasin).

With the exception of the Penthouse Suite, located forward on the starboard side, the bathrooms in the other suites and "mini-suites" are a little disappointing—neither as spacious nor as opulent as one would expect. All outside-view suite and cabin bathrooms feature a bathtub/shower while interior (no view) cabins have a shower only. Also, note that the 23 cabins for the physically challenged feature a roll-in shower enclosure for wheelchair users (none have bathtubs, no mater what the category).

Part Two: The Cruise Ships and Ratings

Dining: The Rotterdam Dining Room (the ship's main dining room) is quite a grand room, and is spread over two decks, with ocean views on three sides with a grand staircase to connect the upper and lower levels. There are two seatings for dinner, open seating for breakfast and lunch, and both smoking and no smoking sections are provided. Fine Rosenthal china and cutlery are featured (although there are no fish knives). Unfortunately, Holland America Line food isn't as nice as the china it's placed on. It may be adequate for most passengers who are not used to better food, but it does not match the standard found aboard other ships in the premium segment of the industry. While USDA beef is of a good quality, fowl tends to be battery-tough, and most fish is overcooked and has the consistency of a baseball bat. What are also definitely not luxurious are the endless packets of sugar, and packets (instead of glass jars) of breakfast jam, marmalade, and honey, and poor quality teas. While these may be suitable for a family diner, they do not belong aboard a ship that claims to have "award-winning cuisine." Dessert and pastry items are of good quality (specifically for American tastes), although there is much use of canned fruits and jellies. Forget the selection of "international" cheeses, however, as most of it didn't come from anywhere other than the US, a country known for its processed, highly colored slices, and not fine cheese-making.

The alternative, casual dress Marco Polo Restaurant seats 88, and there is no charge, although reservations are required. It has been created in the style of a California artists' bistro and serves Italian cuisine from a set menu together with nightly specials. Passengers thus can have more choice and an occasional change of venue. Anyone booking suite-grade accommodation gets priority reservations.

In addition, there is the Lido Buffet, a self-serve café that has proved popular aboard all Holland America Line ships for casual breakfasts and luncheons. There is also an outdoor grill serving hamburgers, hot dogs, and other grilled fast-food items. The Lido Buffet is also open for casual dinners on each night except for the last one, in an open seating arrangement. Tables are set with crisp linens, flatware and stemware. A set menu is featured, and this includes a choice of four entrees.

Other Comments: Her hull is dark blue, in keeping with all Holland America Line ships. Although similar in size to the line's flagship *Rotterdam*, this ship has a single funnel, and she is a sister ship to *Volendam*.

The ship's interiors carry on the same flow and comfortable feeling as most other ships in the fleet so that repeat passengers will immediately feel at home aboard almost any ship in the Holland America Line fleet.

Zaandam features three principal passenger stairways, which is so much better than two stairways, particularly with regard to safety, accessibility and passenger flow. There is a magrodome covered pool on the Lido Deck between the mast and the ship's funnel. The health spa facilities are quite extensive, and include gymnasium, separate saunas and steam rooms for men and women, and more treatment rooms (each has a shower and toilet). Practice tennis courts can be found outdoors, as well as the traditional shuffleboard courts, jogging track, and a full wrap-around teak promenade deck.

The interior decor is best described as restrained, with much use of wood accenting, and the design theme of music incorporated throughout. Music memorabilia is scattered throughout the ship, in fabrics, posters, and — believe it or not—real instruments. The musical instruments and other memorabilia were acquired from the "Pop and Guitars" auction at Christie's in London in 1997. They include a Fender Squire Telecaster guitar signed by Mick Jagger, Keith Richards, Charlie Watts, Ronnie Wood, and Bill Wyman of The Rolling Stones; a Conn Saxophone signed on the mouthpiece by US President Bill Clinton; an Ariana acoustic guitar signed by David Bowie and Iggy Pop; a Fender Stratocaster guitar signed in silver ink by the members of the rock band Queen; a Bently "Les Paul" style guitar signed by various artists, including Carlos Santana, Eric Clapton, B. B. King, Robert Cray, Keith Richards, and Les Paul.

As a whole, the decor of this ship is quite refined, with much of the traditional ocean liner detailing so loved by frequent Holland America Line passengers. Additions are children's and teens' play areas, although these really are token gestures by a company that traditionally does not cater well to children. Popcorn is even available at the Wajang Theatre for moviegoers, while adjacent is the popular Java Café. The casino, which is located right in the middle of the principal passenger flow, now features blackjack, roulette, stud poker, and dice tables alongside the requisite rows of slot machines. The casino bar is also known as the ship's sports bar.

The ship's focal point is a three-deck-high atrium, around which the ship's main offices can be found (reception desk, shore excursions desk, photo shop, and photo gallery). It also houses a fanciful pipe organ, complete with puppets that move in time with the music.

As in *Volendam*, the Lido Deck swimming pool is located one deck higher than the S-class ships, offering convenient direct access between the aft and midships pools unavailable aboard the S-class ships. This provides more space on the Navigation Deck below for extra cabins to be accommodated.

This ship is perhaps best for older passengers who seek conventional, pleasant surroundings and food. Holland America Line provides complimentary cappuccino and espresso coffees, and free ice cream during certain hours of the day aboard its ships, as well as hot hors d'oeuvres in all bars, a nicety other major lines seem to have dropped, or charge extra for.

642

She is an extremely comfortable ship in which to cruise, with some fine, elegant, and luxurious decorative features. However, these are marred by the poor quality of dining room food and service, and the lack of understanding of what it takes to make a "luxury" cruise experience, despite what is touted in the company's brochures. Refreshingly, the company does not add an automatic 15% gratuity for beverage purchases.

The ship operates Caribbean cruises year-round (the first Holland America Line ship to do so).

Weak Points: Standing in line for embarkation, disembarkation, shore tenders, and self-serve buffet meals is an inevitable aspect of cruising aboard all large ships. With one whole deck of suites (and a dedicated, private concierge lounge, with preferential passenger treatment), the company has in effect created a two-class ship. The charge to use the washing machines and dryers in the self-service launderette is really petty and irritating, particularly for the occupants of suites, as they pay high prices for their cruises. Communication (in English) with many of the staff, particularly in the dining room and buffet areas, can prove very frustrating! Room service is poor. Non-smokers should avoid this ship, as smokers are everywhere.

SHOPPING

→ Many cruise lines that operate in Alaska, the Bahamas, the Caribbean, and the Mexican Riviera openly engage a company that provides the services of a "shopping lecturer." The shopping lecturer promotes selected shops, goods, and services heavily, fully authorized by the cruise line (which receives a commission from the same). This relieves the cruise director of any responsibilities, together with any question about his involvement, credibility, and financial remuneration.

→ Shopping maps, with "selected" stores highlighted, are placed in your cabin. Often, they come with a "guarantee" such as: "Shop with confidence at each of the recommended stores. Each merchant listed on this map has been carefully selected on the basis of quality, fair dealing, and value. These merchants have given Cruise Line X a guarantee of satisfaction valid for thirty (30) days after purchase, excluding passenger negligence and buyer's regret, and have paid a promotional fee for inclusion as a guaranteed store."

→ When shopping time is included in shore excursions, be wary of stores recommended by tour guides; the guides are likely to be receiving commissions from the merchants.

→ Shop around and compare prices before you buy. Good shopping hints and recommendations are often given in the port lecture at the start of your cruise.

→ When shopping for local handicrafts, make sure they have indeed been made locally.

→ Be wary of "bargain-priced" name brands, as they may well be counterfeit and of dubious quality. For watches, check the guarantee. Some shopping information may be available in information literature about the port and this should be available at the ship's shore excursion office.

→ Remember that the ship's shops are also duty free and, for the most part, competitive in price. The shops on board are closed while in port, however, due to international customs regulations.

→ Know in advance just what you are looking for, especially if your time is limited. But if time is no problem, browsing can be fun.

Zenith
★★★★ +

Large Ship:	47,255 tons	Cabins (for one person):	0
Lifestyle:	Premium	Cabins (with private balcony):	0
Cruise Line:	Celebrity Cruises	Cabins (wheelchair accessible):	4
Former Names:	-	Cabin Current:	110-volt
Builder:	Meyer Werft (Germany)	Full-Service Dining Rooms:	1
Original Cost:	$210 million	Elevators:	7
Entered Service:	April 1992	Casino(gaming tables):	Yes
Registry:	Liberia	Slot Machines:	Yes
Length (ft/m):	681.0/207.59	Swimming Pools (outdoors):	2
Beam (ft/m):	95.1/29.00	Swimming Pools (indoors):	0
Draft (ft/m):	23.6/7.20	Whirlpools:	3
Propulsion/Propellers:	Diesel (19,960kW)/2	Fitness Center:	Yes
Passenger Decks:	9	Sauna/Steam Room:	Yes/No
Total Crew:	670	Massage:	Yes
Passengers (lower beds/all berths):	1,378/1,800	Self-Service Launderette:	No
Pass. Space Ratio (lower beds/all berths):	34.2 /26.2	Dedicated Cinema:	No
Crew/Pass. Ratio (lower beds/all berths):	2.0/2.6	Library:	Yes
Navigation Officers:	Greek	Classification Society:	Lloyd's Register
Cabins (total):	689		
Size Range (sq ft/sq m):	172.2–500.5/16.0–46.50	**OVERALL SCORE:**	**1,623**
Cabins (outside view):	541	(OUT OF A POSSIBLE 2,000 POINTS)	
Cabins (interior/no view):	148		

Accommodation: There are 12 grades of accommodation, including outside-view suites and cabins, and interior (no view) cabins, but even the smallest cabin is considerably larger than most of the standard outside and interior (no view) cabins aboard the ships of sister company Royal Caribbean International.

All of the standard interior (no view) and outside-view cabins have good quality fittings with lots of wood accenting. They are tastefully decorated and of an above average size, with an excellent amount of closet and drawer space, and reasonable insulation between cabins. The bathrooms have a very generous shower area, and a small range of toiletries is provided (the bathroom towels are a little small, however), as is storage space for personal toiletry items. The lowest grade outside-view cabins have a porthole, but all others have picture windows.

The largest accommodation consists of two Royal Suites on Deck 10. These suites feature a separate bedroom and living room/dining room with glass dining table (with VCR and CD player in addition to the TV), and a large bathroom with whirlpool tub. Butler service is standard.

Another 20 suites on Deck 10 are very tastefully furnished, although they are not as large as the suites aboard the company's four larger vessels, *Century*, *Galaxy*, *Mercury* and *Millennium*, and they have a generous amount of drawer and other storage space. They also have excellent bathrooms and come with butler service. All accommodation designated as suites have European duvets on the beds instead of sheets and blankets. Unfortunately, all suffer from noise generated on the swimming pool deck directly above. Butler service is standard.

The standard interior (no view) and outside-view cabins are reasonably well insulated, have twin beds that convert to a queen-size bed, and a good amount of closet and drawer space. They are nicely appointed and spacious enough for 7-night cruises, much larger than cabins aboard the ships of sister company Royal Caribbean International, for example.

The bathrooms are very practical and well laid-out, with large shower areas. Various toiletries are provided (soap, shampoo/conditioner, body lotion, and shower cap). Note that most outside cabins on theBahamas Deck have lifeboat-obstructed views. The cabin soundproofing is fair to very good, depending on the location. All suites and cabins have interactive Celebrity TV, including pay-per-view movies.

Dining: The Caravelle Dining Room (nonsmoking), which features a raised section in its center, has several tables for two, as well as for four, six, or eight (in banquettes). The chairs do not have armrests. There are two seatings. The cuisine, its presentation and service are really extremely good. There is a separate menu for vegetarians and children. An extensive wine cellar means that the wine list features a fine selection of vintage and non-vintage wines and champagnes from around the world. The wine sommeliers are knowledgable, and wine suggestions are provided on all dinner menus.

For informal meals, the Windsurf Café (nonsmoking) features good buffets for breakfast (including an omelet station) and luncheon (including a pasta station, rotisserie, and pizza ovens). At peak times, however, the buffets are simply too small. At night, the dining area changes into an alternative dining spot for passengers who want good food, but in a more casual setting than the main restaurant, with items such as grilled salmon, steaks, and rotisserie chicken, as well as specialties that change frequently.

The Grill, located outdoors adjacent to (but aft of) the Windsurf Café, serves typical fast-food items. And for those that cannot live without them, freshly baked pizzas (in a box) can be delivered, in an insulated pouch, to your cabin.

Other Comments: This ship has a smart, contemporary profile that gives the impression of power and speed owing to her blue paint striping along the sides, separating the hull from the superstructure, as in her two-years-older sister *Horizon*. The funnel is instantly recognizable in royal blue, with a white "X," the company's logo.

Inside, there is a similar interior layout (to sister *Horizon*) and elegant and restrained decor that most find a little warmer, and an enlarged and enhanced forward observation lounge with a larger dance floor.

The feeling is one of uncluttered surroundings. Intelligent, well-chosen artworks adorn the vessel. Soothing pastel colors and high-quality soft furnishings are used throughout the interiors.

The principal deck that houses many of the public entertainment rooms features a double-width indoor promenade. Facilities include an excellent show lounge (with very elegant shows), with main and balcony levels, and good sight lines from almost all seats (however, the railing in the balcony level does impede viewing).

There is a good-sized library, which was relocated and enlarged in a mid-1999 refit. A good program for children and teenagers, with specially trained youth counselors is provided on a seasonal basis. There is a large, elegantly appointed casino with its own bar, while outside is a satellite-linked BankAtlantic ATM machine (there is a $5 access charge) in case you didn't bring enough cash. An Art Deco-style hotel-like lobby (reminiscent of hotels in Miami Beach) has a two-deck-high ceiling and a spacious feel to it.

The refurbishment in mid-1999 added the delightful Michael's Club cigar smoking lounge (complete with fireplace and bookshelves containing leather-bound volumes) in what was formerly an underused discotheque, as well as the enlarged library, and a small business center. A popular martini bar, a room dedicated to the display of art (for art auctions), an expanded health spa (this now includes a rasul treatment room, AquaJet and dry flotation bath), and an enlarged beauty salon with ocean-view windows; and a fine Cova Café (named for Cova Café, located near the La Scala Opera House in Milan, which opened in 1756) were also added.

This ship will provide you with a well-packaged cruise vacation in elegant, calming surroundings, with finely presented food in a formal dining room setting, and service by a well-trained service staff that include a large percentage of Europeans. Almost all passengers feel that the company exceeds their expectations of a 7-night cruise experience.

Weak Points: Standing in line for embarkation, disembarkation, shore tenders, and self-serve buffet meals is an inevitable aspect of cruising aboard all large ships. Unlike the company's larger ships *Century*, *Galaxy*, *Mercury*, and *Millennium*, no suites or cabins have private balconies. Trying to get Cabin Service, or the Guest Relations Desk to answer the phone (to order breakfast, for example, if you don't want to do so via the interactive TV) is a matter of luck, timing, and patience (a sad reminder of the automated age, and lack of personal contact). The doors to the public restrooms and the outdoor decks are rather heavy. The public restrooms are clinical and need some softer decor. There are cushioned pads for poolside deck lounge chairs only, but not for chairs on other outside decks. Participation activities are amateurish and should be upgraded.

OCEANGOING CRUISE SHIPS TO DEBUT: 2002-2005

CRUISE LINE	NAME OF SHIP	TONNES	COST
2002			
Aida Cruises	*AIDAvita*	42,200	$350 million
Carnival Cruise Lines	*Carnival Conquest*	110,000	$450 million
Carnival Cruise Lines	*Carnival Pride*	88,500	$375 million
Carnival Cruise Lines	*Carnival Legend*	88,500	$375 million
Celebrity Cruises	*Summit*	85,000	$350 million
Festival Cruises	*European Dream*	58,600	$250 million
Holland America Line	*Zuiderdam*	85,700	$400 million
Norwegian Coastal Voyages	*Finnmarken*	15,000	$105 million
Norwegian Coastal Voyages	*Trollfjord*	15,000	$105 million
Norwegian Cruise Line	*Norwegian Dawn*	91,000	$400 million
Princess Cruises	*Star Princess*	108,806	$425 million
Princess Cruises	*Coral Princess*	88,000	$360 million
ResidenSea	*The World of ResidenSea*	50,000	$262 million
Royal Caribbean International	*Adventurer of the Seas*	137,300	$500 million
Royal Caribbean International	*Brilliance of the Seas*	88,000	$350 million
Royal Caribbean International	tba	88,000	$400 million
2003			
Aida Cruises	tba	42,200	$350 million
Carnival Cruise Lines	*Carnival Glory*	110,000	$450 million
Celebrity Cruises	*Constellation*	85,000	$350 million
Costa Cruises	*Costa Mediterranea*	85,700	$377 million
Costa Cruises	*Costa Fortuna*	105,000	$418.5 million
Crystal Cruises	tba	68,000	$350 million
Cunard Line	*Queen Mary 2*	150,000	$700 million
Holland America Line	*Oosterdam*	85,700	$400 million
Mediterranean Shipping Cruises	tba	60,000	$266 million
Norwegian Coastal Voyages	*Trollfjord*	15,000	$105 million
Princess Cruises	*Island Princess*	88,000	$360 million
Princess Cruises	*Diamond Princess*	113,000	$460 million
Radisson Seven Seas Cruises	*Seven Seas Voyager*	46,000	$200 million
ResidenSea	*The World of ResidenSea 2*	50,000	$288 million
Royal Caribbean Internatonal	tba	88,000	$400 million
Royal Caribbean International	tba	137,300	$600 million
United States Lines	*American Classic*	72,000	$440 million
2004			
Carnival Cruise Lines	*Carnival Miracle*	85,700	$375 million
Carnival Cruise Lines	*Carnival Valor*	110,000	$450 million
Costa Cruises	*Costa Magica*	105,000	$418.5 million
Holland America Line	tba	85,700	$400 million
Mediterranean Shipping Cruises	tba	60,000	$266 million
Norwegian Coastal Voyages	tba	15,000	$105 million
Princess Cruises	*Sapphire Princess*	113,000	$460 million
Royal Caribbean Internatonal	tba	88,000	$400 million
Royal Caribbean International	tba	137,300	$600 million
United States Lines	*American Classic*	72,000	$440 million
2005			
Celebrity Cruises	tba	85,000	$350 million

NOTES:This chart shows ships under firm contract. It is given in alphabetical order according to cruise l
tba = to be announced

LENGTH (feet)	LENGTH (meters)	PASSENGERS (lower bed capacity)	BUILDER
662.7	202.0	1,270	Aker MTW Werft (Germany)
951.4	290.0	2,974	Fincantieri (Italy)
957.0	291.7	2,100	Fincantieri (Italy)
957.0	291.7	2,100	Fincantieri (Italy)
964.5	294.0	1,950	Chantiers de l'Atlantique (France)
824.1	251.2	1,566	Chantiers de l'Atlantique (France)
957.0	291.7	1,848	Fincantieri (Italy)
444.5	135.5	674	Kleven Werft (Norway)
444.5	135.5	674	Kleven Werft (Norway)
964.9	294.1	2,400	Chantiers de l'Atlantique (France)
951.4	290.0	2,600	Fincantieri (Italy)
948.1	289.0	1,950	Chantiers de l'Atlantique (France)
629.9	192.0	400	Apuania (Italy)
1019.7	311.0	3,114	Kvaerner Masa-Yards (Finland)
961.9	293.2	2,188	Meyer Werft (Germany)
964.5	294.0	2,170	Chantiers de l'Atlantique (France)
662.7	202.0	1,300	Aker MTW Werft (Germany)
951.4	290.0	2,974	Fincantieri (Italy)
964.5	294.0	1,950	Chantiers de l'Atlantique (France)
959.6	292.5	2,114	Kvaerner Masa-Yards (Finland)
893.0	272.2	2,720	Sestri Cantieri Navale (Italy)
777.8	237.1	1,080	Chantiers de l'Atlantique (France)
1131.8	345.0	2,800	Chantiers de l'Atlantique (France)
957.0	291.7	1,848	Fincantieri (Italy)
824.1	251.2	1,600	Chantiers de l'Atlantique (France)
444.5	135.5	674	Kleven Werft (Norway)
948.1	289.0	1,950	Chantiers de l'Atlantique (France)
964.5	294.0	2,600	Mitsubishi Heavy Industries (Japan)
708.6	216.0	720	Fincantieri (Italy)
711.9	217.0	396	Fosen MEK Versteder (Norway)
964.5	294.0	2,170	Chantiers de l'Atlantique (France)
1019.7	311.0	3,114	Kvaerner Masa-Yards (Finland)
840.0	256.0	1,900	Ingalls Shipbuilding (USA)
957.0	291.7	2,124	Kvaerner Masa-Yards (Finland)
951.4	290.0	2,974	Fincantieri (Italy)
983.0	272.2	2,700	Sestri Cantieri Navale (Italy)
957.0	291.7	1,800	Fincantieri (Italy)
824.1	251.2	1,600	Chantiers de l'Atlantique (France)
444.5	135.5	674	Kleven Werft (Norway)
964.5	294.0	2,600	Mitsubishi Heavy Industries (Japan)
964.5	294.0	2,170	Chantiers de l'Atlantique (France)
1019.7	311.0	3,114	Kvaerner Masa-Yards (Finland)
840.0	256.0	1,900	Ingalls Shipbuilding (USA)
964.5	294	1,950	Chantiers de l'Atlantique (France)

"Delivery/debut dates may be brought forward or put back, therefore precise months are not listed."

INDEX TO SHIPS' RATINGS

SMALL SHIPS (LESS THAN 500 PASSENGERS)

111 Ships/104 Rated

Ship	Score	Rating
Europa	1857	5+
Seabourn Legend	1791	5
Seabourn Goddess II	1792	5
Seabourn Goddess I	1790	5
Seabourn Pride	1790	5
Seabourn Spirit	1790	5
Silver Shadow	1765	5
Hanseatic	1740	5
Silver Cloud	1729	5
Silver Wind	1729	5
Sea Cloud II	1709	5
Sea Cloud	1704	5
Hebridean Princess	1701	5
Clipper Odyssey	1678	4+
Seven Seas Navigator	1653	4+
Song of Flower	1651	4+
Paul Gauguin	1645	4+
Le Levant	1609	4+
Radisson Diamond	1591	4+
Wind Surf	1567	4+
Clelia II	1551	4+
Club Med 2	1546	4
Le Ponant	1540	4
Royal Clipper	1540	4
Wind Song	1518	4
Wind Spirit	1518	4
Wind Star	1518	4
Renaissance Seven	1506	4
Renaissance Eight	1506	4
Minerva	1476	4
Bremen	1461	4
Nippon Maru	1397	3+
Star Clipper	1390	3+
Star Flyer	1390	3+
C. Columbus	1383	3+
Orient Venus	1382	3+
Fuji Maru	1371	3+
Galapagos Explorer II	1365	3+
Sovetskiy Soyuz	1292	3+
Yamal	1292	3+
Kapitan Dranitsyn	1287	3+
Kapitan Khlebnikov	1287	3+
Kong Harald	1285	3+
Nordkapp	1285	3+
Nordlys	1285	3+
Nordnorge	1285	3+
Polarlys	1285	3+
Richard With	1285	3+
Delphin	1279	3+
Yorktown Clipper	1267	3+

Ship	Score	Rating
Nantucket Clipper	1265	3+
Endeavour	1263	3+
Vistamar	1262	3+
Switzerland	1245	3
Sapphire	1220	3
St. Helena	1219	3
Polaris	1210	3
Clipper Adventurer	1175	3
Black Prince	1144	3
Funchal	1097	2+
Explorer	1095	2+
Grande Caribe	1095	2+
Grande Mariner	1095	2+
Midnatsol	1093	2+
Narvik	1093	2+
Vesteralen	1093	2+
Niagara Prince	1087	2+
Royal Star	1080	2+
Stella Oceanis	1079	2+
Odysseus	1071	2+
Calypso	1066	2+
Kristina Regina	1052	2+
Legacy	1029	2+
Spirit of '98	1018	2+
Silver Star	1009	2+
Bordeaux	1006	2+
Princesa Amorosa	970	2+
Akademik Sergey Vavilov	963	2+
Professor Khromov	947	2
Professor Molchanov	947	2
Professor Multanovskiy	947	2
Spirit of Endeavor	946	2
Sea Bird	943	2
Sea Lion	943	2
Harald Jarl	940	2
Lofoten	940	2
Wilderness Adventurer	939	2
Wilderness Discoverer	939	2
Spirit of Alaska	936	2
Spirit of Columbia	936	2
Spirit of Discovery	946	2
Spirit of Glacier Bay	913	2
Flying Cloud	902	2
Mandalay	902	2
Polynesia	902	2
Yankee Clipper	902	2
Arion	859	2
Olvia	842	2
American Eagle	827	2
Dalmacija	821	2

Ship	Score	Rating
Arcadia (Golden Sun Cruises)	724	1+
Atalante	666	1+
Ambasador I	620	1
Cape Cod Light	NYR	NYR
Cape May Light	NYR	NYR
Hebridean Spirit	NYR	NYR
Silver Whisper	NYR	NYR
Spirit of Oceanus	NYR	NYR
Sun Bay	NYR	NYR
The World of ResidenSea	NYR	NYR

MID-SIZE SHIPS (500–1,000 PASSENGERS)

61 Ships/58 Rated

Ship	Score	Rating
Crystal Symphony	1769	5
Crystal Harmony	1755	5
Seabourn Sun	1725	5
Seven Seas Mariner	1703	5
Asuka	1658	4+
Pacific Venus	1647	4+
Caronia	1649	4+
R One	1548	4
R Two	1548	4
R Three	1548	4
R Four	1548	4
R Five	1548	4
R Six	1548	4
R Seven	1548	4
R Eight	1548	4
Astor	1547	4
Arkona	1532	4
Saga Rose	1460	4
Olympia Explorer	1434	4
Black Watch	1420	4
Olympia Voyager	1409	4
Marco Polo	1406	4
SuperStar Aries	1396	3+
Maxim Gorkiy	1385	3+
SuperStar Gemini	1385	3+
Pacific Princess	1370	3+
Norwegian Star	1355	3+
Victoria	1323	3+
SuperStar Taurus	1278	3+
Ocean Majesty	1274	3+
Albatros	1253	3+
Olympia Countess	1240	3
Costa Allegra	1210	3
Costa Marina	1209	3
Flamenco	1203	3
Bolero	1197	3
Rhapsody	1194	3
Stella Solaris	1193	3
The Emerald	1177	3
Seawing	1165	3
Universe Explorer	1159	3
Costa Riviera	1152	3
Van Gogh	1111	3
Valtur Prima	1102	3
Princess Danae	1101	3
World Renaissance	1096	2+
OceanBreeze	1095	2+
Independence	1092	2+
Monterey	1087	2+
Azur	1069	2+

651

Ship	Score	Rating
Triton	1047	2+
Ausonia	1006	2+
Aegean I	972	2+
Regal Empress	962	2+
Serenade	946	2
Aegean Spirit	906	2
Princesa Marissa	901	2
Princesa Victoria	895	2
Princesa Cypria	691	1+
Finnmarken	NYR	NYR
The Iris	NYR	NYR
Trollfjord	NYR	NYR

LARGE SHIPS (OVER 1,000 PASSENGERS)

96 Ships/86 Rated

Ship	Score	Rating
QE2 (Grill Class)	1763	5
Infinity	1707	5
Millennium	1707	5
Galaxy	1697	4+
Mercury	1697	4+
Century	1696	4+
QE2 (Caronia Class)	1625	4+
Zenith	1623	4+
Horizon	1618	4+
Disney Magic	1553	4+
Disney Wonder	1553	4+
Golden Princess	1549	4
Grand Princess	1549	4
AIDAcara	1548	4
Amsterdam	1548	4
Aurora	1548	4
Rotterdam	1548	4
Volendam	1548	4
Zaandam	1548	4
Radiance of the Seas	1546	4
Explorer of the Seas	1545	4
Voyager of the Seas	1545	4
Dawn Princess	1539	4
Ocean Princess	1539	4
Sea Princess	1539	4
Sun Princess	1539	4
Royal Princess	1536	4
Maasdam	1533	4
Ryndam	1533	4
Statendam	1533	4
Veendam	1533	4
Oriana	1530	4
Mistral	1529	4
SuperStar Virgo	1522	4
Enchantment of the Seas	1521	4
Grandeur of the Seas	1521	4
Rhapsody of the Seas	1519	4
Vision of the Seas	1519	4
Legend of the Seas	1511	4
Splendour of the Seas	1511	4
Crown Princess	1509	4
Regal Princess	1509	4
Norwegian Sky	1507	4
SuperStar Leo	1498	4
Crown Odyssey	1471	4
Carnival Spirit	1469	4
Carnival Destiny	1455	4
Carnival Triumph	1455	4
Carnival Victory	1455	4

Ship	Score	Rating
Costa Atlantica	1438	4
Costa Victoria	1406	4
Majesty of the Seas	1394	3+
Monarch of the Seas	1394	3+
Westerdam	1394	3+
Norway	1393	3+
Norwegian Sea	1392	3+
Paradise	1390	3+
Elation	1387	3+
Imagination	1387	3+
Sovereign of the Seas	1387	3+
Norwegian Majesty	1386	3+
Ecstasy	1385	3+
Fantasy	1385	3+
Fascination	1385	3+
Inspiration	1385	3+
Sensation	1385	3+
QE 2 (Mauretania Class)	1383	3+
Norwegian Dream	1381	3+
Norwegian Wind	1381	3+
Arcadia (P&O Cruises)	1374	3+
Pacific Sky	1372	3+
Costa Romantica	1369	3+
Costa Classica	1368	3+
Nordic Empress	1355	3+
Noordam	1350	3+
Patriot	1340	3+
Viking Serenade	1320	3+
Celebration	1318	3+
Holiday	1318	3+
Jubilee	1318	3+
Sunbird	1275	3+
Melody	1259	3+
Star Pisces	1247	3
Costa Tropicale	1239	3
Carousel	1226	3
Sundream	1226	3
Topaz	1096	2+
Oceanic	1093	2+
AIDAvita	NYR	NYR
Adventure of the Seas	NYR	NYR
Brilliance of the Seas	NYR	NYR
Carnival Pride	NYR	NYR
European Stars	NYR	NYR
European Vision	NYR	NYR
Norwegian Star 2	NYR	NYR
Norwegian Sun	NYR	NYR
Star Princess	NYR	NYR
Summit	NYR	NYR

CRUISE LINE ADDRESSES

MAJOR CRUISE LINE HEAD OFFICE ADDRESSES

NORTH AMERICA

Abercrombie & Kent
Abercrombie & Kent
1520 Kensington Road
Oak Brook, IL 60523-2141USA
web site: www.aandktours.com

Alaska's Glacier Bay Tours and Cruises
Glacier Bay Park Concessions, Inc.
520 Pike Street, Suite 1400
Seattle, WA 98101USA
web site:
www.glacierbaytours.com

American Canadian Caribbean Line
461 Water Street
Warren, RI 02885 USA
web site: www.accl-smallships.com

American Cruise Lines
One Marine Park
Haddam
CT 06438 USA
web site:
www.americancruiselines.com

American Hawaii Cruises
1380 Port of New Orleans Place
New Orleans, LA 70130-1890
USA
web site: www.cruisehawaii.com

Carnival Cruise Lines
3655 NW 87 Avenue
Miami, FL 33178-2428 USA
web site: www.carnival.com

Celebrity Cruises
1050 Port Boulevard
Miami, FL 33124 USA
web site:
www.celebrity-cruises.com

Classical Cruises
132 East 70 Street
New York, NY 10021 USA
web site: www.classicalcruises.com

Clipper Cruise Line
7711 Bonhomme Avenue
St. Louis, MO 63105 USA
web site: www.clippercruise.com

Club Med Cruises
75 Valencia Ave.
Coral Gables, FL 33134 USA
web site: www.clubmed.com

Costa Cruises
World Trade Center
80 SW 8 Street, 27th Floor
Miami, FL 33130-3097 USA
web site: www.costacruises.com

Cruise West
4th & Battery Building, Suite 700
Seattle, WA 98121USA
web site: www.cruisewest.com

Crystal Cruises
2049 Century Park East, Suite 1400
Los Angeles, CA 90067 USA
web site:
www.crystalcruises.com

Cunard Line
6100 Blue Lagoon Drive, Suite 400
Miami, FL 33126 USA
web site: www.cunard.com

Delta Queen Coastal Company
30 Robin Street Wharf
New Orleans, LA 70130 USA
web site: www.deltaqueen.com

Disney Cruise Line
210 Celebration Place, Suite 400
Celebration, FL 33747-4600 USA
web site:
www.disney.com/DisneyCruise

First European Cruises
95 Madison Avenue, Suite 1203
New York, NY 10016 USA
web site: www.first-european.com

Great Lakes Cruises
217 E. Wisconsin Avenue
Waukesha, WI 53186, USA
web site: greatlakescruises.com

Holland America Line
300 Elliott Avenue West
Seattle, WA 98119 USA
web site:
www.hollandamerica.com

Lindblad Expeditions
720 Fifth Avenue, Suite 605
New York, NY 10019 USA
web site: www.expeditions.com

Marine Expeditions
890 Young Street, 3rd Floor
Toronto, Ontario
CANADA M4W 3P4

Mediterranean Shipping Cruises
420 5th Avenue
New York, NY 10018 USA
web site: www.msccruisesusa.com

Norwegian Coastal Voyage
405 Park Avenue
New York, NY 10022 USA
web site: www.coastalvoyage.com

Norwegian Cruise Line
7665 Corporate Center Drive
Miami, FL 33126 USA
web site: www.ncl.com

Orient Lines
1510 SE 17th Street
Ft. Lauderdale, FL 33316 USA
web site: www.orientlines.com

Princess Cruises
10100 Santa Monica Blvd, #1800
Los Angeles, CA 90067-4189 USA
web site:
www.princesscruises.com

Quark Expeditions
980 Post Road
Darien, CT 06820 USA
web site:
www.quark-expeditions.com

Radisson Seven Seas Cruises
600 Corporate Drive, Suite 410
Ft. Lauderdale, FL 33180 USA
web site: www.rssc.com
Raymond & Whitcomb
400 Madison Avenue
New York, NY 10017 USA

Regal Cruises
300 Regal Cruises Way
Palmetto, FL 34220 USA
web site: www.regalcruises.com

Renaissance Cruises
350 East Las Olas Boulevard, Suite 800
Ft. Lauderdale, FL 33335-0307
USA
web site:
www.renaissancecruises.com

ResidenSea
45 Rockefeller Plaza, Suite 2079
New York
NY 10111, USA
web site: www.residensea.com

Royal Caribbean International
1050 Caribbean Way
Miami, FL 33132-2096 USA
web site: www.royalcaribbean.com

Royal Olympic Cruises
One Rockefeller Plaza
New York, NY 10020 USA
web site:
www.royalolympiccruises.com

Seabourn Cruise Line
6100 Blue Lagoon Drive
Suite 400
Miami, FL 33126 USA
web site: www.seabourn.com

Silversea Cruises
110 E. Broward Boulevard
Suite 300
Ft. Lauderdale, FL 33301 USA
web site: www.silversea.com

Society Expeditions, Inc.
2001 Western Ave., Suite 300
Seattle, WA 98121 USA
web site:
www.societyexpeditions.com

Star Clippers
4101 Salzedo Avenue
Coral Gables, FL 33146 USA
web site: www.star-clippers.com

Temptress Adventure Cruises
6100 Hollywood Boulevard, Suite
202
Hollywood, FL 33024 USA
web site:
www.temptresscruises.com

United States Lines
1380 Port of New Orleans Place
New Orleans
LA 70130-1890
web site:
www.unitedstateslines.com

Voyager Cruise Line
520 Pike Street, Suite 1400
Seattle, WA 98101 USA
web site:
www.voyagercruiseline.com

Windjammer Barefoot Cruises
1759 Bay Road
Miami Beach, FL 33119 USA
web site: www.windjammer.com

Windstar Cruises
300 Elliott Avenue West
Seattle, WA 98119 USA
web site:
www.windstarcruises.com

World Explorer Cruises
555 Montgomery Avenue
San Francisco, CA 94111 USA
web site: www.wecruise.com

REST OF THE WORLD
Aida Cruises
Am Seehafen 1
Siemenstrasse 90
63203 New Isenberg
GERMANY
web site: www.aida.de

Airtours Sun Cruises
Parkway Four, Parkway Business
Centre
300 Princess Road
Manchester
M14 7QU
UK
web site: www.airtours.co.uk

Canodros
Guayaquil
Ecuador
web site: www.canodros.com

Costa Crociere (Costa Cruises)
Via Gabriele D'Annunzio, 2/80
16121 Genoa
ITALY
web site: www.costacruises.com

Croatia Cruise Lines
Riva 16
51000 Rijeka
CROATIA
web site:
www.globalquesttravel.com

Delphin Seereisen
Blumenstrasse 20
63004 Offenbach/Main
GERMANY
web site: www:delphin-cruises.com

Festival Cruises
99 Akti Miouli
GR 185 38, Piraeus
GREECE
web site:
www.festivalcruises.com

Fred Olsen Cruise Lines
Fred Olsen House
White House Road
Ipswich
Suffolk 1P1 5LL
ENGLAND
web site: www.fredolsen.co.uk

Golden Sea Cruises
Filonos 64
Piraeus 185 35
GREECE

Golden Sun Cruises
85 Akti Miaouli
Piraeus
GREECE 185 38
web site:
www.goldensuncruises.com

Hapag-Lloyd Cruises
Ballindamm 25
D-20095 Hamburg
GERMANY
web site: www.hlkf.com

Hebridean Island Cruises
Acorn Park
Skipton
North Yorkshire BD23 2UE
ENGLAND

Kristina Cruises
16 Kirkkokatu
Kotka 48100
FINLAND
web site:
www.kristinacruises.com

Louis Cruise Lines
54-58 Evangoros Avenue (P.O. Box
1306)
Nicosia
CYPRUS
web site:
www.louiscruises.com

Mitsui OSK Passenger Line
Shuwa-Kioicho Park Building
Kioicho 3-6
Chiyoda-ku
Tokyo 192-8552
JAPAN
web site: mopas.co.jp.com

**NYK Line (Nippon Yusen
Kaisha)**
Yusen Building
3-2 Marunouchi 2-choime
Chiyoda-ku
Tokyo 100-0005
JAPAN
web site: www.asukacruise.co.jp

New Paradise Cruises
P.O. Box 50157
3601 Limassol
CYPRUS
web site:
www.paradise.com.cy

Orient Lines
Michelin House
81 Fulham Road
London SW3 6RD
ENGLAND
web site: www.orientlines.com

P&O Cruises
77 New Oxford Street
London WC1A 1PP
ENGLAND
web site: www.pocruises.com

P&O Cruises (Australia)
P.O. Box 5287
Sydney 2001
New South Wales
AUSTRALIA
Web site: www.pocruises.com.au

Phoenix Seereisen
Kolnstrasse 80
53111 Bonn
GERMANY
web site:www.phoenixreisen.com

Plantours
Obern Street 69
Bremen 28195
GERMANY

Ponant Cruises
60 Boulebard Marchal Juin
44100 Nantes
FRANCE
web site: www.ponant.com

St. Helena Shipping
The Shipyard
Porthleven
Cornwall TR13 9JA
ENGLAND
web site: rms-st-helena.com

Saga Cruises (Saga Shipping)
Folkestone
Kent
ENGLAND
web site: www.saga.co.uk

Sea Cloud Cruises
Ballindamm 17
D-200095 Hamburg
GERMANY
web site: www.seacloud.com

Seetours International
Frankfurterstrasse 233
63263 Neu-Isenburg
GERMANY
web site: www.seetours.de

Star Cruises
Star Cruises Terminal
Pulau Indah
PO Box No. 288
42009 Pelabuhan Klang
Selangor Darul Ehsan
MALAYSIA
web site:
www.starcruises.com.my

Star Line Cruises
P.O. Box 81443
Mombasa
KENYA

Swan Hellenic Cruises
77 New Oxford Street
London WC1A 1PP
ENGLAND
web site: www.swan-hellenic.co.uk

Thomson Cruises
Greater London House
Hampstead Road
London NW1 7SD
ENGLAND
web site:
www.thomson-holidays.com

Transocean Tours
Postfach 10 09 07
28009 Bremen
GERMANY
web site: www.transocean.de

Transtours
49 avenue de l'Opera
75002 Paris
FRANCE

Valtur Tourism
web site: www.valtur.com

Venus Cruise
Umeda Hanshin Daiichi Building
5-25, Umeda 2-chome
Kita-ku
Osaka 530-0001
JAPAN
web site: www.venus-cruise.co.jp

Other Cruise Line Web Addresses

Canodros	www.canodros.com
Captain Cook Cruises	www.captcookcrus.com.au
Cruceros Australis	www.australis.com
Eurocruises	www.eurocruises.com
KD River Cruises of Europe	www.rivercruises.com
Victoria Cruises	www.victoriacruises.com

SHIP INDEX